S0-AEI-138

THE HAPPY ISLES OF OCEANIA

HAWAIIAN ISLANDS

WESTERN
SAMOA

AMERICAN
SAMOA

GROUP

TONGA

COOK ISLANDS

TAHITI

MARQUESAS

TUAMOTU
ARCHIPELAGO

EASTER ISLAND

0   500   1000   Statute miles

THE HAPPY ISLES
OF OCEANIA

BY THE SAME AUTHOR

FICTION

Waldo
Fong and the Indians
Girls at Play
Jungle Lovers
Sinning with Annie
Saint Jack
The Black House
The Family Arsenal
The Consul's File
A Christmas Card
Picture Palace
London Snow
World's End
The Mosquito Coast
The London Embassy
Half Moon Street
O-Zone
Chicago Loop

CRITICISM

V. S. Naipaul

NONFICTION

The Great Railway Bazaar
The Old Patagonian Express
The Kingdom by the Sea
Sailing Through China
Sunrise with Seamonsters
The Imperial Way
Riding the Iron Rooster
To the Ends of the Earth

THE

HAPPY ISLES

PAUL
THEROUX

LIBRARY
COLBY-SAWYER COLLEGE
NEW LONDON, NH 03257

OF OCEANIA

Paddling the Pacific

G. P. PUTNAM'S SONS

New York

DU 23.5 .T47 1992
OCLC 25009523
The happy isles of Oceania/
Theroux, Paul.

G. P. Putnam's Sons
Publishers Since 1838
200 Madison Avenue
New York, NY 10016

Copyright © 1992 by Cape Cod Scriveners Company
All rights reserved. This book, or parts thereof, may not
be reproduced in any form without permission.
Published simultaneously in Canada

The author gratefully acknowledges permission from Faber and Faber Ltd.,
for the lines from "Brother Fire" by Louis MacNeice.
Reprinted from *The Collected Poems of Louis MacNeice.*

The text of this book is set in Times Roman.

Library of Congress Cataloging-in-Publication Data

Theroux, Paul.
The happy isles of Oceania : paddling the Pacific / by Paul Theroux.
p. cm.
ISBN 0-399-13726-2 (alk. paper)
1. Oceania—Description and travel. 2. Theroux, Paul—Journeys—Polynesia. I. Title.
DU23.5.T47 1992   91-39687 CIP
919.504—dc20

Designed by MaryJane DiMassi
Endpaper maps by Lisa Amoroso

Printed in the United States of America
1 2 3 4 5 6 7 8 9 10

This book is printed on acid-free paper.
∞

To Mei-Ling Loo & Sheila Donnelly

Contents

God bless the thoughtful islands
    Where never warrants come;
God bless the just Republics
    That give a man a home . . .

                    —RUDYARD KIPLING, "The Broken Men"

        Come, my friends,
'Tis not too late to seek a newer world.
Push off, and sitting well in order smite
The sounding furrows, for my purpose holds
To sail beyond the sunset, and the baths
Of all the western stars, until I die.
It may be that the gulfs will wash us down;
It may be we shall touch the Happy Isles . . .

                        —TENNYSON, "Ulysses"

THE HAPPY ISLES
OF OCEANIA

Part One

MEGANESIA

Chapter 1
NEW ZEALAND: THE LAND OF THE LONG WHITE CLOUD

There was no good word in English for this hopeless farewell. My wife and I separated on a winter day in London and we were both miserable, because it seemed as though our marriage was over. We both thought: *What now?* It was the most sorrowful of goodbyes. I could not imagine life without her. I tried to console myself by saying, *This is like going on a journey,* because a journey can be either your death or your transformation, though on this one I imagined that I would just keep living a half-life.

From habit, when I was alone, I slept only on the left side of the bed, and so I felt lonelier when I woke up with a big space beside me. At last I felt so woeful I went to my doctor.

"Your blood pressure is fine," she said, "but I don't like the look of that."

She touched a discoloration on my arm. She used the misleadingly sonorous name "melanoma" to describe it. I heard melanoma and I thought of Melanesia, The Black Islands. Eventually she gouged out the black spot and put in four stitches and said she would let me know if this piece of my arm, this biopsy the size of an hors d'oeuvre, was serious. "I mean, if it's a carcinoma."

Why did all these horrors have pretty names?

Needing to be reassured by the familiar sights and sounds of the place where I was born, I went to Boston, but I felt too defeated to stay. And home is sometimes so sad. One day a message came from Melbourne: *Are you free for a book promotional tour in New Zealand and Australia?* I thought, *Any excuse.* So I continued on my journey, carrying a tent, a sleeping bag, and a collapsible kayak. I headed west, by plane, to Chicago, San Francisco, and Honolulu where, to cheer myself up, I took the big bandage off my stitched arm and put on yellow Garfield the Cat Band-Aids.

I went farther away, deeper into the Pacific, thinking: *Planes are like Seven League Boots. I could be in New Zealand or Easter Island tomorrow.* And yet the Pacific was vast. It had half the world's free water, it was one-third of the earth's surface, and it was the balmiest place on earth, too.

More than an ocean, the Pacific was like a universe, and a chart of it looked like a portrait of the night sky. This enormous ocean was like the whole of heaven, an inversion of earth and air, so that the Pacific seemed like outer space, an immensity of emptiness, dotted with misshapen islands that twinkled like stars, archipelagoes like star clusters, and wasn't Polynesia a sort of galaxy?

"I've been all over the Pacific," the man next to me said. He was from California. His name was Hap. "Bora-Bora. Moora-Moora. Tora-Tora. Fuji."

"Fiji," his wife said.

"And Haiti," he told me.

"Tahiti," his wife said, correcting him again.

"Oh God," he said. "Johnston Island."

"What was that like?"

This sinister little island, with the Stars and Stripes flying over it, is 800 miles west of Honolulu, and was formerly a launching site for H-bombs. More recently, nuclear waste was stored there, along with nerve gas and stacks of hydrogen bombs. A recent accident had left one end of Johnston Island radioactive. Few Americans have heard of it. The antinuclear New Zealanders can tell you where it is and why it terrifies them.

"Who said I got off the plane?" Hap said.

"We're members of the Century Club," his wife said. "You can only join if you've been to a hundred countries."

"What does 'been to' mean? Pass through the airport? Spend a night? Get diarrhea there?"

"Guess he's not a member!" Hap said, joyously.

Tourists don't know where they've been, I thought. *Travelers don't know where they're going.*

Then it was dawn, but it was the day after tomorrow, a narrow band of ochreous light like sunrise in the stratosphere. In this part of the Pacific, at the 180th meridian of longitude, the world's day begins. When the plane arrived in Auckland, New Zealand, it was like touching down on a distant star.

"What's that?" It was the inspector: Immigration and Ethnic Affairs, poking my big canvas bags.

"A boat," I said. "Collapsible."

"What's wrong with your arm? Hope it's not contagious."

It might be cancer, I wanted to say, to wipe the smile off his face.

"Welcome to Na Zillun," he said quietly.

It was nine in the morning. I had an interview at ten ("Is your novel based on real people?"), and another at eleven ("What does your wife think of your so-called novel?"), and at noon I was asked, "What do you think of Na Zillun?"

"I have been in New Zealand three hours," I said.

"Go on."

Provoked, I said, "This is a wonderful country—or would you call it an archipelago? Most New Zealanders seem to wear old shapeless hats. You see a lot of beards and knee socks. And sweaters. You also see an awful lot of war memorials."

I was led into a ballroom where I gave a luncheon speech. It was the first meal I had eaten in thirteen hours, but I had to sing for my supper. They wanted autobiography; I gave them Chinese politics.

A person in the audience said, "Are you working on a book at the moment?"

"No, but I'd like to write something about the Pacific," I said. "Maybe the migrations. The way the people went from island to island taking their whole culture with them, until they found a happy island, and spread it all out, like a picnic that would last until the end of the world."

Saying it aloud made it seem like a promise, something I ought to do. I needed a friend. There was always the possibility of friendship in travel. It was an odd place for such an observation, yet in *The Secret Agent* Joseph Conrad wrote, "But does not Alfred Wallace relate in his famous book on the Malay Archipelago how, amongst the Aru Islanders, he discovered in an old and naked savage with a sooty skin a peculiar resemblance to a dear friend at home?"

The great naturalist Wallace had been looking for specimens of the Bird of Paradise on the Aru Islands, which are off the southwestern coast of New Guinea. He had written about "one funny old man, who bore a ludicrous resemblance to a friend of mine at home . . ."

That was not very surprising. The oddest part was that it had happened only once in the entire book. It happened repeatedly to me. In Africa, in India, in South America, in China and Tibet, I had constantly run into indigenous people who rang bells like mad and reminded me of old school friends at the Roberts Junior High, and Medford High, of Peace Corps buddies. People who bore a resemblance to members of my own family popped up from time to time.

Suddenly, I wanted to see the extreme green isles of Oceania, unmodern, sunny, and slow, with trees to sit under and bluey green lagoons to paddle in. My soul hurt, my heart was damaged, I was lonely. I did not want to see another big city. I wanted to be purified by water and wilderness. The Maori people of New Zealand called the Pacific *Moana-Nui-o-Kiva,* "The Great Ocean of the Blue Sky." And the image of the night before came to me again, of the Pacific as a universe, and the islands like stars in all that space.

Auckland has the largest Polynesian population of any city in the world—fully half the people are dusky islanders, and looking at them you might think: They all come from Fatland. Many of them were organized into street gangs with names like The Mongrel Mob and The Black Power Gang, the Tongan Crypt Gang, the United Island Gang, and the Sons of Samoa. Where were the women? The ones I saw were potbellied men, some of them so fat they had an odd twisting walk, like penguins waddling down a plank. Their skin had gone gray in the chilly New Zealand climate. Their swollen cheeks gave them squinty gimlet eyes. It was hard to imagine any of them paddling a canoe. Roughly ten percent of them, the Maori, had arrived from Tahiti via the Cook Islands about a thousand years ago and named these islands *Aotearoa,* "The Land of the Long White Cloud."

Plenty of them are nice as pie, people said, but lots of them are rapists. Everyone had an opinion about them: You should see the thighs on some of them, people said. You should see their tattoos. Your Maori just doesn't want to work, they said. And they're not really full-blooded. The half-castes, the quarter-castes—they're the troublemakers. Your Tongan is a decent chap, but your Samoan can be a terror when he's the worse for drink. If you see a Samoan full of grog, just turn around and walk the other way. Your Fijian? Let's face it, they're cannibals, simple as that, and your Indian is a terribly hard-working person—work like dogs, most of these Hindus. Your Mohammedan is another story. They're randy wee buggers—I hate to say it. But while we're on the subject, a lot of these island women are root rats. They bang like a dunny door. Your Rotuan, your Nuiean, your Cook Islander—oh, it's a mixed bag, no question about it. Some of them are doing very nicely, thank you, drive flash cars, own tidy houses and land. But you just go to one of their bloody wee islands and try to buy a block of land and see what happens. They'll laugh in your face.

Islanders were religious, islanders were gamblers and drinkers, islanders were devoted to their families, islanders were dole scroungers, islanders fought among themselves, islanders were economic refugees, islanders were villains. They towed your car away at night and the next day called you up and demanded money to return it. They practiced extortion,

protection rackets, mugging and racial violence in this pastoral republic—seventy million sheep farting in the glorious meadows.

But these days the gang violence of islanders had been pushed off the
front page by the news that the prime minister, David Lange, had just left
his wife and run off with his speech writer, Miss Margaret Pope.

LANGE'S MOTHER DENOUNCES HIM, the headlines said. CLAIMS SHE RE-
GRETS THE DAY HE WAS BORN. Mr. Lange's wife, Naomi, was screeching
on radio and television, demanding her rights and trying to get even. In
what seemed the direst threat of all she said that she intended to publish
a book of her own poems.

The papers were full of separation and divorce, the whole world was
splitting up. The sheep shearers were on strike. They wanted $46 for
shearing 100 sheep.

Carrying my collapsible kayak, I went to Wellington, where a television interviewer gloated to me that old Mrs. Lange had been on his very
program saying that her son should never have been born, and why had
he run off with this scarlet woman, and marriage was supposed to be
sacred. Did I have any views on that?

No, I said, I was just passing through.

Another man I met said, "This Lange. He's got some Maori blood in
him."

It wasn't true but it was supposed to explain why he had ditched his
wife.

I sat in my hotel room reading *The Sexual Life of Savages* by Bronislaw
Malinowski. When I ordered room service, the man in the hotel kitchen
snapped at me, "Did you order this yesterday?"

I said no, but why?

He said, "We need one day's advance notice on room service orders."

What a bungaloid place, I thought. It is bungalows and more bungalows and little fragile chalets in Wellington, and none of them is higher
than the trees around it, so that at a distance all you saw were roofs,
mostly tin roofs painted browny red. The rest was bare hills and a wind
so strong it seemed to have shape and substance. The wind scoured the
streets and whipped the dark waters of the harbor.

I read Malinowski. I tried to imagine the Trobriand Islands. I noticed
that most stores in Wellington sold camping equipment, and I bought
some more. I sat in my hotel room with my collapsible kayak, feeling
morbid. I also worried about David Lange. What if I ended up with
cancer and a divorce? I was now onto the Betty Boop bandages. One
night, with nothing better to do, I did my arm—took off the Betty Boop
bandage and cut and tweezed out the stitches with my Disposable Suture
Removal Kit.

Among the Trobriand Islanders, Malinowski said, *The formalities of divorce are as simple as those by which marriage is contracted. The woman leaves her husband's house with all her personal belongings, and moves to her mother's hut, or to that of her nearest maternal kinswoman. There she remains, awaiting the course of events, and in the meantime enjoying full sexual freedom.*

The next day I went to Christchurch, on the South Island. It looked prim and moribund, like the sort of South London suburb I had mocked in England on Sunday outings with the kids, driving through on the way to Brighton thinking: This is the English death, the indescribable boredom that makes you desperate to leave. Life is elsewhere, I thought in Christchurch, but in this purgatory I began reliving my past. I saw frightful bungalows and dusty hedges and twitching curtains, and at last in front of the California Fried Chicken Family Restaurant on Papanui Road in the district of Merivale I saw a family of four, Dad, Mum, and the two boys, eating happily in the glary light and joking with each other, and at the sight of this happy family I burst into tears.

Still, nearly everyone I met asked me, "What do you think of Na Zillun?"

"It's wonderful," I said.

They always shrugged and denied it. New Zealanders, smug and self-congratulatory about David Lange's nonnuclear policy, seemed to me the hardest people in the world to compliment. There was something Calvinist in this refusal to accept praise, but it was so persistent it was almost as though in their stubborn humility they were fishing for compliments.

If you spoke about their well-maintained cities they said they were actually very disorderly. Tell them their mountains are high and snowy and they retorted that yours were higher and snowier. "New Zealanders are fitness fanatics," I said to a man. "That's a myth," he said. "We're very unhealthy as a nation. We're poofs." If I said New Zealand seemed prosperous they claimed it was dying on its feet. Mention the multiracial aspect of the North Island and they said, "We hev ithnic unrist. There'll be a blowup any munnit."

"But it's much better than Australia, I hear."

"Bitter by a long chalk. Your Aussie's an enemal."

Secretly, I said to myself: Everyone's wearing old ill-fitting clothes and sensible shoes. They carried string bags. They shopped in places with names like Clark's General Drapers and Edwin Mouldey Ironmongery. It was the indoor suburban culture of the seaside suburbs of 1950s England, Bexhill-on-the-Pacific, with strangely colored plates *(Souvenir of Cheddar Gorge)* on the mantelpiece and plump armchairs and an electric fire where there used to be a hearth. The older people were dull and decent, the younger ones trying hopelessly to be stylish, and the students—Kiwis to the tips of their pinfeathers—aggressively scruffy and gauche. Here and there you saw a Maori, often working a cash register. They were supposed to be clubby and faintly menacing, but they were all smiles and inhabited big solid bodies; Maoris were the only people in New Zealand who looked right at home.

I went to Dunedin, which was cold and frugal, with its shabby streets and mock-gothic university and talked to the students.

"They're very shy," I was told.

Really? They seemed to me ignorant, assertive, and dirty. It felt like the end of the world, and when I looked at a map this seemed true: We were only about 20 degrees north of the Antarctic Circle—leave the southern tip of New Zealand and the next upright animal you are likely to see is an emperor penguin.

Back in Christchurch, I sat in my hotel room, staring at my feet. I watched a New Zealand version of *This Is Your Life,* paying tribute to a middle-aged Maori singer, and when the man wept openly at seeing his family traipse into the studio, I became so depressed I drank most of the mini-bar. The hotel was in the Tudor style, with fake beams and mullioned windows. I was consoled by my luggage, the boat I had carried with me but not yet paddled.

What was the Pacific Ocean like? I rented a bicycle and rode it about five miles to Sumner Bay, where surfers were lazing like seals and the cold blackish breakers were much too big for me to penetrate with my boat. There was another harbor—Lyttelton, over the hill. I cycled a steep circling road and after an hour came to another surfy harbor, but it wasn't Lyttelton—it was Taylor's Mistake.

In 1863, Captain Taylor thought this was Lyttelton after a round-the-world voyage, and ran aground, losing his ship. It was my mistake too. I cycled back up the Port Hills and over another range of hills to Lyttelton Harbor, which was lovely and long, a safe anchorage, with Chinese shops and pretty houses. There was a shortcut back to Christchurch, a tunnel under the hills, but bicycles weren't allowed in it. Procrastinating in the town, I passed a bloody sanitary towel, where someone had thrown it on the street and I thought: *Because of that disgusting thing I will never come here again.*

Pushing and pedalling I made it back over the hills to Christchurch, tired after my forty-mile cycle ride and frustrated by not having found anywhere in the nearby Pacific to paddle my boat.

I called my wife and told her what an awful time I was having. We both cried. She was miserable, she said. I said, So was I!

"But it's better that we stay apart," she said.

Then she begged me to stop calling her.

She said I was like a torturer, calling her out of the blue and making her feel like a prisoner being given a cup of tea by a quixotic jailer. But all I could think of was myself tearfully pedalling the wonky bicycle, all alone, in the wind, up the steep hills at the edge of Christchurch.

And I probably had cancer. In the seedy Tudor-style hotel I looked up from *The Sexual Life of Savages* and saw that the people in the next room had gone, and left the door ajar, and a new set of people were sitting in the same chairs and laughing, having displaced them. Life was like that! The tide came in and went out. People died and others took their place, not even knowing the others' names. They sat in your chairs, they slept in your bed. And you were probably lost somewhere in the Pacific—gone and forgotten. *I wonder where this thing came from?* someone said, scribbling at your beautiful desk.

The next day, Sunday, still feeling morbid and stunned by the sunny emptiness and indifference and the almost indescribable boredom of sitting alone in front of a fan heater in Merivale, in a transported culture of houses named "Oakleigh" in suburbs called Ponsonby, that looked secondhand and small and seedy, ill suited and mediocre—the most terrible aspect of which was that the New Zealanders themselves did not seem to know what was happening to them in their decline—there stole upon me the sort of misery that induces people in crummy hotel rooms to make sure the cap is on the toothpaste and the faucet is turned off, and then they kill themselves, trying not to make too much of a mess.

Get me out of here, I thought. And I headed for the wilderness.

Chapter 2
NEW ZEALAND: SLOSHING THROUGH THE SOUTH ISLAND

As long as there is wilderness there is hope. I went southwest, from Christchurch to Queenstown, at the edge of the waterworld of Fiordland. Even today it is one of the world's last real wildernesses. But a thousand years ago, before the arrival of any humans, it was like the world before the Fall.

Then, there were no predators except falcons, hawks, and eagles—no other meat eaters. There were no browsing mammals, no land mammals at all, apart from two species of small bat. Everything grew and flourished, and the weather came up from the Roaring Forties, watering this corner of New Zealand with twenty-five feet of rain a year. It is still one of the wettest places in the world.

It was once so safe here that the birds lost their sense of danger, and without enemies some stopped flying—among them, the flightless New Zealand goose and the Fiordland crested penguin, now extinct. Others evolved into enormous and complacent specimens, like the spoiled and overfed children I had seen in Auckland—the giant rail, more than a yard tall, or the feathered long-necked moa, a distant relative of the emu and the ostrich and Big Bird, which grew to be ten feet tall.

In that old paradise the trees grew abundantly and the moss was two feet deep—a perfect seedbed for new trees. The creatures lived on roots and insects, and not on one another. The foliage grew without being cut or grazed. Fiordland, which had been created by glaciers, was the Peaceable Kingdom.

After the Maori arrived, probably in the tenth century, from the Cook Islands in tropical Polynesia, with the dog *(kuri)* and the rat *(kiore)* they kept for food, they made forays into Fiordland from the north. They had a great love for decorative feathers, and in their quest for them, and for food, they hunted many birds into extinction. The Maori dogs and rats preyed on the ground-dwelling birds. For the first time since its emergence from the Ice Age, Fiordland's natural balance was disturbed. The arrival of these predators produced the ecological equivalent of Original Sin.

There were always treasure seekers in Fiordland—Maori looking for feathers and greenstone, *pakehes* (whites) looking for gold—but such people were transients. Fiordland never had any permanent settlement, only camps and way stations and the temporary colonies of sealers and whalers at the edge of the sea. People came and went. Fiordland remained uninhabited—a true primeval forest.

But the humans who passed through left many of their animals behind. They introduced various species either for sport or food, or in the mistaken belief that one animal would stabilize another. The pattern is repeated all over the Pacific—there are wild goats gobbling up Tahiti, and wild horses chewing the Marquesas to shreds, wild pigs in the Solomons, and sneaky egg-eating mongooses, presented to the islands by missionaries, all over Hawaii. The rabbits and wild dogs in Australia did so much damage that a Vermin Proof Fence was put up across New South Wales that is longer than the Great Wall of China.

The foreign animals brought a subtle chaos to Fiordland. When the rabbits went wild, the stoats and weasels were introduced to keep them in check, but instead they ate birds and bird eggs and the rabbits increased. Every other non-native creature was similarly destructive. The New Zealanders I met hated these foreign animals even more than the islanders, but they hated them for the same reasons—because of their indecent fertility and their breeding habits and their excessive greed, eating everything in sight.

The greatest threat to vegetation was the red deer. Deer breed quickly and can go anywhere. Helicopters flying over almost inaccessible hanging valleys could spot three or four hundred deer in the steepest places. The Norway rats that came to New Zealand on ships have multiplied and reduced the native bird population. There are American elk in Fiordland, the only herd in the Southern Hemisphere.

"They're a nuisance," Terry Pellet told me. He was the district conservator of Fiordland. "There are so many exotic species that thrive here and harm the local flora and fauna—possums, chamois, and hares."

And the Germans, he said, were terrible about paying hut fees.

What is native and what is alien is a Pacific conundrum. In New Zealand all strangers were suspect, whether they were animal or vegetable. You can shoot a red deer any day in Fiordland and it is always open season on elk. Foreign trees are regarded as unsightly weeds, whether they are Douglas fir, silver birch, or spruce, and no growing things are hated more than the rampant gorse and broom planted by sentimental and homesick Scots.

Nearly all the people I met said they wanted to reclaim their hills and make them bald and bright again, ridding them of these alien plants and animals, to bring about the resurgence of the flightless birds, vegetarians and insectivores, and to preserve the long valleys of native conifers and beeches. There have been some pleasant surprises. One guileless, ground-dwelling bird, the plump beaky takahe, which the Maori hunted, was thought to be extinct. In 1948 some takahes were found in a remote region of Fiordland. Although protected, the bird faces an uncertain future.

Old habits of contentment, curiosity, and trust—the legacy of paradise—remain among the many bird species in Fiordland. Anyone taking a walk through the rain forests will be followed by the South Island robin, the fantail, the tomtit, and the tiny rifleman, New Zealand's smallest bird. These birds seem absolutely without fear and will flutter and light a few feet away, pecking at insects the hiker has disturbed. The kea, or mountain parrot, is so confident it becomes an intruder, squawking its own name and poking into your knapsack.

So, in magnificent Fiordland, far from the dreary frugality of Christchurch and its suburbs, the birds were unafraid and all the water was drinkable; the bird-watcher didn't need binoculars and the hiker had no use for a canteen.

I cheered up and decided to go for a one-week hike over the mountains and through the rain forest. I would paddle my kayak somewhere else.

The best-known long-distance walk in Fiordland is the Milford Track, but it is now a victim of marketing success, and "the finest walk in the world" is simply tourist board hyperbole. It has become crowded and intensively regulated, and as a result rather hackneyed.

The Routeburn Track was my choice, because—unlike the Milford, which is essentially a valley walk with one high climb—it rises to well above the scrub line and stays there, circling the heights, offering vistas of the whole northeast corner of Fiordland. I decided to combine the Routeburn with the Greenstone Valley Walk, so that I would have a whole week of it and so that I could enter and leave Fiordland the way people have done for centuries, on foot.

There is an intense but simple thrill in setting off in the morning on a mountain trail knowing that everything you need is on your back. It is a confidence in having left all inessentials behind, and of entering a world of natural beauty which has not been violated, where money has no value, and possessions are a deadweight. The person with the fewest possessions is the freest: Thoreau was right.

Even my recently gloomy mood had lifted. I felt a lightness of spirit, and the feeling was so profound it had a physical dimension—I felt stronger and that eased my load. From the age of nine or ten, when I first began hiking, I have associated camping with personal freedom. My pleasure has intensified over the years as equipment has improved and become more manageable and efficient. When I was very young, camping equipment was just another name for "war surplus." Everything was canvas. It was made for World War II and Korea. It was dusty, mildewed, and very heavy. I struggled with my pup tent. My sleeping bag was filled with cotton and kapok and weighed fifteen pounds. Now all the stuff is light and colorful and almost stylish.

And hikers are no longer middle-aged Boy Scouts. A violinist, a factory worker, an aspiring actor, a photographer, a food writer, a student, and a grumpy little man with an East European accent made up our Routeburn hiking party. We were, I suppose, representative. Some dropped by the wayside; the photographer stayed on at one hut to take pictures, and the man who kept interrupting discussions with, "Hah! You sink so! You must be choking!" at last went home, and when we finished only three of us pushed on to the Greenstone. Isidore, the violinist, cursed the water and mud and apologized for being a slow walker, but he was better at other pursuits—he was concertmaster of the New Zealand Symphony Orchestra, and he had a knack for beating me at Scrabble during the long nights at the trackside shelters.

We started walking up a muddy track at the north end of Lake Wakatipu in sight of deer and majestic stags.

"I find it hard to view these creatures as pests," I said. "Vermin is not the first thing that comes to mind when you see the monarch of the glen."

"Vermin!" Isidore said, mockingly. He had the northern Michigan habit of talking with his teeth clamped together. He soon stumblingly fell behind.

He caught up at lunch, while we ate beside a stream (which we drank from). We were bitten by sand flies there and we set off again. After a horizontal stretch across Routeburn Flats, among the tawny blowing tussocks, we climbed steeply on a track that took us through gnarled and ancient beeches to Routeburn Falls. This was a succession of cataracts which cascaded over black rocks on about six levels of bouldery terraces.

From this level, it was possible to see clearly how the glaciers carved Fiordland, creating the characteristic U-shaped valleys, whose sheer walls gave them the illusion of even greater height. The dragging and abrasive glaciers smoothed the valleys' walls, but here the ice had been about 5,000 feet thick, and so the tops of the mountains were jagged and sharp where the glaciers didn't reach.

That night we stayed in a hut. A hut on the Routeburn Track, I discovered, is essentially a small drafty shelter erected over a Scrabble board. At the Falls hut that night we talked as the rain began to patter on the roof.

"How did the Maori withstand this cold?" Isidore asked, massaging life back into his sensitive violinist's fingers.

James Hayward, the aspiring actor, did not have the most accurate explanations, but they were always memorable.

"The Maori kept warm by catching keas," he said, referring to the mountain parrots. "They hollowed out these birds and strapped them to their feet and used them for slippers."

"I sink you are choking," came a voice. "Hah!"

James merely smiled.

"You're talking crap, Jim," someone said. "They've found Maori sandals on the trails."

"You see a lot of interesting things on the trails," James said. "I once saw a man on the Routeburn in a bowler hat, a pin-striped suit, a tightly rolled umbrella, and all his camping gear in a briefcase."

He had had to raise his voice, for the wind and the rain had increased. It kept up all night, falling fast and turning to sleet and making a great commotion, with constant smashing sounds, pushing at the side of the hut and slapping the windows.

I played Scrabble with Pam, the student. She said that she beat most of her friends.

"You won't beat me," I said. "Words are my business."

She was a big strong girl. She had the heaviest rucksack in the group.

"If you beat me, I'll carry your pack over the Harris Saddle tomorrow."

She beat me easily, but in the morning I felt sure that I would be spared the effort of carrying her pack. The rain was still driving down hard. Visibility was poor. Between swirling cloud and glissades of sleet, I could see that the storm had left deep new snow on the summit of Momus and other nearby mountains. From every mountainside, cataracts had erupted, milky-white, spurting down the steep rock faces.

"Let's go walkabout," James said.

The narrow footpath near the hut coursed with water, and I had wet feet before I had gone ten yards. We tramped up the path in the snowy rain and wind, marvelling at how the Routeburn Falls was now about twice the torrent it had been the day before. We climbed for an hour to a hilltop lake that lay in a rocky bowl, a body of water known here, and in Scotland, as a "tarn." ("Burn" is also Scottish, for that matter, meaning "stream.") The storm crashed into the tarn for a while, but even as we watched, it lessened and soon ceased altogether. Within fifteen minutes the sun came out and blazed powerfully—brighter than any sunlight I had ever seen.

The photographer, Ian, said, "This sunlight is three-quarters of a stop brighter than anywhere else on earth I've taken pictures."

It seems that the greenhouse effect can be measured with a light meter.

In this dazzling light, Pam helped me strap on her fifty-pound pack and we climbed upward. Lake Harris a few miles up the trail was greeny blue and enclosed by cliffs. Then we were above it, tramping through alpine scrub and the blowing spear grass they call spaniard. Staggering under the weight of Pam's pack, I tottered towards Harris Saddle (4,200 feet), which stands as a glorious gateway to Fiordland. Beyond it is the deep Hollyford Valley, which winds to the sea, and high on its far side the lovely Darran Mountains, with glaciers still slipping from their heights and new snow whipping from their ridges.

The Harris Saddle was worth the long climb for the sight of the panorama of summits to the west, a succession of mile-high mountains—Christina, Sabre, Gifford, Te Wera, and Madeline. I could not imagine mountains packed more tightly than this—a whole ocean of whitened peaks, like an arctic sea.

Apart from the wind whispering in the stunted scrub, there was silence here. At this height, among powerful mountains, I felt that I had left mean and vulgar things far behind, and entered a world without pettiness. Its counterpart, and a feeling it closely resembles, is that soaring sense of well-being inspired by a Gothic cathedral—not a nineteenth-century New Zealand imitation, of which there were many, but a real one.

Walking along the ridge of the Harris Saddle, I had a clear recollection of the London I had left, of various events that people talked about: a steamy affair between a literary editor and one of her younger assistants; of a famous widow, an obnoxious Anne Hathaway type, who gave parties—drinkers jammed in a room full of smoke—that people boasted of attending. I saw people—writers—talking on television programs, and partygoers smoking, and snatching drinks from a waitress's tray, and shrieking at each other, and talking about the literary editor and her younger lover, and then they all went home drunk.

From this path blowing with wildflowers and loose snow these far-off people seemed tiny and rather pathetic in their need for witnesses.

"Bullshit!" I yelled into the wind, startling Isidore until he discerned that I was smiling.

I needed to come here to understand that, and I felt I would never go back.

Walking these New Zealand mountains stimulated my memory. My need for this strange landscape was profound. Travel, which is nearly always seen as an attempt to escape from the ego, is in my opinion the opposite. Nothing induces concentration or inspires memory like an alien landscape or a foreign culture. It is simply not possible (as romantics think) to lose yourself in an exotic place. Much more likely is an experience of intense nostalgia, a harking back to an earlier stage of your life, or seeing clearly a serious mistake. But this does not happen to the exclusion of the exotic present. What makes the whole experience vivid, and sometimes thrilling, is the juxtaposition of the present and the past— London seen from the heights of Harris Saddle.

Leaving the others behind, I started the long traverse across the high Hollyford Face—three hours at a high altitude without shelter, exposed to the wind but also exposed to the beauty of the ranges—the forest, the snow, and a glimpse of the Tasman Sea. It was more than 3,000 feet straight down, from the path on these cliffs to the Hollyford River on the valley floor. The track was rocky and deceptive, and it was bordered with alpine plants—daisies, snowberries, and white gentians.

Ocean Peak was above us as I moved slowly across the rock face. It was not very late, but these mountains are so high the sun drops behind them in the afternoon, and without it I was very cold. The southerly wind was blowing from Antarctica. As the day darkened I came to a bluff, and beneath me in a new valley was a green lake. I was at such a high altitude that it took me another hour to descend the zigzag path.

Deeper in the valley I was among ancient trees; and that last half hour, before darkness fell, was like a walk through an enchanted forest, the trees literally as old as the hills, grotesquely twisted and very damp and pungent. A forest that is more than a thousand years old, and that has never been touched or interfered with, has a ghostly look, of layer upon layer of living things, and the whole forest clinging together— roots and trunks and branches mingled with moss and rocks, and everything aboveground hung with tufts of lichen called "old man's beard."

It was so dark and damp here the moss grew on all sides of the trunks—the sunlight hardly struck them. The moss softened them, making them into huge, tired, misshapen monsters with great spongy arms. Everything was padded and wrapped because of the dampness, and the boughs were blackish green; the forest floor was deep in ferns, and every protruding rock was upholstered in velvety moss. Here and there was a chuckle of water running among the roots and ferns. I was followed by friendly robins.

It was all visibly alive and wonderful, and in places had a subterranean gleam of wetness. It was like a forest in a fairy story, the pretty and perfect wilderness of sprites and fairies, which is the child's version of paradise—a lovely Disneyish glade where birds eat out of your hand and you know you will come to no harm.

I began to feel hopeful again about my life. Maybe I didn't have cancer after all.

It was cold that night—freezing, in fact. I woke in Mackenzie Hut to frosty bushes and icy grass and whitened ferns. There was lacework everywhere, and the sound of a far-off waterfall that was like the howl of city traffic.

There were keas screaming overhead as I spent that day hiking—for the fun of it—to the head of Lake Mackenzie. The paradise shelducks objected to my invading their territory, and they gave their two-toned complaint—the male duck honking, the female squawking. I continued up the valley, boulder-hopping much of the way along a dry creek bed. It was steep, most of the boulders were four or five feet thick, so it was slow going. I sheltered by a rock the size of a garage to eat my lunch. The wind rose, the clouds grew lumpier and crowded the sky. The day darkened and turned cold.

I climbed onward, and the higher I got the freer I felt—it was that same sense of liberation I had felt on Harris Saddle, remembering the trivialities of London. At the highest point of the valley face, an uplifted platform just under Fraser Col, the clouds bulged and snow began to fall. I was in a large quarrylike place littered with boulders the size of the bungalows in Wellington, in a gusting wind. I decided not to linger. The commonest emergency in these parts is not a fall or a broken limb but rather an attack of hypothermia. I descended quickly, moving from rock to rock, to whip up my blood and warm myself, and I arrived back at the hut exhausted after what was to have been a rest day.

That night was typical of a stop at a trail hut. Over dinner we discussed murder, race relations, AIDS, nuclear testing, the greenhouse effect, Third World economies, the Maori claim to New Zealand, and Martin Luther King Day.

The Czech, whom I thought of as The Bouncing Czech—he had emigrated from Prague to become a businessman somewhere in California—said, "I never celebrate Martin Luther King Day at my plant. I make my men work."

"How long have you lived in America?" I asked.

"Since sixty-eight."

"Do you know anything about the civil rights movement in the United States?"

"I know about my business," he said. That was true—he spent a great deal of time boasting about how he had made it big in America.

"But you're doing it in a free country," I said. "When you left Czecho-slovakia you could have gone anywhere, but you chose America. Don't you think you have an obligation to know something about American history?"

"As far as I am concerned, Martin Luther King is not significant."

"That's an ignorant opinion," I said.

Isidore said, "Does anyone want to play Scrabble?"

The hut was small. I was angry. I went outside and fumed, and through the heavy mist an owl hooted, "More pork!"

I woke early and left the hut quickly the next morning, so that I wouldn't have to talk to the Czech. He was a rapid walker and what is known in camping circles as an equipment freak: very expensive multicol-ored gear.

It was raining softly as I set off, and roosting on a branch above the path ahead was a New Zealand pigeon. It was like no other pigeon in the world, fat as a football, and so clumsy you wonder how it stayed aloft. It does so with a loud thrashing of wings. In the past, the Maori who walked this way snared these *kereru* and ate them. They needed them to sustain themselves in their search for the godly greenstone, a nephritic jade hard enough to use for knives and axes and lovely enough for jewelry. They dug this rare stone all over the Routeburn Track. On that same stretch, from Mackenzie to Lake Howden, I heard a bellbird. This remarkable mimicking bird trills and then growls and grates before burst-ing into song. It was much admired by the Maori. At the birth of a son they cooked a bellbird in a sacred oven in a ritual of sacrifice meant to ensure that the child had fluency and a fine voice.

The light rain in the morning increased to a soaking drizzle, turning the last mile on the Routeburn Track into a muddy creek. I passed under Earland Falls, which splashes 300 feet down—the water coursing onto the rocky path. There was water and mist and noise everywhere, and it involved a sort of baptism in order to proceed. Farther down the track the woods offered some protection from the rain, and yet we arrived at Howden Hut drenched. That is normal for Fiordland. Photography can-not do justice to rain, and so most photographs of Fiordland depict a sunny wilderness. But that sunshine is exceptional. At Lake Howden, for example, there are roughly 200 rain days a year, producing twenty-five feet of rain.

It was still raining in the afternoon, and yet I was looking forward to three more days walking, down the Greenstone Valley to Lake Wakatipu. It was the sort of rain that makes local enthusiasts start their explanations with *if only*—

"If only it weren't so misty you'd be able to see wonderful—"

LIBRARY
COLBY-SAWYER COLLEGE
NEW LONDON, NH 03257

Wonderful peaks, lakes, forests, cliffs, waterfalls, ridges, saddles, and ravines. They were all obscured by the rain. But the wonderful woods with their mossy grottoes were enough. This was a famous valley, one that had been pushed open when a glacier split off from the Hollyford Valley and flowed southeast about thirty miles to Lake Wakatipu. It was another Maori route to the greenstone deposits at the top of the lake. Its presence so near the rivers and lake confirmed them in their belief that the stone was a petrified fish. Greenstone had both spiritual and material significance and was cherished because it was so difficult to obtain.

Isidore still struggled along, humming Brahms. The Czech evaporated—we never saw him again—and we were joined by two New Zealanders, a courting couple, who were terrific walkers and who tripped and pushed each other, threw blobs of mud, splashed each other in the icy streams, wrestled at lunch in the tussocky meadows—Kiwi courtship. And there was an elderly lawyer and his wife, from somewhere in Oregon.

Seeing the mixed bunkroom at one of the Greenstone huts, the man said, "Oh, I get it. It's bisexual!"

Not exactly, but we knew what he meant.

The Greenstone was a walk down a river valley—no snow and sleet here. After breakfast we set off together but since everyone walked at a different pace we ended up walking alone, meeting at a rest spot for scroggin (nuts and raisins) and then onward through the forest for lunch—on the Greenstone it was always a picnic by a drinkable river; and finally slogging throughout most of the afternoon towards one of the riverside huts. As the river widened to a mile or two the river became louder and frothier, and the soaked graywacke stone that lay in it made it greener.

Cataracts poured from the mountains above the trail, but they were so high and the wind so strong that they were blown aside, like vaporizing bridal veils—a gauze of mist that vanished before it reached the valley floor. We were followed by birds and watched by deer and hawks and falcons. The weather was too changeable and the prevailing westerlies too strong to assure one completely rainy—or sunny—day. Clouds were always in rapid motion in the sky and being torn apart by the Livingstone Mountains at the edge of Fiordland—for we had now left the park proper and were making our way through Wakatipu State Forest to the lake.

The silver beeches of the high altitudes gave way to the thicker, taller red beeches of the valley and the slender and strange young lancewood trees with their downward-slanting leaves at the margin of the valley floor. We walked across the sluices of long-ago rockslides and through a forest of whitened trunks of trees killed by a recent fire, and by a deep gorge and a rock (called a *roche moutonée*) too stubborn for the glacier to budge, and through cool mossy woods, and knee-deep in a freezing creek—the courting couple shrieking and kicking water at each other—always followed by birds.

At the last swing bridge that trembled like an Inca walkway near the mouth of the Greenstone, where the Caples Valley converged to form an amphitheater of mountainsides, the foliage was of a European and transplanted kind—tall poplars in autumnal gold, standing like titanic ears of corn, and dark Douglas fir and the startling red leaves of copper beeches—the trees the New Zealanders call foreign weeds and would like to destroy, root and branch.

I was sorry to reach the end of the trail, because there is something purifying about walking through a wilderness. To see a land in the state in which it has existed since it rose from the waters and let slip its ice, a land untouched, unchanged, its only alteration a footpath so narrow your elbows are forever brushing against ferns and old boughs, is greatly reassuring to the spirit.

Bush-bashing on these tracks had stimulated my imagination, and the vast landscape had a way of putting human effort into perspective. The smaller one feels on the earth, dwarfed by mountains and assailed by weather, the more respectful one has to be—and unless we are very arrogant, the less likely we are to poison or destroy it. In the Pacific the interlopers were doing the most damage—bringing nuclear waste to Johnston Island, digging a gigantic copper mine at Panguna in the North Solomons, stringing out miles of drift nets to trap and kill every living creature that came near its ligatures, testing nuclear devices at Moruroa Atoll in the Tuamotus.

But this too was Polynesia—this rain forest, these Southern Alps. *Te Tapu Nui,* the Maori called their mountains. "The Peaks of Intense Sacredness."

Chapter 3
WAFFLING IN WHITE AUSTRALIA

Australia, the gigantic Pacific island in Meganesia, is an underdeveloped country that is bewildered and at times terrified by its own emptiness. People shout as though to keep their spirits up. *G'day! How's your rotten form! Good on yer!*

As on every other Oceanic island, most of its people live at its shores and beaches, so its edge is bricked and bungaloid, the rest an insect-haunted wilderness of croaking wind and red desert.

And the whole place is fly-blown. "It seems an unfortunate habit of Australians to speak through their teeth as if they came from the fly country," a Sydney judge remarked about fifty years ago, and he went on, "afraid to open their mouths for fear of flies." People there blink at the flies and turn their backs to the desert, showing total native imbuggerance, and say, *Go and have a roll!* or *Who gives a stuff?*—in snarly voices. And maybe Australians talk a lot louder because they are so far away from the rest of the world. How else will anyone hear?

The Australian Book of Etiquette is a very slim volume, but its outrageous Book of Rudeness is a hefty tome. Being offensive in a matey way gets people's attention, and Down Under you often make friends by being intensely rude in the right tone of voice. Australian English (one of Australia's glories and its greatest art form) is a language of familiarity. *Goodoh! How yer doin', mate, all right? How's your belly where the pig bit yer?* Understanding the concept of mate-ship is the key to success in Australia; and mockery is the assertive warmth of mate-ship.

Australians are noted for the savage endearments in their mockery, and as for self-criticism, no one is more mocking of Australia than the Australians themselves.

"This is the arse of the world," I heard an Australian say on television.

He was from Melbourne, which some Australians call "Smellburn." He was commenting on the Bicentenary, the anniversary of the ignominious arrival of the first convicts at Botany Bay. "Look at us on the map," he went on. "The country resembles a bum. And, look"—he was pointing to its contours—"two sagging bum-cheeks!"

I brought my collapsible boat to the coast of Western Australia, which is a state the size of Mexico, a place which that man would have termed the left buttock. This was Perth, and you never saw such wind.

"We're on the edge of the earth," a woman said to me in the nearby harbor town of Fremantle. "And guess which other writer was here?" she said. "D. H. Lawrence. For two weeks."

"Australia is outside everything," D. H. Lawrence said in *Kangaroo,* the novel he wrote while he breezed through Australia in 1922. It took him less time to write this book than I took to read it, because it is practically unreadable. He started writing the thing, anatomizing and fictionalizing Australia, about ten days after he got to the country, and he finished it less than a month later. Five weeks to write a 400-page novel. Lawrence is flat-footed in this book, but never mind! You have to admire his speed. And now and then he surpasses himself, describing a plopping wave or a jellyfish.

My idea was that my trip, beginning as a publicity tour on which I would be speaking—or more properly, waffling on—about my own work, would end as a trek in the wilderness. Perth was the first of the five Australian cities I had agreed to visit, to give lectures at literary lunches and submit to interviews. For me, it was total immersion from the first, because Australia is a country of readers and viewers, among the best-informed and most outward-looking people in the world, and with the most predatory journalists in the business—they rejoice in being "journos" and hacks in a place that is saturated in newspapers, magazines, radio, and television. Australia is full of news media but generates very little national news; so the media are hungry, they retail the world's news and culture and any newcomer—author, actress, politician, fellow hack— is pounced upon. Anyone is fair game—anyone from beyond the Great Barrier Reef.

And it was total immersion for another reason: Australians have the American habit of greeting most outsiders as though they are potential immigrants. They reserve some of their most picturesque mockery for such people, referring to Jewish refugees as "refujews," Italians as "ding-bats," "eyetoes," "spiggoties," and "spagies." New Zealanders are "pig islanders," and the English are "poms," "pommies," or "pongos." They seem to have invented the word "chink" for Chinese—they were certainly the first to use it, in 1879, twenty-two years before it was recorded in

America; but they also refer to Chinese as "canaries," "dinks," and "chow-chows." Americans are universally "yanks" or "yank wogs," and the English are occasionally "pom wogs." This distinguishes them from the real McCoy, known in Australia as "wog wogs." This is not to be taken as abuse, but rather as an obscure but nonetheless genially Australian form of hospitality.

Here I was among the "sandgropers"—the term the rest of the country uses to describe Western Australians—in Perth, a big brand-new boom city surrounded by empty bush, tall buildings in the middle of nowhere, with the scale and optimism and much of the brightness of a place like Portland, Oregon. It was a good place to start a life in, which was what a lot of the people I met seemed to be doing—they had come from South Africa, from Europe, even from America.

Australia is the only country in the world I have visited where Americans in large numbers have made serious efforts to put down roots. Thirty years ago, when the so-called White Australia Policy was in full swing, they—and other nationalities—set sail because it was a country of white exclusionists; and any number of pale jug-eared boofheads were eager to become migros and have their passage paid by a desperate government grateful for white workers. Now they go for the opposite reason, because Australia seems politically even-handed and has become, racially, a free-for-all. Many Americans there said to me, "I consider myself an Australian." Not once in eighteen years of living in Britain did I ever hear a transplanted American say, "I consider myself British."

I traipsed around Fremantle harbor, right next door to Perth, wondering whether I should launch my collapsible kayak. But the wind blasting off the Indian Ocean was much too strong for me. Out past the surf zone the strangely shaped sheep-carrier ships toppled in the heavy swell. They were like floating ten-story buildings, and packed closely into open wire cages were thousands of live sheep, off to the Persian Gulf to be slaughtered by the halal method—throat slashed, facing Mecca. It is a fact that most of the mutton in Arabia comes from Meganesia. Australia supplies the jumbucks for stews; and the majority of New Zealand lambs end up on shish-kebab skewers in Iran and Iraq.

My books made a sea voyage to Australia, and two editions had just arrived, a novel and a travel book. I was beginning my Australian tour by publicizing both of them. And so I did the rounds of interviews.

"What's your opinion of the Chinese people?" a woman journalist in Perth asked me on behalf of her magazine, and I reminded her that this was not an easy question, as there were one billion Chinese people.

"How long does it take to write a book?" was another question I pondered over until I realized that I did not have the answer.

.The supplementary question to this was, "Do you respect the main character in your novel?"

That puzzled me. Was this a sample of the sort of question I could expect in the rest of Australia? I said yes, I respected all the characters in my books, and I thought: *Even you, Digger, if ever you become a character.*

But there were questions I could easily answer.

"What's the main difference between a novel and a travel book?" a man asked me over lunch in Fremantle, holding a tape recorder under my chin.

It seemed to me an easy matter to be a journalist in this part of Australia. For example, one day I was wakened from a nap in Fremantle (I had been having a nightmare about suffering from cancer), and hurried to a Perth newspaper, an easy-to-remember tabloid called the *Daily Mail,* for it had made itself famous by printing a big beefcake picture each day, entitled "Your Daily Male."

I was asked to wait for ten or fifteen minutes, and then I was escorted to a cubicle where an eighteen-year-old boy was sitting at a tidy desk. One feature of this cubicle interested me: There were little snipped-out pictures of Elvis Presley taped to his blotter, his notice board, his calendar, and even on the dial of his telephone.

"Been in Perth long?"

No, I said. I had just flown at great expense and enormous personal inconvenience from America via New Zealand to join him at his desk here in a big building off the Mitchell Freeway, on the outskirts of Perth, Western Australia. He made no comment on this, didn't even make a note on his clean pad; so I asked him about the Elvis pictures.

He smiled—glad that I had asked. He said, "I just fell for him."

He turned his gaze onto the snipped-out and yellowing pictures of the doomed American singer. In the long silence that ensued I wondered whether I should ask another question. Then the boy looked at me, as though remembering where he was.

"Well, where shall we begin?" he said smoothly.

It was not a rhetorical question, so I said, "Have you read anything I've written?"

"No," he said with hearty confidence—it was as though he was boasting.

"Perhaps you saw the movie of *The Mosquito Coast?*"

"Oh, yes. I liked that." And he doodled on the pad.

"Now you can read the book!" I said, and felt I had made a breakthrough.

"No. I'll never read that book. Because I really liked the movie. I

mean, I liked it too much. What if I read the book and didn't like it?"
I was staring at him, but he had leaned over urgently to divulge a confidence.

"Then the movie would be spoiled for me," he said, and tapped his pad. "It's too much of a risk."

"Too much of a risk. I see."

We got nowhere. Perhaps there was nowhere to get? I turned the conversation to Elvis, and we chatted about him.

The young man saw me to the door and asked me the only literary question of the interview.

"How do you get your characters? You just think them up?"

"Sometimes I think them up," I said. "And sometimes they appear before my eyes."

"Good on yer!"

These clumsy encounters sometimes left me feeling alienated and depressed. That night I was the guest speaker at a literary dinner at the Fremantle Town Hall, a lovely gilded building—like many in this beautifully preserved harbor town—put up to celebrate Queen Victoria's Jubilee in 1896. I felt wobbly with sleeplessness and I began to worry that I would burst into tears if anyone mentioned my wife.

Almost the first thing anyone asked me at the town hall was, "So you didn't come with your wife!"

I went to the men's room and sighed and almost sobbed, and then I washed my face and joined the others at the head table. I thought, *I am the shakiest person in this entire room and I'm the one who has to get up and speak.*

The woman on my left said, "Roald Dahl was here last month with his wife."

I went quiet. The meal was served. Four hundred and fifty people, all talking at once, and drinking, and having a wonderful time. Looking at them and hearing their laughter I lost my appetite.

The woman on my right said that she worked in a bookstore and that I was one of her favorite authors. She said, "You should write some short stories!"

Was this another Australian leg-pull? I said, "I've written some."

"Why don't you publish them?"

Australians are famous for being familiarly sarcastic in this obvious way, but in my solemnity I became very literal.

"I did."

"I mean publish them in a book."

"I've published four collections. About eighty stories."

The woman on my left said that she had lived in Perth for about fifteen years.

"It seems very nice," I said. "Fremantle is very pretty, and Perth reminds me of an American city in the Pacific Northwest. All this clean air."

"I hate it," she said. "This is like another planet. The people in Perth are so strange. I can't describe it. I felt happier in Africa, among Africans."

The next sound I heard was a man clearing his throat loudly into a microphone, and enthusiastically introducing me.

I did not have a prepared speech. I made some remarks about traveling in general and I spoke anecdotally about China, which was the subject of one of the books I was supposed to be promoting. This sort of speechifying is an awkward business. You feel you are being scrutinized, like someone looking for work. You feel that you are standing here talking your head off so that at the end of it they will say, *He seems an awful nice bloke, Fred. Let's buy his book.*

As I stood there, speaking, I noticed a large man lurch out of his chair at a table at the back of the hall. He still had a glass in his hand, but he put it down as he staggered forward. He was well over six feet tall and very heavy—fat as a poddy, as he himself might have put it. He wore a long overcoat, and there was anger in the way he moved towards me—for that indeed was his direction. The hall was so spacious that it was quite a while before anyone else saw him. I watched him advancing upon me, as I spoke about the death penalty in China. And now a woman, much smaller than he, took hold of his arm and tried to restrain him. The way he tipped her over and dragged her told me that he was an engine of determination.

Was he going to throw up? Was he going to shout? Perhaps he was going to attack me?

I faltered and stopped speaking when he broke free of the woman and stood menacing me before all the diners. He thrust his fingers at me, making obscene gestures and gargling, while the woman—surely an embarrassed companion?—heaved herself at his coat.

"You're a wanker, mate!" he said. "You're a fucking wanker!"

There were hisses of distress and clucks of disapproval from the uneasy audience. Yet no one rose to eject him. Only that tiny tenacious woman was doing anything—now she was dragging him sideways, as he fought to shake his fat fingers at me.

By this time I had abandoned any pretense of continuing my talk, and I simply waited for him to rush forward and bash me and throttle me in front of the Fremantle Literary Dinner. I prayed that the woman tugging at him would be strengthened. My prayer was answered, as she pulled the huge brute to the door. Then he was gone. But not for long. A moment later, like the corpse that springs alive to scare you in the horror movie, he lurched powerfully through the door and shouted, "You fucking wanker!" And he was dragged away once again.

"People like that call the Chinese 'chinks' and say they have awful manners," I improvised nervously. I mumbled some more and then I abandoned the effort.

He was just drunk, people said later. *Probably hates books. His missus made him come to the dinner. Probably thought you were boring. Couldn't take any more of it.*

One recent migrant explained to me, *They're pretty frank, the Aussies. They don't mind telling you to fuck off if they don't like you. I mean, they'll just look at you and say, "Get stuffed"—right to your face.*

Another said, *I had my eye on that big bloke. I was watching him. Hey, I could have handled him. I've done martial arts.*

I did not dare to confess that I had been afraid, and that I had fully expected him to attack me. His being drunk didn't seem like much of an explanation in a country where most of the men seemed drunk most of the time.

I heard even odder things, as I sat at a table and signed copies of my books. It is impossible to anticipate the oblique and nervous utterances of readers jostling. *I thought you were taller,* they say. *I thought you were younger. When did you shave off your beard?* or *My husband and I are going to India next month—can you recommend an inexpensive hotel in Darjeeling?* or *You should use a word processor* or *You're my mother's favorite author—will you come to her birthday party? It's Tuesday.*

A scowling woman, with the face of an emu, stared me down at Fremantle town hall and shook a copy of my book at me.

"I've never read anything by you," she said. "This better be good."

Another peered at me pityingly and said, "Why do you hate Australians?"

And while more people filed past, with books for a signature, or with non sequiturs, a man stood just behind me and breathed into my ear, "You're pissed off, aren't you? Admit it—go on. You hate doing this. You hate these people. You're pissed off."

I turned to him and said, "Friend, this is my living."

When I was done I walked the windy streets of Fremantle, and it did seem to me a very precarious place, half a town on a little surfy strand, between the ocean and the desert. White Australia.

"Where are the Aborigines?" I asked any number of people in the days that followed.

Most of them shrugged, some of them jerked a thumb in the direction of the outback.

"In Woop Woop," one said, explaining that it was the generic name for the uttermost place in Australia.

After that, whenever anyone asked me where I really wanted to go in Australia, I said, "Woop Woop."

But first I had to finish visiting these cities. I went to Melbourne by plane, 2,000 miles away, across the great Australian emptiness, where Australians say nothing at all lives.

They call this the Paris end of Collins Street, someone said to me in Melbourne. Many people told me how European-looking it was: the brownstone churches, the venerable railway stations and the marshalling yard and the trams and the soot.

But no, I didn't think so. It was more spacious, much younger, and had more the aspect of a city in the American Midwest. European cities have a damaged and repaired look. Melbourne's most American feature was that it was obviously a city that had never been bombed.

My various encounters in Perth had given me pause, just as though I had been stung. I became wary. And after that, my overriding feeling, facing a large seated crowd of people in Australia, any gathering at all, or dealing with these people in banks or restaurants or on street corners or in taxis—buying something or just passing the time of day—my feeling, as I say, or to be more precise, my fear, was that they were not being polite to me but simply restraining themselves. Nothing personal. They just wanted to hit me.

Australians (it seemed to me) were people who appeared to be at ease when in fact they were simply controlling their emotions, and being on good behavior, because the slightest relaxation of this stiffened vigilance would have them howling. They were like people who had only recently been domesticated, like youths in their late teens sitting among adults, rather upright and formal and wooden, because as soon as they loosen their grip or have one beer too many they slip into leering familiarity and all hell breaks loose. What you took to be good manners was simply the forced, self-conscious behavior of someone holding on. Much of the time Australians had the exaggerated and unconvincing manners of drunks pretending to be sober.

A friend of mine had emigrated in the sixties to Monash ("The Farm"—it was a country of fond nicknames), a university near Melbourne. He told me, "Australians are aggressive and envious, but they'll end up liking you."

In Melbourne I saw my first Aboriginal. He was at a street corner, pushing the button at a crosswalk, waiting for the WALK sign to click on before he could venture across. I watched him from a little distance and wondered why I found this solitary man so strange. It was not his smooth face or matted hair, his lopsided posture or broken shoes. It was the very fact of his being there on the curb. Because there were no cars on the street. Because it was his country. Because this nomad was seeking permission to walk.

"They hate the Abos, really hate them," a newish immigrant from the north of England said to me. "The things they say amaze me—the hate, I mean. Me, I don't care one way or the other. Sometimes I look at them and feel really sorry for them, though—"

People talked about them; and I looked for them; but they seemed not to exist. They were less than shadows. They were lost in the crowd, and those Aborigines who had become city dwellers lived in locations that were given a wide berth by everyone else.

My question "Are there many Aborigines here?" was usually answered by an Australian saying, "Too bloody many." But where were they?

Meanwhile, I was the one who was supposed to be answering the questions.

"With all this traveling of yours doesn't your wife miss you?"

My wife and I are calling it quits.

"Yes, I think she does," I said.

"You go to such strange places, how do you stay so healthy?"

As a matter of fact, I might have cancer.

"I never drink the water," I said.

"Don't you ever get diarrhea in these countries?"

Constantly.

"No. Usually constipation," I said.

"You're so cheerful. But your books are so depressing at times."

Exactly. Because I feel alienated and depressed. Particularly now.

"Are you planning to write a book about Australia?"

Yes.

"What do I know about Australia?" I said.

Melbourne, settled and social, looked especially prosperous in bad weather, its buildings darkened by rain and its streets shining with the reflections of busy crowds. There, as elsewhere, the papers were full of harsh self-analysis. The Australian image abroad is one of swaggering confidence and contented good humor, but in Australia itself there is nagging self-criticism, a constant theme of *What's wrong with us?* The visitor is frequently asked for a frank assessment of the country. If you praise it they jeer and call you a poof or a gussie (their language abounds with abusive expressions for gays: quince, queen, spurge, pood, sonk, and Are you Arthur or Martha? are just a few). What most Australians seem to want in the way of a response is something funny and familiar, such as *You bloody diggers are rough as pig's breakfast, but that's what I like.*

I did my lunchtime spiel for 500 people in Melbourne's Regent Ballroom, as they tucked into their meal of lamb and potatoes. I wondered whether a crowd this size would have turned up in an American city to hear me stammer. This was an odd crowd, my Australian readers, ranging from very elderly fiction buffs and railway enthusiasts, who invited me to tea, or to trips on train junkets, to furtive youths with tobacco-stained fingers and tattoos, who leaned over, reeking of dope, and proffering dog-eared paperbacks. Two of these younger readers were musicians, who handed me an invitation to their concert that night.

Fred Fenton and The Fellow Travellers, Debut Gig and Record Launch at Fred's Hashish Centre—Serving You the Best Nepalese Hash and Ganja—Wed. Free.

"I love to see young people reading," someone said, as Fred Fenton packed his books into his Balinese shoulder bag and glided out on a cloud of smoke.

"I seem to have a very wide spectrum of readers in this country," I said.

When it came time to head for Sydney there was an airline pilots' strike, and no planes were flying.

"This strike is shocking," a man said to me. "This place is ridiculous. We're going down the gurgler."

"You're the great railway traveler," a reader told me. "You should have taken the Indian-Pacific from Perth to Melbourne across the Nullarbor Plain. This is your chance to take the train to Sydney."

I had two objections. One, I had vowed that I would not board a train in the Pacific. Two, I was in a hurry to begin my real trip, going walkabout in Woop Woop and paddling beyond. I was still reading Malinowski's *The Sexual Life of Savages* and was playing with the idea of going to New Guinea after Australia.

But I kept careful notes on the people who interviewed me, and I asked them questions, too. I had the idea of writing a little portrait about everyone who was writing about me. *Theroux has a rather strange taste in leisure wear,* an English interviewer, in a stained tie and a checked shirt and a rumpled sweater, had written, filling me with an urge to have the last word. I wondered what these frank Aussies would say about me and my clothes. Several of them had asked what these two canvas bags in my room were, and when I said, "A boat," they simply made ambiguous noises that put me on my guard. Perhaps this publicity-tour prologue was also part of my trip?

When I finally decided to take the train I was warned against it and urged to take another instead—"a lovely old atmospheric train." Well, I didn't say so, but they are frequently the worst ones. I didn't want atmosphere, I wanted a train with privacy and comfort, and when I boarded this sleeper I was happier than I had been since arriving in Australia.

This train had the sort of dining car that had just about disappeared in the rest of the First World: tables, chairs, clinking cutlery, and servers hurrying back and forth with platters of food on tin trays. The menu of the day was tomato soup followed by grilled flounder and two vegetables, and stodgy pudding for afters. No one ever ate this satisfyingly on an airplane. My waitress was Lydia, a small brisk woman with a pencil jammed into her hair, who had recently arrived in Australia from Poland, but was already using Aussie vowels and converted the simple word *now* into a triphthong. She intended to stay forever, she said.

And at the next table a man was offering a bag of candy to his son and saying, "Want some jolly boins?"

Mark Twain took this train in 1896, on his lecture tour through Australia. He remarked on the good berths and the bad coffee (he suggested improving it by adding sheep dip). He spent much of his trip staring out of the window, trying to get a glimpse of a kangaroo or an Aboriginal. At about the same time, Dame Nellie ("Sing 'em muck") Melba was a frequent traveler on this line, going back and forth for concert engagements. She took her last trip, too, as she was carried in her coffin on this train from Sydney to Melbourne.

It had always been a busy line. Before the promotion of Canberra to nation's capital, Melbourne was the administrative center, and I was told by older Australian civil servants that a great deal of government business was transacted on these railway carriages. One man told me that just a few years ago, prostitutes worked these coaches, turning tricks in the sleeping cars—the whole train heaved with bag-swinging chippies, while their lookout men, called gigs and cockatoos, warned them of the approach of the train conductors.

So I went headfirst, horizontally, 500 miles in my swaying berth, through Euroa, Benalla, Wangaratta, and Wodonga, and across Father Millawah, the Murray River, to Wagga Wagga, Junee, Cootamundra, Yass, Goulburn, and Mittagong. Towards dawn I lifted my window shade and looked at the bush—the stringybarks and the blue gums and the mulga trees at the edge of pebbly yellow gullies. The land was stony and eroded and when the train slowed down, the bungalows began, and the first large settlements and suburbs—Campbelltown with its jammed level crossing and inevitably a sign saying TRUSSES, and then Liverpool, Lidcombe, Homebush, and finally, Sydney.

"Mr. Theroux, I am your butler."

This was the presidential suite of the Regent, thirty-eight floors above the Sydney Opera House, facing east to the mouth of the magnificent harbor and beyond to the Tasman Sea. My butler was an upright man,

with a hint of Oz in his middle European accent, and he wore a white bow
tie, a white bib-like dickey, a black tailcoat, and striped trousers. He had
delivered me my luggage and was holding my collapsible boat, a bag in
each hand.

"May I unpack your bags and put your things away?"

My camping clothes for Woop Woop, my kayaking shorts and
T-shirts, my sleeping bag, my water bag, my tent, my cookstove and pots,
my two-part paddle, first-aid kit, compass, bilge pump, insect repellent,
and assorted tools.

"Shall I start with these?"

He heaved my kayak bags over to the closet and began fumbling with
the knots on the drawstrings.

I said, "That's not necessary."

He straightened himself and said politely, "I am at your service. If there
is anything you need just ring eight."

There was a bottle of Dom Perignon in an ice bucket with a pleasant
note from the general manager. In the living room—I had four rooms
altogether—there were baskets of fruit and more flowers. There was a
drinks trolley, with bottles of scotch, bourbon, port, vodka, sherry, gin,
each wearing an identifying silver necklace. A bowl of candy, another of
nuts. And the best touch of all, a powerful telescope.

I trained the telescope onto Sydney Harbour, conning east to the
Pacific. It was the most beautiful harbor I had ever seen in my life, long
and wide, spangled with sunshine and filled with coves and bays. I
focused on the little white tiles on the Opera House roof, and farther to
Port Jackson and the ferries and sailboats and the mansions and tower
blocks on the cliffs of the gorgeous bays, the breakers smashing against
the low black headland at the harbor mouth at North Head. Down below
me at Circular Quay, where the ferries docked, commuters mingled with
guitarists and conjurers, and an Aboriginal sat with his knees together on
a bench on Sydney Cove, nearer the Harbour Bridge. I toyed with the
frivolous idea of writing a detailed profile of Sydney and its people by
sitting here in this penthouse drinking champagne and looking at the city
through this telescope.

The butler came and went, taking away laundry to be done, bringing
me food and faxes, and rehearsing his Jeeves role for the benefit of the
reporters.

"I was in this room once before," a woman said, "to do Lord Litchfield."

And there were the standard questions: "Doesn't your wife miss you?"
one said, and another, "I'd like to ask you about the novel you wrote
about yourself—"

I spoke at the literary luncheon, another ballroom, another meal, another head table, but in spite of all the good will, I wished with all my heart that I could simply sit there and eat and listen to someone else. By that time I had read enough of Lawrence's *Kangaroo* to discuss its presumptions about Australia, but the only questions people asked me were about railway trains.

"I look like you," a man said afterward at the book signing.

I said, "Do you?"

He was middle height and rather Latin-looking, with a beaky nose, scraped-down hair, and tinted glasses, and he frowned at me.

"I very seldom read books," he went on, "but about fifteen years ago when I looked at your picture on your book jacket and realized that I resembled you I bought the book. As a result I have read every one of your books. And I still look like you, don't you think so?"

I said, "You're much better-looking."

He said, "May I take you to lunch?"

I had other plans, I said, but that was the first of many invitations, often scribbled on a card, or in a note that was pressed into my hand—

—*Come to dinner* . . .

—*My wife and I would like to have you round for drinks* . . .

—*If you're at a loose end please call me* . . .

—*I'd like to show you Sydney* . . .

—*May I interview you this weekend? It might be fun* . . .

—*You are the funniest man I've ever read. Please don't waste your comic gift. Write a book about Australia* . . .

They were eagerly, spontaneously hospitable. But I kept to myself. I bought more camping equipment. I went to concerts and an opera, *The Pearl Fishers,* at the Opera House; and I drank champagne and searched the city through my telescope. *You're the funniest man* . . . Now and then I thought about my life, about cancer and divorce, and became maudlin.

The room was my refuge. Of course, my first experience of such luxury—isn't everyone's?—was to wallow in it and wolf it all, gobble the fruit and the chocolate mints, drink the champagne, unwrap the soap, smell the flowers, take long bubble baths with the cobalt-colored bath crystals. But after a day or so, I became abstemious. I woke early and ordered porridge and green tea and a grapefruit. I spent the day doing publicity ("How long does it take to write a book?") and when I returned to the security of this penthouse I read Malinowski and studied maps of the Trobriands. I annotated travel guides to the Solomon Islands, and Tonga and Vanuatu. How odd, I thought, to be reading about the vast and dangerous estuarine crocodiles of Guadalcanal and North Queensland, and the orgiastic yam harvest in Kiriwina, as I sat here in the Lord Litchfield Suite sipping champagne.

One night I was at my telescope when the phone rang. "It's a call from London," the operator said.

I said hello but there was no greeting or salutation from the other end.

"I just got your medical report." It was a familiar voice, distorted by distance and emotion. "You don't have cancer."

"Thank God for that."

The contours of the harbor and every object in it collapsed before my squinting eye and the odd liquefied light of my tears.

A button came off my shirt, and I sewed it on myself, rather liking the thought of such a mundane chore amid all this luxury. At eight the maids came to turn down the bed. They placed a bottle of cognac and a snifter and a bottle of mineral water on the bedside table. I drank the water. I read until I fell asleep, and I woke, exhausted by my dreams.

With breakfast, the butler brought me messages on a silver salver.

—*If you're at a loose end, please call* . . .

—*May I take you hacking? My horse farm is not far* . . .

—*My husband urged me to get in touch with you* . . .

But I was happy with my telescope, and never went nearer any of these people. One day I went out, past the swimming pool and the five-star restaurant, and rented a beach chair at Bondi Beach, and I ate fish and chips among the surfers hanging five on the screamers and greenies and watched by lounging surf bunnies baking their bare tits before the startled gaze of Japanese tourists, who gave a convincing demonstration of never having seen such tits before, crowding out of their pausing tour bus, and madly snapping pictures of them with all the concentration they would have given photographing prize jumbo melons. Elsewhere on the beach, there were weight lifters and big hairy men and sufferers from melanoma. Bondi, something of a cliché in Australia, is a lovely beach. The people who go there praise it and defend it; the ones who stay away claim that it is unsafe and dirty, and that if the undertow doesn't yank you under forever, you'll gag on the raw sewage.

I was happy to return to my luxury suite in this penthouse with my camping equipment. But deeper than the sense of isolation I felt in all this luxury was a feeling of vulnerability, verging on paranoia, every time I left it. I couldn't wait to get back to the paintings, the sofas, the champagne, and the cool fruit, and my boat. I liked this comfort and quiet solitude. Sluttish comfort is one of the most corrupting things of all, and it easily becomes a dependency, even an addiction. At first I had wanted to share it; and then I saw it as my refuge and wished to keep it for myself; finally, I regarded it as a necessity, and I dreaded losing it. After even a short experience of luxury, anything less is like punishment.

Obviously it was time to leave.

* * *

In Brisbane, a celebrated trial, "The Vampire Murderers," had riveted the city's attention. "Vampire" was not newspaper hyperbole. Witnesses in Brissie testified on oath that three youthful lesbians who spent their evenings sucking blood from each other's arms had grown tired of this tame domesticity and gone out, abducted a man, and killed him by stabbing him in the back. His throat had been slashed and one of the women had drunk his blood. "I have fed on him," one of the women said—she was grossly fat and had piggy cheeks and a crew cut and was eventually convicted of the crime.

This riverside city was large and sunny, but my impression was of a great sadness in this sunshine and heat. Or was it me? The interviewers were more aggressive and blunter.

"I wonder about all these crazy people you meet," one reporter said. "They seem a little improbable."

"More improbable than that book that just appeared here, called *Australian Thinkers?*" I said. "More improbable than your monthly magazine *Australian Gourmet?* More improbable than your vampires?"

He squinted at me as though I had unmercifully bowled him a googly. It was odd. They could be so thin-skinned. The very mention of a funny name like Wagga Wagga could make them cross.

A note of archness had crept into some women's questions.

"In what ways are you different from the main character in your novel?"

"He is a sexual athlete," I said.

"And how do you know you're not?" the woman said, tossing her hair.

Several of them asked me, "What does your wife think of your book?"

Exercising restraint, I asked, "Is that a literary question?"

My throat ached from all this talk. My eyeballs felt swollen and boiled. The interviewers went on twitting me. I sat in empty studios that smelled of musty rugs, broadcasting my opinions to Hobart, Tasmania. My roomboy called me "Mr. Thorax." When I confided to a journalist that I had no intention of writing a book about Australia, but only wanted to go walkabout in Woop Woop, and paddling my collapsible boat in North Queensland, she said, "If the sharks don't get you, the crocodiles will."

Everyone in a jeering, mocking, we-know-better way warned me of the dangers in the outback—of the snakes and lizards, of the biting flies, of the heat and the blinding sun and the thorns and the terrible roads. The coast was much worse, they said: There were sea snakes, and sharks, there were sea wasps, poisonous box-jellyfish, venomous stonefish, and seagoing crocodiles fourteen feet long. They warned me of the plants and the wildlife.

There is a great fear of natural things in Australia. But no one mentions the drunks, who are everywhere and are a great deal more dangerous.

There were many croc stories in Cairns, my last city in white Australia, but there were even more drunks, and drunks gave me the most persistent and colorful warnings.

"You have to carry a gun and shoot their nose off," one man said. "Bullets won't penetrate their thick skin."

"If you see one, *shout* at it," another said.

"Once they submerge you you're dead," yet another said. "They can't swallow you. They come up under you and whack you with their tail, and then they hold you under in their jaws and drown you. When your body begins to rot, they eat you."

The more people warned me, the more determined I was to set off— first into the fly-blown outback I remembered from Patrick White's novel *Voss,* and the Nic Roeg movie *Walkabout,* and then up to North Queensland, beyond Cooktown, to a part of the coast that was nearer New Guinea than Sydney, a part of the map which no one had written about.

For some people Cairns was the outback. It was not, but it was on the very edge, and it was a pleasant place. It seemed to me an overgrown town on a muddy estuary. It had become prosperous because of its wonderful weather and its boat charters to the Great Barrier Reef for scuba divers and snorkelers. Most of its signs were bilingual, English and Japanese. It had the greatest concentration of shops selling T-shirts and opals of any I saw in Australia.

From the publicity point of view, this was my last stand. I was interviewed by seventeen-year-old Sandra from the *Cairns Post.* She was nervous, she said she had not read anything I had written, she was serving what she called her cadet-ship at the paper, she said, "I've never interviewed anyone before." She was stumped for questions, so we talked about her family. She said she loved her parents, her new baby sister, her house in Cairns, her bedroom with her posters and her records. She said, "I'd hate to go to Brisbane to work. Then I'd have to leave home." I decided not to disillusion her with stories of my traveling. Later, I gave what I felt was a spirited talk at another literary lunch, and when I described how the Chinese government frequently sentenced thieves, arsonists, and racketeers to death an older woman in the front row grinned and burst into applause.

Queensland is known for its conservative views and its gun-owning rednecks. Politically, it resembles a state in the American Deep South, and with these attitudes it even produces similar crops—tobacco, sugarcane, cotton, bananas, mangoes. The farther north you go in Queensland the tougher the views. And in Cairns, as in the South before Martin Luther King, there are somber gatherings of benighted-looking blacks— odd, soft, misshapen folks, with soft pretty eyes and long lashes. Even the fattest of them have skinny shanks and all of them look bowlegged. None looks alike and they shamble around in town clothes and dusty slouch hats locally known as Cunnamulla cartwheels, the broad-brimmed diggers' delight.

From a distance Aborigines were a menacing smudge at the roadside; but up close they seemed oblique and fearful or else very shy, and their clothes seldom seemed right for their odd shapes—they were either rail-thin or very fat, and many were barefoot. None of them ever came to my lectures. They were never at the literary lunches. They never entered the bookstores—not even the bookstores that featured Aboriginal literature. They never interviewed me. I saw them, but they never returned my gaze. It was as though they did not exist. Some were not locals at all, but rather Thursday Islanders from the Torres Strait.

"More like your blokes," a man in Cairns told me, meaning that these smooth-faced Thursday Islanders were like black Americans, and when I asked why he claimed this was so, he said, "Well, they're further down the tree, aren't they?"

I had been traveling in white Australia. I wanted to see more of the country, if for no other reason than to look deeper into the lives of the Aborigines. Now that I was done with this waffling I could go walkabout.

Chapter 4
WALKABOUT IN WOOP WOOP

Ask white Australians what "walkabout" means and they will tell you it is an Aboriginal's furious fugue, shambling off the job or out of the shelter of the humpy, and heading into the outback. It is a sudden departure, a bout of madness almost—after which the Aboriginal chases his tail. But is that so?

Back in Sydney, I looked for an Aboriginal to ask. "Don't call them Abos," people cautioned me—not that I ever called them that—but privately they muttered a dozen or more different names for them, of which "boong," "bing," and "murky" were just a few. Yet those Australians who were bigoted were completely impartial: "A boong with boots on" was a Japanese and "a Yank boong" was a black American.

Searching for Aborigines in Australia was a bit like bird-watching. Birds are everywhere, but only real birders see them clearly. Without warning, bird experts lean slightly forward, then stiffen and whisper, "Yellow vented bulbul," and you see nothing but fluttering leaves. In a similar spirit, making a point of it, developing a knack, I began to spot Aborigines. They were so often camouflaged by gum trees or splotches of shadow. They were frequently motionless, usually in the shade, often in city parks, nearly always under trees. There were many.

"So poor," as the saying went, "they were licking paint off the fence."

Perhaps they were visible to everyone, but if so, Australians never pointed them out. I began to think that Aborigines were only visible to those people who were looking for them. I kept track of my sightings, like a birder.

Mark Twain was in Australia for more than a month in 1895 and regretted the fact that he never saw either a kangaroo or an Aboriginal.

"We saw birds, but not a kangaroo," Twain wrote, in one of the

Australian chapters of his round-the-world tour, *Following the Equator,*
"not an emu, not an ornithorhyncus [sic], not a lecturer, not a native.
Indeed, the land seemed quite destitute of game. But I have misused the
word native. In Australia it is applied to Australian-born whites only. I
should have said that we saw no Aboriginals—no 'blackfellows.' And to
this day I have never seen one."

"I would walk thirty miles to see a stuffed one," he sighs towards the
end of his Australian tour.

It seemed to me that the people and the problem were unavoidable.
There was a tidy Aboriginal settlement in La Perouse, at Botany Bay,
near Sydney's airport. I walked through it one wet afternoon with a man
from Sydney who had told me about it, and we looked at the hundred or
so prefab houses—down Elaroo Avenue, up Adina, across to Goolagong
Place. There were very few people outside and, seeing us, some Aborigines who were gathered around their motorcycles mounted the machines
and roared away, scowling into the wind.

"They're strange people," Tony said. He was Italian—first-generation
Australian. He was small, the sort of man Australians describe as being
so short he had to stand on his head to get his foot into a stirrup. He
didn't hate Aborigines, he said, but he pitied them—and he didn't understand them. "They never fix anything. If they break something it stays
broken. If they knock a tooth out they don't bother to replace it."

Certainly there was a dark fatalism about many of the Aborigines I
met; sometimes it made them seem sad, at other times it made them seem
indestructible.

"There's no trouble here," Tony said. "It's not like Redfern, where
there are pitched battles with the police."

Many of the Aborigines in the Sydney district of Redfern were notoriously scruffy. "Rough as guts," said the white Australians—these could
be last month's immigrant Turks, or last year's Sicilians, or the pompous
people who snobbishly boasted about their convict ancestry—and they
went on to generalize about Aborigines on the basis of these rather
derelict urban specimens. The Aborigines aroused pity or disgust, they
provoked feelings of violence or mockery. They were joked about, especially by schoolchildren.

> Q: Why are the garbage bins in Redfern made of glass?
> A: So that the Abos can window-shop.

Everyone had an opinion and no one had a solution.

I tried to reach Patrick White, Australia's greatest living writer, who
was a vocal advocate of Aboriginal rights. He had created a memorable

portrait of an Aboriginal, Alf Dubbo, in his novel *Riders in the Chariot*—Alf's walkabout, his vast vivid paintings, his confusion, his culture shock, his drinking, his martyrdom. What about the word "walkabout" as a sudden departure, I wanted to ask him; indeed, what about *Walkabout,* the classic film by Nicolas Roeg, which—with Mr. White's novels—had been my only previous experience of Australia? I was having trouble with the meaning of the word and wished to leave white Australia for the distant outback that is summed up in the name Woop Woop. I felt that Patrick White could help me. In his advancing and opinionated old age he had been pronouncing on most subjects.

"I can't meet Paul Theroux. I am too ill to meet celebrities," the Nobel prize winner said, from his home in a Sydney suburb.

He died two days later—speaking of sudden departures—and the Australian obituarists went to work on him. Nothing made national traits more emphatic than a victory in an international sport or the death of a prominent citizen. In this case, the obituarists kicked Patrick White's corpse from Maggoty Gully to Cootamundra. There was almost no evidence that any of these people had actually read the man's novels. The vindictive philistines on Rupert Murdoch's national paper *The Australian* put a portrait of Patrick White's old enemy, A. D. Hope, on the front page instead of a picture of the man himself, and in any number of other papers White was depicted as a meddlesome old poofter.* Never mind his novels, what about the dreadful things he had said about Australia? True, he had been characteristically crisp.

"After I returned to this country," Mr. White had written, "one of the most familiar sounds was the heavy plop-plop of Australian bullshit."

In a public lecture he had called Bob Hawke, the prime minister, "one of the greatest bull artists ever," and said he had a hairstyle like a cockatoo. He had been cruel about the British Royal Family—"Queen Betty" and "The Royal Goons." He had ridiculed Dame Joan Sutherland.

But on the day the Nobel laureate was cooling quietly in his coffin in Centennial Park, La Stupenda was being draped with paper streamers, the sort you fling at ships. They were strung out from all tiers of the Sydney Opera House, and her vast preponderant bulk could have been

---

*From the Sydney *Daily Telegraph Mirror,* 21 Feb., 1991: "A magistrate has outraged police by ruling that it is acceptable to describe them as 'f——— poofters.' . . . On Tuesday, magistrate Pat O'Shane dismissed a charge of offensive language against Geoffrey Allan Langham, 43. Sitting at Lismore on the State's north coast, Ms. O'Shane said the words 'f——— poofters' were not as upsetting as the term 'collateral damage,' used by military officials to describe human casualties. In the past three months, the NSW magistrates have ruled it acceptable to call police 'pigs' and to use the word 'shit' in public."

mistaken for an ocean liner as, after her final bow in Meyerbeer's religious farrago "The Huge Nuts" (as I heard it jocosely called), she said she was proud to be an Australian, sang "There's No Place Like Home," announced that she would never sing again, and flew back to her mansion in Switzerland. It was all walkabouts that week.

Reminding myself of the details in the movie, I used Nicolas Roeg's *Walkabout* to guide me around the city, and beyond it to the outback, because that is precisely the direction of the movie's plot.

No one I met in Australia or elsewhere who had seen *Walkabout* had forgotten the film's power or denied that they had been enchanted by it. After being released in 1969, it soon vanished, and had never been rereleased. It was not available on video anywhere in the world. It was never shown on television. It languished, the victim of Hollywood infighting, in some obscure and spiteful limbo of litigation.

Yet it still existed as a notable conversation piece in the "Did-you-ever-see?" oral tradition among movie buffs, and it endures that way, because it has a simple tellable story. Those who have seen *Walkabout* always speak of their favorite scenes—the opening, a salt-white tower block in Sydney with its swimming pool smack against the harbor; the frenzied picnic in the outback where the father tries and fails to kill his two children; the father's sudden suicide against a burning VW; the desperate kids faced with an immensity of desert; the girl (Jenny Agutter, age sixteen) peeling off her school uniform; the shot of an ant made gigantic in front of tiny distant kids—and every other creature in the outback crossing their path—snakes, lizards, birds, beetles, kangaroos, koalas, camels; the discovery of water under the quondong tree, after which the ordeal turns into a procession into paradise, as they all swim naked together in the pools of sunlit oases; the close call with the rural ockers; the wrecked house and its curios; the lovestruck Aboriginal's dance, ending in his suicide; the madman in the dainty apron in the ghost town howling at the children, "Don't touch that!"—and no rescue, no concrete ending, only a return to the tower block (it seems to be years later) on a note of regret.

And that is the film, really, almost all except the spell it cast on me. In a seemingly modest way it encompassed the whole of Australia, nearly all its variations of landscape, its incomparable light, its drunks and desperadoes, all its bugs—from its most beautiful city to its hot red center. A work of art, and especially a film or a novel, with a strong sense of place is a summing up, fixing a landscape once and for all in the imagination.

The director was an adventurer who relished the difficulties and improvisations of filmmaking on location. His was a triumph over mud, dust, rain, heat, impassable roads, and deserters from the crew.

"A few went apeshit in the night and started smashing things," he had told me. "They couldn't take the isolation. One of the toughest sparks [electricians] deserted. The grip freaked out. The cook went crazy one night, and crept off and sat on a chair near the airstrip. This was in the outback. He flew off without speaking. It was his fear of all that empty space."

The movie seemed to me to contain the essential Australia, even its bizarre and rowdy humor—most notably in the scene in an abandoned mining town, miles from anywhere, where a loony man, hanging on, stands in a ruined building wearing an apron and ironing a pair of pants.

"It doesn't have Ayers Rock in it," Roeg said. "Everyone expected that it would. I was determined to make a film in the Australian outback that didn't show Ayers Rock. But it has everything else."

And it was the first feature film in which an Aboriginal played a starring role. David Gulpilil had had no training as an actor—had probably never seen a film in his life. He had been about fifteen years old, a dancer on his Aboriginal reserve somewhere in the north, in Arnhem Land.

I wanted to look at Aboriginal Australia. Going on the trail of *Walkabout,* in Woop Woop—the remote outback—meant going walkabout in the Aboriginal sense of the word—setting off in search of old visions and sacred sites.

The Botanic Gardens in Sydney were easy enough to find, and it is possible to sit under the spreading tree where the little boy hurries towards Woolloomooloo Bay after school in one of the early sequences. But his home on the harbor, the tower block with the swimming pool, was harder for me to locate. I knew it lay next to the water, and there is a glimpse of Sydney Harbour Bridge in the distance, but there are no other landmarks.

Thinking the tower block might be at the far edge of the harbor, I took the Manly Ferry and on the way scrutinized the shoreline: south side going out, north side on the return. Any visitor to Sydney would be well advised to take the Manly Ferry soon after arriving in the city, just to get the lie of the land. It is a long inexpensive ferry ride that takes in the entire length of the harbor, from Sydney's Circular Quay to distant Manly—an Edwardian township by the sea, with tea shops and palm trees, its back turned to the harbor, and facing the breakers of a beautiful bay.

Manly's smug and tidy little houses have names like "Camelot" and "Woodside." The town was named by an early settler who regarded the local Aborigines as fine specimens of manhood. But no Aborigines are found there today. Manlyness in the municipal sense is the epitome of the Australian good life: a snug bungalow of warm bricks by the sea, with a privet hedge and a palm.

Here and there on Manly beach were delicate dying jellyfish, small and blue, and so thin, so bright, so finely shaped, fluttering on the sand, they reminded me of little hanks of Chinese silk. Beyond them, some boys were surfing the waves, which was appropriate, because the first surfing—body surfing—was first done here at Manly around 1890 by an islander from the New Hebrides. (It was not until 1915 that surfboards were introduced to Australia, when the technique was demonstrated by the great Hawaiian surfer and Olympic swimmer Duke Kahanamoku.)

Manlyites who commuted from here to their jobs in the city had the best of both worlds, but the despairing father in *Walkabout* was obviously not one of them. I walked from one end of Manly to the other and could not locate the white tower block. Nor was it apparent on any of the bays on the harbor.

"You're looking for a needle in a haystack," a woman on a bench said to me one day as I searched nearer the city, among the bobbing sailboats.

And she explained. In the twenty years since the film was made, Sydney had become extremely prosperous—there were plenty of stylish tower blocks now, there were lots of swimming pools by the sea. It might have been torn down, she said. That is another aspect of a movie with a strong sense of place: It is an era in history, it is the past.

I was told by Grahame Jennings, a Sydney movie producer who had helped *Walkabout* get made, that the tower block was out by Yarmouth Point, past Rushcutter's Bay.

My taxi driver was Cambodian, six years in Australia, where he had arrived as a political refugee ("I would have gone anywhere except China"), but less than a year behind the wheel. He had struggled to pass his driving test. And his knowledge of Sydney's streets was shaky. He agreed that he was somewhat handicapped as a cabbie. Australian passengers often berated him.

"They say, 'You fucking stupid.' But I smile at them. I don't care. This is a nice country."

I roamed the harborside back streets, I detoured up Yarranabee Road and saw a familiar tower block—the one from the movie, with improvements; and beneath it, at the water's edge, the greeny-blue swimming pool. I congratulated myself on this little piece of detection, but I was also thinking how lucky all these people were who lived around Sydney Harbour. Because of the jigs and jags of its contours it is one of the most extensive pieces of real estate in the world.

The taxi driver who plucked me from Rushcutter's Bay was an economic refugee from Pakistan. We talked about Islam, about the similar stories in the Old Testament and the Koran—Joseph (Yusof), Jonah (Yunis).

"This is the first time I have ever spoken of religion with one of my passengers," he said—he was pleased.

But this was merely ice-breaking on my part. I came to the point. Had he heard of Salman Rushdie?

In his monotonously singsong Pakistani accent, he said, "Salman Rushdie must be punished with death."

"I don't agree with you," I said. I leaned forward, nearer his hairy ears. "And no one in this nice law-abiding country agrees with you."

"Rushdie is a bad man—devil, I should say."

"—And you know why people in Australia don't agree with you?" He was still muttering, but what I said next shut him up. "Because they're not fanatics."

The man's bony hands tightened on the steering wheel, and when I got out of his taxi he gave me the evil eye.

"Walkabout was quietly released," Grahame Jennings told me. "I collected the reviews. Of the thirty-odd I saw from around the world, four were negative. Three of those negative reviews were written by Australian critics."

"Why Australians?" I asked.

"Tall poppy syndrome."

Anyone who spends even a little time in the country hears this odd phrase, which means simply that people who succeed in Australia—or who distinguish themselves in any way—can expect to be savagely attacked by envious fellow Australians. It is also used as a verb: To be "tall-poppied" means to be cut down to size. That was the reason that Patrick White, in spite of his Nobel prize—or perhaps because of it—was spoken of as an insignificant and nagging old gussie. This merciless national trait is regarded as the chief reason for gifted Australians emigrating to countries where they are—or so they say—properly appreciated.

" 'What right does this foreigner have to come and make a film about Australia?' was one criticism."

"That's ridiculous."

" 'Too many contradictions about the geography in the film,' was another. 'You can't get to the outback by driving from Sydney—' "

But you can. You might be the desperate alcoholic father leaving Yarranabee Road with his kids, intending to shoot them, or you might be a visitor to Syndey with a rental car, yearning for the open spaces. In either case, you head up George Street and keep driving, first following signs for Parramatta. In this sprawl of sunburned bungalows, each one with its own lizards and its own dead hedges and its own peculiar-smelling lantana (but this bush usually smelled of cats); the discount stores and bad hotels and bottle shops and used car lots with tacky flapping banners, through Emu Plains and Blacktown—almost until the

road rises into the first wooded slopes of the Blue Mountains, you begin
to understand the disgusted snarl with which people in Sydney always
utter the phrase *the Western Suburbs.*

Ascending the escarpment that winds towards Katoomba, I was in a
different landscape—mountainous, cool, green, with ravines and can-
yons, the gum trees having given over to pines. After these heights, it is
a long slow descent to Lithgow, and not many miles farther on I felt I was
truly in sunset country. Here, near Wallerawang on the Great Western
Highway, less than two hours from Sydney, the proof of it: a big brown
kangaroo, lying dead by the side of the road.

Dubbo, where Alf the Aboriginal in *Riders in the Chariot* could have
come from, is two or three hours more, and Bourke four or five. But out
there in the west of New South Wales—Bourke in one direction, Wil-
cannia in the other—you will have achieved your simple goal of driving
from Sydney to the outback in a long day.

"Back o' Bourke" is an Australian expression for any out-of-the-way
place, and there are dozens more—perhaps more euphemisms in Australia for remoteness (outback, wayback, back o' sunset, behind death
o'day, Woop Woop, and so forth) than in any other language; but this
is obviously because there is more remoteness in Australia than in most
other countries—more empty space. These words are like little lonely
cries of being lost, speaking of a solitude that is like exile on this huge
island.

Somewhere before Dubbo I was distracted by bewitching names on the
map and found myself detouring to places like Wattle Flat or Oberon or
Budgee Budgee (turn right at Mudgee), just to look at the small round
hills, the frisky sheep, and the gum trees. It is hard to imagine anywhere
on earth so pretty and peaceful as these hamlets in Australia's hinterland,
green and cool in springtime September.

I was halfway to Woop Woop. I continued the rest of the way, to Alice
Springs in the dead red center of the island of Australia, leaving my
collapsible kayak behind in Sydney with my butler, who still believed the
two big bags contained clothes.

I have usually yawned at travelers who describe landscapes from the
window of a plane passing overhead, but the Australian landscape is well
suited to such treatment, the bird's-eye view.

After the hills and square patches and pockets of farmland just west of
Sydney, the greeny-yellow crops vanish, the rivers and lakes turn white
and great gray ribbons appear and fade like enormous drips and spills of
a red so red that they seem like bloodstains a hundred miles long. This
is the beginning of the Simpson Desert, and there is so much of it that it

takes hours to cross it flying in a jet at 500 miles an hour, and even at that you are only halfway over the country. With every passing minute the colors change from gray to mauve to pink and to a bleached bone-white that is chalky enough to pass for the Chinese color of death. No road, no water, no life, not even names on the map. I remembered Bruce Chatwin in 1983 stabbing his finger excitedly onto a map of the outback, thrilled by its emptiness, and saying to me, "Nothing there! Nothing there! Nothing there! I want to go there!"

(Later that year, Chatwin sent me a postcard from the outback: *All going well down under. . . . Have become interested in a very extreme situation—of Spanish monks in an Aboriginal mission, and am about to start sketching an outline. Anyway the crisis of "shall-never-write-another-line" sort is now over. As always, Bruce.*)

The Australian surface is stubbly, the gravelly texture a wilderness of boulders and wind. Then there is the so-called Dingo Fence, or Vermin Proof Fence, put up by the Wild Dog Destruction Board to keep the dingos out. This structure is such a serious effort it is longer (they say) than the Great Wall of China, and much more secure, and more clearly visible from the moon.

Farther on, below the flight path the land is scooped out and whitened. It is drizzling with sand—vast streaks of it. It becomes a rucked-up and striped horse blanket, a thousand squares miles of wool. And soon after there are ridges of red hills and black patches of trees and the gouges of dry creeks, literally billabongs (dead creeks).

And it occurs to me that this is not like another planet but like the bottom of the sea after an ocean has drained away. It is Oceania after someone has pulled the plug. And sure enough a few days later I was hiking in the cliffs of those same mountains, in the Macdonnell Ranges, and found small broken fossils in the red rock—"nautiloids," the distant cousins of squid deposited here when this was an inland sea.

Alice Springs is here in the middle of these red ranges, a jumbled little one-story town, which is a railhead and a road junction and the confluence of three rivers—billabongs once again, because there is not a drop of water in them, only hot sand and tilted gum trees and Aborigines squatting in family groups in the splotches of shade. The Todd River is the widest, and the driest. Like many Australian rivers—few of them contained water—it looked like a bad road, but wider than others I had seen. It is said that if you've seen the Todd River flow three times you can consider yourself a local.

I walked around town, noting the meeting places of Aborigines and generally chatting.

"I'm not a racist—I just hate Abos."

This neat and commonly uttered absurdity was put to me by a woman on my first day in Alice Springs. When I said that I had come to the town to meet some Aborigines she began seething. It is probably worth putting down what she said, because so many people I met said the same things, and only the tone of voice varied—ranging from sorrowful to apoplectic. Hers was outraged.

"They drink—they're always drunk and hanging around town. They're slobs, they're stupid. Their clothes are in rags—and they have money too! They're always fighting, and sometimes they're really dangerous."

I always smiled ruefully at this rant, because it was a true description of so many white Australians I had seen. I could never keep a straight face when I heard one of these leathery diggers turn sententious over the drinking habits of Aborigines, for whom they themselves were the alcoholic role models.

"There was a blackfella, worked for Kerry's father as a stockman outside Adelaide. He went walkabout. He comes back after aideen months and says, 'Where's my job?' "

The speaker, Trevor Something, was barefoot, twisting his greasy hat, a tattooed and ranting ringer, snatching at his three boisterous kids, and snarling at Kerry. He had a stubbie of Castlemaine Four X in his fist.

I wanted to laugh, because he was another one, a white Australian imputing slovenly habits to Aborigines and then behaving in precisely the same way, except the white Australian always did it wearing a hat—a Sewell's Sweat-Free Felt for preference, and in certain seasons in a brown, ankle-length Driazabone raincoat.

"We're not racists anymore," Trevor said. "They're the racists!"

It was true that Trevor was a ringer, an ocker—a redneck—but I had heard the same twanging sentiments more prettily phrased from the mouths of accomplished and well-educated people in Sydney and Melbourne, and a well-bred woman from Perth had said to me, "All Abos are liars."

When I encouraged Trevor to reminisce, he said, "We used to come up here to Alice Springs and get into fights with the blackfellas. Mind you, there are some first-class blackfellas. Some of the nicest blokes you'd ever want to meet."

"They've got some funny ideas, though," his wife Kerry said. "We just come up from Ayers Rock. Blackfella we met said he wouldn't set foot on it. It would be like climbing over a pregnant woman's belly. He says to me, 'That rock is the pregnancy of the earth—swelling up, see.' Yairs, but there were plenty of drunken blackfellas all around Ayers Rock, and they didn't look too bothered."

"Maybe they had gone walkabout?" I asked.

"Yeh. They disappear," Trevor said. "They go mental."

The notion was that the Aboriginal lost his grip and in a severely manic mood whirled out of sight, endlessly perambulating the outback.

The Aborigines I met denied this, and they were unanimous in agreeing on the meaning of "walkabout."

"It means walking," Roy Curtis said. Roy was an Aboriginal of the Walbiri people in Yuendumu, 400 dusty kilometers to the northwest.

It is in that simple sense of walking that the word is used in, for example, Psalm 23 in Aboriginal Pidgin: *"Big Name makum camp alonga grass, takum blackfella walkabout longa, no frightem no more hurry watta."* ("He maketh me to lie down in green pastures: he leadeth me beside the still waters.")

Big soft potbelly, skinny legs, long eyelashes, whispering Roy Curtis was a part-time painter of dot pictures, waiting under gum trees in Alice Springs for compensation from the idiot who cracked up his car.

"It means going home," he said, and sounded as though he yearned to do that very thing.

"The word has a specific meaning," Darryl Pearce, director of the Institute of Aboriginal Development, told me. "It is when a person leaves to go to the outback on ceremonial business or family business, to visit sacred sites, to be with people of his own nation."

I had left my car and walked across a wide dry riverbed in Alice Springs to reach Darryl's office. This river, a tributary of the Todd, was crammed with cast-off beer cans and wine jugs from Aboriginal drinkers, and here and there against its banks, under the gum trees, were little abandoned camps, tattered blankets, and a litter of torn paper.

Two Aborigines were sitting impassively under a gum tree like people cast in bronze, a man and woman holding hands. I talked to the man, who was named Eric, about a scheme to dam one of the rivers. It was one of the explosive Aboriginal issues in Alice Springs at the moment; if the scheme went ahead it would mean that an Aboriginal sacred site would be underwater.

"How would you like it if Westminster Abbey were destroyed?" some people argued, fumbling about for an analogy.

They were often greeted with a reply something like, "That site's about as sacred as fly's arse."

There were sacred sites all over town. One was a fenced-off rock protruding, like a small fallen asteroid, from a parking lot of a pub that had borrowed its name: The Dog Rock Inn.

What was more important—I asked these two people sitting on the bank of the dry river—saving the town from flooding, or preserving the sacred site?

Eric said, "Preserving the site, I reckon."

Then I walked on to the Institute and heard a fierce version of this view from Darryl.

As for the word "walkabout," Darryl said he understood the concept well, because he himself was an Aboriginal. He could have fooled me. He was pasty-faced, freckled, somewhat stocky, with brownish hair cut short. I would have guessed Irish. He looked like any number of the drinkers and shopkeepers and taxi drivers who denounced Aborigines as boongs and layabouts.

"The expression 'part-Aboriginal' is bullshit," Darryl said. "Either you are an Aboriginal or you aren't. It's not a question of color but of identity. We are all colors."

His mother had been a full-blooded Aboriginal, one parent a Mudbara from the Barkly Tablelands, the other an Aranda from near Alice Springs.

"People ask us why we're angry," he said.

I had not asked him that. Angry was not a word I associated with any Aborigines I had met, who had seemed to me more waif-like and bewildered.

"We've been in Australia for forty thousand years, and what good has that done us? Before 1960 it was illegal for a white Australian to marry an Aboriginal. We had no status. Until 1964 it was illegal for an Aboriginal to buy or drink alcohol—and anyone supplying an Aboriginal with alcohol could be jailed. We weren't even citizens of Australia until 1967."

"If Aborigines weren't citizens, what were they?"

"We were wards of the state. The state had total power over us," Darryl said. "The 1967 Referendum gave us citizenship. Wouldn't it have made more sense to ask us whether we wanted to be citizens? Yet no one asked us."

"Isn't it better to be a full citizen than a ward of the state?"

"We don't want to be either one. Something was taken away from us in sixty-seven. It was the blackest day in our history."

Before I could ask him another question—and I wanted to, because I did not understand his reasons for seeing the citizenship issue as sinister—he went on, "We pay for things we don't use. Lots of things are offered to us, but what good are they? We're entitled to so many services that mean nothing to us. We don't access the mainstream. It doesn't matter whether roads and schools and hospitals are built for us if we don't want them."

I said, "Then what do you want?"

"Our aim is to control our own future," he said. "We want to make our own decisions."

In a word, Aborigines had no power. Keeping the Aborigines power-less, he said, was the hidden reason behind many government policies.

"Look at the Aboriginal languages—what do you know about them?"

I said I had been to the Central Land Council in Alice Springs, because so many of the Aboriginal issues related to land questions. I had asked an official there about Aboriginal languages. How many were there in the Northern Territory—his own area?

"Umpteen," he said. Then, "Maybe two hundred and fifty?"

In fact he had no idea. I subsequently learned that when the first colonists arrived in Australia 200 years ago, there were 500 different Aboriginal languages in use. Only a fraction of these are still spoken.

"Aboriginal languages are not taught in Australian schools," Darryl said. "Why not? Because it would empower us. We would have to be taken seriously. It's ridiculous. An Australian student can choose be-tween French, German, Italian, Greek—even Japanese, for God's sake!—but not any Aboriginal language."

This powerlessness he saw as the condition of many other native peo-ples—Maoris, Fijians, Inuits, black South Africans. But Maori was taught in New Zealand schools (and, ironically, the highest marks in it had been attained by white Kiwis); ethnic Fijians had recently taken control of their islands—with illegal force and the imposition of martial law; and as for black South Africans, Nelson Mandela was very shortly to be visiting Australia on his round-the-world tour after his release from a South African prison, and Darryl was going to meet him with an Aboriginal delegation.

"Indigenous peoples all over the world get shit land that can't be farmed," Darryl was saying. "And then someone discovers minerals on it and the government wants it back."

"I've heard Australians say that in the course of time assimilation will occur and—"

"Assimilation is a hated word. We don't want to assimilate. Why should we?"

It seemed to me that Darryl himself—Irish-looking Darryl—was al-ready assimilated. But I said, "I don't know the arguments. But do you really want apartheid—separate development?"

"This whole country is our land," Darryl said. "White people need permits to go on our land. Now they're saying that we'll need special permits to come into town. And it's all our land!"

The lack of water in Alice Springs was no deterrent to the annual Henley-on-Todd Regatta, which is held in the dry riverbed. When I heard that it was happening I headed for it, in a walkabout way—you couldn't miss it: I followed the roar of the crowd and the plumes of dust rising like smoke from the gum trees.

The events were in full swing, "Eights," "Yachts"—bottomless boats carried by running men, "Oxford Tubs"—six people carrying a bathtub with someone sitting in it, "Sand Shovelling"—a relay race to fill a forty-four-gallon drum with sand, and men racing each other lugggging sacks of wet sand.

The announcer was yelling himself hoarse, but there was no cheering. The large audience—thousands, it seemed, looking like jackeroos and jillaroos and the sort of cattle rustlers known locally as poddy-dodgers and cattle duffers—stood in the blinding sunlight and dust, wearing sweaty T-shirts and wide-brimmed hats and rubber flip-flops, drinking beer. Like many another outback event—the Birdsville Races, the rodeo in distant Laura—the Henley-on-Todd was merely another excuse to get plastered in the most good-humored way.

"This place is a dump," a photographer friend confided to me in Alice Springs. He was doing a photographic essay about Australia, and the stress was beginning to become apparent. "Birdsville is a madhouse. I hate the cities. I get depressed in the suburbs. I can't win. To me, Australia is one big beer can."

By midafternoon the spectators at the Henley-on-Todd were so drunk they hardly seemed to notice who was competing, and they paid no attention to the skinny biting flies that are a plague in the outback. These flies are pestilential but much too small to show up on photographs of Australia. If they did, prospective tourists might think twice about going.

From where I stood, in the sand in the middle of the Todd River bed, I could see dark clusters of Aborigines under the distant trees. They were no more than insubstantial shadows. Two of those shadows were Michael and Mary, an Aboriginal husband and wife. I introduced myself to them that day and met them again a few days later in town. They told me that when they were in town they slept under the gum trees. Today they were standing mute and barefoot not far from the Dreamtime Art Gallery. They were covered in buzzing flies and looked quite lost. Michael had a rolled-up painting under his arm. They were both drunk but reasonably coherent. I looked at the painting.

"It's a kangaroo," Michael said. "I painted it."

"Do you paint, Mary?"

"I help with the dots," she said.

It was almost all dots, an amorphous pattern—perhaps a kangaroo but one that had been squashed by a truckie with a 'roo bar on the road to Tennants Creek. Michael said he would sell me the painting for $200.

He turned towards the art gallery and said, "They know me in there."

He took me inside. The gallery owner was a white Australian woman in a bright dress, sorting Aboriginal drawings in a folder.

Michael approached her. He said shyly, "You have my painting?"

"I think we sold it," she said.

"It was there," Michael said, pointing to a space on the gallery wall.

His wife in her torn dress stood on the sidewalk, staring through the plate glass and somewhat unsteady on her feet, sort of teetering.

The gallery was full of paintings in a similar pointillist style, dots on canvas, some showing identifiable creatures—kangaroos, lizards, crocs, and other paintings depicted the collapsing geometry of Aboriginal designs, which occasionally had the look of those dotty eye charts that are used in tests for color blindness.

I said, "You understand these pictures?"

Michael nodded. He blinked. The flies had followed him into the gallery. Some flies hurried around his head and others rested on his shoulders.

I pointed to a painting showing two crescents and a blob. "What's that?"

"People sitting in a circle."

I pointed to one showing just a blob, dots of two colors.

"An egg."

"That's a goog?" I said, trying out an Australian word. Chooks laid googs.

"Yah."

"What's this?" I said, in front of a large canvas covered in squiggles.

"Water. Rain."

"And that?" It looked like an irregular horizon of dots.

"A snake."

Michael said he bought canvas and paint here in Alice Springs and took them back to his house in the reserve near Hermannsburg where he did the paintings. Many of the canvases in the gallery were priced in the thousands.

"How much do you get for your paintings?"

"Not much," he said. "But enough."

I wanted to go to a reserve. I had been told that I would need an official permit to enter an Aboriginal reserve, but in the event I simply drove into Amungoona, a reserve outside Alice Springs, and asked the man in charge—Ray Satour, formerly a bulldozer driver, now a headman—if I could look around.

"Sure thing, mate," he said. He said I should pay special attention to the tennis courts, the swimming pool, the gymnasium, and all the new houses.

Why had he said that so proudly? Amungoona Aboriginal Reserve was fenced and ramshackle and looked like a cross between a free-range chicken farm and a minimum security prison. It was very dirty. The tennis courts were derelict, there was no water in the swimming pool, the gym was a wreck and so were the houses. This was all something of a conundrum to me.

I thought: *Perhaps rather than build swimming pools, the authorities should plant more gum trees for Aborigines to sit under?* There was surely something amiss when almost no white person spoke an Aboriginal language, and this in a country where a good two-thirds of the place names had Aboriginal roots. It made for alienation and hard feelings.

My intention was to go to Palm Valley, which was part of Michael and Mary's Aboriginal reserve, beyond Hermannsburg, about a four-hour drive west from Alice Springs.

"I wouldn't go if I were you," the clerk at the car rental agency told me.

A half a dozen times I was told this same thing, about other places. Some of my informants were Americans. There seemed to me many Americans in Alice Springs—they said they loved it there and wanted to stay as long as possible. They were the dependents, wives mostly, of the American soldiers who worked at the Joint Defense Facility at Pine Gap—a satellite tracking station or perhaps a nuclear missile base: It was secret, so no one knew.

"Whites aren't welcome in Palm Valley."

I could not determine whether these warnings were sound. I felt that much of it was just talk. After all, I had simply waltzed into the reserve at Amungoona—my being polite and respectful had worked. And I had made a point of saying that I was not an Australian. But that warning worked—in the end, I decided not to go to Palm Valley.

Being a foreigner helped me in so many ways. It sometimes provoked Australians to give advice. I kept noticing how Australians—the most urbanized people in the world—were full of warnings, full of anxieties about the sun and the sea and the creep-crawlies and what they call "bities," snakes, spiders, box jellyfish, crocodiles, kangaroos bursting through your windshield, wild pigs eating your lunch. It is apparently a fact that the Australian desert contains more species of reptile (250— many of them venomous) than any other desert in the world, and it has been proven scientifically that the Australian inland taipan is the most poisonous snake on earth—its bite will kill you in seconds. But none of this ought seriously to deter anyone from confronting the outback on foot, or even on all fours.

I was doing this very thing, perambulating on my hands and knees, at Glen Helen Gorge, 130 kilometers from Alice Springs, climbing the red cliffs, looking for the shy black-footed rock wallaby. Beneath this magnificent ridge of crumbly russet sandstone was the Finke River—one of the few rivers in the outback that actually had some water in it—and there was a large cold pool of black water at the gorge itself. I climbed to the top of the hill, a hot two-hour trek up a fissure in the cliffs, and wandered around and then lost my way—couldn't find the return fissure, only a sheer drop to the valley floor. But just when it seemed to me that *Walkabout* was turning into *Picnic at Hanging Rock* I saw a way down and followed it.

There were Australians swimming at the pool at Glen Helen. They were shrieking at their kids, they were munching sandwiches, they were drinking beer, they were sitting under trees with their white legs thrust out, and they had hiked up their T-shirts to cool their bellies. The T-shirts said *Freddy Krueger* and *These Here Are Strange Times* and *I Climbed Ayers Rock*. It was all families. They were having a wonderful time.

These white Australians were doing—perhaps a bit more boisterously—what Aborigines had always done there. Because there was always water at Glen Helen it had been a meeting place for the Aranda people, who wandered throughout the central and western Macdonnell Ranges. This water hole was known as Yapalpe, the home of the Giant Watersnake of Aboriginal myth, and over there where Estelle Digby was putting sun block on her nose (and there was something about the gummy white sun block that looked like Aboriginal body paint) the first shapeless Dreamtime beings emerged.

The pool at Ormiston Gorge was even prettier—shadier, more secluded, with pure white tree trunks looking stark against the cracked and branched red rock. It looked as serene as Eden, even under the bluest sky. And here too kids were yelling and adults snoozing and a few old women with scowling emu-like faces, totally unfazed, were kicking through the loose gravel. They happened to be white, but they could easily have been Aborigines. It just so happened that Aborigines chose to gather at other water holes—the large dark pool at Emily Gap, east of Alice Springs, was one. There I saw Aborigines swimming or snoozing or dandling their babies, doing what they had done for tens of thousands of years, but now wearing shorts and T-shirts.

It is perhaps oversimple to suggest that white Australians are Aborigines in different T-shirts, but they are nearer to that than they would ever admit, even though they are rather trapped and blinded by the lower-middle-class English suburban culture they still cling to. After all, a bungalow is just another kind of humpy.

About twenty or thirty miles northwest of Alice Springs on the road to Tanami, I stopped the car to look at a lizard squatting by the roadside, and heard the wind plucking at the thorn bushes and moaning in the telephone lines. And then I realized that some cattle behind a fence were looking up, with rapt expressions. It was the music I had on the cassette player, Kiri Te Kanawa, singing *"I know that my Redeemer Liveth."* I played it louder, and the cattle crowded closer, listening to that glorious voice.

I got out of the car and walked up the road. It was a typical outback road, with dust and corrugations, hardly distinguishable from a riverbed except that it was straighter.

A tin sign was nailed to a tree:

This plaque in memory of Jonathan Smith
who if he hadn't jumped the fence in Darwin
would have been able to do kaig. 13-8-88.

I had no idea what it meant, but I was sure that Jonathan Smith had been an Aboriginal, and this was one of those gnomic expressions of Aboriginal grief.

Going walkabout myself had led me here, looking hard at some of Australia's empty places, and I realized it was not just a dramatically beautiful land but a unique one, full of wild creatures which were just as strange as its people—its skinks and snakes and adders and wasps. Some I saw a few feet off on a track of red dust, others squashed in the middle of the road to Tennant Creek, and many were the subject of horror stories.

Some of the ugliest creatures were harmless, such as the thorny lizard, a horrible-looking but innocent spiny and scaly harlequin. Yet the Eastern brown snake—second most toxic in the world—was an unprepossessing reptile. There was Spencer's goanna, with its baggy yellow belly and black tongue, the gidgee skink, a spiny lizard with a fat prickly tail, and the shingle-back lizard that was so flat it looked as though it had been mashed by a car even when it was fully alive. The frilled-neck lizard looked like a lizard's version of Bozo the Clown, and the desert death adder tricked its prey with its grub-like tail. And if you went down the road slowly you might see, watching by the roadside, the military dragon, a patient creature that squatted on the shoulder of the road, scoffing up insects that had been smashed by oncoming cars. As for the carpet python, which hunted at night, it had heat receptors in its head and a whip-like response that allowed it to catch a bat blindfolded.

Aborigines had learned to live with these creatures. Some they caught and skinned and ate raw, others they chucked into a fire and left them until they were black and bursting like sausages, and then they stuffed them into their mouths. They were not frightened of snakes. They believed they were related to snakes—to kangaroos, to the whole earth; and they did not see the place where the earth began and their lives ended. It was all part of a continuum, a natural process, in which with the blessings of the gods they whirled around with the rocks and stones and trees.

They coped well with the inland taipan and the death adder. It was the white Australian who presented problems.

"Very little has been done to give [Aborigines] a sense of security in the country we invaded," Patrick White wrote on Australia Day in 1988, the year of the Australian Bicentenary. "In spite of a lot of last-minute face-saving claptrap from the Prime Minister—one of the greatest bull artists ever—Aborigines may not be shot and poisoned as they were in the early days of colonization, but there are subtler ways of disposing of them. They can be induced to take their own lives by the psychic torments they undergo in police cells. It's usually put down to drugs or drink—and some of them are on with these—they learned it from the whites. In a town like Walgett, prestigious white characters can be seen reeling about the streets on important occasions. In my boyhood when I used to go there to my uncle's sheep station on the Barwon, and he drove me in his buggy past the shanties on the outskirts of town, he said, 'There's nothing you can do for these people.' "

The statistics for Aboriginal suicides in jail are terrifying, because a jail cell is an Aboriginal's idea of hell on earth, and waking up sober after being hauled in for drunkenness—or for possession (being found with alcohol within 100 yards of a bottle shop)—the realization of being penned in is such a nightmare to a nomadic soul that many hang themselves in these hot little holding cells before guilt or innocence can ever be determined. But drinking was not the main reason for younger Aborigines entering the criminal justice system. They were usually arrested for petty nuisances—for breaches of "good order," or for property offenses, burglary, and vehicle theft. But seldom for traffic violations or shoplifting, offenses in Australia which were monopolized by whites. In the normal way, Aborigines did not kill themselves, though you would have expected them to be hanging themselves left and right from gum trees on the basis of the jail suicides—somehow deducing that they had a propensity for it. But no, it was the result of their having been taken captive.

There was no question that Aboriginal drunks had become a problem. But were they more of a problem than white drunks? With the possible exception of Finns in winter, I had never in my life seen so many people, black and white, dedicated to intoxication than I did in Australia. And

it was not socially disapproved of, not any more than football rambunc-
tiousness, or obscene rugby songs, or the peculiarly insulting manner that
in Australia was taken to be a form of mateyness—"mate-ship" being the
concept that helped Australia operate. In Australia generally a non-
drinker was regarded as a much greater irritation, not to say a threat,
than a shouting, puking drunk.

So why in a drinking and drunken land were Aborigines blamed for
being drunks? Perhaps it was their cheerlessness. All the Australian boredom and desperation was evident in Aboriginal drinking. They didn't
sing when they were drunk, they didn't dance or become matey. They
simply hurled up their supper and fell down and became comatose in a
pool of their vomit. There was a furious singlemindedness about it all,
and it was not unusual to see Aborigines under the gum trees getting
through a four-liter box of Coolabah Moselle in a morning, and when
money was short it was time for a "white lady"—methylated spirits and
milk. All I had was anecdotal evidence, but statistics were available, and
they were surprising. An authoritative report (by Pamela Lyon, for Tan-
gentyere Council; June, 1990) on alcohol abuse by all racial groups in
Alice Springs stated that Aborigines drank less than whites but were more
affected by it, suffered more physical disability, and died earlier as a
result.

I was told that David Gulpilil might have a thing or two to say on the
subject of Aboriginal drinking. As the first Aboriginal movie star, he
might also have views on fame and fortune. I had wondered about his life
since that movie. He had apparently been given rather a raw deal by the
makers of the movie *"Crocodile" Dundee,* his only other movie effort.

"He's gone walkabout," a woman in Sydney told me. That word again.
Then I was told that he had been sighted in Darwin, and in Alice Springs.
Everyone knew him.

"I saw him the other day walking down the street," someone else told
me in Sydney. "A tall skinny bloke. Couldn't mistake him. He's such a
beautiful dancer."

I was given a telephone number for him—the phone was in a reserve
up north. I called but there was no answer. I tried a number of times, and
then I was told that it was a public call box, somewhere on the reserve in
Arnhem Land, another Woop Woop place. I had seen call boxes like
that—dusty vandalized stalls, scratched with dates and nicknames and
obscenities, baking in the sun, the phone almost too hot to hold. I never
spoke to him—no one picked up the phone. Is it any wonder? But I kept
imagining the phone ringing on a wooden post in Woop Woop, under a
cloudless sky—ringing, ringing—and a tall black figure in the distance,
not deaf, just not listening to the thing, and walking away.

Chapter 5
NORTH OF THE NEVER-NEVER

I picked up my collapsible kayak, flew north almost 2,000 miles to Cairns, kept going by road to Port Douglas, caught a boat to Cooktown—which is spitting distance from New Guinea—set up the kayak, and started paddling the thing offshore, near the mouth of the Endeavour River, fishing for mackerel with a handline—bliss. But for nearly everyone in Australia this area is regarded as Crocodilopolis.

The wind was strong, a gusty twenty-five knots from the southeast, the sort that whips your hat off and stretches a flag straight out and lifts a sea into a short stiff chop with breaking waves. Everyone had warned me of sharks and man-eating crocodiles; no one had mentioned this wind. That seemed to me the proof that they didn't know what they were talking about.

All the way from Port Douglas to Cooktown the Hovercraft *Quicksilver* had been buffeted. Port Douglas was a newly Nipponized resort, with golf courses and spruced-up shopping malls. Japanese tourists in silly hats flew here from Tokyo to buy designer merchandise and to hit golf balls. They said it was cheaper to do this than to join a Japanese golf club. I was happy to board the big boat and take off, but I was suprised by the way the white foam was blown alongside by the wicked wind.

"It's always like this," one of the deckhands had said. "It's the worst place for wind. Going up to Cooktown, eh? It's bloody awful there."

The headlands and bays that Captain Cook named were a record of the emotions in his progress up the coast—Weary Bay, Cape Tribulation, Hope Island. The hills were arid and scrubby, the headlands rocky and scoured smooth by the wind. This same wind had blown Cook's ship, the *Endeavour,* onto a reef just here in June 1770, and then he had limped to shore to patch the boat. He slid up the river, watched from the bushes by the Aborigines of the area, who called the river *Wahalumbaal,* which meant "You will be missed," a word of farewell, for these Aborigines paddled canoes out of this place.

"People up in Cooktown get crazed by the wind," the deckhand said. "One bloke couldn't take any more of it. Started screaming about the wind—raving, actually. Went mental. Climbed onto the roof of his house and started firing his shotgun into the wind."

Windy conditions are the very worst for a paddler—much worse and more wearying than high waves or a big swell. But I was so impatient to be paddling, so glad to have a chance to do so, that I spent most of the day fighting the wind. I caught no fish.

"You're bloody lucky you didn't get a fish!" a man shouted at me when I got to shore. "Some of the mackerel here are a hundred and eighty pounds. They'd sink your little boat in short order. Some of those buggers are as big as me!"

He was very fat and had (as they said in Cooktown) a face like a gumnut. His T-shirt advertised a brand of beer, and he was smacking his lips. He clearly loved telling me how I had almost lost my life to a giant fish.

"I was more worried about the wind," I said.

"Never stops," he said.

I was about to ask him how many calm days they had at this time of year, and whether I should wait for the wind to slacken. I knew there had to be flat days, but if I asked him this he would have laughed and mocked me for being a bloody Yank and a tourist.

There were mangroves at the bank just below the town, and there I left my boat, tying it bow and stern so that the tide wouldn't take it away. I had spent my first night at a hotel in Cooktown, but I had wanted to make camp, so I pitched my tent on the far bank on the Endeavour River, which was just bush and dunes, and wild pigs. And as for the river, everyone said—of course—that it was full of crocs. A fourteen-footer had just been trapped and sent to the croc farm at Cairns, where it was called George and photographed by tourists.

Cooktown, the classic dust-and-bungalow settlement of the Never-Never, or distant outback, was one main street and not much more. It resembled an African town out of the 1950s, complete with barefoot, beaten-looking blacks, and those who were not downright lugubrious were roaring drunk in one or another of the town's many pubs. It was payday for the Aborigines—they got money every week, like a welfare check, but it was also compensation for the use, by miners and exploiters, of their reservation or their traditional lands and stomping grounds. Just up the coast the Japanese had started a silica industry, turning the Aborigines' sand into Japanese sake bottles, and paying for the privilege.

"It's drip-feed money," a drinker at the Sovereign Hotel bar told me. He was a local electrician, self-sufficient and somewhat a loner, like many men I had met in outback towns. "It's intravenous money. They just sit on their arses and they get it."

Cooktown was full of wild white men—fuller than any Woop Woop I had seen in the whole of Australia—and they were not just dirty and drunken, but sunburned and pugnacious as well, with filthy bare feet and torn T-shirts. Locally they were known as "ferals," they too were on the dole, and they poked their sunburned noses and whiskery faces into mine and warned me of the Aborigines in Cooktown, as they warned me of the sharks and the crocs and the poisonous box jellies.

"There seem to be a lot of bars in this town."

"Not that many, mate," the man said. "But every place has three bars inside it. There's the animal bar, the regular bar, and the snobs' bar."

"What's this?" We were at the Sovereign.

"This is the regular bar. Around back—that's the animal bar. The ringers, the ockers, the ferals, and the Abos."

He didn't like the ferals much but he resented the Aborigines even more.

"They're paid for being black. They get drip-feed money and two percent loans. They borrow money and buy fancy trucks and Jeeps. And maybe they forget about the loan. If they default they still keep the vehicle, and their organization comes in and pays it off."

He was drinking slowly and eyeing two Thursday Islanders playing billiards—they were bald beefy Melanesians with the look of boxers, and they were watched by some rather gaunt and drunken Aborigines who were waiting for their turn at the table.

"They're demoralized," he said. "Why work if people are paying you not to?"

He asked me where I was living in town.

"I'm camping on the other side of the river."

"Got a gun, mate?"

"No."

"You should have one. Everyone who camps out here needs a gun of some kind." He thought a moment. "There's pigs, crocs, all kinds of things."

If he had been like the others—warning me away from the bush, trying to frighten me with tales of giant fish and mammoth crocs, I would have dismissed this. But he was of a different sort—encouraging me but suggesting that I go armed. He recommended a gun dealer on the main street, Charlotte Street.

Padlocked and fortified against thieves with iron grids—standard protection for a rural gun dealer—the shop was dusty and temporary-looking, with most of its merchandise in cardboard cartons. The man inside was middle-aged—a tough man with graying hair and a sensitive and watchful gaze.

"New in town?" he said.

"Yes," I said and told him where I was camping and that I was planning to kayak up the coast.

"I have just the rifle for you," he said.

It was no more than the black plastic stock of a rifle, but nesting inside (you pulled off the shoulder rest to find them) were the barrel, the action, and a magazine. It was easy to assemble—screw on the barrel, clap the action on underneath, and secure it with a wing nut, shove in the eight-shot magazine. Not only waterproof and foolproof, it was also semiautomatic: One pull of the bolt and then you could fire as fast as you pulled the trigger.

"It floats, too."

"But do I really need it?"

"Ever see a feral pig? The wild ones? They have big tusks and they root around the beach looking for oysters." He smiled at me. "I've seen two-hundred-pound pigs. Terrible tempers. What would you do if one of those came at you?"

I bought the rifle and thought: *Two-hundred-pound pigs, hundred-and-eighty-pound mackerel, fourteen-foot seagoing crocodiles, man-eating sharks. Some camping trip this was going to be.*

"I'd like to try out this rifle," I said.

"No problem."

We drove just outside Cooktown to a little quarry that served as a rifle range. On the way he told me about himself—his name was Fred Hardy and he had come to Cooktown because he liked the open spaces. He was not a native-born Australian. He said he made a point of never using the word "mate." He ran several businesses and, as he was able to repair most machines and do electrical work, his skills were in demand. Cooktown was a place where motors were always breaking down and spare parts were in short supply. Any welder or mechanic could find work here. It was the frontier in many senses, a new start for some people, an escape for others, a fortune for a few of those prospecting for gold in the outback.

A hundred and twenty years ago, there had been a real gold rush, and Cooktown had swelled almost to the size of a city, with 30,000 people—

half of them Chinese prospectors wearing pigtails. This being Australia, a Chinatown sprang up by the river. The town was famous for having 163 brothels and ninety-four bars. Goldseekers traipsed over Aboriginal land to get to the Palmer River goldfields and to look for areas with more gold; there were pitched battles between prospectors and Aborigines (who were suspected of being cannibals). Not far away was the settlement of Battle Camp, the name a reminder of a well-known slaughter of Aborigines by white gold miners. Some great fortunes were made from gold in just a few years. Then the gold ran out and Cooktown reverted to being a little spot with a tiny population, at the far edge of the Never-Never.

"But it's funny," Fred Hardy said. "A fellow came in the other day and asked me to fix his cradle. Know what a cradle is? For sluicing gold. And his was huge. He's got a bloody great gold operation going on somewhere in the bush—no one knows where—and for all I know he's got bags of gold, too. I fixed his cradle. I didn't ask any questions. You learn not to ask where the gold prospecting is going on. Showing too much interest could be fatal."

We riddled half a dozen targets with bullets, and when the sun went down and the light was too poor to shoot by, we packed up our guns.

Fred said, "Want to see a bit of the outback tomorrow? I have a few errands to run. You could come with me."

I said I would, and the following morning I left my camp and paddled across the river to town once again to meet him. He said that because of the rutted road we would have to weigh down his pickup truck to keep it from jouncing. We loaded it with fourteen sacks of cement—about half a ton—and set off.

In the yellowy bush of thin gum trees and pale dry soil just ten minutes out of Cooktown, Fred peered at the wheel tracks in the straight flat road ahead and said, "It's all like this—for hundreds of miles. This is what we'll see all day. This is Australian bush."

Then why not turn back? I wanted to say. I hated the narrow track and the way the pickup slewed in the ruts, and whenever another truck passed us we were overwhelmed with choking dust. There was no shade here— the trees were too thin, the leaves too small. Sunlight slashed through the woods.

Several hours passed. He asked what I did for a living. In a rare burst of candor, I told him I was a writer. Normally, this admission makes the listener self-conscious; it strikes people mute or else makes them talkative—nonstop questions, unedited monologues about unforgettable trips or colorful characters. When they don't know you are a writer most people tell much better stories and converse more naturally. Fred was unfazed. He had read three of my books, and we talked about them, but he was as eager to tell me about Australia as I was to listen—and this was a guided tour of one of its strangest corners.

We went through Battle Camp and at the Normanby River we had lunch—he had brought a picnic basket—and had target practice: shooting the bolts off an old boiler that had become mired at the river's edge. He was a crack shot with his .38. He described a trip he dreamed of taking down this river in a croc-proof boat of his own design. He had actually seen crocodiles here; he was not afraid of them, though he said that on any trip down this river you would have to take them into account. He told the sort of sensible, rational croc stories that I liked to hear. His point was always: Be careful of crocodiles but don't let them dominate your life.

"I have a greater problem with sharks," I said.

"I don't know much about them around here," Fred said.

"Peter Benchley told me to be careful of sharks on the Queensland coast," I said. "When the author of *Jaws* tells you something about sharks, you listen and take heed."

"I suppose it's a bit like you telling someone about railway trains," Fred said.

More miles into this dry yellow bush took us to Laura, a small cattle station deep in the Never-Never, which contained one pub and several houses, and rumors of Aboriginal cave paintings. It was too small to be a town, too small for a village—"station" was about right. It was a proper Australian word, meaning a farm with the status of village; it was larger than a "property" or a "run." Laura was very tiny in the silence and the heat. There was no breeze; the only movement was that of the flies.

Lakeland Downs was farther on. Each station had a gas pump and a pub. Soon we were on the main road north to Cape York. Max, a peanut farmer whose crop had failed, was directing traffic on a construction site on this empty and dead-straight Cape York road. He was terribly sunburned. He said, "There's a car about every fifteen minutes."

Fred gave him a cold beer.

A kangaroo, pumping its legs, dashed in front of us, moving fast through the trees on a gravelly back road. I marvelled at its speed. Fred just shrugged and said there were millions of kangaroos around. Paradoxically, kangaroos are listed under the United States Endangered Species Act as a threatened species, but in Australia they are not protected. In fact, the Australian government encourages the slaughter of kangaroos, and in 1991 sanctioned the killing of 4,208,800 kangaroos to be made into dog collars, stuffed toys, sports shoes, and whips. In the shops selling tourist curios in most of Australia you can buy a little leather purse made from the kangaroo's scrotum. Down the road, we saw magpie geese. We saw vultures. Towards the end of the afternoon we saw big pale turkey-like birds pecking in a field, browsing among the corn shucks.

"Bustards. Endangered species," Fred said. "They taste fantastic."
"You eat them?"
" 'Don't shoot them!' people say." Fred derided the thought and mimicked again in a nasal nagging voice. " 'They mate for life! The poor mate will grieve!' " And then he smiled. "But I have the perfect answer to that."
"You do?" I said, because he was staring knowingly at me.
"Yup. Shoot 'em both."
At sundown, after this long dusty day of sunshine and buzzing flies, we found a bar back in Cooktown.
"Can I tell you something—and promise you won't take it the wrong way?"
It was an awkward moment—I could see that Fred Hardy was a man not given to exchanging confidences—but I said, "No problem."
"You're the only person in the world that I envy," he said.
I then realized how little I had told him of my life.
"See those ringers?" he said, abruptly changing the subject. He indicated a table near the back of the bar.
There were four people sitting together—two heavily tattooed men who were bearded and barefoot, wearing dirty shorts and torn T-shirts, and two Aboriginal women. The women, in faded, shapeless dresses, had scraggly hair and big soft faces; they sat with cans of beer resting on their skinny thighs.
"Gin jockeys," Fred said.
And he explained it was the local expression for a white Australian who lived with an Aboriginal woman, a so-called "gin." All Aborigines got a weekly check, and so the relationship, which might very well have been a fulfillment of true love, was regarded by most white onlookers as easy money for the man in question.
Think I'll go round back and bang a boong, Fred once heard a drunken man say in a bush bar. In the outback Aboriginal women were often abducted for sexual purposes. "Gin burglar" was another term. They looked for what they called "creamies" or "halfies," preferably a *lubra,* a girl.
"Tell you something, Paul," Fred said. "Some of these Abo women are all right. They buy guns from me and shoot pigeons—they like four-tens or twelve-gauge shotguns. They're good shots. The men couldn't care less. The women shoot, the men drink."
There were six or seven drunken Aborigines at other tables, swigging beer together, and they looked miserable—red-eyed, skinny, and very dirty, with matted hair. It was almost frightening the way an Aboriginal's bones were so obvious, and some of them looked like skeletons wrapped in crushed velvet, like zombies, or like their own horrific water monsters, the bunyips.

"They own a lot of guns," Fred said, "but they don't shoot each other. Matter of fact, they have a low crime rate. They drink and fight—the ones that come to town. I can't blame them. I've been in a fair few fights myself. By the way, I've been meaning to write a letter to someone in Hollywood. Why is it that fights in movies last so long? You see these blokes punching each other back and forth for ten or fifteen minutes." He thought a moment and then said, "Ever been in a fight?"

"A fistfight? No," I said.

"I've been in lots of them and they were all settled with the first punch. *Bang,* right in the face, *splat,* and it's all over. Never more than one punch. I'm not saying I'm tough or anything—all the fights I've seen have been settled with one punch. What are you grinning at?"

"At the idea of you punching one of these ringers in the face."

"I did that very thing not very long ago—a man made a remark about my wife. I gave it to him in the face and that was that. See, I have a problem. I suffer from a medical condition known as a very short fuse."

"Would you say these Aborigines are pugnacious?"

"One or two. But there are plenty of quiet respectable blacks in Hopevale, on the reserve, across the river," Fred Hardy said. "Listen, did you know you're camped on their land?"

I had not immediately realized how much land these Hopevale Aborigines possessed, but it turned out that everything north of the Endeavour River was theirs, a large notch of North Queensland. This included the little place I had hacked out for myself, which I called Windy Camp. After what Fred had told me about my trespassing I had an urge to go farther up the coast—it had been my original intention in any case—so that I would be smack in the middle of the Aboriginal reserve.

It took me three trips to town to carry enough food and drinking water for another week on the coast. The heavily loaded kayak sat well in the ocean, stabilized by all the food jammed fore and aft in waterproof bags. The weather that day was similar to that on all the other days I had been on the coast—sunny, temperature in the low eighties, southeasterly winds twenty-something, gusting to thirty. Beyond the harbor mouth there were waves breaking all over the sea, a short breaking chop, as the wind whistled around Anchor Point, Cooktown's headland.

The stiff wind annoyed me, but I was determined to stay afloat, and on this coastal run I could go ashore at any time and make camp, write something, listen to the radio. Or eat a meal—I vastly preferred my own cooking to the Australian tucker I had found in hotels and restaurants— flyswisher stew, fried barramundi, snorkers and googs, roast chook; bewitching names for uneatable meals. I had never in my life felt more portable or self-sufficient. I had shelter, food, water, medical supplies, and a seaworthy boat. No one was waiting for me at either end.

There were three-to-four-foot breaking waves all over the ocean, as far as I could see. I set off for the headland I could see, Saunders Point—a high hill and at the foot of it foaming surf. It was clumsy paddling in a beam wind, the waves breaking against the side and twisting the boat. But it was well known that both crocodiles and sharks avoided such suds—it was much too exhausting for them—so at least I didn't have to worry about being eaten.

My problem lay in trying to stay upright in the kayak with the wind and waves beating against me on one side. Being heavily loaded was a help—the kayak moved slowly but smoothly; and just the thought of leaving Cooktown, the last settlement of any size in Queensland, lifted my spirits. Most people I had met in Australia regarded Cooktown as the limit, the real bush, the Land of Wait, the Never-Never—few had actually been there. Now I was going beyond it, and going north of the Never-Never was like going off the limit of the known world.

I paddled in this beam wind until early afternoon when the gusts became more frequent, and then taking a compass reading, I was caught broadside by a boomer that turned the boat. Before I could recover—I was bracing myself with the paddle—another wave sent me surfing towards shore. I struggled to balance on the wave and shot down, picking up speed. To my right were the spiky rocks of the headland, but just ahead, on shore, there was sand beneath the breaking waves. Nearer the beach, I managed to slow myself and turn, and I went into shore backward—doing a backshoot, a surfer would say—and beached the boat without a wet exit.

It was too surfy at that moment to reenter the ocean and go around the headland—anyway, what was the hurry? I dragged the boat through the shallow water, found a sheltered spot to sit and rest, and beached the boat, tying it to an enormous log. I walked to Saunders Point and climbed high enough to see where the good camping places were—and I also saw a beachcomber's shack (or was it an Aboriginal's humpy?)—which I decided to avoid. Walking on, I came to a cluster of logs, a sort of picnic site, with a fire smoldering at the center of it. This was obviously where the Aboriginal fishermen cooked their food. The fact that the fire was still smoking unsettled me—it seemed to indicate that whoever had lit it would be back fairly soon and might object to my presence.

There were rusted cans near the fire—food cans, beer cans—and bits of plastic. Looking closer I saw that on every yard of this stretch of beach there were bottles and fragments of plastic debris: sandals, torn nets, lengths of line. There were cast-off aerosol cans, rubber tires, hunks of cork and wedges of Styrofoam. The plastic net-floats were inevitable, but what of all the plastic bottles, the beer cans, the empty oil drums? They had obviously been chucked off boats sailing the Coral Sea, they had been blown from the islands of Vanuatu and New Caledonia, and the trade winds had swept them to this shore. There was an enormous and ugly tidewrack of this indestructible stuff that gave this long windward coast a look like the rim of a junkyard.

It was too depressing to camp within sight of the junk, so I walked down the beach, found a good camping place behind a dune, and set up my tent. It was so hot, and I was so tired from the effort of paddling in the high wind, that I crept inside and napped for an hour. Afterwards, I removed all my gear from the boat and got organized: hung up my water bag, set out my stove, unpacked my sleeping bag and let it swell and loft, sorted my food and hung that out of the way of foraging pigs.

There were pig tracks and lizard tracks all over the sand beneath the trees. In the cool of the late afternoon, I assembled my rifle, filled my pockets with bullets, and looked around. Fred had assured me that I would meet an enraged pig. At least I had protection from that ignominious end—not that I relished killing an animal. I had owned a gun of some kind since the age of ten, but I had not shot any living thing since my early teens, and I hated anyone who killed animals for sport. I regarded this rifle as a form of self-defense and recreation. I practiced on a tin can and then walked on, listening for the snuffling of pigs.

This is perhaps the place to say that in a year and a half of traveling in the Pacific I did not kill any animal and only ate a few—I remained a fish-eating vegetarian except on the rare occasions when it would have been an unforgivable insult to refuse to eat meat ("We killed this pig in your honor, Mister Paul"). Why should any animal have to die in order for me to make my trip?

Beyond the coastal fringe of trees there was a huge stinking swamp, and this I guessed—from the tracks and the situation—was where the wild pigs lived. Overhead and in the trees were birds of all kinds—fish eagles and kites, plovers and whimbrels and curlews, and nameless whistlers and twitterers.

At sundown I made couscous and had it with beans and tuna, and a pot of green tea. I regretted that I had no beer, but beer cans were heavy. As I ate I listened to the radio—and when darkness fell and the night grew buggy I got into my tent and, by the light of my overbright flashlight, read *The Sexual Life of Savages*. After that I listened to the BBC World Service in the darkness: news of the other world, all of it sounding inconsequential.

The wind blew all night and it reached me even in this depression behind the barrier dunes. My tent flapped, and the boughs above me, which were all thin pines, swished and howled. The wind affected everything here, living and dead. It washed junk and driftwood onto the beach, it whipped up the sea and made it beat the rocks into spikes, it piled the sand into dunes, and it made these trees grow at an unnatural angle—all of them leaning away from the wind.

Dreaming hopelessly, I slept until dawn, when certain birds—I never found out their name—began their wolf whistles.

The strong wind made cooking difficult—no matter where I placed my stove the wind reached it and blew the gas jet sideways. I peeled an orange and ate it and eventually the water boiled for my noodles and a pot of green tea, a nutritious breakfast vouched for by farmers all over China.

While I was eating, sitting cross-legged on the dune, my tent rose up like a kite and blew into the boughs of a small pine tree. I intended to look for a new place to camp that day so I packed and stowed the tent with the rest of my gear, hung it from a tree, and set off with my rifle. I saw pig tracks, but no human footprints. In the shadows of the trees at the edge of the denser woods I sometimes heard a giggle or a loud squawk, but I never saw the birds that produced these sounds.

Beyond Saunders Point was a steep hill—Mount Saunders—and dotted on its slopes were giant boulders. But after I climbed halfway up I saw that these boulders were in fact anthills, seven and ten feet high. There was no path; I scrambled from one rain gully to the next, and in a shallow one a dark snake crossed my path, taking quite a while to do so. I tried to calculate its length, as I watched it slowly sliding through the depths of the tussocky hill grass. I am not afraid of snakes but I cannot rid myself of the African notion that it is very bad luck for a snake to cross your path once you have begun a journey. Caving in to this superstition, I changed direction and almost immediately stumbled upon an Aboriginal's humpy hidden in some bushes in the saddle of the hill, out of the wind.

"Hello," I called out, startling myself with my own voice. All around me were bees and butterflies. I looked closely at the humpy. (This small windowless shelter made of sticks and rubbish is also known by other names—a *mia mia,* a *wurley,* or a *gunyah.*)

There was no one home.

From here I had a wonderful view of Indian Head farther on and the long crescent of white sandy beach beneath it. One of the greatest features of Australia were these tropical beaches all the way north of Never-Never—miles of lovely sand and surf, and no one swimming anywhere near it. There are many large empty countries in the world, but few are as lovely or as habitable, or in a certain sense, as happy, as Australia.

The beaches were nameless, because people so seldom used them. Anyway, this was all Aboriginal territory. If they had a name for it they had not divulged it to the cartographers. The mountains and headlands had all been named by Captain Cook, 200-odd years ago: He had only been able to pick out the higher ground from his ship.

Back at my camp I carried my gear to the kayak and went farther along the coast, looking for a less windy spot. I struggled to get free of the surf zone but I saw—with dismay—that there were breaking waves all the way to the horizon: a wide, foaming sea. Nearer shore I dragged the kayak along and just ahead was a four-foot shark—the sort of sand shark that turns up every now and then on Cape Cod beaches. I splashed my paddle and he took off: no need to spear the poor creature.

I had lunch on a sandy shelf on the steep back side of a dune: no wind at all, but because it was so still the dune was very hot and rather smelly and it was teeming with mosquitoes.

Kicking along the beach, pondering where to camp that night, I saw a figure in the distance coming towards me. When he came nearer, I saw it was a small grubby man, moving slowly, looking down: beachcombing. His shirt was torn, his trousers rolled to the knees. Every so often he picked up something, examined it, then either put it into his satchel or chucked it away. A dejected-looking dog trotted beside him.

I said hello. We talked about the wind. He was eyeing my boat.

"Collapsible," I said.

He said, "Want some home-brewed beer?"

One of the warnings I had received in Cairns was: "Don't trust anyone who's very friendly. A mate of mine did. He ended up with broken bones." At the time I had put it down as just another strange Australian warning, in a class with the fat man shouting: "Those mackerel are bigger than me!"

But this beachcomber was small and weedy.

"Lead the way," I said.

He blundered straight up the dune and through a dense thicket, going a very circuitous route.

"There's no proper path," he said.

We walked on, bush-bashing.

"I don't want to make a path."

The pine boughs were snapping in my face and even the dog looked confused.

"Then everyone visits," the beachcomber said. "Especially official-dom."

He had a rather formal way of speaking, and I thought I caught a whisper of London in the way he swallowed the "L" and said, *Offi-shoodum.*

Finally we came to his camp. It was a patch of disorder in the bowl between two dunes. At the center was a pallet, with the dimensions of a queen-size bed, with a tattered canvas canopy suspended over it by guy ropes. This sleeping place was surrounded by immense clutter, but what looked like junk and debris at first glance was, if you looked closer, a collection of glass bottles and containers arranged by size and shape— stacks of them, and ones in long rows set up against the sandbanks, cups and tubs nested together. There were also net-floats—the large plastic balls that broke free from the wicked, turtle-strangling, dolphin-killing drift nets of the Japanese. A rusted wood stove had been set up next to the bed—I could see how this beachcomber might recline and cook at the same time—the beachcomber's economy of effort.

"This is what I call home," he said.

There were blackened bones, animal bones, on top of the stove's grille. To the side of the stove a heap of magazines—the *Reader's Digest* dominating the heap; and on a log, looking prim, a large pink plastic radio.

The man fossicked among the bottles and drew one out, while the dog yapped at me. I hated being barefoot here; I had thought that the camp was nearer the shore. But it was quite a distance from it, obviously to avoid the scrutiny of officialdom.

"Try this," the beachcomber said, and jerked the cap off the bottle.

I said, "Oddly enough, I'm not thirsty."

He took a swig. "Not bad." He took another, and wiped his mouth. "I made this batch last week." He swigged again. There was froth on his lips. "Thing is, the bottles have been exploding."

I distinctly heard him say *bottoos*.

"You're English," I said.

"From Kent," he said. He licked the froth from his lips. "Which is near London." He took another swig. "I was born in Gravesend. It costs six dollars to make about forty bottles of this beer. You just use a tin of this"—he indicated an empty can—"and a few pounds of sugar."

He became very intent on finishing the bottle of beer. He drank the rest of it in sips, neatly, staring between sips at the mouth of the bottle.

"And now you live here?"

"That's right," he said, and glanced around at the clutter. "In actual fact, I'm constructing a raft. That's why I have those pipes and those plastic balls. That's all my flotation, see."

Any purpose or design of those balls and pipes had been hidden by all the clutter.

"What will you do with the raft?"

"I'm aiming to build this raft and sail it in a northerly direction," he said with a certain precision.

"How much more northerly can you get than where we are now?"

"Around Cape York."

Good God, I thought. "Through the Torres Strait?"

One of the worst currents in the world—twelve turbulent knots of ocean rushing like white water squeezed between New Guinea and Australia.

"Yes. Through there."

"Any particular reason?"

He was smiling. His hair was wild. He was unshaven.

"That way I can go to Darwin."

"On a raft across the Gulf of Carpentaria."

"And the Arafura Sea. Yes." He had finished the beer. He put the bottle neatly away with the empties and said, "I'm not in any hurry. I've sailed rafts before. Down the Cabrera River in Colombia. I spent six months in South America. That was about eight years ago. Lots of adventures. Some dangers, too."

"Dangerous Indians?"

"No. I traveled with the Indians. In the South American bush you can't do anything without Indians." He seemed a little tipsy now. He struggled towards the bottles, rearranging them. "Kept a diary. I always said I should write a book about it."

Somehow, even standing barefoot in his beachcomber's camp on the shore of an Aboriginal reserve in North Queensland, it did not seem so odd that he should express this writing ambition. After all, I had the same ambition, and I was barefoot and whiskery too.

"Why don't you write a book about your South American trip?"

"I would," he said, "if I was in a hospital."

He was scratching his dog behind the ears as he spoke, and looking into the middle distance.

"In a hospital, with two broken legs. Then I'd do it," he said. He reflected on this a moment. "But I probably wouldn't want to do it if I had two broken legs."

"You seem to have plenty to drink here," I said. "What do you do for food?"

"Fish. Plenty of fish in these waters. I've got a crab pot. That's what I do with these bones." He poked the blackened bones on the stove. "Put them in the pot. Crabs love them. Also onions."

A bag of onions hung from the limb of a tree.

"Onions will keep for months."

We both looked at his bag of onions.

"Also 'roo meat," he said. "Plenty of that around. Here—have some."

He handed me a brown strip of meat that had the look of leather, exactly the shape and size of the tongue of an old shoe.

"That there is smoke-dried. Done it meself. Lasts for a long time. Years, actually." He became reflective again. "I found some 'roo meat under a box once. Forgot I had it. Two years old, it was."

"What did you do with it?" I said, trying to egg him on.

"Ate it."

"Two-year-old kangaroo meat?"

"Smoke-dried. It was delicious. Wonderful in soups."

"You make soup here?"

"All the time," he said. "Lovely stuff."

"Do the Aborigines mind you camping on their reserve?" I asked.

"They don't make a fuss. The ones in town are a bit rough. But the Abos here are good people. They're losing their old ways, though. They caught a big turtle the other week down where your boat is. They took some of the meat and left the rest to the wild pigs. Years ago they would have eaten the whole thing."

That was very much a beachcomber's point of view, the obsession with other people's wastefulness.

I told him I was camping myself, but that I was looking for a place out of the wind.

"Have you tried Leprosy Creek?"

"No. But I kind of like the name," I said.

He gave me directions to the inlet. I paddled there and at a little bend in the creek, I found a good spot—no wind and quite sheltered, and there I pitched my tent and spent the night. My only moment of anxiety came in the dawn, when I heard big feet crashing through the leaves. I grabbed my rifle as the noise came nearer—very loud now. I peered out of the tent flap and saw two wild turkeys—brush turkeys, with bald heads and yellow wattles, sleek black feathers, handsome, strutting past my tent.

"You can eat them, you know," the beachcomber said, when I saw him at the shore the next morning. He had just checked his crab pot: nothing inside. "You pluck the turkey and put it into a pot with a brick. You put some water and boil the whole thing, until you can shove a fork through the brick. Then you throw the turkey away and eat the brick."

He did not smile.

"That's very funny," I said. "What is your name?"

"You can call me Tony," he said.

I was sure that Tony was not his name. He was, in spite of his apparent friendliness, deeply suspicious of strangers, and from time to time he lapsed into silence, self-conscious because of my persistent questions.

He was very interested in my gear—my well-made tent and boat: He examined the stitching and the fittings. He looked closely at my pots and stove, the water bag I had bought in Sydney.

He said, "That's just what I need for my trip around Cape York on my raft."

I said, "Where do you get your water?"

There was no drinking water anywhere to be found on this sunbaked coast; the pools of water I had found were brackish.

"I go to Cooktown in my canoe when the wind drops," he said. He made a face. "But the Cooktown water is no good. They put fluoride in it."

It was completely in character for this beachcomber to be very fussy and complain about the quality of water in the town. Most tramps I had met in my life believed there was something profoundly unclean about towns and cities, and many of the homeless men I had run across in London—the ones who slept on the common land outside London in camps very similar to Tony's here in Queensland—many of them had spoken with disgust about the beetles and the filth in the charitable wards and dorms. The grubby beachcomber invariably believes he is living the cleanest life possible on earth, and personal hygiene is always a popular topic with tramps, who invariably boast of their fastidiousness.

I said, "Aborigines aren't very popular in Cooktown."

"That's because Australians are racists, aren't they?" Tony said. "If it wasn't the Abos it'd be the Italians or the Yugoslavians. They need someone to hate."

This lucid statement from a barefoot wild-haired man with a dog in his arms, standing in torn pants in the wilds of Queensland.

"There's some towns in Australia, like Katherine"—in the Northern Territory—"where whites and blacks actually fight all the time. But Cooktown is mainly a peaceful place. I get my beer ingredients there. When the road gets bitumenized it will all change."

"Tony, it seems you're well set up here."

"I reckon I am," he said, looking pleased. "I've got all the necessaries."

"See any crocs?"

"Only little buggers. There are pigs around but they don't bother me."

"Mosquitoes?"

I had mosquito net on my tent. Tony slept in the open air.

"When the wind drops there's mozzies. But the wind don't usually drop."

He hesitated a little—it was a sign that my questions were making him anxious.

"Catch you later," he said—the Australianism that means: This conversation is at an end. And he appeared to be heading back to his camp.

"Aren't you going for a walk today?"

He was carrying his beach-combing satchel. His shoes were inside, with his water bottle, his hat, and something to eat wrapped in paper. He never went out on the beach without this survival kit, and it gave him a look that was at once shabby and respectable.

He said he had been on a walk but that he had turned back. "The beach was getting a little crowded."

I looked down five miles of beach on the great sweep of bay and saw no one.

"I saw someone else on the beach. Besides you."

This was too much for him. He went back to his camp, and I fished from my boat. I caught nothing but it was a good excuse to bob in the ocean all afternoon. At one point I thought I saw some Aborigines fishing in the surf about a mile farther up the beach—perhaps they were the people Tony had seen?—but when I paddled towards them they vanished.

At dusk I made my dinner to the sound of pigeons' wings—they were making for the trees to settle for the night. There was wind in the upper branches, but it was quiet down below in my camp. Just before I crawled into my tent I saw, clinging to the fly, a large brown spider, about two or three inches long. I flicked it away ("You got some of the most poisonous spiders in the world here, mate. One bite and you're dead as a mutton chop") and zipped myself in for my nightly ritual: drinking tea, writing my notes, and after lights out, radio programs from distant lands. This sound of bad news was mingled with the frog croaks from Leprosy Creek.

Dawn was sudden and hot in the still air of Leprosy Creek, the sun striking my tent the second it rose over the mangroves on the distant bank. The sunlight turned the surface of the creek into a blinding sheet of tinfoil. And with this heat and light the birds in the mangrove boughs over my head giggled and whistled. These trees had wet, twisted root systems that held the sandbank together, and the murky pools beneath them teemed with mosquitoes. This was a tidal creek and at high tide I was at the creek's edge. I could not leave my tent without spraying myself with insect repellent. Still, I was happier here at Leprosy Creek than I had been in any Australian city, and I preferred camping in these lumpy dunes to sitting in the Sydney Opera House.

After breakfast (more noodles, green tea, a Queensland banana) I paddled out of the inlet and up the coast. The great sweep of beach was empty all the way to the point, and I paddled along under a sunny sky, thinking how lucky I was to be here, and laughing when I remembered Tony the beachcomber praising the taste of two-year-old kangaroo meat and saying, when asked if there were any crocodiles around, *only littoo buggers.*

Some supine humans a mile up the beach turned out to be Aborigines, reclining against a log, kicking their heels—an elderly black man, a full-blooded woman, and a boy of about six. The small boy was combing nits out of the woman's hair. He did it with solemn attention, searching the hair, fingering it, and pinching the nits and lice in his nails, while the woman sat slightly turned away from me. The old Aboriginal man simply sat looking at the sea.

From their patch of shade on the beach, they watched me come ashore. I dragged my boat onto the sand and said hello, and asked them—only making conversation—whether it was all right for me to camp on their reserve.

"No worries, mate," the old man said. His accent was pure Australian, with more strine in it than almost any of the people, natives and immigrants, whom I had heard abusing Aborigines. "You can do it. Now, your boat—we don't call that a dinghy. That's not a dinghy."

"What would you call it?"

"It's a *wongka.*"

This was the first time I heard this term for canoe: I was pleased to get it from an Australian Aboriginal. Later, I was to hear it, or a variation of it, again and again, throughout the Pacific. It is one of the proofs that the Pacific was populated from Southeast Asia and not (as Thor Heyerdahl claimed) from South America. In *Canoes of Oceania*—the three-volume authority on the subject, published in the 1930s—the authors provide extensive detail in describing canoe terms; they write, "The *wangka* or *waka* term is . . . widely distributed over the whole Malayo-Polynesia area. . . . It is found in Indonesia, the Philippines, Micronesia, Melanesia, Polynesia . . ."

I said, "You speak the language."

"I do speak it," the old man said. He was completely toothless.

He was wearing blue jeans and a shirt. He was eighty-two (though he looked much younger) and his name was Ernie Bowen. The woman—wearing a torn dress—was his wife, Gladys. She was thirty years his junior, but she was toothless as well. The boy was their grandson, Shawn, and he wore blue shorts. He remained intently combing and picking through the woman's loose hair.

"What language is that?"

"Guugu Yimidirrh."

He had to say it five times before I could hear the words clearly enough to write down. The word "Guugu" sounded like "Koko." He explained that the expression meant simply "Our Word" or "Our Language," and it was the name for the people who lived here in the area north of the Annan River and south of the Jennie, beyond the headland of Cape Flattery.

Meeting the three folks was a stroke of luck for me, because these people are historically unique in Australia. The Guugu Yimidirrh were the ones whom Captain Cook referred to on 16 June 1770 when in his crippled and leaking ship he wrote tersely in his ship's log, *Some people were seen ashore today.*

Captain Cook found them very timid. At first, with a sense of apprehension resembling that of Robinson Crusoe in precisely the same circumstances, he noted, "their footmarks upon the sand below the high tide mark prov'd they had very lately been here." Soon he encountered them in the flesh but they were not interested in his presents of cloth or nails or paper. They were delighted when he gave them a fish, which they regarded as a symbolic gift. They worshiped fish, they painted pictures of them on the walls of their caves—they were great painters, of their other totems, turtles, demons, naked people, dugongs.

"They were clean limn'd, active and nimble," Cook wrote. "Cloathes they had none."

A misunderstanding over some turtles provoked some musket fire from Cook's men, then peacemaking. And they told Cook some of their words. Fifty words were taken down in Cook's detailed log, and in this way it was the first Aboriginal language to assume written form.

"What is this?" one of Cook's men had said, showing an animal he had shot that morning as it had jumped past the camp.

"Gangurru," an Aboriginal informed him, and a Guugu Yimidirrh word became known to the world. They were particular in their nomenclature. It happened to be a big brown animal that was shown. They had eleven words for the different varieties of kangaroo and wallaby, from the small swamp wallaby *bibal,* to the *galbaala,* the large red kangaroo.

They were hunters and fishermen. They had weapons, they made dugout canoes. They had lived in this area for thousands of years. They did not practice circumcision or tooth extraction. Their great fear was of *Yigi,* an evil spirit which went about at night. For this reason they seldom went out after dark.

They had no word for love. For the Guugu Yimidirrh, friendship was everything, the strongest bond in the world. Marriage was regarded as a bond of friendship, not love. This surprised the missionaries, who thumped them over the head with the Christian Bible and turned many of them into Lutherans. Yet even the missionaries could not change the language, and the expression "I love Jesus" they rendered "Jesus is my best friend."

Cook was deeply impressed by these people. And even though he had just come from Tahiti, islands of "dissolute sensuality," he was startled by the Aborigines' utter nakedness: "They go quite naked both men and women without any Cloathing whatever, even the women do not so much as cover their privities." Joseph Banks, the botanist on the *Endeavour,* reflected that the Aborigines were like people before the Fall—peaceable, well fed, nomadic, naked: "Thus live these I had almost said happy people, content with little nay almost nothing."

After repairing his ship, a process that took six weeks at the riverside, Captain Cook set sail, the Guugu Yimidirrh watching him, and he took up his log again.

"From what I have said of the natives of New Holland they may appear to be some of the most wretched people on Earth," he wrote. "But in reality they are far happier than we Europeans, being wholly unacquainted not only with the superfluous, but with the necessary Conveniences so much sought after in Europe; they are happy in not knowing the use of them. They live in Tranquility. The Earth and the Sea of their own accord furnish them with all things necessary in life . . ."

A hundred years passed. Then gold was found on their land. They were slaughtered for being cannibals. They fought back but when their numbers were reduced they dispersed. It was assumed that they would die out. They fled to the north shore of the river, and to the coast where I was camped: "Swampy stony country that no white man would want."

One day in the 1880s, in the town of Oberfalz in Bavaria, a Lutheran pastor read a German edition of *Cook's Travels.* The Guugu Yimidirrh people were described ("clean limn'd . . . cloathes they had none"). This pastor, Johann Flierl—his name and mission were eventually known to every Aboriginal in the area—received God's summons to seek out "a totally untouched heathen people." The fate of the Guugu Yimidirrh was sealed, and it was *wahalumbaal* to their customs and habits.

German missionaries descended upon these innocent people and this stony Cape Bedford coast. Fifty-one hymns were translated into Guugu Yimidirrh. Luther's *Catechism* went into the language. And a missionary named Pastor Poland started on the New Testament, but before he got to Luke the catastrophic 1907 cyclone hit the coast, levelling the mission and scattering the pages of the translation.

The Guugu Yimidirrh people prayed. Nothing happened. Then in the 1930s a great shortage in China of sea slugs—so-called sea cucumbers and bêche-de-mer—and trochus shells gave the people something to provide for the outer world. The Cape Bedford Aborigines revived and, in a small way, prospered.

When the war came, and Japanese planes flew over the heads of the Guugu Yimidirrh people, they were evacuated, and their German missionaries were interned as possible Nazi spies.

In 1942 Ernie Bowen was in that evacuation to Rockhampton—so he told me. Born on Cape Bedford in 1907, the year of the great storm, he had spent most of his early life fishing and diving. Diving was his real trade, for the trochus shells—the source of all the buttons on fine clothes until the plastic industry rendered them unnecessary.

I asked Ernie to tell me about the evacuation which uprooted nearly 600 Aborigines from this place.

"See, Lutheran is a German religion," Ernie said. "And the war was on, mate. Some of your mob was here, too. Yanks. They was all over. They thought we might spy for the Germans—there were real German missionaries here."

"What was the trip to Rockhampton like?"

It was a distance of some fifteen hundred miles, for people who had never left their traditional land.

"Terrible, mate. One day and one night on a ship. No food. People crying—didn't know where they was going." He stopped speaking and looked at the sea. He had an old man's clouded eyes. "After the war we came here—not to Cape Bedford but to Hopevale Mission."

"Where is that?"

"Just inside."

He explained that this legacy of Johann Flierl was an Aboriginal settlement of a hundred or so houses at the end of a dirt track in the reserve.

"May I pay the place a visit?"

"You're welcome, mate," he said, and looked closely at me. "Where is your swag?"

"My swag is behind that point," I said, showing him. "Do you own some land around here."

"I don't own anything except these clothes and a vehicle. If the white man wanted to walk in and take the reserve he could do it, like he did in Cape Flattery."

"But you're being paid some money by the Japanese who are mining up there, aren't you?"

"Yes."

"Is it enough money?"

"Yes."

Gladys looked up from the busy hands of her grandson—he had tangled her hair and he held the skeins of it in his little fingers. She said, "The government is on our side. The white people were much worse before."

"In what way?"

"They were very rough."

Ernie glanced down the coast and said, "It's all hooligans in Cooktown. Some of those Aboriginal boys drink too much."

I told them I had seen a humpy on the slopes of Mount Sanders.

"Must be a fisherman," Ernie said.

"You call it a humpy?"

"No. We do call that a *bayan.*"

"See many crocs around here, Mr. Bowen?"

"Lots of crocs in Leper Creek."

"That's where my swag is," I said. "I was told the crocs there are little buggers."

"There's some big buggers too."

"Is it Leper Creek or Leprosy Creek?"

"Leper Creek. Because long ago there were some lepers there, with the disease."

"Do the crocs bother you?"

"The salt-water ones we call *kanarrh* and they grow very big. They took some people here—they usually take women. Don't know why, mate. Maybe because they're weak."

I said, "Or maybe because the women are doing the laundry in the creek."

"Maybe," he said. "If there's four or five people swimming the croc won't take anyone, but when they get out of the water the croc will take the last one."

"What would you do if you saw a croc when you were swimming, Mr. Bowen?"

"If I saw a croc, heh, I wouldn't swim."

Gladys said, "Sit with us. You can sit here." And she patted the end of the big log.

I sat with them and said, "Do you speak English when you're with your people?"

"No," Ernie said. "We do speak Guugu Yimidirrh, mate."

"That's good."

"Yes. It is good to have a language. Now listen. I can say"—he spoke some words quickly, a muttered rumbling that sounded like *worrojool gangaral*—"and you wouldn't know."

As he had spoken, Gladys jerked her head out of her grandson's hands, and blinked hard, and looked away.

"What wouldn't I know?"

"I said, 'Kill that white man,'" Ernie said, looking pleased, "and, see, you didn't know what I said."

He had a twinkle in his eye.

"It is good to have a language," he said.

Gladys still looked pained.

"American Negroes, what language they do speak?"

"English."

"They don't have their own language?"

"No."

"What a shame. It's only right that they should have one. What language people do speak in America?"

"English mostly."

This perplexed him a little. He said, "In Germany the white people speak German."

I said, "Mr. Bowen, are you a Lutheran?"

"Yes, mate."

"Still diving?"

"I left that years ago."

"Did you kill turtles and dugong?"

"So many times."

"How do you kill a dugong?"

"Spear it with a harpoon, turn it up and hold it against the boat and drown it. Oil is good for your aches and pains. Good meat, too."

I later found out that the Guugu Yimidirrh are among the last people in Australia still allowed to hunt the endangered sea cows, the dugong, and the endangered green sea turtle.

We talked a while longer, and I asked for directions to the Hopevale settlement. I would have no problem visiting, I felt, if I knew someone there; and Ernie and Gladys said that I could come anytime.

"I'll drop in sometime," I said.

"That's good, mate."

"I think I'll get back to my swag," I said.

But Ernie was not listening to me. He was staring in the direction of the point, where there was a single palm tree.

He said, "That palm. Never seen that palm before."

I met another beachcomber the next day. He said hello, then thought better of it and ducked into the woods. This was another mile up the beach. I later learned that he had a sailboat moored out of sight, in a tidal creek. These people, beachcombers and Aborigines, were miles apart, but even so they seemed to think they were too close. Tony certainly believed that. I saw Tony over the next few days, and I had the idea that he coveted some of my equipment for his voyage around Cape York.

I encouraged Tony to visit my camp. I wanted to know more about his beach-combing. I began to see a kind of luxury in his life that would be very hard to buy—it was not just comfort but privacy. I was interested in his periods of activity, his plans, his days of total idleness; his total self-absorption, and in his pleasures.

There was something deeply respectable and orderly about him. There was his satchel, containing his day's essentials—shoes, hat, food, water. He always wore a shirt and trousers, though buttons were missing from his shirt, and his trousers were torn in half a dozen places. He never went anywhere without his dog, which was a tiny mutt with a hoarse and timid bark.

I asked him one day whether the dog had a name.

"No," Tony said. "Well, he's so small"—as though his size did not justify having a name. He went on, "Sometimes I say 'chop chop' meaning hurry up. Maybe that could be his name."

The dog loved him, needed to be picked up and hugged. I was especially interested in the idea of Tony's trying to survive in this difficult place, and needing to find food for a dog, but when I mentioned it to him he simply shrugged.

Tony's routines and opinions, and the way he ran his life, suggested respectability. He could not bear the proximity of other people, and I knew from his reactions to my questions that he had a real aversion to anyone's discovering where or how he lived. He was entirely self-sufficient, contemptuous, and selfish. The fact that he was a beach-comber did not mean that he was an exile. He had a place in the world, which was wherever he happened to be. Beach-combing, though, was his preoccupation: He needed bottles for his beer brewing, floats and cast-up line for his raft, driftwood for his stove. The rest of the time he went after fish, oysters, and crabs. He was proud of his soup making and his bread making. He was often very busy, involved in the process of survival—and he managed this without spending any money at all—but he also had immense leisure.

He said to me one morning, "I drank eight or twelve bottles last night, listening to the radio. I slept late. Had a bit of a hangover. Then I put out my crab pot. Now I'm going for a walk."

This was his whole life on the hot windy coast of Cape Bedford, and it amazed me, because it combined the most rigid discipline with an utter disregard for time.

And sometimes I seriously wondered: *Am I like him?*

The night before I left my camp, I asked him whether he had been back to London.

"Oh, yes, I went back once. About ten years ago. Didn't have no money, so I got a job in the post office, the central one, in West One." He smiled. "It was all Indians and Jamaicans. Blacks from the West Indies on my right, Hindus from India on my left. I couldn't understand a word they said, and they were always jabbering. I said to myself, 'What's this country coming to?' "

He was in his early fifties, small and rather slender, scorched by the sun that always burned in a cloudless sky.

"That's why I couldn't see any point in staying."

I was tying my boat to the mangrove roots so that the tide wouldn't take it away.

"And I'm not even a racist," he said, in a complaining way.

I aimed to set off for the Aboriginal mission, and I wanted to lighten my load, so I gave him some food I would not need and my spare water jug that held two and a half gallons.

"I'll use it on my raft," he said, "when I go north."

"I wish you luck."

"I'm not bothered," he said, and then in a casual way he summed up what I took to be his guiding philosophy, "What I find is that you can do almost anything or go almost anywhere, if you're not in a hurry."

After so many warnings about crocodiles, I was determined to see one. I had read the pamphlet *Living with Wildlife: Crocodiles,* published by the Queensland National Parks and Wildlife Service, and that seemed to contain sensible advice: "Avoid murky water . . . Don't trail arms and legs from boats . . . Pitch camp at least 50m from the water's edge [that was inconvenient; I took the risk] . . . Don't leave food scraps around your camp . . . Be careful during the breeding season, October through April . . . Never feed crocodiles . . . Never approach them: Crocodiles have been known to charge boats and canoes . . . Be particularly wary of any large crocodile floating high in the water or with its tail arched out of the water. This is often a sign that the animal is likely to be aggressive . . ."

If I had a nightmare it was based on that last warning, with the image of a large bobbing croc, his tail erect and arched, coming at me like a monster scorpion.

I paddled up Leprosy Creek to where it became narrow, and almost a mile from the creek's mouth, I saw two small crocs at rest at the edge of a sandbank, their bug eyes and their snouts just above the surface. Maybe their mother would get crazed and attack me!

I looked around, but of course I saw nothing.

"You will never see the croc that eats you," a man in Cooktown told me. This sounded true. "You'll never hear it. You'll never know what hit you. You see nothing. They are simply not there. And in the next second you'll be in its mouth. They have this incredible capacity for sudden movement. And of course, they don't eat you. They twist you underwater and hold you there until you drown. Then they hide your corpse in the mud, and when your flesh is rotten and falling off your bones, they'll devour it."

I paddled back to the creek mouth and in the Cape Bedford direction to the point. At least now, if someone asked me if I had seen any crocs, I could say casually, *A couple.*

* * *

The Hopevale Mission was some miles inland. I started walking through the pig and lizard tracks, found a path, and after a while came to a road. I was picked up by a man in a fairly new four-wheel-drive vehicle—many of the Aborigines in Hopevale seemed to own them.

This man was a fat, cheery man named Paul Gibson. "G'day—where you headed?" He was coffee-colored, frizzy-haired, and wore a trimmed beard. He was extroverted in a way that I had not seen in any of the Aborigines I had met. I asked him his business.

"I'm a disc jockey."

"Is there a radio station here on the reserve?"

"Everyone listens to it."

"What's the most popular music on your show?"

"Country music. Aborigines love country music."

"Willie Nelson? Dolly Parton? Loretta Lynn? That kind of thing?"

"Too right, mate."

So we discussed country music until we came to the settlement.

No one was quite sure just how many Aborigines lived here. Some people said 600, other people said 700. They lived in houses that ranged from gunyahs or glorified humpies, to large well-maintained brick-fronted bungalows, with planted trees, and vegetable gardens and fences. The last thing I ever thought I would see in an Aboriginal reserve was a fence. But these were Lutheran Aborigines.

It was a flat place of wide streets and low dwellings, all sunstruck and dry, with the look of a camp that was evolving into a village. It had that company town sense of order: The stores on the main street hadn't sprung up—they had been imposed, according to a designer's scheme. The store, the post office, the community center, the gas station—someone had put them here. Some Aborigines were working on the roads, and some were leaning on their shovels. But the work was slowly being accomplished, and there was no question but that the curbs and sewers and roads were superior to those in Cooktown.

I lurked at the community center. I had now been among Aborigines long enough to see that they carried silence with them. They didn't shout, they chatted softly when they chatted at all, they moved keeping themselves very straight, loping quietly along on big flat feet. When I said hello they didn't speak to me but only nodded.

On the bulletin board a large notice read PIG DOGS FOR SALE SEE STEVE LEE. Pig dogs were ferocious hounds that went after pigs in the bush.

Another notice read, COULD OWNERS OF THE HORSES WHICH IS WONDERING ABOUT THE COMMUNITY PLEASE COLLECT THEM BY NEXT WEEK AND PUT THEM IN YOUR PADDOCKS. IF YOU CANNOT DO THAT, WELL YOUR HORSE WILL BE TRUCKED AWAY AND SOLD.

One of the notices concerned the Aborigines' weekly payments: THOSE PEOPLE WHO HAS MISSED OUT ON WAGES WILL NOT BE PAID BY CHEQUE UNTIL NEXT WEEK'S WAGES. "Wages" was a euphemism for their share of the money paid to the community by the mining company, and the implication of the notice was that some of them were too lazy to pick it up on the appointed day.

ANYONE WANTING THEIR DOGS TO BE SHOT, another notice ran, PLEASE SEE GOOMBRA JACKO.

A half a dozen surnames dominated in the community—Flinders, Gibson, Deemal, Woibo, Cobus, and Bowen. The place was full of Bowens, but I could not find Ernie or Gladys.

"Probably off fishun," Lynton Woibo said.

This was in the store that was run by the mission, and it was more thoroughly stocked than any food store in Cooktown. The only thing missing was alcohol—the reserve was dry. That was the primary reason for any of the Aborigines going to Cooktown: to buy liquor. I was surprised that the Aboriginal store had such expensive and fancy food— duck liver pâté, Sara Lee Black Forest Gâteau, frozen quiche lorraine, Birds Eye Chinese Vegetables, and Papa Giuseppi's Microwave Pizza. And, in a reserve that had tillable soil and irrigation, canned vegetables. I kept trying to imagine the spear-throwing, dugong-drowning Aborigines I had seen in the bush, coming back from an unsuccessful expedition and flinging a Papa Giuseppi's pizza into the microwave.

Microwaves were on sale in the dry-goods store, along with toasters, video machines, radios, and axes. The butcher shop was well stocked and also expensive (rib fillet at $12 a pound).

This settlement, as Ernie Bowen had told me, was started after the war, when the Aborigines had been taken back from Rockhampton. The history was recorded on a plaque at Pioneer Hall, but it was a short history—three lines, about its beginnings in 1949 and IN MEMORY OF OUR PIONEERS, with a column of the familiar surnames.

There was no single color, or face, or racial type in the community. They were all colors, from the deepest, purplest black to plain pinkish white.

Barry Liddie was a great deal paler and more civilized than most of the white Australians I had met elsewhere, yet he had several Aboriginal grandparents. His house at the edge of the settlement was low and rambling and rather littered, with a clutter of dead and rusted machinery all over the garden and the porch. He was sitting on his veranda. He had locked himself out of the house. Instead of looking for his wife, he simply sat down. She'd be home later to let him in.

He was stocky, with reddish hair, and handsome in a beefy way. He came from the hot far northern town of Coen in the deepest outback.

After marrying Lynette Deemal, who had been born right here at the mission, they had come here to live. He fished. She worked at the council offices. Besides this house they owned a boat and two large four-wheel-drive vehicles.

To kill time waiting on the veranda for his wife's key, Barry had a few beers. I declined the beer—too early: It was about eleven in the morning. "It's never too early," he said, but he drank furtively, hiding the bottle with his hand. The place was supposed to be dry.

When Lynette arrived and let him in he disappeared, and Lynette told me about their twelve-year-old daughter, whose name was Sacheen—pronounced "Sha-heen." I asked if that was a Guugu Yimidirrh name.

"No. Don't you remember that Indian girl who collected the Academy Award for Marlon Brando? She was called Sacheen. The name just stuck in my mind, and when we had a daughter I knew that was what I wanted to call her."

"Does she go to school here?" I asked.

"No. She's at school in Cairns. I think she's better off there than in the reserve," Lynette said. She was articulate and poised; it was hard to tell what proportion Aboriginal she was. She had the features and the complexion of a Tamil, from south India. "Sacheen is studying hard. She might do hairdressing later on, or business."

"Would you like to see her get involved in the life of the reserve?"

"I don't want to influence her. I want her to do whatever she wants to do. I'd like her to stand on her own two feet."

It was an admirable sentiment, because here on the reserve, where every Aboriginal was a landlord, money was free: No one ever had to work. I remarked on what a quiet place Hopevale seemed.

"It's noisy here on Fridays, when the people get their money," Lynette said. "Then all the drunks are out."

I said I had to get back to the coast—to my boat. Barry helped me find a lift, and when I left him I shook his hand. He took my hand without gripping it, one of the strangest handshakes I have ever experienced—stranger even than that of the most tepid non-handshaking Englishmen.

I mentioned to an Australian that I found it odd that Barry claimed to be an Aboriginal. He was white, after all.

"How can you tell he's really an Aboriginal?"

"Did you shake his hand?"

"Yes."

"Did it feel like a dead fish?"

"Yes."

"That's the proof. They don't shake hands."

This was back in Cooktown. I had not had a shave or a hot bath for a week. As an experiment I walked into the so-called Animal Bar to see whether I would blend in. My disguise worked: No one took a second look at me.

"Quiet tonight," I said to the young man next to me.

He was not quite as grubby as I was, but he was barefoot.

"Wait till check day," he said. "The Abos'll all be in here. They love fire water. They get their money and then go on the piss."

"Is it dangerous?"

"They're not too violent," he said. "No knives. Nothing like that. They might use the broken end of a glass stubbie. Yeah, some of the younger footballers are tough, but most of the Abos just drink and fall down."

Then he started the old refrain: government money, land royalties, free cash, land rights, two percent housing loans. "And what have I got?"

It seemed to me that he had a very great deal if he lived in this lovely climate on the dole and could sit on his ass drinking beer throughout the night, chatting to the pretty barmaid, seemingly without a care in the world. But I said nothing.

"Ever heard of this bloke," he said, becoming warmly vindictive, "down in Melbourne who's trying to prove that the first people in Australia weren't the Abos?"

"Never heard of him," I said. "But if the Aborigines weren't the first people here, who was?"

"That's just it. According to this bloke, it was the Jews."

"The Jews were here first?"

"Right," he said, and he was triumphant. "And if he proves it, then these Abos are up the creek."

I said, "Then Jews will be collecting money from the mining companies. They will control the sacred sites. And they will be getting two percent loans."

His eyes became very small. He swallowed some beer. He saw my point.

"Yeah. Rather have the bloody Abos."

He had been counting on disinheriting the Aborigines, but this conclusion made him thoughtful. He was glassy-eyed anyway, but his eyes grew glassier. After a while, realizing that I had not moved or spoken he piped up again.

"Have I seen you in town before?"

"Probably not. I'm camping up the coast, Cape Bedford way."

"Place is full of Abos. And bloody crocs."

I smiled harmlessly, conveying the thought *That's obvious!*

"You seen any crocs?" And he put his whiskery face closer to my whiskery face.

"A couple," I said casually. "What do you call them—estuarine crocodiles?"

"A couple! Good on yer!"

Part Two

MELANESIA

Chapter 6
BUOYANT IN THE PEACEFUL TROBRIANDS

I was nearer to the mangrove coast of Papua New Guinea when I was up among the Aborigines and beachcombers of Cape Bedford than I was to Brisbane or any other Australian city of any size. And now that I knew I wanted to see The Islands of Love, described in graphic detail in Malinowski's *The Sexual Life of Savages,* couldn't I simply get in my collapsible kayak and paddle there from here?

A map of the Torres Strait, the passage between Australia and New Guinea, made the trip seem pretty straightforward. I would paddle to Cape York, camping on the way, and then I would go island-hopping across the strait—no island involved much more than a twenty-mile, or one-day, crossing: from Thursday Island, to Moa Island, and from one rock to another, heading for the New Guinean depot of Daru near the mouth of the Fly River; across that estuary and up the coast, where there were little stations and muddy harbors to Port Moresby—a couple of weeks. If you're not in a hurry you can go anywhere, as the man said. Then I would figure out how to get to the Trobriands.

Maps, especially simple ones, can offer very hospitable and kindly portraits of a place. Maps of the Torres Strait cannot depict the powerful current rushing between the islands, the strong wind, the numerous reefs, the few real refuges in case of trouble, the absence of fresh-water sources, the miserable insect-ridden mangrove coast of the far side, and—in the vast muddy estuary of the Fly River—the crocs. I did not get my information from townies; I asked old black Thursday Islanders, and fishermen, and boatmen in Cooktown who had cruised and worked in the Torres Strait. They didn't tell me scare-stories, they told me what they had seen. And they didn't try to discourage me. Don't go alone, they said, and they told me to allow a month or six weeks for the trip. And on no account was I to spend a night among the savage and desperate (so they said) mud men in the unfriendly stilt villages of the Fly.

I collapsed my boat and took a plane from Cairns to Papua New Guinea. It was a little over an hour's flight to the capital, Port Moresby, one of the most violent and decrepit towns on the face of the planet. Dusty and falling apart, it had been thoroughly vandalized before it could ever be finished, and so it looked like an enormous building site, slums and flimsy bungalows scattered across a number of ugly hills. It was full of ragged bearded blacks, New Guinea highlanders, most of whom bore an exact facial resemblance to the distinguished jazz pianist Thelonious Monk.

"Wonem dispela?" asked the New Guinea customs officer, a wild-haired woman in a filthy dress at the terminal. She began pinching my canvas sacks.

This was incidentally the first time New Guinea Pidgin rang against my ear. "Neo-Melanesian," as it is known by linguists, is one of the fascinations of the Western Pacific: ". . . many commentators err in thinking of Pidgin as static baby talk . . . This is quite wrong . . . Pidgin is both complex and precise." That is the opinion *(ting)* of a distinguished *(gat nem)* teacher *(tisa)* who has given this language *(tok)* a great deal of thought *(tumas tingktingk)*.

Later, speaking it—saying the days of the week for example—I felt that I had talked my way onto the pages of *Finnegans Wake,* where Joyce writes the days as moanday, tearsday, waitsday, thumpsday, frightday, shatterday. In Pidgin, they are *mande, tunde, trinde, fonde, fraide, sarere, sande.*

"This fellow is a boat," I said.

"Yu tingk dispela bot? How long dispela bot blong yu?"

"Four years, approximately."

"You taking dispela away wit' you when you lusim hia?"

"I imagine so."

"Wonem dispela bek?" Now she was gesturing to the lunch bag I had intended to throw away.

"Trash," I said.

"Samting-nating," she said, using a precise Neo-Melanesian expression, as she looked inside. *"You pas."*

She made a chalk mark on my canvas sacks.

I said, "I'm looking for the plane to the Trobriands."

Hearing me, one of her colleagues said, *"Balus I laik go nau."*

"Does that mean the plane is leaving?"

"Yesa."

In fact, it was leaving in fifteen minutes from the domestic terminal, a

shed up the road reeking of fruit peels and urine. I was forcibly helped by
a dwarfish highlander in a wool hat. His teeth were black, his feet and his
hands were huge, and he was wearing one of the dirtiest shirts I had ever
seen. We struggled with my boat and my camping equipment.

"Yu kam olsem wonem?" he asked. He was grinning. He was sweating.
He himself was from Mount Hagen, he said, *"Yu kam we? Yu go we? We
yu stap long?"*

"I'm just visiting," I said.

"Wat dispela bikpela kago?"

"It's a boat."

"Kago bilong yu, putim long hap, klostu long dua." And he dropped my
bags near the door.

"Where's the plane?"

"Balus i bagarap."

"It's buggered up?" I said.

The man smiled, he pulled off his wool hat and wiped the sweat from
his face, and he then demanded oysters. But the word for oysters in Pidgin
was also the word for money. I handed some over and he saluted me.

The Twin Otter wasn't buggered up, it was only out of gas, and the
Australian pilot was saying to a bearded highlander, "I can't go to Losuia
without fuel now, can I?"

The Men's Room *(Haus Pek Pek)* outside the terminal was almost too
disgusting to use. A prominent warning was printed in two languages: DO
NOT MISUSE THE TOILET/NO KEN BAGARUPIM HAUS PEK PEK.

In the end, I was the only passenger on the little plane to the Trobriands.

After an hour of high clouds and blue ocean, the green islands shimmered into view. They were in the middle of nowhere: it was another
experience of the Pacific being like the night sky, like outer space, and of
island-hopping in that ocean being something like interplanetary travel.
In the Solomon Sea below, there were about a dozen islands big and
small; and they could not have been flatter. Only a few feet above sea
level, without a single hump or mound, they appeared to be floating, like
a thin layer of green weed rippling upon the sea. At the center of each of
the larger islands was a bright boggy swamp, and I could see the tall
coconut palms lining the dirt tracks, their long shadows stretching across
the low bush. The pattern of each village was the same, just as Malinowski described—the lovely huts ranged around the stately carved and
painted yam house. A great deal was obvious from the air: no cars, no
paved roads, no power lines, no billboards, no tin roofs, no motorboats.
The promise of this simplicity thrilled me.

The airstrip was a grassy swathe that resembled the fairway at a public golf course—rather trampled and untended. The terminal was a shed slightly smaller than a one-car garage. Two battered vehicles were parked near it, and about two hundred brown people were ranged around it. They wore shorts, and the sarongs they called lap-laps; some wore flowers behind their ears, or coronets of white wilted frangipani blossoms. About half a dozen carried carvings—walking sticks, salad bowls, war clubs, statuettes; the rest simply gaped as the plane taxied to a stop. This was one of the group activities of Kiriwina—the main Trobriand island— watching the Moresby plane land and take off.

On the evidence of this crowd, there was no Trobriand face: These people had few features in common. The people ranged from black, smooth-skinned Nat King Cole Melanesian, to light-skinned straighter-haired Polynesian types who would not have looked out of place in a hula competition in Waikiki. And every racial gradation and hair type in between. Here and there was a woman with sun-scorched hair, almost blond; and there was a handful of redheads, who looked as though they had overdone it with the henna treatment. It was a very odd assortment of people—there was even a scattering of albinos—and much odder for representing the population of a relatively small island in the middle of the ocean.

I was approached by a fat little Trobriand woman. The pencil bristling from her frizzy hair gave the appearance of being stuck into her skull.

"You can get in," she said, and motioned to a rusted pickup truck.

She worked at the lodge, a tumbledown seaside inn, which was the only place to stay on the island—or in the entire archipelago, for that matter. It was assumed that any visitor who got off the plane was headed for the lodge. I had planned to get a lift to the shore, and camp there, but this arrangement suited me even better.

"What is in all this luggage?"

"A boat."

She shrugged, sighed, and made a face. On the way she sat clutching the steering wheel and glowering at the rubbly track ahead, hardly speaking. After a while I coaxed from her the information that her name was Amy and that she had spent some time in Australia. I put her sulkiness down to the fact that she had probably been treated rather badly there— or in the same offhand way as she was treating me.

"Is there any sort of administration center on this island—a town, or a market?"

"We just went through it," she said.

I had not seen anything but palm trees and wooden sheds.

"Is there anyone else at your lodge?"

"Some *dim-dims,*" she said, using the local word for white person. "Australians."

They were seven expatriates who had flown from a town on the north coast of New Guinea on a private plane for a weekend of heavy drinking and horsing around. They had with them—it seemed to be their only luggage—a number of cases of beer. It was midafternoon and they were already drunk, in the state of clumsy geniality that I had come to recognize from my stay in Cooktown.

They were sunburned and glassy-eyed, all of them fleshy, and they were as friendly as they knew how to be. They became hearty, seeing me and sizing me up, and one handed me a beer, for drunks love companions and hate sober witnesses. I shook hands with the fattest one.

"G'dye. I'm Mango. That's Fingers. That's Big Bird—he owns the plane. That's Booboo. That's Ali—"

It was all nicknames. We had another beer and sat on the veranda, watching the tide drain out of the flats of the lagoon.

"Fingers saw a croc here just a minute ago."

"Unless it was a fucken *meri* out swimming."

Meri was Pidgin for woman.

"I had three national *meris* last night."

"Fingers is a fucken animal."

Fingers was freckled and had close-together eyes, and the odd set of his jaw—his underbite—gave him a moronic expression when he smiled.

"They're all looking for white husbands," Booboo said.

"Do you find them madly attractive?" I asked.

"Some of them are pretty and others are ugly as hell," Mango said. "But they all fuck."

This was one of their topics of conversation, but in their telling they were always passive, the women always the aggressors: *So I hear this fucken noise at the window and I look out and it's a* meri, *lifting up her lap-lap—*

Other topics were the laziness of highlanders, the high crime rate, particularly destructive car crashes, good meals, the horror of Port Moresby, and the good fun of heavy drinking. They were loud and jolly and fairly harmless. They said as much.

"We're all going troppo."

"What are the symptoms?" I asked.

"The first one is that you don't want to go home," Fingers said. "You go a bit round the twist, see."

"And the national *meris* look bloody marvelous," Booboo said.

"And you sit in places like this with a stubbie in your hand," Mango said.

Big Bird stood up and walked to the veranda rail. "That's a croc," he said. "That's definitely a croc."

A low log-like shape darker than the water around it trembled in the muddy lagoon and then sank, leaving subtle ripples.

"Ugly bugger," Mango said, staring at the widening ripples.

"That one was eight foot at least," Ali said.

"Ten is more like it," Booboo said.

They discussed the length of the croc, and it kept growing, until Amy appeared on the veranda and sulkily announced dinner.

We were served by two barebreasted girls in grass skirts, who managed to look demure, even as Fingers was blatantly leering. The girls were small—Trobrianders were small of stature anyway, but these could not have been older than thirteen or fourteen. Their grass skirts were short and dense and fitted them like dancers' tutus. Malinowski remarked on how the grass skirt "is very becoming to fine young women, and gives to small slender girls a graceful, elfish appearance."

"Elfish" was just about perfect. And the shell anklets and bracelets and necklaces they wore made pretty wind-chime chuckles as they walked. No one spoke—there were only sighs and murmurs of concentration from the Australian men—as the girls glided near the table, padding around it on bare feet.

The food was unappetizing and uneatable—fatty meat and boiled white tubers, served with hunks of Spam.

"What do you think of this food?" I asked.

"It's crap," Mango said, stuffing Spam into his mouth.

There was dancing afterwards, by the barebreasted waitresses and some drummers who had been hauled in from the road. A crowd of people always gathered there under the lights; they crouched and chattered. The rest of the island seemed to be in darkness but people habitually sat outside the lodge at night because it had a generator and a few electric lights.

When the music was over, and the Australians stumbled outside to look for women, and after Amy had firmly put me in my place ("We don't have coat hangers"), and I found out where I could get food and supplies for tomorrow, I went to bed, vowing to paddle away in the morning.

"Waga," I heard them say. *"Waga. Waga,"* as the kayak took shape. A crowd of about fifty men and boys were squatting at the edge of the lagoon watching me assemble it. Most of them were gaping, some were mocking me, some fooling with the kayak pieces, and two or three were in my way, competing to help me put the thing together.

After that, whenever I put the kayak together, or took it apart, a crowd of males gathered (the women had better things to do) to watch me, or to fool. On this sort of occasion—a hot humid day on a muddy Trobriand foreshore, picking my way among the broken coral, and hearing the laughter of the islanders and their certain mockery ("What is the *dim-dim* doing now?"), I was often reminded of how Malinowski, the most sympathetic of anthropologists, would spend a day among these laughing people and then go back to his tent and scribble vindictively in his private diary.

"The natives still irritate me, particularly Ginger, whom I would willingly beat to death," he wrote. "I understand all the German and Belgian colonial atrocities." Or: "Unpleasant clash with Ginger . . . I was enraged and punched him in the jaw once or twice." Or: "I am in a world of lies here." Or worse. Publicly he called them "the Argonauts of the Western Pacific," but in his diary he had his own private name for the Trobrianders. "The niggers were noisy . . . General aversion to niggers . . ."

The entries could have come from the intimate journals of Mistah Kurtz in his hut at the Heart of Darkness, but no, they are those of the founder of the modern discipline of social anthropology, the man who had made it a highly literate, observational science. There was a general outcry when Malinowski's private diaries were posthumously published in 1966, but they were harmless enough—just trivia, ranting, loneliness, insecurity, and self-pity. What is clear in them was that what he hated most—what all travelers hate—was not being taken seriously.

They teased him and they teased me. It is irritating, but so what? The Trobriand children are rambunctious; they are seldom scolded. No children I had ever come across lived a less repressed existence. The youngest played all day, and on the moonlit nights they all went frolicking—I was often to hear little kids' laughter at midnight. Yet they do what they are expected to—work in the gardens and pick coconuts and go on fishing expeditions. There are schools, but though half the village children never see a classroom, they are skilled in the arts of the island and have an intimate knowledge of their own stories and traditions. This attitude of self-possession, which seemed like arrogance—the teasing of *dim-dims*—had kept the Trobriand culture intact and was perhaps the key to their survival.

And after I pulled the pieces out of my two bags and assembled the kayak, I stowed my food and the rest of my gear, and—as they watched, still muttering and laughing—I simply pushed off and paddled away. This was on the east coast of Kiriwina, near the village of Wawela. On my chart I saw a break in the reef marked "Boat Passage"—and I paddled to it. A strong riptide was moving through it and waves were breaking just outside it, so I stayed inside the lagoon and paddled south along the reef in pretty, greeny-blue water, across shelves of brightly colored coral.

I paddled about five miles south, until the lagoon narrowed, squeezing me into a small neck of water between the reef and the beach. I looked onshore and saw a crowd of people, seemingly camped—there were no huts or shelters of any kind. I thought perhaps they were killing time, waiting for a boat to Kitava Island, which lay about five miles in the sea beyond the reef.

Seeing me, several men began waving and whistling, gesturing for me to come over. Having nothing better to do, and wishing to add a little coastal detail to my rather stark fifty-year-old chart, I paddled towards them.

A green sea turtle lay on its back on the sand near the men, gasping and feebly working its flippers. From time to time, whenever the turtle tried to turn itself over, a man would kick it.

The men who had called me over did not speak English, but another fellow, named Sam, spoke English fluently. Pidgin would have been of little use. It is regarded as pig-English in the Trobriands and is spoken self-consciously and with great reluctance. Sam had learned English in Port Moresby, where he had worked in a bank. But he hated the city and when he had earned enough money returned to his Trobriand village, Daiagilla.

"It is in the north of this island, near Kaibola, but not on the beach," he said. "That is our problem. We have trouble fishing there. So many people, and all of them fishing."

The solution was to come here, fifteen miles away, and establish a temporary fishing camp, which was what this group of thirty-three men and boys comprised. They wore ragged bathing suits. One was feebleminded. One was deaf and dumb. They lived in complete harmony. They had made an arrangement with the village that owned this beach, and they fished day and night, using spears and nets, until they had enough fish to bring back.

"Why is this village willing to help you?"

They said that the local village was given some of the catch, and in return they brought vegetables and drinking water to the fishermen.

"There is no trouble," Sam said. "We don't fight. We want to live in peace."

They had been there for four days, and when they weren't fishing they were processing the large (eight and ten pounders) coral trout, smoke-drying them on a sort of rickety table erected over a smoldering fire. Fish hung from lines that stretched from palm trunk to palm trunk.

"We catch more at night," Sam said, and showed me the long waterproof flashlights they used for night fishing. He showed me a wooden spear with a rusty barbed point. "And these harpoons are good, too. This is a good place for fishing. But we don't come here much. This is only the second time this year."

"What do you eat the rest of the time—yams?"

"Yam is for feasts. It is special. We don't eat it when we are in our huts, but when we are together at a feast we eat it. We eat other vegetables. Taro. Sweet potato. Pumpkin tops."

"I don't see any women here," I said.

"The women don't fish. They are home tending the gardens, looking after the little children, and preparing for us to return." He glanced at the struggling turtle and gave it another kick. "When we return there will be a great feast. We will eat most of the fish. We have to eat it—there is no way to keep it."

I said, "Have you ever heard of Malinowski?"

"I have heard of him," Sam said, and he laughed. " 'The Islands of Love.' I have never read his books, but someone told me about him when I was in Moresby."

"What did they say?"

"He came here. Maybe he came during the Yam Festival. So he thought we were like that all the year. I think he generalized about us."

"Tell me about the Yam Festival," I said. Malinowski had compared it to a bacchanalia and had given graphic examples of sexual license.

"The Yam Festival"—Sam smiled and looked at the others, who were picking through my boat, examining my own fishing spear, knotting and unknotting my nylon lines. "It is in June and July. The women do silly things. And the men do silly things. And I also do silly things. It is a funny festival."

They invited me to stay at their camp. It was only midafternoon, but the day was hotter than I had expected, and when they brought out a big smoked fish, steaming on a palm leaf, I ate with them and abandoned any plans to go farther south that day. They expressed an interest in my food. I was happy to give them a loaf of my bread, which they passed around, and some fruit and cookies.

I often had this frustrating experience of handing out goodies. I would take a whole box of cookies or a giant chocolate bar and I would see it subdivided and wolfed down so quickly it was as though I had given them nothing at all. They always shared the food, they never fought over it, and yet food—especially cookies—seemed to vaporize in their eager hands. This stuff was a frivolous and insubstantial present anyway. I had brought spear points and spear rubbers and fishhooks to give as gifts.

That night around the fire, Sam asked me the questions the others relayed to him—where was I from? What was my name? Was I married? Did I have children? How had I heard about the Trobriands?

I answered the best way I could, and I told them about Malinowski. Sam said, "I don't want to read his books. Why should I?"

"You seem to be happy people," I said. "But what if you had a chance to improve your lives. What would you do?"

He thought a long time, and he consulted the others before he answered. Then he said, "If only we had a vehicle. It is so expensive for us to come here on the government truck"—two or three trucks passed for public transport on Kiriwina, and there were no vehicles at all, nor any roads, on the other islands. Though this seemed to me a delightful situation, Sam disagreed. "But we will never have the money. We get some money by selling carvings and selling food at the market. It is so little."

I told him that I thought the virtue of the Trobriands was that it did not have a money economy. He said, Yes, but there were some items you just couldn't barter for—school fees, canned meat, good clothes, and the sort of vehicle his village craved but would never have.

In the darkness beyond the camp fire, the younger men and boys fussed with spears and flashlights. Sam had once or twice referred to the chief. It turned out that he was with them, a toothless, betel-chewing man in a torn T-shirt, named Goody, or perhaps Gudi.

"He owns the land of our village," Sam said.

Because of the steady wind there were no mosquitoes, so I dug out my sleeping bag and found a patch of sand to sleep on. It was a night of their muttering and splashing, and when the wind shifted I got a face full of wood smoke. In the morning I could see clearly what a mess the camp was, a great litter of smashed coconuts, fish bones, crab shells, smoking fires, reeking fish, and the same gasping, dying turtle.

Through Sam, Gudi said, "Let me paddle your boat."

The shoreline was all coral and I was afraid he would puncture it, so I said, "Not today. Maybe when I come back for the Yam Festival."

Towards the bottom of Kiriwina Island, at Gilibwa, there was another boat passage which I paddled through to cut over to the swampier, western side. Here there was no wind inshore, but the water was shallow, and in some places I had to get out and drag the boat along by its bow line. I sloshed along in rubber reef shoes because of the stonefish and the sea urchins and the sharp coral, but listening to Mozart on my headphones and feeling safe among these hospitable people, I found the whole trip around the south end of the happy island of Kiriwina extremely pleasant.

The lodge was empty except for a sunburned French couple in green army fatigues who complained that the fan in their room didn't work.

I restocked with food and water and prepared to head west out of Losuia on about an eight-mile paddle to the next island, Kaileuna, which I intended to circumnavigate.

"A woman was taken by a croc near Boli Point," Bill, the Australian manager of the lodge, told me just before I left.

I would be passing Boli Point in a few hours.

"When are you planning to be back?" he asked.

"Tuesday afternoon."

"If you're not here then we'll come looking for you," he said in a neighborly way. "One other thing. Don't camp at random. Get permission from the village nearest the beach. They might charge you a few kina, but not more than that. The person who does all the talking is usually the least trustworthy. It could cost you a lot if you're not careful. Don't go along with them if they say, 'Never mind—we'll settle it tomorrow' because by tomorrow you could be in deep shit. They could charge you a hundred and you'd have to pay."

Just before I got into my boat the sky grew black and rain came down, such a heavy downpour that I was prevented from leaving for another hour. The men and boys laughed when they saw me dripping in my wet clothes and fussing around my boat—the sudden storm had dumped an inch of water in the bottom. They stopped laughing and came closer, seeing me working my bilge pump—just a simple hand pump, but quicker and more effective than the wooden scoops they carved to bail out their canoes.

"You give this to me," one of the men said.

"Sorry," I said, and stowed it.

He fooled for his friends. "The *dim-dim* no give to me!"

"Because you laughed at me," I said.

Steam was rising from the lagoon, and the air was heavy and humid, all the big trees on shore drizzling, as I set off across the flats of Losuia Bay, picking my way among the muddy chunks of coral. Fish were jumping, and birds squawking, and kids screaming and splashing at the bank.

There was little wind at first, but I was fighting an incoming tide. I left the shallow area and paddled to the main channel of dark blue water, deep enough to take the trading boats that crossed Milne Bay with supplies from the New Guinea mainland port of Alotau.

Approaching Boli Point, I thought of Bill's croc story and kept about a mile offshore in a freshening wind and three-foot waves. I could see the muddy inlet where the crocodiles were reputed to be. There is a certain stagnancy and opaqueness to crocodile-inhabited water, a sheltered quality to the vegetation, stillness and stinky shadows. I could well believe there were crocodiles in this smelly estuary.

Beyond the point I saw Kaileuna Island, flat and deep green, about two miles away, across a stretch of open water. I paddled across to the far point, Mamamada, which was a chunk of spiky coral and a narrow beach. By then it was early afternoon—lunchtime—and as I ate I congratulated myself on having reached one of the smaller islands in the group. There were no villages here that I could see, though I had seen some huts farther up the eastern shore. I decided to avoid them, to paddle along the south side of the island.

I came to a white sandy beach, protected by a pair of jutting cliffs. There were green parrots in the trees, a big eagle overhead, and terns strafing the lagoon. There were no human footprints, only lizard tracks, and it looked like a perfect camping place, but while I was sizing it up a dugout canoe went past, two barebreasted women paddling it, and they called out, sort of yodelling at me. So now my presence was known. I got back into my boat and paddled in the direction they were headed. Soon I saw a plume of smoke about a mile away and the light outline of some roofs of huts lining the beach. The village was not marked on my chart.

I first came to a little thatched pavilion at the end of a pier, and I nearly beached my boat there. It was a good thing I didn't, because this was the toilet for the women of the village—the men's was on the beach at the other side of the village. As I paddled parallel to the shore a group of boys began following me, running along the beach, whooping and hollering. I waved back at them.

By the time I got to the village's main beach a large number of people had gathered to watch me drag my kayak onto the sand—jeering boys, frightened infants, boys in lap-laps and bathing shorts, topless women, muttering men—some of the older men were holding lime gourds and sucking betel juice from sticks.

"As soon as an interesting stranger arrives," Malinowski wrote of a typical reception in the Trobriands, "half the village assembles around him, talking loudly and making remarks about him, frequently uncomplimentary, and altogether assuming a tone of jocular familiarity."

This was the general impression I had of my arrival, but what distracted my attention was the good health of the villagers, in particular their good teeth.

"Does anybody speak English?" I asked.

"Everybody speaks English here," a man said.

An older man came towards me and shook my hand. He said that he was the chief, and asked where I was from, and what kind of a boat was this?

I told him and explained that I was paddling around the islands and that I had found a camping place about a mile away. Could I have his permission to camp there?

"Why don't you stay here in the village?" a man standing beside him said. "The missionary will show you a place."

"Where is the missionary?"

I expected to see a *dim-dim* in a black frock, but instead I was greeted by a Trobriander in a T-shirt and bathing suit.

"I am the missionary," he said.

He said his name was John. He was a tall brown skinny man with frizzy, gingery hair, and close up I saw that his skin was reddish. He was holding a small naked child, and for some reason the child was clutching a long carving knife and slashing the air with it and snorting through his snotty nose.

Some small children trooped after us, as John led me through the village. The rest of the villagers had gone back to their chores—seven or eight of the men were building a large sailing canoe, some women were tending smoky fires, and a soccer game resumed nearer the edge of the clearing.

Toddlers, seeing me from their mothers' arms or from where they were playing on straw mats, howled and pissed in fear. To torment them further, people picked the kids up and pretended to hand them over to me, and the more the kids screamed at the sight of the *dim-dim* the louder people laughed.

John said that he was from Alotau and that God had sent him here to Kaisiga—which was the name of this village. This was a very fortuitous choice on the part of the Almighty because it so happened that John's wife, Esther, was from the next village, Bulakwa, just along the coast. John and Esther had two children—the snotty one in his arms, and another one torturing a cat under the ladder to their hut: Cleopas and Waisodi. Esther was heavily pregnant and she sat in an open-sided shelf by the sea cutting vegetables.

"I would like to have a little girl," Esther said. "What is your wife's name?"

Whenever my marriage was mentioned, even in the most casual way, I grew sad and fell silent. At first I pretended I had not heard, but Esther persisted and eventually I gave her the information she wanted.

"I like that name," Esther said, placing her hands on her belly. "If we have a girl we will call her Anne."

Meanwhile, John was telling me about his conversion.

"I was blind. I spent many years as a blind man," he said. "Then I became a Seventh Day Adventist and I learned to see. Paul, would you like to learn how to see, like your namesake on the road to Damascus?"

So they were Seventh Day Adventists: that obviously explained their good teeth. They did not smoke or drink, the younger ones did not chew betel. No pig-eating.

"Do you want to convert me?"

"Yes. I do."

"I'll have to think it over, John. It's a pretty big decision in any person's life."

"That is true," he said, and then looked doubtful. But his mind was on other matters. "The trouble with camping here is that the small children will bother you. They are very curious and troublesome."

"Why don't we tell them not to be curious and troublesome?"

"They will just laugh at us."

Another man confirmed this. "Yes," he said. "They just come and go as they wish, the small boys."

"What time do they go to bed?"

"Whenever they like," the man said. "At eleven or twelve, or even later."

"And the other problem for you," John said, "is that I will beat the drum early in the morning to call people to the morning service. So don't put your tent close to the drum."

"What do you call early?"

"Maybe six o'clock."

"I think I'll put my tent way over there," I said.

I went back for my kayak and dragged it through the shallows of the lagoon to the edge of the village, and when I unloaded it a crowd gathered—forty-seven people, big and small, I counted as I started to set up my tent. The little kids were touching everything—feeling the tent cloth, the kayak skin, twisting the ropes and stakes, most of them hindering me and getting underfoot in their attempts to help me. The naked, dusty munchkins rather fearlessly fingered my gear, and yelped and gabbled and passed various items to their parents for inspection.

"They are impressed with your tent," John said.

I shot out the shock-corded poles and, as they clicked together into their nine-foot length, there was applause and laughter. The people sat down around me, awaiting more. I hung up my water bag on a tree, turned the kayak over so that the kids wouldn't get in, and then distracted by all the people, took a walk down the beach. When I returned at dusk the villagers had gone away. I crawled into my tent, took three swigs of sherry from my bottle, so as not to demoralize the Adventists, and started cooking my dinner.

Before leaving Losuia I had bought some kerosene for my camp stove. I got the stove going and boiled some water and made tea and then noodles, which I had with beans and canned mackerel.

While I was eating, John came over, still holding his snotty child.

"They think you are strange," he said. "But I told them you are not strange."

"I appreciate that, John."

"They have never seen anyone eat alone, but I told them that Western-ers do it all the time. When you arrive in a place you make your own food."

"Very true, John," I said. "Have a cookie?"

He took a handful and we wandered back together in the fading light, to the thatched pavilion they called a *bwayma* by the sea, and I passed out cookies to the others there and we sat and talked while the kids still chattered and splashed at the edge of the lagoon.

"What do these kids do until midnight?"

"They play. They sing. They tell stories," he said. "No one tells the children to go to bed."

It was suppertime, a bright fire blazing in front of each hut, the woman poking it and cooking, her husband sitting on the porch of the hut eating.

"We share everything here," John said. "If the men catch fish, every family will get some. We have the same garden. We cook for each other. Whatever someone has, he shares."

Five of us were sitting in the breezy pavilion, eating the last of the cookies. John wanted to tell me about the Seventh Day Adventists, but I headed him off, asking him about the Yam Festival.

"The Yam Festival is very unChristian," John said, and the others smirked at me. "The girls and the women just rush at you. They grab at you anywhere"—and he gestured at his groin and frowned.

The others shrieked with laughter.

"It is not funny," John said, sadly.

"It is unusual," I said.

"It is worse than unusual," John said. "The women can hold you down. There might be seven or eight of them. They hold you and one of them sits on your face and laughs at you and she presses her waist against you."

"Presses her *waist?*"

"Her thing," John said.

"Her *wila,*" someone said, and there was more laughter.

"I get it," I said.

"There is much fornication, and even rape," John said, with great solemnity. "Yes, I tell you, five or six girls can rape a man. They take a man and they sit on him, and they touch him and when his—"

"*Kwila!*" someone said.

"Yes, when his *kwila* gets hard the lucky one sits on it. What do you think of that?"

Everyone looked in my direction. I was smiling. I said, "Honestly, it sounds like traditional fun."

The men began to laugh at John, and I thought, *Tennyson, anyone?*

I will take some savage woman, she shall rear my dusky race.
Iron jointed, supple-sinew'd, they shall dive, and they shall run,
Catch the wild goat by the hair, and hurl their lances in the sun;
Whistle back the parrot's call, and leap the rainbows of the brooks,
Not with blinded eyesight poring over miserable books—

The men were poking John and demanding that he speak up.

John said, "The Bible says that your body is the temple of God."

"It does say that," one man said, and was jeered at by the others.

"But God is love," I said. "And the Yam Festival is love, isn't it?"

"Yes! Yes!" the men and boys were chanting at their missionary, who was looking miserable.

He said, "Adultery can break up a marriage."

"Do the marriages of these people get broken up by this Yam Festival fornication?"

"No," John said, frankly. "For two months the husband goes this way, the wife goes that way. Then after the Yam Festival is over they come back together and all is the same as before."

"So there is no problem," I said.

"But the body is the temple of God," John nagged despairingly. "And there are worse things."

"I would love to hear them."

"The *mweki-mweki.* Tapioca dance," someone said. "It is shameful."

"And tug-of-war," John said. "They challenge the other villages. Boys from this village challenge the girls from that village. The girls from here tug-of-war against the boys from there. They are half-dressed. Only bottoms. They pull the vines, and whichever side wins chases the other, and when they catch them they fornicate on the grass, just like that."

"Then what happens?"

"Then they put their pants on and have another tug-of-war."

"That really sounds like fun," I said.

Everyone laughed except John, who left the pavilion and went to his hut. He returned a moment later with a copy of an Adventist magazine, *The Voice,* which he urged me to read. Then he said he wanted to tell me how it happened that he came here to Kaisiga Village.

"This village was all United Church once. But one morning the people saw that a very big whale had come to the beach and was just lying there at the edge of the sand. The chief of the village had a dream. In the dream a voice told him about the whale. 'Because you asked for food,' the voice said. They got ropes and they pulled it out to sea. But the next day it came back. The chief had another dream. This time the voice said, 'Not physical food but spiritual food.' So instead of pulling the whale to sea, they took it and buried it on the next beach. The chief had a dream and he was told the meaning of the whale. 'You are asking to be fed another religion.' So they left the United Church and they invited the Adventists and I was sent from Poppondetta to lead them."

It was now dark over half the sea, though a pinky seashell light still lingered where the sun had set, making looming shadows of the high humpbacked islands on the horizon, Fergusson and Normanby and Goodenough, in the distant southwest. Part of the lagoon was a great pink lake, and the more shadowy ocean close by sloshed against the edge of the village.

"How do you say 'good night'?"

"Bwoyna bogie," John said.

"Bwoyna bogie," I said, and left them and crawled into my tent.

And most of the night, under the brilliant half moon that lighted the starry sky and the jungle treetops and the high clouds breezing across it and made silhouettes of the coconut palms, the children sang and laughed, by the surge of the sloshing lagoon.

The banging of the drum came early—it was a steel oil drum and made a hell of a noise and went on for ages, because the drummer was another village kid, having fun. It was five-thirty in the morning—first light. Then I heard whispering and laughter, and padding feet on the hard tramped earth of the village, and then the creaking planks of the church floor, and then the sweet harmony of children's voices singing,

> *Weespa a frayer in da morning,*
> *Weespa a frayer at noon.*
> *Weespa a frayer in da evening*
> *So keep your heart in tune.*
>
> *Jesus may come in da morning,*
> *Jesus may come at noon,*
> *Jesus may come in da evening*
> *So keep your heart in tune.*

And then I heard part of John's sermon as he read some verses from the Bible and began explicating it, saying, "Now that is not alcoholic wine. It is pure wine. It is, let us say, something like grape juice—"

I was up, making green tea, when the people from the morning service left the tin-roofed building that served as the church—it was nearly all children, and some women, and a few of the hecklers from last night at the seaside pavilion.

Seeing John, I said, "You were up early."

"Six-thirty, every morning," he said.

I said, "You mean five-thirty."

"Was it?" he said. "Well, we don't have a watch in the village. But that's a nice watch."

As he was looking at mine and seemed to be on the verge of breaking the Eighth Commandment, I thought how wonderful it was to have so little idea of the right time.

"What is this you are making?"

"Green tea."

"We don't drink tea," John said. "Or coffee. The body is the temple of God."

He was speaking as a Seventh Day Adventist, but it seemed odd to be making a virtue out of something that was untraditional on these islands anyway.

I drank some tea and almost choked. John took this as a sign from God, but I realized that I had accidentally filled my water bag with brackish water back in Losuia. I was angry at myself for having lugged three gallons of undrinkable water in my kayak.

He invited me for breakfast. The mashed taro cooked in coconut milk and the bananas led us to a discussion of the pleasures of vegetarianism.

"Also we don't eat pigs or bats. Or Tulip," John said.

Tulip was not his pet chicken but rather a brand name, generic for any fatty pork in a can.

"Or coneys," John said.

"Did you say *coneys?* Rabbits? Are there any rabbits here?"

"No," John said.

"Which book of the Bible talks about food?"

"Leviticus. Chapter Eleven," he said. "Also something in Deuteronomy."

He showed me his Bible and, reading the chapter in Leviticus, I concluded that it was like an environmentalist's charter and probably had done more to protect endangered species than all the nature charities put together.

"I can see you are interested," John said, sensing my imminent conversion.

While I was sitting there, eight or ten older boys came over, one with a lei of frangipani blossoms they called a *katububula*. The boy, whose name was Wilson, said, "The old man asked, 'Why didn't you give him flowers yesterday?' But we said, 'We didn't see him coming.'"

"Are you through with that?" a boy named Zechariah asked me, seeing that I had put my plate aside—I had eaten half of the stodgy mixture.

"I'm done," I said.

He snatched up the plate and ate what I had left. Then he smiled and said, *"Sena bwoyna!* That was very good!"

They asked me what I was doing. I said I was on vacation and that I was just paddling around the islands. This to them seemed a perfectly natural way of passing the time. A man named Micah said, "But do not paddle to Tuma Island."

"Why not?"

"It is where the dead people go."

I found it on my map, a slender island, about five miles long, to the northwest, and questioning them further I learned that it was a haunted place where no living person went because it was where the dangerous spirits of the dead resided. In Malinowski's description it was the Trobrianders' heaven, a place of eternal youth and perpetual copulation—an erotic paradise, if you were a *khosa,* a spirit. Even the Seventh Day Adventists of Kaisiga Village did not deny this, though they said that the *khosas* flitted around tormenting and tricking living people.

I put Tuma high on my list of destinations of places to paddle.

One of the boys was the son of the master canoe builder, Meia. I was taken to where they were working on the large outrigger canoe I had seen when I arrived. This labor had occupied them for almost a year, they said. I sketched a picture of it, so that I could remember the names of all the parts—the splashboard and prow were beautifully carved and painted, and clusters of little cowrie shells had been strung along the gunwales. They had given it a name, which translated as *Sailing with the Wind.*

"Will you take this fishing?"

"No," the old man Meia said through an interpreter. "This is for playing."

It was to be used in the *kula* expeditions, as the men from Kaisiga sailed from island to island giving and receiving the elaborate arm shells *(mwali)* and necklaces *(soulava)* that were involved in this enigmatic game. It was outwardly a ceremony of exchange, with people taking shell ornaments from island to island and passing along to friends (the *kula* partners), who, in turn, took ornaments to other islands. The so-called *Kula* Ring was partly social and partly magical, a game that has been played in the Milne Bay area for thousands of years, as the players—all of them expert sailors—traveled among the islands. The arm shells went counterclockwise around the islands, the necklaces clockwise, and they were valuable because of their history, and their power deepened as they passed from person to person over the years. That supernatural power in Polynesia was known as *mana*—it was soul and strength. Each one (there are hundreds in circulation at any one time) has its own name and

pedigree and personality. It is not owned by anyone. It would be unthinkable to sell any of these shell artifacts.

Joining the *kula* voyages was not for all Trobrianders. I had the impression that only a minority of the islanders were actually *kula* people, and
that they were brought into the small circle of *kula* society by friends and
relatives, the way one might be asked to join a bowling club in another
culture—the comradeship was the important thing, and—this being the
Trobes—women were also included.

All this I learned from Meia, the master canoe builder. The seagoing
canoe, the *masawa,* was essential to the *kula* expedition, since the islands
were so far-flung.

As he spoke to me, Meia was mixing betel with lime in his little pot and
sucking red globs of it off a stick. He was one of the few people in Kaisiga
who was addicted to this stuff, a mild intoxicant.

"What is that?" I asked.

"Beer," he said, and smiled his toothless lime-rotted smile.

It was impossible to tell how old Meia was, but I could estimate his age.
He remembered helping American soldiers carry boxes of food and am-
munition after their amphibious landings in the Trobriands. (General
MacArthur had thought the grass airstrip on Kiriwina might be useful in
the Allied air war against the Japanese.) That was in June 1943. If Meia
had been fourteen then, he was sixty-one now. His toothlessness and his
skinny withered face and cloudy eyes made him look a great deal older
than that.

No one I met in the Trobriands knew his or her exact age, and many
could not even guess at it. A birthday, or year, was simply not recorded
or remembered. Little breastless girls said, "Feefteen!" and big buxom
ones said, "Seex!" "I am one hundred years old," a schoolboy told me in
his teasing way, but when I promised him some candy if he told me his
true age he could not do it. Speaking of their parents they would say,
"Forty—or maybe fifty—or something."

I explained what a birthday was to Zechariah, who was in his early
twenties.

"It is an interesting idea," he said. "But I don't know. My father and
mother don't remember when I was born."

I had not planned to stay long at Kaisiga, but once my tent was pitched
and I had ceased to be an oddity I decided to stay. Kaisiga was a good
place to set off from to visit the rest of the villages on this fairly large
island; and it was a good place to return to in the evening. There was
drinking water here, the village was clean and orderly, the villagers were
hospitable—they didn't importune, they didn't borrow, they didn't steal,

and after a few days they didn't stare. Most of all they were gentle and peace-loving. That was what impressed me most, the peacefulness of the place. I decided to stay longer.

My food supplies were gone, but by a happy accident I discovered that I had an appetite for their food. Their staples were steamed or boiled taro roots and sweet potatoes and yams, and the greens they called "pumpkin tops," and a spinachy green they referred to as *ibica.*

They cooked with coconut milk—shredding the coconut meat and squelching it with fresh water. Now and then they had fish, smoked or steamed. Bananas and guavas were plentiful. For religious reasons they never had meat. They never fried anything, they used no salt or spices. It was a nearly perfect diet—in fact, it closely approximated the no-fat, high-energy diet that had been advocated in America and turned into a best-selling book by Nathan Pritikin.

"Obesity is extremely rare, and in its more pronounced forms is called a disease," Malinowski had written seventy years ago on the Trobriands. This was still true. One Saturday when there was nothing to do in the village—no one could cook or work on the Sabbath—I persuaded a small group of villagers to come on a nature walk with me so that I could learn some of the island's names for these creatures (most of them proscribed in Leviticus—herons, snakes, lizards, turtles). I quizzed them on the topic of obesity, and with real emotion Lyndon (Leendon) said, "It is horrible."

The rest of them agreed. It was almost unknown in the Trobriands for anyone to be *napopoma* (potbellied), they said, and a fatty was as unerotic, in their opinion, as an elderly person, a cripple, a leper, or an albino.

The Saturday Sabbath in Kaisiga was a day for eating cold yams and clammy greens; for sitting around and talking; for sleeping, while the younger villagers sang and prayed or listened to Pastor John's Biblical texts—he called them "Memory gems." However distant and solitary I felt all week in this little eventless village on this little humid island, I felt even more so on a Saturday. It made me jumpy and watchful. But by my second Saturday I had learned to glide along, and when John asked me to speak I decided to give a vegetarian sermon. I read from the Book of Daniel, of how Daniel had refused to defile himself with Nebuchadnezzar's meat and wine, and how he had grown healthy and wise insisting on his diet of lentils and water.

John felt that I was ripe for conversion, and whenever we were together he preached the Adventist message. One day I expressed an interest in seeing the communal gardens, which were a mile or so in the interior of the island. We trekked in on a path that was partly mud and partly coral, and in the jungle the air was still and humid. I tried to leap from one tree root to another over the black shiny millipedes and the mud, as I was stung by no-see-ums and mosquitoes—here and there was an eight-inch spider clinging to a web the size of a wagon wheel, bits of the web smeared on my face, and I was hot and thirsty and gasping and my feet hurt from my stumbling on the coral—and all this time John was sermonizing.

"Jesus said, 'No man can serve two masters: for either he will hate the one, and love the other; or else he will hold to the one and despise the other. You cannot serve God and mammon.' Now what does that mean when Almighty God says that? It means—"

And perspiring and stung and covered with mud, I staggered onward, batting the spiders away, and each time I brushed past a tree trunk the ants leaped from the bark to my skin and began biting me.

"Wide is the gate and broad is the way that leadeth to destruction," John was saying.

The gardens, when we reached them after an hour of bush-bashing, were rubbly and helter-skelter, the yams, the sweet potatoes, the taro, the pawpaws thriving among chunks of coral and tree roots on uneven ground.

"I tell them not to waste food," John said, standing on a coral boulder. "There are people in this world who are starving to death!"

I saw a chicken scratching in the garden. I said, "Do you eat chickens?"

He frowned at me. "The body is the temple of God."

This was his text for the return trip.

"The Yam Festival is terrible," he said, clucking. "Everyone commits fornication."

"In the village?"

"Yes, they do it right in the village."

"Can you see them?"

"Yes, they do it while people's eyes are on them!" he said, batting branches. "Yes, you can see them going up and down! Oh, it is terrible."

"I don't even like to think about it," I said, and I clucked in disapproval as he gave me more details.

At night the church services were held in the dark—there were no working lanterns in Kaisiga; the flashlights were used only for fishing. In the early evening I went to my tent and drank sherry and wrote my notes, and heard the children singing *Weespa a frayer in da morning*. I knew the service was ending when they sang,

Lord keep us safe dis night,
Secure from all our fees
May ainjoos guard us while we sleep
Till morning light appees.
Amen!

And then they left the church and hurried into the dark, where they ran and played and sang, giggling and fumbling and sometimes—in spite of all their apparent piety—raising hell, and often singing,

> *London Bridge is palling down*
> *Palling down, palling down,*
> *My pair lady!*

The best beach on the island was on the western side, in an uninhabited cove, a two-hour paddle from Kaisiga. It was a white crescent of sand with clear water and shady trees. On some days I brought my lunch here and swam and watched the parrots and fish eagles.

But that was only part of it. The rest, and in a way, the most blissful, was sitting in the pavilion at the Kaisiga shore, among a dozen softly chatting villagers, as the sun went down and the cool breeze wafted from the lagoon. We drank the sweet water from green coconuts.

When you come back bring us chocolate, they said. Bring us spear rubbers, bring us spear points and fishhooks and fishing line. Bring us T-shirts. Bring me a lantern, Micah said. Bring me baby clothes, Esther said. Bring me a watch, John said.

And on those nights we talked in whispers about ghosts. So many ghosts in the Trobriands! It was the reason people lived in huts that had no windows—they barricaded themselves in at night, even as their children were out playing. They told me about the *khosa,* the spirits of the dead. "They come and trick us!" About the *mulukwausi,* the invisible flying witches who perched in the trees and on the hut roofs and then swept to the ground and penetrated people's bodies, and lived in their hearts and lungs, killing them that way. Or the *bwaga'u.* No, they are not ghosts, they whispered: They are real men who kill at night. The *bwaga'u* were sorcerers.

"Give me an example," I said.

This was on one of those moony nights at the pavilion by the lagoon when the bliss of the south seas dream was palpable—the breeze on my face, the sound of the sea, the aroma of blossoms, the last squawks of the birds settling in the branches for the night.

"Two years ago," Lyndon said, "there were two small children in the village who were thought to be evil. They were causing bad things to happen. That's what people said."

The breeze ruffled the thatch on the pavilion roof, and I could hear the low breathing of the villagers.

"So what happened to the children?"

"They were killed."

"How?"

"Poisoned."

"By whom?"

"A *bwaga'u.* Someone in our village."

"Do you know who?"

No one replied. There was darkness and silence. *Someone in our village.* A sorcerer. But it was a very small village.

Chapter 7
AGROUND IN THE TROUBLED TROBRIANDS

"We cannot take the shortcut. I saw some naked girls this morning on that road," Simon said, smiling—but there was a tremble of anxiety on his purplish lips.

This was my second visit to the Trobes—I had just been dropped at the airstrip by the Moresby plane and Simon, barefoot and toothless, had met me at the airstrip in his rusty pickup truck. Simon disproved Malinowski's observation: "They give at first approach not so much the impression of wild savages as of smug and self-satisfied bourgeois."

The surprise to me was that Simon was smiling at all. At the roadside a little earlier an elderly Italian priest wearing a straw hat and shorts had asked him for a ride. Simon said, "You Catholic mission?" and when the priest nodded, Simon said, "No, no, no!" and gunned the engine. The mission was next to his village. "They are bad people," he explained to me. "They are troubling my village."

My collapsible kayak was in the back with all my camping gear, and a large bundle of presents—the T-shirts, the lantern, the spear points and fishhooks, and all the rest of the stuff the people from Kaisiga had asked me to bring.

"I saw the girls doing the *mweki-mweki*," and he giggled at the thought of it. He had dusty hair and a brown scarred face. "Wearing short skirts." That meant the brief, bristly grass skirts. "They lifted their skirts up. They show their arse and private parts."

"What will happen if we go there?"

"They will rape us."

"How can they rape us if we just lie there? It's physically impossible."

"They will"—and now he smiled his red-toothed betel-juice smile—"sit on our faces."

"Does that frighten you?"

"Very much."

"They wouldn't attack a *dim-dim* like me."

"Yes. One was attacked some years ago. And Dennis"—Dennis was the local Member of Parliament, but a *dim-dim*—"they chased Dennis last year."

"The Yam Festival isn't supposed to start until next week," I said.

"It started today," Simon said. "This is the first day of yam harvest."

Perfect, I thought.

The Trobrianders who hung around the lodge, or who worked there— it was never clear who was who—greeted me in a friendly way and helped me carry my gear. "This is your boat, Mr. Paul!" In places where the passage of time is unimportant, where there are no deadlines, where there is little sense of urgency—Pacific islands, the landlocked countries of Africa, the clearings in the South American jungle—people seem to have excellent memories. And they seldom remark on how long it has been since your last visit. You are welcomed, not effusively but warmly. You are fed. It is as though you had never left.

"Anything new?" I asked them.

"No," they said.

The food at the lodge was much worse than before. I sat down to the first course, which was a dish holding one orange segment, a small withered carrot, some brown disks of banana, and a cold gray cut-open hot dog.

"The cook is on strike," Gertrude said. She was skinny and wizened, though she was no more than thirty-five. In a place where the average life expectancy was forty-something—because of malaria, TB, and bacterial infections—Gertrude was regarded as (and looked) rather old.

I asked her to bring me fish, yams, and sweet potato, and if they didn't have it in the kitchen, I said, why not get it at the village next door? She brought it, and then sat with me while I ate, and we talked about the yam harvest. Just that morning some girls had accosted a man as they were leaving the gardens with some yams. The yams were special, magical; the carrying was always done by women, and in this matrilineal society the women had power.

"They took him on the ground," Gertrude said. "They scratched him on his arms."

"Girls or women?"

"Just the girls. Not the women. The girls are young. They can do as they like. They are public property. But even some women wear short skirts at this time of year. Their husbands cannot do anything about it."

"Do you wear a short skirt sometimes?"

"If I want to!" she said, and laughed hard. "What do they do in America?"

"Men and women chase each other all year, not just at harvest time. But it's not so much fun. Also they pay the women sometimes."

"They pay here, in some villages. Five kina. Or two kina, if the man doesn't have a job."

I loved that.

"They call it the 'Two Kina Bush.' You pay the money and do it in the trees."

The wind had blown all night and it was still blowing hard in the morning, which would make for rough paddling conditions. It was cooler than on my previous visit, with scattered clouds. But I wanted to set off, so I carried my gear to the shore and—as men and boys wandered over to watch (*"Waga,"* they muttered)—started assembling my boat. Nine of the men carried bunches of betel nuts. They were from the island of Munawata, which lay a few miles to the west of Kaileuna. They sat and watched and spat blood-red betel juice, and they laughed each time they saw me stumble or heard me curse, as I put the boat together.

Two Chinese men joined them. They said they were from Malaysia and I guessed they were here in the Trobriands to buy some bêche-de-mer, the sea slugs the Chinese regard as a delicacy and call sea cucumbers. Local divers found the best of these creatures in deep water, and got about fifteen cents apiece from island traders, who processed them. The fat squishy sausages were smoke-dried and turned into hard little dicks, then bagged into forty-pound sacks and exported—with carvings, sea slugs were one of the few Trobriand exports. (Trochus shells for buttons and pretty butterflies—sold to lepidopterists—were others.) Selling sea slugs was the only thing to do with them. Most Trobrianders laughed at the thought of anyone eating them, though when there was not much food available some people ate them.

Mr. Lim and Mr. Choo watched me loading my boat.

"You are going out in that little boat alone?" Mr. Lim asked.

"Yes."

"That's adventurous," he said.

"If you say so."

"But you don't look adventurous," he said. "You look like a professor."

"Thank you, Mr. Lim."

Mr. Choo said, "I am adventurous."

"Good for you," I said.

"But I wouldn't go alone. It is dangerous to go alone."

Mr. Lim was scowling at the group of men from Munawata.

"But the Aborigines seem friendly," he said.

Andrew, a dark sturdy fisherman who worked at the lodge, was talking to the men. When they spoke to him, he laughed, and he said, "They told me, 'Tell the *dim-dim* to be careful.'"

"Why do they say that?"

"Because the water is very rough around Kaileuna," Andrew said. "That's why they are here. They are waiting for the weather to improve."

It might have given me pause, but I knew their canoes well enough now. They were well built but did not have much freeboard and in a heavy sea they shipped water. They could go anywhere, even in fairly poor sea conditions, but there was often a lot of bailing to be done, with their wooden scoops. My boat could go anywhere, in almost any weather: that was the great virtue of a kayak.

But I had never paddled this boat so heavily laden. Besides my food and my gear, I had bundles of presents, and some of the presents—the fifty T-shirts and the fishing tackle, for example—I had crammed into a big canvas sack about the size of a mailbag and tied to the stern deck of my boat, where it sat like a carcass.

The weight thrust the boat into the water and all this wetted surface gave it stability. But it was harder to paddle and, beyond the clay-colored channel and the weedy shallows and the crocodile nostrils poking up at Boli Point, where the open water began there was a strong wind blowing and four-foot breaking waves.

And the high lump of cargo lashed to the boat caught the wind and I was turned like a weather vane. I seriously wondered whether I should go back, or camp on this western side of Kiriwina Island and wait for better weather. As I pondered this—Kaileuna Island lay in the distance—the wind was still spinning my boat sideways, and waves were breaking across the bow deck, and I realized that in my indecision I had been blown quite far from shore.

So I kept at it. If you are stuck in chop and wind, kayakers say, just stay upright and paddle through it. I had the entire day ahead of me, there was no hurry, all I had to do was plow on to Kaileuna. The breaking waves were the worst of it, and every now and then I was drenched— being slapped in the face by a cold frothy wave inspired a nervous dread in me, the feeling (as the water ran down my neck) that there was worse to come.

I headed for the nearest part of Kaileuna, which was a point of land, so that I could shelter and have a drink before pushing on along the coast to Kaisiga. It took me three hours to reach this rocky nose, but before I had time to celebrate my little achievement with a swig of water, two boys appeared on the beach, carrying spears—straight shafts with homemade rusty points.

"We will not hurt you," one said. He was wearing a pair of goggles that gave him the pop-eyed appearance of a villain.

But that in itself was a kind of warning. I took out my own spear—a long fiberglass one with a wicked-looking trident on the business end.

"Want to see my spear?"

They admired it, looking suitably respectful. "Where are you going?" I said, "To Kaisiga."

"We do not like those people," said the boy with the goggles. "We are from Giwa."

I said, "Are the girls in Giwa raping the men this week?"

"On the mainland the girls rape men. Not here."

"Mainland" meant Kiriwina. This larger island was always called "the mainland." And the real mainland they called New Guinea.

"Come to Giwa," they said, as I paddled away. "We will show you our village."

It was another hour or so to Kaisiga and, in a stretch of water where there were normally lots of fishing canoes, little dugouts and larger outriggers, there were no boats at all, only a sea of rough water. And there were no people on the beach, only the sweeping wind and the thrashing of thatch and the loose panels of the woven huts.

I was spotted—first by some children, then by some men sheltering behind a hut—and they helped me ashore, Micah, and Josiah, and Lyndon, who called himself Leendon.

Josiah said, "You came from the station?"—meaning Losuia—"In this wind? Eh! Eh!"

I could see that they were pleased. They themselves had planned to go fishing today, but instead stayed ashore because of the stormy weather. They were flattered that I had come all this way in the wind and the waves to see them—and, more than that, risked getting wet in order to bring them T-shirts and fishing tackle.

John was at the garden, but Esther was at her hut. She was sitting cross-legged, suckling her infant.

"This is Anne," she said. "As I told you. We named her after your wife."

"It's a nice name," I said.

It was simply impossible for me to explain to her, or anyone on these happy islands, the derangement in my life.

I gave Esther the pressure lamp I had brought her from Moresby, and then I unloaded my boat. As I was setting up my tent, the wind rose, gusting madly and lashing the coconut palms. Meanwhile, about ten children were kicking a football nearby—every so often the ball would bash into my tent. I waved the kids away, but they just laughed at me—they were fearless. And when the rain started they kept kicking the ball and screeching, as they ran and splashed.

The frenzied kids, and the rain and wind, exhausted me. I went into in my tent and made notes about my morning paddle in the high wind, while sipping the sherry that I hid from these prohibitionists. Every so often the children booted the ball into the side of my tent, but they laughed when I told them to play somewhere else. Finally I dozed off.

The gong woke me. I heard the kids hurrying in the pattering rain, and then,

> *Weespa a frayer in da morning,*
> *Weespa a frayer at noon . . .*

The sweetness of their voices was undeniable, but in it was a note of mockery. They no longer sounded innocent to me. These prayer rituals were no more than momentary pauses in their relentless teasing, and indeed seemed to make their teasing worse.

Pastor John had come back from the gardens in order to conduct this evening service. I met him amid the blowing trees a little later and told him that I had brought the things they had asked for—the watch, the lantern, the T-shirts, the fishing tackle.

A number of villagers gathered in the wind and drizzle to watch me unpack the bundle of T-shirts which I had collected from friends to bring here. I let them choose the ones they wanted, and they immediately put them on—*Boston Celtics, Hard Rock Cafe, Me and My Girl, Punahou School, Great Wall Hotel Beijing, Dream Girls, Braves,* and so forth. They took them without ceremony. Though there was gratitude in the way they accepted them, it was wordless thanks, yet it was so muted and perfunctory it seemed to verge on disappointment.

I gave Leendon some fishing hooks. He smiled at me. "But where is the line? What good are hooks without line?"

Zechariah thanked me for the spear point. He said, "Now I need a spear rubber"—meaning the tube of surgical rubber they fastened to the shaft of the spear to give it propulsion.

"You can borrow Micah's," I said. I had given Micah a length of rubber.

But Zechariah had seen that I had several more—ones I had planned to use for trading in other villages.

"I want my own rubber," he said.

"Did you get me extra batteries for my watch?" John asked.

"This shirt does not fit me," Derrick said, exchanging a *Braves* T-shirt for one that said *A Day in the Life of Canada.*

In a society that operated on a principle of continuous gift-giving, what I had done was merely to perform a ritual, fulfilling an obligation, which was why they felt free to nag me. And when I showed myself completely indifferent to their nagging, they changed the subject.

"There is a feast at Sinaketa tomorrow," Leendon said. "I am sailing there. You could come with us."

"What if the weather is bad?"

"I am a good sailor," Leendon said, and laughed. "I am big-pela, strong-pela. Ha!"

"I might paddle in my boat," I said.

The wind blew so hard that night it lifted the fly of my tent and soaked the mosquito net. And the pelting of raindrops and the sound of the wind in the trees woke me and made me anxious. Hearing the waves loudly hitting the beach, I poked my head out of the tent, but in the blackness I saw nothing. So I switched on my flashlight and disturbed a dusky crab twice the size of my hand clawing at my tent flap.

I made green tea with my little stove, and had this for breakfast with Esther's rice, and pumpkin tops boiled in coconut milk. The wind was still blowing hard and I could see that the whole lagoon was frothy with chop and breaking waves. Was this a day for sailing or paddling anywhere?

Leendon said, "We are going. Come with us."

This man had once told me: *We sail out, and if it gets dark, we find an island and stay there for the night. There are islands everywhere in this sea, and there is always an empty island at night.* So I trusted him.

The whole village turned out to launch Leendon's outrigger canoe into the surf. I carried my binoculars and my compass. There were nine of us on board, including just one woman, who crouched at the bow. I sat on the gunwale of the canoe and the seven men were occupied as crew members, two adjusting lines and trimming the rigging, two using the steering paddles jammed between braces, one on the main sheet, one standing at the bow and yelling about the heading, and Leendon alternately grunting orders and bailing the canoe. It would have been hard to sail this twenty-foot canoe with fewer than seven men. We began to ship water as soon as we left shore, and when we burst over the reef, seawater streamed in. Most of it came through the uncaulked seam in the longitudinal planks that had been added to give the vessel greater height and volume. No one seemed worried by this, least of all Leendon, who bailed with an old wooden scoop they called a *yatura.*

We had a lateen sail made of thick blue plastic sheeting and we sailed with the wind striking us on our outrigger side, which lifted the platform towards the body of the boat and almost submerged the seam of the plank on the opposite, down-tilted side. We could not sail very close to the wind, and at the beginning everything seemed very chaotic to me; but after a while I saw that each person on board had a specific role to play and in this rough sea was very attentive to his task.

The canoe was slow to respond to any trimming, even slower to turn, and was sluggish in the waves. We were all soon soaked to the skin as soon as we were past the reef.

"Leendon, does this canoe have a name?"

He said the name, *Toiyokwai.* "It means, 'Too Big-Headed.' You say, 'Do this,' 'Do that' but the person don't listen. They got their own way. You can't tell them a thing."

Pompous, arrogant, overconfident. "I know the type."

"But why are we heading out to sea?"

"It is better in this wind."

We looked back at the disappearing islands, where another canoe was struggling against a lighter wind.

"We're going to beat him," I said.

They laughed, and clearly it was what they intended, and they continually fine-tuned the paddles they used variously as leeboards and rudders.

"Look at him," Micah said.

The other canoe rocked and slewed in the wind, and a half a mile of choppy water lay between us. We were heading southeast towards the sea-arm of Kiriwina, to the coastal village of Sinaketa.

Micah spoke in Kiriwina to the other canoe, a voice of casual contempt and glee, which made the others laugh.

"What did he say?"

"Micah say, 'Go fuck your mother.' 'Go fuck your sister.'" And I must have frowned, because he added, "We are just joking him."

The wind was now tearing at our sail and straining the ancient-looking lines.

I said, "This is what we call a steep and confused sea."

"The current is running *this* way, and the wind is blowing *that* way," Leendon said, enunciating an immutable law of the sea. "That is why there are waves."

"Does the village have a motorboat?" I asked.

"Yes, a dinghy, but the motor is buggered," one of the oarsmen said. "And there are problems."

Leendon changed the subject. We talked about crocodiles. They had no fear of them. *They used to come to the village to eat the dogs,* one of them said. And another put in, *You see them at low tide at Boli Point looking for something to eat.* Leendon said, *One* dim-dim *shot a big crocodile that had killed a small girl. They cut it open and found her bones and the earring from her ear.*

We were now way past Kaileuna and almost out of sight of the main island, all the lines tightened and the various sticks and braces in the canoe creaking. Leendon kept up a running commentary on the adjustments, while at the same time answering my questions about marriage in the Trobriands. Not marrying was unthinkable, he implied. ("The Trobriander has no full status in social life until he is married," Malinowski had said.) There was a partner for everyone. Wasn't that true of America?

"Some people never marry," I said. "I know a man who is fifty-something. He was supposed to marry a woman but at the last moment she changed her mind. He found another. Just before they were to be married she met another man. A third one dropped him—*bwoyna bogie,* bye-bye, and she was gone. A fourth one agreed to marry him but they argued one day and she went away and sent his ring back in a little parcel."

"He is very sad," Leendon said.

"He says he hates women now."

"He has no wife. No kids. That is terrible. What does he do all day?"

"He writes things."

"He is wasting time. He should come here. We will find him a wife."

I said, "A fourteen-year-old girl in a grass skirt with flowers in her hair?"

"Maybe fifteen," Leendon said.

The rest of the way to Sinaketa they told me what I should bring them the next time I came (waterproof watch, a tent like mine, a water bag like mine, more fishing tackle) and we trolled for fish, using fragments of a plastic bag for bait.

"I ran out of plastic last month when I was out fishing," Micah said. "I just cut my shirt and used little rags for bait. I caught many fish."

At Sinaketa we beached the canoe and went ashore, where the feast was in progress. Our little canoe party found the large number of decorated and dancing people rather overwhelming, and we stayed together. Leendon pointed out Puliyasi, the Paramount Chief of the Trobriands, from the powerful Tabalu clan, who lived in Omarakhana with a number of wives. Sir Michael Somare, the former New Guinean prime minister, was seated under an awning. And a man as black and as hip as any American rapper was a Melanesian nutritionist from New Ireland in the Bismarck Archipelago.

Frowning, barebreasted girls in straw tutus danced in a sort of conga line, egged on by sweating drummers. Some of the girls wore kula artifacts—jangling arm shells and necklaces. They were followed by boys with talcum on their faces—strange white masks—who did the *mweki-mweki,* the so-called "tapioca dance." This was an explicitly sexual, buttock-slapping bump and grind, with lots of shouted grunts, and it made the audience scream with approval.

The dancers wove their way among tall towers made of branches and containing yams which had been provided for the guests of honor. There were flags and flowers, and here and there were hairy black pigs tied up and whimpering as they struggled against their knots.

I fell into conversation with a man named James from Sinaketa, and asked him about burial customs.

"There isn't much burial here," he said. "The people die and their bones are put into clay pots and hidden."

Now I saw that Leendon had led Micah and the others to the little shelters that had been erected for the occasion. On long tables there were heaps of rice and boiled yams and bananas, and the sailors from Kaisiga were snatching handfuls of it and stuffing their mouths.

"But on Kitava," James was saying, "they take the dead man and butcher him while the widow is lying underneath the body. The blood spatters her clothes. She wears the clothes for three days while the village cleans her husband's bones. The bones end up in a clay pot."

This village was wilder and so much more festive than any I had seen elsewhere. I pestered Leendon on the way back for an explanation. And it became clear to me that this main island, where there were a few schools and the only vehicles, was also the most traditional island. It was the Paramount Chief's island, it was where the strongest clans and the wealthiest villages were located. This was where the yam harvest rituals were strictly observed, and although there were missions here, the missionaries had little influence.

Normally, traditions were strongest the farther I had been from the center of things, but in the Trobriands, the hinterland, the outer islands, the little atolls regarded the big island as a throwback, full of primitives. That was why the villagers from Kaisiga were so eager to leave the big royal island of Kiriwina. Anything could happen to you there.

I had a vivid demonstration of that a few days later. Oppressed by the solitude of the village—everyone was working in the hot, mosquito-infested gardens—I had paddled to a swampy mangrove island called Baimapu to go bird-watching. The wind had died, and the morning was lovely and peaceful, the sea a mirror of limpid light all the way to the horizon, all pinky-blue pastels. Red and black parrots were chasing each other through the trees, and the herons and other fish eaters were wading in the shallows.

The water here was shallow and muddy, but a channel ran around the island. I tried to stay in this deeper water, away from the shadowy mud flats where there could have been crocs and where paddling was difficult—in places the water was only a few inches deep.

Ahead I saw seven or eight boys sloshing through the shallows, occasionally chucking spears into the water in front of them, going for fish. Seeing me, they changed direction and came near.

"Where you come from, *dim-dim?*" one said. He was a boy of thirteen or so, and his long spear—he wagged it at me—had a rusty point.

He was challenging me and being intentionally rude, so I said, "Don't call me *dim-dim*. I come from America."

Another said, "Give me PK"—the brand name was a generic term for chewing gum.

The others pestered me for gum, and then some of them began fingering the boat.

"We want to ride in your *waga.*"

One tried to sit on the stern, another pressed his spear point against the fabric of the boat.

"Don't touch it," I said sharply. "Get away from it."

By this time I had drifted out beyond the edge of the channel and was wedged in the shallows. The boys surrounded me, lifting their spears. They wore ragged shorts and their legs were muddy and there were smears of mud all over their bodies.

Shaking his spear at me, one of the smaller boys began running back and forth, shrieking, "I keel you! I keel you!"

As he jabbed the spear at me he made a hideous face, scowling and sticking his tongue out.

I dipped my paddle blade but my boat was stuck in the mud and I could not move it. I tried not to show my nervousness. In a tone of forced calm I said, "Don't be silly."

But seeing that I couldn't move, the others took up the chant, "Keel the *dim-dim!* Keel the *dim-dim!* Keel heem!"

The smaller boy came close to me and shook his spear and hissed at me, "Run you life, *dim-dim.*"

"Keel heem!"

All this time I was smiling my rigid smile and speaking slowly and trying to move myself off the mud bank with my paddle. I did not want to get out of the boat, nor did I wish to show my alarm.

It was a nightmare—the shrieking youngsters, the way they pranced and plopped in the water, threatening me, their fierce dirty faces, their hideously dangerous spears. I was seated, they were standing. And of course I was stranded—they saw that I was helpless. I could not understand whether it was merely a macabre game or genuinely hostile. But I decided not to antagonize them—only to ignore them and get myself out of there.

Turning my back on them, I dislodged the boat. It moved slowly, but still they pranced and chanted ("Run you life!"), and cried out, "Look at me!"—they wanted me to see their threatening spears. I deliberately kept my back turned to them and, disguising my effort (I was sure that if they saw that I was nervous they would pursue me), kept my boat sliding away from them. I went on talking monotonously to myself in an unconcerned way, "There is no reason for you to be shaking those ridiculous spears at me . . ."

"Look!" One of them was holding a small dead, discolored stingray—a despised fish in the Trobriands, eaten only in the poorer inland villages. "Eat it, *dim-dim!*"

They ran in front of me, so that I could see them with their spears, but I tried to appear calm, and I paddled past them. They threw the stingray at me and kept yelling, working themselves into a fury—horrible boys, with rusty spears and dirty faces.

In deeper water I dipped the paddle and took hard strokes. The boys followed me for a while—I was holding my breath, I had a sense that one of them would fling his spear at me—but I sprinted away and I did not stop paddling until I saw that they were astern, at a safe distance.

They had threatened me because I had been alone and had not given them any gift, and because they outnumbered me. I had left my fishing spear at the village. If I had shaken my own spear at them, or on the other hand if I had been a total wimp, they might have been much more hostile. I was the perfect victim: an outsider. It would not have been hard for them to injure me, even kill me. Just the bacteria on one of those rusty points would have done the job. What had surprised me most was their sudden cruelty.

I paddled to the wharf at Losuia, where a number of canoes were tied up. I was feeling unsteady and simply wanted to get out of my boat and sit down. If the little trade store was open I would buy myself something to eat.

A fisherman at the wharf said, "You want to tie up your boat?"

I said yes. I had tied it there many times.

"It will cost you thirty kina," he said.

What was this? Over thirty dollars, for something that had never cost me a cent. A crowd gathered behind the man.

"In that case, I won't tie up."

"What will you pay?" the self-appointed extortionist asked me.

"Nothing."

The rest of the people stood gaping at me from the wharf, no one saying anything. Again, I felt a sense of threat. Everyone I ran into seemed hostile. As I paddled away someone called out, "Come back! We will help you!" but I was sure they only wanted to torment me, so I kept going, back to my camp at Kaisiga.

Even the people at Kaisiga were acting strangely. One day I paddled to the eastern shore of the island, to Koma Village—a spooky inland village full of black snorting pigs—where I swapped a couple of silk scarves for some carvings (a canoe prow, an ebony lime pot). *Don't go to Koma,* they said afterwards. *The people in Koma are bad.*

The villagers seemed restless and preoccupied. I suggested that we all go fishing in Leendon's canoe.

Zechariah said, "I will go if you let me have your goggles and your spear."

"I'll share them with you," I said.

In the end, twelve of us set off in Leendon's canoe and as soon as we were a mile or so offshore they all stood up in the canoe to look for submerged rocks, where there would be fish. The water was so clear the rocks were visible for some distance, and when we found one—it was actually a cluster of rocks and coral—they all dived in and began thrashing towards the bottom.

The clarity of the water had disguised the depth. I slipped into the water but the others were way below me—thirty feet down, among the twinkling yellow and green tiddlers and the hordes of plump parrot fish. I had never seen people dive so deeply, and they stayed at the bottom, hanging on the rocks with one hand and jabbing with the other. When they needed a breath they kicked to the surface, leaving their spear wedged in the coral; and then they swam down and resumed. I got within about ten or twelve feet of the bottom and then felt pain in my eardrums and had to hover nearer the surface. The others were oblivious to the depth and they stayed down for two or three minutes at a time. They were deadly with the spears, too, for soon after we arrived at the spot they were bringing up fish—parrot fish, reef trout, and a dark surgeonfish with a poisonous spur near its tail they called a blackfish.

Noticing that the canoe had begun to take on water, I sat in the sunshine, amid the flopping fish, and bailed, scooping with Leendon's *yatura*—and the water was pink from the blood of the speared and wounded fish. We had brought coconuts—to drink, to eat, and as a native skin remedy (the others rubbed crumbled coconut meat over their shoulders and arms for protection and to ease the scorching). From time to time they brought up fish.

When I dived back into the water I saw that the others were ranging all over the broken reef, chasing fish until they cornered them in the cleft of a rock and then jabbing fiercely. I took several deep dives and I was about to take another when I saw—unmistakably—the silvery snout and torpedo body of a shark, drifting downward in the long shafts of sunlight that penetrated the deep water, towards some of the swimming spear carriers.

It was the smooth wickedly smirking shark of scare stories, huge and hungry-looking, surveying the naked swimmers with a kind of monstrous patience. The dark cigar shape of our canoe was just above me. With the fewest strokes ("sharks know when you're scared") I made for the canoe and in one motion shot out of the water and tumbled into it, among the frantic fish.

Wiping fish slime from my arms and hands, I tried to see beneath the water. The breeze rippling the surface was like a curtain being drawn across it, and nothing was clear to me.

Leendon was the first to surface. He snatched the canoe and took a great gasping breath. Then Derrick and Zechariah did the same, and others followed, clinging to the boat.

"Did you see the shark?"

Leendon said, "There were three sharks. The big one and two behind him. They were swimming to Zechariah, but he was on the rocks and he did not see them. So I shouted to him."

I could just see Leendon howling twenty-five feet underwater.

"I turned around and they were near me," Zechariah said. He was smiling.

I said, "Were you frightened?"

"No. I shout at them. 'Hoop! Hoop! Hoop!' That scared them away. They are stupid fish."

"Why didn't you swim away?"

"If they see you are scared they eat you."

"Leendon," I said. "Aren't you scared of sharks?"

He laughed at me and said, "No!"

"Do you know anyone who was bitten by one?"

"No one."

"But you can kill sharks."

Now he looked indignant.

"No. I am a Seventh Day Adventist."

And he referred me to Leviticus 11, where fish without scales are proscribed as an abomination.

We continued to dive, though I stayed close to the canoe. I was certain that the fish blood I had bailed out had attracted the sharks, and I was not comforted by the serenity of the others. I was afraid. And I disgraced myself again when, seeing a yellow sea snake moving sinuously through the water above me, I hurried into the canoe.

Leendon had seen me. "Why you fearing?"

I said, "Big-pela snake. Long pela. Yellow-pela."

"They not hurt you," Derrick said. "We play with them."

Later, looking for better fishing grounds, more tumbled coral rocks, we saw what could have been a coconut bobbing about thirty yards away.

"Turtle," Leendon said.

"It is a big one. We can chase it," Micah said.

"Do you eat them?"

Leendon said, "No. We are SDA. But the old men in the village eat them. They have a good taste."

It was a green sea turtle, with a shell the size of a manhole cover. We went after it, but it slipped away.

"It is better to catch them at night, when they are sleeping under the reef," Leendon said.

We were sitting cross-legged on the platform of poles that had been lashed across the outrigger of his canoe—a comfortable spot that could accommodate eight or nine people. He was watching the others count the fish. *Porty-pive,* someone said—Ps and Fs were interchangeable in the Kiriwina language.

"The current is too strong," Leendon said, signalling to the others to prepare the rigging for the return trip. "That is why we get pew pish."

Forty-five was quite a few—it was sixty pounds, or more, of fish. But the whole village had to be fed—that was his point. They would need twice that amount of fish to be able to smoke them and keep them for tomorrow.

On the way back we ate bananas and drank coconut water, and they eviscerated one coconut and rubbed the crumbled meat on their skin to ease their sunburn.

Out of the blue, Leendon said ruefully, "I am sorry we did not catch that turtle."

When we got near to shore the fishermen threw the fish out of the canoe into the water and the children splashed around snatching them up and washing them. Then they carried them to the village where another group of children had made a windbreak and erected a grille over a fire. There were twenty children involved in grilling the fish, many of them the boys and girls I had thought of as the village brats. When it came time for a village chore to be done, everyone lent a hand, even the brats.

The women, who had been awaiting the return of the fishing party, were steaming yams, bananas, and sweet potatoes by the underground-oven method that is used all over the Pacific, from New Guinea, where it is called *mumu,* to Hawaii, where it is known as *imu.* The Trobriand word, which is almost certainly cognate with these, is *kumkumla.*

I tried to get the fishermen talking about the *kula* expedition after we had sat with our food—we were all in a long row on the ground, eating off of palm leaves. Leendon was the most serious *kula* man in the village, but he was reluctant to talk about the arm shells and necklaces he had in his hut. Finally he said, "I don't want to show Faul my *bagi.* He will want to buy all of them."

I persuaded him to show me the best necklace, which was a long beautiful string of tiny polished shells, and then I said, "I don't want to buy it. It is not nice enough. In fact it is very ugly. It is nogut, samting-nating."

"He say it samting-nating! Ha!"

They all laughed. Heavy sarcasm was just the sort of clumsy teasing that they loved.

John was revolving his sister-in-law's six-month-old daughter, Primrose, over a smoldering coconut shell as he listened to all the banter. There were so many words in Pidgin for worthless things. ("It is bullseet . . . It is rabis . . . Namba-ten . . .")

They also found Pidgin as funny as I did, and because they seldom used it in the Trobriands the effect was always comic. And speaking Pidgin I could often ask questions that were awkward in plain English

Dog eaters always interested me, so I used this little feast as an occasion for asking, *"Yu-pela kai-kai dok?"*—Do you people eat dogs?

"SDA-pela no kai-kai dok," Leendon said.

"Yu traiem kai-kai dok—nambawan, moa beta," I said, patting my stomach.

John was smiling, still rotating the naked infant in the smoke. *"Alotau people traiem dok tumas. Tu, kai-kai pusi."*

The Kaisiga women stared at him and the men began to shriek with laughter.

"Why are we speaking Pidgin?" I said. "Let's talk normal English. We are all normal English speakers, aren't we?"

"I am the most normal," Leendon said, and everyone laughed.

But I was looking at John. "Let me get this straight. You say that people in Alotau eat pussycats?"

"Some of the people," he said. "But not our own dogs and cats. We get other ones from the bush or running in the roads, and we cook them just like any other meat. Yes, sometimes it is sad, because a dog is man's best friend. But they taste good."

"Are dogs and cats mentioned in Leviticus?"

"No," John said, still dipping the infant into the smoke. "And not in Deuteronomy."

"What are you doing with that baby?"

He lifted the coconut shell and showed me a smoldering object beneath it, the size of a walnut.

"You see this grasshopper's egg?" he said, indicating the smoky walnut. *Grasshopper's egg?* "We burn it and when the smoke comes through the coconut shell we let the baby smell it. It is so the baby will walk straight."

"Do you believe that?"

"Yes. I have seen it."

I had found him monotonously Biblical—his lengthy way of saying grace was so sententious it set my teeth on edge; so, seeing this Christian islander espousing magic and superstition, I encouraged him.

I had promised myself that I would paddle to the tiny islands at the edge of the Trobriand group. I could not interest anyone in Kaisiga in coming with me—visiting another village or another island involved a complex ritual of gift-giving and they couldn't be bothered. It was easier for me to show up, shoot the breeze, and placate them with some sticks of tobacco or fishhooks: A *dim-dim* was hardly human in any case.

It took a day to paddle to and from the island of Munawata. The sailors at Munawata remembered me from the days of bad weather when I had paddled off and they had stayed on shore. Their lovely island had only their village on it, and when I praised its beauty they said, "But we have no water."

The penalty of living on this island paradise, with sandy beaches and fertile soil, was that whenever they needed fresh water they had to get into their canoes and sail over a mile to Labi Island, where there was a spring. And when there was a northwest wind blowing they couldn't get there at all. This might last for days.

"Then we eat green coconuts and try to save rainwater and wait for the wind to change."

On Munawata there were traditional bachelor houses, in which young boys lived and where they brought their girlfriends. The girls might stay with them for weeks, though they always had their meals with their parents—a very civilized arrangement, I felt. The boys on Munawata wore flowers in their hair and the teenaged girls and women were bare-breasted and had deeply rouged cheeks. The girls were assertively sexual in their manner and the way they dressed because the yam harvest was in progress.

It was so strange to paddle from that village of free love back to

Kaileuna, where the pious folk in Kaisiga laughed at these old ways and clung to their newfound Adventist beliefs. But even they were rooted enough in Trobriand culture not to find a trip to the forbidden and haunted island of Tuma too spooky for words. No one would go with me, and they urged me not to go—the island was full of voices and shadows, the ghosts of everyone who had ever died in the Trobriands lurked in Tuma, and if I spent the night there I would get no sleep. I paddled there—it was another lovely island, empty and overgrown because of its reputation—but in the event I did not camp there. I camped back at Kaisiga and then kept going the next day to the main island of Kiriwina. On the way a motorboat came alongside—a German anthropologist, Dr. Wulf Schievelhovel and his son Fridjtof. Wulf said he had recognized my collapsible kayak as German.

"I have never seen anyone paddling a kayak here before," he said.

We tied our boats together and shared a Pepsi he brought from his cooler and talked about the Trobrianders. He had been studying them for twenty years. They had an almost perfect diet, he said, they had no heart disease or coronary problems at all. Their blood pressure went down as they grew older, and yet he confirmed what I had heard, that they didn't live long: Their life expectancy was less than forty, because of the high risk of bacterial infections.

"But so little has changed here, it is as though these people have walked straight off the pages of Malinowski," he said.

He urged me to see more of the main island and to visit Omarakhana, the village of the Paramount Chief. Then he snapped my picture—I had found it inconvenient to carry a camera—and we continued on our separate ways, he to his village on Kaileuna, I to Kiriwina, in the blinding afternoon sunshine.

The heart of the Trobriands, its chieftainship and culture, is Omarakhana. "Ever since we came out of the caves," Trobrianders say, "our chief has lived here." They never said that their ancestors might have migrated from other islands; indeed, they firmly do not believe it. Long ago, their people emerged from the the caves of coral rock near Kaibola at the top of the island and they divided into separate clans. One of the most respected is the Tabalu, clan of the present Paramount Chief, Puliyasi, who had been chief for about three years.

Because of the danger of rape—and rape wasn't a joke; it was exactly what it was anywhere, a violent assault, a humiliation—I went in a truck with a friendly villager named Matthew. On the way he told me that this chief was better than the last one. Traditionally the Paramount Chief controls the weather. The previous chief, always in a foul mood, gave them miserable weather—too much rain, then too much sun, and then days of wind.

"If I say, 'Please make it rain, Chief,' will he do it?"

"If he want, he do it."

It seemed wonderful to live in a place where you could actually blame someone you knew for the weather.

The royal village was muddy and humid, in the center of the island, far from the sea breeze, two miles or more from its beach, at the end of a bad road and an overgrown path. It was nowhere near as tidy or pleasant as the villages I had seen on the outer islands. It seemed neglected and rather haunted, with shabby huts and bad thatching and ramshackle pavilions. Pigs rooted and snorted near the huts and the snotty-faced children, and the scruffy dogs fought one another for scraps. The chief's hut was one of the flimsiest-looking, but Matthew said that he had several, because he was still acquiring wives—he had three at the moment.

A balding man in torn shorts and a dirty T-shirt lettered *Coca-Cola Fun Run 1988* came out of the hut, and spat. He was smoking acrid Trobriand tobacco in a rolled-up tube of newspaper. He was barefoot. He approached me and smiled a stained betel-juice smile and beckoned to a boy who hurried towards him and set up a rickety beach chair in one of the wall-less moldering pavilions. And then he sat and the frayed blue plastic webbing creaked. This was Paramount Chief Puliyasi.

I sat at his feet—it would have been unthinkable for me to sit at the chief's height and look him straight in the eye—and introduced myself as a traveler and a grateful guest on the Trobriands. I then gave him twenty dollars' worth of sticky black tobacco.

And the chief, who knew no English, mumbled something to one of his courtiers.

"The chief wishes to know how did you hear about the Trobriands."

"I read some books about the Trobriands, by a famous *dim-dim* named Malinowski."

"He lived in this village," the man said. His name was Joseph Daniel and he wore a pair of torn brown trousers. "The people could not pronounce his name, so they called him *Tolibwoga,* which means 'Master of Stories' or 'Historian'—something like that. He was always telling old stories."

Hearing the name, the chief smiled and puffed his newspaper cheroot. I asked where Malinowski lived.

"Over there, where you see the string and the clothes."

"Near that clothesline?"

"Yes. He lived near Chief To'uluwa. That man was Chief Puliyasi's mother's grandfather."

In this matrilineal society all titles and lands passed through the mother's line, and a woman's brother was closer to her children than their father, who was hardly even regarded as a blood relation (but there was no question about the link of the uncle to his sister's kids).

"Do they tell stories about Tolibwoga?"

"No. But the chief knows some stories."

"Did Tolibwoga travel to other islands?" I asked, and my question and the reply were translated.

"He never traveled, because they could not guarantee his safety. At that time there were quarrels on the other islands. The people were fighting. Tolibwoga stayed here."

I pretended to write this in my notebook. What I wrote was: *Fun Run T-shirt, beach chair, shaven-headed women, spider webs on all houses, pigs and dogs, neglected houses in need of repair.*

The chief mumbled to Joseph, who said, "The chief wants to know if you have any questions for him. He wants to help you. You are welcome to ask all questions."

I asked a few harmless questions and then decided to risk the one that had been nagging at me.

"Is it true that Chief Puliyasi has magic that lets him control the weather?"

When this was translated, the chief chuckled condescendingly and mumbled and puffed his burned tube of newspaper and plucked at his filthy T-shirt.

"Yes, he can control it."

"He has magic?"

"Yes."

"Did someone give him this magic when he became chief?" I asked. I had been told that the chief had advisers who were sorcerers, who could bring about a person's death. If Chief Puliyasi raged, "Who will rid me of this turbulent priest?" the clergyman was as good as dead.

Joseph said, "No. The chief has had this magic for many years. He was doing the weather even before he became chief."

And Puliyasi smiled. He had chubby cheeks. He was one of the rare plump men I had seen in the Trobriands. It was the confident smile of someone who can arrange it so that you will be rained on if you ask too many obnoxious questions.

He was happy to talk about his wives—his courtiers were smoothing the way for a young girl to be sent from each of the major clans in the Trobriands, and he would probably end up with a dozen wives, like his predecessor. The brothers of these women would all work for the chief, tending their own gardens and bringing him the harvest. Yes, it was hard work and it was a job for life, but it was also useful to be able to remind people that your brother-in-law was the Paramount Chief.

"How long have there been chiefs here?"

"Since we came out of the caves."

That answer reminded me of a question I had been meaning to ask. Had the Trobrianders of long ago sailed off in their canoes to live on other islands in the Pacific?

"Yes. In Fiji," one man said. His name was Patimo Tokurupai and he spoke English well. "We know that because of the facial resemblance. Some Fijians visited us and they said, 'Our ancestors came from here.' "

I was getting stiff from sitting cross-legged on a loose plank, so I asked whether I could see the chief's yam house. Only the Paramount Chief can decorate his yam house in an elaborate manner, and this was festooned with shells, pictures of birds and fish, and was surmounted by a strange head—the only head I ever saw carved in the Trobes—at the apex of the roof, a black-and-white glowering face that looked like that of Mister Punch.

On my way out, I asked one of the men from Omarakhana why the village seemed so neglected. He told me that it had been deliberately neglected—no one was allowed to repair the huts or cut the grass, because one of the chief's brothers had died. The widow shaved her head and each day she smeared her face with mud and ashes—I caught a glimpse of her kneeling in the mud, and she looked corpse-like herself. After this five-month period of mourning was over they would repaint and rebuild the village and restore it to its former glory. In the meantime, it looked hideous.

It was stifling there, and so I was glad to leave a few days later for Kaisiga. But this time, even after I had paddled for four hours, I was given only a perfunctory welcome by Leendon and the others. They were in no mood for joking in Pidgin, or sitting in the *bwayma* by the sea and chatting. This was uncharacteristic, but I could see that the villagers were preoccupied. They made rather a point of asking me to buy things for them (duct tape, rope, plastic sheeting, another lantern, spear points, knives, fishing line) and then seemed to suggest that I ought to be on my way.

They did not ask me to stay, which was the classic villagers' way of telling me to go.

They were laconic, thoughtful, apprehensive. I was struck by this wholly different mood, and especially by their eagerness for me to leave. I had not planned to stay long in any case—I would be flying out the day after tomorrow—but I regretted the muted goodbye. Perhaps it was not muted. It was deep emotion, a mood of bewilderment and sadness when words are no use at all, the sort of silent summing up that is a final farewell. I now knew that sort of farewell.

I paddled away thinking how I had once seen these islands as idyllic. I had been wrong. An island of traditional culture cannot be idyllic. It is, instead, completely itself: riddled with magic, superstition, myths, dangers, rivalries, and its old routines. You had to take it as you found it. The key to its survival was that it laughed at outsiders and kept them at arm's length. And although it seemed strange that they thought of themselves as human and me as subhuman, a *dim-dim,* I could now see the utter impossibility of my ever understanding the place. On this second visit I had felt an undercurrent of violence—and it was not only because I had been threatened. It was something in the air—a vibration, the cries of certain birds, the way the wind whipped the trees, the stifling darkness of some jungle paths, and the sudden noisy jostling in the leaves that shocked me and left me breathless.

"What was that?" I would ask.

"A leezard."

A two-hundred-pound lizard?

"Maybe a wild pig."

But sometimes even they seemed worried.

Two days after I left Kaisiga, on the night before I was to take the plane to the Solomons, I ran into an Australian shopkeeper in Losuia. He said, "Did you hear about the battle? Koma Village marched on Kaisiga. There was quite a fight, I understand. They've sent boats to take some of the people to hospital. About thirty people were injured and some of them are in very bad shape."

Before catching the plane out, I mailed a letter to John at Kaisiga, asking for details, and eventually his reply, in neat mission-school handwriting, caught up with me:

SDA Mission Kaisiga,
Trobriand Islands PNG

Dear Paul,
    You've asked about the fight between Koma and Kaisiga. Well, the fight was about a dingy that belongs to Kaisiga Community. After an agreement that has been made by the 2 villages, Koma people began to run the dingy for 2 weeks. After the 2 weeks were over they (Koma) refused to return the dingy to the Kaisiga people and planned to hold it back for a year. Therefore the Kaisiga men went to Koma beach on Monday night and pulled it back to Kaisiga—the dingy.
    Early on Tuesday morning, all the Koma men, with Giwa

and Lebola, came to fight us, on Kaisiga beach about ¼ mile away from the village. They were blowing a shell very loud. They came with bush knives, short sticks, iron rods, and even a few diving spears. The fight began at about 6:30 A.M. and lasted until 11:30. I went to stop the fight, but could not. After the fight finished, the police from Losuia came for investigation. We all went for court. The court fine for Kaisiga was K1920. The fine for Koma was 7 months imprisonment, for all people about 30 in all, including the women who brought food to the fighting ground.

There were some men from Kaisiga who were injured, people like Micah, Lyndon, Peter and others. Two men from Koma who were seriously injured were flown to Alotau Public Hospital. After a week one died. When the Koma men return from prison there will be a big party [a feast to reconcile the warring villages].

Please Paul I need a new watch, because the old one is no more in use. My Mrs needs a wrist watch. Also when you are shopping at Port Moresby when coming, please could you buy us about 3 bolts with flowers on. Nothing much to say, so better pen off from here. May God richly bless you,

And then his scribbled indecipherable signature, an English name rendered in a twitchy Trobriand hand.

But that bloody battle was not the whole story. I kept remembering my happy days and nights on these islands, and they became emblematic of the Pacific. It was in the Trobriands that I had realized that the Pacific was a universe, not a simple ocean.

I especially recalled how one day sailing back to an island we were delayed, and night fell. There were stars everywhere, above us, and reflected in the sea along with the sparkle of phosphorescence streaming from the bow wave. When I poked an oar in the ocean and stirred it, the sea glittered with twinkling sea life. We sped onward. There were no lights on shore. It was as though we were in an old rickety rocket ship.

It was an image that afterwards often came to me when I was traveling in the Pacific, that this ocean was as vast as outer space, and being on this boat was like shooting from one star to another, the archipelagoes like galaxies, and the islands like isolated stars in an empty immensity of watery darkness, and this sailing was like going slowly from star to star, in vitreous night.

Chapter 8
THE SOLOMONS: DOWN AND DIRTY IN GUADALCANAL

The great canoe route of migration, which was my itinerary, cut through the mountainous islands and coral atolls of Milne Bay and headed east to the Solomons. I wished to follow this old oceanic thoroughfare. The nearest Solomon islands to me were just off the eastern tip of New Guinea—the so-called North Solomons, which were, confusingly, a province of Papua New Guinea. I had the idea of paddling there, and then onward to the vast archipelago—992 islands and atolls—that is the Republic of the Solomons, named by a fanciful Spaniard, four hundred years ago, after King Solomon.*

Before I was able to do this, I met Takaku, an islander who confirmed the rumor that the North Solomons had seceded from New Guinea and that his fellow islanders, under siege, had taken up arms. These guerrilla fighters called themselves "Rambos," and generally modelled themselves and their hit-and-run killings after the ugly bulgy little palooka they had seen in videos.

Takaku frightened me. It was not just his great size but his anger, and his threatening T-shirt depicting a Solomon Islander Rambo celebrating his freedom, rather prematurely I felt, dancing wildly with a machine gun.

"Dim-dims say I look like Idi Amin," Takaku said.

I was another *dim-dim* who agreed. He had two blazing bloodshot eyes in a rich rubbery face of astonishing blackness. His teeth were sharp, his gums were the color of tar. His belly was vast, and his enormous feet had crushed the life out of his rubber sandals. He was the sort of man teasing

---

*The captain, Álvaro de Mendaña, had sailed from Peru, inspired by Inca stories that islands of gold lay 600 leagues to the west. This seemed to me a brilliant way for the Incas to rid themselves of another conquistador.

Trobrianders (who thought of themselves as white) called *Tabwaubwau*—
"Blackie."

Takaku said he believed that the New Guinean province of North
Solomons, its rich copper deposits exploited by foreign interests, ought to
be a sovereign state. Having recently declared themselves independent,
the local people had killed some foreign-born miners to show they were
serious, and driven the rest back to Australia. The armed rebellion was
led by one Francis Ona, a nationalist, who was seen by the islanders as
a visionary, and the miners as an opportunist and a rabble-rouser. A
nationalist is nearly always a pest.

"Ona is a great environmentalist," Takaku told me. "He wants to give
the land back to the people. You see, our land was raped by the minority
interests in Panguna."

Panguna was the capital of the main island, Bougainville.

"You mean the local people don't want money from the mining firms?"

"No. If we show my people gold and silver they will say, 'What is this?
It is just metal. We don't want it. We want taro and cassava. Why are they
digging up our land and sending it overseas?' "

This was not a time to remind him that most New Guineans, even
Trobrianders, needed money occasionally to buy necessities (fishhooks,
rope, cloth, pots) and occasional luxuries. They had put me in my place
by telling me so. For one thing, they preferred the taste of Japanese
canned mackerel to any fresh fish they caught themselves. But the territorial problem was, at the moment, a standoff. The North Solomon secession had become a military issue.

"Is it true that the government of New Guinea has blockaded Bougainville?"

"Yes, but it will have no effect," Takaku said. "People say to them,
'You will have no energy or lights.' But my people say, 'Can you keep the
sun from rising? Can you prevent the rain from falling?' They give very
poetic answers. It is a wonderful poetic language. It is not an Austrone-
sian language."

"Will this new republic have a new name?"

"Francis Ona wanted to call it 'The Sacred Land' but so many languages are spoken there he thought it was better to call it Bougainville."

"Does it seem to you to be a sacred land?"

"Yes. We don't need radios and cars and money. My people say, 'We
will drive our cars until we run out of petrol and then we will push them
into the sea to make homes for fishes. We have canoes, we have food, we
will dance and sing.' "

But Takaku had a complaint. He said that he had been trying to rally
support for the new republic and had not made any progress.

"I went to the New Zealand High Commission in Moresby and asked, 'Why don't you recognize us?' He said, 'If we do, we will be the laughing-stock of the world.' But why don't they?"

I said, "Because they don't need you. If you don't reopen the copper or gold mines, and if you don't buy anything from overseas, why would anyone want to recognize you? What's in it for them?"

"We want to protect our land," he said.

"But the more solitary you are the more vulnerable you will be."

"It doesn't matter. We will be weak. But we will have our own country. We don't want foreigners. You see what happened in Fiji—the Indians tried to take over. But they will be kicked out."

We talked for a while more, and as I became firmer in my resolve not to go to this rebellious province of New Guinea—I had no wish to risk death among these quarrelling islanders—Takaku told me of his Melanesian uniqueness and how proud he was not to be a Polynesian.

The North Solomons were not happy islands. It did seem to me strange that this little group of islands belonged to New Guinea and not to the Republic of the Solomons, the hundreds of islands just south of it, with whom they shared both language and culture. But that was just another anomaly of history.

Taking my collapsible boat, I bypassed Panguna and flew with it to Honiara, the capital of the Solomons, the harbor city at the edge of the island of Guadalcanal. The name was Arabic, from *Wadi el Ganar,* which was the name of the hometown of its first European discoverer, the Spanish explorer Mendaña.

A definite sense that the world is elsewhere, I wrote in my notebook in Honiara.

My first impression was of a place so ramshackle, so poor, so scary, so unexpectedly filthy, that I began to understand the theory behind culture shock—something I had never truly experienced in its paralyzing and malignant form. The idea that this miserable-looking town could be regarded as a capital city seemed laughable.

And I also wrote, *Why would anyone come here?*

It was not only hideous, it was expensive. Nearly all the food in Honiara's stores was imported—from Australia, New Zealand, Japan, and America. It is often possible to gauge the prosperity of a place by looking at the central market. Honiara's central market was pathetic—a few old women selling little piles of blackened bananas and wilted leaves and some tiny flyblown fish.

"If I were a king, the worst punishment I could inflict on my enemies would be to banish them to the Solomons," Jack London wrote in his

Pacific travel book, *The Cruise of the Snark*. He added, "On second thought, king or no king, I don't think I'd have the heart to do it."

The Solomons and Melanesia in general frightened and inspired London much more than the Klondike had done. The Solomons were synonymous with horror, in his view; the most savage islands in the Pacific.

You consider that a moment, and then you want to see more.

I walked farther, past the wrecked and vandalized buildings, and the gangs of teenagers in dirty T-shirts. Honiara had the decrepit and resentful look of Haiti, or one of the plundered coastal towns of West Africa. There were a few hundred yards of wide paved road before it gave out and became a broken road, full of potholes. Even the trees were shabby. The ships tied up at quayside, or moored in the harbor, were rusty hulks. Most of the shops were owned by Chinese and contained identical merchandise: cloth, soap, shoes, tin pots, lard, matches, and the Ma Ling range of canned goods—luncheon meat, chicken feet, lychees in syrup, corned beef, goose meat in gravy. A Japanese store advertised its offer of big money for endangered species, and urged islanders to bring in turtle shell, giant clams, and rare birds. Before I had gone fifty yards an islander sidled up to me and showed me a necklace made of about 300 teeth—they were dolphins' teeth, pretty little pearly ones, and he urged me to count them, because such necklaces, representing the slaughter of perhaps twenty dolphins, were sold at so much a tooth.

I walked to the harbor. A little wooden fishing boat was grandly named *PT-109* in homage to the boat that had been torpedoed under John Kennedy near an island not far from here. The wicked-looking spikes and rusty guts of World War II wreckage—abandoned landing craft and the hulks of larger vessels—poked up from the water, posing severe hazards. Garbage and raw sewage sloshed against the shore, and what I had first taken to be a beach toy was the gray corpse of a pig, swollen in death and bobbing on the dirty water and seemingly on the point of bursting. Watching that dead pig impassively were three fat Melanesian boys in torn shorts sharing a bag of Cheez Doodles.

The Solomon Islanders in Honiara were among the scariest-looking people I had ever seen in my life—wild hair, huge feet, ripped and ragged clothes, tattoos on their foreheads, ornamental scars all over their faces, wearing broken sunglasses. They loped along in large groups, or else idled near the stores that played American rap music and looked for all the world like rappers themselves.

That, as I say, was my first impression of Honiara. Yet as time passed and I shopped for expedition food and asked directions and bought maps and generally hung around, this impression softened. The town had been a village that the war had turned into a capital; it had only existed since the war, less than fifty years. Knowing this, I did not regard the place with less horror, but I came to realize that these wild-looking people were friendly and approachable.

Gude apinun, mistah, yu stap gut?

Yes, they spoke Pidgin here.

Ples bilong yu we? Wanem nem bilong yu? Mi laikim America tumas. Yu savvy Michael Jackson himpela sing-sing?

As for crime, I decided to talk to someone who might know about it. This was Officer Saro of the Honiara Police. His Christian name was Marcelline—the name had been suggested to his parents by a French priest in Malaita, the Western Province. Malaita was a traditional place, Saro said. Some men still wore bones in their nose. Some villages attacked any outsider who came near. Some villages worshipped sharks—his did, as a matter of fact.

"But Honiara is a safe place," he said. "Guadalcanal is quite safe. Just petty crimes—mostly drinking and fighting. Some driving offenses. Maybe one murder in two or three years, caused by drinking. That's about all."

We were drinking beer under the trees at the edge of Honiara's stinking harbor, looking out upon the channel called The Slot, and Iron Bottom Sound, which got its name from the great number of ships—sixty-odd—that were sunk in the battle of Guadalcanal, a six-month ordeal that ended in an American victory in February 1943. It had been one of the crucial Pacific battles in World War II. The Japanese headquarters had been at Tulaghi, across Iron Bottom Sound, at the northern side of the Sealark Channel—The Slot. This battle was perhaps the turning point in the war, at the great cost of 30,000 lives.

Marcelline Saro had discovered that people elsewhere knew the name Guadalcanal. He had been an amateur boxer and then became a coach on the Solomon Islands Olympic boxing team.

"I went with them to the Los Angeles Olympics," he said. "I liked Disneyland the best. People asked me if I was from Africa. I said no, but when I told them I was from Guadalcanal everyone recognized the word. Because of the war."

"Did they know where Guadalcanal is?"

"No," he said, but he did not mind that.

He had also gone to the Seoul Olympics.

"What impressed you in Korea?"

"I realized how lucky I am to speak English. They don't speak it at all there."

His own children, he had five of them, learned English at school. He and his wife spoke their own language—she was from Malaita—and he also spoke Solomon Pidgin to his kids.

When he had saved enough money he would take the whole family
back to Malaita and have a farm. He disliked cities, he said. He could
never have lived in Los Angeles or Seoul. If he had the chance of going
to another country he would travel to the countryside and see how the
farmers lived.

"My island is traditional," he said. "We have no electricity. It is dark
at night."

And, he implied, the missionaries had lost their grip. At that point I
asked him about traditions and he told me about the shark worship.

"We respect the shark, that is why we worship it," he said. "And that
is why we never eat the shark. We believe it will save us and protect
us—the shark has magic—"

In the same spirit, the ancient Russians of the steppes venerated the
fierce brown bear and called it *medved*—"honey wizard."

"Every year," Saro said, "we have the sacrifice ceremony of the roasted
piglet. No woman may come near the altar, ever. The shark caller summons the shark—he stands at the edge of the sea and calls the fish. When
he sees it swimming towards him, he throws the piglet to it. And the shark
eats it, and then protects us."

Saro saw his friend William Fagi walking along the seafront and called
him over, to share another beer with us. William was a cook in the Happy
Cafe in Honiara, and he had just knocked off work. He too was from
Malaita—another part of the island, but just as traditional as Saro's
village. Both men used the Pidgin word *kastom* to describe how traditional the places were. They believed in *kastom*.

Fagi said, "In our *kastom* we worship the eagle. Eagles deliver messages—they are strong. No one may kill or eat the eagle."

It was nearing sunset and at that time of day, as so often seemed to
happen in this part of the Pacific, the wind dropped and the horizon in
the new light of early evening became lumpy and irregular with the
pronounced shapes of islands which the haze of day had obscured. Seated
comfortably under the trees, we could see the Florida Islands, the two
Nggelas, big and small, across the channel, and in the northwest the
simple hump of a volcano rising from the sea. This was Savo Island.

"That is an active volcano," Saro said. "I have never been there but
they say that the volcano erupts now and then. There is a scrub duck that
lives there and lays eggs in the sand. It is a strange place, but I think the
people are friendly."

As he spoke I began to calculate how long it would take me to paddle
there if I started here, went along the coast, and then struck out across
the channel—twenty-odd miles.

Meanwhile, Fagi must still have been ruminating on his village in
Malaita, and the creatures worshipped there, because he said, "A certain

snake is also important to us, especially when we travel. It is the *baeko*—
black with white spots. This snake can save you and bring you back
alive."

"Tell me about it," I said, because—traveling—I often felt the lingering
anxiety that I was doomed.

Traveling would kill me, I felt. I had always had the idea, and still do,
that my particular exit would be made via an appointment in Samarra:
I would go a great distance and endure enormous discomfort and trouble
and expense in order to meet my death. If I chose to sit at home and eat
and drink in the bosom of my family it would never happen—I'd live to
be a hundred. But of course I would head for the hinterland, and pretty
soon there would be some portion of a foreign field that would be forever
Medford, Mass. And I imagined that this overseas death would be a silly
mistake, like that of the monk and mystic Thomas Merton at last leaving
Gethsemane, his monastery in Kentucky, after thirty secure years, and
popping up in Singapore in 1970 (while I was there) and accidentally
electrocuting himself on the frayed wires of a fan in Bangkok a week later.
All that way, all that trouble and fuss, just to yank a faulty light switch
in a crummy hotel.

I wanted to hear about this snake which might save me that fate.

"Before we go on a trip," Fagi said, "we go to the *baeko*'s hole and put
our hand in and touch all the snakes. Then we reach for the fattest one
and hold it."

"This is a poisonous snake?"

"Oh, yes, very poisonous. And when we hold it we take a good hold
and squeeze it."

Later I found out that this *baeko* snake is the venomous and fanged
Loveridgelaps elapoides, one of the deadliest snakes in the Solomons. This
might have been the Malaita way of breaking the appointment in
Samarra, but I found it unlikely that I would ever get on my knees and
stick my hand deep into a black hole and grasp one of these creatures by
the waist.

I asked Saro and Fagi where they thought the Solomon Islanders had
originated from. Had they come from Australia?

Fagi said, "No, not from Australia. We are nothing like the Aborigines. They have rounded noses and wide faces and soft hair. They are
more like Indians, from India."

"Sometimes I see people from Israel and the Middle East and I think—
'They are like me,' " Saro said. "But if you ask me who in the world looks
like us and has our *kastom* I would say Ethiopians."

"Is there any connection at all between the Solomon Islands and Ethiopia?" I asked, and I thought, Yes, there is a certain resemblance.

"I will tell you a story," he said. "There was an Ethiopian on a certain ship. He was there illegally—"

"A stowaway," I said.

"Indeed. And when they found him after some days at sea they wanted to send him ashore. They said, 'Who are you? Where do you come from?' And the Ethiopian looked straight at them and said, 'I am from the Solomon Islands.' "

Fagi said, "I have heard this story myself."

"The ship continued onward and when it arrived in Honiara the man was put off. We took him into custody in the police station. He spoke perfect English. He looked exactly like us, and he lived here for over a year. While he was here, no one ever questioned him or asked him where he came from. The people looking at him believed he was from the Solomons. He wanted to stay longer, but his government was notified and he was sent back to Ethiopia."

It was now dark, and the channel was silvery black, like a sea of ink. The islands we had been looking at for the past hour, while we had been drinking, had vanished, blackened, and become part of that depthless night.

"Savo's gone," I said.

"They have no lights," Fagi said. "They have no electricity, no roads, no telephone. Only those funny scrub ducks they call megapodes."

It sounded a wonderful place.

"Megapode means 'big foot,' " I said.

"I think you are a teacher," Fagi said.

"Do I need permission to go to that island?"

"Yes. It is a good idea. You must ask permission to go to such places. But you always get it. And I know the man you should see." It was the minister of housing, one Allen Kemakeza, whose home village was on Savo Island. I did not imagine that a government cabinet minister would see me at short notice to discuss the possibility of my paddling to an obscure island for the purposes of camping and examining the nesting habits of the Big Foot Bird. But as this was the Solomons I gave it a shot the very next day, calling his office the first thing.

"He is not here," his secretary said.

"When do you expect him?"

"He usually comes to the office at nine. But you could call him at home."

It was eight-thirty in the morning, and I was a perfect stranger—nevertheless, she did not hesitate to give me the minister's home telephone number, so that I could ask him to do me a favor. From my point of view, this seemed a happy way of running these islands.

I called the minister's house and asked if I could see him.

He said, "I have a little problem here, but I will be at my office in an hour. Meet me there and we can talk."

He had no idea who I was or what I wanted, yet at a moment's notice he was prepared to meet me.

The new six-story Ministry of Housing, in which Mr. Kemakeza's office was located, was the most obvious building in Honiara—it was four stories higher than any other building in town, and contained the country's only elevator. Barefoot youths in T-shirts and sunglasses sneaked in and went for joyrides on the elevator, leaving timid graffiti behind on the walls as a testimony that they had been there.

This building was so inappropriate it had to have been a result of foreign aid—one of those self-serving boondoggles in which a western country gives money in the form of a contract to one of its own builders to put up an expensive structure no one really needs. It was dungeon dark inside this strange building—strange, because in spite of its newness doors were broken, locks hung loose, doors were off their hinges, floors unswept, and all the signs were scribbled on pieces of paper and taped to walls. Few lights were working. Most of the offices were empty. It was clearly a building no one had gotten used to, but it was being broken in—neglected and vandalized in a way that would make it seem habitable to a resident of Honiara.

I followed a scribbled sign and its arrow to an office that was bare except for a Melanesian boy sitting in a chair. He had golden skin and fuzzy blond hair, worn in an Afro the dimensions of a basketball.

"I have an appointment to see the minister," I said.

"Dis way," he said.

Allen Kemakeza was in an office that was equally bare of furniture. He was seated at a desk, initialling tattered file folders. Stocky, about forty or so, he wore an old faded shirt and shorts. Later he told me that he had been a policeman for about twelve years, and that he had risen in the ranks of the People's Rights Party. But he still had the look of a policeman—tough, skeptical, ironic, physical, resentful, suspicious, not particularly talkative but very attentive; the sort of man who looks as though he has survived a few fights. He had a cop's hard gaze.

I introduced myself, told him where I was from, that I had been traveling around the Pacific and that I was interested in going to Savo, preferably by paddling my collapsible boat, to look at the egg fields of the megapode birds.

"Are you a teacher?"

"Do a little teaching, do a little writing," I said, smiling fatuously and trying to sound like a harmless pedagogue.

"What made you start traveling around the Pacific?"

"My wife and I separated, and it seemed a good way of, um"—I thought fast—*"no getum bikpela bagarap in hia,"* and I tapped my skull.

"Mi savvy tumas," he said. "I can make arrangements for you on Savo." Then he fidgeted and hesitated, and finally said, "What do you know about this Iraq business?"

"Only what I hear on the radio. I listen every day—to Radio Australia, the Voice of America, or the BBC, whichever comes in clearest."

This was at the time President Bush had given Saddam Hussein an ultimatum for withdrawing Iraqi troops from Kuwait; the multinational force was in place, and the deadline was a few weeks away. It was that period when everyone speculated about what might happen in a shooting war—when people said that casualties on both sides could run in the tens of thousands, that Israel would be attacked, that a nuclear device might be detonated by the Iraqis, and so forth. In fact, no one had any idea at all what would happen in the event of a war, and so anything was possible, even Doomsday.

"You think there will be a war?"

"I have no idea. I hope not."

He pushed his file folders aside. He said, "It will be terrible. Already we are noticing the effects of the trouble in the Middle East. The price of fuel in Honiara has skyrocketed."

There were very few motor vehicles in town, and just a handful of trucks and buses on Guadalcanal, but the overloaded boats and rusty ferries that ran among the islands needed fuel. Even the short trip to Tulaghi in a little boat with an outboard motor cost the equivalent of about five American dollars, which represented a week's pay for a Solomon Islander.

"If there is a war, do you think it will lead to World War Three?"

"No. Because the Soviets wouldn't be able to afford it. They seem to be on our side, or at least neutral, because they need economic assistance from the U.S. and Europe."

"They are poor now."

"Everyone is poor except the Japanese."

"But why are they the only rich ones?"

"Because it is a one-race, one-language, one-family island of desperate overachievers who have a fascist belief in their own racial superiority," I said, and I could see that I had struck a chord, because Mr. Kemakeza clasped his hands and smiled. "These little people have a palpitating need to dominate the world and will do anything at all to sell their stuff. In the nineteen-seventies when the rest of the world refused to trade with South Africa because the whites there were treating Africans like scum, the

Japanese were so eager to do business they had themselves reclassified as white and made billions. They eat whales, they strew drift nets all over the Pacific, and they accept no immigrants. They are frugal, too—the largest money-savers in the world, which means they have the richest banks. Everyone on earth owes them money."

"They are doing business here."

"*Bikpela no lilik?*"

"*Bikpela pis bilong tins,*" he said. "Fish cannery. I am also minister of taxation, and I have been dealing with a complaint from this Japanese company here, Solomon Taiyo, fish business. They heard that I was giving a tax concession to a Canadian company. They said, 'Why don't you give us a tax concession?' I pointed out to them that they had a tax concession twenty years ago, when they started. It is an incentive to new businesses. They said, 'But we have been losing money for twenty years.' "

"What do they do with their canned fish?"

"Some they sell locally and some they export."

"How can they have lost money all this time and still be in business?"

"I don't know. But they say so. It is a joint venture, with the Solomons government."

"So you haven't been earning any money from it?"

"It is hard to say. Their bookkeeping methods are complicated. For example, it is all done in Japan. We never see their records."

"Fish in Japan is expensive, and everyone eats it. I should say that they have been making a fortune. They are using you—probably cheating you. Why don't you consider the fact that they need you much more than you need them?"

It seemed to me grotesque but typical that the wrinkleproof executives in this Japanese company were taking advantage of this poor barefoot country, robbing them of one of their few valuable commodities and staple foods, fish.

The minister said, "Solomon Islanders are too kind." He looked out the window at the patched and broken roofs of Honiara. "But when we lose patience—then, you will see."

"What will I see?"

"We will ask questions."

"Don't ask questions. Threaten them, close them down, freeze their assets," I said. "Or why not demand that they allow you to send a delegation to Japan to start a business there?"

I could just imagine the welcome they would get in Japan, these black bushy-haired Solomon Islanders, with bones in their noses and the raised welts and scars of Xs cut into their foreheads and cheeks. Even an unscarred minister like Kemakeza would be treated as though he was subhuman and offered shiny trinkets in return for his country's natural resources of timber and fish. And what laughs of derision would greet the islander's request to start a business in Nippon: *Mi laik opim kwiktaim kampani bilong bisnis.*

"Why do you let them manipulate you? You're a government minister. You deal with taxes. This is your country. Summon the bookkeepers and accountants to your office and *mekim long pinga long*—point that out."

He was smiling broadly now. "Yes, yes."

With a flourish, he wrote a letter and folded it and slipped it into an envelope marked *On Her Majesty's Service.*

"When you go to Savo, give this to my brother. His name is Nathaniel Mapopoza."

On the way to the elevator he told me that, as a policeman, he had gone to England, to Bradford in the north to take a course in police tactics. He had liked England, he said.

"You can walk at night. Go to a pub. Go to a disco. The people are friendly. In New York it was the same. I was safe."

"So you liked New York?"

"Yes. But New Guinea is *wuss*," he said, slipping mildly into Pidgin. "There it is more dangerous. Why is it more, Mr. Paul?"

I told him why I thought Port Moresby was dangerous—too many homeless people from the highlands, no common ground, no shared culture; and he inquired further, listening carefully to my answers.

At last he released me, saying, "Go to Savo. Stay as long as you like. I hope I will see you again, and we can talk."

"I have to buy some food now to take with me."

He then uttered a strange sentence: "There are many eggs in Savo."

Chapter 9

THE SOLOMONS: IN THE EGG
FIELDS OF SAVO ISLAND

A large group of gaunt and hollow-eyed Solomon Islanders watched me set up my boat under the palm trees at Honiara. Untypically for Melanesians, they made no move to help me. It was hard to tell whether they were pirates or castaways—they could have been either. At times like this, laboring under the unfriendly gaze of pitiless islanders, I seriously wondered whether my solitary island-hopping was such a great idea. But I knew that if I were home I would be cursing the traffic and wishing I were here, on a sunny day under the palms, preparing to launch myself across the open water.

I left my boat in the care of a sympathetic-looking old man, and set out to buy a week's provisions in town—the standard items. Afterwards, seeing that I still had spare room I bought a few extras—two six-packs of beer and some five-pound tins of Australian cookies labelled "Conversation Biscuits."

Outside one of the stores a ragged boy was showing some passersby a bird squashed into a narrow basket and so I joined the curious group. The bird was green and red, the size of a small thrush, and cheeping miserably.

I said, "Where did you catch this bird?"

The boy did not understand.

I said, *"Dispela pisin where you gettim?"*

"Inna boos." In the bush.

"Wanem nem bilong dispela pisin?"

"Dispela 'laru.' "

A lorikeet, one of the twenty-one species found in and around the Solomons.

"Is gutpela pisin?"

"Ya, dispela numbawan. Dispela pisin savvy totok, savvy sing-sing. Eve-ryting numbawan."

But trapped in the basket it certainly was not talking or singing now.

I was torn between interfering, buying the bird and liberating it (as I had once done to an edible owl in China), and simply observing the daily life of a Solomon island poacher—seeing what would happen. Within a few minutes a Melanesian man wearing bangles and earplugs stepped forward and thrust the equivalent of nine American dollars into the poacher's hand and carried the protesting lorikeet away.

Back at the shore, the group of fifteen bedraggled men with wild hair, wearing only shorts, still stared at me with hollow eyes but now they were on the deck of a battered sailboat anchored just off the beach.

"They are from the weather coast," an islander named James told me. That explained their piratical faces: They had a weather-beaten, wind-ward look.

I was glad to be heading off the lee shore, in a calm sea, with plenty of time to paddle to Savo. James came from Savo himself, from the village of Monagho, where he urged me to stay. But I told him that I was going to Kemakeza's district. I told him I would visit him.

"That is the north of the island, where the eggs are."

Another gnomic utterance.

"Is there a strong current out there?"

"Not bad."

"Any sharks?"

"During the war, when all those boats were sunk, there were *planti tumas sak,* because of the bodies," James said. "And for years *planti moa.* But these days not many."

Rather than head straight out from Honiara, paddling across fourteen miles of open water, I kept near to the coast, using an excellent nautical chart showing the whole of the Sealark Channel. I paddled west about twelve miles to the village of Visale at Cape Esperance, where I had a rest on the beach, and then struck out north for a six-mile crossing. I was always somewhat wary of these channels, because of the current, or a sudden change in weather, so I paddled hard for an hour and did not ease up until I was near the island.

Savo, which from Honiara had seemed like a small hump in the ocean, was on closer inspection a mountain in the sea, a gently rounded volcano, with green slopes. The southern end was rocky, but I could see palms and white beaches along its eastern side. I chose to paddle along it because I was tired, and I knew that I could safely go ashore at any point.

The villages were small, set just inland, and I was reassured by the pretty huts. People who wove huts out of split bamboo and thatched them and lashed them as carefully as these Savo Islanders had done had to be hospitable traditionalists. If I had seen tin roofs and cinder blocks, the sort of sheds with swinging doors and padlocks that aid agencies often built for such people—in the innocent belief they were doing them a favor—I would have been very worried. I regarded such dwellings and such violated villages as unpredictable, full of nuisances. Villagers living under tin roofs stencilled *A gift from the people of the United States of America,* and eating food aid, regarded people like me as a soft touch. I was all for foreign aid, but there was a certain type of aid that undermined people and made them dangerous.

In Savo there was no apparent sign that any village had been penetrated by the west. And just offshore men and boys fished from dugout canoes. Seeing a settlement on a great sandy beach, I paddled to one of these canoes.

"Wanem nem bilong dispela ples?" I asked a fisherman, pointing to the huts.

"Dispela Pokilo," he said.

"Balola Village i stap we?"

He waved his hand to the west and said, *"Klostu liklik. Go stret."*

He was right. Balola was very near, but when I landed and dragged my kayak up the sand I was surprised by its air of desertion. No one watched me come ashore, no children shrieked at me, no dogs barked at me, no women were dumping trash on the beach, nor were any men fishing in the low surf. I passed from the early evening light of the beach to the cool crepuscular darkness of the small village that lay damply beneath the dense foliage of trees. Some chickens hurried and clucked on the path, but it was only after walking from one end of the village to the other that I found a person—a man named Aaron, who had bushy side whiskers and a gammy leg.

"Hello. Yu savvy tok Inglis?"

"Pisin," he said.

"Plis yu nap halpim?" I asked and showed the letter the minister had given me. *"Mi laik toktok Nathaniel Mapopoza. Mi givim dispela pas."*

"Yumi go," he said. *"Mapo i stap long ples"*—and he pointed down the muddy path.

"Emi longwe o nogat?" I asked, because if it was far I was much happier simply waiting here.

"Klostu liklik," he said, setting off, and I followed.

It was a forty-five-minute walk along a narrow path; it was the only thoroughfare, and it circled the island. I could see at once that it was an island without a road, or a motor vehicle, or electricity. We passed through six or seven small villages and in each one Aaron called out in the local language that he was taking me to see Mapo.

Mapopoza was seated under a pawpaw tree, chewing betel and stuffing his mouth with lime, at a village called Bonala. The village presented an odd spectacle. About a hundred people were milling around whispering and examining great stacks of bananas, baskets of potatoes, and more coconuts than I had ever seen piled in one place. And three fat pigs, whickering and squealing, because their feet were tightly bound.

"Feegs," Aaron said, attempting English. He gave me to understand that a wedding was about to take place, but that this was the fixing of the bride price. No money was involved; there was little money on this island.

I handed my letter to Mapo. He shrugged—did not meet my gaze—and looked away. He was a bit dazed from the betel nut, but that was not the only reason for his obliqueness. It soon became clear to me that he could not read, but it was not odd that his brother should write him a detailed letter. Mapo simply handed the thing to a boy nearby, who clawed it open, and as people gathered round, the boy read the letter in a superior way, as though he was rather stuck on himself for being so literate.

I stood there with salt in my eyes and my arm muscles screaming from the long kayak trip.

My name was mentioned—*Mistah Foll*—and the listeners turned to me and stared. And then, *Amerika.*

Mapo was vague. Not only was he illiterate, he did not speak English. But none of this mattered. I only needed his blessing, I didn't need his hospitality. What I wanted most was his permission to put up my tent, my *haus sel,* in Balola Village.

So I said, *"Plis, mi laik putim haus sel long Balola na stap long?"*

"Orait," he said. *"Mi kam bai."*

He gestured, showing me that he was being detained. I could see he had a role to play in this betrothal, but still he urged me to sit down and sip some coconut water from a freshly hacked nut. He said nothing. He had a crooked smile. A few feet away the tied-up pigs were quivering with thirst and suffocation. To amuse themselves, some village boys went near and began kicking the poor creatures.

Women with streaks of white paint on their cheeks wandered around muttering—part of the betrothal, I guessed—and others were talking and spitting betel juice and slurping lime. I noticed another group of people crowding into an open-fronted hut, and asked Aaron what was going on. He didn't know, but he asked a Bonala man, who spoke directly to me.

"There is a man from Africa in there."

"Africa?"

It was a bit like Saro's story of the Ethiopian stowaway who had claimed to be a Solomon Islander. But who could this man be, and what was he doing? I thought he might be a preacher or a healer, granting an audience to these villagers.

I sidled up to the hut, wondering how I might introduce myself, and came face to face with a sturdy fellow who greeted me, "Hey, man."

This was Bilal Mohammed, an American Peace Corps volunteer from Brooklyn, New York, shaven-headed, and very black from the Solomon sun, wearing a jolly T-shirt and baggy Bermuda shorts.

He was a teacher on another island, Makira, but as he was on vacation he had come here to Savo in a motor launch to visit some friends. He asked me whether I knew anything about the standoff in the Gulf.

"Just sabre-rattling so far," I said.

"I've got a bet with a guy in Honiara that there won't be a war," he said. "Because no one is that stupid."

"It looks bad," I said, and yet I had no idea where I would place my bet. It was a period of great uncertainty. "There are more than two hundred thousand troops in Saudi Arabia, waiting for the word."

Bilal said, "People think they are making plans, but they don't realize that God has his own plan, and we can't outwit God."

It was spoken with true Islamic fatalism and a rueful smile. We shook hands, and both of us said that we hoped it would all end peacefully. Then he went back into the hut and I walked three miles back to Balola Village with Aaron and put up my tent in the dusk, at the edge of the beach.

Before I had finished making camp, a fat man in a dirty lap-lap stepped out of the bush—clearly a busybody—and told me that I would be much happier camping near his hut. Before I could react, he was scooping up my gear and helping me move.

"I am president of Savo," he said in a lordly way.

I had been in Melanesia long enough to know that even if this were true it did not mean a great deal. As it turned out, his being president did not mean much more than that his T-shirt was slightly less dirty than other people's.

This man was Kemakeza's other brother, but they were not on speaking terms—nor was he on speaking terms with Mapo, who he quickly told me was an ignorant villager. His name was Ataban Tonezepo—there were no common surnames here—and he was well spoken. He said he thought Pidgin was a silly language.

"But it is useful," I said, "because people speak it."

"That is a very wise observation," he said, and I suspected on the basis of this obsequious turn of phrase that he might turn out to be a royal pain.

When we had settled on a place where I might put my tent—it was a free-standing Moss tent, we just swung it fully pitched, twenty feet along the beach—Ataban said, "I am former premier of Central Province, but I lost at the last election. So here I am, back in Balola."

"But your duties as president must keep you busy."

"That is very true."

In the growing darkness people had begun to gather, trying to help me. There were now twenty-eight of them—I counted as I set out my gear, hanging my food from trees, so that the rats wouldn't get it. As we were facing north, there was no dramatic sunset, only a diminishing glow on the water, and the shapes of the distant islands of Nggela, Isabel, and Russell.

"We used to sail there," Ataban said.

"You might be sailing there again, if the fuel prices rise."

"That is very true."

The twenty-eight men and boys sat down and watched me start my kerosene stove and eat my hurried supper of beans and mackerel and fresh bread from the bakery in Honiara. I gave Ataban a beer and some "Conversation Biscuits" to the others. And when I had finished eating, Ataban demanded that four of the boys take my pots to be washed.

"Do you think there will be World War Three after January?" Ataban asked.

"Frankly, no."

"We think it will come here. Everyone is worried."

"Believe me, you are safe here," I said.

"World War Two came here," he said. "Right here. To this island."

"Yupela bigpela, strongpela," I said. *"Yupela nogat pret"*—you guys aren't afraid—*"Yupela kilim i dai."*

They laughed at me, and then Ataban sent everyone away and told them to let me sleep in peace.

"In the morning you can't go down to the beach," he said. "The women will be using it. Doing shit there—right there. And the men will be over there, doing shit."

The village beach was the toilet in the Solomons; it was where people shat. Even in simple grubby New Guinea people said *Mi go haus pekpek,* and looked for the privy or the thunderjug. In the Trobriands they had a pavilion on a pier, with a long drop into the sea; and there was a word for toilet in Kiriwina. But in the Solomons things were different. *Mi go nambis*—"I'm going to the beach," in Pidgin, meant one thing only, a B.M. by the sea. It never meant swimming—that was *waswas,* and anyway only little kiddies did that, frolicking in the excrement and the fruit peels—for the beach was also the village dump, littered with rusty cans and plastic bottles.

It was extraordinary how the islanders fouled their beaches, always expecting the tide to purify it twice a day. But I preferred to camp on the beach. The fact that it was generally regarded as a toilet made it emptier—no intruders—and I disliked the mosquitoes, the human gabbling, and the cockcrows in the damp shadowy villages.

The beach was also a graveyard. One of the keenest nineteenth-century observers of the Melanesians was R. H. Codrington, a missionary-turned-anthropologist, who wrote, "In Savo . . . common men are thrown into the sea, and only great men buried." Codrington also remarked on the fact that the people of Savo were renowned in Melanesia as poisoners.

That night while I lay in my tent writing notes, under my swinging flashlight, I heard children just outside whispering. After I switched the flashlight off they went away.

For hours after that I heard them singing and strumming, making their way around the village from hut to hut, like carollers at Christmas.

Large crabs gathered against my tent at five in the morning and their scratching woke me—the rising sun gave them distinct silhouettes. Remembering what Ataban had said about the women *doing shit* I stayed in the tent and listened to my shortwave radio for the Gulf update. The Voice of America, which sounds like a local radio station, had hardly altered its programming schedule to take account of the crisis—it still ran its trivial music and frivolous features, interspersing them with little bursts of solemn news, delivered by credulous-sounding journalists. Radio Australia and the BBC had actually changed their whole news format—they reported news, scoops, rumors, and in-depth pieces, and in the mounting suspense gave a plausible commentary of the crisis.

Yet I listened to it all feeling that I was a million miles away, on another planet, lost in the galaxy of Oceania.

After the news I crawled out and shooed the crabs away, made tea and noodles, and sat listening to music and looking at the sea until Mapo came by, to ask me the news. It was hardly past five-thirty in the morning.

"Sapos ol bigpela kaontri pait," he said, *"mi tingting ol kam na pait long Solomons."*

Which in fact was everyone's fear: If the superpowers went to war they would eventually fight in the Solomons. This lurking fear was evident in the questions of nearly everyone I spoke to in that period, and for some it was an absolute terror—the complete disruption of their way of life and a brutal disorder imposed upon them.

They had not felt liberated by World War II; they felt as though a succession of cyclones had passed through their islands—first the Japanese one, the invasion, the takeover, the occupation; then the Allied bombing, the firefights, the battle of Guadalcanal, and the destruction of villages, the sinking of scores of ships, the deaths, the arrival of the sharks to feed on the bodies.

The aftermath—the postwar chaos—had been just as bad. American troops attempting to disentangle themselves from the islands and demobilize had been nearly as disruptive. During the war, there was little fishing, and very little farming was done—three years' crops were lost. With no harvests the islanders had become dependent upon the foreign soldiers, and had developed a dreary taste for canned food, in particular for the corned beef and pork luncheon meat that persists to this day.

I gave him my now standard reassurance in Pidgin: If the war started it would not come here. For emphasis I said, it was *Tru tumas.*

Mapo smiled. He did not believe me.

He said, *"Yu laik lukim megapode pisin?"*

Savo was not an island that was short of strange features—it had an active steaming volcano, it had hot springs, it apparently had a president—but the megapode birds were the strangest of all.

The local word for the birds was *ngero;* in Pidgin they were called *skraeb dak;* ornithologists called them "mound builders"; but most people on Savo, when speaking to strangers, called them by their scientifically correct name, megapodes, from their family, *Megapodiidae.* It was a fairly rare variety of big-footed bird, of which twelve species were known from Indonesia to Vanuatu. Its distinguishing habit was that it relied entirely on environmental heat to incubate its eggs. The bird laid its eggs in sand that was always warm because of its nearness to the volcano. The megapode had the most precocious hatchlings of any bird—the birds did not sit on the eggs, they did not feed or tend their young. After they dug a deep hole in this unnaturally warm sand, they laid the egg, covered the hole, and flew off.

Three weeks later the bird hatched, dug itself out of the hole, and fully fledged in a matter of minutes, started running. Within hours of its birth the baby bird had learned to fly, and—if it had managed to elude the pariah dogs and the bush pigs—it made for the trees.

But relatively few of the eggs ever hatched. Mapo told me in Pidgin that they were disinterred by egg diggers later in the morning. We walked through the bush, parallel to the beach, for about half a mile and down a narrow path to a stretch of fenced-off beach where, in the dawn light, I could see hundreds of squawking, strutting moorhen-like birds digging holes or kicking sand with feet the size and shape of salad tongs.

Mapo sat on a rock in the shade and smoked a cigarette, while I crept forward on my belly and watched, fascinated, relieved that I did not have a camera. The sight was unphotographable—the birds were too deep in the holes, a camera could not do justice to the noise, and clearly the birds were skittish—they would have run from a photographer. All you heard were squawks, and all you saw were bunches of sand being flung out of the holes. Now and then a nervous bird would emerge from a hole, fill it hurriedly, and flap away, like a startled coot.

In the rising heat of early morning—even in the palmy shade I was perspiring heavily—I watched for almost an hour, and by the time I was ready to leave many of the birds had finished burying their eggs and flown.

I wondered whether they ate the birds, and so on the way back to the village I asked, *"Yupela kaikai megapode pisin?"*

Mapo said, *"Sapos dok i gat long tit, mipela kaikai."*

If a dog gets it in its teeth, we eat it.

But it was forbidden to kill the bird, he said, and he said rather obscurely that once *tambu* ceremonies were held in which the bird was worshipped.

Mapo took me to his house and introduced me to his wife, Rebecca, who served us each a megapode egg omelette with rice. And he showed me an egg from his kitchen. It was an extraordinary size—the thing was large—about four inches by two, larger than any duck egg I had ever seen, and heavy.

People on Savo really depended on the eggs, he said. They collected them, they ate them, they sold them in Honiara for a Solomon dollar apiece. I began interrogating him, as best I could in Pidgin, about the history of the island, the worship of the birds, the mythology of the eggs. He answered in a halting way.

But then he said that I would have to ask someone else, and he said shyly—it was a try at English, it was not imperfect Pidgin—"I no have education. No school." And he smiled sadly. "Now I too old to go school."

One of his children was nearby, and Mapo swept the little boy onto his lap and pushed his half-eaten megapode omelette aside.

"Dispela pikanin savvy toktok Inglis!"

Because of the megapode eggs this half of the island was prosperous and well fed. The eggs were greatly in demand on Guadalcanal. The opposite side of the island was well off, too—it had a reef and plenty of fish. The whole of Savo was rich in fruit trees—oranges, lemons, guavas. There were betel nut trees and *ngali* nuts (which were similar to macadamias) and coconuts. But gardening was basic—cassava, taro, beans—fairly easy crops. The result of this abundance was that life was undemanding, a little sweeping, a little weeding. The villages were very quiet and had little of the harum-scarum that I had grown used to in the Trobriands. Most of the time Savo slumbered.

What terrors would the Japanese have had in store for these happy, indolent folk if they had won the war? At the very least there would have been a golf course here, and someone like Mapo would have been a caddy, and Rebecca would have had a job in the kitchen of the golf club, rustling up megapode omelettes for the hungry Sons of Nippon.

In the first few days I camped on Savo the stillness and inactivity were profoundly apparent, and there was even something lugubrious about it, as though the place were haunted.

I paddled south to Mbonala, a village in a little bay, where children were splashing, and boys were spearfishing, and women were washing clothes. The men of the village sat under trees, chewing betel nut. A screeching crowd gathered on shore as I asked directions to Monagho. Savo on my chart was a yellow disk, showing topographical lines and a few elevations. Whenever I spoke to someone I added detail, and filled in the blanks, noting the names of villages, and bays, and streams.

The village of Monagho turned out to greet me. It was—like Balola and Mbonala—a village of topless women, many of them smoking briar pipes. Soon James joined them—he had been thatching the roof of his house. He introduced me to his family. His pretty sister Mary, who was about sixteen, wore a necklace of dolphin's teeth. James said he was looking for a husband for her.

"You marit pinis?" he asked me—but the fact that he spoke in Pidgin meant that he really did not expect an answer.

"It's a long story," I said.

He showed me his house, which was large and well built like most of the houses and huts on Savo—thickly woven palm leaves on a strong frame of poles, with an ingeniously woven roof that was both waterproof and graceful. While I sat talking with his family he borrowed my kayak and amused the village, as he paddled up and down the shore.

I paddled three miles farther to Kaonggele, the village which had the right of way to the volcano, and when I came ashore I was helped by twelve boys, who put my kayak on the village canoe rack. I told them I wanted to see the volcano.

"You will have to pay that old man," one boy said. "He is our chief."

He was sitting on a log under a tree, listening to an early-model transistor radio the size of a Kleenex box. It was bruised and dirty and patched with tape, but a buzzy voice was murmuring in the speaker.

The old man's name was Marcel Devo—this was another Catholic village: St. Theresa's Church was on the bluff just above it—and he said he thought he was seventy-seven. He did not speak Pidgin or English, only Savosavo.

"Ask him if he remembers the war," I said to one of the boys.

"I was already married when the war started," he said, and the boy translated.

"What do you remember?"

"Everything," he said, in a croaky voice. "I helped carry the American food and equipment. I worked hard. You see this road?" He gestured to a rutted path that sloped from the beach. "The Americans built it. It was the only road we had in Savo."

"Did you see fighting during the war?"

"There was fighting everywhere." And he raised his red eyes to me. "Smoke and fire. And loud noises. Ships all over the water."

Putting his radio down he nearly dropped it. He was very feeble, but I had reminded him of the nightmarish years of the war.

"It was terrible"—the boy was still translating—"Some bodies washed ashore and others were eaten by sharks. We were frightened. We did not know what to do."

"What were you listening to on your radio?"

"The news," he said. "The war will start in Iraq and it will come here. Either the Iraq people will come first and then the Americans will drive them away, or else the Americans will come and the Iraq people will fight them here."

"Tell him I don't think that will happen," I said.

When he heard this he muttered to the boy, who said, "You are wrong."

Normally the chief was paid five Solomon dollars by anyone who wanted to use Kaonggele's path to hike up to the volcano, but the old man said I did not have to pay.

"I saw you paddling your canoe here, so you can go for nothing."

Eight of the boys came with me—they had nothing else to do, they said. It took an hour to reach the rim of the crater where I looked down and saw the gray steam blowing out of the cracks down below. That to me was a less impressive spectacle than the hot springs here and there on the upward path—little boiling pools, where people gathered to cook their food. I hung around one group which was simultaneously steaming cassava and sweet potatoes and ears of corn—the vegetables were thickly wrapped in leaves. A man offered me an ear of corn, which I ate, and looking for a place to fling the cob after I had finished I stepped into a puddle of sulphurous water and scalded my foot.

Cooking on free hot water on the slopes of a volcano! These people had everything! Birds flew in and gave them hundreds of huge eggs a day, and all they had to do was carry them up the hill and boil them. They had nuts and oranges and lemons and breadfruit and papaya—the trees required no care at all. Their pigs looked after themselves, so did their chickens.

It seemed an almost unimaginably pleasant life.

"Do you have missionaries here?"

"No. But a priest comes once a month for mass."

They showed me the church. It was wooden, and rather roughly put together, and big and musty and empty.

"What about mosquitoes?"

"They don't trouble us."

But they troubled me. The only aspect of this island I did not like was its pestilential insects—fleas and midges and mosquitoes, and most of all its skinny biting flies that never left me alone, in spite of my insect repellent.

I gave the boys some chocolate cookies and made a point of saving three or four for the chief, Marcel Devo. In return they climbed the coconut palms and hacked open some nuts. I drank a whole one and filled my water bottle with the sweet water from the others.

A few days later I paddled back to Kaonggele, but instead of a somnolent village I found boys and men engaged in furious activity on the beach, setting out piles of yams and bananas on palm leaves. One boy, whom I recognized from my previous visit, was hacking a dead pig to pieces with a bloody machete.

"What is this all about?" I asked.

"For peace," the boy said and smiled knowingly.

"Do you mean there was trouble here?"

"There is peace now," a furtive man said.

"This man Phillip make trouble," the boy with a machete said.

Phillip, the furtive fellow, was skinny, about thirty years old. He had a pinched and rather anxious face, and did not look at all like a troublemaker. He squirmed and said, "Sha-sha-sha," trying to shut the boy up.

"That is Phillip's pig," another boy said teasingly, and laughed.

"There was fighting," the first boy said.

"Did you fight?"

"No. Ask Phillip."

Phillip was sorely embarrassed. He said in a low voice, "I made the trouble with that other village. I made a fight. So I do this to stop the trouble."

This feast was a *zokule,* a peacemaking meal. Phillip had quarrelled with a man from a neighboring village, and caused bad feeling. To bring peace he had offered his pig and the others had provided vegetables. When the food was all set out the offended village would walk down the beach and eat it and in that way, having shared this food and especially Phillip's pig, would be placated.

That day and other days, when I encountered men or boys in canoes— not outriggers, but the slender dugouts they used for fishing and playing—they challenged me to races, and I beat them. Their canoes were sleek enough but their paddles were single-bladed and rather heavy and hard to handle. I had a carbon-fibre double-bladed paddle—the usual for kayaking. When I loaned it to any of them, and I used that person's paddle, I always lost. So I encouraged them to use my paddle and tried to convince them to carve long double-bladed paddles for themselves, using this design.

They usually said they would try. They were certainly open to suggestions. Ataban's schoolgirl sister Agnes, who was a plump and mature fourteen, had a large fresh set of scars on her cheek—a circle radiating wiggly lines.

"Dis da sun," she explained.

Yes, a radiant sun, carved into her cheek.

"Is that a custom here on Savo?"

"No. On Malaita. It is not our custom. I asked the Malaita people to do it to me. They came here to dance. One month ago."

"Did it hurt?" I asked.

"Yes. Very much. They did it with a fork and a knife. Afterwards they put salt water on it."

I thought, *How strange.* Because another group of people in the Solomons had a tradition of scarring their faces, this Savo schoolgirl had offered hers, and had her cheek painfully knifed open with an obnoxious disfigurement she would carry on her face for the rest of her life.

"You like it?" she asked.

I told her what she wanted to hear.

The nights were so starry they lit the island even before the moon had risen. The children played and sang until midnight. I thought they were bratty, but one day they brought me a chair and I felt ashamed of myself. I could actually sit comfortably under a palm tree, writing or reading, while I swatted flies. I usually waited until the shore was empty of people and then I went *nambis,* feeling like an utter fool, so exposed. You squatted at the tidemark, facing inland.

Except for the insects, and the occasional snake, life for me on Savo was idyllic. But I soon realized that I was caught between the feuding of two brothers—Ataban, the fat former politician, who spoke English well if a bit pompously; and Mapopoza, the skinny illiterate who did little except stuff his mouth with betel and lime. Both men were capable of being jolly. But of course, Mapo, who had no pretensions, who had never left the village, had the most power.

Ataban, however, controlled the egg fields—actually owned a quarter mile of beach where the eggs were laid. It was strange that these wild birds were in a sense privately controlled. This was an almost inexhaustible source of wealth, and it was obvious that he was rather resented for it—but what could anyone do? He charged the diggers five eggs a day in order to go on digging for more eggs. On successive days I met Ataban in the egg fields, and what I had thought to be easily won food turned out to be hot, dirty, tiring work.

So as not to risk breaking the eggs, the men began digging with a small flat piece of wood, but after they had dug about eighteen inches they lay on their bellies and used their bare hands. The volcanic sand was heavy and the men labored in the full sun, sometimes digging to three or four feet before they came upon the egg. It amazed me to think of the bird digging that deep, laying the egg, and then pushing all the sand back in with its scratching feet. All morning, in the egg fields of Savo, there was the curious spectacle of men stuck in holes, chucking sand out, and all you saw were their sweaty kicking legs smeared with sand grains.

A young man named Walter told me he was saving up his eggs. He had eighty-five at the moment. He wanted to take 100 eggs to market in Honiara. It would cost him twenty-four Solomon dollars for the round-trip on the motorboat, and a few dollars to hire a table at the market. His profit for fourteen days of laborious egg-digging would be less than thirty American dollars.

Peter from the village of Alialia presented a strange sight. He had been to London in the 1970s on a parliamentary delegation. He had met the British foreign secretary and the Queen, and had worn a borrowed suit, and here he was lying on his belly in his Foster's Beer T-shirt, sand in his springy hair, his arms filthy, his face gleaming with sweat, scrabbling in the sand with his bare hands, searching for a megapode egg.

The egg fields were sort of a men's club—women were not allowed to dig or even to set foot in the place. The diggers joshed each other and gassed with me, while Ataban sat plumply in the shade of a tree, accepting his tribute of five eggs from each man—he collected between twenty and a hundred eggs a day in his cloth bag. When he had three hundred or so—a week's accumulation—he sent his son to Honiara to sell them at the market.

"Everyone wants them," Ataban said.

One day I said, "Do you have the same number of megapode birds as years ago?"

"No. We have less."

It was predictable enough. "So why don't you give the eggs a chance to hatch? That way you'd end up with more birds and more eggs."

"The young people would never accept it, although that was done in olden times, when the bird was worshipped with sacrifices."

That day he showed me the grave of the man who was the last person to carry out sacrifices. The man, Kigata, had died in 1965. The usual sacrifice was the burning of a pig to ashes in a tabu grove on the cliff behind the village. But Ataban explained a sort of Manichean idea that the bird was also associated with a certain snake, its "devil" or spirit.

On the way back to the village, I said, "What month do you harvest the yams?"

"Usually in June."

"You have plenty of food that month. Why not forbid the digging of eggs then? Set June aside for hatching. A few weeks later you'd have megapodes hatching all over the place, and you'd have more eggs."

"That is a very wise observation," Ataban said.

It was hard to tell whether he was satirizing me.

"I will put that idea to the council," he said. "We will make it a byelaw."

It was in the egg fields, in the breather between eggs, that they became very chatty. They asked about the price of oil in other countries, about the power of the Soviet Union and Japan, about the greenhouse effect (this question raised by a very old man who said, "A man in Honiara told me—"), the cost of living elsewhere, and how much you would have to pay for a house in various countries. Invariably the talk in the egg fields turned to the standoff in the Gulf, and after Ataban demanded my assurance that in the event of a war the Americans would win ("No problem," I said. "But men will die"), he began teasing me.

"Put away your guns!" he said. "Put away bombs and planes and bullets. Fight with your hands. We Melanesians can beat you—with our hands!"

"*Rabis. Bullseet,*" I said, and the others tittered. "That is all *nambaten.* You wouldn't have a chance. We are *bigpela, strongpela.*"

"No! We are Melanesian!" Ataban said. "We are warriors, and we have magic."

"Ya, ya," the men said, and began jeering at me.

"Where was your Melanesian magic in 1942?" I asked.

"Oh, dear," Ataban said in a squeaky voice. "We no have no magic at that time. We just ran into the bush and let the Americans fight the Japanese. Ha-ha."

After that particular discussion a twenty-year-old named Edward sidled up to me and said, "But Rambo is very strong. He can fight without guns."

Rambo is one of the folk heroes of the Solomons—indeed, his fame pervades Oceania. Anyone hastily condemning this credulity as simple savagery must recall the utterance of the American President Ronald Reagan in which he mentioned how he had seen a Rambo movie at the

White House, and how the witless brute in this worthless movie had inspired him.

Over dinner at his hut one night (megapode eggs, the Spam they called "Ma Ling," and *kumara,* sweet potatoes), Mapo asked me, *"Mi laik lukim* Rambo *video tumas. Yu lukim* Commando? *Nambawan man long* Commando."

"Yu lukim video long ples Balola?"

"Ya. Mi kros. Dispela generator bagarap."

The one generator on the island had no use except as a source of energy to show videos here.

Pidgin was in fact rarely spoken on Savo, except to outsiders. The island language, called Savosavo, was said by linguists to be Papuan—not Melanesian at all. Ataban denied this, but there were many Polynesian-sounding words in the language. For example, the Savosavo word for "island" was *molumolu,* undoubtedly a cognate with Polynesian forms (*motu* in Tahiti, *moku* in Hawaiian, and so forth).

"Where did Savo people originally come from?" I asked Ataban.

Before he could answer, Peter the egg digger said, "Asia."

"I don't think so," Ataban said. "We believe that we were always here. That we came from a bird or a snake. The bird—maybe it was a frigate bird—laid an egg, and a woman came out. That is what I think."

"What about the people on other islands? What about those people who live on Ontong Java?"

They were Polynesians on this small atoll in the north of the Solomon Group.

"Maybe they sailed there," Ataban said. "But we came from birds and sharks and snakes."

And, he explained, after death they turned back into sharks. It was a belief on Savo that sharks were the ghosts of dead people. For this reason sharks were often spoken to and given food.

There was no fear of sharks in the Solomons, but then there was no fear of sharks anywhere I went in the Pacific. This was not so strange. It is a statistical fact that only twenty-five people a year are killed by sharks. Many more people are killed by pigs.

Most of the time, paddling around Savo, I wore earphones and listened to my Walkman, the same tape—because I had only one at the time—which was of Puccini and Verdi arias sung by Kiri Te Kanawa: "Vissi d'arte" from *Tosca,* "O mio babbino caro" from *Gianni Schicchi,* "Un bel di vedremo" from *Butterfly,* "Ah, fors'è lui" from *La traviata,* and others. It is almost impossible to describe the peculiar poignancy of being close to a small, lovely island, passing under the high cliffs surmounted by

slender palms, the strange lumpy hills and calderas created by the vulcanism of the fairly recent past (the explorer Mendaña saw Savo in eruption
in 1568), the surf whitening the rocky beaches, and the children with
sunburned hair running from the bamboo huts and playing in the waves,
all of them—the people, their huts, their canoes, their little gardens, the
women gaping up at me from their washing—dwarfed by the active
volcano just behind them, as I listened to the rich soprano voice singing
"Quell', amor," with piercing sweetness as I paddled on.

Or, more appropriately, "Se come voi," the aria of the pretty flowers—because the flowers were visible from where I paddled. If I were as
pretty as they, then I could always stay close to my love, and would say
"Don't forget me"—

> *Se come voi piccina io fossi,*
> *O vaghi fior, sempre sempre*
> *Vicina potrei stare al mio amor . . .*

Under the pink and purple sky of early evening, paddling in a sea the
color of rose water, while the cockatoos flashed from tree to tree and the
frigate birds soared, I felt lucky. I had found this island by chance, and
it seemed to me that if the people were not interfered with by tourists or
bureaucrats, the island would remain intact and the people would be able
to manage well on their own. It daunted me to think of the permanence
of that strange simple life, but it must have been a fruitful life or else the
people would not have been so generous and unsuspicious.

When I perceived this place as sad, as I sometimes did, listening to
those arias and watching this green island revolve past my boat, I realized
that the sadness was mine. I had brought it here. It was part of my mood
in the day. It affected my dreams, which were of gray chaotic London and
steep stairs leading to thick locked doors—no doors here, no locks, no
stairs even—and dreams of delay and missed appointments, almost meeting my wife and then bamboozled by a sudden orgy of naked people on
a street corner or a bolted back door, and arriving and whimpering *Too
late,* and waking up in a sweat, hearing the sloshing surf and remembering I was in Savo, in the Solomon Islands, alone in a tent on the beach.

I paddled because it was a way of being alone. I paddled because I liked
listening to music. I paddled because the water was too filthy for swimming in. I also paddled to give the day a shape, because I usually wrote
my notes in the morning, exerted myself in the afternoon—only eight or
ten miles, but in that equatorial heat the sun shone from a cloudless sky.
I paddled because it was often the only way of getting from one place to
another.

If Mapo was not with me at sunset, Ataban (who hated him) stopped by for a chat. One day he asked whether I thought it was odd that he should regard his brother as an enemy. I said I found it much more understandable that he should dislike or pity his brother than feel that way towards a vague acquaintance.

"In a way, you can only really dislike a member of your family or someone you know well," I said. "But I think Mapo is a good fellow."

"That is because you do not know him," Ataban said. "Ha!"

He usually greeted me with, "You had a good pandle?"

"A very good paddle."

"You like to pandle," he said. "And I am so busy!"

"You mean busy sleeping under a tree while people bring you megapode eggs?"

He took this mockery well, and even seemed to regard it as a gesture of friendliness. "No. I am a poor Melanesian. I have to work. I am not lazy like you Americans. I have to feed my feegs."

Then he would sit down and talk until it was dark. Usually I pestered him to show me the tabu groves, where the megapode birds were worshipped, but he said it was too *tambu,* and that it would be very bad for me to go there. After a week, I stopped asking him.

"Tomorrow I will show you the place where we sacrifice to the megapode birds," he said one night. "And I will tell you the story of the bird and the devil."

"Tell me now, Ataban."

He made a face. "It is too long. And my feegs are waiting."

"Yu go we tude?" Mapo asked me the next day. *"Yu wokabaot Kwila? Yu laik samting, yu laik kaikai?"*

It was a charade, but so as not to make the brothers' feud any worse I said I was simply going for a walk and did not need any food.

Ataban met me at the edge of the village and introduced me to an old man—he said he was seventy-four—who had brought him some eggs. Whenever I met someone that old I asked them about the war. The man had lived on Savo his whole life. He said that nothing had changed, and the only interruption had been the war. Ataban acted as translator.

"The Japanese came here. One Japanese man said, 'We are powerful and we are staying here—in Tulaghi. We will never leave. Go to your fields. Pick coconuts, make copra, grow bananas. Cultivate vegetables. Go fishing. We will buy everything you have to sell.' "

"Did they mention the Americans?"

"They said, 'The Americans are very strong. They will come and try to fight. But we will beat them.' We were frightened of them."

"But why?" I said. "The Japanese are little bowlegged people who can't see without glasses. They are smaller than you. Why were you afraid?"

The old man laughed and spoke again, and Ataban translated. "It's true, they looked strange to us. But some were tall. And they had guns. A little while later the Americans came and it was all different. There was fighting. Many people died. I was afraid. And I still think about it."

"But this was a long time ago."

"No! It was recent. It was just a little while ago. I was already married and had children," the old man said.

After the old man left us, Ataban changed his mind and said that it wasn't such a good idea for him to take me to the place of sacrifice, because it was too *tambu.* But I urged him and when he still seemed reluctant, I asked him why.

"Because I believe in *kastom.* I am not a Christian. This place is *tambu.*"

"I won't step on it. I won't touch it. I won't even go near. I just want to look."

"That's better," he said. "Look at a distance."

We set off on a steep overgrown path and immediately saw a brown snake, the thickness of a garden hose—a four footer—and according to my handbook, *Reptiles of the Solomon Islands,* probably a venomous land snake of the genus *Salomonelaps* (it flattened itself when provoked, and hissed, and made a chewing movement with its jaws; "The toxicity of its venom is unknown but could be regarded as potentially dangerous to humans . . .").

Farther on, there was a big clumsy crashing in the bush, and I had a glimpse of a creature I took to be a dog.

"No. It is a lizard," Ataban said.

A lizard as big as a cocker spaniel? The reptile handbook suggested a monitor lizard.

How different it was just half a mile inland from the breezy beach! Here it was still and hot and steamy, and the air stank of wet and rotten leaves. There was a spider on every bough, and even in the daytime the air was thick with mosquitoes. Merely by grazing a tree trunk with your elbow you picked up a mass of biting ants. We had not gone fifty yards when the ants had worked their way to my neck.

Fat Ataban walked ahead, slapping his arms.

We came to a rectangle of stones.

"This is the grave of the man who first welcomed the birds to Savo," Ataban said. "He was on the hill. The bird came and wanted to stay. But the devil—the snake—would not allow it. Then the bird laid an egg. The man ate the egg and said, 'This is good.' So the bird was allowed to stay, as long as it promised to go on laying the eggs."

We walked farther, all the while Ataban was muttering in a complaining way, "This is *tambu*," and waving his arms.

"No trees may be cut here," he said. "No ropes"—he meant vines—"may be cut."

And because the bush had never been cut, and was seldom visited, it was vast and green and dark—very dense and tall. The megapodes were squawking like chickens in the tree branches. This was their haunt.

A large black spider hung in a web just in front of the tabu grove. The spider's body was about the size of a silver dollar and the legs were each about three inches long. Passing it, Ataban punched the web.

"Did you see the spider?"

"Yes. It will not hurt you."

We did not go very far into the grove. There was no path, for one thing. The whole place was overgrown, and the trees were thick—their trunks averaging about two feet in diameter. It was so strange to see such old trees on a small island: Normally they would have been cut for firewood or for houses. The bamboos which grew everywhere here in dense clusters were deep green and fat, the thickness of a drainpipe.

Ataban was nervous. He said, "It is just there. And I tell you it is very *tambu*. Look at it, but do not go near."

I saw a pile of boulders.

"That is where they burn the feegs to ashes in the sacrifice."

"I can't see very well. There are too many trees."

"We believe that if anyone cuts down a tree here he will get sick. He will probably die."

The word *tambu*—taboo—had a definite meaning in this creepy place. The sunlight hardly penetrated the trees, and because there was no path we had to push the bamboos aside in order to move—and the whole place hummed with insects and the *kuk kuk kuk* of the roosting megapodes. And as we moved slowly through the grove a pig blundered out of the sacred place and Ataban kicked at the startled creature and yelled *"Yu gettim bek!"*—as though the only proper way to address a pig was in Pidgin.

We crashed through the bush a bit more, he showed me another sacred hill, and I asked, "Why don't you have ceremonies these days?"

"If a person carries out a sacrifice and burns a pig to ashes he can't go to church. But I could do it, because I believe in *kastom.*"

When I pressed him, saying that the megapodes were in danger of not being respected, and might fly away forever, he said that an old woman came once a year and sacrificed a pig to the birds.

Back on the path, badly bitten, after two hours of that tangle of spiders and vines—we were both drenched from the wet leaves and the heat—Ataban said protestingly, "I tell you I have shown many people the megapode fields, but I have never taken anyone to the *tambu* place. You are the first one, ever."

I told him that I appreciated the trouble he had taken.

"Now you will go back to your camp and write about it in your notebook."

"How do you know?"

"I see you sitting and writing all the time."

I thought I was alone on the beach, but I should have known better. There is no privacy in a village.

"Don't be silly, Ataban. I can keep a secret. Of course I'm not going to write this down."

But as soon as he was out of sight it was exactly what I did.

I stayed on Savo longer than I intended, and after I ran out of food I simply ate yams and megapode eggs, which were the yolkiest eggs I had ever seen. One day James came by in his motorboat and after a little bargaining—I gave him my fish spear and a full tank of gas—we went fifteen miles across The Slot to Nggela, to look at Tulaghi. The town had been captured by the Japanese in January 1942. It was retaken by the Americans in August, and because of its deep harbor, this was the headquarters for the invasion of Guadalcanal. There were rock walls at the harbor entrance. Once they had been painted with American war cries, on the instructions of Admiral "Bull" Halsey.

". . . we steamed into Tulaghi Harbor," an American sailor wrote, remembering his first sight of the place in 1944. "There were great tall bluffs, palisades towering out of the sea on both sides of the entrance, and there painted on the bare rock in letters that were maybe a hundred and fifty feet high was a message. The top line read *KILL . . . KILL . . . KILL,* second line, *KILL MORE JAPS,* third line signed, *HALSEY.* We all cheered, because we were all trained killers, parts of a powerful killing machine. But later, it made me think about the ways we had been settling differences with the Japanese."

Now the town of Tulaghi was even more deserted and derelict than it had been in the war—beer cans everywhere, paper blowing, broken bottles, empty houses.

As we walked around, James told me stories of his days on a Japanese longline tuna boat, earning forty dollars a month. The boat brought the fish directly to Japan, where in Yokohama, James had fallen in with American blacks, who asked him whether he was from the States. "They didn't know where the Solomon Islands is. But they took me to bars and bought me beer." He found Japan expensive. He swapped cuts of tuna with bartenders for bottles of whisky. Japan bewildered him. "It is all Japanese people. There was no one like me there."

Eventually I loaded my boat and said goodbye to the people at Balola. I gave the men fishhooks and the women some silk scarves. It was a perfunctory goodbye. Only the children came to the beach, and when I saw Rebecca hurrying towards the beach I greeted her, but she didn't look up. She chucked a basket full of garbage into the water and walked away.

Back in Honiara, I visited Bloody Ridge, where thousands of men died in 1942. I paddled up the gray-green Lungga River for five miles, but it was a much more noxious sewer than the sea, because it ran more slowly, and wherever I looked there was trash, or shit, or dead animals. The people looked wild, yet they were unfailingly courteous, and everyone I greeted said hello.

The town was dreadful. I wanted to get out of it, but not leave the Solomons. And remembering how I had circled the green volcano in my boat, paddling slowly, and listening to Puccini, I had a strong desire to return to Savo.

The night before I left Guadalcanal I fell into conversation with a Solomon Islander named Kipply and told him I was off to Vanuatu.

"You will enjoy it. They are like us there," he said, and I felt better.

Chapter 10
VANUATU: CANNIBALS AND MISSIONARIES

I soon found myself in White Grass Village on the island of Tanna, in Vanuatu (formerly the New Hebrides), living in a three-room bamboo hut with four burly, bearded New Zealanders. They murmured all night and sometimes yelped, sounding as though they had hit on an idea.

When Glen, the battiest one, confided to me that the impending Gulf war might be Armageddon, and that all over the world silicone chips were being inserted under people's skin—"the Mark of the Beast, see, foretold in the Book of Revelations"—I suspected that they were born-again Christians, come to save Tanna, an island with a past rich in cannibalism. I was right, and they read their Bibles by the light of a kerosene lantern— we had no electricity—and when it rained the hut leaked. But there was nowhere else for me to stay.

The fundamentalists loved the rain and regarded the dark clouds with dull slow smiles of approval.

"Behold!" said Douglas cheerfully one rainy morning. Douglas was nearly as batty as Glen. He had a suppurating sore on his leg that he bathed in seawater every day, not realizing—though I told him—that he was only adding to the infection. "He's putting obstacles for us!"

Now they were all outside the bamboo hut, getting drenched, but agreeing like mad.

"Who's putting obstacles?"

"The Devil," Douglas said.

"Why would the Devil do that to you today?" I asked.

"Because we're walking to north Tanna to preach," Douglas said. "It's an all-day hike. Very tough bush. He doesn't want us to preach."

Later that morning, Glen hurried back to the bamboo hut. He was soaking wet, his face was muddy, his hair was plastered against his scalp, his hands were greasy. He told me delightedly that their Jeep had broken down on their way to the path.

"Obstacles!" he cried.

The rain, the breakdown, the native hostility, my indifference—the Devil's obstacles—it all seemed a testimony to the sanctity of their mission. And I was sure that Tanna's long anthropophagous history, its people-eating, was another factor—rumors of cannibalism are like catnip to missionaries, who are never happier than when bringing the Bible to savages. Missionaries and cannibals make perfect couples.

Just the swiftest glance down the library shelf devoted to the New Hebrides had to be enough to convince any evangelist that these happy islanders were in need of the Christian message. A partial chronology included *Missionary Life Among the Cannibals* (1882), *The Cannibal Islands* (1917), *Cannibalism Conquered* (1900), *Two Cannibal Archipelagoes* (1900—the Solomons included), *Cannibals Won for Christ* (1920), *Cannibal-land* (1922), *L'archipel de Tabous* (1926), *Living Among Cannibals* (1930), *Backwash of Empire* (1931), *Backwaters of the Savage South Seas* (1933), *The Conquest of Cannibal Tanna* (1934), *Savage Civilization* (1936), Paton's *Thirty Years With South Seas Cannibals,* and Evelyn Cheesman's *Camping Adventures on Cannibal Islands.*

I had found circumstantial evidence for cannibalism—the liking in Vanuatu (and it had been the case in the Solomons too) for Spam. It was a theory of mine that former cannibals of Oceania now feasted on Spam because Spam came the nearest to approximating the porky taste of human flesh. "Long pig" as they called a cooked human being in much of Melanesia. It was a fact that the people-eaters of the Pacific had all evolved, or perhaps degenerated, into Spam-eaters. And in the absence of Spam they settled for corned beef, which also had a corpsy flavor.

But cannibalism was less interesting to me than cargo cults. Most of all I wanted to visit Tanna because I had heard that a cargo cult, the Jon Frum Movement, flourished on the island. The villagers in this movement worshipped an obscure, perhaps mythical American named Jon Frum who was supposed to have come to Tanna in the 1930s. He appeared from nowhere and promised the people an earthly paradise. All they had to do was reject Christian missionaries and go back to their old ways. This they did with enthusiasm—booting out the Presbyterians. Jon Frum had not so far returned. The Jon Frum villages displayed a wooden red cross, trying to lure him—and his cargo of free goods—to the island. This iconography of the cross was not Christian, but rather derived from the war, from the era of free food and Red Cross vehicles.

The believers sat in hot little box-like structures and prayed to Jon

Frum. Some had visions of the strange American. They sang Jon Frum ditties in Bislama, the local Pidgin.

I mentioned this to the God-bothering New Zealanders.

"Obstacles!" they cried.

I had come here from Port Vila, on the island of Efate, because I had found Port Vila too tame and touristy. It was a pretty town built against a hill, and its harbor was deep. Cruise ships from Australia anchored and then went on to Nouméa and other sunny islands, which retailed baskets and T-shirts and shiny shell necklaces and five-dollar bottles of Perrier. The shops in Vila were full of goods, the place was clean and tidy and had at least a dozen comfortable hotels, two or three of them luxurious. They held pig roasts. Their guests went snorkeling in the lagoon. Islanders serenaded them at night, strumming ukeleles and singing "Good Night, Irene" in Bislama.

I was convinced that the town was profoundly civilized when I saw multiple copies of my books displayed in the Port Vila Public Library. In addition the islanders were pleasant and not at all rapacious.

Tipping was discouraged in Vila, and throughout Vanuatu. This was usually the case in countries where most of the tourists were Meganesians—New Zealanders and Australians. Living far from Europe, they had had to be self-sufficient. No tipping was the rule in Meganesia. They had learned frugality and were eager to teach it.

"It's a bit of luck that you're here, Paul," a Vanuatu soldier named Vanua Bani said to me. "You will be safe from the Gulf War."

"Very true," I said. Then we talked about the possibility of war.

"I don't think there should be a war," he said, "because too many people would die."

"Would you fight, if Vanuatu were in the Multinational Force?"

He was evasive, and then said, "I would fight for my own country, but I would not let myself get killed for another country."

His was not in uniform. He wore a T-shirt that said, *Vanuatu—Ten Years of Peace and Prosperity 1980–1990.*

"Did you fight the British?"

"Oh, no," he said. "We wouldn't do that. We like the British."

But it had been a circuitous route to independence. After a free-for-all by French and British land-grabbers in the nineteenth century, both countries agreed to joint responsibility and they turned the islands into a condominium government. The local wags called the condominium "the pandemonium." It wobbled along largely because, in the words of an English settler named Fletcher, "these poor beggars have more manners and more virtues than their masters."

The settler-missionary structure was altered by the Second World War, when the New Hebrides was a base for U.S. troops fighting in the Solomons and elsewhere in the Coral Sea. But afterwards life resumed and the islands reverted to fishing, timber cutting, and mining (manganese mostly). In the late 1960s and early 1970s decolonization began in a series of conferences but the sides (British, French, islander) were too self-interested to find common grounds for agreement.

Two leaders emerged in the 1970s—Jimmy Stevens, a charismatic figure with a Moses beard and an Old Testament manner, who called himself Moses; and Father Walter Lini, a Presbyterian—a shrewd, English-speaking, conservative missionary product. Lini had a broad base of support. Stevens's followers were mostly on his home island, the large island of Espiritu Santo, with its French planters, opportunists, bush folk, upstarts, and eager secessionists. Stevens also had the support of a meddling right-wing American organization, dedicated to eradicating communism, called The Phoenix Foundation. Stevens's threats to make Santo independent worried the electorate on the other islands, and after several national elections Lini was elected prime minister. At Independence, Stevens led an unsuccessful armed rebellion which became world news as "the Coconut War" for a few days in 1980, until the bearded one was jailed.

After ten years, Lini was still prime minister and Jimmy Stevens was still in jail.

Vanua Bani assured me that Father Walter, as he called him, was very popular and much loved.

He confirmed that the Jon Frum Movement was flourishing on Tanna, and he also said that if I was going there I ought to make a point of seeing Chief Tom Namake, who knew a bit about it.

I packed my boat and left the tourists—Gloria and Bunt ("the blacks here are ever so sweet—not like ours") and their kids Darrell and Shane, from Adelaide—the cruise passengers, the snorkelers, the Women's Conference on Nuclear Policy in the Pacific (moved from New Guinea because the women's safety could not be guaranteed in Port Moresby), and I took a small plane to Tanna.

Chief Tom happened to be elsewhere on the island, and while I waited for him I had the New Zealand born-again Christians to contend with. It so happened that camping was not allowed on this part of the island, and the bamboo hut was the best I could find.

Whenever they were not having a prayer meeting or a preach-o-rama in a village, the born-agains lay in wait for me and ambushed me. It was not hard. The driving rain made it impossible for me to go very far. At first I was more or less supine and let them preach, but I retired to a corner with the Bible and found passages that I asked them to explain. For example, Matthew 10:35, in which Jesus says combatively, "For I am come to set a man at variance against his father, and the daughter against her mother—"

They said I needed faith. I needed to be born again, and they flipped pages until they came to John 3:3 ("Except a man be born again—").

I noticed that they were indiscriminate and passionate carnivores. At breakfast they made greasy bacon sandwiches, at lunch they fried sausages, and on some days they spooned tuna fish straight from the tin. My experience among the Seventh Day Adventists of the Trobriands stood me in good stead here.

"The Bible says you shouldn't eat that meat," I said.

Their smiles were torpid and condescending, but they went on munching.

Glen said to the others, "Paul's got spirit. But he needs the holy spirit. He needs Jesus."

"Leviticus. Chapter Eleven. Also Deuteronomy. It's all forbidden—pork, fish without scales and fins, all of it."

"There have been directives about that," Douglas said vaguely.

"He needs the name of Jesus," Glen said.

I said, "You told me that you believed in the strict word of the Bible. What about all that stuff you told me about the flood?"

The previous night Douglas had asserted that the flood had covered the earth. They had found evidence of it in Australia for example. He believed in Adam and Eve, and in Noah's Ark. He believed that Mrs. Lot had been turned into a pillar of salt. Why didn't he believe in the prohibitions of Leviticus?

I nagged them for a while, because it was raining and I had nothing better to do. Later that day I read them parts of the Book of Daniel, which had wonderful arguments for vegetarianism: Daniel refused Nebuchadnezzar's meaty feast, and insisted on eating his usual diet of lentils, which gave him a rosy complexion and helped make him a healthy magician.

"Don't you think you could learn something from that, Glen?"

"You need Jesus," Glen said, tucking bacon into his mouth.

"There is nothing in the Bible that says that Jesus ate meat," I said, and wondered if that were so. They did not dispute it. I liked talking to them on this subject of vegetarianism while their mouths were stuffed with bacon sandwiches.

"Don't get so intellectual about it," Brian said.

Brian worried me. He had a loud shouting laugh that was like a warning. He could be rather sulky, too. Brian was the hairiest one, the most bearded, the leader. I was wary of him most of all because whenever he told me how he had found Jesus it was accompanied by stories of how he had been a violent and wicked sinner. *I did terrible things,* he said, and gave me a hard look, and I took this as a warning that he would do terrible things to me if I didn't listen to him. I had a feeling terrible things had happened to Mrs. Brian, back in Auckland. *I defiled the name of Jesus—I wouldn't even tell you half the things I did. I was horrible.*

And he sometimes still looked horrible when we sat at the wobbly table, with his enormous Bible between us. In the margins were his notes, written in ballpoint. Handwriting—just its contours—can look violent. I found his blue scribble alarmingly slow-witted and threatening.

Still the rain came down.

Brian insisted (and the others closed ranks behind him) that nothing on earth was older than 4,000 years. Not dinosaurs, trilobites, Chinese tombs.

"Carbon dating has been totally disproved."

"You're saying that Tyrannosaurus rex was running around less than four thousand years ago?"

"It certainly couldn't have been more than four thousand years ago, because the world hadn't been created," Brian said. He pretended to smile in triumph but if you looked at his teeth and his eyes you knew that he wanted to bite you.

Glen then told me about the silicone chips.

"And the Mark of God will appear on the foreheads of those who are saved," Douglas said.

"But obviously not on mine, is that what you're saying?"

I did not push these paranoiacs too far. The trouble with such Christians was not their faith in God but their hearty, adversarial belief in the Devil. It seemed to me that it could be a fatal mistake for me to dispute too strenuously with them. There were no doors on this bamboo hut. I heard the men murmuring at night. *I did terrible things.* They were completely convinced that the Devil himself was at large, roaming to and fro, around White Grass Village, perhaps in their very hut, trying to confound them. They might get it into their heads that I was the incarnation of the Antichrist and drive a bamboo stake through my heart.

They were "God-swankers"—one of the paradigmatic types that Elias Canetti describes in his strange book *Earwitness:* "The God-swanker never has to ask himself what is correct, he looks it up in the Book of Books. There he finds everything he needs . . . Whatever he plans to do, God will endorse it."

Because of the storms we had each night, the villagers were spared our nighttime disputations. In times of high wind and rain everyone in the village ran into a specially constructed hut—rounded and very tightly woven—and there they huddled, one on top of the other, until the storm passed. There was no room in their emergency hut for the shouting, praying New Zealanders.

The Melanesian people of Tanna were small scowling knob-headed blacks with short legs and big dusty feet, and some of them were the nakedest I saw in the whole Pacific, the women in tattered grass skirts, the men and boys in "penis purses" (in the words of a Tanna man). These little pubic bunches of grass were about the size and shape of whisk brooms and were worn over their dicks. This bunch of grass, secured by a vine, a belt, or a piece of string, was a male's entire wardrobe. The Bislama word for this item was *namba,* literally "number." In Vanuatu one group of people were known as the Big Nambas and another as the Small Nambas.

Most of these grass-skirted and namba-wearing folks were happy heathens living in *kastom* villages in the muddy interior of the island. Whether or not they were cultists in the Jon Frum Movement was something I hoped to establish, and so I went by Jeep to one of the *kastom* villages to find out.

It was raining in Yakel Village, and it looked as though it had been raining for two thousand years. The huts were soaked, the thatch was soggy, the sky was black, the air was chilly, the ground was a quagmire, and the naked people were huddled—men under one tree, women under another—hugging themselves to keep warm. Rain ran down their backs and dripped from their bums. The women had hoisted their grass skirts around their necks, wearing them for warmth, like cloaks; the men squatted so close to the ground, their nambas drooped into puddles. It was a village of runny noses. In the persistent drizzle it was a gloomy little glimpse of the Neolithic Age, complete with muddy buttocks.

The men smoked bitter-smelling tobacco and passed coconut shells of kava back and forth, and when they smiled at me—which they did often; they were extremely friendly—they showed me black stumps of teeth.

"Yu savvy Jon Frum here?"

They grinned and waved me away. "No Jon Frum."

It was strictly a *kastom* village—no Christians, no politics, no Jon Frum—and there were many such villages on the island, though this was the only one which allowed contact with outsiders. The other *kastom* villages, deeper in the interior, were fierce and xenophobic, and—I had the impression—nakeder, though a namba made you nearly as naked as it was possible to be. In Yakel, a namba was called a *kawhirr* in their language, which was Nahwal. The language had never been written down and was one of the few languages in the entire world into which the Bible had never been translated.

At the center of the crouching group was the chief, a tiny skinny man with a bushy grizzled beard and clouded eyes and tufts of yellow-white hair over his ears. He was entirely toothless. I took him to be about seventy. I asked him in Pidgin how many Christmases he had had—which was the standard way of asking someone's age—but he said he had no idea, and added that his Pidgin was none too good.

His name was Chief Johnson Kahuwya. He hadn't a clue as to where the Johnson came from. He was spokesman and leader. He led the dances. He directed the planting of the gardens. He gave advice. He was the father of the village.

Using a man from a nearby village as my interpreter, I asked the chief how long he had allowed outsiders to come to his village.

"Since 1983. That was when we first saw white people."

"What did you think of them?"

"We decided not to chase them away," the chief said.

The Melanesians did not have any organization larger than a village, nor did they have any conception of themselves as branches of a major race, Austin Coates writes in *Islands of the South,* a book about the attitudes and movements of Pacific populations. *When a Melanesian encountered someone not of his group, though he denoted a likeness, he did not think, "It is a man." The word "man" applied solely to his own group, or tribe. Between his own tribe and others he made an enlarged distinction, much as he would between a pig, a bird or a fish, or between himself and any of these animals. The concept of mankind was absent.*

This was also an explanation for the Trobrianders' belief that they were human and that *dim-dims* were not. A non-Trobriander was of a different species.

"What about Christian missionaries?" I asked the chief.

"We have no missionaries here."

"But did Christian missionaries come here?"

"Yes. Long ago. They came." He was puffing a cigarette—tobacco rolled in a withered leaf. The rain kept dousing it. "They held a service. We watched them. They were talking and singing."

"Were you impressed—did it seem a wonderful thing to do?"

"No. We watched them. That was all."

"What did they tell you?"

The chief laughed, remembering, and then he imitated the missionaries talking, " 'After we go, you do this—what we have been doing.' "

"Did you do it?"

"No."

Now the other men laughed and slapped their wet goose-pimpled arms. "Why not?"

The chief said, "We are not Christians."

Nor were they Muslims, or Hindus, or Buddhists, or Jews. They were totally traditional and wished to remain so. I had never met such confident animists in my life—neither in Africa, nor South America, nor Asia. They had no interest whatsoever in changing their way of life. I found the whole setup heartening, muddy buttocks and all.

"We are *kastom* people," the chief went on.

"But the missionaries might come again," I said, thinking of the four New Zealanders over at White Grass.

"It is okay for them to worship as they want," the chief said. "But we have different ways. We go our own *kastom* way."

"Do you pray sometimes?"

"Yes. We pray for food."

"How do you do that?"

"We sing for harvests," the chief said.

All this time the snotty-nosed boys laughed among themselves and the dripping men murmured and passed the kava. And I crouched with them, making notes. I was wetter than they, and more uncomfortable, because I was wearing clothes and I was soaked. Their nakedness made complete sense.

"Where did your ancestors come from long ago?" I asked. "Did they travel from another island?"

"No. They came from this island."

"Maybe you came from birds and snakes?" I asked, thinking of what the Solomon Islanders had told me of themselves.

"No. We are people. We have always been men."

In Melanesia, creation stories were always intensely local. The tribal name usually meant "man." The people of the tribe had either always been there or else had emerged from the land—from live creatures or from trees. Melanesians never said they had arrived from another island, and they never made reference to boats or the sea journeys when telling creation stories.

The rain with its crackling drops swept through the towering trees and dense bush around us and coursed through the sodden hillside. The grass huts were so wet they looked as though they were in a state of collapse— heavy and toppling.

"You live far from the sea. Do you ever go fishing?"

"Yes. There are *kastom* villages near the sea. They let us fish."

"How do you return the favor? Do you give them some of the fish you catch?"

"No. But we give them our trees for wood, and sometimes we make canoes for them."

"Do you go to other *kastom* villages in the bush?"

"We do," the chief said, still sucking on the cigarette. "For weddings and circumcisions."

A wedding was a straightforward feast, he said, but a circumcision was rather more complicated. He told me about it. It took place when a boy was four or five, and it began first as a great feast—many pigs being killed. There would be a dozen or so boys involved. After the snipping—a sharp knife was used—the boys were sent into the bush for two months. They could not be seen by any woman. They could not touch food with their hands—they used a certain designated leaf, scrunched up, to eat with, scooping the food. They were not allowed to touch their hair, or pick out lice, and if they wanted to scratch their head they had to use a twig. Men were appointed to cook for them. After the two months were up, when the cut had healed, they went back to the village wearing a namba they had made.

I asked the chief, "What food do you like to eat?"

"Taro. Yam. Leaves. Pigs."

"If you get money, what do you buy in the trade store?"

"A knife or an axe. Or rice. Or corned beef."

"How many wives are you allowed to have?"

"In the past, two or three. Now we have one, usually."

"Have you ever left this island of Tanna?"

"Yes. During the war. I helped to build the airfield at Vila."

It was now called Bauer Field, named after the valiant Lieutenant Colonel Harold Bauer, a fighter pilot in the U.S. Marine Corps who, in 1942, battling against great odds, downed eleven Japanese planes and was eventually killed in Guadalcanal. Posthumously, Bauer was awarded the Medal of Honor, and a brass plaque at the airport recorded his courage and his deeds. Bauer Field was presently being enlarged and improved by a Japanese–Vanuatu joint venture, to accommodate Japanese planes and tourists, and I was very curious to know what the Japanese construction company would do with the plaque when the airport was complete. Would they hide it; would they lose it; or would they hang it in the new terminal to enlighten future generations—and the visiting Japanese—of Bauer's war effort? Time would tell.

"Did you wear a namba when you were building the airport?"

"No. I wore a *kaliko.*"

"Why not wear a namba?"

"I wanted to. But the American said, 'Don't wear this thing.' "

Although the rain had not let up, they took me—the chief leading the way—on a tour of the village, which was nestled against the hillside in tall grass that was shoulder height. Cross-faced men squatted under the drooping eaves. Naked women knelt in smoky huts. The children shrieked at me, their faces smeared with snot. Everyone in the village had filthy muddy legs. They showed me the large round hut they hid in when the weather was very bad: They had spent the previous night in it, all of them piled in, nearly eighty of them.

Later, under a dripping banyan, they did a loud stamping dance, pounding their big flat feet hard into the mud, slowly at first, then quickening their pace, and each time they brought their feet down they yelped and their nambas flopped up and down. The mud dried on their buttocks, giving them brighter smears on their bum cheeks, like perverse war paint. They skipped in a circle, and shouted hoarsely—egged on by the chief—and clapped, and stamped again, heavily, a thumping that seemed to make the forest tremble and shook droplets from the boughs.

They were not much bigger than pygmies, and they were blacker and more naked. They had terrible teeth—stumps and canines broken into fangs. They looked like cannibals. Indeed, they had been, although on Tanna cannibalism was a privilege usually reserved for chiefs, nobles, and dignitaries.

Once, in Christie's auction rooms in London, I had seen a large and horrific painting titled *Cannibal Feast on the Island of Tanna, New Hebrides,* by Charles Gordon Frazer, a widely traveled English landscape artist. It had been worked up in 1891 from a sketch he had made of a jungle scene he had actually stumbled upon on Tanna in the 1880s. It has been claimed that Frazer was the only white man ever to witness a cannibal ceremony. He recorded the scene faithfully in his celebrated painting, which showed two victims being brought into a shadowy jungle clearing—just like this—on poles; the gloating villagers (there are almost 100 figures in this enormous canvas), the muscled, tufty-haired warriors, the women preparing the cooking fires.

"The bodies of the two victims, slung on poles, are painted in a masterly style," an English critic wrote when it was first exhibited, "the one being evidently dead, the other in stupor approaching death in its growing muscular relaxation." Another critic, Australian, described Frazer's painting as a "walkabout by a load of washed-out niggers."

Put on the defensive by alarmed and nit-picking gallery-goers, Frazer explained in an essay why he had chosen to paint the cannibal feast. "It was not from any desire for sensation," he wrote, "but from the fact of having by accident witnessed a scene of superstition so ancient, a custom that must soon become extinct all over the world before the great march of civilization, that I considered it my duty to illustrate this dark and terrible phase in the history of man . . ."

He was certainly telling the truth about having been an eyewitness—it was obvious in the painting's shocking details; and now, on Tanna, I knew that Frazer had been on the island, sketching in the gloomy light of this dense forest. It seems that Frazer's jungle clearing was farther east, at Yanekahi, near Tanna's volcano—and near Port Resolution, where Captain Cook landed in 1774.

Frazer also wrote, "If it were not for their superstitious rites [by which he meant cannibalism], these black people are no more cruel than the white men. If a boat lands and treats the natives brutally it is not unnatural that the next white man who lands will be revenged upon." And he went on, "There is much that is beautiful in these black savages . . ."

I left Yakel and went a hundred years or so across the island, to White Grass. Chief Tom Namake had returned from his trip to the bush. He had a fat sweaty face and a big belly. He spoke quickly—so quickly he sounded as though he was being evasive. He wore a dirty T-shirt that said *Holy Commando,* with the motif of an archer, and motto from Isaiah 49:2, *He made me into a polished arrow.*

He was not only a Christian, he said, he also believed in the spirit world, and Jon Frum and *kastom*. He believed in magic stones and magic dances. He believed that all the people on Tanna Island had sprung from the twigs of two bewitched trees. His strongest belief was in traditional magic. But the T-shirt seemed the appropriate thing to wear around the New Zealanders. "Everyone must be allowed to do as he wishes, even them," he said of the Kiwis. At that moment they were preaching nearby. And they were planning some late-night prayer meetings in the village. It struck me that they held their services at very odd times of day, favoring nighttime.

"I have just come from Yakel," I said.

"What do you think?"

I hesitated and then said, "Were those people cannibals at one time?"

"Oh, yes," Chief Tom said, and seemed pleased to be disclosing it. "Many people were cannibals. But cannibalism on Tanna stopped about a hundred years ago. It was mostly over land disputes that they killed and ate each other. The Big Nambas were the last people to be cannibals."

"What about *kastom* people like the ones in Yakel. Are there people like that elsewhere in Vanuatu?"

"In Santo and Malekula you will find them. If they see you they will chase you around. What are you writing?"

"Nothing," I said. But I had been scribbling in my tiny notebooks, *Big Nambas chase you around.* I tucked it into my pocket.

"If you promise not to write it down I will tell you something," he said.

"Look, I'm not even holding a pen!"

Chief Tom glanced around and then looked at me with his bloodshot eyes and said, "I think some of those *kastom* people are still cannibals today, but they wouldn't tell you."

Chief Tom's son Peter was reading the Australian weekly magazine which had a lurid cover showing a grinning young woman in a bikini. She had freckles on her shoulders and she looked deeply unreliable.

Peter suddenly snatched up a sharp knife and slashed out a page and stuffed it into his pocket.

Later I asked him why he had cut the page out of the magazine, and he shyly showed it to me. It was a full-page advertisement, which I read closely.

BODYWISE
the Female Attractant that makes 9 out of 10
men more attractive to women.
With Bodywise Spray you can become
a walking magnet to women!!
You will be amazed at the results!! Only $39.95!!

COMMENTS:
"Your product really works!"—CG, NSW

"A much younger beautiful lady sitting next to me
at a formal dinner whispered that she
wanted to make love to me!"—MF, Pomonia

"As a professional chauffeur, I find
my clientele has increased!"—BC, NSW

Peter took the torn page back, and folded it and put it into his pocket. He was smiling.

Then he said in a low voice, "Me want dis."

The following day, Chief Tom said in an accusatory tone, "I saw you writing."

"Just a letter to my mother," I lied.

"That's all right then," he said. "If you promise not to write it down I will tell you a true cannibal story."

"Why can't I write it?"

"You will take my magic if you do! Don't fool with such things! Oh, I don't think I will tell you after all."

"Please," I said. "Look, no pen. No paper."

His expression was untrusting. We were sitting on a bluff above the chop of the windblown sea. It was a rocky coast, with rough ledges instead of beaches. There was nowhere here that I had found where I could launch or beach my kayak, and yet I remained hopeful.

Chief Tom squinted into the wind and then stole a glance back at me, as though he expected to find me sneaking out my notebook. He had become suspicious of my writing. Out of boredom I had been doing a great deal of writing at White Grass, describing the New Zealanders, making notes on the Bible for future disputations, noting down the conversation I had had at Yakel Village. Chief Tom regarded all writing with alarm, because it was a way of stealing someone's magic. I understood exactly what he meant, and I agreed with him. It was a fact, not a savage superstition. If he told a story, and I wrote it down, the story became mine. I did not have the guts to tell Chief Tom that writing was my business.

Wiping his hands on his *Holy Commando* shirt, he began.

"It was just down the road here, near Imanaka Village, about a hundred years ago. A certain European trader came in a ship looking for—what? Some things—food, water, whatnot.

"The Tanna people saw him at the beach. They listened to him and said they could help him. They tell him to follow them and still talk to him in a friendly way, and when they get down into the bush they take out bush knives and kill him, then stab him with spears. He is dead.

"They carry him to their village and prepare the fire and the stones for the oven to cook him. And then they take his clothes off. One man feels the arm and says, 'I like this—I eat this!' And another says, 'I want this leg.'

"And another and another, and so on, until they have the whole body divided, except the feet.

"The last man says, 'I want these'—meaning the feet."

Chief Tom smiled and smacked his lips and poked his thick black forefinger into my chest.

"The dead man is wearing canvas shoes!" he cried. "They never seen canvas shoes before! They take the shoes off and say, 'Hey, hey! This must be the best part!' So they throw the body away and keep the shoes. They boil them for a while, then they try to eat them, the canvas shoes!"

I interrupted at this point and said, "I don't understand why they threw the body away."

"Because it is nothing to them, but the feet you can remove—that is special."

"The feet you can remove are the shoes, right?"

"They never see such things before," Chief Tom said. "That is why they boil them. After they take them out of the pot they chew and chew. Cannot even bite the canvas shoes. They try to tear them with their teeth. No good.

"Everyone has a chew.

"What is this? Cannot eat his feet!

"They take the shoes to another village and those ones try to eat the canvas shoes, but it is impossible.

"So they dig a big hole and throw in the canvas shoes and cover them. Then they plant a coconut tree on top of it. That tree grew up very tall—and when the storm came in eighty-seven it blew the tree down, so they planted another tree. It is still growing. I can show you the tree tomorrow."

Chapter 11
THE ODDEST ISLAND
IN VANUATU

Looking for the cannibal palm, and the burial place of the canvas shoes late on one hot afternoon, I discovered a wonderful thing: Imanaka was a Jon Frum village—there was the red cross, in wood, at the center of the lopsided woven huts. A cargo cult flourished within.

Imanaka, wreathed in smoke from cooking fires, was in the woods, on a stony hillside, behind a broken fence, at the end of a muddy track. It was easy to see how such a hard-up village would take to the idea of deliverance and develop faith in the idea that one day an immense amount of material goods would come their way, courtesy of Jon Frum, only if they believed in him and danced and sang his praises. But it was also an article of faith that Jon Frum villages had to neglect their gardens and throw their money away: When Jon Frum returned he would provide everything.

I had no idea what sort of reception I would get. I was watched from a distance by a group of dusty women, and the first men I met spoke neither English nor Bislama—which was simply a version of Pidgin (the word Bislama being a corruption of bêche-de-mer—it had started as a trader's language).

It occurred to me that this visit might be an error of judgement. I was alone. It was obviously a poverty-stricken village. Hungry people can behave unpredictably. Who knows—they might get it into their head to kill me and eat my shoes. Smoke swirled around the village and the smoke alone, the way it straggled this way then that, gave the village a profound look of dereliction.

Men came forward and stared at me. One was clearly a mental case. He giggled in bewilderment. Another had a rag tied around his head. There were six more. They carried sticks and bush knives. Behind them were the women. Every one of them looked very dirty. Still I wondered: *Is this a mistake?*

"*Yupela savvy tok Bishlama?*" I asked, and when they shook their heads and grinned, I asked, "*Yupela savvy toktok? Chief bilong yupela i stap we?*"

One boy stepped forward and said, "*Parlez-vous français, monsieur?*"

"*Je parle un peu,*" I said. What was this, a French-speaking village? "*Les gens de ce village—parlent-ils français?*"

He said some of them did and others didn't. The chief didn't, for example. He would be joining us soon, the boy said, but in the meantime perhaps I would like to sit on this log in the shade of this thatched shelter.

I did so, and while we waited he asked me whether I had news of the war in the Gulf. I bumblingly explained what I had heard that morning— that there were diplomatic missions flying back and forth in the hope of averting war.

The chief, whose name was Yobas, shambled over to the shelter. He was old and feeble, carrying a stick that was smooth where his hand gripped it. He wore a torn undershirt and a dirty cloth tied like a sarong, and he had the oppressed and wincing expression of a chief who was probably being blamed by everyone, including his own people, for presiding over such a miserable village.

"*Yu savvy tok Inglis?*"

Incredibly, he nodded: yes, he did.

I greeted him by making an insincere speech saying what a delightful village it was and how happy I was to be in it, and I hoped that this would put all thoughts of killing me out of their minds.

"So this is a Jon Frum village?"

"Yiss. All dis. Jon Frum." And he motioned with his stick.

"The village dances for Jon Frum?"

"We dance here"—it seemed that we were sitting in the open-sided dance hall. "For Jon Frum. Also sing-sing. For Jon Frum."

"Sometimes do you see Jon Frum?"

"Nuh. But the old fella they see him."

"What does Jon Frum look like? Is he black or white?"

"White like you. From America. He is a beeg man—very fat! He strong!"

"What does he wear?"

"He wear clothes. He wear everything. He wear hat."

I was wearing a baseball hat. I said, "Like this?"

"Nuh. Big hat. Like a missionary."

I took out my notebook and drew a picture of a wide-brimmed hat. He said, Yes, that's the one. And when he spoke the other men and the children crowded around me and jostled for a look at the notebook page.

Later, when I had spoken to more Jon Frum adherents, I discovered that I might have confused the chief with my questions, because he seemed to be describing a Jon Frum emissary who was known as "Tom Navy." This Floridian was a Seabee who had turned up on Tanna in 1945 and briefly had the island at his feet. Another Jon Frum had appeared in 1943 and proclaimed himself "King of America and Tanna"—and an airfield was cleared on the north of the island, so that when his cargo planes arrived they would have a place to land.

I wondered about the prayer houses, in which certain Jon Frum prophets, called "messengers," knelt and had visions of their benefactor. I asked the chief about this.

"Old fella talk to him," he said, "but me no talk."

The crucial question—crucial for the Vanuatu government, at any rate—was the extent to which the Jon Frum Movement displayed American paraphernalia. The most egregious aspect, from the government's point of view, was whether these villages flew the American flag. The notion was that since Jon Frum was an American, the cargo would come from America, and mixed up in this iconography of the red cross and the mysterious vanishing American, was the Stars and Stripes. In some villages the American flag was flown often; in others, every February. The Vanuatu government frequently lost patience with the Jon Frum people and actively persecuted them, jailing them or confiscating their American paraphernalia.

I decided to be blunt. "Do you have an American flag?"

Chief Yobas hesitated for a while, but finally made a sheepish face and nodded. I asked him why the flag was necessary.

"During the war he come again and he give an American flag to an old fella."

"Do you raise the flag on a pole?"

This was too much for him. He said, "You go to Sulphur Bay. See Chief Mellis. Isaac One. He tell you everything."

I pretended not to hear him. I smiled at the men with knives and sticks who hovered around me. It was about five in the afternoon. The sun was just low enough to slant through the thin tree trunks and it seemed to be much hotter at this hour than it had been at noon. I was reminded of how dreary such a village could seem, and this was—dusty and flyblown and poor, clinging to its belief in Jon Frum—sadder than most I had seen. It was silent, except for the clucking of chickens and the crowing of an occasional rooster.

Gesturing at the thatched shelter in which we sat I said, "You sing-sing here?"

"Yiss. We sing-sing."

"Please. Sing-sing for me."

The old chief considered this, and then hitched himself forward and in a whispering voice that rustled and hissed like tissue paper he began to sing.

> *Jon Frum*
> *He mus come*
> *Look at old fellas*
> *Give us some big presents*
> *Give us some good tok-tok*

He wheezed and riffed, sounding a good deal like the groaning blues singer he much resembled—John Lee Hooker came to mind—and he continued.

> *Jon Frum*
> *He mus come*
> *Mus stap long kastom*
> *Mus keep kastom*

He looked squarely at me and rolled his head and whispered again,

> *Jon Frum*
> *He mus come.*

When he had finished I fossicked in my knapsack for my gift bag, a plastic sack of fishhooks and spear points and trinkets and scarves that I gave to people who were hospitable. I had made several rules on my trip. One was that I would not kill or eat any animal. Another was that I would not give anyone money in return for a favor.

Chief Yobas spread his fingers and clutched a slightly used but still radiantly colored Hermès silk scarf. He touched it to his face.

"Handkerchief," he said.

"They were lying to you," Chief Tom told me that night. "Jon Frum was not fat. He was small, very slight. A small man. This is the truth. If you write this down I will not tell you anything. He could speak all the languages. He saw one man and spoke that man's language. He saw another man and spoke to him in his own language. And so on."

"How do you know this?"

"You promise not to write it? You promise not to steal my magic?"

"I could never steal your magic, Chief."

"My grandfather met him and shook his hand. This was my mother's father—he was prominent in the Jon Frum Movement. My father's father was a Presbyterian minister."

We were alone. I no longer disputed over the Bible at night with the evangelists from New Zealand. They had now based themselves among some tenacious heathens at the north of the island. The great number of obstacles they had encountered on the way convinced them that the Devil did not want them to go there; and so, wishing to defy The Prince of Darkness, they had hotfooted it to North Tanna, to preach.

"How did Jon Frum get to Tanna?"

"In a plane. There was no airstrip. He landed his plane in the tops of trees."

"Where was this?"

"At Green Point."

Examining the map, I saw that if I had a lift past this rocky part of the coast, where there was no break in the reef, I could launch my kayak and paddle to Green Point.

I managed this the following day. Peter—Chief Tom's son—gave me a ride in his Jeep on the understanding that when I was back in Vila I would send him any information I could find on Bodywise, the female attractant that made you "a magnet to women."

"Listen, Peter, do you have trouble meeting women?"

"No trouble," he said. "But me want dis."

He regarded the stuff as a sort of magic that would give him power over women. I said I would do what I could.

The wind was discouragingly strong, and the absence of any canoes offshore was the unmistakable sign that it was a bad day for small boats: not even the local fishermen dared to go out. But I found that by staying just inshore, paddling along the cliffs, I was out of the strongest wind and waves. I crept around the black walls of the island, past the blowholes, and found a dark gravelly beach near Green Point, where I went ashore and ate the bananas I had brought for lunch.

I had the absurd thought that I might be seen by a Tanna person and mistaken for Jon Frum, and I was half-fearful and half-eager that my arrival at this significant place might provoke that reaction in an onlooker.

As it turned out, some children fishing there asked me to give them my Walkman. I was listening to Chuck Berry—rock and roll here made paddling as pleasurable as opera had in the Solomons. I said to the children, No, I needed it, and so they simply ignored me, and went on fishing.

It was not until I was on the point of leaving (I had been procrastinating, because there was so much paddling ahead of me) that I ran into a man. He asked me the usual questions about my boat. Where did it come from? How much did it cost? How had I brought it here?

The man's name was Esrick—at least that was what it sounded like. He was a teacher at one of the schools on Tanna. He was presently on vacation. He said he neither believed nor disbelieved in Jon Frum.

"I think he was one of our old speerits appearing in the shape of an American white man."

"Why would one of your spirits want to come back and visit you?" I asked.

"Because at that time Presbyterianism was very strong. So he appeared at the right time, because the foreign missionaries had banned kava drinking, magic stones, and dancing. Jon Frum said, 'Destroy what the missionaries gave you. I will give you goods.' "

It was a fortuitous visitation. Just when Protestantism had taken hold of the islanders and the missionaries had begun to write their *Cannibalism Conquered* and *Cannibals Won for Christ* memoirs, the strange little man with piercing eyes had popped up here at Green Point and said: Lose those Bibles. He urged the people to revive the important traditions— kava drinking, dancing, and the swapping of women for sexual purposes. About three years after Jon Frum's first appearance in 1938, half the island had abandoned Christianity

"They forsook Christianity," Esrick said. "Because he said he would be back with plenty of goods if they went back to their old ways."

I said, "So when do you think this will happen?"

He laughed at me. "It has already happened! In spirit! Jon Frum's spirit is everywhere. He is in every village."

"But you said you didn't believe in him."

He accused me of being literal-minded, without using that expression.

"You see," Esrick explained, as though speaking to a moron, or one of his schoolkids, "he has come back in the form of development and progress. We have goods now. Go to the shops. Go to Vila. You will see that we have what we want. We have kava. We have dancing. He is back in spirit. He knows he has won!"

Was Jon Frum a friendly American pilot who had brought supplies here and shared them around? And perhaps he had said, *I am John from America.* And then had the war convinced the villagers on Tanna how wealthy America was?

It hardly mattered now. The dogma of the movement seemed to suggest that Jon Frum was a sort of John the Baptist, preceding the savior, which was a redeemer in the form of cargo—every nice and useful object imaginable. And the important aspect was that it had come to the island directly, without the help of missionaries or interpreters. No money, no tithing was involved; no Ten Commandments, no Heaven or Hell. No priests, nor any imperialism. It was a Second Coming, but it enabled the villagers to rid themselves of missionaries and live their lives as they had before. It seemed to me a wonderfully foxy way of doing exactly as they pleased.

On my way back along the coast, the wind was behind me.

I was still listening to Chuck Berry on my Walkman.

> *Get a house*
> *Get married*
> *Settle down*
> *Write a book!*
> *Too much monkey business!*

I rode the swells, slipping forward on the faces of the waves—and rather breathlessly, too: If I turned over here with the surf breaking on the rocky shore I was out of luck. I was fearful until I was past the shoaly headlands and the biggest breaks, and then something just as bad happened.

I felt a sharp knifing against my fingers, like ten beestings, and I saw a gooey, spittle-like substance that had wrapped around my hand and was dripping like snot from my paddle shaft. Blobs of it hit my arm, stuck to my elbow, and stung me there, and when I tried to flick it off it became molten and blistering, hurting me more.

It took me only a short time to work out that it was a cluster of jellyfish tentacles—they were so misshapen and long it was impossible to tell how many. I had picked them up with my paddle blade and they had slipped down the shaft and over my right hand and forearm and elbow, shooting stingers into me. A neurotoxin, marine biologists say; and if a swimmer gets wrapped in one of these creatures it is serious illness, if not certain death.

Probably a Portuguese man-of-war—just my luck, in this wind, on a rocky coast, in a heavy swell off Cannibal Island. My whole arm burned with pain, and I could not flex my fingers. The folk remedy is urine. I clawed my earphones off and pissed into my left hand, and rubbed the burning area. There was a slight momentary relief, but the pain returned.

It was a good thing the wind was at my back. I was able to steer the boat with my good arm. After an hour or more I saw the headland where I had put in, and when I landed I looked for a papaya tree. This is folk remedy number two for jellyfish stings. Papaya sap is generally reckoned to be good medicine for much of what ails you in the tropics—the flesh and seeds are good for diarrhea, the leaves contain an enzyme that acts as a meat tenderizer, and the sap is said to ease the pain of stings. I found a tree, I squeezed the sap onto my arms, and again I noticed a slight lessening of pain. But it came back, and it burned for three hours more, and then it was gone.

Hearing that the Kiwi God-botherers had returned to White Grass Village, I decided to stay on this southeastern part of the island. Here I ran into a mad Irishman, Breffny McGeough. Breffny was a yachtsman who had come ashore here with his girlfriend; and they were in the process of creating a resort hotel of little bungalows from what had been a rather derelict venture run by a man known as Bungalow Bill.

One day, in a heavy rain, Bungalow Bill had heard a strange noise. Leaving his wife in bed, he had rushed out of his bungalow and listened hard. The sound came nearer and nearer—a rumbling, like a tremendous herd of wild pigs moving through the forest. The sound soon revealed itself to be a wall of water, tumbling down the creek bed towards his bungalow. Bill jumped back and saw the water smack the side of his bungalow and carry it off its foundations and into the bay, where it sank, with Mrs. Bill and everything he owned.

"Hell of a way to go," Breffny said. "In bed, in a bungalow, in a bloody gale. Poor old thing probably never knew what hit her."

Breffny had recently given up smoking and drinking. But when the urge was on him he drank kava (which was not the same as beer—quite the opposite), and smoked the sort of local reefer I had seen being passed around by the naked Little Namba people in Yakel Village.

I let Breffny play with my kayak and for a small fee he let me sleep in a deserted house, full of dead flies, at the top of a hill nearby, where the only sound in the day was a bird that peeped like a microwave timer, and at night barking dogs in the woods and the odd but unmistakable lolloping and thrashing, in bushy boughs, of fruit bats.

"We eat them," a villager named Carlo told me. "We boil them or throw them on the fire. They taste like birds a bit."

"Tanna kava is the greatest drink in the world," Breffny said a day or so later. "There's of course the two-day kava which puts you out for twenty-four hours—I mean, you're paralytic. Nothing like it. And there's the village stuff. We'll go up there sometime, what? Have ourselves a few shells, what?"

And he winked his Irish wink.

"Seen the volcano, have you?" he asked. "It's marvellous, it really is."

Near sundown one day, he arranged a ride across the island for me with a Tanna girl named Pauline who came from a village near the volcano. The volcano was called *Yasur* in her language (there were twenty-nine different languages spoken on this small island), and this meant "God." The winding bumpy road soon came to a strange, poisoned-looking area of smooth bald hills—it was downwind from the crater, where the prevailing wind flung the hot, sulphurous ashes from the volcano, killing every living thing. In the distance I could hear the volcano grumbling and eructing, the amplified belches like those of a fat man after an enormous meal; and these sounds of digestion were accompanied by distant crepitating rumbles like those of loosened bowels. The expression "bowels of the earth" just about summed it up.

We parked in a lava field upwind of the slope and walked to the rim of the crater. Here the farting and belching of the thing was explosive— more like cannon fire. It was a far cry from the steaming cone of Savo Island, where grinning villagers harmlessly boiled megapode eggs.

The crater of Yasur the godly volcano was almost a mile wide and half a mile deep, and at times it was like a vision of hell. It was full of smoke and fumes, and at its deepest point, like two malevolent eyes, were a pair of fiery holes, each of them gurgling wickedly and tossing out red gobs of molten lava.

Under me, against the steep side of the crater, about halfway down near a ledge, there was another hole that was hard to see. But roughly every five minutes it gave forth a thunderous explosion that echoed inside the crater's hole and this mighty crack cast forth a shower of lava, all red and orange, that twisted and lighted the entire crater, and then flopped and blackened as it cooled. This eruption added to the plume of ash that continuously rose from the volcano and wandered off, enlarging the blighted area of the island.

Later I heard that there is a theory that Jon Frum lives deep in the maw of the volcano with an army of 5,000 men.

There were no other islanders here. I mentioned this to Pauline.

"The local people don't come here," Pauline said. She knew—she had grown up only three miles away in one of these benighted, African-looking villages. "They are afraid. They say that when you die you come here and you remain inside."

So the volcano was God, Heaven, and Hell, all at once; like Tuma Island in the Trobriands—the bourne from which no traveler returned.

"Did the people in your village talk about how this volcano started?"

"Yes. They say that two ladies, Sapai and Munga, were making laplaps one day"—the New Guinea Pidgin word for a sarong was the local Pidgin word for vegetables wrapped in palm leaves—"and then an old lady appeared and talked to them. She said she was very cold. Could she sit by their fire, she asked. Sapai and Munga pitied her, so they said yes. The old lady sat near the fire. After a little while she began to make noises. She was growing. She was bigger and bigger. She covered the two ladies and turned into the volcano."

"What was the old lady's name?"

"We do not know," Pauline said.

Meanwhile, the volcano was filled with cannon booms and such diabolical fire and noise, and the frightening thing prompted Pauline (perhaps without her realizing it) to ask me whether I knew anything about the situation in the Persian Gulf—did I think a war was going to start?

It was a difficult coast for paddling; the wind was strong, usually blowing twenty-five knots and roughing up the sea. Tanna was just a rock in the middle of the western Pacific. And there were not many places to launch the boat from—Breffny's was one of the good sheltered coves. But I had brought my boat, so I was determined to use it.

One of the advantages of paddling was that I could listen to music as the shoreline unfolded—and the lava sections of this shoreline were full of blowholes: An incoming wave washed under the lava shelf and burst through the hole, making a twenty-foot spout of water. Another advantage was that, in my boat, I did not have to swat flies. Tanna was as flyblown as the Australian Woop Woop and the Solomons had been. Flies were the curse of villages. Insect repellent did not have a noticeable effect on them. It was a relief to be in a kayak, away from these tiny biting flies.

I was dismayed when no fishing canoes were out—when I saw them upturned on the cliffs of black porous stone.

Encouraged by the sight of some boys paddling small canoes and dawdling in a little bay I asked them how far out they went. They said they didn't go out far at all.

"Who made these canoes?"

"My father made them," one boy said, speaking English clearly. "He goes out far."

"How far?"

"Sometimes he goes outside"—and he pointed.

He meant outside the reef, in the open sea, the water that has a different name.

Usually I thrashed into the headwind, knowing that if I got tired or if something went wrong, I would have this same wind to bring me back. Often I got to where I wanted only to find that, because of the heavy dumping surf, it was impossible for me to land my boat. On two successive days I tried to get to a place called Imlao, but on reaching the beach had to turn back, not daring to risk a surf landing. The waves were high dumpers, and if I miscalculated, my boat would be smashed. Since the only intention I had in landing was to eat and then shove off again, I ate in my boat, and then headed back. Captain Cook landed here on his first Pacific voyage. The Tanna people defied him: "One fellow showed us his backside in such a manner that it was not necessary to have an interpreter to explain his meaning."

One day I saw a man in an outrigger canoe riding the swell about a mile offshore. He was not paddling—he was simply letting the wind take him, and fishing with a handline.

I headed towards him and when he looked up I waved. Nearer, I said hello, and asked him whether he wanted a drink of water.

"Me have water," he said. He showed me the corked bottle lying in his dugout. But when I took a drink of mine, I offered him some and he had a swig.

"Where are you from?"

"Me stap long Tanna." Then he hesitated. "My home Futuna."

Futuna is an island east of Tanna, a small rock with not more than 300 people on its eight square miles of surface. And yet it is a distinguished place, for this tiny spot in the middle of Melanesia is inhabited, like the atoll of Ontong Java in the Solomons, by Polynesian-speaking people. In his book about Pacific migrations, *Islands of the South,* Austin Coates explains that wandering Austronesians avoided large, mountainous islands, preferring smaller and more isolated atolls.

"Such was the people's prestige that these dots on the ocean map became more important than the substantial islands, including New Guinea, which they embraced like a chain of distant sentinels. In the framework of an ocean civilization, these dots were the centers, mountainous islands the periphery."

They had settled on small wild islands that had been considered uninhabitable (because of course the islands had been known to Melanesians). And they regularly conducted family business and contracted marriages between islands a thousand miles away—from Futuna to Ocean Island, from Ontong Java to the Gilberts. There was a good reason for their being fearless on these lone rocks and atolls. They were brilliant navigators, they were great seamen and skillful canoe-builders.

"Never before or since was there an age when people were so at ease in the ocean."

Wishing to talk to this Futunese fisherman I rafted up, tying a line to his outrigger. He did not mind—my rafting up did not hinder his fishing; and what else was there to do, a mile or so from shore on this windy day, except drift and talk?

His name was Lishi. He had some Melanesian features but not so strong as those of the Tanna people. I might have assumed that he was part Polynesian if I had had time to consider the matter, but really the physical aspect was minor compared to the language.

I said, "Do you say *moana* for this?" And I slapped the ocean with my paddle.

"This *tai*," he said. He pointed out to sea, beyond the reef. "That is *moana.*"

I said, "What is this?"—indicating my kayak.

"Wakha," he said. A version of the Aboriginal word I had heard in Australia, and in the Trobriands and elsewhere.

I said, "You're Polynesian?"

"Yes," he said.

"Where do your people in Futuna come from?"

"From Samoa, I think. Maybe from Tonga."

Quite a different reply from the Tanna people saying, *We come from two magic sticks,* or the Solomon Islanders claiming ancestry from sharks or snakes.

"Is Futuna a nice place?"

"Is small. Few people."

"What is good in Futuna?"

"Good *kaikai.* Good fish. Good wind."

I reached into my waterproof bag and took out my notebook and pen, and while we were blown along, side by side, over the curving blue belly of the swells, and sometimes riding the crest of the breaking waves, I asked him certain words and he told me the Futunese equivalent. Many of them were identical to, or cognate with, the languages spoken in Hawaii and Tahiti.

Often, Oceania seemed not one place but many—a universe of distant islands. But sometimes—like today, with Mr. Lishi translating these words for me—it seemed like a small area, with a common language.

Apart from the deep sea being *moana,* and the lagoon being *tai,* big was *nui,* water was *vai,* and hand was *rima,* the same as the word for five. Fish was *ika,* house was *fare.* A Samoan, a Maori, even an Easter Islander from 7,000 miles across the open ocean would have been able to converse with Mr. Lishi, here in western Melanesia. Thank you was *fafatai*—the same word in Samoan. I wrote down others, and they too sounded familiar: Sun was *ra,* moon was *mrama,* and the numbers one to five were *dasi, rua, toru, fa, rima.* Dugout was *porogu,* probably from pirogue, and hello was *rokomai.* Heaven was *Rangi,* exactly as in Tahiti (*lani* in Hawaiian), and woman was *finay,* cognate with the Tahitian *vahine.*

I made notes, marvelling at the linguistic similarities, and we drifted. Meanwhile, Mr. Lishi caught some fish, but most of them were tiddlers, fewer than six inches long.

He wore a crushed straw hat and tattered shorts. He was wrinkled. His outrigger canoe did not look at all seaworthy. He was a small Futunese fisherman and we seemed to be in the oceanic version of outer space—beyond time—drifting on this dazzling blue day in the chop some miles off Tanna, the oddest outside-time island in Vanuatu.

That was the setting. That was the mood. I mention this because of what Mr. Lishi said next.

"Yu savvy war long Iraq, long Gulf?" he asked.

I was startled by the question, but I recovered and said, "No war yet."

But I was wrong. After I got to shore I turned on my radio and heard the Pidgin broadcast—the Bislama news on Vanuatu Radio. This was about noon on the seventeenth of January, Tanna time, which was early morning in Iraq. The first attack had come in the early hours of the morning, at roughly the time Mr. Lishi, the Futunese fisherman in his outrigger canoe, had asked me the question. It was not telepathy on his part: The matter was on everyone's mind.

"Fait blong Persian Gulf we i brokaot finis," the broadcast began, the announcer jabbering very fast. *"Mo plante pipol oli stap ting se bae hemi savvy lid i go long wan wor bekegen sapos ol bigfela kaontri—"*

The superpowers.

"—oli no stopem quik taem, hemi holem, wan bigfela kwesten mak i stap se bae who nao i winim fait ia—"

The fear was that it would turn into a world war, involving the superpowers.

I then tuned my shortwave to Radio Australia, which had a strong signal in the daytime, and I heard that the United States had attacked first by flying 400 missions against sixty targets in Iraq. The newscast spoke of the mood of euphoria surrounding the aerial attack, and even I who had hoped there would be a diplomatic solution felt that same unholy energy, which is the emotion in Louis MacNeice's poem "Brother Fire," in which he describes the blitz in London:

> *O delicate walker, babbler, dialectician Fire,*
> *O enemy and image of ourselves,*
> *Did we not on those mornings after the All Clear,*
> *When you were looting shops in elemental joy*
> *And singing as you swarmed up city block and spire,*
> *Echo your thoughts in ours? 'Destroy! Destroy!'*

Five men on the beach saw me listening to the radio. They had heard their own Bislama broadcast. They knew what was happening.

One said, *"Plante pipol heli kilim ded?"*

I said there were no casualty figures yet. There was a major difference between *kilim,* which meant hit, and *kilim ded,* which meant killed.

They were very concerned and they knew a great deal about the lead-up to the fighting—the invasion of Kuwait, the aggression of Saddam Hussein (and they knew his name), and the dangers of Israeli intervention. It impressed me that ragged fishermen in such a remote island on the Pacific should know so much or care so deeply; but of course a war had come this way before, and it had involved everyone, and had caused a convulsion in their lives.

"Rambo hemi faet nao—Rambo stap long, long Gulf," another man said, somewhat lessening my respect for the accuracy of their views.

"Where did you hear that?"

The fellow swore that Radio Vanuatu had disclosed the fact that Rambo had been hurried to the Persian Gulf, to help win the war.

"I strongpela tumas," another said.

"How true."

I saw Breffny McGeough and told him about the aerial bombardment. It was the first he had heard of it. His reaction was characteristic.

"A drop of kava would help."

We went on his motorcycle to a *nagamiel,* a village clearing that was also known as a *yimwayim,* about five miles in the bush. The clearing was surrounded by elephantine banyan trees.

"And this is me friend, the chief," Breffny said, greeting a toothless grubby old man squatting on the damp ground with four other men. Three men stood nearby, chewing.

The chief and the others greeted him as a friend, while Breffny said that I was in for a treat—the real McCoy—some shells of Tanna kava, probably the best in the Pacific. It was certainly the best Breffny himself had tasted, and he had sailed all over Oceania. Fijian kava and Tongan kava was piss compared to this, he confided.

I had brought my little radio to keep up with the news of Brother Fire. I listened as I watched the kava being prepared. It was being done from scratch.

—missile installations were attacked and destroyed. B52 bombers flew numerous missions and damaged Iraqi airfields—

One man was cutting the kava plant, *Piper methysticum,* a dusty little cluster of dry twigs and spindly roots. As he hacked with a bush knife, making a pile of roots, another man scraped and peeled each root, while a third man worked on the half-peeled root with a coconut shell, rubbing off some—by no means all—of the red dust.

The coconut-rubber handed the piece of root to the men who were standing. They opened their mouths. They had black teeth and gummy, coated tongues. They stuffed the woody kava roots into their mouths and with a crunch like chicken bones, they began to chew them.

These chewing men—one in a straw pie-plate hat, another wearing a T-shirt that said *Alaska–The Last Frontier,* the third in a sensationally filthy sarong—walked in circles, chewing seriously, their cheeks bulging.

I heard *Many eyewitness reports of bombs falling on the Presidential Palace in Baghdad.*

At that moment, one of the men leaned over and spat a big wet wad of masticated wood, the size of a scoop of ice cream, onto a green leaf that had been spread on the ground, apparently for this purpose.

—*Bombs also fell on Baghdad Airport, destroying runways*—

Splat went another blob of kava and spittle, as the man in the T-shirt bent from the waist like a bobbing duck and released it onto the leaf.

Splat—more mush hit the leaf: It was like a kid spitting up baby food he hated. That was the consistency of the stuff—a cowpat of Gerber's baby food.

"Bloody marvellous stuff," Breffny was saying, as he sucked on a stinking cigarette. "What's the news, Paul?"

I had the radio to my ear. I said, "Bombing."

Splat. Another disgusting cud hit the leaf. It was pale and juicy, and it turned my stomach just to look at it.

Now, with a leaf of three blobs of masticated kava root, the chief went to work. With his dusty fingers he picked up the blobs and placed them onto a small, finely woven square of matting. This he held over a chipped enamel bowl, and while a man poured a few cups of water onto it the chief twisted the mesh, twisted the whole mixture—chewed and pulped kava root, saliva, water, dirt—and forced a trickle of water into the bowl.

"Tanna kava," Breffny said, smiling in anticipation.

The chief filled half a coconut shell for him, and the jaunty Irishman lifted it, and drank, and sighed with pleasure.

He wiped his mouth and said, "In Fiji they pound the roots and stew it. But this—it's all in the chewing, you see."

I was still listening to the bombing, and the chewers were still masticating ostentatiously, and splatting it onto the leaf.

"Now you're sure you won't have a shell?"

He was whispering. It was one of the rules of Tanna kava ritual that none of the drinkers was to speak loudly.

It was a feeling like novocaine, he said. And he claimed that his whole body was going numb, as we headed back to the shore, in twilight, in an explosive sunset that was appropriate to the first day of war.

* * *

The next day I went out paddling again. I brought my radio and listened with my earphones. Israel was hit by eight missiles. Two people were taken to the hospital, with heart failure. Some others were treated for shock. An Israeli woman's kitchen was destroyed. There was general outrage. You could hear it in their complaining voices. Meanwhile, in Iraq and at the borders of Kuwait, the first of 150,000 people began to die: the nameless, faceless enemy.

Paddling in that day, I saw a couple on shore. They stepped into the surf and grabbed my bowline and helped me beach my boat.

They were from New Zealand, they said. Odd place Tanna, they said, wasn't it? I agreed. We talked about the *kastom* people, the volcano, the Jon Frum cargo cult, the rumors of cannibals, the unbridled attentions of missionaries. But the Solomon Islands, I said, were equally interesting.

"You travel all over," the woman said. "Do you write about your travels?"

I said, Yes, I did. Articles. Books. Whatever.

"You must write Paul Theroux–type travel books," she said.

I said, Exactly, and told her why.

Eventually I went back to the island of Efate, another happy isle. I paddled out to Pele Island and Nguna. These were protected waters on the lee side of the island, nothing like the gales of Tanna. Off Nguna I could see Epi Island, and the islands in the Shepherd Group. I fantasized about staying and paddling and camping on these happy islands, watching the men make copra and the women doing laundry in streams.

I paddled to an island called Kukula, only a mile or so at the edge of the lagoon. It was idyllic, although there was no fresh water there. And when I landed I stepped into the water and saw a whitish snake, with black bands, floating near the sandy bottom. I poked him with my paddle and the thing recoiled and bit my paddle blade, before it took off.

Some of the smaller islands were uninhabited, but the rest were populous. The people I met were cheerful and friendly. There was no theft, nor any stories of it. The villages were rather empty. The weather was perfect. Business was terrible, people said, but no one seemed seriously to mind.

Most days I had enough of the news. I left my radio onshore. I listened to my Walkman. But Chuck Berry was too cheerful for me. For the hundredth time, among the pretty islands, I paddled slowly and listened to a Puccini aria of hope, how one fine day a white ship would appear on the sea and then sail smartly into harbor, and all would be well—

Un bel di, vedremo
Levarsi un fil di fumo sull'estremo

Confin del mare.
E poi la nave appare.
Poi la nave bianca
Entra nel porto . . .

I ate the local delicacy, coconut crab. At night, when the airwaves were louder, I monitored the news. I shared what I knew with the islanders, who always mentioned Rambo. Some people said that after the war was over the American troops would head for Tanna and liberate all the people, in the name of Jon Frum.

When I heard that, I was reminded of Tanna—how I had known almost nothing about it before I arrived, and what an odd and pleasant island it had been. I hoped to find another, but that night I had a dream, a rather mournful one, of one of my children writing a story that began: *Long after he died—for weeks, for months—we kept receiving postcards from Dad, because he had traveled so far and to such small and insignificant places.*

Chapter 12
FIJI: THE DIVIDED ISLAND OF VITI LEVU

At the very frontier of The Black Islands lies Fiji, the edge of Melanesia—so close that some of its tinier islands, Rotuma and the Lau Group, for example, overlap Polynesia. In these transitional straddling dots of land, the people are regarded as Polynesian. There is a strong Tongan influence in the Lau culture. They make and sail canoes in the Lau Group. They wear crunchy mats around their waists, Tongan-style. They paddle. They fish. They dance. They recall their great sea ventures. In a village on the Lau island of Lakeba they hold an annual ceremony in which sharks are summoned—a "shark caller" up to his or her neck in the lagoon is circled by a school of sharks, attracted by the person's chanting.

On the Lau islands, you see Mormons. In Oceania, where Mormons regard Micronesians as the sons of Cain, and Melanesians as the dark, scruffy descendants of Ham, the surest sign that you are on a Polynesian island is the sight of Mormons.

The American Mormons who evangelize on these islands can seem rather fearsome and intrusive, like the worst sort of door-to-door insurance salesmen—black tie, white shirt, dark trousers, breast-pocket nameplate *(Elder Udall)*, all the answers, clutching copies of the book that the Angel Moroni gave in the form of golden tablets to Joseph Smith in 1827. Smith put "peepstones" on his eyes and a blanket over his head and translated the tablets, dictating the text to Emma, the first of his fifty wives. ("When I see a pretty woman I have to pray," Smith once said.) These prophetic books in the *Book of Mormon* not only foretold—if belatedly—that Columbus would discover America but also described how American Indians, descendants of the Lost Tribes of Israel, had got it into their heads to sail across the Pacific and settle these islands. It was not a question of Polynesians becoming Mormons. They have, according to the *Book of Mormon*, been Mormons all along. They simply needed to be reminded of the fact.

Yet the Lau Group is one of the pretty little star clusters in the universe of Oceania. Melanesian Fiji is another story. Fiji is like the world you thought you left behind—full of political perversity, racial fear, economic woes, and Australian tourists looking for inexpensive salad bowls (though why anyone would think a race of Queequegs, proud of their cannibal past, might excel at making salad bowls is not only a cultural mystery, but proof that tourists will believe almost anything as long as they are comfortable). Fully half the population is ethnic Indian—Muslims, Parsees, Buddhists—wearing turbans and skullcaps and Hindus with big staring red dots on their foreheads. They run shops that sell overpriced "duty-free" merchandise and native curios, spears, napkin rings, the salad bowls, and other nameless-looking bits of hacked wood.

"What is this wooden spindle?" I asked an Indian shopkeeper.

"Gannibal imblement, sah."

"Did you say 'cannibal'?"

"And gannibal glub," he went on, showing me a shiny skull-crushing bat of the sort that had once been used to bash out an enemy's brains (and then you ate them, so that you would be as intelligent as he was).

He showed me the section on cannibal artifacts from the catalogue of the Suva Museum. Yes, they somewhat resembled this tourist stuff. And they proved the truth of the travelers' tales about cannibal Fiji—colorful accounts such as that of the swashbuckling Irishman Peter Dillon, who in the 1820s made a narrow escape from a Fijian cannibal feast but not before witnessing two of his fellow crew members being baked in ovens and gobbled up. There is a lurid summary of Fijian cannibal practices in the usually authoritative Eleventh Edition (1911) of the Encyclopædia Britannica: "The Fijians were formerly notorious for cannibalism, which may have had its origin in religion, but long before the first contact with Europeans had degenerated into gluttony. The Fijian's chief table luxury was human flesh, euphemistically called by him 'long pig,' and to satisfy his appetite he would sacrifice even friends and relatives. The Fijians combined with this a savage and merciless nature. Human sacrifices were of daily occurrence."

You want to say *Really?* The same entry mentions how many Fijians are a racial blend of Polynesian and Melanesian, with "the quick intellect of the fairer, and the savagery and suspicion of the dark." On such ludicrous assumptions, the Pacific was evaluated and plundered by the missionary, the trader, and the planter—an unholy trinity who were, it must be said, often the same person, neatly illustrating one of the central mysteries of the religion they crammed down these cannibals' throats.

When I inquired about cannibalism, Fijians never denied the anthropophagy of their ancestors—on the contrary, they talked with lip-smacking enthusiasm, reminding me of Australians revelling in stories of how their distant relatives had been convicts.

"Fahmerly this island was all ferocious gannibals, sah," the Indian said, glancing furtively behind him. "Feezee pipple, sah."

But the reason he looked so nervous and lowered his voice was because the Fiji people—most of them, and the government, which was only one man, Lieutenant Colonel Sitiveni Rabuka, known to all as "Steve"—wanted to send them back where their grandparents, and in some cases, great-grandparents, had come from, the Indian subcontinent. (The first Indians arrived in Fiji as indentured laborers to work in the cane fields over a century ago.) In another age, they might have wanted to eat the Indians. Now they wanted to return them—something like disgusted diners sending unappetizing food back to the kitchen.

But it was a mistake to think of the Fijians as angry.

"Just because we're not as intelligent as Indians," Steve said, in a widely quoted observation, "doesn't mean that Indians can take advantage of us."

"We have the land—you have the brains," he said on another occasion, addressing Indians directly. "Why should you be richer just because you've got a bit more brains?"

He was no more subtle when he came to write about the affair in his book, *No Other Way*. In it he described the Indians as "an immigrant race" who "wanted complete control of the government." A coup d'état was the only solution "for the survival of the Fijian race. As simple as that."

But wasn't the coup racist? he was asked on a New Zealand news program. He cheerfully admitted that this was so. He said, "It is racist in the sense that it was in favor of one race."

The Indians were equal in numbers to the Fijians, who had only recently begun to worry about their being overwhelmed. And even now the Fijians' spirits were not dampened. They laughed and numbed themselves with kava (they called it *yanggona* here) six days a week and spent the seventh in Methodist chapels—every village had one—singing deeply lugubrious hymns and generally condemning the behavior of the heathenish Muslims, Hindus, Buddhists, and Zoroastrians who had, they said, hijacked their country by outbreeding them and voting Melanesians out of office.

Then God spoke to the Fijian, who assembled his God-fearing commandos and led them masked into the Fiji Parliament, and marched the newly elected prime minister and most of his cabinet out at gunpoint.

After this 1987 military coup in which Colonel Rabuka took power (he had been alarmed by an election which had produced—in his view—the nightmarish prospect of a multiracial government), he immediately decreed that Sunday was a holy day which had to be observed by everyone—no commerce, no travel, no buses, no cane cutting, no games, nothing but solemnity and Methodist hymns.

Later he played himself in a starring role in a Fiji government video about the whole business. An early scene went like this:

INT—RABUKA HOUSE—MORNING:
A room in the Fijian household of *"Steve" Rabuka.*
Mrs. Rabuka and little *"Skip" Rabuka* are seated at the breakfast table, eating a traditional Fijian breakfast of tea and porridge.
Enter Steve Rabuka in military uniform.

Skip Rabuka: Where are you going, Daddy?
Steve Rabuka: I am on a mission from God.
Mrs. Rabuka: What do you mean, husband?
Steve Rabuka: God has told me to overthrow the government.

This was revenge on the worshippers of Allah and Hanuman the Monkey God and gold calves and elephantine Ganapati with his snout and his smile. And for a time this decree gave Sundays in Fijian villages and towns the atmosphere of desertion you associate with cholera epidemics or nuclear holocausts or Welsh Sundays.

"Fiji is a Christian country," Rabuka said repeatedly, and he spoke of Fiji's solemn traditions and strict morality—quite funny, really, when you thought how he had come to power by gun-toting commandos, declaring martial law, and tossing out an elected government.

Ethnic Fijians had gotten even with the Indians by shouting hymns at them—overwhelmingly fat Fijian women in Mother Hubbards, and enormous, skirt-wearing, bushy-haired Fijian men with Bibles the size of paving stones stood there and bellowed *Come to Jesus* in A-flat at the top of their lungs. This of course terrified the Indians.

I rented a car and put my kayak and camping equipment inside, so that I could drive around the island of Viti Levu ("Big Fiji"), looking for the best place to paddle.

"Do you sell maps?" I asked the Fijian at the car rental agency in Nandi. I had nautical charts of Fiji but no road maps.

"Why you are needing a map?"

"So I'll take the right road."

"You don't need a map. There is only one road."

This was not strictly true, and anyway the idea that I might have needed it for other reasons had not occurred to him.

"You American?" he asked. And then he marvelled in a gloating way about the violence in the Gulf War, now in its second week looking more and more like a punitive mission of the most destructive kind. In the Solomons and Vanuatu the fear was that the war would come to their islands. The Fijians would have ridiculed that notion. But they had no political views. Theirs was a simpleminded fascination in the spectacle of it all—the pyrotechnics, planes taking off, bombs dropping, sirens wailing, bloody people trundled in stretchers through smoke and flames. News reports were like Rambo videos, and they seemed to give all Fijians pleasure.

I had a slight problem. I had picked up a fungal infection in Vanuatu—I blamed it on unwashed sheets. It could hardly have been anything else. I was nearly always a model of rectitude. Oceania was full of AIDS posters, and an AIDS poster in Pidgin was an explicit and frightening warning.

"Do you have the name of a doctor?" I asked at my hotel, the Regent in Nandi.

"What's the problem?" the desk clerk asked—impertinently, I felt.

"Fungal infection," I said. "Nothing serious. It's on my foot."

This was a lie, of course. But I did not have it in me to say *It's on my willy* to a Fijian woman who was a Methodist.

"Athlete's foot. You can get some powder for that at the chemist shop."

The next day was Sunday. *Nothing is more pacific than a Pacific Sunday,* I wrote in my notebook later. I suspected from the first that it was a deliberate Fijian ploy to make the non-Christians feel like heathens and aliens. The attitude was one of *Shut up and let us pray* as the uncompromising Fijians beat the non-Fijians over the head with the Bible.

Nandi was full of doctors' offices, but none were open—and by the way, every one of them had an Indian name on the door.

The very settled, messy, and domesticated look of Viti Levu was an effect of the fields of sugarcane, the floppiest and most ragged crop imaginable, and one which becomes floppier as it matures. And when it is harvesttime the cane is shaggy and peeling, yielding a very messy harvest. All over coastal Fiji the trees have been cut down to make room for the crop, and so the slopes were either bare or else they supported ill-assorted pines and scrubby bushes. The roads were also in a state of decay, some of them falling apart. I had been used to the underdevelopment and jungle of western Melanesia. But this was a heavily populated and prosperous place that was urgent to attract tourists. All together it was a landscape under stress, and many of the hills looked denuded, their muscles showing just beneath the grass.

On Queen's Road, the main street of Nandi, were rows of Indian shops, with signs saying PRICES SLASHED and STOCK CLOSE-OUT and SALE. This was not cynical salesmen's hyperbole. The Indian merchants really wanted to sell their inventory and emigrate—to Canada, to Australia, to New Zealand, to wherever they could buy land and start again. There was a hint of panic in most Indian signs, and though some shopkeepers professed to be optimistic, no one sounded more desperate than an Indian protesting that things were rosy.

The fact was that under the newly rewritten Fiji constitution—proposed, but so far unratified—ethnic Fijians would not only be guaranteed control of the government forever, but also all the old leases and land deals would be renegotiated, so that no land would be in non-Fijian hands. Even the leases were being rejiggered—an Indian with a 100-year lease would end up with a twenty-year lease and a Fijian partner. It made no difference that the Indian had Fijian citizenship.

This seemed laughable but the Fijians were in deadly earnest.

"We see what has happened to our Maori and Hawaiian brothers elsewhere in the Pacific," ran a letter in the *Fiji Times* while I was there. "Second-class citizens in their own islands."

"I understand the Indians are experiencing difficulties," I said to Vishnu Prasad, a Nandi storekeeper airing his guard dog.

Vishnu went silent, and when I pressed him he giggled in terror.

"I am knowing nothing about politics. Hee! Hee!"

At the time of the coup in 1987, indigenous Fijians rioted in the streets of Nandi and Suva, attacking Indian shops and looting them. A number of shops were burned. After a caretaker government was installed, Steve lost patience again and staged a second coup four months later.

An Indian *yanggona* seller said to me, "This was a happy and good place before the coup, but they spoiled it."

"But the money has been devalued and business is terrible and the future looks bleak, so the Fijians are worried, aren't they?"

"No. They are looking backward. This is a return to the chiefly system."

"But who wants the chiefly system?"

"The chiefs," he said.

That dead Sunday I drove east from Nandi to Singatoka, a largely Indian town, where I was told a doctor's office might be open. This was not the case, but when I asked for a vegetarian restaurant—one of the great attractions of any Hindu town—I was directed to "Go Kool Hot

Snax," where I met Subhash, who stuffed a curry puff into his mouth and told me he disliked Fijians.

He had just come from church. Yes, on Sunday. He was an Indian Christian.

"I go to Church of Christ," he said.

He wasn't married, he said, so I asked him whether he would want to marry a Christian or a Hindu.

"When I get married it will be to an Indian or a European—never to a Fijian," he said.

"Why not?"

"Because they have no morals," he said, practically exploding. And then he spoke with the singleminded conviction you hear in the monologues of bigots. "Even the schoolgirls behave like prostitutes, taking men to the beach and sometimes robbing them. Ha! A Fijian wife would commit adultery with other men while you are away. They go with anyone. They don't care. Even though they are Christians they still behave like heathens. I would never marry one. Never!"

The Indians were hardly conservative-looking, though. The girls wore dresses and cut their hair, they had loud liberated-sounding laughter, and they stared at me. Staring at men was something that women in India never did. I was told that marriages between Muslims and Hindus were common, though there were few Fijian–Indian marriages. This was nothing new. A turn-of-the-century English writer observed, "The Fijians show no disposition to intermarry with the Indian coolies."

Driving onward from Singatoka, I picked up a hitchhiker named Akiwila. He was Fijian, a Methodist. Like Subhash, he too had just come from church. He carried his Bible. The Sunday roadsides were crowded with these Bible-carrying men, and I imagined they seemed rather menacing to an unbeliever.

He was black, his head surmounted by a bush of thick kinky hair. He had a snub nose and a heavy jaw—the classic virile mask that was a Melanesian face. He was like many male Fijians I met, a big breezy specimen, all smiles, with a mustache that made him look older, and more serious and somewhat formidable. Yet he was friendly—and respectful rather than shy. He wore the gabardine skirt Fijians call a *sulu,* a white shirt and tie—you were not considered well dressed in Fiji unless you wore that garbardine skirt and a necktie.

Akiwila was on his way to his brother's house for a meal, before the next church service. No, he said, they were not allowed to cook on Sundays, but the food had been prepared yesterday. I tried, and failed, to imagine a Deity that would be deeply offended by someone's cooking. But of course Methodism in the Pacific was stuck pretty much in the nineteenth century, when fat furious hypocrites from England and America laid down the law—no cooking, no dancing, no games, and two church services on Sunday.

After a little while I said, "Akiwila, what is your opinion of the military coup?"

"It was very good," he said, smoothing the leather cover of his Bible.

"But it was against the Indians, isn't that right?"

"Yes." And he smiled. "You see, they are now almost half the population."

"You have to keep the Indians in their place, is that what you mean?"

"Yes. Very much so."

He went on smiling and nodding his head and tugging his *sulu* modestly over his knees.

After I dropped him, I drove on. I gave a ride to Joe and Helen, two homeward-bound Fijians who worked at a local hotel. They were so pleasant, I was seized with uncharacteristic reticence and did not ask them how much they earned. Of Americans, New Zealanders, and Australians, I asked, who were the most obnoxious guests? "They are all nice," Joe said, mildly, and when they got out Helen offered me a dollar for the ride. A mile farther on, I was flagged down by some boys who were also headed home after a Sunday service. They were teenagers—Moses, Yakobi, and Kamwela (Fijian for Samuel). They agreed that everything ought to be closed on Sunday, especially Indian shops.

"Sunday is for church," Moses said.

This sanctimonious insistence on desecularizing Sundays was expressed with the greatest friendliness. The Fijians were calmly assertive, while the Indians either falsely claimed to be unworried or frankly expressed their hysteria. Both sides seemed to be equally bigoted, and each dismally ignorant of the other's culture.

The most sustained vilification of Indians in Fiji was that of James Michener in *Return to Paradise*. It is a rehash of his *Tales of the South Pacific,* and it is superficial and dated and rather poorly written. But his attack on Indians (this was in 1951) has a definite horror interest:

"It is almost impossible to like the Indians of Fiji. They are suspicious, vengeful, whining, unassimilated, provocative aliens in a land where they have lived for more than seventy years. They hate everything: black natives, white Englishmen, brown Polynesians and friendly Americans. They will not marry with Fijians, whom they despise. They avoid English ways, which they abhor. They cannot be depended upon to support necessary government policies. Above all, they are surly and unpleasant. It is possible for a traveler to spend a week in Fiji without ever seeing an Indian smile."

Now set his overwhelming dislike of Indians beside his jolly acceptance of Fijians: "It is doubtful if anyone but an Indian can dislike Fijians. They are immense Negroes modified by Polynesian blood. They wear their hair frizzed straight out from the head . . . They are one of the happiest peoples on earth and laugh constantly."

These judgements are much too silly to discuss. Michener is just another in the long parade of explorers and travelers and tourists who felt a need to invent the Pacific and to make it a paradise. How misleading it all is. The very name of the Pacific is a misnomer. But I should say that the very fact that so much written about the Pacific is inaccurate—indeed, most of it is utter crap—intensifies the pleasure of traveling there and gives it so much unexpectedness.

My visit to the doctor became urgent—I had run out of fungal cream—and so on Monday I hurried back to Singatoka where I chose a doctor at random—Dr. S. K. Naidoo, near the market. It was a hot, dusty office, with a calendar showing Hanuman the Monkey God, and advertising an Indian electrical goods shop in Suva.

The receptionist was Fijian. She broke off an animated conversation with a girl who was sitting next to her and asked me why I wanted to see the doctor.

"Infection," I said. "Sore foot."

She leaned over and looked at my feet.

"Which one?"

"Right one," I said, wagging it.

I took a seat and picked up an old tattered Australian *Cosmopolitan* magazine, and became engrossed in a quiz entitled *How Good Is Your Sex Life?* The preface said, *Work your way through the four-part questionnaire and you'll learn a great deal about yourself,* but it seemed to me that the further I read the more I learned about the sort of people who made up these titillating quizzes. *Do you find sex boring?* was a question in Part One, and in Part Two, "Rating Your Partner's Sexual Skills," I had to evaluate my partner's "ability to see the funny side and laugh about it" on a scale of one to five, and I thought, *Funny side of what?* Part Three asked me whether I had "anxiety about the size and shape of a particular part of my body," and though it didn't specify I thought only of my nose. Part Four was blunt: *Do you ever go to sex orgies?* and *Do you take part in sex photo sessions?* and *Do you make love with other people watching?*

Ha! I could just imagine what these puritanical Fijians would make of this, and how they would whisper about the sexual savagery of Australians in much the same way as Australians whispered about Fijian cannibalism.

"The doctor will see you now."

I entered the next room, pushed a greasy curtain aside, and found myself face to face with Dr. Naidoo, a small and rather young Hindu woman in a sari, fingering a clipboard.

"You are having a problem with your foot, Mr. Thorax?"

"A slight problem," I said, moistening my mouth. "My main problem is a fungal infection on my, um, genital area."

Dr. Naidoo did not blink.

"I caught it—or rather *got* it—in Vanuatu. Strange sheets, I think. It wasn't from sexual contact."

"Though it can be transmitted that way," the doctor said—pedantically, I thought. Hadn't I just told her how I'd got it?

"I'll have to have a look at you," she said. "Step behind the screen, please."

I did so. She joined me. With trembling fingers, I exposed my weepy member, and she crouched and squinted at it. Though she was thoroughly professional—or perhaps that was the reason—we seemed for a split second to be enacting exhibitionistic Position Forty-five ("Admiring the Lingam") from the *Kama Sutra.*

As she prescribed a cure, scribbling on a pad, I asked her where she had gone to medical school. I had asked her the question nervously, simply to fill the silence, but I must have sounded skeptical, because she seemed defensive when she replied, "In Suva. It is a highly respected medical faculty."

Ten dollars for her, two dollars for ointment. Then I bought a tape for my Walkman, the sound track from *The Big Chill,* which an obliging Indian at the music store copied from a master tape, an act of piracy that did not worry anyone in Fiji (videocassettes were similarly pirated). It was yet another Fijian bargain.

Recession, devaluation, the low sugar and copra prices, Indian fears, and tourist anxieties had all combined to make Fiji rather empty and pleasant. That was obvious as in the next few days I explored the island east of Singatoka, working my way towards Suva. Business was terrible. In the competitive atmosphere of Fiji it made traveling rather inexpensive. And Fiji was well set up for travelers. The efficient airport was at Nandi, the busy harbor—said to be the best in the Pacific—was in Suva. There was extensive development in between. What I had seen so far of Viti Levu was uninspiring—muddy beaches, messy crops, too many hotels, too many duty-free shops, ugly villages of huts that looked like prefab chicken houses—but I could not complain: The people were friendly and the place was cheap, as well as safe.

I rattled around the bad roads, looking for a campsite on a pretty beach. The beaches were undramatic—the lagoons too shallow, the reefs too surfy for launching a kayak. And there were settlements everywhere.

All the land was spoken for. This was fine in theory but it made camping on this Nandi-to-Suva stretch impossible. And anyway I did not want to camp within hailing distance of the Golden Sands Motel or the Coral Coast Christian Camp. There was either a house or a village or a hotel on every mile of the southern coast, which was both densely populated with locals and also tourist-ridden—Aussies and New Zealanders, mostly, with sunburned noses, seeming somewhat disappointed by the tameness of this part of Fiji and wearing T-shirts that said *My Job Is So Secret Even I Don't Know What I'm Doing* and *It's Not Beer, Mate, This Is Just a Fat Shirt.*

I found a launching place near the town of Nasavu and set up my kayak, intending to paddle across the five-mile channel that separated Viti Levu from a largish oyster-shaped island called Beqa (pronounced *Benga*), where there were said to be firewalkers.

No sooner had I cleared the reef than I was battered by a strong wind from the east. I found I was expending most of my energy trying to keep myself upright—the wind was hitting me broadside—and so after less than two miles I abandoned the effort, and with great difficulty (because I had been pushed some distance to the west) I paddled back to my beach.

I was sorry I had missed the firewalkers—and my kayak trip had been an experience of wind and slop. But that night I met a man who said that he had mastered the art of firewalking and that I could do it too. He would teach me how to walk on hot coals.

We were drinking South Pacific beer in the grim lounge of one of the tacky hotels on the way to Suva. The man, Norman, was American, originally from California, but he had left home to wander in the Pacific. Like me, he had been in the Peace Corps in the 1960s. We talked about that and then I had mentioned how I had been frustrated in my attempt to reach Beqa to see the firewalkers. Forget it, he had said—firewalking is simple.

"What is it, then, mind over matter?"

"No, no, no"—and in his impatience Norman started to get cross. "It's simple physics. You just walk across the hot coals. They're very bad conductors of heat. You don't need thick foot soles or anything like that. You just walk."

"And get charbroiled."

"Bull," Norman said. "You can stand the heat for up to five seconds. Say you're in a twelve-foot firepit. You just walk down it—you don't even have to go fast. You could do it—I guarantee you wouldn't get burned."

"Have you ever done it?"

"Yes. Lots of times."

"Hot coals?"

"Hot coals!" Norman said. "Of course hot coals."

"Done it lately?"

"I did it in"—and he mentioned the name of a village that I could not quite catch. "The guys there almost shat when they saw me."

"And you didn't get burned?"

Norman stared at me, as though this was the dumbest question imaginable.

"But charcoal fires are hot," I said. "You stand next to one and you get burned."

"See, that's the strange thing," Norman said. "Charcoal fires are much hotter when you're standing next to them than when you're walking across them in your bare feet."

"How did you get interested in this?"

"Read an article. 'The Physics of Firewalking'—something like that." He put his face close to mine. "Anyone can do it," he said, and hissed, *"You can do it."*

"Walk on glowing coals in my bare feet?"

"Oh, God, what did I just tell you?"

I did not do it, but his certainty made me want to try.

"Suva reminds me of an aunt of mine who drank too much," a Canadian woman, resident in Fiji, said to me. "She was delightful. But she was prone to stumble. Her clothes were a little askew, and there was always a strap of her slip showing."

Yet seedy, friendly Suva, with wet green mountains behind it, and sloping on twisting lanes of cheek-to-cheek shops down to the sea, was probably the most habitable and busiest harbor city I saw in the South Pacific (Honolulu is in the North Pacific). A settled place, with a look of comfortable monotony, Suva was a city to live in, not to visit. And it was not for tourists—tourists seldom visited anyway, because it rained so often there, and it was more than a three-hour drive across the island from Nandi, and it had no beaches or hotels to speak of. The nearest resort, Pacific Harbor, was thirty miles away. In any case, tourists tended to avoid Suva. The Fiji experience for tourists was a week or so in a resort in the drier part of the island near Nandi, where they stayed behind the hedges, sipping drinks, playing tennis, and if they penetrated Melanesia at all it was in small talk with dusky, smiling room attendants and waiters.

"I like Fiji, because this is one of the few places in the world I've been where the blacks didn't hate me," a woman from Los Angeles told me in a Nandi resort hotel—and it seemed to me one of the silliest summaries of Fiji I had heard.

Suva was an Indian city, not only in its population but in its layout as well—it had compounds, and tenements, and back alleys, and the hectic atmosphere of a bazaar. There were many benefits of Suva, because it was a city of shopkeepers and rooted families, where everyone was local and as urbane as it was possible to be in Oceania. Tourists become lonely and uncomfortable in such places, seeing residents so preoccupied with their own lives—work, school, bills, friends. It was the sort of place where you could buy a screwdriver or a teapot or a roll of duct tape, but you'd never find clothes or a pair of shoes you liked. Suva people themselves ate in the restaurants, which were inexpensive and served good plain food. This was a wonderful change from the mock-coconut-isle Fijian hotels that made inedible attempts at nouvelle cuisine such as Carpaccio of Slack-Jawed Sea Bass (thirty-seven dollars and fifty cents) and Goujons of Owlet's Thighs Presented on a Bed of Warm Lettuce (forty-five dollars, subject to availability).

The city had grown up around the harbor of its large bay, and it had prospered through its shipping when Nandi was just a village. Even now Nandi was no more than a scruffy small town—one main street and a market. Suva's market was vast and noisy, teeming with activity, full of vegetables, fish, and fruit—and shells. "I can give you a good deal on some shells," an Indian said to me with a desperate wink. The shell and curio business was terrible, but it was interesting to see how Indians, who never drank kava, had more or less cornered the kava market. They did a brisk trade in *yanggona,* selling dusty roots or bags of high-quality powdered root to Fijian men who did little else but squat around a bowl and guzzle it. I bought four pounds of the stuff—roots and powder— because I was told that it would come in handy if I wished to ingratiate myself in a Fijian village. I give you *yanggona,* you let me camp here.

As in Nandi, nearly all the shops in Suva were Indian, displaying panicky-looking hand-painted signs saying CLOSE-OUT SALE! and PRICES SLASHED!—and though the city had the look and feel of a provincial town in India, looking closer anyone could see that it was a polyglot place. It was a mishmash of Muslims and Hindus, representing most of the larger provinces in the subcontinent. There was a Chinese community in Suva, too, and Australian franchises, and a residue of British commerce.

The sidewalks were crowded with shoppers and strollers—Indians mostly, with a scattering of Fijians. The merchandise in the stores looked rather old and shopworn, and even the duty-free goods for which Fiji was famous looked a bit old hat, overrated, old-fashioned. Why order a shipload of new models if you were about to lose your lease and Doomsday was just around the corner? There was such a variety of prices that I didn't buy anything except a map of Ovalau, an offshore island where I hoped to paddle. I went back and forth to Natovi Landing to launch my boat, but I was always facing the teeth of the wind that blew from the east. I decided to suspend paddling for now, and to pursue it when I got to the lee of this island, or to the larger island to the north, Vanua Levu.

In the steamy, humid interludes between the bouts of cold drizzle, Suva looked miserable and friendly. I liked the vegetarian restaurants—where else in carnivorous Oceania would I find others? It could be pleasantly informative to eat in the Hare Krishna vegetarian restaurant on Pratt Street, and over a healthy meal, listen to Indians complaining about the Fijians. I said nothing; I felt they needed each other.

If Fiji had been an Indian island it would have been charmless and frenzied, a hotbed of litigious warring sects, at each other's throats. As a homogeneous Fijian island it would have been something like the sleepy Solomons, hospitable but hardly functional. As a multiracial place (Indians in towns, Fijians in villages) it seemed to work. What surprised me was that the Indians wanted to live there at all, since they had no political future, were frankly hated, were forced to pay lip service to a military government, and had to make do with minimal profits.

"Situation is stagnant," an Indian named Kishore told me in a gloomy voice, and then attempted to bamboozle me into buying an overpriced wristwatch.

Perhaps the hustle-bustle of the packed streets in muddy claustrophobic Suva explained it. This was obviously an easy place for an Indian to live because it was predominantly Indian, a bunched-together place that had a life of its own. It was unlike any other town in Fiji, or the Pacific, for that matter. You could imagine someone arriving and seeing all the people and the built-to-last buildings and the busy quays at the harbor and thinking: *There's money to be made here.*

Fijians were in the minority in Suva, and the few that loitered in town shopping or eating kept to themselves. They tended to prefer porky Chinese food over Indian curries. Apart from the market stalls, there were no Fijian restaurants. In my days in Suva—waiting in vain for the weather to break: but it did nothing but drizzle and blow—I noticed that when Fijians dined out they gorged themselves on fatty meat and gravy, with taro or rice. As with other former cannibal islanders—"reformed cannibals" was the missionary phrase—they loved Spam and corned beef.

Their carnivorous appetite alone could have been the reason they were so much out of key with the Indians. It was hard to see what Fijians and Indians had in common culturally, and though there were moderates in Fiji from every racial group (a moderate coalition had won the election), the loudest people in Fiji were those who exploited the conflict and eagerly exaggerated their differences—the Indians boasting of their ancient culture and complex family structure and their skill at arithmetic, the Fijians smilingly reminding them that they were here first, on this tight little archipelago of cannibals and Christians.

Having just come from wild but coherent islands which had resisted the pressure of colonials and aliens, and where race was not an issue, I found this Fiji strife a tiresome novelty. It also tested the patience of all right-thinking New Zealanders who smugly condemned apartheid and championed human rights in South Africa, but hadn't the slightest idea of how to react to this racial conundrum. After a hundred years, the Indians in Fiji—fully half the population—had found themselves a politically oppressed and soon-to-be disenfranchised people. Yet they were prosperous!

Go home, the Fijians said to Indians who knew no other home but Suva.

Other foreigners in Fiji avoided the pickle that Indians had found themselves in by buying islands outright. After they became wealthy, the Banaban people of Ocean Island (little more than a three-mile-wide lump of coral and phosphate in the Gilbert and Ellice Group) came to Fiji and bought the island of Rambi, off eastern Vanua Levu, because mining had made their own island uninhabitable. A number of other islands in Fiji are also privately owned. On a whim, Malcolm Forbes bought Lauthala island off Taveuni, and at least six whole islands in the Northern Lau Group were bought by aliens—one by a Japanese hotel company, another by an Australian export firm, one by an American messiah named Jones who after colonizing the island with his acolytes began calling himself Baba Da Free John. A number of other islands are owned by obscure millionaires—there are 300 islands and atolls in the Fiji group. Paddling off the north shore of Viti Levu I often landed on a small pretty island only to see a sign saying PRIVATE ISLAND—NO TRESPASSING. Private islands in Fiji change hands for a million and a half and up.

Here are some Fiji island offerings—"Entire Islands Freehold/Fee Simple"—from a current (1991) real estate brochure called South Pacific Opportunities:

> TIVI ISLAND—NE of Labasa, Vanua Levu: 204 acres, white sand beaches. US $1,500,000

> ADAVACI ISLAND—104 Acres, superb beach & anchorage, perfect for small exclusive resort or private estate. U.S. $1,500,000

SAVASI ISLAND: 52-acre plantation, 2 nice residences & related, lovely residential estate or
major resort. US $2,000,000

KANACEA ISLAND—Near Vanua Balavu: Operating copra plantation, over 3000 acres, suitable
for major resort. U.S. $4,500,000

I heard there was a private island, called Mana, in the Mamanuca
Group—owned by Japanese, so I was told—where if I played my cards
right I could visit. "Playing my cards right" simply meant paying a large
sum of money to an excitable Fijian who owned a small speedboat. I
would not have dreamed of paddling across those eighteen treacherous
miles in a high wind and six-foot waves, though Mike the Fijian was not
fazed in his boat, even when we were on the point of being swamped.

Smacking his boat into the steep faces of waves, he denied that the sea
was rough.

"What's rough then?"

"Waves more than two meters!" he shouted. "This is a bit less!"

We wallowed in the troughs of waves and then banged forward with
such force that fixtures fell off the boat—the binnacle compass hit the
deck, and then its bracket, and then the lug bolts from a bench. For an
hour and a half, Mike fought the breaking waves, skirted the reefs and
shoals, and plowed into the headwind. We arrived at Mana Island soaked
to the skin.

I had expected to find a Nipponese outpost, full of little Japanese
vacationers in floppy hats snapping pictures of each other. All I saw were
sunburned Australians sleeping off their lunch on the beach and playing
with their scorched-looking children.

"You should have come this morning," Geoffrey, the general manager,
said. "We were full of Japanese. We'll get another batch tomorrow."

There was a weekly plane, he said, Tokyo to Nandi, and then the
people were shipped out to the island, where they were dispersed among
a hundred little tidy bungalows. There were three or four beaches, some
restaurants—one was Japanese—and various sports facilities. Many of
the Japanese were honeymoon couples. New Japanese brides, horrified by
what marriage entailed, regularly flung themselves out of the windows of
Honolulu hotels, but Geoffrey said his honeymooners were no problem
and anyway could not harm themselves by jumping out of the windows
of his bungalows.

"Is there a language barrier?"

"Not really. I encourage my Fijian staff to learn Japanese," he said. He sent a dozen or so of his workers every few months on a Japanese language course. And in the staff rooms at Mana as in the equipment sheds and dive shops of resorts elsewhere in Fiji, there were blackboards chalked with Japanese phrases and their English (but not Fijian) equivalent: *Konnichiwa*—hello. *Arrigato*—Thank you. And so forth.

The Mana Resort was owned by a Japanese company, Nichiman, which had negotiated a ninety-nine-year lease from the island's owners, the Fijians who lived in Aro Village at the eastern end of the island. The Fijian village was ramshackle but no worse than any other slaphappy Fijian village of flat-roofed prefab huts. One proviso in the lease was that first preference for jobs had to be given to the villagers living in Aro.

There were no gardens on Mana Island, there was no fresh water, no fishing. The Fijians in the village lived off the money they got from the Japanese tenants. They did a little fishing, but only for their own amusement.

"Do you collect rainwater from roofs?"

"No. We barge it in," Geoffrey said.

Twice a week a water barge made the forty-mile round-trip from Lautoka, the western harbor of Viti Levu, and the water was stored in big ugly tanks.

Solar power was not used. They had, instead, a generator that ran on diesel fuel. That too was barged in from Lautoka. In fact, everything was barged in—food, water, fuel, guests, equipment, and the majority of the workers, because most of the people in Aro were unwilling to work at the resort.

It was a strange artificial way of inhabiting the island—totally dependent on barges, boats, and the occasional sea plane. Nothing at all was generated locally, and even the coconut trees were seen as something of a liability.

"One of our guests was hit by a falling coconut," Geoffrey said. "He was hurt really bad. We flew him to Nandi for X rays. Thank goodness, he was all right in the end. Those coconuts can be lethal."

One day in Fiji a man I knew vaguely said, "Want to meet the governor-general?"

He meant of New Zealand, but I said yes anyway. The nights could be long and very quiet in Fiji.

A curious aspect of my traveling in Oceania was that I found most people accessible, and I met everyone I wanted to meet. In New Zealand I had wanted to speak to the new governor-general, the first woman to hold the post, Dame Cath Tizard. She also had the reputation for being enormously shrill and good-hearted. She was notorious for having called one of her political opponents a "fuckwit." And when asked to apologize, she refused, saying that in fact the man was demonstrably a fuckwit. I left New Zealand before I was able to arrange to see her, but she turned up in Fiji when I was there—she had just come from the United States on a junket ("I think you Americans call it a freebie"), where she had been the guest of a company that sold expensive diet food.

We met for dinner at a resort restaurant near Nandi—Dame Cath, my friend Andrew, and Jock and Helen, a husband and wife who had fled Scotland some years ago to set up a fitness program in Auckland. I was struck by Jock's involvement in health matters because he was a heavy smoker and had downed the best part of a bottle of wine not long after we sat down.

"And you say you're a mastermind of fitness programs?" I said.

With a cigarette bouncing in his lips, he said, "What does it matter if you die at the age of sixty, as long as you die with a smile on your face."

"I want to die with a smile on my face at the age of a hundred and twenty," I said.

"Bloody Americans! Obsessed with extending their lives!"

Still, I pestered him about his smoking, because with all his talk about health he was such a contradiction, not to say a hypocrite. At first he denied that smoking was bad for him. He said he was more stressed when he didn't smoke. Then he twisted his face at me and said in a rather pathetic way, "I *have* to smoke. I'm addicted. I can't stop. I've tried everything."

"Americans are always going on about smokers," Dame Cath Tizard said. "But have you seen how fat they are? Some of them are just incredible."

"Fat's as bad for you as smoking," Jock said irritably.

This topic seemed unfortunate since both Jock and Dame Cath were hefty people, but they seemed oblivious of that and indifferent to the anomaly of wolfing down huge helpings of dinner while they talked about fat Americans. Dame Cath paid little attention to Jock and when she did speak it was in a drawling Scottish manner that is a variety of Kiwi speech.

Dame Cath had an odd, coarse way of eating. She scraped food onto her fork, but before she heaved it she nudged more onto the fork with her thumb. And after she ate the forkful she licked her thumb. Once I caught her grinning at me, but she was not grinning. She was trying to dislodge a bit of food that had found its way between her teeth, and still talking to me and grinning, she began picking her teeth. Having freed the food from her teeth, she glanced at it and pushed it into her mouth.

Eating in this manner, she said, "People kept telling me I was going to be chosen governor-general, but I couldn't believe it, so I just put it out of my mind."

"How does one get to be chosen?"

"Well, that's just it." *Will, thet's jest ut.* "The Queen does the choosing."

Her finger was in her mouth, fishing for bits of trapped lamb sinews.

"When I got the news—in effect, here was the Queen asking me to be governor-general."

And she slurped the food off her finger, and then began again scraping her plate in the waste-not, want-not manner of a Kiwi who had been through the war.

Jock said, "I know what I'd do!" and raised a glass to the absent Queen of the United Kingdom, Northern Ireland, and Overseas Territories and Commonwealths such as New Zealand.

"Yes," I said. "If the Queen asked me to be governor-general, I would say, 'As Your Highness commands.' "

"It wasn't that simple," she said, obviously wanting to make a meal of her dark night of the soul when she received the Royal Command. "I thought about it for two weeks."

"I'd think about it for about two seconds," Jock said.

"My daughter said, 'Don't be so effing silly, Mum—take it!' "

She smiled, enjoying this chance to tell the story of her ennoblement, and I realized I disliked her politician's vanity and her interminable way of telling this simple story. She was picking her teeth again, and baring them at me.

"I was mayor of Auckland," she said, somewhat defiantly.

"More Polynesians in Auckland than in any other city in the world," I said.

"And some very sad Indians from Fiji, I'm afraid," she said. "We're getting an awful lot of them. But they're no trouble. I had other problems." One problem widely reported was that she had been faced with repeated calls for her resignation following a government investigation that a project for an entertainment center in Auckland, in which she had been involved, had quadrupled in cost from $25 million to $106 million. In a threadbare and overtaxed country this was not merely excessive, this was egregious and stupid. The opposition and her critics—many of whom had once been her supporters—were eager to see her humiliated before she took up the post of governor-general.

"What finally decided you?" I asked, hoping to cut this short.

"After six years of mayor I was really tired of the hassles," she said. "And this way, as governor-general, I could get my superannuation."

It seemed to me rather a mundane notion that one would agree to such a post simply in order to qualify for a state pension, but then the New Zealanders are a practical people.

At that point, out of the blue and fairly tipsy, Jock said he loved New Zealand for its rugby.

"I hate rugby," Dame Cath said. "I think it is violent and that it inspires violence. That's one of the reasons New Zealand is such a violent place. I'm sure rugby," she went on, though I could not follow her reasoning, "causes a lot of rape."

"I was born in Glesgie," Jock said. "Know how they deal with rapists there? Aw, there was one wee lad raped a girl. They took this lad and kneecapped him. Hammered five-inch spikes through his knees."

He waited for a reaction. I put down my fork. No one said anything.

"He's not raping anyone now, I can tell you," Jock said. "He's in a wheelchair."

"I wonder how those men who did it feel?" Dame Cath said, and you knew she thought: Those men were brutalized and remorseful!

"Bloody happy, I think," Jock said.

I said, "Do you think they should introduce kneecapping in New Zealand?"

"Kneecapping is too good for some of these rapists!" Jock said.

Mrs. Jock, meanwhile, did not say anything.

The subject of rapists and rugby turned into a discussion about South Africa, which New Zealand had boycotted because of the way the teams were selected. When I introduced the subject of New Zealand playing Fiji in rugby—what about the undemocratic government here?—they winced at me, as though I had farted in church. No one had an answer to this quite simple matter of political oafishness.

"Anti-apartheid people say they're for freedom," Jock said. "I want to watch my rugby, but I'm not allowed to! What about my freedom?"

"It's not a question of freedom," Dame Cath said. "It's a question of justice. Apartheid is an injustice."

"What do you think of the Fiji constitution?" I said.

"It's a proposed constitution," she said. "Who knows what will happen? Did you say you're a writer? What sort of books do you write?"

"All sorts," I said, but already she seemed bored.

"I am reading a marvellous book at the moment," she said. "About John F. Kennedy. It is very naughty—he committed every indiscretion you can name. And with Marilyn Monroe!"

"I hate those books," I said.

"I think it has historical value," she said.

Oh, sure you do. It irritated me that this New Zealander, and politician to boot, was gloating insincerely over a sensational book.

"But of course you have to admit that your interest in this book is almost purely vulgar," I said. "That's the fun of it, right? It's a cheap thrill, isn't that the whole point?"

She began yammering sanctimoniously about politicians not being above the law and so forth.

"But you're a politician," I said. "And you were a human being before you became a politician."

She glared at me and said that politics was her life—well, anyway, until she had been appointed governor-general. There was something formidable about the way she commanded the table, doing nearly all the talking, being right all the time.

"So you approve of this type of Kennedy book," I said. "How would you like it if someone wrote one about New Zealand politicians. Would you write that sort of book?"

"New Zealand politicians are too bloody boring. They don't even have sex lives."

"Isn't your husband a politician?" I said.

"I left him," she said.

"I read somewhere that David Lange has recently run off with his speech writer and left his wife. What if someone wrote a book about his libido?"

Dame Cath said, "What do you mean 'libido'? You mean screwing around?"

"So to speak. I mean, you say you approve of this type of book, right? It's a historical document, right? Well, I'm sure you know all sorts of dirt about New Zealand politicians. So would you write a book like this about New Zealand indiscretions?"

"I can't write," she said.

"I am being hypothetical," I said, trying to pin her down. "You are in the know. All sorts of secrets. You love to read books about sexual revelations. All I'm saying is—would you be prepared to spill the beans and write the kind of trashy book you like to read?"

This threw her. She fussed and mumbled, and finally said, "If I thought it would help," blah-blah-blah.

"And what if someone wrote a vicious little portrait of you?"

"Let them," she said.

She seemed in the end rather silly and shallow and unimaginative, as well as bossy, vain, and cunning, but principled in a smug and meddling way. A New Zealander to her fingertips, worthy of the Queen's Honour's List.

In a silence after the meal she hitched her skirt and suddenly spoke up.

"I once called a man a fuckwit," she said in her governor-general's voice, dredging up one of her political victories. "Of course I didn't apologize. He *was* a fuckwit."

Chapter 13
FIJI: VANUA LEVU AND THE ISLETS OF BLIGH WATER

In Viti Levu, there was no avoiding the tourists. I kept hoping for something wilder, more remote, a bit emptier, no golfers. Yes, here and there, in an isolated part of the island was a valley of dark green jungle, but really what sort of jungle was it when you went for a hike and after a few hours ran into an Indian family picnicking? They had driven there, all eighteen of them, by car on a back road; they left empty squash bottles and orange rinds and cookie wrappers behind—and sometimes chicken bones. It was a fact that some Hindus, especially in Fiji, hid themselves and secretly gobbled meat, the way teenagers in America sneaked illicit cigarettes.

I heard there was a ferry that sailed from the north coast of Viti Levu, across the twenty-mile-wide channel called Bligh Water, to the much emptier and reputedly rather strange island of Vanua Levu.

"There are no tourists in Vanua Levu," an Indian in Nandi told me. "It is too far and too primitive."

Perfect. Taking my collapsible kayak and all my equipment, I went there on another paralytic Fijian Sunday, stopping for a curry in Lautoka and, out of curiosity, attending a Methodist church service in the northeast town of Mba. The church was full, but many in the congregation were coughers and fidgeters, and during the long, hectoring sermon—in Fijian—a number of people dozed off. Dealing with the sleepers, a smiling Fijian man in a traditional sulu skirt walked up and down the aisle with a long pole, prodding the sleepers and waking them.

In Rakiraki at the top of the island I visited the grave of a nineteenth-century chief of this area—the Province of Ra—Ratu Udre Udre, who had distinguished himself by eating 800 humans. In a hotel nearby, a drunken Australian, seeing my boat, accused me of being a CIA agent. This seemed a reasonable presumption, so I did not deny it. That night, even drunker, he sang tunelessly in the hotel bar while Fijians on the veranda sniggered among themselves and sneaked looks at him through the window. The village nearby was full of aggressive and hysterical dogs; they fought all night, and their barking woke the roosters.

In the morning I found the ferry landing, Ellington Pier, a rubbly platform near a sugar mill. In the blue distance was Vanua Levu. A sugar worker told me I would have to buy my ticket in the next town, Vaileka. The ticket-seller said the ferry would be at the pier at noon and that I could take my rental car.

Vaileka, this small town on the north coast of Viti Levu, had a narrow main street and one row of shops. On this hot day the dust on the dry street seemed to blaze. At the shops and the open-air market—no more than twenty fruit-sellers squatting under an enormous fig tree—I bought provisions for a week. It was not a bad place, but it was very small, it had an air of discouragement about it, the rather sleepy atmosphere of an outpost, and in the silence, with so little stirring, it seemed about as out of touch as a town could possibly be. The world was somewhere else.

That was how it seemed to me: another world. Before I left London, I had been in touch with Salman Rushdie—I wrote to him, he phoned me—and commiserated with him. I considered him a friend; and his confinement pained me—it was like house arrest. I had suggested that he remove himself to a town like this in Mexico or South America or Australia or the Pacific. I had specifically mentioned Fiji. He could be safe, he could be free, he could write in such a place.

"You know Salman Rushdie?" I asked several Muslims in this distant place, Vaileka.

"Yes," one said. "He must die."

And the other said, "Rushdie is a devil."

There were pairs of Mormons in Vaileka, too, which was proof that the town was not as Melanesian as it seemed.

Back at the pier I waited for the ferry. Lizards skittered on the pilings. Birds of prey came and went. Fish jumped. There was no ferry at noon. I listened to news of the Gulf War on my shortwave: more bombing missions, no invasion, a great anxiety over the possible use of nerve gas.

An Indian fished from the pier.

I asked him, "Where is the ferry?"

"Him leave ready. Ten clark."

I thought, *Damn,* but when I questioned him further he appeared not to understand English. He also began to clamber among the rotten pilings humming to himself and I thought he might be demented.

Another Indian sauntered by. He had been burned black by the sun. He was whistling through the gap in his teeth. I asked him about the ferry that was supposed to have come at noon. It was now nearly two.

"Fiji time," he said.

This was a frequent response in Fiji—no offense was meant or taken. Most people laughed about lateness or irregular hours. It simply meant: wait.

But then I saw the black smudge on the horizon, which swelled into a top-heavy ferry, its white hull streaming with rust stains. It was a typical Pacific ferry, down to its greasy decks and broken fixtures and its pretty name painted over Chinese characters—Pacific ferries were always castoffs, secondhand vessels from Hong Kong or Taiwan that someone had managed to sell to a coconut kingdom instead of to a scrapyard.

This one was called the *Princess Ashika.* It docked; six timber trucks heavily laden with logs rolled off it and headed down the dirt road that led away from the pier. I drove on board. I was the only passenger. Within fifteen minutes we were at sea—no time-wasting at all.

The *Princess Ashika* was soon rolling across Bligh Water in a twenty-knot headwind and bright sunshine. With a steady wind like this blowing west across this part of the Pacific it was not hard to see why Captain Bligh had made such good progress on his epic forty-eight-day journey in an open boat, with eighteen of his men, after the mutiny on the *Bounty.* They had been cast adrift by Fletcher Christian off Tonga, and had sailed among these islands, between Viti Levu and Vanua Levu. Captain Bligh was the first European to map this part of Viti Levu. Bligh had sailed onward, through the Coral Sea, past the Queensland coast and Cape York, squeezing through the Torres Strait, and finally reaching landfall at Kupang in Timor. It had been a voyage of almost 4,000 miles, and his men had been frightened for most of the way—a fear of cannibals, mostly, and amply justified. In fact, just after their longboat passed this point several canoes crewed by fierce Fijians gave chase and kept after them almost until Bligh had cleared the Yasawas, about twenty odd miles west of here.

Passing this way, Bligh had looked at the islands and described the landscape in his log, remarking on the "cockscomb mountains." It was an accurate image. The mountains were high and green, with gently rounded lobe-like peaks. Clouds gathered around the summits of the old volcanoes inland, but the coast was bright, and even on this north coast of Viti Levu, which was as quiet as the island could be, it was possible to ascertain that Viti Levu had been spoken for. It was not that the island was crowded, but rather that it was settled. It was farmed and deforested. In a word, it was possessed.

I hoped for better in Vanua Levu. This ferry was headed for a small pier at the southwestern tip of the island, Nabouwalu. No one I had spoken to knew anything about Nabouwalu—so I was heartened.

Since I was the only passenger—this ship was used mostly for ferrying timber to Viti Levu—the crew had little to do en route. They sat on the broken benches in an upper-deck lounge watching a video. The movie, ostensibly a costume adventure about a band of pirates looking for treasure in the West Indies, was a thin excuse for showing sex and violence—two rapes, the beating of a woman, lots of cleavage, a simulated act of sodomy (a pirate and a busty, gasping woman in a hiked-up prom gown), and a number of whippings. Dungeons and rats figured in a number of scenes. The Fijian deckhands laughed delightedly at the rapes and were so riveted by the floggings that they almost missed the docking procedure and had to be summoned by the captain.

The sun was setting beneath Coconut Point as we docked. I could take in the whole place in one glance. Nabouwalu was the pier, two shops, some scattered huts, and a stony road. Little wonder no one had said anything about it. What was there to say? Driving in the darkness on such a bad road was ill-advised, so I asked a strolling Fijian where I might camp. He directed me to the Rest House. This bungalow was fully occupied—three or four Fijians in residence—but one of them, a strapping fellow in a skirt named Jone Kindia, said that the only really safe place to camp was at his workers' compound. He took me there and he explained on the way that Fijians were funny about their land. They were suspicious of strangers who showed up without an introduction, wishing to camp.

"They wonder how long you are going to stay," Jone said. "Maybe you will want to stay for years. That is what they worry about."

"I just want to stay for a few days," I said.

"But how do they know that?"

"Good point."

The workers' compound was a clearing on a hillside outside Nabouwalu—a few flimsy huts, a wooden bungalow that served as an office, and an unfinished building in which day and night the local Fijians sat around a bowl drinking kava. They did not call it kava, nor even *yanggona.* They called it grog.

"Where is Masi?" Kindia asked a woman in a field.

She mumbled a reply.

"Drinking grog," Kindia translated.

He was sitting around the bowl with Yoakini and they both had the stupefied, slightly stunned and smiling expression of kava drinkers. Kava drinkers were never aggressive. They looked numb, like hypothermia victims, or patients who had just been dragged from a dentist's chair. Kava drinkers were weak and compliant; they whispered; they swayed when they tried to stand straight. Kava was like chloroform. "He's not feeling any pain" was truer when spoken of a kava drinker than an alcoholic. And because kava deadened the lips and tongue one never heard a harsh word from one of these men.

Yoakini said, "You stay at my *bure.*"

"That's all right. I have a tent."

Masi wore a slaphappy smile. He looked at me through heavy-lidded eyes and said, "Do not go to the beach."

Kindia muttered impatiently.

"Never go to the beach," Masi said. He was on his feet and swaying.

"Why not?"

"Alfred Hitchcock is there," Masi said and stopped smiling.

"Did you say Alfred Hitchcock?"

The fellow simply stared at me.

I set up my tent away from the coconut palms and hurriedly ate dinner—it was a starry moonless night. Just before I turned in, Masi came by. He teetered for a moment and then spoke.

"Remember, Alfred is at the beach," he said, and then staggered into the darkness.

Yoakini was a soldier in the Fijian army. "I am about twenty-eight," he said. He described himself as a "sapper"—a military engineer. Carpentry was his specialty. He was very black, with thick hair and a fierce mustache, and he was bulkily built, his body like a fortification. He said he drank grog every night when he was off-duty. He showed me where I could get fresh water, where I could take a shower, and where the best latrine was located.

He was shy, but not timid, and though he was quiet, he answered my nosy questions. When he said that he had been in Suva during the coup and the ensuing riots in 1987, I asked whether he had found it exciting to be in the thick of a battle on his own island (he was from a village in Viti Levu): the Fijians storming the Indian shops, burning and looting.

"Yes, it was exciting," he said. "It was very exciting."

"Have you traveled overseas?" I asked.

"I was in Lebanon twice."

"Lebanon?"

"In the peacekeeping force. In 1982 and in 1984," he said. "I was in Cairo, in Beirut, and in South Lebanon. I visited Israel, too. It was nice."

"Weren't you afraid to be in a place where there was so much fighting?"

"No. The worst is the weather. Very hot in the day. Very cold at night."

"Did you have grog?"

"They flew in *yanggona* sometimes—the roots. We pounded it and drank it in our tents. Some we saved for Christmas. We had a good Christmas in Lebanon, drinking grog."

"What did you think of the situation there?"

"It is a mess. I don't know the answer. I was a soldier in Sinai. The Arabs asked us for food, the Israelis asked us where are we from? Then they said, 'Where is Fiji?' "

Yoakini laughed at the memory of it—of the ignorance of the Israelis, these embittered and confused civilians living at the edge of the desert. "In Fiji we study geography. We know where all countries are. We know where Israel is."

"Were you doing carpentry in Sinai?"

"No carpentry. In Sinai they gave me a weapon," Yoakini said.

"But isn't it ridiculous that a Fiji Islander should be in the Middle East, risking his life because of a local conflict?"

"Maybe. But the money is good," he said. He told me what he was making. I estimated that he was earning ninety dollars a month.

"Are you willing to risk dying to earn that?"

"I don't know," he said. "Thirty Fijians have been killed there—by single bullets, by accidents, from sickness. It is a mess."

What he did not say—something I discovered later—was that Lieutenant Colonel Rabuka had served twice in the Middle East with the Fiji Army, in the same places Yoakini had been posted, in Lebanon and in Sinai.

I asked Yoakini whether he would serve in the Gulf War. He said it depended on whether the Fiji Army was involved, and if it was a question of volunteering, the money had to be good—though his idea of good was ninety dollars a month. I had heard that the Fijian soldiers had been highly effective in World War II—they had the essential military virtues, a legacy of the British colonial past: They were ferocious, loyal, politically disinterested, impervious to bad weather, and would eat anything. They fought when they were ordered to. They were professionals. They soldiered for money. They were the perfect mercenaries—not elite troops and janizaries, but workhorses and warriors.

I gave Yoakini some of the *yanggona* roots that I had brought with me, and he invited me to drink grog with him. Because it was considered rude to refuse I joined him that night around the kava bowl, the *tanoa*—which was about twice the size of a salad bowl and beautifully carved. These bowls were the only accomplished carvings I saw in Fiji.

With my lips going numb and my tongue thickening, I said that what I really wanted was to go paddling.

"But where will you stay?"

"I'll just ask someone in a nearby village."

"It is better you stay here."

When I explained that my boat was collapsible and that I could take it back here to this campsite—something he urged me to do—Yoakini showed me a good place to paddle that was east of the little town, beyond Solevu Point. The water was muddy and shallow near shore, but out at the reef I could make headway. I realized that this was what I had missed on Viti Levu. Though the Fijian resorts were pleasant, there was a fence around each one, and people could stay for weeks and never know Fiji. Even people who had lived in Fiji for a long time told me that they had not been to this island, Vanua Levu. There was nowhere to stay on this western end of the island, they said. There were no restaurants. It was just jungle and scattered villages. The beaches were muddy and thick with mangroves. The people were simple and suspicious. The roads were appalling.

This was music to my ears. And these perceptions of the island proved to be true. But I had a tent, and a stove, and food, and a boat. I even had a car, so I could tote all this stuff around. But I paddled during the day, exploring the large bay and the inlets west of Nabouwalu; at night I went back to my tent and stayed put in Kindia's compound.

Long after night had fallen, and often until quite late, I heard the villagers pounding the *yanggona* root in their big wooden mortars. This thudding was continuous, like the sound of a stirrup pump, and it was always a woman using the pestle. The Fijian method was different from the Vanuatu way. In Fiji they sluiced this pounded root through a piece of cloth and the narcotic drink was squeezed into the kava bowl.

"We don't chew," Masi said.

But I now knew that human saliva reacted with the root and made a stronger drink—that was why they called Tanna product "two-day kava": You were stupefied for two days on a few shells of the stuff.

At one time, village girls in Fiji had prepared the root by chewing it and spitting it out. Having a winsome Fijian girl smilingly masticating by my side seemed infinitely preferable to me than a filthy man with black tooth stumps munching and drooling. But as Masi said, *We don't chew*. Non-chewing islands in the Pacific were invariably the islands where the missionaries had exerted the strongest grip, for nothing was more disgusting to a European than drinking someone else's saliva. Missionaries had encouraged the use of mortars and pestles.

I usually dropped off to sleep to the rhythm of *yanggona* being pounded. One night in my tent in that compound I dreamed that I was going home—"home" was the concept I had in my dream, but it was not my house. It was a mansion set amid parkland, very serene as I approached it, but chaotic and filled with people when I stepped inside the ornate front door. There were a number of women in the mansion: All of them at one time had been married to me. And there were many children, all mine. It dawned on me that I had been away a long time, and these wives and children had multiplied in my absence. They were all having a wonderful time, and yet there was great confusion. I wandered outside, to the swimming pool, on which floated chunks of blue ice.

Jone Kindia was the *Roko*, or head of the Fijian Affairs Board. This was a glorified name for an agency that spent most of its time settling local disputes. The burden fell upon Jone. He was the dispute-settler. He set off each morning for his office in his starched shirt and his wraparound garbardine skirt and his polished sandals. There were usually a dozen people waiting at the veranda of the wooden bungalow which housed his office, and one by one Jone listened to their tales of woe. On the walls of his office were lithographs of British coronations, a large one of George V, and other portraits of George V and VI. Jone said they dated from before independence, when an Englishman had had this office. Jone had not taken them down. He said he thought they were very pretty, and they took his mind off his wearying job. He said sometimes he spent days or even weeks on just one dispute.

"What sort would that be?"

"Land dispute. They are the worst," he said, smoothing his mustache. "There is no end to them, and I find it very hard to straighten them out."

Fijians were intensely territorial. But of course all the islanders in the Pacific were territorial: Land was their birthright, their wealth, and in Melanesia it was the origin of their creation—they had sprung from this soil. *We came out of the caves at Kaibola,* as they said in the Trobriands. They could account for every foot of land, and because it was family land it had been extensively subdivided—that also made it unsaleable, for how could you get all these people to agree to sell? If you made the mistake of camping without permission on an uninhabited island, God help you—because someone owned it, and camping on it meant that you were attempting to claim it. Fijian territoriality was at the heart of their animosity against the Indians. Fijians did not mind being outnumbered—in fact, Fijians had been outnumbered by Indians off and on for as far back as 1946—what they minded was losing their land to these pagan aliens.

"I own this beach," a Fijian said to me, up the coast at Nasavu. "You go two chains and that is Tumasi's. Three chains and it is Alesi's."

They often used this old English measurement, too. A chain is equal to 100 feet. Ten square chains is an acre.

Jone, Masi, and Yoakini became protective of me in a way that puzzled and irritated me. I know they were trying to prevent misunderstandings, but I felt I could handle myself—hadn't I managed in Vanuatu and the Solomons, reputedly much wilder places?

They always wanted to know exactly where I was headed. I would find a place on the map and say, "I am going to Wailiki."

Jone or one of the others in the compound would then say, "Where will you stay?"

"I'll pitch my tent. I'll ask permission."

They would go silent, or else mumble among themselves.

"It is better you stay here."

"I want to go to Wailiki."

Then they would giggle, and this meant that going to Wailiki was difficult. Loud laughter was the Fijian way of conveying the bad news that something was impossible.

"Someone can go with you."

"I want to go alone. Why does someone have to go with me?"

"To introduce you."

"Can't I introduce myself? I'll give them some *yanggona.*" I still had three dusty bunches of the horrible stuff.

"Yes?" they would say, meaning no.

They weren't kidding, and after a while I knew that their anxiety was justified. At three villages I was asked the same insulting question: "You're a businessman?"

The feeling was that I had come to diddle them out of their birthright, when all I really wanted was to pitch my tent and paddle my boat.

I paddled down the coast, and at Sawani, Solevu, and other coastal villages, I presented myself to the *Yaganga ni Koro,* "Master of the Village" (*Yaganga* was also the word they used for Almighty God), who was a sort of chief or headman. I had a message from the *Roko.* This cut little ice. They were not used to seeing travelers here. They had heard about them.

They winced at me. They smiled—this was an expression of disagreement—and they said: It is not nice here. It is not even clean. This is a poor village. You would do better to keep moving and to go somewhere else.

"Can't I put my tent here?"

Their bewilderment seemed to say: Why would you want to do that?

When I camped I did not stay longer than a night. Their suspicion and anxiety made me uneasy—although I should add that they were pleasant people, gentle, unthreatening, helpful to each other.

But an encounter could be an unusual experience. One day after paddling three or four miles I stepped onshore and saw a bushy-haired man and woman. The woman was carrying a dog in her arms like a baby. The man wore a filthy T-shirt lettered with the slogan *Nibble Nobby's Nuts.*

He carried a wicked-looking bush knife, a slasher that was about two feet long. They were both very dirty and rather apprehensive.

"Where is Nakawakawa Village?" I had found it on my map, but there were no huts in sight.

"Just here," the man said.

"Can I get there on this path?" I asked.

"You want to go there?"

"Yes."

"Yes?"

"If it's all right"—a man carrying a knife like that could make me very circumspect. "Otherwise, I'll just paddle away."

"Yes," he said, which I took to mean: *That is what I advise you to do.*

And then—and this was also typical—the man asked whether he could be my pen pal.

Farther up the coast I paddled into a little bay where there was a large cathedral-like church, made of wood and gray plaster. A horse cropped grass in the churchyard, and there were school buildings behind the church. But there were no people anywhere. I crept into the church and in the large dusty nave there were no pews, only wall-to-wall mats, and over the altar verses from the gospel in Fijian.

I found two Fijians sitting on the floor of a nearby wooden building. There were chairs in the room, which had the look of an office, but the men were drinking kava. It was unthinkable to engage in kava drinking while sitting in a chair. You had to sit cross-legged, around the bowl.

"What are you doing?"

"Drinking grog."

They must have started early. It was nine-thirty in the morning and both men had the dazed and somewhat anesthetized expression of kava drinkers who had knocked back a dozen shells.

"Where is the priest?"

"At the priests' conference in Savusavu."

This was obviously the priest's office—his desk, his papers, his crucifix. It was a good secluded place, perfect for kava drinking.

"Very nice," I said, watching the bigger of the two men working a coconut shell around the bowl, stirring the opaque muddy liquid. This dishwater color was standard, no better or worse than any other I had seen.

The man filled the shell and offered it to me.

By now I knew the ritual. I sat and clapped a little as he handed me the shell—and drank it down in a gulp—then handed the empty shell back and clapped again. It had a revolting taste. It was lukewarm, and it had the slightly medicinal flavor of mouthwash to which some mud had been added. There was nothing alcoholic in it, though there was a mild after-burn and a hint of licorice.

With the first shell my lips were numb and my tongue was furry. The second shell deadened my tongue and killed my facial nerves. Successive shells paralyzed my legs, reaching my toes first then numbing my shanks.

"It is a good safe drink," an Indian told me in Nabouwalu. Though Indians themselves didn't touch the stuff. "People just get very sleepy and tired. They are slow. There is never any violence. They are too weak to fight."

No one ever went haywire and beat up his wife after bingeing on *yanggona*. No one ever staggered home from a night around the kava bowl and thrashed his children, or insulted his boss, or got tattooed, or committed rape. The usual effect after a giggly interval was the staggers and then complete paralysis.

These men were at the giggly stage. They answered a few simple questions I had about the church—it was called the Immaculate Conception Church, it had been founded by French priests, and they said it was 120 years old, which seemed unlikely; and then they smiled and passed the shell.

This was the last thing I wanted to do. The kava sapped my energy and made it a chore to paddle. But I did not wish to be offensive, so I sat for a while and asked them about it. They told me about the girls who had once chewed the root and they said that in some places the root was still chewed. But they had little conversation. This was not an activity that induced high spirits. Most men sat around the bowl mumbling. Initially a kava ceremony was an occasion to gossip, but the more people drank the less coherent they became.

These men said they would be there most of the day. They had nothing else to do. When I asked them how much they could drink they said, "Two kilos"—they meant of the pounded root, which was gallons of the muddy liquid.

It was a struggle to paddle onward from there, but I had no choice. I had intended to reach the far side of the bay, where a town showed on the map. The effects of the kava did not wear off until midafternoon, and then I made better time, reaching the settlement just before sunset. But the name on the map was misleading—as names so often were on maps of Pacific islands. It was simply a crossroads, and a small store, run by a small grizzled Indian named Munshi.

Munshi said I could camp on his land, a little clearing just inland from the mangroves. He claimed to own it outright. He said his grandfather had bought it—his grandfather had come to Fiji to work on a sugar estate in the 1890s. Munshi had been born in the same house where his father had been born, on the other side of the island at Votua.

He watched me pitch my tent and to make conversation I asked how he was getting on.

"This is a bad place now," Munshi said. "This is no place for Indians. We are suffering."

I found this all depressing—the undercurrent of resentment, the silliness of the tourists, the fact that no one in the world paid the slightest attention to it. It was a lost cause, the kava-drinking Methodists on the one hand and the cliquey puritanical Asians on the other. All they had in common was a love of videocassettes—a shared fondness for *Rambo* and *Die Hard* and *Predator II*. Apart from that, there was no sympathy much less any intermarriage. Here and there—and sometimes in the wildest, emptiest places of Vanua Levu—was a Chinese shop, its owner looking like a Martian behind the counter, utterly indifferent to it all.

The next day, a hot humid morning, Munshi sold me some Shell-Lite fuel for my stove and explained his predicament. I had asked him what he wanted to do.

"I want to leave. To go anywhere."

"Have you ever been away from here?"

"No," Munshi said. "But my father went to India. He made the *Haj* pilgrimage. I would like to do that."

He was barefoot and dirty. His wife, who never spoke, swept the yard with a twig broom, shifting garbage from one side of the yard to the other. His kids squawked on the porch, and some Fijian boys sat on the steps, one holding a loaf of bread, the other a can of corned beef, listening without understanding.

Munshi said, "Where do you come from?"

"America."

"I would like to go to America."

Munshi handed me my fuel and replaced the bung on his oil drum.

"This is a bad place." He snatched off his greasy skullcap and scratched his head. "Why you come here?"

"Just looking around."

"You like?"

"Very nice."

He shook his head.

"No," he said.

The Fijian boys on the porch began to eat their breakfast. They knifed open the can of corned beef, tore the loaf of bread into hunks, and took turns scooping smears of corned beef out of the can with the bread hunks. These they stuffed into their mouths, until the can was empty. There was little fresh fish here. People ate canned fish, as they had in New Guinea and the Trobriands—pilchards, mackerel, "tuna flakes."

Munshi had baked the bread. He made it fresh every day, with flour that came on the ferry and that he trucked to his kitchen. His shop was the only source of bread on this entire end of the island, for fifty miles or more. All the Fijians ate bread. None of the other shops—the other Indians, the Chinese man—made bread.

I was certain that he would leave—he said his land was for sale, his shop was for sale. If he couldn't go to Canada or America he would go to New Zealand. Then there would be no bread. I imagined that his bread would be missed, even if he were not; but the Fijians would learn to do without it. They would eat crackers instead—cream crackers. There was a traditional diet in Fiji, as there was on other islands; but along with this was another kind of food, the sailors' diet which was standard on many Pacific islands and was eaten with relish: ships' biscuit, corned beef, Spam, tinned fish, and for sweets, jars of marmalade and canned plum duff.

No fishing canoes were made or used in Viti Levu nor even in simpler and more traditional Vanua Levu. I never saw anyone fishing beyond the reef. Inshore, they waded up to their thighs and cast small nets. They threw dinky spears. They caught tiny fish. Off the beaten track, there were some thatched huts on Vanua Levu but mostly the roofs were corrugated tin, and the villages tended to be ramshackle—no evidence of weaving, carving, or lashing poles. It was the apotheosis of missionary effort, a great evangelical success. All the people went to church. But they had lost most of their traditional skills. Even their gardens were unimpressive— they only grew enough for themselves, and they still patronized the Indian shops. They needed Munshi more than they realized.

When the tide was out—and it went very far out on this Bua coast—the place seemed even more remote and abandoned, a distant muddy shore. In so many words, Munshi told me he was simply going through the motions; he was waiting for his chance to leave.

I was grateful for his letting me camp on his land. He expected nothing in return. When I offered him *yanggona* he just laughed at me. We were sitting on his veranda. He repeated that this was an awful place. What should he do? Where could he go?

"I am like a prisoner," Munshi said.

This reminded me. "You know Salman Rushdie?"

"I have heard of him."

"What did he do?"

"Bad things."

"Is he a bad man?"

"I think so, yes," Munshi said.

I said, "The Ayatollah wants to have him killed."

"Yes," Munshi said, and smiled, and made a harsh noise as he scraped at his whiskers with his skinny fingers.

"You want to kill him?"

"Maybe not me. But it is better if he die."

I paddled back to Nabouwalu and camped up at Yoakini's and drank grog in the kava circle. When Masi got stiff he began warning me about Alfred Hitchcock. I thought I would load my boat and drive north eighty miles to Labasa, where there was a sugar town and some offshore islands. I asked them what it was like there.

They said, *It is like this.*

I went to bed feeling as though I had just been at the dentist's, my mouth full of Novocain.

It was another hot day in Nabouwalu. I was in the car. My gear was packed—my tent folded, my boat collapsed. I began driving through town and out of the corner of my eye I saw that the ferry was docked at the jetty. An immense timber truck was waiting to drive on board. Another was trundling down the stony road to the pier.

The wind lifted, and an overwhelming stink of rotting vegetation rose from the shore to the west and blew past me. It carried with it muddy beaches and buggy mangroves and decrepit tin-roofed villages. It even carried with it a glimpse of the big bushy-haired man with the wicked cutlass and the T-shirt that said *Nibble Nobby's Nuts.* I looked up and saw the rutted road, and envisioned how bad it would be after fifty or sixty miles—the dust, the potholes, the hairpin curves above the sludgy lagoon. *It is like this.*

On a sudden impulse I swerved onto the road, jounced towards the pier, and a Fijian stepped out of the way and waved me on board. Within minutes we were out of there, and then Vanua Levu was astern, just another Fiji island smothered in cloud and haze.

Paddling in the cluster of reefs and islets and remote villages, off Viti Levu, in Bligh Water, I met Ken MacDonald, who was building a hotel for scuba divers on the island of Nananu-i-Ra. He suggested that camping might be misunderstood on the island and said that I could stay at his bungalow while I explored the islands in the area—and I might find an island to camp on later.

MacDonald, who looked as Scottish as his name, surprised me by saying that he was partly Tongan and Samoan. This ancestry was unfortunate, he said. Though nothing specific was mentioned about it, he felt that it had been the reason he had been unable to marry the daughter of the Fijian nobleman Ratu Sir Kamisese Mara. He had romanced the woman for nine years. If he had been part Fijian, or wholly Scottish or English, he thought he might not have been rejected. This was an insight into the Melanesian social system—and it was true that behind this facade of religion and tourism and sugarcane and the rather decrepit modernism of Fiji was an inflexible and ancient infrastructure of chiefs— the *ratus,* and real power, where caste and blood mattered.

I wondered what Ken might mean when he warned me that he could be moody, with sudden lapses, and odd humor, unpredictable opinions and slight tetchiness. He seemed very pleasant, if a bit quiet. It was an advantage to me that he was somewhat remote, and preoccupied with the building of his resort. I hated being anyone's house guest. I disliked being shown around, cooked for, and patronized. It suited me that Ken was too busy for this, and I could see that his diving resort, Mokusiga (the word meant goofing off), had been designed to be as unobtrusive as possible on this pretty island. It was taking all his savings and most of his energy to see it through.

His house was crammed with books and cassettes, and the shelves in the kitchen lined with cans of mackerel, the sort I always brought along when I was camping.

"So you eat this stuff too," I said.

"That's for the cats," Ken said.

But he said that there were very few people who went fishing in a serious way. Now it was all vegetables and corned beef and soft drinks; a pretty awful diet.

"Fifteen years ago you saw outrigger canoes," Ken said. "The men went fishing beyond the reef. Now you might see some people with nets, but not much more."

In the evenings after I had returned from paddling we sometimes sat in the darkness, under his trees, slapping mosquitoes and drinking beer. He said that it seemed to be simply a standoff between Fijians and Indians. But it was much more complicated than that. There were all shades of political opinion—very right-wing Fijians, very nationalistic parties, like the Taukai. It was during the second coup that this party emerged— significantly, the word *taukai* in Fijian means "landowners"—and Fijians from all classes became members.

"The Taukai burned shops and beat up Indians," Ken said. "And some of the Indians were militants. Arms—all sorts of guns and ammo were found in some Indian areas. And a boat with arms for Indians tried to slip in here—through the channel. But there were soldiers watching from the hills and they intercepted it."

"Do you think the Indians will leave?"

"Some have already left. The ones that stay are not persecuted. They are just left out," Ken said. And it seemed to me that this was so. "Anyway, they never had a lot of faith in the Fijians."

"For Fijians the feeling is mutual," I said. "So, what if the Indians are forced to leave, as they were in Uganda? It was an economic catastrophe for Uganda. If that happens in Fiji, there will be very few shops, poor supply lines, a scarcity of goods and services, a shortage of skilled man-power—teachers and medical people, for example. Then Fiji would be in a very bad way. It will be an island of ghost towns."

Ken said, "Yes, that's a possibility."

He was being realistic, but had no sense of urgency. He was not alone. The general feeling among Fijians and other aliens was that the Indians would stay as long as there was business to be done and money to be made—the idea of profit overrode any political consideration.

Personally, I did not agree. It seemed to me that Fiji had an uncertain future and that there was a great deal of bitterness and resentment. Unless a democratic constitution was enacted, there would be trouble—if the Indians stayed they would be bitter and angry, and if they left there would be economic collapse.

Some neighbors of Ken's were old soldiers—part-Fijian—who had served during World War II, in the Western Pacific. They had been part of the struggle to take Bougainville Island, in the north Solomons. Every night they met Ken under the trees, and sat in the darkness, chatting amiably and drinking beer. I asked them about their part in the war.

"You Americans had a small beachhead, about six miles wide, on Bougainville," a man named George told me. "The rest was held by the Japs. We were trying to get them out. I am not boasting but I can say that we were well trained and we were used to the jungle. We knew better than to wear helmets and we knew how to be very quiet."

He was laughing, perhaps wondering whether I would be insulted by what came next.

"I am sorry to say but your American troops weren't used to the jungle. And there was one of these Negro battalions. All black. Very scary."

It seemed unusual that a Fijian soldier would say this. "You were scared by black soldiers?"

"No. Only by soldiers who shoot at every sound they hear. An Ameri-can said to me, 'We had to chase them and put shoes on them, and then we sent them over here.' They shot at birds. They shot at each other. They never hit anything! And every morning they did the heebie-jeebies. Hee-bie-jeebies! Up and down!"

He stood up from his canvas chair, mimicked a prancing minstrel, and made his friends laugh.

"One American colonel saw us going into the jungle. He said, 'These men will protect you on your way out.'

"I said, 'No sir! I am going the other way! I don't want these men protecting me!'

"We went on patrol. I was with my men, about six of us. Of course we never talked. We stopped to rest at noon and were lying there, no talking, when I heard a loud click—a helmet hitting a rock. We never wore helmets. If you see pictures of soldiers wearing helmets in the Solomons they are untrue—they are posed.

"Hearing this click, I got up slowly and looked through the bushes. And about fifteen feet away, just on the other side of the bushes, were some Jap soldiers, resting, like us."

George was still on his feet, showing us how he had moved in that jungle clearing, still gesturing and whispering hoarsely.

"I signalled to my men to fan out—to the right and left. Just hand signals, no talking. Then I gave the signal for—you know what enfilade fire is? Sweeping them with bullets? We did that, caught them in a cross-fire you might say. We killed six of them. We wounded more. We followed the trails of blood but those Japs escaped."

"How did you feel at the end of that day?" I asked.

"Lucky. And tired," George said. "We buried their bodies. We were not savages. We gave everyone we killed a decent burial."

It was said that the Fijian soldiers were so tough, and were preceded by a reputation for such ferocity, that surrendering Japanese sought out American Marines for fear of being used brutally by Fijians.

There were six or eight other islands, small and large, around Nananu-i-Ra. One, Dolphin Island, was privately owned and on the market for a few million. Another private island was a coconut plantation. I was making a sixteen-mile circuit of Nananu-i-Ra, and had my tent and food with me in case the weather suddenly turned foul. Yet it brightened, the clouds dispersed, the wind dropped, and I was paddling on an incandescent mirror, watching the plopping terns and the patient herons and the kite-like motion of the frigate birds.

Although I was well protected, wearing a shirt and a hat and sunglasses, the blinding light on the ocean drove me into the shore of a bay at noon, where I looked for a shady spot to rest, before pushing on in this circumnavigation of the island.

There were two other people on the beach. I said hello. They had just gone snorkeling on the reef and they too had been driven onto the shade of the beach by the blazing sun.

They were the Garstangs, originally from South Africa but now living in Virginia. Michael was a meteorologist who had been one of the first people to work on the change in the world's weather pattern and the possibility of a greenhouse effect. He had recently been teaching in New Zealand and was about to embark on a weather expedition to Borneo.

Michael said, "People mainly think about Brazil—the rain forest—when they worry about the ozone layer. But there are three hot spots that determine the world's weather. Brazil, Borneo, and Congo-Zaire, the middle of Africa. They produce the heat and the force"—and he pushed upward with his fist—"that drive El Niño."

"Is it just Borneo that's the hot spot?"

"No. New Guinea—the whole region. You probably noticed how warm the water was there. That's another factor."

"Does it bother you that everyone claims to be an expert on global warming?"

He smiled and said, "Not really. But accurate data is very hard to obtain. You might have a calculation on warming, but if there is just the slightest amount of cloud cover your calculation can be thrown off by an enormous amount. The fact is that no one really knows the answer."

"Michael has been studying this for years," Mrs. Garstang said.

Michael said, "Did you know there is an ozone surplus in the South Atlantic?"

"I was under the impression there was ozone depletion—an ozone hole," I said.

"Yes. Over Antarctica. But I'm talking about the South Atlantic. This ozone surplus has just been discovered and has only recently been studied."

We stood knee-deep in the lagoon talking about the world's weather, and then about the changes in Fiji—he had first seen the island many years before and said that it had deteriorated. And it struck me that the people who knew Fiji best removed themselves to be as far from Nandi and Suva as possible. The Garstangs had begun their life in America at Woods Hole, when Michael had worked at the Oceanographic Institute, and so we chatted about Cape Cod—places we knew and liked—and we were so engrossed on this sunny day that it was as though we were there, in a little cove, passing the time of day.

At one point Michael said, "The nineties will be a hot decade"—he seemed to mean by it, lots of action—volcanic activity, earthquakes, storms.

In New Zealand, I had noticed how my memory was provoked by travel—I think this is perhaps true of many people—and how remote places could induce in me the most intense reveries of home. This little conversation at the edge of the lagoon cast a spell upon me. I paddled on

in this Cape Cod reverie, my mind was in Nantucket Sound, and so I was
startled a few minutes later to see naked Fijian boys with water droplets
glistening in their hair, clambering on rocks and flinging coconut husks
at each other.

Soon I was in open water, being driven by that same stiff wind that had
sped Captain Bligh on his way. I found an empty beach at the western tip
of the island, and had lunch, cat food—as this Japanese mackerel now
seemed to me—and fruit. I had a nap in the shade of a tree and afterwards
went snorkeling. About sixty yards offshore there was a ledge and then
great black depths of cold water. Parrot fish and tiny fish, brilliant yellow
and blue, glittering like jewels, massed along the ledge of coral and
crown-of-thorns starfish, nibbling and darting with a thousand other fish.

I drifted and watched the fish, but I did not linger. Now I knew enough
about the features of Oceania to recognize a perfect habitat for sharks.
Normally when I snorkeled I kept looking behind me for a shark and this
day I was especially careful. And I did not press my luck. I soon swam
back to my camp on the beach, and when it was cooler I continued
around the island.

Just at dusk, in a lovely orangey-pink lagoon off the last point in the
island, wavelets lapped against black rocks. Lingering here, before my
last push to circle the island, I marvelled at the play of light and shadow,
the way the water glowed, and I soon realized that two of the waves were
a pair of sharks, with spots on their dorsal fins—epaulet sharks. They
were mottled and elegant, and I had a sense that they were playing—
simply fooling in the water.

I reached for the spear that I kept tied down on the deck of the kayak.
The sharks were each about five feet long, and they were side by side in
only a few feet of water. How could I miss? Already I could see myself
paddling into the bay, and Ken under his tree with a beer would stand up
and goggle at me in my kayak, with two plump sharks slung on my
thwarts. Fijians would be dumbstruck seeing my prowess with the spear,
my fearlessness at facing sharks. I would say to them, *I learned to deal
with sharks in the Trobriand Islands.*

I threw the spear as hard as I could at the nearer shark, and it hit the
thickest part of the creature's long body just behind its head. Both sharks
thrashed and were gone. No damage was done: In my hurry I had not
removed the lump of coconut husk I had rammed on the end of my spear
point—I had been afraid that this sharp trident would puncture my boat.
I might have given one of the sharks a bad bruise, but nothing worse than
that—and when I thought about it I was glad. The sharks had not
menaced me nor even bothered me. They were apparently enjoying themselves. But in trying to kill them—so impulsively, from a sense of power

and domination—I was behaving with the sort of malicious wickedness that we always attributed to sharks.

One island in this north coast group was often on my mind, because it was visible even at night. This was Malake. It was constantly on fire. During the day it smoked—gray and black smoke billowing from the steep sides of its hills, and at night it was lighted with the flames of circling fires, creeping sideways towards the summits. On my map the island was not much more than a mile long and half a mile wide. The parts of it that were not on fire were already black.

"They're always burning that bloody island," an old-timer said to me. "They got nothing to do, so they set fires."

I wanted to visit the arsonists of Malake. It was ten miles downwind—too far to reach and get back on one of these very hot days. So I decided to make an expedition of it, and bring water and food and my tent, and a bunch of *yanggona*. I left early one morning, and helped by the wind I moved swiftly along, listening to the old rock-and-roll songs on my *Big Chill* tape.

It had seemed an unpopulated island—its fires had given it a strange character—but nearer I could see a little settlement, where the arsonists lived, and that it had a distinct reef. The tide was ebbing and the coral protruded so near the surface that in places my boat bumped and snagged. Closer still, I could see signs of cultivation—taro patches, papaya trees, cassava plants. But these were small and they were in the isolated parts of the island. The rest had been burned. I could see the blackened grass, the new erosion, the scorched trees, and the newly dead pines with orangey needles.

The settlement faced the north shore of Viti Levu, but what had seemed a busy village of huts was up close no more than a cluster of tin shacks on a littered beach. I paddled behind the island—the northern slope of the mountain and the foothills that were black from the grass fires.

I paddled out to sea, to avoid the sharp coral that I thought might tear the hull of my boat. And, paddling, I began to feel weary. Until then I had felt healthy, but I had caught a cold somewhere—perhaps at my campsite in Vanua Levu, perhaps from that damned kava, where we all drank from the same coconut shell. Anyway, I was sure that I was coming down with a cold—I had a headache, my eyes hurt, my throat was sore, my nose was blocked, and my muscles ached. The best thing, I felt, would be to go ashore and make camp and simply stay there, resting and keeping out of the sun. I had enough food and water for three days.

Looking for deep water on this coral shelf, I heard a chopping sound from shore—like that of someone cutting wood—and so I paddled away and put in farther down the coast, on a little bay. As I was tying up my boat on a mangrove root five men materialized from the bushes, brandishing the bush knives that looked like pirates' cutlasses. So these were the arsonists of Malake. They had come out of nowhere.

I was about to get into my boat and paddle away when they surrounded me. I felt foolish. If I tried to escape from them they could easily have stopped me—the water was shallow for some distance, I would have to paddle carefully because of the coral. One swipe of a knife would sink my boat anyway. So I brazened it out. I said hello. I smiled.

They were ragged Fijians, with the jutting cannibal teeth of the rural Fijian, and the sloping forehead, the tiny eyes, the crow-black mustache. They wore torn shorts and T-shirts.

"Where you come from?"

"Nananu-i-Ra—over there."

"No. What country?"

"America."

"America is very rich."

I was unshaven. I felt ill. I had a collapsible boat. I slopped along in soggy reef shoes, wearing a baseball hat.

"You think I'm rich?"

They stared at me. They were among the poorest Fijians I had seen— they were dirty, their clothes were rags, several of them had teeth missing, which is not only a sign of poverty but suggests violence. Most of all I was wary of their rusty cutlasses.

I said, "Look at me. I am not rich. No money."

They were touching my boat, poking their fingers at its canvas and rubber hull. They could have chopped it—and me—to pieces in a few seconds.

"What are you doing with those knives?"

They did not answer.

"Cutting trees?"

They smiled, meaning no.

"Cutting coconuts?"

The stockiest and toughest and dirtiest one of them had done all the talking so far, and I guessed that only he knew English. Pidgin was not spoken here.

This grubby little man said, "You want coconuts?"

I said yes.

"You come."

Two walked in front of me, three walked behind, and once we were off the beach, walking through the dry yellow bush, the breeze was cut off and without a breeze it was very hot and buggy. There was no path, just the semblance of a track, littered with rubbish from the trees, dead boughs and piles of leaves.

I had not wanted to go with them, but somehow I had agreed. I had thought it would seem unfriendly, not to say cowardly, to refuse. And I had been curious—I had a fatal nosiness in places like this. This was in a sense the ultimate Fiji—the offshore island of an offshore island, where nothing grew except vegetables. No sugarcane, no tourists, no cars, no roads, no electricity. Just a heap of grassy hills burned black and still burning, because the people had nothing better to do. Like the Trobrianders, they called the big island that they could see "the Mainland."

These strange silent grubby men had a disconcerting habit. Whenever we passed a particularly shapely bush they assaulted it, and hacked it to pieces. Even before we had left the beach one of the men had attacked a mangrove, smashing his cutlasses against the frail branches, whipping at the leaves and the trunk—his nostrils flaring—and finally demolishing the tree, leaving the white slashed bits of it lying in the mud.

He had cut it for the sheer wicked hell of it, just like that, vandalized it, the way kids in big cities snap the trunks of saplings that have recently been planted.

I found that alarming, the suddenness of it, a filthy little man going to town on a tree with his rusty knife. It was nasty-mindedness, and a show of strength, and ill will. They weren't clearing a path or anything like that—it was just dicking around. But it also reminded me of that moment in the Melville story *Benito Cereno* when the mutineers smile and sharpen their knives—and come to think of it, these men looked malevolent enough to have been members of that mutinous crew.

I was dizzy from the heat, and it was odd to be with five other people when I was usually alone. This part of the island was penetrated with a smoky odor and I could see some of the burned hillsides—the burned areas looked much worse up close. The landscape looked devastated. It was as though they were simply destroying their island.

"Why do you burn the trees?"

"Yes, we burn the trees. We burn. We burn." The little man gestured with his knife.

We were well into the island now, walking across the lower slopes of the hills. I thought about turning back—inventing an excuse and taking off. That was when I saw the palms.

"There are the coconuts," I said.

This seemed to confuse them. It was as though they had forgotten why we had come here.

"Who will climb the tree?" I asked.

There was some mumbling.

"That boy will climb."

But the boy was hacking at a stunted tree, whacking its fragile trunk apart. He turned, he looked up, he spoke some words—mumble, mumble—in the sulkiest way.

I am not climbing that tree for anyone.

The stocky little man said something more, and the young man mumbled again and hacked the stunted tree with his cutlass.

If that white man wants a coconut he can climb the tree himself.

The funny thing was that I actually did want a coconut. I was thirsty, and I still felt faint. But we stood in silence in the heat. I tried to take a deep breath and realized that my lungs were congested. So I had creeping bronchitis. I wheezed and sat down. I hated this. I thought of the time in the Trobriands when I had had a paronychia—infection of my thumbnail—and I had had to boil my thumb twice a day to keep the infection down. And small children would gather round, watching me pump my stove, and fill my pot, and boil my thumb.

I put my head in my hands.

"No. We go."

It was another one, speaking English—a fat man, with teeth missing, slashing with his knife.

I said, "I can't go with you."

"Yes," he insisted.

"No. Because," and now I was thinking hard, "I want to bring you *yanggona.*"

They chewed their lips and smiled, recognizing the word.

"And my *yanggona* is at my boat. In my *waga,* see."

I pointed through the yellow bushes towards the shore.

"You give us?"

"Yes. I give you. But first"—and I was smiling in terror, like a hostage promising his ransom—"I have to get it for you."

I kept talking, promising, smiling, trying to sound reasonable—I had an irrational thought that as long as I kept talking they wouldn't kill me. It seemed rude and unsporting to stab someone to death while he was talking to you. Still, I felt uneasy with these men walking behind me, and the idiots kept whacking innocent trees.

I handed over a bunch of *yanggona* wrapped in *The Fiji Times,* and while they clawed it open, I untied my boat. One of them called out, "Come back!"

"I'll be right back!" I said, and climbed into my boat.

Sure, I thought. But I still felt rotten. Instead of heading away from the island I paddled towards its western tip, where there was a rocky headland. Near shore I heard someone mumbling, not to me, or about my approach; it was the monotonous yammering of someone talking to himself—just blabbing aimlessly. I kept going until, on an isolated beach, surrounded by rock, I found the sort of sheltered area that had the look of a campsite that fishing parties probably used. It was secluded, a cubbyhole against a cliff, with part of it open to the sea.

Thinking that hot liquid might be good for my cold, I boiled some water and made green tea and soup. After that I began to perspire. I lay down and went to sleep I was so tired.

When I woke, it was too late to go back. I carefully made a circuit of the perimeter of the little beach. I looked and listened for strangers. There was no one. And I knew no one would come out at night—no one wandered out in the dark here.

I waited until the last moment, sitting, listening carefully, and just before night fell and the mosquitoes swarmed, I pitched my tent and crawled in and slept for nine hours, waking just before dawn to the smell of burning and then I remembered that I was on Malake, island of arsonists. The sleep had restored me. I made more green tea, and had beans and bread for breakfast and set off around the other side of the island, to pass the settlement of Malake Village.

I paddled near it, but when I saw the ragged people waving me to shore, and the old men, and the small children, their faces shining with snot, I turned my boat to catch the incoming current that would take me east and away from here.

Farther on, feeling freer, I experienced something that had happened to me in the Trobriands, in the Solomons, in Vanuatu, and again and again in the offshore waters of Fiji. Paddling along, the sound of the paddle or the slosh of the boat would startle the fish, and they would leap from the water and skim across the waves, shimmying upright, balancing on their tails—more than one, often eight or ten fish dancing across my bow as I paddled towards a happy island. It entranced me whenever it happened, because it was comic and unexpected, as though the fish had been bewitched into unfish-like behavior, walking upright on the surface of the water.

But I had not been wrong about feeling unwell. Soon after, I ran a temperature of 103 and the doctor diagnosed pneumonia.

"Bloody Indians, what do they know?" a Fijian said.

I suffered for a few days, and then took antibiotics and simply felt frail and lonely, but after a few weeks I was breathing normally. Oceania was a wonderful place if you were healthy, but it was the worst place on earth if you felt sick.

Part Three

POLYNESIA

Chapter 14
TONGA: THE ROYAL ISLAND OF TONGATAPU

A big square-headed Tongan official in a blue skirt with a hem below his chunky knees, after asking me the usual questions about my boat bags, said, "You must pay wharfage."

Wharfage? He had to repeat it several times before I understood. And then I jibbed. Wharfage was payment for a boat's use of a wharf, surely, but my boat was in two canvas bags and where was the wharf?

We were standing in a wooden shed at the Fua'amotu Airport on the island of Tongatapu with other burly jostling Tongans, many of them wearing big crunchy mats around their waists to celebrate their arrival home. Some of them carried Desert Storm videos—the war so far—that they had bought in Fiji, from Indians who had pirated footage from CNN television news and then sold for sixty Fijian dollars each.

I told the man that it was a rather small collapsible boat, and I described it.

Ignoring me, he began to fill out a form which was headed *Kingdom of Tonga* and under "Description of Goods" he wrote *"1 boat"* and under "Wharfage" he wrote *"Two pa'anga, fourty cents."* Two dollars. That calmed me. I paid in Fiji dollars, the handiest cash I had.

Then I declared in my printed form that I had no "potable spirits . . . fruit or microorganisms . . . used bicycles . . . obscene books . . . indecent photographs . . . fireworks . . . noxious, stupefying or tear gas."

What struck me was how sturdy these Tongans were and what a filthy little place this terminal was. That contrast continued to puzzle me in Tonga, the physical power of the people—their big solid bodies, in great contrast to the decrepitude of their flimsy houses and island structures.

"What are you doing in Tonga?"

"Just looking around," I said. "A little paddling."

I want to see the king, I almost said. I intended eventually to go to the northern archipelago, called Vava'u, and camp on a desert island—there were many in that group. But what I wanted to do on this island was meet His Majesty, King Taufa'ahau Tupou IV, the king of Tonga.

Salesi and Afu Veikune and their friend, Mrs. Vahu, I was told, might be able to help me in my royal audience. Like many Tongans, Afu had spent some years as a house servant for a family in Honolulu. Salesi had been a driver for Budget Rent-a-Car—his sign read YOUR COURTEOUS DRIVER IS SALESI VEIKUNE. Mrs. Vahu had worked for Budget in San Francisco.

Menials and drivers, you would say. But that was in America. In Tonga they had royal connections. Afu, a mediocre cook, scorching eggs and Spam in Honolulu, had been the lady-in-waiting to the famous and much-loved Queen Salote of Tonga, the present king's mother. Afu's father was a *Tui,* a chief, and a considerable landowner. Their son had married a royal cousin. The king had come to the wedding. They were closely acquainted with princes and princesses. The present queen often visited their house. Never mind that in Hawaii one drove a bus and the other did housework; in Tonga they were highly regarded, they had land, they had power, and they owned more fat black pigs than I had ever seen snorting and oinking in one place.

"Maybe you talk to Mister Mo'ungaloa," Afu said. She did most of the talking. Even after many years in America, Salesi was uncomfortable speaking English. Perhaps that was a result of the occupational hazard of his work. DO NOT SPEAK TO THE DRIVER WHILE THE BUS IS MOVING, another of his signs had said.

"Who is Mister Mo'ungaloa?"

"The king's secretary."

"Putt dee no workeen now," Mrs. Vahu said. "Dee haveen lanch."

We were traveling at fifteen miles an hour along Taufa'ahau Road, the main thoroughfare of Nuku'alofa ("Abode of Love"). From the airport to the capital we passed twenty-seven Mormon churches—some of the villages had two of them. This was Polynesia for sure. The road was riddled with potholes, which accounted for our slow speed. No one drove fast anywhere in Tonga. The roads were appalling. The buildings were grim, too. You would look at this Royal Capital and probably sum up its stricken look by guessing, *Severe shortages.*

But this was not so. The place was unattended to and beneath notice. Islanders on Tongatapu were personally neat and tidy, though of a dour temperament, and they lived in a state of continuous disorder. Certainly, Nuku'alofa was in greater disrepair than any island capital I had seen since Honiara, back in the Solomons. Not long ago, perhaps at the time of King Tupou's coronation in 1967, this might have seemed a charming place, with its crumbling stucco churches, its wooden shops, its wooden Royal Palace—the only wooden palace on earth. It had lost whatever charm it had had. It seemed simply neglected, but like many neglected backwaters in the world it had the great virtue of very little traffic.

Nuku'alofa had no visible industry. It looked dusty and down-at-heel. Even its singular building the Royal Palace resembled nothing so much as a Christian church, wooden and white, with a bulky steeple and a prospect of the sea—indeed, Christianity came into full flower with the approval of the monarchy. Nothing locally made was for sale in Nuku'alofa except postage stamps. What money it had came from the remittances of Tongans in Meganesia—Auckland in particular—and in America, mainly Hawaii, where Tongans were employed as domestics, gardeners, car-washers, and tree-trimmers. Pretty stamps and family remittances were the standbys of other destitute countries in Oceania, such as the Philippines and Samoa, which produced immigrants.

Another source of revenue in Tonga—a bizarre one—has been the sale of Tongan passports. This was the brainchild of a Hong Kong Chinese man, one Mr. George Chen, who was asked by the Tongan king for advice on how to raise revenue. "Sell passports," Mr. Chen said, knowing that many would be sought after by Hong Kongers who watched with horror the approach of the People's Republic takeover of the colony in 1997. For $10,000, someone who was otherwise stateless could become a Tongan Protected Person (TPP) and carry a Tonga passport, which conferred the freedom to travel to any country in the world except Tonga, where a TPP was forbidden to settle.

When some countries considered these passports invalid the king was informed and a new model Tongan passport went on sale for $20,000 (or $35,000 for a family of four). This gave the holder Tongan nationality and a right to settle. South Africans and Libyans, as well as hundreds of Hong Kong Chinese, were quick to snap up these passports. Imelda Marcos bought one, and in the process became a Tongan citizen. In the past seven years this has produced $30 million for Tonga as well as a constitutional crisis—angry Tongans demonstrating their opposition to the sale of Tongan nationality, calling for the limitation of the king's powers (because His Royal Highness approved the whole thing) and demanding to know what happened to the money.

And another source of wealth was the returning Tongans, like Afu and Salesi, who had made a few dollars overseas, and who had come back to retire and sit under the trees and raise pigs.

"That is Queen Salote's grave," Afu said, pointing across a weedy field to what looked like a war memorial surrounded by a large iron fence.

Queen Salote (Tongan for Charlotte) had more or less upstaged Queen Elizabeth at her own coronation in 1953. It rained hard that day. Tongan custom insists that in order to show respect you must demonstrate humility, and you cannot imitate the person you are honoring. At the first sign of rain, Queen Elizabeth's footmen put the hood on her carriage as it rolled towards Westminster Abbey. Hoods were raised on the rest of the carriages in the procession—all but one, that of the Queen of Tonga. She sat, vast and saturated and majestic, her hair streaming with rain, in a carriage that was awash; and from that moment she earned the love and affection of every person in Britain.

Only one person mocked the queen of what had once been cannibal islands—Noel Coward. Queen Salote sat in the carriage with a tiny retainer. "Who is that person with the Queen of Tonga?" someone asked, and Coward quipped, "Her lunch."

"But what shall I tell Mr. Mo'ungaloa?"

"Tell him who you are," Afu said. "He wishes to check your background."

"What does he want to find in my background?"

"Nice tings," Mrs. Vahu said.

Salesi chuckled in a wheezing way at the thought of this. Did he know something? He was big and slow, and when he uttered a word, he was soft-spoken. He was fat and fifty-eight. As we wobbled through the holes in the road, the car jounced and the mat around his waist made crunching noises, like a cow chewing hay. I found the crunching of his waist mat oddly satisfying. Sometimes it sounded like a cookie being crumbled.

We went to a small red-roofed building in another weedy field. This was outside the high fence of the Royal Palace and was the secretary's office. We all entered the building together, and they were like parents on my first day at school. There was an open room with some desks and perhaps ten fat men in skirts sitting and bantering with one another in Tongan. You could almost determine a person's social status from his obesity—these chunky men were all nobles. They also wore layers of fraying mats around their midriffs.

Though they hardly knew me, Afu and Salesi and Mrs. Vahu energetically testified to my fine character, and at last Mr. Mo'ungaloa agreed to see me.

"Yes?"

Mr. Mo'ungaloa was a small bespectacled man in a cramped side office. It was an unprepossessing cubicle for the royal secretary, but perhaps no stranger than the outer office with its hooting fatties.

"You wish to see the king?"

"Very much," I said. And I went on to say that about fifteen years before I had met Crown Prince Tupou'toa in London. He was about my age. He had been to the Military Academy at Sandhurst. He played the piano. He had formed his own jazz combo called The Straight Bananas.

"Prince Tupou'toa is now the foreign minister," Mr. Mo'ungaloa said. He had winced at my innocent mention of The Straight Bananas.

The prince was unmarried and it was said that he could often be found in one of Nuku'alofa's clubs, an easy task to find him therefore, since there were not more than two clubs. His family was still pestering him for an heir.

A photograph of the prince showed him to be wearing a much larger size uniform than in his London days. There were also photographs of Queen Salote, and old Tongan kings—including the first Christian king George Tupou I (baptized in 1831), and of the British Royal Family. A framed letter from the president of the All-Japan Karate-Do stated in English and Japanese that King Taufa'ahau Tupou IV had been created an "Honorary 7th Dan" in Karate. There were other obsequious letters, and a friendly one from Betty herself, the Queen of England, in which she was described as Queen of the Realm and Defender of the Faith, and addressed to His Majesty.

"Sendeth Greeting! Our Good Friend!" this one began, which interested me as a salutation—so this was how one amiable monarch wrote to another. In this letter she was introducing the British high commissioner, praising his accomplishments, and wishing him well, and she signed off with a formula to the effect that it was 1970 *in the 17th Year of Our Reign* and ended, *Your Good Friend, Elizabeth R.*

Why frame that letter and not all the others she must have sent? But I didn't ask Mr. Mo'ungaloa. I was busily trying to impress him with my seriousness.

I wrote books, I said. I was traveling in the Pacific. Had he ever read the *National Geographic* magazine? I sometimes appeared in those pages. I was very interested in the peoples of Oceania—in their voyages (Mr. Mo'ungaloa stifled a yawn), and their arts and crafts. I had once been a university professor. Mr. Mo'ungaloa's eyes were glazing over. I had recently been to Fiji, I said, and before that, the Solomons.

"Which university do you teach at?"

"Used to teach," I said. "Oh, several."

"And you are presently working for?"

"I am unemployed at the moment," I said. "I mean, I write for a living, but I don't have a job. One with a salary, that is. This sounds much worse than it actually is."

But I thought: *An unemployed middle-aged foreigner in a sun-faded shirt shows up unannounced, claiming to be a writer, and asks to see the king.* If I had been the secretary I would have sent me away.

Incredibly, he said that the king would see me. What did I wish to discuss with His Majesty.

"Nuclear policy in the Pacific? Polynesian migration? The future of tourism?"

Mr. Mo'ungaloa seemed satisfied.

"The king will talk freely," he said, with confidence, and we settled on a date and time for my royal audience.

After they vouched for me at short notice, saying how well they knew me and what a splendid person I am, it seemed only right that we give some reality to this sudden fiction. I made an effort to know the Veikunes and Mrs. Vahu better. They told me that although they had spent many years in the United States they had always intended to return to Tonga.

Afu said, "We came back because Tonga is our home."

They showed me a picture of an Eskimo. He was dark, his cheeks gleamed, he was squinting out of a fur hood, he was wearing a thick parka, and snow and ice were crusted to the fence post just behind him. Was this Jerry Amlaqachapuk, an Inuit? No it was not.

"This is our son. He lives in Alaska," Afu said. "Ketchikan."

Salesi whispered, "It is very cold there. I no like."

Mrs. Vahu, who was only in her middle thirties and was chubby and very cheerful, had six children, ranging in age from three to fourteen. All the children had been born in the United States and had American passports, and yet Mrs. Vahu had decided to head home.

"I came here because I want my children to know *faka tonga,* the Tonga way. It is more expensive, and very little work. But it is better for them."

They were not unusual in their having returned. It was a proven fact that of all the islanders in the Pacific, Tongans found it hardest to adapt to other cultures—to the work, the stress, the deadlines, the moods and way of life—and a very high proportion returned to Tonga. They told horror stories about New Zealand and Australia and America to their relatives who had wisely stayed on the islands. Tonga was simply Tongans. Tonga had never been colonized or conquered, except in the profoundly ambiguous way that Christian missionaries managed. This involved preaching against evil and nakedness, and solemnly convincing people that they were sinners, their bodies were shameful, and generally encouraging the intense and rather joyous hypocrisy that you find among God-fearing people.

Tongans did not know the world, nor did the world know them. Even their king, one of the last absolute monarchs on earth, was known only as a very fat man—his weight was given whenever his name was mentioned. This made about as much sense as regarding the British Queen's small stature as important: "Five foot two inches high Queen Elizabeth," such a sentence might begin. There were few expatriates and hardly any tourists in these islands. The tourists who did visit saw that Nuku'alofa, the royal capital, was a backwater, just a small seedy town, and became visibly depressed. And seldom have I felt more unwelcome at a hotel than when checking into what is regarded as Nuku'alofa's best hotel, the International Dateline. (The smaller grubby places were full.) I carried my own bags, including my boat, although the lobby was thronged by able-bodied Tongan hotel staff. And when I asked for someone to show me to my room, the desk clerk snorted and pointed and said, "Up dey! Too-oh-tree! Turd flo!" as though to an imbecile. When I remarked on this to people who knew the place I was told that Tongans were renowned for their unhelpfulness, unless they knew you, in which case they made you one of the family. Yet one of the family was a condition I had no wish to enter into, here or anywhere.

There was little understanding of—and no interest in—the outer world, apart from the worst of its popular culture, rock music and violent videos (there was as yet no television in Tonga). Tongans regarded non-Tongans with a kind of pity and disdain, as though they were all sinners and suckers, and people who foolishly worked their heads off. Tongans had a reputation for thievery that exceeded even that of the light-fingered Samoans, but only in Tonga did I suffer serious theft—a rather nice pen, my Walkman, my three-hundred-dollar cowboy belt with the silver buckle. Towards each other, Tongans seemed to have more complex attitudes—different from anything I had seen so far. Quite early on in my travels in Tonga I found that Tongans regarded each other with a certain amount of envy and suspicion, and these were the only islands in Oceania where I discerned an attitude that I could describe as haughty.

"Honolulu was nice," Afu said. "Good work, good money. Plenty of Tongans there."

That seemed consistent: Tongans could not live or operate in a place where there were no other Tongans.

"But California," Mrs. Vahu said, heaving a sigh.

"You didn't like it?" I asked.

"Well, Los Angeles, sorry to say, is full of colored people," Mrs. Vahu said. "They just sitteen around. Watcheen you. Hey, you can get scared of them! You see them standeen. So many colored people!"

I guessed that the snobberies, the racial confusion and suspicion I detected in Tonga might have arisen because of the Tongan class system in which there was a king and nobles and an aristocracy at the top and landless peasants at the bottom. And when I inquired, Afu said that there was indeed a strict class system and each class had its own language. Royalty had its own language, and a Tongan fortunate enough to speak to the king had to use an archaic tongue, which was totally dissimilar from the language spoken by all Tongan commoners. In between, the nobles had their own language, which bore no resemblance to either of the other two languages.

"But can you tell a noble people when you see them?"

"We know them," Afu said. "And we also know their children. And when they have girlfriends, and those friends has children, we know who they are."

Afu went on to say that Tonga was full of noble—and in some cases royal—bastards. Some of the Tongan kings had had mistresses who had borne them children, and so there was an illegitimate line, much as there was in Europe, but unlike Europe these secret nobles occasionally became useful. If a nobleman had one child, a daughter, who was rather hopelessly single and there was a danger of the line dying out with her childlessness, one of these royal bastards would be rustled up—everyone would know that though his mother was common his antecedents were regal—and a marriage would be arranged. His children would inherit his father-in-law the nobleman's title, because this bastard's blood was noble enough—and everyone knew it. This was, after all, a small group of islands, with a total population of less than 100,000. Being noble could be a meal ticket. Among other things it could get you a seat in the king's rubber-stamp Legislative Assembly, half of which was noble and nonelective, chosen by other nobles.

The commoners tended to emigrate or else become Mormons, though this often amounted to the same thing.

"They think if they become Mormons they will go to America," a Tongan told me.

And it was true, many were sent to Salt Lake City to delve deeper into the sanctities of Mormonism. But the Mormons also looked after their flocks in Tonga and they took up a lot of social slack, built clinics and schools, as well as their interminable Latter Day Saints' churches, all of which looked like Dairy Queen franchises.

My audience with the king was still almost a week off, and so I tried to make the most of being in Nuku'alofa. It was the sleepiest, the dustiest, the slowest, and one of the poorest of the Pacific ports. Honiara was uglier, Port Moresby much more dangerous, Papeete tackier, and Apia more sluttish and decrepit, but there was something extraordinary and unmoveable about Tongan torpor—it was both regal and lazy. Some Tongans were friendly, but few were cooperative, and it was maddeningly difficult to make onward plans. Phones didn't work, offices were empty or locked when they should have been open, and in some places I was simply waved away—too much trouble, it seemed. It was a society that was used to dealing with beachcombers, who had all the time in the world.

I was trying to make arrangements to travel to Vava'u, a large archipelago about 170 miles north of this island, Tongatapu. There were fifty islands in the Vava'u group and many of them, I had been assured, were uninhabited. A boat left Nuku'alofa once a week for Vava'u.

"It is better you take plane," Salesi said.

"I want to catch the boat."

"Plane is better."

"I prefer the boat," I said.

"Boats make you seasick," Salesi said.

"I don't think so."

"I get sick every time."

That was a familiar refrain. In Polynesia I rarely met anyone who did not claim to get horribly seasick on a boat, no matter how short the trip. Even on the brief interisland ferry rides this race of ancient mariners puked their guts out.

Again I was surprised by the Tongans as physical specimens. The girls and women were the most attractive I had seen so far—not just winsome and willing, as Melanesians had been, barebreasted, with their shrieking laughter and their splayed feet, nudging you in the guts after each wisecrack or snatching with tough hard hands. These Tongans were elegant—it was something in their posture, in their features, many actually looked noble—a prince here, a princess there. Something in their very languor (a nice word for laziness, after all) was sensual. Of course, many were fat and jolly, the big soft women, the chunky web-footed men, each fat Tongan packed with Pacific Brand corned beef, with salt, fat, natural juices, and nitrites.

Men and women, old and young, walked slowly and very erect. Each person wore a mat tied around his or her waist, and some of these mats were no larger than a cummerbund, though some were enormous flaking carpets, crunched and wound clumsily around a person's midsection, making them look even fatter, and some of the mats twisted and dragged and frayed against the ground.

Nonetheless, in these days of preparation in Nuku'alofa, I could not remember having seen a people so bereft of enterprise, so slow of speech, so casual in manner, so indifferent to a schedule, so unable or unwilling to anticipate. Being inattentive, they were physically clumsy and had little manual dexterity. They dropped things, they forgot things, they broke promises. They drove slowly—who else in the world did that?

Salesi had a friend, Alipate. He had done Alipate a favor—something connected with land. By way of returning this favor to Salesi, Alipate looked after me for a while. Alipate was a wily bird, and rather unwilling. Sometimes after we agreed to meet, because I needed a ride—which he had offered—he didn't turn up. The concept of face-saving was nearly as important in Tonga as it was in China. I could not mention that he had let me down. I had to pretend to be grateful to him, and Salesi, for a favor neither of them had done me. In fact reneging on the promise had complicated things for me—I had had to get a taxi, not an easy matter in a place where phones seldom worked. I visited the sacred flying foxes of Kolovai—feathery casuarina trees draped with great shitting fruit bats—without Alipate's promised ride.

"We are going to be late," I said one day to Alipate.

We were on our way to the airline office. Since the boat wasn't going this week to Vava'u I would have to fly.

"Yes, but they will be late," Alipate said.

This was *faka tonga,* the Tongan way.

Desperate to involve myself, I took an interest in Tongan graves. These were not the ancient pyramids and terraces and stately mounds that I saw elsewhere in the Pacific, but rather small earth mounds ringed with beer bottles shoved into the dirt. Granny's grave, Mom's grave, little Taviti's grave. Some were in fenced-off plots, under large cloth canopies, with embroidered tapestries flapping in the wind—Jesus, the Last Supper, crosses. And underneath them, rows of Foster's Beer cans, arranged symmetrically; or red banners and bunting; or tinsel—Christmas decorations were popular on Tongan graves, and Christmas was a long way off. They were everywhere, by the roadside, in cemeteries filled with big flapping banners and the funereal beer bottles, and in the yards of little huts, the grave being an adjunct to the house. Some were strung with tassels, or plastic flowers, or bunches of yellow ribbon; some had bottles as well as beer cans on the periphery; some had wind chimes. Chinese funerals sometimes looked like this, but in a few days the ribbons were gone and the banners removed. In the case of Tonga the graves were everlastingly decorated.

Here and there was a tiny bungalow on a lawn, with windows, a little dwelling that you might mistake for a doghouse. But no, it was a mausoleum—there was a grave inside.

While I was out visiting graves, someone stole my pajama bottoms. I had moved to a different hotel in the meantime, but it seemed you were robbed wherever you went. (And isn't hotel-room theft the worst? The thief sees you leave the room and they have all the time in the world to take what they want.) I was fond of the pajama bottoms. The great thing about camping on islands was that you could wear your pajama bottoms all day.

I went to three tailor shops in Nuku'alofa and asked whether they could make me some more pajama bottoms. The women in these shops sat idly, propped against their sewing machines, not working. "We are too busy," was the excuse at one shop. At another: "We are making school uniforms." At the third: "Come back in a month."

But I persevered and found a willing woman and her assistant, a boy who in the Tongan way had been raised as a girl—because there were no girls in the family, and a girl was needed. He was known as a *fakaleiti* ("like a lady") and he was helpful—responsive, competent. He conferred with his boss, who did not speak English. Yes, he said, they could make two pairs of pajama bottoms in a few days, for twenty dollars.

I decided to suspend judgement on Tonga—I would not generalize from what I saw in Nuku'alofa, and I wrote in my diary: *Tonga is itself.* It had no investors, no immigrants, no history of occupation by foreigners. It had no desire to see strangers. Long-termers were actively discouraged. They did not even issue tourist visas to Fijian Indians (Fiji was only an hour away by jumbo jet) for fear they would stay and contaminate this Christian kingdom with Islam. I wondered whether there was another group of islands in the Pacific that was so much itself—one people, one language, one set of customs, one way.

Or was it changing? Viliami Ongosia, who lived in a lopsided hut outside Nuku'alofa, had once been a Methodist. But recently he had switched his allegiances to The Assembly of God. I asked him why. He said, "Because it has more spirit."

"Methodists drink and Methodists don't do what they say"—hypocrites, he implied, without using the word. These happy-clappy religions were gaining ground, and even the Jimmy Swaggart ministries had a following in Vanuatu, on the island of Efate. They sold videocassettes of Swaggart himself, the old whore-hopper preaching his head off, and of course they solicited funds.

Viliami, like Salesi, became so seasick that although his mother was from Vava'u and most of his relatives lived there, he never went to the islands—the boat was out of the question, and he couldn't afford the plane fare. He had sailed there once. He said, "I was so seasick I thought I was going to die. I could not hold my head up straight. It was terrible."

I liked hearing stories of Polynesian seasickness. It was like discovering people you had always regarded as cannibals to be vegetarians.

In fact, the Tongans had once been nearly as cannibalistic as the

Fijians, but unlike the Fijians, who gloried in their cannibal past, the Tongans made nothing of it and seemed to resent any mention of it.

One year, seeking work, Viliami had gone to Fiji. He found no work, though he had gotten on well with the Fijians.

"But the Fijians are Melanesians and you are a noble Polynesian," I said.

He smiled, he knew I was being sarcastic. He said, "I like them. They are good people."

"What about the Indians there?"

"I never talk to them. They just look at me, and I look at them. They know how to save money."

"How?"

"They carry their lunch to work. Just some curry. Never go to restaurants, never spend money."

"Tongans go to restaurants all the time, of course," I said, watching him closely. "Nuku'alofa is full of wonderful restaurants and delicious food."

He shrugged. "But we don't carry our food in a bag." And he explained, "We too lazy to cook at home. We don't care about saving money. But the Indians, they don't eat meat—no pig, no cow, no horse."

Vegetarianism was a way of saving money: It was not only a Tongan point of view. I had heard Fijians say as much. Vegetables were cheap. The expense in any of these island households was the meat supply. In a word, it was the high price of corned beef, imported from New Zealand. But if money was plentiful what these Tongans wanted was to get their teeth into a roast pig.

"And the Indians don't eat dogs," I said.

"Yes. No dog."

"And no fruit bats."

"Yes. No fruit bat." He smiled. "You like fruit bat?"

"Never ate one, Viliami."

"Taste good."

"I'm sure," I said. "In a soup?"

"No. *Umu.*" The underground oven had a similar name all over the Pacific.

"What about dogs? You stew them or *umu* them?"

"Always *umu*. I like to eat dogs but I don't like to look at it when they are cutting it. I don't want to see it. But it is all right in the oven. And I like to eat the dog meat."

We were at the seafront, on a bench, watching some young girls swimming. A group of boys were also watching. This being Tonga the girls swam and thrashed in the water with all their clothes on. It was unheard of—because it was sinful—for any girl to wear a bathing suit. And because wet clothes could be so revealing, the girls wore several layers—two shirts, two soggy skirts, trousers. They shrieked, mimicking suicide, and rolled off the pier, then thrashed and climbed back onto the pier, streaming with water, wearing every article of clothing known to man, and grinning with great big booby faces. It was a wonder they didn't drown.

After a while, Viliami, who had a strong Tongan accent, uttered an incomprehensible sentence.

"Tocks putt not gets."

Perhaps this was Tongan? No, what he meant was, *Dogs but not cats.*

"But does anyone in Tonga eat cats?"

"Plenty people in the bush eating cats. Not in Nuku'alofa, they don't eat," implying the enormous sophistication of not indulging in cat stew, "but in the bush, they do eat them and they say, 'We eat gets!' "

The Tongans talked about food a great deal of the time. I was sheltering in a doorway one night during a drenching rain on my way back to my hotel (where, because of the terrible service, I swore I would never eat). In this same doorway was a Tongan name Koli, a man of about thirty.

After a while he said, "Boll, you like Tonga girls?"

"Yes," I said. "Do you like American girls?"

He thought a moment, and then said, "No, I don't like."

The rain fell. The road was flooded. You could not walk—the potholes brimmed, the monsoon drain was clogged. The rain had brought darkness to Nuku'alofa.

"Boll."

"Yes?"

"You like Tonga food?"

"Do you mean dogs and cats and horses and fruit bats?"

"Everyting."

"I have not eaten much of that food."

"Boll. You come to my house. You eat Tonga food. My wife cook it."

"Maybe sometime," I said, and thought: Perhaps I have them wrong. Perhaps they are friendly and warm and hospitable. But I had never found them nasty—that wasn't the issue; I had found them unpredictable.

A Tongan Sunday was even deader than a Fijian Sunday. It began at midnight Saturday, when everything shut until Monday morning. At 5 A.M. on Sunday the church bells rang, and soon after a dirge-like harmonizing was heard from every Methodist chapel and every Free Wesleyan church. At 10 P.M. that same night the voices were still raised in song, in praise of the Lord. And once during the day. Tongans went to church three times on Sunday, and they roundly condemned anyone who failed to. If you wanted to go snorkeling or swimming you had to make arrangements to do it on an offshore island.

The Sabbath, an official government handout stated, *from midnight Saturday until midnight Sunday, is a day of rest in Tonga. The law says it 'shall be kept holy and no person shall practise his trade or profession, or conduct any commercial undertaking on the Sabbath.' Any agreement made or document witnessed on the Sabbath shall be counted null and void of no legal effect. Please do not date your cheques on a Sunday . . .*

No planes land or take off on a Tongan Sunday. No one is allowed to play games or to swim—Tongans are fined or given three months in jail for violating this law.

"Would it be appropriate for me to jog today?" an American asked—rather delicately I felt—at the hotel.

The answer was no: It was sacrilegious. If anyone was observed enjoying themselves on a Sunday there was hell to pay. Yet I never saw any evidence, in Tonga or elsewhere, that the Sabbath exertion of three church services, three sermons, umpteen hymns, and all those prayers made them better people the rest of the week. They were usually late, unapologetic, envious, abrupt, lazy, mocking, quarrelsome, and peculiarly sadistic to their children. On small islands where there were two different churches, the church members fought.

They claimed to observe the proprieties. It was, for example, unthinkable (and illegal) in Tonga to be without a shirt in a public place, and their crunchy waist mats were always neatly tied, and they constantly alluded to their loyalties towards *faka tonga,* the Tongan way. And yet they spat, they swore, they shouted, they razzed outsiders, they threw my change at me in shops, they seemed to consider it an indignity to carry anything for me, and certainly not my heavy bags.

"They often let air out of my tires," the captain of a sailboat told me. He was a New Zealander who had been in Nuku'alofa for a short time, and his present means of livelihood was ferrying people back and forth to the outer islands on Sundays. On these islands you could swim undisturbed. But the penalty for this was that he frequently came back to his van and found the tires flat. Who did it?

"Church people," he said.

They were the Tongan equivalent of the *mutawwaain,* the religious police of fanatic Arabia, who throw paint on unveiled women, and who once pushed my brother Peter into a mosque to pray because infidel horoscopes ("the evil work of credulous infidels") appeared in the pages of the newspaper he worked for in Riyadh.

Still waiting for the day of my audience with the king, I went on one of these Sunday day trips with Big Jim, skinny Dick, and their wives. They were from San Diego, California. Bob was retired from the auto parts business. We talked about the drought in southern California. I said that it was odd that the government did not supply water to every household. Jim said, "That's socialism!"

Why was it that Republicans traveled all over the world, shouting their views, and that it was so seldom that one found oneself listening to a fellow American deploring, say, capital punishment?

Dick was more reasonable. We talked about the Gulf War and skeet shooting.

As for their wives, "They love shelling. They're happy as long as they're shelling," Jim said.

Shelling was what a lot of people did on luxury vacations.

Jim, I discovered, simply liked to be blunt, if not downright crude. He was fairly stupid and rather prided himself on his vulgarity. Later, he walked by me while I was eating alone and slapped me on the back, jostling the plate on my lap, and said, "How do you like that mess?"

The only other people on this Sunday jaunt were Steve and Anne. We were talking about Japanese honeymooners in Hawaii, where they had just been, and Anne said, "Just like us."

They wore identical baseball hats that said *Oregon,* though they themselves were from Burbank, California. "They were a gift from a friend," Steve explained. They were a small-sized couple and seemed ill-at-ease— still getting acquainted with each other. Anne was the talker, Steve a self-confessed introvert. They had met at a community choir—they were both singers—on the 30th of October, 1989. By Christmas, Steve had marriage in mind. Anne took a bit longer to decide. It was more or less settled by March of the following year that they would marry. A year of seeing each other, as the expression goes, and they were married two weeks ago—two weddings, one small Saturday nuptial at a Russian Orthodox church (Anne: "I converted. I used to be a Methodist") and a big one, a hundred and fifty-odd people, on Sunday at Steve's Episcopal Church. Their community choir had sung at the service. Then early the next morning to Honolulu, two nights at the New Otani Hotel near Waikiki and—possibly a mistake, Steve felt—a luau at Germaine's.

"It was an hour-and-a-half bus ride," he explained in his gentle way. He had a high voice and was a small, sweet-tempered man. "The bus ride was more or less dominated by the other people."

"Who were they?"

"An Australian rugby team," he said, "and they were drunk."

"Good God," I said. And then, as he smiled, perhaps recalling the ordeal of listening to the rugby team's singing, I said, "What line of work are you in, Steve?"

He cleared his throat and adjusted his slightly-too-large baseball hat and said, "I'm a nuclear astrophysicist."

It said as much on his business card: *Stephen E. Kellog—Nuclear Astrophysicist,* a Pasadena address, a Caltech address (his lab), and a little quotation from Walt Whitman that ran, *I believe a leaf of grass is no less than the journey-work of the stars.*

"Is that a kind of motto for you?"

"Yes."

I said,

> *"To see a world in a grain of sand*
> *And a heaven in a wild flower,*
> *Hold infinity in the palm of your hand*
> *And eternity in an hour.*

"William Blake. That kind of thing?"

"I believe that, too."

"I speak French," Anne said. "In France I was taken to be a French person. That's how good my French was. I've got a good ear, I guess."

Jim from San Diego said, "I have trouble with English!"

This was the truth. He said *fillum* for film, for example. He said *nucular* for nuclear.

"What sort of nuclear astrophysics do you do?" I asked Steve. "Stephen Hawking generalizations about the nature of the universe? And by the way, did you hear that Hawking's wife has just left him? Amazing. The guy's a genius, slowly wasting away in a wheelchair, and she ups and leaves."

"Are you married?" Anne said.

"No. I upped and left," I said. "Kind of."

"Hawking is interested in the big questions," Steve said. "I deal with particles. Nuclei. But they contain what human life contains—helium, oxygen—"

"He told me that on our first date," Anne said.

I said, "You do research?"

"Yes." And he frowned. His hat was slightly crooked, his shirt hung out. "Mainly the nucleosynthesizing of tantalum-one-eighty."

I may have seemed a little slow—at least I had no immediate response to this.

"It's the rarest of the stable isotopes," he said.

"Of course."

"We were trying to find out how it was made." He smiled a scientist's smile. "We found out how it wasn't made."

"Tantalum-one-eighty?" I said.

"Yup."

Jim said, "Looks like rain, Dick."

After we reached the island, Atata, which was about eight miles off-shore, we went snorkeling. We had lunch. It rained. We looked in the gift shop. Postcards, T-shirts: *Tonga—Paradise in the Pacific.*

"Steve, do you have a necktie I can borrow?" I asked on the way back. "I have to meet the king."

"And you need a suit to see the king," Afu said, the night before my audience. Nor was she much impressed with Steve Kellog's dark Mormon-style tie. She said Salesi had better ones.

"I don't have a suit."

The virtue of traveling in the Pacific is that a suit and tie is never necessary. True, a tie is required in some restaurants but you can always be assured that the food in those places (always served by candlelight) is pretentious, saucy, overpriced, and strictly for honeymooners.

"But you have a lounge jacket."

"I don't have any jacket," I said. It was often ninety in the shade here.

"You try Salesi's jacket," Afu said.

Salesi was a short stout man. I am not a short stout man. The shiny ill-fitting jacket made me look like a bum. That odd jacket with the neatly knotted tie made me look like a mentally defective bum.

I tried on the tie and jacket for Afu's inspection. She was dissatisfied but resigned. I was staring at my reflection in a mirror.

"It is the best we can do," she said.

"I look like a Mormon," I said.

They had invited me to their house—"farm" was the word they would have used—for dinner. They had said dinner, but I did not see any food. We spent an hour or more drinking Kool-Aid and going through their son's wedding pictures, all seven albums. It had apparently been a very grand affair—great rolls of finely woven mats, and dead pigs everywhere. I remarked on the pigs.

"You want to see some pigs?" Salesi said.

We went outside. The pigs were active. I counted thirty-three porkers, big and small, under one tree. Some of them resembled the wild pigs I had seen on the Hopevale Aboriginal reserve on the Queensland coast—hairy, snouty, narrow-eared creatures.

"Yes. It is related to the wild pig," Salesi said.

"So what you've got here, really, is a kind of pig farm."

The pigs screeched and snuffled. They butted each other. They trotted from one patch of grass to another. They sucked dirty water out of puddles. They jostled, hoofing it in and out of the shed under the tree.

"Yes. You can say that. I eat them. I sell them."

"Do you kill them yourself?"

"Yes," Salesi said sadly. "But I don't like to. A pig can be your friend."

We were joined by Afu.

"They sleep in that shed?" I asked.

"Sometimes," Salesi said.

"That was our first house," Afu said.

It was a tiny wooden-plank hovel. They kept it, they said, to remind themselves of the days when they had been struggling. They had married against the wishes of their parents; their early married life had been made difficult by this disapproval.

"How did you meet?"

Afu said, "At the palace."

Salesi said, "I just sneak in and want to talk to her."

This was when Afu had been eighteen, the lady-in-waiting to Queen Salote.

"The queen was very cross when I marry Salesi. She did not know he was visiting me. I just say to her, 'I'm getting marry.' But she had another man picked out for me, with an education. And she had a girl picked for Salesi, a girl with an education—"

I got the idea of Queen Salote as a meddler, an arranger, a manipulator—and Afu confirmed this was so. She was after all an absolute monarch. She made a point of teaching Afu simple household chores—how to clean a room properly, how to dust shelves, how to sew, how to make dresses.

"She didn't think I would be happy," Afu said, and she beamed. "I wish she could see us. I wish she could see that we have been so happy."

Afu told me the coronation story, how Queen Salote had distinguished herself by showing respect for Queen Elizabeth.

"If someone has an umbrella you stand in the rain, to show respect," Afu said. "If someone is on a chair, you sit on the floor." Then she told me a detail that no one else had mentioned. Apparently there had been another foreign dignitary in the carriage—not "her lunch" but another head of state.

"He was from some country," Afu said. "He don't speak English good. He say, 'Up! Up!' He getting wet. But Queen Salote say no. He very cross!"

At last, quite late, we had dinner—chicken and taro and cassava and a delicious bowl of soupy greens, which were taro leaves cooked with coconut milk, a Samoan specialty called *palusami*. The chicken came from America. Most chicken eaten in the Pacific came from America—from Tyson's Chicken Farm in Arkansas, to be precise. Even on distant islands in the Marquesas, which are among the most remote islands on earth, they were cheaper than the local birds.

Afu was still talking about her years with Queen Salote, how she had traveled with her, how she knew her moods ("She pretended to be cross sometimes, so we would be frightened"). In New Zealand, the local people recognized the queen and waved to her. Afu had panicked. "Wave at the people, Afu!" Queen Salote had said sharply.

"So I wave," Afu said and put on a goofy, small-girl face and flapped her hand. "Hello! Hello!"

Before I left, Afu reminisced about how sorry she was that Queen Salote had not known what a happy marriage they had had. But Queen Salote had not been healthy. She had had diabetes. "She could not eat pigs." Yet she respected their families. Afu's elderly mother was coughing and spitting in a side room just off the dining room, where we were eating. And Salesi's father, Afu said, had real power.

"He is a chief. He owns land," Afu said. "He gives land to people, and then he does nothing. He finds a tree. He goes under it. He sleeps."

"People bring him food," Salesi said. "He does nothing."

"Is that good?" I asked.

"That is what I want," Salesi said.

That was what I kept noticing in Tonga, its traditional class system of nobles and commoners, of landlords and peasants. The first Europeans who had ventured into Tonga had remarked on this same stratification, and the way commoners tried hard to please the nobility, and usually failed. The nobility paid little attention. Why should they? Nothing would ever change. Even the Englishman of humble birth like Captain Cook, who knew the niceties and grovellings of the English class system, was astounded by Tongan servility and he remarked on how the commoners stooped to show respect and touched the sole of a chief's foot as the great man ambled past.

And soon it would be my turn.

Early on the morning of my royal audience I walked down to the palace, just to look at the flag. The king's standard was not flying on the flagpole, which meant he was not in the palace. I began to think that the audience was not going to happen.

Some Tongan soldiers were drilling with fake guns near the palace cannons. This was one of the most ragtag armies in the Pacific—not more than 200 men. By comparison, Fiji was a superpower—indeed, in the U.N. Peacekeeping Force, posted between the Israelis and the Palestinians, the Fijians had proven themselves courageous and resourceful soldiers. It was unimaginable that the Tongan army would be capable of anything even remotely similar.

I asked the drill sergeant about the king's flag. He said, "The king only comes to the palace on business. He lives at Fua'amotu, near the airport."

By the time I had changed into Salesi's jacket and Steve's Mormon tie, and walked back to the palace, the flag had gone up, though it did not fly. The flag drooped heavily on the pole in the windless, sticky heat.

Perspiring, I entered the office of the king's secretary and saw my name chalked on a board and after my name, *Author, former university professor*. I was shown to a waiting room, which was full of red plush chairs and dusty glass cases which contained labelled items and bizarre memorabilia. An old sextant, a rhino beetle encased in plastic, a cane—*The Walking Stick of King Taufa'ahau I (1797–1893)*, five feathers stuck into a crumbly piece of coral, *Worn by Queen Salote at the Coronation of Elizabeth II*, a silver-plated shovel, a black war club labelled *A War Stick*, photographs of bewildered-looking royal personages, and a jumbled heap of dirty shards: *Pottery pieces found at the hospital site of Haveluloto, 1969*.

That glass case was unlocked. Discovering this, I was seized with a desire to steal an artifact—anything—in revenge for the things that had been stolen from me in Tonga. As I jiggled the door sideways, fully intending to swipe something, I heard footsteps—heavy heels.

"Mr. Paul?"

It was an army officer.

"I am the king's aide-de-camp. Call me Joe. How do you pronounce your name?"

I told him.

"Because I have to announce you," he explained.

We walked through the tall grass and the weeds that lay outside the high palace fence, and we then squeezed between a pair of gates that were ajar and across through more tall grass, still wet with the morning dew.

The king's new Mercedes was parked in the portico out front. Joe led me past it to a ground-floor room on the right—with a buffet and a heavy refectory table, it had the look of having once been a dining room. It was strewn with gifts—an inscribed crystal punch bowl, a framed key, a toy Thai temple, a silver-plated telescope, a lamp with a label on it, a ceremonial dagger, a samurai sword, and a large framed photograph of Tonga's many islands, snapped from space, with a long laborious inscription and the signature of Ronald Reagan in ignorant wobbly handwriting.

A throne-like chair stood at the head of the table. Joe showed me to a chair next to it. I was surprised to see that the throne was the same height as my chair, because I had been told that I would be seated lower than the king, out of respect. I sat and practiced crouching to look humble.

There came a wheezing and a shuffling from the hallway. It was a bit like being in a well-furnished boardinghouse—it even looked and smelled like one, with wooden panels, varnished banisters and stairs, and armchairs with doilies.

In his black bombazine skirt, thumping along with canes, the king had the distinct appearance of a landlady, the same bossy authority and eccentric dress, his smocklike shirt buttoned to his neck and a great braided mass of cords around his belly. He had an aluminum cane in each fist, and in each breast pocket a pair of glasses, and a gold watch on each wrist—two of everything. But the details of his person were overwhelmed by the king's size.

One day in Suva, a settlement he called "the white folks' town," Mark Twain reached the conclusion that "in Fiji, as in the Sandwich Islands [Hawaii], native kings and chiefs are of much grander size and build than the commoners." And he might have added that it was true of Tonga— where it is still the case.

Whenever Tonga was mentioned, the king's weight figured. The guidebooks gave it importance: *The current king, Taufa'ahau Tupou IV, may be the world's most powerful (as well as largest!) reigning monarch . . .* Or: *. . . The King is known worldwide for his ample girth . . . (Lonely Planet Guide to Tonga)* Or: *The present monarch is a 1.9-meter, 22-stone* (308 pounds) *giant . . . (South Pacific Handbook).* Travel books also gave the king's weight when dealing with Tongan issues, for example, *Cruising in the Friendly Isles: The King of Tonga weighs 375 pounds . . .* Foreign newspapers described it: *The King—who once weighed in at 210 kilograms* (464 pounds) *. . . (South China Morning Post,* 31 March 1991).

His actual weight (and no one seemed to get it right) seemed irrelevant to me. He was vast, he was slow, an enormous shuffling man whose heavy-lidded eyes and whopper jaw gave him the huge froglike face you sometimes saw on ancient carved Polynesian tikis. A tiki is a statue, but Tiki is also a god—the greatest in Oceania. A suggestion of divinity is attached to the Tongan monarch, as it is to the British one. Tonga was a kingdom of big men, and this man was the biggest of all—you would have known instantly that he was the king. He also had presence. Superficially his bulk made him a bit of a caricature, a sort of Pacific island version of Jabba the Hutt from *The Empire Strikes Back.* But his size also gave him a mythic quality. I had never seen anyone so politically powerful who was at the same time so physically overwhelming.

Tongans could seem oddly inert creatures, and they smirked a great deal when you asked them questions; but the king possessed a monumental serenity, and he had a watchfulness about him—an intelligence and sensitivity—that I had not seen in any Tongan. Tongan silence was like the stillness of a lizard—a waiting to snatch at an insect. But the king's silence was not predatory like that. It was like a supreme indifference, as though he was a titanic spectator—impassive, perhaps wise. There was something oriental in his aloofness, in the detachment of his presence, and at times when we were speaking he seemed like a sultan or an emperor, an eastern potentate. Not the effete and inbred monarch of Europe, but a bigger, rougher version, the king of cannibals and coconuts, regal in a distinctly physical sense.

He put his big warm hand in mine and when he said, "Sit"—I heard it, though the sound was deformed by his jaw or his speech defect—the word stayed in his mouth.

"He is known for his long silences," an Australian expatriate in Nuku'alofa had told me the day before.

I was close enough to see that each of his wristwatches showed the same time.

To prove I was bona fide I had brought the king a book I had written. This I now handed him, telling him so. The king picked it up. His hands were big and plump, each one like a baseball mitt. His fingers were thick, his fingertips blunt—too blunt to assist him in separating pages. The book looked helpless in his hands, but neither could the king peruse it. It was too delicate a task for those fat royal fingers.

I made a short speech, saying how grateful I was that I had been welcomed so warmly in the kingdom.

Perhaps it was the false suggestion of monotony in his froggy eyes, but he seemed very bored by what I was saying. Minutes had passed and the only word I had heard the king utter so far was "Sit."

"In the 1890s," I went on, "the Hawaiian King Kalakaua had the idea of uniting the Pacific into a large federation of island nations—a great community of like-minded people. It never happened, of course. But does such an idea interest you, Your Majesty?"

And I immediately wondered whether I should have said *Your Highness* instead.

"I have already started," he said, "though it is not the whole Pacific. It is Polynesia."

I had been right about the speech defect—he had rather a slushy way with S's and with consonant clusters. He hardly opened his mouth. His words remained echoey in his mouth and some of them stuck to his tongue. It was a growly voice, exactly that of someone protesting as he swallows his mashed potatoes. Perhaps it was a dented palate? Certainly

there was little effort in the voice. It was languid and somewhat impre-
cise—not an accent but a difficulty enunciating—bobbling the words, and
snuffling whole sentences. Each time he spoke I made a desperate effort
to translate. Probably the greatest difficulty in his speech was that it had
no emotion in it. Emotion was superfluous to royal speech, anyway. He
had known the luxury of never having to persuade anyone of anything;
he spoke and was obeyed; he was the king.

"The chairman was a minister from the Cook Islands," the king said.
("Minister" had been a real mashed potato.) "But this man was voted out
in the last election, so I am taking charge."

"What is the aim of your Polynesia group? Is it political, Your Highness?"

"It is not political. How could it be? The Cook Islands is a republic.
Hawaii is a state. French Polynesia is a colony. Tonga is a monarchy.
There are too many differences. No, it will be concerned with culture and
society. With language and the arts." He took a deep breath. "We will
publish a magazine."

"And Melanesia is not a part of it, Your Majesty?"

He was silent. At last, without opening his mouth, he produced the
word *no* and it went on rumbling inside his body.

"Yet Ontong Java in the Solomons and Futuna in Vanuatu are inhabited by Polynesia people," I said.

"We will provide some pages for them in the magazine."

The king now seemed thoroughly bored and I thought for a moment
that he was going to send me away.

I said, "Your Majesty, will you deal with questions such as nuclear
testing?"

"That is a political matter—"

Not only did he not move his mouth, he did not move his head either,
nor his body. He simply sat, huge and immoveable, like a great lumpish
oracle or the sage in a children's story, the wise old giant of the cannibal
isles.

"—but nuclear testing in the Pacific is very bad."

There came one of his silences. It is a TV interviewing technique to say
nothing after a question is answered; then the interviewee often tries to
fill the silence by babbling, and often this is confessional stuff. I decided
to wait.

"I have been to Moruroa," the king said after a while. "I saw the holes
in the reef. They drilled down and put the bomb inside, and then filled the
hole with cement. They had made so many holes they had very little room
left on the reef to dig more. So they had started to dig into the bed of the
lagoon, which is of course very dangerous."

On the king's face was something like a smile, the sort of mirthful expression that beholds abject stupidity.

"Your Majesty, did you make your opinion known?"

"At the time I had no opinion," the king said.

"What is your opinion now, sir?"

"Nuclear testing must stop in the Pacific," the king said without any feeling, and in the same monotone he went on, "The French must leave. They import everything from France. It is ridiculous. Although it will be hard financially for the people of those islands, they must decolonize French Polynesia."

"Do you mean soon, or all in good time?"

"Soon," the king said. "Soon."

He was staring at me.

"The atom bombs can be tested elsewhere. Testing is needed. And bombs are needed to stop people like Hussein. To frighten him. He is like Hitler."

"Are you saying, Your Majesty, that they should use an atom bomb on Saddam Hussein?"

"They should put a bomb under him," the king said.

"And you trust the French to test their nuclear devices elsewhere in the world?"

"I don't trust the French at all!" he said, and saying so, he roared with laughter. It was so unexpected that I twitched with surprise.

Intending to exploit this sudden emotion, I said, "The French are usually self-interested, so they are—in foreign policy at any rate—insincere, unprincipled, and unreliable."

"Totally unreliable!" he roared and he laughed again. "I have been rereading the history of the Franco-Prussian War. Do you know how that war started?"

But it was a rhetorical question; he then summarized the events of 120 years ago that led to the outbreak of war, specifically the so-called Ems telegram sent by King William I of Prussia to his chancellor, Otto von Bismarck. After deliberately editing and publishing the telegram so as to offend the French government, Bismarck succeeded in outraging the French, who declared a war that the Germans wanted (and so did Napoleon III of France, to boost his sagging popularity). In the end the Germans won a humiliating victory over the French.

All this, and more, the King of Tonga told me of the Franco-Prussian War.

"So it was on that little detail of the telegram that the French started the war, which they lost," the king said.

"The French make a detail into a principle," I said, "but they are just as likely to make a principle or a murderous event into a detail. Look at the sinking of the *Rainbow Warrior* and the murder of the photographer on board by the French saboteurs in New Zealand. The French government said it was nothing—they regarded it as nothing. Yet if it had happened to them they might have used it as a pretext for a war."

"But New Zealand can't go to war with France," the king said. "There was nothing that New Zealand could do."

"No one went to bat for New Zealand, though," I said. "The British have a rather ambiguous attitude towards the French. They like the food, they feel somewhat intimidated by the French people."

"The English overlook the French weaknesses," the king said, "and so do your people in the United States."

"Since we are generalizing about national characteristics, what about the Japanese, Your Highness?"

"They are building a new terminal for us at the airport."

"Do they mention wanting to buy islands from you?"

"We will never give our land away," the king said. "That is the worst problem in Hawaii—the loss of land. It now belongs to other people, and the Hawaiians have so little left."

Another silence ensued; I simply listened to its drone.

"The Japanese work very hard," the king said. "It is strange—they think they are pure but they are not pure at all. Their culture is derived from the Chinese. Their language is full of foreign words."

He gave me the foreign derivations of *arrigato* and *tempura* and I gave him *kasteru* and *pagoda*.

"Would you like to see Tonga develop into a great tourist destination?"

"Already we receive many tourists—"

Twenty thousand a year—nothing.

"But when the terminal is in place there will be many more." He clasped his hands, making a great meaty pile of fingers on the table. "We will soon have three television stations. And oil. We have oil in Tonga."

"Oil, Your Highness?"

"Yes. I have seen it myself—gushing from the reef. We will soon have someone drilling."

And not a moment too soon: Fuel oil was very expensive in Tonga, and also very scarce. But this could not have been much more than a seep hole from an oil pocket under the reef—hardly a commercial proposition.

We returned to the subject of Polynesia, and I asked whether he felt an affinity with other Polynesians.

"I do. The Samoans are very close. My second son is married to a Samoan. And of course we have a common origin. There is a fellow here at our university who is from Sumatra, and he has told me that there is a village in Sumatra where the language is very similar to Tongan."

I said, "The Polynesians have a sense of having come from a distant place. The Fijians are muddled about that. The Melanesians I've met speak of having come from sharks and snakes and birds. Some people say they came out of the ground."

"We have a sense that our ancestors were voyagers and explorers, that is true."

"But of all the Polynesians you are the last absolute monarch, Your Highness."

He laughed his roaring laugh. "I am not an absolute monarch."

"With all respect, Your Highness, surely you are. In what way are you not?"

"I have a," he said and produced a mashed potato word. It stayed in his mouth, it had no echo, it was a swallowing sound.

"Excuse me, sir?"

He repeated the word three times. The word was *parliament*. But of course the assembly was no more than a rubber stamp, and half of it was appointed by his allies the Tongan nobles.

Soon after this I asked him whether he had committees that were looking into tourism and oil and television.

He said, "I am the committee!" and he laughed very hard.

"We always have a majority!"

Another laugh, and I of course obsequiously joined him.

"No dissenting voices!"

By any account, the King of Tonga is one of the few absolute monarchs in the world.

He asked me—it was his only question to me—whether I had any news of the Gulf War. I told him what I had heard on the BBC that morning.

The king said, "America could use this as a chance to put their resentment aside and make an ally of the Iranians. America needs allies in the Middle East. Iran is not the same country that humiliated America during the hostage crisis. They have a new government—a good one, I think."

"The Israelis tend to dominate our thinking on the Middle East," I said.

"America should be objective. And Israel has a big responsibility to be fair to the Palestinians. The Israelis should leave the occupied territories and stop killing Palestinians. Israel is strong and the Palestinians are weak. They are a problem because Israel has made them a problem."

We talked some more, about his children, about his liking for French food, about his exercise (he cycled up and down the runway at the airport—he was trying to get his weight down). He then lowered his massive head and said, "I have another appointment."

I scrambled to my feet and thanked him, and then Joe was summoned to lead me away across the weedy lawn.

* * *

A day or so later, Afu and Salesi killed and roasted a piglet in my honor and the burned creature was hacked apart and distributed to a number of Tongan men sitting under a mango tree. The women were under a different, smaller tree.

There was no beer. I drove with a man named Meti to the next village and bought a case. He said we would share it—that was the Tongan way. But he kept the beer in his car. I had three bottles, he had two, none was offered to the others, and in the end Meti went off with nineteen bottles of my beer.

"Me I don't drink beer," Alipate had said. He was stuffing his mouth with a pig's muscley bum. "I am a Methodist." And in almost the same breath he said, "You try any Tongan women?"

No, I said, I hadn't.

"I like *palangi* pussy," Alipate said, and rubbed pig fat from his mustache with the back of his fleshy fist.

"What a delicate fellow you are," I said. It annoyed me that this slob should say that to me. "I'll bet *palangi* women are devoted to you."

"I be careful! I got da wife! She cut da neck! She cut da ball!"

This word *palangi,* the euphemism for white person, was interesting. It meant "sky-burster." In the seventeenth century, Tongans and Samoans believed that their islands lay in a great and uncrossable ocean. The story of a long overseas migratory journey was conjectural in Tonga and absent in Samoa, where the local creation myth described how they had risen from a knot of twitching worms in the soil of their islands. So when the first Europeans appeared in this part of western Polynesia—Tasman in 1643, and later Roggeveen and Cook—the only possible way for them to have arrived was from the sky, exploding from the heavens.

It is one of the paradoxes of language as living culture that a vulgar man like Alipate used this poetic and allusive expression all the time—there was no other word for white person except "sky-burster." Alipate was a stonemason. He frequently boasted of the money he had made laying bricks in Hawaii. He liked hoisting his shirt and cooling his belly with the night breeze, and talking about women he had had, or money he had made.

"What you talkeen to da king?" he asked me. His T-shirt was hoisted. His brown hairy belly glistened with sweat.

"He told me you're going to have television."

"In his dreams," Alipate said. He translated this into Tongan and everyone laughed. "Da king all the time dreameen."

They mocked the king for a while. They were like a different race of people altogether. Socially they were another species. A little over a hundred years ago such Tongans had been slaves—King George Tupou I had abolished slavery in Tonga. Alipate saw that I had not touched the clutch of pig ribs on my plate and without saying a word he reached over and snatched it, and when he finished chewing it he went on cooling his belly and jeered at the king some more.

Chapter 15
TONGA: ALONE ON THE DESERT ISLANDS OF VAVA'U

In the way that tardy and negligent people are often blame-shifting and chronically mendacious, many of the Tongans I met in Nuku'alofa were unreliable, and some outright liars—or, to put it charitably, they meant very little of what they said. This could be tiresome in a hot climate. My solution was to take my boat to a part of Tonga where there were no Tongans.

I resolved that I would find a desert island in the middle of nowhere and live a beach-combing life for a while. My ideal island would have a sandy beach, and coconuts, and jungle, and no people. About fifty islands, remote and empty, fitted this description, and they lay in Tonga's northern archipelago, called the Vava'u Group. I knew somehow that there would be fruit bats. There were bats on every Tongan island. It was said that these islands were among the most beautiful in the Pacific, and many of them were desert islands, utterly uninhabited but pristine—dream islands, each one like a little world.

"The trouble is," a Tongan on the small plane to Vava'u told me, "you'll have to find someone to take you out to the islands."

I did not tell him about my boat, that I could assemble it and paddle to any island, and that I had a nautical chart of the whole group, and survival gear.

This man, Aleki, had with him a videocassette of the Gulf War that had been taped four days before from news footage shown in New Zealand. The war was still being fought, but the Tongan interest in this sort of footage was not very different from their interest in *Rambo* videos. Aleki gave me his address and said that if I cared to, I was welcome to come over to his house in Neiafu—Vava'u's main town—and watch the video of American planes raining bombs down on Iraq and Kuwait. This seemed hospitable enough, though I did not take him up on his offer.

Everything about the Vava'u Group pleased me—the islands were not far apart, there were plenty of sandy beaches on them, there were stores in Neiafu where I could stock up on food, and although it was windy I could paddle in the lee of a long chain of islands and stay out of trouble. Most of all, the Tongans on the main island in Vava'u seemed friendly. If they had airs the airs were different from those I had had to contend with in Nuku'alofa. This was not a place of nobles and landlords and peasants, but of hard-pressed islanders—apparently one class—who managed by fishing and farming. Most of the Tongans I met in Vava'u said they hated Nuku'alofa—"The fast life, the noise, the always hurry-hurry," one named Siole said, summing up the Vava'u objections to the royal city. Though I hardly recognized this frenzied Nuku'alofa of their description—it had seemed to me a place without any events, except for church services and the occasional funeral or coronation—I came to see that, by comparison with Neiafu, which was very nearly fossilized, semi-moribund Nuku'alofa could seem a trifle hectic.

Siole (Tongan for Joel) had a car, a prized possession in Neiafu, where there were never more than two or three in sight—people tramped the dirt roads of the main island confident that they would never be run down. Siole also had gas, and this was amazing, because there had been no fuel at all in Vava'u for almost a week. No one knew when the next shipment would arrive. Everyone blamed the delay on the Gulf War, which was probably not the reason, though the Gulf War was certainly to blame for the high price—about six dollars a gallon, and rising.

In his old car, Siole took me to the market and the stores, so that I could buy provisions.

We passed a fat pig—very fat, perhaps hundreds of pounds.

"What is a pig like that worth, Siole?"

"Six or seven hundred." He meant *pa'anga,* and this amounted to about five hundred dollars.

"How would you eat it?"

"At a feast. Maybe a funeral," Siole said.

"Only when someone dies you eat it?"

"If someone, say your mother, gets bad sick, you feed your pig a lot of food. Get him fat."

"Because you might need him for your mother's funeral?"

"Right."

I could just imagine a sick Tongan's sense of doom when he or she looked out the hut window and saw the family pig being fattened.

"Also your horse."

"To be in the funeral procession?"

"Not the procession but the feast. We eat the horses."

He was driving slowly along the dirt road of the main street—slowly, to avoid flattening a dog that was sleeping in the patch of shade thrown down by the leafy bough of a tree.

"What about them—you eat dogs?"

"Yes."

"You eat flying foxes—fruit bats?"

"Yes."

"How do you cook them?"

"Pigs, horses, and dogs we put in the *umu* oven. It makes the meat very soft. But flying foxes we can just barbecue."

It seemed to be a general rule on Pacific Islands that there were few, if any, food taboos. Wherever I went I asked about diet, and except for the Seventh Day Adventists in Kaisiga Village in the Trobriands, no one was very fussy. In Oceania you ate every living thing that fitted into your mouth.

Dogs had been cooked and eaten in the Pacific from the moment the Pacific was inhabited. The dogs had come in the canoes of the voyagers from Southeast Asia (where they were—and still are—also eaten). There was no game to be found on the Pacific islands, and so the dog was prized—for its taste, its food value, its scarcity (pigs greatly outnumbered dogs). Its fur was used for decoration, its skin was turned into articles of clothing, its teeth into necklaces and ornaments, its bones into implements—hooks and needles. On various islands, Hawaii in particular, dogs were fed with vegetables or *poi*—thus the term "poi-dog" still current—to sweeten their flesh, and some were breast-fed by women. Gobbling the leftover sweet potatoes or scraps of greens, snuffling in the undergrowth for an edible root, most of the dogs and cats I saw on my Pacific travels seemed to be vegetarian.

All the early European explorers in Oceania mentioned dog-eating. These men had come from societies in which dogs had status as sympathetic companions with precise personal names—in Claude Lévi-Strauss's description, "metonymical humans." Invited to feast on dog meat in eighteenth-century Hawaii—the Sandwich Islands—a scandalized Englishman wrote, "The idea of eating so faithful an animal as a dog prevented any of us joining in this part of the feast." He added, "Although to do the meat justice, it really looked very well when roasted." Some tried eating dogs—Georg Forster, the German scientist and chronicler who accompanied Captain Cook, said dog meat was indistinguishable from mutton. On one occasion in the last century a group of Hawaiian jokesters served up a dog with a pig's head replacing the head of the mutt, in order to fool the American visitors who happily devoured the animal. In the Pacific, a dog might be a household pet but never the sort of companion that possessed an implied taboo against its being eaten.

In *Man and the Natural World,* the Oxford historian Keith Thomas lists three features that distinguish eighteenth-century pets in England ("privileged species") from other animals: they were encouraged to enter houses and churches; they were given individual personal names; and they were never eaten—"Not for gastronomic reasons . . . it was the social position of the animal as much as its diet which created the prohibition." In 1616, the first Dutchmen to reach the Tuamotus, Le Maire and Schouten, who had earlier named Cape Horn, called one island Honden, because of its dogs, and they noted that the dogs caught and ate fish and were themselves on the menu and did not bark.

None of these early dogs barked. This was also remarked upon by European visitors. Apparently, wild dogs never bark—they howl and whimper, as dingoes in Australia do—but only the domesticated dog goes woof-woof.

Right here in Vava'u, a young English castaway (fifteen years old when he first arrived), William Mariner, was adopted by a Haapai chief, Finou 'Ulukalala the First, and went native. He lived in Tonga from 1806 until 1810. Much of what we know about early life in Tonga comes from a detailed account of his adventures taken down by a London physician and published in 1820. In this book he remarks on his benefactor Finou's love of cooked dog meat,

> but he ordered it to be called pork, because
> women and many men had a degree of abhor-
> rence at this sort of diet. The parts of the dog in
> most esteem are the neck and hinder quarters.
> The animal is killed by blows on the head, and
> cooked in the same manner as a hog.

My new pal Siole agreed that dog meat was delicious. He was a friendly fellow—relaxed, and helpful, and not rapacious. I needed to buy food, and then to find a place to stay the night and launch my boat. We had struck a simple bargain—for ten dollars he would ferry me around the small rambling town. He took me to the Oceanic provisioners—Burns Philp, Morris Hedstrom—and then to the market, where I bought a basket of small pineapples. Because there was no gas in town I bought kerosene for my camp stove. All this took an hour or more, but Siole did not complain, not even when the rude Tongan woman at the hotel said, "Your taxi driver can carry your bags."

The hard part about arriving in such a place, with little prior information, was that I did not know what the hazards were—the winds, the reefs, the shoals, the tides, the currents, the unfriendly villages, the bad beaches, the creatures—if any. Some hazards were obvious—the pounding surf, the frothing chop of a channel that looked like a river in spate; others might not be apparent until it was too late. I always remembered those awful boys in the Trobriands who shook spears at me and said, "Run you life, *dim-dim!*" or the island of arsonists in Fiji. I made a point of bringing detailed maps and charts. I often had a guidebook. But there was no substitute for local knowledge.

So I was lucky in meeting Leonati, a sturdy Tongan who was also a diver and a fisherman. He watched me put my boat together beside the little pier, under the limestone cliff where my hotel was situated.

"How much water do you draw?"

"A few inches," I said, unrolling my chart.

"Why not go this way?" he said, and put his finger on a tiny break between two islands on my chart. I would not have seen it had he not pointed it out.

"I was thinking of going this way out of the harbor," I said, and showed him my proposed route through the Port of Refuge, named by Don Francisco Mourelle, the Spanish discoverer of this place, in 1781.

Leonati made a face and said, "It's all villages there."

He was the first person I met not just in Tonga but the whole of Oceania so far who had said anything like that.

"This island is empty," he said, and circled a small island. "And this one—no people there. This one is small but very beautiful. And this one"—he tapped another—"paddle there and the wind will take you back."

Everyone else had said: Make for the villages. I liked Leonati, the only loner I had come across. He said he sometimes took his own boat out and camped on those islands.

"Who owns them?"

He shrugged.

"No one will bother you," he said.

It was a hot and steamy morning in the Port of Refuge, and the yellow light of early dawn slanted through the haze, hanging like smoky vapor on the water, where thirty sailing yachts lay at anchor, their wet laundry drooping where their sails should have been. I was stowing gear in my little boat and swatting mosquitoes that had been vitalized by the humid heat. The mosquitoes frisked around my ears.

It had rained hard in the night, and when I commented on this to an American on the pier coiling a line, he said, "Of course," and seemed surprised that I had bothered to mention it. This was after all the hurricane season—and it was also why there were yachts in the harbor. Most of them had come in November and they would remain moored there until April, when the weather moderated. No one sailed the South Pacific in this dangerous weather.

"I used to work on Cape Cod," the man said, when I told him where I was from. "Camp Seascape in Brewster. It was a summer camp for fat girls. I helped run it." He became reflective, as though he had not thought about this for years. "The average weight loss was twenty pounds."

He drifted away, while I finished loading my boat. My heaviest single item was water, because I was not sure whether fresh water would be available on my desert island. I carried it in two- and three-gallon bags, a week's supply, which I stuffed under the bulkheads, with my waterproof bags containing food, my dry clothes, my stove, my pots, my tent. On the deck, in a plastic holder, I had my map of the whole archipelago, and a water bottle, and a compass. Close to hand I had emergency flares.

I had given my life jacket to the old Kula man, Meia, in the Trobriands. I had swapped my spear in the Solomons. The last of my fishing gear I had handed out in Vanuatu. My Walkman had been stolen in Nuku'alofa. I had broken my spare paddle. I was now so worried about having only one canoe paddle that I usually put on a leash, a line running from its shaft to the deck. It was not theft that I feared but rather the thing being blown out of my hands by a strong wind.

Unnoticed, I slipped away from the shore and paddled south along the inside of the harbor, which was walled by high cliffs and surmounted by tall wet trees. Small boys were jumping from the black rocks, swimming in the early morning. About a mile farther on was a narrow break in this jungly wall, just a slice of air, with birds squawking and flitting on the steep green sides, and water so shallow that the bottom of my boat rubbed against the rocks. This was Leonati's suggested shortcut, Ahanga Passage.

Once I was through it I was in the wind and waves, and I saw surf breaking out on the reef and in the distance a chain of islands. I used my map to keep to the deeper parts of this bay, and paddled out far enough so that I could identify the islands. There were islands everywhere—close to me and on the horizon at various distances, and I knew from what Leonati had told me that most of them were uninhabited. Just to keep my bearings I headed for one called Tapana Island.

I chose that island because it was distinctly noted on my chart. There were islands in this archipelago that were not on it. Fafini and Fanua Tapu, shown as insignificant reefs, were a pair of high, hefty islands. My chart had been drawn "from a British survey in 1898"—but was it possible that islands could form and grow in just under a hundred years?

The wind was blowing about ten to fifteen knots, brisk and steady enough to whip up the waves and give them frothy peaks. With only one paddle I worried that it might be blown out of my hands, so I dug out my line and tied it on, as a tether, and I put on the secure storm spraydeck, so that I was completely watertight. This was just as well, because I could see in the distance billowy black clouds, and long gray curtains of rain.

The rain crept nearer and was soon on me, and I was paddling among the faint outlines of islands in a heavy downpour.

Leonati had said, "We had a drought until December, but it has been raining ever since—"

It was no fun paddling in the rain, but the worst of it was the possibility of losing my bearings. Now, in the heaviest rain, a solid sheet of slashing water, all the islands were eclipsed. It was as though I were paddling beneath a waterfall, like the *Maid of the Mist* under Niagara. I used my compass to get to Tapana—following the needle until the gray island emerged. There was no shelter, no beach, only cliffs, so I headed through the crackling rain to a nearby island that I could just discern among the flailing drops of rain. This was Lautala, which Leonati had told me was deserted. It was, but there was no beach, I had no way of landing.

Each island in Vava'u is a limestone block that has been pounded into a dangerous and unapproachable shape by the waves and wind, giving the island straight sides, spikes and crags, a ten-foot wall of sharp stone around most of its edge. But on some the wave action had pushed sand behind them—I could see sandy beaches at the backs of other islands farther into the archipelago.

I found a little cleft at the side of Lautala where I sheltered, with water dripping from the peak of my hat. And sitting there miserably dripping I was approached by curious birds—brown noddies that looked like dark terns, and big fearless shearwaters.

Trying to spot these birds with my binoculars I looked around, into the rain, and saw two canoes—four men in each—making directly for me, or perhaps for the island: I would soon find out.

The canoes were ten-foot dugouts with outriggers—vessels for paddling rather than sailing—and experts said they were "the only surviving seacraft of indigenous origin in Tonga." I usually made sketches of the dugouts on particular islands—and I noted the islands where canoeing and canoe-making had been abandoned. These Tongan canoes had a feature I had never seen before—the outrigger attachment (securing the outrigger float to the booms extended from the dugout) was U-shaped. I had never seen this before—all other canoe-makers used a V-shaped attachment, or just a pair of lashed struts. It may seem a small thing, but after seeing so many canoes made in much the same way, this difference, and especially such an elegant object, appeared remarkable to me. And

Tonga was a place where no one carved with any precision or troubled themselves to make anything substantial in a traditional way.

When the canoes drew up beside me—they too were sheltering from the sudden storm—I said hello and pointed to the well-made fixture. What was its name?

The men laughed. One mumbled something—mockery, I was sure; *fucking palangi,* something like that—and the other men laughed again.

The rain came down. I asked how they had bent the wood into this U shape. They shrugged, they mumbled again, more laughter.

You think: They don't speak English. But I was sure they did—most people in Tonga did; and Vava'u with its influx of *palangis* in yachts was even more English-speaking than the main island, Tongatapu. Along with the precepts from the Golden Tablets, Mormons also taught volleyball and English to all the islanders they converted.

"Are you fishing?" I asked plainly.

"Yes," one said, and turned his back on me.

This is not necessarily a hostile gesture, but considering that we were sheltering from a heavy rainstorm at the edge of a remote, deserted island in the distant Tongan archipelago of Vava'u—miles from anywhere—it seemed a trifle unfriendly from an inhabitant of The Friendly Isles.

They had no interest whatsoever in me, nor in my reactions to the storm—they did not inquire (islanders sometimes did) as to whether I was okay, or my boat was leaking, or the waves were too high for me. They talked among themselves. They were incurious, indifferent, probably mocking—because I was alone, and a *palangi,* and posed no threat to them. Had I been big and dangerous, or well connected, they would have grovelled and paid fond attention to my butt, exclaiming upon how the sun shone radiantly out of it.

We sat bobbing in the heavy rain, saying nothing to each other, though they muttered obscurely to themselves from time to time. My consolation was that if they posed a threat to me (Tongans had a reputation for violence) I could quite easily outpaddle them—my light kayak was by far faster than their clumsy outrigger canoe.

"Up yours," I said to them, smiling, when the rain eased, and I paddled away.

Later I found out that Vava'u was the only place in the Pacific where this lovely outrigger attachment existed and that it was called a *tukituki.*

I headed across a two-mile stretch of water for a crescent-shaped island which, when I came close, turned out to be two distinct islets joined by a spit of sand: Taunga, where there was a village, and Ngau, which was uninhabited. Beyond it, according to my map, was another uninhabited island, named Pau.

As I approached Pau, two fat fruit bats flew erratically overhead, making for the island. And now I could see through the gently falling rain that the island was small, uninhabited, jungly, and had a narrow sandy beach on its protected western side. It was just what I was looking for. It had another pleasant feature—a grove of coconut palms only eight or nine feet tall, with clusters of green coconuts on top, each nut containing the best drink in the world.

I paddled to the beach and pulled my boat above the tidemark, but before I could locate a campsite the rain increased, pouring straight down, the heaviness of its fat, stinging drops making it fall vertically. I found a large green leaf and put it on my head, and there I stood, dripping under a dripping tree, watching the black sky, the churning sea, listening to the deafening tattoo of the rain, and feeling miserable.

Two hours passed in this way, very slowly. To add to my discomfort, clouds of mosquitoes, loving this cool rain-sodden thicket, emerged and began to bite me all over. I had insect repellent but it made no sense—and it was ineffective—to spray it on while I was standing in the rain.

The nearby islands had disappeared in the rain and mist. I was on a tiny corner of Pau Island. There was nowhere to walk to: Ahead was a wall of jungle, dense with thorn bushes; behind me was the sea. I stood on a strip of land, with that silly leaf on my head, and began to shiver.

To whip up my circulation I took my paddle and cleared the branches and rubbish—and spiders—from the area around me. I awaited a break in the rain, so that I could unpack my boat and put up my tent without getting everything wet.

When the rain eased, I hurriedly set up camp, stuffing the items that needed to be dry (clothes, sleeping bag, radio) into the tent, and hanging up the food sack and the water bag. Then I took off my wet bathing suit and T-shirt and got into the tent naked and warmed myself in my sleeping bag, until the raindrops ceased to patter on my tent.

I had had no lunch. I had planned to eat on the water, but those unfriendly fishermen had prevented me from eating at that halfway point on Lautala Island. I unpacked my stove, intending to light it to boil water for noodles. But my matches were wet, my lighter wouldn't spark. I began to curse out loud—after all, this was my island.

It would be impossible for me to live on this island for a week or more without matches, and I remembered the village I had seen on Taunga. I got into my boat and paddled two miles to that village, which was a pleasant place—about fifteen simple houses at the sloping edge of a pretty cove. Two motorboats were drawn up to the Taunga beach, giving the place a look of prosperity. But there was no one in sight.

I walked to the nearest house, where, just inside the front door, an enormously fat woman was weaving a mat from pandanus fronds. Her skirt was hiked up and I could see that her vast thighs were gray and dimpled, and hideously bitten, with many open sores on her legs—perhaps from her scratching them. She was a woman of about sixty and her name was Sapeli.

"Is there a store on this island?" I asked, knowing there could not possibly be.

"Nudding," she said.

"Do you have any matches?"

Without a word, and without rising, she reached to a shelf and picked up a matchbox, removed half the matches in it, and handed the box to me.

She called out, "Lini!"

A group of children, led by two pretty girls, emerged from a nearby house.

The oldest girl introduced herself as Lini Faletau.

"Faletau means 'house-something,' " I said.

"House-war," she said. "People fighting in the house."

"A delightful name."

Since I had paddled all the way there I thought I might as well ask permission to camp on Pau, which—being so near by Vava'u standards—was probably their island. Lini said the chief was in Nuku'alofa, but we could ask someone else.

We traipsed into the bush—girls in front, kids in back, me in the middle—and along the path encountered barking dogs which tagged along, howling and snapping at my bare legs.

"Please eat those dogs," I said.

Lini laughed. She was seventeen. Her sister Deso was fourteen, but taller, with a long elegant face and a slender body and a guffawing way of laughing—deep in her throat. Deso's looks reminded me that the prettiest women I had seen in the Pacific had been here in Tonga; the loveliest, and also the ugliest—fat, hairy things with bad skin. And many of the men were hulking and horrible.

After a fifteen-minute walk through the wet grass we came to a house. Like the others it was a simple box, with a porch and a flat roof. A woman inside was weaving a mat—the room was strewn with dead palm leaves. I said hello. The woman looked at me in an uncertain manner.

"Ask her if I can sleep on Pau Island."

This request was conveyed.

"She says yes."

"Who is this woman?"

"She is my wife," Lini said.

Deso gave one of her deep attractive laughs.

"Your mother surely?"

"My mudda."

"Thank her for me, and tell her that I have brought a present for her from the United States."

I gave her a silk scarf. I had given Sapeli one, too. I never entered a village, no matter how suddenly or how small, without bringing a bag of presents—usually these scarves.

Deso began to bawl out one of the little kids. It was a small boy, who began to cry. Tongans could be very fierce with one another—screeching and scolding.

On our walk back to the beach we were joined by an obviously effeminate young man, possibly a *fakaleiti,* who demanded a scarf. He asked me my name, and then I asked him his.

"My name is Russell Go-For-Broke."

"Liar!" Deso shouted at him. "Your name is Ofa."

"But I changed it. Because of Cyndi Lauper."

I had no idea what he was talking about. He had a lisping voice and a coquettish manner and he asked me to stay awhile.

"I'll come back sometime," I said. "You have a nice village."

The beachfront and the boundaries of the village were lined with the bleached valves of the giant Tongan clam.

"The Queen of Tonga came here on December second," he said.

The queen and king had spent Christmas at their house in Neiafu—the queen was a native of Vava'u.

"Did the queen stay long?"

"Two days," Lini said.

This surprised me. They pointed out the house in which she had stayed. It was a simple place, and it reminded me how Marie Antoinette of France had dressed up as a shepherdess and danced with peasants.

"What did you do for her?"

"We danced. We sang."

"Did she enjoy herself?"

"Yes. She went swimming."

The seventy-year-old monarch had swum in this little lagoon.

"Did you see her?"

"We swam with her!"

"What did the queen's bathing suit look like?" I asked.

"She wore a Tongan cloth wrapped around her."

"The Queen of England would never swim with English people at the beach," I said.

"The Queen of Tonga is very kind."

I gave them more of my silk scarves. They did not take much interest in them. One knotted hers around a small girl's head.

"I am called Russell Go-For-Broke because I always go for broke."

"But his name is Ofa."

"Shut up." Seeing me launching my boat, he said, "Please come back. We will give you a present. Maybe a shell."

Lini said, "Bye for now."

Russell said, "Goodbye for now but not forever." He repeated this, and then he said, "Are you going back to fight for the freedom of Kuwait?"

This they found hilarious, and with their laughter ringing in my ears I went back to my own island and cooked my dinner while it was still light. But more rain drove me inside and the whole black night was filled with dripping and blowing.

The rain continued for the next two or three days, sometimes very heavy and just as often a light drizzle. Before the hard rain fell on me I could hear it beating noisily on the trees at the southeast end of the island, traveling towards me like a monster in the forest; and then it was on my head and all over me.

So far there was no sun. That was the downside of this island life in Vava'u, and added to it were the mosquitoes, my damp clothes, the impossibility of walking anywhere on this jungly piece of land. On the plus side, the island was mine, the offshore coral was thick and full of fish, I had plenty of food, and radio reception was excellent. Sometimes the rain came down so hard that it drowned my radio. The other inhabitants of the island were crabs, herons, and a tree full of hanging, squeaking fruit bats.

Mealtimes were irregular because of the rain, and this was irksome, because I always tried to keep to a schedule when I was alone, so that my day would seem sensible and structured. *Now it's time to tidy the campsite,* I would say to myself. *Now it's time for tea. In two hours I will begin writing my notes.*

I hated paddling in the rain. It was not easy to cook in the rain. It was no fun to swim in the rain. As there was nowhere to go, I stayed inside the tent during the storms, listening to news of the Gulf War; and at night I lay there scribbling in my notebook, feeling damp and miserable under the dangling flashlight, hoping the next day would be sunny enough to dry all my wet gear.

In that sort of mood, feeling lonely and clammy, I felt a sense of regret that my married life had ended—I missed dull predictable London, my little family, the ordinariness of my old routine. In that isolation, I saw that my life had been broken in half, and I wrote on a damp page, *Travel is very hard alone, but hardest of all when there is no one waiting for you to come back.*

Usually, seeing a scrawled thought like that in black and white, I closed my notebook and simply prayed for sunshine, and in the mornings, out of loneliness, I fed the bluey-gray ghost crabs chocolate cookies and pieces of cheese.

When the sun finally came out after three days my mood lifted and I was energized by the light and heat. I harvested a few coconuts—knocked them down by poking them with the blade of my long paddle, and gouged a hole in them and drank the sweet water. In this good weather I dried my clothes and the rest of my gear, and stowed it, and planned a kayak trip to other uninhabited islands in the Vava'u Group, and I made a circuit of Pau Island.

Pau was uninhabited but it was not quiet. The bats made a racket, the birds whistled and squawked, the trees rattled and flapped, the fruit bats lolloped in their branches. The reef heron went *kark! kark!* The water lapped at the shore, and on the large exposed reef that lay between Pau and the next island, Fuamotu, there was a constant roar of breaking waves. I could see eight islands from where I sat slurping noodles or eating fish and pineapples, but not a single person was visible—no village, no boat.

After that day of sun it rained in the night, lashing the tent. I had left a cooking pot out in my hurry to get into the tent. There were almost three inches of water in it in the morning, and it had been sitting under a tree.

I usually woke early, at five or so, and listened to Gulf War news on Radio Australia or the BBC. The war euphoria of the first days had worn off and now it seemed as though it would go for a long time.

That was what Leonati had said in Neiafu: "They say the war will finish fast. But I think it will go on for a long time. They say they did a lot of damage in the first few days. I don't think they did much damage."

My island was as far as it was possible to be from the Middle East, and yet the war was on everyone's mind. And I heard on the radio that on the Pacific island of Kiribati (a corruption of its former name, Gilbert), prisoners had gone on strike, refusing to enter the exercise yard, for fear they would be hit by an Iraqi Scud missile.

There was more speculation than news—where were the eyewitnesses?—and so I always crawled out of the tent into a hazy dawn wondering what the world was coming to, and rather enjoying the idea that I was so far away, living the life of a beachcomber. The following days were warm, humid, cloudy with sunny periods and a light breeze.

On these good days, in the dazzling light of sunny mornings, I saw many more islands than I had before—they stretched like stepping-stones into the southwest, and I saw that by island-hopping I could get to most of them. None of them were inhabited, all of them had pretty shapes—humpbacked with good-sized hills, some with cliffs, some with saddle ridges, all of them densely wooded with old-growth forest as well as coconut palms.

It was a perfect area for paddling a kayak—perhaps the best in the Pacific. The islands were well defined and visible for some distance. The wind was strong in the afternoon but by setting out and returning early that was avoided or minimized. There was a surfy side and a safe side to each island—the lee shores usually had the beaches—all were secluded, all were lovely. There were no tourists, no signs at all, and no litter—no indication that human beings had ever set foot on these outer islands. It seemed to me that a person could spend weeks or months in Vava'u, making occasional trips to Neiafu, the town, to restock with provisions. It was a world apart, and solitude was available, because Tongans were not terribly interested in outsiders. Tongans did not take people to their bosoms as Melanesians did; Tongans did not pretend to be friendlier than they were.

My only question regarded the currents: I wondered how strong they were between these outlying islands, and if I paddled eight or ten miles to one of those distant places on my chart, would I risk being swept into a strong current?

I paddled back to Taunga to ask a fisherman. All of them were out this lovely day, but I found Lini and she inquired among the women of Taunga. None of them had the slightest idea about the currents. This was not so surprising—women did not paddle or sail in Tonga.

"The beach at the tip of your island is very beautiful," I said.

"Yes. We swim there."

"Do tourists visit you?"

"Sometimes, in boats. A cruise ship came once. There were many people. They loved our village. They admired our houses and the flowers we planted."

"What did the cruise ship look like?"

"I don't remember," Lini said. "But they loved our beach."

"Where did the people come from—what country?"

"I don't know," she said impatiently, as though it was a silly question.

Just like a Tongan: She remembered only what the strangers had said about her village. She had taken no interest at all in the strangers.

"There is no one swimming on the beach today," I said.

"It is so far to go"—it was about a ten-minute walk. She smiled and added, "A man from overseas told the king that he wanted to build a hotel on the beach. A very big hotel, so that tourists will come."

"What did the king say?"

"He could not say anything to the man until he asked us."

"So the king asked the village about building a hotel?"

"Yes."

"What did the village say?"

"We don't want it," she said, and turned away.

"Why not?"

"We don't want those people."

By *those people* she meant strangers.

Tongan snobbery, offensiveness, incivility, and rampant xenophobia has kept the great glorious archipelago of Vava'u one of the least spoiled places in the Pacific.

That day and the next I paddled to the west, making a circuit of the deserted islands and keeping close track of the currents. The limestone cliffs of these places, pounded by the sea, were vertical and the texture of the stone like that of monastery walls in England—the same browny-gray color, the same venerable look, like gothic ruins, as though if you excavated further you would find an abbey or a cloister or the boney relics of medieval saints.

The white beaches on the lee shores were bright in the sun, and hot and beautiful and empty, with greeny-blue lagoons shining below them. On most of the islands there were coconut palms, and birds. These islands were so lovely that it was hard to be alone on them—it was not that I required company, but rather that I wished that someone else had been there to see them: I wanted another witness, someone to share them with. If the place had been miserable I would have coped—during the days of rain I had not been lonely. ("I can endure my own despair, but not another's hope.") But the good weather had changed my attitude. I did not feel adventurous or lucky alone under sunny skies; I felt selfish, in all this splendor.

Most people who sail the Pacific know Vava'u—Neiafu is the destination for many of the yachts, the Port of Refuge regarded as one of the best places to pass the hurricane months from November to April. And these yachts plied around some of the Vava'u islands. But it was a place with many reefs and shoals, and most of the islands were off limits except to a shallow draft boat like mine.

Paddling past Eua'iki Island I heard a great racket of birds, like a chorus of cockatoos, and went ashore. The area was rich in bird life—herons and egrets, noddies and swallows and terns. But this bird screech was almost deafening.

I beached my boat and climbed the cliff for a better look, and there massed on the branches of one tall tree high on a bluff were several hundred fruit bats, hanging and twittering and quarrelling and negligently micturating in slashes and squirts. One broke loose, and looking precisely like Bruce Wayne in disguise, and twice as ugly, it flapped in a great circle and then returned to the tree and reattached itself, hanging upside down.

The other bats, still hanging, flexed their membranous wings, looking like a black array of windblown and broken bumbershoots.

On my desert island, Pau, I needed to make specific plans, or else I might lose my bearings and begin brooding. So I ate three meals every day. I had a morning and afternoon paddling objective. I always did the dishes and hung them on my tree. I carefully kept my gear dry. I allowed myself a certain amount of fresh water each day, even though I knew I could get more drinking water at Taunga. I had a nap after lunch and usually went snorkeling in my own lagoon. There were lots of plump pretty fish, but I had swapped my fish spear in the Solomons—and just as well: The islander could use the thing to feed himself.

I had a taste of what it was to be a beachcomber on a happy empty island. It was mostly pure idleness, with the invented urgencies of having to carry out various duties. And then I came to believe in these fictions, and so the day was filled. It meant being alone and self-sufficient. It meant that I got plenty of sleep and perhaps a bit too much sun and more mosquito bites than I had ever known. It meant keeping close track of my food and eating coconuts whenever possible. Most of all, because I had very little fresh water for washing, it meant a perpetual state of being sticky and salty.

One day I returned to my camp to see a rental sailboat, a thirty-five-footer from the Moorings outfit in Neiafu, anchored in the channel between my island and Ngau. That stretch was a sandbar at low tide. Did this yachtsman know that in an hour or so he would be aground?

I paddled over and saw four adults on deck, two couples—American, from their greeting.

"You're in very shallow water," I said.

And I wondered whether my warning was also stimulated by the feeling that I did not want to wake up the next morning and see this boat willfully trespassing on my lagoon.

"We were just leaving," the man at the wheel said. "This is a lovely spot. You American?"

"Yes. From Cape Cod."

"We spend summers in Osterville."

"Small world."

The two married couples had rented this sailboat a week ago, and were cruising in the Vava'u Group. They took vacations every year in interesting places—hiking in Alaska one year, biking somewhere else another.

They seemed happy and fulfilled people—their homes were in Georgia—and I was touched by their close friendship.

They asked me to come aboard, but I said I had an errand to run. I didn't, but I was self-conscious about being unshaven and grubby and they looked so shipshape in their trim craft.

We talked awhile about Tonga and Tongan traits.

One of the women said, "We walk down the street and no one sees us. The Tongans don't look. Everywhere else, people look."

"You worried about being alone?" one of the men said, when I told him I was camping on a desert island.

"I'm happy."

We exchanged names, and it seemed that my name had reached their households. More than that, one couple had known one of my older brothers at Harvard.

"He was having woman trouble," one woman said. And then she began to describe him in intimate detail.

She tried hard but it was not he. It never was. Whenever someone who was not a member of my family described my brother, no matter how well they knew him—or whether they were praising or blaming—I never recognized this person in their descriptions as Mycroft. They always had him wrong. Does anyone know your family better than you?

"What's he doing these days?"

"He lives alone with a cat named Rat on the Cape, rearing turkeys," I said. "Now and then he exhibits them. And he dedicates books to his cat."

The sun was setting by the time I paddled back and got my boat into a safe place under the trees. I was wary of being seen—my tent was behind bushes, my boat was hidden; and taking such care to hide myself I remembered Tony the beachcomber on the coast of North Queensland in his secluded camp, refusing to make any sort of path, so as not to arouse what he called "officialdom." This beach-combing experience was making me similarly furtive.

Each evening I had to write my notes and eat my dinner before night fell, or else I would be stumbling around in the darkness. And that was when the mosquitoes emerged. It would have been an unbearable island without mosquito repellent or netting on my tent; there were masses of them, morning and evening, breeding fast in the rain-swollen pools.

I sat on a log of driftwood writing notes while two gray herons stood in the shallows waiting for the tide to ebb so that they could more easily find fish. All along the beach crabs dug holes, bringing up clawfuls of sand. As the tide went down, the reef a mile out was exposed and the waves grew louder, sounding like the traffic roar on a highway.

Because of the mosquitoes and the night rain, I spent nearly all the hours of darkness in my tent, writing, drinking green tea, or lying in the dark listening to the nightmarish news. *You worried about being alone?* the yachtie had asked. No, I felt perfectly safe.

And I loved the stars—big beaming planets and small single pinpricks, fat blinking stars and masses of little peepers but also glittering clouds of them—the whole dome of the sky a storm of light over my island.

One day, about noon, going towards my boat, I was exceedingly surprised with the print of a man's naked foot on the shore, which was very plain to be seen on the sand, said Robinson Crusoe.

I had an identical experience, except that it was dark—the tide had ebbed all afternoon, I looked up from my meal and saw footprints everywhere. They led down the beach and into the woods; up to the cliffs, along the shore, across the dunes, all around the camp, desperate little solitary tracks.

There were hundreds, perhaps thousands of footprints, suggesting vast wandering mobs of idle strangers, and what frightened me—what eventually impelled me to break camp soon afterward and head for the nearest inhabited island, where I was assured of a welcome—and what sent a chill through me, was the thought that every single footprint, every urgent little trail, was mine.

So, with this hint of rock fever, I left my little island, and for the first time on my travels there was no one to say goodbye to. I left this secret place silently—this small mute island in the mist, the haunt of pissing bats and watchful herons. I simply slipped away and made off across the reef, going clockwise among the islands, past Euakafa to the big island of Kapa. I saw a wide reef being lashed by waves on the channel so I stuck close to the shore.

Three miles along I saw a stone jetty and a man struggling with a net while another steadied a dinghy.

The net was underwater, and it seemed to be very heavy. The man was having no success in lifting it.

"You have fish in the net?" I asked.

The fisherman groaned and heaved and muttered yes.

I paddled near and hovered, watching. The men seemed to be blundering, one almost swamping his boat, the other tangling himself in his net. At last the man with the net dumped the catch, a mass of sardine-sized fish, into the dinghy. Then they beckoned to me and offered me a bucket of them, the first time in Tonga anyone offered anything to me. When I politely declined the fish, the men lost interest in me.

More men were fishing under the cliffs of Kapa, catching larger fish on handlines. When I said hello they returned my greeting but without moving their heads, without any expression, just an impassive "Huh."

To keep away from the yachts—I could see a half dozen here and there, bobbing at anchorages—I decided to paddle through a lagoon, which was too shallow for anything bigger than a canoe. The island just to the west of the lagoon was Utungake, where I intended to camp, and near the shore, women—fifty or sixty of them—were standing waist-deep, holding buckets and gathering—what?

A woman called me over. Like the rest of the women she was fully dressed and completely wet. She was sitting in water to her armpits with four other women, gutting sea creatures—eels or slugs.

"Where is your wife?" she said, by way of salutation.

"Not here," I said. "Where's your husband?"

"I no gat none." This was Enna, and she was very fat, her hair hanging into the lagoon, her fingers smeared with eel guts the color of butterscotch.

"Why not get one?"

"You can hee-hee be hee-hee my husbeen!"

Another named Melly said, "What is your name?"

"Paul."

"Like dis?" She made a sphere with her fat hands. "Ball?"

"Not ball," I said, but she was tittering—they all were—"but Paul. Like Saint Paul."

"Thank you, Meestah Ball."

"What are you doing?"

"Cutting dese," Enna said. *"Lemas."*

Now I could see that they were sea slugs, but limper than any I had seen, the shape and color of bulging condoms. The women were gathering them from the bottom of the lagoon—there were thousands of these creatures in the mud—and cutting them open, and extracting a long orange organ, sticky and dripping, which they dumped into the plastic bucket.

"You like?" Enna asked.

"We don't have *lemas* in America."

"You eat."

"I no eat," I said.

Enna twirled the raw gooey thing around her finger and sucked it like a noodle into her mouth and said, "Yum!"

Melly did the same. Then Melly picked up a gelatinous eel from the lagoon mud with her knife and held it dripping in my face.

"You afray of dis?"

"No," I said.

"You eat it den."

It was what bratty schoolchildren did to the school wimp, or the new kid. Melly held the long limp creature on the blade of her sharp knife, while I sat in my kayak smiling at her.

"Put it down, Melly," I said.

"You afray," she said, and jerked the knife at me.

I tried not to blink.

"Why no no eat dis?"

"Because I'm not hungry," I said, and thought, *Fatso.*

I paddled farther into the lagoon, going faster than any of these people could walk. Most of the villagers on Utungake struck me as being incredibly stupid and slow, and they seemed to take only a cruel interest in other people. Everyone was digging for slugs. No one looked at me. A woman carried a big water jug through the lagoon. Like everyone else she was wearing all her clothes. They always swam in dresses and skirts and blouses, like Victorians. The boys wore shirts and trousers. But everyone was barefoot, in spite of the coral and the sea urchins.

I went swimming myself at the head of the lagoon and in the late afternoon got permission from a nearby village to camp on this deserted beach, distributed some silk scarves, and settled down for the night, which was full of lantern light and laughter and barking dogs.

The next morning I paddled back to civilization.

"And yet the sea is a horrible place," Robert Louis Stevenson wrote in 1888 to a friend in London. He had been wandering the Pacific in a chartered schooner, *Casco,* looking for a happy island on which he would spend the last six years of his life. He liked islands. He hated the sea. Sailing the sea was "stupefying to the mind and poisonous to the temper; the sea, the motion, the lack of space, the cruel publicity, the villainous tinned foods, the sailors, the captain, the passengers—but you are amply repaid when you sight an island, and drop anchor in a new world."

Those were my sentiments exactly: Sailing the sea was a monotony of doldrums interrupted by windy periods of nightmarish terror. No desert was ever deadlier or more tedious than an ocean. Then—after weeks or months of your thinking *Life is a reach, and then you jibe*—landfall.

I had never loved a boat enough to want to spend a year in it, and the fact is that yachties loved their boats—every cupboard and binnacle. Yachties were also finicky, orderly, conservative, and yet haters of authority; they were self-sufficient—capable menders and fixers of things; they could be peevish; they frequently shifted the topic of conversation to Doomsday. They had little in common with landlubbers—was it this that had driven them offshore? And had these people always been so orderly or had yachting, with its limited space, forced them to become such fussbudgets?

Whatever, I saw them everywhere in Oceania, and they seemed to me truly a breed apart. They were not intrusive. They were great live-and-let-livers. Yachting involved certain complex courtesies. If you didn't bother them they would not presume on you. They wanted mainly to be left alone—that is why they had weighed anchor in the first place. They spent years and years in their boats. They had sold houses and businesses and cars; they had quit jobs and put their life-savings into this venture, the all-consuming occupation of being Flying Dutchmen.

In the Port of Refuge of Vava'u were thirty-four yachts, all bobbing at moorings, waiting out the hurricane season. Most had been there for three or four months, some for several years. On good days the yachties ventured out and might spend a night at an anchorage, near one of the islands; but mostly they stayed here, going ashore from time to time, for water at the dock, or food at the Neiafu shops, though generally they hated the shops for being expensive. (Yachties never threw money around—partly out of frugality but mostly out of a desire to be anonymous: Spenders were always noticed.) They bought bananas and coconuts at the market, bread at the bakery, and they checked the post office or the Moorings agency for mail from home.

They did not often call each other by their proper names, but rather referred to the boat.

"*Windrift* is a plumber," a yachtie told me gesturing to the vessel. "*Southern Cross* is a builder. *Sourdough* is a doctor, though you'd never know it—he's a very nice guy. *Gungha* used to be a lawyer and now he's a salmon fisherman during the season up in Alaska—there's money in that. You get all kinds of people, a real cross section, you know. Of course in the season people fly in and meet their yachts. 'Take the boat to Tonga—we'll meet you.' They cruise a little, then they fly home. 'Take the boat to Fiji—' "

We were on the dock at Neiafu, talking about cruising. I had come in with a week's growth of beard, in my salt-flecked kayak, and a group of yachtsmen had taken an interest. Mine was clearly a seaworthy craft, even if it was only a little more than fifteen feet long. Yachties admired anything functional that was well made and compact, because the best yachties were enemies of superfluity.

Sundog said, "We try to spend a year in each place."

And he added that he and his family—two little girls—had been cruising the Pacific for the past seven years.

"We had a great time in Tahiti—not Papeete, but Moorea and Tahiti-

Iti, the little island just behind Tahiti. That's another world. Very sensual. Then you come here and everyone's going to church."

"We've been cruising since eighty-six," *Glory* said. "This is our second time in Tonga, and I can tell you it's really gone downhill. This used to be the cleanest harbor in the Pacific."

"I studied history and Polynesia navigation," *Dancer* said. "When I came here I discovered that no one knew a damn thing about it."

Sundog was still talking about Tahiti: "Your Polynesian doesn't really have a problem with nakedness the way they do here. They're very welcoming—you see all these smiles."

"Now there I have to disagree with you," *Glory* said. "We brought needles and fishhooks to the Marquesas. We always try to leave a place a little bit better than we found it. That's our way. But they weren't interested. They couldn't care less. They didn't want our needles and fishhooks."

"The thing is"—this was *Dancer* speaking—"you always judge a place by the last place you were in. We were last in New Zealand. Everyone talks to you in New Zealand. Great people. Great sailors too. It's blowing a Force Ten and you hear some Kiwi on the radio saying calmly, 'We're okay—just out here with the missus' and the fucken Tasman Sea is like hell on earth."

I introduced the topic of Tongans, because I had been wondering whether I had been imagining their xenophobia and bad temper. It is quite easy in travel to project your own mood onto the place you are in; you become isolated and fearful and then find a place malevolent—and it might be Happy Valley!

"Tongans? They're surly," *Sundog* said. "They're unhelpful. They're resentful. They don't care about you."

"They pretend not to see you—don't even look at you, right?" *Dancer* said. "But they're always looking at you sideways. They see everything."

"I blame the church," *Glory* said. "The Free Wesleyans especially—they're always collecting money. They get thousands from these people, but what do these people have? They're tithing like crazy and in hock to the church."

"Tongans are unteachable," *Sundog* said, beginning to rant. "Hey, they just don't want to learn. They're slow, they're lazy, and a lot of them are real wise guys."

"Your Fijian is pretty affluent," *Dancer* said. "But if you have business to do in Fiji you always do it with some downtrodden Indian."

"I'm headed for Samoa," I said.

Glory said, "Now I wish—I really wish—there was something good I could say about your Samoan. But I can't." *Glory* smiled a gloating smile.

"Oh, sure, your Western Samoan has to scratch a little harder, so he might be a worker. But I was in Pago for two years and I thought the people were horrible—they steal, they lie, they're lazy, they hate you, they're takers. We give them seventy-five million and what do we get for it?" He smiled again. "They're violent, too."

"People get involved there, though," *Dancer* said.

"See, a lot of your so-called expatriates are not very bright lights," *Glory* said. "But they shine more brightly in places like that."

"And this," *Gungha* said. He had just stepped onto the dock and was tying up his tender.

"Your Tuamotuan is a delightful person," *Sundog* was saying. "They'll *umu* a dog or a pig and make you feel very welcome."

So it went, our discussion on the dock. They often had such confabs on this neutral ground. But they also visited each other, rowing from yacht to yacht in their little dinghies, paying calls. Sometimes they yelled from rail to rail. But each boat occupied its own specific area of water. There were no close neighbors. When it was windy they battened down.

"It's funny," Mike of *Gungha* said. "You often find in a place like this the very problems you thought you left behind—pollution, bureaucracy, all that."

Glory told me how proud he was of his self-reliance. He had left Honolulu a year or so ago with four thousand dollars' worth of stores—canned his own meat and fish, made his own chutney.

"My wife bakes bread once or twice a week. It's fantastic bread. We give it out," he said. "The one thing we have is time."

Who, in the world they had left, could say that?

They also read books, and *Glory,* the most manic, sententious, and domineering yachtie in the harbor, told me how much he disliked *The Mosquito Coast.*

"I hated the guy in it. I couldn't stand him. You wrote that book? I really didn't like that book at all."

I said, "I'd probably hate your wife's bread."

"My kids think I'm just like the guy in that book," Verne Kirk of *Orion* said. "So I think that book's a masterpiece."

And that was the end of that discussion. The yachties were soon in their dinghies, rowing home; all except Verne.

"I like that book because it's true," Verne said. "People do that. They leave the States, just like he did. You see them here all the time."

He was the archetypical Pacific wanderer, down to his last whisker and eccentricity. He was nearly always barefoot, with a bandanna around his head; he smoked heavily—yachties were frequently heavy smokers, I found—and played Rolling Stones music on his boat. He had spent years tacking back and forth in Oceania. He was in his mid-to-late-fifties—funny, friendly, and crotchety. "Life is a two-edged sword," he often said. His *Orion* was a battered trimaran that he used for charters, taking people out for a day of snorkeling or a week of cruising. But *Orion* was also his home. He had sailed it from Samoa. It contained all his possessions, the most valued of which was his library. He was always quoting—Margaret Mead, Captain Cook, William Mariner, various historians, and me. Freud's *Totem und Tabu* was a great favorite. He showed me his extensively underlined and annotated copy.

"Business is pretty bad here, but the place is nice," Verne said. "It's true that I have a few enemies—*palangis* naturally. Machiavelli says you should judge a man by his enemies. That's all right with me. My enemies are dipshits."

He had spent five years in Samoa and was alone in my experience in putting in a good word for the Samoan people.

"I liked them," Verne said. "American-ness is only skin deep. They're funny and they left me alone. I pretended to be crazy. I guess I am a little crazy. If people think you're whacko they keep their distance."

"People say Samoans are violent," I said.

"Oh, sure, they are. But that didn't bother me," Verne said. "I had a pretty good job there."

"How was the money?"

"Five bucks an hour—chicken feed. But I lived on my boat. I didn't have any expenses."

Verne said that "for reasons too complicated to go into now"—he often used the expression when speaking of his exploits, and I liked the "now" most of all—he had been a staff engineer at the Department of Public Works in Pago Pago.

Verne confirmed that Vava'u was one of the great yachting destinations. People sailed from Hawaii to Pago and then here. Or they came from Fiji or New Zealand. But where to go from here was a difficult decision from the navigational point of view. If they continued west to Vanuatu and Australia they then had to sail north into Micronesia and more northerly still into cold waters in order to pick up the westerlies that would take them back to Hawaii. The alternative was to sail east out of Tonga and go as far east as necessary, beyond the Tuamotus, heading towards Easter Island, in order to pick up the southeast trade winds for the run back to Hawaii.

It all sounded like hell to me. And for most people in the Port of Refuge leaving Vava'u was the last thing on their nautical minds. Verne had been in the harbor for two years and said he was here more or less for the duration. If you asked what that might be like he would reply by saying that life was a two-edged sword.

I told Verne that one of my canvas boat bags was coming apart at the seams, as a result of being thrown around by baggage handlers. It was the size and texture of a mailbag and I had repaired it with layers of duct tape.

"I know just the man who can fix that," Verne said.

"It has to be done with an industrial sewing machine," I said.

"Andy on the *Jakaranda* has got an industrial sewing machine."

The *Jakaranda* was a sleek green schooner at a mooring some distance from the dock. Andy and his companion Sandy had been coming to Tonga since the mid-eighties. Andy said they had become somewhat disenchanted by the Virgin Islands—the selfishness and rapacity of the locals, the numerous yachts. They liked the pace of life in Vava'u, they liked the people, too.

"Where is your home port?" I asked.

Andy said, "This is. *Jakaranda* is our home. We've been living in this boat for the past twelve years."

It was a beautiful boat, made twenty years before in Holland, lying deep in the water because—Andy said—of the stuff they had accumulated: artifacts from around the world, the sewing machine, a big *tiki* from the Marquesas. Even so, there was plenty of room to ramble around in.

"I just got a Tongan work permit," Andy said. And he explained that he would be making and mending sails—all kinds of sewing. "In the season this harbor will be full of boats."

I showed him my boat bag.

"I can fix that," he said.

He tore out all the stitches and mended it expertly in fifteen minutes. It was a brilliant stitching job, and his willingness and his skill made it an even greater act of kindness.

We had coffee and chocolate cookies that had been sent to Tonga by Sandy's mother in Pennsylvania. Sandy was mellow, pleasant, good-tempered, and like many yachties easygoing because she was on her own boat. That was also a yachtie temperament. You spent years and years in a confined space in all sorts of weather and you either coped and developed a cheery positive outlook, or else you headed home. Andy and Sandy expressed a genuine liking for the Tongans, and echoed other yachties in saying they had no immediate plans.

"In a way, this is the best place to be," Sandy said. "I mean, with the war on. If the worst happens, we could just settle down and plant taro."

As someone who needed space, I marvelled at their capacity for living at such close quarters—and the marriages and friendships that prevailed over these conditions seemed to be as solid as it was possible for a human relationship to be, totally interdependent.

I remarked on this to Sandy, who said, "This is the way I want to live."

"Going from one strange hotel room to another can be traumatic," Andy said. "But in this boat we can go anywhere and still have our own bed, our own food." He thought a moment. "Our own toilet."

But it also meant years on the water, years making crossings, long periods in terrible harbors, always sleeping in a narrow berth, often banging your head, a whole life in which the world was elsewhere. To live such a life you needed a companion who was handy and healthy and optimistic and who didn't get seasick, and who was willing to renounce his or her country; and then you went where the wind took you.

You had to live in a certain way in these island harbors. Yachties could not live too intensely among the local people or they would be destroyed. It was the reason for their watchfulness. It was why they spoke to me only after I had been in the area for more than a week. They bobbed offshore, making the odd foray into town. Who in marine history, or in the history of oceanic exploration, ever lived like this? Either they went ashore and conquered, claimed the island, and left; or they stayed ashore, anthropologizing, botanizing, evangelizing, being a complete nuisance to the locals, whom they wished to subvert.

The yachties at their moorings had the equivalent of a gypsy camp at the edge of town, slightly exotic, occasionally insinuating themselves into the life of the place.

"The tourists do as they like—they wear bikinis—but they leave in a few days," one of the yachties had told me. "We have to keep to the rules, because we're staying."

They had to acknowledge the fact that they existed there for months or years because of the hospitality of the Tongans. They did not abuse that hospitality. They didn't litter, they wore modest clothes when they were in town, they endured the Tongan Sabbath. The yachties' generally compassionate attitude made me look harder at my own opinion of the Tongans.

I told Verne this—that I felt a bit guilty for distrusting them, and that I had found very little hospitality here. Or was I being too harsh on these people?

"People here—they may not be friendly but they leave you alone," Verne said. "It's a two-edged sword."

We were sitting on the dock at the Port of Refuge, among the perfect little islands of Vava'u, each of which was a perfectly rounded piece of land, many of them just like drops of batter on a hot griddle, the ones that cook quickly—simple little places with no people—that was the thrill, the innocence of it, and anyone with a little boat like mine could play Robinson Crusoe here. Each one was just what you imagined a tropical island to be—palms, woods, surf on the bright beach, limpid green lagoons. I was so glad I had come, and I felt that I had discovered an island that few others knew and had found a way of going there and living on it. That was the realization of the South Seas dream—and I had seen how the dream had been deficient. It was not the mosquitoes or the rain. But really I had wished that there had been someone else with me in that pint-sized paradise—a woman.

Meanwhile, Verne was talking about Doomsday, because a moment ago I had asked.

"The Doomsday thing is very common among yacht people," Verne said. "You hear it all the time. 'The world's going to hell,' 'This used to be a great country,' 'This place is awful,' 'The end is nigh.' So they buy a boat and ship out. They come here and talk about it."

He was quiet a moment, and then glanced up and looked across the lovely harbor to the green wall of Pangaimotu.

"This is a fabulous place to sit around, talking about the end of the world."

Chapter 16
IN THE BACKWATERS OF WESTERN SAMOA

Apia, the squalid harbor town of Western Samoa (but it was also squalid a hundred years ago in the heyday of its most famous resident, Robert Louis Stevenson) seemed to me mournfully run down, with broken roads and faded and peeling paint on its ill-assorted wooden buildings, and Samoans rather gloatingly rude and light-fingered, quoting the Bible as they picked your pocket. There were hardly any beaches here, too. But no matter how misbegotten and wayward an island in Oceania happened to be, it always had stars in its sky.

On the nights without rain I sprayed myself with insect repellent and went out to the shore to look at the stars.

Even in Africa I had never seen such a profusion of stars as I saw on these clear nights on Pacific isles—not only big beaming planets and small single pinpricks (plently of fat blinking stars and masses of little peepers), but also glittering clouds of them—the whole dome of the sky crowded with thick shapes formed from stars, overlaid with more shapes, a brilliant density, like a storm of light over a black depthless sea, made brighter still by twisting auroras composed of tiny star grains—points of light so fine and numerous they seemed like luminous vapor, the entire sky hung with veils of light like dazzling smoke. Even on a moonless night you could read or write by these stars, and they made night in Oceania as vast and dramatic as day.

That was how people had migrated here to Samoa, from Vava'u in Tonga, culturally its nearest neighbor: The old Polynesian voyagers had made complex charts of these stars—star maps—and traveled great distances with them in their canoes, stargazing and navigating. This was accomplished 1,000 years before the Europeans—Portuguese in this case—ventured out and discovered the Azores 900 miles into the Atlantic.

The Polynesians would have guffawed at such timidity, though these days, they are a seasick-prone people.

With daybreak the starry enchantment vanished from Apia, and once more it looked rusted and neglected. And it was much starker on Sundays, a day observed as fanatically in Samoa as in Tonga, for on Sundays the town was deserted. Elsewhere on Upolu, Samoans with big brown chins and fleshy noses, carrying Bibles, and dressed all in white—white dresses, white shirts—headed for church. In Samoa, as in other Polynesian places, I found myself muttering against missionaries and generally rooting for heathens. Pacific Christians were neither pacific nor Christian, nor were they particularly virtuous as a result of all their Bible thumping. Religion only made them more sententious and hypocritical, and it seemed the aim of most Samoan preachers to devise new ways for emptying people's pockets.

I had arrived on a Sunday—day of obstacles. It was impossible to rent a car or do much else on a Samoan Sunday—the Sabbath had to be kept holy. Somehow, taxis circumvented this restriction, even if buses could not.

I took a taxi and I looked around the island for a place to launch my boat. I was eager to paddle to a smaller island or even a village. I could not blame Apia for being awful. Apia was miserably typical. Except for bright little Port Vila in Vanuatu, no city or town in the whole of Oceania was pleasant. Islanders were not urbanized at all—they became antsy and deracinated in anything larger than a village, and without the means to be self-sufficient they generally made a mess of their towns. They were habituated to their own fruit trees and to crapping on the beach and flinging their garbage into the shallow lagoon. Disorderly towns were not so surprising. Apart from Meganesia, where immigrant islanders were considered a nuisance and a social problem, no island in Oceania was industrialized and, except for tourist hotels, few buildings on Pacific islands were higher than three storeys.

Pacific islanders of the traditional sort, as Samoans were, seemed to function best in families, and in order to thrive they needed a hut or a bungalow with a little vegetable patch by the sea. Samoan towns were worse than most, and included Carson, a suburb of Los Angeles, where there were more Samoans than in the whole of the Samoan islands and obnoxious posses (there were also branches in New Zealand) of the violent street gang S.O.S—the Sons of Samoa. The Samoans' large physical size served them well in football (nearly every professional football team in the NFL had its Samoan tackles), and some 500-pounders had succeeded as *ozeki,* champion sumo wrestlers, or musicians—the Boo-Ya Tribe, a quintet of shaven-headed fatties, had made a fortune in Los

Angeles imitating black rappers. Samoans were whispered about in the Pacific for being big and bull-like and, though placid by nature, were said to be capable of extreme violence.

Samoan stories are retailed throughout the Pacific—the Samoan who casually snapped someone's arm in two, the Samoan who ripped off a man's ear, the Samoans who sat in front of a house and then mooned the occupants when they were told to push off, the Samoan who bit off an assailant's fingers, the Samoans who went haywire in the disco, crushing a hairdresser's skull ("Because she touched my plastic toy," the Samoan explained in his defense, in court). In the "Samoans Too Big to Fit" category, there are endless tales of airlines having to unbolt seats or remove armrests in order to accommodate Samoans; too big for telephone booths, too big to fit through doorways, too big for bar stools, for bicycles, for toilet seats. A truthful friend of mine traveling on Hawaiian Airways out of Pago Pago witnessed the mounting terror of flight attendants when a Samoan man, urgently wishing to relieve himself, could not fit through the lavatory door. The employees' desperate remedy was to hold up blankets to create a wall of privacy for the Samoan, who stood just outside the lavatory and pissed in a great slashing arc through the door and into the hopper.

The sympathetic Robert Louis Stevenson liked the Samoans for being unpretentious family people, and he managed them by cozying up to the chiefs and patronizing his hired help. The islanders liked being taken seriously by this raffish and yet respectable *palangi,* who said "some of the whites are degraded beyond description," but it is clear that Stevenson kept his distance.

"He says that the Tahitians are by far finer men than the Samoans," the bumptious New Englander Henry Adams wrote, after he had visited Stevenson in Apia in 1891, "and that he does not regard the Samoans as an especially fine race, or the islands here as specially beautiful."

Yet Stevenson had done more than put Samoa on the map. He was the magician that some writers are—people who, by using a specific location as a setting, lend it enchantment.

A place that is finely described in a novel by such a person is given a power of bewitchment that it never really loses, no matter how much its reality changes. Not only Samoa, but other islands and, in a sense, the whole of the South Pacific is a clear example of this sort of transformation because it has been used so effectively as a setting by writers as various as Melville, Stevenson, Somerset Maugham, Rupert Brooke, Mark Twain, Jack London, Pierre Loti, Michener, and even Gauguin in his only book *Noa Noa.* Fiction has that capacity to make even an ordinary place seem special. The simple mention of the name of a place can make that place become singular, never mind what it looks like.

I sometimes felt as though I was part of that process of improvement or transformation, too—in spite of my natural skepticism—because I felt such relief, such happiness, paddling my boat through a lagoon under sunny skies. And I suspected that when I came to write about having come to the Pacific in such distress, needing the consolation of blue lagoons, that my subsequent relief would perhaps transform a buggy, drowsing island into a happy isle.

But Robert Louis Stevenson had the whole world to choose from. He had traipsed through Europe and Britain, he had bummed across America, he had sailed throughout the Pacific, from California to Australia and back. The King of Hawaii, Kalakaua, personally urged him to settle on O'ahu. Instead, Stevenson chartered a schooner and sailed to scores of islands, seeking the perfect place, which he had depicted long before, as a young man, in a verse he had written in Edinburgh.

> *I should like to rise and go*
> *Where the golden apples grow;*
> *Where below another sky*
> *Parrot islands anchored lie.*

No golden apples in Samoa, and no parrots. There were quarrelling islanders and drunken *palangis*. The Stevenson family arrived in the rainy season, when Apia is at its most dismal—hot, clammy, humid, muddy, with gray skies. Yet Stevenson homed in on it, knowing that he had few years left to live (in the event, only four). So what was the attraction of Samoa?

In a word, the postal service. Other islands were prettier; the high islands in the Marquesas overwhelmed Stevenson with their rugged beauty, and the atoll of Fakarava in the Tuamotus was bliss—the Stevenson family rented a cottage on the lagoon. But on those islands it could be many months between mail boats. In Samoa the mail came regularly, at least once a month, via New Zealand, or else from ships in the Sydney-to-San Francisco run. Stevenson was a zestful letter-writer and, as a novelist who depended on serializing his books in magazines, he needed a reliable postal service in order to make a living. That settled it, because the mail was his lifeline.

Afterwards, when he became acquainted with the island, he found ways of fitting in and even becoming predominant. The Samoan social structure of clan chiefs and drones and hangers-on and peasants and pot-wallopers was familiar enough to an upper-middle-class Scotsman. Partly through insinuation and partly through recruitment, Stevenson became important in Samoan society. This allowed him to live like a Scottish laird among obsequious chieftans—and that suited him best of all. He was not a snob, though he had the Scottish love of stern affectation and obscure formality, and especially the highland proclivity for fancy dress at ceremonials: All the household staff at his house, Vailima, wore a Royal Stuart tartan lavalava—the nearest thing in Oceania to a kilt.

The power and the dignity of lairdship Stevenson found very handy. He made the most of his four years in Samoa—the late 1880s and early '90s were years of disruption on the islands (Britain and Germany vying with America for control of the archipelago), and Stevenson—who was partisan, on the Samoan side—recorded it all in his *A Footnote to History*. The Samoans were masters of manipulation—they had made a fine art of obligating outsiders as part of the family and then taking them for all they were worth, while at the same time, making these suckers feel important. Blending Samoan traits with those of the Scottish highlands, Stevenson returned the favor and bamboozled them into believing they were part of his big tangled family—his elderly widowed mother had joined them, his wife's two children by her first marriage, his step-daughter's drunken husband—it was all *fa'a Samoa*. He was Laird of the Manor as well as their historian and *Tusitala*, "writer of stories." Stevenson in Samoa is a tremendous success story, a masterful example of forward planning—and everyone profited by his perfect choice of island: his family, his readers, the Samoans, and Stevenson himself. As Byron had done in Greece, he had found a great place to die.

I stopped by Vailima, Stevenson's house, but was sent on my way by an officious sentry who told me it was occupied by a paramount chief and not open to the public.

"You can visit his grave," the man said.

"Gravestones depress me," I said. They were for pilgrims and hagiographers.

I wanted an inkling of his spirit. It was the house he had built, and where he had lived, that I wanted to see—there were always vibrations of past tenants in houses. Why should I want to climb all morning up Mount Vaea to see the little plot which contained his moldering bones?

After a tour of the north coast, the taxi driver dropped me back on Beach Road, the empty main street of Apia, and demanded extra money.

"Because I waited for you."

He meant he had waited while I had walked fifty feet to a possible launching place on the coast.

I said, "Don't be silly," and gave him only the taxi fare.

"You not paying me," he said, muttering darkly. "I going to the police station."

"What are you going to do at the police station?"

"Tell them. I waited."

"How long did you wait?"

"A long time," he said, and looked away. Finally he said, "Fifteen minutes."

"What is your name?" I asked.

"Simi."

"Is fifteen minutes a long time in Apia, Simi? I would have thought it was a very short time."

Simi said nothing.

"How much more money do you want?"

"Two *tala.*"

I handed it over.

The next day, I drove to the ferry landing on the northwest corner of the island, Mulifanua Wharf, but there was no ferry to Savaii that morning and no one knew when it might leave. I went farther west and at a little bay was set upon by five fierce guard dogs—German shepherds, the sort that, spitted and grilled, would be considered the high point of a Tongan feast. A German in an expedition hat appeared and called them off.

His name was Stefan. The company he worked for had been granted a lease on this neck of land by the owner, the head of state for life, Malietoa Tanumafili II, who lived in Stevenson's grand house, Vailima. Stefan was supervising the building of ten traditional huts, called *fales.*

"I saw this beach from the road yesterday," I said, "when everyone was at church. They pray a lot here, eh?"

"If you steal a lot, you pray a lot," Stefan said.

He confirmed my impression that there were very few beaches on Upolu. There were more on Savaii, he said. I told him that it was my intention to paddle there, across the Apolima Strait.

"That's very dangerous," he said.

It seemed to me that people on Pacific islands were inclined to say a thing was dangerous when they knew very little about it, but I intended to ask a local fisherman just the same.

Stefan showed me around the thatched-roof huts at the edge of the lagoon. He said the huts were not finished but that I could stay, for a fee. The sky was gray and the lagoon was dark and muddy, but it was a pleasant enough place to stay—quiet, remote from Apia—and a good spot to launch from.

I moved in and assembled my boat, and that became my base for a time.

My first paddling objective was an island, Manono, across a three-mile channel. There were 1,500 people on Manono, but no dogs, no roads, no vehicles, no electricity. I thought of it as 100 years offshore.

There was a legend about Manono, how it was not a fixed island at all, but rather a piece of land, a sort of floating fortress owned by Chief Lautala of Fiji. The chief had sailed it to Samoa in the year dot in order to fight and conquer the Samoans. It was a bloody battle, and though he lost it he inflicted so many fatalities on the Samoan side that the numerous dead gave an identity to the floating piece of land—Manono means "numerous."

I drank beer that night in my hut and listened on my shortwave radio to what turned out to be the collapse of Iraqi resistance in Kuwait—an all-out rout of a raggle-taggle, underfed, and demoralized army of cowards and persecutors. And after that, when the clouds parted in the sky, I looked at the stars—ignorant stargazing providing for me one of the most vivid experiences I had, traveling through Oceania. And I was reminded that such stars were the best part of being in a wilderness or an ocean—and could take the curse off even so sorry a place as Apia.

It was windy when I slipped into my boat the next morning, preparing for Manono. Stefan repeated that my real problem was the current in the middle of the channel—because of an incoming tide I might be swept onto the reef to the southeast.

At such times in Oceania, I always reflected on my paddling between Falmouth and Martha's Vineyard in the summer—a greater distance, stronger wind, less predictable current, and much more irascible and inhospitable natives.

With that thought in mind I set off and paddled hard for an hour or so until I was within half a mile of Manono—I had passed through a strong but not obnoxious current. Beyond it I could see the tilted volcano cone, which was Apolima Island. In the distance, about nine miles away, was the island of Savaii—another good paddling trip and a place I wished to see.

All that was visible on Manono from my kayak were a profusion of outhouses on stone jetties—some of them hanging over the sea, others poised above the shoreline. They were called by various names—*fale ki'o,* "shit house," or *fale sami,* "sea house," *fale laititi,* "little house," or the more euphemistic *fale uila,* "lightning house."

Closer to the island, the Samoan houses that were visible were traditionally made and as symmetrical as on Upolu, with open sides, but the whole thing with the general shape and contours of a Spanish conquistador's helmet. A breeze wafted through the hut in the day, and at night the rolled-up woven blinds were let down, and served as walls. The huts of Western Samoa were attractive and comfortable structures, and were stronger than any huts I saw elsewhere in the Pacific. It has been said—by

Margaret Mead, among others—that the Samoan extended family, the *aiga,* is a closely knit and effectively interdependent household; and I wondered to what extent this well-made hut played a part. Certainly it was able to house many people—and with these open sides it was always possible to see children playing inside, or women weaving, or people talking or napping—an atmosphere of activity or repose, seemingly at times almost idyllic.

I heard roosters crowing and children screeching, but—unusually for a Pacific island—no barking dogs. About eight or ten children met me on the rocky shore as I paddled to the edge and got out, below the village of Faleu. They were chanting *"Palangi! Palangi!"* and they quarrelled among each other as they vied to help me put my boat on the village canoe rack.

Foreigners walking, cycling or riding motorbikes through [Samoan] *villages will frequently be considered moving targets by village children, and stones will fly,* a current guidebook to Samoa advised. *They will often surround you mockingly and demand money or sweets and will make great sport of trying to upset you.*

This gratuitous hostility I found to be generally the case, from that day onward, and throughout my time on whatever island in Samoa. Samoans could be merciless to outsiders. It was bad for a man and worse for women. A stranger was persecuted precisely because he or she was a stranger—alone, unprotected, unfamiliar with the language, uncomprehending, easy to confuse, not part of any family, unconnected, weak, an alien, the perfect victim.

You were mocked if you became angry with your persecutors (who always outnumbered you), and if you attempted to be conciliatory they took this as a sign of weakness and were worse. The conflict—a wicked game—was unwinnable.

These children pestered me from the moment I stepped ashore on Manono, but I thought it was probably better not to warn them about stealing or damaging my boat, because I didn't want to give them any ideas—knowing that I was concerned, I guessed it might be the very thing they would do.

I walked east, counterclockwise, around the island, ignoring the screeching kids and making a point of talking to older people. The teenaged boys I passed were fairly monotonous in their mockery, but I walked on, leaving these Christians behind.

In spite of their ill nature, the islanders seemed traditional—and very likely there was something in their ill nature that was traditional, too. All explorers in the Pacific, from Abel Tasman in 1642 onward, had to confront thievery, silliness, aggression, greed, and rapacity. Perhaps Samoan mockery was nothing new, but it was rather boring to have to endure this and then have to listen to either a travel writer or someone at the Samoan Vistors' Bureau extolling the virtues of Samoan hospitality. Of all the places I had traveled in my life, Samoa was one in which one needed letters of introduction or the names of natives. Otherwise, you were condemned to being alienated.

But alienation was my natural condition. As for their hostility, I kept strolling and watched my back.

"We are traditional here on Manono," a man told me, when I asked him to characterize the island. "We relate the stories of our ancestors."

This sounded fine, but when I asked him to tell me a few, he went blank—I suspected he meant family histories rather than island legends or myths.

Another said, "Manono is a good place, because we have no air pollution."

We were looking in the direction of Upolu. I said, "Is there air pollution on Upolu?"

"No," he said.

The fact was that the nearest air pollution was perhaps five thousand miles away in Los Angeles.

"And we have no buses."

"Is that good or bad?"

"Good. Buses have fumes. They cause dust."

It would have been something of a miracle to find a bus on an island with no roads. The path around the island was at its widest not more than twelve inches.

A man I met on this circumambulation said he was a minister of the church. But his necktie—ties were required among the clergy—was lettered *Malua Theological College.* He admitted that he was still a divinity student and that he had come to Manono to practice his preaching.

While the younger people were almost uniformly mocking *(Palangi! Palangi!)* the older ones were correct—neither friendly nor distant. There are complex rules governing greetings in Samoa, as well as extensive aspects of etiquette, including many prohibitions. A stranger, unfamiliar with the Samoan way, is therefore a sitting duck. The Samoans had not seen many tourists, and their attitude seemed to be that if you were part of the family you were left alone, and if you were a stranger you were fair game.

I was followed by more kids, and always I heard the word *palangi* in their muttering. I usually turned to face them.

"Yes. I am a *palangi.* Do you have a problem?"

In a shouting, jeering way one would say, "Where are you coming from?"

"I think Japan," one would say.

This they regarded as very funny.

"Do I look Japanese?"

"Yes! He Japanese!"

A woman sidled up to me at the edge of a village and said, "What you religion? You a Cafflick?"

I said, "Yes, in a way."

"Come with me," she said, and brought me to her house and showed me little shrines and holy pictures tucked into the eaves of her *fale.* She was like an early Christian in the furtive way she revealed these items to me.

"I am the only Cafflick in Salua," she said. "Please stay with me."

This seemed rather awkward, but she said that her husband was on his way back home and that he would be pleased. Her name was Rosa, she was twenty-five, and had five children. Her husband returned soon after, and though I half-expected him to be angry over finding me alone with his wife—it is very bad form in most societies—he did not take it amiss. He repeated the invitation to stay.

I said I had other plans, and when he told me he had just been fishing, I asked him whether he ever went to Apolima, the island beyond the reef, two or three miles from Manono.

"We don't fish at Apolima. It is too deep."

They poled their canoes through the shallow reef and never ventured into water deeper than the length of their poles.

Continuing my walk, I was accosted half a dozen times and asked "You have a wife?" and "What is her name?" and "Where is she?"— questions that always presented difficulties to me.

But I could see that the island had a pleasant side. It was backward-looking, with its coconut palms and its mango trees, its well-tended gardens and its tidy huts set on well-made house platforms, all of black boulders, the sort of stonework that is found in the most traditional parts of Polynesia. The wood carvings in Polynesia did not interest me. The music I found ineffectual—though the drumming could be attractive, when it was strong and syncopated. The cannibalism was just a story of goblins, meant to give you the willies—very few people could vouch for it, and little of it had been documented. But two aspects of Polynesian culture always impressed me: the old navigational skills of the sailors (and canoe building in general) and the magnificient stonework—altars, dancing platforms, house foundations, plinths for statues, and the statues themselves (though there were no statues in Samoa; there had never been). In Samoa, both of these skills had vanished—there were no more navigators nor any stonemasons. These boulders had survived from an earlier time.

After two hours of circling the island, I sat on a stone near the shore and began scribbling notes, when I was approached by a woman—I took her to be in her twenties. She was friendly. We talked in general about Manono. Then she said her *fale* was nearby and did I wish to see it?

I equivocated until she said, "I want you to see something very important."

"Show me the way," I said.

Her name was Teresa, and although she was twenty-seven, she was not married. The kids fooling around the hut were her brothers and sisters and more distant affines.

Was I hungry? Was I thirsty? Was I tired? Teresa galvanized the household and I was given a cup of tea and, when I said I had liked the *palusami* I had had in Tonga, I was served what I was told was the real Samoan thing—taro leaves mixed with coconut cream, then wrapped and steamed in banana and breadfruit leaves. With this was a disk of hard gray taro.

"In Tonga they put corned beef inside," I said. "But I prefer this."

"Sometimes we make with *pisupo,*" Teresa said, using the Samoan word for corned beef, an adaptation of "pea soup," which was also shipped to the islands in cans.

While I was eating, Teresa changed her clothes, from a dress to a T-shirt and shorts. The light was failing, too—it was certainly too late to paddle back to Upolu—and rain was softly falling, whispering against the triangular leaves of the taro plants and making them nod.

So far there had been no further mention of the thing she wished me to see. But after a while Teresa removed it from the pocket of her shorts. It was an American Express traveler's check for a hundred dollars—quite a lot of money in Manono Tai.

"Where did you get this, Teresa?"

"A man gave it to me. But the bank refuses to cash it."

Of course: The check lacked the necessary second signature. As for the first, even holding the check near the bright pressure lamp I could not read the name.

"Who was the man?"

"He was staying here. For a week."

"Palangi?"

"Yes. From Germany."

We talked about the check. I explained the niceties of traveler's checks—the need for another signature—and that she would have to send the check back to the man so that it could be cashed.

"He said he wanted to marry me," Teresa said, in a tone of complaint.

"Maybe that's why he gave you the money."

"No. He was here more than a week. He did not give us anything," Teresa said.

"What about this check? You said he gave it to you."

"Yes. But I did not want to marry him," she grumbled.

That was another trait of the Samoans—evasion that expressed itself as tetchiness.

"Why not?"

"He was too old. Born in 1946, something like that."

It was now very dark beyond the reach of the lamp, but in that darkness children were seated with older people, all of them watching me with bright eyes.

"How old is too old?"

Teresa gnawed her lower lip, and then said, "He was too old for games."

"What kind of games?" I asked. Though I knew.

The lantern hissed, leaking light everywhere.

"Night games," she said softly, her voice just a whisper more than the sound of the lantern.

After that, again and again, I remembered the way she lowered her head, but still watched me closely, and spoke those words deep in her throat.

I asked her again about the man. His name was Kurt, she said. He was a teacher, and he did his teaching in various countries. (*Cheechah,* she said, and *cheeching.* I was trying to get used to the Samoan accent.) He loved her, she said, but she disliked him.

I said, "He might be too old for some night games but not for others."

This observation interested her greatly.

"Which ones do you mean?"

But at this point her father interrupted me and asked where my boat was.

I told him it was in Faleu.

"The children will destroy it," he said, without much concern.

"Why would they do that?"

"Because you don't have a family."

I heard that explanation many times in Samoa: Having a local family gave you status and protection. Samoans quite freely co-opted strangers and made them part of the family, and you didn't need to be dusky, with webbed feet and a big belly—*palangis* qualified, as long as they were endlessly generous—but if you were alone on the islands and did not know anyone you would be victimized.

"And because they are stupid in that village," the father went on.

It was a Samoan trait for them to speak ill of each other; I was not convinced that my boat was in danger. But it was too dark to go looking for it, in any case. That would have to wait for the morning.

"Everything is so espensive here," Teresa said, apropos of nothing—or perhaps apropos of the check.

She was looking at the lantern.

"The fuel. So espensive."

I said, "There is a Chinese proverb that says, 'It's no use going to bed to save candles. The result will be more children.' Get it?"

Then, seeing the others drifting away, she asked me again about the other games that the man might or might not play.

In the end, the sleeping arrangement was modest, though all night the *fale* purred with the snores of her large family. I slept beside the small boy Sefulu, whose name meant Ten.

In the dark I worked it out. The man, Kurt, had stayed for a week or ten days. He pestered Teresa to marry him, though he had come empty-handed and had not given them any money for his stay. At some stage, Teresa had boosted the traveler's check—extracting it from his ruck-sack—but it had been in vain: The bank would not cash it without the other signature. She now realized that she needed a signature. Was she asking me to do that?

Yet I was more concerned about my boat than her possible thievery, and so at dawn I hurried back to Faleu to look at it. Children were playing near it, as though waiting to pounce, but the boat was undisturbed.

Over breakfast—more taro, mashed this time—Teresa took out the check and frowned at it.

I said, "Do you want me to sign it?"

"If you don't mind."

There was no date, and the man's own signature was no more than a squiggle.

What to do? They had been kind to me, even if they had had an ulterior motive. And though the money had been thieved, it had in a sense been owed by a tight-fisted *palangi* who had lived with them. Indeed, I had accepted their hospitality too. So perhaps I owed? Forgery seemed a small matter, and yet it interested me. Without the signature, the check was worthless. And there was always the chance that the forgery would be detected, in which case Teresa would be in trouble—and was that my affair?

I could be a totally disinterested forger, a sort of philanthropic felon.

I sat there on the steps of the *fale* practicing the squiggly signature in my notebook, and then I placed the check on my lap and, watched by her family and the neighbor kids, I executed the signature on the traveler's check—very well, I felt.

"It's perfect," I said.

"It is close." She squinted critically at it.

Everyone crowded close to have a look.

"Put the date," Teresa said.

I wrote the date, as Kurt might have.

"Will it get stale?"

"Did you say 'stale'?"

She said yes, she had, and so I explained the nature of traveler's checks, how they never went stale, how she could wait a while before cashing it—thinking that I could be safe and out of the way on another island by then.

The fishermen said a strong current ran through the Apolima Strait, which separated Upolu and Savaii, the two largest islands of Western Samoa. If I had not been alone I would have risked the trip—I was almost halfway across when I had been at the far side of Manono: I didn't see a problem. The fishermen did not cross the strait in their canoes, and yet they warned me. Did they know something? I heeded the warning, and with regret took the rusty ferry across to Savaii, with my packed-up boat among my other bags.

"The worst Samoans and the worst *palangis* come to Apia," a schoolteacher named Palola told me. "All the failures. But they never get together."

His description made the place sound more interesting than it was. Its Third World dereliction—and it was alone in the Pacific in possessing it—made it look simply unsightly, neglected, abused, and even the sea was hidden from it. From the harbor's edge, where water lapped feebly at the shore, the reef was a great distance and the lagoon was gray and turbid, the water the ghostly gray color of dead coral.

"It is worse in Pago," Palola said. He was polite and well spoken, on the ferry to visit his folks in Papalaulelei.

No sooner had I made my mind up that these people were brutes than I met a person who was decent and restrained, dignified and helpful, among the most hospitable I had ever met in my life.

"The main difference is in the attitude of people," he said, trying to answer my question comparing Western Samoa, an independent republic, with American Samoa—a territory belonging to the United States. "Take the attitude towards money. If we get money we spend it on our family, on our house, or food and necessities. In American Samoa they use it to buy a car, or for entertainment. They spend it on themselves. They care less about the family."

"Why is the family so important?" I asked, pressing him.

"Because it helps you—it looks after you. It is your life," Palola said.

"Is the house part of your life?"

"Yes. If you go to Pago and see a fine house you will probably discover that the people in that house came from Western Samoa. We are still following our old ways."

"But why is Apia in such bad repair? And the rest of the island isn't much better."

"It is getting worse. We had a hurricane last February—"

Everyone spoke of this three-day gale which wrecked houses and uprooted palms and destroyed roads with high tides and floods. But that was over a year ago and the wreckage remained.

"—we have not rebuilt it," Palola was saying. "We have no money. And the government is also to blame."

The family looked after itself but was indifferent to the plight of other families, and it was no concern of a family if there were tree trunks and splintered houses up the road. The breakdown of the family in American Samoa (the main island of Tutuila was only forty miles east of here) was said to be the cause of the strife there. Depending on whom I was talking to, Samoans either said they were one people, or else as different as they could possibly be. "We have a different language!" one man insisted. *"Sapelu* means bush knife in Western Samoa and shovel in American Samoa. *Ogaumu* means an oven here but it means a pot over there. We have different words for east and west!" Great stress was laid on the fact that money mattered more in American Samoa than here, its poor cousin.

I had a standard island question, which I tried to remember to ask everywhere I went: Why are islands different from the mainland?

Palola said, "Because you are free on an island, and you can control your own affairs."

He went on to say that he had visited his brother in Auckland and that he had been too frightened to drive his brother's car. "Everything was so fast there," he said, meaning the traffic, the marching people on the sidewalk, the way they spoke and did business. He had found it unendurable.

No one was seasick on the ferry—I had assumed that, being Polynesians, they would be puking their guts out, even on this half-hour run. On the other hand, they were none too healthy, and they made their way onto the jetty with a side-to-side duckwalk that was characteristic of these obese people.

They valued fatness, and to make themselves physically emphatic they ate massive amounts of bananas, taro, breadfruit, and such snacks as were on the menu of the eateries in Apia. *Toasted spaghetti sandwich* was one I noted. (The New Zealanders have a lot to answer for.) They ate the cuts of mutton that were whitest with fat. Meat that the Kiwis and

Aussies refused to eat, unsaleable parts of dead animals—chicken backs, parson's noses, trotters, withers, and whatever—were frozen and exported here. A scrap of meat on a chunk of fat attached to a big bone they found toothsome. The imported canned corned beef they called *pisupo* was up to 90 percent fat. It was not the solid meaty thing that we sliced with a knife in the United States and made into hash; this Pacific corned beef was often like pudding it was so loaded with fat, and it could easily be eaten with a spoon. Not only was beef tallow added to it, but some brands contained hippo fat.

Heart disease was endemic and people died young, but still there were only two doctors on the island of Savaii (population 46,000)—one was Italian, the other Burmese.

I met the Italian doctor, Peter Caffarelli, in a roundabout way. He lived just outside the village of Tuasivi where my younger brother Joseph had been a Peace Corp volunteer. Tuasivi was a number of *fales* on both sides of the coast road, near a headland occupied by a college, where my brother had taught English. The settlement—a large village—had none of the raddled run-down look of the comparable places on Upolu that I had seen. The *fales* were well made and there was a busy air to the place, people gardening, feeding their chickens, and a profusion of lavalavas flapping on clotheslines. The wreckage of last year's hurricane lay farther down the coast—tipped-over trees, broken culverts, washed-away roads.

Tavita Tuilagi, one of Joe's former colleagues, was building a new *fale*, not only in a traditional style but by a traditional method: None of the men working on the house were paid. They were relatives, part of the extended family, and friends. In theory this was all a labor of love; in practice it could be expensive, since Tavita—Samoan for David—was obliged to supply all the men at all times during the construction with food and drink—and the better the food the harder the men would work. Indeed, if the food and drink ran out, the men might decide to work elsewhere.

"This man Tavita has just been given a title," said the Samoan who had shown me the way to Tuasivi. "He is now *Oloipola.*"

"It is not much," Tavita said, sounding suitably modest, and hardly looking titled and chiefly in his L.A. Lakers T-shirt.

But saying it was nothing was not modesty. It was the truth. This title, which meant "matai chief"—head of the family—had once been a powerful position. But lately such titles had been handed out willy-nilly by chiefs as a way of getting themselves reelected to positions of power.

"Sio was a good boy," Tavita said, giving Joe his Samoan name. "He was a good teacher too. I want him to come back."

"Why don't you write him a note and say so?" I asked. And I found a blank page in my notebook and gave him a pen. "You could invite him back, and I will make sure he gets it."

"That is a good idea," Tavita said, and began scribbling.

"I doubt whether I'll get a chance to read it," I said, when he had finished. I put the notebook into my pocket and walked up the road.

The note said: *Dear Joe Theroux, I'm so happy to meet your father* (crossed out) *brother. Remembering you for the past years since you were here. I am building a new fale. If you could give me a donation through finance I would like to accept it. May God bless you. Thank you. Tavita Tuilagi.*

On my way back through the village I gave Tavita thirty Samoan *tala,* which he accepted without ceremony.

The Italian doctor, Caffarelli, lived up the road, near the beach in a straggling village beyond Tuasivi. He was skinny, burned dark by the sun, wearing a lavalava patterned in red flowers. I took him to be in his late-sixties. His wife was Samoan. Children seemed to be scattered everywhere around his house, and we were outside, strolling around his tussocky grass, among lanky pawpaw trees. The house was badly mildewed stucco in the European style and (so he said) it stood on one of the few plots of freehold land in the whole of Samoa. It had apparently been doled out by a chief on the understanding that as long as the doctor lived on that land he would look after the chief's health.

When I asked the doctor direct questions about himself he became unhelpful and vague—vague even about the number of his children. "Ten," he said in a tone of uncertainty, and then, "Eleven." Answering my questions about Samoan life he spoke with greater confidence.

"The family is very important here, yes," the doctor said. "But when we say 'family' we are talking about a very large number of people. Times have changed and that has made it all more complicated. There are obligations, but that is not so bad when you are in a non-money economy. When someone offers to work, or gives you fruit, you offer food at a later time."

"I noticed. There are always gifts in circulation here," I said.

"But when money comes into the picture"—the doctor made the Italian hand-weighing gesture which signifies tribulation—"it can be expensive. Money for this, money for that. And the rule is that you don't refuse."

"Does that mean you give it every time it's asked for?"

"You look after children," the doctor said. "But how far does your obligation extend if the father of those children is out chasing a bar girl in Apia? Do you go on pretending that he's just doing his duty and turn a blind eye?"

"Does this happen often?"

"All the time," the doctor said. "And there's a moral dimension. Why should I give money to someone if all he plans to do with it is waste it on prostitutes. The rule is that you give, if someone asks. But it raises moral questions sometimes."

I asked about stealing, since it was mentioned by many other travelers I had met, and all the guidebooks contain warnings. I had not lost anything, but the fact was that so much had been pinched from me in Tonga I had little else of value that could be stolen.

"When this was truly a non-money economy, when cash didn't come into it at all, everything was shared," the doctor said. "So my bush knife was also yours. A person would come and take it. There was no concept of private property. There was perhaps a little pleasure in a person's taking something. Nothing was privately owned, there was no idea of personal property."

He went on to say that money had complicated this traditional arrangement—everyone in Samoa blamed money for their problems: the lack of it, the greed for it, the power that wealthy people had.

"People steal all the time now," the doctor said. "Yes, it is the old habit, but it is stealing. Yet no stigma is attached to it. They even admire trickery."

"What if you steal from them?"

"In theory, that is what you are supposed to do. But they are not always so tolerant, eh? They are communal-minded when it suits them, but there are plenty of instances when a person gets something and never shares it."

I told him that it wasn't the stealing, but the inconsistency and the hypocrisy that caused the problems.

"Yes. I will give you an example," he said. "A man I know had a very big mango tree. He noticed that everyone was stealing his mangoes as soon as they were ripe. By the way, he was an Australian, but he had lived here for some years. He didn't say anything to the people, but he thought, 'Ah, so that is what they do.' Thus he began picking bananas from the trees of these people. And they didn't like it!"

"What did they do about it?"

"There was a hell of a fuss."

"How bad?"

He shrugged and made the Italian fishmouth that signified a paradox was in the air.

"They wanted to kill him."

We talked about the birthrate. It was very high—but although 60 percent of the births were illegitimate, the children were well looked after and always part of a larger family. Still, the government authorized the use of birth-control remedies—Depo-Provera.

"Isn't that a dangerous drug?"

"Yes, it is bad, but who is sentimental here? You might be sterilized for life, you might die—but isn't that the motive of the people who give out contraceptives? They want to bring down the birthrate, at any cost. They are not sentimental." After a moment he said, "I don't have anything to do with contraceptives."

He walked me to the road, his lavalava flapping, his numerous children frolicking around us.

"You must like it here to have lived here so long." Twenty-five years he had spent in Samoa.

"A doctor here is a despised person," he said, smiling. "The great thing is to be a minister in the church. People give you food and money. You have status. You can be rich. But they regard me as ridiculous, because I am a doctor. When my surgery building blew down and was demolished in the hurricane everyone stood near it and laughed. 'Look at what happened! The doctor's house is down!' The Samoans thought it was very funny."

There are not many wild creatures in Samoa, and most are near the road, so just walking home I saw nearly every one of them—the black rats, the endangered bats, the pigs, the rails, swiftlets, reef herons, and crazed limping dogs.

I was staying in a *fale* myself, at Lalomalava. It often rained in the dark early morning, three or four o'clock, the downpour drumming on the thatch and tin roof—a lovely sound, half-roar half-whisper, and it made a tremendous slapping on the big broad leaves just outside the blinds. Then dawn broke, the gray sky lightened, and the rain still fell and finally, when the sun's rim appeared against the palm trees at six or so, the rain pattered to a stop.

I lived among a farrago of aging expatriates and more youthful Samoans. In the near distance there was always the full-throated sound of mocking laughter—always children. This sudden explosive laughter I found unaccountably jarring and demoralizing, but it seemed to bother only me—no one else. The expatriates more or less assumed that they would be buried here eventually, though the Samoans all expressed great homesickness for places like Auckland and San Francisco.

Loimata was typical.

"*Mata* means 'eye' in Malay," I said.

"And also in Samoan," she said. "Loimata means tears."

She had relatives in Hawaii, Los Angeles, San Francisco, New Zealand, and Australia. Visiting some of them, she had lingered to work, and for a while lived in the Samoan enclave outside Honolulu, called Wahiawa. She had been traveling with her mother, who missed Samoa, and so mother and dutiful daughter had returned to Savaii.

"I miss the work," she said.

Her friend twitted her and said, "You don't miss the work. You miss the money."

"Yes, I miss the money."

Warren Jopling, a New Zealander in his mid-sixties, had simply come to Samoa and become so entangled in his newly acquired Samoan family that he had stayed. He said he liked Samoa. And of course the family had adopted him—but two or three Samoans were attached to twenty more, and in the end they took possession of him and moved wholesale into his house in Apia, occupying it so fully that he moved out and came here to Savaii.

I had wanted to see an ancient stone mound, called Pulemelei—a great stepped pyramidal structure, the largest mound of its kind in the whole of Polynesia. I asked a number of Samoans about it. Most knew nothing of its existence. The two who had heard of it had never seen it. I asked Warren whether he knew about it—and of course he, a *palangi* living on the fringes, had visited it many times and knew this obscure ruin in the jungle intimately.

No one has any idea what this enormous ruin was used for—whether it was a tomb, a fortress, or a so-called bird-snaring mound. It is all the more intriguing for that—for its size and its mystery. It lies in the depths of the Samoan jungle behind the village of Vailoa and it is so seldom visited that there are no paths around it. Even Warren Jopling, who knew it well, became a trifle confused on our approach through the bush.

Built against the brow of a hill, it was covered in jungle greenery—vines and bushes—and yet its architectonic shape in two great steps was vivid: With the contours of a titanic wedding cake it had the look of a ceremonial mound, but it offered a wonderful prospect of the sea. In its day, before any of the palms had been planted, it must have had the grandeur of the great Mayan pyramid at Chichén Itza, the so-called Castillo, a structure it somewhat resembled in size and complexity. Some archaeologists have conjectured that there was a large dwelling on the top of it, which would truly have given it the look of a castle. It was forty feet high, and about 180 feet wide and over 200 feet long, with battlements and parapets and flights of stone stairs.

"You know the oddest thing about this place?" Warren said. "This is an island that is rich in legends. They have stories about the blowholes and the waterfalls and the caves. They have stories about things that don't even exist. Giants, dwarfs, ghosts, spirits. How this volcano appeared, where that island came from. But there are no stories about this, not even fanciful ones. Don't you think that's strange?"

He showed me a number of other rock mounds—graves, house platforms, altars, all covered with jungle, buried in ferns and vines, all unknown, none of them excavated.

"A great civilization lived here," he said. "It must have been here, because there was a great deal of available water—two rivers, the only real year-round rivers on Savaii."

The volcanic nature of the soil helped all water to percolate through very quickly, Warren said—he had spent a career as a geologist. Rain fell and then it disappeared, he said. There were a few pools, but no lakes. Yet just here there were springs and rivers.

One of these rivers, the Faleala, ran over a high ledge farther into the jungle and turned into Olemoe Falls. Warren had brought along two Samoan boys in case we should have an emergency—a blowout, a wreck, whatever. They would come in handy. They were frisky and willing—one named Afasene ("Half a Cent") the other Siaki (Jack). We sat by the pool and they wove crowns of fern for me and put them on my head, making me feel like The Unbearable Bassington in the Saki novel.

And then they splashed and dived.

"Look at me, Paul!"

"I will get a stone from the bottom!"

"I will jump!"

"Don't look at him—look at me!"

Into the falls, down the sluice, diving backwards, fooling and loving it. They were fourteen and sixteen, but seemed much younger.

So this was what it was all about. You came here and frisked with brown boys, and slept with their sisters, and gave money to their parents, and lived and died. You slept and ate and laughed.

Savaii was a maddening place from the paddling point of view—either surf crashing on rocks and nowhere to launch from, or else a lagoon so shallow that my paddle blade struck bottom with each stroke. The Samoans were not boat people themselves—only the oldest ones could remember ever crossing from island to island paddling in a canoe or sailing an outrigger. This skill of using small craft, by which I tended to judge Pacific islands, had just about vanished in Samoa.

The Taga blowholes were not far from the mysterious stone mound of Pulemelei. The blowholes, locally know as *pupu,* were volcanic fissures in the cliffs of black lava that made this part of the coast of Savaii so dangerous. The swell crashing into the cliffs traveled through the sea caves and the hollows and shot into the vertical holes, producing a waterspout that made a plume of water eighty feet in the air.

We stood by one of the dozen or so blowholes and chucked coconuts into the hole just as the swell hit the cliff, and within a few seconds the coconut was shot into the air like a cannonball. The kids did the same with palm fronds and watched them flung upward, twisting and turning in the spray.

The whole place was deserted. It was one of the great natural phenomena of the Pacific. We stood under sunny skies and big puffy clouds, by the lovely sea, the boys fooling, the coconuts shooting skyward, and I thought, *My God this is stupid.*

But it was a feeble protest. By then a lazy sort of boredom had taken possession of my soul, the Oceanic malaise. I never saw anyone reading anything more demanding than a comic book. I never heard any youth express an interest in science or art. No one even talked politics. It was all idleness, and whenever I asked someone a question, no matter how simple, no matter how well the person spoke English, there was always a long pause before I got a reply, and I found these Pacific pauses maddening.

And there was giggling but no humor—no wit. It was just foolery. The *palangis* were no better. Warren got up a picnic with an American named John, who had started his own farm in the Midwest, and with Friedrich, who told me, "I am studying the smell of roast beef." He meant just that: He roasted a chunk of beef every day in his laboratory in Munich and then distilled its essence and tried breaking the flavor down into its chemical components. "This has many applications," he explained. In our party there were also the usual contingent of Samoan youths, clambering and laughing.

We were sitting under the palms at Asuisui, and when Warren passed out the sandwiches, I said, "I can't eat Spam. Hey, that reminds me. Ever read Descartes—René Descartes?"

Silence from John, silence from Friedrich, silence from Warren, giggles from the Samoans.

"As in 'Don't put Descartes before the horse'?"

In the ensuing silence, Warren cleared his throat. "I've read him," he said, "but it was years ago, and I don't have a retentive memory."

"I was just going to make a joke."

They stared at me.

"Descartes—didn't he say, 'I'm pink, therefore I'm Spam'?"

A look of apprehension settled over them, and only Manu broke the silence.

"What you tink?"

"What do I think about what?"

"Da wedda."

So we discussed the wind and clouds.

Later in his car Manu said, "I got a wife."

We were driving towards Lalomalava. His car was a jalopy which contained an expensive cassette player, and reggae music was blaring from his stereo speakers, mounted with some stuffed toys on the back shelf.

"Any kids?"

"I got a kid in here," he said, and banged the glove compartment. He was having trouble opening it, until he thumped it very hard. "Kid—in here—somewhere."

Finally he took out a crinkled photograph of a fat brown baby wrapped in a clean blue blanket. The picture had not been snapped in Samoa.

"My son," Manu said proudly.

"What's his name?"

"I dunno."

"Where was this picture taken?"

"Auckland."

"You want to go to Auckland?"

"No," Manu said, and tossed the picture back into the glove compartment and hammered it shut with his fist.

What exactly was the story here?

I traveled to the northwest of Savaii, to Asau Bay, to paddle and there I met Fat Frank, who had recently arrived from California and was scouting the island. He was an alcoholic, and he had taken up residence at a motel at Vaisala. Apart from Fat Frank there was only one other guest at the place, a Finn from a freighter in Apia, who complained bitterly about Frank. His habit was to rise at eleven, drink a bottle of Vailima Beer for breakfast, follow it with a half bottle of tequila, and then paw Samoan waitresses until he passed out. He was a chain-smoker and his huge pendulous belly hung over his belt. He sat hunched over, breathing hard. I met him in the late afternoon, after his second snooze, when he was wheezing and on whisky.

He grumbled about his feet swelling up. He hated the heat. He said he didn't sleep well. He was one of those fat people who when they are horizontal begin to breathe irregularly and snore in a choking, strangling manner all night, *Aaarrrghh!*

"I'll be here six weeks or so," he said.

"That seems such a long time for such a small island."

"Thing is, I'm thinking of relocating."

"Moving here to Samoa?"

"Yeah. Changing my whole life-style. Why wait until you retire? Why not do it now?"

He was only in his thirties, but had a certain swollen look that made him seem much older, like a fat elderly baby.

"Ever been here before?"

"No, but I think I could fit in. The people here are very friendly—very warm. Not like Pago. That's a dump. I was supposed to stay there a week and I stayed one night. But these people take you into their family."

"I think they expect something in return. I mean, wouldn't you have obligations?"

"We could work something out. I'll look around. Look for a house. Look for a village. Then find the chief and talk it over."

He was looking for a life and he made finding it seem simple. *A Somerset Maugham character,* people say, but in the flesh Somerset Maugham characters could be such slobs and bores.

"And I might do some business."

He had a very furtive way of lighting a cigarette, palming it, turning his lighter on it, sucking it hard, then spitting the smoke out. He was from Mile City, somewhere north of San Francisco.

"Want to know the trouble with business here? You can't make any money in a country where the people have no money."

Delivered of this wisdom he took a long pull on his bottle of hooch.

"But I figure a dive shop might make it. The Japs will come here eventually."

"Why would they come here? They want golf. Beaches. Luxury. Mickey Mouse logo shops. They like to shop. God, you can't even swim here. I'm just managing because I have my own sea kayak."

"I can make out."

"You might be a teeny bit bored."

"Go back"—he wasn't listening to me, he had a slow wheezing way of talking, and this sentence had begun long before—"get my toys. Motorcycle. Hi-fi. Diving equipment. Scuba gear."

Heavy people are often divers. Was it the sense of weightlessness that attracted them—the experience of being light and buoyant, as they chubbily made their way among the coral and the flitting fish?

"What do you do?" he asked me, wiping his mouth.

"I do a little writing."

"That's why you got all the questions!"

He looked around and laughed. He was laughing at the blazing sun, the palms, the wrecked beach—the worst of the hurricane had come here. His laughter showed in the rolls of flesh on his gut.

"I knew I was going to meet a writer here. As soon as I saw this fucked-up place I said to myself, 'I'm going to meet a writer.' And a painter. Where's the painter? There must be a painter here."

So he was thinking of leaving the vastness of northern California, and the friendliness of his small American town, and settling here in a jumbled family, taking up residence in a *fale* in a Samoan village, with all its Christians. I said this to him in so many words.

"It's a trade-off, isn't it?"

He wanted a new life. He wanted the pleasure of retirement now—not when he was arthritic and unhealthy. That in itself was sensible: At this rate he wouldn't last—fat and tanked up and chain-smoking.

"I got the answer. People will buy anything from someone they like."

"Meaning you?"

"Yeah. Like me. A real character," he said. He rested the bottle on his belly. "An interesting guy."

And then I understood, and I saw him in America, on his Harley-Davidson. He was one of those terrifyingly fat fellows in a Nazi crash helmet that are seen roaring down the highway, sitting behind the immensity of his belly, that shoot out in front of sober motorists who say, "Look at him, Doris. Hogging the road!"

"Don't make him mad," Doris says. "Please don't honk the horn."

And you don't.

Fat Frank was looking for an indulgent family, and it was possible that he would find one in Samoa, where you could develop a relationship with a family that had strong ties. I was not worried about Frank taking advantage of them; in the end, they would take him for all he was worth. But it was a paradoxical society. Outside the family there seemed to be no driving force, no loyalties; and the interdependency that was limited strictly to the family made it seem less like a society than like a simple organism, a certain type of jellyfish, perhaps, the hydrozoan that was a little colony of tentacles, some for stinging, some for eating, that sways and bloops along the surface of the sea.

Whenever I attempted to do something in Samoa—buy a ticket, rent a car, obtain information—the Samoan I asked looked a bit surprised and seemed totally unprepared to help. In their own lives, Samoans managed to scrape along with a little farming and a lot of remittances. It was the most cohesive society that I saw in the Pacific, but the least individualistic—perhaps the most traditional in Polynesia. But apart from the immediate needs of the family, nothing was achieved—where were the doctors, the dentists, pilots, engineers, architects, and skilled people? Many Samoan teachers fled to better-paying jobs elsewhere, and their positions were filled by Peace Corps volunteers. Even the grubbiest road supervisors and heavy machinery operators—driving bulldozers and augering holes for power lines—were from New Zealand and Australia.

Or was I taking the whole business too seriously? Perhaps it was all a comedy. But if you weren't in the mood for that sort of low hilarity it was the wrong place to visit.

"I tone like Tonga," a Samoan said to me.

"Why not?"

"Pecause it is too much sandy."

"Too sandy?"

"Yes. And dey tone like Samoan people."

"What a pity."

"Because a Samoan kai cut off da head of a Tonga kai."

"Is that all?"

"And cut off his leck."

"I see. The Samoan guy cut off his head and his leg."

An ancient quarrel, shrouded in myth? No. It happened in Auckland, he explained, just a few months ago.

Some of these wild cannibal-looking youths were very sweet. The surliest-seeming ones, obstinate one minute, could be unexpectedly helpful the next. The policemen were ineffectual but in their white helmets and epaulets they were at least picturesque. Was it because I was in Samoan backwaters? But in Samoa it was all backwaters. And at those moments when I was most exasperated I would look up and see the oddest things—a man holding a pig in his lap, or a man standing up to his neck in the lagoon, smoking a cigarette—and I would laugh the witless Samoan laugh and think: *Take this seriously and you're dead.*

Chapter 17
AMERICAN SAMOA: THE LITTERED LAGOON

No one in the Pacific has a good word for American Samoa. This alone predisposed me to liking these islands and finding them habitable and bounteous, the sort of carefree archipelago I might want to fling myself into and be happy as an Oceanic clam.

The place was generally hated, but what was the problem? Six little islands and one biggish one, Tutuila; a total population of 37,000 people—American Samoa had only half the population of the town where I was born, Medford, Massachusetts, which I had always thought of as unbearably small. And every year the United States government handed over roughly seventy-five million dollars to American Samoa. You couldn't get much more carefree and bounteous than that, though politically it is perhaps a kleptocracy.

On the face of it, there was no reason why these islands should not be paradise—indeed, they are, in their own potbellied way: The islanders are very happy. Life in American Samoa is one long Yankee boondoggle, and the people are so hoggishly contented that they cannot stand the idea of ever forming an independent political entity with their brothers and sisters in Western Samoa, just across the water, because that reunion might diminish the money supply. The average per capita income in Western Samoa was $580 a year; in American Samoa it was almost ten times that. But it was all funny money in any case—intravenous, drip-feed cash, as they said in Australia—most of it foreign aid. New Zealand had gone on financing its former territory of Western Samoa, and America still stumped up money for its indigent islands which, politically, had the same status as Puerto Rico.

So much for all the guff about the sacred concept of familyhood in the two Samoas. "Corrupted" is the perfect word, though an American Samoan can revert from being a fat guy in a Bart Simpson T-shirt, with a can of Coke Classic in his hand, watching the Super Bowl; and, at a moment's notice, turn into a big dark fire-breathing islander, confounding you with obscure incantations and unfathomable customs. When Samoans have their backs to the wall they put on a lavalava and pretend to be islanders. The rest of the time—it seemed to me—they were fat jolly people, with free money, having a wonderful time.

The last sight I had had of real life in Western Samoa was that of some women at dawn on the coast of southern Savaii, washing their clothes and themselves at the edge of the Faleala River—the soap suds vivid as surf against the black rocks. Virtually the first thing I saw in American Samoa were four enormously fat women sitting in Danny's Laundromat in Pago Pago, watching their clothes being tossed in washers and yakking about the high cost of living. They were an extraordinary size, guzzling Cokes and glowing with perspiration, and sitting with their chubby knees apart, Samoan-style.

Houses in Western Samoa are true *fales,* shaped as though modelled on the humpy helmet of Hernando de Soto, and enhanced with mats and blinds and thatch; in American Samoa the so-called *fales* are little boxy bungalows, prefabs made in California—flat roof, single walls—plopped on a slab. Poverty in Western Samoa has forced people to build in a traditional way, because it is cheaper. And the *fales* there are better suited to the climate than the cinder-block bungalows of Tutuila, which are unendurable without a rusty, howling air conditioner propped in a window. Even the churches are less impressive in American Samoa, because of their dreary modernity.

But in both Samoas dead ancestors are buried in the front garden, or next to the house, in a colorful sarcophagus. Samoans had all sorts of explanations for this burying of the dead beside the hibiscus hedge on the lawn—grief, affection, tradition, ancestor worship, the vulgar love of a good in-ground necropolis, a wish to be near Auntie Ida, and so forth. But the true answer seemed obvious to me. On an island where land tenure was always subject to lengthy deliberation, wasn't it a way of taking possession of the land? You could evict anyone from a house, but how did you go about ridding the place of a dozen dead relatives, sealed in coffins deep in the ground?

Kind of a crazy place, Verne in Tonga had told me. *But I'm kind of crazy, so I liked it there.*

The ferry from Apia to Pago Pago had been full ("We sell three hundred and twenty-one tickets, because we have three hundred and twenty-one life jackets," the man in the office explained) so I took the short airplane ride.

"You are overweight," the 350-pound Samoan at the check-in desk said.

It was nothing personal—it was my boat and my gear, but the chunky airline employee said that it was too much trouble to collect the additional charge, and so he waved me through.

Pretty was not the word for Tutuila; it looked fabulous, with green steep-sided mountains that had black peaks—dark splintery antique volcanoes—and precipitous valleys plunging down to seacliffs and rocky headlands. It was a high vertical island, with a wide lagoon and many fine bays and the deeply indented harbor of Pago Pago—a lovely place, more vertiginous and dramatic, steamier, much lusher than its sister islands to the west. Not pretty at all, but hot, languorous, ravishing, dangerously attractive, like the person you pass on the sidewalk—what is it about these lucky people?—who makes you feel flustered and breathless and forgetful. You could fall in love at first sight with Tutuila.

But on second glance, a moment later, looking closer, you recover and decide not to throw your life away. Pago Harbor is muddy—it doesn't get properly flushed by the tides—and it reeks of the tuna canneries on the eastern side, Star Kist and Van Camp's. The rubbish on the beaches, flung everywhere and seldom collected, is worse than anywhere else in the Pacific and would make any sort of beach activity in Samoa depressing— but the lagoon is too shallow for swimming, the coral is broken and dead, there is a sensational litter of old soft-drink cans underwater, so there is not much beach activity.

When an American Samoan is finished with a can or a box or a bag, he or she flings it aside. In the past such items were palm fronds and coconut husks and banana peels: biodegradable. These days the trash is beginning to accumulate. The island is noisy, vandalized, and all somehow familiar—it is not the seedy poverty and squalor of Apia, where there is no money and nothing seems to work; it is the fat wasteful American-style conspicuousness epitomized by much-too-big, much-too-expensive, rusted cars. Greedy, wasteful, profligate, and proprietorial, American Samoans are living on large handouts, forever pushing supermarket shopping carts full of junk food, packages and cans, the Cheez Ball diet of fat-bellied Polynesia—seedy prosperity.

The two Samoas are close together, but while Western Samoa looks to New Zealand and Australia, American Samoa looks to Hawaii and mainland America. New Zealanders have taught Western Samoans the elements of thrift—the roadsides and lagoons are dreary but noticeably tidier in those islands. What America has accomplished in its Samoan islands—and this is instantly visible—is the removal of the cultural props, by creating a cash economy. The worst effect of this has been a kind of competitive selfishness which has fragmented the family. Most people I met in American Samoa spoke with regret about the loosening of these family ties, which has meant a decline in traditional formality and courtesy and a widespread casualness that borders on insult and disrespect.

I tended to evaluate Pacific islanders by the way they related to the ocean around them. Did they swim? Did they fish with nets or spears? Did they build boats, and paddle and sail? Could they go from one island to another on their own in one of these boats? Once, these people had been among the greatest sailors in the world. But what now? I wondered whether they were afraid of the sea—whether they knew anything about it, whether they cared. Did they know which way the wind was blowing, could they forecast weather from the patterns of the clouds and the color of the sky? Did they ever venture beyond the breakers on the reef?

On some islands, it was possible to say that the islanders were still people of the sea. Western Samoans did some fishing and boating in a limited sense, and in a Christianized pigheaded way, they were traditional. In American Samoa some subtle and obscure customs were still practiced in their dull bungalows, but the people seemed indifferent to the ocean. No one went sailing. No one paddled. They jumped into the water and splashed—but they hardly swam. Now and then you saw a fat kid on a jet ski. The rest of them hid from the sun. They stayed away from the lagoon. Their fish came out of cans. It had been years since anyone had made an outrigger. It was as though the entire population (and this seemed pretty odd in the Pacific) was possessed by the most virulent form of hydrophobia.

The tradition is that the first Samoans—the first real Polynesians—arrived from Tonga and Fiji, in about 600 B.C., at the eastern tip of Tutuila, near the village of Tula. Never mind that it was now an unprepossessing village of flimsy bungalows and littered roads and stray dogs; it was the ancient landing place of the canoes. I decided to paddle around there and set my sights on the only island I could possibly paddle to, Aunu'u, off the southeast corner.

"You'll never make it," a Samoan told me.

This was a true landlubber's point of view: The island was only a few miles. Even with a rip-roaring current I could have made it, I felt.

Later, I was looking around Alofau, having just come on the coast road. In an equivalent place in Western Samoa the people would have been watchful and circumspect. Here they were talkative and pushy.

Kenny, a big brown man, said to me, "You are new here."

It was not a question, so I asked whether he meant here in Au'asi, or on the island.

"On the island," he said. "In Samoa."

"How do you know that?"

"By your face."

"I look new to the island, you mean?"

"We know all the faces. I haven't seen you before," Kenny said. "I think you have arrived very recently."

"That's true. But I'm surprised you know that."

He said, "We can know everything, because we know everyone on the island."

Elsewhere in Oceania, and in Western Samoa in particular, such a conversation would have been essentially friendly, but in American Samoa it seemed intrusive and aroused my suspicions—the man seemed determined to nose around and probe, to find something out. And even the most innocent-seeming remark put me on my guard.

I made my way around the island. I looked at Tula, I scoped out the island of Aunu'u. At night I returned to my hotel in Pago. I came to think of it as a soggy, good-hearted town. Like most other visitors I reflected on Maugham's "Rain." Maugham was another writer who had sanctified a place by using it as a setting; he had done the islands a great favor—made them seem exotic and interesting. Camping was out of the question here—all the land was owned, accounted for, and heavily protected against any intrusion. A camper seemed like a squatter—indeed, that was how the Samoans themselves sometimes staked their claims—he or she might never go away. And it must be said that not one square foot of land in American Samoa could be owned by a non-Samoan. The Samoans were noted for not being particularly fastidious about other people's rights, but they were fanatics about their own—being selfish and infantile seemed appropriate to their clumsy obesity, like children who are always insisting It's mine!

I was assembling my boat on a beach one day—a futile-seeming operation: The lagoon was inches deep and littered with rusty cans, there was no break in the reef, the surf was high and impenetrable. But I soldiered on, just to see what I might find. And, having left one small item in my rented car (the stoppers for my inflatable sponsons), I found I could not finish setting up the boat until I got them. I had been talking to two fellows—any activity at all seemed to interest people here. No one ever offered to help me, nor did anyone refuse when I asked them to lend a hand.

I had parked my car discreetly, so that it couldn't be broken into (the island was rife with break-in stories), and I was in two minds about whether to get the items out of the car. I decided to be oblique.

"I have to buy something at the store," I said.

I went down the street, into the store, bought a drink, went out the back way, tiptoed behind the building, and slipped past some thick trees, ducked down, and opened the car door, retrieved the stoppers, crept back to the rear of the building, and left through the front door, still sipping the can of Fanta.

"Is that your car?" one of the men said when I got back to the beach.

How had he seen me? And of course the question worried me, because he knew I was just about to set off into the lagoon, where I could be seen. It would have been so easy for them to break into my car.

"Where are you going in that boat?" the other man asked.

"Just paddling."

"How long will you be out there?"

What was this? Again, their nosiness seemed to give them away. In Western Samoa they would simply have watched me. Here, artless and intrusive at the same time, they seemed to reveal their intentions in all their nosy questions.

But in the event, the lagoon was too shallow for paddling, and that was the day I planned my trip out of historic Tula, to make for the offshore island of Aunu'u.

I was continually worried about Samoans stealing my gear. Everyone—even Samoans themselves—spoke of the predilection for theft here in the islands; and everyone had a theory as to why it happened—ranging from *It's-an-old-Samoan-custom* to *They're-natural-kleptomaniacs*. It was always assumed that if you left something sitting idly by it would be instantly pinched, and no one was very subtle about it. If someone stole a shirt from you, he would probably be seen wearing it the next day; if someone stole a hammer or a knife, the thief would be observed using the item very soon after. "And if you say, 'That's mine!' they'll laugh at you." So I was told.

I was careful, but any traveler is vulnerable. In Tonga my hotel room had been plundered while I was out. Yet nothing was stolen from me in Samoa.

I paddled from Tula to the little hamlet of Au'asi, where there was a breakwater, just to verify that there were motorboats that plied back and forth from Aunu'u Island at a dollar a trip. I thought I would ask one of these motorboaters about the sea conditions between here and the island.

A boatman was hunkered down on the jetty, so I asked him, "Is there much of a current out there?"

It seemed calm enough, but there were waves breaking on all the reefs and shoals, and there was about a three-foot swell—not bad-looking, but the sea is a riddle.

"The sea is move," the man said.

"You mean, the sea is moving—a current?" And I made the appropriate gestures with my hands.

"The sea is move," he said placidly.

I muttered it to myself.

"The sea is smooth?"

"Yeh. Is move."

It was too late that day to paddle out, so I returned the following day and set up my boat. Seven boys—big bulky teenagers, just out of school—sat under the palms at Au'asi, watching me struggle with my boat parts. The scene could have been idyllic—healthy youths in the shade of the coconut palms, by the beach, on a sunny day in Samoa. But the tussocky grass was littered with paper, the fence was broken, the beach was scattered with broken glass, and in the shallow water there were bottles and cans and soggy sunken blobs of paper. Dogs barked nearby, overloaded buses wheezed past (because the shoreline in Samoa is a road), and music played—reggae or rap, from each bus.

The boys wore T-shirts with various motifs—one showed a black Bart Simpson making an obscene gesture and was captioned *Fucking Bart,* another showed an angry duck—*I Got An Attitude!* it said. One said *Hawaii,* another—the most preposterous—*Samoa: People of the Sea;* and still others were simply numbered and colored athletic shirts.

"What's that—a tent?" one said.

I was unfolding the canvas hull. Before I could answer, another said, "Is a pig boat. Is a chip."

I said, "It's a boat."

I was trying to assemble it quickly and get out of there.

"What kind of boat? You can give us a ride?"

"It's for one person," I said.

"He don't want to give you a ride, you stupid shit."

They hovered around me.

"Did you just come from school?" I asked.

"We just come from fucking these guy's girlfriend."

"Shut up, you stupid."

I found their insolence remarkable, because on arriving at Pago Pago Airport I had been given a pamphlet with no less than a dozen admonitions on how to behave in American Samoa. One concerned general behavior: *It is hoped that you will take extra care to ensure that none of your actions is misinterpreted as dissatisfaction with your host;* and the reason was given: *The Samoan people are, by nature and culture, extremely anxious to please their guests.*

"Where you come from, mister?" asked *People of the Sea.*

"I'm from the States. What about you?"

Would they say "American Samoa"? "Samoa"? "Tutuila"? or what?

"I'm from Compton," one said, naming a black area in Los Angeles—the name frequently occurred in the violent songs of a rap group that called itself N.W.A. or Niggers With Attitude. Needless to say, this group was immensely popular in American Samoa.

I said, "Are you really from Compton?"

"He lying," another said.

"I'm from Waipahu."

"Isn't that in Hawaii?" I asked.

"He never been to Hawaii!"

"Me, I'm from California, man."

"Dis a lie!"

And so they went on, giggling and yakking, and none of them told me where they were really from, the offshore island of Aunu'u.

"I think you're waiting for the boat to Aunu'u," I said. "What do you do out there?"

"We kill people!" the one in the *Fucking Bart* T-shirt said.

"Ya, we do dat!"

Tedious little bastards, I thought, but I said, "You are being very rude to me. Do you think it's funny?"

They were silent a moment, and then one jabbed his finger sideways. "He tink so."

It seemed to be one of the oldest Samoan customs to victimize the person without a family, the individual, the outsider, the stranger, because it was a society where, if you had no family, you had no status. Perhaps this was the reason they had achieved so little, either here or on the mainland. They did not want to stand out. They were the most pathetic conformists, and so the greatest bullies, in the Pacific. Who was I but a middle-aged oddball on the beach, trying to assemble a foreign-looking object that they did not recognize as a boat. They mocked me because I was an outsider, and they mocked me because they outnumbered me. None of them would have had the guts to face me alone, unless he had been suffering the Samoan affliction of extreme bad temper, a sort of hideous Black Dog mood called *musu.* A Samoan with *musu* was a man to avoid.

When my collapsible boat was once again set up, one of the youths stood and said in a demanding way, "You give me a ride."

"I don't think so," I said.

"Where you going?" another asked.

"I think I'll paddle out there."

"You go to the island?"

"Maybe. Do you live there?"

"I live in Hawaii. Hee hee!"

"You're all very funny guys," I said, and turned my back on them.

Some older people, eight or nine of them, were sitting nearby, also waiting for the boat to Aunu'u—fat women, fat men. They heard this bantering, but took no interest in it; they looked hot, and bored, and irritable. They carried parcels of food, and when they walked to the water's edge to look for the boat they crunched old crumpled soft-drink cans.

I vowed that I would not leave the beach until the boys did, because I suspected that such cranky kids might find my car and break into it. The launch came and went. The boys stayed. I wondered what to do. And, waiting, I slapped on some suntan lotion, because of the dazzling sun.

"What dat stuff?"

"So I won't get sunburned," I said. I knew if I ignored their silly questions it would be worse: They would consider it a victory to irritate me.

"Looks like sperm," one said.

"He putting sperm on."

I said, "Is that funny?"

"You got sperm on your face."

I said calmly, as though seeking information, "Why are you saying that to me?"

He laughed at me, but I pursued it, and finally said, "What's your name?"

"M.C. Hammer."

More insolence—another name from the rappers' Parnassus.

This was ridiculous, but it was wrong to think that it could have happened anywhere else in Oceania. I had traveled enough in the region to realize that this was a uniquely American Samoan experience. They were victimizers, they were oafish, and lazy, and defiant and disrespectful. Would they be different when they grew up? It was impossible to say. Perhaps, like so many others, they were just waiting for a chance to go to Honolulu or Los Angeles like a hundred thousand other Samoans whose culture had become degenerate.

Eventually, they boarded their motorboat, and were swept away, jeering, and the oafs I had met in Western Samoa now seemed to me the very picture of innocence.

Paddling out to the island of Aunu'u I thought again of the pamphlet that had been given to me, with the rules that all visitors were urged to observe:

When in a Samoan house, do not talk while standing.
Do not stretch your legs out when seated.
Do not carry an umbrella past a house.
Do not drive through a village when chiefs are gathering.
Do not eat while walking through a village [it seemed to me that
    Samoans ate no other way, and usually were munching a very
    large jelly donut].
Samoans are deeply religious—pray and sing with them.
Do not wear flowers in church.
When drinking kava, hold the cup in front of you and say "manuia."
    ["When drinking Coke" would have been more apposite, since
    that seemed firmly part of the culture.]
Bikinis and shorts are not considered appropriate attire in Samoan
    villages or town areas.
Ask permission before snapping photos or picking flowers.
Be extra quiet on Sundays.

And there were more. How odd that this joyously piggy society should
be so obsessed with travelers' etiquette, or apparently so easily offended.
    No, I told myself, *this is a comedy.*
    I continued paddling out to this small low crater in the sea. I was
always concerned, in one of these stretches of open water or channels,
whether a current would pick me up and sweep me sideways, into the blue
moana. I had left the safety of a shallow lagoon, cut through a break in
the reef, and now I was between a large peaky island and a small green
islet.
    It was a lovely day. My consolation on such a day was that if something
went drastically wrong I would still have plenty of time to get straightened out, either by paddling hard for shore or sending up flares. But so
far it seemed easy paddling to Aunu'u, and as I glided down the back of
the swell towards the island, I congratulated myself on having found in
this somewhat degenerate and tentative territory a good place to go.
    And where would I have been without my boat? At the mercy of
mocking and xenophobic islanders, or worse—people who hated boats.
An astonishingly large number of people in American Samoa seemed to
hate the water, or at the very least were indifferent to it—didn't go near
it. How odd for them to be islanders, and to live on a small island at that.
    I set my compass for a low white building and when I drew nearer to
the island I saw a pair of breakwaters below it. A launch was just leaving
this enclosure—so this was the place to go. I was there in twenty more
minutes, and paddling into this tight harbor I saw eight or ten boys
swimming and diving—jumping from the little stone jetty. Three of them

immediately jumped into the water and swam towards me and tried to tip my boat over.

The Samoan people are, by nature and culture, extremely anxious to please their guests, the pamphlet had said. This might well have been true of some villages, of the attitude of elders or chiefs. If so, I was not privileged to encounter it in American Samoa. It was all foolery and antagonism for no good reason.

"Go away," I said. "Let go of my boat."

Brown hands were fumbling and snatching at my lines.

"Bugger off!" I said, very loudly.

It worked. They splashed back to the jetty. But I still had a problem. The wharf was too high for me to land. I could tie up, but I would have to climb a ladder and leave my boat to the frenetic attention of these jumping, screaming kids and some lurking adults.

Some coconuts were being unloaded from another boat. I asked a man what they were used for here.

"To make *palusami,*" he said.

Sticking to that traditional dish of steamed taro leaves and coconut cream seemed old-fashioned and civilized, and it reassured me. It made me curious and encouraged me to look for a landing place on the island.

I had a good nautical chart of the whole coast of American Samoa, and it showed me the particular jigs and jags of this little island. I paddled out beyond the breakers and then went counterclockwise, past a shipwreck and another beach and reef. But the beaches were too steep for a landing—they all seemed to be ledges of pale crushed coral bashed by waves. I needed a more sloping beach.

Farther on, at the eastern shore of the island, was an inlet, Ma'ama'a Cove, where I thought I might land, until at the last moment I saw surf roiling and smashing on rocks. And so I paddled on.

There was a lake of quicksand near the northwest coast, or so I had been told. I continued paddling towards this part of the island, still looking for a landing place. I was now approaching another reef, and more breakers, but I could see how I might squeeze myself in between them, and did so, leaping out at the beach and hurrying out of the path of the waves just before they broke over my boat.

How odd, among all those awful teenagers, and the junk food, and the suspicion, to have been subjected to these tricky sea conditions. But that was the paradox of Samoa: American bad food and popular culture, on a lovely volcanic island that was set in turbulent and reefy seas.

This small island of Aunu'u was a beautiful place, with a good view of Tutuila and its easternmost point, Cape Matatula. I also suspected that it might be one of the best places in American Samoa, since there were no cars here, no amusement arcades, no fast food, no laundromat or take-aways. There was one village and in it, one shop. Like other tiny offshore islands I had seen, this too was a quiet preserve, still living partly in the past. Given the state of American Samoa, this was amazing.

I pulled up my kayak and hid it, and then walked to the Pala Lake to look at the quicksand. I found it easily—it was sludgy red sand, covering the whole of the lake's surface, and it shimmered in the sun. But how was I to know that it really was quicksand? I had read that men hunting ducks swam in the quicksand by lying horizontal, keeping themselves perfectly flat. I was alone and decided not to test it by trying this. But these stories about quicksand were the first ones that had ever stirred my imagination when I was ten or so and considering travel to distant places: the idea of being sucked down and smothered by depthless sand the consistency of cold Quaker Oats.

The idea here was that a stranger was supposed to ask permission before making camp here—the old fear of people squatting on your land and never leaving. But I decided not to announce myself. I wanted to be on my own, and I knew that if I asked I would either be forced to stay in one of their *fales* with an inquisitive and imprisoning family, or else I would be made conspicuous in my campsite and perhaps robbed.

I walked around looking for a place to pitch my tent, and nearer dusk found a sheltered spot in a grove of trees and set up camp quickly. I did not bother to make tea. I did not light my stove. I ate sardines and bread and listened to the BBC, and did not switch on my flashlight. When it was dark I crawled in and spent a fitful night, wondering whether I would be discovered, or my kayak stolen. And, meanwhile, what about my car on Tutuila? That was the terrible aspect of American Samoa—I could never tell for sure whether I was in America or Samoa.

At dawn I crept out and checked the boat. It was still well hidden, but a woman walking along the beach saw me. She said hello and I greeted her.

"How did you come here?" she asked.

"By boat," I said, trying to be ambiguous, and to change the subject I asked her the meaning of the island's name.

"I dunno," she said, and laughed, and walked on.

That morning, after I had packed and hidden my gear—so that it would not be seen and stolen—I walked along a circular track to a marsh and back to the cove where I had seen the thrashing surf. It looked much worse from here on shore than it had from the backs of the waves.

I killed the day swimming and then walked to the village, hoping not to meet the boys who had been so irritating the day before. The older people were polite, although the kids were still a nuisance, preening themselves and trying to be defiant. It was wonderful to be in a place with no cars, and yet most of these older people and all the schoolkids made a daily trip to Tutuila. And that afternoon, when I paddled back across the channel to Tutuila, I was both uplifted by the mountains and the glorious vistas along the south coast, and also depressed by the seedy modernity of this seemingly spoiled society.

The next day in Leone, the second town of Tutuila—a shopping mall, a school, supermarkets—I met a woman who was visiting her family. She said she lived in Las Vegas. She was half-Samoan and looked very weary but not old. "I love Las Vegas," she said. An islander in the desert. It seemed incredible to me, and I remarked on that. "I miss Las Vegas," she said.

And that same day, getting a haircut, I asked the barber where he was from.

"Western Samoa," he said. "But my wife is from here."

His two children had American passports. He said that they would almost certainly end up in the United States, while he would probably go back to his home village on Savaii. So American Samoa was like a convenient ship which people boarded to get them where they wanted to go.

"I don't want them to stay here," he said. He was very polite—and he did not put into words the other thought that must have been in his mind: that there was nothing for them in Western Samoa.

The traveler's great fear in Samoa is of *musu*—the ferocious mood that turns a Samoan man into a brute. You can see it in their eyes, people say, and if a Samoan behaves like a bear with a sore head he is in the grip of *musu*. My apprehension had made me overly cautious in Samoa, but just before I was about to leave I sat down and examined my Samoan experience, and I realized that most Samoans, on whatever island, had been kind to me—generous, good-humored, and helpful. I felt bad about carping, and was it wrong to make so much of their physical size? It was a race of giants, with big flapping feet, and when they walked their thighs rubbed and made a chafing sound that was audible ten feet away. I could only conclude that when Samoans were good they were very very good, and when they were bad they were horrid. But most of the time they were indifferent.

It was when I was in Samoa that American troops flushed the remaining Iraqis from the suburbs and rode in triumph through Kuwait City. This was a news item in the Samoan newspapers, but it was not a topic of conversation; there was no air of celebration, and not even much interest in it. There was no flag-waving, but was that so surprising?

American Samoa wasn't a political entity. It was a social phenomenon—a rescued orphan, a fat feckless child that we had adopted. The arrangement perfectly suited *fa'a Samoa,* the Samoan way and its family ideal in which everyone was looked after. If you didn't have one you found one. I met many foreigners who had attached themselves to Samoan families, and were perfectly happy to support everyone. The Samoans remained hospitable as long as someone else paid their bills. They sat by the littered lagoon, cooling their bellies, and eating.

Samoa had become part of the American family and was content. Samoans were generally unenthusiastic, but similarly they were uncomplaining, and this little-brown-brother relationship would continue as long as America fed them and paid for their pleasures.

Chapter 18

TAHITI: THE WINDWARD SHORE
OF THE ISLAND OF LOVE

One day in 1768 a barebreasted Tahitian girl climbed from her canoe to a French ship under the hot-eyed gaze of 400 French sailors who had not seen any woman at all for over six months. She stepped to the quarter-deck where, pausing at a hatchway, she slipped the flimsy cloth *pareu* from her hips and stood utterly naked and smiling at the men. Up went the anchor, and in that moment the myth of romantic Tahiti was conceived, a paradise of fruit trees, brown tits, and kiddie porn. Like Venus rising from the waves—that was how the naked girl was described by the captain of the ship, Louis-Antoine de Bougainville, the first Frenchman in Tahiti, who believed he had discovered heaven on earth ("I thought I was transported into the garden of Eden"), the abode of Venus, the Island of Love.

Now I had a similar experience in Tahiti, involving stark nakedness, the lagoon, the hot-eyed gaze, and an outrigger canoe, but in its suddenness and coloration this incident was more up to date and more represent-ative of Tahiti today. And I was the one in the outrigger canoe.

After a day or so rattling around the streets of Papeete, Tahiti's capital, I rented an outrigger from a Frenchman (he called it his *"petite pirogue"*) and paddled for a day to Tahiti-Iti—"Little Tahiti," the volcanic bulge that is attached to the eastern shore of the island. The ancient name of the island of Tahiti is *Tahiti-nui-i-te-vai-uri-rau,* "Great Tahiti of the Many-Colored Waters."

The name is apt. The lagoon beneath Tahiti's dead green volcanoes is a luminous varying blue, not seawater-colored, but with glittering opales-cent depths, and elsewhere shallow coral shelves, white and knobbed like bones, rippling with fish. Overall the water is limpid and unexpectedly bright, like those candy-colored liqueurs made from berries, cordials that are so pretty in the squat glass bottles in a bar that just looking at them cools you and takes away your thirst. The surface of Tahiti's lagoon was spangled with stars of sunlight. A mile or so offshore was the reef, being pounded by surf that was so heavy it had the muffled boom of distant cannon fire and it ringed the entire island with a white flash of foam.

Tahiti has its drawbacks—it is expensive, traffic-choked, noisy, corrupt, and Frenchified—but it is impossible to belittle its natural physical beauty, and in spite of the car exhausts there is nearly always in the air the fragrant aroma—the *noanoa*—of flowers—the *tiare* especially, a tiny white gardenia that is Tahiti's national blossom. Visitors are full of complaints, though. Just that morning, on the public vehicle they call *le truck* (a cross between a mammy wagon and a school bus, and Tahiti's only bargain) I had fallen into conversation with a man from Maryland. His name was Don Kattwinkel—he wore a get-acquainted badge—and he was obviously a sucker for carvings, from the look of his war club and his letter opener. He was on the three-day tour, just arrived at Faa'a a few days ago—today Tahiti, tomorrow New Zealand. And he tried to sum up Tahiti for me.

"No one smiles here," he said. "And you can't drink the water."

I broke it to him gently that both were half-truths. The locals smiled at each other, even if they didn't smile at us, and they boiled their water before drinking it.

Don made no comment on that. He said, "You sound like you're from Australia."

I wanted to tell him that people have been killed for uttering an uncalled-for libel like that.

"You're sure not from Mass," he went on. "I know that dialect."

I was thinking about this irritating fart while I was paddling my canoe—nothing like meeting a man like that to preoccupy yourself. There was a current campaign put on by the Polynesian Tourist Board called *Put On A Smile!*—encouraging Polynesians to smile at tourists, mostly Japanese, none of whom smiled themselves. Is there a Japanese smile that does not seem like an expression of pain?

By midafternoon I had paddled halfway around this part of the island, and was nearing the village of Atimaono. It was not much of a place, but it was the setting of one of Jack London's masterpieces, his story "The Chinago." In the story some Chinese laborers—"Chinagos"—are accused of murder, and though all are innocent of the crime, they are found guilty by the French magistrate and one, Ah Chow, is sentenced to hang. Another, Ah Cho, is given twenty years in a prison colony, but one morning he is taken to this village, Atimaono, and told that he is to be beheaded. He protests to the various gendarmes—it is a case of mistaken identity, because the names are so similar—and at last, pleading for his life and proving he is not the condemned man, he is believed. But the French officials confer. They have come a long way from Papeete. The guillotine is ready. Five hundred other laborers have been assembled to watch. A postponement to find the right man would mean being bawled out by the French bureaucrats for inefficiency and time-wasting. Also it is a very hot day and they are impatient.

All this time Ah Cho listens and watches.

At last, but knowing they have the wrong man, one French policeman says, "Then let's go on with it. They can't blame us. Who can tell one Chinago from another? We can say that we merely carried out instructions with the Chinago that was turned over to us . . ."

And, still making excuses, the French strap down the innocent Chinese man and strike off his head.

"The French, with no instinct for colonization," London writes at one point, and that is the subject of the grim story.

An hour past Atimaono was the harbor of Port Phaeton. In a lovely garden by the sea was the Gauguin Museum, but in spite of its name it contained no paintings by Gauguin, only a haunted grimacing tiki. Farther on, the village of Papeari was said to be the first settlement of the seagoing people who originally landed on Tahiti and it lay next to the piece of land, like a pinched waist, where Little Tahiti was attached to Big Tahiti. But it was all so suburban.

One of the curious facts of Tahitian life was that strictly speaking there were few usable beaches on the island—the public ones were dismal and littered, the others were the property of proprietorial Tahitian villages. Looking towards the island from the lagoon, I could see that the coast was an unbroken stretch of bungalows and villas, one enormous attenuated suburb that encircled the whole of Tahiti. Undermined by French aid programs, and besieged by French construction companies, the Polynesians have abandoned their traditional house-building. The houses were extremely unattractive and they were packed cheek by jowl along the coast, surrounded by chain link fences and walls and high hedges. Most Tahitian bungalows had signs saying TABU, which needed no translation, and the French houses had security cameras and signs saying ATTENTION CHIEN MÉCHANT! (Beware of the Fierce Dog!)

Earlier in the day, paddling near Punaauia, I had passed a pair of *fares*, or traditional huts, but there were not many others like them in the whole of French Polynesia. I was so interested in them that I went ashore there and was told that these two at the edge of the beach at Punaauia were owned by the Swede Bengt Danielsson, who had run aground in Polynesia forty-odd years ago on the raft *Kon-Tiki*. In his book recounting the adventure, Thor Heyerdahl wrote, "Bengt was right; this was heaven," and Bengt stayed in Polynesia.

"Monsieur Danielsson is on holiday in Sweden," a Tahitian woman on the lawn told me.

I was sorry to miss him, because Danielsson and his French-born wife Marie-Thérèse have courageously fought a vocal battle against French nuclear testing in the Pacific, and in this small and politically incestuous French colony Danielsson has been threatened, obstructed, and shunned. Yet he perseveres in publishing to the world the fact that the French have been continually detonating nuclear devices—160 so far—in one of the world's most fragile ecosystems, a coral atoll, nuking it to pieces, killing fish, and causing cancer.

Perhaps it was just as well that I did not engage Danielsson on the subject of French colonialism, because just a short trip to any French territory in the Pacific is enough to convince even the most casual observer that the French are among the most self-serving, manipulative, trivial-minded, obnoxious, cynical, and corrupting nations on the face of the earth.

Et c'est vous qui parlez! a French person might reply. *Look who's talking!*

It is true that America has overwhelmed its own territory in Samoa and made it a welfare state, but Samoans have emigrated wholesale to the mainland United States, where they flourish or fail, according to their abilities. There is no profit in Samoa for us. But Polynesia is all profit for the French; they need the land and the distance to capitalize on world air routes for French airlines, and they need Polynesia as a military garrison, and—most profitable of all—they need nuclear testing facilities for their arms industry. As an old-fashioned colony it is a racket. The French effort is devoid of idealism.

Only a minuscule number of Polynesians ever make it to metropolitan France to qualify as doctors or administrators—the French run the entire show. But the patronizing racism inherent in French colonial policy has not had the demoralizing effect that was intended. They planted themselves in the islands and consistently discriminated against Polynesians and refused to learn their language—there was a law passed in French Polynesia in the 1960s forcing Polynesians and Chinese to take French names so they could be more easily pronounced. In this way, the French turned most of these friendly people into sullen adversaries and some into lapdogs. But though they have lost most of their traditional skills of weaving and house-building and fishing and sailing, the Polynesians have retained their oral culture—and that is a good thing, because no one needs their culture more than colonized people. What else do they have?

The Polynesians paid lip service to the French and so the French truly believed they had subverted the islanders. But in fact they only made a greater burden for themselves. By encouraging the islanders to be "colorful" they distanced themselves. The French are at their most obvious, their most bourgeois and sentimental when they are dealing with people they regard as savages, but it seems to be a fact that sentimentality is a trait one always finds in bullies and brutes.

The honest thing, in dealing with Tahiti, would be to discuss French Polynesia as a depressing political problem, because it has been a French colony for 150 years. Everything else ought to be irrelevant—that is, whether the beaches are pleasant and the food is tasty, and the hotels are comfortable, and what's the music like? The very fact of politics mattering in the Pacific seems strange—few people on other islands care about politics—yet it is the only place in the Pacific where there is a political situation. It is a characteristic of colonies that unless political life is manipulated or made ineffectual the place won't work.

But it is all so boring. I liked Pacific islanders generally for the way they guffawed at politicians—I admired their sense of family, their practicality, their usual indifference to world events. They were out of the mainstream, on the other side of the world—the brighter, happy side. For those with televisions, "Operation Desert Storm" had been to them not much more than a nightly entertainment video. That attitude seemed informed by a healthy combination of wisdom and vulgarity, and a taste for sensationalism—but most of the world's couch potatoes are much the same.

There was always a mixture of motives among Polynesians: They made you feel at home and then they stole from you. If you complained, they would say that it was nothing personal—and if you couldn't afford it, what were you doing here, so far from home, in the first place? Colonial politics was just another complication. Yes, the French built courthouses and schools, but the French colonialists needed such institutions far more than Tahitians did. I just kept wishing that the French were a bit nicer and more generous, and weren't so keen on nuking everything in sight. They said they had to—for world peace, but that was *merde.* The French arms industry, third largest in the world, and exporter of nuclear technology, now more than ever depended on extensive nuclear testing.

I paddled past Bengt Danielsson's two thatched-roof *fares.*

Buffeted by the trade winds—the wind never ceases to blow in Polynesia—I kept within the reef, glorying in the sight of the lovely island of Moorea, its mountains looming dark and spiky—local myths claimed they were the dorsal fins of giant fish, but the island looked to me like a seagoing dragon, crossing the channel known as the Sea of the Moon.

It was then, squinting into the intense glare of a cloudless oceanic afternoon—the sun slanted into my eyes—that I saw a small raft drifting perilously near the reef. There were some inert specks on it—humans probably—but it was the oddest possible place for a raft to be. If it went on drifting it would be smashed to pieces by surf. It had no mast or sail, nor was anyone paddling it. I had the idea that it had broken free of a ship and that somehow it had floated through a break in the reef. What was beyond question was that it was hardly visible from shore. The only reason I could see the raft was because I was in a seaworthy outrigger canoe and paddling along the margin of the reef.

You sometimes heard stories of the ordeal of the people on such rafts, how their expensive yacht had been sunk by a killer whale, and how the quarrelling castaways had clung to the wreckage for days or weeks, praying for deliverance until, one sunny morning, the battered thing hove into view on a tropical shore, where holiday-minded families frolicked with beach balls, the raft looking as though it had floated straight out of Poe's *Narrative of Arthur Gordon Pym,* and it was immediately, grotesquely clear that the survivors had made it through by using each other with the utmost barbarity—human bones, scraps of flesh, and the evidence of cannibalism. "Daddy, what's wrong with those people?"—one of those rafts.

That made me paddle faster, and I could see that there were only two figures on board and that I was gaining on the raft. It excited me to think that I might be the first person to witness the arrival of this desperate craft in Tahiti, and I alone would hear their ordeal—what a piece of luck for someone like me, who intended to write about these islands where in the normal way nothing much happened.

Now I could see that the two figures on the raft were lying flat, as though prostrate from the sun, and there was something melancholy about the solitariness of their situation—within the reef and yet still so far from shore. You could drown, or starve, or die of thirst, or suffocate with heat exhaustion, even in this bewitchingly lovely place.

I had a water bottle and the remains of my lunch in my boat—enough to revive them, I was sure. They were upwind, so they did not hear the thrashing of my canoe, but I was soon close enough to recognize the strangeness of this simple raft. It was not drifting; it was tethered to a mooring. Apart from the two people, there was nothing else on it, not an object of any kind—no flag, no scraps, no bones, no bucket, nothing—nor any clothes.

There were two skinny women on the raft and they were naked. As I drew near—I was only thirty feet away—some warning vibration of my maleness must have charged the air: Suddenly each woman sat up straight. Or had they heard my paddling? They were young, in their twenties, rather pretty and, from their demeanor, French. They were browner than any Tahitian I had seen—the gleaming darkness of the most lizard-like sunbather. It was the sort of tanning that made you think of leather. Seeing me, they arranged their bodies compactly, as modestly as they could, folded themselves with ingenious economy, their knees drawn up under their chins, and their feet jammed together, and they hugged themselves, like monkeys squatting in the rain.

To preserve their modesty, I did not go much closer, and yet I was close enough to be able to marvel at their nakedness, at the exoticism of this sight—a pair of nymphs on a bobbing raft in the Tahitian lagoon.

"Hello," I said, trying to be jaunty, so as not to alarm them. But it had a hollow sound—and I realized it was just the sort of thing a rapist or voyeur might say to give false reassurance to his victim.

They narrowed their eyes, their gaze did not meet mine, and their tense postures, with this grim indifference (which I took to be fear and apprehension), was meant to shame me. They wanted me to go away, of course. And now I saw a Tahitian fisherman, trolling from a small motorboat. He looked up and leered at the crouching sunbathers. They shrank from him, too, and wished him away.

It irritated me that they felt we had no right to go bobbing past them—that, simply because they had taken all their clothes off, they regarded themselves as inviolate, and treated this part of the lagoon (which belonged to everyone) as their private property. For that reason I lingered and then I left, paddling onward towards Papeete. There I was told that this was a fairly common practice—a French thing, women sunbathing nude in order to eliminate bathing-suit silhouettes on their skin. A speedboat dropped them on the raft and returned two or three hours later to take them back to their hotel.

It was dangerously silly to lie naked under this blistering Oceanic sun, and there was not a single Polynesian who would dare it. Apart from being bad for the skin, and a cause of premature wrinkling, if not cancer, it was blatant immodesty.

Once upon a time the Tahitians had revelled in nakedness and seduced European sailors and tempted them from their stern duties on shipboard. ("For when we were sent away, 'Huzza for Otaheite!' was frequently heard among the mutineers," Captain Bligh wrote bitterly, after seeing his ship the *Bounty* headed back to Papeete and the local women.) But these days only the tourists went naked, and the bare tits you saw were always those of visiting sunbathers. The Tahitians were all covered up and decent; history's wheel had taken a complete turn, the fantasies were reversed, and now it was the Christian Tahitians who leered, and the pagan French who were naked.

* * *

As soon as the nameless Tahitian girl on Bougainville's ship dropped her flimsy cloth in full view of the impressionable sailors, Tahiti's fate was sealed, and the South Sea Island myth was born. Ogling a woman's private parts is the Frenchman's version of a glimpse of paradise in any case, but to these horny and fanciful sailors this was even better—the woman was a dusky maiden, just the sort of uncorrupted savage living in her natural state that Rousseau had described only fifteen years earlier.

Captain Bougainville was ecstatic. He paid Tahitian women his highest compliment: "For agreeable features [they] are not inferior to most European women; and who on the point of beauty of the body might, with much reason, vie with them all." He wrote that the naked girl on board "appeared to the eyes of all beholders, such as Venus showed herself to the Phrygian shepherd, having indeed, the celestial form of the goddess."

From that moment—and Bougainville encouraged the view—Tahiti was known as The New Cytherea, the abode of Venus. When Venus Aphrodite rose from the sea foam she stepped ashore (according to the poet Hesiod) at Cytherea, in Ionia. This naked Tahitian girl was Venus made flesh, a goddess of love and beauty, the physical embodiment of the life force. But there was more. Every detail of Tahiti excited Bougainville, and when he settled down to write about his voyage he described how like the world before the Fall this island seemed, and he used Rousseau's precise expression "the golden age" for this uncorrupted place: Polynesia was one of "those countries where the golden age is still in use." Even the creatures associated with the mythology of Venus could be found in Tahiti. The dolphin, the tortoise, and the gentlest birds were sacred to Venus—and there the captain had found them in the very spot where this dusky Venus smiled upon him.

More than that, more rousing than the unashamed nakedness, were the sexual practices—and they were of the most unfamiliar kind. This seemed to be an island of exhibitionists. Officers and sailors invited into the islanders' houses were given food and afterwards the Tahitians "offered them young girls." Neighbors crowded into the house, music was played, the floor was spread with leaves and flowers, and the Europeans were encouraged to strip naked and make love to the girls, there and then, under the approving eyes of the islanders. "Here Venus is the goddess of hospitality, her worship does not permit of any mysteries, and every tribute paid to her is a feast for the whole nation." In short, public copulation, group sex, fruit trees, and freedom.

The islands were bountiful and lovely, and what distinguished them from all other happy islands on earth was their dedication to free and joyous and unsentimental sexuality. Captain Cook was shocked by what he saw in Tahiti, and he wrote, "There is a scale of dissolute sensuality which these people have ascended, wholly unknown to every other nation whose manners have been recorded from the beginning of the world to the present hour, and which no imagination could possibly conceive." On one occasion in Tahiti, in a presentation that was organized by the islanders for the amusement of the foreigners, Cook and some of his men watched a naked six-foot Tahitian man copulate with a fourteen-year-old girl, and he noted that neither was embarrassed—indeed, the young girl was sexually skillful.

Bougainville's extremely well-written *Voyage Around the World* (1771) made Tahiti a byword for everything beautiful. The book was quickly translated into English, and it delighted and inspired—and stimulated— its readers. Just a few years after the book appeared, James Boswell got a hankering to go to Tahiti, and he mentioned this to Doctor Johnson, who told him not to bother, because "one set of Savages is like another."

"I do not think the people of Otaheite can be reckoned Savages," Boswell said.

"Don't cant in defense of Savages," Johnson replied.

"They have the art of navigation," Boswell said.

"A dog or a cat can swim," Johnson said.

Boswell persisted: "They carve very ingeniously."

"A cat can scratch, and a child with a nail can scratch," Johnson said.

But Boswell was right, and he went on yearning to go to Tahiti, in order to "be satisfied what pure nature can do for man."

The Tahitians were anything but primitive. They were among the greatest navigators the world has ever known. They had been brilliant stone carvers and masons. At Papara they had raised a large eleven-step pyramid, the Mahaiatea Marae, and there were more temples and altars at Paea and on the island of Moorea. The people whom Wallis, Bougainville, and Captain Cook met (these captains visited Tahiti within three years of each other) were skilled in the arts of war, of boat-building, and navigation. And far from depending on the fruit trees of the island for their food, they practiced complex and organized cultivation, growing yams, sweet potatoes, gourds, and sugarcane; they raised pigs and chickens, and dogs—they preferred dog meat to pork. Speaking of the first Europeans in Polynesia, Fernand Braudel wrote (in *The Structures of Everyday Life*), "But were the savages they described really primitive people? Far from it." Yet to nearly everyone, the sophistication of the Tahitians was the least interesting thing about them.

Because of its reputation for innocent sex, for pretty people in a pretty place, Tahiti has been one of the most inspirational pieces of geography in the world. Even writers who never saw it praised it—Lord Byron, who wrote a poem about it ("The Island"), and the philosopher Diderot (cribbing from Bougainville) set a novel there. Melville made his reputation by writing about it in *Typee* and *Omoo,* and Robert Louis Stevenson vastly preferred it to Samoa. Most of the people who subsequently wrote about it described it in much the same terms as Bougainville. Pierre Loti went one better and in the purplest prose imaginable described his marriage to a Tahitian; after reading this book, Paul Gauguin was encouraged to set sail. They were all male writers, of course; it would have been interesting if someone like Edith Wharton or Simone de Beauvoir had gushed in quite this way about Tahiti.

Even the sexually ambiguous Somerset Maugham regarded Papeete as pleasant—but he had reason to feel lucky for having gone there. He had sailed to Tahiti after Samoa (which he hadn't liked much) in order to collect material about Gauguin for his novel *The Moon and Sixpence.* This was in 1917, and only thirteen years after Gauguin's death, and so memories were still fresh. Indeed, one old woman remembered that the obnoxious Frenchman had painted the glass panels of a door in a decrepit village house. Maugham went immediately to the house, where the door was still hinged and swinging, and bought it from the innocent owner for 200 francs (he later sold it for $37,400). Years later, Gauguin's son Emil, an overweight buffoon, was a colorful local character. Emil hung around the bars of Papeete, and visitors bought him drinks and badgered him for information about his father (whom he had never known), and for ten francs he let you take his picture.

For literary reasons, Maugham regarded Tahiti as a seductive place (Gauguin certainly didn't, which was why he abandoned it for the Marquesas). It is questionable whether all Tahitians were ever as sexy as Bougainville described—he was only on the island a matter of days, his ship anchored off Hitiaa—but proof of the power of his book is the fact that Tahiti in particular and Polynesian islands in general are still regarded as Cytherean. Yet, manifestly, they are not. Pleasant and feckless, yes; paradise, no.

Bougainville's descriptions stimulated two quite different sorts of people, polar opposites actually—adventurers eager to taste the Cytherean delights of willing women; and missionaries determined to clothe and convert the islanders to Christianity. Over 200 years later, these people are still contending for the souls of Polynesians. But for every Melville or Gauguin, or Don Kattwinkel on the six-day Polynesian package tour ("Features include welcome flower leis"), or anyone else searching out a seductress, there are many more zealots with fire in their eyes who have made it their life's work to convince these people that they are imbued with Original Sin. No adventurer's book is complete without an attack on missionaries—Melville despised and ridiculed them for their subversion and hypocrisy; no missionary's memoir omits to mention the sinfulness and opportunism of beachcombers and remittance men. Each saw the other as a corrupter.

It is almost axiomatic that as soon as a place gets a reputation for being paradise it goes to hell. Tahiti seemed to me dramatically beautiful, but its population lived entirely on the fringes of its steep and inaccessible slopes; and so it seemed small and crowded. It was full of French soldiers and expatriate bureaucrats cashing in on the fact that overseas salaries were double what they were in France and here there was no income tax. The businessmen wore a perpetual scowl of disappointment, because business was so poor. The hotel owners and tour operators complained that tourism was off 20 to 30 percent. Even in its great days Tahiti prospered because of French aid rather than from the receipts of tourism, but if it was ever to become independent it needed to make a show of self-sufficiency. By the 1980s it had become noticeably poorer and more careworn. The bureaucrats were overpaid, but the place itself was under-capitalized, and the locals were penetrated by the aimlessness and vague resentment that characterizes most colonial people. Treat people like children and they become infantile and cranky. The clearest evidence of this was the government's official *Put On A Smile* campaign.

Another campaign—the Tourist Board was unimaginative but desperate to please—was a contest to find "the most hospitable Tahitian" who would qualify for a *Mauruuru* (Thank You Very Much) Award. Visitors to French Polynesia were encouraged to write letters to the *Tahiti Sun Press* recommending a person who had impressed them. I found the letters laughable but engaging, as they described a particularly helpful bellhop or swimming pool attendant or taxi driver. One day, I read a laudatory letter from some visiting Americans (Mr. and Mrs. Albert Crisp, from Los Angeles) who had spent a week in Moorea.

> Since our stay at the Hotel Bali Hai in Moorea we have enjoyed meeting and getting to know Helene ("Mimi") Theroux, a sweet girl who tends bar.
> Mimi Theroux is extremely friendly and helpful, and we would like to show our gratitude by nominating her for a Mauruuru Award. She works very hard and this is to show our appreciation.

Seeing your own strange, hard-to-spell name correctly printed on the pages of a Tahitian newspaper can give you a powerful sense of belonging to the islands. And it is a belief in my family that every person with that surname is a relation—a descendant of Peter Theroux (1839–1915) of Yamaska, Quebec, who had nine prolific sons, Henri, Louis, Ovide, Leon, Dorel, Joseph, Peter, Alexandre, and my grandfather, Eugene. I immediately called the Hotel Bali Hai and asked to speak to my cousin.

"Mimi Theroux doesn't work here anymore," the manager told me.

He thought I might find her somewhere in Moorea, but he wasn't sure. He promised to find her address for me.

I planned to paddle around Moorea sometime soon, and I vowed that I would seek out Mademoiselle—or was it Madame?—Theroux, when I got to that island.

Two things kept me in Tahiti for the moment—the arrangements I was making to go to the distant Marquesas on a freighter, and the prospect of watching the Bastille Day parade. I also wondered whether I ought to get a tattoo in this the homeland of tattoos—even the word was Polynesian (*tatu* means "puncture"). The idea of a tattoo on my ankle seemed an inoffensive way of satisfying my curiosity, but the sight of the only tattooist in Papeete, an excitable Belgian in a bloodstained room, made me change my mind.

Papeete is a rather ugly, plundered-looking town. Its buildings are scruffy, and flimsy and ill-assorted, and they clutter the lower slopes of the extinct volcanoes, Aorai and Orohena, that rise six or seven thousand feet behind it. Tahiti's road—there is only one narrow one, inevitably a speedway, that encircles the island—is quite famously bad and dangerous. To complete this unromantic picture, I found Tahiti to be one of the most expensive places I have ever visited—a pack of cigarettes is $5, a liter of petrol $5, the simplest cotton shirt $50, and a meal in a good restaurant almost prohibitive, but as there are few good restaurants this is academic; and yet if you decide to have a pizza instead you will be paying about twice what you would at the Pizza Hut in Boston. There is no income tax in French Polynesia, yet indirect taxation can be just as brutal. You may congratulate yourself that you don't smoke or drink alcohol, yet even the most frugal vegetarian is in for a shock when he sees the Tahitian cabbages (grown in California) priced at $8 in Papeete's central market.

But for the Tahitians themselves the price of cabbage was academic. The islanders, who were always tidy and clean—impressively so, in a place where fresh water was scarce—managed to survive, and even to flourish, by cultivating small vegetable gardens and applying for welfare and using the extended family. They were a chunky breed, and I felt that there was perhaps something assertive in their obesity. They seemed to revel in being a different size and shape from their colonial masters or mistresses; apart from enthusiastic teenagers, who were imitative, there was almost no emulation among Tahitians of French physical types or styles—no joggers, no fashion casualties, no snobs or socialites. Few of them were even smokers.

The Tahitian's most obvious indulgence was a kind of relentless snacking—they were forever munching and manipulating Planters Cocktail Nuts, potato sticks, Porky Snaks *(Porc Frites),* "Rashuns" *(frites au bacon),* Kellogg's Corn Pops, Figolu Fig Newtons, Champagne Crispy Sponge Fingers, Cadbury's Crunchies, Pinkys, Moros, and Double Fudge Chocolate Biscuits, Toscas, Millefeuilles, and Tiki *crousti-legers,* and Cheez Balls at five bucks a five-ounce can. To pay for this they spent their welfare checks or else got jobs catering to the dwindling number of tourists, few of whom were big spenders. But even the poorest, scrounging Tahitian did not solicit tips and regarded tipping as one of the more insulting of foreign habits.

Tahiti was typical of Oceania generally in the frugality of its long-term expatriates—it seemed a kind of caution, not to say fear, that these people saved their money. Because people were so vulnerable, they made a point of not appearing to be well off—it was altogether too easy for anyone to be burgled. There were retirees here, but they had gone to ground—they hid in bungalows deep in the valleys of Tahiti and Moorea. There were always yachties in Papeete harbor, but yacht people the world over are notoriously careful with their money—circumstances forced them to be self-sufficient.

Elsewhere on the island, the villages were fenced off and seemed contented, and the most conspicuous people in Papeete—apart from Japanese tourists and French soldiers—were the two sorts of folk who had been there since Bougainville described it as paradise—the adventurers and the missionaries; the drunks and the God-botherers. At any time of day in downtown Papeete it was possible to see a sanctimonious clergyman passing a bar where a wrecked-looking Frenchman was sitting glumly over a bottle of Hinano beer. It was still possible to go to pieces here, and any number of Frenchmen had married teenaged Tahitians, given them six kids, and turned them into twenty-year-old hags, thus keeping alive the South Sea Island myth.

I had longed to be in Tahiti for Bastille Day and I made a point of lingering on the island to witness the parade. Rather disingenuously the French authorities on the island had converted Bastille Day into a gala they called *Heiva Tahiti,* the Tahiti Festival—they hadn't the guts to come clean and celebrate their independence day in full view of people who had yet to gain their freedom. I expected it to be a wonderful example of colonial comedy and hypocrisy and it was, "Sponsored by Toyota."

To make matters even more puzzling, the posters announced in French *The 109th Tahiti Annual July Festival,* and to work this out you had to go to a history book and establish that it was in 1880 that Ariane (Pomare V), the son of the intransigent Queen Pomare (IV), was pressured by the French into abdicating and handed his entire administration over to France, who proclaimed the island a French colony. With an astounding insensitivity the French had conflated the dates, and the Tahitians were being persuaded to celebrate the anniversary of their subjection on the very day the French celebrated their own freedom.

At eight o'clock on Bastille Day morning I joined the crowd of impassive Tahitians and frisky French people on the Boulevard Pomare, wondering what I would see, and fifteen minutes later I heard the first distant syncopation of the parade, a French army band playing the World War I song *"Auprès de Ma Blonde" (il fait beau blah-blah . . .)*—strange in almost any circumstances but especially bizarre on an island of dusky, dark-haired people.

There followed a regiment of Marine Fusiliers carrying a French flag lettered *Honneur et Patrie* and about fifty men from the Special Forces holding hi-tech weapons. The "Regiment du Tonkin" band seemed harmless enough, but the oncoming ranks grew increasingly menacing— three units of legionnaires with fixed bayonets, and one with a French flag down the muzzle of his rifle; a black beret regiment with fierce dogs in personnel carriers, and more infantrymen, followed by men from the Foreign Legion, all of them bearded and wearing white leather aprons and white gauntlets and each man had shouldered—because this was the symbol of this unit of sappers—a wicked axe.

The word *Camerone* was inscribed on the flag of these marching men, commemorating a battle in Mexico in 1863 in which a detachment of sixty-five legionnaires with their backs to the wall faced an army of 2,000 Mexicans and, refusing to surrender, were wiped out by the admiring yet remorseless enemy. This was the battle in which the famous Captain Danjou lost not only his life but his wooden hand (it was later retrieved and became a sort of Foreign Legion relic and talisman). "Life—not courage—abandoned these French soldiers," was the official summing up, and the event entered the language in the form of a colloquialism— *"faire Camerone"* means to fight to the end.

I had the feeling that these parading regiments had been chosen for their ferocity. Anyone watching them pass by would think twice about mounting a revolt or starting an uprising, and so the Bastille Day parade, the so-called Fesitival of Tahiti—this part of it, at least—was unambiguously intimidating to the Polynesians who watched in complete silence, even when the wives and children of the French soldiers were applauding.

The French Foreign Legionnaires are very thick on the ground in Polynesia. Their toughness and intransigence is needed in such a sensitive place, and the romantic pose suits their swashbuckling image. I was told that they often take Tahitian mistresses. Owing to an indifferent diet and their love of snacks and sweet drinks, Tahitians frequently have bad teeth. The legionnaires' first—or perhaps second—demonstration of their love is to buy their Tahitian girlfriends a set of false teeth. You can often spot these spoken-for girls on the public trucks, sitting and smiling a lovely white smile.

When the legionnaire goes back to France (and it might well be to revisit the wife and children he left behind) he takes his girlfriend's teeth with him, so as to leave her less attractive to men.

"Sometimes the girl does not want to give her teeth back," a legionnaire told me in Papeete. "Then we turn her upside down and shake them out of her."

The second part of the parade was much friendlier and less deadly-looking. It began with fire trucks and local school bands, and continued with majorettes and kids in cowboy hats and Miss Tahiti, who was carried in an outrigger canoe by six muscular men.

"Smile, woman," the islander in front of me called out in French to Miss Tahiti.

Twenty-eight women in white muumuus, twelve in purple, a gang of drummers, dancers wearing feather headdresses and coconut-shell brassieres, trick cyclists, the fat and wicked-looking men on motorcycles, flying a skull-and-crossbones flag reading "Le Club Harley-Davidson du Tahiti," and local kids doing handstands on skateboards—and now the Tahitians cheered, yelling from balconies and clinging to tree branches beside the boulevard. And I kept imagining a painting—full of oceanic color and tropical light, and packed with chubby islanders and children and large laughing families, and severe and authoritarian-looking French soldiers, called "Bastille Day in Papeete," illustrating the paradoxes of French colonialism.

This happy back half of the parade put me in a better mood and I followed a sniggering group of Tahitians through the side streets and into the fenced-in garden of the French High Commission, where a garden party was in progress under a huge Polynesian tree. Half of us had clearly crashed the party, and the rest—the VIPs, the beefy-faced *faranis* and *colons* in tight suits and the threadbare old soldiers wearing heroic clusters of medals and battle ribbons, and one conspicuously decorated with the Legion of Honor—were too drunk to notice us. "This *France Libre* was given to me by General de Gaulle," one elderly man told me, and other old soldiers—some were African and some Vietnamese—had seen action in Indo-China in the 1950s. The Tahitians especially were having a grand time: They ignored the waitresses with drinks and made a beeline for the hors d'oeuvres, which they managed with wonderful dexterity, scooping up three or four at a time, squeezing them between two fingers, and cramming them into their mouths.

A French army band set up their music stands in the shade of the tree and perspired and played rousing songs, *"Sang et Or,"* and "Tenth Festival," and *"Adios Amigos,"* and the stirring *"Marche des Mousquetaires Noirs,"* while the bandleader conducted them without a baton, using only his hands, the slapping gestures of a man making a sandcastle.

For the people watching the parade or in this festive garden, Bastille Day in Tahiti was an excuse for a party, to play games at the fun fare in the park, and buy balloons and amuse the kids. But walking back to the wharf along the Rue du General de Gaulle I saw a wall urgently spray-painted with the word *INDEPENDENCE.*

The next day I went to Moorea, in search of Mimi Theroux. The ferry left from a wharf on Papeete Harbor—and as it entered the Sea of the Moon I looked back and saw the great greeny-black crags of Tahiti's volcanoes. They weren't rounded and plump and undulant, but like a starved sierra, like the corpses of mountains, with bony protruding ridges and hard sharp hips and shoulders, narrow valleys with hollow sides, knobs and angles on the escarpments and an intense steepness all over them, as though in their ancient years of vulcanism they had hurled out their life and left themselves exhausted.

The peaks and slopes of Tahiti—and of volcanic islands all over Oceania—are so steep and dark and so thoroughly wicked-looking that the coasts by contrast are gentle, and their pale pretty lagoons seem unutterably sweet. There is always a scrap of mist around the peaks, and sometimes a great torn pillow of black cloud hovering. The vertical roughness is visible on these islands, but so is the mildness of their fringes. "Seen from the sea, the prospect is magnificent," Melville wrote of this same view of Tahiti. His words are still true. "Such enchantment, too, breathes over the whole, that it seems a fairy world, all fresh and blooming from the hand of the Creator."

It cost seven dollars each way for the one-hour trip, and no charge for my collapsible boat. Most of the passengers were Polynesian, either full-blooded or else part-French, the people known locally as *demi orafa.* There were Chinese, too, and a smattering of *faranis,* the French who have attached themselves to the islands. The Polynesians were of two

distinct physical types—either slender and nimble—the children and teenagers, or else (the over-twenties) fat and rather shapeless. Girls and boys
were equally winsome, and men and women were precisely the same
shape and almost indistinguishable.

It ought to have been possible to paddle my own boat from Papeete to
Moorea, but the wind discouraged me, a strong current ran between the
islands, and apart from the ferry landing at Vaiare there was only one
break in the reef, Avarapa Passe, on the northwest side of the island. The
reefs of these islands were a great disincentive to any sort of casual
boating, and as I intended to sail for the Marquesas within a week I could
not mount the sort of expedition that had gotten me safely around the
archipelago of Vava'u in Tonga. I planned to make camp on Moorea, to
paddle within the reef, and to seek out Mimi Theroux.

There is no town near the ferry landing, there is hardly a village, and
after the trucks had taken the ferry passengers away Vaiare seemed
deserted.

"I'm looking for a place on the shore to camp," I said to a Moorean
at the roadside.

"Not possible," he said—and he was sympathetic.

It was a Polynesian problem: All the land was spoken for. I did not
argue. I rented a motorcycle and went in search of a hotel with a beach,
but this was an easy matter. Moorea had many hotels, and business was
so terrible I could take my pick. When I had settled this, I went back to
the rental place for my boat. But I kept my motorcycle.

I rode to the Hotel Bali Hai and found the manager, who seemed to be
American. Yes, he said, Mimi Theroux had worked here not long ago,
but she had left.

"She lives with her mother at Paopao."

That was Cook's Bay, not far off.

"Is she married?"

"I never saw any husband," the man said, and he described her house
so that I could find it.

It was a white building, but it was not a house. Large and square, two
stories, with verandas above and a restaurant below, and with a flat roof,
it had the geometric look of a commercial structure. But it was in good
condition, freshly painted, gleaming in the sunshine, and facing directly
onto the bay.

I parked my motorcycle and walked around. A Tahitian was tinkering
behind the building, but as it was high noon and very hot there were few
other people in sight.

"Mimi Theroux?" I asked the Tahitian.

He pointed upstairs, to the porch where laundry was hung. I knocked
on the door at the foot of the stairway, but there was no response. I

knocked again and excited a dog in the next yard. I called out, and a young woman appeared at the top of the stairs.

This was Mimi. She was Chinese. I told her my name and she invited me up the stairs where at the top, a small dark child was playing with an older girl.

"This is Moea," Mimi said, hoisting the smaller child.

"Your daughter?"

"Soon she will be." She spoke English with a slight American accent.

We were walking through the cool interior of the upper floor where, at the far end on the front of the building, I could see the blaze of the sea and the glary sky of Cook's Bay—one of the most beautiful spots in the whole of Oceania, lovely, secluded, dramatic, and rather empty. But this was French Polynesia. Because it was secluded it was neglected; the beach was no good, the shore was littered, and if you didn't have a motorcycle how would you get there?

It seemed to me that Mimi had a tincture of Polynesian blood. She said that this might have been so—she vaguely remembered seeing an elderly Tahitian relative, but she was not sure whether this was a blood relation. I rather liked her for not being sure and for not caring much about it.

"I'm sorry to drop in on you like this," I said.

"It's okay. Jim has spoken about you."

She explained that she was married to James Theroux, who was a distant cousin and, as he had spent years sailing back and forth across the Pacific, from Samoa to Fiji and Tonga, to Port Vila and Australia, Jim was well known in Oceania. He was an expert surfer and experienced sailor and navigator. His name had been mentioned to me and sometimes, introducing myself to a yacht owner, I was mistaken for him. People knew his boat in the way they knew my books: just names that had become familiar.

"He is in Australia, at the moment, in the Whitsundays, taking charters," Mimi said. "I saw him seven months ago. Maybe I will see him again in a few months. He is like you, always traveling."

"Does he look like me?" I asked.

"No. He is more handsome," Mimi said, and went to chase Moea, who was throwing toys at the wall.

Mimi was relaxed, she seemed capable, she was slender and barefoot, wearing a *pareu* on her hips; a loyal and energetic Chinese who did not make a fuss about a seven-month separation. She was small, quick, and attractive. After she told me a few details of her life I figured her age to be thirty-four.

She had met Jim when she was twenty-one, at the girls' college in Puunuaia, on Tahiti. Her maiden name was Chanlo.

"Jim said, 'Come with me,' so I went. Yes, it was romantic," Mimi said.

"He had a boat. I had never been on a boat like that before. First we went to Pago, and I was sick, from the sea. Then we went to Fiji, Vava'u, Vila, Australia. We were in Vila for a couple of years, but when independence came there was trouble"—the Jimmy Stevens uprising—"and we left. In Vava'u the Tongans stole our laundry from the lines. But we liked it. Jim fished with the local people in the night."

"Do you still get seasick?"

"No. Now I am a good sailor. I have done it for more than ten years," Mimi said.

Each phase of her life had been different, and she was one of those people who seemed to have been strengthened and made confident by the sudden changes. It seemed to me Chinese tenacity, but in this Polynesian setting—in the beauty of Paopao—it had no edge to it. She had traveled from Moorea to Tahiti; she had gone off and married this impulsive American; and they had sailed the seas together. In Australia, Jim sold his boat and then hearing that Alan Bond's twelve-meter yacht *Southern Cross* was for sale they flew to Perth and bought it. It was a wonderful boat but it was empty. They rigged it and sailed it across the top of Australia, through the Torres Strait and past Cape York to Cairns. That took a year, because they had spent all their money buying and refitting the boat.

"We stopped in many places—to work and make money. But they were interesting places," Mimi said. "In Darwin we stopped for months. I worked as a waitress and Jim was a gardener. We didn't mind. It was an adventure."

Moea was still running around the room with her little friend. The room was large and breezy, with a few pictures—Jim's yacht was one— and some calendars and plain furniture. It was clean and more pleasant for being mostly bare.

"Moea is very pretty," I said.

"Soon she will be a Theroux," Mimi said.

Seeing the impish face of this little islander and hearing my own name made me glad.

"Her mother is a Marquesan," Mimi said. "My sister knew her mother when she was pregnant, and she knew that I could not have a child myself and that I wanted to adopt one. The woman already had two children and no husband. You know how it is here. Anyway, as soon as she had the baby she gave it to me. She told me the father is French, but look at her—that baby is Marquesan—very black hair and dark eyes and skin."

Mimi turned to the child with admiration. Moea was a very sweet, very strong and upright two-year-old; and happy, her laughter ringing in the room, as she played.

"The father went afterwards to the woman and asked, 'Where is the baby?' " Mimi went on. "But the woman said, 'You didn't come the whole time I was pregnant. I gave the baby away.' "

"Where had the man been?"

"The man just left her and ran after a young girl when the baby was in the stomach," Mimi said. "That was two years ago. I have been happy. But now I am getting worried. In the past weeks the mother has been calling me. I know that if she sees Moea she will take her. She signed the document for adoption but it does not become final until two months more. I have to hide. The woman does not know where I am, but somehow she knows my telephone number. I would never give Moea away. She was such a lot of work when she was small, but she is so intelligent and she understands everything I say."

We were seated at a table, looking past Paopao to the bay.

"It is so lovely here," I said.

"It is a picture postcard view," Mimi said. "You should have seen the sunset last night. The sky was all pink—no sun, just clouds and sky. I sat here and watched it with Moea."

I was touched by the thought that after seeing twelve and a half thousand sunsets in the Pacific she still marvelled at one.

Suddenly she said, "How did you find me?"

"I asked at the Bali Hai. You know you were nominated for a *Mauru-uru* Award?"

"No," she said without much interest. And then she called out to her mother. Was she conveying this news?

Her elderly mother, Madame Madeleine Chanlo, was seated silently on the porch, looking off to sea. Mimi did not know the old woman's age—she said it was impolite to ask. Madame Chanlo had had nine children, of which Mimi was the youngest ("I am the runt"). All the rest were married—to French, American, Tahitian, Chinese—and they lived all over, in many countries.

The old woman smiled at me and spoke in Cantonese to her daughter.

" 'Give that man some food,' she said."

Mimi went to the kitchen and brought me a plate of vegetable stew—carrots from New Zealand, potatoes from France, rice from China. You needed a garden in order to live, Mimi said. There was no work, she said, but many people got by on breadfruit and taro and mangoes. Talking about food, Mimi remarked on the high cost of living.

"We have the most expensive electricity in the world," she said. "Every month I can't believe the bill. It costs me fifteen thousand francs a month, for just a TV, a freezer, a fridge, and lights."

That was $160.

"They want to give us income tax, but everything is taxed! That is why it costs so much to live here."

The reason there was no income tax was because people were taxed on the things they bought. Tax had been reduced on alcohol in order to encourage tourism, but that had not done the trick.

"Three weeks ago there was a roadblock in Tahiti, because they raised the petrol ten cents and the diesel twenty cents."

This was a few days before I had arrived but people were still talking about it and marvelling at the disruption it had caused. The roadblock of bulldozers and trucks had been put up just outside of Papeete, between the town and the airport, so that in order to get to the airport it was necessary to take a ninety-mile (117 km) detour around the island. No one was arrested. There were negotiations, and at last the government reduced the price. What was clear in most people's minds was that if it happened again, if the government passed an unpopular measure, road-blocks were the answer—though in the past (as recently as 1987) the government had used riot police against protestors.

"What about the French?" I asked. "Do you think they'll hang on here?"

"Good question," Mimi said. "Eventually we will be independent, I suppose."

I left Mimi, admiring her strength and her filial piety, and I mounted my motorcycle and went the rest of the way around the island. It was a stormy month—three or four times I was caught in a downpour, either in my boat or on the motorcycle—and so I was not sorry to be denied the chance to live in my tent. The raindrops pelted so hard they stung my skin. And after the rain there was always a lovely aroma of *tiare* and oleander, and enormous complete rainbows, every color in a whole archway.

One day I paddled to Maatea. Melville had lived for a while here in 1842, and he mentions it a number of times in *Omoo* ("Fair dawned, over the hills of Martair, the jocund morning"). It had been a long trip for me, because I had stopped at a little island called Motu Ahi. And when I was caught in the rain on the way back I headed for the shelter of a little beach, where—sheltering with me under a tree—was a cyclist, Dominic Taemu, who was in his twenties and pedalling around the island.

We talked about Bastille Day and the *Heiva Tahiti.* He laughed.

"Bastille Day. That is a French festival. That is historical. It is not our day."

"Do you want Polynesia to be independent?"

"How can we be independent? We have no resources," he said. "The Japanese have taken all our big fish—they come in their big ships and use drift nets. We had lots of fish before, but now they are small and few. The coconuts and the copra are nothing. We have nothing."

"What about other work?"

"There is no work, because there are too few tourists," he said. And he thought awhile. "We know other places are cheaper. For us this is a big problem. We don't know what to do."

It was the fear of destitution; the fear of losing French protection and aid. But it was perhaps like a woman anxious about divorcing, fearing to be alone, without support—even though the husband is an opportunist and an exploiter.

"Independence—yes, certain people want it. It might come. But what will we do then?" And it dramatized the paradox of French Polynesia that Taemu, a native of what has been called the most beautiful place on earth, then said, "We have no means to live."

Chapter 19
A VOYAGE TO THE MARQUESAS

It was very hard for me to board a ship for the Marquesas Islands, where Paul Gauguin lay buried, and not squint at the passengers and recall the title of the painter's enigmatic picture *Where Do We Come From? What Are We? Where Are We Going?*

Perhaps it was premature to size them up, but I couldn't help attempting to spot the smokers, the drinkers, the boasters, the fanatics, the Germans. This looked like a honeymoon couple and surely that one was an escapee and why was that skinny old man—Gandhi to his fingertips—wearing such a skimpy bathing suit and nothing else? The two butch women looked rather fearsome in their iron pants and their tattoos. The mother and her middle-aged son seemed rather touching, sharing a cigarette by the rail. But those big beefy Australians with the flowers behind their ears were certainly a bit worrying. The more nervous among us reverted: It became an assertion of national characteristics, the French pushing, the Germans snatching, the Australians drinking, the Americans trying to make friends, the Venezuelan couple holding hands.

How wrong I was about most of them. The "honeymoon couple" had been married for three years, the "escapee" was simply a dentist, "Gandhi" was an elderly fresh-air fiend, the "butch women" were mother and daughter, the "mother and son" were a married couple—Americans; and the fellows from Melbourne lovably challenged me with their tolerance. I would say something critical of a passenger and when I was through they'd disagree, saying, "We think she's *fabulous!*"

But that was later. In the meantime we were settling in for a longish voyage of eighteen days in the Marquesas. True, Herman Melville was in the islands for about ten days longer, but he wrote an entire book about it—his first, and by far his most successful, *Typee*.

Named after a valley on the island of Nuku Hiva where Melville claimed to have lived (the exaggerated subtitle of the book is, "A Four Months Residence"), *Typee* appeared in 1846 and was an instant hit. It had everything—sex, nakedness, fresh fruit, warfare, and cannibalism. It was the ultimate South Sea island adventure and further confirmation that Polynesia was paradise. Melville, thinly disguised as the narrator Tommo, flees a brutal captain by jumping ship at the Marquesan island of Nuku Hiva. He first travels among the friendly Happar people, but soon finds himself among the cannibalistic Typees, and being pursued. The book combines anthropology, travel, and adventure, and even today it is not merely enjoyable but informative. Melville practiced a little cannibalism himself in writing the book, by hacking out and serving raw and still bleeding many passages and incidents from other writers who had published eyewitness accounts of the Marquesas.

The most compelling feature for most of its readers was that it was also a love story, Melville's passion for the dusky, delectable Fayaway. The book was frankly physical, particularly in the unexpurgated first edition—scenes of Tommo swimming and frolicking with island girls, smoking and eating with Fayaway who sometimes wore a piece of bark cloth, but was usually clothed in the "garb of Eden"—starkers. The incident that whipped up the blood of most readers was the one in which Tommo takes Fayaway on an idyllic canoe trip across a lake in the Typee valley. Feeling impish, Fayaway stands erect in the canoe, unknots her tapa cloth robe, and unfurls it until it fills with wind and becomes a sail. And there she stands, this naked "child of nature," her naked body a "little mast," and holding the sail with her arms upraised, making the canoe glide along, and "the long brown tresses of Fayaway streamed in the air."

I did not know much more about the Marquesas than this, and the fact that Gauguin had more or less chosen another island in the group, Hiva Oa, as a place to die.

The Marquesas were far and few: way beyond the Tuamotu chain, three days' sailing from Tahiti, a dozen high islands, six of them populated, and only 7,000 people on them altogether. These details don't make a picture, but I heard better arguments for going there. With greater justification than Tahiti and Moorea, it was said, the Marquesas had the reputation for being the most beautiful islands on the face of the earth. Because of their steep cliffs and poor anchorages and few good harbors, only a handful of yachts called there. The islands were filled with the same so-called "tabu-groves" that Melville had described: They had never been excavated and so the islands were an archaeological treasure house. Distant, and difficult to traverse, the Marquesas were seldom visited. That did it. The fact that few people go there is one of the most persuasive reasons for traveling to a place.

* * *

The *Aranui* was one of several ships that made the inter-island trip; there were two other cargo ships that carried some passengers, there was a luxury vessel, the *Wind Song*—very chic, very expensive, nice boutiques, no cargo. The *Aranui* had a hold full of cargo, forty-odd passengers amidships in cabins, and an indefinite number—it varied according to the run—sleeping on mats on the stern decks and sharing a rudimentary head. But nothing is cheap in French Polynesia; the fellows from Melbourne were paying almost $1,400 apiece to sleep on the Bridge Deck and although this included meals their nights were noisy with humming ventilators, winds in the ratlines, the sloshing sea—and one said to me, "Earplugs are a must." I was paying about $2,000 to share a tiny cabin near the Plimsoll line, with Señor Pillitz, a young man from Argentina. On rougher days when the porthole was awash with the sudsy ocean it was like being in a launderette.

I had so little space in my cabin that I was told that I could not bring my collapsible boat, but it was emphasized that this was a handsome favor to me, because it removed a fatal temptation: If I tried to paddle anywhere around these islands, with their notoriously bad anchorages and rough seas, I would probably drown.

The lights were twinkling on the slopes of Orohena as we left Papeete Harbor and headed northeast through Matavai Bay. A few miles farther on, we rounded Point Venus. Captain Cook camped here in 1769 in order to observe the transit of Venus across the sun, and this was also the spot where Captain Bligh collected the breadfruit trees he stowed on the *Bounty*. As soon as we were at sea I went below and raided the ship's library. By this time the South Equatorial Current rose against the hull of the *Aranui*, and the wind picked up, and my stomach rose and fell.

The movement of the ship convinced me to eat sparingly, and after dinner I went back to the library and read *An Angel at My Table*, the second volume of the autobiography of the New Zealand novelist Janet Frame. The central part of the book concerns her committal to an asylum, and I was held by her story, which was written entirely without bitterness or self-pity. As I read on about her suicide attempt, her treatment, her matter-of-fact madness—she uses the word "loony" to describe her condition—the ship pitched and rolled. Some other passengers discovered the seclusion of the library, and when one of them gulped, went glassy-eyed, and then noisily and messily puked onto the floor I went on deck for air.

We had sailed straight into a gale, and all night the ship rolled in a figure eight. In the morning there was a certain amount of hopeless hilarity.

"Whoops! There we go again!"

"I spilled my tea."

"I'll be spilling more than that if this keeps up!"

"That woman's laugh is diabolical," I muttered.

"We think she's *fabulous!*"

Bad weather and heavy seas inspire facetiousness and intensify the confinement: Passengers stay below and giggle insincerely. That day and most of the next, people kept staggering and falling; and they talked disgustingly about being sick. Most wore—uselessly—seasickness bandages behind their ears. The folk wisdom is probably true: "The only cure for seasickness is to sit on the shady side of an old brick church in the country."

Señor Pillitz said that he had suffered badly in the night, that he had felt desperate, as they said in Argentina, "between the sword and the wall" *(entre la espada y la pared)*. He was full of robust wisdom and pithy sayings. Later, at a dismal place in the Tuamotus, he glanced around and said, "All you would ever find here is three crazy cats" *(tres gatos locos)*.

I did not feel so wimpy when Señor Pillitz added that he had worked his way on a ship, chopping vegetables, from Buenos Aires to Rotterdam, so he knew a thing or two about sea conditions.

During breakfast, dishes slid to the floor, bottles fell and smashed, Mr. Werfel tripped and fell at the feet of Dennis and Bev, from Vancouver. Later in the morning, a man who had been full of complaints ("How do I get my faucet to work?" "Suppose I want to shut off my hot water?" "What's the story with my fan?") fell off his chair in the library and moaned. He lay on his side. He said he could not get up.

"I musta cracked a rib or somesing."

He was middle European, with American in his Teutonic accent.

"Breathe deeply," I suggested.

He did so, and winced.

"Does it hurt?"

"Sorta."

It was my distinct impression that he was faking, and when people began to ignore him he crept to his feet and went away. He was happier after the captain gave him a tour of the britch and on most days he was the first to examine what he called the vezza shart to see whether we were in for another gale.

That second day, as the sea moderated, a succession of green stripes appeared on the horizon. These were the outer islands of the Tuamotus, a chain of flat coral atolls of which Moruroa is one. Since 1966, the French have been using Moruroa as a testing site for their nuclear devices and they have just about succeeded in making that atoll unsafe for human habitation for generations to come. More than 160 nuclear devices have been detonated, atomic and hydrogen bombs as well as neutron bombs; and there have been atmospheric tests—fastening nuclear devices to French balloons and exploding them over the atolls. Recently the explosions—averaging eight a year—have taken place in the core of the coral reef, or underwater, and the more France has been criticized for the danger and contamination, the less willing the French government has been to allow any sort of inspection to take place. There have been leakages of plutonium and radioactive debris, notably in 1979 and 1981. But the French did not abandon testing at Moruroa when they saw how they had damaged the atoll; they simply detonated fewer bombs there and switched their heavy testing to the neighboring atoll of Fangataufa.

Even the most user-friendly travel guide becomes Francophobic when the question of testing is raised. "French radioactivity will remain in the Tuamotus for thousands of years," David Stanley writes in *The South Pacific Handbook* with justified indignation; "the unknown future consequences of this program are the most frightening part of it. Each successive blast continues the genocide committed by the Republic of France against the people of the Pacific."

Elsewhere on the Tuamotu archipelago, the many shoals and poor anchorages have given it the reputation of being one of the most notorious ship-swallowers in the Pacific.

Under a cheddar-colored moon that rose through black shreds of cloud and glimmered in shattered light on a rippling tropic sea, the crew began emptying clattering barrels overboard—waste paper and plastic bottles and crushed tins and vegetable peelings—but it hardly disturbed the sea, because the radiant rubbish was bobbing in the moonglow in this remote and peaceful place, and the junk and detritus had a lively phosphorescence all its own.

I woke to shouts and the sound of cranes the third day. I could see the whaleboat through my porthole, ferrying cargo to the tiny village on the harbor at the croissant-shaped atoll of Takapoto. It was too deep to anchor, and there was no harbor here, and so we were pitching just offshore, as the whaleboats came and went. In the whole voyage only once was the ship moored alongside a quay, with a gangway from the deck to dry land. In every other instance we were brought ashore in the whaleboats, which necessitated a delicate (and at times wet) transfer. It should have been hell for the elderly passengers but it wasn't: The powerful Marquesan crew members lifted the feebler ones bodily into the whaleboats and at the edge of the pounding surf hoisted them again like kids and carried them to shore—little twittering women and men in big tattooed Marquesan arms.

These same crewmen also hauled the cargo—thirteen hours repeatedly going from the ship to the quay and back again, that same quarter mile—the twenty-foot whaleboats always piled high. The cargo covered all aspects of human activity—loaves of bread, sanitary napkins and toilet rolls by the crate, mineral water, breakfast cereal, a large pea-green three-piece suite, and in a place that teemed with live fish, crates of canned fish. Two whaleboat loads contained cardboard boxes of Tyson's frozen chicken pieces (from Arkansas). The rest was predictable—building materials, lumber, bricks, pipes, cement; and rice, sugar, flour, gasoline, and bottled gas. (Many of these staple items were heavily subsidized by the French government. The rice, for example, cost $12 for ten kilos, which was not much more than 36 cents a pound.) There was crate after clanking crate of soft drinks, Budweiser beer, bottles of Hinano, Arnott's "Cabin" Biscuits in ten-pound tins, and cartons of snacks, including immense quantities of Planters Cheez Balls.

A cloying odor of decayed copra hung over the quay at Takapoto, where it was stacked in bulging sacks, quietly humming, like a mountain of last week's dessert. Copra has the look of brown rinds and is in fact chunks of dried coconut meat that is later processed into coconut oil. The French heavily subsidize the copra crop (paying $650 a ton), making it profitable for the grower. But the islanders shrug, the harvest is in decline and the shortfall is made up by copra imported from Fiji (where growers are paid $100 a ton).

Forget copra, the locals say—the great business today in Takapoto is black pearls. The seed pearls are slipped between the valves of the giant black-lipped oyster which is happiest in the lagoons around Takapoto, and if the transplant is successful, in about three years a pearl fisher could become very wealthy.

The Japanese have thrust themselves into the black pearl industry and now—to no one's surprise—almost totally dominate it, from seeding the oysters to stringing the pearls and selling them. Even so, fortunes have been made by Tuamotuans on some atolls that are little more than desert islands—a coral beach, a few palm trees, and cringing dogs.

I had hardly been in Takapoto an hour when a woman named Cecile sidled up to me and asked me in French whether I wanted to buy some black pearls. She said they were from Takaroa, a neighboring atoll where the best-colored pearls are found.

"This is my son," Cecile said.

But he didn't hear anything: He was listening to a rock music cassette on earphones, and it was presumably turned loud—I could hear it—to overwhelm the sound of the pounding sea. And the dogs—we were being followed by nine barking dogs.

Cecile was in no hurry, nor was she interested in bargaining—haggling is not a habit in Polynesia. She slid open a matchbox and showed me the four pearls—a tear drop, a polyp, and two round ones—and she mentioned the price. That same amount would have bought three loud Tahitian shirts or two meals in Papeete.

"Done," I said, and handed over the money. As we walked back to the quay, where the atoll's whole population ("Four hundred—plus children," Cecile said) had gathered, we were still followed by the dogs, about fifteen of them now.

"About those dogs," I began. We were speaking French.

"So many of them," Cecile said, not looking.

I wanted to be delicate. "In the Marquesas the people eat dogs."

"We eat them too!" She seemed to be boasting, as a way of setting me straight.

Now I began to see something canine in Cecile's features, her teeth more doglike than is usual, her nose looked damp, her jowls a bit loose, her eyes rather soulful.

"What does dog meat taste like?"

"Like steak."

Most dog-eaters stew it, the meat is so tough, but the French had made steak and chips so popular in their colony this had obviously influenced the manner of serving up woof-woof.

"Entrecote of dog, dog steak, and what about dog stew?"

She shrugged and said, "Sure."

"Do you eat sea turtles?" I had noticed that the shells of this endangered species were hung up to decorate many of the boxlike houses on Takapoto.

"We love turtles," Cecile said. "We make them into soup."

Food was not a problem on an atoll like this, where fish and coconuts were plentiful. There were pigs in the place too. They could have managed without dogs, but as Cecile said, they ate them because they tasted good. The rest of the time they subsisted on fish and rice and coconuts. When the *Aranui* called they had carrots and onions. No one on Takapoto had a garden—the soil was too poor; it was hardly soil at all, but rather crumbled coral, and all that grew were palms and feathery Australian pines.

I met an American named Tim at the landing stage. He had the look of a surfer. He was from California and was making his way from atoll to atoll, any way he could. He had been on Takapato for several months. He liked it more than any other atoll, so far. I asked him why.

"The sharks are smaller, and there are fewer of them, for one thing," he said. "And the people are really friendly. As soon as you arrive they sit you down and give you food, even if it's the only food they have—even if their children haven't eaten."

"I was thinking that it doesn't look as though there is much food here," I said.

"There's more than you might think," Tim said. "These houses look poor, but in each one there's a TV, a video machine, a gas stove, and a freezer. They freeze the fish they catch and sell it to the boats that stop by. The *Aranui* will pick up a lot."

"Is that how they get their income?"

"That's it, mainly. Apart from the child allowance, they don't get handouts from the French. The copra price is subsidized. Otherwise they provide for their own needs."

"I noticed that quite a few cases of whisky were unloaded."

"Drinking is a problem here," he said. "And it really has an effect on them. They get very violent—their whole personality undergoes a change. There were four serious fights last Saturday night."

The cargo, including booze, was still being carried past us by men who were so heavily laden they sank up to their ankles in crushed coral.

Tim said, "They say that if you hand someone a bottle of Jack Daniel's you can get anything done—anything."

"What if you had a whole case of the stuff?"

"You'd probably get a handful of black pearls."

Such a strange, recent-looking piece of land, a few feet above sea level in the middle of the ocean, so flat, so thinly wooded—no grass, few people. If it were not for the pearls it might have been forgotten long ago and left to itself. Seeing the entire population gathered there at the landing in the failing light I thought of people clinging to coral, frail people holding on to the frailest and most crumbly living rock. The whole place was like a small fragile organism.

It was dark when the last of the copra was brought aboard and by then I was sitting with some of the Marquesan passengers—Thérèse, a medical worker; Charles, a powerfully built former soldier in the French army with tiny white *tiare* blossoms in his shoulder-length hair (he had seen action in Chad and had the scars of bullet wounds to prove it: "The Africans are real savages"); and Jean, who claimed that he was descended from the last king of the Marquesas and was just returning from Tahiti where he had been combing through the birth records and genealogies to establish his royal connection.

They had not known each other before the voyage, but had fallen in together and they agreed on most things—hated Tahitian politics, were against French nuclear testing ("Everyone is against it. It poisons all of nature, the sea, the fish, and it causes sickness," Thérèse said), and they wanted the Marquesas to be independent of the rest of Polynesia.

"We want a free Marquesas," Charles said, and then confusingly added, "It doesn't matter whether the French are there or not. We just don't want Tahiti politics."

He also repeated what many Marquesans said: His islands were a family, a large Catholic family. The rest of French Polynesia was rather despised for having abandoned the faith and gone over to the Mormons and the Jehovah's Witnesses.

Just before I went below I saw Patrick, one of the fellows from Melbourne, looking over the rail.

"Did you see that movie *Cocoon,* where all those people got into the boat and then the boat was beamed up to another planet?" He was smiling. "When I saw these people hobbling on board the first day I thought to myself, 'Oh God, hold on, we're off to outer space!' "

In a way it was true: The Marquesas were a world apart. It was a thirty-six-hour run from Takapoto to the first of these high islands.

In that time I got acquainted with more of the other passengers. Señor Pillitz had once trained as a waiter at the Ritz in London, but one night he spilled an entire tureen of onion soup down a woman's back ("She was wearing a lovely green dress") and that convinced him that he should take up photography. The Germans kept to themselves and hogged the best seats, the most food, and with an instinct for invasion went up and down the ship, claiming the prime areas for themselves. Carmelo and Amelia from Venezuela had been around the world several times. India was their favorite country, "for cultural reasons." Ross and Patrick, on their first foray out of Melbourne, found everything just fabulous. Horace, a neurosurgeon from Sarasota, held me spellbound when he described the process of removing a brain tumor, which was his business. After a person's head was opened (the cut was made behind the ear, at the base of the skull) the tumor was taken out with unbelievable slowness, "like removing sand, one grain at a time, and at the end of the operation, when you are very tired, there's a chance you might slip and cut vital nerves." Philippe, who was also a doctor, was doing his National Service at Papeete Hospital, and had a Tahitian grandmother. Pascale, a young and pretty French woman, who was usually topless except at mealtime, worked as a nurse at the Papeete hospital and had helped deliver Cheyenne Brando's little boy. "This Brando is a strange woman—she will not let anyone touch her. You think it is possible to have a baby and not be touched?" A woman from Chicago who called herself Senga (she hated the name Agnes and so spelled it backwards) said she was seventy years old and had come on this trip "because I want to do everything before I die." There was a sunburned Frenchman we called Pinky, who, when he got drunk, which was every evening at eight in the bar on C Deck, praised the racist French politician Jean-Marie Le Pen. Pinky's nemesis was Madame Wittkop, whom we called The Countess; she often said, "I'm outrageous" but so far she had seemed unprepossessing. That was most of them.

* * *

Four and a half days after leaving Papeete, we raised the first of the Marquesas, the little island of Ua-Pou.

Several passengers on board said that Ua-Pou did not look anything like a South Seas island. Melville had anticipated that reaction. "Those who for the first time visit the South Seas, generally are surprised at the appearance of the islands when beheld from the sea. From the vague accounts we sometimes have of their beauty, many people are apt to picture to themselves enameled and softly swelling plains, shaded over with delicious groves, and watered by purling brooks," he wrote in *Typee*.

"The reality is very different," he went on, and he was speaking of Nuku Hiva but it might have been Ua-Pou he was depicting: "Bold rockbound coasts, with the surf beating high against the lofty cliffs, and broken here and there into deep inlets, which open to the view thickly wooded valleys, separated by the spurs of mountains clothed with tufted grass, and sweeping down from the sea from an elevated and furrowed interior."

The rock, most of all, and the way it was arrayed in pinnacles—that was the most unexpected feature. It was high and where it was wooded it was dark green. Some of the mountains were shaped like witches' hats and others like steeples and domes—everything eroded and slender and perpendicular, and the cliffs of black rock plunging straight into the sea and foaming surf. Where are the sandy beaches? Where are the translucent lagoons? There are not many in the Marquesas, and they are hard to find. It is almost impossible to overstate the ruggedness of the islands— the almost unclimbable steepness of their heights or their empty valleys. And at the head of every valley was a great gushing waterfall, some of them hundreds of feet high.

We went ashore at Hakehau—a tiny town on a snug harbor—and Señor Pillitz and I, egged on by a Frenchman desperate for customers, went for a two-hour ride to the stony beach at Hohoi, where we saw a brown horse. "And two crazy cats," Señor Pillitz said, snapping a picture. Several minutes later the Frenchman said we must leave. The road was muddy. The Land Rover got bogged down. I wrenched my spine helping to push the thing. Back in Hakehau he charged each of us twenty dollars and tried to sell us for another twenty dollars framed photographs he had taken of the volcanoes. We were just in time for the dancing—fifteen young men doing "The Pig Dance"—snuffling and oinking and nimbly hurrying on all fours. They finished with a great shout and then we feasted on langouste, and octopus, breadfruit, bananas, and raw tuna marinated in lime juice and coconut milk, the raw fish *(ia ota)* that the French call *poisson cru*.

Strolling back to the ship I found myself walking among flowering bushes which exuded a delicious fragrance, a *noa-noa,* and then I came upon a big family behind a hibiscus hedge hacking a dead cow apart with axes and machetes. They were skinning and butchering it at the same time, while seven dogs fought over the scraps. Just before we set sail I saw these same people running up the gangway, with bulky sacks of the butchered cow slung over their shoulders. They were off to another island with enough meat to last them a month.

In the afternoon, the *Aranui* sailed to the other side of the island, to another village on a bay, Hakehetau, where whaleboats brought bottled gas and provisions ashore. The sky was full of birds—brown noddies, white terns, grayish-yellow finches, and—two or three at a time—the slowly soaring frigate birds. On the high slopes of Ua-Pou there were flocks of wild goats, which had nibbled the mountainsides bare.

Then, in a puddly golden sea that was calm and mild in the same golden sunset, with the scent of flowers carrying from shore, we sailed to Nuku Hiva, and at night we anchored off Taipi, where there was a bay—but no mooring, no quay, no landing stage, nothing but a stinking sandbar at the river mouth.

We went ashore the next day to the village of Taipivai, the whaleboats sputtering up the deep river valley. This was in the southeast of Nuku Hiva. At the sacred site nearby, the passenger I thought of as Gandhi displayed for the first time his uniquely obnoxious habit. At every ancient platform, and at all the stone tikis, he turned his back on the rest of us and yanked his swimsuit down and, sighing with pleasure, relieved himself against the noble ruins. I noticed this first at Taipivai, and thereafter, for reasons that are still obscure to me, Gandhi desecrated every *marae* in every tabu grove we visited in the Marquesas.

"That man is so disgusting," I would say.

"Isn't he *fabulous?*"

Perhaps he was no worse in his way than the missionaries who had castrated these very statues. There is not a dick that has not been hacked off, nor a statue that has not been tipped over, in the name of God Almighty. "But what matters all this?" Melville remarks sarcastically. "Behold the glorious result! The abominations of Paganism have given way to the pure rites of the Christian worship—the ignorant savage has been supplanted by the refined European!" Some of the people struck back, and even statues were said to be rebellious. All tikis are "live" and they can be vindictive, the Marquesans say. Anger these fat black demons that look like the gods of constipation and you will be cursed with bad luck or death.

It was up this path in Taipivai that Melville had spent most of his month. Here it was that he had got the title for his book: Typee was just another way of writing Taipi, and "vai" or a variation of it means "water" all over Polynesia.

The ruins and the tikis in the *marae* just above the village were only part of the story. There were ruins all over the valley, which was fragrant with wild vanilla, and they were practically invisible until you looked closely into the jungle. Then you could see stone walls, platforms, altar-like structures, carvings, and petroglyphs tangled in the vines, and with trees—very often a banyan, associated with sacredness in the Marquesas—bursting through them.

And this was true of the Marquesas generally. Entire hillsides, covered in jungle, hid enormous ruins made of black boulders. It was in this respect like Belize or Guatemala—full of huge tumbled structures, strange statues and walls. Where the walls were intact the construction was like Mayan stonework. These jungles had once been full of villages and big houses, the population must have been immense—estimates are that it was more than ten times larger (80,000 is one guess) at the time of their initial contact with the outside world. This first emissary was Captain Ingraham of Boston, Massachusetts, though the islands were first sighted by the ubiquitous Spaniard Mendaña and named Las Marquesas after his patron, the Marquis of Mendoza.

What had happened to all those Marquesans? The Pacific historian Peter Bellwood has an explanation in his book *The Polynesians.* "The Marquesans, together with their close cousins the Maoris, were by all accounts the hardiest and most robust of the Polynesians, and life was never pervaded with the indolence associated with an island such as Tahiti. Heavily dependent on the breadfruit—a tree which fruits seasonally and not all year round—they were subjected to famines of devastating proportions, and these naturally increased the incidence of warfare. Many early visitors reported that impoverished and defeated Marquesan families would set off in canoes to find land over the horizon."

Now most of the ruins were buried and all of them overgrown; some had been documented, but very little had been excavated. Except for the jungles of Belize and Guatemala, I had never been in a place where the foundations of so many stone structures existed, covered with moss and ferns. All around them were petroglyphs, of birds and fishes, and canoes, and turtles, finely incised in the rock. In the damp shadows of the tall trees, and teeming with mosquitoes, the sites had all the melancholy of lost cities. It was exciting to see them sprawled in the gloom, on those muddy slopes—the immense terraces, the altars, the scowling, castrated tikis. To anyone who believed that all the great ruins of the world have been hackneyed and picked over I would say that the altars and temples of the Marquesas await discovery.

A woman I met in Taipivai, Victorine Tata, had just bought a pickup truck. She drove, riding the brake like my grandmother, but never mind; what bothered me most was that she had floated a loan from the bank and financed the vehicle on the installment plan, and it had cost her $35,000. Would she ever pay off her debt? Victorine just laughed.

The *Aranui* sailed to the administrative center of Nuku Hiva, Taiohae, where it would be unloading cargo for a few days, and so I stayed in Taipivai, and asked Victorine, for a fee, to drive me around Taipi in her new truck. She said she would be delighted. She was a big bulky woman, with a square jaw and heavy legs. She was impassive, but she was honest, and seated in her truck she was so huge and immovable she seemed to give the vehicle enough extra weight to hold it firmly on the precipitous narrow curves of Taipi's heights.

"Melville lived over there," she said in French, and pointed to Taipivai, about two miles above the estuary, near a large *marae* on the eastern side of the valley.

We were now driving up a steep muddy path.

"My uncle traveled with him for a while. He showed him tikis and taught him about the flowers and the trees."

"Do you mean he traveled with the real Melville?"

"Yes. The American Melville." She pronounced it Melveel. "My uncle liked him."

Her uncle had given Melville many a helping hand.

"Wasn't this a long time ago?"

"Eighteen twenty-something," Victorine said. "Long ago. My grandfather also knew Melville. He showed him the island—all around."

"How do you know this?"

"My father told me many stories about my relatives and Melville."

It was not clear to me whether there was even a grain of truth in what she said, but she was a good sober person, and she believed it, and that was what mattered.

"The Marquesans were anthropophagi, weren't they?"

"What's that?"

I had hesitated to use the word "cannibal," but I steeled myself and rephrased the question.

"Oh, yes, before—long before. They ate people. But not now."

The word "Typee" in the Marquesan dialect signifies a lover of human flesh, Melville had written. True? Victorine said no.

"Now, I understand they eat dogs here," I said after a while.

"No. The Tuamotus—that's where they eat dogs. We eat goats and cows."

The Taipi hills were empty. In Tonga and the two Samoas, in Fiji and on other islands, I had become used to seeing concentrated populations—

crowded towns, and hillsides filled with huts, and every twenty feet of shoreline claimed and occupied. This place was extraordinarily depopulated—there was no one in sight. This was simply a great empty island of dense trees and the deserted magnificence of the black stone ruins.

We sometimes enjoyed . . . recreation in the waters of a miniature lake, into which the central stream of the valley expanded, Melville had written. *This lovely sheet of water was almost circular in figure, and about three hundred yards across. Its beauty was indescribable.*

That was where the naked Fayaway had mischievously played at being Tommo's mast, and where Tommo had splashed among the dusky bathing beauties.

"What about the lake?" I asked.

"There is no lake," Victorine said, and another illusion was shattered.

Although Victorine's pickup truck had a radio-cassette player, there was no radio station in Nuku Hiva—there was none in the Marquesas—and she had no tapes. But I had replaced the Walkman that had been stolen from me in Tonga, and I still had the Kiri Te Kanawa tape *(Kiri—A Portrait)* that had soothed me in the Solomons. I popped the cassette into Victorine's tape deck as we chugged across the Taipi mountains.

There was a sudden plangent burst of Kiri singing "Dove sono" from *Le Nozze di Figaro.*

"That is a song from an opera."

"Opera, yes. I have heard of opera."

The next aria was *"Je dis que rien ne m'épouvante"* from Bizet's *Carmen.*

"That's French," she said—we were still speaking French. "But do men sing like that, in that sort of voice?"

She pretended to be a man singing in falsetto.

"Sometimes they do, but they don't sing exactly like that."

"Vissi d'arte" was issuing from the loudspeaker of the muddy truck.

"Do you like that one?"

"I love it," Victorine said.

"I'll tell you something interesting," I said. "That singer is a Polynesian—a Maori, from New Zealand."

"I am happy to know that."

Her face was blissful. I imagined Victorine traversing these roads, from Taipi to Taiohae and back, dropping off eggs, picking up passengers, and on every trip, listening to these arias, and "Rejoice Greatly" and "I Know That My Redeemer Liveth" from the *Messiah,* and the others—perhaps looking forward to listening, and mumbling the words that might become familiar.

And so after a while I said, "You can have the tape. A present."

She was pleased; she started to speak, then thought a moment. Finally, she spoke in English, "Sank you."

Victorine dropped me nine miles above Taiohae, because after the confinement of her little truck, I craved a walk. I hiked across a high ridge and on a switchback road down to the main town of Nuku Hiva, where the *Aranui* was still discharging cargo. Although it was also the main administrative center of the Marquesas, it was a small settlement, a few grocery stores selling expensive canned food and some imported vegetables. In Taiohae I saw nine-dollar cabbages, from California; and that same day there appeared carrots and onions from the *Aranui*.

The ship was headed to a village on the north coast of the island, Hatiheu, and as I could get there myself by road I lingered in Taiohae, enjoying the novelty of walking. I had begun to dislike the sedentary voyage, and all the meaty food. In Taiohae I felt better for missing meals, and although I stayed in a hotel, I occasionally bought a liter of fruit juice (from Australia) and a can of baked beans (from France) and a baguette (from Papeete), and sat under a tree on the seafront and made my own meal.

All canned goods were luxuries in the Marquesas. The people grew breadfruit and mangoes, and they caught fish. If they had spare money they treated themselves to a can of Spam or one of the crunchy snacks they liked so much.

"A girl might work as a waitress simply to be able to buy cigarettes," Rose Corson told me. She ran a small hotel on the western side of Taiohae's pretty harbor. "At five dollars a pack the cigarettes would take most of her salary."

The Marquesans I met were big and ponderous. They were noted for their gloom and their heavy moods, and unlike the Tahitians they were not at all quick to play music and sing. At sundown, fat men in T-shirts gathered at the seafront in Taiohae, near the jingoistic French memorials, and cooled their toes in the breeze and shared family-size cans of Cheez Balls.

One plaque said, *A la Mémoire des Officiers, Soldats et Marins Français morts aux Marquises 1842–1925,* but no mention of the thousands of Marquesans who had died fighting in vain to keep possession of their homeland. Another, ignoring the fact that the islands had been discovered by brave Polynesian navigators who had probably crossed the ocean from Samoa about 1,800 years ago, extolled the spurious claim of a "discoverer"—*Au nom du Roy de France le 23 Juin 1791 Etienne Marchand découvreur du groupe N.O. de Marquises prit possession de l'isle*

Nuku Hiva. This also took no account of the fact that Captain Ingraham had claimed it two months before.

Nuku Hiva was annexed in 1813 for the United States by Captain David Porter. He put up a fort and renamed Taiohae after James Madison, who was president. But Madisonville was no more than an impulsive gesture, and as Congress never ratified the act it had no force. The French would have fought us for it in any case, battling just as fiercely as they did in 1842 when they slaughtered thousands of islanders in order to gain possession. Melville witnessed the shelling. His Marquesan jaunt coincided with the French adventure, and in his book he mocks the French part in the affair: "Four heavy doubler-banked frigates and three corvettes to frighten a parcel of naked heathen into subjection! Sixty-eight pounders to demolish huts of coconut boughs, and Congreve rockets to set on fire a few canoe sheds."

After my two days alone in Taiohae, I made my own way across the island to Hatiheu, where the *Aranui* was moored in the pretty bay—there was no dock for the ship: The whaleboats brought the cargo through the surf to a crumbling pier.

Hatiheu was a small exquisite village at the foot of three steep mountains, and in a meadow at the center of the village was a large church, with two steeples and a red tin roof, dedicated to Joan of Arc. Horses cropped grass in the churchyard. And standing under a tree outside Hatiheu's tiny post office, with dogs barking and the waves breaking on the black sand beach, I made a telephone call to Honolulu.

Later, I found Señor Pillitz, and we walked into the woods behind the village, through the palm plantations—and the palms were interspersed with kapok trees, laden with bursting pods; kapok had once been cultivated commercially here. But now all this farming was outdated. Beyond the plantation was a ceremonial area, called a *tohua,* which was about the size of a football field, and enclosed stone platforms, and altars, and carved statues. Such an area tended to be avoided by the local people, who believed the *tohua* to be haunted and that it had a *mana,* or spirit, that was at odds with their Christianity. There was an enduring fear if not horror among locals of these ancient sites. Most of all it was a fear of the spirits of the dead that haunted these glades after dark, the malevolent *tupapau.*

Deeper in the forest there was another site that was larger but much harder to see, because it had all been tumbled apart—the terraces, the altars, the boulders cut with petroglyphs. It was overgrown with banyans, several of them giant trees. In an earlier time, the Marquesans had placed the skulls of their enemies among the exposed tree roots, and on a higher slope there was a round pit, lined with stone, where captives were held in order to be fattened before they were killed and eaten.

"Zey wair cooking zem wiz breadfruit," a Chinese woman told me later. Her name was Marie-Claire Laforet. Her father had dropped his Chinese surname ("The French didn't want foreign words," Marie-Claire said) in the great Tahitian name change of 1964. It was an appropriate choice. His Cantonese name, Lim (Lin in Mandarin) is the character for wood or trees.

That same day I went with Philippe and Señor Pillitz across a ridge beside Hatiheu to Anaho Bay. Well enclosed, with extensive ruins, a white sand beach, and a coral shelf—one of the few reefs in the Marquesas, the only lagoon—it was the loveliest spot I saw in these islands, combining the color and gentleness of a tropical beach with the ruggedness of surrounding mountains. Robert Louis Stevenson had stopped in this very bay in 1888 in the *Casco* with his wife and his two stepchildren and his elderly mother. It was the sight of Anaho Bay, and his dealing with the tattooed Marquesans, whom Stevenson believed still to be cannibals, that convinced him of the rightness of his decision to spend the rest of his life in the Pacific. Anaho had a profound effect on him—and on his mother, too: For the first time in her life this fastidious Edinburgh matron gave up wearing stockings, "and often shoes as well." Bewitched by Anaho, the whole family went native. Anaho was—and still is—the apotheosis of the South Seas: distant, secluded, empty, pristine—ravishing in fact.

"Are there sharks here?" I asked two spear-fishermen, wading out to the edge of the reef.

"Many sharks."

"Big ones?"

"Very big ones."

"Do they bother you?"

"No."

They left a machete behind. I knocked some coconuts from a low palm tree and slashed them open. We drank the sweet water and ate the meat. Walking back past the scattering of fishermen's shacks and through the humid forest we were followed by a small so-called *demi,* a Chinese-Marquesan boy, about ten years old.

"I am happy here in Anaho," he said stumblingly in French. "I would not like to go to France. There are no langouste there and no breadfruit. Here we have food. We have fish. We can build a house anywhere in the woods. I can swim, I can fish from my father's pirogue. I would not be happy in France."

In the early evening we sailed to the island of Tahuata, anchoring off the black sand beach of the village of Vaitahu. In the morning we were taken ashore by whaleboats. Vaitahu was typical of most of the larger Marquesan towns in a number of respects: a Catholic church, a canned-food shop, wonderful ruins at the edge of town, steep green valley walls, flowering trees, and fruit trees—avocadoes and grapefruit trees in the gardens of little wooden bungalows, hairy black pigs, fretting mongrels, a new church, and an insulting plaque on the seafront speaking of all the Frenchmen who had given their lives battling to take possession of the place.

The monument in Vaitahu spoke of the French soldiers and sailors who had "died on the field of honour," in the battle for Tahuata in 1842. Melville had ironized about this very place, and how the French had prided themselves on the good order they had brought to the Marquesas, though it had caused human fatalities; and "to be sure, in one of their efforts at reform they had slaughtered about a hundred and fifty at Whitihoo [Vaitahu]."

I was overheard jeering at the plaque by the woman known on board as The Countess. She was half-French, half-German and often strolled along, holding a tape recorder to her lips and nagging into it. She said she was somewhat struck by my sarcasm. It so happened (she went on) that she was a travel writer. Thus the tape recorder.

"I am writing a story about this trip for the best and most brilliant newspaper in the world"—and she named a German daily paper. "They respect me so much that in seventeen years they have changed only one sentence of mine."

"What was the sentence?"

"It was very reactionary you will think," The Countess said.

"I'll be the judge of that."

"All right then. 'Three hundred years of colonialism have done less harm to the world than thirty years of tourism.'"

I smiled at her and said, "That's brilliant."

Thereafter whenever she felt the need to unburden herself she sought me out.

"My husband was a genius," she said later. "I myself have written many books about clothing."

"I hate children," she told me another day. "I love doggies."

I told her I had seen some puppies with wire on their necks being taken out of Vaitahu to be used as shark bait by some Marquesans in a canoe.

"They should use babies instead," she said, and laughed like a witch in a pantomime.

Speaking with some youngsters in Vaitahu, one of them asked me, "What are you? What is your country?"

"I am an American. And you?"
"I am a Marquesan."

Dolphins riding our bow wave preceded us the next day as we plowed into Traitors Bay, to enter Atuona Harbor, on Hiva Oa. Tahuata was clearly visible beyond the bay, in a nameless channel, and to the southeast was the tiny Marquesan island of Mohotani.

An old red Citroën was swung out of the hold of the *Aranui* and driven away. Then the crates were unloaded—sacks of farina, cases of beer, gasoline, building blocks, snack food. A Hiva Oa nun picked up a parcel that had been shipped to her and then drove off in her Toyota.

Three Mormons, two of them islanders, watched the unloading, and surveyed the disembarking passengers as though looking for possible candidates for conversion.

I asked them whether they had saved any souls.

"In a year and a half I have not converted too many people," Elder Wright (from Seattle) said. "Two families. But we also help in other ways. We teach games. We play basketball."

"I saw you talking to those Mormons," Ross said, sidling up to me as I was walking into town. "They're supposed to be so holy, but some of them are unbelievable root rats."

"Do you have any scars to prove it?"

"Isn't he fabulous!" Ross called out, but he was soon confiding his proof. "A couple of Mormon chaps came to the door of a gay friend of mine in Melbourne. They had some cold drinks—nonalcoholic—and about ten minutes later they were all in bed together!"

Hiva Oa was Gauguin's last island.

Gauguin is often represented as a bourgeois stockbroker who suddenly upped and left, abandoning his job and his wife and five children and recklessly fleeing to Tahiti, where his artistic genius flowered. But he had always been reckless, and he began painting only a few years after his marriage. And he knew something of the wide world: He had spent part of his childhood in Peru (his mother was half Peruvian Creole); he had gone to sea at the age of seventeen and sailed as an ordinary seaman for six years. His marriage was unhappy, and it was not he who quit the stock market but rather the other way around, for when it went bust he began painting full-time—there was a stock market crash in 1883. By then he was already accepted an an Impressionist.

Rejecting Europe, he tried Martinique, in the West Indies, and when that didn't work for him he went to Tahiti, thinking it to be Cytherean. It was the opposite: Papeete was bourgeois and westernized, full of puzzling colonial snobberies and irritating bureaucrats, sanctimonious missionaries and corrupt townies; and people were generally as unsympathetic towards him there as anyone might have been, seeing a long-haired Impressionist, in metropolitan France. His hair was long—shoulder length—and he wore a velvet cowboy hat. They loathed him for his repulsive manners and his mode of dress. The Tahitians were more tolerant but still they called him *taata-vahine,* "man-woman," because of his hair. He moved to a seaside village, painted madly, and wrote letters home grumbling about the colonials and about life in general. After two years he packed his things and went back to Paris, where the exhibition of his paintings was a critical and financial disaster.

In *Noa-Noa,* he celebrates island life and the beauty of the people, but *Noa-Noa* was written by a man who was eager to convince himself, and others, that he had been resident in paradise. It is vastly at odds with his letters. But the love affair in *Noa-Noa* had a basis in fact, for Gauguin had met his Fayaway in Tahiti. Her name was Tehaamana and she was thirteen ("this was an age Gauguin was greatly drawn to in females," the Pacific historian Gavan Daws has observed); and Gauguin painted her over and over until she became the embodiment of his South Seas fantasy.

In his two-year interval in Europe he was miserable. "Literally I can only live on sunshine," he said and returned to Polynesia, and although he intended to head straight for the Marquesas he procrastinated. He still hated the colonial life in Tahiti, the bureaucracy, the tyranny of the church—hated these aspects of Tahitian life so deeply that they never appear on his canvases. You look in vain in a Gauguin painting for anything resembling details of the colonial life he must have seen most days in Tahiti: no ships, no sailors, no traders, no officials—nor their wives or children; no roads or wagons, or mechanical contraptions; no books or lamps or shoes; no *faranis* at all—and the place was full of white folks, and not only whites but Chinese. The islands had endured sixty years of colonial rule, and yet in Gauguin's paintings—in the fragrant vision he created for himself—Polynesia is inviolate. The only indication we have of foreign influence is the bedstead in several of the paintings. Tahitians slept on mats, not on beds.

"In Gauguin, a need to persuade always went hand in hand with a desire to offend," one of his biographers has written. Living in the bush with yet another Tahitian teenager, Pauura, he quarrelled constantly with the authorities (his starting a little newspaper did not endear him to them either), and eventually—still seeking savagery—he set sail for the Marquesas, leaving Pauura and their son, Emil, who was destined to become a tourist attraction.

He arrived in Hiva Oa in 1901 and died less than two years later, having spent ten years altogether in Polynesia—two extended visits, during which he fathered numerous children between painting masterpieces. Here in the little village of Atuona, under the great green Matterhorn of Temetiu, he had built a fine two-story house, which he called The House of Pleasure, and having carved on the wooden frames his favorite maxims, *"Soyez mystérieuses"* (Be mysterious) was one, and *"Soyez amoureuses et vous serez heureuses"* (Be in love and you will be happy) was another—he took a fourteen-year-old girl, Vaeoho, as his mistress. He had come to some sort of arrangement with her parents. Gauguin was in his mid-fifties, and Vaeoho was soon pregnant. Their child, who had become an old woman, was still living in the valley in the 1980s.

It is surprising, given the heat, the disorder, the difficulties of living, all his enemies, and the simple necessities of stretching and preparing canvases—never mind buying materials—that Gauguin painted at all; yet his output was large, and he was a steady worker, sometimes turning from his painting to wood carving or pottery. Gauguin was also plagued by bad health—he drank, he took drugs, he had syphilis and stress and a fractured leg. The church authorities in Atuona hated him, and he had protracted legal problems there, too—a libel action against him. He suffered; and one day a Marquesan neighbor, Tioka, ventured into his house and found the *farani* stretched out and apparently lifeless. Following Marquesan custom, Tioka bit Gauguin's head. The man did not stir.

Gauguin lies buried high on a slope in the cemetery above the village. Near him are the graves of Thérèse Tetua, David Le Cadre, Jean Vohi, Josephine Tauafitiata, Anne Marie Kahao, and Elizabeth Mohuho, who were alive at the turn of the century and died in Atuona and must have known the strange, wild painter. Gauguin's grave is simple, made of pockmarked volcanic rocks and shaded by a large white-blossomed frangipani. Garlands of flowers were strewn over the grave. The grave marker was his own statue of a wild woman, lettered "Oviri."

Some children were playing nearby. I spoke to them in French, and then asked them, "What does *oviri* mean?"

They said they didn't know. I had to look it up. It is a little ambiguous but appropriate. The word means "savage." Gauguin applied the word to himself in his bronze self-portrait of 1895–6, his face in profile. He wrote in 1903 to Charles Morice (who had collaborated with him on *Noa-Noa*), "You were wrong that day when you said I was wrong to say I was a savage. It's true enough. I am a savage. And civilized people sense the fact . . . I am a savage in spite of myself." But the goddess Oviir-moe-aihere is not only a savage; it is she who presides over death and mourning.

As with his paintings, the grave was a colorful mixture of truth, imagination, suggestion, and rough brilliance. The faces in the paintings can be encountered all over Tahiti and the Marquesas, but the backgrounds and landscapes are idealized and dreamlike. Gauguin needed to believe he was a savage—and perhaps he was, but of a different kind entirely from the gentle islanders he had wished himself upon.

Gavan Daws tells a lovely story about Gauguin in *A Dream of Islands,* his wonderful account of the numerous men who came to Oceania to revisit and verify their fantasies.

"One night at sunset [Daws writes] Gauguin was sitting on a rock outside his house on Hivaoa, naked except for his *pareu,* smoking, thinking about not very much, when out of the gathering darkness came a blind old Marquesan woman, tapping along with a stick, completely naked, tattooed all over, hunched, tottering, dry-skinned, mummy-like. She became aware of Gauguin's presence and felt her way toward him. He sat in inexplicable fear, his breath held in. Without a word the old woman took his hand in hers, dust-dry, cold, reptile-cold. Gauguin felt repulsion. Then in silence she ran her hand over his body, down to the navel, beyond. She pushed aside his *pareu* and reached for his penis. Marquesan men—savages—were all supercised, and the raised scarred flesh was one of their great prides as makers of love. Gauguin had no savage mark on his maleness. He was uncovered for what he was. The blind searching hand withdrew, and the eyeless tattooed mummy figure disappeared into the darkness with a single word, '*Pupa*' she croaked— White man."

The ship was anchored for the night, so I walked with Señor Pillitz over the ridge to the next wide bay, Taaoa, about four miles up and two down, but by the time we came to the archaeological dig the day had grown too dark for us to see anything. Walking back in the dusk to Atuona we passed two parked cars. There were half a dozen people in them, Tahitians and Marquesans and French, having a wonderful time. Footsore, we asked for a lift.

They said no. It was inconvenient.

"We want to look at the airport," one of them explained.

Señor Pillitz said, "You are visiting Hiva Oa?"

"We are officers, with the Department of Tourism," one of the women said.

"What a coincidence. We are tourists," Señor Pillitz said, "and we need a ride back to our ship."

Someone muttered in the backseat. They laughed and drove away.

"He eats it doubled up," Señor Pillitz said. It was an Argentine term of abuse: *Se la come doblada.*

We saw them later in the bar of the *Aranui.*

"You say you're a writer," one of the tourism officials said. "What do you write about?"

"Everything I see."

* * *

We sailed to the north coast of Hiva Oa, and anchored and went ashore. There at Puamau, at a *marae* at the end of a muddy path in the jungle, was a vast ruin. Finding such a place unmarked in the jungle behind a remote village was one of the singular pleasures of cruising the Marquesas. This one was a jumble of overgrown and scattered stones, and many carvings, some beheaded and castrated by souvenir hunters or missionaries. Others were fiercely intact, one of which is the largest tiki in Polynesia—a seven-foot monster, grimacing and clutching its belly— and another the strangest and most beautiful frog-faced creature, horizontal on a pedestal. It had a jack-o'-lantern mouth and donut eyes and fat extended legs, and it was apparently flying.

"It is a tiki woman," a Marquesan told me.

The giants [tikis] *of the cliff-girt Puamau Valley displayed such a contrast to the lazy people on the beach,* Thor Heyerdahl writes fatuously in *Fatu-Hiva, that the question inevitably came to mind: Who put these red stone colossi there, and how?*

His answer, refuted by every archaeologist of any reputation, was: People from South America.

Farther west on Hiva Oa the *Aranui* provisioned the village of Hanaiapa, and I hurried up another muddy path in a light mist until heavy rain began to fall—so heavy I had to shelter in a deserted building. It was a rickety wooden church, with vines reaching through the windows and a crude pulpit, and a quotation painted high on one wall, *Betheremu* ("Bethlehem") and *Miku 5:4-5,* a gnomic reference to the text from Micah in which the prophet mentioned Bethlehem and foretold the coming of the Lord: "For now shall he be great unto the ends of the earth. And this man shall be the peace, when the Assyrian shall come into our land—"

Through the tilted doorjamb I could see coconut palms and breadfruit trees, mangoes, papayas, grapefruit, avocadoes—and the wet straggling village next to the gurgling stream.

Walking back to the beach (muddy gray water washing muddy gray sand) I passed a house where three young Marquesans were listening to music from a boom box.

"Who is singing?" I asked.

"Prince."

And farther on I met a woman walking hand in hand with a young girl. The woman was attractive, in a green blouse and wearing a flower-patterned *pareu*. She smiled at me and stood with her feet apart, blocking the path.

"Hello. My name is Mau," the woman said in English, and she showed me her name tattooed on her wrist.

"Where did you learn English?"

"From the boats." And she pinched the little girl's cheek. "This is my daughter, Miriam."

The woman was wearing a lei—a Marquesan one, with mint and other fragrant herbs entwined with flowers.

"That's very pretty."

She immediately took it off and put it around my neck and kissed me on each cheek, more like a French formality than a Marquesan custom.

"Where are you going?"

"Back to the ship."

"Too bad."

She smiled a little ruefully, but the ship would be back, and perhaps next time it would stay a bit longer, and she would meet someone else, someone more willing.

She was as near as I came to finding Fayaway. But she was much like the other people I had met, who seemed decent and hard-working and happy. She was the one who seemed to possess just a flicker of coquettishness, and none were flirts. Most of the people were tough and down to earth, a little gloomy and very religious. Where was the romance? I had no idea. Even the islands, so dramatic at a distance, were quite another story close up—muddy and jungly and priest-ridden, and the beaches teeming with no-see-ums they called *nonos*.

Instead of painting the great rocks, the black cliffs, the crashing waves, the deep Marquesan valleys, the sea-washed crags, the cataracts and mountainsides, the hypocrites and colonials—instead of dealing with this reality, Gauguin decided to test his own theories of color and perspective. He painted pink beaches, yellow fields, Buddhist images, Javanese statues. He created a tropical horse culture in which France did not figure. He invented Polynesia. So people came. They don't find his Polynesia, but what they do find is just as magical, though undoubtedly forbidding, and just as *luxe, calme et volupté,* as Baudelaire wrote in *L'invitation au voyage,* one of Gauguin's favorite poems.

But some of the islands were anything but voluptuous. Ua Huka was one of these. The harbor at Hane was so narrow, no more than a pair of granite jaws, and the *Aranui* lay tethered between them, on short lines, and bouncing in the swell. The island was bereft of trees, and in the interior wild goats and horses and wild donkeys were desperately foraging. The island, the smallest in the Marquesas, looked nibbled to death. There were only 500 people on Ua Huka. Some were carvers, and they came forward, trying to sell expensive tikis, and war clubs, and bowls that cost $350.

After looking at the ruins—muddy path, boulders, the shattered buttocks of a tiki—I found a place to eat and had a feast—breadfruit, and *miti hue* (river shrimp in fermented coconut milk), *poe* (sweet starchy pudding flavored with papaya), *poisson cru* made with tuna, and sweet potato, *umara*.

I walked until the hard-driving windblown rain forced me inside. The post office in Hane was a small bare room—about the size of the average bathroom. The postmistress, Marie-Thérèse, a hibiscus flower in her hair, sat at a trestle table with a telephone and a cash box. Here, while Marie-Thérèse read a French magazine, *La nouvelle Intimité,* I made a telephone call.

I sat beside Marie-Thérèse, who was reading a section called *Dossier,* which was headed, *Le Plaisir au Féminin—Pour une sexualité sans tabous.* What a coincidence, that word that had found its way back to Polynesia in an article about uninhibited women's pleasure. It spoke of orgasms, sexual response, diseases, and sexual variations *(mille et une),* and Marie-Thérèse was so engrossed she hardly noticed when I hung up the phone.

Waiting for the whaleboat to take me back to the ship, I fell into conversation with some youngsters who were seated near the beach for this monthly event, the visit of the *Aranui.*

"Are there any *tupapaus* here?" I asked one of them, Stella, who had been listening to the lambada on her brother's Walkman.

"Not here, but beyond the restaurant."

"At the *marae?*"

"Yes. And in the forest."

"Are you afraid of the *tupapaus?*"

"Yes."

And the whaleboats came, and the older passengers were carried in the arms of the Marquesans. It was accomplished quickly, but I was struck by these arrivals and departures through the surf: Most of them were exactly like rescues, just as wet and urgent and precarious.

There were more stone terraces and house platforms on pretty Fatu Hiva (pop. 500), the smallest, the prettiest and most vertical island in this group. Thor Heyerdahl's account in *Fatu-Hiva: Back to Nature*—how he got away from it all by coming here—resulted in an influx of people to Fatu Hiva similarly trying to get away from it all. There were so few habitable valleys that these foreigners were concentrated in only a couple of places and produced a rash of thieving and conflict: a period of intense xenophobia among Marquesans, and disappointment among the foreigners. Everyone had been misled. Characteristically, Heyerdahl's book was fanciful and inaccurate and self-promoting, with many narrow escapes and improbable incidents (in one, the ponderous Norwegian buys Gauguin's rifle, and it is obvious to even the most casual reader that he is being bamboozled), and long misleading chapters about cannibalism as well as tendentious detail—Heyerdahl's hobbyhorse—about the peopling of Polynesia by South Americans.

The *Aranui* first stopped at Omoa, and the walkers among us trekked seventeen kilometers over the high ridges among wild horses and wild goats to Hanavave and the Bay of Virgins. The interior of the island was perfectly empty. Walking was something Marquesans seldom did. They sat, they hung out, they rode four-wheel-drive vehicles and sometimes horses; but I never saw any islanders hiking the upcountry paths. Some frankly said they were afraid of the *tupapaus* that lurked in the dense upland foliage. That could have been one reason. But Marquesans also seemed a sedentary lot and were never happier than when sitting under the palms on the seafront, near one of the pompous and vainglorious French plaques ("To The French Dead"), holding a big blue can of Cheez Balls between their knees and munching.

The Bay of Virgins was a misnomer, but deliberate. The bay is surmounted by several unmistakably phallic basalt pillars, and was originally called Baie des Verges—Bay of Dicks is a fair translation of that. But outraged missionaries slipped an "i" into the word, making it *vierges,* virgins. If they had been English missionaries they might have slipped an "r" into the word, turning Dicks into Dirks ("because they resemble knives").

At the tight little harbor of Hanavave there were children and dogs running in circles—I counted twenty dogs in one place alone—and big bulky Marquesans waiting for the ship's cargo. They had been without beer for two weeks, they said. They had run out of gasoline. The snacks had been gone for some time. The whaleboats came and went, leaving provisions, taking away fish. A Marquesan woman watched wearing an *AC/DC* T-shirt, a man watched in a baseball hat that read *Shit Happens.* As Gauguin indicated in the androgyny of his portraits, the men and women physically resembled each other, and became almost indistinguishable as they grew older.

The island of Fatu Hiva was without doubt the most beautiful of the Marquesas, not just for its great vistas, and the wild horses scrambling on the slopes, the sheerest cliffs, the greenest ledges, and the beautiful bay. It was its greenness, its steepness, its emptiness; the way daylight plunged into it only to be overwhelmed by the darkness of its precipitous valleys, and the obvious danger of its entire shoreline gave it the look of a fortress or a green castle in the sea.

The Marquesans were gloomy and laconic, and they lived quietly, out of the sun, in the depths of their damp valleys. They seemed to be gentle people. They harvested coconuts. They fished. They raised kids. On Sun-

days they went to church and sang the whole mass. They tattooed themselves and ate breadfruit and fish. They grew fat, and then their children
served them. It was not a bad life.

Still, the islands seemed paradoxical to me. The soil was fertile, but the
vegetable gardens were small and insufficient. The people were intensely
proud of their ancient Marquesan culture, but they were also God-fearing
Catholics. They spoke proudly of their ruins and carvings in the jungle,
but did nothing to preserve them, letting them fall into greater ruin. They
said they disliked the French, but they let the French run all their affairs.
It made no difference to them that 85 percent of their food was imported
as long as the few really important items like rice were subsidized. They
loved eating loaves of French bread, but there were only a handful of
bakeries in the islands; they let the *Aranui* deliver bread from Tahiti—it
was stale and expensive coming by ship but that seemed preferable to
their baking it themselves. They lived hand to mouth but no matter how
hard-pressed they were for money they would not accept a tip. They were
eager for tourists, but there was hardly a hotel on the islands that was
worth the name. The Ministry of Tourism—no doubt this is a blessing—
is almost wholly ineffectual where the Marquesas are concerned.

There are all sorts of little guidebooks to the Marquesas, but the
liveliest and the most informative, for all its fiction and inaccuracies, is
Herman Melville's *Typee*. Give or take a few roads, and one video store,
the little post office and the usual curses of colonialism, not much has
changed in Nuku Hiva since Melville fled the cannibal feast almost 150
years ago. There is no cannibalism in the Marquesas anymore—none of
the traditional kind. But there was the brutality of French colonialism.
Gauguin had noticed the peculiar hypocrisy, and Gavan Daws quoted
him as hectoring the bourgeoisie of French Polynesia.

"Civilized!" Gauguin cried. "You pride yourself on not eating human
flesh, [yet] every day you eat the heart of your fellow man."

Now the islands are emptier, the valleys are silent, the tabu groves more
ghostly, and at the head of most valleys there is an enormous waterfall—
and sometimes three or four—coursing hundreds of feet down from the
cliffs.

About that water. Seeing those cataracts often made me thirsty. One
day in Nuku Hiva I went to a bar and asked for a drink of water. A half
liter of Vittel was opened for me, and I paid—$2.50. It was unthinkable
that I should want the vile water from the pipes of Taiohae, and no one
questioned the absurdity of buying this little bottle of Vittel from halfway
around the world. That it is available at all is something of a miracle; that
it might be necessary is a condemnation of this lovely baffling place.

The French praise and romanticize the Marquesas, but in the 1960s they had planned to test nuclear devices on the northern Marquesan island of Eiao, until there was such an outcry they changed their plans and decided to destroy Moruroa instead. It is said that the French are holding Polynesia together, but really it is so expensive to maintain that they do everything as cheaply as possible—and it is self-serving, too. Better to boost domestic French industries by exporting bottled water from France than investing in a fresh water supply for each island. That is what colonialism is all about. You can hear the bureaucrats say, "Let them boil their water." The French have left nothing enduring in the islands except a tradition of hypocrisy and their various fantasies of history and high levels of radioactivity.

So what is this part of Polynesia today except France's flagpole in the Pacific, and a devious way of testing nuclear devices?

"The people are helped, but the help is not handed over—it is bounced to them," Señor Pillitz said—another Argentine expression, *La agarro de rebote,* meaning that something is grudgingly given.

When France has succeeded in destroying a few more atolls, when they have managed to make the islands glow with so much radioactivity that night is turned into day, when they have sold the rest of the fishing rights and depleted it of fish (already Tahiti and the surrounding islands have been overfished), when it has all been thoroughly plundered, the French will plan a great ceremony and grandly offer these unemployed and deracinated citizens in T-shirts and flip-flops their independence. In the destruction of the islands, the French imperial intention, its *mission civilisatrice*—civilizing mission—will be complete.

Chapter 20

THE COOK ISLANDS: IN THE
LAGOON OF AITUTAKI

I was paddling in the huge lagoon of Aitutaki, which was green sea ringed by tiny islands and a reef that was like a fortification made of coral and sea foam. An old man fishing from a dugout canoe called out to me.

"Why are you paddling there, listening with those earphones?"

I was listening to Chuck Berry.

"Because I am unhappy," I said.

"Where is your wife?" he yelled.

Then the wind took the rest of his talk away, and it also separated our boats.

I had come to this lagoon in the Cook Group from the Marquesas for a reason. The Marquesas were the dispersal point, from about A.D. 300 onward, for people who populated the three corners of the Polynesian triangle. They sailed to the top of it, the Hawaiian Islands; to the Cooks and beyond, to New Zealand; and to Easter Island. No one is certain why the Marquesans embarked on these long and difficult voyages, some of them over 2,000 miles. The people were skilled in the arts of warfare, gardening, navigation, and boat building. They had found every island of any size in the eastern Pacific, bringing to it their arts, their gods, their chiefs, their domestic animals, and their favorite vegetables. They worked in stone, they made tools, they wove ingenious baskets, but they did not make pots. They civilized these islands with a peculiarly harmonious culture that combined a reverence for flowers, a fondness for music and dancing, and a predilection for cannibalism.

Letting these old discoverers determine my itinerary, I had decided to leave the Marquesas to paddle in the Cook Islands. After that I planned to paddle around Easter Island, and finally Hawaii.

It was a short flight from Papeete to Rarotonga, the main island in the

Cook Group. I arrived late at night in a cold drizzle and was watched by heavy Maori-looking people with big fleshy faces, large and not very dexterous hands, and bulky bodies. They looked like unfinished statues and were handsome in the same sculptural way, with broad open faces and big feet. Every adult, whether man or woman, had a rugby player's physique.

"This is camping equipment?"

"It's a boat." I had checked "camping equipment" on my arrival form.

"Is it clean or dirty?"

"Very clean."

"You can go."

Two different New Zealanders, seeing my boat bags and my gear, said sarcastically, "You travel light!" But the Cook Islander heaving them off the baggage cart said, "My woman weighs more than that."

It was like landing at an airstrip in the middle of Africa—one plane, three small buildings, few formalities, only one person around, seeing to everything. It was easy to get information because there was so little to know. It was nearly midnight. I asked the only person there whether I could fly the next day to Aitutaki.

"The first flight's at eight o'clock. I can put you on it."

The speaker was Mr. Skew, a New Zealander. He told me about the political system, which seemed simple enough. Then he asked where I was staying. I saw the name of a hotel on the wall, and said, "There." He drove me to the place ("And that's the Cook Islands Parliament House," Mr. Skew said, as we passed a very small wooden shed beyond the airport).

Viv, the dour New Zealand clerk at the hotel, at first pretended she wasn't glad to see me, and then said, "We have plenty of rooms. Do you want a sea view?"

"I'm getting up at six." It was now twelve-thirty.

"You should get one of our cheap rooms," Viv said. The room had a Soviet look, chipped paint, plastic chairs, easily-tipped-over lamps, and a blocked drain in the sink. And it was barely furnished. I had last stayed in a room like this in Wellington, but this made pretty Polynesia seem chilly and frugal. The Cooks were still informally linked to New Zealand, but the smug and self-denying Calvinism of Kiwi-land was at odds with everything Polynesian, and the Kiwis themselves looked rather out of place here, so beaky and pale, with short pants and knobby knees.

"I'm from Aitutaki myself," a Cook Islander said to me the next morning at the airport. He had a strong New Zealand accent. His name was Michael Rere.

"There's supposed to be a great canoe maker in Aitutaki," I said.

"Probably my father."

"Is his name Rere?"

"Yes, but they call him 'Blackman,' because he's always out fishing. That makes him black."

Cook Islanders were standing in a light rain, holding garlands and crowns of flowers, watching passengers disembark from a flight that had just arrived from Auckland, watching lots of bundled-up and brightly dressed people hurrying through puddles towards the arrival building. Fat people greeting even fatter arrivals—happy families.

Inter-island planes began to arrive. Besides the high volcanic island of Rarotonga, the most populous (10,000) and developed, there are fourteen other islands in the Cook Group, ranging from coral atolls like Suwarrow (with six inhabitants) to Mangaia, which is nearly as large as Raro. Small planes flew to most of these islands. Aitutaki had been recommended to me as a friendly and pretty place, and so I decided to go there with my collapsible boat.

A woman was yapping in Maori, and among her unintelligible muttering I caught the phrase *no place like home.*

That same hour I was flying in sunshine over the lagoon at Aitutaki, looking down at its wonderful configuration of reefs and *motus,* and after lunch I was paddling there.

It was then the old man called out to me, "Where is your wife?"

I spent the night at a small seedy house by the shore called Tom's. Camping was forbidden, because all the land was spoken for and constantly being quarrelled over, subdivided, and renegotiated. Mr. and Mrs. Tom were islanders; they were out but their daughter had shown me around. The walls of the house were plastered with religious pictures, and copies of *The Book of Mormon* were lying about, bristling rather ominously with bookmarks and dog-eared pages.

"You can cook here," Winnie said, showing me a greasy stove. "You can put your food here." She opened a dusty cabinet. "You can share this bathroom," and she shoved a plastic curtain aside, "with the others."

But what I felt most keenly was the absence of beer. And even if I found some in town, how could I guzzle it in front of this pious family of Mormons?

It was next to the lagoon, so I stayed awhile, and I became friendly with the three fearfully solemn evangelists who could usually be found conferring on the porch, their black ties dangling—a Cook Islander, a Maori from Auckland, and Elder Lambert, from Salt Lake City.

"I'm from Massachusetts," I said on first meeting them, and when they gave me blank looks I added, "which is not far from Vermont."

The big booby faces of the islanders were in marked contrast to the consternation on the face of Elder Lambert.

"And you know who was born in Sharon, Vermont," I said.

"Who was born there?" the Maori asked.

After an uneasy pause, the Cook Islander laughed. "I doon know eet!"

Elder Lambert said, "Joseph Smith was born in Sharon, Vermont."

They were so transfixed by the fanciful details of their absurd millennialism (Jesus's visit to the Mayans in Guatemala, golden tablets buried in New York, the prophecies of the Angel Moroni, God encouraging polygamy, and so forth), that they had lost sight of the simplest facts, such as where the founder of their church, their prophet, was born.

I urged them to read *No Man Knows My History: The Life of Joseph Smith,* by Fawn Brodie, and they said I should look into *The Book of Mormon.*

"I will," I said. "I want to read about the Lost Tribes of Israel sailing into the Pacific."

This made Elder Lambert hitch his chair forward and begin pointedly tapping the air with his finger.

"In the first chapter of Nephi, Lehi went east from Jerusalem. His descendants are in the Pacific. And in the last chapter of Alma—sixty-three—Hagoth and many others built ships and sailed into 'the Western Sea.' Those are the very words. The Pacific, in other words. They were Nephites."

"Sailed from where?"

"America. Central America." Tap-tap-tap went his finger. " 'A narrow neck of land.' "

"And they made it to Polynesia."

"Yes. The Polynesians are descendants of these people."

The Maori was beaming. His expression said: *Take that!*

"What about the Melanesians?"

"Sons of Ham."

"What about the Micronesians?"

Elder Lambert narrowed his eyes at me. He said, "Corrupt defilers."

After all this disputation I needed air. I thought: You had to admire Joseph Smith for trying to come up with a homegrown faith—it was the most Americanized religion. (Christopher Columbus and the American Revolution made appearances in *The Book of Mormon.*) But Mormonism was like junk food: It was American to the core and it looked all right, but it wasn't until after you had swallowed some that you felt strange.

I strolled into Aitutaki's town, Arutanga. It was a very small town—hardly a town at all, more a village, and its small size and its dullness kept it pure. It was the post office, two shops, four churches, a muddy harbor, a school, some houses. The shops sold only canned goods: fish, beans, corned beef, cookies, crackers—the South Pacific standbys.

Poo, the postmaster, was sitting on the post office steps. He told me he disliked Rarotonga for being too busy and stressful.

"Are you busy?"

"Not really," he said.

Eleanor at Big Jay's Take-Away fried a fish burger for me, a chunk of wahoo in a bun, and said she had lived her whole life on the island, and that she was trying to make a go of this business.

"Are you busy?"

"Not really," she said.

It began to rain very hard, and walking back to Tom's I had to take shelter under a big tree. A girl of about twenty, who had been headed out of town on her motorbike, was doing the same thing. The rain crashed through the branches and leaves.

"You mind this rain?"

"Not really," she said.

But it let up after an hour, and the sun came out, and I went paddling again.

On the beach, near Tom's, I met two enormous women, Apii and Emma. They looked elderly, but they were exactly my own age. They referred to me as a *papa'a*—a white man.

"What if I were black—what would you call me?"

"Then you would be a *papa'a kere kere.*"

"What if I were Chinese?"

"You would be *tinito.*"

"What if I were from another island?"

"You would be *manuiri*—a stranger."

I asked them whether there were community activities on the island. They said there were the churches and sometimes there were festivals.

"We used to have a cinema in Aitutaki, but videos are better," Emma said.

"Do you think that videos from America make the young people violent?" I asked.

Emma said, "Maybe. But the young people in Aitutaki are all right. The problem is with these Cook Island kids who come home for the holidays. They live in New Zealand and they learn bad habits. They are troublemakers. We call them 'street kids.' They give a bad example. Cook Islanders go bad in New Zealand."

"I like watching videos," Apii said. "Most people in Aitutaki have a video machine. We have had them for four years. Or maybe three."

"And blue movies," Emma said. "Did you ever see blue movies?"

"I have seen some," I admitted. "What about you?"

"We have," Emma said. "One called *The Tigress*—something like that."

"Naked *papa'as,*" I said. They laughed. "Do young people watch them?"

"No. Only adults," Apii said. "Men like them."

"Women find them silly," Emma said.

I asked, "Why do you think men like them?"

"They get ideas. They like to watch. And sometimes"—Emma raised her large hands to her face and giggled behind them—"sometimes they end up."

"What does that mean, 'end up'?"

"They end up doing what they are seeing," Apii said.

"Because the blue movies make them hungry," Emma added.

We were standing under some palm trees. It began to rain again, but still they shifted themselves and said they had to go. Before they left, I gave them some chocolate.

"I would rather have nuts," Emma said, and laughed.

The next day I got tired of the Mormons and the tiny mildewed house, and I moved to a bungalow at a lodge another mile up the road, but also on the lagoon. Not long after I moved in, I switched on my shortwave radio and, searching for world news, I heard a familiar voice.

I am a little incredulous still, that I am the representative of Her Majesty the Queen in New Zealand—

It was Dame Cath, whom I had met in Fiji. She was back in Auckland, and still harping with false modesty about carrying out the queen's wishes.

—and that the daughter of poor Scottish migrants should be standing here today, is testimony to—

I switched the thing off and somewhere in the palms a cockatoo shrieked.

That day I paddled to the edge of the reef, a place marked Nukuroa on my chart, where a father and son were fishing.

Toupe, the father, said, "I can only live here in Aitutaki. It is small. Rarotonga is big. If you have a small place you have few people. But in a big place you get Samoans, Tongans, and all different people. I don't like that."

I pointed to one of the little islands south of us. "Do you call that a *motu?*"

"Yes."

Then I pointed to Aitutaki, which was low and green and glimmering in the sunshine. "Is that a *motu?*"

"No. That is *enua.*"

Enua was land. *Fenua* in Tahitian. *Vanua* in Fijian. An island was a little parcel in the sea. It was something you could see the whole of in a glance. But land was something else—it had a sense of home, it had size, it was divided, it contained more than one family. I asked Toupe for a definition.

"*Enua* is not an island. It is a small land," he said, and then he asked, "Are you married?"

"That's a long story," I said.

"But where is your wife?"

"That's what I mean."

"Not with you?" He was very persistent.

"No," I said.

"That is bad." He looked genuinely annoyed. "You will go with girls from bars."

"Not a chance," I said. "I am too old."

"They like older men."

"I am not interested."

Anyway, where were these girls? Where were the bars, for that matter. They were mentioned in Tahiti, too. I never saw them. In Taiohae in Nuku Hiva one night a man said to me, *All the boys have gone to the bar to pick up girls.* I did not see any bar in Taiohae that had a woman in it. Fast women were muttered about in Fiji. What a shame—all the prostitutes, people said. I looked and did not see a single one. Rarotonga was reputed to be a hot place. You could have fooled me. It was jolly, but in a hearty unambiguous way. Bar girls were mentioned in Nuku'alofa, in Tonga. There were two bars; I looked; no one. I never saw anything vicious on the streets or bars of Polynesia, and my only brush with the local libido was in the Trobriands, where I had sometimes been woken with a drunken cry, *Mister Paul, you want a girl?* but I usually assumed it was a clumsy attempt to rob me and always went back to sleep.

Before I left Toupe I asked him about sharks. Yes, he said, there were plenty of them in the lagoon. I showed him the four-foot spear I kept beside the cockpit of my kayak.

"That will do nothing to the sharks we have," he said. "They are bigger than your boat."

That gave me pause. My boat was almost sixteen feet long.

On the other hand, Aitutaki was famous for not having any dogs on it. No one had an explanation for this, but I was glad in any case, because Polynesian dogs were bad-tempered scavengers. It was as though they knew that human beings were not to be trusted: and that the fate of all dogs was to be cooked and eaten.

I went back to my bungalow that day and found six ripe mangoes on my table. Somehow the two fat ladies, Apii and Emma, had found out where I was staying and had brought the fruit to me.

My intention was to paddle to the *motus*. Because it was forbidden by custom for any stranger to stay overnight on them, these involved round-trips of anywhere from eight to twenty miles. But I had to be prepared for emergencies: I might get stuck on a *motu* if there was a storm. I bought food at the local shops—beans, sardines, raisins, cucumbers, bread—and set off, launching into the shallow lagoon. There was no local market. The meat in the shops was canned, and one store sold frozen New Zealand lamb and mutton.

"What about chickens? Don't you raise chickens?"

An islander said, "We have wild chickens."

"Do you eat them?"

"Sometimes. But they are too tough."

I loved the expression *wild chickens*.

At low tide great bristling shelves of coral were exposed in the lagoon, and fighting the wind I was sometimes blown onto the spikes. Then I had to get out and disengage my boat and tramp away, pulling it carefully, before getting in. I always wore reef shoes in Aitutaki for this reason. After a few days the rubber bottom of the boat was terribly gouged, but I had no leaks.

The skipping fish seemed to be stirred by low tide, too, and they sometimes surfaced in a silver sheet—hundreds of sardine-sized fish—shimmering seventy-five feet across my bow, dancing on their tails, and into the distance, a lovely sight.

One day, making for a little *motu* called Papau at the eastern edge of the reef, I realized that I was low on drinking water. If I happened to become stranded on Papau I would have no water at all, except for the coconuts I might knock down (and that was never easy). Spotting a village called Tautu marked on my chart, on the east side of Aitutaki, I paddled there and went ashore.

Two naked boys watched me drag my boat onto the sand.

"What is that?"

"That's my boat," I said.

They laughed. The kayak did not look like any boat they had ever seen.

I walked up a path and over a jungly hill and found some houses. There was no one home at any of them, though the houses looked cared for and the gardens well tended. On the veranda of one of the empty houses, a washer was going—a washtub, which was open and agitating clothes, this way and that, *shlip-shlop, shlip-shlop,* with a laboring motor. It was a sound from my past, my mother's washer going most of the day, it seemed—all that distance to hear that evocative noise and recover a memory of early childhood.

Farther along the road, I saw an islander. I said I needed some water. He pointed to a house.

A white man came out, followed by a small grubby child.

"What is it?" the man asked in what was perhaps a New Zealand accent. He seemed tetchy.

"I wonder if you could give me some drinking water, please."

Without a word, he took my bottle and went into the house. Then he was back, handing it to me, again in silence.

"I came by kayak," I said. "I saw this village on the map. My boat is on the beach."

He simply stared at me, without any interest.

"Have you lived here long?" I asked.

"Eighteen years."

"You must have seen some dramatic changes," I said.

He pressed his lips together, then said, "No paved roads then."

Yet I had not seen any paved roads even now.

"This was all jungle," he said.

Wasn't it still jungle, except for the odd little bungalow?

"That kind of thing," he said.

I said, "Do the high prices bother you?"

This seemed to irritate him.

"It's all relative, isn't it?" he said defiantly.

"That it costs three dollars for a cucumber?"

"You learn to live with high prices," he said, and now he was cross, though I could not explain why. "Just like you learn to live with low prices. You go to Australia"—perhaps he was an Australian?—"and the prices are low, and you learn to live with them. And you come back and the prices are high and you learn to live with them."

I said, "I suppose if you have a garden you can reduce some of your costs."

"A garden?" he said, sneering in incredulity. "Do you know how much time a garden takes? You could be at it all day, weeding it, watering it. Time—that's the rarest commodity here. Time."

That was news. I would have thought that time was plentiful on this little island—that the one commodity everyone had in abundance was time.

The man had a rising tremor of mania in his voice as he said, "You wake up and you're off and there's never enough time to do everything that needs to be done, and if it's not one thing it's another. Time is scarce here"—and he leaned forward at me: He was barefoot, in a dirty T-shirt, the grubby child nuzzling his legs. "I never have enough time!"

"I'd better be going," I said.

"And another thing," he said. "I'd rather pay three dollars a pound for tomatoes than thirty dollars and all the time it takes to grow them."

"Of course. Well, I'm off—headed out to that island"—Papau, in the distance, was partially misted over.

"It's two miles, you know. Maybe more."

"I've just come six miles from Arutanga. I can manage."

"And the wind's against you," he said.

"True. But it will be an easy paddle back, or to that other island."

"Unless the wind shifts. Then it'll blow you straight out to sea or onto the reef."

Now I saw that he had a stubbly face, and bitten nails, and spit in the corners of his mouth.

"I was under the impression this was the prevailing wind—southeasterly."

"It shifts at times. Not usually at this time of year. But it shifts."

I had a sudden urge to push him over, but I resisted, and turning to go I said, "At least it's not raining."

"It might rain," he said eagerly. "We need rain. I hope it does rain." He grinned horribly at the blazing sky. "And it's four miles to that island, Papau."

"Then I'd better get started," I said.

"The reef's at least three," he said.

"I was told there's an ancient *marae* on the island."

"There's said to be. I haven't been out there."

And he had lived here for eighteen years?

"Haven't had the time," he said, as though reading the query in my mind. "There's never enough time." He looked extremely harassed. He clutched his T-shirt. He said, "Now, I'm sorry, but you're just going to have to excuse me. I haven't got all day for chatting. I've got masses of paperwork to get through. That's what I was doing when you came. You interrupted me. You see? Time. Not enough."

"Thanks for the water."

"It's good water. From an artesian well. It's all drinkable here," he said, as though I was on the point of accusing him of poisoning me.

It took me an hour, paddling into the wind, to get to Papau. There were herons and egrets wading in its shallows. From a distance it looked as though it had a white sand beach. Close up it was broken coral and bleached rock, and it was littered with rubbish and flotsam that had floated from Aitutaki or had been chucked from ships.

As I sat on a log, eating my lunch, the whole beach got up and started walking sideways. Shells, big and small, were bobbling all over the place. This was amazing, like a Disney cartoon, where nature starts to frolic—singing trees, nodding flowers, dancing shells. The hermit crabs I had startled earlier had begun to move, and I had never seen so many of them in action at one time.

I tramped around the island, looking for the ancient site, but saw nothing. It was a deserted island, with dense jungle at its center, and the remains of campfires at the edge. I had told myself that I had come here to look at the *marae* but once on the island, faced with thorns and tall grass and spiders, I could not be bothered, so I went for a swim instead, and after that knocked down some foul-tasting coconuts.

It occurred to me that I might work my way down this long chain of *motus,* starting here, and then going on to Tavaeraiti and its sister *motu* Tavaerua. The fifth one along was in the far corner of the lagoon, almost out of sight of land. I could get close to it tonight, hit it tomorrow, and then head back.

The idea of trespassing excited me, and there was enough daylight for me to make it to the largest of the *motus,* Tekopua, where I could hide.

The wind helped me by beating against the beam of my kayak and slipping me quickly past Akaiami and Muritapua, and by then Aitutaki was almost lost on the horizon. It was a low island and at this time of day no fishermen came out this far. My only problem might be a fisherman who had come to the same conclusions as me and decided to spend the night—but there was none. I went ashore at the top end of Tekopua and dragged my boat off the beach. I had everything I needed: water, food, mosquito repellent, and enough canvas to keep the rain off my sleeping bag.

Darkness was sudden. No sooner had I finished eating than night descended. There were no stars. No lights—not even any on the distant island. The palms rattled and the surf broke on the far side of my *motu.* That sound of surf and thrashing palms woke me throughout the night—there were no real silences on Polynesian nights: At the very least it was wind or waves. But this sound was noisier than city traffic.

I woke very wet, not from rain but from the residue of heavy mist, and after breakfast began to worry about having camped. Now I had used up most of my water and food. If I had a problem, I'd be stuck.

The last *motu* in the chain, Motukitiu, was only an hour away. I started paddling for it before the sun was up, before the wind had begun to rise; and after I had landed and had a quick drink I headed north across the widest part of the lagoon, to catch the rising wind that would take me west to the safety of Te Koutu Point.

There were turtles on the way, and more dancing fish, and spikes of slashing coral. I realized that I had not rested well in the night when, after I had reached the shore of Aitutaki, I lay back and fell asleep. It was not even noon. But after I woke, I felt refreshed, and more than that, felt that I had accomplished something in seeing each of the islets on this entire side of the huge lagoon—the desert islands of Aitutaki.

I swam at Te Koutu—this whole part of Aitutaki was empty, except for screeching birds; and then I headed back, with a tailwind, to Arutanga.

Although I stayed a mile offshore, because of the jagged coral, I could hear loud singing as I passed the beach below a village that appeared on my chart as Reureu. I could just make out a group of men under a wooden shelter that was next to a large tree. I paddled nearer, avoiding the coral, and was debating whether to go ashore when I heard shouting. The men were waving me towards the beach.

I parked my boat and joined them. There were about fifteen men. Most were drunk and all were singing. One man had a guitar, another a ukelele.

"Please, come," one man said. He was wearing a T-shirt that said *Rarotonga*. "Have some kava."

He gestured to a cutoff metal drum that sat in the middle of the group of men. One of the men worked a coconut shell around in it, slopping the brown opaque liquid.

"Is this *yanggona?*"

"No. This is Aitutaki kava. Made from malt, sugar, and yeast. This is beer, my friend."

"Bush beer."

"Yes. Have some."

I was handed a black coconut shell brimming with it. The taste was sweetish and alcoholic. I sipped. They urged me to gulp it all. I did so and almost hurled.

"So you're out paddling that little boat?"

"Yes. I was out to the *motus,*" I said. And then, to confirm that I had indeed trespassed, I asked, "But what if I wanted to spend the night on one?"

"If no one sees you, what is the harm?" one of the men said.

They all wore filthy T-shirts and were squatting on logs.

"You come from?"

"America. But not in that boat."

They laughed. They were drunk enough to find this hilarious. Then they began to tease one of the men, who appeared to be very shy and possibly mentally disturbed.

"This is Antoine," the man in the Rarotonga T-shirt said. "He comes from Moruroa, where the French test the bombs. He is radioactive. That is why he is so strange."

Antoine lowered his head.

"Antoine speaks French."

I addressed Antoine in French, just saying hello. All the men laughed. Antoine left the group and mounted his motorbike and then rode away.

I said, "Is this a bush-beer school?"

That was the Aitutaki term for a drinking party, I had read.

"Yes. He is the teacher."

The man dipping the filthy coconut shell into the metal drum smiled and went on dipping and slopping.

"But it is more like a ship," another man said. "He is the captain. He is the first mate. He is the second mate. He is the engineer—"

"It is a club." This man was standing against the tree. "We call it Arepuka Club. This is a *puka* tree. And this is an *are*." He meant the little wooden shelter.

"He is chairman."

The standing man smiled: The only man sober enough to be able to stand up had to be chairman, I supposed.

"How long has this club been in existence?"

"Three years."

"You come to drink every day?"

"Excuse me. We have meetings every day."

"What do you do at your meetings?"

"We drink beer."

"And then?"

"We sing."

"How long do you stay here each day?"

"Until we are drunk and cannot stand up."

All the men laughed hard as this unsmiling man explained the workings of the club to me.

"And then we go home."

"What songs do you sing?"

"About the island."

"Is it a nice island?" I asked.

"It is like paradise," he said.

"Why do you say that?"

"Because we have everything we want—food, beer, vegetables, fish—"

Suddenly the man next to me snatched my hand and began reading my palm.

"You are thirty-six years old," he said, squeezing my hand. "I can see it here."

Another man said, "It is better here than in New Zealand."

"Have you been there?" I asked.

"Yes. It is too fast there. Too much busy."

"Some Cook Islanders come back to Aitutaki from New Zealand and go to the latrine and say, 'It is dirty. There is no flush. Look at all the cockroaches.' But there is much water in New Zealand for flushing. We have little water."

"After two or three weeks they stop complaining," someone said.

"What do you think of New Zealand people?" a man asked me, handing me another shell of beer.

"They are very careful people," I said. "They obey the law. They eat carefully. They speak carefully. They spend money carefully."

"Because they have no money!" one man cried out, and the others laughed. "They are poor."

"Are you rich?" I asked.

"No."

"Being poor doesn't mean you spend money carefully. Poor people can often be very generous."

"And rich people very mean with money," a man said.

We discussed this and I became so engrossed in this topic I soon realized that I was drunk and that my head hurt. When I shut up for a while they began to sing.

"What was that song about?" I asked when it was over.

"About Ru. Our ancestor. He found Aitutaki. With his four wives and his brothers."

That legend was mentioned in my guidebook, how Ru had voyaged from the island of Tupuaki, in what is now the Society Islands, which had become overcrowded. The first name of Aitutaki was *Ararau Enua O Ru Ki Te Moana,* "Ru in Search of Land Over the Sea."

In spite of the missionaries, local legend was alive and well. And the Cook Group had been one of the first in the Pacific to be converted by the passionate clergyman John Williams: He had left Aitutaki a Polynesian convert named Papeiha, in 1821, and the Aitutaki Christian church, oldest in the Cooks (1828), had a tablet in the churchyard, one side extolling Williams, the other extolling Papeiha.

I said, "Where did Ru come from?"

"Maybe the Society Islands. Maybe Samoa."

"And before that?"

"Not Asia. I think Asia Minor. Where Adam and Eve came from."

Ah, that was the link between Polynesian legend and Christian tradition. Ru the voyager had sailed his canoe from the Holy Land.

I said, "What do you like best about living on an island?"

"We are free," one said.

"We can do whatever we like," another said.

I said, "But what if other people come? *Papa'a*. Or *Tinito*. Or *manuiri*. Or Japanese?"

"We would kick them out."

"This is our island. We have everything."

They sounded fierce, but they were merely tipsy, and they followed me staggering to my boat and urged me to come back the next day. They promised to sing for me.

I could not explain why, but in the waning light of day, the sun going down beyond the lagoon, and paddling past one of the prettiest—and friendliest—islands I had seen, I felt very lonely. I heard that man saying *Where is your wife?* and the fact was that I no longer had one.

Soon I was paddling in night-blackened water, splashing like mad towards the lights on shore.

Being alone was the oddest aspect of my traveling in Oceania, because the island people of Oceania were never alone and could not understand solitude. They always had families—wives, husbands, children, girl-friends, boyfriends. To the average person on a reasonable-sized island, nearly everyone was a relative. Wasn't this extended family one of the satisfactions of being an islander? Living on an island meant that you would never be alone.

There was no concept of solitariness among the Pacific islanders I traveled among that did not also imply misery or mental decline. Book-reading as a recreation was not indulged in much on these islands either—for that same reason, because you did it alone. Illiteracy had nothing to do with it, and there were plenty of schools. They knew from experience that a person who cut himself off, who was frequently seen alone—reading books, away from the hut, walking on the beach, on his own—was sunk in deep *musu,* and was contemplating either murder or suicide, probably both. Now and then, people would mention that a place had a much higher suicide rate than I could possibly imagine, and in truth I was usually rather surprised to hear the figures. Then they would describe the method—nearly always taking a dive off the top of a palm tree.

Marriage was seldom stressful, because the rest of the family was usually so supportive—the husband had his male friends, the wife had her female friends, the children were raised by all these uncles and aunties. When a marriage was that complex and seemingly casual, divorce was somewhat irrelevant. (And lots of people stayed married by having abso-lutely nothing to do with each other—by rarely being in contact.) This big family was circumscribed by the island, and so an island family was like an entire nation.

I met divorced people now and then. In the Trobriands a divorced woman was permanently eligible for marriage and was regarded with horror by single men: "I might have to marry her," they said. The Presbyterian stigma of divorce which had been imposed on the islands by severe missionaries in the nineteenth century was harsher than tradition had ever been, and was like the Mark of the Beast. Often a divorced person simply left the island—he or she had disappointed too many people or made enemies. They were the women who worked in hotels in the capital; they were the men who emigrated. Generally, it was not easy to become divorced without seeming like a traitor.

All this made my position awkward: Being solitary made me seem enigmatic, paddling alone made me seem like a true *palangi* "sky-burster," reading and writing made me look like a crank, and my being wifeless was a riddle. My condition was hard for anyone to relate to and impossible for me to explain. And I seemed to be challenged a lot in the Cooks. *Where's your wife?* Oh, God, let's not go into it. I could only approximate my feelings to them, and it would be like explaining something like Westminster Abbey but using only their references: "This very big *are* has a *marae* inside, and petroglyphs on the walls—"

I sometimes felt like the only person in Oceania who had wrecked his marriage, and I was reminded of that overwhelming sense of remorse I had felt that dark night in New Zealand, when I looked through the front window of the California Fried Chicken Family Restaurant on Papanui Road in Merivale and burst into tears at the sight of a happy family.

My solution was to keep paddling.

One evening, musing in this way, I was dragging my boat up the beach and saw a man strolling among the palms. He was white, probably a tourist, but something about his physique commanded my attention. He was an unusual shape—he was tall, with a full belly, and narrow shoulders, thin arms, rather spindly legs, and a large head; he was as unlike an islander in his general shape as it was possible to be. He looked like an English squire or ship's captain, who never missed a meal but seldom walked anywhere; well fed but underexercised.

I turned my boat over and parked it under a palm. The man had paused and was looking back at it. He was gray-haired, with thick glasses, and rather dainty hands that matched the slenderness of his arms. He was alert, perhaps restless, but he had a ready smile. For all I knew it was the simple good will and fellow-feeling of one *papa'a* for another, but it was a bit more penetrating than that, not just an acknowledgment but a welcome.

"You look familiar," I said.

"David Lange," he said. "I used to be prime minister of New Zealand."

"How about a beer?"

"Lovely."

Now you are not alone, I told myself.

I had admired David Lange from a distance for helping to make New Zealand antinuclear. Here was one of the poorer industrial nations, needing world markets for its butter and lamb and wool, risking the economic retribution of America and Europe by lecturing them on the dangers of nuclear dependency, and going further and not allowing warships carrying nuclear material into New Zealand's harbors. It is usually expensive and lonely to be principled; this seemed like political suicide. But Lange stuck it out and won friends, and more than that he became an example for many world leaders. There were some exceptions. It was well known that the prime minister of Australia hated Lange for taking a stand, but then Bob Hawke—as Lange himself might have put it—had uranium on his breath.

And there was Lange's separation. It had been the current topic when I was in New Zealand—his estranged wife yelling her grievances, his mother denouncing him, and the combined snipers in the Kiwi press doing their best to destroy him. I had felt for him. His turmoil had come at the time of my own separation. I had identified with him, and in a quiet way felt he was an alter ego. We were almost exactly the same age. I read items with headlines like "DAVID DECEIVED ME," SAYS LANGE'S WIFE and I would cringe for him and for myself.

Yet what a funny old world it was. Here we were under the trees of Aitutaki, by the lagoon, in the failing light of day, the former prime minister and the former writer—which was how I felt—two clapped-out renegades taking refuge on a remote island.

I told him my name.

"Really? The writer?" and he named some of my books. "Are you writing something here?"

"No, just paddling."

But he of all people had to understand how a writer's denial was not very different from a politician's denial.

"I'm glad to hear it," he said, though he didn't seem convinced. "I'd love to write something about Aitutaki. I've been coming here for years. I've thought of writing some kind of book—like one of yours, about this place. Aitutaki is full of wonderful characters."

While we were seated having a beer, he said suddenly—his manner of speaking was rapid, he had a restless impatient intelligence—"You write about trains," and gulped his beer, and said, "Ultimate railway story. I was traveling from Delhi to Bombay in 1967. I was a student. In those days it took thirty-seven hours, but they had a wonderful dining car, with heavy silver and cloth napkins and waiters running to and fro. I had beef curry. The meat tasted strange, but of course it had been heavily spiced. I was violently ill afterwards, and I spent days in bed. I have never been so ill with food poisoning. And I wasn't the only one. Most of the people who had the beef curry on that train ended up in the hospital."

He chuckled at the memory and then went on. "About a month later I read that one of the waiters on the Delhi-to-Bombay run had been arrested for supplying dismembered human corpses to the dining car, claiming they were fresh beef. They were hardly recognizable, of course, after they had been turned into curry."

The nature of a politician is to talk; the nature of a writer, to listen. So here we were on this lovely island, the public man and the private man, with plenty of time to practice our peculiar skills. Lange talked often and well, and was affable. He greeted strangers, he had a good word for everyone, he introduced me around the island. If a small group congregated he took charge, and to simplify matters he would launch into a long humorous monologue as a substitute for a halting conversation. He had a parliamentarian's talent for avoiding all inter-ruptions—rain, falling coconuts, loud music, pestering strangers, awk-ward questions; and he had the successful politician's gift for being able to repeat himself without sounding bored. I could vouch for Lange's ability to tell the same complex story (involving accents, mimicry, his-torical detail, and mounting suspense) three times in as many days with the same gusto.

I had gotten a sunburn on my jaunt down the chain of *motus*. I needed to stay under a tree for a while, and so the next three days I spent on and off with David Lange, who knew Aitutaki well, and we discussed (he talked, I listened) the *Rainbow Warrior* affair, the future of New Zealand, ditto of Australia, Ronald Reagan's senility, Saddam Hussein's paranoia, Margaret Thatcher, the Queen, Yoko Ono, Lee Kuan Yew of Singapore, Rajiv Gandhi, Chandra Shekhar, the characteristics of various Pacific islanders—Tongans, Samoans, the Cooks, the characteristics of various Christian religions.

The most unsatisfying international gatherings Lange had ever at-tended, he said, were Commonwealth heads-of-government meetings. It was not just Margaret Thatcher nannying everyone and swinging her handbag, or Bob Hawke of Australia being personally abusive. It was the utter waste of time. The Bahamas meeting of 1985 was notable for its host, the prime minister of the Bahamas, "a remarkable character who came unscathed through an inquiry as to why in the past year he had put in his bank account an amount eighteen times greater than the total of his salary." At a similar meeting in Vancouver, Lange discovered that the

Botswana delegation had made $1,300 worth of phone calls and charged them to his hotel bill. The Ugandans at that same conference "took advantage of their leader's absence at a retreat to invite a fair number of Vancouver's prostitutes to their hotel. They refused to pay and had the police evict the women. Those were the greatest excitements of the conference."

I liked his frankness, and I found him funny. Lange was on familiar terms with the entire world and with its events. He had spent his working life making the acquaintance of powerful people. Who had I met? I fished around and mentioned my trip to Fiji. Lange brightened. "Rabuka's a bully, and Kamisese Mara the prime minister is a stooge of the military government."

"I want to ask you about Dame Cath Tizard, your governor-general," I said.

"She won't be doing much governor-generaling," Lange said, talking a mile a minute and never ceasing to smile. "She'll be in court most of next year in a libel suit—she called someone an incompetent, and she's being sued for fourteen million dollars."

I began to explain my impression of her extraordinary table manners, but Lange rumbled on, still smiling.

"Her ex-husband's quite a character—caused an amazing fuss in Japan after the Emperor died and various world leaders were sending their condolences. He said the Emperor of Japan should have been cut into little pieces after the war. Unquote."

Any conversational lull was my cue for asking a question, and he always gave me a straight answer, and this included questions about the breakup of his marriage and his relationship with his speech writer, Miss Pope, and his mother's sticking her oar into the whole affair.

"Your mother apparently denounced you."

"Yes!" He was smiling. "She went on television! You should have heard her!"

"Was it one episode that ended your marriage or—?"

"We had been drifting apart," he said. "It happens so subtly you hardly notice. Then one day you look up and your marriage is over."

"But there's a woman in your life now?"

"Oh, yes. Margaret. Lovely person—you must meet her."

"What did your children say about the divorce?"

"Older child's in India, studying. That's my son. My daughter said, 'I suppose I'll have to get used to being spoiled, the way children of divorced parents always are.' She doesn't miss much."

"Did you ever get sad afterwards, thinking of the happy days of your marriage?"

"We had rather a turbulent marriage. Didn't you?"

"No. It was pretty quiet most of the time," I said. "I often find myself looking back and feeling awful."

"You've got to look ahead," he said, sounding decisive.

"Do you think you'll ever go back to your wife?"

"It's much too late for that," he said. "She's not doing too badly. She's just published a book of poems."

"What about you?"

"Here I am at the age of forty-eight and I don't have a bed or a chair. My wife got the lot."

He laughed out loud—not a mirthful laugh, but not a bitter one either. I was inexpressibly grateful to him for not evading my questions. He was not whining or blaming or trying to turn the clock back. I wanted to be as resolute as that, and in a way I wanted to stop paddling and reacquaint myself with the sort of contentment I had known in my early life—loving and being loved.

This divorce conversation produced the only silence that occurred between Lange and me.

And then he was back on world leaders, Oliver Tambo of the African National Congress: "When I met him he tried to justify 'necklacing.' "*

"As prime minister of Britain, Harold Wilson was a tricky man," he said, "but what's the future of the Labour Party of Britain? Bryan Gould? He's a New Zealander. He was my roommate at college. How could he lead the Labour Party—he's not even British!"

He had just finished a book *Nuclear Free—The New Zealand Way,* about his antinuclear policy in the Pacific and he was full of stories about sinister French plots.

"The French are swine," he said. "The night before the arbitrator in the *Rainbow Warrior* affair delivered his verdict to the tribunal his house was broken into. Only one item was missing. The word processor which contained his files of the proceedings had been stolen, and a carving knife was left in its place."

In his book he wrote, *The testing at Moruroa still continues. Nothing in French history suggests that it will stop until countries more powerful even than France put a stop to it. I can only look forward to the day when they will want to.*

We talked into the night. The nights were starry on Aitutaki. It was an ideal island; it had one of the largest and most beautiful lagoons I had

---

*A violent mode of aggression between political rivals in South African townships in the 1980s, this involved the placing of a gasoline-soaked rubber tire over an opponent's upper body and setting it and the live person on fire.

seen in Oceania. Its people were friendly and gentle, its food was plentiful; it had no telephones, no cars, no dogs.

More than once, after a peroration or an anecdote, Lange leaned over and said, "Are you sure you're not writing about this island?"

Towards the end of that week, I bumped into Lange on the beach again, and he said, "The Queen's Representative is leaving the day after tomorrow. There's a sort of do for him in town. Want to come along as my guest? Might be fun, even if you're not writing about this place."

"What is a Queen's Representative?"

"In this case an anachronism named Sir Tangaroa Tangaroa."

I spent the next day spear-fishing, using my mask and snorkel, and dragging my boat behind me. My idea was that I would make my way along the reef, and when I got sick of fishing I could paddle the remaining distance to the only *motu* I had not visited, Maina ("Little Girl"). There was the hulk of a ship near it that had been wrecked on the reef in the 1930s with a cargo of Model-T Fords.

Beyond the twists of plump black sea slugs and tiny darting fish were the lovely parrot fish. I swam between the bulging lumps of coral, pursuing fish. *After you have seen the lovely colors of live fish, and how gray they look when they're dead on a slab, how can you eat them?* a vegetarian had once said to me. Soon I lost all interest in spearing fish and just snorkeled, and then—remembering there were sharks around this reef—I got back into my boat, and put on my Walkman and paddled.

On this lovely morning in the lagoon of Aitutaki I was listening to *Carmina Burana*. It was one of those days—I passed many in Oceania—when I forgot all my cares, all my failures, all my anxieties about writing. I was exactly where I wanted to be, doing what I liked most. I was far enough offshore so that the island looked distant and mysterious and palmy, and I moved easily through the greeny-blue lagoon, and I could hear the surf pounding on the reef between the movements of music.

The wind strengthened and I paddled on and saw more wrecked ships. They were strange monuments to the danger of this reef, and seemed fearsome and skeletal. They had a look of frozen violence—so large and rusted black. The oddest aspect of that was that there was no sense that anything was happening on shore. It seemed so absurd that a captain should even steer his ship to Aitutaki, much less risk his whole enterprise on this reef. The island seemed to slumber dreaming its green dreams in its green shade. There was no industry, no traffic, no smoke even. It was the simplest, quietest society I had seen. I seldom saw anyone cooking or gardening, or doing anything energetic except fishing. The island was almost motionless in the still hot mornings, and only at night after the drumming and dancing started did it come alive. The people were alert and could be talkative. It did not surprise me that life proceeded at the slowest possible pace, but rather that it proceeded at all.

Something about Cook Islanders (there were only 20,000 of them altogether) made them seem special. Even with all the patronage from New Zealand, and their passionate interest in videos, the people remained themselves. They were not greedy. They were not lazy. They were hospitable, generous, and friendly. They were not violent, and they often tried to be funny, with little success.

One day early in my visit I had speared a parrot fish. I showed it to a man on shore, when I was beaching my boat.

"What do you think of this?"

"It is a fish," he said, deadpan.

"A good fat fish?"

"A normal fish," he said.

"But it's a good one, don't you think? A big one. Good to eat."

"A normal parrot fish," he said, refusing to smile. "A normal parrot fish."

Meanwhile I was still paddling to Maina. I had asked David Lange about the distinctiveness of the Cooks, and his explanation was that it had retained its character because it was still owned by the islanders. Not one acre had been sold to a foreigner. The land was sometimes leased, but it had not left their hands. This was also the basis of an anxiety—that the Japanese would come and somehow wrest the land away from them, trick them somehow. They hated and feared the Japanese, and I saw no Japanese tourists in the Cooks. "We don't want them!" a man in Aitutaki told me. "We will send them away!"

The wind was roaring in my headphones, blowing waves across my deck and slewing me sideways. I paddled on, feeling happy in this vast green lagoon, among turtles and glimmering coral, and at last reached Maina. Isolated and empty and hardly ever visited, in a distant corner of the lagoon, it was one of the most beautiful islands I walked upon in Oceania.

On the way to the feast for the Queen's Representative, David Lange showed me some new trucks parked in the Ministry of Works depot.

"They can't use them. They've been here for months. But they're using that dangerous old banger"—he indicated a jalopy, dumping logs—"you'll never guess why."

"Someone put a curse on them?"

"Close. They haven't been dedicated. They need a proper ceremony. It might be months before they manage that."

It was a God-fearing archipelago. Mormons, Jehovah's Witnesses,

Seventh Day Adventists, Catholics, and the local outfit, Cook Island
Christian Church, the CICC. The plaque to the martyr John Williams
(eaten by Big Nambas in Erromanga in Vanuatu) should have been a
tip-off, but there were churches everywhere, and crosses, mottoes, Bible
quotes, grave markers, and monuments. The history of the Cook Islands
was the history of missionaries—that, and a small trade in fish and
coconuts. But mostly it was people's souls that were sought after, and
some of the earliest photographs of Cook Islanders showed the men in
long pants and women in Mother Hubbards, the modest all-embracing
muumuu. The Mormons didn't drink, the Jehovah's Witnesses didn't
smoke or vote, the Seventh Day Adventists didn't dance, the CICC didn't
fish on the Sabbath.

Still, life went on in its passive Polynesian way and somehow people
managed still to dance, to drink, to smoke and sing and fish and make
love. There was a local woman who had a reputation for simply appearing on the beach, offering herself, welcoming any and all fishermen, who
made love to her. As for the dancers, they cleared their consciences by
saying a prayer before every dance—then they drummed and twitched
their bums and shook their tits; and afterwards they said another prayer.

There were prayers in the garden of the small tin-roofed bungalow that
was the residence of the administrative officer of Aitutaki. Just a simple
hut with a pretty garden. About thirty men and women joined in the
prayer, and they all wore colorful shirts and dresses—there was no clothes
snobbery at all in the Cook Islands. You wore a T-shirt and shorts, a
bathing suit, a lavalava, and that was it. No socks, no shoes, no ties, no
dress code at all.

Another day in Fatland—fat men, fat women. The fattest was the
Queen's Representative, an older man—perhaps seventy—in a very tight
Hawaiian shirt, a button missing where his belly bulged. This was Sir
Tangaroa Tangaroa, QR. In spite of his titles he was a simple soul. But
I had heard this word *tangaroa* before, in connection with Polynesian
cosmology.

"What does 'tangaroa' mean?" I asked the mayor.

The mayor was the brother of the prime minister. *It's all nepotism here,*
Lange had told me.

"His name is the name of god."

"God in Heaven?"

"No. One of our old gods."

"Which one?"

The mayor's own name was Henry and he looked a bit flummoxed.

"God of the sea? I think god of the sea."

This man Henry was very vague altogether. There was a big *marae* in the south of the island. I asked him where it was. He said, "Somewhere in the jungle. You will never find it."

Aitutaki was less than two kilometers wide at its widest point, and it was less than six kilometers long. *Somewhere in the jungle* had no meaning when dealing with a place this small, unless one was an islander and considered this island an entire world.

"Can't you tell me how to get there?"

"No. It is not easy. Someone will have to take you."

That was another thing about islanders: They were almost incapable of giving clear directions, because they had never needed to encapsulate directions by giving the location of a particular place. An island was a place where everyone knew where everything was, and if you didn't you had no business there.

I said, "But this is not a very big island."

"The *marae* is in the jungle."

"Even so, there's not much jungle. Do you ever go there?"

"I am so busy."

But this was merely an expression: No one was busy in Aitutaki.

I then approached the Queen's Representative.

"Have you spoken to Her Majesty?"

"Yes. For hours," he said, and blinked at me. "For many hours."

His English was very limited—in fact this was the whole of our conversation, for he soon lapsed happily into Maori—but he insisted that he had had long talks with Queen Elizabeth.

Lange had heard me quizzing the man. He said, "If you get the Queen alone she's very good—very funny. Loves New Zealand."

He said that he had spent some time with her alone when he'd been awarded the title CH, Companion of Honour, which was more coveted than a knighthood.

After the prayer in the garden the food was uncovered—and men and women stood near it, fanning away the flies, while we filled our plates with octopus in coconut milk, taro, sweet potato, pig meat, marinated raw fish (with skin and bones), banana fritters, fruit salad.

Lemonade was served, and then there was dancing—young men and women in grass skirts. The drummers sweated and smiled, and people wandered into the garden from the dirt road to watch, gathering at the hedge or sitting on the grass. Children who had been playing on the grass since before the party began—they had no connection with the party—went on playing. It was all amiable. There were no ructions here.

The Queen's Representative smoothed his shirtfront—it was now splashed with food—and accepted his gifts, a woven mat and a piece of nice-stitched cloth. He spoke briefly but in a formal, chiefly way, in his own language, Maori. He was from the little island of Penrhyn, an almost inaccessible atoll in the far north of the Cook Group. He had spent six years making the rounds from island to island. Now he was on his final round, collecting gifts. A new QR would soon be sworn in—someone's relative.

Leaving the party, Lange turned to me and asked again, "Are you sure you're not writing about Aitutaki?" and he smiled, but instead of waiting for an answer he began to describe for me his recent experiences in Baghdad.

When I left Aitutaki it was Lange who saw me to the plane and we agreed to meet again. I went to Rarotonga, a pretty island entirely ringed by bungalows and small hotels. You couldn't paddle without paddling in someone's front yard. But there I had a sense of the murmurs of island life.

A New Zealand couple from Aitutaki recognized me on the road in Rarotonga and told me about the woman who wandered the beach and was such a rapacious fornicator with the Aitutaki fishermen.

When I tried to verify this story with an Australian he told me that the gossiping New Zealand couple had been heard quarrelling loudly and abusively in their bungalow.

"He's the world's authority on giant clams," someone said of the Australian.

"You could get killed for fooling with fishermen," someone else said.

The gossips were gossiped about, and everyone had a story.

"Never guess who's in Aitutaki," another Australian said to me in a bar in Avarua, Rarotonga. "David Lange. Someone saw him get on the plane. He split up with his wife. He's out of office. He's fucked-up and far from home."

I said, "I have the feeling he's going to be fine."

Chapter 21

EASTER ISLAND: BEYOND THE
SURF ZONE OF RAPA NUI

It was too dark to see anything, even at seven in the morning when I arrived on Easter Island, but there were the insinuating smells of muddy roads and damp dog fur, wet grass, briny air, and the sounds of barking and cockcrows, the crash of surf, and people speaking in Spanish and Polynesian. The customs inspector had been drinking. Someone muttered *"Borachito"*—tipsy.

On winter days on Easter Island the sun rises at eight in the morning and by five-thirty in the afternoon the light has grown so crepuscular there is not enough to read by—not that anyone reads much on this lost island of damaged souls. Long before sundown, the horses are tethered (there are few vehicles); the motorboats are moored (there are no canoes, and haven't been for a hundred years); and anyone with money for a bottle of *pisco*—hooch—is quietly becoming *borachito*.

The island goes cold and dark, and except for dogs barking and the sound of the wind in the low bushes, there is silence. There are not many trees, there is only one town—a small one, Hanga Roa—and as for the *moai,* the stone statues, no one goes near them after dark. They are associated with *akuaku*—spirits—and are the repository of the island's secrets. Many, many secrets, you have to conclude, because there are hundreds of stone heads on the island—upright and staring, lying down and eyeless, shattered and broken, some with russet topknots, others noseless or brained—more than 800 altogether. They are also known as *aringa ora,* "living faces."

The rest of the island is yellowing meadows with thick wind-flattened grass, and low hills, and the weedy slopes of volcanoes. Its landscape looks in some places like the coast of Wales and in others like Patagonia yet it is totally itself, the strangest island I saw in the whole of Oceania—a place penetrated by gloom and anarchy. And a spooky place, too. *Te Pito o Te Henua,* "The Navel of the World," the early inhabitants called their island, and more recently *Rapa Nui.* Easter Island is smaller than Martha's Vineyard, and probably has fewer stony faces.

I passed through the airport building, which was just a wooden room with signs in Spanish, and went through Chilean customs (Easter Island, Isla de Pascua, is part of a province of Chile).

An attractive woman, obviously Polynesian, approached me.

She said, "May I offer you my residence?"

It takes an hour to fly from Rarotonga to Tahiti, and five and a half from Tahiti to Easter Island. But connections in Oceania are seldom neat. I had two days to kill in Rarotonga, and three days in Papeete before I could head to this little island, the easternmost outpost of Polynesia.

My traveling time must be compared with that of the original migrants to Easter Island. They might have sailed from Rapa—now called Rapa Iti—in the Austral Islands, 2,500 miles away. Or it might have been from Mangareva in the Gambier Group. In any case, the journey in double-hulled canoes took them 120 days. This was sometime in the seventh century (though some archaeologists have dated it earlier). On the other side of the world the Prophet Mohammed was fleeing to Medina (in the year 622), the start of the Moslem Era. The Dark Ages had taken hold of Europe. The glorious Tang Dynasty had begun in China. In the Pacific, people were on the move, for this was the most active period of Polynesian expansion, which one Pacific historian has called "the greatest feat of maritime colonization in human history."

Before I left Tahiti I had called on the airline representative. He was Chilean. We conversed in Spanish. He spoke no other tongue.

"The plane is half full, maybe more," he said.

"All those people going to Easter Island!"

"No. Only four passengers are getting off there. The rest are going to Santiago."

"Will the weather be cold on Easter Island?"

"Sometimes. Especially at night." He flapped his hand, equivocating. "You have a sweater? That's good."

"What about rain?"

"It can rain at any time. And wind. You will have some wind. But not too much." He smiled at the ceiling and he blinked for effect as he chanted, "Sun. Cloud. Sun. Cloud."

He was trying to encourage me.

"Now the hotels are interesting," he said. "I know you don't have one. You never have one before you go. But at the airport, the island people will look at you and offer their houses to you. You will see them and talk to them. That way you can find the most economical one."

He then searched for my reservation.

"Your name is not on the passenger list," he said. "But come tomorrow. If you don't have a ticket we will sell you one. There is space. There are always seats to Easter Island."

That was my preparation for the journey—that and a vast tome entitled *The Ethnology of Easter Island,* by Alfred Metraux, and the writings of other archaeologists, and much colorful and misleading information by the enthusiastic Thor Heyerdahl, who is regarded by many Pacific historians and archaeologists as of minimal consequence to serious archaeology. Scientifically, his books have as little value as those of Erich von Daniken, who theorized that the Easter Island *moai* were carved by people from outer space.

I found a place to stay, a guest house, and agreed on a price—$65 a day, which included three meals a day. I planned to camp, too—no one seemed bothered, as they had on other islands, by the threat of my pitching a tent.

Stretching my legs after arriving, I walked to the Easter Island Museum. It was one mute room on a hillside at the edge of town. There are some carvings, and some dusty skulls with drawings scratched on the craniums, and artifacts, but no dates have been assigned to anything in the room. There are old photographs of melancholy islanders and hearty missionaries. There are ill-assorted implements—axes, clubs, knives. One exhibit shows how the *moai* had carefully fitted eyes, most of them goggling—the sclera of the eye made of white coral, the iris of red scoria, and the pupil a disc of obsidian, which gave the statues a great staring gaze.

Many of the *moai* had been ritually blinded by the islanders themselves. The archaeologist JoAnne Van Tilburg mentions how "specific, probably ritual damage was done to only certain parts of the figures, in particular the heads, eyes, and occasionally the right arms."

That first day, I ran into an island woman who was secretary of the Rapa Nui Corporation for the Preservation of Culture, known locally as *Mata Nui o Hotu Matua o Kahu Kahu o Hera* ("The Ancestral Group of Hotu Matua of the Obscure Land"). She confirmed various stories that I had read about the island.

Hotu Matua was the leader of the first migration to Easter Island. Descended from ancestral gods, this first king had *mana,* great spiritual power, and is credited with the founding of this civilization. Much of the early history is conjecture—there are so-called wooden *rongo-rongo* tablets, with strange figurative script incised on them, but no one has ever been able to decipher them. In spite of this, most of the stories regarding Hotu Matua agree on the salient points. That he sailed from an island (Marae-renga, perhaps Rapa) in the west commanding two ninety-foot canoes. That he brought with him "hundreds and hundreds" of people. That some of these people were nobles *(ariki)* and others skilled men and women *(maori)*—warriors, planters, carvers—and still others common-ers. That the captain of the second canoe was a noble named Tuu-ko-ihu. That on board these canoes they had "the fowl, the cat, the turtle, the dog, the banana plant, the paper mulberry, the hibiscus, the ti, the sandal-wood, the gourd, the yam," and five more varieties of banana plant. (Later generations gave Hotu Matua credit for introducing animals which early explorers introduced, such as pigs and chickens.)

After sailing for two months in the open sea, the voyagers came upon the island and they sailed completely around it, looking for a place to land. After their tropical home, this windy treeless island must have seemed a forbidding place: then, as now, black cliffs being beaten by surf. They found the island's only bay, its only sandy beach. They went ashore there and named the bay Anakena, their word for the month of August. It was an island of seabirds and grass. There were no mammals. The craters of the volcanoes were filled with *totora* reeds.

Another happy incident, which occurs in all versions of this first-arrival story, is that shortly after Hotu Matua's canoe reached the shore of the island, one of Hotu Matua's wives, named Vakai, gave birth to a baby boy, Tuu-ma-heke, who became the island's second king. The cutting of the infant's navel cord caused the place to be called *Pito-o-te-henua,* "Navel of the Land."

The woman who was telling me these stories said that she was a teacher of the Rapa Nui language. But was there such a language? She claimed there was, but linguists said that the original tongue had been lost, and that the language spoken on Easter Island now was the Tahitian the Christian missionaries had brought—because that was the language of their Bible and hymn book. Because this Tahitian had many similarities to the old Rapa Nui it had displaced it. Easter Islanders were identified as Polynesians when they boarded Cook's ship in 1774. As soon as they spoke, Cook recognized that their language was similar to Tahitian.

Looking for a place to launch my boat, I walked down the main road of the town, a dirt track called in the local language Navel of the World Street, past grubby little bungalows—they had the shape and dimensions of sheds: flat roofs, single walls—to Hanga Roa harbor.

It was not like any harbor I had ever seen, and it explained why if you totalled the time all the early explorers spent ashore on Easter Island, it would amount to very little. Few of the nineteenth-century explorers,

Metraux says, "stayed on the island for more than a few minutes." Some of the explorers, having made the 2,500-mile run from Tahiti (and it was nearly as far from South America) were unable to go ashore—too windy, too dangerous, too surfy. In 1808, for example, Captain Amasa Delano of Duxbury, Massachusetts, (and of Melville's story "Benito Cereno"), arrived at the island and sailed around it, but could not set foot on the island, because of the heavy surf off Hanga Roa.

Some ships did land, to the sorrow of the islanders. In 1804, the men on an American ship, the *Nancy,* kidnapped twelve men and ten women from the island after a fight—the intention was to use these captives as slave laborers at a seal colony on Más Afuera, a rock halfway to Chile. When the islanders were allowed on deck after three days at sea, they jumped off the ship and began swimming in the direction of their island, and all drowned. Whaling ships plying the southern oceans often abducted Easter Island girls, for their sexual pleasure.

"In 1822 the skipper of an American whaling ship paused at Easter Island long enough to kidnap a group of girls who were thrown overboard the following day and obliged to swim back to the island," Metraux writes. "One of the officers, simply for amusement, shot a native with his gun."

After more raids of this sort the islanders became hostile to any foreigners. But the foreigners persisted, either fighting them or employing more devious means to subvert the islanders, using gifts as bait, as in this raid in 1868: "The raiders threw to the ground gifts which they thought most likely to attract the inhabitants and . . . when the islanders were on their knees scrambling for the gifts, they tied their hands behind their backs and carried them off to the waiting ship." The king, Kaimakoi, was kidnapped with his son and most of the island's *maori* (experts). These and later captives were sent to work, digging on guano islands, where they all died.

The history of Easter Island in the nineteenth century is a long sad story of foreign raiding parties (mainly American and Spanish), of slavery and plunder, leading to famine, venereal disease, smallpox outbreaks, and ultimately the ruin of the culture—the place was at last demoralized and depopulated. In 1900 there were only 214 people living on Easter Island, eighty-four of them children. A hundred years of foreign ships had turned Easter Island into a barren rock.

The island had flourished by being cut off, and then it became a victim of its remoteness. Since the earliest times, it had never been easy to land on it, but it was so far from any other port, and in such a rough patch of ocean, that every ship approaching it took advantage of it in some way—looking for water or food, for women, for slaves.

How was it possible for even a small ship to land here? In fact it had never been managed. No more than a scooped-out area, with boulders lining the shore and surf pounding beside the breakwater, the harbor was a horror, and it was difficult even to imagine a ship easily lying at anchor offshore, with a whaleboat plying back and forth with supplies. Problem one was mooring a ship in the wild ocean off Hanga Roa; problem two was getting the whaleboat through the surf to shore and, since there was nowhere to land, steadying it long enough to unload it.

I saw that I could paddle through the surf zone. But it was usually easier to get out than to paddle in. The danger here was that the surf was breaking on large rocks at the harbor entrance. Even if I surfed in I might be broken to smithereens on the rocks.

The most ominous sight for a potential kayaker was that of Rapa Nui boys surfing into the harbor on big breaking waves. This surfing, locally known as *ngaru,* had been a sport here since the earliest times, and was the only game that had survived all these years. They had abandoned the ancient games of spinning tops, flying kites, and going to the top of volcanoes and sliding down "tracks on which they had urinated to make the path more slippery." But surfing had been useful in the early innocent days of foreign ships anchoring off Hanga Roa in a heavy sea. Surprising the seamen, the islanders swam out to the ship, using "swimming supports"—a plank or a rush mat. Some of the islanders were observed surfing back to shore afterwards, riding the waves using the planks as surfboards.

In the Rapa Nui language there was a complete set of surfing terminology, which described the board, the surfer's waiting for the wave, allowing the wave to crest, and settling on the wave; what in current surfing jargon would be the banana or the pig board (or sausage board), the pickup and takeoff, the cutback on the hump, hotdogging, hanging ten, and walking the plank. In the olden days there had been surfing contests and some men, real Rapa Nui beachies, had gone far from shore to surf a long distance on the large ocean swells.

But the sight of surfers convinced me that this was not a good area to paddle from—and it was the harbor!

A place called Hanga Piko, a rocky bay farther along, looked slightly more promising, but studying it closely—I walked along the shore and watched the breakers for about twenty minutes—I saw that it would be tricky here, too. Big rollers tumbled in from the deep sea without anything to stop them or modify them.

I walked another mile to Anakai Tangata, an ominously named cave (meaning "The Cave Where Men Are Eaten") with petroglyphs on the walls, and nearby some stone foundations of ancient houses still existed. The stones had holes in them, where poles were inserted, for the tall tent-like structure, which was then thatched. Below this place were sea cliffs, and beyond was the volcano Rano Kau. In the sky here and all over the island were hawks—the *cara-cara,* which the Chileans had introduced to rid the island of rats. The hawks were numerous, and highly competitive—they flew close to the ground, they perched fearlessly, they swept down on anything that moved, they were fearless raptors.

There were groves of thin peeling eucalyptus trees rattling in the wind on the lower slopes of the volcano. These had been planted by the Forestry Commission. I followed the dirt road that wound through them, seeing no one, only hawks. At the top, I had a lovely view of the crater, and because this volcano was at the edge of the sea, beyond the crater's rim was the blue ocean. In the depths of the crater was a lake, with totora reeds, papyrus thickets, and steep walls, and in the most protected part of the crater—the lower edge, out of the wind—there were banana trees and an orange grove.

Orongo, the site of the Bird-Man Cult, was at the lip at the far side of the crater, high above the sea. That was another mile onward, and on the way I ran into a Rapa Nui man, Eran Figueroa Riroroko.

Riroroko was about thirty, a handsome stocky man who lived in a hut near Orongo and passed the time carving hardwood into animal shapes. In halting Spanish, he explained the Bird-Man Cult—how in the ancient times the men gathered on the cliffs here every September (the austral spring). At a given signal they went out to the island Motu Nui, about two kilometers offshore. It was not far, but the water was notorious for sharks.

"They went in canoes?"

"Swimming." *Nadando.*

Every ship that called at Easter Island in the eighteenth and nineteenth centuries remarked on the brilliant swimming skills of the islanders, but these *hopu,* candidates for the title Bird-Man, had to bring food with them. They scrambled up the ledges of Motu Nui to bivouac and wait for the first sooty tern's egg of the season. When the first egg was laid and seized, the lucky man who held it called out his victory, and then tied it to his head in a little basket and swam to shore. He had no fear of sharks or waves, for the egg contained powerful *mana.* And his capture of the sacred egg meant that for a year he was Bird-Man: He had great authority, he lived in a special house, gifts were brought to him, and with this sudden assumption of power he settled any old scores he had—*I'm the king of the castle, and you're a dirty rascal,* as a schoolchild might put it—for now, with this *mana,* he had warriors on his side, who would do as he bade.

Bird-Man petroglyphs—a beaked creature of grotesque strength—

were incised in the boulders and cliff faces all over Orongo, along with portraits of the great god Makemake, who was on Easter Island what Tiki or Atua was elsewhere in Polynesia. Smaller, broken ovals cut into the rock were depictions of vulvas—all over the island, on cliff faces and in caves, there were old carvings of vulvas *(komari)*, which were cut by priestly elders when a girl reached puberty. These priests comprised a special class and were given the title *ivi-atua*, "kinsmen of the gods."

The Bird-Man Cult with its eggs, and the vulvas, and the solstice, all suggested that Orongo was associated with sexuality and fertility. On the bluff at Orongo there were also small stone dwellings built into the cliffs, dry-stone burrows and pillboxes with crawl-in openings, in which people had lived when this cult flourished.

"Do you get frightened at night up here by the ghosts?" I used the local word for ghosts—*akuaku*.

Riroroko said, "Yes, there could be *akuaku* here. Devils, I mean."

"Are you a Christian?"

"Yes. Catholic."

"Have you traveled away from the island?"

"I have been to Tahiti. To Santiago. To Venezuela."

"Were you tempted to stay at any of those places?"

"No. Tahiti was unbelievably expensive," he said *(tremenda-menda caro)*, "but I was just looking. I just wanted to get to know them. I would never live in those places. Santiago is full of people, traffic, and bad air. I needed to come back here where the air is clean."

"What language did you speak in Tahiti?"

"I spoke Rapa Nui and people understood me. Tahitian is very simi-lar—close enough so that they can understand. I liked the people."

I walked down the volcano five miles, taking a shortcut through the eucalyptus plantation, but on the outskirts of Hanga Roa I was footsore, and now from every roadside hut crazy hostile dogs ran at me.

A beat-up Jeep, with music blaring, shuddered along the road. I stuck out my hand.

"I'm Rene," the driver said. "He's Mou."

They were two grinning wild-haired youths.

"You speak Spanish?"

"Yes. But Rapa Nui is better."

"What's that music?"

"AC/DC." An Australian rock group.

They dropped me on The Navel of the World Street and sped away.

When night fell at six or so, the island went black, and apart from wandering boys and homeward-bound drunks, no one stirred. I went to bed early and listened to my shortwave radio in the dark. The news was of floods in south China, which had drowned 2,000 people. That was the entire population of Rapa Nui.

The west coast seemed as unpromising for paddling as the south coast. There was a heavy swell, and high surf dumping on black bouldery shores. The islands marked on my chart were not islands at all, but like Motu Nui in the south—slick black rocks, washed by foaming breakers. God help anyone who tried to land a boat on one.

I hiked along a road, which narrowed to a path, then degenerated and lost itself among the grass on the high cliffs. I liked the island's obscurity. It resembled the Marquesas in having no signposts, no information at all. Half a mile from town there was an *ahu* with a lineup of five heads. I knew this was Tahai because of the paddling chart I had with me. Farther on there were more *moai* and some of them had had their eyes reinserted and were staring inland—in fact, all the statues on the island had their backs turned to the sea. They were carved from brownish volcanic stone, they averaged five or six tons apiece, some had topknots or hats carved from red scoria.

Their size would have been overwhelming enough, even if they had been badly carved. But these were brilliantly executed, with long sloping noses and pursed lips and sharp chins. Their ears were elongated, and the hands clasping the body had long fingers, the sort you see on certain elegant Buddhas. Some of the statues had a mass of intricate detail on their back. And although there were similarities among the statues' profiles, each one had a distinctly different face.

When the first Europeans came to this island in 1722 all these "living faces" were upright. The first chronicler (Carl Beherns, who was on Roggeveen's ship) wrote, "In the early morning we looked out and could see from some distance that [the islanders] had prostrated themselves towards the rising sun and had kindled some hundreds of fires, which probably betokened some morning oblation to their gods . . ." And this veneration might also have been related to the fact that the islanders had just had their first look at a Dutch ship and a mass of pale jug-eared sailors.

A little more than fifty years later, Cook recorded that many of the statues had been knocked over. And by 1863, all the statues were flat on the ground and broken—a result of warfare, competition, and an iconoclastic frenzy that periodically possessed the islanders.

Stranger than the towering statues that stood and stared were the enormous fragments of broken heads and faces, tumbled here and there on the cliffs—just lying among the cow shit and tussocky grass.

Every rock on Rapa Nui looks deliberate, like part of a wall or an altar or a ruin. Many of them are carved or incised—with mystical symbols, with images, with vulvas. Most are black basketball-sized boulders and have the character of building blocks, as though they have been shaped for some structural purpose. I wondered whether it was ignorant of me to imagine this. Hiking alone all day can inspire fanciful thoughts. But at lunchtime, sitting among a mass of boulders, I saw that they led to a cave entrance, and I crawled into one that was walled, big enough to hold three people. (Islanders had hidden in these caves to escape the attention of slavers, the so called "blackbirders.")

I walked along the high cliffs of the west coast, to Motu Tautara and the caves near it, in which lepers had once lived, and beyond to where the island's highest volcano, Mount Terevaka, sloped to the sea. There were *moai* on this northwest coast, too—isolated heads, some of them fallen and broken. Heads like these, looking complete and final, were so far from any habitation that they had that hopeless and rather empty gaze of Ozymandias.

You come to a place you have read about your whole life, that is part of the world's mythology of mystery and beauty, and somehow you expect it to be overrun—full of signs and guidebooks and brochures, and other similarly rapt pilgrims and individuals. That very anxiety can forestall any real anticipation, and so you might procrastinate, fearing that it might be another Stratford-on-Avon with Willy Shakespeare souvenirs, or Great Wall of China packed with tour buses, or Taj Mahal, entrance fee ten rupees. Instead of risking disappointment, isn't it better to stay away?

But Easter Island is still itself, a barren rock in the middle of nowhere, littered with hundreds of masterpieces of stone carving, blown by the wind, covered in grass, and haunted by the lonely cries of seabirds. It is not as you imagine it, but much stranger, darker, more complex, eerier. And for the same reason that it always was strange: because it is so distant and infertile an island.

Late in the afternoon, there was a sudden downpour, and as the heavy rain persisted I ran for shelter, taking refuge under a cliff. I crouched there for about twenty minutes before it dawned on me that other people had done exactly what I had done: I was crouching in an ancient shelter, which had been hollowed from the cliff and decorated with petroglyphs, and the sides shored up by bouldery walls. If it hadn't rained I would not have found it.

Walking up this west coast, looking for an ancient canoe ramp or a place to launch my boat, I marvelled at the emptiness of the island, and lamented the decline of its ancient culture. It is not as though it was swept away. The material culture was so substantial that now more than 1,200 years after the first *moais* were carved (Tahai I, just down this coast, was dated and shown to have been in use around A.D. 690) they still exist and still look terrifying, their expressions sneering, *Look on you mighty and despair.*

I didn't find a place on this coast to launch from but I was heartened nonetheless by the utter emptiness—just me, and the staring heads, and the soaring hawks.

On my way back to Hanga Roa I took an inland route and first met a man herding cows who said hello in Spanish, and then ran across a younger fellow, a Rapa Nui named Iman, about twenty-five or so, who had recently arrived back from Paris where he had been supervising his grandfather's business. He had agreed to look after his aging parents on the island.

"How do you like Rapa Nui?"

"I hate it."

I asked him why.

"There is nothing here," Iman said. "Nothing to do. Nothing happens."

Near sunset we walked towards town. There were cacti and palms growing near some of the houses, and others had banana trees in their gardens. In spite of these plants the island did not feel tropical. It could be warm in the day, but it was cool at night. Always there was the smell of damp or dusty roads and the stink of dog fur.

We came across the carcass of a horse. The thing had died on the road and it had lain there all day. Children were pitching stones at it, but timidly, as though at any moment they expected the corpse to scramble to its feet and neigh at them.

"Look at that," I said.

"It is a dead horse," Iman said. "It collapsed this morning. It belongs to the man Domingo. I saw it fall over."

"And yet you say that nothing happens here."

I rented a Jeep and drove with my tent and collapsible boat to the top of the island, to Anakena, where Hotu Matua and the first canoes had arrived, where the first true Rapa Nui person had been born. It was a lovely protected bay, with a sandy beach, and just above the beach seven *moai,* some with cylindrical topknots, others decapitated.

Camping there I dreamed of the writer Jerzy Kosinski, who had killed himself a few months before, how he laughed when I told him that I liked camping. Perhaps the dream had come to me because I had read an article about him recently. The piece said that he had had no writer friends. But I had known him and regarded him as a friend. He seemed a bit paranoid and insecure, and vain in an unexplainable way. One night in Berlin he had gone back to the hotel and put on a type of male makeup, giving his pale Polish complexion an instant tan. What was that all about? He told me that he was afraid of assassination attempts, of being the object of sinister plots.

But it was the opposite that he feared—not notoriety. He was afraid of being ignored, not taken seriously; he could not stand being regarded as insignificant, or of his gifts being belittled.

"He likes to camp," Jerzy said to his then girlfriend (and later, wife) Katarina. His Polish-Jewish accent made what he said sound like sarcasm, but I didn't mind. He seemed to find my life negligible. I found his horrifying. Oh, well.

He could not understand my incessant travel. I could not understand his need to be a Yale professor, hurrying up to New Haven to give lectures on the evils of watching television. He needed to be an intellectual. East European writers use that word all the time to describe themselves. I hated the word. He liked power. He wanted to be respectable. When he ceased to be respected—in the end he had actually been mocked for being a lightweight and suspected plagiarist—he killed himself.

I woke up in my tent under the palms at Anakena thinking: A traveler has no power, no influence, no known identity. That is why a traveler needs optimism and heart, because without confidence travel is misery. Generally, the traveler is anonymous, ignorant, easy to deceive, at the mercy of the people he or she travels among. The traveler might be known as "The American" or "The Foreigner"—the *palangi;* the *popaa,* as they said here in Rapa Nui. But there was no power in that.

A traveler was conspicuous for being a stranger, and consequently was vulnerable. But, traveling, I whistled in the dark and assumed all would be well. I depended on people being civil and observing a few basic rules. Generally I felt safer in a place like Anakena than I would have in an American city—or an American campsite, for that matter (mass murderers were known to lurk around campsites). I did not expect preferential treatment. I did not care about power or respectability. This was the condition of a liberated soul, of course, but also the condition of a bum.

A small Rapa Nui boy watched me setting up my boat later that day on the beach at Anakena.

I pointed to the seven carvings on the huge *ahu* and asked him in Spanish, "What do you call those?"

"Moai," he said.

"Are they men or gods?"

"Gods." *Dios.*

The water at Anakena was no colder than that in Cape Cod Bay in

July. Because there was no one here to tell me anything about the hazards—the current, the tides, the submerged rocks, the sharks—I paddled out in stages, to test the current and the wind. There was a light northerly wind blowing onshore, into the bay, and moderate surf. I made it to the opening of the bay and paddled east for a few miles and saw only waves crashing against the black rocks of the island. Once past Ure-Mamore Point (Punta Rosalia on my chart) I could see all the way to the far eastern headland of the island, more high cliffs rising to another of Rapa Nui's four volcanoes, this one was Pukatike on Poike Peninsula. There was a surf break nearer shore, which meant that I had to stay about a quarter mile from the island to avoid being tipped over and dashed against the rocks. But still I felt pleased having come this far, and justified in having brought my boat.

I had water and food in the boat, but the sea was so rough—the wind bashing my beam—that I could not put my paddle down long enough to eat anything. Instead, I went out farther (it was a safe wind: If I had tipped over I would have been blown back into shore) and then in a westerly direction, past Anakena again, and onward, blundering towards another headland, Punta San Juan. The wind picked up and the sea was filled with breaking waves and crosswinds, and once again, looking along the whole coast towards another corner of this triangular island—Cabo Norte—I was amazed by what a rocky, inhospitable shore it presented: nowhere to land, nothing but breakers and black boulders.

I was listening on my Walkman to a Charlie Parker tape, *Apex of Bebop*—it suited the surf, the tumbling clouds, the chop, the waves, every soaring bird: "Crazeology" and "Yardbird Suite" and "Out of Nowhere" and "Bird of Paradise."

Standing in the sunshine on the grassy slope of a volcano, among big-nosed stone heads, sniffing the heather, I had had no real idea of what an intimidating island this could seem. It was cows and meadows and huts, and smashed statuary. It was bleary-eyed and rather grubby Polynesians, and Chileans from the hinterland.

From my boat the island seemed truly awful and majestic, a collection of grassy volcanoes, beaten by surf, and surrounded by more than 2,000 miles of open water. It was not like any other island I had seen in Oceania. Tanna had been rocky, Guadalcanal had been dense and jungly, the Marquesas had been forbidding—those deep valleys, full of shadows. But Rapa Nui looked terrifying.

The tide was ebbing in the late afternoon when I returned to Anakena—the water had slipped down to reveal protruding rocks. I beached my boat and saw a woman walking along the beach. Her name was Ginny Steadman, and she was a painter, who had come here with her husband, Dave, an archaeologist, who was digging near the *ahu* above Anakena.

I talked awhile with Ginny, about islands we had visited, but I found it hard to concentrate, because all the while, I was thinking of how about six or eight months previously I had had a premonition of this exact moment, the way everything was positioned: how the sunlight hit the water, the slope of the beach, the angle of the boat, Ginny herself, the sight of the bay, even the air temperature and the swooping birds, so vivid a déjà vu—*I have seen this before,* I thought—that I resisted telling her, afraid the poor woman would be startled.

Dave Steadman was up to his neck in a symmetrically stepped pit. He talked without interrupting his digging and sifting and sorting. He had spent years traveling the Pacific, looking for the bones of extinct birds. Later, I read about him, how he had discovered new species of rails, of gallinules, of parrots, and as one of the world's authorities on the extinction of species he had published many articles—"Extinction of Birds in Eastern Polynesia," "Holocene Vertebrate Fossils in the Galapagos," and others. He told me he was looking for bone fragments, but he said he picked up anything that looked interesting.

"Here's some flakes of various kinds—obsidian—and a drill."

It was a chipped stick of stone, about two inches long.

"That was for drilling wood or bone—or making tools."

He had small plastic bags of sorted bird bones.

"These might be shearwaters or petrels." He pointed to the pit he had dug. "There's lots of extinct birds down there. Not many up here on the surface. What have you got here? No trees. Hardly any birds. The *caracara* was introduced. They've got that gray finch. A few terns. Masked booby. Frigate bird. That's about it."

He did not stop digging, and now Ginny was sifting through the sand he shovelled into mesh-bottomed boxes.

"You can always tell what a place was like when you dig," Dave said. "Polynesians got to an island and they started eating. And they didn't stop. Within a hundred years or so they ate everything—all the birds are gone. That's the first level—extinct birds. At the next level you find different bones—dogs, pigs. Then another level and, hey"—he glanced out of the pit, just his head showing—"they start chowing down on each other."

"Was there much cannibalism here?" I asked.

Metraux had said there was, but he had done no digging. He had collected old stories about the *kai-tangata,* "man-eaters," on Easter Island: the way that victorious warriors ate their slain enemies after a battle, though sometimes people were killed to provide a special dish for a feast. Human fingers and toes "were the most palatable bits." On at least one occasion some Peruvian slavers were ambushed and eaten.

"Yes. Human bones have been found here, mixed together with fish bones and bird bones," Dave said. "There was cannibalism all over Polynesia. In the Cooks, in Tonga, the Marquesas. Everywhere. You see the evidence when you dig. As soon as the population gets to a certain level people start chowing down on their neighbors."

He had returned to his digging, but he was still talking.

"Some guy's taro patch is bigger than yours? You want his *mana?* You kill him and you chow down." After a moment, he added, "Cannibalism was big here in the sixteenth century."

Inevitably, our discussion turned to Thor Heyerdahl.

Dave, who as an archaeologist was the straightest talker I had met, as well as the most down to earth, said, "Thor Heyerdahl is the most fanciful adventurer ever to hit the Pacific."

This made Ginny wince, but then she smiled and nodded agreement.

"Many things he says about Easter Island are incorrect," Dave said. "He dreams something one night, makes a connection, and the next day he puts it into his book. See, he already has his theory. He just looks for ways of proving it. That's not scientific. And he commits the worst sin of an archaeologist—he has been known to buy artifacts from the locals. If you dig them up you get proveniential information. But when you buy them you know nothing."

He dumped another bucket of sand for Ginny to sift.

"I guess you could say that because of him, Easter Island is on the map," he said. "There's been more archaeology done here than on any other single place in the Pacific. But want my opinion of it? It's shitty archaeology. It's some of the worst excavation in the Pacific. No one knows anything here. They get a big bag of bones and chips, and they don't know where the stuff comes from. It's all a mystery."

Dave pointed with his trowel at the *ahu* with the seven *moai* on it, their backs turned to us.

"Look at that *ahu.* To rebuild it, they had to move tons of sand—right here, a whole mountain of it. What was in it? Where did it go? Think of all the information that was lost! And you can't criticize the guy who did it, because he's an archaeologist."

"What about the reed-boat theory?" I asked. "That was disproved, wasn't it?"

"Yes. By Flenley's pollen studies. He proved that the reeds in the crater are twenty-eight thousand years old. How could they have been brought by South Americans? And the thing is, Heyerdahl was here when Flenley read his paper. He just sat there. He didn't say anything. It was completely ridiculous."

But closely questioned, Dave became less rambunctious and more scientific. He even stopped shovelling to explain.

"See, the lake sediment contains pollen, and the anoxic mud preserves the pollen. So you do a core, for x number of meters, and then you radiocarbon-date it. They're good tests. They're real diagnostic."

The Steadmans covered their hole and left, and when they were gone it began to rain. Then the clouds blew past, and I was alone in pink late-afternoon sunshine. And I thought that, even without the *moai*, it would be a lovely island, because of the volcanoes—the craters and hornitos—and the long grassy sweep of their slopes.

The sunset, purple and pink, altered slowly like a distant fire being extinguished, and then cold black night fell for thirteen hours.

Everyone goes home and shuts the door when darkness falls, and at night on Easter Island I had a sense of great suspicion and separation, of distinct households, of a competitive, feuding society, full of old unresolved quarrels, in which there was quite a lot of petty theft, suspicion, envy, evasion, and insincerity. The toughness and self-reliance of the people made these traits even more emphatic.

The next morning I went across the island, into town, to send a fax. It was simple enough. It went through the only phone in town, at the Entel/Chile communications center, where there was a large satellite dish. It was also possible to receive a fax there, for a dollar a page, or to make international phone calls (Easter Island was in the same time zone as Denver). Every day that office received by fax the news pages of the Santiago newspaper, *Las Noticias,* and these pages were tacked to the wall of the office: This wall newspaper was the nearest Easter Island got to having a paper, but in any case people only read it when they were making a long-distance call.

The Steadmans were back at Anakena digging again the following day, sifting for bird bones and chips, and they seemed to me among the unsung heroes of Pacific archaeology. Their fieldwork, like most scientific research, was laborious and undramatic, but it yielded indisputable results. And nearly every shovelful had something of value in it.

Dave picked up a small bone from the screen. He blew the dust from it.

"This is a bone from the inner ear of a porpoise."

"Did it swim here?"

"No. Someone chowed down on it. This is a habitation site," he said, gesturing at the pit he had dug. "It's all food here. And there's enough organic material in that bone to date it."

"Is this what you've done in other places in the Pacific?"

"Pretty much so. We dig, we collect what we can. Most people ignore us. We don't care about that."

Ginny said, "Except for Tonga."

"We got some hostility in Tonga," Dave said. " 'Fucking *palangi*'—that stuff. We kind of liked the Cooks."

"Women don't get hassled in the Cooks," Ginny said. "They left me alone."

"There's a rain forest in Eva, in Tonga," Dave said. "When we were there in eighty-seven we said, 'Take care of it. Eco-tourism is the big thing now. People will want to come here and experience this rain forest.' They said, 'Yeah. Yeah. Great idea.' "

He was digging again—digging and talking.

"We went back two years later. Now the Japanese want to build a hotel and golf course in Eva, right in the rain forest."

It was pleasant to talk with people as widely traveled and knowledgeable as the Steadmans. I proposed that they write A Book of Extinct Birds. They said they had thought of it already, and might just do it. I asked Dave about the megapode birds I had seen in the Solomons. He was full of information, and had seen megapode skeletons—an extinct one as big as a turkey—but never a live bird. I described for him the pleasure of eating a megapode egg omelette.

He found the Easter Islanders an even greater riddle than their artifacts, but in their own way just as ruined.

"I've seen more hard-core debauchery on this island than anywhere else in the Pacific."

"Like what?"

"You name it."

It was the drinking most of all that alarmed him. A bottle existed to be emptied. Even a full bottle of whisky was gone by the following morning.

"Their attitude is, 'If you've got 'em, smoke 'em.' " After I had chosen a spot and set up camp, I saw that I was only a half a mile from the famous *moai* quarry at the volcano Rano Raraku. I walked there and spent the rest of the day wandering among the stone heads. From a distance, the heads look like the stumps of enormous trees, but walking closer you see how distinct they are. Most of them were two or three times my height. I counted thirty of them, then walked a bit farther and counted a dozen more. There are over a hundred of them here, on the slope of the volcano, from which they were carved. They have enigmatic faces, highly stylized, like the characters in old Virgil Partch cartoons, or like attenuated Greeks, or gigantic chess pieces.

On these slopes, they are standing, lying on their faces, on their backs, broken, and seemingly walking down the slope—some have a whole trunk, a thick upper body, attached to them, buried underground. The inside of the crater had a number of them. And outside, some are half-sculpted, lying horizontal in a niche in the side of the volcanic rock. One of these was forty feet long—a head and body, lying like an unfinished mummy. Another was a kneeling figure. Yet another upright *moai* had a three-masted schooner carved on its chest.

There were no other people at the site, which made the experience eerie and pleasant. It was without any doubt one of the strangest places I had ever been. From the heights of the volcano, I could look south and see more figures, twenty or thirty, strung out along the meadows, as though making their way towards Hanga Roa.

The questions are obvious. Why and how were they carved? Who are they? How were they moved? Why were so many destroyed?

The long Norwegian shadow of Thor Heyerdahl falls across every archae-ological question on Easter Island. Even the simplest people I met on the island had an opinion about their history, and they all had views on Thor Heyerdahl.

Drunk or sober, nearly all were skeptical about the man. The drunkest was Julio, a fisherman who, because of bad circulation brought on by his continual state of inebriation, was always shivering, and this in spite of wearing a winter coat and woolly hat (with earmuffs). Although the rest of the men went around in shorts or bathing suits, I never saw drunken Julio take off either the thick hat or the coat.

"You have heard of Thor Heyerdahl?" he demanded. "I worked for him for six months. I don't like him. Listen, he gets publicity all over the world and what did I get for six months' work? *Nada!*"

Anna, a young mother in a torn T-shirt, also had views. She spoke a little English. She had been to Los Angeles in 1982, but hadn't liked it. "Too many Mexican people."

We were near Rano Raraku, in view of the quarry, and so I asked her about the *moai*. She said she had taken her little daughter to see them and that the little girl had wondered how they had been moved.

"What did you tell her?"

"Thor Heyerdahl says that the statues 'walked'—that the people used ropes and lines to move them, while the statues were upright. But the stone is very soft and Tahai is nineteen kilometers away. So they would never have made it. I think Heyerdahl is wrong. There were palm trees here at one time. They could have used those trunks as sleds. The people must have pulled them that way."

In *Easter Island: The Mystery Solved,* Heyerdahl writes how a man telling him that "the statues walked" made perfect sense. (It was an island legend, this walking by means of the divine power of *mana:* Metraux heard the same tales.) Of course, ropes must have been affixed to upright *moai* and the great things rocked back and forth, one set of ropes yanked, then the other. Heyerdahl experimented, moving one *moai* twelve feet. This is something less than fifteen miles, but the more convincing argument was put in the magazine *Archaeology* by Professor van Tilburg, who examined all the statues for "wear patterns" on the bases, necks, and upper torsos and found none. If ropes had been attached to this soft stone and the statues joggled for fifteen miles, the stone would have been abraded.

Much more likely is the sledge theory—the figures were dragged "on a frame or a sledge, to which ropes were attached . . . using a crew of approximately 150 individuals, over specially prepared transport roads." Metraux's conclusion is similar, though he says that skids must have been used, Tongan-style, as they had when the forty-ton pillars of the trilithon had been moved across Tongatapu. The average weight of the Easter Island heads (because the stone is so porous) is only four or five tons.

Thor Heyerdahl is shrill but mistaken in many of his assumptions. Far from solving the Easter Island mystery, he has succeeded in making the solution more difficult for qualified scientists and made something of a fool of himself in the process. He is an amateur, a popularizer, an impresario, with a zoology degree from the University of Oslo. And his efforts in the Pacific greatly resemble the muddling attentions of, say, the hack writer of detective stories when faced with an actual crime scene—someone who ignores the minutiae of evidence, hair analysis, or electrophoresis (for typing bloodstains) and in blundering around a crime scene muttering "The butler did it!" makes a complete hash of it for the forensic scientists.

The mention of Heyerdahl's name in academic circles frequently produces embarrassment or anger, and even villagers on Rapa Nui find Heyerdahl ridiculous. The Rapa Nui know they are the descendants of Polynesian voyagers and regard themselves as the creators of the monumental figures, which they claim are representations of various prominent ancestors. The figures are not gods, but men. (Forster, who went with Cook, claimed that the statutes were of "deceased chiefs.") Historians back up the Rapa Nui beliefs, even if Heyerdahl sneers at them. In an important article in *Scientific American* in 1983, "The Peopling of the Pacific," P. S. Bellwood writes, "At least one thing is now quite certain: the Polynesians are not of American Indian ancestry, in spite of some evidence for minor contacts with the Pacific coast of South America."

"There is absolutely no hard data known from the cumulative effort of nearly 100 years of investigation," Professor van Tilburg writes, "which would archaeologically link the island to the mainland."

This view is supported by other Pacific historians and scientists, by Professor Sinoto of the Bishop Museum in Honolulu, who has carried out excavations throughout French Polynesia and who has studied Easter Island; by P. V Kirch in *The Evolution of the Polynesian Chiefdoms,* regarded as the best documented study of Polynesian settlement; indeed, the view is supported virtually by everyone except Heyerdahl himself, who clings to his absurd theory that Peruvian voyagers carried their culture—their stonework, their gods, their sweet potato—into the Pacific. Polynesians came later, he says, and brought these thriving cultures to an abrupt halt.

What about the totora reeds in Rano Kau crater lake, upon which Heyerdahl places so much emphasis in attempting to prove his reed-boat theory? As David Steadman said, pollen studies such as John Flenley's have proven that the reeds have been growing in the craters for about 30,000 years. Thor Heyerdahl claims that they were brought from South America about a thousand years ago, and this is one of the cornerstones of his reed-boat theory—that South Americans with reed-boat technology sailed to Easter Island bringing sweet potatoes and creating masterpieces of stonework.

Why, you may ask, does the authoritative *Encyclopædia Britannica* disagree with the botanists and support the conclusions of Thor Heyerdahl? The *Encyclopædia Britannica* text supports all of Thor Heyerdahl's assertions: "boggy crater lakes are thickly covered in two imported American species." The answer is that the lengthy entry "Easter Island" in Volume 6 of the Macropædia bears the initials "Th.H." and was written by the egregious Norwegian.

Probably the most obnoxious aspect of Heyerdahl is that he appears to display a deep bias, bordering on contempt, against Polynesians. In *Fatu-Hiva,* he maintains that the Marquesans are too lazy to have created the ambitious stonework and carvings on Hiva Oa. In *Aku-Aku,* reflecting on the stonework of Easter Island, he writes, "One thing is certain. This was not the work of a canoeload of Polynesian wood carvers . . ." In *The Mystery Solved,* he rubbishes the Rapa Nui people even more: "No Polynesian fisherman would have been capable of conceiving, much less building, such a wall." Too lazy, too uncreative, too stupid.

This extraordinary prejudice is not only without foundation, but is the opposite of the truth. A review of his last book in the magazine *Archaeology* called it "a litany of hypocrisy, superciliousness, and prejudice against Polynesians in general and the inhabitants of Easter Island, the Rapa Nui, in particular." One of Heyerdahl's most offensive theories is that the Rapa Nui were brought to Easter Island from another island, possibly as slaves, by ancient Peruvian navigators who were cruising and being artistic elsewhere in Oceania.

In a lifetime of nutty theorizing, Heyerdahl's single success was his proof, in *Kon-Tiki,* that six middle-class Scandinavians could successfully crash-land their raft on a coral atoll in the middle of nowhere. That book made him a folk hero. And it focused attention on the Pacific. I have not read a learned article or met a scientist who did not regard Heyerdahl as a nuisance, an obstruction, and a pest. Heyerdahl's theory has also been disproved by scientists studying human genetics and DNA.

"In the Pacific there are two distinct branches [of the human family]," stated Dr. Steve Jones of University College, London, in the BBC Reith Lectures for 1991. "One—the peoples of New Guinea and the Australian Aborigines—is genetically very variable, and differs greatly from place to place. They have been there for a long time. The other—which fills the vast area of the Pacific islands—is more uniform and is related to east Asians. These people arrived after the origin of agriculture, a few thousand years ago. In spite of Thor Heyerdahl's crossing of the Pacific on a raft, there is no evidence of any genetic connection between Pacific islanders and Peru. Population genetics has sunk the *Kon-Tiki.*"

In the face of this scientific evidence, one could easily reach the conclusion that Heyerdahl, in clinging to his silly theory that Hagoth-like voyagers set sail from South America to civilize Polynesia, is in the pay of the Mormons.

Meanwhile, Easter Island remains a mystery.

Chapter 22
EASTER ISLAND: THE OLD CANOE RAMP AT TONGARIKI

Lovely Anakena was penetrated by the past. Although it was a remote beach, the whole history of the island revolved around it. But it was whipped by wind, and I craved to paddle a long stretch of coast. So I folded my tent, packed my boat, said farewell to the Steadmans, and drove across the eastern peninsula to Hotu-Iti Bay, which was protected—the towering cliffs of the Poike Peninsula were its windbreak. One of the stranger *motus,* Maro-Tiri, lay about two miles from the head of the bay, on the way to Cape Roggeveen.

I wandered around this new bay, in the ruins of a settlement which was called Tongariki, and found a large broken *ahu* with fifteen smashed stone heads. The *moai* were lying every which way, with tumbled red topknots, and I later learned that they had been battered to pieces by a tidal wave that had engulfed the whole of Tongariki about twenty-five years before. There was also an ancient canoe ramp here, which had been in regular use for centuries, though it was last used, according to historians, a hundred years ago. I thought I would put it to use once again.

Where once there had been a village at the edge of the bay, there was now a tin shack, and when I approached it and called out, some people emerged—about six or seven girls and perhaps five older men. Several of the men were drunk. I asked whether I could camp nearby.

One of the girls said, "I'll ask my father."

The man next to her looked up from his fish heads and sweet potato, and he muttered in Rapa Nui.

"Of course," the girl said.

Later, I heard the others—the girls, the men: laughter—but did not see them, and so I ate alone, boiling some noodles, and eating them with bread and cheese, and a can of fish. Another feast in Oceania. I slept, waking every so often by the breaking waves and the surge of the sea.

At dawn, the men were mending nets, but they stopped when I began assembling my boat.

"That's not a boat," one of them said to me in Spanish. "That's a canoe."

"What is your word for it? A *waga?*"

"Not *waga*, but *vahka*. How do you know this Rapa Nui word? We don't use this word anymore."

I did not tell him that the word was similar in the Trobriands, on the Queensland coast, in Vanuatu and Tonga—all over. Their word *vahka* was used in the Cook Islands. Later in the morning, one of the girls brought me a boiled sweet potato. I amazed her by saying, "You call this a *kumara?*" In the Solomon Islands, 7,000 miles away, the villager Mapopoza had said to me, *"Nem bilong dispela kumara—"*

The other men gathered and watched me putting my kayak together.

"What are they saying?" I asked the girl, whose name was Jimene.

"They like your boat," she said. "They want it."

"If I give it to them I won't have a boat."

"They say they will trade you something for it."

"What will they give me?"

The men conferred and muttered to Jimene.

"They will give you a *moai* for it."

"How will I take a *moai* away?"

"Other people have taken them. That one near the road was taken to Japan and then brought back."

It seemed to me that the men were only half joking, and would have slipped me one of the fallen heads from the *ahu* at Tongariki, fifty feet away, if I had provided the means to dispose of it. Their outhouse had been plunked on the sacred *ahu* site. You could sit on their toilet and gaze upon exquisite carvings.

The men were lobstermen. I asked them through Jimene how big their lobsters were, and speaking in Rapa Nui, she asked them the size *("Nui nui?")*.

"One or two kilos."

From the ancient canoe ramp here, they went out in their twenty-five-foot motorboat, plowing through the surf, to check their lobster traps. I engaged them in a discussion about sea conditions and with their encouragement I set off that day for Motu Maro-Tiri, a tall rock stack down the coast.

Large waves were beating the base of the peninsula, but there were few waves breaking offshore. There was a moderate swell and a light wind.

Inside the bay there was high surf, but I skirted it, heading out to sea and then turning back when I got past the surf zone. I was now several miles from shore, and heading towards one of the more notable offshore islands of Rapa Nui. Here it was that people cowered from cannibals, having swum from shore, and in the old stories it was described how the cannibals went out in canoes and captured the people who had fled from them, who were clinging to the heights of Motu Maro-Tiri, how they were hacked to pieces and brought back to shore to be eaten.

I was listening to my Walkman, and with Vivaldi's Oboe Concerto in C playing, I paddled under the cliffs of the Poike Peninsula, onward towards the island, very happy that I had brought my boat, feeling a total freedom of movement. Seabirds flew from cliff to cliff as I made my way to the rock pillar that they called an islet.

It was like a gigantic grain silo, made of granite, with perfectly vertical sides—so steep that there was no way I could get out of my boat and climb it. The sea-facing side was dashed by waves, and behind the stack of rock the swell continually lifted and dropped me. I touched it with my paddle, adding it to the list of forty-something islands I had visited in Oceania.

On the way back to Tongariki, in the failing light, I was startled by a sudden thump against my boat—*dumpf!* I stopped and turned to see whether I had hit a submerged rock, but there was nothing but black water. There was always the possibility of a shark, and sharks were said to be stirred by thrashing paddles—*Here is a panicky creature that is afraid of me,* the shark reasoned instinctively, *I think I will eat it.* So I made an effort to paddle fairly evenly, without any fuss, and when I got to shore I asked Carlos, one of the fishermen, whether he had encountered any sharks in these waters.

"There are lots of sharks," he told me in Spanish. "Big ones, too. Six or seven feet long. They surround us when we catch a fish."

It seemed a little late in the day for me to start worrying about shark attacks, and so I told myself that perhaps a turtle had bumped me.

The patriarch of this fishing camp was a dignified old gent named Andres, who spent most of the day pulling nails out of wooden planks and cutting pieces of driftwood to manageable size. These he lovingly stacked near the tin shed, to be made into articles of furniture—he was planning a table, he told me. Every early traveler had remarked on the absence of trees on Easter Island, and the great value placed on wood by the islanders: "They made their most precious ornaments of wood. Even today the islanders do not despise the least plank."

"This wood would cost a lot," Andres said, and he mentioned the peso equivalent of a dollar fifty for a small piece. "All wood is expensive here because we have no trees. The Chileans prefer to sell their wood to the Japanese, who have more money."

He went on thoughtfully yanking nails with his claw hammer.

"The Japanese are very intelligent people," Andres said.

"Do you really think that?"

"Well, not compared to you or me, but just in general," he said.

I asked him whether he had spent his whole life on the island. He said no, he had gone to the mainland to work.

"I worked on the railway in Valparaiso, and then I came back here. This is a good place, it's a good life. I like the sea, the fish, the lobster. You live near the sea? So you know what I mean."

"Can I leave my boat here?"

"Yes. There are no thieves. Oh, maybe someone drinks something and takes one or two things. But this is not like the continent. You can take off your clothes, leave them there, and when you come back they will be here. There are no real thieves on Rapa Nui."

"Why not?"

"Because we have no money. Nothing to steal. We're not Japanese, eh?"

The girl Jimene stopped by my little camp that evening. She was nineteen, but had visited the United States—she had a relative in Seattle.

She said, "We were out fishing today. We saw you paddling. We started talking about you. We said how nice it is that you came to our camp."

That inspired me to stay longer. I had to tell the owner of the Jeep I had rented that I would need it a few more days. I drove into Hanga Roa and found him. He was not bothered.

"You're at Tongariki," he said.

"How do you know?"

"Someone saw you."

The owner of the Jeep was Roderigo. He was a medical doctor and part-time businessman. He wanted to buy my baseball hat. He wanted to buy my Patagonia jacket, my Walkman, my tent.

His assistant was Mou, whom I had met my first day on the island—he had picked me up on the road.

Mou said, "Give me your Walkman and I will get you some real *rongo-rongo* tablets."

I swapped Mou my *Apex of Bebop* tape for Bob Dylan's *Infidels*, which I had been meaning to buy. (A few days later, Mou said, "Can you find my father for me? He is somewhere in Colorado. I haven't seen him since I was very young.")

I asked Roderigo about health problems on the island.

"The worst, the principal problem on Easter Island is drinking," he said. "Not from the medical point of view, but psychological. The drinkers have severe psychological problems. People go crazy. Their livers are all right, but it makes them strange and lazy."

"What do you do about them?"

"We are getting a rehabilitation center," he said. "Also, there are respiration problems, from the dampness and the humidity."

I made it back to my camp just as night fell, as it always did, with a thud. I had so little light I ate quickly and crawled into my tent, and I spent the next few hours listening to the BBC, first the news, then a program called "Brain of Britain."

Who was the first Christian martyr?

Saint Stephen.

What is the center of the best cricket ball made of?

Cork.

What was a "louison"?

A guillotine.

What do we call the descendants of Meganeura, which had a two-foot wingspan and lived in the carboniferous age?

Dragonflies.

And then I was overtaken by sleep.

Some days traveling in an odd place there is nowhere else I would rather be. I had this feeling now and then in Oceania, as you know. I felt it every day on Easter Island. I wondered why. The island seemed haunted. The people were unpredictable and inbred, which made them by turns both giggly and gloomy. It was a difficult and dangerous place to paddle a kayak. Some of this strangeness added to its attraction. But it was also the smallness of the island, and its empty hinterland, the symmetry of the volcanoes, the extravagant beauty of the stone carvings, the warm days and cool nights, the tenacity of the people, and all the island's mystery, still unsolved.

There was also something wonderful about waking up in a tent, on a beautiful morning, with the great masked noddies hovering and swooping overhead, and looking over the bluff at the ancient canoe ramp at Tongariki and five miles up the island to the cape and thinking: *I will paddle there today.*

"What do you call that cape?" I asked Andres, pointing towards Cape Roggeveen.

"Vakaroa."

"Do you know the name Roggeveen?"

"No."

Jacob Roggeveen was the first European to sight the island, on Easter Day, 1722, and it was he who named it.

"What about the cape beyond it to the north?" On my chart it was Cape Cumming.

"We call it Kavakava."

At that point I saw one of the girls returning to the camp with one of the older men, along the grassy path that led down to the caves and inlets at the edge of the bay. They were carrying nothing. They walked in silence. Andres said nothing to them—obviously they were father and daughter.

I saw more of this furtive behavior, and I was so unused to it—on other Oceanic islands it was taboo for a father to isolate himself with his daughter—I watched closely and I asked oblique questions. I knew from Metraux's ethnology that there was a horror of incest on the island. There had always been. But it did not stop close cousins from marrying. I had met some married cousins in Hanga Roa. A brother and sister had not long ago fled the island—eloped was what actually happened, one of the weirder tales I heard about Rapa Nui. The graphic expression for incest on the island was *Eating your own blood.*

At this camp, the daughters seemed to serve many functions. They cooked the food and tidied the place. They untangled and spread the nets (but did not mend them: that was man's work). They fetched and carried. They played among themselves, but when they were called they kept their fathers company. The fathers went fishing and lobstering with their daughters. Often there was a group: the brothers, their daughters, and nieces. But just as often the father and daughter were alone. There was always activity, always movement—"He's going for a walk with his daughter"—the men always in bathing suits and torn T-shirts, looking grubby. The girls were mostly fattish adolescents with bad skin. The eldest was nineteen. Her father was thirty-six, but looked much older. She was born when her mother had been fifteen. That until recently was about standard childbearing age.

"My father goes to the disco with us on Fridays," she told me.

"What about your mother?"

"She stays home."

"Where is your mother now?"

"In town, selling fish."

"With your aunties?"

"Yes."

Another vivid sight was that of a father putting some sort of lotion on his daughter's back, the father being roughly affectionate, the daughter giggling.

I trusted Andres' instincts. If something was amiss, he would sort it out. He was the most reliable person at the fishing camp, and because he was always sober I brought him a present of a bottle of vodka. I gave the girls a large box of chocolates. But nothing was said about these gifts. They were never referred to. They were squirrelled away as soon as they were handed over.

But Andres was always courtly.

"I like being here," I said in Spanish.

"Good to have you."

"It is my pleasure."

"Equally."

In the pleasantest circumstances, like this, I tended to procrastinate. I planned an expedition for the day, but then I would fall into conversation with someone, and find it interesting, and say to myself: *I'll go on my expedition tomorrow.* Normally, I was not a time waster—being busy kept my mood bright—but here I adjusted my pace, and I realized that I was living as they were. On a given day they would say they were going fishing, and they would sit around, talking and laughing until nightfall, the fishing trip forgotten.

When I was alone with an islander I enlarged my list of Rapa Nui words. On each island in Oceania, I made a list of thirty-odd words, the same in each place: moon, sun, day, fish, food, big, small, sweet potato, woman, man, water, canoe, land, island, and so forth, as well as the numbers from one to ten. I did it mainly for my amusement, to compare the language on one group of islands with another. The results were always revealing. Fiji was technically Melanesia, but the standard Fijian language was full of Polynesian words. And I marvelled at how islands as far apart as Hawaii and New Zealand shared a common Polynesian tongue that was mutually intelligible.

I wondered about Easter Island. The language was said to be corrupt. I had not read anything definitive about the impact Tahitian had had on Rapa Nui. There had been times when the entire island had been removed to Tahiti for economic reasons (there was still an acrimonious land dispute regarding the ownership by Easter Islanders of a portion of Tahiti).

On my days of procrastination I developed my word lists, and I discovered that many words were not Tahitian at all, and may well have been part of the original vocabulary, which had been traced to the Tuamotus. The numbers were different from Tahitian, though they resembled Samoan. Their word for sun, *tera'a,* was unique to the island (it was *la* in Samoan). Their word for man, *tangata,* differed from Tahitian *tane,* but was similar to Tahitian for human being, *taata,* and identical to the word for man in Tongan. Woman in Rapa nui was *vi'e,* cognate with *vahine* but obviously different. The word for sweet potato, *kumara,* was universal in Oceania and the prevalence of the vegetable had given rise to one of Rapa Nui's more melancholy proverbs for life on the island: "We are born. We eat sweet potatoes. Then we die."

There was no reef around Easter Island, but there was still a concept of *inshore* and *deep sea*. Their word for the deep blue sea was *moana*—the word is known all over Polynesia. But "inshore" water, the Rapa Nui equivalent of inside the reef, was *vaikava*, "where the green water is," Carlos explained.

I would not have paddled in the far *moana* around Easter Island for anything. If something went wrong I would be lost in cold water, in a high wind, with no possibility of rescue or of being swept to any other island. About a mile and a half was as far as I ever got from Rapa Nui, but that was enough—perhaps more than enough, since there was nowhere else to go. The islands, those vertical rock pillars, were less than a mile from shore, though they were never accessible from the nearest point on shore. You set out and had to paddle perhaps four miles along the coast to reach them.

I planned for my last long paddle—a trip past Motu Maro-Tiri to the eastern tip of the island, beyond Cape Roggeveen. I brought food and water, my chart and my compass. I told Andres where I was going and that I would be back before evening. As I had been about a third of the way along this coast a few days before, I knew that if something went badly wrong—tipping over and having to swim to shore was about the worst—I could find a cave or a ledge somewhere in the rock wall of the Poike Peninsula. When I did not return, I assumed someone would look for me in one of the lobster boats.

The Dylan tape *Infidels* that Mou had swapped me was playing in my Walkman as I paddled out of the bay. I skirted the surf zone, watched for shark fins, and made a mental note of the configuration of cliffs on the peninsula, looking for a funk hole.

The sea caves beneath the 300-foot-high cliffs were lashed by surf which engulfed the cave entrance and then, after a long pause, and squirts from cracks and blowholes, that same wave was spewed out, foaming. These waves made the front side of Motu Maro-Tiri inaccessible, and it was only there that it was possible to climb to a ledge or a cave. I made a feeble attempt, but gave it up, afraid that I would tip over.

For the next hour and a half I paddled northeast, about a mile or less from the peninsula, sometimes in choppy water, sometimes in high swells. If I paddled too close to the shore I was the victim of reflected waves, which tossed my boat; but farther out I had to contend with a stronger wind and a swell. I found it simpler, but slower, to paddle into the face of waves than in the direction they were traveling, because going downwind there is always the possibility of the boat broaching, turning sideways, or of your losing control because of the speed of your surfing.

I was just confident enough in this water to have a quick cheese sandwich and a swig of water, and in the meantime I was paddling to the beat of Dylan's guitar riffs. Musically, this was a different and less uplifting experience than the baroque oboe concertos of a few days before, but there was no time to change the cassette.

It seemed to me that a mile past Cape Roggeveen was as far as any sensible person would go on a winter day off Easter Island in a choppy sea. There were light winds behind the peninsula, but around the corner it was blowing twenty-odd knots.

The worst of it was the heavy surf, which resulted in reflected waves and a confused sea just offshore. I tried to find a middle ground to paddle in, between the chop and the deep blue sea. To take my mind off this, I marvelled at the big waves breaking against the sea caves and spilling down the ledges—with the foam and the spray whitening the air at the base of the cliffs. It was a lovely and dramatic sight, the dumping sea and the whiteness of the waves.

All this to the sound of music.

And then I took the headphones off, and heard the immense roar of waves and the screaming wind, and I became frightened. The music had drowned the sounds of the beating sea, and without music I felt only terror. My boat immediately became unstable. I paddled hard to give myself direction and stability, and I pushed onward, past the cape to the corner of the island—the edge, round which the wind was whistling. Unwillingly I was thrust out, where I got a wonderful view—much better than I wanted—of Kavakava, Cape Cumming, and then I turned and spun my boat over the crest of a wave and began surfing back to the lee of the island, with a big wet following sea.

I stayed beyond the surf zone, which was especially dangerous on Easter Island because the waves broke on a rocky shore, yet I was curious to see some of these *moai* from the sea. I paddled across the mouth of the bay in a southerly direction, to Punta Yama, where there was a smashed *ahu,* and half a mile farther down the coast there were deep sea caves. Rapa Nui people were fishing near the caves, a family with some horses were camped on the grassy cliff not far away, and there were more fishermen (and more broken statuary) another mile on.

It was odd to be hovering here, between the surf zone and the *moana,* the deadly emptiness of the enormous ocean behind me, the fatal shore in front of me. Landing was impossible. But being here, bobbing in a small boat, demonstrated how resourceful these people had been. They had found ways in and out of the surf (swimming, surfing, using reed floats). They had made canoes ingeniously sewing scraps of driftwood together in much the same way the Inuit had done to make kayaks in the Arctic. They had incorporated every geographical feature of the island— caves, ledges, cliffs, hills—into their cosmology. And they had done much more than merely survive here—they had prevailed over the inhospitable place and shaped it, made altars and temple platforms and houses with its boulders, and carved from its volcanoes some of the greatest, most powerful statues the world has seen, artistic masterpieces as well as engineering marvels.

They were also known as quarrelsome and competitive people, and there is evidence that warring groups on the island smashed each others' *moai* and some also smashed their own, ritually decapitating them and building better ones. Many of the statues that were standing when Captain Cook visited had been tipped over and broken a few years later.

About five miles away at a bay called Rada Vinapu I saw marked on my chart the abbreviation *Lndg,* but it was impossible to tell what that landing might be. I was afraid it might be a jetty—one that a ship could slide against, in spite of the waves that hit it, but impossible for me. I had been almost around the entire island and had found only two places to launch and land from; the rest was surf breaking on rocks.

Still outside the surf zone I paddled back, and when I got nearer to Tongariki I put in my tape of baroque oboe concertos and watched the island slip past me, and I felt joyous.

Above the bay at Tongariki there was an unusual ditch-shaped land feature that seemed to cut across the peninsula. One of the island's more colorful stories concerned an ancient battle between two distinct groups of islanders, the Long Ears and the Short Ears, in which the Short Ears had been victorious. The violent battle, involving flaming ditches and fierce pursuit, is part of the island's oral tradition. But it seemed no more based on fact than the arrival—also here at Tongariki—of Tangaroa, who took on a useful incarnation *(ata),* the form of a seal, and swam from Mangareva to this very spot, where he revealed himself as the God of the Sea.

When I returned, I asked Carlos, Andres, and Jimene about these particular island legends. The men just smiled. Jimene said, "There are so many stories here, it is really wonderful."

There was a different man sitting there near the tin hut that evening. He was Juan Ito, a Rapa Nui man, who was caretaker of the great *moai* quarry across the long meadow at the volcano Rano Raraku. Had he heard those old stories?

"Yes. I know those stories and I believe them," Juan said.

He was one of many people who told me that he would never stay anywhere near the *moai* after dark, because of the existence of supernatural beings. But I was impressed by his fear, because he was among the *moai* nearly every day.

He asked me whether I was driving into Hanga Roa. Realizing that I would need some food, I drove Juan and his son, Roberto, the twelve miles into Hanga Roa. Roberto was about eight. Roberto was a skinny and rather undersized and neglected-looking boy—he had just come from school, he said. His hair was matted, his face was smudged. He looked very hungry and when I found an apple and a boiled egg from the lunch I had only picked at he wolfed them in the backseat.

"How do you usually go from Hanga Roa to the volcano?" I asked Juan.

"Walk. Sometimes I get a ride," he said. "There is no bus. I have no car. If I walk the whole way it takes two or three hours."

Juan's Spanish was like mine, clumsy and functional, which encouraged me to converse unself-consciously.

"What about a bike?"

"No money."

"Have you got any other children?"

"Three boys altogether. Aged five, seven, and eight."

We were driving along the cliffs I had paddled past that afternoon and they looked lovely and rubbly under the pink sky, with the waves breaking at the foot of them.

"But the mother is gone," Juan said. "She went to Santiago."

"To work?"

"I don't know. I never hear from her. She drank—she drank everything, whisky, pisco, beer, wine, anything. Then she just left."

"Do you cook the food?"

"Yes. And I clean the house. I do the laundry, too." He laughed. "At first I didn't know anything about looking after a house. But after a while I learned."

He was a small rather sad figure, in his early thirties, and I felt sorry for him, for his having been abandoned. He had a badly paying job, and three young children, and a long walk to work. But he was honest and forthright.

We talked about politics. He volunteered that he hated Pinochet, who had come to power in a military coup that of course had been welcomed by the United States—Pinochet being the sort of bullying right-winger the CIA had found easy to work with.

"Why do you hate Pinochet?"

"Because he's bad. Because he's corrupt. Because he was tough on this island," Juan said. "I liked Allende. I hate militarists."

I spent another night and day at Tongariki, still wondering what the real relationships of my neighbors were. Nor could I understand their reserve. They were tolerant but inhospitable, and without any curiosity. Now and then one of them had said, "Come fishing with us sometime."

I said, "Fine," but the invitation was never more explicit than that. Their indifference forced me to look after myself, which was what I wanted, but I was not sure whether I could ask anything of them.

That was one of the trickier aspects of camping on a Polynesian island. Anyone who is not a member of a family is in an awkward position and somewhat suspect. There are only two categories—Family Member and Other. "Other" includes guest, and the responsibilities, though they are never apparent, are complex. For one thing, because a guest was an outsider he or she was never totally trusted. This ambiguity alone was like proof that Easter Islanders were Polynesians.

I finally left Tongariki because after four nights camping by the sea I needed a bath. My hair was salty, I felt grubby. What did these people do? They did not take many baths. There are no rivers at all on Easter Island, and there is a serious shortage of fresh water.

Carlos said to me, "Come back sometime."

After this vague salutation, the whole fishing camp of fathers and daughters went back to their own affairs.

The rest of the time I spent in Hanga Roa. The wind changed and blowing now from the south, from Antarctica, it was much colder, and I was glad that I had done my paddling in the fairer winds.

I wanted to buy carvings—some were very well done indeed, so well done that people said they had slipped them to Thor Heyerdahl and fobbed these copies off to him as ancient artifacts. The carvings were expensive. *Two hundred dollars,* a person would say, and when I walked on, *How much will you offer?* I hated haggling, so I kept walking. I wanted a rubbing of the Bird-Man petroglyphs, of the god Makemake or one of the more winsome and presentable vulvas. I wished I had brought the simple materials with me that would have allowed me to make rubbings (and I suggest that anyone who goes to Easter Island, or to the Marquesas, do this). Some of the shops had cloth printed with the Bird-Man motif, and this pattern had originally been a rubbing. I saw the same cloth in four shops (Hanga Roa had a whole street of curio shops, identical souvenirs, no customers), and prices ranged from $65 to $150 for the same simple item. Each person who offered the cloth claimed that he or she had actually painted it. *I did this with my own hand!*

Nothing had a price. It was all haggling—what the market would bear. This was Chilean influence; in the rest of Oceania haggling was regarded as insulting.

Then I was offered one of those cloths for $45. The woman who was selling it said that she had painted it, but this time the claim was true. Her name was Patrizia Saavedra, she was a Chilean, and she had come to the island nineteen years before, "because I am an artist and this is an island of artists."

After nineteen years she had to know the place well.

"It doesn't suit everyone, but it suits me," she said. "The main problem is social conflict. Yet the people are not violent. They might shout at you one day, but the next day they will be kind."

"How do you explain that?" I asked.

"They have a habit of forgetting quarrels. They don't store up their grievances. There is little fighting."

I said that I had an intimation of anarchy and mistrust on the island. Had she felt that?

She thought a moment and then said, "You know, dictatorship is bad in many ways—some that you don't expect. It changes people's minds. It affects their thinking. It affected the people here." She intimated that the people had become rebellious and selfish. Pinochet had put his friends and flunkies into positions of power on Easter Island. The local people resented it, and as a result—yes—they were mistrustful. The young people didn't study.

"Now that democracy has come and the military rule has ended, everyone wants to be king of the island." She smiled a pretty, toothy smile and added, "Yes, that is not a bad thing, but *everyone* wants to run for office." She began pointing. "This man. That man. That woman. Him. Her. Everyone wants to be governor, or *alcalde* [mayor], or whatever. Elections are coming soon. They will be funny, with everyone's name on the ballot—a big long ballot!"

Some months before, elsewhere in Oceania, I had heard on Radio Australia's reliable program "Pacific News" that there had been a large demonstration on Easter Island. For reasons I could not remember, people had gathered at the airport and, holding an airplane hostage, had prevented it from taking off.

"It was last March," Patrizia said. "The whole island was united, the islanders and the Chileans together. There was a radical group behind it—The Society of the Old Chiefs, *Mata Nui o Hotu Matua*. But everyone supported them, two thousand people, in rotation. They went to the airport after the plane landed—the governor was in Santiago—and they claimed it. They would not let the plane take off. It was not violent—no guns. But the people were very determined."

I asked her why they had done it.

"The cause was a two-hundred-percent increase in prices—fuel, water, electricity."

"And so the islanders united?"

"Yes. And they won. The increase was dropped. The plane took off."

The important detail was that the core of the rebellion had been a Rapa Nui cultural group. Asserting their Polynesian identity was a way of giving their cause legitimacy. All along the Chilean government had encouraged the people to be colorful, to dance and sing, to recall their past. The effect of this cultural submersion had been similar to that of Tahitians and Marquesans, who had been urged to dance and sing and who had done so, faced with pervasive Frenchness. The Rapa Nui dance troupe dressed up, the girls in grass skirts, the boys in loin cloths. They found that they were welcomed in Tahiti, in Hawaii and New Zealand. They realized that they were part of the great Polynesian diaspora. And dancing and singing was inimitable and became their way of resisting Chilean influence. It had also led to more overt political acts.

For a while in Hanga Roa I fell in with the drinkers. Their objective each evening was to drink themselves into a state of paralysis, and I was fascinated by their methods. They drank anything alcoholic—beer, wine, whisky. And they combined the drinks.

Martin and Hernando, who were Chilean, made Carlos and his brothers seem positively abstemious by comparison. Martin had been on the island for twelve years, Hernando only four. Both were from farms in the Chilean hinterland, and they had an old leathery and weather-beaten look, though Martin, the elder of the two, was only forty-one. They drank every day, from the moment they got out of work—they were in the Forestry Department. Given the small number of trees on the island, this did not seem an exacting occupation.

They sat at a table in a small bar overlooking Hanga Roa harbor. They bought cans of beer and cartons of wine. They drank some beer and then poured some wine from the carton into the beer can, and mixed it, and swigged. They staggered, they shouted, they became absurdly affectionate, then they quarrelled and went stiff.

There were two discotheques in Hanga Roa. Paralysis was the objective in those places too. The Tokoroko was the more notorious of the two. "That is Sodom and Gomorrah," a woman told me. That made me hopeful, but I was disappointed. I visited and saw only youths stumblingly dancing. Their drinking was done with more seriousness. When they were truly rigid, like Martin and Hernando, they went home.

Life in Hanga Roa made me miss my camp near the canoe ramp at Tongariki, but my time on Easter Island was coming to an end. I was headed for another corner of the Polynesian triangle—Hawaii.

"You will have to get up early tomorrow," the owner of my guest house said the night before I left. "We leave for the airport at six in the morning."

Afraid that I might not get up in time, I hardly slept. I dozed, dreamed of missing the plane, and then woke up in a panic. I was fully awake at five. I was loitering in the driveway at five-thirty. At six, no one appeared. At ten past I began knocking on doors. It was another cold, black Easter Island morning. I went on waiting. Where was everyone?

I dragged my collapsible boat, my camping gear, and my bag of clothes out to the dirt thoroughfare, The Navel of the World Road, and I prayed to the great god Makemake for assistance.

A small truck trundled down the road, waking the dogs. I flagged him down.

"Are you going to the airport?"

He could only have been, at that hour. He said he was from the post office. This heavyset Rapa Nui man in his beat-up truck continued down the bumpy dirt road. It struck me that this was the only island in Oceania I had been where people wore lots of clothes, old filthy clothes, and boots, and torn sweaty hats. Their mode of dress gave them a downtrodden, hopeless look. The man asked me where I was going.

"Tahiti, then Honolulu."

"I would like to go there," he said.

Part Four

PARADISE

Chapter 23

O'AHU: OPEN ESPIONAGE IN HONOLULU

The two most obvious facts of Hawaii are the huge sluttish pleasures of its Nipponized beachfront hotels and, in great contrast, its rugged landscape of craggy volcanoes and its coastal headlands, where lava has been pounded by heavy surf into black spikes. Hawaii is smooth, but it can also be rough. I went intending to sample this fearful beauty. On my first swim in Hawaii, on the north shore of O'ahu, off a gorgeous beach, I was yanked by the undertow, carried past the surf zone, and swept into a strong current almost a mile from my towel. I swam hard upstream for an hour and finally struggled ashore on sharp rocks, where I was lacerated and shaken. Was this outing a mistake? I wondered whether I should leave because of that, but people said this happened to newcomers all the time.

Soon after, I was introduced to a dignified old man at a party. He began to tell me about a book he had written, and then he asked me my name and what I did for a living.

"I'm a writer."

"What restaurant do you work in?"

"Excuse me?"

"Where are you working as a waiter?"

He was not hard of hearing, simply logical—there were so many waiters and so few writers. Never mind. As time passed, I felt I might stay there for the rest of my life.

"There's Arthur Murray," someone said, in a restaurant.

It was he, in the flesh, ninety-three years old. Decades ago he had sold the dance-lesson business. He had a collection of French Impressionist paintings and lived in a luxury penthouse overlooking the beach at Waikiki.

"She slipped on a shrimp," I heard an anguished person say at another party. "Hurt her leg real bad. Plus she's real stressed," giving it the slushy Hawaiian pronunciation, *shtressed.* People also said *shtrength,* and *shrtreet.*

You expected someone to ask, *What happened to the shrimp?* but no one did.

I procrastinated about paddling my boat, because I wanted to get the hang of this complicated city.

Probably the best view of Honolulu is from the top of the city's mountainous backdrop, Aiea Heights. We have Takeo Yoshikawa's word on that. He was one of the spookiest and most important of history's phantoms and was part of the plot to destroy Hawaii. It was in Aiea, in what were then cane fields (now mostly bungalows), that Yoshikawa, a Japanese spy, watched the movements of ships in Pearl Harbor and, in general, gaped at the life of the friendly city.

No one suspected this man of engaging in open espionage—Honolulu was, and is, a city where Japanese are in the majority. Yoshikawa was twenty-nine. Some days he disguised himself in cane cutter's clothes. On other days he wore a suit and worked under a false name at the Japanese Consulate—as prettily housed today on the Pali Highway as it was in 1941, looking just as it did when the impostors inside supplied information for Admiral Yamamoto's master plan of bombardment. "If you want the tiger's cubs," the admiral was fond of saying, "you must go into the tiger's lair."

Yoshikawa arrived from Japan in March 1941 and, prowling Aiea, spied assiduously on the city and harbor for eight months. He was still on the job the day the planes were strafing, and the bombs were falling and ships sinking and the first of the 2,403 people were dying from Japanese bombs.

When he had scoped out the strategic locations, Yoshikawa had noted that the ships were generally moored in Pearl Harbor on the weekends, and the planes were parked at Hickam Field then too. From his tootling around the north shore of the island in a borrowed 1937 Ford, Yoshikawa was pleased to see that North O'ahu was very lightly defended—a safe direction for the kamikazes. Admiral Yamamoto had worried about balloons—barrage balloons that would impede attacks by fighter planes. No balloons, Yoshikawa reported, and less than a day before the Sunday morning bombing of Pearl Harbor, Yoshikawa cabled from the consulate: *There are limits to the balloon defense of Pearl Harbor. I imagine that in all probability there is considerable opportunity left to take advantage for a surprise attack . . .*

Fifty years later, I went to the *Arizona* Memorial in Pearl Harbor to pay my respects. This area of Pearl is a national park. Everyone watches the short documentary beforehand, which describes the events of the morning of December 7, 1941. It is not a flag-waving film and is the more moving for its cruel factuality. After that sobering experience, the visitors are ferried into the harbor to the memorial itself, which is a white shrine-like structure built over the rusty hulk of the sunken battleship in which 1,200 Americans lost their lives when a Japanese bomb scored a direct hit on the *Arizona*'s number two turret. Research is so detailed on the attack that the bombardier's name is known. It was Noboru Kanai, who, like the others in the attack force, wore a white cloth around his head reading *Hissho,* "Certain Victory."

"Do Japanese tourists come here?" I asked the park service guide.

"Not many," he said. "And the ones who do sometimes laugh and snap pictures of each other. I don't think they realize how important this place is to us."

Looking out from the spymaster's vantage point, the heights of Aiea, after arriving in Honolulu from the Western Pacific—from the far corners of the Polynesian triangle, from travel in small simple islands—I was overwhelmed by the city's prosperity and its modern face. It is the most visible city in the Pacific.

You can take in the whole busy panorama of Honolulu by glancing from right to left, beginning at Waianae and Pearl Harbor—the cranes and ships, Hickam's planes painted in green camouflage, Downtown with its banks and skyscrapers, and Chinatown's meaner streets, where the less motivated prostitutes tend to linger, the scarcity of open space, its heavy traffic, the Bishop Museum, the suburbs on the slopes of its volcanoes, bungalows magnetized to old lava flows and in green drenched valleys, the high-rise hotels like goofy dentures and the surf breaking on the reef at Waikiki, the streets of Korean bars and strip clubs, Punchbowl volcano, and the pretty parks, the green cliffs and peaks that enclose the city, a prospect of the sea, and at last Diamond Head, which, a vast and Sphinxlike sentinel, can be seen from almost anywhere in the city. After Diamond Head, your eye is traveling to windward, towards the far side of the island.

Where are the pedestrians? Outside of the seaside honky-tonk of Waikiki (less than a mile long) few people walk. Honolulu, a city of drivers, is dense with private cars, and of two- and three-car families. Even the poorest in Honolulu, the recently arrived Pacific islanders—Samoans, Tongans, people from Christmas Island and Yap—have at least one vehicle, usually a new four-wheel-drive pickup truck. In fact, the pickup truck seems part of the personality of these islanders, just as an expensive usually European car is an aspect of the personality of Honolulu's affluent families. It is a point of pride among Filipinos to buy a truck as soon as the down payment can be scraped together. The middle class drives Japanese cars, the military buys American. No one walks.

One of the paradoxes of Hawaii, yet one of its most American features, is that it quickly—recently—became a car culture. Why is this a paradox? Because, apart from the beaches and shopping malls, all within a small radius, there is nowhere to drive—no hinterland, no open road. A car is regarded as a necessity not simply because a bus passenger is stigmatized as one of the sadder and more poverty-stricken citizens but, more than that, a car in Honolulu is the badge of one's class. I think the car is the key thing. In such a hot city, where nearly everyone rich and poor dresses identically, clothes cannot possibly be a status symbol.

The semiotics of Honolulu, its signs and symbols, are complex and highly colored; the city in particular and Hawaii in general have more class divisions and more subtle aspects of social difference than I have ever seen before. The local idiom is crammed with who's-who designations and signifiers: *Malihini* (newcomer), *kama'aina* (old-timer), *pake* (Chinese), *katonk* (mainland Japanese: It is an onomatopoeic word, the sound a Japanese head makes when it is struck by a hard object), *kachink* (mainland Chinese, same definition), *buk-buk* (Filipino; also "Flip" and *monong*), "moke" or *blalah* (young tough), *tita* ("sister," moke's girl-friend), *popolo* (black person, sometimes the word is playfully inverted as *"olopop"*), and all the gradations of *haole* (Caucasian)—new *haole,* old *haole, hapahaole* (half-*haole*). The Portuguese (of which there are many in Hawaii) are not regarded as *haoles,* but rather are universally known as "Portugees." A Latin or a Jew in this society of fine racial distinctions is not seen as Caucasian. There is no colloquialism for a Hawaiian person, though "part-Hawaiian" or variations of *hapa* are the usual descriptions, since so few are full-blooded. There are peasants, and there are aristocrats and royals—that they were overthrown and pensioned-off is a meaning-less quibble, for the fact is that Hawaiian ex-royalty, some of it *hapahaole,* are still among the wealthiest people in the islands.

With all these divisions, you would expect trouble, but Honolulu does not have the conflicts usually associated with strict class-ridden societies. Even the ritual "Kill-a-*Haole* Day" popularized at some of Honolulu's public high schools is merely a macabre (and toothless) prank rather than a piece of racial vindictiveness meant to inspire terror in whites. In the sense that many races work harmoniously together, with only the softest undertones—the murmurs of racial memory—and that the races also habitually intermarry, producing startlingly good-looking offspring,

Honolulu may be the most successful multiracial culture in the world. At least, I have not seen another to rival it. One of the proofs of its success is that people in Honolulu are contemptuous rather than envious and resentful about the clubs (the Outrigger Canoe Club, the Pacific Club), which until recently did not admit Orientals, or the banks that discriminated against certain races in giving loans.

And oddly, in a city of so many races, there are seldom racial jokes in circulation. The few I heard were almost incomprehensible. They were never about Orientals or Hawaiians, or even islanders; nearly always the joke victim was a Portuguese or Filipino. Filipino jokes are almost entirely concerned with the Filipino reputation for eating dogs.

> Q. What did the Flip say when he was shown his first
>   American hot dog?
> A. "That's the one part of the dog we don't eat."

There is a certain slang idiom, loosely based on Hawaiian Pidgin, which conveys a heavy humor and is almost exclusively concerned with eating, drinking beer, being fat, being lazy, being slow-witted, surfing, playing loud music, taunting tourists, and owning a four-wheel-drive vehicle. This is purely local and almost untranslatable. It is a manner of speaking, not joking, but joshing, and only "mokes" engage in it. Like English cockneys, who in temperament and lingo they greatly resemble, mokes are at the bottom of the social ladder, but have such a well-defined place in society that they are proud of it. Some are islanders, some are Hawaiians, some are a complex racial mix, but they are all dark and chubby, and they are ambiguously regarded as both cuddly and lethal. Mokes constitute a fraternity and even greet each other *"Brah"* (brother). They are self-mocking, and they ham it up in their baseball caps and T-shirts, crowding the beaches like the Tons-of-fun, but anyone foolish enough to laugh at them, or even to make sustained eye contact, is quickly in danger.

The so-called mokes, when gainfully employed, work as mechanics or manual laborers, but no matter what the job there is a race in Honolulu which has monopolized it. Tongans are tree cutters and yard workers, though the more detailed landscaping is done by Filipinos, who are also field workers—accounting for most of the pineapple pickers. Agriculture was formerly an occupation of rural Japanese. Samoans wash cars. Doctors and lawyers are Chinese and Japanese. A surprising number of *haoles* are engaged in real estate. Yet class distinctions, unlike job descriptions, are not strictly racial but rather economic and, in Honolulu, always geographic.

"We were involved in product transitions," someone told me at a party, explaining why business was bad. "We descoped the high end of our line."

It seemed to me that people in Honolulu talked business most of the time. Business or golf. They rose early—though no matter how early they got up they never managed to beat the freeway traffic, which was dense even at six in the morning; they worked hard, they hustled; they went home and hid—privacy being something that is greatly desired in Honolulu.

Each class has its own turf, from the low-income areas of Kalihi, and Makaha in Waianae, and the middle- and upper-class serenity of Manoa and Nu'uanu, to the super-rich in Waianae-Kahala. All of Hawaii's beaches are public, yet each class sticks pretty much to its own shoreline. Some of the most beautiful beaches in the islands are found on the Waianae stretch of coast, but they tend to be avoided because of the intense territoriality of the locals. *Haoles* are cheerfully tormented and sometimes attacked in Waianae. And each class sticks to its own sports, ranging from surfing to golf, and to its own depravities—the poor using "ice," crystal methamphetamine (*pohaku* in moke slang), the middle-class youth smoking pot (*pakalolo,* crazy smoke), the wealthy snorting cocaine. There is no crack and, indeed, no perceived drug problem. Gambling is illegal, and so naturally is very common in a clandestine way, but the preferred games also have class associations—cards for Chinese, cockfights for Filipinos, dice for Japanese, trips to Las Vegas for those who can afford it, and so forth.

This exclusivity is also the case with the military, who exist in the tens of thousands in and around Honolulu, on bases and in married quarters. Soldiers are known to locals as "jar-heads." They constitute a subclass and they keep to themselves. They don't want trouble. They know they are lucky to have been posted here. They swim at their own beaches, shop at the PX, attend their own churches and schools. Unlike other cities which have bases nearby, Honolulu has little casual fighting between soldiers and locals. The military is known only by its violent crimes—a rape, a stabbing, a shooting: typically a young jar-head from Schofield Barracks or Fort Shafter committing an offense against a local woman.

Violent crime is always reported in detail in the daily paper, because in this basically humane and gentle society it is still considered extraordinary. Handguns are outlawed on the islands. Not many rifles are privately owned. There is no capital punishment. The population's predominantly Oriental cast means that it is not a confrontational society. It is not a horn-honking society, either—anyone leaning on a horn is immediately seen as an ignorant newcomer or a tourist. Drivers are polite. It is essentially Christian, and not a litigious society. In a patient way, scores are settled over the long term. Revenge is a dish best eaten cold, might be a Honolulu motto. The Chinese who were blackballed at the Outrigger Canoe Club started their own golf club, Waialae, and now *haoles* are lining up to join this exclusive club.

Once in a great while there is a meaningful murder or suicide in Honolulu: Everyone seems to understand. *Oh, he had gambling debts,* someone will say, or *She was involved in a really hot scandal.* Anyway, these are islands. People are intensely visible and nothing is forgotten. The person you are rude to today might be your golf partner tomorrow. In the absence of satirical magazines or good newspapers or investigative reporting, there is the island standby of gossip, and in Honolulu rumors travel with great rapidity.

Middle-class Honolulu society is law-abiding, churchgoing, and rather sanctimonious—in fact everything but racialistic. A family that has married completely within its own race is the exception, not the rule. Anyway, the Honolulu bourgeoisie is not a racial group but an economic entity, and in spite of its ethnic sentiments, is Christian and has much in common with the aspirations of mainstream America. There is a strong sense of family, and an even stronger sense of the extended family. Within the bourgeoisie, old Japanese are bumpkins (but friendly), new Japanese are jovially regarded as uptight (and shrewd), Chinese as niggardly (and independent), Koreans as tough (and cruel), Hawaiians as indolent (and mellow), Filipinos as self-serving (but hard-working), Portuguese as excitable (but buffoons). But in Honolulu race is not an indication of class.

The clearest and most concise indicator of your class in Honolulu is your high school, because until very recently this was the highest educational level you were likely to have attained.

"You find out who someone is in Honolulu by asking them where they went to school," a local woman told me.

And it's true. It is the key question in any introduction.

"Never mind college," she went on. "Once you know their high school you know everything. Where they live. How much they make. Their politics. Their outlook, their expectations. If they went to Farrington they're mokes. If they went to St. Louis they're bourgeois Catholics. If they went to Radford they're probably military or new *haole.* If they went to Roosevelt, they're mainstream. And at the top is Punahou."

Punahou students are seen as Hawaii's achievers. The school is highly regarded academically and, founded in 1841, was the first high school to be established west of the Mississippi. It produces community leaders, but it also produces obnoxious prep-school pushies, smug and preening and forever gloatingly recalling their school days. Like many of Honolulu's institutions, Punahou has its roots in the Protestant missions. There is something pervasively old-world in Honolulu, which Punahou—with its colors of buff and blue and its tribalism and its cultivated silliness—seems to epitomize.

This is undiluted New England Anglophilia; Yankee missionaries had a profound influence on the islands—on the class structure, the culture, even the architecture of wooden white frame and shingled houses. In Honolulu, and in Hawaii in general, Anglophilia amounts at times to Anglomania. The Union Jack boxed-in on the Hawaiian state flag is an ominous sign of this, and at times Hawaii seems more like the Sandwich Islands of yore than the fiftieth state. It is a fact that the upper class—old family, Republican, mainly *haole*—resisted statehood and saw it as a slippery slope. Nearly everyone else agrees that it was statehood that brought racial equality to the islands.

Well-heeled Hawaii, with its garden parties and its snobberies, its cultural affectations, is deeply Anglophile (and still resentful of statehood). This ought to make a new *haole* a sure bet for fitting in; but Hawaii's complexities do not ensure that. The word *haole*—which means "of another breath [or air]"—carries with it many ambiguous associations and qualities, and because of that it is an enigmatic word, describing an unknown quantity, with a suggestion of someone who is "not one of us." I seldom heard this word without imagining it written as it is spoken, like an angry complainer: *howlie.*

And there are the tourists, but they come and go, and apart from people working in the tourist industry, no one takes much notice of them.

There are six million tourists a year, each one staying on average eight and a half days. Two million are Japanese, and many of those are in the marriage package—room, white limo, nondenominational service, champagne—at $10,000 a pop. Every so often a new bride leaps to her death from an upper floor of a luxury hotel. *These arranged marriages,* local people mutter, as a Shinto priest hurries upstairs to exorcize the ghosts in the room with chants and howls and incense. The room is soon reoccupied. Tourism is the largest industry and the mainstay of the entire state. But tourists, even without realizing it, are also territorial. They keep to Waikiki. Except for the beach, the hotel, the luau, the pineapple tour, they do not stray far afield. They are undemanding, they are generally smiled upon, they are seldom ridiculed, they are hardly even mentioned, except by people who are paid to look after them. It is acknowledged that they have brought prosperity to the state. A local person who kept away from Waikiki could form the impression that tourists do not exist. In no sense do they enter the life of Honolulu, which is not a city really but a highly complex small town, Main Street running into Polynesia, America-by-the-Sea, the splash of surf at the shore, *Lovely Hula Hands,* the roar and monotony of traffic, and inland the eternal snapping sound of the Weedwacker.

But tourist Honolulu and town Honolulu not only coexist; each makes the other possible—sometimes in unexpected ways.

One night, I went to the "Don Ho & Friends Polynesian Extravaganza" at the Hilton Hawaiian Village—a profusion of leis, muumuus, fruity drinks, white shoes, and sunburned noses—and Don came on singing *Tiny Bubbles* (*in da wine*) in his bored and growling way.

He was applauded.

Shuffling peevishly, he said, "I am so sick of that song. God, I hate that song. I gotta sing it every night!" Then he sang an encore.

Don Ho had been a permanent fixture at the hotel for twenty years. But even his churlishness did not dampen the ardor of the audience. There were dancers, there were more Hawaiian songs, including *Pearly Shells* (*in da ocean*), *The Hawaiian Wedding Song* (the singer accompanied herself using deaf and dumb signs), and a young male singer, a local fellow, joined Don in singing *I'll Remember You* (*long after dis endless summer is gone*).

A week later I went to *Aida,* well staged by the Hawaii Opera Theater, with an imported soprano and tenor. The baritone was Les Cabalas, the man who had sung with Don Ho & Friends. And since the opera is mainly by subscription, no tourists could have known that the colorful Hawaiian local guy in the ugly shirt with Don Ho was moonlighting, with a powerful voice and a strong presence, as Amneris in a Verdi opera.

Eventually I unpacked my boat and paddled out from Kailua on the windward side of O'ahu. Kailua, over the volcanic ridge from Honolulu, is famous for being residential, middle-class, and military, mainly *haole.* It is a safe haven of one-story bungalows, and it is filled with loitering U.S. Army kids—brats on bikes. It has one of Hawaii's most pleasant beaches and, in addition, several picturesque islands a few miles offshore but part of the great sweep of coast, which takes in three bays and is contained by two magnificent headlands. Even when the trade winds are strong the surf is tolerable for a small craft, and I happily paddled out from Kailua, past Lanikai, to the Mokuluas ("Two Islands").

They are a pair of rocky peaks standing in the lagoon, near the reef, on a ledge of coral. I saw an endangered green sea turtle as soon as I was half a mile offshore, and of course it was brown—the "green" crept into their name when they were still being eaten, because their fat is green. The windward sides of the Mokuluas were being beaten by surf, but on the lee shore, waves were breaking more gently on a small sandy beach.

I saw other kayakers for the first time in the whole of my trip through Oceania. They were surfing their boats through the waves behind the Mokuluas, they were skidding down the swell between the two islands, they were fighting the chop nearer the reef. I had never felt safer.

I waited for the lull between waves and landed on the small beach of the north island. Signs at the edge of the sand explained that this was a sanctuary for seabirds, ground-nesting shearwaters, and that it was forbidden to venture up the slope of the hill. The reason was obvious—the birds had dug nesting holes all over the slope and were compactly occupying them. Because it was such a small island, visitors and birds coexisted uneasily. There were a few picnickers—one from a kayak, half a dozen from a motorboat. Every so often a startled shearwater would take off, mutter *ka-kuk,* and fly swiftly away.

This island was a microcosm of Hawaii. It was lovely, it was lush, it was heavily visited, it was threatened, it seemed doomed. Everything had been fine until recently, but then great numbers of people began going to the Mokuluas on weekends. I paddled here half a dozen times, and I noticed that on weekdays there were birds sitting quietly all over the island; on Saturdays and Sundays there were no birds, and there was sometimes litter and the remains of fires—although both were expressly forbidden. Camping is also forbidden. But because the island is so pretty—just like O'ahu, you might say—people tend to break the rules.

"Lanikai residents say they frequently see people camping overnight there in tents," *The Honolulu Advertiser* reported recently, "walking beyond the no-trespassing signs and into the bird-nesting areas and climbing to the summit of each island.

"The worst intrusion . . . was two rock concerts . . . held on the small beach," the article went on, and it described the illegal crowds, the loud music, the beer drinkers on this fragile piece of land. There were strict rules governing the islands, but Hawaii's Department of Land and Natural Resources did not have the manpower to enforce them, and so it seemed—at this rate—that the Mokuluas were doomed, the birds either dead or gone, the beach crammed with pleasure boats, the hill with campers, the air filled with rock music.

It's seventy-eight degrees in paradise, the disc jockeys say in Honolulu, without a trace of irony.

It often seemed to me that calling the Hawaiian Islands "paradise" was not an exaggeration, though saying it out loud, advertising it, seemed to be tempting fate. They are the most beautiful, and the most threatened, of any islands in the Pacific. Their volcanic mountains are as picturesque as those in Tahiti, their bays as lovely as the ones in Vava'u; the black cliffs of the Marquesas are no more dramatic than those on Molokai and Kaua'i. The climate is perfect. And Hawaii is highly developed, with great hospitals and schools and social services and stores. But modernity has its price. There is beach erosion. There is pollution. There is a constant threat of water shortage or contamination. The traffic problem seems at times overwhelming. O'ahu is overbuilt and so expensive that young people leave, unable to believe that they will ever be able to afford to buy even the simplest house. Maui is overdeveloped—spoiled, some people say—with more hotels than it will ever need. The little island Lana'i is losing its pineapple industry. Ni'ihau is an ecological catastrophe, according to environmentalists. The Big Island is wrestling with the issue of development. There is still hope on Kaua'i, under an enlightened mayor who made campaign promises to limit hotel development and to put islanders' interests first.

The Hawaiian Islands are the most remote—the farthest from any mainland—on earth, and this remoteness made their living things unique. Hawaii's only land mammal was a small bat, and in its waters the monk seal. Both precariously still exist. The islands' birds and plants, which existed nowhere else, have not been so lucky. The impact of humans on Hawaii was catastrophic—Hawaii has lost more indigenous species of birds and plants, driven more creatures into extinction than any other single place on the globe.

"The tragedy of the oceanic islands lies in their uniqueness, the irreplaceability of the species they have developed by the slow process of the ages," Rachel Carson wrote in *The Sea Around Us,* thirty years ago. "In a reasonable world, men would have treated these islands as precious possessions, as natural museums filled with beautiful and curious works of creation, valuable beyond price, because nowhere in the world are they duplicated."

It would have been difficult even with foresight to preserve these fragile ecosystems, but who could have predicted the destruction that followed? For some of the smaller Hawaiian Islands, Doomsday happened quite a while ago—the islands of Lana'i and Ni'ihau, for example, do not even physically resemble the islands they once were, having been plowed, planted, overgrazed, and generally blighted, the haunt of immigrant animals and restless humans. The once-pretty uninhabited (and sacred to Hawaiians) island of Kahoolawe, just off Maui, has for fifty years been a target for bombing practice by the U.S. military; although bombing has now ended, the island is off-limits because of the danger of unexploded bombs lying all over. One end of Johnston Island in the Hawaiian chain is a depot for toxic waste, the other end is radioactive because of a nuclear accident.

Most people go to Waikiki. One in ten of them is a victim of crime, according to a statistic released by the Honolulu Police Department. The sidewalks in Waikiki are heaving with prostitutes and their pimps. In the middle of Waikiki, smack on the beach, is the ugliest and most pointless American Army installation imaginable—Fort De Russy, an eyesore the Defense Department refuses to remove. Much of the sand on Waikiki is trucked in from elsewhere and dumped. Dangerously high bacteria levels exist at the eastern end of Waikiki, near the zoo, because of monkey shit being flushed directly into the sea.

Three of America's billionaires and numerous millionaires live in Honolulu, but even the wealthiest people have to contend with Honolulu's plagues—rats and cockroaches. No house is free of them— you hear the rats squeaking and quarrelling just below the windows, or sometimes nimbly flashing up the trunk of a tree—and it is one of the realities of Honolulu life that once a month Rat Patrol will visit and set out bait and remove corpses. Pest control is one of Honolulu's growth industries and, because of the fastidious nature of the city's inhabitants, includes exterminating unwanted birds and bees.

Now and then, in the belief that the artist Christo is at work in Hawaii, tourists excitedly point to a large house or a church or a tall building entirely swaddled in a billowing blue tent—these dwellings under great soft buntings are among the strangest sights on the island. But no, they are not the wrapped-up creations of Christo, it is only the fumigator at work, his last desperate measure, zipping up and tenting the house in order to kill every live thing.

This same fastidiousness extends to the city's attitude towards strip clubs and prostitutes. In the Narcotics and Vice Division of the Honolulu Police Department there is something called Morals Detail. Essentially, this is a posse of undercover policemen who work at night either in Chinatown or in the streets around Waikiki, the male cops hoping to be propositioned by hookers, the female cops hoping to be importuned by a so-called john. There is no law against loitering, and under the city's new "John Law" a person cannot be arrested unless a deal has been made—but both the man and the woman can be collared.

It all sounded very strict to me until one night I went to Waikiki and examined the matter firsthand. Except for a glimpse I had had of whores braying at passing cars from the sidewalks of Kings Cross in Sydney, and *Meestah Boll, you wanna gull?* at night in the Trobriands, this was my first experience of vice in Oceania. Kuhio Avenue was busy in the early evening, but towards midnight there were about equal numbers of tourists, prostitutes, and policemen, each category in an unmistakable uniform, whether it was an aloha shirt, a tight skirt and high heels, or a blue suit. And here and there, up and down the avenue, all three were sharing the same slab of sidewalk.

Even without the tight skirts the prostitutes would have been highly visible. There is something in their alertness, the way their gaze travels from man to man, and their overbusy walk.

"They walk like they're not going anywhere," Bill said. "That's what Lieutenant Lum told me."

I had arranged to meet Bill in Waikiki. He was writing an article about prostitution for *Honolulu* magazine and had interviewed a woman who had been arrested for soliciting. He had gone to her trial ($100 for the first offense, $500 for the second). He knew about an older woman, a Baptist preacher they called "The Condom Lady," who had made it her mission to hand out free contraceptives to the streetwalkers. He had made friends with some of the people on Morals Detail.

We watched the prostitutes, who usually seemed to travel in twos, strutting and twitching like herons. They took no notice of us, we were invisible to them, and every now and then they would stiffen and make a beeline for the men behind us—Japanese. On Koa Street, where many girls lurked, a pair of girls pushed past us and pounced on two Japanese, and if you happened to be of a sensitive turn of mind you could find something awfully depressing about the girls ignoring us in favor of two callow sauntering youths in baggy shorts and T-shirts.

After a while, Bill spoke with a girl in a tiny orange skirt, but it was a brief conversation. The girl hurried away from him.

"I told her I was from *Honolulu* magazine and she just took off," he said.

"I don't think these girls want to get their names in your magazine."

"Sometimes saying you're a reporter opens a lot of doors," Bill said.

"Not whorehouse doors."

"I guess not."

Walking past me a skinny girl in a skintight dress said, "You want a date?"

"How much?"

"A hundred dollars."

"I'm not Japanese, you know."

The girl laughed—and all her youth was in her laugh, she could hardly have been more than sixteen.

"If you were Japanese I'd charge you double that!"

"So I give you a hundred bucks, and then what happens?"

"We go to my hotel. It's the Holiday Surf, just down there. And you have a great time—"

But the instant she saw me vacillating she walked away. Hustling was the perfect word for this activity.

"There's one wearing a beeper," Bill said. "That's for escort calls, a hotel job. The pimps have beepers, too."

The pimps were much in evidence. The beeper was only one point of identification. Pimps were also stylishly dressed, and they carried leather handbags in which, you gathered, a lot of money was stuffed. Most of the pimps were young black men who walked with a kind of menacing confidence.

"When I started I wanted this to be a real upbeat American story about free enterprise," Bill said. "But it's depressing. These pimps meet girls in Canada or wherever and say they love them. The typical girl is a runaway. She's been sexually abused as a child. The pimp says he loves her. They come to Honolulu. Then after a week he puts her on the street. It's exploitation, coercion, abuse, and disappointment. I'm real unhappy about that."

In the absence of a heavy mob in Honolulu, rackets like gambling and prostitution are a free-for-all. The Japanese mobs, the *Yamaguchi Gumi,* and the *Yakuza,* are involved in other long-term investments, like real estate and building contracts. This leaves vice somewhat unorganized and even amateurish, and the pimps are very obvious dudes—all *olopops* are in Honolulu—as though they rather like playing the role of superfly, bobbing between the pair of whores they are currently running.

A pale girl, standing by a lighted doorway, handed us a bilingual (English-Japanese) leaflet reading *Foxy Lady! Girls! Girls! Girls!* and invited us upstairs.

"What have you got for us?" Bill asked.

"Naked girls who love to party."

"Will they sit with us?" Bill asked. He was trying to find out the varieties of sexual experience, for his article. What would they do? How far would they go? What would it cost?

The girl in the doorway began to frown.

"Wanna tip?" she said. "Wanna get laid?"

Bill was smiling through his big beard.

"Crawl up a chicken's ass and wait," the girl said, turning her back on him. "You'll get laid."

"What are you writing?" Bill asked me, but he knew. "My magazine won't print that. I can't put it in my piece. Rats."

"Then I'll put it in mine," I said.

We went to Chinatown, in a corner of Downtown; what had seemed amateurish and depressing in Waikiki looked dirty and dangerous here. "That there's a safe bar," a prostitute called out to us, pointing to a doorway. She accurately saw that we were simply passing through. "The rest of them are bad." There were no cars. Lining the streets were ragged, muttering men and bad-tempered women. The only people smiling were the *mahus,* obvious transvestites, who regard Hotel Street and Mauna Kea Street in Chinatown as their natural habitat. They walk the streets, not going anywhere, waiting for a passing car to pick them up—and they might well be politicians or tycoons living their secret lives. Many scandalous stories originate in Honolulu's Chinatown—and that includes Maugham's story of Sadie Thompson, who began her career here and ended up in Samoa.

"This was going to be a great story," Bill said, surveying the dereliction of Chinatown. "Maybe even funny. But it's not. A whore got stabbed to death in that parking lot last week by a soldier. It's depressing."

On another night, still in search of Honolulu, I went to clubs and I remembered what Bill had said of the hookers—you expect hilarity, you look around, you end up depressed.

There are Japanese clubs, very sedate, where each patron keeps a bottle of Chivas Regal with his name on it behind the bar, the carry-over of a practice common in Japan. At these clubs, which are no more than dimly lit rooms, neatly dressed Japanese hostesses join rowdy Japanese men and smile and act submissive while the men, becoming drunker, grope them. It is all chilly and sexless and overpriced, but the massive number of new Japanese have made it a booming business. So much for the Club Tomo, and Mugen, and the others.

Apart from The Club Mirage, which was empty—perhaps this name was a deliberate joke?—the other clubs were a little livelier. Club Cheri had one naked girl doing knee bends on a table. In Club Top-Gun three overdressed Japanese men screamed songs into a *karaoake* mike in front of a television set, and in Club Hachi Hachi one man was doing that. In the Butterfly Lounge young soldiers heckled a fattish dancer, and in Exotic Nights and Club Turtle, naked dusky girls posed on a small stage for sweaty men in baseball hats, who were encouraged to buy beer at five dollars a bottle.

Saigon Passion had a successful theme: the last days of the Vietnam War. It was soldiers from Schofield and Vietnamese hostesses, dressed casually, in jeans and T-shirts, and lots of army memorabilia. It was one of the few clubs that held my attention, because the music and the faces made it seem such an atmospheric time warp. A young girl sat with me—Ruby, from Saigon, lived with her mother in Waipahu, and was about twenty or so. I began asking her questions until finally she fell silent. Then I prodded her.

"You undercover?"

"No. Of course not. I'm not a policeman."

"I think you undercover."

"Why do you think so?"

"Questions. Questions."

I went to the Carnation Lounge, to The Misty II Lounge, Kita Lounge, Les Girls, Club Rose, and Club Femme Nu. There were twenty within a three-block area. Some were run by Vietnamese women, most were run by Korean women—because of this, their generic name in Honolulu was "Korean bars."

At one time they had been famous for the tricks women performed in them—one club was put on the map because a woman in it picked up coins with the skillful manipulation of her vulva, another boasted a woman who inserted a cigar between her labia, and puffed it (men crowded near to see the tip of the cigar brighten), and that same woman could play a clarinet in a similar way. There was a club where a woman stood behind a transparent shower curtain while men groped her (introducing another sort of club in Honolulu, the "feelie bar"), and there was one on Keeaumoku (known as "Korea-Moku" because of the nationality of the proprietors) where an agile woman came onstage, leaned back, parted her legs, and expelled Ping-Pong balls from the depths of her vaginal cavern—and the balls, still warm and damp, were fought over and clutched by grateful men.

This last example at conjuring had been popular at a club called the Stop-Light, but the place had since changed hands, it was now called the Rock-Za, and in its way it was typical: loud music, expensive drinks, naked girls. The bouncer, John—an enormous Samoan, from Pago Pago—said it was a gold mine. It was his job to prevent patrons from touching girls.

"They get one warning, and the next time out they go," John said.

But he was ambivalent about the honor of the performers. He said the girls were spoiled and overpaid. Now and then a Japanese tour bus would stop and sixty or eighty tourists would pile into the bar—aged men, old crones, couples, honeymooners—and they would sit, have a few expensive drinks, and would marvel at the big white women displaying themselves stark naked at very close range.

Men—all sorts—sat on low stools, with their elbows on a twenty-foot table. The young women, posturing more than dancing, struck poses and squatted. I sat a while, watching everything. And what seemed at first like a fantasy realized, a centerfold coming to life, turned into a raucous gynecology class, in which proximity was everything. There was a certain amount of comedy in that.

People say, *You have to see this,* and they think you'll see exactly what they do. I went, trying to be open-minded, but my reaction to these clubs (after I had a little time to reflect on it) was quite different. The clubs were so ritualized I came to see them as temples in a pagan rite, in which the women were priestesses, like the women in ancient Babylon who whored in the temple of the goddess Ishtar.

There was something undeniably strange and solemn and even somewhat religious in the fervor of the men who sat like intense votaries waiting for a woman to come near. The man's patience, the woman's confident movements, edging nearer and nearer on the altarlike table, squatting, opening her legs very wide, her thighs enclosing the man's head, and the man staring hard in a frenzy of concentration as though a mystery were being revealed to him that he must memorize. It was public, and yet highly personal—only the chosen man could see clearly. There was as much veneration in this man's goggling at a woman's everted private parts as you would find in most church services. The man slipped a dollar or more into the woman's garter, and she lingered, and the man stared straight on, serious and unsmiling in his own private vision. From this sort of ardent behavior, it was a very short step to the Hindu worship of lingams and yonis, or to the cultism of the *komari,* the vulvas carved in stone all over Rapa Nui.

Still, it was easy to forget in the flux of Honolulu that I was in Oceania. Sometimes O'ahu seemed an offshore island of America, sometimes of Asia. Yet it was the only real crossroads in the Pacific, the junction of every air route, and in many senses the heart of Polynesia. This was noticeable in trivial ways—when Walt Disney World in Florida looked for performers for their "Polynesian Luau Revue" ("One-year contracts with relocation will be offered . . ."), they auditioned in Honolulu; whenever a serious piece of Pacific scholarship was undertaken it was invariably under the auspices of the Bishop Museum or the University of Hawaii or the East-West Center, or more significantly the Mormon church, passionate about converting the whole of Polynesia to Mormonism, and which had its Pacific headquarters, as well as its banks, on O'ahu.

Whenever I inquired about an archaeological ruin in Polynesia I was told that it had been catalogued, or studied, or excavated, or written about by one man, Professor Yoshiko Sinoto, the senior anthropologist at the Bishop Museum in Honolulu and one of the world's authorities on the Eastern Pacific cultures. *Ask Sinoto,* was the reply I got to most of my Polynesia questions.

The professor is diminutive but muscular, and from his strong accent and his bearing obviously not local. Clearly an academic, but with the restlessness and vigor of someone used to working outdoors, he inhabited a small, cluttered office at the back of the museum. On the walls of his office were charts and photos of sites, stacks of files and artifacts—bone fishhooks, stone implements.

I went to see him one afternoon, simply to put my *Ask Sinoto* questions to him. He said he had been to the Marquesas recently, and we chatted about the ludicrous necessity for having to drink imported mineral water on these islands of waterfalls and freshwater lakes.

"It is the case all over French Polynesia," Professor Sinoto said. "I was working on a dig in Huahine. While I was there, the mayor of Huahine got a grant of money. He used this money to pave one road, he built a television station, he put streetlights in the town. But he did not spend any money at all to provide drinking water. Can you imagine?"

I asked him about the great number of bouldery ruins I had seen in the Marquesas.

"Every valley in the Marquesas is full of sites," the professor said. "Yet when the first surface survey was done in 1918–19 they thought there was nothing left—no wooden implements, nothing but stones. They thought that the weather was so hot and the climate so difficult and damp that only stone structures could survive. Real excavations were carried out by Robert Suggs in 1956 and '57. I disagreed with his conclusions. I went with Thor Heyerdahl's group in 1963."

"And what did you think of his conclusions?"

"He reached his own conclusions," the professor said, tactfully. "As for me, I am convinced that the Marquesas were the dispersal point for Eastern Polynesia. The migration and settlement was very rapid. The canoes seem to have come from the Admiralty Islands"—in northeast New Guinea—"around one thousand B.C., and they found Samoa, Tonga, and Fiji. They stayed in those islands, and by staying they developed Polynesian culture."

"That's the point, isn't it? That they became more Polynesian by living on their islands and not venturing farther," I said. "But why didn't they go on navigating and sailing? Is it possible that they lost their nerve, or lost their technology and had to reinvent it?"

"Yes. Possible. They stopped making pottery in three hundred to five hundred—there was no pottery in Hawaii. We have not found even one shard. They sailed to the Marquesas in about three hundred, probably from Samoa. From there they dispersed. Heyerdahl said that the South Americans brought the sweet potato to the Pacific, but I disagree. It is much more likely that the Marquesans sailed to South America and brought it back."

"But the canoes would have been sailing very close to the wind—and is that voyage possible?"

Professor Sinoto was hypothesizing a voyage that went in the opposite direction from that of the *Kon-Tiki.*

"Many canoes must have set sail. A lucky canoe reached Easter Island and later found its way back," the professor said. "I was on Easter Island just a few years ago and met a man who told me a story of how he had sailed away in a small canoe with two boys. They brought a big bunch of bananas and twenty gallons of water. He reached the Tuamotus after three weeks or so, and there he stayed for ten years."

I had heard a similar story on Easter Island, about this same man who had sailed to the Tuamotus.

"Other people might have been put into canoes with some food and deported—the chief ordering them away," the professor said, describing how the voyagers might have been banished.

"What about migrants being refugees from tribal wars?"

"Yes. After about 1500 there were many tribal wars in the Marquesas, one valley against another, or one island against another. The choice was whether to stay in the valley and fight—or else leave. I excavated many fortifications and found many sling stones. The people were very accurate in throwing the sling stones—they could throw them two hundred feet or more. Missionaries have written how the people always had bumps on their head from the fighting."

"So they lived in small groups?"

"They isolated themselves," he said. "I am very interested in fishhooks. I have found that as the time passed the fishhooks grew smaller. They were catching smaller and smaller fish. They didn't want to go out so far—perhaps they were afraid of the sea, or else of their enemies. They stayed nearer to the shore."

He showed me a set of fishhooks diminishing in size.

"The Little Ice Age was another factor that isolated the people," he said. "And as you say, these cultures always developed after they were isolated. The Little Ice Age was between fourteen hundred and fifteen hundred. There was a colder climate and rougher seas, so the people tended to stay on their islands in this period. That produced local culture. All the Marquesan tikis are post-fifteen hundred, for example."

"I am planning to go paddling along the Na Pali Coast of Kaua'i," I said. "Is it true that the Marquesans sailed there and brought their stonework and techniques of building?"

"Hawaii was settled between five hundred and seven hundred, by Marquesans," he said. "You will see in Nualolo Vai—which I excavated, by the way—the people worked with much smaller stones than in the Marquesas, where the stones are very big."

"Why do you suppose they set sail for Hawaii?" I asked. "I mean apart from the tribal wars and the famines that forced them out to sea?"

"It is a good question, considering the distance," he said. "But when I was in the Marquesas some years ago I remember seeing migratory birds arrive—first two or three, then fifteen or twenty. And then many, many birds. I am a scientist, but I am also somewhat romantic, and I began to imagine the people saying, 'Look at those birds! Where do those birds come from? Let's go!' "

"Have you found any evidence of cannibalism in your digging?"

"I once found fifty skulls on a Marquesan site. In some places people say, 'Don't touch the skulls.' But in the Marquesas the people say, 'You want these skulls? Take them.' "

This question of cannibalism animated him. He rose from his chair and began to describe other circumstantial evidence.

"I would sometimes be digging and find—mixed together—dog bones, pig bones, and human bones, all thrown into the same garbage pit, as though they had just been eaten. Why else mix human bones with pig bones?" he said. "There was human sacrifice everywhere in Polynesia—for big events, to bring rain because of a drought, or for whatever reason."

"What is the most Polynesian island in the Pacific—the most traditional?"

"Polynesia is gone," he said. "Western Samoa is probably the most traditional place, and perhaps Tonga. The Solomons and the New Hebrides are also traditional. But even so it is spoiled in those places. Fiji and Tonga still have chiefs."

This tallied with my amateur observations: the graceful huts of Savaii, the nobles and commoners of Tonga, the egg fields of Savo, the cross-faced tribes and muddy buttocks on the island of Tanna.

"But I remember Atiu," the professor said, speaking of a small island in the Cook Group, not far from Aitutaki, where I had paddled. "I was working there and as recently as 1984 Atiu was totally traditional. Everything was intact. I returned for several years, and then in 1989 the culture was gone. It was finished, just like that. How did it happen so quickly? You know what caused it? The video. I don't know why the government doesn't regulate videos. They are terrible. Rape. War. Violence. Drinking. They give bad ideas to young people, and they destroyed the culture in Atiu, which had lasted for over a thousand years."

Then he began to talk about his dig in Huahine, how he had worked on the lovely island for twenty years—the uniqueness of the place, with aquaculture in the lagoon, and farming beyond it, and the chiefs living along the shoreline. He had uncovered thirty-five sites behind the lagoon, one of the richest archaeological finds in Polynesia.

"But what do my fellow countrymen do?" Professor Sinoto said. "Some Japanese businessmen want to buy this whole end of Huahine. They want to put up three large hotels and use the lagoon for swimming and waterskiing. They want to put up an airport and have three jumbo jets a week from Tokyo."

It was wonderful to hear a Japanese person becoming indignant over the acquisition and exploitation of Pacific islands. For once, I could shut my mouth and listen to someone echo my sentiments.

"The Japanese are looking for playgrounds in the Pacific," the professor said, barely controlling his fury. "What kind of benefit will this bring to the locals? They hire a few people to work in the hotels for the lowest wages. The first big hotel on Huahine was the Hotel Bali Hai. Local people became drunk in the bar. Because of their drinking they needed money. They began to steal money from the bungalows. When I heard that the Japanese were planning to buy this area I hoped they would be turned down. Their application was temporarily denied. After that, I saw someone in the government and said, 'We must preserve this area,' and he helped arrange it. So it might not happen in Huahine, but it has happened in many other places."

He let this sink in. We sat among the artifacts, in front of a great chart with arrows showing the ancient migration routes in Oceania.

Professor Sinoto said, "Everyone is looking for playgrounds in the Pacific."

Chapter 24
KAUA'I: FOLLOWING THE DOLPHINS ON THE NA PALI COAST

There are distinct seasons for everything in the Pacific, though this is not always so obvious to the tourist on dry land. Look at all the people lounging on the beach in Hawaii, remarking on the balmy weather, the wonderful hotels, the funky music, the ya-yas at the local clubs, the great food. They haven't the faintest idea what month it is, because paradise hasn't got a calendar, or seasons. *Aloha,* they say to each other, and after a while they learn to say *Mahalo* (thank you).

They bandy these two words all over the place, and some people laugh at them for it, but why? It is rare—almost unheard of—to find anyone who speaks Hawaiian in complete sentences. This is tragic, because when the Hawaiians lost their language—when it was debased and bowdlerized by missionary literalism—they lost their identity. The movement for reviving the old language, which is melodious and highly metaphorical, is (like the movement for sovereignty) still struggling. What you hear in normal speech is jargon, conversational color, a matter of vocabulary, of knowing twenty or thirty words and scattering them in your English sentences.

The more Hawaiian words you know the more easily you can pull rank. It is exactly what missionaries do in simple societies to ingratiate themselves. In Hawaii this manner of speaking comprises a local idiolect, or lingo, in which every hole is referred to as a *puka,* and all talk as *namu,* and every toilet as a *lua,* and all children as *keikis,* and so forth. Directions are full of Hawaiian jargon—seaward is *makai,* towards the mountains is *mauka,* and west is *ewa.* Like Hawaiian Pidgin, with which it shares many words, it is often used jokingly. Of course, there are words which only native-born Hawaiians know, but they keep them to themselves: Why give everything away?

This lingo has a certain charm, though no one forms sentences. No one ever says "Hello, how are you?" in the language, and when I asked some old-timers, who would have called themselves *kamaainas,* they couldn't tell me that the simple greeting was *Aloha kakou. Pehea'oe.* Hawaiian is used simply to gain credibility. In Africa it has an exact counterpart in so-called kitchen Swahili.

Travel writers in Hawaii interlard their prose with this island jargon to give it verisimilitude. Travel writers in Hawaii write about the room service at the hotels, and the efficiency of the valet parking, and whether the hollandaise on the eggs Benedict has curdled. Brunch is quite an important subject for the travel writer. So is golf. So is tennis. They are mainly junketers, people on press trips; and they often travel with their spouses—one scribbles, the other snaps pictures—making travel writing one of the last mom-and-pop businesses in America. I thought of such people when I was in my campsite at Vava'u, or paddling in the Trobriands, or squatting on the beach in the Solomons, or sheltering from the driving rain in a ratty cave on the west coast of Rapa Nui.

"I'm a travel writer, too," one named Ted said to me on Kaua'i. "I'm here covering some hotels. I'm covering some restaurants, too. Pacific Cafe? It's Pacific Rim cuisine. We're at the Waiohai here. My wife Binky is with me—we always travel together. She's an astrologer. Have you stayed in the bungalows at Mauna Lani? We had three nights there. I'm covering it for a paper back home. We mainly do upscale hotels. Last time I was here I was covering the block party at Waikiki. It was kind of fun."

I asked Binky to tell my fortune.

"I couldn't read your stars unless I had lots of astral information," Binky said. "I do a little writing myself. I like the hotels. But it's funny about Hawaiian hotels. Some of them serve only American wine. And I can only drink French wine. I love Cristal. They made us feel very welcome at the Four Seasons in Maui. They gave me a gold pendant and Ted got a fabulous shirt from the logo shop. They hydrated our faces with Evian atomizers as we lounged by the pool. My real favorite place is St. Bart's. Ever been there? I love French food."

I was proud of being a travel writer in Oceania. I stopped seeing it as a horrid preoccupation that I practiced only with my left hand. But when I got to Hawaii I changed my mind. I was not sure what I did for a living or who I was, but I was absolutely sure I was not a travel writer.

As a matter of fact, travel writers seldom wrote about the seas that lap Hawaii. The Pacific was something they squinted at over the rim of their pineapple daiquiris. They gushed about the waves breaking on the reef, but apart from that water sports are not a frequent subject for travel writers. The proof of this was their love of surf. And yet boat owners are never so sentimental about surf, which is like a vision of death and destruction.

Boating in Hawaii's waters can be rather uncongenial. Just offshore, prevailing conditions are unpredictable much of the time, and fierce (and of course prettiest) in winter months—frothy seas, stiff winds, and strong currents. The sailor with a problem looks onshore and sees a rocky coast or a reef, heavy surf, or one of the great horrors for anyone in a small boat—surfers having a wonderful time.

"It's not too great when you see surfers," Rick Haviland told me in Kaua'i. He was a master of understatement. "That's kind of a bad jelly-fish," he said one day of a Portuguese man-of-war, and "Kind of neat" always meant breathtaking. Rick was in the kayak and bike business, rentals and sales, and as a former surfer he confided to me that the presence of surfers always means high waves and the worst conditions for the rest of us. It was Rick who gave me a crash course on Kaua'i's sea conditions, and it was Rick whom I successfully bullied into accompany-ing me on an off-season jaunt down the coast, which has the most beauti-ful cliffs in the Pacific.

If you try to paddle a kayak in the wrong season off the glorious and almost inaccessible Na Pali Coast of Kaua'i you can get into deep trou-ble—no one does much paddling between October and April, though some of the tour boats run throughout the winter. I was apprehensive, because it was November and I was looking for a window of good weather to make the trip paddling my own little boat. I had a special reason for wanting a closer look at Kaua'i, because I had traveled in the Marquesas in French Polynesia. There is a great cultural connection between those two places.

Of course there are connections and relationships all over the Pacific—words spoken in Tahiti are also spoken in New Zealand and Samoa, food items and cooking methods are shared in island groups thousands of miles apart, and so are dances and deities. It seems at times—and it is often argued—that this enormous body of water is a single oceanic family of like-minded people with a common culture.

But, as Professor Sinoto had said, one of the closest connections that exists is between the Marquesas and the Hawaiian islands. In fact, the Hawaiians are the descendants of the Marquesans who sailed to Hawaii and settled there sometime around A.D. 700. But it is generally reckoned that the last place in the Pacific to be settled was here, on the almost inaccessible Na Pali Coast. They could not have chosen a more appropri-ate place. Nuku Hiva in the Marquesas and Kaua'i in Hawaii might be neighbor islands: They look similar, with volcanic mountains shaped like witches' hats and vegetation as dense and dark green as spinach, the same deep valleys, the same furrows of cold lava flows. Their ancient ruins—patterns of boulders, rock platforms, and walls and petroglyphs—are almost identical, and they are just as dangerous to anyone who travels offshore in their peculiarly tricky waters.

"I guess we should kind of angle out here," Rick murmured, looking up at the surf as we set off in our kayaks from Haena Beach Park near where the Na Pali begins. To the right were surfers frolicking in the ten-foot breaking waves of "Tunnels," a well-known surfers' spot; to the left was a reef and more waves nearer shore—another version of sudden death.

I followed him; I liked his mellow mood, the way he relaxed and rode the waves. The happiest campers are imperturbable. So what if the wind was blowing fifteen knots or more? At least it was at our back, helping us along in a big following sea. The outlook was good, but so what if the weather turned foul? We had camping equipment, we had food and water, we had survival gear, we even had a quart of margaritas.

We paddled on, past the first of the cliffs—Na Pali means "The Cliffs"—a corner of the coast, which was the place where Hawaii's best-known deity, Pele (goddess of the volcanoes), fell in love with a mortal, the chief Lohiau. It is a hidden and in many respects a spiritual coast, full of *mana;* a place of temples and burial grounds—a holy coast. This coast and much of Kaua'i is a byword for the exotic. It is the source of many Hawaiian legends, ancient and modern, as well as some of our own sweetest myths: Just above us, the Makana Ridge was the location of Bali Hai, in the movie *South Pacific;* a bit farther on, Honopu Valley was seen by millions as the home of King Kong, and across the mountains the opening of *Raiders of the Lost Ark* was shot, and farther along the coast Elvis Presley fooled with Ann-Margret in *Blue Hawaii.* Talk about legends!

An eight-foot swell with a strong push to it ("Kind of a surge—feel it?") was dragging us sideways towards the first of the deep Na Pali valleys. This one was Hanakapiai, with a small but lovely beach, which is swept away each year by the powerful winter seas and then is piled up again in the spring and summer. The footpath passes here and then continues on to about a third of the length of this coast, the eleven-mile Kalalau Trail. It is only for the strongest hikers, but is well known among outdoor people as one of the most scenic in the world.

The rocky cliff face a bit farther along was being battered by waves, and these reflected waves smashing against oncoming ones created a choppy sea and a phenomenon called clapotis—vertical standing waves—which were making me seasick. I had never felt pukesome in a kayak before but, bobbing like cork in this chaotic chop, I felt distinctly nauseous.

Coincidentally it was lunchtime, but paddling out a mile in the wind and streaming sea I was able to settle my stomach. Rick and I divided up our lunch and, eating it—a sandwich, an apple, a bottle of water—we drifted apart, and there we stayed, for an hour or two.

There is a mystical element in paddling a kayak which might be described as the trance induced by the rhythm of paddling, lifting, and stroking continuously and gliding along. The paddler concentrates, and falls silent, and without fanfare but with a relentless steadiness goes forward, rising and falling in the waves. It is an effort, of course, but because of this trance the effort is almost unnoticeable. I suppose hikers and joggers must enter that same state of mind, because it becomes a very peaceful and healthful way of breathing, and here it was intensified by the beauty of Na Pali, with its long narrow fluted valleys, and cliff rims rising to 4,000 feet.

This spell is hard but not impossible to break. In my case it was shattered by the bite of a poisonous jellyfish. In my paddling trance I had spooned up the tentacles of a floating Portuguese man-of-war, and one tentacle—a long gelatinous noodle—slipped down the shaft of my paddle and flipped around my forearm. The pain was almost immediate: The poison is a neurotoxin, attacking the nerves the way the jellyfish immobilizes its prey. My arm was fiercely stung as I plucked off the tentacle, and then I summoned Rick.

He reminded me gently that the folk remedy is urine. I had tried that without any success in Vanuatu. Papaya leaves or meat tenderizer would have been more effective, and would have spared me three hours of numbing agony.

But the spectacular landscape eased the pain—it had that capacity to bewitch. They were not simple ledges, but rather a multitude of sharp green pinnacles all over the face of the cliff. The whole mountainside had the look of a gothic church in a fantasy—hundreds of steeples and cupolas. Even with my stinging arm in this choppy sea, I felt that I would rather be here among the cathedral-like contours of the cliffs on this high island than seeing its architectural equivalent in Europe—and I knew that the next time I saw Westminster Abbey or Notre Dame I would be instantly reminded of the soaring Na Pali Coast and miss it terribly.

The ancient Hawaiians must have known how strange and magical these pinnacles seemed for, down to the last green cone, they called the whole lot of them keiki o ka 'aina, "children of the land," and gave each one a different name.

We passed "a flower-throttled gorge, with beetling cliffs and crags, from which floated the blattings of wild goats. On three sides the grim walls rose, festooned in fantastic draperies of tropic vegetation and pierced by cave entrances." This is Jack London's description of the Kalalau Valley and beach, which is the setting for his powerful story "Koolau the Leper" (and it is true in most of its details). This valley is as far as anyone can get on foot. The rest of the coast is reachable only by the various tour boats, big and small, which trundle back and forth. And there are helicopters buzzing on high—dipping into the valleys, hovering over the cliffs. Two today were passing the lovely stone arch at the mouth of Honopu Valley, the so-called "Valley of the Lost Tribe," where a pre-Hawaiian people (their origin is the subject of archaeological dispute) flourished.

Opinion is divided on the choppers of Kaua'i. Except for the operators themselves, most people on Kaua'i would like to see them vanish into the sunset. But there is no question that the chopper, the most versatile of aircraft, offers an unusual way of seeing the Na Pali Coast. They are numerous and intrusive and noisy, but their worst fault is not the noise pollution to others but the way they deafen their own passengers—the sound of the rotors drowns out the wind whistling through the valleys, the water music of mountain cataracts, the crashing of the waves against the sea cliffs; and it gives the false impression that this hidden coast is easily accessible.

"They're kind of a pain," Rick said. This was as close as he ever came to stating his anger, but modest as these words seemed they represented for him blind fury. "I don't want to think about them."

On some days, Zodiacs—huge rubber dinghies—took tourists along the coast, splashing back and forth, mercilessly wetting the passengers and giving them the impression they were on a do-or-die expedition. But the Zodiacs, though noisy and just as intrusive as the choppers, are very safe. If you listen carefully to one boatman talking to another you might hear the following exchange.

"How many burgers you had today?"

"Twenty-three burgers this morning, eighteen this afternoon."

"Lenny had thirty-some-odd burgers all week."

It was their way of referring to boat passengers, and although it was utterly dismissive, there was something horribly appropriate in calling a big sunburned tourist a "burger."

We passed Awaawapuhi Valley, the narrowest and most dramatic of the valleys and where, on the tight strip of the valley floor, there had been an extensive old Hawaiian settlement.

There was also once a large settlement of Hawaiians living in a traditional way at the next valley, Nualolo Aina. In fact, so hidden was this valley that the people remained as they had been for centuries, living undisturbed into the early twentieth century. They were *alii*, or nobles, in the valley, and just outside it, a shoreside village called Nualolo Kai was inhabited by commoners. The foundations of the dancing pavilions, the houses and temples, garden walls, and many other structures—excavated and catalogued by Sinoto—still remain, inside and outside the valley. We returned to them the following day and I was astonished by how closely they resembled the ones I had seen 2,000 miles away in the Marquesas.

Under the cliffs, which were like black turrets, we made for the valley of Miloli'i. Off in the distance the sun was setting behind the privately owned island of Ni'ihau and its neighbor, the little lumpy volcano of Lehua. We were paddling in a headwind. I hate headwinds. I had thought that everyone hated headwinds.

Rick said, "It kind of cools you," and paddled uncomplainingly onward.

That night we camped on the sand of Miloli'i—baked potatoes and grilled fish over an open fire. Afterwards we talked for a while, and then Rick crept down the beach.

I sat by the fire, stirring the coals and feeling drowsy. I had had some happy times paddling through the Pacific, but their origin had been sights and sounds. I had not experienced much comfort. The hardship had been necessary to the discoveries I'd made. But this was different, this was one of the most pleasant interludes in my trip. It was luxury—the meal, the fire, the night air, and most of all my fatigue, which was like the voluptuous effect of an expensive drug. I loved being numb, utterly senseless, and sitting there dead tired on the soft sand, and then simply easing myself down onto my sleeping bag, and subsiding.

It was a magic, memorable slumber. I slept under a full moon that was as bright as an arc light. All night the surf dumped and slid on the steeply shelving sand. In the early hours of the morning I was wakened by something tickling my nose—a fat and overambitious ghost crab perplexed by the task of eating my face, or perhaps wondering how to drag me into its hole in the sand. I slapped the thing away and went back to sleep.

I had thought that nothing could equal the thrill of those cliffs seen from a kayak. I was wrong, for the next day we headed back to Nualolo Kai to look at ruins; we saw some splashing out at sea—probably dolphins—and we headed in that direction. I was totally unprepared for what we were about to see—dolphins, in every direction, dolphins. There were sixty or seventy of them, a variety called spinners, four or five feet long, and some babies. They were jumping clear of the water, swimming upside down, frolicking in groups, and swimming in a vast irregular circle about a quarter of a mile in diameter. And they were gasping. I had always seen dolphins from a bigger noisier craft, so I had not known anything about the sounds they make—how they breathe and sigh and blow. Every time they break the surface they gasp, like a swimmer sucking air, and hearing this laboring breath, which is the most affecting and lovable human noise, I was struck by how much we miss when we can't hear the creature we are looking at.

"Kind of neat," Rick said.

Even the experienced guide was amazed. He had been down this coast hundreds of times and he had never seen anything like it, he said. For the next hour and a half we played with them, paddling among them, and they performed for us. We made no sound, we posed no threat, we merely watched appreciatively—and they seemed to realize that.

After this, who wouldn't paddle into Nualolo Kai, and put ashore, and walk to the great *heiau,* or temple, against the cliff face and leave an offering? We wrapped round stones in freshly plucked *ti* leaves, and placed them on the wall with a wish that we would have a safe trip and would return.

At the end of the trip, riding the surf into Polihale, I was very happy, with the pure joy that comes to the traveler whose efforts are rewarded— in my case handsomely, with the sight of those cliffs and ruins, and the antics of those dolphins. Our little boats had given us the greatest freedom. The Hawaiians had always known that simple fact. And it was as true of the dead as it was of the living. In the cliffs above the broad white sand of Polihale hundreds, perhaps thousands, of corpses had been found, and the luckiest—the most noble—had been buried in their canoes, like the greatest Vikings in the bogs and burial places of England.

Chapter 25
NI'IHAU AND LANA'I: SOME MEN
ARE ISLANDS

"What you see ahead is Ni'ihau, the Forbidden Island," the chopper pilot said, as his flying machine went *quack-quack-quack* across the seventeen miles of channel that separated this small arid place from the friendly green island of Kaua'i.

"We'll be landing pretty soon," he went on, "but I just want you to know that I can't show you any of the people, we can't enter the village—you won't even be able to see it, I'm afraid. In fact, most of the island is off-limits, and it has been for over a hundred years."

And then he steered us south, through the clear Hawaiian air, into the nineteenth century.

Hawaii is full of marvels, but one of the strangest aspects of this chain of eighteen islands is that two of them are private property, and neither of them is owned by an ethnic Hawaiian. Some characters in literature also have private islands: They take possession of islands in much the same spirit that they head into exile—in Shakespeare's *The Tempest*, Prospero does both. Usually, a person seeking an island craves simplicity and glories in a world that is still incomplete, and therefore full of possibilities. Anything can happen on an island—guilt can be expiated *(Robinson Crusoe)*, the forces of good and evil can emerge in the breasts of castaways *(Lord of the Flies)*, love can be discovered *(The Blue Lagoon)*, so can a great fortune *(Treasure Island)* or a true paradise *(Typee)*, or a kind of hell (Conrad's *Victory*); it can be the setting for a great departure (the Nantucket of *Moby Dick*), or for the oddest landfalls on earth *(Gulliver's Travels)*. It is impossible to imagine these episodes unfolding on the mainland.

The common denominator is not the landscape of the island, nor its location on the globe, but rather the fact of a place being surrounded by water—the character of the water itself is the magic element, offering the islander transformation. The water, seemingly nothing, is everything—a moat, a barrier, a wilderness, the source of food and hope, the way out. The ocean—as any true seagoing person will testify—is not one place but many. The sea has specific moods and locations as any landscape of hills and valleys does. It even has thoroughfares. Oceania is full of ancient named waterways—the paths to other islands or archipelagoes. A piece of water off the Big Island is known as Kealakahiki, "The Way to Tahiti" (2,500 miles away), one of the great canoe routes.

A person who emigrates to an island is obviously different from a native islander. There is something rather suspect about a person who seeks to recapture island innocence. But in any case it is a futile search, because no one really can take possession of an island. Being the monarch of all you survey is in reality a mainland conceit; on an island it is you who are possessed. Islands have a unique capacity to take hold of their inhabitants, whether they be natives or castaways or potential colonizers, and that is perhaps why islands are so rich in myths and legends.

An island ought to seem fragile and isolated, and yet I visited fifty-one islands in Oceania and every one of them seemed like a thing complete in itself, self-contained and self-sufficient, because of the surrounding water. Whether that was an illusion or not I don't know, but this sense of mystery and power must communicate itself both to those who are native to the islands and those who seek them. There is something princely in the very situation of someone who builds a house on an island and lives in it. But an island is much more than a principate. It is the ultimate refuge—a magic and unsinkable world.

Owning an island is something like having this entire world to yourself, where you can do as you like—making your own rules, fulfilling a vision or a fantasy. The two private islands of Ni'ihau and Lana'i are dramatic examples of that, but they are moving in totally different directions.

Ni'ihau is quite small and so obscure and so seldom visited it is called "The Forbidden Island." Hawaii's second private island, Lana'i, is fairly large and has not been much on the tourist map and is hardly known, except as a Dole plantation. Its nickname is "The Pineapple Island." Each place is extraordinary in its own way. The owner of Lana'i is just now ending its seventy-year tradition of pineapple growing and has invested heavily, with two luxury hotels, in the tourist industry. In great contrast to this, the owner of Ni'ihau long ago decreed that nothing would change on his island and his descendants have kept to that promise—forbidding any outsider from entering the community of Hawaiian-speaking people, or looking closely at the land or its inhabitants.

* * *

"If any island is inviolate, it is Ni'ihau," Hawaii's historian Gavan Daws wrote almost thirty years ago; "if any man is an island, it is Ni'ihau's patriarch."

One of the pleasures of the Hawaiian islands derives from the fact that no beach is private. A tycoon might have a mansion jammed squarely against the sand, but the law allows you to use that same beach, sunning yourself and swimming in the surf. The beaches belong to everyone. And even on the most remote or exclusive beaches there is public access.

The single exception to this is Ni'ihau. I wanted to take my collapsible kayak there. I was told that this was out of the question, that the sand and even the water around the island—to ten fathoms—was private.

Because of its isolation, Ni'ihau has acquired an extensive mythology—the unknown always passes for something particularly wonderful. The very idea of Ni'ihau fascinates people in Hawaii, and to nearly everyone it suggests Shangri-la. Tell someone you've been to Ni'ihau and their face becomes brilliant with curiosity.

"What was it like?" they say. "I'll bet it was fantastic."

A NO TRESPASSING sign is like catnip to a travel writer. I was determined to find out about the island, and to visit if possible. I discovered that there were occasional helicopter tours, but—to maintain Ni'ihau's low profile—the service was never advertised. In the end, interviewing informants, and finding the chopper, and making the trip turned out to be a bit like mounting an assault on Alcatraz, another Pacific island that Ni'ihau physically resembles.

Ni'ihau was sold for $10,000 to a family of wealthy wandering Scots by the Hawaiian king (Kamehameha V) in 1864. The family successfully transformed this Polynesian volcano into a Scottish estate, turning the islanders into tenants and themselves into lairds. They were muscular Christians. They decreed that everyone on the island would attend church. They discouraged smoking. They forbade the drinking of alcohol. They fortified the church and distributed Bibles, in the Hawaiian language. Even today, on an island on which the main language is Hawaiian, the only reading material in that language is the Bible and the hymn book, and the same prohibitions persist. Little wonder that (as a former resident wrote in 1989), "a favorite pastime of the children is trying to stump each other by reciting phrases from the Bible"—guessing chapter and verse. Fishing, manual work, and games are forbidden on the Sabbath.

In theory it is a sober and pious island of twelve Hawaiian families (inevitably related). Ask anyone in Hawaii and they will tell you that it is a unique preserve of native culture, of people living in the old way, fishing and farming, preserving the island traditions.

This is of course ridiculous. At best the island is a throwback to the days of soul-saving missionary paternalism in which the hula was banned and singing generally disapproved of and islanders seeking work were allowed to look after the owner's livestock. It is an insular ghost from the age when Polynesia was condemned as lazy and needing to atone for its Original Sin. Oddly enough, the island and the stubborn, backward-looking Robinson family, which owns it, have more defenders than attackers, because casual onlookers enjoy the fantasy that an island has been trapped in time—indeed, that traditions have been preserved. Although last year the islanders voted Democratic (for the popular and progressive mayor of Kaua'i, JoAnn Yukimura) the Ni'ihauans have usually been as staunchly conservative as the Robinson family—they voted against statehood in 1959, the only precinct in the islands to reject joining the United States. Yet it is not possible to stop the clock, even on an offshore island.

So what is Ni'ihau tradition now? It is the language—perhaps the only community in the entire state whose daily conversation is Hawaiian. It is the preservation of family units—and extended families—which are said to live in harmony. It is the practice of fishing—but only by the men and boys; the women are homemakers, and many of them search the island's beaches for the tiny Ni'ihau shells, which they pierce and fashion into precious and exquisite necklaces—much coveted by people the world over who appreciate their rarity. And it is churchgoing.

Apart from all that piety, Ni'ihau tradition is now also welfare checks, food stamps, soda pop, and canned food. In the houses with electrical generators, it is video machines. The windward side of Ni'ihau is so horrendously littered with plastic rubbish that has floated from the other islands that it was pictured as a sort of spoiled Eden in a recent *Time* magazine. There is no hula, there are no canoes. And their racial purity is another myth, for there is a strain of Japanese blood on the islands.

"They don't live as Hawaiians," cultural historian Sol Kahoohalahala told me. "They have a poor diet and as a result they have severe health problems."

If the culture had been intact and the people had retained their old island skills and pleasures, the experiment of isolating these Hawaiians might have succeeded. But it has been a failure. What remains is the language, and the Robinson family prevents any outsider from studying it there. It is possible that, with such a small number of people speaking Hawaiian in Ni'ihau, the language will degenerate as the people have and become extinct.

It was once the rule that when a Ni'ihauan left the island he was regarded as tainted and was forbidden to return. This is no longer the case. Ni'ihauans regularly cross the channel in a Vietnam War surplus landing craft to Kaua'i to work on the Robinson estates, to collect their welfare checks, to buy food and visit relatives (there are large communities of Ni'ihau families on Kaua'i), or to attend parties—where drinking and smoking are cheerfully tolerated.

On my furtive flying visit to the island I traveled in a helicopter which was the property of the Robinson family—at $200 per person a trip this is obviously a way of paying the upkeep of the chopper, which is also used for medical emergencies (there is no hospital on Ni'ihau).

We banked past the cliffs that rose to 1,000 feet and we landed on the deserted southern end of the island, where some of Captain Cook's sailors (including his first mate William Bligh) spent one night in 1778. They were the first white men to step ashore in the Hawaiian Islands. Cook had unexpectedly discovered the Hawaiian Islands—and this unexpectedness was strange for him, because Cook had a genius for anticipating islands. Like the Polynesian navigators, he could read the pattern of the sea, the configuration of waves, the movements of seabirds, the sight of turtles, the quality of light. But Hawaii—his first sight was of O'ahu—loomed up out of the ocean, without any warning. And he had not expected to see high islands in the North Pacific. He then spotted the islands of Kaua'i and Ni'ihau, and while he was still reflecting on whether they could be inhabited, he saw canoes, three and four men in each one.

The islanders spoke, "and we were agreeably surprised to find them of the same nation as the people of Otaheite [Tahiti] and the other islands we had lately visited." Cook's meticulous collection of word lists came in handy, and even the crew knew enough of this Tahitian-like language to ask for food—hogs, breadfruit, yams, water. The words were the same.

"How shall we account for this nation spreading itself so far over the vast ocean?" Cook wrote, deeply impressed. But he was aware of the fragility of the culture he had encountered, and knowing that his men were carrying venereal disease he had made a rule that his men were not to fraternize with island women. Offending men were ordered by Cook to be flogged.

The encounter could not have been stranger if Cook had come from outer space, and more than anything it resembled the meeting of Martians and Earthlings—indeed, Cook was seen as possibly supernatural, the embodiment of the God Lono (Orongo in Rapa Nui), whom they believed would appear to them on a floating island, which was exactly what the *Resolution* looked like. There was iron all over the ship, and the metal was like treasure to the islanders. Reckless greed and impatience overcame the islanders' fears—and besides such creatures, being foreigners, were outside the *kapu* (taboo) restrictions, which were severe in Hawaii. Pilferage was immediate, anything made of metal was stolen; this led to quarrels, one of them fatal, when one of Cook's lieutenants shot an islander.

Two days after sighting the islands, and in spite of Cook's strict precautions, a few of his men got ashore on Kaua'i and infected some island women. This also happened on Ni'ihau, and there was soon an epidemic of syphilis and gonorrhea on the islands, which vastly reduced the population. Ironically, many of the men had picked up the diseases in 1777 from women in Tahiti, who had caught it from the French sailors.

The Ni'ihauans who visited Cook's ship asked the captain whether they could leave a token behind. Cook agreed and the islanders cut locks of their hair and left them on the ship, as an act of faith, for having something so personal as hair (or nail parings) empowered the owner to cast deadly spells. Cook took on drinking water from the springs of Ni'ihau and set off to look for the Northwest Passage.

I walked down an ancient lava flow to lean over the steep rock walls and listen to the crashing of surf and the cries of seabirds in Keanahaki Bay.

In the distance I could see the simple wooden structures of the island's only village, Puuwai, as we made the hop to the rocky plain at the northern end. Ni'ihau is very arid—the island recently suffered a seven-year drought—but if there is rainfall it descends on Puuwai, where it is collected in cisterns. Beneath the chopper I could see what is actually a devastated ecosystem—the effects of hungry cattle and sheep, wild pigs and herds of wild horses—many of them visible. The browsing animals had started the damage, wind erosion had done the rest. The whole place has the rather tragic look of a utopia gone wrong, and it has the curiously dusty and deprived atmosphere of a penal colony.

Even in 1863 the Hawaiian staple food taro would not grow on the island because of poor soil, and good trees were so scarce they had to be shipped from Kaua'i. The situation is much worse now. There has been no apparent reafforestation. It is an island without any visible topsoil. The vegetation that exists is kiawe tree, a thorny bush akin to mesquite. Charcoal made from this wood by the islanders is greatly in demand elsewhere in Hawaii, and the kiawe flower results in delicious honey that is collected by Ni'ihau's beekeepers. But these remain cottage industries.

The protected anchorage at this northern end of the island, just inside Puukole Point, is where the landing craft—with its food and its passengers—creeps from the sea to the sand. The great black volcano just offshore is Lehua Island, a state seabird sanctuary, on which Hawaiian structures and caves and fresh-water springs have been studied.

Walking the beach at the northern end of Ni'ihau I kept wondering what I would do with this island if I owned it. I knew that I would not want to see it nibbled to death by wild animals or blown, grain by grain, into the ocean. It was admirable that its people still spoke their mother tongue; Ni'ihau Hawaiian is regarded by some linguists as the purest form of the language. But it was a pity that they could not share it, nor did they know the history of their people before the traders and cattle farmers, and the vengeful God of the Old Testament, and the missionaries who convinced them that they were sinners.

Isolation had not worked. There is something fundamentally subversive about the master-servant relationship, and a *haole* family lording it over dusky islanders is hardly likely to be a blueprint for utopia. Even if that had worked, corruption had set in with the first video machine, if not with the first transistor radio. The intention was that the island would not change, but of course it has, inexorably. Just as mice can nibble a mansion and turn it into a ruin, the animals and alien plants have caused the ecology to degenerate; the people's diet has altered; and perhaps their outlook has adjusted, too, as their trips across the channel have become more frequent.

An island can be owned; but people cannot be owned nor can they be managed as though they were cattle or, worse, as though they were vaguely animate and supine museum exhibits. So the answer is obviously that the Ni'ihauans themselves would have to be consulted about the future. They are notoriously wary of strangers' questions, as I discovered—even on Ni'ihau they regarded my questions as *niele*—nosy. They are said to be intensely proud of their difference, their separateness.

Ideally, the islanders would choose not to be invaded by tourists, but to be put in touch with other Hawaiians—poets, dancers, ethnographers, linguists, farmers—in the hope that their community might be rejuvenated, and gain a measure of self-sufficiency. That could eventually lead to revitalizing the Hawaiian language in the rest of the islands.

The island of Lana'i is a different experiment altogether. No one objected to my collapsible kayak—the little airline that flies in from Honolulu is used to dealing with kayaks, surfboards, scuba gear, and high-powered rifles (there is hunting on Lana'i), as well as Louis Vuitton golf bags and Chanel hatboxes: Lana'i has some of the simplest as well as the most sumptuous accommodations in Hawaii, and the island is unique in welcoming the backpacker as well as the billionaire.

Like Ni'ihau, Lana'i passed from the control of the Hawaiian monarchy into private hands—in fact, it was once owned by the same family that now owns Ni'ihau. After several incarnations—as a ranch, as a promised land (the Mormons owned it for a while), as a glorified botanical garden and game park—James Dole bought it in 1922 and planted

15,000 acres of pineapples. The company town, a cluster of simple houses on a grid of narrow roads, rejoices in the name Lana'i City and for seventy years nearly all its 2,200 inhabitants—largely of Filipino or Japanese ancestry—worked for Dole, in the labor-intensive business of pineapple growing.

Because of high labor costs, pineapple is ceasing to be a commercially viable crop in Hawaii—such enterprises are cheaper and simpler in the Philippines and in Central America. But there was no serious suggestion that the Dole plantations would close until five years ago, when the swashbuckling investor David Murdock took control of Castle & Cooke (which had owned Dole, and the island of Lana'i since the 1950s). Realizing that the pineapple plantation had no future, Murdock sized up Lana'i and concocted a scheme on a grand scale for the entire island. He was uniquely privileged to do this; after all, he owned the island. The island had one hotel—a modest and charming old building with ten rooms, at the top end of Lana'i City, called inevitably the Lana'i Hotel.

Taking advantage of the island's vistas and two distinct climate zones, Murdock specified that his first luxury hotel would be built in the cool hills above Lana'i City, amid the mists and the Norfolk pines. This, the Lodge at Koele, has turned out to be, in style, a sort of turn-of-the-century Anglo-colonial hunting lodge, with verandas and vast fireplaces, that would not look out of place in the highlands of Kenya. The second hotel, Manele Bay, Murdock placed fifteen miles distant, on a spectacular sweep of bay, above a sandy beach, and it has the look of a grand Mediterranean villa—stucco, tile roofs, elaborate gardens.

In the beginning, the sudden change bewildered the people of Lana'i City, who had known only the pineapple business and the company routine. There was an *Over-our-dead-body* faction, advocating the status quo—this group has diminished in size but is still vocal, because the nearest island to Lana'i—Maui—has seriously and seedily degenerated into a destination that in large part looks like a suburb of San Diego. There was a *We-don't-want-rich-people* faction, which wondered aloud about the implications of luxury hotels on the island. There is a more moderate *Lana'ians-for-sensible-growth* faction, which wishes to have a say in determining the island's future. Mr. Murdock has listened to all the contending points of view, sometimes with patience and forebearance, sometimes with the blustering megalomania and single-mindedness one associates with General Bullmoose. There is a strong feeling that Mr. Murdock has everything to gain if the islanders are happy and prosperous, even if it means change. And there is an undercurrent of anxiety—terror is perhaps a truer word—that Mr. Murdock might get sick of spending his money and sell the whole operation to the Japanese, who would ruthlessly Nipponize it, subdivide it, and turn it into a golf paradise and labor camp, a combination that has worked well for them elsewhere.

But in all this turbulence an unexpectedly serene thing has happened. The children of these pineapple pickers, who had fled the island for more congenial and better-paying jobs on other islands or on the mainland—most of them young people—began to return home, to work in the hotels, literally rejuvenating an island of aging plantation workers. The manager of Koele, Kurt Matsumoto, is a native of Lana'i and so are nearly all his staff.

"I would never have come back here to pick pineapples," Darek, a van driver, told me at Manele. "But this is different. This is a job I like."

"My parents wanted me to come back to Lana'i," Linda told me. "But I didn't want to. There was just the plantation and working in the fields for five dollars an hour." And she laughed, thinking about it. But as soon as Linda, who had been working as a waitress in San Diego, heard about the hotels, she returned to her island home and her parents and a job in the dining room at Manele.

I heard that same story over and over. Some people, like Perlita, had been working in the pineapple fields for ten or fifteen years and were now on the hotel staff.

"My father worked in the fields for forty-five years," a Lana'i teacher, Dick Trujillo, told me—we were in the S&T, one of Lana'i City's platelunch establishments, having fish burgers. "He was against the changes. But there was a plantation mentality on Lana'i, the sense that you can't better yourself, that there are managers and field workers—two classes—and if you are the child of a field worker you have no right to go to college or better yourself."

After graduating from the University of Hawaii he had worked for a while in Honolulu, but the traffic, the high cost of living, and the stress of city life had caused him to gravitate back to Lana'i, with its quiet pace, a luxuriant garden in the yard of each tidy bungalow.

"We are a throwback, about twenty-five years behind the times," Henry Yamamoto said up at the ranger's office of the Lana'i Company, where he supervises the hunting on Lana'i—particularly the monthly Damage Control Hunt. He said that they were trying to keep the deer to a controllable level, about 4,000. As for the ending of pineapples and the beginning of the hotels, "We were due for a change."

Nearly every person I spoke to on Lana'i mentioned the strong sense of community on the island. That neighborly spirit is not a myth. The friendliness is evident in the casual good humor of the people and their candor with strangers.

"I want to return to Lana'i when I finish college," Roderick told me. His major was recreational leadership, but his summer job was waiting on tables at Koele. "I'd like to give something back to the community." That expression of loyalty and gratitude is not a sentiment that is voiced much these days on other islands, and I felt sure that it was inspired by the good feeling of Lana'i.

The ethnic Hawaiians on Lana'i are actively interested in their history and culture, studying traditional music and dance, as well as art. Under a supervised program set up by Castle & Cooke, the skilled people of the town did nearly all the artwork—the murals, the decorations, the painted flowers on the new hotels.

Hawaiians date their history on Lana'i from about the fifteenth century, and the island is rich in old Hawaiian sites—temples, house platforms, and petroglyphs carved into rock. No extensive archaeological digging has been carried out, and so whenever I walked through the tall grass or across a windblown hillside to one of these bouldery ruins I felt a sense of excitement. Though any number of guidebooks, or the directions of islanders, can lead you to these sites, the places themselves are unimproved and look undisturbed—there are as yet no signs, no arrows, no plaques. The silence and the look of abandonment gave me the illusion of being a solitary discoverer.

After experiencing the gourmet cooking and the sybaritic life at the hotels at Koele and Manele Bay, I set up camp near Shipwreck Beach, on the northern shore of the island. I pitched my tent in a grove of the kiawe trees, out of the wind, at Halulu. This windward side was very surfy but absolutely deserted and wonderful for snorkeling and hiking. In the night the branches of the kiawe trees rubbed and muttered, sounding like live creatures. To the east I could see the bright lights of Maui, and across the moon-whitened surf of the channel the towering dark shape of Molokai.

In the mornings, before the wind intensified, I paddled along the reef. About two miles up the coast there was a rusted hulk of a Liberty ship that ran onto the reef. I paddled to it and closer I saw that the remains of many other ships were evident—the wooden decks of smashed ships lay on the beach, twisted in frayed fishing nets, and farther on were the beached and dented containers that had been flung from the decks of more recent wrecks. This is said to be the best area of the island for beach-combing—for glass floats and shells and messages in bottles. There were deer tracks all over these beaches, though I did not see any of the cautious creatures, and for a day and a half I did not see a single human being.

Beaching my kayak and wandering across the dry cliffs that were blasted by the wind—this side of Lana'i has the look and feel of a Scottish moor—I came across petroglyphs and stone terraces that could have dated from the reign of Kamehameha, the king who succeeded in unifying the Hawaiian islands in 1795. It is said that he spent his summers on the opposite side of Lana'i—and it is a historical fact that he lived from time to time on Lana'i. He is strongly associated with Kaunolu—an eerie and extensive site on the southern side of the island—but as a Hawaiian historian told me on Lana'i, "That could be just a case of 'George Washington slept here.' "

I loaded my kayak on my Jeep and traveled down dirt roads to other beaches, to paddle; and then across the island to look at the strange rocky plateau in the northeastern part of the island called The Garden of the Gods, a place where the wind moaned through the long needles of drooping pines and the great boulders that had been exposed by erosion had the look of altars and temple ruins. Crossing the Munroe Trail at an altitude of 2,000 feet I needed to put on a sweater against the cold drizzly air.

The stereotype of a Hawaiian island is sunny beaches and funny shirts, palm trees and surfers. Lana'i has those, but Lana'i has much else. Passing the pineapple fields and heading down Fraser Avenue, past the numbered streets into Lana'i City—the simple houses, the grocery stores, the lunch rooms, the bakery, the launderette: all wooden buildings—it is difficult to rid yourself of the impression that you are in some ingenious theme park of the Hawaiian past.

But the oldfangled appearance of the town is not an illusion, and not a fake. With the simple sepia look of an old photograph, it is a living, breathing remnant of old Hawaii—a plantation town of the sort that flourished all over the islands before the Second World War, and before mass tourism. Almost every building in Lana'i City looks as though it could be dated 1935. Remaining true to their past, conservative by nature, the Lana'ians never saw much point in modernizing, and anyway the company owned most of the houses. Lana'ians with money bought expensive, sturdy vehicles—the only conspicuous sign of material wealth is a person's pickup, and the island is a four-wheeler's dream.

The $300 million that Castle & Cooke has invested in the island is not immediately obvious. The excellent high school is at one side of town, the new housing at the other side. In Lana'ian terms the luxury hotels and the golf courses are remote and hidden—as they should be. It would be a shame if the pleasant homely character of the place changed, and Eighth Street was turned into a shopping mall. It could still happen—nothing is more expensive than preserving the past—but so far it looks as though the owner has found a way of rejuvenating the island without spoiling it.

Chapter 26
THE BIG ISLAND: PADDLING IN THE STATE OF GRACE

I was nervous about asking how much Orchid Bungalow, my luxury dwelling by the sea, was going to cost me—it was said to be the most expensive, the most sumptuous in Hawaii, and that was saying a great deal, because already I had felt Hawaii to be the most orchidaceous place on earth.

Still, I risked the question when I saw Ms. L'Eplattenier, the Bungalow manager.

"It's two thousand five hundred dollars a day," she said, flinging back the drapes to show me my swimming pool.

I must have winced, because she turned back to me and smiled.

"That includes Continental breakfast," she added.

This was the Kohala Coast, just north of Kealakekua Bay, where Captain Cook was clubbed to death in February 1779. It is impossible to travel in the Pacific, even for a short time, and not develop an admiration for this hero of navigation and discovery, who was—amazingly, for a great captain—a thoroughly good man.

Having sailed from Ni'ihau some nine months before to look for the Northwest Passage—a sea route to the Atlantic—Cook had been resting in Hawaiian waters after finding only dangerous ice and mountainous shores. His two ships had returned to Hawaii, but this time to Maui, and Cook bitterly logged the fact that the venereal pox they had left in Kaua'i and Ni'ihau had reached this island. They sailed on to the island of Hawaii and made contact. The islanders were harder to read than any Cook had met before—their reputation threw him. The Hawaiians still seriously wondered whether this was the god Lono on his floating island.

What followed was a chaotic interaction, a clash of cultures, with blundering on both sides, which made violence almost inevitable. Was this *haole* really Lono? Were these sailors dangerous? Cook met the aged king, Kalaniopu'u, who treated him as an equal. Meanwhile William Bligh and others were making charts, collecting artifacts, sketching pictures of landscapes and ceremonies. But the pilferage by islanders—their passion for pieces of iron undiminished—was unceasing. There were random desecrations and casual cruelty by Cook's men. The ships were besieged for iron, and the islanders even devised ways for winkling nails out of the timbers.

This situation continued for just under four months and then at last, with the theft of his best cutter—an important boat to the expedition—Cook was so exasperated he went ashore to take the king hostage until the vessel was returned. The king was at first friendly. There was a conversation. But a misunderstanding arose, and soon panic. The islanders became menacing—Cook's frightened men fired their muskets. A thousand islanders had gathered on the beach. Many of them began to throw stones. Cook was struck by stones, and then clubbed and held underwater, and stabbed, and drowned.

"Justifiable homicide," Mark Twain snarls in the Big Island chapter of *Roughing It*—he felt that Cook had been ungrateful and belligerent, that he had asked for it by pretending to be Lono. But poor Cook had died in an almost meaningless scuffle, an incoherent event, an accident of panic and riot. It was an unacceptable way for a hero to go, and yet human and horrible, a bit of bad timing, just the sort of end you predict for yourself. And though the conflict was later patched up, the next day some islanders dressed in the breeches and shirts of the men they had killed and they went to the beach and showed their buttocks to the seamen, mooning being a traditional Polynesian way of taunting an enemy.

The beach at Kealakekua Bay is still strewn with stones, the right size and shape to use as weapons.

Beyond the bay, and above it, is a lava field—great browny black cinders and clinkers the size of boulders, called *a'a,* as far as the eye can see, interrupted by the occasional grove of palms or stretch of meadow. Because of that landscape there has not been much building here. There are three large resort developments, but they are self-contained, like small green islands, isolated on the coast at the end of the lava flows. On this leeward side, it hardly rains (ten inches of rain a year)—it is a great sloping desert of black volcanic rock, the Kaniku Lava Flow on the west coast of the Big Island.

Orchid Bungalow was one of four luxury bungalows at the Mauna Lani Resort, and because a golf tournament was in progress, my neighbors were Arnold Palmer (in Plumeria), Lee Trevino (in Hibiscus), and Gary Player (in Bird of Paradise). Jack Nicklaus had just moved out of

Orchid. Golfers were the only people swinging clubs on this coast these days.

"A strange thing happens to our guests in the bungalows," the resident manager of Mauna Lani told me. "They get what we call 'bungalow fever'—they check in and eat all their meals in them. They use their twenty-four-hour butler service. They give parties, they have cookouts. They don't leave. And when it comes time to check out they don't really want to go."

The current record for staying in one of these $2,500-a-night bungalows is held by the actor Dustin Hoffman, who checked in and did not emerge until twenty-eight days later.

The sun was shining on the snowcapped crater of Mauna Loa the day I checked into Orchid Bungalow, and almost the first thing I saw from the veranda (or *lanai*) was an enormous humpback whale, which breached and slapped its tail throughout the afternoon.

That night I was invited to a party at the hotel—something to do with the golf tournament. The moonlit Pacific lay just beyond the raw bar, where Bryant Gumbel stood, beaming expansively. The president of Rolex, lifting a grilled prawn to his lips, displayed his wristwatch, a Rolex El Presidente—he had handed out at least one that day to a successful golfer. I was in conversation with a man wearing an ugly shirt.

"I've got a twin-engine jet with a Harley-Davidson on board. I can go anywhere in the world. Where should I go? Don't say Yerp. I hate Yerp."

"Know where his money comes from?" someone said to me later. "He's a multimillionaire. His father invented the supermarket shopping cart."

"It's like inventing the spoon," I said. "Or the can opener."

"Charro and Sylvester Stallone have houses in Kaua'i," someone else was saying. "She was married to Xavier Cugat. We used to see Willie Nelson jogging on Oahu."

"If you understand Japanese banks you understand Japanese investment in Honolulu. People just off the plane were getting mortgages of between two and five percent, and they could borrow up to a hundred and twenty percent of the purchase price."

"The Japanese love Disney memorabilia—Mickey Mouse, especially. But they're also into quality. Hermes opened a store in Honolulu strictly for the Japanese market. We're talking silk shirts at thirteen hundred dollars a pop."

"They used to pee in the sink," a hotelier was reminiscing, smiling at the memory. "This was only ten or fifteen years ago, in a good hotel—well-to-do guests. They stood on the toilet seat to do number two. I guess they were used to poor sanitation in their country. They stretched out on the lobby seats and had naps. They walked in the public rooms in their pajamas—kimonos, whatever. We had to print notices. 'Please do not pee in the sink.' "

Across the lawn, Japanese tycoons looking deceptively childlike were clustered around Arnold Palmer—his name was impossibly difficult for them to pronounce. They had flown in from Tokyo for the tournament, and here they were proffering their caps and visors for him to sign, which he did without a protest.

One of those Japanese gentlemen moved into Plumeria Bungalow after Arnold Palmer had moved out. Each day a stretch limousine drew up to the front door and the family—father, mother, four children—disappeared inside and, hidden by its black windows, were whisked away. But they were soon back in the bungalow garden, sniffing flowers and thrashing in the pool.

A sort of bungalow fever afflicted the golfers. Gary Player wanted to bring the butler with him to South Africa, and he was so taken by the bungalow's design that he asked the management for a copy of the architect's plans. One of the other golfers—Nicklaus, I was told—also insisted on a copy of the floor plan. And all of them said they would be back, as soon as possible: The luxury had not been exaggerated, nor had the daily rate put them off. Or did they get it free? Some of them were walking billboards. Lee Trevino had a contract to wear a hat advertising a Japanese make of car—and he never took the hat off. A prominent golfer like Trevino could get half a million dollars to wear one of those hats. They wore patches on their shirts. They had big visible logos on their golf bags. They would have called themselves sportsmen, but some of them were merely glorified sandwich boards.

Gillian, the woman who had told me the price of the bungalows and added memorably, *That includes Continental breakfast,* stopped in at Orchid Bungalow to make sure I was comfortable.

"I am very comfortable," I said.

The bungalow had two enormous bedrooms, each with its own spa area—steam bath, whirlpool bath, orchid garden; a central lounge area was about half the size of a basketball court, with a cathedral ceiling, and the entertainment center in the southwest corner of the lounge was supplied with a television, VCR, tape deck, and CD player.

I could have added, *I often sleep in a tent.*

This bungalow had recently figured in an episode of the popular television show "Lifestyles of the Rich and Famous," she said. She pointed out how the tables and some of the furniture had been cut from solid blocks of Italian marble, that the carpets had been loomed in England using the designer's marble-matching pattern of burgundy and gray. Had I noticed the bar—seventeen full bottles of liquor? She wondered whether I had any questions about the pool, which was exclusively mine, as was the outdoor Jacuzzi nearby.

"We put out some CDs we thought you might like," she said.

Kenny Rogers, Fleetwood Mac, Eric Clapton, Cher. Never mind. I had a whole catalogue to choose from.

"The chef will be over shortly to take your instructions for lunch and dinner," she said, and she vanished.

That was something I was to take for granted—the sudden apparition of a butler or a maid, setting out fruit juice or caviar, skimming the pool, bearing flowers or fruit. It was all accomplished without a sound, as though these people trembled a few inches above the floor. Any request I made was carried out instantly, gracefully, and without any pomposity—no Jeeves nonsense, but rather speed and a smile, from Richard, my personal pool attendant, to Orrin my butler, who served the meals and opened the champagne.

Each morning before I did anything else I strolled from the bedroom to the lounge and opened the sliders to the lanai, walked around the pool to the edge of my domain, where a fish pond, my own fish pond, with appropriately big fish circulating in it, separated me from the beach. There were coconut palms leaning over the sand, and the lagoon at the edge of the bay was greener than the sea. The beach was mine, the whole Pacific was mine, all the happy isles of Oceania; and so was this luxury bungalow. But wasn't my chef a trifle overdue? When I saw a human being on the beach I became slightly miffed and pouted in my luxury bungalow, wondering whether I should summon my security guard, until I remembered that in Hawaii the beaches are for everyone.

That momentary sense of violation at seeing another person on the beach, the glimpse of Friday's footprint, in a manner of speaking, helped me to understand how quickly I became habituated to this billionaire's life. *Hey, I could get used to this!* people say, when something unexpectedly pleasant comes their way. They are telling the truth. To rephrase Tolstoy, All luxury is the same, but misery for each person is miserable in its own way. And it is the easiest thing in the world to become corrupted by the good life. Once you have flown first-class in an airline an economy seat is intolerable: After you have tasted luxury you are changed, and there is no cure for it. Pain does not create a long-lasting memory, but the memory of luxury exerts itself forever. That is wonderful, the memory of happiness being so strong, but I can imagine circumstances when it might become a curse. It could be a crueler punishment than torture—giving a person a taste of heaven, creating a habit, and then whisking the victim away to suffer without it.

The hitch at Orchid Bungalow was that the day was not long enough. I wanted to read, lie in the sun, exercise, swim, sit in the Jacuzzi, eat lengthy sumptuous meals, drink champagne, and listen to music all at once. I discovered that some of these activities could be combined. Now I understood why many multimillionaires—Axel Springer and Somerset Maugham were but two—received annual injections of longevity potions. The science of life extension is funded by a large number of very wealthy individuals, who have the most selfish motives. There is something about the pure effortless pleasure of being hoggishly, sluttishly rich that must make you want to live longer.

The fact that the sun was shining on me out of a cloudless sky in what was by any reckoning one of the most beautiful places in the world only enhanced what was already wonderful. It is hard to improve on bliss, but Orchid Bungalow proved that it was possible. The only way I could imagine myself happier, more comfortable or contented, was to have someone else to share this bliss with.

"What if I wanted to have a dinner party?" I asked the chef, Piet Wigmans, when he came to take my order one day. "Say six people."

"Anything you like," he said. He suggested the food we might have— the various local fish, tuna and opakapaka (snapper), shrimp from O'ahu, crabs, and so forth. There were also Maine lobsters, New Zealand mussels, Chilean asparagus, fresh avocados, and passion fruit—and he was a master chef; he had run great kitchens in San Francisco and Dorado Beach. ("How did you make out in Puerto Rico?" I asked. He replied, "Fine. I have a whip.")

I chose spicy Dungeness crab soup, followed by spinach salad with avocados. The main course would be sautéed opakapaka with citrus sauce and stir-fried baby asparagus and snow peas and garlic potatoes. For dessert, chocolate Grand Marnier soufflé. As soon as any chef mentions baby vegetables you know you're into three figures.

"And now shall we discuss the wines?" Chef Piet asked.

We settled on the wines—four altogether—and then feeling slightly weary from all these decisions I reinvigorated myself with a swim and a little nap on my sunny lanai.

The guests, my new Hawaiian friends, were delightful—intelligent and shining with health and accomplishment, all of them residents of this little paradise and suitably impressed with my bungaloid version of Xanadu.

One of the guests was the distinguished trial lawyer George Davis, still brilliant and active at the age of eighty-three, looking a bit like Robert Frost. At one stage in the dinner he recalled the last night he spent with his doomed client Caryl Chessman, which was Chessman's last night on earth, in 1960. Chessman had not killed anyone. He had been convicted

of being involved in a bungled kidnapping—he had protested his innocence in a famous and eloquent book, which had been utterly convincing.
The crime was not serious by today's standards, and even if he had
committed the crime today he would not have been executed for it—it
was no longer a capital offense.

That night Chessman said goodbye to his attorney. His parting words
were, "George, you're shaking hands with a dead man." A few hours
later he was electrocuted.

After dinner, when I was alone, I walked outside. The pool was glowing, the palms rattling, the moonlight lay liquefied on the Pacific. I sat
under a jewelled sky having difficulty imagining what death row must be
like. I took out my pocket calculator and began tapping away—peep,
peep, peep. Ah, yes. At $2,500 a day, it would cost me 32 million dollars
to live in Orchid Bungalow until the year 2015, when I would be eighty-
three years old.

It had taken only two days for this luxury to affect me, but it did so
profoundly. It was a shock to my system that in a very short time
transformed me, as luxury will—like a drug. It was wonderful being
supine and semi-comatose in the sunshine, but it was also a bit like being
a zoo animal—wallowing in the sort of captivating comfort that I felt
would numb me and then make me fat and crazy. On the other hand, I
wasn't terribly worried: At these prices there wasn't an earthly chance of
this luxury lasting much longer.

I resisted it a little. I became reclusive and abstemious. I began living
in a corner of the bungalow and working hard to break the day into three
distinct parts—morning (tea and writing), afternoon (light lunch, swimming, then poaching myself into exhaustion in the hot tub), and evening,
which was built around one of Chef Piet's dinners, an elaborately choreo-
graphed event, no matter what was on the menu—usually a hundred
dollars' worth of sealife so deliciously prepared that I stopped asking the
butler for the Tabasco sauce.

The sun shone unceasingly upon the sea, and the humpback—my daily
whale—bucked and slapped just offshore. I was living in all this Hawaiian
splendor, and yet I was also a spectator to it, enclosed by a bungalow so
protective it was like a complicated organism, feeding me, cooling me,
lulling me to sleep with maternal caresses. It was an existence just about
summed up in the expression "splendid isolation."

What was strictly Hawaiian about this? I kept asking myself whether
I could have mistaken this place for another sunny paradise in the Carib-
bean, or the Mediterranean, or the coast of Africa. But no—the flowers
and the fragrance were Hawaiian, the great rolling waves could only have
been breaking and dumping on a Pacific reef, the high clouds, the coral,

the vast dark landscape of lava, some of it gigantic *a'a* cinders and some of it the buckled *pahoehoe* that looks like a melted parking lot; the hospitality, the smiles, the sense of abundance—it was all Hawaiian in its very essence.

The nagging reality of it was the price, $2,500 a day. I began seriously to wonder what the opposite of this might be. What would life be like if I were living as cheaply as possible in paradise? Indeed, how much fun would you have here in Hawaii on one one-thousandth of that, say about $2.50 a day?

I still had my Oceanic camping gear: tent, sleeping bag, cooking kit, water bag, and Swiss Army knife. I had left my collapsible boat in Honolulu, but I had had the good fortune to meet one of Hawaii's best-known kayakers, who had lent me an inflatable kayak and a paddle. My idea was to check out of the luxury bungalow at Mauna Lani before my bungalow fever became incurable, and paddle down the coast—find a sheltered cove, go beach-combing, and live on next to nothing.

I averaged the cost of the noodles, couscous, fruit, and vegetables I packed into the kayak and it came out to $2.18 a day. So I had thirty-two cents a day to play with, but that was purely theoretical—the nearest shops were in Kona, thirty miles away.

My original plan had been to go to the north shore of the island and paddle from one coastal valley to the other—from Waipio to Waimanu, where the steep valley walls allow only helicopters or the sturdiest hikers to enter. But of course a kayaker could enter from the sea, paddling around the headlands. But the seas were bad—everyone warned me against them.

Nainoa Thompson was one of the leaders, and the navigator, of the *Hokule'a* expedition—helping to sail successfully a double-hulled canoe from Hawaii to Tahiti and New Zealand in 1986. He took me aside and said, "I was out in that channel in a sea like this and the glass on the steering house was smashed by a wave—that thing is fifteen feet up, and it's very strong. Don't paddle there now."

Some other time, I thought. I was patient in Hawaii. I would be here a long time, I felt. There would be time for everything.

Instead of at Waipio, I paddled about seven miles south of Orchid Bungalow and camped among the palms at the edge of Keawaiki Bay. An estate nearby comprised of a dozen rambling stone buildings had been built in the 1920s by Francis I'i Brown, champion golfer, bon vivant, millionaire, and direct descendant of one of King Kamehameha's advisers—in other words, in one of the smallest and most select classes in Hawaiian society, an *alii,* a nobleman. The family had once owned a very large slice of O'ahu, including Pearl Harbor.

One day at Keawaiki I pressed my nose against the window of one of these stone buildings and looked at the framed photographs on the near wall. One was a picture of Francis Brown standing with Babe Ruth, both of them in golfers' duds, knickers and long socks, and cloth caps. In another he posed with a young man still recognizable as Bob Hope. Stories were told in Honolulu and the Big Island of Brown's eccentricities and friendships, and how this strange little seaside estate—accessible only by water—had been visited by celebrities. "Wild parties," people said. In the center of one of Keawaiki's brackish fish ponds was a semi-ruined dwelling, which had been a little pavilion once upon a time, where Francis Brown—who had never married—kept the girl of his dreams, known as one of the most beautiful hula dancers of her time, named Winona Love.

The buildings were empty and locked, and had the sun-faded moribund look of neglected houses by the sea. But I had no need of them. I cooked my dollar's worth of dinner—couscous and lentils, fruit and tea—and sat at the edge of the cindery dune above the black lava beach under the same crescent moon that had bewitched me at Orchid Bungalow. I had had air-conditioning there and a pool; here I had a soft breeze and the sea, and for a bath a brackish pool that had been scooped out of the lava, fed by a spring. It is not hyperbole to say that I felt a greater sense of wealth, greater happiness, and a more powerful sense of well-being camping here than I had living in the luxury bungalow. It was the same sense of liberation I had felt on the desert islands of Vava'u and in my little camp at Tongariki, beneath the crumbled *ahu,* at the edge of Easter Island.

I was not only safe and very comfortable, but most of all nothing interruptive like a wall or a carpet or a pane of glass stood between me and this natural beauty. There was nothing to fear—in fact, I felt supported and protected by the palms and the dunes, and that encouraged me and raised my morale. At the bungalow I had only wanted to mooch around the pool—I had become fairly dopey and unambitious. But here, living outdoors, I was filled with a desire to get into the kayak and paddle beyond the bay.

I paddled north into the next bay and around Weliweli Point, where waves were smashing onto the black heap of lava. I paddled a few more miles to Anaehoomalu Bay, where there were two luxury hotels and no one swimming in the sea, much less boating. I found a secluded beach at the south end of the bay, had lunch, and headed back. The wind had picked up and the waves had heightened, but this inflatable kayak bobbed along, twisting and sliding.

The humpback whale appeared early the following morning, just offshore, near enough for me to see the blast from his blowhole. He surfaced and slapped his tail and turned, plowing the sea like a dithering submarine. I paddled out in his direction, and I saw him dive one last time:

He did not breach again that day. So I turned south, where a lava flow a mile wide formed the coastline. Just beyond Ohiki Bay was Luahinewai, vividly illustrating the Hawaiian conundrum that most beauty spots on the islands are haunted with grisly memories—this particular area of outstanding natural beauty was associated with the slaughter of Chief Keoua and twenty-four of his retainers by King Kamehameha in 1790.

My bay, Keawaiki, was particularly rich in fish, which were gold and emerald and silver, surgeonfish and parrot fish and the small, colorfully striped state fish (humuhumunukunukuapua'a). They twinkled like jewels among the coral. Because of its protection and its steep beach I could dive in from the shore and go snorkeling and float on the fringes of the tide rip to the edge of the bay, weightless and warm. Here in my little camp exercise required more initiative than at Mauna Lani—no health club, no golf course—but because of that was more rewarding. I swam, I walked.

One of the strangest trails I have ever hiked lay just inland from the palms, a hot narrow path through the lava flow, called The King's Trail, and cut centuries ago by Hawaiians long before *haoles* like Cook ventured ashore. The path is a groove three feet deep, like a single wheel track that runs for miles down the side of the island. Like the Inca Trail and Watling Street, it is one of the great thoroughfares of the ancient world. I hacked at coconuts, I searched for petroglyphs—the rock carvings that are numerous on the Big Island.

One day I went north to one of the most sacred places in Hawaii, and one of its oldest sites, the Mookini Luakini Heiau. Built on a high point overlooking the sea, the temple is a vast rectangle of cannonball-sized stones. It looks like a crumbled monastery, the Hawaiian version of Tintern Abbey, just as ghostly, with altars and fallen walls, and a nobility that is lent an even greater magnificence by the sight of the waves breaking on the point just beneath it. It was similar in its position and its shape to structures I had seen in Samoa and the Marquesas, but to think that these other ruins were thousands of miles away, across the dangerous *moana,* that made it even more fascinating. Wind and trees, the flattened grass and black rocky shore gave this part of the Big Island an uncanny resemblance to Easter Island—even to its colors and grassy odors.

A ten-minute walk across the meadow was the birth site of King Kamehameha. A signboard nearby read in part, "His prowess as a warrior-statesman destined him to unite the Hawaiian Islands and bring peace and prosperity to his people . . . He was true to his own religious beliefs." And there was a regal quotation from the controversial eighteenth century king who was known as "The Lonely One"—*E oni wale no oukou i ku'u pono 'a'ole pau*—"Endless is the good that I have given you to enjoy."

My days were sunny and pleasant. My nights were luminous with stars. I slept as I had on Kaua'i, pleasurably drugged with fatigue. In the morning I was woken by the mewing and screeching and the ratchet-like scrapings of birds in the palms above me. The exercise and the simple food and the frugality of this enterprise made me feel smugger than when I had been living like a millionaire, and in that gloating mood I slept like a log in my tent, at the edge of the lagoon.

Time passed—months. I was still in Hawaii, I had not left Oceania. I was paddling my collapsible boat, marvelling at the way its canvas hull had faded in the punishing sun. Some days I paddled rented outriggers off Honolulu, and open hardshells off windward O'ahu. The places I had paddled to write about I was still paddling, for pleasure. There were more seacoasts I wanted to paddle: off Maui, to the bombsite of Kahoolawe, and along the north coast of Molokai to Father Damien's old leper settlement of Kalaupapa, and eventually—in good weather—from one island to another. Paddling had taken the place of writing. I thought about my book and then muttered, *Oh, never mind.*

Normally, at this point in the trip—in this chapter, say—the traveler is heading home. Or the traveler is already home, reflecting on the extraordinary trip, looking at slides, sorting notes, perhaps wishing the trip had not ended, or at least saying so. But that nostalgia can sound so insincere. You read it and think: *No, you're delighted to be home, dining out on your stories of megapode birds and muddy buttocks and what the king of Tonga told you!*

Isn't one of the greatest rewards of travel the return home—the reassurance of family and old friends, familiar sights and homely comforts?

I used to go back home and be welcomed, and find months of mail stacked on my desk and spilling to the floor, and after I opened it all, I would answer some and pay bills and burn the letters and envelopes. It could take half a day at the incinerator in the garden, as I stirred the ashes of all the mail I had received. And when I was done and caught up, the routine of home would reassert itself. I would begin writing, spending the day at my desk reliving my trip, and when the pubs opened at five-thirty I would buy an evening newspaper and sit reading it with my elbows on the bar, drinking a pint of stout, thinking: *A month ago I was in a tent by a riverbank, swatting flies.*

Sitting there under the timbers of the cool musty pub, I would receive a clear recollection of someone like Tony the beachcomber on the Aboriginal coast of North Queensland—Tony saying, *I found some 'roo meat under a box once. Forgot I had it. Two years old, it was. I ate it. Wonderful in soups, y'know.* And, feeling blessed, I would give thanks that I had returned, that I had a home, that I was safe, that I had been missed, that I was loved.

A trip like that had a beginning and an end; it was an experience in parentheses, enclosed by my life. But this trip, paddling through Oceania, had turned into my life. Now I was in Hawaii, living in a valley full of Honolulu rainbows, writing about the Trobriands and the Solomons and Australia, writing about Tony the beachcomber. I thought of the watchful Aboriginal Gladys as her grandson searched her hair for nits. The Kaisiga children singing *Weespa a frayer* in the darkness. The old man on Savo holding a big old radio to his ear, listening for news of the Gulf War. Mimi in Moorea saying of her Marquesan child, "Someday she will be a Theroux." There were good people in the waterworld of Oceania. I thought often of Easter Island, the haunting stone faces, the scouring wind, and because I had seen so little hunger in Oceania, I thought of the hunger of little Roberto, muttering his thanks in Rapa Nui, as he clawed the shell from the hard-boiled egg I had not wanted, and wolfed it, his eyes bulging.

I spent a great deal of time wandering the beaches of Hawaii. I kept paddling too. One morning, paddling off Kaua'i, I saw two humpback whales, and I slipped into the water and spent an hour or more with my ears submerged, listening to this happy couple sing and grunt. I was still going, like the man who steps out for a paper and never comes back. I was that man. I had vanished. And there was no reason to go back now. No one missed me. Half my life had been eclipsed.

And then all of it was eclipsed. One morning in July, the Path of Totality lay over the Big Island. I woke at five A.M. and foraged around for my welder's mask. It had a density factor of fourteen—the most opaque obtainable. I put it on and was in darkness. If I stared at the sun (so I was told) I would see the same darkness, and a dim wafer.

The last total eclipse in Hawaii had been in 1850, and at the time the Hawaiians had felt that their chiefs had abandoned them, that the gods were angry, and that the sun—the great *La*, which they worshipped—had lost its *mana*. The stars appeared in daytime, the temperature dropped, flower blossoms closed, birds stopped singing.

People flocked to Hawaii to experience this total eclipse of 1991. There would not be another one like this for 142 years. Fifteen hundred Japanese crouched on the first fairway of the Hyatt Waikoloa, clutching "sun peeps" which would prevent them from being blinded.

The astronomer Edward Krupp said, "Eclipses are the most awe-inspiring event on earth. No one should go through life without witnessing one."

It was also a marketing opportunity. The hotels were serving a special omelette called an "egg-clipse." There were eclipse towels, eclipse mugs and jewelry, T-shirts saying *Eclipsomania!* and *Totally Umbra!* and *I was there!* A young man named Miles Okimura of Honolulu sold specially sealed commemorative cans of tinned darkness. The *Honolulu Advertiser* pointed out that "the darkness had been canned before the eclipse."

Walking groggily to the roof of my hotel in the early morning darkness I bumped into a man with a flashlight, who was unmistakably Portuguese.

"It's cloudy," he said, sounding vindictive.

Louis Schwartzberg, time-lapse photographer, had been on the roof since four, assembling two 35mm cameras. He had brought fourteen large crates of equipment.

"I usually bring thirty," he said. "But I'm alone."

We ate grapes. Louis looked anxiously at the cloudy skies over Mauna Kea.

"You're not going to need that," he said, indicating my welder's mask.

"What time will sunrise be?"

"It happened twenty minutes ago," he said.

A cloudless day had been forecast. Most days were cloudless here. This freaky haze was connected with the volcanic ash from the eruption of Mount Pinatubo in the Philippines. Louis fell silent. I walked to the edge of the roof and saw people assembling on the driving range half a mile away.

"What can we do?"

Louis said, "Pray." I thought he was going to scream; his jaw tensed. Screaming is uncool. Louis (from Los Angeles) said, "I accept the clouds. I won't get a good shot. I accept that. At least the eclipse brought all these nice people together."

I hurried to the driving range where little family groups squatted on the grass, peering at the bright clouds, aiming cameras. Bryan Brewer, a tall, pale man from Seattle wearing an *Eclipsomania* T-shirt, paced the grass. He was the author of a book about eclipses called *Totality*. He had seen his first eclipse in 1979 and was hooked. He traveled the world, observing eclipses. This, he had predicted, would be one of the greatest. I greeted him, I asked him how he was.

"Nervous," he said.

It was as though he was personally taking the blame for this Act of God.

"We won't see this cloud cover for another hundred and forty-two years," a photographer said.

No one laughed, though I found this very funny.

A woman named Charlene had come to Hawaii to give lectures on cosmic consciousness and solar vibrations linked to the eclipse—*mana* in fact, emanating from the shadow of the sun. Charlene had long hair and a gown-like dress, and she had attached herself to a group of chatty photographers. She had a sense of urgency, and she walked among the group of men and women saying, "Listen, guys" or "I've got an idea, guys."

The sky was filled with pearly gray clouds and on the ground the gloom was palpable.

"Guys, there's an answer," Charlene said. "When the Dalai Lama escaped from Tibet he needed cloud cover. He and his followers linked their arms together and chanted *'Om'* over and over."

Having nothing to lose we tried this, and the clouds seemed to thicken. Wasn't that what had happened in Tibet? No one said so, but nearly everyone had spent thousands of dollars to come here. Besides the Japanese there were French and Germans, there were people from Brazil, from California, from Canada.

A photographer said, "Mike's in Baja. That's on the Path of Totality. There are never any clouds in Baja—"

Another photographer said, "We should go back to the hotel and watch this on CNN."

On the roof, Louis Schwartzberg was saying, "I accept this."

"So what happened to the eclipse?" a man asked Bryan Brewer.

"I don't know," Mr. Brewer said, guiltily. "I'm still hoping."

"Did you see the sign in Kona?" a woman asked. "The eclipse has been cancelled due to unforeseen difficulties."

"The eclipse has been eclipsed."

Tedious early morning jollity had begun.

Someone said breathlessly, "The cloud's moving."

People were willing the clouds to shift. And some of the clouds were shifting—sludgy layers of them jostled, allowing sunlight to burst from their seams. It was ten minutes to seven.

Hopefully, I put on my welder's mask and was in total darkness. I took it off and saw that clouds were passing across the sun, ravelling like great hanks and skeins of wool.

No one spoke, there was scattered applause and intense concentration, as the sun burned through the fragmenting cloud, illuminating the woolly shreds. And when it emerged, still in haze but visible, it was not a perfect disc. There was a smooth measured bite out of the top of the sun. And while we watched, the bite grew, until the sun looked like a moon crescent, a fat one, glimmering in daylight.

"What's your setting?"

"One-twenty-fifth at F-eight, a hundred ASA."

It was like a command to fire, for as soon as the words were spoken there was a sucking sound of shutters and winders, a shooting that was like bolts being shot from crossbows in furious gulps.

"Check the focus."

"Look at that shadow."

"Anybody got an exposure?"

I was putting on and taking off my welder's mask. With it, I saw a dim crescent. Without it, the glare dazzled and almost blinded me. I scrunched my eyes and glanced and then looked away, as though peering at a forbidden thing. The time was 7:24 and the sun was a golden banana, and two minutes later, the air had already begun to grow cool, and the banana had narrowed to a bright horn that kept thinning and was soon a brilliant splinter, and finally a sliver of intense whiteness. The rest was a dark disc, with specks of light glimmering at its edges, a phenomenon known as Bailey's Beads.

At last the sun was in total darkness, as though a dinner plate had been slid across it—the hand of God, someone had predicted, and that was how it seemed, supernatural. There was brief, hesitant applause, some worried whooping, and then silence, as a chilly shadow settled over us. In Hawaiian Pidgin, the expression for goose pimples is "chicken skin," and I could hear this word being muttered: *cheecken skeen.*

By 7:29 the world had been turned upside down. Again the stars appeared in daytime, the temperature dropped, flower blossoms closed, birds stopped singing, and we sat transfixed on our cooling planet, watching light drain from the world.

We stared blindly at the black sun until there was a sudden explosion at its top edge that showed a flare of red light.

Our amazement was not pleasurable—not fascination; it was compounded of fear and uncertainty, a feeling of utter strangeness. It was like the onset of blindness. I looked around. There was just enough light to scribble by if I held my little notebook near my face. It was not pitch darkness, but the eeriest glow around the entire horizon, a 360-degree twilight. The silence continued, and in the large crowd, all looking upward, the mood was somber, though the morning air was unexpectedly perfumed by night-blooming jasmine.

It was a world of intimidating magic in which anything could happen.

Before the sun emerged again from its shadow, making the earth seem immeasurably grander than it ever had before, I kissed the woman next to me, glad to be with her. Being happy was like being home.

Honolulu, January 1992

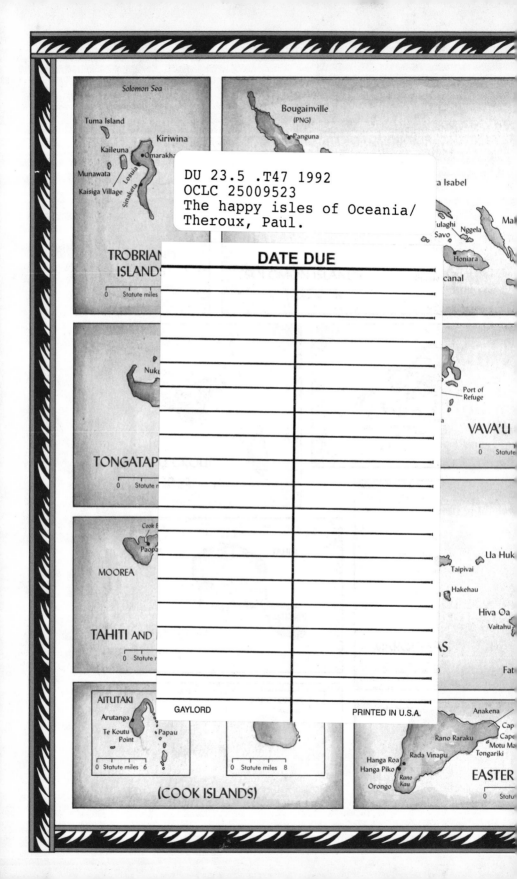

DU 23.5 .T47 1992
OCLC 25009523
The happy isles of Oceania/
Theroux, Paul.

DATE DUE

GAYLORD   PRINTED IN U.S.A.

SO-AIA-058

More Praise for *The Civil Sphere*

"This subtle and hugely informative work . . . offers not only acute theoretical discussion of the civil society concept, but also generous and expansive accounts of social movements of race and gender, and the theory and practice of multiculturalism and assimilation (two chapters on the Jewish experience are especially compelling)."   —*Contemporary Sociology*

"*The Civil Sphere* offers a bold and original thesis about the culturally important role that civil societies play in Western democracies. Although I will challenge Alexander's thesis, it is important to state at the outset that *The Civil Sphere* is a valuable book packed with rich social histories, lively engagements with ancient and contemporary theories, and novel interpretations. There is much to be learned here about the historic and sociological nature of racial, gender, and ethnic oppressions, and the struggles waged to overthrow them."
                    —Aldon Morris, *Sociological Quarterly*

"*The Civil Sphere* is truly a masterful and groundbreaking work, the rare and ambitious kind that does not just contribute to one of the many ongoing conversations in sociology, but brings them together and reorients them. It will undoubtedly confirm and reinforce Jeffrey Alexander's reputation as one of the foremost sociological theorists of our day. Indeed, reading *The Civil Sphere* generated the same sense of intellectual excitement that I experienced the first time I read Durkheim or Weber or Habermas—and for similar reasons: *The Civil Sphere* addresses big and important questions about freedom, inequality, and solidarity."
                    —Chad Goldberg, *Sociological Quarterly*

"*The Civil Sphere* is . . . rich in its empirical descriptions and resourceful and suggestive in terms of its conceptual and theoretical framework. The book will challenge and shape its discussions in cultural sociology for many years to come."   —*Cultural Sociology*

"*The Civil Sphere* is a major work that is going to change the state of the debate in many fields . . . It aims to provide a new theory of contemporary society, based on a new interpretation of solidarity [that] is a radical challenge to political economy."   —*European Journal of Social Theory*

"A tour de force of sociology, political science, and philosophy, [its] repercussions might be felt for decades to come . . . This is a book worth reading by both social scientists and the general public, for its persuasiveness can inspire us to imagine that another world is possible"
                    —*Mediterranean Quarterly*

"All sociologists, social scientists or writers probably nurture some secret ambition of writing a mega book that will immortalize them by its originality, the persuasiveness of arguments, impact, or its sheer size. For Jeffrey Alexander, this is it. A magisterial book, a contribution to social theory that will be talked about, criticized and never overlooked."
                    —*Asian Journal of Social Science*

"Jeffrey Alexander's *The Civil Sphere* is nothing less than an attempt to create a new theory of civil society for the 21st century through an almost equally ambitious attempt to reground the discipline of sociology."   —*Journal of Communication*

"A major work of cultural and political sociology, exploring the possibilities of civility as action and civil sphere as a public domain . . . *The Civil Sphere* can be taken as conclusive evidence that sociology is alive and well, and more importantly relevant to modern social action."
                    —*Citizenship Studies*

"*The Civil Sphere* is the best book in sociology that I have read in many years . . . It will find its place on the shelf with the other great classics of sociology. [A] great work."
                    —*Perspectives: Newsletter of the Theory Section of the American Sociological Association*

"The book is an exercise in forging theory as a tool for democratic practice." — *Thesis Eleven*

"Arguably the most probing and insightful examination of civil society in America since Tocqueville's *Democracy in America*. He offers a penetrating and original causal interpretation of the success of the Civil Rights Movement, and addresses with understanding and fresh perspective the question of Jewish assimilation in post-civil rights America. Alexander's long awaited book establishes a new benchmark for cultural sociology and social theory with its rigorous theoretical and historical analysis of transformative societal change."
—Victor Nee, Goldwin Smith Professor of Sociology, Cornell University

"Jeffrey Alexander's *The Civil Sphere* is the most important, effective, and readable book in his distinguished career. A powerful and provocative account of civil society, this brilliant piece of theorizing is fueled by an expansive moral vision. Alexander punctures the overblown claims of other thinkers both left and right, and stunningly combines theoretical vigor with a subtle, becoming humility in the face of the best achievements and most compelling aspirations of the civil sphere."
—Michael Schudson, Professor of Communication, University of California at San Diego

"An original portrait of civil society which addresses issues which must be addressed if we are to live in peace with those unlike ourselves. *The Civil Sphere* is remarkable for its clarity and depth of exposition. All readers will benefit from Alexander's ideas: he does not try to batter the reader into submission; instead, he embodies the very ideal of civil society, by inviting the reader to argue with him. In sum, an extraordinary and necessary book."
—Richard Sennett, Professor of Sociology, The London School of Economics

"This is a Herculean labor in which Alexander not only deconstructs the discourse of 'civil society' but reevaluates the entire tradition of political and social thought which attempted to establish, justify, and actualize this abstract idea."
—Hayden White, Professor Emeritus of the History of Consciousness,
University of California

"Long recognized as one of the world's foremost intellects, in *The Civil Sphere* Jeffrey Alexander delivers a masterpiece. In this breathtakingly erudite tour of literature, history, philosophy, and social science scholarship, from Hannah Arendt to Woody Allen, Alexander takes on in a single volume both foundational questions of the human condition and the political exigencies of our day. The result is a book that will wholly transform the conceptual landscape; from this point forward we will recognize that the civil sphere's potential for social justice can only be an ongoing project, never a finished achievement."
—Margaret R. Somers, Professor of Sociology, University of Michigan

"*The Civil Sphere* is at once an energizing ideal for democratic society, and a source of violations of its own ethos. Jeffrey Alexander's well-argued book identifies this crucial level on which liberal democratic societies must operate and offers an insightful and non-reductive account of the struggles against such violations, for what he calls 'civil repair'. He provides fascinating analyses, among other events, of the civil rights movements, and of modern anti-Semitism."
—Charles Taylor, Professor Emeritus of Philosophy, McGill University

The
Civil Sphere

JEFFREY C. ALEXANDER

OXFORD

UNIVERSITY PRESS

OXFORD
UNIVERSITY PRESS

Oxford University Press, Inc., publishes works that further
Oxford University's objective of excellence
in research, scholarship, and education.

Oxford   New York
Auckland   Cape Town   Dar es Salaam   Hong Kong   Karachi
Kuala Lumpur   Madrid   Melbourne   Mexico City   Nairobi
New Delhi   Shanghai   Taipei   Toronto

With offices in
Argentina   Austria   Brazil   Chile   Czech Republic   France   Greece
Guatemala   Hungary   Italy   Japan   Poland   Portugal   Singapore
South Korea   Switzerland   Thailand   Turkey   Ukraine   Vietnam

Copyright © 2006 by Oxford University Press, Inc.

Published by Oxford University Press, Inc.
198 Madison Avenue, New York, New York 10016

www.oup.com

First issued as an Oxford University Press paperback, 2008

Oxford is a registered trademark of Oxford University Press

All rights reserved. No part of this publication may be reproduced,
stored in a retrieval system, or transmitted, in any form or by any means,
electronic, mechanical, photocopying, recording, or otherwise,
without the prior permission of Oxford University Press.

Library of Congress Cataloging-in-Publication Data
Alexander, Jeffrey C.
The civil sphere / Jeffrey C. Alexander.
p. cm.
ISBN 978-0-19-516250-9; 978-0-19-536930-4 (pbk.)
1. Civil Society.   2. Pluralism (Social sciences).   3. Social interaction.
I. Title.
JC337.A47 2006
300—dc22   2005027349

2 4 6 8 9 7 5 3 1

Printed in the United States of America
on acid-free paper

To the memory of my mother and father,
Esther Leah Schlossman Alexander and Frederick Charles Alexander,
who believed in the possibility for civil repair

As we look at the problem, we see that the real tension
is not between the Negro citizens of Montgomery
and the white citizens, but it is a conflict between justice
and injustice, between the forces of light and the forces
of darkness, and if there is a victory—and there will be a
victory—the victory will not be merely for the Negro
citizens and a defeat for the white citizens, but it will be a
victory of justice and a defeat of injustice. It will be a victory
for goodness in its long struggle with the forces of evil.
—MARTIN LUTHER KING

We know of no scientifically ascertainable ideals. To be sure,
that makes our efforts more arduous than those of the past,
since we are expected to create our ideals from within our
breast in the very age of subjectivist culture; but we must
not and cannot promise a fool's paradise and an easy road
to it, neither in thought nor in action. It is the stigma of
our human dignity that the peace of our souls cannot be as
great as the peace of one who dreams of such a paradise.
—MAX WEBER

PREFACE

I T IS HARD to know what Wittgenstein means when he concludes his preface to the *Philosophical Investigations* by remarking, "I would have liked to produce a good book," but "this has not come about." It is not difficult, however, to understand exactly what he is getting at when he follows this lament with the assertion that he cannot delay the publication of his *Investigations* any longer, for "the time is past in which I could improve it."

In 1979, I received a John Simon Guggenheim Memorial Foundation Fellowship for a project titled "Watergate and the Crisis of Civil Society." With this topic, whose title must have seemed more than slightly recondite at that time, I meant to signal my interest in solidarity as central to democracy. Interest in "civil society" had emerged from my earlier interest in Gramsci's cultural Marxism, which later had become filtered through Tocqueville's democracy, Durkheim's civic morals, Weber's fraternization, and Parsons's societal community. I published some papers from this Guggenheim research, but not a book. The project plunged me deeply into television and newspaper archives and produced in me a conviction that there is a cultural structure at the heart of democratic life. It is this paradoxical and contradictory language, I came to believe, that provides a reference for assertions about social solidarity and the putative obligations immanent to it, for demands about economic equality and political responsibility, for scandals over the abuse of office power, and for repairing the rent structures of social life.

In the middle 1980s, as I was beginning to think about what a cultural sociology might look like, I spent a year at the Institute for Advanced Studies in Princeton at the invitation of Michael Walzer, who had been an inspiration in my days as an undergraduate social studies major at Harvard. Fifteen years later, he had become my tutor once again, this time in philosophy and political theory. From that time onward, I saw clearly that, far from being confined to interpretive social science, hermeneutics could be central to normative political philosophy.

In the spring of 1989 I spent a month in China at Nankai University in Tianjin teaching a course on democracy and sociological theory. The linked topics grew in importance as I experienced the rush of excitement from the students, who filled every seat and cranny in the lecture hall. As I departed from China, the pro-democracy student movement gathered force in Beijing's Tiananmen Square. Its defeat was traumatizing. Upon my return to UCLA, I spoke with Adam Seligman about my sense that I had seen something new, something that sociological theory could not explain. He pointed me to the new literature on civil society. Six months later, I had written a lengthy draft essay that laid the foundations for this book. A year later, in the fall of 1990, Ivan Szelenyi invited me to speak about civil society to the Hungarian Sociological Association. It was on the flight to Budapest, worrying over whether I had anything new to tell those who were actually participating in the construction of a new civil sphere, that the theory presented here crystallized in its final form.

During the academic year 1993–94, I lived in Paris and worked under the auspices of CADIS, the center created by Alain Touraine at the *Ecole des Hautes Etudes en Sciences Sociales*. The interests of this group stimulated a greater appreciation for the role of social movements in civil society, a topic that Ron Eyerman had first placed on my intellectual horizon. With the assistance of Michel Wieviorka and François Dubet, I spent spring 1994 teaching a course on sociological theory and the racial underclass in America at the University of Bordeaux. This experience made race central to my thinking about the possibilities for justice in the civil sphere.

Over the course of five years during the 1990s, I participated in the annual Prague conference on Critical Theory, Philosophy and the Social Sciences, and engaged in discussions about aesthetics and morality with the Mexican philosopher Maria Pia Lara. It was during a fellowship at the Swedish Center for Advanced Study in the Social Sciences in 1997 that I clarified the relationship between my emerging sociological theory of civil society and some recent developments in political philosophy.

At UCLA in the winter of 1996, under the auspices of the interdisciplinary Social Sciences Collegium, I participated in a course titled Beyond Enlightenment: Jews, Jewishness and Modernity, organized by David Myers and co-taught with David Ellenson, Arnold Band, and Rabbi Chaim Seidler-Feller. The format, readings, lectures, and discussion convinced me that anti-Semitism could not be left out of the history or sociology of civil society, and that realization helped to frame the approach I have taken here. Adinah Miller, a graduate student in Jewish history at Yale, helped guide me through secondary literature.

In 1998–99, I organized a research group at the Center for Advanced Studies in the Behavioral Sciences in Stanford. Over the course of that year, I met weekly with Ron Eyerman, Bernhard Giesen, Neil Smelser (the center's director), Piotr Sztompka, and Bjorn Wittrock to discuss the dynamics of cultural trauma, how feelings of moral responsibility depend on symbolic extension and psychological identification and respond to the constructions of carrier groups. These discussions in general, and Eyerman's and Giesen's work on African-American and German memory construction in particular, triggered my investigations that year on the American civil rights movement and the Holocaust, which informed Parts III and IV of this book. Nancy Cott, who was also a Fellow at the center that year, helped me think through some of the contemporary literature on American feminism. My interest had earlier been stimulated by conversations with Ruth Bloch and by her work.

This book took final shape after I moved to Yale University in 2001, as I helped rebuild the sociology department and created, with Ron Eyerman and Philip Smith, the Center for Cultural Sociology. Yale's seriousness and purpose proved critical for finally bringing this long project to a close. I am grateful to the leaders of this great institution and to my colleagues in the sociology department and the Whitney Humanities Center for their support and interest, and also to Ann Fitzpatrick for her clerical assistance during my years as Chair. Nadine Casey has proved invaluable to the task of putting the manuscript into final form and helping to track down references and books. Dedi Felman, my editor at Oxford, was as creative as she was assiduous in her efforts to bring *The Civil Sphere* to publication.

Over the years, I have shared my understanding of democracy and civil society with several generations of students, and through their master's theses and Ph.D. dissertations they have more than paid me back in kind. They will see their own work, in published and unpublished form, cited in the pages that follow, but I should like to mention Philip Smith, Ronald Jacobs, Eyal Rabinovitch, and especially Isaac Reed for research and critical feedback. And there are some critical academic-cum-personal friendships I should like to mention as well: Nick Entrikin for his cultural geography lessons; Ken Thompson for Durkheimian collegiality; Steven Seidman for steadfastly criticizing modernity; and Roger Friedland for insisting on institutional power.

As the ideas in this book took shape, I published some of my initial findings in journal articles and book chapters. For providing these opportunities, I would like to thank Charles Lemert, in whose *Intellectuals and Politics* appeared the first run-through of chapter 3; the editors of *Mondoperai*; Carlo Mongardini, who edited *Due Dimensioni delta Societa l'Utile e la Morale*; and Marcel Fournier and Michele Lamont, editors of *Where Culture Talks*, for publishing early versions of chapter 4; Andreas Hess and the other editors of *Soundings*, for publishing the first version of chapter 8; Marco Diani and Jon Clarke, who solicited an early version of chapter 9 for their *Alain Touraine*; Jonathan Turner, who welcomed the first renditions of chapters 10 and 17 in *Sociological Theory*; and Mark Jacobs, for publishing the analysis of the Birmingham campaign in *Culture*. In my own edited book, *Real Civil Societies*, I published much of the material that appears in chapter 2. The material in these earlier publications has been modified in more and less significant ways as they became transformed into chapters for this book.

My wife, Morel Baquié Morton, provided the grace, serenity, and stimulation that I needed to complete this book. My parents, Frederick Charles Alexander and Esther Leah Schlossman Alexander, provided the sense of moral seriousness and intellectual engagement without which it would not have been started. They were deeply interested in the fate of the civil sphere and were devoted to its sustenance and repair. It is to their memory that I dedicate this book.

CONTENTS

PART II
STRUCTURES AND DYNAMICS
OF THE CIVIL SPHERE

The
Civil Sphere

INTRODUCTION

W E LIVE IN a cynical age. Some people think might makes right, and sometimes they are the leaders of powerful countries. So-phisticated intellectuals sometimes think there is no right, and relativism becomes the order of the day. The gap between philosophy and empirical social science threatens to become a chasm. Once mired in analytic and technical concerns, philosophy has sprouted new branches. Today, it has become again a great moral science, filled not only with normative stipulations but with empirical assumptions about the world. Sociology has begun to grow out of its pseudo-scientific ivory tower theories and methods, and a newly cultural sociology allows us to speak centrally to the issues of public and everyday life.

In this book, the normative and empirical sciences meet, and they do so on the terrain of civil society. The premise of *Civil Sphere* is that societies are not governed by power alone and are not fueled only by the pursuit of self-interest. Feelings for others matter, and they are structured by the bound-aries of solidarity. How solidarity is structured, how far it extends, what it's composed of—these are critical issues for every social order, and especially for orders that aim at the good life. Solidarity is possible because people are oriented not only to the here and now but to the ideal, to the transcendent, to what they hope will be the everlasting.

Our new moral philosophies underscore the vital significance for justice of broader and more inclusive social ties, but that they do not, in fact, tell us much about solidarity itself. When we examine the masterworks of classical and modern sociological theory, we find the same thing. Solidarity is pointed to, but it is nowhere systematically interpreted or explained.

Where can we look for a better theory? In 1980, a momentous and

3

effervescent social movement arose in Poland. It was called Solidarity. After a year and a half of extraordinary success, it was repressed, but it marked the first chapter of a democratic narrative that has continued to this day. The theorists and leaders of Solidarity said they were fighting for a civil society, and those who followed them in time often followed their civil society banner as well.

Civil society is an idea that has been heard from before. In the wake of Solidarity and its successor democratic revolutions, there has been a great revival of civil society talk, but too much of it echoes earlier times. We need a new concept of civil society as a civil *sphere*, a world of values and institutions that generates the capacity for social criticism and democratic integration at the same time. Such a sphere relies on solidarity, on feelings for others whom we do not know but whom we respect out of principle, not experience, because of our putative commitment to a common secular faith.

The idea that there can be a secular faith has been anathema to modern sociology, which has falsely equated being modern with being beyond belief. I challenge this old-fashioned perspective of modernity. In its place, I introduce the idea of democracy as a way of life. Democracy is not a game governed by technical rules. It is a world of great and idealizing expectations, but also overwhelming feelings of disgust and condemnation. It is a competitive scene of partisan conflict, but also cosmopolitan disinterest and love. Democratic life shifts back and forth between a transcendental language of sacred values of the good and profane symbols of evil, but these shifts are mediated by institutions that push for agreement in difference, such as voting, the rule of law, and the ethics of office.

Civil society is not a panacea. Modernity is strewn with the detritus of civil societies, shipwrecks, such as the Third Republic in France and the Weimar Republic in Germany, whose carcasses came near to suffocating the twentieth century. The discourse of civil society can be as repressive as liberating, legitimating not only inclusion but exclusion.

The structure of civil society may rest upon a cultural structure, but it is hardly merely discursive in its shape and form. It is filled with institutions, organizations of communication and regulation. To see what these institutions are up to, we need to recognize first the world of public opinion, which is the sea inside of which the civil sphere swims. Public opinion is the middle ground between the generalities of high-flown discourse and the ongoing, concrete events of everyday life. It is filled with collective representations of ideal civility, but it is also defined by strong expressions of negativity. For every "yes" and "I agree" there is, in every poll, the responses of "no" and "strongly disagree." There are often, in fact, "feeling thermometers" to register, in numeric terms, just how strongly are the passions of civil life. It is no wonder that public opinion has a real, if nonbinding, force.

The communicative institutions of civil society are composed in part of mass media. Newspapers and television news are factual media; they record, but they also select and reconstruct in civil terms what "actually goes on" in a society's life. Fictional media—such as novels, movies, and television comedies and dramas—do much the same thing, but at a temporal remove from immediacy and under the guise of high and popular art. Mass media institutions respond to opinion, but they also structure and change it. Public opinion polls seem merely to measure opinion, to make it scientifically factual, but actually they construct it in a palpable way. Civil associations, such as Mothers against Drunk Driving or Moveon.Org, are also vital communicative institutions in civil life. It is traditional to equate such civil associations with voluntary associations, but I am skeptical about taking this path. Voluntariness characterizes the Girl Scouts, hospital volunteers, and the PTA. Each of these is a good thing, but they do not project communicative judgments in the wider civil sphere.

The representations that pour forth from the communicative institutions of civil society have influence but not power in the more instrumental sense. This is why, even in the quashed and confined civil spheres of authoritarian societies, communicative institutions can often project representations that have some communicative force. To the degree that a society is democratic, however, the broad solidarity that constitutes "the people" must have teeth in it. There must, in other words, also be institutions of a more regulative kind, which means they need access to the violence monopolized by the state. Voting and party competition create civil power. They allow representatives of civil society not only to insert themselves into state bureaucracy but to formally control it. To represent civil power, however, is not necessarily to serve it. It is because power potentially corrupts that we speak of the duties and ethics of "office." Office can be thought of as a regulative institution. A product of centuries of religious and political conflict, office functions as an invisible kind of control that warns and periodically publicizes and pollutes actions of the powerful when they slide toward self-interest alone.

Voting, party conflict, and office are essential in the construction of social solidarity, and they go beyond merely persuasive force because they have access to the law. It is of more than passing interest that law has rarely been a compelling subject for either empirical or theoretical sociology, still less for social theory more broadly defined. When law has been discussed, moreover, it has usually been treated merely as the means to gain some economic interest or political end, not as a means for establishing civil solidarity. Drawing on certain trends in jurisprudential philosophy, I propose to rethink law as a form of symbolic representation. Law highlights, stereo-types, and pollutes actions that are considered threatening to civil society. The regulatory power of such legal representations is extraordinary. They constitute simultaneously symbolic constructions and normative judgments, and, in the name of the civil community, they can draw upon coercion and even control the bureaucratic state. Even while such control is exercised for the civic good, it often legalizes exclusion and domination at the same time. Law applies the sacred principles of civil discourse case by case, in real historical time; in order to do so, it must identify and punish the profane.

Civil society can thus be thought of as an independent sphere. It has "its own" ethics and institutions. But the civil sphere is not separated and ideal; it must exist in the real world. It must be located in time and space. As civil society settles down into everyday social systems, its contradictions become apparent. Real civil societies are created by social actors at a particular time and in a particular place. These founders and their qualities are lionized. It might perhaps be thought one of the abiding misfortunes of civil society that this founding, the actors who did it and the place where it occurred, tend almost always to be seen through a sentimental and nostalgic gaze. The qualities of the founders and the place of their creation are sacralized; they are taken, somehow, as the very essence of civility. The founders' ethnicity, race, gender, class, and sex are essentialized, and so is the city, region, or nation in which these qualities were first displayed. By an alchemy that is less mysterious than it is mystifying, these arbitrary qualities become trans-formed into necessary qualifications. Those who follow are judged as worthy or unworthy in relation.

All this contradicts the utopian aspirations of civil society, but there is

6

more. The civil sphere is bounded by what might be called "noncivil" spheres, by such worlds as state, economy, religion, family, and community. These spheres are fundamental to the quality of life and to the vitality of a plural order, and their independence must be nurtured and protected. At the same time, their concerns and interests often seem to threaten the civil sphere. The goods they produce and the powers they sustain are sectoral not societal, particularistic not universalistic. The hierarchies in these non-civil spheres often interfere with the construction of the wider solidarity that is the sine qua non of civil life.

Real civil societies are contradictory and fragmented. These dynamics create the conditions for suppressing the very existence of the civil sphere. They also create the possibility for its civil repair. The ideals of civil society are never completely negated. They hold before us alternative possibilities, and from these general principles there emerge counterproposals for reform. It is the idea of civil solidarity that allows divisions to be reconstructed. That solidarity can be broadened is the project of civil repair.

But civil repair does not happen just like that. Ideals don't just realize themselves. In considering the dynamics of civil societies, social movements must be given pride of place. They are accordions that inflate and deflate civil contradictions, instruments that supply the melodies, in major and minor keys, for expressing its divisions and for repairing or suppressing them. To see how this accordion is played, social movements must be rethought. They are not motivated simply by cognitive perceptions of rational interest, and their success hardly depends on mobilizing resources in the material sense. Social movements are rooted in subjectivity and dependent on symbolic communication. Anchored in the idealized discourses and communicative institutions of the civil sphere, social movements have one foot in some particular injustice and the other in promises about the general good. This reflects the duality of social position in complex social systems and fragmented civil spheres. The civil rights and feminist movements were not only about the particular interests of racial and gender groups. They were about the reconstruction of social solidarity, about its expansion and repair. To be successful, they had to convince people outside their groups; they could do so only by interweaving their particular struggles with universal civil themes.

Those who are excluded from civil societies do not gain entrance through the struggles of social movements alone, but through more indirect and incremental processes of incorporation. In the recent life and times of social theory, "assimilation" has become almost a dirty word. In fact, however, it represents, in terms of the promises of civil society, a tremendous achievement. Members of out-groups are, in principle, allowed to become members of the society on condition that they keep their stigmatized qualities hidden behind the wall of private life. Allowing persons to be separated from their qualities, assimilation gives members of stigmatized groups an out. If they learn to wear the primordial camouflage of the core group, they can become members. This is a cruel paradox, but over the last centuries it has often been accepted as the price for entry into civil life. In the course of the twentieth century, other options have emerged. Hyphenation suggests a more horizontal, if still asymmetrical, relationship between the qualities of core and out-group. With multiculturalism, there emerges the possibility that out-group qualities can be purified—that they can, in fact, become objects not only of tolerance but of respect and even desire. As the multicultural mode of incorporation becomes more than merely a theoretical possibility, the language of incorporation changes from integration to diversity. But the siren song of difference can attract only if it represents a variation on the chords of civil society.

If the initial story I tell is relatively uplifting, it is the dark side of civil society that dominates the latter part of the book. For two thousand years, the "Jewish question" bedeviled the history of Western civil societies. Because of the early civil ambition of Christianity and its later political, social, and legal domination, Western antagonism to Jews has never been only religious. Jews have been constructed as anticivil, as the ultimate threat to broad solidarity and the good life. When Jews were emancipated after the early modern democratic revolutions, their millennia-long demonization became ever more closely intertwined with the contradictions of civil society. Despite what seemed the rapid progress of assimilation, for European Jews these contradictions became, eventually, an iron cage, and then an inescapable chamber of death. This mass murder was not because Europeans suffered from ineradicable anti-Semitism, but because in the most powerful and aggressive European society, Germany, the civil sphere collapsed, and it became impossible to keep state violence at bay. In America, Jews did not suffer the same fate, but this was not because their qualities were acceptable. Indeed, until almost halfway through the twentieth century, the status of Jewish Americans was precarious, and in the 1920s and '30s they were increasingly excluded from civil and noncivil life. World War II changed everything. In the aftermath of the Holocaust, the relationship of Jews to the American civil sphere shifted dramatically. For the first time in history, Jewish qualities became respectable, and sometimes even attractive, to masses of non-Jewish people.

Civil society is a project. It cannot be fully achieved, even in the fullest flush of success. Nor, despite tragedy and defeat, can it ever be completely suppressed. The contradictions of civil society, divisions of race, religion, gender, and class, can seem like arbitrary and destructive intrusions into its ideal of social solidarity. In fact, however, they are civil solidarity's other side. We would not be so indignant about these contradictions if we were not so fiercely committed to the ideal of a broadly solidaristic humanity, to brotherhood and sisterhood. These contradictions, in other words, are the price of civil society. The idea of civil society is transcendental. Its discourse and institutions always reach beyond the here and the now, ready to provide an antidote to every divisive institution, every unfair distribution, every abusive and dominating hierarchy. Let us grab hold of this old new concept and theorize and study it before it is too late.

PART I

CIVIL SOCIETY
IN SOCIAL THEORY

CHAPTER I

Possibilities of Justice

THIS BOOK IS about justice and about the democratic institutions and beliefs that can sustain justice in our massively complex and highly stratified world. *Justice depends on solidarity, on the feeling of being connected to others*, of being part of something larger than ourselves, a whole that imposes obligations and allows us to share convictions, feelings, and cognitions, gives us a chance for meaningful participation, and respects our individual personalities even while giving us the feeling that we are all in the same boat.*

What could be more important than justice? What has been more important to the dynamics of our societies? But what has been more difficult to conceptualize in social theory and philosophy, and what more difficult to explain in social science?

Let us begin with philosophy. Because of the hopes unleashed by the defeat of Nazism, because of the Cold War competition with state communism that followed, and, last but not least, because of the unexpected and explosive black social movement for civil rights, justice became central to the revival of political theory in the early 1960s. In his major work *Theory of Justice*, John Rawls, the central figure in this revival, advanced the simple but radical claim for "justice as fairness."[1] We must be so fair that social goods will be distributed only if they can be justified in the "original position." In this hypothetical world, we disencumber ourselves of our existing social status and encrusted beliefs, imagining ourselves in a new world where we don't know what we have or who we are. This is a wonderful and liberating standard of high principle. To employ it is to subject distribution to an extraordinary sense of obligation to the whole, to think of others as we would ourselves; it is to act on a principle of true solidarity.

The problem, from a philosophical but even more emphatically from a sociological point of view, is why? Why should people act in this way? Why should they put themselves into such an original position? Now, if a philosopher's job is simply to develop searing moral principles, then Rawls succeeded. Still, he has a good deal left to explain: the how, the who, and the why. Without understanding such things, how could we institutionalize his wonderful principles in everyday life? How could we understand why people fight for them and against them?

Rawls answers that we need to put on the "veil of ignorance." Only with this piece of metaphorical clothing can we think ourselves back into the original position. We can be fair, in other words, only if we willingly cover our eyes. If we cannot see where we are, who we are, and who others are, then we will be unable to discriminate, and we cannot fail to accept any standard other than a truly humanity-wide solidarity. If we can't see the stick, then how would we know that we might not ourselves be grabbing the short end?

But such ignorance is exactly what does not characterize real life. People never willingly put on the veil. Life is about meaning, and it is discrimination that makes meaning possible. Our distinctive identities, as individuals and collectivities, are central to our projects for life. Identity is meaning, and the meaning of our life gives us vitality. Meaning defines us, and it defines those around us at the same time.[2]

| Rawls can define justice in such a high-minded manner only by avoiding the messiness of life, the work that we must do as members of real societies. His theory is not very helpful to social scientific thinking about justice, and it is also, at the very least, implausible philosophy.|

In his later work *Political Liberalism*, Rawls tries to make up for these problems.[3] He acknowledges right off that we all have particular beliefs, indeed, that they are often so particular as to be irreconcilable. Because no one set of beliefs can be proven more truthful than another, they are irrational. This is a big step for a philosopher of high and abstract principles to take. Rawls quickly goes on to say, however, that if we want to have a chance of realizing these ideals, we must be "reasonable" about them. Despite the irrationality and irreconcilability of our beliefs, as reasonable people we must be able to reach an "overlapping consensus" about the principles that we share. Only by virtue of such an overlap will we then be able to pursue our distinctive values to the maximum degree.

But how do we get to be reasonable about the pursuit of beliefs when we are fundamentally *un*reasonable in finding them? How can we be rational about them when we irrationally "cherish" them as sacred? Rawls's answer is simple. We will be reasonable if we live in a society that has liberal political traditions, not only fair laws and a constitution but a deeply tolerant and humanistic political culture. So we can get there, to an overlapping consensus, if we already are there! But if we are already there, then we do not, in fact, have to get there after all. We would not be so irrational as to keep hold of extreme and possibly divisive beliefs in the first place.

In the problems of Rawls I and Rawls II we find an unsatisfying theoretical pattern that has broadly marked thinking about justice and the good society. Rationality and irrationality, principles and creeds, universalism and particularity are treated as resolutely separate, whether they are things, activities, measures, or beliefs. Good comes from abstracting away from the particular, from getting away from who we are and setting our sights on the "view from nowhere." Bad comes from the other side, from beliefs we cannot or will not give up, from things that are meaningful in a deep and irreconcilable way. If we are to be moral, according to these philosophical beliefs, we must find a way of staying inside of principle, inside the good, inside of abstraction, and of keeping away, as much as possible, from the concrete messiness, the irrationality of everyday life.

When Jürgen Habermas moved to communication theory, he introduced this pattern of thinking, for the first time, into the Marxist tradition of critical theory.[4] He attached reason and principle to the public sphere, and all three to democracy. By doing so, he succeeded in pulling neo-Marxism away from its tendency toward economism and romanticism, and its often casual attitude toward democratic politics. He pushed it from Hegel to Kant, from Marx to Rawls, from Lenin to Dewey.

This was an extraordinary achievement. In the course of making these transitions, however, Habermas lost his sociology. The greatness of more traditional Marxist theory was its intertwining of normative and empirical thinking. This combination is notoriously difficult to maintain, and the effort can distort both sides. At its best, however, the Marxist tradition allowed critical and utopian philosophy to connect with the contradictions of social life. This isn't there in Habermas after he turned to discourse ethics.

Every philosophy, however, has a sociology, even if only implicit, and in the later Habermas, this empirical theory is no more convincing that in the later Rawls. It is fine to say that democracy must be deliberative and reasonable, that there are principles that should guide public discussion. But it's simply not true that such idealizing principles actually grow out of speaking, deliberating, or being active in the public sphere, which is exactly the contention of discourse ethics. In fact, something more like the opposite is closer to the truth. Speaking is encased in language games. Deliberation is a second-order decision, which does not challenge but elaborates presuppositions. Publicness is a social and cultural condition, not an ethical principle; it points to symbolic action, to performance, to projections of authenticity.[5]

Like Rawls, Habermas senses these problems. We see increasing, if ad hoc references to culture and tradition even as he moves into his later, more abstract and more normatively concentrated work. Public discourse, he allows, does require a background of democratic culture.[6] Yet, such an acknowledgment, however welcome, undermines the insistence on the purely deliberative nature of public life. Habermas tries to save his rationalist theory in a manner that is similar to Rawls. He claims that although cultural commitments are vital, they belong to the messy sphere of the ethical, not to the high end domain of morals. Culture, identity, and socialization are lifeworld issues; they are not the objects of democratic philosophy and social theory.

But if identity and meaning constitute critical background for democratic society, shouldn't they be topics for democratic philosophy as well? We do not have to be followers of Nietzsche or Heidegger to think so. Any discussion of democratic morality must be connected to the discussion of culture and tradition, if only to understand why morality is so often the claims of the strong, so often falsely universal, and so prone to camouflage and cover-up rather than to upholding reciprocity and claims to truth. To investigate these negative tendencies has been difficult for the theory of communicative action. Neither Habermas nor his disciples has systematically discussed the Holocaust, let alone integrated an analysis of racism and genocide into critical democratic theory. Was this tragic, world-historical event just the lifeworld or the marketplace illegitimately interfering in the otherwise pristine moral sphere? Does it not indicate systemic problems of discourse, and of the public deliberation it informs, in the conception of "right thinking" that is fundamental to the moral sphere itself?

This points again to the limitations of theories of justice whose vitality depends on keeping some putatively higher sphere separate from lower order contamination. On the internal grounds of theoretical logic and the external grounds of history and society, such a position is not only implausible philosophically but sociologically as well.

Communitarian philosophy aims to avoid these problems by embracing, rather than rejecting, the concrete. In *Spheres of Justice*, Michael Walzer brings normative thinking down to earth.[7] Employing hermeneutic methods to move from the interpretation of meaning to principles of justice, he argues that the plurality and difference of actually existing communities constitute viable moral standards. Walzer celebrates, not denigrates, the fact that it feels good to feel solidarity with particular others, in particular spheres, in particular ways. In order to sustain this immanent morality, Walzer explains, we must be relativistic, tolerant, and truly respectful of other values. The alternative is to dominate other spheres, extending illegitimately the reach of our own sphere-specific morality, which means to allow one sphere to control the production and distribution of goods in others.

What Walzer does not explain is why justice would ever prevail. Why would the dominating intrusion of one sphere over another not always take place? Walzer has normative arguments that it should not, but he does not offer a sociological explanation of why it will not. Nor does he explain why, and how, domination and monopoly are so often fought against. Are domination and intrusion really confronted in the name of pluralism and the protection of one's own sphere? Or is it not more likely that such confrontations are carried out in the name of some solidarizing abstraction, in the name of "society" and the interests and rights of the "people"? How would this be different from the kind of universalizing sphere that Rawls and Habermas laid out?

These are the paradoxes that haunt moral philosophy. Theories of imperative abstraction turn resolutely away from the meanings that define everyday life. Hermeneutic philosophy cultivates meaning but cannot envision its expansion beyond particular communities.

It is tempting to suggest that empirical social theory could solve these paradoxes in moral philosophy. But when we turn to the social science disciplines, to sociological theory, we run into theoretical problems of a similar kind.

Contrary to the antiseptic claims of the positivist persuasion, concerns for justice have marked sociology from the beginning of its great traditions. This is vividly the case for Karl Marx, though he cloaked his moral concern in immanent economic laws. Yet, in less apocalyptic ways, justice motivated the writings of the founders of sociology as well. In Emile Durkheim's first book, *The Division of Labor in Society*, he wrote about the moral superiority of restitutive over punitive law, and the unfairness of industrial society's economic order. His central concern throughout his early writings was moral regulation.[8] It is the task of society, Durkheim maintains, to construct, impose, and continuously sustain appropriate boundaries between right and wrong. Agreements between persons, no matter how voluntary, are regulated by what Durkheim calls the "noncontractual" elements of contract. You cannot knowingly sell damaged goods to an unsuspecting customer, and you cannot marry somebody if you are already married. In these and many other ways, the moral force of society makes itself felt. Individual desires and actions must defer to prevailing standards of justice or be stigmatized as a result. In a real empirical sense, one is sociologically compelled to have obligations to others.

Durkheim knew all this, but he did not very well conceptualize how it actually happened, or even what "society" itself is. In his early work, he spoke about the "growing abstraction of the collective conscience," and later about the central role of powerful modern substitutes for traditional religious life—totemlike symbols, public rituals, and postmetaphysical versions of the rational sacred and profane. In modern societies, Durkheim suggested, the individual has become the only really sacred thing: people worship the "cult of the individual."[9]

These ideas are enormously suggestive; they are also metaphorical and empirically vague. How is such modern morality actually connected to social action, to institutions, and to social groups and movements in our complex, fragmented, and stratified societies? This Durkheim hardly begins to explain. How can moral regulation be squared with the rot and murderousness that have marked so much of modern life? Durkheim died in 1917, in the middle of the first great military conflagration of the twentieth century. Two decades later, as the modern world prepared for a second horrendous war, his closest collaborator remarked that the Durkheimians had never imagined totems as swastikas. They had believed that social morality would be transcendent, universal, and abstract, and that social obligations would reinforce sacred good, not sacred evil.

The mid-twentieth century social theorists Talcott Parsons and T. H. Marshall have typically been understood as representing antagonistic traditions, the former the systems-building functionalist, the latter the social democratic utilitarian. Each in his own way, however, developed the connection between justice and solidarity that Durkheim opened up. In his concept of social citizenship, Marshall politicized Durkheim by broadening legal membership in the polity to collective moral obligation for members of subordinated economic classes.[10] In his notion of societal community, Parsons carved out for Durkheim's diffuse solidarity a distinctive institutional sphere, defined its primary purpose as inclusion, outlined the boundaries it shared with other spheres, and described the inputs and outputs it needed to sustain.[11]

But with these later sociological approaches to justice we are also left asking how and why. The cultural and social structures of neither societal community nor social citizenship are well explained. Do they have their own cultural languages other than legal rights? Do they gain their social traction because they are separated from power, or do they have distinctive powers of their own? Why do these solidarizing forces emerge here and not there? Why have they been disfigured in such persistent and striking ways? What about the vicious underside of modern life, the oppression that has marked modern history? Parsons barely touches on the Counter-Reformation and the Holocaust; he takes the relative success of the "American experiment" as his lodestone for estimating the possibilities of justice in modern life.[12] Marshall does not write about the civil wars of twentieth century modernity, about the antidemocratic triumphs that have shamed Western civilization. Under the cover of universal history, he is really writing about Britain alone. In the end, both Marshall and Parsons rely on the mechanisms of social evolution—which must, perforce, be shrouded in obscurity—to explain why solidarity must develop and justice will prevail.

Into these yawning chasms in philosophical and sociological thinking about justice stepped Michel Foucault. In Foucault's philosophical histories, we come face to face with the dark side of modernity, with its corruption and authoritarianism, and in a more culturally sensitive, less economistic manner than Marx. Foucault systematically theorizes *injustice*, not just acknowledging it as a possibility but insisting upon its central place. He shows how it emerges from the abstraction and universalism of modernity, those very qualities which, according to the philosophical and sociological traditions, make justice possible.[13]

Foucault turns moralizing modernity inside out. The generalized and abstract principles of modernity are bad, not good, the problem, not the solution. They allow us to treat one another as things, to homogenize and thus ignore the distinctiveness of each human being. Professionals, whether scientists, journalists, doctors, judges, lawyers, or priests, use abstract knowledge not to help others but to reinforce their power. Foucault looks at law, civil organization, and government, and he sees not moral regulation and justice but social surveillance and oppression. At the end of his life, he illuminated a path that led away from abstract knowledge and morality. Justice could be found in the personal aesthetic realm. It would unfold in a kind of infinite concreteness in the cultivation of a unique self. There would no longer be the need for abstraction to some broader and imagined whole. In his *Postmodern Ethics*, Zygmunt Baumann articulates this understanding well.[14]

Foucault provided a voice, in philosophy and the human studies, for the awful underside of modernity. Once hidden or residual, this dark side now becomes the primary interpretive or explanatory goal.\Foucault does not convict modernity of some historically specific pathology, of a distinctive crime committed by one of the usual suspects—capitalists, imperialists, orientalists, Christians, males, heterosexuals, or the white race. He insists, rather, on a fundamental malady, on an excluding otherness produced by rationality itself.\ It is ironic that from this systemic indictment emerged postmodern thinking about the other. Race and sex theory, biopolitics and cybertheory, radical feminism and postcoloniality—all came to situate themselves under the sign of Foucault. Yet each has reduced power-knowledge to particular interests and their ideologies. This move has been socially and politically productive, but its theorizing is more instrumental and "progressivist" than the Foucauldian vision allowed.

The dialectic moves on, the negation is negated, and Foucault becomes the object of interrogation in turn. What about the other side of the other? How could Foucault's theory think himself? How could Foucault explain the social movements in which he so actively participated—the struggles against state communism, for prison reform, against abuse of the mentally ill, and for homosexual rights—if rationality were indeed so closely tied to power and exercised in such a dominating and excluding way? Is modernity no more than the Holocaust? Has democracy been only a fig leaf for domination and deceit? Can knowledge only reinforce hegemony? Are the social movements for economic, racial, sexual, and gender equality, for human rights and ecology, somehow outside of modernity and democracy, or are they not, in fact, critical movements that are immanent to them?[15]

It is not enough to consider only modernity's dark side, any more than the theoretical imagination can dwell exclusively on its progress. There has been tragedy but also triumph. We have experienced not only despair but hope.

There are thinkers who have seen ambiguity and contradiction inside modernity itself. What would Max Weber have said to Foucault's assertion that rational knowledge is only enslaving, that power produces domination alone? Weber theorized these tendencies in his critical discourse about the "iron cage." But this was not the only thrust of rationalization, Weber believed. He understood that subjugation and emancipation, exclusion and inclusion, the ascetic and the aesthetic all were deeply intertwined.[16] Still, Weber's fin-de-siècle pessimism convinced him that contemporary modernity was tilting toward the darkened side. It was in part for this ideological reason, but also for more technical theoretical ones, that Weber failed to conceptualize the social and cultural structures that could sustain justice and democracy in anything other than a formal way.[17]

The same insight onto the ambiguities of modernity marked the explorations of Sigmund Freud and Norbert Elias.[18] They illuminated the paradoxes of the civilizing process and the multilayered, continually conflicted character of emotions and mind. Neither Freud nor Elias believed that the modern self-control could be achieved without severe cognitive, moral, and emotional strain. The repercussions for expressive rationality would be violent and punitive. The pressing abstraction, preening consciousness, and insistent moralism of modernity were rooted in the primitive and concrete. Transgressive desires are hidden inside the modern unconscious; they exert their social force in more insidious because less publicly available ways.

Such considerations point to S. N. Eisenstadt's writings about the implications of the Axial Age, the period during the first millennium B.C.E. when transcendental philosophy and monotheistic religion first arose.[19]

When universalism and abstraction are institutionalized, according to Eisenstadt, they produce not only the possibilities for emancipation and inclusion but tension, alienation, and a restless duality. The articulation of an abstract ethics, and increasing efforts to apply them to the regulation of social life, can never eliminate the dangers of moral violation, social contradiction, and institutional constraint. The tension between the transcendent and the particular cannot be avoided. Modernity is fundamentally multiple and ambiguous. There is no going back from abstraction; it defines the very essence not just of modern but all post-Axial time. But neither is there a place for homogeneity. There will always be fragmentation in the post-Axial age.

In this book, I explore the territory between the abstract and the concrete. It is in the theoretical space between them that we can give voice to the heroics and the tragedies of modernity. We must find this voice, because brotherhood and otherhood must always exist side by side.

CHAPTER 2

Real Civil Societies:

Dilemmas of Institutionalization

VITAL CONCEPTS ENTER social science by a striking process of intellectual secularization. An idea emerges first in practical experiences, from the often overwhelming pressures of moral, economic, and political conflict. Only later does it move into the intellectual world of conceptual disputation, paradigm conflict, research program, and empirical debate. Even after they have made this transition, vital concepts retain significant moral and political associations, and they remain highly disputed. What changes is the terrain on which they are discussed, compromised, and struggled over. The intellectual field, after all, has a very distinctive specificity of its own.

This secularization process created such basic concepts as class, status, race, party, religion, and sect. More recently, we can see a similar process at work with the emergence of such concepts as gender, sexuality, and identity. The subject of this book, civil society, is being subjected to the same kind of secularization today.

Civil society enters into intellectual discourse from the ongoing tumult of social and political life for the second time. We must make every effort to refine it in a theoretical manner so that it will not disappear once again. If we fail, the opportunity to incorporate this idea might disappear from intellectual life for another long period of time. Not only normative theory but moral life itself would be impoverished if this opportunity were missed, and empirical social science would be much the worse as well. There is a new theoretical continent to explore, a new empirical domain waiting to be defined. But we will not be able to make out this new social territory unless we can look at it through new theoretical lenses. Our old conceptual spectacles will not do.

To forge these spectacles is the aim of this book. Its ambition is to develop a set of concepts that can illuminate a new kind of social fact and open up a new arena for social scientific study, one much closer to the spirit and aspirations of democratic life.

Civil society has been conceived in three ideal-typical ways. These have succeeded one another in historical time, though each remains a significant intellectual and social force today. After situating these ideal-types temporally, and evaluating them theoretically, I will introduce the analytical model at the core of this book, a model which aims to define the relationship between civil society and other kinds of institutional spheres. Only by understanding the boundary relations between civil and uncivil spheres can we push the discussion of civil society from the normative into the empirical realm. And only by understanding civil society in a more "realist" manner can we lay the basis for a critical normative theory about the incompleteness of civil society in turn.

Civil Society I

It is well known that in its modern, post-medieval, post-Hobbesian form, "civil society" entered into social understanding only in the late 17th century, with the writings of figures like Locke and James Harrington.[1] Developed subsequently by such Scottish moralists as Adam Ferguson and Adam Smith, by Rousseau and Hegel, and employed energetically for the last time by Tocqueville, "civil society" was a rather diffuse, umbrella-like concept referring to a plethora of institutions outside the state. It included the capitalist market and its institutions, but it also denoted what Tocqueville called voluntary religion (non-established Protestant covenantal denominations), private and public associations and organizations, and virtually every form of cooperative social relationship that created bonds of trust—for example, currents of public opinion, legal norms and institutions, and political parties.

24

It is vital to see that in this first period of its modern understanding, civil society was endowed with a distinctively moral and ethical force. As Albert Hirschman showed in *The Passions and the Interests*, the civilizing qualities associated with civil society most definitely extended to the capitalist market itself, with its bargaining and trading, its circulating commodities and money, its shopkeepers and private property. Identified by such terms as *le doux commerce*, the processes and institutions of the capitalist market were benignly conceived—particularly by the progressive thinkers of the day—as helping to produce qualities associated with international peace, domestic tranquility, and increasingly democratic participation. Capitalism was understood as producing self-discipline and individual responsibility. It was helping to create a social system antithetical to the vainglorious aristocratic one, where knightly ethics emphasized individual prowess through feats of grandeur, typically of a military kind, and ascriptive status hierarchies were maintained by hegemonic force. Montesquieu provided high ethical praise for capitalism in this early phase.[2] Benjamin Franklin's influential *Autobiography*, which identifies public virtue with the discipline and propriety of market life, might be said to provide an equally important example of a more popular, more bourgeois, but perhaps not less literary kind.[3]

The decidedly positive moral and ethical tone that CS I attributed to market society underwent a dramatic transformation in the early middle of the nineteenth century. The development of capitalism's industrial phase made Mandeville's famous fable of capitalism's bee-like cooperation seem completely passé.[4] The pejorative association of capitalism with inhumane instrumentality, domination, and exploitation first emerged among radical British political economists like Thomas Hodgskin in the 1820s and 1830s.[5] Marx encountered this Manichean literature in the early 1840s, and he provided it with a systematic economic and sociological theory. His voice, while by far the most important in theoretical terms, was for contemporaries only one among many.

The emerging hatred of capitalism, its identification with all the evils of feudal domination and worse, was expressed among a wide and growing chorus of utopians, socialists, and republicans. It is noteworthy that, for their part, the new industrial capitalists and their liberal economic spokesmen did not shy away from this new view of capitalism as an antisocial force. Brandishing the doctrine of laissez-faire in a decidedly un-Smithean way, their motto seemed to be, "society be damned!" There exists no better representation of this self-understanding of the supposedly inherent and ineradicable antagonism between an evil, egotistical market, and "society" in the moral and collective sense, than Karl Polanyi's *The Great Transformation*,[6] which dramatically took the side of "society" against the market. Despite its interpretive power and normative force, however, Polanyi's influential book has reinforced the very theoretical understandings I wish to make problematic here.

Civil Society II

In social theory, this dramatic transformation of the moral and social identity of market capitalism had fateful effects on the concept of civil society. As Keane[7] and Cohen[8] were among the first to point out, the connotations of this fecund concept became drastically narrowed. Shorn of its cooperative, democratic, associative, and public ties, in this second version (CSII), civil society came to be pejoratively associated with market capitalism alone.[9] Marx's writings between 1842 and 1845 reflected and crystallized this reduction in a fateful way. Not only does civil society come to be treated simply as a field for the play of egoistical, purely private interests, but it is now viewed as a superstructure, a legal and political arena that camouflages the domination of commodities and the capitalist class. For Marx, industrial capitalism seemed only to consist of markets, the social groups formed by markets, and market-protecting states. Society in the collective and moral sense had dissolved into a morass of particularistic interests. Only the submerged and repressed cooperative ties that defined the proletariat's true economic interest could provide a counter-balancing universalism. Only the collectively-binding social organization of the bourgeoisie's class enemy could sustain a social alternative to selfishness that the ideals of civil society provided only in name.

As Cohen[10] observed in her devastating critique, in Marx's theory of civil society "social, political, private, and legal institutions were treated as the environment of the capitalist system, to be transformed by its logic but without a dynamism of their own." Nothing more clearly illustrates the paradigm shift from CSI to CSII than the accusations Marx made against Hegel, namely, that he had sought, in a reactionary manner, to justify just such a privatized, selfish vision of civil society, that he had identified the civil sphere only with the 'system of needs' that became the mode of production Marx's own work.[11] But Hegel actually never did any such thing. To the contrary, he sought to rework the liberal line of CSI in a more communal, solidaristic way. It is true that the available linguistic resources and the peculiarities of German history had led Hegel, as it had led Kant before him, to translate the English term, civil society, as *Burgerlich Gesell-schaft*, literally 'burger' but more broadly 'bourgeois' or 'middle class' society.[12] But Marx's contention that Hegel, and non-socialists more generally, had identified civil society simply with capitalist class structures was an ahistorical distortion reflecting the sense of crisis that marked the birth of industrial society. For Hegel, the civil sphere was not only the world of economic needs but also the sphere of ethics and law, and other intermediate groupings that we would today call voluntary organizations.[13]

It is not surprising that in this social and intellectual situation, in the middle of the nineteenth century, civil society as an important concept in social theory shortly disappeared. If it was no more than an epiphenomenon of capitalism, then it was no longer necessary, either intellectually or socially. In the context of the ravages of early industrial capitalism, social and intellectual attention shifted to the state. Substantive rather than formal equality became the order of the day. Issues of democratic participation and liberty, once conceived as inherently connected to equality in its other forms, became less important. Strong state theories emerged, among both radicals and conservatives, and bureaucratic regulation appeared as the only counterbalance to the instabilities and inhumanities of market life.[14] In the newly emerging social sciences, mobility, poverty, and class conflict become the primary topics of research and theory. In social and political philosophy, utilitarian and contract theories assumed prominence, along with the neo-Kantian emphasis on justice in terms of formal rationality and proceduralism at the expense of ethical investigations into the requirements of the good life.

The legacy of this century-long distortion of the capitalism-civil society relationship has had regrettable effects. Identifying society with the market, ideologists for the right have argued that the effective functioning of capitalism depends on the dissolution of social controls. Secure in the knowledge that civil society is the private market, that economic processes by themselves will produce the institutions necessary to promote democracy and mutual respect, they have labored righteously to disband the very public institutions that crystallize social solidarity outside the market place. Such efforts have continued to this day.[15]

Yet if, for the right, the capitalism–civil society identification suggested abolishing society, for the left it suggested abolishing markets and private property itself. If civility and cooperation were perverted and distorted by capitalism, the latter would have to be abolished for the former to be restored. In this way, the big state became the principal ally of the left, and progressive movements became associated not only with equality but with stifling and often authoritarian bureaucratic control.

This was by no means confined to the Marxist left. For thinkers from Walter Lippman and John Dewey to C. Wright Mills, Hannah Arendt, Jurgen Habermas, and most recently Robert Putnam, the disappearance of public life became axiomatic to any thoughtful consideration of twentieth century modernity.[16] Captives of the historical shift in intellectual presuppositions which I have described as CSII, these influential thinkers were unable to think reflexively about it. They were convinced that capitalism was destroying public life, that in democratic mass societies an all-powerful market was pulverizing social bonds, converting citizens into egoists, and allowing oligarchies and bureaucracies full sway. Capitalism and mass societies were conceived as social worlds in which privacy ruled. That this was, in fact, far from the case had become for even the most acute social observers very difficult to see. Because CSI had given way to CSII, they could no longer draw upon the idea of an independent civil sphere. The social conditions that had triggered the demise of CSI still held sway.

In a paradoxical manner, the civil society thinking of Antonio Gramsci, which differed significantly from the reductive understandings of traditional CSII, actually seemed to buttress these fateful lapses in critical democratic thought, whether liberal or socialist. Drawing on a less reductive reading of Hegel, in the early decades of the 20th century Gramsci had developed his own, thoroughly anti-individualistic and anti-economistic approach to civil society. He defined it as the realm of political, cultural, legal, and public life that occupied an intermediate zone between economic relations and political power.[17] With this idea, Gramsci meant to challenge the evolutionary line of Marxist thinking, which held that socialist revolution would be triggered automatically, by a crisis in the economy alone. Broadening Lenin's earlier critique of economism, Gramsci suggested that civil society itself would have

28

to be challenged, and transformed, independently of the strains created by capitalism's economic base. Yet, even while Gramsci challenged the instrumentalism of Marx's thinking about the civil sphere, he reinforced CSII by insisting that, within the confines of capitalist market society, there would never be the space for institutionalizing solidarity of a more universalistic and inclusive kind. Gramsci did not associate civil society with democracy. It was a product of class-divided capitalism understood in the broad sociocultural and economic sense. The values, norms, and institutions of civil society were opposed to the interest of the mass of humanity, even if they did provide a space for contesting their own legitimacy in a public, counterhegemonic way. Civil society was inherently capitalist. It was a sphere that could be entered into but not redefined. Its discourse could not be broadened and redirected. It was a sphere that would have to be overthrown. In this book, my argument is directed in an opposite way.

Return to Civil Society I?

In recent decades a series of social and cultural events has created the circumstances for a renewed intellectual engagement with civil society. Big state theory has lost its prestige, economically with the falling productivity of command economies, morally and politically with the overthrow of state Communism and bureaucratic authoritarian regimes.[18] Within social science, there is now more interest in informal ties, intimate relationships, trust, cultural and symbolic processes, and the institutions of public life.[19] In political and moral philosophy, there has not only been a return to democratic theory, but renewed interest in Aristotle, Hegel, critical hermeneutics and Pragmatism—all marking a return to investigations of the lifeworld ties of local culture and community.[20]

The problem is that this re-engagement with civil society has largely meant a return to CSI. In *Democracy and Civil Society*, a path-breaking work in many ways, John Keane defines civil society broadly as "the realm of social activities," a realm that includes "privately owned," "market-directed," "voluntarily run," and "friendship-based" organizations, phenomena that are by no means necessarily theoretically complementary or practically congenial. Keane goes on to assert, moreover, that such civil activities are at once "legally recognized" and "guaranteed by the state," even as they form an "autonomous [sphere of] social life." Civil society is said to be "an aggregate of institutions whose members are engaged primarily in a complex of non-state activities–economic and cultural production, household life and voluntary association," seemingly private activities that Kane identifies as distinctly "sociable" and at the same time "public spheres."[21] Similarly, when Andrew Arato[22] first employed civil society in his important articles on the Solidarity movement in the early 1980s, he suggested that the civil sphere in its Western form was tied to private property, a traditional understanding that not only contradicts the broad range of references employed by Keane but threatens to render the concept useless for distinguishing democratic from nondemocratic capitalistic societies. A decade later, in their major philosophical rethinking of civil society theory, Cohen and Arato[23] severed this connection, and in its place they offered a substantially improved three-part model of society that went well beyond CSI and CSII. Nonetheless, perhaps by relying so heavily on Hegel, this major work failed to define the civil sphere as distinctive vis-a-vis such arenas as family life, and neglected entirely the relation between the civil sphere and such arenas as culture, religion, ethnicity, and race.[24] Here they were following Habermas, who insists on separating rational discourse in the public sphere from the traditions of cultural life.[25]

The same tendency toward diffuseness marked Alan Wolfe's[26] identification of civil society with the private realm of family and voluntary organization, and Adam Seligman's[27] insistence that it corresponds to the rule of reason in the Enlightenment sense. Carole Pateman[28] claims civil society to be inextricably linked to patriarchal family relations, and Shils[29] and Walzer[30], while disagreeing with Pateman in virtually every other way, likewise revert to an understanding of civil society that reflects its earlier diffuse and umbrella-like form. Victor Perez-Diaz[31] argues, indeed, that only such a 'maximalist' approach to civil society can maintain the necessary linkages between a democratic public sphere and particular forms of economy, state, family, and cultural life. Though Robert Putnam's model for strengthening democracy through voluntary associations does not focus explicitly on the civil society idea, this neo-Tocquevillian approach looks backward to CSI in very much the same way.[32]

It is most definitely a good thing that the destructive and overly narrow understandings of CSII have been undermined by the recent revival of democratic thought. But social life at the beginning of the twenty-first century is much more complex and more internally differentiated than the early modern societies that generated CSI. The old umbrella understanding will no longer do. We need a much more precise and delimited understanding of the term. Private property, markets, family life, and religious ideals might all be necessary at some point or another to create the capacities of the civil sphere, but they are by no means sufficient to sustain it. Rejecting the reductionism of CSII, but also the diffuse inclusiveness of CSI, we must develop a third approach to civil society, one that reflects both the empirical and normative problems of contemporary life.

Toward Civil Society III

We need to understand civil society as a sphere that can be ⌊analytically independent⌉ empirically differentiated, and morally more universalistic vis-à-vis the state and the market and from other social spheres as well. Building upon important directional signals from empirical theoretical traditions in sociology and normative traditions in political theory and philosophy–which I have discussed in chapter 1 and will elaborate further in chapter 3—I would like to suggest that civil society should be conceived as a solidary sphere, in which a certain kind of universalizing community comes to be culturally defined and to some degree institutionally enforced. To the degree that this solidary community exists, it is exhibited and sustained by public opinion, deep cultural codes, distinctive organizations—legal, journalistic and associational—and such historically specific interactional practices as civility, criticism, and mutual respect.[33] Such a civil community can never exist as such; it can only be sustained to one degree or another. It is always limited by, and interprenetrated with, the boundary relations of other, non-civil spheres.

The solidarity that sustains the civil sphere amidst the complex and highly conflictual spheres of contemporary life draws from long-standing cultural and institutional traditions that have sustained individual and collective obligation. CSII theories were quite mistaken to link not only individualism (its emergence) but the collective sense of social obligation (its decline) with market society. The individuality that sustains civil society has a long history in Western societies, as a moral force, an institutional fact, and a set of interactional practices. It has a non-economic background in the cultural

31

legacy of Christianity, with its emphasis on the immortal soul, conscience, and confession; in aristocratic liberty and Renaissance self-fashioning; in the Reformation's insistence on the individual relation to God; in the Enlightenment's deification of individual reason; in Romanticism's restoration of expressive individuality. Institutions that reward and model individuality can be traced back to English legal guarantees for private property in the eleventh century; to the medieval parliaments that distinguished the specificity of Western feudalism; to the newly independent cities that emerged in late medieval times and played such a powerful historical role until the emergence of absolutist states. The economic practices of market capitalism, in other words, did not invent either moral or immoral individualism. They should be viewed, rather, as marking a new specification and institutionalization of it, along with other newly emerging forms of social organization, such as religious sect activity, mass parliamentary democracy, and romantic love.[34]

Just as individualism in its moral and expressive forms preceded, survived, and in effect surrounded the instrumental, self-oriented individualism institutionalized in capitalist market life, so did the existence of "society." Civil ties and the enforcement of obligations to a community of others were part of the fundamental structure of many British towns centuries before the appearance of contemporary capitalist life.[35] The notion of a "people" rooted in common lineage, of the community as an ethnos, formed the early basis for an ethically binding, particularist conception of nationhood from at least the fifteenth century.[36] Karl Polanyi well described the "double movement" that characterized the emergence of industrial capitalism in the nineteenth century, pitting "moral forces" representing "the moral entity 'man' " against the egoistical, impersonal, and degrading practices of the market. The upshot of this struggle was that the "general interests of the community" created "protectionist measures" regulating the conditions of land, labor, and productive organization inside the very bowels of economic life. "Once we rid ourselves of the obsession that only sectional, never general, interest can become effective," Polanyi writes, "as well as the twin prejudice of restricting the interests of human groups to their monetary income, the breadth and depth of the protectionist movement lose their mystery."[37] Still, Polanyi is wrong to describe this "countermovement" as of a "purely practical and pragmatic nature," as producing measures that "simply responded to the needs of an industrial civilization with which market methods were unable to cope."[38] The protectionist movement did not simply grow naturally in response to a moral violation that was there for all to see. Rather, this defensive moral response emerged precisely because there had already existed strongly institutionalized and culturally mandated reservoirs of non-market, non-individualistic force in Western social life. It was from these sources that there emerged protests against capitalism on behalf of "the people."[39]

To identify civil society with capitalism (CSII) is to degrade its universalizing moral implications and the capacity for criticism and repair that the existence of a relatively independent solidary community implies. The civil sphere and the market must be conceptualized in fundamentally different terms. We are no more a capitalist society than we are a bureaucratic, secular, rational one, or indeed a civil one. Yet, to suggest the need to acknowledge the environment outside of economic life is not to embrace the kind of relativism that the pluralism of CSI implies. Michael Walzer has argued eloquently that there are as many spheres of justice as there are differentiated social spheres.[40] Luc Boltanski and Laurent Thevenot, in a parallel argument, suggest that complex societies contain several "regimes of justification," each of which must be respected in its own right.[41] As these American and French theories persuasively remind us, no social sphere, not even the economic, should be conceived in anti-normative terms, as governed only by interest and egoism. They have immanent moral structures in their own right. It remains vital, nonetheless, to specify and differentiate the "regime of justification" or the "sphere of justice" that makes a clear and decisive reference to the common good in a democratic way. This is the criterion of justice that follows from ideals that regulate the civil sphere. The codes and narratives, the institutions, and the interactions that underlay civil solidarity clearly depart from those that regulate the world of economic cooperation and competition, the affectual and intimate relations of family life, and the transcendental and abstract symbolism that form the media of intellectual and religious interaction and exchange.

When the domination of one sphere over another, or the monopolization of resources by elites within the individual spheres themselves, has been forcefully blocked, it has been by bringing to bear the cultural codes and regulative institutions of the civil sphere. This, at least, is the thesis that informs this book. Civil and noncivil spheres do not merely co-exist in a kind of harmonious interchange, as functionalist theories of differentiation from Spencer and Durkheim to Parsons and Luhmann imply. It is not only the pluralization of spheres that guarantees a good society, nor the free play and good will of interlocutors willing to compromise their interests in the face of competing and persuasive claims for moral justification. To maintain democracy, and to achieve justice, it is often necessary for the civil to 'invade' noncivil spheres, to demand certain kinds of reforms, and to monitor them through regulation in turn. In modern times, aggrieved parties have demanded justice by pointing angrily to what they come to see as destructive intrusions into the civil realm, intrusions whose demands they construct as particularistic and self-serving. In response, the forces and institutions of civil society have often initiated repairs that aim to mend the social fabric.

In terms of the normative mandates established by democratic societies, it is the *civil* sphere of justice that trumps every other. The universality that is the ambition of this sphere, its demands to be inclusive, to fulfill collective obligations while at the same time protecting individual autonomy—these qualities have persistently made the civil sphere the court of last resort in modern, modernizing, and postmodernizing societies.[42] For the last two centuries explicitly, and implicitly for many centuries before, it has been the immanent and subjunctive demands of the civil sphere that have provided possibilities for justice.

As we will see in our later analysis of the tense and shifting boundaries between civil and uncivil spheres, CSIII allows us to revisit the 'capitalism problem' in a more productive way.[43] When exploitation leads to widening class conflict, it signals strains and inequalities in economic life. When class conflict leads to wide public discussion, to the formation of legal trade unions, to urgent appeals for sympathy and support, to scandals and parliamentary investigations, such expansion signals that market conflicts have entered into the civil sphere. In such situations, the mandate of solidarity, the presumptions of collective obligation and autonomy, come face to face with the demands for efficiency and hierarchy. These conflicts are not accidental; they are systematic to every society that opens up a civil sphere, and they make justice a possibility, though not in any sense a necessary social fact. In real civil societies, extending solidarity to others depends on the imagination. As I have suggested in chapter 1, the counter-factual "original position" that inspired Rawls' philosophy of justice is assumed in fantasy, as an idealization, via metaphor and symbolic analogy, not through pragmatic experience or logical deduction. It is a matter of cultural struggle, of social movement, of demands for incorporation, of broken and reconstructed dialogue, of reconfiguring institutional life.

Such tense and permeable boundary relationships between capitalist markets and the civil sphere, barely visible during the early reign of CSI, were denied in principle by CSII. Only if we develop a new model, CSIII, can we understand why capitalistic and civil society must not be conflated with one another. If these realms are separated analytically, we gain empirical and theoretical purchase, not only on the wrenching economic strains of the last two centuries, but on the extraordinary repairs to the social fabric that have so often been made in response. Markets are not, after all, the only threats or even the worst threats that have been levied against the democratic possibilities of civil life. Far from the mere existence of plural spheres providing the skeleton key to justice, each of the diverse and variegated spheres of modern societies has created distortions and undermined civil promises. Religious hatreds and repression, gender misogyny and patriarchy, the arrogance of expert knowledge and the secrecy of political oligarchy, racial and ethnic hatreds of every sort—each of these particularistic and anti-civil forces has deeply fragmented the civil domain. The identification of capitalism with civil society, in other words, is just one example of the reductive and circumscribing conflation of civil society with a particular kind of non-civil realm.

Social and cultural movements of every kind, whether old or new, economic or religious, have organized to expose the pretensions of civil society and the hollowness of its promises. The theorists and ideologists who have led these rebellious and critical movements have often concluded, in their desperation and frustration, that civil society has no real force at all. Whether such radical arguments focus on class, gender, race, or religion, their argument is much the same. Justice is impossible; revolution and flight are the only options left. In this book, I will suggest that these radical, and radically despairing, arguments for emancipation from civil society are not empirically accurate, even if they are sometimes morally compelling. Generalizing from distorted and oppressive boundary relations, they draw the false conclusion that the civil sphere must invariably be distorted in this manner, not only now but in the future as well. Building on this faulty line of reasoning, they have outlined utopian projects that reject universalizing solidarity as a social goal or have proposed a reconstructed social order in which only peaceable relations will reign. I will suggest in the chapter following why the aspiration to universalism simply cannot be dispensed with, and in Part II of this book I will explain why continuous conflicts over the structuring of solidarity are the inevitable result. There is no way to avoid conflicts over boundary relations. They reflect the pluralism and complexity that mark modern and postmodern life, especially in its democratic forms. Between civil society and the other social spheres there is a theoretically open and historically indeterminate relation. Sometimes, the power of noncivil spheres has overwhelmed the universalistic aspirations of the civil sphere. At other times, its relative autonomy has provided the possibility for justice.

CHAPTER 3

Bringing Democracy Back In:
Realism, Morality, Solidarity

A NY DISCUSSION OF the civil sphere is inextricably intertwined with an analysis of democracy as a political form. Indeed, it was to provide some rationale for political democracy that the early modern approach to the civil sphere (civil society I) emerged. Yet, the promise of civil society III is to take us beyond such political forms as narrowly conceived. Democratic politics, in the sense of voting and associational liberties, rests upon a broader, suprapolitical base, just as it helps give life to these social and cultural dynamics in turn. As we develop an approach to civil society III, we move from the restricted, if vital, concerns of democratic government to the broader problem of a democratic social life, a terrain that points not only to freedom in the exercise of political rights but to social and cultural freedoms, to inclusion and recognition, and to the problem of justice itself. "Democracy is more than a form of government," John Dewey insisted. "It is primarily a mode of associated living, of conjoint communicated experience."[1]

In order to get to this broader understanding of the civil sphere, however, we must work through the issues that are raised by democracy as more traditionally conceived.[2] We begin by reviewing the two broad approaches that marked the social scientific treatment of democracy in the last half of the twentieth century. After suggesting the limitations of each, I will argue that democracy depends on the existence of solidary bonds that extend beyond political arrangements.]Solidarity is civil only if it combines collective with individual obligations.\ Civil solidarity can be sustained only by a democratic language, a discourse that allows the abstract and universal commitments of the civil sphere to take concrete and imagistic forms. Justice is possible if there is civil solidarity, which itself depends on the vitality of a fluent and provocative moral discourse.

Utopianism: The Fallacies
of Twentieth-Century Evolutionism

In recent decades, as one nation after another has embarked on the long, difficult, and precarious effort to build a more liberal and responsive social order, democracy has once again become a fashionable term. It is ironic that, fifty years ago, in the early days of the Cold War, social scientists considered democracy to be something rather easily achieved, a heritage that the world deserved and would eventually receive. It was conceptualized as a necessary implication of the classical dichotomies that structured the field, of *Gesellschaft* as compared with *Gemeinschaft*, of organic versus mechanical solidarity, of rational-legal versus charismatic authority, and, most broadly, of modernity in contrast with traditionalism. We would become democratic by default, simply by virtue of being modern. Systematic distinctions were rarely made within the concept of modernity itself. Non-democratic societies were understood, rather, as not yet modern enough.

The classical founders of sociology hardly ever spoke of democracy, because they conceived it either as unlikely (Weber) or presumed it in the short or long term to be inevitable, part of the evolutionary package of modern life (Durkheim and Marx). In the postwar period that marked the birth of modern sociology, there was a new concern for democracy, and this discourse took two forms. One language stressed efficiency. Democracy was adaptive because it was flexible. Because it was flexible, it would survive. In Parsons's inimitable phrase, democracy was an evolutionary universal.[3] The other vocabulary was taken from the more intentional rationality of Enlightenment thought. In the postwar world, the victors had forcefully introduced democracy to their defeated enemies, and former imperialists to their soon-to-be-emancipated colonies. Constitutions were put into place,

38

legal guidelines established. These normative expectations, it was fondly believed, would be cherished and followed in due course.[4]

We can now see that these earlier efforts failed to fully understand the requisites of democracy. They were often technocratic and deterministic,[5] or hopelessly rationalistic and optimistic.[6] To continue such theorizing in the present day would not merely be anachronistic; it would be irresponsible.[7] We have learned that democracy does not come easily, that the universalism of modernity has often provided a fig leaf for particularity and exclusion. This education has been a salutary one. In normative theory, it has been reflected in the renaissance of democratic thought.[8] The shift which these developments have produced in social scientific understanding has not been as positive. Late modern and postmodern cynicism, materialist and world-weary realism, these have too often replaced the earlier, simplistic faith in democratic morality. Instead of exploring politics, social scientists began to explore society. They investigated the so-called social origins of political arrangements,[9] and they downplayed the effects of constitutions and political norms.[10] Conflict models replaced theories about the possibility of social integration.[11] When the specificity of politics was acknowledged, moreover, the independent state was still conceived in a purely instrumental way, as simply another, more independent power bloc within which egoistic interest could be pursued.[12]

Realism: The Tradition of Thrasymachus

This did not mean that political ideals disappeared from the sociological discourse about politics. It meant, rather, that they were now pursued in a tough-minded way. Democracy has come to be considered merely a formal arrangement. It is the distribution of power and force, the balance of material resources, that is important. Equality now becomes the central focus; class conflict and power structure the topics of elaborate analysis.[13] If there is unequal economic or political power, it is assumed that dominant groups will pursue their interests by any available means. It is the availability of means that counts, not the nature of ends. It is concrete goals that matter, not the moral frameworks that can encapsulate them.[14] Citizenship results from class struggle, rather than class struggle being mediated and channeled by citizenship. Rights are not conceptualized in an independent way. Democracy is explained as the product of a truce between conflict groups that have achieved relative but temporary parity,[15] a political manifestation of a capitalism whose function is to provide "the material bases for consent."[16]

In fact, despite the return of democracy in recent decades, critical theories about the political condition of contemporary societies have persistently demonstrated little confidence in the possibilities for its realization. When Marcuse attacked capitalist democracies as one-dimensional and totalitarian, he was considered a radical iconoclast.[17] Thirty years later, Foucault gained wide acceptance for a historical and social theory that, though less economic and more cultural-political, emphasized the same repressive qualities in Western societies while virtually ignoring the meaning of a democratic state.[18] Citizens of Western societies are seen as monitored, as subject to surveillance.[19] They are selfish and do not engage in public life.[20] No possibility for binding ties of a horizontal kind—much less the idea of a normatively regulated, constitutional democracy—appears in the work of Bourdieu, who created the most expansive sociological theory of recent times.[21] When democratic ideas have become the focus of recent social analysis, they are conceived as ideology, not as values, which is to frame them as a cultural means of pursuing strategic ends.[22]

Such debunking rhetoric, of course, has the distinct merit of cutting pretentious authority down to size, and for this very reason it has been a mainstay of democratic politics in modern times. In this manner, social science thinking about democratic societies becomes merely an extension of democratic practice. Without gaining more theoretical distance on democracy, however, neither intellectual nor moral reflexivity about the political process can be achieved. The development of a realistic theory of democratic societies becomes impossible. Only the possibility of a realist theory remains.

We are left with the tradition of Thrasymachus, an object of praise in an essay written by one of the first sociological conflict theorists.[23] Thrasymachus provided the foil for Plato. Against Socrates' vision of an ideal and transcendent justice, Thrasymachus insisted on base motives and the necessary cruelty of political life: " 'Just' or 'right' means nothing but what is in the interest of the strongest party. . . . In all states alike, 'right' has the same meaning, namely what is for the interest of the party established in power, and that is the strongest."[24]

Such hardheaded caution about idealism clearly is important. In fact, it sometimes seems that the entire tradition of normative political theory has been written with Thrasymachus in mind. In his *Politics*, the ever-practical Aristotle argued, against Platonic idealism, that well-ordered constitutions would have to be divided against themselves.[25] Montesquieu, in *The Spirit of Laws*, suggested that, if independent institutions were not pitted against each other, the natural tendencies of human beings for tyranny, arbitrary control, and uncontrolled violence would triumph.[26] In his arguments supporting ratification of the U.S. Constitution, James Madison eloquently said much the same. Assuming that base motives and self-interest ruled all politics, he dismissed solidarity as a starry-eyed dream and argued that American democracy could rely only on the separation and balancing of inveterate antagonists.[27]

Classical social scientific theories of democracy largely followed a similar path, which helps explain the powerful resurgence of realistic thinking in our own day.[28] Marx economized Thrasymachus when he argued that democracy was a sham, reasoning that unequal class power ensured that economic interest would dominate political life.[29] Weber sociologized Thrasymachus when he argued that democracy depended on the creation of powerful counterweights to state bureaucracies, on the emergence of political demagogues and ruthless party organizations.[30] Following upon Marx and Weber, Michels argued that socialist parties and unions became oligarchical because their leaders could monopolize an organization's material resources.[31] When Lipset, Coleman, and Trow wrote *Union Democracy*, they followed in Michels's footsteps.[32] They argued that democracy could be defined only organizationally, as a differentiated system of rewards and sanctions sustaining opportunities for effective group competition.

This line of thinking is certainly essential to any realistic thinking about democracy. The return to it has been an important antidote to the ideological innocence and theoretical simplification of midcentury social thought. It has also functioned as an antidote to the democratic rhetoric in which state socialist regimes so often engaged. In a world where the idea of democracy has too often been merely an ideological subterfuge for leveling dictatorship, we would do well to remember the separation of powers and the kinds of formal procedures that guarantee it. The self-interested dimension of human action must be firmly respected, as must the significantly self-aggrandizing character of every social group. Even the most idealistic democrats acknowledge that fully participatory decision making is impossible to sustain over an extended period of time.[33] Oligarchies do form in every organization. If these elites are not given what they consider their due, they will respond in destructive ways. Democracies depend on social structures that allow egoism to be pursued but that make the aggregation of egoism impossible. No society can prevent the formation of elites, and a society can be democratic only to the extent that the interests of these elites are differentiated in a manner that makes them competitive rather than convergent.[34] If society cannot prevent elite formation, it can at least prevent the widespread monopolization of power and resources by any one among them.[35] This is not an elitist theory of democracy; it is a realistic one.

It is no accident that the virtues of this narrowly institutional approach were most recently renewed by theorists on the post–Marxist Left, who wished to save socialism from the clutches of totalitarian thought. In Germany, Habermas left the Marxism of his early work on the public sphere, studied the evolution of universal morality, and created a democratic theory that emphasizes dialogue and legal forms. In Italy, Norberto Bobbio defended the democratic aspect of socialism by insisting on "mainly procedural mechanisms." In Britain, John Keane returned to the traditional understanding of democracy as "a differentiated and pluralistic system of power," and David Held brought socialist economic thinking and democratic political thought together in a particularly sophisticated way. In France, Claude Lefort pointed to the "institutional apparatus" that creates democracy, the "disentangling of the sphere of power" that "prevents governments from appropriating power for their own ends." In an American inflection of this post–Marxist political turn, Robert Alford and Roger Friedland insisted that class structures were mediated, not only by autonomous states, but by plural groups in civil society.[36]

Morality and Solidarity

The premise of this book is that a realistic social theory of democracy need not be so narrowly construed. It must, indeed, be hard-headed, focusing on real as compared to ideal civil societies.[37] But it need not be realistic in the mechanistic and reductionistic sense. It need not presuppose cynical and instrumental actors, nor imagine a democratic order that is only external and institutional. Cynicism and pessimism need not be the only order of the day.[38]

To understand democracy realistically, elite conflict and structural differentiation cannot form the exclusive point of our interest. However well intentioned, and however important a window on critically important aspects of democratic life, the tradition of Thrasymachus is not adequate to understand politics, much less the phenomenon of democracy more broadly, more sociologically, and more culturally conceived. Within the narrow confines of Thrasymachus, we have no access to the interior domain, to the "structures of feeling," the "habits of the heart," and the worlds of moral sense and perception that make living together possible. We cannot illuminate the mysterious process by which citizens so often agree, willingly and without coercion, to uphold rules whose utility they scarcely understand and whose effect may be detrimental to their self-interest narrowly understood.[39]

It is not only difference and antagonism that sustains democracy, but solidarity and commonality. We need to develop a model of democratic societies that pays more attention to shared feelings and symbolic commitments, to what and how people speak, think, and feel about politics and, more generally, about democratic social life. We need a theory, in other words, that is less myopically centered on social structure and power distribution, and more responsive to the ideas that people have in their heads and to what Tocqueville called the habits of their hearts.[40]

It is for this reason that I stress the critical role of social solidarity. But as I emphasized in the last chapter, I wish to understand civil society as the arena not of solidarity narrowly defined in a communitarian and particularistic way but in universalistic terms. It is the we-ness of a national, regional, or international community, the feeling of connectedness to "every member" of that community, that transcends particular commitments, narrow loyalties, and sectional interests. Only this kind of solidarity can provide a thread, not of identity in the narrow sense, but of the kind of mutual identification that unites individuals dispersed by class, race, religion, ethnicity, or race. Edward Shils once wrote, following Durkheim, that every functioning group needs a collective self-consciousness.[41] What must be added is that a collectivity so constituted supports a civil sphere only to the degree that collective self-consciousness can extend so widely and deeply that it can, in principle, include as full members every grouping and individual composing it. Identification over a widely dispersed territorial space can be sustained only by universalizing ties, bonds that transcend particularistic interest groups and identity communities alike.[42] Paradoxically, only when there is such a common and unifying thread, one that is supraindividual and extraparticular, can the individuals who compose the various social groups be freed from compulsions of a hierarchical kind. Only through the existence of a universalizing social solidarity can individuals become free and responsible for their putatively "natural" autonomous rights.

Civil society is a form of social and cultural organization rooted simultaneously in a radical individualism and a thoroughgoing collectivism, a combination best captured in Habermas's notion of "the sphere of private people come together as a public."[43] The phrase "We, the people," which begins the U.S. Constitution, is a reference that constitutes the "civil" in every struggle to broaden social participation and extend equality.[44] Yet if solidarity were extended only to the collectivity as such, it would become a particularism supporting repression, not liberty. Indeed, by understanding civil solidarity only in its purely collective sense, twentieth-century totalitarian regimes justified their governments as "people's democracies."[45] In his reflections on the social dimensions of modern citizenship, T. H. Marshall underscored the fundamental importance of complementing the collective, communal component of solidarity with the institutionalized protection of individuals. Distinguishing "Socialism II," exemplified by the postwar British welfare state, from "Socialism I," the Bolshevik's communist model, Marshall emphasized the former's insistence that welfare be distributed on the basis of individual rights and obligations rather than according simply to collective membership in the national group.[46]

The liberal tradition that largely informed civil society I has often been accused, and often also praised, for approaching the civil sphere in an emphatically individualistic way. It is important to recognize, however, that the major theorists of civil society I understood that such democratic individuality depended on solidarity as well. In his *Second Treatise on Government*, for example, Locke traced the creation of an independent sphere of fellowship, a "commonwealth" that emerges from the state of nature and is extended, via the social contract, to the civil law regulating social life. This solidarity rests, in turn, upon the capacity for individuation. It is because human beings are "all equal and independent," according to Locke, that "no one ought to harm another in his life, health, liberty or possession."[47] The Scottish moralists elaborated precisely this interrelation of solidarity and individuation. In Adam Ferguson's *History of Civil Society*, a response to what he considered the overly rationalistic individualism of contract theory, he argued that an increase in self-control and "subtlety" and a decrease in brute impulse were necessary for the emergence of civil society. At the same time, Ferguson identified civil society with the social bond that establishes "fellow feeling" among the members of a nation.[48] Similarly, while Adam Smith, in his *Theory of Moral Sentiments*, emphasized the role of shared values in constituting the "impartial spectator," a kind of third-party observer that ensured universalism and fairness, he also highlighted the individualistic search for recognition and prestige that lay at the base of this newly civil sphere.[49] An effort to connect individual and collectivity also lay at the base of Tocqueville's conception of the sphere of democratic public life. Describing it as based on "self-interest rightly understood," he expressly anchored individualism in the collectively binding, extrapolitical world of legal regulation and, more important, in the cultural mores that undergirded American individualism in his time.[50]

Complexity and Community

In the tradition of normative political theory that most emphatically objects to the consideration of politics in exclusively utilitarian and individualistic terms—the postwar republican tradition that extends from Arendt and Wolin to Unger, MacIntyre, Walzer, Sandel, and, in a rather ambiguous way, to Habermas[51]—democracy is understood as a participatory political community whose citizens display commitments to a public interest that transcends private and egoistic concerns. From the perspective of these ideal, and idealized, democratic forms, these thinkers have called for a politics of vision, a vision in relation to which contemporary political life often seems mean-spirited and instrumental. According to this republican and sometimes communitarian ideal, democracy can be sustained only if a sense of altruistic civic virtue permeates political life.

The problem here is not with such an emphasis on shared internal commitments and solidarity, which provided a welcome antidote to the tradition of Thrasymachus, much less with the interjection, against purely realistic empirical theories, of considerations of an explicitly normative kind. The problem is with the manner in which these commitments are understood. Too often, the republican tradition has conflated its normative aspirations with behavioral possibilities. Certainly, the moral ought must inform investigation into the empirical is, but this commitment to idealized standards should not obfuscate the existence of norms and values that have a lesser but still significant effect. If political life is not fully participatory, the republican tradition too often judges it to be egotistical and instrumental, as if it were ruled only by interests, not values. If it is not virtuous in a liberal democratic or socialist sense, it too often is judged to be without reference to any conception of virtue at all.[52] Similar problems have detracted from sociological reactions to political utilitarianism. When Robert Bellah and his colleagues demanded new habits of the heart, and Daniel Bell called for a new public household, they too drew upon this idealized republican vision of the possibility for a powerful and controlling civic virtue.[53] While morally admirable and politically provocative, such utopian thinking neglects the heartfelt habits that contemporary societies do sustain and the civil accounting that continues to regulate privilege and power, though never in a fully satisfactory way.

If we wish to develop an approach to democratic social life that acknowledges the role of solidarity and moral ideals, we must start from a more realistic conception of the difficulties and challenges faced by complex societies. Self-interest and conflict will never give way before some all-embracing republican or communal ideal. Indeed, the more democratic a society, the more it allows groups to define their own specific ways of life and legitimates the inevitable conflicts of interest that arise among them. Political consensus can never be brought to bear in a manner that neutralizes particular group obligations and commitments. To think that it can be is to repeat the fallacy of Rousseau's belief in a communal consensus like the general will distinct from the actual will of particular individuals and groups.[54] A much more complex and internally differentiated conception of solidarity and political culture is needed, one that will be more tolerant of individual differences and more compatible with the pluralization of interests. We must recognize that the communal ties that underlie civil solidarity are constructed in something quite other than an overtly communitarian way.

In fact, one of the enduring normative-cum-empirical contributions of the structural-functional tradition was its insistence that broadly shared moral ties do not mean that individuals and groups pursue similar or even complementary goals and interests.[55] At the same time, the pursuit of divergent and conflictual goals does not mean, contrary to the more individualistic strands of the liberal and rationalist traditions, that shared understandings are not highly significant. Generalized commitments inform and influence goals even if they do not create them. Concrete situations have their own exigencies, but they do not create goals and interests out of a whole cloth. The articulation of this more specific level is always informed by the logic of more generalized patterns, by norms and by cultural codes and narrative structures that can provide a common medium of communication between conflict groups despite their often strategic and divisive aims. Without returning to communitarian earlier innocence or liberal-rationalist naiveté, this cultural dimension must be studied if any plausible sociological theory of democratic social order is to emerge.

This critical insight was hardly confined to the structural-functional school. Hegel also forcefully criticized the theoretical illusion, so common to mechanistic theories, that individuals and institutions are entirely separated from some broader *Geist*. The reasons actors offer for their actions, he insisted, are in fact deeply embedded in moral conceptions of which they are often unaware. Simmel, too, suggested that social conflicts are embedded in concepts, in implicit, idealized, and highly generalized notions that define the rewards for which conflict groups fighting, and even their conceptions of others and themselves. Walzer has argued that the structure of political obligations is much the same. Justifications for political actions and opinions may be forcefully expressed in the language of free will and individual desire; yet the very fact that actors feel obligated to speak or act in these ways reveals that they do so as members of communities. The groups to which they belong impose these obligations in the name of their "higher" ideals. Individuals must act at the level of situationally specific demands; in doing so, however, they implicitly invoke the more general understanding of their groups. This does not mean, however, that such actors may not feel themselves bound by communities that are broader and more abstractly defined than those that define their immediate, everyday lives.[56]

Cultural Codes and Democratic Communication

Particular goals and even the most strategic of actions are framed and sometimes bound by commitments to cultural codes. The tradition of Thrasymachus explores the base of politics. But power is also a medium of communication, not simply a goal of interested action or a means of coercion.
It has a symbolic code, not only a material base.[57]

It is, in fact, precisely because politics has reference to a symbolic code
that it can never be simply situational, for it will always have a generalized
dimension as well. This generalized reference makes politics not only contingent and rational but stylized and prescribed. To understand it, we need
to employ semiotic theories of binary codes, literary models of rhetoric and
narrative, and anthropological concepts of performance and myth. The
symbolic medium of politics is a language that political actors themselves do
not fully understand. It is not only situationally motivated speech, but deep
symbolic structure. In his riposte to functionalist and other equally reductive
anthropologies, Levi-Strauss once insisted that kinship exists "only in human
consciousness; it is an arbitrary system of representations, not the spontaneous development of a real situation."[58] This seminal insight is not only
anthropological, nor does it apply only to archaic worlds. Wittgenstein
placed this notion at the basis of his later, and most profound, language
philosophy.[59] In the chapters that follow, it will inform my sociology of the
modern civil domain.|For I wish to insist on the significance of language in
political life, even if I will follow neither structuralism nor Wittgenstein
in suggesting we can focus on language alone.|As Arlette Farge has written
in her investigation of the plebian public sphrere in prerevolutionary France,
"the words which give opinions—this will do, that will not do—are a reality
and show very clearly that the people of Paris did not blindly accept the
conditions under which they lived." It is their "speech whose meaning we
must strive to discover," she argues, for "words spoken and opinions pronounced could open up distances, cause displacements and organize something which was new to the spheres of saying and doing." It is for this
reason, she concludes, that historians "have to cleave to words so as to
extract their meanings."[60] So must social theorists and sociologists as well.

Civil society is regulated by an internally complex discourse that allows
us to understand the paradox by which its universalistic ideals have so easily
been institutionalized in particularistic and anticivil ways. The breadth and

scope of a civil community led Kant and other Enlightenment philosophers to identify civil ties by such abstract terms as "reason" and "right."[61] In his discourse ethics, which has done so much to sustain the normative idea of universalism in the present day, Habermas has translated this Enlightenment philosophical vocabulary into a theory of rational speech acts. Making the willingness to cooperate immanent to the efforts that speakers make to gain understanding in conversations, and generalizing from this thought experiment to the macrosociological sphere of civil public life, Habermas has effectively limited analysis of public discourse to such concepts as reasonableness, reciprocity, and fairness. Only such references, he has insisted, can create completely "transparent" communication. As I also mentioned in chapter 1, similar strains of abstract universalism permeate Rawls's theory of justice, which rests on the hypothesis that actors can develop solidaristic distributive principles only by denying any actual knowledge of their own particular personal fates. Durkheim's discussion of the growing "abstraction of the collective conscience" and Parsons's of "value generalization" and "instrumental activism" reveal the same effort to tie civil solidarity to an abstract and contentless conception of rationality.[62]

Universalistic ties, however, do not have to be articulated by abstract references to reason or right, to a discourse that transcends the arbitrary in a completely transparent way. Such references do, of course, inform foundational documents like the American *Declaration of Independence* and the French *Declaration of the Rights of Man*. But to limit our thinking about democratic discourse to such symbols alone is to commit what might be called the fallacy of misplaced abstractness. Strange as it may seem, universalism is most often articulated in concrete rather than abstract language. Reworking the narratives and codes of local and particular cultures, normative demands for civility and mutual respect express themselves in figurative images, salty metaphors, hoary myths, and binary oppositions. Universalism anchors itself, in other words, in the everyday lifeworlds within which ordinary people make sense of the world and pass their time. For the French revolutionary *sans-coulettes* and the colonial American patriots, the civil society they fought for was not abstract. For the French, it was the "beloved nation," often portrayed iconically as a woman, Marie, the goddess of liberty.[63] Revolutionary Americans metaphorically inscribed critical reason in the prophetic narratives of the Old Testament and freedom in such icons as the Liberty Tree.[64]

That civil language is symbolic and experiential, not only rational in the moral or strategic sense, that the very effort to speak universalism must always and everywhere take a concrete form, opens our consideration of civil society not only to the particularistic but also the repressive dimensions of modern democratic life. Because meaning is relational and relative, the civility of the self always articulates itself in language about the incivility of the other. This paradox in the very construction of the language of civil society is intensified by the contradictions that inevitably accompany organizational efforts to institutionalize it. There remains the possibility of justice, but it is devilishly difficult to obtain. These are the dilemmas we take up in the chapters that follow.

PART II

STRUCTURES AND DYNAMICS
OF THE CIVIL SPHERE

CHAPTER 4

Discourses:

Liberty and Repression

S OCIAL SCIENTISTS HAVE written much about the social forces that create conflict and polarize society and about the interests and structures of political, economic, racial, ethnic, religious, and gender groups. But they have said very little about the construction, destruction, and reconstruction of civic solidarity itself. They are generally silent about the sphere of fellow feeling, the we-ness that makes society into society, and even less about the processes that fragment it.

For reasons I suggested in Part I, civil society is conceived here as a sphere or subsystem of society that is analytically and, to various degrees, empirically separated from the spheres of political, economic, family, and religious life. Civil society is a sphere of solidarity in which individual rights and collective obligations are tensely intertwined. It is both a normative and a "real" concept. It allows the relationship between universalism and particularism, so central to philosophical thinking, to be studied empirically, as a condition that determines the status of civil society itself.

Civil society depends on resources or inputs from other spheres, from political life, from economic and political institutions, from familial and religious life, from territorial organizations, and from more narrowly constructed primordial communities. In this sense, it can be said that civil society is dependent on these spheres, but this is true only in a very partial sense.

Civil society—and the groups, institutions, and individuals who articulate their "interests" in civil society terms—pulls together these inputs according to its own normative and institutional logic. This is to say that the solidary sphere we call civil society has relative autonomy and can be studied in its own right. It is homologous with, to some degree independent of, and sometimes a match for the other "societies" that constitute the subject of contemporary social science—the economic, the political, the familial, the ethnic, the religious.[1]

Against the new utilitarianism, and other recent installments in the tradition of Thrasymachus, I wish to defend the position that there is, indeed, such a thing as "society," and that it can be defined in moral terms.[2] In the chapters that follow, I will show how the liberating and repressive stipulations of this moral community articulate with organizational power via such regulatory institutions as party and legal systems, voting, and "office," on the one hand, and with such communicative institutions as mass media, public opinion polls, and civil associations, on the other. Civil society is also constituted by its own distinctive structure of elites, by the institutional oligarchies that direct the legal and communications systems, the influentials who exercise persuasion through civil associations, and the "movement intellectuals" who lead social movements.[3]

But civil society is not merely an institutional realm. It is also a realm of structured, socially established consciousness, a network of understandings creating structures of feeling that permeate social life and run just below the surface of strategic institutions and self-conscious elites. To study this subjective dimension of civil society, we must recognize and focus on the distinctive symbolic codes that are critically important in constituting the very sense of society for those who are within and without it. These codes are so sociologically important, I would argue, that every study of social division and conflict must be complemented by reference to this civil symbolic sphere.

Pure and Impure in Civil Discourse

Binary codes supply the structured categories of pure and impure into which every member, or potential member, of civil society is made to fit. It is in terms of symbolic purity and impurity that centrality is defined, that marginal demographic status is made meaningful, and high position understood as deserved or illegitimate. Pollution is a threat to any allocative system; its sources must either be kept at bay or transformed by communicative actions, like rituals and social movements, into a pure form.

Despite their enormous behavioral impact, however, pure and impure categories do not develop merely as generalizations or inductions from structural position or individual behavior. They are imputations that are induced, via analogy and metaphor, from the internal logic of the symbolic code. For this reason, the internal symbolic structure of the civil code must become an object of study in itself. Just as there is no developed religion that does not divide the world into the saved and the damned, there is no civil discourse that does not conceptualize the world into those who deserve inclusion and those who do not.[4] Members of national communities firmly believe that "the world," and this notably includes their own nation, is filled with people who either do not deserve freedom and communal support or are not capable of sustaining them (in part because they are held to be immoral egoists). Members of national communities do not want to "save" such persons. They do not wish to include them, protect them, or offer them rights, for they conceive them as being unworthy and amoral, as in some sense "uncivilized."[5]

This distinction is not "real." Essentialism is a contingent social attribution that, in theoretical terms, must be emphatically rejected. Actors are not intrinsically either worthy or moral: they are determined to be so by being placed in certain positions on the grid of civil culture. When citizens make judgments about who should be included in civil society and who should not, about who is considered a friend and who an enemy, they draw on a systematic, highly elaborated symbolic code. This symbolic structure was already clearly implied in the very first philosophical thinking about democratic societies that emerged in ancient Greece.[6] Since the Renaissance it has permeated popular thinking and behavior, even while its centrality in philosophical thinking has continued to be sustained.

While this symbolic structure is a structural feature of every civil society, it takes different forms in different nations and regions, and its elements are specified and weighted differently in the more conservative and more radical versions of its ideological forms.[7] The nature of these civil codes can be generated speculatively by a kind of thought experiment: Upon what kinds of motives, relations, and institutions would a self-regulating, democratic community be likely to depend? I will speak from within such speculative philosophical reasoning in my presentation of the details of the civil code below. It is important to recognize, however, that the code's symbolic contents are, in fact, the historical residue of a long and diverse series of nitty-gritty movements in social, intellectual, and religious life—of classical Republican ideas, of Judaism, Christianity, and Protestantism, of Enlightenment and liberal thought, of the revolutionary, socialist, and common law traditions. Despite their historical diversity, however, the cultural implications of these variegated movements have been drawn into a highly generalized symbolic system that divides civic virtue from civic vice in a remarkably stable and consistent way. It is for this reason that, despite divergent historical roots and variations in national elaborations, the language that forms the cultural core of civil society can be isolated as a general structure and studied as a relatively autonomous symbolic form.[8] Richard Rorty observes that "the force of 'us' is, typically, contrastive in the sense that it contrasts with a 'they' which is also made up of human beings—the wrong sort of human beings." From this follow certain understandings about democracy as a way of life. If "feelings of solidarity are necessarily a matter of which similarities and dissimilarities strike us as salient," then "such salience is a function of a historically contingent final vocabulary."[9]

The basic elements of this "historically contingent final vocabulary," or cultural structure, can be understood semiotically. They are sets of homologies, which create likenesses between various terms of social description and prescription, and antipathies, which establish antagonisms between these terms and other sets of symbols. Those who consider themselves worthy members of a national community (as most persons do, of course) define themselves in terms of the positive side of this symbolic set; they define those who are not deemed worthy in terms of the bad. It is fair to say—indeed, it is vital to insist—that members of a community "believe in" both the positive and the negative sides, that they employ both as viable normative evaluations of political communities. For the members of every democratic society, both the positive and the negative symbolic sets are thought to be realistic descriptions of individual and social life.

The binary discourse occurs at three levels: motives, relations, and institutions. Motives are attributed to political actors in response to the question that seems always to be immanent in civil democratic life: What kinds of people are necessary for viable democracies to form? Social relations are conceptualized as legitimate and illegitimate in response to the question: How do such civil and uncivil people get along? Finally, institutions are categorized in response to the question, What kinds of organizations would be formed by these kinds of persons, with these kinds of relations?[10]

The Binary Structures of Motives

Let us first discuss motives. Code and counter-code posit human nature in diametrically opposed ways. Because democracy depends on self-control and individual initiatives, the people who compose it are described as being capable of activism and autonomy rather than as being passive and dependent. They are seen as rational and reasonable rather than irrational and hysterical, as calm rather than excited, as controlled rather than passionate, as sane and realistic rather than fantastical or mad. Democratic discourse, then, posits the following qualities as axiomatic: activism, autonomy, rationality, reasonableness, calm, control, realism, and sanity. The nature of the counter-code, the discourse that justifies the restriction of civil society, is already clearly implied. If actors are passive and dependent, irrational and hysterical, excitable, passionate, unrealistic, or mad, they cannot be allowed the freedom that democracy allows. On the contrary, these persons deserve to be repressed, not only for the sake of civil society, but for their own sakes as well.

CIVIL MOTIVES	ANTICIVIL MOTIVES
Active	Passive
Autonomous	Dependent
Rational	Irrational
Reasonable	Hysterical
Calm	Excitable
Self-controlled	Wild-passionate
Realistic	Distorted
Sane	Mad

The Binary Structures of Relationships

On the basis of such contradictory codes about human motives, distinctive representations of social relationships can be built. Democratically motivated persons—persons who are active, autonomous, rational, reasonable, calm, and realistic—will be capable of forming open social relationships rather than secretive ones; they will be trusting rather than suspicious, straightforward rather than calculating, truthful rather than deceitful. Their decisions will be based on open deliberation rather than conspiracy, and their attitude toward authority will be critical rather than deferential. In their behavior toward other community members, they will be bound by conscience and honor rather than by greed and self-interest, and they will treat their fellows as friends rather than enemies.

CIVIL RELATIONS	ANTICIVIL RELATIONS
Open	Secretive
Trusting	Suspicious
Critical	Deferential
Honorable	Self-interested
Altruistic	Greedy
Truthful	Deceitful
Straightforward	Calculating
Deliberative	Conspiratorial
Friendly	Antagonistic

If actors are irrational, dependent, passive, wild-passionate, and unrealistic, on the other hand, the social relationships they form will be characterized by the second side of these fateful dichotomies. Rather than open and trusting relationships, they will form secret societies that are premised on their suspicion of other human beings. To the authority within these secret societies they will be deferential, but to those outside their tiny group they will behave in a greedy and self-interested way. They will be conspiratorial, deceitful toward others, and calculating in their behavior, conceiving of those outside their group as enemies. If the positive side of this second discourse set describes the symbolic qualities necessary to sustain civil society, the negative side describes a solidary structure in which mutual respect and expansive social integration has broken down.

The Binary Structures of Institutions

Given the discursive structure of motives and civic relationships, it should not be surprising that this set of homologies and antipathies extends to the social understanding of political and legal institutions themselves. If members of a national community have irrational motives and distrust social relationships, they will naturally create institutions that are arbitrary rather than rule regulated, that emphasize brute power rather than law and hierarchy rather than equality, that are exclusive rather than inclusive and promote personal loyalty over impersonal and contractual obligation, that are regulated by personalities rather than by office obligations, and that are organized by faction rather than by groups that are responsible to the needs of the community as a whole.

CIVIL INSTITUTIONS	ANTICIVIL INSTITUTIONS
Rule regulated	Arbitrary
Law	Power
Equality	Hierarchy
Inclusive	Exclusive
Impersonal	Personal
Contracts	Bonds of loyalty
Groups	Factions
Office	Personality

These three sets of discursive structures are tied together. Indeed, every element in any one of the sets can be linked via analogical relations—by homologous relations of likeness—to any element in another set on the same side. "Rule regulated," for example, a key element in the symbolic understanding of democratic social institutions, is considered homologous with "truthful" and "open," terms that define social relationships, and with "reasonable" and "autonomous," elements from the symbolic set that stipulates civil motives. In the same manner, any element from any set on one side is taken to be antithetical to any element from any set on the other. According to the rules of this broader cultural formation, for example, "hierarchy" is thought to be inimical to "critical" and "open" and also to "activistic" and "self-controlled."[11]

Civil Narratives of Good and Evil

When they are presented in their simple binary forms, these cultural codes appear schematic. In fact, however, they reveal the skeletal structures on which social communities build the familiar stories, the rich narrative forms, that guide their everyday, taken-for-granted political life.[12] The positive side of these structured sets provides the elements for the comforting and inspiring story of a democratic, free, and spontaneously integrated social order, a civil society in an ideal-typical sense. People are rational, can process information intelligently and independently, know the truth when they see it, do not need strong leaders, can engage in criticism, and easily coordinate their own society. Law is not an external mechanism that coerces people but an expression of their innate rationality, mediating between truth and mundane events. Office is an institutional mechanism that mediates between law and action. It is a calling, a vocation to which persons adhere because of their trust and reason. Those who know the truth do not defer to authorities, nor are they loyal to particular persons. They obey their conscience rather than follow their vulgar interest; they speak plainly rather than conceal their ideas; they are open, idealistic, and friendly toward their fellow human beings.

The structures and narratives of political virtue form the discourse of liberty. This discourse is embodied in the founding documents of democratic societies. In America, for example, the Bill of Rights, which constitute the first ten amendments to the U.S. Constitution, postulates "the right of people to be secure in their persons, houses, papers, and effects, against unreasonable searches and seizures" and guarantees that no person shall "be deprived of life, liberty, or property, without due process of law." In so doing, it ties rights to reasons and liberty to law. The discourse of liberty is also embodied in the great and the little stories that democratic nations tell about themselves, for example, in the venerable American story about George Washington and the cherry tree, which highlights honesty and virtue; in English accounts of the Battle of Britain, which reveal the courage, self-sufficiency, and spontaneous cooperation of the British in contrast to the villainous forces of Hitlerian Germany; in the reverent French folklore about the heroic, honest, and cooperative resistance against the Nazi occupation.

Whatever institutional or narrative form it assumes, the discourse of liberty centers on the capacity for voluntarism. Action is voluntary if it is intended by rational actors who are in full control of body and mind. If action is not voluntary, it is deemed to be worthless. If laws do not promote the achievement of freely intended action, they are discriminatory. If confessions of guilt are coerced rather than freely given, they are polluted.[13] If a social group is constituted under the discourse of liberty, it must be given social rights because the members of this group are conceived of as possessing the capacity for voluntary action. Political struggles over the status of lower-class groups, of racial, ethnic, and religious minorities, of women, children, and homosexuals, of those who are constructed as criminals and as mentally, emotionally, and physically handicapped—these conflicts have always involved discursive struggles over whether and how the discourse of liberty can be extended and applied. Insofar as the founding cultural myths and constitutional documents of democratic societies are universalistic, they implicitly stipulate that the discourse can always be further extended, and that it eventually must be.

The elements on the negative side of these symbolic sets are also tightly intertwined. They provide the elements for the plethora of taken-for-granted stories that permeate democratic understanding of the negative and repugnant sides of community life. Taken together, these negative structures and narratives form the discourse of repression.[14] If people do not have the capacity for reason, if they cannot rationally process information and cannot tell truth from falseness, then they will be loyal to leaders for purely personal reasons and will be easily manipulated by them in turn. Because such persons are ruled by calculation rather than by conscience, they are without the honor that is critical in democratic affairs. Since they have no honor, they do not have the capacity to regulate their own affairs. It is because of this situation that such persons subject themselves to hierarchical authority.

These anti-civil qualities make it "necessary" to deny such persons access to rights and the protection of law.[15] Indeed, because they are conceived as lacking the capacity for both voluntary and responsible behavior, these marginal members of the national community—those who are unfortunate enough to be constructed under the anticivil, counterdemocratic code—must be silenced, displaced, or repressed. They cannot be regulated by law, nor will they accept the discipline of office. Their loyalties can be only familial and particularistic. The institutional and legal boundaries of civil society, it is widely believed, can provide no bulwark against their lust for personal power.

The positive side of this discursive formation is viewed by the members of civil communities as a source not only of purity but also of purification. The discourse of liberty is taken to sum up "the best" in a democratic society, and its tenets are considered to be sacred. The objects that the discourse creates seem to possess an awesome power that places them at the "center" of society, a location—sometimes geographic, often stratificational, always symbolic—that compels their defense at almost any cost.[16]

The negative side of this symbolic formation is viewed as profane. Representing the "worst" in the national community, it embodies evil. The objects it identifies threaten the core community from somewhere outside it. From this marginal position, they present a powerful source of pollution.[17] To be close to these polluted objects—the actors, structures, and processes that are constituted by the repressive discourse—is dangerous. Not only can one's reputation be sullied and one's status endangered, but one's very security can be threatened. To have one's self or movement identified in terms of these objects causes anguish, disgust, and alarm. Collective representations of this polluting code are perceived as a threat to the very center of civil society itself.

Everyday Essentialism

Public figures and events must be categorized in terms of one side of this discursive formation or the other, although, when politics functions routinely, such classifications need not be sharply articulated or explicit. Hegel put it this way in *The Philosophy of Right*: "In an existing ethical order in which a complete system of ethical relations has been developed and actualized, virtue in the strict sense of the word is in place and actually appears only in exceptional circumstances when one obligation clashes with another."[18] Even in routine periods, however, it is their specification within the codes of this underlying discourse that gives political things a civil meaning and allows them to assume the role they seem "naturally" to have.[19] Even when they are aware that they are struggling over these classifications, moreover, most political actors do not recognize that it is they who are creating them. Such knowledge would relativize reality, creating an uncertainty that could undermine not only the cultural core but also the institutional boundaries and solidarity of civil society itself. Social events and actors seem to "be" these qualities, not to be labeled by them.

The discourse of civil society, in other words, is concrete, not abstract. It is elaborated by narrative accounts that are believed to describe faithfully not only the present but also the past. Every nation has a myth of origin, for example, that anchors this discourse in an account of the historical events involved in its early formation.[20] Like their English compatriots, early Americans believed their rights to have emerged from the "ancient constitution" of eleventh-century Anglo-Saxons whose primordial qualities guaranteed that the structures they forged would take a civil form.[21] The specifically American discourse of liberty was first elaborated in accounts of Puritan saints and later in stories about revolutionary heroes. It was woven into the myth of the independent and democratic yeoman farmer, then into tales about upright cowboys and law-making sheriffs, and still later into pulp fiction about doggedly determined and honest detectives and the dishonest and deceptive malcontents they eventually ferreted out.[22] Likewise, the American discourse of repression was made palpable through early religious accounts of miscreants and antinomians and scurrilous stories about selfish and authoritarian loyalists and aristocrats in the Revolutionary War. Later, it was elaborated in accounts of wild Indians and "papist" immigrants and then in regional myths about treason during the Civil War. Such accounts seemed to justify not only exclusion but violence.[23]

For contemporary Americans, the categories of the pure and the polluted discourses seem to exist in just as natural and fully historical a way. Democratic law and procedures are seen as having been won by the voluntary struggles of the founding fathers and guaranteed by historical documents like the Bill of Rights and the Constitution. The qualities of the repressive code are embodied in the dark visions of tyranny and lawlessness, whether those of eighteenth-century British monarchs; Soviet, Chinese, or Vietnamese communists; or Islamic rulers or terrorists. Pulp fiction and highbrow drama seek to counterpose these dangers with compelling images of the good.[24] When works of the imagination represent the discursive formation in a paradigmatic way, they become contemporary classics. For the generation that matured during World War II, for example, George Orwell's *Nineteen Eighty-Four*, so filled with gothic tales of suspicion, disloyalty, calculation, and secrecy, made the discourse of repression emblematic of the struggles of their time.

Within the confines of a particular national community, the binary codes and concrete representations that make up the discourse of civil society are not usually divided among different social groups. To the contrary, even in societies that are rent by intensive social conflict, the constructions of both civic virtue and civic vice tend to be widely accepted by all sides. What is contested in the course of civic life, what is not at all consensual, is how the antithetical sides of this discourse, its two symbolic sets, will be applied to particular actors and groups. If most of the members of democratic society accepted the "validity" and "reality" of *Nineteen Eighty-Four*, they disagreed fundamentally over its relevant social application. Radicals and liberals were inclined to see the book as describing the already repressive or at least imminently antidemocratic tendencies of their own capitalist societies; conservatives understood the work as referring to communism alone.

The Conflict over Representation

Some events are so gross or so sublime that they generate almost immediate consensus about how the symbolic sets of civil society should be applied. For most members of a national community, popular national wars clearly demarcate the good and the bad. The nation's soldiers are initially taken to be courageous embodiments of the discourse of liberty; the foreign nations and soldiers who oppose them are deemed to represent some potent combination of the counterdemocratic code. In the course of American history, this negative code has, in fact, been extended to a vast and variegated group, to the British, native peoples, pirates, the South and the North, Africans, old European nations, fascists, communists, Germans, Japanese, Vietnamese, and Islamic terrorists. Identification in terms of the discourse of repression is essential if vengeful combat is to be pursued.[25] Once this polluting discourse is applied, it becomes impossible for good people to treat and reason with those on the other side. If one's opponents are beyond reason, deceived by leaders who operate in secret, the only option is to read them out of the human race. When great wars are successful, they provide powerful narratives that dominate the nation's postwar life. Hitler and Nazism formed the backbone of a huge array of Western myth and stories, providing master metaphors for everything from profound discussions about the final solution to the good-guy/bad-guy plots of television dramas and situation comedies. Whether "terrorism" and "September 11th" will have the same narrative power remains to be seen.

For most events, however, discursive identity is contested. Political fights are, in part, about how to distribute actors across the structure of discourse, for there is no determined relation between any event or group and either side of the cultural scheme. Actors struggle to taint one another with the brush of repression and to wrap themselves in the rhetoric of liberty. In periods of tension and crisis, political struggle becomes a matter of how far and to whom the discourses of liberty and repression apply. The effective cause of victory and defeat, imprisonment and freedom, sometimes even of life and death, is often discursive domination, or hegemony, which depends on just how popular narratives about good and evil are extended. Is it protesting students who are like Nazis, or is it the political authorities who are pursuing them who are like Nazis? Are members of the Communist Party to be understood as fascist, or does this describe the members of the House Un-American Activities Committee who are interrogating them? Are Islamic militants engaging in violent, antidemocratic behavior, or does this behavior belong to the American military pursuing them?

When the Watergate crisis exploded inside American political life in autumn 1972, only the low-level functionaries who burgled the Watergate building were labeled conspirators, polluted by the discourse of repression, and arrested.[26] The presidential candidate of the Democratic Party, George McGovern, and his fellow Democrats were unsuccessful in their efforts to apply this discourse to President Nixon, who was the Republican candidate for reelection, to his executive staff, or to the Republican Party. Each of these entities succeeded in maintaining the purity of their civil identities. At a later point in the crisis, however, such a reassuring relation to the cultural structure no longer held. Staff, party, and eventually the president himself were re-represented and polluted. As a result, they became subject to humiliation, displacement, arrest, and incarceration.

The general discursive structure, in other words, is used to legitimate friends and delegitimate opponents in the course of real historical time. If the independence and autonomy of the civil sphere were to be fully maintained, of course, the discourse of repression would be applied only in highly circumscribed ways, to such groups as children and those who commit serious crimes, to categories of persons, in other words, who are not in sufficient possession of their rational or moral faculties to participate freely and autonomously in civil life. It has often been the case, indeed, that subordinated, rebellious, or marginal individuals and groups have sustained civil representations over significant periods of time. In such ages of equipoise, conflict groups can understand one another as rational individuals without indulging in moral annihilation.

In normative terms, this sympathetic representation articulates the moral aspiration of a civil society. Over any extended historical period, however, the strains and fragmentations that mark real civil societies are bound to take their toll. It is impossible for the discourse of repression not to be brought into significant play and for opponents not, at some point, to be represented as dangerous and even as enemies of the most threatening kind. It may be the case that such opponents are, in fact, ruthless enemies of the public good. The Nazis were morally heinous killers, and it was wrong to deal with them as potential civic participants, as Neville Chamberlain and the other appeasers did. What is important to understand, however, is that the discourse of repression is applied whether or not its objects are really evil, with the result that a social fact—an objective reality—is created even if none existed before. The symbolism of evil that had been applied by the Allies in an overzealous way to the German nation in the course of World War I was extended indiscriminately to the German people and governments during the interwar period. It produced the debilitating reparations policy that helped establish the economic and social receptiveness to Nazism.[27]

The social application of polarizing symbolic identifications must be understood in terms of the internal structure of the discourse itself. Members of rational, individualistic, and self-critical societies experience themselves as vulnerable because these very qualities make them open and trusting. Beneath the surface, there lurks the fear that such trust will be abused if the other side is devoid of redeeming social qualities. The potential for dependent and irrational behavior, moreover, can be found even in good citizens themselves. Secret conspiracies by dishonest persons disseminate misleading information that might lead even the best intentioned citizens, on what would seem to be rational grounds, to turn away from the structures or processes of democratic society itself.[28] In other words, the very qualities that allow civil societies to be internally democratic—qualities that include the symbolic oppositions that allow liberty to be defined in any meaningful way—mean that the members of civil society do not feel confident that they can deal effectively with their opponents, from either within or without. The discourse of repression is inherent in the discourse of liberty.[29] This is the irony that tears at what Rogers Smith calls "the divided heart" of civil society. It must somehow be managed for the project of democracy to succeed.[30]

CHAPTER 5

Communicative Institutions:

Public Opinion, Mass Media, Polls, Associations

C IVIL SOCIETY IS defined by a particular kind of social relationship, one that has to do with universalistic solidarity. In a complex, far-flung, and relatively anonymous social order, this historically unusual kind of relationship can be widely accessible only if it is articulated symbolically, as a generalized language that can be spoken by many different kinds of people. Hence the importance of the discourse of civil society, the language of binary oppositions I have just described. At the same time, however, these collective representations of an imagined community can and must be articulated in more specific and mundane ways. Members of civil society act not only within a cultural environment but within an institutional one.

In comparison with generalized symbolic patterns, institutions focus on goals and norms, rewards and sanctions; in a word, they constitute social organization. Social organization operates inside of a cultural milieu: An institution can think only inside of the categories that culture provides.[1] At the same time, organizations are as strongly oriented by pragmatic as by ideal concerns. The actions that unfold inside organizations are much more specific and contingent than the generalized categories of culture. As a result, although the structures and activities of institutions are oriented by the discourse of civil society, they cannot be determined by them.

The institutions of civil society crystallize ideals about solidarity with and against others in specific terms. They transform general conceptions about the purity and impurity of motives and relations into specific, normative, sometimes sanctioned, one-time-only social relationships. They articulate specific claims and binding demands for inclusion and exclusion, for liberation and for repression. In so doing, they issue orders, arrange bargains, make exchanges, produce statements, create interpretations, offer rewards, threaten and often confer punishments. The institutions of civil society make it possible for the pure and impure criteria of civil society to permeate the other, noncivil spheres of social life. Civil institutions intrude into noncivil institutions and groups; they are continuously restructuring them and being restructured by them in turn.

Institutions such as law, office, party organization, and "free and fair" elections articulate solidarity in concrete and specific ways, not only through the definitions of moral behavior they project but by sanctions and rewards. These form what I call the regulatory institutions of civil society, and we will discuss them in chapters 6 and 7 below. These more "material" forms, however, by no means exhaust the organizational structures of the solidary sphere. The inclusive and exclusive relationships established by civil society are articulated by communicative institutions as well. It is important to lay out their structure and process before we move on to consider civil institutions of a more regulative kind.

From the cultural and symbolic lifeworld of civil society, intuitive criteria are created that shape behavior in more organized and formal domains. Civil society in this sense should be understood not merely in terms of contrasting symbolic categories but as structures of feeling, the diffusely sensed obligations and rights that represent, and are at the same time evoked by, contrasting solidary ties. Collective representations of such social relationships are broadcast by civil society institutions specializing in communicative, not regulative tasks—by the mass media, public opinion polls, and voluntary organizations. The structures of feeling that such institutions produce must be conceptualized as influence rather than authoritative control, or power in a more structural sense. They institutionalize civil society by creating messages that translate general codes into situationally specific evaluations and descriptions.[2] Before we analyze these organizations of influence, however, we must discuss the lifeworld of public opinion which anchors communicative and regulative institutions alike.

The Public and Its Opinion

There is an intuitive, phenomenological sense of civil society. This structure of feeling, which is at the same time a feeling of structure, is evoked and objectified by the notion of "the public." In the minds of most democratic theorists, it seems, the notion of the public points to the existence of an actual group, to actual deliberations, and to an actual place. According to this concrete notion of the public, members of a closely knit polity meet with one another in the same physical environment, vigorously debating the events that affect their lives. Inspired by the ancient Greek polis, Arendt insisted on the importance of such a concrete understanding—on "being seen and being heard by others"—in her republican analyses of democracy.[3] Influenced by Arendt and the classical aspects of the socialist tradition, the early Habermas also laid heavy emphasis on the public as a concrete space.[4] In his normatively informed historical reconstruction, Habermas claimed that the republican inclinations of the bourgeoisie first emerged in opposition to the private and hidden activities of the king's private household in patrimonial absolutist regimes. This bourgeois preference for open, transparent, and public relationships culminated in the conversation-filled coffeehouses and salons of the eighteenth-century British and French commercial centers. According to Habermas, it was in these public houses that the emerging middle classes debated plans for democracy in a straightforward, rational manner.

This republican equation of public with face-to-face interaction has extended well beyond the normative and Marxist traditions. Max Weber, in his neglected essay on the critical significance of the Western city, and other observers of early modern Europe as well,[5] have drawn attention to the manner in which the Renaissance city-states sustained remarkably high degrees of concrete public life, constructing open places for political discussion that objectified and focused the postmedieval experiences of expanded solidarity. Meetings of the aroused publics of these city-states not only exposed official corruption but allowed demands for greater economic equality to gain normative legitimation for the first time. The preference for thinking of publicness in concrete, face-to-face terms extends, in fact, well beyond the rationalist tradition of Enlightenment thought. Walzer and Mayhew, for example, have argued for the religious origins of the early modern public, demonstrating how the dualistic, dialogic nature of Protestant religiosity and the egalitarianism of its sect organization opposed the secrecy and hierarchy of medieval life.[6]

As my earlier analyses of symbolically articulated solidarity indicate, however, the civil spheres of large, differentiated, and plural societies can no longer be understood in such concrete terms.[7] This does not mean that the traditional idea of the public no longer plays a role in contemporary societies, but that it now assumes a symbolic rather than concrete form. The symbolic representation of traditional public functions is a regulating idea, one that carries with it an obvious force. But it is not the concrete public as a face-to-face association that is fundamental to contemporary civil societies. It is the idea of that public as it has inserted itself into social subjectivity as a structure of feeling. In order to gain influence, actors must speak the language that makes the democratic public into a regulative ideal.[8] The normative reference of the public sphere is a cultural structure, the discourse of civil society.

It is as "public opinion" that public space has its most fundamental repercussions in the present day. Tocqueville insisted that it is the peculiar force of public opinion vis-à-vis the political sphere—not the force of the concrete public composed of face-to-face associations—that distinguishes democratic from authoritarian rule. In a democracy, he wrote, "public opinion is in effect the dominant power." It is because this "guiding power," for example, "asserts itself through elections and decrees" that "in exercising executive power, the President of the United States is subject to constant and jealous scrutiny."[9]

Public opinion articulates the cultural structure of civil society, defining democratic and antidemocratic opinions, publics, representative figures, and regulative institutions. Such binary structuring marks the history of political thinking about the role that public opinion can play. Theorists ambivalent about democracy have conceived the public's opinion in both ways, as gullible and easily swayed, irrational and emotional, and as constituting the potential for tyranny, even as, at the same time, they have found inside public opinion a deep reflection of the rationality, individuality, and independence that marks democratic life. In *The American Commonwealth*, James Bryce recognized in public opinion a "din of voices" that "talks incessantly" and "complains," has an "inability to recognize facts," an "incapacity to imagine a future," and is "swayed only by such obvious reasons as it needs little reflection to follow." He claimed to observe that, "quick and strenuous in great matters" and "heedless in small matters," public opinion has "dulled the sense of responsibility among the leaders in political life" and "is a danger to the people themselves." In the next breath, Bryce asserts that "public opinion is a sort of atmosphere, fresh, keen, and full of sunlight [that] kills many of those noxious germs which are hatched where politicians congregate." He continues that "selfishness, injustice, cruelty, tricks . . . of all sorts shun the light," that "to expose them is to defeat them," that "it is the existence of such a public opinion as this, the practice of freely and constantly reading, talking, and judging of public affairs . . . that gives to popular government that educated and stimulative power which is so frequently claimed as its highest merit."[10] Though Tocqueville preferred democratic opinion to the particularism of aristocracy, he also spoke darkly of the potential tyranny of the majority as the unforeseen product of the influence of public opinion. Emphasizing the binary of dependence-independence, he complained "I know of no country in which there is so little independence of mind and true freedom of discussion than in America."[11] More optimistic democratic thinking, by contrast, grants to public opinion the civil qualities that democracy requires. In his idealistic celebration of the public opinion poll, published in 1940, George Gallup evoked the central category of truth. "Public opinion listens to many propagandas, most of them contradictory," he writes, insisting that in the clash and conflict of argument and debate public opinion tries "to separate the true from the false."

> Public opinion is critical, not submissive; experimental, not dogmatic; and oriented to the individual, not the mass. It needs criticism for its very existence, and through criticism it is constantly being modified and molded. It acts and learns by action. Its truths are relative and contingent. . . . Its chief faith is a faith in experiment. It believes in the value of every individual's contribution to political life, and in the right of ordinary human beings to have voice in deciding their fate. Public opinion, in this sense, is the pulse of democracy.[12]

To the degree that civil society exists, the taken-for-granted, apparently mundane but enormously important phenomenon of public opinion emerges. To refer to public opinion is to indicate, to invoke, and to represent the pure and impure ideas, feelings, and evaluations that members of society hold about one another. Commenting upon the ongoing, unpredictable, and seemingly unstructured events and figures of social life, public opinion consists of factual accounts, emotional responses, and moral evaluations of their extent and effect. Tocqueville saw this clearly, but he limited the phenomenon to American political life. Marx did not see this at all, and Weber was unable to give to public opinion a theoretical place in his descriptions of modern life. By contrast, Durkheim insisted on the omnipresence of opinion, though he ascribed it to the influence of "society" and identified it with the "collective consciousness" rather than with the civil sphere and democratic life.[13] Gabriel de Tarde, similarly affected by the effervescence of the new Third Republic in France, also emphasized the centrality of opinion, relating it the dynamics of fashion, the currents of conversation, and the institutions of newspapers, all clearly associated with the communicative domain.[14]

American social thinkers in the early twentieth century, such as Walter Lippmann and John Dewey, also recognized the centrality and independent power of public opinion, but too often their deeply republican normative suspicions and their insufficiently developed social theories made them believe this independence to be on the wane.[15] Since these early formulations, and indeed in part because of them, the social scientific discourse about public opinion has been reduced to quantitative surveys of individual attitudes. Public opinion is rarely seen as a highly significant macrosociological topic in its own right. The tradition of Thrasymachus makes it hard to see this kind of invisible source of influence; only the visible exercise of power is given free reign.[16]

Within the constraining yet at the same time nubile structures of public feeling there flows the economic divisions, ethnic segments, and ideological polarities that fragment democratic social life. Groups with diverse power, interests, and capital of various kinds produce and compel sharply differing views of one another. It has been the stock-in-trade of social scientists to demonstrate that public opinion depends upon—in technical terms, "varies in relationship with"—more particularistic groups and concrete structural processes, such as class formations, ethnic and regional groupings, education, race, and mobility rates. Even in segmented and multicultural societies, however, there remains an element of public opinion that orients itself to the society qua collectivity, to an audience of citizens and to institutional actors only insofar as they are members thereof. To elaborate this proposition in theoretical and empirical detail is, indeed, one of the main ambitions of this book.

Members of different and conflicting groups certainly have their own opinions about many things, but it is only their "public" opinions that make these ideas evident. If they are to have broader influence, these opinions have to be couched in terms of the regulatory idea that a broader society exists, both as a normative and a real audience, outside of their particular groups. Publicly broadcast opinions may be expansive or restrictive in their attribution of the capacity to engage in the discourse of liberty; they may appeal to the public fact of civil solidarity in order to demonize significant segments within it and reduce the civil community's size. In either case, the social role of public opinion is pretty much the same: it mediates between the broad binaries of civil society discourse and the institutional domains of social life. Public opinion is the sea within which we swim, the structure that gives us the feeling of democratic life.

The Mass Media

The media of mass communications—radio, television, newspapers, the Internet, magazines, best-selling books, and movies—constitute one fundamentally significant articulation of the imagined and idealized civil domain. In both fictional and factual forms they create the characters that people civil society and establish what might be called its communicative boundaries with noncivil domains.

Fictional Media

The symbolic forms of fictional media weave the binary codes of civil society into broad narratives and popular genres. They provide a continuous flow of representations about ongoing social events and actors. Yet in comparison with factual media, such fictional forms operate at a temporal remove from these other representations of daily life. What they gain in return is a much greater cathartic impact on the self-understandings of civil society, on the structures of feeling that define its identity as a civil place. Though their avowed purpose is entertainment, not enlightenment, this very distinction ignores the necessarily aesthetic framing of rational acts.[17] Fictional media create long-lasting frames for democratizing and anticivil processes alike. They constrain action by constituting a teleology for future events, even as they seem merely to be telling stories about people and life in an ahistorical and fictional way.

Expressive media stipulate events and figures that are relevant to members of civil society. Drawing on the repertoire of dichotomous categories, their plots make these events and characters "typical," placing them into revealing and easily interpretable situations that represent civil and uncivil motives and relations. Insofar as television, movies, and popular fiction depict action in particular social spheres, they do so by communicating an image of these actions—sometimes idealized, sometimes extremely harsh—in relation to the standards for participation in civil society, and they broadcast these narratives to some of the individuals and groups that compose society at large.[18]

Historically, it has been the media of high culture that have played this aesthetic-educative role. It was through the narrative structures of its fiction, in the works of writers like Balzac and Flaubert, and not only through their own actual life experiences, that educated members of French society came to form an understanding of the harsh class relations and cruel authoritarianism that distorted French institutions, both civil and uncivil, in nineteenth-century industrial society. It was through Dickens's extravagant and wildly popular novels that the English middle classes were not only informed about the crushing poverty of early capitalism but were taught to sympathize with the plight of the poor and to support sentimental social reform. The structures of these and other popular narratives, including those by such influential, socially oriented women novelists as Jane Austin, have often been called realistic, and their observational detail and down-to-earth qualities certainly made them seem so at the time. In retrospect, however, we can see that they were decidedly melodramatic and moralistic in their representations. The social forces responsible for restrictions on participation, differences of wealth, and cultural prejudices were explained by narratives that constructed and punished selfish, greedy, and irrational antagonists. In so doing, the novels mobilized public opinion against polluting threats to the ideals of civil society.[19] In her enormously influential novel, *Uncle Tom's Cabin*, Harriet Beecher Stowe represented race relations to antebellum Americans in exactly the same melodramatic and empathy-provoking way.

Her narrative greatly affected public opinion. "Less than a year after its publication in March 1852," writes historian Doris Kearns Goodwin, "more than three hundred thousand copies of the novel had sold in the United States, a sales rate rivaled only by the Bible." Beecher's novel stimulated the formation of antislavery civil associations and social movements. Frederick Douglass, the abolitionist leader, described it as a "flash" that lit "a million camp fires in front of the embattled hosts of slavery." In this cultural but very real manner, this fictional reconstruction helped to trigger the Civil War, and thus to abolish the slave relationships that so severely undermined the civil pretensions of American society.[20]

Such sociological students of literature as George Lukacs, Leo Lowenthal, and Ian Watt have argued that novels like these merely reflected actual social life. Nineteenth-century novels were realistic, or moralistic, because they depicted the nature of capitalist society, its class domination, patriarchy, poverty, and racism. Such a perspective, however, ignores the existence of civil society as a differentiated social sphere. If fictional writers were indeed deeply affected by the deprivations of economic, racial, and familial life, they were responding not only to actual situations outside of themselves but to their own inner desires, as members of the civil sphere, to speak on behalf of oppressed groups to society at large. Through their fictional work, in other words, they gave voice to the idealized aspirations of civil society itself. As Peter Brooks writes in *Realist Visions*, "The discovery of the ugly is part of the process of disillusioning in which realism deals," with the result that "realism as the ugly stands close to realism as the shocking, that which transgresses the bounds of the acceptable." This exploration of the aesthetically profane fuels the nineteenth-century novel's broader social and moral ambitions.

> England develops a recognizable "industrial novel," one that takes
> on the problems of social misery and class conflict, and France has
> its "roman social" . . . Balzac and Zola, for instance, both write their
> principle works following a revolution that . . . confronts them with
> the stark question: To whom does France belong?[21]

Elizabeth Long studied the fictional heroes that peopled post–World War II American best-sellers.[22] She found that these collective representations reflected not only the economic strains in American society, but also broad cultural themes of individual achievement and independence. In the 1960s, she found, these characterizations gave way to heroes who experienced anguish about this very individualism and who wanted to live in a more collective and socially involved way. These representations contributed to the turn toward more activistic and critical interpretations of American culture at a time when the boundaries of civil society were being aggressively challenged as unfairly restrictive.

Until recently, scholarly attention remained focused on such high culture. To understand the expressive media of contemporary civil society, however, one must see that popular folklore and folk dramas have always performed similar kinds of sentimental education for the less educated members of society. In the postmodern era of television and digital communication, in fact, the long-standing relation between high and low culture has been inverted. Mass entertainment has increasingly displaced high culture as the principal medium of expressive communication for members of contemporary civil societies, a fact that postmodern concerns with "mediatization" have identified but understood in an overly critical way.[23]

The racially bifurcated civil society of America in the 1950s was symbolized, and reinforced, by such family television dramas as the *Ozzie and Harriet Show*, which represented the idealized qualities of American civil life in the dramas of white families only. At the same time, such satiric comedies as *Amos and Andy* represented African-Americans in polluted terms that implicitly justified their exclusion from the civil sphere. During this same period, the violent colonization of the native peoples of North America, which had created the grossly unequal relations between white European settlers and American Indians, was represented by the Western genre. Because these plots largely associated Indians with violence and cunning and allowed civility to be represented primarily by white settlers, they implicitly justified the exclusion of Indians, their subjugation, and even their murder by representatives of white civil society. As Americans experienced the shocks of the 1960s and 1970s, the conflicts between movements for liberation and the repressive backlash movements against a more inclusive society found their symbolic expression, and explanation, in such popular evening sitcoms as the *All in the Family*, which depicted the conflict between a conservative and prejudiced white working-class male and his long-haired, rebellious, but ultimately sympathetic son. During the years of the highly polarizing Vietnam War, anticolonial and antiwar sentiments were broadcast not only through rational arguments and social movements, but through such expressive and popular television entertainments as *M.A.S.H.*, which featured the cynical portrayal of Army physicians in the Korean War and interpreted American military intervention in comedic and often critical terms.

Americans experienced the protagonists and antagonists of such televised dramas as personal acquaintances. Iconographic symbols of collective sentiments, they became part of everyday speech in those turbulent years. Such representations communicated in direct and emotionally powerful ways, allowing Americans to express their civil judgments in figurative rather than intellectual language, which made it easier, in turn, to identify with one or another solidary group. When the patriarchal distortions of American civil life were being challenged in the 1970s, the *Mary Tyler Moore Show* provided an attractive, widely influential representation of the new woman in the form of the comedy's doughty, resilient, anxious but always independent and competent heroine. Thirty years later, when the incorporation of women had deepened, the stars of *Sex and the City* celebrated a female version of civil society in which personal autonomy and moral obligations were continuously recombined. New understandings of gay and lesbian Americans were symbolically configured through increasingly insistent and normalizing fictional reconstructions of their civil competence. Sometimes these were assimilative and normalizing, as in *Will and Grace*, but often, as in *Queer Eye for the Straight Guy*, they were multicultural and pluralistic.[24]

In the wake of the Civil Rights movement, and its transforming effects on the class structure of the African-American community, *The Cosby Show* emerged as the dominant American entertainment program of the 1980s. Sympathetically interpreting the greatly expanded black middle and professional class to white Americans, this televised entertainment can be seen as critical to the civil reconstruction of a group that had earlier been seen in almost entirely repressive terms. For the first time, an African-American adult male was represented as the warm, wise, loving, intelligent, and highly successful breadwinner of a "normal American family." The contrast to the restrictive racial representations of the family broadcast by *Ozzie and Harriet* three decades earlier could not have been more evident. During the same decade, Alex Haley's television miniseries, *Roots,* watched by record audiences in 1977 and rebroadcast several times since, performed a similar civil-aesthetic function. Reconstructing black Americans as rooted rather than

79

rootless, as resistant victims of oppression fiercely committed to self-improvement and worldly success, the drama allowed white ethnic Americans to experience a new solidarity with their black contemporaries.[25] Two decades after Cosby, the Latino family comedy *George Lopez* became the longest-running series with a Hispanic cast in television history. Interviewed by the *Daily News* about the show's success, the actress who played the main character's wife suggested that "people just see us as people" and "funny is funny."[26] In the midst of this new interracial climate, the Western genre pitting cowboys against Indians virtually disappeared. Its themes of violent race-based conflict and civilizational vulnerability were displaced into battles between democratic Americans, or earthlings, and threatening invaders from imperial, anticivil empires located somewhere in outer space.[27]

Factual Media

In contrast to this fictive manner, the news side of the mass media articulates public opinion and specifies the solidarities of civil society in a less visibly constructivist and much more immediately influential manner. For most members of civil society, and even for members of its institutional elites, the news is the only source of firsthand experience they will ever have about their follow citizens, about their motives for acting the way they do, the kinds of relationships they form, and the nature of the institutions they might potentially create. The factual as compared with fictional status of the news media makes them more significant in affecting immediate social decisions, from the formation of social movements to affairs of state. The reputation of news media—their very ability to represent the public to itself—depends on the belief by their audiences that they are merely reporting on the social world, not constructing it, that they are describing the social world factually, in an objective manner, rather than representing it in artistic or moral terms. In creating the world of society immediately and without remove, news draws upon what the French film theorist André Bazin called the ontology of realism.[28] Emphasizing speed, accuracy, and neutrality, news presents itself as homologous with the real world, as the *New York Times*' slogan, "All the News That's Fit to Print," so vividly suggests.

Yet every news judgment remains an interpretation of significance, one that is achieved by typifying previously unrecognized events in discursive categories that are already understood.[29] News media select a tiny range of sites from the enormous onrush of people and events that characterizes everyday social life./Merely by informing members of society about what events "exist," they have already made decisions about which events matter, about what is happening and what is at stake in social life. In their very representation of social facts, in other words, the news media represent public opinion as well.[30] In answering their famous four questions—"who, what, where, and why"—the lead paragraphs of news reports characterize the people who make these events, why they acted in the way they have, and what effect their actions will have on the structure of society. Do these newly observed actors deserve to be inside or outside of civil society? Do they threaten "us"—the news audience—in a manner that suggests we should mobilize against them, or do they allow us to feel good about ourselves, so much so that we might wish to reach out and lend them a helping hand? The role of binary oppositions is critical here. Contrasts between purifying and polluting motives, relations, and institutions permeate news accounts, linking the presuppositions of civil society to the seemingly random outpouring of social events. Sensationalist, yellow journalism presents overtly exaggerated judgments, emphasizing the negative and frightening figures and events of social life. It would be a mistake, however, to think that more professional and sophisticated journalism fails to adhere to the structured pathways of civil society discourse as well.

From the structured and generalized categories of civil society discourse to the diffuse but more historically and socially directed phenomenon of public opinion to the institutions of news, there stretches a continuum from synchronic to diachronic, from structure to process, from inflexible to flexible, from general to specific, and from unresponsive to flexible. Even in regard to an ongoing event, news media may shift in their interpretations, moving from civil to uncivil framing devices from one week to the next, from one day to another, even from hour to hour.[31] These discursive constructions create reactions in civil society itself. They can trigger violent actions, or the formation of social movements. They can reach deep into the inner workings of noncivil spheres and prepare the path for reconstructive repair. Media interpretations can roll back and make more restrictive the solidarities of civil society in turn.

Because they control such vital interpretive tasks, the factually oriented institutions of mass communication, more than the fictional ones, create chronic tensions between the utopian aspirations and relationships of civil society and the powers and authorities outside the civil sphere. When they apply polluting categories to an event or actor, news reports create public relations problems for "sectarian" religious institutions, "abusive" family relationships, "secretive" or "greedy" corporations, "elitist" scientific institutions, and the "partisan" or "manipulative" actors of political life. To broadcast news reports that construct groups and institutions in such profane terms is to problematize their relation to civil society.[32] Even the occasional news report, or exposé, can lead to a torrent of public demands for internal reforms. Once the reforms are made, factual media often monitor the affected institutions to make sure that their reconstructed relationships remain congruent with the idealized standards of civil society.

The argument over whether news media first emerged from the bourgeois sphere, from private economic life, during the early days of capitalist society is controversial and important precisely because it calls into question the very capacity of such communicative media to create tension between civil and noncivil spheres. If news originated merely as a means to promote commerce, how could it function as anything other than a commodity, particularly inside the advertising-saturated milieu that marks television and print news today? Habermas may be the best-known critical theorist to have tried this strategy of genealogical deflation, but he is by no means the only influential voice who has taken aim at the news media in this way. From Karl Marx to C. Wright Mills and Pierre Bourdieu, social scientists have proclaimed that the news media cannot be factual, that they cannot obtain the relative autonomy from market demands that would allow this potentially critical interpretive medium to sustain the moral autonomy of the civil sphere.[33]

In fact, however, news media first emerged as a means to advance not only economic claims but political, religious, and ethnic ones.[34] As early modern societies began to cohere in wider and more inclusive communities, moreover, public declarations about the factual nature of social life did, in fact, come to have much greater effect. As diverse and competing publics— plebian, Catholic, Protestant, Jewish, immigrant, black, socialist, and conservative—formed to contest particularistic and restrictive forms of social control, they created more independent news media in turn.

Far from being a threat to the civil and solidarizing function of the media, bourgeois commercialization actually encouraged it. News media that could sustain themselves in their own terms, by their own sales, were more independent of particularistic publics. Such financially independent media allowed the members of civil society, who were also members of these particular groups, to participate vicariously in an anonymous civil collectivity and, at the same time, to articulate their individual wills as consumers. So the creation of increasingly large commercial markets for news from the early nineteenth to the early twentieth centuries actually pushed the process of media differentiation further along.[35] The project of professionalizing journalism did so as well. Without market sales and mass advertising, independent media would have had to continue to depend on private individual wealth or on the financial resources of such particularistic noncivil spheres as churches, trade unions, and political parties. The emergence of professional norms of objectivity, while in no sense eliminating the journalist's interpretive function, relegated the more dogmatic and explicit political opinions of private media owners to the editorial page.[36]

To the degree that civil society becomes independent, which marks the degree to which there is a democratic social life, the audience for media of mass communication, whether fictional or factual, becomes the broad "society" rather than particular interests within it.[37] This more inclusive social reference depends, in turn, on the institutional differentiation of mass media organizations. This involves, on the one hand, impersonal markets for information and fictional forms, which allow communication to be acquired via negotiated exchanges among buyers and sellers rather than through more personalized and clientalist relations that involve political and ethnic loyalty, class relationships, or ideological control. Differentiation also depends on the emergence of professionalized occupational ethics emphasizing objectivity and creative autonomy. Such ethics, along with self-regulating guilds, allow producers, writers, directors, and reporters more freedom to offer flexible interpretations responsive to shifting events. They can focus simply on "what is real and accurate" and "what will seem believable and dramatic" rather than on more dogmatic interpretations that merely authenticate loyalties to particular groups and particular institutional spheres. As the messages they formulate relate to society at large, they become more truly media of persuasion and less masked instruments for hegemony and domination. To the degree that this occurs, fewer groups and categories of person are polluted by the categories that justify exclusion from civil society.[38]

Even in this more differentiated and civil situation, however, dichotomous evaluations of persons and events continue to be made, for pollution and purification are structural features of civil society as such. Even when media take society as their reference, their understandings of it are subtly fused with particularistic ideas and influenced by pressures from other spheres. Political parties, social classes, economic exigencies, religious faith, ethnic and racial animosities, gender and sexual groupings—these and other fissures continue to segment even the most differentiated civil societies. Institutions of mass communication crystallize the stereotypes and misunderstandings such fragmentation implies, even when they idealize some social event or institution in civil societal terms. The very differentiation of media, moreover, makes them the focus of continuous efforts at manipulation by elites in other spheres. Their independence makes them vulnerable to "public relations," to staged events, and to more direct forms of corruption like bribes. For in the mass markets for influence and symbolic capital, media are not only sellers but buyers at the same time.

Already in 1835 Tocqueville could discern the intrinsic connection between newspapers and the independent public opinion upon which democracy depends. The press, "lays bare the secret springs of politics and obliges public men to appear before the court of public opinion." It is "through the press that the parties speak to one another without meeting face-to-face and understand one another without direct contact." While an "individual newspaper has little power," the power of the press "in general" is "second only to that of the people."[39] Critics of the media have always insisted, to the contrary, that their independence gives newspapers and television license to violate civil norms, to misrepresent, to distort, to pander, and to stereotype. Not long after Tocqueville's defense of their civil status, for example, a Virginian congressman objected strenuously to the role played by Northern newspapers in promoting the antislavery cause, associating media effects with antidemocratic passions and violence. "Newspapers, pamphlets, tracts, and pictures," he complained, were "calculated, in an eminent degree, to rouse and inflame the passions of the slaves against their masters, to urge them on to deeds of death, and to involve them all in the horrors of a servile war."[40] In response to such efforts at pollution, journalists have identified their professional autonomy with the positive attributes of civil discourse, emphasizing the truthfulness of their reporting and its promotion of rational thought and independent action. In 1731, when Benjamin Franklin was attacked for printing what was considered an offensive advertisement, he published an "Apology for Printers" that made the case in precisely these terms.

> Printers are educated in the Belief that when men differ in Opinion, both sides ought equally to have the Advantage of being heard by the publick; and that when Truth and Error have fair Play, the former is always an overmatch for the latter: Hence they cheerfully serve all contending Writers that pay them well, without regarding on which side they are of the Question in Dispute.[41]

Public Opinion Polls

Public opinion as an active social force is a relatively recent phenomenon in human societies, as are the media of mass communication that inform the public about the "facts" of social life. Public opinion polling is a more recent institution still. More directly and explicitly than the media, polls define the contours of the public even as they take the measure of "its" opinion.

Perhaps because polls are so ubiquitous in contemporary life, their broad theoretical relevance has rarely been conceptualized; when they have been subjected to attention, their communicative role has scarcely been appreciated. By aggregating individual opinion into a group form, polls give objectivity to "public" opinion. In making it visible and numerical, they also make it constraining, allowing this ephemeral, materially invisible cultural phenomenon to become a much more specific, politically more powerful communicative force. Publicized polls provide "hard data" about the lifeworld of the civil sphere, allowing it to be construed independently of other exigencies and institutions. Polls represent this lifeworld as filled with reflection, as based on the responses of independent and thoughtful people. The very process of polling attributes to its interviewees rationality and sincerity, converting the members of civil society from a passive, voiceless, and potentially manipulable "mass" into a collective actor with a voice and intelligence of its own.[42]

In 1940, George Gallup published an intellectually ambitious defense of polling, a few years after his own polling institutions had surfaced as a major factor in America's national political life. Gallop addressed "the various questions and criticisms" that had been generated by this "new instrument," for example the claim that it undermined democracy by making the public appear "stupid and unreliable."[43] Gallup replied by linking the new technique to the liberating rather than the repressive side of civil discourse. The method of random sampling, he suggested, provides a set of "factual observations" that are more "realistic" than the merely subjective claims about public opinion projected by this or that activist group.[44] What endangers public opinion is the possibility that it can be "controlled."[45] "One can never be sure that the letter, telegram, or petition avalanche is the product of a genuine protest, or merely the organized effort of a small but powerful pressure group parading as a majority."[46] The issue of outside pressure acknowledges that anticivil motives and relations can pollute the play of communicative institutions. "When aggressive minorities are on the march," Gallup asks, "how is the Congressman to decide where the truth—or where the greater truth—lies, especially when, as so often happens, the minority represents itself as the majority?"[47] This danger can be addressed, Gallup argues, only by scientific polling. It purifies public opinion by supplying truthful information to the people's representatives: "The sampling referendum offers a gauge of strength for the claims and counterclaims which reach the American legislator."[48] This "new instrument" can "bridge the gap between the people and those who are responsible for making decisions in their name," he wrote.[49] "The public-opinion polls provide a swift and efficient method by which legislators, educators experts, and editors, as well as ordinary citizens throughout the length and breadth of the country, can have a more reliable measure of the pulse of democracy."[50]

In his second book, a decade later, Gallup once again responded to critics who tried to frame polls in an anticivil way. Acknowledging that a "good many" of those polled were "ignorant and uninformed"—character traits that would suggest the necessity of antidemocratic institutions—Gallup argues that these weaknesses can be overcome by random sampling. Polls reveal that a majority "usually registers sounds judgment on issues." Polling is legitimate because "democracy . . . requires merely that the sum total of individual views add up to something that makes sense."[51] Polls allow the collectivity to achieve rationality even when individuals are not rational themselves.

In reality, of course, polls not only reveal but construct "the public's" shifting attitudes toward the continuous, fragmented, and difficult-to-

interpret flow of ongoing social events. Their forced choice questions organize the public's opinion in a manner that makes it seem homologous
with, and therefore responsive to, the binary codes of civil society. Do whites
think that African-Americans are lazier than whites? More inclined than
whites to steal and to engage in violence, often of a sexual kind? Are Jewish
Americans loyal to their country? Are Communists? Is the president trustworthy or faithless, deceitful or honest? Is he his own man or likely to rely
on the judgments of others? Clearly these are as much simplifying constructions of public opinion as measurements of it; they simultaneously mirror
and apply the pure and impure categories that the discourse of civil society
provides.

It is precisely this circularity that makes polls so fundamentally important
to the independence and self-understanding of civil society. It is also what
allows them to exercise such a diffuse but often decisive form of communicative control over economic, political, and even cultural spheres. During
the two-year Watergate crisis in American society, an upheaval that decided
the fate of so many powerful individuals, institutions, and elites, decisions
about the precise wording of poll questions triggered large-scale political
effects.[52] If it was not literally true that "the public," as revealed through
public opinion polling, ruled during this crisis, it is certainly true that other,
more traditional collective actors could exert their force only by presenting
themselves as acting in the public's name. Political parties, lobbying groups,
institutional elites, and powerful individuals could appeal for their just deserts
only if they evoked the public's opinion.[53] When public response registered
in small but fateful numerical shifts in the polls, seismic changes in state
institutions would follow.

Insofar as the news media themselves rely increasingly on polls to report
on public opinion, polls become an even more powerful, doubly objecti-
fying social force. There develops a kind of sub-rosa dialogue, what literary
theorists call intertextuality,[54] between these two communicative institutions.
Because pollsters rely upon news-mediated constructions of recent events,
they are formulating questions not about the public's opinion in some open-
ended sense, but about what the public wants to know about a situation
that has already been communicatively constructed in reference to the binaries of the civil sphere. Polls are asking, in this way, about what the public
wants to know about itself, insofar as this self has already been symbolically
defined by the news. Rather than asking what people know about a situa-

tion, polling questions are directed to what people can be expected to know in the current situation, given the context of opinion as it has developed already. The questions of pollsters, then, are not neutral or detached, in the scientific sense of value-neutrality, but typifications, in the phenomenological sense, based on information that is already known.[55] Polling questions are collective representations that try to extend the horizon of civil ideas, the structures of feelings that the public have already expressed, to information and events that have not yet been processed. It is this already familiar quality of polling questions that ensures the relevance of polling results to the diffuse and anxious concerns of public opinion more broadly defined. It also ensures that polling results will be relevant to news media in turn, that they will be able to examine polls and report back to civil society about what "it" thinks about itself.

In a detailed study of Hong Kong newspapers and polling agencies during the high-stakes battle between mainland Chinese officials and the island's British governor general, Christopher Patten, Agnes Ku has documented such intertextual dynamics in a crisis that seemed to threaten Hong Kong's very existence as a civil society.[56] Drawing upon long-standing codes and narratives in Hong Kong political culture, leading newspapers tended initially to portray Patten as an honest democrat, despite his colonial associations, and China as an oppressive and threatening force. Polling agencies relied on these constructions and formulated forced choice questions that "discovered" increasing public support for Patten's demand that China make promises about ensuring Hong Kong's democratic status after its ties with Britain ended. However, as the tension between China and Britain mounted, and its destabilizing implications became more evident, public anxiety increased. Newspapers reported Chinese accusations that British demands for democracy were hypocritical, that they merely masked Great Britain's continuing colonial intent, and China's suggestions that Patten was determined to proceed no matter what the consequences for Hong Kong's economic well-being. In the midst of these new factual representations from the mass media, opinion polls began reporting that Patten's sincerity was being more frequently questioned and that he was being connected much more frequently than before to the antidemocratic themes of colonialism. The percentage of "don't knows" on questions about support for Patten's suggested reforms increased dramatically. This "fact" was immediately highlighted by leading newspapers, which now began to represent the crisis not as a last-ditch effort to protect Hong Kong's emerging democracy but as an indication that the island's economic future, and even its long-term social viability, was now under siege. The result was a gradual if grudging acceptance of the authority and strategy of the People's Republic of China in the transition, an authority that was, in fact, fundamentally ambivalent on the matter of Hong Kong's democratic aspirations.

Because polls are so often taken as crystallizations of the opinion of civil society as a whole—no matter what the actual fault lines created by the civil sphere's internal stratification—publishing poll numbers constitutes an event to which democratically elected politicians must offer a response, either in words or deeds. In democratic societies, the effects of these public representations happen quickly, primarily because the electoral franchise, which I will later discuss as a basic regulating institution, allows public opinion to directly intrude upon the state. In France, in 1991, only six weeks after assuming office as the nation's first female Prime Minister, the socialist Edith Cresson confronted a shocking decline in civil support. The *International Herald-Tribune* headlined "Cresson Meets Enemy: Public Opinion Polls" on its front page. Despite her close association with French President Mitterand, Cresson's initial moves had "fallen flat," constructed in dangerously anticivil terms. Her maiden speech to parliament had been "tedious and unfocused" and her economic policy had "alienated" both workers and middle class professionals. It was no wonder that, according to the subhead, "Only a Fourth of Electorate Approves Her Performance in First Six Weeks."[57] Cresson left office shortly thereafter.

In the summer of 2005, U.S. news media sympathetically broadcast, as "factual information," the drama of Cindy Sheehan staging an antiwar vigil outside the Texas White House of President Bush to protest her son's death in Iraq. The palpable effect of their construction on the American civil sphere, however, became apparent only with the nation-wide publication of opinion polls. The lead story in the *Philadelphia Inquirer* broadcast "Public's Support of War Faltering," reporting that support for the war had fallen from two-thirds to 44 percent in just one year. Large pictures of "average citizens" with block quotations indicating their skepticism were splashed artfully across an inside page. "These sentiments are mirrored in the polls," the paper assured its readers, providing copious charts and graphs that documented the public's change of mind. The *Inquirer* reported as fact the growing separation between state power and civil sphere: "Bush is losing his domestic battle for hearts and minds." If in a democratic society politicians are representatives of the civil power, they must win not only the heart but the mind of the public to their side.[58]

In antidemocratic societies, political officials use their power to prevent the influence of civil society and its opinions from being separated from the state. They make polling illegal or, if that is impossible, they repress or manipulate poll results, or pollute and undermine their claims. For more than half a century, Mexico had been essentially a one-party state, ruled by the Institutional Revolutionary Party, or PRI. As the date approached for the modern nation's first freely contested Presidential election, in July, 2000, the PRI made it impossible for accurate polling data to be published, making it more difficult for the civil sphere to be organized against the state. When pollster Rafael Gimenez's surveys suggested merely that challenger Vicente Fox was running strongly against the PRI candidate, the government allowed the results to be published in the newspaper *Milenio*. In April, however, when Gimenez's survey found that Fox has taken a surprising lead, *Milenio* announced that they had found a new pollster. Gimenez's results were never published, and he was denounced as either inept or careless, or as having sold out. When a second pollster did report Mr. Fox in the lead, PRI officials ridiculed him and publicly criticized his technical abilities. After a third pollster was blocked, she published her anti-PRI results in the *Dallas Morning News*. She later recalled the results, "suddenly my phone went silent" and "the PRI put out the order to the radio and TV stations: bury that witch."[59] Despite these efforts to block this key communicative institution, however, Fox won the election. The other communicative institutions, most notably the newspapers, but also civil associations, were able to sustain the independence of the civil sphere in a still powerful way.

In the Soviet Union's transition to democracy, the establishment of public opinion polls also played a fundamental role.[60] During Perestroika, the sociologist Yuri Levada, once a disgraced dissident, was allowed to establish the All-Union Center for the Study of Public Opinion on Social and Economic Issues. In February 1989, the center inserted a full-page questionnaire on social and political conditions in the Soviet Writer Union's weekly newsmagazine, the *Literary Gazette*. The poll triggered an immediate reaction among *Gazette* readers, who considered themselves part of the emerging civil sphere. The magazine received two hundred thousand responses, whose aggregated opinions described degradation in a wide range of different services and called for fundamental changes in the moral fabric of institutional life. Because it allowed the public to speak in an apparently authoritative, scientific, and measurable manner, these results helped legitimate President Michael Gorbachev in his drive to reform state power.

In the long run, the shock value of this poll had even deeper effects. Employing some of the central categories of the discourse of civil society, an associate director of the All-Union Center attested that the polling process served to crystallize the democratic self-image of the Soviet people. "Through the decades people have never been asked anything," he remarked. "All of a sudden their opinion is being counted—someone is seeking their answers." His conclusion was revealing: "They feel this is some sign of trust toward them, a demonstration of their worth." |Polling suggests trust in the sincerity, honesty, and intelligence of the people,|the interviewees. When public polls are systematically conducted and publicized for the first time, it is hardly surprising that the members of a nascent civil society can experience a new sense of worth. Yuri Levada was subsequently interviewed about the incident, and he emphasized the qualities of active independence that this communicative institution of civil society brings out. "Russia was deep in sleep, nothing was happening," Levada remarked. When the poll results were published, "for the first time we saw that our people are not only ready to answer a bold question but they actively want to speak out."[61]

Even in democratic societies that have institutionalized the regular publication of opinion polls, the results are often distorted in ways that reflect the strains of fragmenting forces like class, gender, race, and internal colonialism. This was illustrated in a particularly dramatic manner in Israel in the summer of 1989, when Elihu Katz, Hebrew University professor and newly appointed director of the Israel Institute for Applied Social Research, and Majid Al-Haj, sociology professor from Haifa University, announced that, for the first time, Israel's Arab citizens would be included in the sample upon which the monthly Continuing Survey of Israel citizens was based. The Israeli public's opinion had until then excluded the views of its subordinated but legally enfranchised Arab group. According to the *Jerusalem Post*, when Israeli-Arabs were included, poll results revealed a striking shift in "Israeli Opinion."

Taking account of the usually unsolicited voice of Israeli Arabs tilts nationwide opinion in a "dovish" direction. If a referendum were held today on the question, "Are you, on the whole, more inclined towards a solution that favors annexation of the territories or towards a solution that favours yielding the territories," 53% of Israeli Jews would favor annexation [and] 44% would favor yielding territories . . . If the Arab vote is added to this distribution, the dominant position shifts . . . from holding the territories to giving them up . . . A majority (52%) of all Israelis would favour yielding territory.[62]

Civil Associations

There is still another source of the situationally specific symbolic communication that permeates the civil sphere. In response to long-term shifts in social structure and short-term alterations in social circumstances, issue-oriented associations form to affect public opinion and its representatives in the civil sphere. These can be long-established lobbying groups that represent private economic or political interests, such as trade associations or the public arm of trade unions. They can be groups more explicitly oriented to public goods, such as environmental and taxpayer lobbies, or city manager associations. They can be large, relatively bureaucratized associations representing broad categories of persons, such as the National Organization of Women (NOW), Mothers against Drunk Driving (MADD), the National Association for the Advancement of Colored People (NAACP), or the American Association for Retired Persons (AARP). They can be much more intimate associations that form in response to a local "issue"—an offshore oil spill, a threatening toxic waste dump, the poisoning of an underground water reserve. They can be middling organizations that, though large in scale, have arisen in more time-sensitive ways, for example, "Historians against the War," a group within the Organization of American Historians that opposed the Vietnam War, or the "Citizens Trade Committee," a group formed to oppose the North American Free Trade Act.

What these groups have in common is that they have stepped outside the role structures of noncivil institutions—outside of economic organizations, families, churches, and local communities—to press their arguments in the "court of public opinion." What defines such associations, in other words, is their communicative intent. One could say they have, in accomplishing a particular task, gone beyond purely functional interests to broader, civil concerns; one could equally say that they have decided that, in order to accomplish some particular interest, they have found it necessary to address civil concerns.[63] In making their case for the particular, functional interests they represent, these associations are compelled to make an appeal to the entire civil community or to those mandated to represent it.[64] In launching these appeals, they will employ whatever clout they can muster, whether financial, political, religious, familial, or ethnic resources. But these resources can be effective only insofar as they allow the group more persuasively to justify its particular interests in universalizing terms.

Issue-oriented associations can make this case only in terms of the binary discourse of civil society. In doing so, they crystallize this broad and general set of ideals about self and others vis-à-vis particular situations, particular conflicts, and particular groups. These associations translate the codes of civil society into specific claims for, and against, the expansion of rights, the execution of new government policies, and the undertaking of new social actions. They may do so by creating conflict and intensifying opposition, or by trying to create greater cooperation and political or social harmony. They may translate and specify these general codes by impugning the motives of the individuals and groups who oppose their claims; the relations that these claims would putatively establish; or the kinds of institutions that would supposedly result. They may also do so by idealizing, even apotheosizing, the motives, relations, and institutions that they claim to be associated with the policies, actions, and rights of their own group.[65]

In September 1993, the newly elected administration of president Bill Clinton proposed a sweeping reorganization of the nation's largely private, and increasingly expensive and restricted, health care delivery system. Armies of insurance, hospital, and doctor associations set out to defeat the Democratic president and his wife, Hilary Rodham Clinton, whose task force had developed the reform proposal. For many members of these associations, the stakes were material and institutional: if the reforms went through, they would lose their jobs. For many others, the interests were political and ideological: they aimed to prevent a significant expansion of the welfare state, the success of which would have increased public support for the Democratic Party at the expense of the Republican Party. Whatever the reasons for their resistance, one thing was clear: they could not block the Clinton reforms by using their resources directly, by disrupting the state or by blocking the measure inside the medical profession or the health care delivery spheres. Instead, they would have to enter into the civil sphere and engage in communicative action. If they had simply presented public opinion with the importance of their particular interests, however, they would have generated little solidarity. Without support from wider public opinion, their particular, functional interests might have been viewed unfavorably by the journalists who articulated factual frames for interpreting the health reforms, by the polls presenting the public's shifting opinions, and by the civil officers, such as congressmen, who acted in the public's name. They would have gained little influence, in other words, if they had simply complained that the Clinton reforms would undermine their organizational authority, reduce their incomes, or challenge their ethical ideals in a narrowly institutional sense. What these civil associations set out to do, instead, was to intertwine their interests and ethics with the broader civil sphere.

When President Clinton unveiled his reform package to the American people, he presented it as a "health *security*" measure that would extend civil solidarity by repairing a deeply stratified, unequal, and unfair distribution of medical care. He was also careful to root this collective theme deeply inside the discourse of liberty. In the run-up to presenting the reforms, the Clinton team had worked hard to avoid any hint of the coercive and bureaucratic, rejecting public characterizations that mentioned such words as "plan," "*managed* care," or even "program," and in the speech proposing his new legislation, the president criticized the status quo as giving the American people "few choices."[66] The success of this initial civil construction was immediately evident. Public opinion strongly supported the measure, and an influential television pollster and political analyst praised the president for his "intellect" and "conviction" and the first lady for her "compassion and concern."[67] Six months later, the tables had been turned, with 15 percent of poll respondents changing from positive to negative. By August 1994, Democratic congressional leaders declared the reform package dead in the water, and the same influential television commentator now accused the Clinton administration of "awesome political stupidity." He polluted the reform plan as "the living embodiment of Big Government—or Big Brother," describing it as having been hatched by a group of "self-anointed experts" in "secret" meetings "chaired by a sinister . . . and a driven First Lady."[68]

This defeat was historic. It set the stage for the neoconservative seizure of power in congressional elections in November of that year.

Pundits during the debacle, and academic analysts for long after, attributed the defeat of the liberal proposal to material force, to the power of the medical and insurance lobbies and the vast sums of money they had at their disposal. The truth was quite different. The most active lobbying group, the Health Insurance Association of America (HIAA), had actually lost power and money in the months preceding the struggle; the "big five" insurance companies had withdrawn from that lobbying association, declaring that the HIAA was "paralyzed by small insurers who are opposed to national health care reforms."[69] The force in this situation was discursive, not material.

In the eleven months between the reform proposal's birth and death, there had ensued one of the most frenzied public relations contests in modern American history.[70] Health plan opponents had prepared rhetorical strategies for months, and hard-hitting advertisements and press conferences appeared virtually the day after the president's speech. By contrast, the administration's own public relations campaign, which could have provided crucial rhetorical leadership, took months to get in gear.[71] In the interlude, opponents succeeded in constructing the reform proposal in repressive, anticivil terms. They argued that the newly proposed health system would be antidemocratic; that it would take control of health decisions away from the individual; that it reflected an authoritarian distrust for common sense and rationality; that its proposed regulations were confusing and opaque. According to a social science student of the debacle, Theda Skocpol, one series of TV ads in particular became "veritable icons" of the conservatives' rhetorical success.[72] Between September 1993, and summer 1994, the HIAA released three waves of advertisements featuring "Harry and Louise," a fictional middle-class couple who gravely discussed the merits of the Clinton reforms and, after much seeming goodwill and erstwhile hesitation, always ended up coming down on the negative side. "This plan forces us to buy our insurance through those new mandatory government health alliances," Louise lamented, to which Harry readily assented, adding that the alliances would be "run by tens of thousands of new bureaucrats."[73] The factual and the fictional media of communication bleed together; both are directed by the binary discourse of civil society.

After the health care measures were defeated, the American health care system still was compelled to undergo drastic change. The difference was that these changes were organized by the private economic sphere alone instead of being subject to the control of civilly regulated state authority. For-profit health maintenance organizations (HMOs) became omnipresent, and they introduced cost-cutting measures without the scrutiny of civil society. When consumers of this reduced yet more expensive care began to feel the strain, local groups formed to protest particular HMO practices, and, eventually, nationwide consumer lobbies arose, demanding regulation and reform. To do so, they entered communicatively into the civil sphere. To gain solidarity with U.S. citizens who did not share their particular concerns, they had to frame the medical and economic interests of their members in the democratic language of civil society. The groups lobbying for HMO reform packaged their reforms as a "patient's bill of rights." They complained to politicians and reporters that HMOs were hierarchical and repressive in the face of reasonable demands for medical treatment; that they were greedy and self-centered; that they were secretive in responding to patients' requests for procedural information and deceitful in their accounting practices and public representations.[74]

Oscillating in this manner between particular interests and cultural coding, civil associations scan public opinion, make efforts to affect the symbolic constructions of the civil sphere projected by factual and fictional media, and gauge the choices and intensities of the public's opinions as measured by polls. They are, in other words, inextricably interconnected with the other communicative institutions of civil life and the phenomenological lifeworld of intuitive civil sensibility—the structures of civil feeling—that supports and restricts them.

By naming these kinds of groups civil associations, I am differentiating them from the much more general category of "voluntary associations," which has played such a pronounced role in democratic theory and empirical debate. In the era of civil society I, when democratic thinkers linked civil society to virtually every association outside of the authoritarian state, associations were defined as voluntary insofar as they were not state-directed. They were voluntary, that is, in the sense that citizens were free to form them, and members free to join them or leave them, without being subject to political coercion. In Democracy in America, Tocqueville made a great deal of such formations, seeming to praise the new American democracy for the fact that its citizens took matters into their own hands by forming associations rather than simply waiting upon the beneficence of a paternalistic state.[75] But Tocqueville was hardly alone. In *The Division of Labor in Society*, and particularly in his preface to its second edition, Durkheim heralded the significance of what he called secondary associations for providing mediations between the impersonal bureaucratic state and the individual.[76] Such face-to-face groupings were also praised by such republican thinkers as Hannah Arendt, who idealized the local and spontaneous political associations of direct democracy, and by Jürgen Habermas, who enthusiastically evoked the intimacy and conversation of eighteenth-century coffeehouses and salons.[77]

This broad and inclusive approach to voluntary association crystallized in American social scientific thinking about democracy that emerged in the mid-twentieth century, particularly in the evolutionary and idealizing strand I criticized in chapters 2 and 3. Against the conservative and radical theories that posited the inevitability of mass society and elite domination,[78] and in contrast to the big-state theories that romanticized state Communism and its totalitarian control, liberals championed the intermediate level of voluntary associations. These were conceptualized very broadly, simply as "voluntary," in the sense of not subject to direct control, either from the state or from other powerful social hierarchies. In *The International Encyclopedia of the Social Sciences*, for example, a leading sociologist defined voluntary associations as a "group organized for a pursuit of one interest or of several interests in common," which could be "contrasted with involuntary groupings serving a greater variety of ends, such as kin groups, castes, social classes, and communities."[79] In the same set of volumes, in an equally broad fashion, the best-known sociological student of this organizational form stressed simply that a group "is voluntary in the sense that it is neither mandatory nor acquired through birth" and, in addition, "exists independently of the state."[80]

In recent decades, this civil society I approach to voluntary association has formed the heart of the so-called "neo-Tocquevillian" theory of civil society developed by the American political scientist Robert Putnam, a perspective that, in the United States at least, has found sympathetic responses in both academic circles and the popular press. From his sweeping empirical study of democratic and authoritarian tendencies in Italy to his attacks on television viewing and his pithy observations about the dangers of bowling alone,[81] Putnam has vigorously argued that such organizations as the Boy Scouts, church support groups, women's clubs, the PTA, and bowling leagues are the key to a lively civil sphere and thus to democracy itself.

The problem with such theorizing, no matter how well-intended and civic-minded, is that, like civil society I theory more generally, it seems rather out of date. Developed to address the possibilities of democracy in earlier and much simpler societies, it suffers from the diffuseness that makes it congenitally unsuited to providing a critical approach to democracy in the present day. Of course, pluralism and diversity remain vital for complex societies, and the legal freedom to form and unform associations essential. But the neo-Tocquevillian approach paints with a brush that is much too broad to delineate the requisites for contemporary civil society.

To include every possible kind of nonstate grouping under the umbrella of voluntary association—to say, in effect, that every such nonstate grouping teaches the art of civil association—is to say little about the variable relation between association and expansive solidarity. Cooking societies, shooting associations, dog training clubs, star-gazing groups, and hunting clubs permeate democratic and nondemocratic nations alike. So do organizations like the Boy Scouts, which not only have nothing intrinsically democratic about them but, rather, teach values and model social relationships that, it might be argued, are anticivil in some vital ways. Though revolutionary secret societies, such as the Weathermen of the late 1960s or the American militia of the 1990s, are much more political in their activities, they do not seek to achieve power by entering communicatively into the civil sphere; they wish, instead, to use force to overthrow it. In other words, it is not the mere fact of associating that defines a grouping as civil, but what is associated with it, and whether these other factors orient an association to engage with the broader solidarity groupings that exists outside itself. As Cohen remarked in her criticism of such neo-Tocquevillian theory, the question is, What generalizes the social trust that exists within voluntary organizations? How does the trust that sustains a particular association "become trust of strangers outside the group?"[82] Of course, this is a normative rather than an empirical formulation. In empirical terms, the generalizing of trust beyond the confines of any particular organization may actually be done in a manner that increases feelings of strangeness and antagonism among broader settings and large groups. But Cohen's critical point remains well taken. It is not the existence of a group per se, even if the associating it spawns is enthusiastic and face-to-face. It is whether the group is oriented to issues outside of itself, and whether in relation to these it displays a communicative intent.[83]

If we revisit Tocqueville, whose writings are so fundamental to the current revival of voluntary association theory, we find that he was much more attuned to these subtleties than the contemporary school that bears his name. Tocqueville did indeed laud Americans for "forever forming associations," as Putnam put it,[84] but he showed much more sensitivity than his contemporary American interlocutors to the fact that such associations could promote not only civil but anticivil solidarities. Tocqueville did not actually praise Americans for frenetically forming nonstate groups. He called attention, instead, to their having "perfected the art of pursuing their common desires in common."[85] It was, in other words, an orientation to wider civil solidarity, not the act of associating per se, that Tocqueville wished to underscore.

This interpretive distinction may seem subtle, but the variable relationship between association and democracy is not. It is instructive to scrutinize Tocqueville's formal definition of associations, for it consists of two parts, neither of which contemporary neo-Tocquevillians emphasize. An association, Tocqueville writes, "consists solely in the decision of a certain number of individuals to adhere publicly to certain doctrines," on the one hand, and in the engagement "to commit themselves to seek the triumph of those doctrines in a certain way," on the other.[86] By public adherence, Tocqueville means that, to be part of the civil sphere, associations must have a civil orientation, a communicative interest in influencing public opinion. By qualifying this definition still further, by emphasizing that these publicly oriented associations must spread their doctrines in a "certain way," Tocqueville draws attention to the binary possibilities of communicative action. Civil associations can articulate their interests in both civil and anticivil terms.

These ambiguous possibilities were illustrated when Tocqueville undertook to demonstrate that, in his time, voluntary associations actually occurred just as frequently in nondemocratic as in democratic societies. By doing so, he shows that the effects of association are not decided only by whether association takes a communicative, public-oriented form, but by whether, and to what degree, they seek to expand or contract social solidarity. It would come as a surprise to his contemporary interpreters to learn that Tocqueville did not argue that civil associations were more prominent in democratic America than in nondemocratic Europe. What he claimed, rather, is that in Europe associations were more particularistic and divisive, tending to short-circuit public discussion in order to engage in more direct exercises in power. European associations, Tocqueville claimed, treated members of other groups not as potential partners in a wider solidarity, but as enemies.

> Most Europeans look upon association as a weapon of war, to be organized in haste and immediately tried out on some field of battle. People do indeed associate for the purpose of discussion, but the thought of impending action weighs on everyone's mind. An association is an army. Discussion offers an opportunity to count heads and stir spirits, after which it is time to march out and meet the enemy. The members of an association may regard legal resources as a useful means of action but never as the only path to success.[87]

The result, as Tocqueville himself put it, was that in nondemocratic Europe, associations "eschew civil norms" and "adopt military habits and principles."[88] In the United States, by contrast, "association is understood differently." Their energies were directed, Tocqueville believed, to challenging the "*moral* ascendancy" of the majority, not its power in the physical or administrative sense. Rather than taking action and seizing power, their communicative actions aimed at engaging the wider solidarity, "to discover which arguments are most likely to make an impression on the majority." Because American associations oriented themselves to public opinion and to creating a wider, more encompassing solidarity, "the minority always hopes to attract enough additional support to become the majority."[89]

In order to explain this fundamental difference between European and American association, Tocqueville must look beyond the simple existence of voluntary association in the civil society I sense of the term. Though allowing that "the obvious differences between us and the Americans in this respect are explained by several things," he ultimately connects the different forms of voluntary association to the extent of underlying solidarity. Whereas in Europe, the associations out of power "are so different from the majority that they can never hope to gain its support," in America "only shades of difference separate one opinion from another." One thing that contributes to the greater solidary feeling among American voluntary associations is widespread voting rights: "Of all the causes that help to moderate the violence of political association in the United States, the most powerful, perhaps, is universal suffrage." It is universal suffrage, which I will later define as one of the principal regulatory institutions of civil society, that allows a majority to acquire "moral force," and it is this moral status that leads civic associations away from extrademocratic violence to engagement in civil communication.[90] Later in his discussion, Tocqueville writes that "the laws do more to maintain a democratic republic in the United States than physical causes do, and mores do more than laws." In a footnote, he "remind[s] the reader of the general sense in which I use the word mores": "I mean the whole range of intellectual and moral dispositions that men bring to the state of society."[91]

Tocqueville's understanding of the necessity for democratic associations to be oriented to public engagement, rather than simply to be voluntary, is critical; so is his perception that even such publicly oriented associations can engage in communicative action that pollutes opponents as anticivil enemies.[92] What mars his argument is its one-sided application. He treats American associations in an idealized way. The national distinction he draws has the effect of camouflaging the empirical variation within civil associations. By the time Tocqueville visited America, there had already been centuries of anticivil efforts by publicly oriented associations. This did not mean that they became *putschist*, violence-oriented conspiracies, as Tocqueville suggested was frequently the case in France. It did mean that, even in America, associations entered the civil sphere, and engaged public opinion, as often to narrow social solidarity as to broaden it. Indeed, whether their ambition was to broaden or to narrow solidarity, associations could accomplish their aims by evoking repressive categories and creating polluting associations, not just by utilizing liberating categories and creating purification.

Tocqueville was by no means the first social theorist to recognize the anticivil possibilities of civil associations, nor was he by any means the last. In Federalist Paper 51, James Madison wrote eloquently about the dangers of factions, and he insisted on the separation of powers as a counterbalancing institutional system of regulatory control. In fact, those who crafted the U.S. Constitution focused on the divisive aggressiveness of civil associations,[93] as have passionate critics of "special interests" ever since. Employing the adjective "special" is designed, of course, to designate a group's narrow and constricting aims.

Sociologists have often related the antidemocratic effects of voluntary associations to their internal organizational form. Seymour Lipset, Martin Trow, and James Coleman made this internal antagonism to democracy the foil for their classic study, *Union Democracy*. At the very beginning of their book, they noted that "the pattern which characterizes almost all voluntary organizations was generalized over forty years by the German sociologist, Robert Michels, when he laid down his famous 'iron law of oligarchy.' "[94] In "their trade unions, professional societies, business associations, and co-operatives—in the myriad [of] nominally democratic voluntary organizations, the experience of most people," Lipset and his colleagues assert, "would tend to confirm Michels' generalization."[95]

> Since Michels first wrote, many books and articles have been written about oligarchy in voluntary organizations, but almost invariably they have documented the operation of his iron law in another set of circumstances. They have shown how control of the organization machinery, combined with membership passivity, operates to perpetuate oligarchic control.[96]

In their effort to find out what might counteract this anticivil tendency in associations, the authors of *Union Democracy* point, as Tocqueville had before them, to the offsetting role that can be played by the other communicative and regulatory institutions of civil society, emphasizing the role of democratic elections and competing outlets for public opinion, such as newsletters and newspapers. If these other institutions are present, they suggest, associations are more willing to reign in their competition, to obey overarching rules of the game, to allow power to change hands in a peaceful way.

The research of social scientists since the publication of *Union Democracy* has confirmed the caution that dampened its authors' enthusiasm for association in its pristine, unadorned form. In the encyclopedia article I noted above, David Sills addressed the prevailing belief that "since voluntary associations can exist only in societies in which freedom of association exists, and since such societies are more or less democratic in their ethos and political structure, there is an expectation that members will take an active part in the affairs of the association and that democratic procedures will govern its conduct." Pointing to a range of different empirical studies, however, Sills warned that "this expectation often is not met; although most voluntary associations have constitutions, bylaws, or oral traditions that call for full participation by the members, the 'iron law of oligarchy' formulated by Robert Michels generally has greater weight."[97]

Camouflaged beneath his influential encomiums for face-to-face associations, Putnam actually himself acknowledges the "need to take into account the fact that closely-knit social, economic, and political organizations are unfortunately prone to corruption."[98] The problem is that, given his emphasis on association per se, Putnam cannot explain why or how this antidemocratic tendency might be counteracted. Without acknowledging that he is doing so, however, Putnam refers to a whole set of nonassociational factors that can critically affect the democratic capacities of associations. In his historical reconstruction of the process that led to the creation of communal democracies in late medieval northern Italy, he mentions "elaborate legal codes" that "confine[d] the violence of the overmighty,[99] and a "public administration" which, because it was "professionalized," allowed "legitimate authority in the North" to be "only delegated to public officials, who remain responsible to those with whose affairs they are entrusted."[100] In my discussion of the regulatory institutions of civil society in chapters 6 and 7, law and office will be presented as fundamentally important forms of social control. In fact, Putnam even points beyond these institutions to the cultural milieu within which associations launch their claims. He stresses the significance in Italy's late medieval period of a "renewed civic morality" that mandated "fraternal assistance" and "hospitality toward strangers," a cultural ethic designed to "prevent the new society from tearing itself apart in internecine strife."[101]

In other words, associations can contribute to democracy only if they are intertwined with the full range of communicative and regulative institutions and the cultural codes, which crystallize the idealizing normative commitments of the civil sphere. The civil potential of voluntary associations is promoted by these other institutions, even as they provide critical inputs in turn. If clubs and associations are merely self-referential, they play no effective role in society's civil sphere, though they may perform important functions in their respective noncivil spheres. Before the feminist movement brought women into the paid workforce, for example, hospitals benefited greatly from their women volunteers. So did elementary and high schools from their largely female Parent-Teacher Associations. To become organs of civil society, however, such groups must direct their particular interests outward, into the broader network of solidary ties and claims.

Historical considerations lend support to these theoretical arguments about the tendencies of contemporary society. As Michael Schudson shows, civil associations first emerged in a democratic context that put a high premium on solidary communication. It was in the run-up to the American Revolution that self-organizing, issue-oriented groups, as compared with state-directed or ascriptive organizations, first achieved prominence on the American scene. "With a political crisis looming," Schudson writes, "the colonists made use of their various means of communication, of which newspapers were only the most visible."

> Colonial elites knew one another through trade; businessmen in one colony might buy real estate in another. They knew one another through college experience. Yale attracted many students from New York and Massachusetts as well as Connecticut [who] did not necessarily return to their home colonies but chose to settle elsewhere. . . . Presbyterian and Congregationalist ministers representing most of the colonies banded together with annual meetings and committees of correspondence. . . . A wide variety of social, economic, educational, and religious contacts transcended colonial borders, and so did common interests in science, medicine, or the arts.[102]

Schudson's point is that this new organizational form emerged in response to demands for greater solidarity and mutual understanding on a national scale. The fragmentation created by the wide dispersement of isolated colonies could be overcome only with the help of civic association. If this was true for the problem of creating civil solidarity between colonies, it was equally the case for breaking down barriers within each colony itself.

> As for communication with a colony, formal and informal organizations operated as well as newspapers. Boston's social clubs and Masonic lodges became centers where people could come together to talk politics (among other things). A caucus system coordinated Boston artisans and prepared them to vote . . . at town meetings.

While New York had no similarly focused system, its taverns were a regular site for political talk.[103]

It is actually this outward civil orientation that provides the benefits that the neo-Tocquevillian civil society I perspective erroneously ascribes to association in and of itself. Putnam traces the striking diminution of some of America's most beloved voluntary associations and decries what he sees as its result: the decline of American civil society.[104] Only such face-to-face interactions, he believes, can "foster sturdy norms of generalized reciprocity and encourage the emergence of social trust."[105] As we have learned from this discussion, however, voluntary associations play this solidarizing role only if they can assume a communicative form. As sources of situationally specific applications of broad civil discourse, lobbying groups, public service associations, and clubs of all sorts do play a singular and irreplaceable role in defining the boundaries of the civil sphere and offering justifications for placing groups inside and outside it. Such associations represent particular interests—economic, political, ethnic, religious, racial—and they employ every possible resource on their behalf. In order to effect such representation, however, they must develop civil influence. In doing so, regardless of their particular interest, and whether or not they evoke polluting or purifying discourse, they reinforce the solidarity of a broader community, contributing to the normative standards that function to hem these particularistic interests in.

This approach to civil associations adumbrates my understanding of the decidedly anti-institutional forces represented by social movements, to which I will devote chapter 9. In the chapter that immediately follows, however, we turn to civil institutions in their regulative form.

CHAPTER 6

Regulative Institutions (1):

Voting, Parties, Office

THE RELATIONSHIP BETWEEN democracy and civil society is by no means clear-cut. Civil society exists even in antidemocratic societies, though in a less differentiated and distinctive form. In such a submerged civil sphere, the "people" may still be rhetorically constituted as a community of autonomous individuals, but it is a community whose existence, functions, and character are publicly defined by the state. The people's construction as an independent community can be glimpsed only partially, at a distance. This fitful solidarity presents itself in clandestine meetings of communicative associations, in carefully nuanced public statements and discussions, in controlled but subtly implicative news stories, in circulating internet and *samizdat* communications, in ostensibly apolitical fiction, and via informal but still audible murmurings of public opinion, which can be heard indirectly through attribution.

To the degree that a society is democratic, the relation between civil society and state is more differentiated. The civil sphere becomes decidedly more self-defining and distinctive as a society becomes democratic. Solidarity becomes palpable, an almost visible force that represents itself via groups, media, polls, and the many diverse and visible channels of legitimate public opinion. What makes this separation possible is the independence of the communicative institutions of civil society from consequential control by state power. Standing firmly inside the civil rather than the state sphere, communicative institutions become free to broadcast interpretations that are not only independent of the state, but can challenge its commands, its capacity for indirect domination, and its potential violence.

All complex societies have states, and they are extraordinarily important, but it is vital not to conflate states and their powers with the institutions of the civil sphere. States are organizations that exercise social control in formal and explicit, if sometimes indirect ways, by requests if possible, by commands if necessary, and by force if nothing else will do. States may themselves be composed of various organizational forms, from such collegial bodies as councils and central committees to such debating institutions as parliaments. Their most distinctive and overriding form of organization, however, is the bureaucratic. Formal, impersonal, and hierarchic, with clear lines of subordination, bureaucracies are, as Max Weber demonstrated long ago, the most efficient and ultimately the most responsible way to ensure that governmental decisions will be carried out.[1] Only bureaucracies can supply political structure to mirror the complexity of social life, developing procedures for coordinating the practical tasks of putting government decisions into play.

The manifest historical necessity for such formal state organization makes it abundantly clear why democracies have had such a difficult time. If democracy is as Aristotle defined it, "ruling and being ruled in turn," the problem seems quite overwhelming. There is, in fact, a "state-centered" tradition in sociology that sees state power as independent of any serious social control. Derived from Weber and his associate Otto Hintz, and revitalized by the writings of Theda Skocpol, such statist theory resists not only liberal but also Marxian ideas that state interests can be defined by forces outside themselves.[2] The problem of state autonomy is particularly acute when the outside force attempting to control the state is itself not of a material kind. How can the most powerful material and organizational force in modern society—the bureaucratic state—be controlled by solidary institutions of such manifestly lesser force? The answer is that bureaucratic states have an Achilles' heel, a structural feature suggesting that state power, while terribly effective as means, can never be an end. As Weber pointed out, every bureaucracy is nonbureaucratic at the top: "The consequences of bureaucracy depend therefore upon the direction which the powers using the apparatus give to it."[3] The goals of government, its ends, are established by forces outside state organization itself. At the head of state organization sits an authority that is instituted by some nonbureaucratic power, which aims to make the bureaucracy work in its own interests and name.

Civil Power: A New Approach to Democratic Politics

Historically, this extraorganizational force has typically emerged from an upper class that controls the resources of economic life, a dominating "social" power whose agents exercise "political" power by collecting taxes, raising armies, and building the administrative infrastructures of public life.[4] In traditional and early modern societies, such rulers are aristocrats. Representing familial networks, they form dynasties to exercise state control. In more developed societies, the class whose representatives sit atop bureaucracies are defined less by familial than by market networks. To the degree that capitalist societies are not democratic, the bourgeoisie has ruled, either directly or in a more mediated manner through its political agents. In communist societies, political representatives of the proletariat have exercised direct and indirect power in its name.

The question is whether such class control continues to mark capitalist and socialist societies in which governments are regulated by democratic procedures. Marxist and neo-Marxist social scientists have remained deeply committed to the view that such continuity exists.[5] How precisely class rule is mediated in so-called "formally" democratic societies, and whether it truly speaks for the interests of the dominant class or is co-opted by oligarchic interests of its own, have been continuous foci for political controversy and sociological research.[6] What concerns us, however, is the central claim upon which all the parties in these disputes agree, namely, that social power does always and inevitably become political power, regardless of whether there is formal democracy.

In terms of the perspective I am developing, it should be clear that this is not the case. To the degree that the hierarchies of social power also become the political hierarchies of the state—directly and indirectly translating themselves into a ruling class or power elite—democracy does not exist. Such a translation can be blocked. The ruled can, in fact, learn to become the rulers in turn. The ability to effect such blockage, indeed to institutionalize it in a systemic manner, is how democracy should be defined.

Democracy rests on the independent production of a new kind of power, which I will call "civil power." In a democracy, the civil sphere, not social power, decides who will sit at the state's nonbureaucratic top. |Civil power is solidarity translated into government control. |How does this happen? To the degree that there is an independent civil sphere, the people "speak," not only through the *communicative* institutions that provide cultural authority, but through *regulative* institutions as well. The civil community regulates access to state power. To do so, it constitutes a new and different kind of power of its own. To the degree that society is democratic, to that degree regulatory institutions are the gatekeepers of political power. It is civil power that opens and closes the gate.

 | This is not to say that social power does not deeply affect the dynamics of democratic politics, both during the contest for state power and after, when civil power is exercised inside the state. It is to say that these dynamics are everywhere subject, not only in principle but also in practice, to the communicative and regulatory powers of the civil sphere. That these soli-darizing processes typically have the effect of excluding certain groups, and of justifying domination over others, does not make the civil mediation of social power less real. Indeed, it is all the more significant for that. |

Revisiting Thrasymachus:
The Instrumental Science of Politics

I will devote this and the following chapter to the regulatory institutions of civil society. Before doing so, however, it is important to recognize how the tradition of Thrasymachus has caused these institutions to be understood in a radically different way. Typically, indeed, they have not been seen as civil institutions at all. Rather than regulate state power, they have been defined as simple manifestations of it, not as conduits for civic culture but merely as instruments of social hegemony, as machines that function either to rationalize political domination or to efficiently translate social into po-litical control.

This understanding is most neatly articulated by the economic theory of democracy, according to which, as Anthony Downs suggested, |"each citizen casts his vote for the party he believes will provide him with more benefits than any other." | But the instrumental science of politics is hardly confined to such a narrowly circumscribed model of rational choice. Writing a few years after Downs, the erudite and classically oriented political thinker Bernard Crick described politics as nothing more than "the market place and the price mechanism of all social demands."[8] Crick's insistence that "there is nothing spontaneous about politics—it depends on deliberate and continuous individual activity" is a presupposition that widely informs contemporary political studies. As Nelson Polsby and Aaron Wildavsky put it in their influential *Presidential Elections*, politics concerns "courses of action consciously pursued toward well-understood goals." Explaining that "the strategies of participants in a Presidential election make sense once we understand the web of circumstances in which they operate," these American political scientists assert that "this principle applies to candidates and their managers, to delegates at nominating conventions, to party workers, and to voters."[9]

If Machiavelli first gave modern voice to this strategic and world-weary approach to power, it was Max Weber who transformed it into the language of combat and struggle that has marked the social science of politics. Describing political parties as simply living in "a house of power," Weber insisted that "party actions are always directed toward a goal which is striven for in a planned manner," one that aims for "the conquest of a community."[10] It was in this martial and instrumental spirit that Weber's student Robert Michels developed his new approach to political parties. Parties emerge, according to Michels, purely for instrumental reasons, because of the "mechanical and technical impossibility" for the democratic citizens of large-scale societies to realize their will. Parties institutionalize a purely strategic logic in turn because of "the technical specialization that inevitably results from all extensive organization."[11] Continuing this reductive approach, one leading post–World War II student of political parties, the French political scientist Maurice Duverger, described parties as a "coordinating machinery" that provides "the machinery for the selection of leaders, and decides their powers."[12] V. O. Key, the highly influential American student of southern politics, converted the professed pragmatism of party politicians into the academic language of marginal utility. In the "battle for control of a state," he wrote, parties "must raise issues and appeal to the masses if for no other reason than the desire for office."[13] Nelson Polsby and Aaron Wildavsky likewise understand parties as "organizations devoted to maintaining or increasing their own opportunities to exercise political power."[14] Parties are necessary because "without coalitions it is impossible to enlist the machinery of government in behalf of the goals of any faction."[15]

In comparison with political scientists, those trained in the sociological approach to the science of politics pride themselves on getting beyond the focus on individual decisions and political institutions and moving toward a more "social" perspective. As I suggested in chapter 3, however, inside the reductive tradition of Thrasymachus, the social tends to become a stand-in for the economic, and the latter need not be understood in only a Marxist sense. Seymour Martin Lipset followed Weber, not Marx, when he famously declared that "in every modern democracy conflict among different groups is expressed through political parties which basically represent a 'democratic translation of the class struggle.' "[16] After Lipset set the theoretical stage, the critical questions for political sociology became instrumentalized, its controversies generated by disagreement over what determines the "cleavages" that are taken to be the indelible markers of democratic life.[17] Did the elections that placed Hitler into power, for example, take their shape from the declining lower middle class of German society, from its impoverished working class, or from the machinations of its aristocracy or the bourgeoisie?[18] Similarly, when Daniel Bell wanted to explain McCarthyism, he pointed to "deep changes taking place in the social structure that are reworking the social map of the country, upsetting the established life-chances and outlooks of old, privileged groups, and creating uncertainties about the . . . structural relations between class position and power."[19] In *The Politics of Unreason*, Lipset and Earl Raab related political extremism to "a sense of power and status deprivation," to "the deprived, the 'never-hads' and the 'once-hads.' "[20] Those who reject such social explanations in favor of a more organization analysis of politics continue to put their findings in a determinedly strategic and instrumental way, as in Friedland and Alford's emphasis on "institutional logics."[21]

Indeed, the power of this language of social reduction is so pervasive that, even when it is falsified empirically, it continues to exert its hold. In a series of closely reasoned and methodologically rigorous empirical studies, Jeff Manza and Clem Brooks have brought the political sociology of voting to bear on the most pressing electoral problems of the present day. They present their project in terms of the instrumental logic of social politics that for so long has defined the field. "How the middle class votes is of increasing consequence for understanding key sources of change in American politics," they assert, and they frame their data on voting patterns as if it reflects changes that are taking place in economic life: "Post-industrial trends have enhanced the electoral significance of the professional and managerial segments of the electorate, as they have grown significantly as a proportion of the population." It comes as a surprise, then, to learn that the actual findings of Manza and Brooks suggest not material but ideal control. The class developments they describe have, in fact, been regulated and restructured by a "new political culture," by the shared commitment to rights expansion that derives from the social movements of the 1960s and 1970s.[22] Could there be a more powerful illustration of how civil power can regulate the social? What is lacking is not empirical evidence but theoretical logic. We need a new theoretical language, one that can conceptualize civil as compared with social and political power. Only a theory of civil power can explain how national cultural configurations create a climate within which the voters in contemporary capitalist societies define and control class interest in more, and less, universalizing ways.

Fifty years ago, C. Wright Mills contended, in an extraordinarily influential book, that America was ruled by a "power elite." Sociologists who have followed up on his pioneering investigations have confirmed that there is, indeed, an economic elite in the United States. Wealth is vastly concentrated at the top 1 percent of the American population. Not only that, but a large part of this wealth is inherited at birth. Many large stock-holding families remain actively involved in controlling the direction of major corporations, through family offices, investment partnerships, and holding companies.[23] Yet, while Mills and his intellectual descendants have demonstrated that social power is distributed highly unevenly, they have never succeeded in making a good case for their more ambitious claim that the economic elite actually controls the state. Indeed, in the often fiercely fought political struggles to influence state power, social elites fail time after time to exercise compelling control not only over civil discourse but over political goals.

Mills himself was keenly sensitive to this possible dilemma. He recognized that the central empirical question for understanding modern politics is not, in fact, about the social or even the power elite but actually about the civil sphere. The only issue that really matters, he allowed, is "the degree to which the public has genuine autonomy from instituted authority."[24] If there exists "the free ebb and flow of discussion," Mills acknowledged—if there are "possibilities of answering back, or organizing autonomous organs of public opinion, of realizing opinion in action"—then whether there is a concentration of social and political power ends up not being very important at all.[25] Mills's theoretical prescience was striking. He speaks precisely to the issue that, almost a half-century later, has now become the order of the day: If "the power elite . . . is truly responsible to, or even exists in connection with, a community of publics, it carries a very different meaning than if such a public is being transformed into a society of masses."[26]

How Mills himself answered this question is history. He asserted that the public has, in fact, been transformed in just this pacifying way. It constitutes a mass, not a civil sphere. The public consists of helpless and hapless victims of media manipulation, not citizens whose discursively constructed autonomy gives them the ability to persuade the mass media to speak in their name.[27] There are no communicative institutions in Mills's theory of the power elite; he rules out of court the very possibility of an independently demarcated civil sphere. Institutional regulation of state power, in the service of public opinion, is a theoretical impossibility.

But it is precisely such a possibility that I will pursue here.

Constructing and Destructing Civil Power (1): The Right to Vote and Disenfranchisement

Civil regulates state power most conspicuously via the electoral process. By casting their votes, the putatively autonomous individuals whose feelings of solidarity with one other create the civil sphere regulate access to state power. They do so by aggregating their legally endowed political voices. "Vote" derives from the Latin *votum*, for "wish." Votes are the political wishes of the individuals who compose civil society. Voting allocates positions of power at the top of the state, and these authorities, in turn, appoint the power-holders immediately below. To the degree that there is democracy, voting breaks up the direction translation of social into political power. Again, the point is not that, in democracies, social powers cease to exist. Certainly, they continue to make every effort to bend and shape the voting process their way. The point is that the translation of social into political power is mediated through the casting of votes. Because voting is a regulatory institution of the civil sphere, those who cast their ballots are conceived as doing so in a manner that is relatively independent of the noncivil constraints of other spheres. That such independence is not only an abstract ideal but a powerful cultural practice can be seen in the dogged, centuries-long resistance to expanding the franchise, which was once described by the political sociologist, Stein Rokkan, in a manner that is highly apposite to the discussion here.

> In the situation of secret voting the individual adult is cut off from all his roles in the subordinate systems of the household, the neighborhood, the work organization, the church and the civil association and set to act exclusively in the abstract role of citizen. . . . The provisions of secrecy . . . make it possible for the voter to keep his decision private and avoid sanctions from those he does not want to know [and] to make it impossible for the voter to prove how he voted to those he does want to know. . . . By ensuring the complete anonymity of the ballots it became possible not only to reduce bribery of the economically dependent by their superiors but also to reduce the pressures toward conformity and solidarity within the working class.[28]

If voting is a basic regulative institution of the civil sphere, then who gets to vote becomes a primary criterion for gaining full membership within it. The less democratic the society, the more is voting restricted to dominant core groups, who legitimate this restriction via the binary discourses that fragment civil communication. The more democratic the society, the more widely extended is the liberating discourse of civil sphere, and the more restricted is the scope of the anticivil discourse that justifies repression. Indeed, the very possibility of democratic government has always been debated in terms of the discourse of civil society. In 421 B.C.E., when Athens was forced to make a temporary treaty with Sparta during the Peloponnesian War, Euripides defended democratic government in his play *The Suppliant Women*. Upon arriving in Athens, the herald from Thebes asks Theseus, the king of Athens, to whom he should deliver a message he is carrying from King Creon of Thebes. "Who is King absolute here?" asks the herald. The reply Theseus makes is structured by a homologous series

STRUCTURES AND DYNAMICS OF THE CIVIL SPHERE

of antipathies, according to which freedom is to subjection as the people are
to personal will, as office is to kingship, as equal authority is to special power
and wealth.

> This state is not
> Subject to one man's will, but is a free city.
> The king here is the people, who by yearly office
> Govern in turn. We give no special power to wealth;
> The poor man's voice commands equal authority.

In his contemptuous reply, the Theban herald defends autocracy by constructing democratic government in terms of the polluted discourse of repression. The common man is associated with impatience and foolishness
and is said to be incapable of reason; subordination to command is linked
with sound policies, experience, and useful knowledge.

> The city that I come from lives under command
> Of one man, not a rabble. . . .
> The common man!
> Incapable of plain reasoning, how can he guide
> A city in sound policies? Experiences gives
> More useful knowledge than impatience. Your poor rustic,
> Even though he be no fool—how can he turn his mind
> From ploughs to politics?[29]

If such an argument twenty-five hundred years ago structured classical
debate over whether or not democracy was possible, it is hardly surprising
to see a similar logic at work in modern times in debates about the shape
of democracy after it was first instituted in nation-states. As Alexander
Keyssar asserts in his powerful revisionist history of American voting, "At
its birth, the United was not a democratic nation—far from it."

> The very word *democracy* had pejorative overtones, summoning up
> images of disorder, government by the unfit, even mob rule. In
> practice, moreover, relatively few of the new nation's inhabitants
> were able to participate in elections: among the excluded were most

116

African Americans, Native Americans, women, men who had not attained their majority, and adult white males who did not own land. Only a small fraction of the population cast ballots in the elections that elevated George Washington and John Adams to the august office of the presidency.[30]

From the origins of modern democracy, then, a major problem for the regulatory institutions of civil society was deciding who could vote. This problem deeply involved communicative institutions.

Arguments justifying and opposing restrictions to the franchise were structured in terms of civil competence. According to the tradition of Thrasymachus, the gradual expansion of the franchise responded directly, and principally, to changes in social power. Certainly industrialization gave a new and powerful role to the working classes, and women's increasing activity in economic and voluntary organizations was far from a negligible factor in their empowerment. But such marked shifts in social power were, in fact, by no means sufficient in themselves. New forms of civil power had to be created first. Expanding access to the regulatory institutions of civil society required the support of public opinion, a shift that involved communicative institutions. What is crucial to understand is that the core groups of American society, its first voters, did not defend their social power directly. Whether for strategic or sincere reasons, they were compelled to legitimate their asymmetrical electoral position in civil terms.

\ Elites argued that *social* disparities caused or were caused by *civil* disabilities. Because the excluded were civilly incompetent, they not only could not, but should not, vote—for the sake of protecting democracy itself. This defense of elite regulation sparked a great conversation inside the nation's communicative institutions, animating two centuries of American political life. Keyssar cautions that we should not dismiss such debates as "simply a self-interested shouting match between the haves and the have nots or between men who owned different types of property." \

Ideas—whether or not independent of interests—mattered to the haves and have nots alike. Participants in debates about the franchise surely were influenced by their own material interest, but they also were trying to grasp or invent ideas that meshed with social reality and harmonized with deeply held values.[31]

In her essay on American citizenship, Judith Shklar stepped outside the rationalist limitations of democratic theory to explain the franchise debate in a decidedly cultural way. While voting is certainly a matter of institutional power, Shklar insisted that it is also, perhaps even more important, a matter of recognition and respect, of "membership" in the community, of "standing" and "civil dignity."[32] Rejecting the idealist mode of normative argumentation, Shklar understood, moreover, that such judgments about civil position involved comparison and difference, purity and pollution. From the nation's beginnings as an independent republic, Shklar recounts, Americans were animated not only by their own positive aspirations for democracy but by deep-seated desires to exclude others. "From the first," she writes, "they defined their standing as citizens very negatively, by distinguishing themselves from their inferiors."[33] For Americans, "the value of citizenship was derived primarily from its denial to slaves"; it was the polluted category of enslavement that gave meaning to the vote, for "to be refused the right was to be almost a slave."[34] What the disenfranchised had to fight against was not, in the first instance, political, much less social, power, but deeply structured attributions of civil incompetence, in which the members of the core group, and not only the core group, widely believed.

> Prevalent beliefs made the struggle for the vote extremely intense . . . Those who demanded the vote were . . . up against . . . a representative democracy that falsely ascribed personal deficiencies to them, in order to treat them as lesser beings than "We the People." The excluded were not merely deprived of casual political privileges; they were being betrayed and humiliated by their fellow-citizens.[35]

If slavery was the polluted image that inspired fear and distance, the sacred value that exercised positive attraction was not hard to find. In contrast with those who were enslaved, it was widely believed, civil power over the state could be exercised only by people who were fully independent. Henry Ireton had made this argument already during the first democratic revolution, in seventeenth-century England. "If there be anything at all that is the foundation of liberty," he declared, "it is this, that those who shall choose the law-makers shall be men freed from dependence upon others."[36] During the centuries of franchise debate that followed, the binary autonomy-dependence allowed every form of social subordination to be converted into a weakness of character.

It was in precisely this manner, for example, that leading democratic thinkers defended the traditional practice of allowing only property holders to vote. Montesquieu insisted that democracy must exclude those who "are in so mean a situation as to be deemed to have no will of their own."[37] The English jurist Sir William Blackstone, whose writings in other respects—for example, on contract and corporations—made singular contributions to the legal regulation of democratic societies,[38] reiterated this principled yet deeply disturbing restriction on democratic life.

> The true reason of requiring any qualification, with regard to property, in voters, is to exclude such persons as are in so mean a situation they are esteemed to have no will of their own. . . . All popular states have been obliged to establish certain qualifications; whereby some, who are suspected to have no will of their own, are excluded from voting, in order to set other individuals, whose wills may be supposed independent, more thoroughly upon a level with each other.[39]

On the eve of America's democratic revolution, in 1776, John Adams, founding father and future U.S. president, roundly agreed. "If you give to every man who has property, a vote," he asked, "will you not make a fine encouraging provision for corruption?" Citing "the frailty of the human heart," Adams concluded that "very few men who have no property have any judgment of their own."[40]

Those who wished to abolish property restrictions had to confront this cultural framing of its civil effects. In 1778, during the Massachusetts constitutional convention, delegates objected to such property qualifications on the grounds that it made "honest poverty a crime."[41] Metonymically equating the civil quality of honesty with lack of property, they threw its polluted status into doubt. Half a century later, when manufacturing was on the rise and an urban proletariat had begun to grow, a group of voteless men presented "The Memorial of the Non-Freeholders of the City of Richmond" to the Virginia Constitutional Convention. In one of the most eloquent protest documents in historical record, its signers denounced the property privileges of "freeholders" for violating the sacred ideal of extended solidarity upon which American democracy was supposed to rest. Property restriction, they declared,

> creates an odious distinction between members of the same community and robs of all share, in the enactment of the laws, a large portion of the citizens, bound by them . . . and vests in a favored class, not in consideration of their public services, but of their private possessions, the highest of all privileges.[42]

It is important to note here the qualification "in consideration of their public services." These protestors were not claiming that the mere existence of democratic solidarity justified the inclusion of every group. To the contrary, they felt compelled to justify their own claim to membership by purifying themselves in civil terms. The possession of land, they went on to argue, did nothing to make a man "wiser or better." Against the argument for elite regulation, they asserted that "virtue" and "intelligence" were "not among the products of the soil."[43]

Racial restrictions on the franchise had to be justified in exactly the same manner. If slavery was the master metaphor of pollution, why should freed African Americans not be allowed to vote? Before the Civil War, this conundrum primarily confronted democratic citizens in the North. In the early years of the nineteenth century, the abolitionist message circulated with increasing frequency and power through the communicative institutions of the Northern civil sphere. Its success with one segment of this community, however, actually increased antagonism with another, and the Northern civil sphere became increasingly polarized around race. At the nation's founding, the number of states that formally excluded free African-Americans from voting was small. From 1790 to 1850, the number steadily increased.[44] This opposition, however, had to be legitimated in the civil sphere. Two discursive strategies were possible. Either the very being of African-Americans was uncivil or their long-suffering history had so degraded them that they could not perform in a civil way.

In the racist climate of the time, both of these arguments could easily be made. In 1821, during the New York constitutional convention, a delegate opposed to black suffrage described African-Americans as "a peculiar people, incapable . . . of exercising that privilege with any sort of discretion, prudence, or independence."[45] Thirty years later, as the number of free blacks increased, the suffrage issue became caught up in party politics, for there was now at least a theoretical possibility that an election's outcome could be swayed by the black vote. Yet, power-political arguments do not, in and of themselves, carry weight in the communicative institutions of the civil sphere. Competence and incompetence were what mattered, and these binaries were continually addressed in a racial way. "No pure negro has wishes and wants like other people," a delegate to the Indiana convention declared in 1850. Another rooted black incapacity in the will of God. "The distinction between these races has been made by the God of Nature," he declared. "The black race has been marked and condemned to servility by the degree of Omnipotence."[46]

National sentiment became even more polarized, though more along geographical lines, after the Civil War. The Fifteenth Amendment to the Constitution promised that "the right of citizens of the of the United States to vote shall not be denied or abridged by the United States or by any State on account of race, color, or previous conditions of servitude." In the fight against its passage, conservative Democrats from Alabama sent Congress a petition that placed freed African Americans on the negative and polluted side of virtually every category of civil discourse. If "negroes" were, indeed, "improvident, disinclined to work, credulous yet suspicious, dishonest, untruthful, incapable of self-restraint, and easily impelled . . . into folly and crime," then it was only logical to argue that their enfranchisement would subject whites to a "blighting, brutalized and unnatural dominion" that would "bring, to the great injury of themselves as well as of us and our children, blight, crime, ruin and barbarism on this fair land."[47]

By virtue of their membership in the "party of Lincoln," by contrast, Republicans stood to benefit from black voting. Yet their racist construction of civil competence often made them suspect that freed Southern slaves would not vote in this predictable, Republican way. One Georgian Republican claimed that "negroes" were "without . . . sufficient intelligence to appreciate the power that *Ballot* gives them, add to which a system of intimidation persistently practiced by the Rebels, appealing to their fears through their superstition, and you have a mass of poverty, ignorance, stupidity, and superstition under the influence of fears both real and imaginary."[48] Eschewing any effort at defending contemporary black competence, proponents of black enfranchisement justified voting subjunctively, arguing that, if it were to be allowed, it would constitute a civil cure. In 1869, the radical abolitionist Wendell Phillips described the Fifteenth Amendment as just such a civil purification. Voting "contains within itself the cure for all its own defects."

A man with a ballot in his hand is the master of the situation. He defines all his other rights. What is not already given him, he takes. . . . The Ballot is opportunity, education, fair play, right to office, and elbow room.[49]

The Fifteenth Amendment eventually became the law of the land. As black voters sent many black officials to office, Southern whites became increasingly enraged, stepping outside civil society and replacing persuasion with force. By the late 1870s, Reconstruction began to be rolled back, and, in the decades following, white Southerners took the black right to vote away. In one sense, of course, this was purely a matter of social power. As one delegate to the Mississippi constitutional convention in 1890 told the *Clarion Ledger*, in Jackson, "The avowed purpose of calling [this] Convention was to restrict the negro vote."[50] Even so, the techniques for disempowerment needed to be legitimated in civil terms. The crowning achievement of that Mississippi convention was putting into place a franchise qualification called the "understanding" clause, which required that a potential elector be able to read from any section of the state constitution, or at least provide a "reasonable" interpretation if it were read to him.[51] Six years later, when the legality of such ostensibly civil provisions came before the Mississippi Supreme Court, they were sustained. The court explained that, because of the passage of the Fifteenth Amendment, Mississippi's state convention, in 1890, had been "restrained by the federal constitution from discriminating against the negro *race*." Needing another outlet, then, the convention had "discriminated against its *characteristics* and the offenses to which its weaker members were prone"![52] According to the discourse of civil society, polluted others threaten democratic *institutions*. If the discursive understanding of motives is distorted in a racist manner, regulative institutions can be "legitimately" employed to support a dominant caste. Insofar as civil power becomes fragmented and unequal, then state power will function in a hegemonic way.

Constructing and Destructing Civil Power (2):
Parties, Partisanship, and Election Campaigns

Communicative conflicts over who should vote are structurally similar to struggles over how these votes should be cast. Election Day is the last act in a political campaign. Though voting in democratic societies reflects individual decisions, these actors do not cast their votes in an organizational vacuum. Voting members of the civil sphere must learn to think about themselves in a political way. Distinctive ideologies develop that allow the civil sphere to organize opinions about how state power should regulate social power and social life, about who should rule and why. Inevitably, this involves confrontation over conceptions of justice and the good life.

Those who wish to assume state power must persuade their fellow members of civil society that they are deserving of their votes, that they will represent their values and their interests, that they will, in other words, exercise state power in their name. They do so by making public assurances as to their own civil aptitude, by remonstrating that they will exercise power in an accountable, honest, and artful manner. Such efforts at persuasion constitute a political campaign, during which individual voters are subjectively incorporated into the electoral process. This is a vast and dynamic opinion-shaping process. Individuals seeking state power engage in intensive symbolic confrontations with one another, even as they try to generate a continuous flow of sympathetic symbolic communication with the voters at large.

Political campaigns unfold within the civil sphere, not the state. Candidates who can assure a majority, plurality, or some legally designated minimum of the national vote, having assured the members of civil society that they will exercise state power effectively and legitimately, are allowed to assume it. | Those who wish to hold power form groups to mobilize civil support, which eventually organize themselves into parties. | Parties propose platforms obligating candidates to exercise state power in relation to shared political values. Election campaigns are dominated as much by parties as by individual candidates. Political parties thus constitute another powerful regulatory institution of civil society. It is individual votes that put state officials into power, but parties form the containers within which these votes are cast. "To be truly democratic," writes political scientist John Aldrich, "it is necessary for any nation's leadership to be *harnessed* to public desires and aspiration." It is "the political party, as a collective enterprise, organizing competition for the full range of offices," according to Aldrich, that "provides the only means for holding elected officials responsible."[53]

That parties regulate state power in the name of the civil sphere is not, of course, how they themselves see their role. Parties want to gain power for their members, for their candidates, and for the ideologies they represent. Groups form parties to create strategic alliances and organizational economies of scale, yet in doing so they also maximize their rhetorical force. Aggregating the multifarious political opinions of civil society into a small number of "fighting groups" simplifies the discursive division between friends and enemies. Only if this division is compelling and broad, and at the same time contained, can it be transformed into civil power. If political campaigns are vigorous, they can successfully project solidary commitments from civil sphere to state. Chantal Mouffe is right to insist that "the novelty of democratic politics is not the overcoming of this us/them opposition." The challenge, rather, "is to establish this us/them discrimination in a way that is compatible with pluralist democracy." Democratic politics is a kind of "democratic agonism," the function of which "consists in domesticating hostility."[54]

The complex communicative process that constitutes an electoral campaign is forcefully structured by the binary discourse of civil society. Because state power has such far-reaching effects, every possible kind of social concern enters into the campaign to regulate it, from pocketbook issues to collective identity and matters of life and death. Though political parties take positions on each of these issues, they try also to weave them together in an ideologically coherent way. Political campaigns consist of practically oriented speech, and situationally defined speech acts must draw upon the broad language of the civil sphere. In the context of a party-driven electoral campaign, the aim of effective political speech is not only to make rational arguments that coolly and deliberately appeal to interest but to symbolically purify one's own party positions and pollute the other's in powerfully affective ways. Parties garner support, not only by proposing idealistic programs, but by declaring the other side's candidates unfit to serve. In this agonistic manner, the binaries of civil discourse become specified in terms of party conflict. Each party links its own positions to the democratic, liberating discourse of civil society, associating the other party's with the antidemocratic, repressive side. The other party's organization is attacked as uncivil, and so is the imagined society their policies propose to create. Their motives are deceitful, their relations are secretive and authoritarian, and their institution corrupt. Under no circumstances must the carrier of such politically repressive motives, relations, and institutions be allowed to control the state.

To understand party politics in this manner is not to embrace irrationality in a normative sense; it is, rather, to recognize culture's empirical sway.[55] Democracy rests inside symbolic and institutional domains that have some autonomy from those of such noncivil spheres as economy, state, religion, and family. Yet the discourse that marks this civil domain, and the ethical actions that result from it, are not "rational" in a purely deliberative way. The ability to engage in rational deliberation is a value commitment that presupposes civil discourse; its truth can be demonstrated only performatively, through symbolic action which involves, at least in part, polluting those who are constructed as pursuing the other, antirational side. There may well be a "reasoning voter" and a "rational public," and it certainly is possible to understand political parties as organizing the "rational actions" of goal-seeking politicians,"[56] but none of this reasoning or rationality can be understood in anything other than a culturally constructed way. They are performative actions, speech acts that draw the meanings of their words from the more general language of civil society.[57]

Critics of contemporary political democracies, whether Left or Right, often posit a golden age in which deliberative democracy and reciprocal dialogue ruled, in relation to which the present constitutes a decline.[58] But the patterns of civil society I have outlined here have a structural status. Boundary relations with noncivil spheres have always been unsettled, civil discourse has always been deeply dichotomized, and its communicative and regulative institutions deeply fragmented from the start.[59]

In Boston in May 1766, supporters of Britain's discredited Stamp Act continued to hold sway in the Massachusetts colony's statehouse. To combat this political power, leaders of the "popular party," the group of colonial Americans who had opposed the act, placed a list of the act's alleged supporters into the *Boston Gazette* and other local papers. The thirty-two officeholders named on this list were identified as enemies of the people, and members of the popular party demanded their ouster. They asked the voters to reject "the old leaven" and to "look out for good and honest and free men—men that are unshackled with posts and preferments; men who will not warp, nor be cajoled into any measures that will tend to impoverish and enslave their country." The maneuver was successful; nineteen of the thirty-two officials were defeated.[60]

By the middle of the following century, this early party politics, having passed through the fire of Jacksonian democracy, had further heated up. In the 1856 Presidential campaign, for example, a New York city illustrated newspaper, *Frank Leslie's*, bemoaned "the strife, the bitterness, the brawl, and the abuse, that characterize our public assemblies, disgrace our legislative halls, and that fill the columns of many of our papers [with] the froth and scum which rise upon the surface of our society."[61]

Modern party politics were no different. In the ferociously contested presidential election of 1948, the Democratic incumbent, President Harry Truman, was in grave danger of being defeated by the Republican challenger, New York Governor Thomas Dewey. In his desperate sprint to Election Day, the president struggled to pollute his opponent, and Republican policies more generally, in the most repressive of civil society terms. Communicative institutions broadcast these partisan broadsides. On October 26, 1948, the *New York Times'* front page dramatically displayed this four-tiered headline:

President Likens Dewey to Hitler As Fascists' Tool

Says When Bigots, Profiteers Get Control of Country They Select 'Front Man' to Rule

Dictatorship Stressed

Truman Tells Chicago Audience
A Republican Victory Will
Threaten U.S. Liberty

The event being reported was a campaign speech that President Truman had given in Chicago the night before. The *Times'* lead reported the president's civil discourse in a condensed and especially frightening way: "A republican victory on election day will bring a Fascistic threat to American freedom that is even more dangerous than the perils from communism . . . President Truman asserted here tonight." President Truman warned of Dewey's being manipulated by "evil forces," suggesting Hitler, Mussolini, and Tojo, the leaders of America's wartime enemies, as examples of earlier "front men." The 1948 campaign, he asserted, was not "just a battle between two parties" but a "crusade" for "the very soul of America." In the days that followed, Truman made the comeback of the century. He won the election and served another four years.[62]

Recent party politics has continued to be fueled by the same binary rhetoric. During the 1992 presidential campaign, in the closely watched vice presidential debate between incumbent Dan Quayle and the Democratic challenger, Senator Albert Gore, Vice President Quayle announced in his opening remarks that he would demonstrate two themes: that the Democrats' economic program would make the economy worse and that "Bill Clinton does not have the strength nor the character to be president of the United States." In the course of what turned out to be a surprisingly successful performance, Quayle repeatedly returned to these two issues, but especially the second, drawing attention to "a fundamental question of trust and character" and claiming that "Bill Clinton has trouble telling the truth."[63] Three presidencies later, in 2004, when the Republican "attack machine" began spending tens of million of dollars on negative television advertising, the Democratic candidate John Kerry called it "the most crooked [and] lying group I've ever seen," warning "it's scary."[64] In the days following, these remarks circulated with great intensity throughout the communicative institutions of American civil society.

It is not that voters do not exercise judgment, but that these judgments occur against a system of background signs. The very meaning of one's own party platform, and those of one's antagonist's, is conditioned, filled in, and limited by the kind of language that political actors can speak./ In their seminal article on symbolic politics, David Sears and his colleagues were quite right to suggest, twenty-five years ago, that "the central elements in political belief systems [are] strong affective commitments to certain symbols, which . . . constrain the individual's political responses to numerous other stimuli, such as policy issues, political events, media presentations, or electoral candidacies."[65] John Zaller put this into more formal, social-

psychological concepts, but he made the same point. "Political predispositions," he insists, "are the critical intervening variable between the
communications people encounter in the mass media, on one side, and their
statements of political preferences, on the other."[66]

Because Sears and Zaller focused on individual, short-term decision
making, neither connected these insights to the kind of structural and long-
term constraints on political judgment that I am considering here. It is
perfectly consistent with their research, however, to suggest that political
parties mediate the symbols and predispositions that structure individual
perceptions by providing "shifters"[67]—broad ideological frameworks that
relate them, in a simplifying and dichotomous manner, to the issues of the
day.[68] Ideological shifters specify and elaborate civil discourse so that it can
mobilize, and polarize, diverse segments of society. Undoubtedly the most
significant ideological shifter is the division between Left and Right, which
allows parties and individuals to connect ongoing, unforeseen events to the
liberating and repressive discourses of civil society in a consistent and coherent way. "The rationale of the party system," Robert MacIver wrote in
the middle of the twentieth century, "depends on the alignment of opinion
from right to left."[69] Though in contemporary, postindustrial society this
division is no longer as focused on class issues, Left and Right polarization
remains the name of the game. Drawing on the discourse of civil solidarity,
parties are partisan and one-sided. They must be if they are to produce civil
power in effective ways.

In a series of influential empirical studies of presidential elections over
the last half-century, one loosely affiliated group of political scientists has
registered strong reservations about the view that party politics are a deliberative, rational affair. In a manner that is complementary to the present
argument, they have rooted partisan commitment in early socialization and
primary groups, and they have likened party affiliation to religious faith.[70]
In one of the most recent and methodologically sophisticated versions of
this argument, for example, Donald Green and his colleagues argue against
"the prevailing way of thinking about partisan identities," which "emphasizes the extent to which they are shaped by rational evaluations of party
platforms and performances in office." Solidarity with one's own party
group, and the "adversarial relationship" with another, are much more
important influences on such political evaluations.[71]

128

Seldom . . . do political events alter the stereotypes of partisan *groups* . . . As people reflect on whether they are Democrats or Republicans . . . they call to mind some mental image, or stereotype, of what these sorts of people are like . . . One's partisan self-conception is guided by a sense of who belongs to these groups and one's relationship to them. . . . Ordinary politics and life experiences . . . leave little imprint on voters' party identities. . . . Elections are . . . forums for intergroup competition.[72]

By focusing on the effects of primary group socialization, these analysts link partisan ideology to emotional stability and group integration. Yet even if it might provide equilibration at intrapsychic and intragroup levels, partisanship is the sine qua non of conflict between groups. Intense hostility and unrelenting competition must certainly be viewed, therefore, as equally significant macrolevel effects. The problem is in part a disciplinary one. From the more individualistic perspective of social psychology, partisanship is viewed as defense against psychic anxiety.[73] But partisanship can also be seen as a cultural structure. In this latter understanding, ideological polarization is normal; it emerges from the basic meaning-making structures of civil life. From the former perspective, by contrast, ideological polarization seems abnormal and irrational, a "strong prejudice" that "operates to make the opponent into more of an 'enemy.' "[74]

The corollary of this emphasis on partisanship-as-distortion is the belief that ideological partisanship has "little 'real' connection with politics,"[75] the latter being concerned with issues of power and distribution which presumably produce perceptions of a more rational kind. But such a separation can hardly be made. State decisions about distribution are tied to the recognition and misrecognition of others. Because recognition is itself "distributed" unequally, conflicts over subjectivity do indeed become central objects of real political life.[76] It is impossible to speak about distribution and its justice or injustice without the utopian and distopian ideas institutionalized in the civil sphere. Partisan divisions are rooted in the structure of meaning, not in the anxieties of the self, and they are basic to everyday political life.

To the extent that the civil sphere has autonomy, solidarity becomes more expansive and universalizing, and there is space to struggle over these ideological interpretations in a democratic way. After election campaigns are concluded, losers express their allegiance to the shared democratic space and promise to respect their opponents when they assume legitimate power in the state. Winners express their humility and promise to serve the entire collectivity, not only their party group. Such assertions are possible only if party opponents experience themselves to be members of the same civil sphere. They employ and crystallize the binary discourse of civil society, but they are "friendly enemies," a relationship described by Mouffe as "persons who are friends because they share a common symbolic space but also enemies because they want to organize this common symbolic space in a different way."[77]

> An adversary is an enemy, but a legitimate enemy, one with whom we have some common ground because we have a shared adhesion to the ethico-political principles of liberal democracy: liberty and equality. But we disagree concerning the meaning and implemen-tation of those principles, and such a disagreement is not one that could be resolved through deliberation and rational discussion . . . hence its antagonistic dimension.[78]

The challenge is to understand how this trick is turned. How can political campaigns confirm this common space even as partisan party confrontations deny it? One reason is that they can have positive functional effects. In a relatively autonomous civil sphere, party conflict allows social disparities and strains to be communicatively crystallized and submitted to reconstruction by state power. But there is more to it than that. The relationship between partisanship and solidarity also is confirmed in a hermeneutic way, in terms of symbolic legitimation. Civil spheres are composed of overlapping circles. Elements that confront one another as separate "parts" at one level, and which are antagonistically constructed in binary discourse, can be interpreted from the vantage point of another level as part of a single whole, one that is construed in terms of only one of the discursive sides. Antagonism at one level, in other words, can be interpreted as civility at another. This is what can happen to even the most ideologically divisive party conflicts, when civil power is created in a relatively democratic way. Individual parties demonize one another, but the system of party conflict itself is purified; it is constructed not in terms of repression but liberty.

Up until the nineteenth century, this was hardly the case. Political parties were viewed in the most negative, anticivil terms. In his classic *The Idea of Party System*, the American political historian Richard Hofstadter observed that, in eighteenth-century Anglo-American writing, "party" was used interchangeably with "faction," and both "carried invidious overtones."[79] Faction and party were listed as synonyms in one widely read English dictionary, and Jonathan Swift wrote that "party is the madness of many, for the gain of the few."[80] In America, critical constitutional debates often hinged on similarly polluted, antidemocratic constructions of the institution of party. Madison's strictures in the *Federalist* Number 10 are well known. Franklin also warned against "the infinite mutual abuse of parties, tearing to pieces the best of characters," and George Washington, in his *Farewell Address*, described "the baneful effects of the Spirit of Party."[81]

Yet as American society become more developed and its social powers more complex, its civil sphere more fragmented and plural, and its political structures less easily subject to aristocratic control, parties organized themselves in ever more frequent and conspicuous ways. There simply was no other manner in which social forces and opinions could be aggregated and linked to the powerful discursive divisions that defined the civil sphere. Changing social and cultural conditions presented new opportunities for political ambition. Political entrepreneurs emerged, and these "party men" were naturally inclined to understand their organizational activities as civil rather than as repressive.

The first really effective party structure was organized by Republicans in early-nineteenth-century New York. Martin Van Buren, one of their leaders and a future U.S. president, suggested that conflicts produced by partisan differences actually were purified by the civil motives of party activists. When "the principles of contending parties are supported with candor, fairness, and moderation, the very discord which is thus produced may in a government like ours, be conducive to the public good."[82] Because civil motivations and civil institutions go together, it is not surprising that an influential Albany newspaper, the *Argus*, opined that the maintenance of parties was "necessary to the just exercise of the powers of free government."[83] Framed in this manner, parties could be conceptualized as a new kind of regulatory institution. "The spirit of party," one Republican activist wrote, was "the vigilant watchman over the conduct of those in power." Rather than polluting and distorted, then, partisanship was a force for the good. The more hardened the partisans, the more would they "expose the crimes, and even the failings, of competitors for the people's confidence. Competitors of this description *force* into notice facts . . . which the people at large could never have derived from the ordinary commerce of thought."[84] New York's governor, Enos Throop, declared that even the simplification of party slogans was helpful; by allowing the public's attention to be focused, it promoted the moral regulation of motives and relations.

> Those party divisions which are based upon conflicting opinions in regard to the constitution of the government, or the measures of the administration of it, interest every citizen, and tend, inevitably, in the spirit of emulation and proselytism, to reduce the many shades of opinion into two opposing parties . . . Organized parties watch and scan each other's doings, the public mind is instructed by ample discussions of public measures, and acts of violence are restrained by the convictions of the people, that the prevailing measures are the results of enlightened reason.[85]

Civil Power in the State: Office as Regulating Institution

Voting and party conflict push representatives of civil society into the state, the sometimes collegial, most often bureaucratic organization that monopolizes the means of violence, makes positive law, and deals directly from a position of material strength with the constraints and maladies of social power. But even here, where the rubber meets the road, civil society by no means entirely gives up its control. James Madison clearly understood this before-and-after quality of regulatory institutions when he thought about the role of constitutions. In the first place, this regulation is needed to select the most qualified political representatives of civil society and put them into the state:\"The aim of every political constitution is, or ought to be, first to obtain for rulers men who possess most wisdom to discern, and most virtue to pursue, the common good of the society."\Once these representatives become rulers, however, regulatory institutions must try to prevent their separation from the community: Constitutions must "take the most effectual precautions for keeping them virtuous whilst they continue to hold their public trust."[86]

Civil institutions regulate political power, then, not only by putting their representatives into the state, but by making efforts to control them when they are there. To exercise such control is an enormous challenge. Even when they have a boundary with civil society, state institutions try to build walls. The horse-trading, organization building, and calculations of social and economic costs and consequences, even the very nature of government decisions themselves—all these dimensions of governing are often exercised in secret.[87] Those who pull the levers of state power would prefer to do so behind the curtain of the state. For the institution of bureaucracy, Weber put the issue of state secrecy very well: "The bureaucracy's supreme power instrument is the transformation of official information into classified material by means of the notorious concept of the 'service secret.' In the last analysis, this is merely a means of protecting the administration against supervision."[88]

To the degree that society is democratic, however, the regulatory institutions of civil society struggle to push the curtain aside, to regulate just how the levers of government are pulled. For one thing, there remains the continuing role of party power.\Rulers remain party members. Even when they forget their promises to voters, \even if their ideological commitments dissolve away, there remains the threat of upcoming elections, the civil power of voters, and the potential accusations of the political opposition. For another, there is the continuing role of communicative institutions, which continuously crystallize public opinions about the behavior of power holders and channel these back to those exercising power in the state. But there is also something else, an institution that almost never comes up in discussions about regulating state control. This is the institution of office.[89]

When those who are elected to power take up their positions in the state, this institution can prevent them from simply becoming another cog in the state machine, from becoming the servant of social rather than civil power, and even from acting in a purely self-interested way. When the representatives of civil society, and their high-level appointees, take up the reigns of state power, they enter into an "office," a publicly defined role regulated by ethical and legal constraints on both corruption and self-interest. Because we take the office role for granted, it seems banal, part of the common sense of social life; but it is this very omnipresence that compels us to make the effort to conceptualize office in a distinctive way. In fact, office is an immensely significant social invention. It institutionalizes a universalistic understanding of organizational authority that has emerged only recently in human history, growing gradually with the creation of the civil sphere.

In societies where social solidarity is greatly constricted, the reach of civil obligation is so narrow that the very idea of "official" duties is difficult to conceive. In his ethnography of a small village in southern Italy, Edward Banfield documented an extraordinary gap between those who produced state power and those who were its recipients. "A zealous official is as rare as a white fly," a retired government worker informed him. "From the President of the Republic down to the last little Italian," a landowner remarked, "there is a complete lack of any sense of duty."[90] Without solidarity, civil power cannot be produced, and without its moral pressure the officeholder will not feel an obligation to civil society in turn. Without such a sense of civil obligation, indeed, officials will not be attentive even to social power.

> The merchants of Montegrano are well aware of the importance to them of good roads. They would not, however, expect to be listened to by the authorities who decided which roads are to be improved. A Montegrano man might write a letter to the provincial authorities in Potenza or to the newspaper there, but it is unlikely that his doing so would make any difference. In fact, the officials would be likely to resent what they would consider interference in their affairs. . . . Official position and special training will be regarded by their possessors as weapons to be used against others for private advantage.[91]

When solidarity is more expansive, and the pressures of "society" become more explicit and powerful, office becomes an outpost of civil society directly inside the state. Office becomes another regulatory institution of the civil sphere, and this distinctive role definition is by no means without weight. In Aristotle's treatise on politics, immediately after offering his famous definition of democracy as ruling and being ruled in turn, he testifies that "from rule thus conceived" follow the "common characteristics of democracies." The first of these characteristics is "election to office," and in all but three of the others "office" is involved in a central way.[92] The institution of office cannot, of course, prevent power from corrupting, but it creates a normative counterideal to the exercise of ruthless power, such that deviation from office standards can be legitimately presented as moral depravation, sometimes even as criminality. Power holders take up offices, not merely jobs. Even when they are inside the state, they are subject, in principle, to civil power.[93] Of course, the structural challenges to making this principle effective are great. Because access to government decision making is restricted and secrecy is the rule, there is a dearth of the kind of factual information that makes legal regulation possible. For this reason, communicative institutions become central to office's regulating control. Normatively oriented "leaks" from inside the state allow journalists to extract "facts" about power's deviation from civil obligation. These facts become "news" when media bring them from the darkness of state secrecy into the public light of day.

When there is a developed civil sphere, communicative institutions can, at any moment, leverage putative office regulation into "affairs" and "scandals." They do so by painting the holders of office in anticivil ways. Rather than acting honestly, they have been duplicitous. Rather than allowing their office to be transparent, they have shrouded their administration in secrecy. Rather than being cooperative with those who opposed them politically, they have been aggressive in exercising their power, treating their constituents not as citizens but as special friends or vicious enemies. Rather than being independent of social power, they have been submissive to it or have been captives of their own bureaucracies. They have been selfish rather than solidary, emotive rather than calm, irrational rather than rational. It is the existence of office regulation that allows such public claims about the deviance of authorities to be broadcast in a legitimate way. While such polluting claims often cannot be sustained, their symbolic damage can be immediate, whether or not legal sanctions follow.[94]

The institution of office demands that particularistic personal and ideological commitments be separated from, and subordinated to, obligations of a more universalistic and collective sort. There is a sense, of course, in which the duties of office are inherently particular, for they are tasks set by the organization at hand. But when an organizational role is an office, it has not only a position in the division of labor but a status in moral terms. There is the obligation to carry out one's duties regardless of the personal stake, and this obligation is not something specific to this or that particular organization but one imposed by society at large. "Office" has a morality in and of itself, and it is one common to every such institutional position, no matter what its specialized task. The moral obligation is to wield power on behalf of others. In this generic manner, office connects power and interest to the conventions and logic of civil society.[95]

Legal sanctions can enforce the incumbent's respect for office, and these sanctions are backed up by punishment and force. But office is much more than a code of law. It is an ethic of responsibility, a norm of impersonal and universalistic behavior in which members of civil society are socialized from their earliest years.[96] In his standard work on public administration, Frederick Mosher calls responsibility "the most important word in all the vocabulary of administration," and he argues that it is sustained not only objectively— "according to the law and the organization chart"—but by "subjective or psychological" reinforcement as well. The "meaning" of responsibility, Mosher suggests, "is more nearly synonymous with identification, loyalty, and conscience that it is with accountability." With the ethic of responsibility, the question becomes not "to whom and for what one is responsible"—a question for the organizational flow chart—but "to whom and for what one *feels* responsible."[97] For those who wield power in an office, the compelling object of responsibility is larger than the specialized task, pointing beyond the organization as such to the community writ large. It is the civil society that ultimately compels the deep sense of responsibility upon which the institution of office depends, and which it regulates in turn.

Within the social sciences, this understanding has scarcely received the attention it deserves. Administrative science and organizational studies have focused on the relationship between means and ends. Their central questions concern whether an organization can effectively carry out its tasks. Are the members of an organization responsive to the goals at the top? What is the relationship between line and staff? Are they tightly connected or decoupled? Modern administrative studies have found organizational rationality not nearly as effective as Weber once claimed, though debates over the sources and consequences of such departures from means-ends efficiency continue to rage.[98] From the perspective of a sociological theory of democracy, however, these are not the central questions. Organization is not only a more and less efficient means; it is also an end, a value commitment that mediates broader cultural patterns in distinctive ways.[99]

Offices are created in response to objective, systemic pressures for accomplishing some goal, but they are more than merely a marker in the division of labor. Through the institution of office, civil society can exercise regulating control on organizational means, on how the ends of political power are actually pursued. When authorities personalize office, its civil character is reduced, and power becomes identified with clique, party, ethnicity, or ideology rather than with the broader solidarity of the community at large. Some sense of a higher responsibility is necessary if political institutions are to be made responsive in broader and more civil ways. Office obligations must be separated from personal ones if organizations are to play a central role in democratic life.

In *Union Democracy*, Lipset and his colleagues made office obligation a critical variable in distinguishing between democratic and undemocratic trade unions. "In most one-party unions," they write, "it is difficult for members to distinguish in their own minds between the organization and the leader or leaders who have controlled it for decades."[100] The result is that "the incumbents habitually use the loyalty that exists for the organization as a means of rallying support for themselves." Financial corruption and political manipulation are the inevitable result. Democratic institutions, by contrast, create an environment that offsets this fusion of person and office. "In a union with a legitimate two-party system," they observe, "it becomes possible and even necessary to distinguish between the current officeholders and the organization as a whole." Though pathbreaking in its articulation of the connection of office obligation to democracy, this analysis interprets the regulatory power of democracy in an overly social-structural way. Because contenders for organizational position in two-party systems "have objective chances of gaining power," Lipset and his colleagues write, they also "have an interest in maintaining the attachment of all members to the organization" rather than simply to the person of the leaders themselves. From the perspective I am developing here, however, maintaining this sense of broader responsibility depends on much more than being afraid of being thrown out of office. The meaning of office obligations also is crucial, whether or not officeholders experience solidarity with the values of the wider community.

Though Weber laid the foundations for the objectivist, social structural approach to organization, it was in his religious studies that the framework for a more culturally oriented understanding of office obligations emerged. In these writings, Weber discovered an intimate historical connection between the sense of office obligation and Protestant, particularly Puritan, notions of a "calling," or *Beruf*.[101] This inward ethic, Weber believed, obligated religious leaders to morally regulated, impersonal forms of action, which were expressed in their commitments to God's will, on the one hand, and their equally fervent sense of obligation to members of their own religious sects, on the other. The failure to bring these insights from his religious studies into his sociology of organization and politics severely limited the contemporary relevance of Weber's work.[102]

Linking justice and interpretation, Michael Walzer has been one of the few social theorists to address this gap between cultural sociology and organizational theory. In both historical and philosophical investigations, he has explored how office can be nested within communal obligations and their cultural presuppositions. As "a place of authority under 'constituted authority,' " Walzer writes, office is a "position which the political community takes an interest in."[103] The Protestant Reformation made the impersonal and moral notion of office central to political life, just as the nineteenth century movement for civil service reform had the effect of restricting partisanship inside the secular democratic state.[104] Walzer explicitly relates these office-transforming developments to the broadening of social solidarity and the inclusion of new members into the community, the "extension of trust or 'friendship' beyond the family and of citizenship beyond race, ethnicity, and religion."[105] Justice in public activities, he argues, can be realized only if officeholders are responsible to the broader community; injustice, correspondingly, can result from the "isolation of office."[106]

Separating "the office from the man," then, should be seen not simply as a functional necessity but as an institution deeply rooted in the culture of democratic society. It can, in fact, be traced all the way back to fundamental understandings within Western Christianity. The Church was the first great "rational" bureaucracy of Western life. What is less widely appreciated, however, is the distinctive manner in which this organization forged with imperial and local European "states" a relationship that adumbrated the regulatory institutions of modern democracies. This ability to control state power came not only from the organizational efficiency of the Church, but from its autonomy and sometimes even opposition vis-à-vis earthly powers that Weber called "hierocratic domination," which made Western church-state relations different from those that existed in other powerful civilizations.[107]

This hard-won autonomy depended, at least in part, on the sacramental understanding of priestly office. In his classic text on the relation between church and state, the cultural historian Gert Tellenbach argued that, already during the Middle Ages, "the clergy as a class owe their position in the main to the fact that they are the instruments of Christ," not to their personal qualities or even to their pastoral skills. "The grace that works within him" is what counts; the priest "passes on what has been given him" to "the people under his charge."[108] It is "the grace inherent in the office which ultimately determines clerical rank," according to Tellenbach, such that "fidelity or negligence in the performance of official duties in general will be one of the reasons for reward or punishment before the heavenly tribunal."[109]

The challenge for Christianity was not only to preserve this separation of earthly incumbent from divine office inside the Church but to spread it throughout medieval society, for only in this manner could humanity's religious salvation be attained. One of the principal obstacles to this expansion was the overreaching powers of feudal social hierarchies. Lordship implied compulsory control in every kind of social domain. On his local estate, for example, the lord "would often build a church, where he installed a priest of his own choosing, either a serf or some other acceptable man."[110] From the churchly perspective, such practices polluted the independence of sacramental office. Not only did lords not consider the qualification of religious grace, but they often neglected to pay their priests, demanded that they devote themselves to such secular tasks as managing feudal property, and let churches fall into disrepair.

The "Investiture Controversy" brought these strains to a head. Investiture refers to the act of establishing religious office, which invested priests with divine grace. It was bad enough for lords to block the religious investiture of local churchly office; when the kings who assumed divine right began to exercise such blocking power on a broader expanse, however, the challenge to Church authority became acute. In 1046, Henry III marched on Rome and deposed Pope Benedict IX, establishing a "royal theocracy" which gave him the right of investiture of priests, bishops, archbishops, and even popes.[111] His successors were able to maintain this practice of "lay investiture" for most of the next seventy-five years, a hegemony that created extraordinary political, theological, economic, and military strife. When Henry V and Pope Calixtus II finally worked out a compromise in 1122, at the Concordat of Worms, it established the cultural framework for office regulation in a permanent way. The emperor conceded to the Church free elections of bishops and popes and gave up investiture of them with ring and staff, the traditional symbols of their spiritual duties. For his part, the pope merely granted to the emperor the right to be present at such churchly elections and to invest bishops with their temporal rights and duties.

This unprecedented separation of office obligations from power hierarchies had far-reaching implications, setting the pattern for making state offices responsive to civil power in secular democratic life. In fact, the matter of the integrity of office obligations became central to the overthrow of absolutism in the French Revolution. When the divine grace regulating religious sacramental power was corrupted by the buying and selling of religious office, it was called the sin of "simony." As Western societies became larger and more complex, and there emerged the first great absolutist states, the buying and selling of office continued, undercutting office obligations of a more secular kind. This corruption was called "venality." For centuries, the French kings had sold offices in the state or offered them on fixed terms for rent. The instability of such arrangements had even produced, in 1467, a royal declaration that made offices into a position for life.[112] This security did not, however, prevent incumbents themselves from reselling their offices to third parties or from passing their offices on as patrimony to sons and heirs. By the eighteenth century, the labyrinth of venality had become so extensive that "men would acquire offices only because they brought tangible and worthwhile advantages."[113] While the continuous exactions of bribes and favors that such a system induced "provoked regular complaints from aggrieved subjects," according to a historian of this practice, such general venality "was grudgingly accepted as inevitable."[114] The sale of judicial offices, however, was quite another matter: "It was repeatedly denounced by estates and other representative bodies as opening power over the lives and properties of the king's subjects to untrained and unsuitable men of wealth, likely to buy and sell justice itself."[115] Venal deviation from judicial office obligations, in other words, seemed to undermine the very possibility of an independent civil sphere. Outrage against this pollution of democratic principles, from many different sectors of French life, permeated the run-up to the revolution of 1789: "Venality was invariably denounced in the preambles to edicts, as an abuse to be eradicated, a burden on the public, the corruption of justice, socially and economically mischievous."[116] On the night of August 4, 1789, when hereditary privileges were abolished and the principles of democracy established, the French National Assembly abolished the venality of offices. The official decree, issued on November

3, 1789, linked purification of office institutions to the possibility of justice: "Venality of judicial and municipal office is abolished from this moment. Justice is to be dispensed freely."[117]

⎮When the civil sphere has real autonomy vis-à-vis the state, office represents the most immediate hands-on institution for controlling the instrumental force of political power.⎮ It constitutes a kind of master role that allows power to be trusted because it is understood to be regulated by the collective-cum-individualistic commitments of civil society. Offices of great power pose potentially great dangers for the civil sphere if that power becomes unregulated and deployed in an anticivil way. For such high offices, there are elaborate rituals of transition that mark the ascension from citizen to ruler. These rituals culminate in "oaths of office." In these public avowals before the mass mediated public, the neophyte incumbent solemnly promises not only to uphold the law but to follow principle, to forgo self-interest and ideology. In the United States, the president-elect stands symbolically before the nation, one hand on the secular scripture of the Constitution, the other raised to God, and swears an oath, administered by the chief justice of the Supreme Court, to "faithfully execute the duties of the office of the president of the United States."

Such rituals of office transition are hardly confined to the "civil religion" of the United States. In 1989, after a decade of revolutionary political struggle, newly democratic Poland installed a member of the Solidarity party, Tadeusz Mazowiecki, as prime minister. After his election by a nearly unanimous vote of the assembled parliament, according to the report by the *New York Times,* "the new Prime Minister then strode to the speaker's platform and, his voice wavering, told the legislators that he was moved by the 'proof of trust.' " Mazowiecki seemed to acknowledge that this trust was on loan from the wider community, which had established this office to carry out its democratic will. "I can count on this moment becoming significant in the consciousness of my compatriots," he declared, "so that we can revive Poland by common effort, not because of my person, but because of the needs of Poland and the historic moment." The prime minister then made a gesture that underlined the role that a broad and inclusive understanding of social solidarity must play in sustaining a sense of office responsibility. Despite his own persecution by the former communist state, which had once declared martial law against his own Solidarity Party, "Mr. Mazowiecki strode to the benches of the Communist cabinet, and shook the hands of its members, beginning with General Kiscak. He [only] then received the warm wishes of Solidarity's leaders, who ascended the steps to the Government bench one by one to shake his hand."[118]

Between the various regulatory institutions of civil society there are some endemic strains. Waging a successful electoral campaign depends on fierce loyalties to particular political parties. When the successful partisan ascends to office, he or she must rule in the name of the entire community. The dividing line between campaigning and governing, however, is not so clean. The staff of the party campaigner tend to become staff of the White House, such that in every effective government there is always something of the permanent campaign. The universalism of the institution of office, then, exists in tension with the particularity of party politics. But if the discourse of civil society can never be fully institutionalized, its idealization constitutes a continuing source of normative tension and control. When the newly elected Republican mayor of New York City, Rudolph Giuliani, endorsed a liberal Democrat, Governor Mario Cuomo, for election to the U.S. Senate, his action was praised as exemplary of universalistic office obligations. Noting the challenge that partisan campaigning presented to office obligation, the *New York Times,* in its lead editorial, noted that "throughout a tough mayoral campaign," Mayor Giuliani had "promised repeatedly that he would put the interest of the city above partisan considerations." That he kept his promise strengthened the link between civil solidarity and office and demonstrated that an inner sense of responsibility can exert powerful controls in democratic life.

> In thousands of dinner-table conversations and man-on-the-street interviews, citizens have wished for officeholders who acted on principle rather than party loyalty or short-term political gain. . . . Mr. Giuliani has lived up to his own strict and demanding definition of the central obligation of his office.[119]

The idea of office is so powerful that the communicative media of civil societies engage in continuous, if often ineffective surveillance of high officials. When anticivil behavior is discovered, its polluting effects are not merely sanctioned but deeply feared. During the Watergate crisis in the early 1970s, John Dean, the president's counsel, warned "there is a cancer on the Presidency." When the disgraced President Richard Nixon was driven from office, two years later, his successor, Gerald Ford, declared that "our long national nightmare is over." Anticivil actions by powerful officeholders are experienced as threatening the sacred center of civil life. "Scandal" derives from the early Greek *scandalon*, which meant an obstacle or "a cause of moral stumbling."[120] When its modern usage emerged in the sixteenth century, it was associated with scurrilous individual conduct. The meaning of scandal, however, eventually developed in a much more collective and social way. "No longer a relation between two people, between someone who scandalizes and someone who is scandalized," writes Eric de Dampierre, it became "rather an event which breaks out at the heart of a collectivity of people."[121] Citizens are scandalized by the affront to office, and this pollution threatens their idealization as citizens and the power and very independence of civil solidarity itself. No wonder that, as scandals unfold, metaphors about pollution abound. Reporters dig up dirt about foul play; officials find themselves mired in a swamp and covered by mud. There are calls for special investigators who are clean as a whistle, for blue ribbon commissions and white papers, for a powerful broom that can sweep the slate clean.[122]

If the movement from sacred to secular power shifted representations of office violation from "simony" to "venality," the institutionalization of democratic society marks this deviation from civil standards as "abuse." The tried and true temptations of power, of course, never really change. High officials in democratic societies are not only tempted to sell their power to the highest bidder, but they have continued to do so in impressively consistent ways. In terms of the theory of civil society, such behavior in itself is not of particular interest. The response to it is. It is constructed as deviance, not norm, as surprising and shocking, as not at all what is expected, and, in every respect, it is represented as the abuse of office. When Joseph Ganon, the mayor of Bridgeport, Connecticut, was sentenced to nine years in jail for organizing a public works payoff scheme, the *New Haven Register*'s five-inch banner headline screamed: "Nine Years for Ganin; judge scolds him for running office 'CONTAMINATED BY CORRUPTION.' "[123]

In June 2000, California's elected insurance commissioner was discovered to have collected bribes and campaign contributions from the insurance companies that his office was supposed to regulate. The *Los Angeles Times* news coverage of the breaking scandal, while presented as factual reporting, reads in retrospect more like a morality play about the rigors of moral regulation in the political sphere. "Somewhere along the way," the *Times* reporter intoned in his front-page story, the commissioner "chose to neglect his duties as a public steward and put his own political interests first." Office authority had failed to control personal power. As one political observer put it, "the seductive quest for power overwhelmed his ability to say no." Other critical politicians claimed that the commissioner had never conceived of himself as a representative of civil society. He "was elected basically as an agent of the [insurance] industry," and he "chose to use the powers of the office of commissioner to extract contributions to . . . engage in a perpetual campaign." It is no wonder that, "on the eve of the toughest questioning yet about his role in the scandal swamping his department," the commissioner chose to resign.[124] It remained to the *Times'* political columnist to draw the civil moral. Though acknowledging there had been "an unseemly feeding frenzy by the blood-sniffing sharks," by the "news media and by political opportunists," he protested, "that's the nature of our democratic system and how we rid ourselves of rotten officials." Better to have scandal than to "knuckle under to his self-serving abuse of power." By abandoning his office responsibilities, the disgraced commissioner had, at one and the same time, abandoned the members of civil society whom he had been elected to represent. He "forgot to represent the people who elected him." Instead, he "tried to enrich himself politically" and "coddle misbehaving insurance companies." For the commissioner to think he could get away with this was "dumb," but it was more than this: "It was an abuse of power."[125]

Less frequent but more serious departures from office regulation occur when power is deployed to pit one segment of civil society against another. In March 1991, news about the police beating Rodney King, an unarmed African American, spread like wildfire across the communicative media of Los Angeles. Though this violence was palpably racial in character, it was represented, most centrally, as a violation of office obligations and was constructed not in racial but in anticivil terms. According to the *Los Angeles Times,* eyewitness accounts "suggested that what should have been a relatively simple arrest . . . escalated wildly out of control."[126] According to Ronald Jacobs, who has made a thorough analysis of news coverage of the affair, the media's extensive use of such adjectives as "violent," "wildly," "pounding," "pummeling," and "brutal" created a set of "symbolic relations" that constructed the confrontation in terms of the discourse of civil society."[127] Initially represented as an abuse of authority by individual police officers, the scandal soon focused on the authority at the top of the police department, the chief of police himself. Criticisms of the chief's racial insensitivity and authoritarianism were at every point connected with his failure to exercise office power in a responsible way.

> The people of Los Angeles have been unable to hold their chief of police accountable for anything—not his racial slurs or racial stereotyping; not his openly-expressed contempt for the public, juries and the Constitution he is sworn to uphold; not his spying on political enemies or cover-up of that espionage.[128]

Whether it is the local police on the city streets or the chief of police, to the degree that a society is democratic, office regulates every level of state power, from the humble to the grandiose. The actions of the president of the United States, who fills an office that is sometimes referred to as "the most powerful job in the world," are subject to continuous scrutiny. His willingness to submit to the moral regulation of his office is a serious source of concern, not only inside American civil society but outside it as well. Indeed, long before the U.S. head of state's actions had global significance, the civil regulation of this executive office was considered a principal challenge for the nation's democratic life. In 1776, when the thirteen British colonies declared themselves to be an independent and democratic nation, the United States of America embarked on an armed struggle against British hegemony. In the decades preceding this conflict, the colonists had fiercely interpreted the economic and political demands of the British king, George III, in terms of the negative discourse of civil society: as arbitrary, abusive, and in every manner corrupt.[129] After the successful conclusion of the American Revolution, the Americans were determined to establish more civil control over political power. In the late 1780s, the new nation's founding fathers created a Constitution. Their aim was to overcome the political weakness of the interregnum period, during which the postrevolutionary Articles of Confederation had allowed individual state governments great leeway at the expense of the national center.

Yet even as they created the position of national president, the constitutionalists sought to regulate this new executive power via office controls. They worried that the autonomy of presidency might open the door to personal and autocratic authority. During the national debate over ratification, James Madison—who was, in fact, to become the new office's fourth occupant—reminded his countrymen that "the overgrown and all grasping prerogative of a hereditary magistrate" posed a potent danger to liberty.[130] The danger was not criminality in the ordinary sense. It was the threat to civil morality. It was this more extraordinary danger that the Constitution's provisions about impeachment were intended to address. Article II, section 4, stipulated that congressional representatives of the American people could remove a president from office on the grounds of "treason, bribery, or other high crimes and misdemeanors," an ambiguous formula that achieved clarity only in its intention to reach beyond the routine compromises of political life and ordinary criminal law.[131] This broadly civil ambition had been highlighted during the drafting convention in Philadelphia. As an influential delegate from Virginia, Madison had asserted that the impeachment provisions must not only cover presidential "incapacity" and "neglect"—problems that refer to administrative deficiencies—but possible "perfidy" as well, an action referring to anticivil motives. In fact, when Madison's fellow Virginian, George Mason, suggested that "maladministration" be added to the impeachment clause, Madison objected. Petty misconduct was not the point. This was too instrumental an understanding of presidential obligations. Administrative failures were about job rather than office; they failed to underscore the issue of civil control. As James Iredell, a future U.S. Supreme Court justice, asserted during the North Carolina debate over ratification, impeachment "must be for an error of the heart, and not of the head."[132] The intention was to compel the holder of presidential office, despite his supreme power as head of state, to keep faith with the civil sphere, to maintain his solidarity with the wider community. As Alexander Hamilton put it, the grounds for impeachment "are those offenses which proceed from the misconduct of public men, or, in other words, from the abuse or violation of some public trust . . . [from] injuries done immediately to the society itself [that] agitate the passions of the whole community."[133]

In the centuries that followed ratification, the impeachment powers of Congress were often evoked but rarely employed. Social conflict and political partisanship frequently made the exercise of presidential power controversial, an object of severe criticism from the institutions of communication and regulation. Only when the integrity of civil society seemed threatened in its fundaments, however, did the regulation of presidential office evoke the civil power of impeachment. The first instance occurred three years after the conclusion of the U.S. Civil War, when President Andrew Johnson, who had succeeded to office after Lincoln's assassination, had deeply alienated the coalition of Northern Republicans that had led the nation into victory over the South. Johnson was impeached by the House of Representatives, which accused him of making "intemperate, inflammatory, and scandalous" speeches and of bringing his office into "contempt, ridicule, and disgrace."[134] With one vote to spare, Johnson escaped conviction in the Senate.[135] When the second instance of presidential impeachment occurred, 106 years later, the occupant of the office resigned before the Senate could record its opinion. For President Richard Nixon, however, the writing was on the wall. He would not have been so fortunate as his predecessor had been in the century before.

The Watergate scandal, which consumed American civil society between 1972 and 1974, followed upon the extraordinary social, cultural, and political polarization of the 1960s, a period marked by intensive and increasingly divisive conflicts over such issues as civil rights, sexual mores, war, the environment, and feminism. In 1968, the backlash against leftward currents had allowed Richard Nixon to gain the presidency. In the course of his first term, Nixon employed his presidential power to suppress not only the extralegal political violence of the fringe Left but legitimate mainstream opposition as well, and he did so by employing methods that, to a growing number of his contemporaries, seemed repressive and antidemocratic.[136] It was eventually revealed that President Nixon had directed his staff to hire teams of secret agents to burglar the private offices and residences of the liberal opposition and that, on the basis of "enemies lists," he and his subordinates intended to blackmail leading political figures and representatives of communicative and regulatory institutions.

These efforts to circumvent the civil regulation of national political power represented an extreme of partisanship, one that moved from agonism to antagonism and exacerbated the already massive divisions of civil society in a dangerously antidemocratic way. When, in the summer of 1972, legal officers inside the executive branch launched preliminary investigations into Watergate-related activities, President Nixon engaged in a cover-up, hiding and destroying evidence and issuing a continuous stream of disinformation to legal authorities and journalists alike. Reporters for the *Washington Post*, a leading communicative institution inside the nation's capitol, eventually gained access to critical insider accounts. News stories narrating polluting constructions of presidential behavior eventually caused a major scandal to erupt.

A leading contemporary journalist was not alone in his identification of the Watergate scandal as "the most profound Constitutional crisis in our history."[137] As the scandal intensified, there was not only great fear and indignation, but growing concern for the institution of office, about whether American civil society would be able to continue to regulate state power. When President Nixon suppressed the early investigations from inside the executive branch, this popular anxiety compelled the U.S. Senate to establish a Select Committee with subpoena power to conduct public hearings. Testimony before this committee, in the summer of 1973, cast a shadow over the president's motives and his political relations, and threw into bold relief the danger his presidency posed to civil institutions. Time and time again, the committee's leading members linked revelations about office abuse to the growing fragmentation of civil solidarity. In one of the summer's most memorable confrontations, a Republican senator dramatically denied that there was, in principle, any connection between partisanship and anticivil behavior: "Republicans do not cover up, Republicans do not go ahead and threaten . . . and God knows Republicans don't view their fellow Americans as enemies to be harassed [but rather as] human being[s] to be loved and won."[138] This passionate rhetorical affirmation of the homology between partisanship and solidarity echoed the efforts of national leaders to legitimate party organization of the electoral process one hundred and fifty years before.[139]

Toward the end of these Senate hearings, a witness revealed that President Nixon had tape-recorded critical meetings inside the Oval Office. The Select Committee voted to direct its chairman, Senator Sam Ervin, to command the president of the United States to release these tapes. When Nixon refused to do so, Senator Ervin called a press conference. In what he later called his "impromptu comments," Ervin emphatically emphasized the separation between role and incumbent, proclaiming that office regulation was critical to preserving the civil power of the people.

> I venerate the office of the President, and I have the best wishes for the success of the present incumbent of that office, because he is the only President this country has at this time. A President not only has constitutional powers which require him to take care that the laws

148

be faithfully executed. . . . Beyond that, the President of the United States, by reason of the fact that he holds the highest office in the gift of the American people, owes an obligation to furnish a high standard of moral leadership to this Nation.[140]

Impeachment was in the air. Defenders of the president repeatedly called attention to the fact that no evidence had been presented of criminal wrong-doing. His critics responded that office obligations answered to a higher standard. Responding to the former treasurer of the Republican Party's Committee to Re-Elect the President, Chairman Ervin demanded: "Which is more important, not violating laws or not violating ethics?"[141] At times, the defense of the higher standard of office obligation even recalled its religious origins, with assertions that the "laws of men" must give way to the "laws of God."[142] The president, for his part, continued to resist not only senatorial demands but court orders to release the tapes, which would later turn out to reveal incriminating examples of office abuse. Finally, Special Prosecutor Leon Jaworski, who had been appointed by the president himself in the wake of a "firestorm" of controversy, accused Nixon of asserting that the president alone possessed "ultimate authority to determine when to prosecute, whom to prosecute, and with what evidence to prose-cute" and of blocking every effort to "take the President to court." Such constructions of executive power as supremely self-interested highlighted the confrontation between personal authority and office obligation. To accept this presidential "contention," Jaworski publicly asserted, "would sharply limit the independence that I consider essential if I am to fulfill my responsibilities as contemplated by the charter establishing this office."[143]

With the president continuing to maintain control over the tapes, and with alarming accusations of repressive power circulating with increasing intensity, the House of Representatives formed an Impeachment Commit-tee. As one of its leading Republican members asserted during the public hearings, "No man should be able to bind up our destiny, our perpetuation, our success, with the chains of his personal destiny."[144] The committee voted out three articles of impeachment. The first charged the president with obstructing and impeding the administration of justice, of violating his constitutional duty "to take care that the laws be faithfully executed." The second charged that President Nixon had, directly or through subordinates, "abused the powers vest in him."[145] As another Republican member asserted, this article "really gets at the crux of our responsibilities here for it directed attention toward the president's oath and his constitutional obligations."[146] The third article accused the president of acting "in derogation of the power of impeachment" by failing to produce materials duly subpoenaed by the House. In a solemn and widely televised roll call vote, these articles were accepted by a bipartisan House majority. Public opinion polls demonstrated that President Nixon's support had plummeted in the course of the impeachment proceedings. The Republican leader of the Senate announced that he considered conviction a certainty, and President Nixon resigned from office.[147]

If the Senate had, in fact, gone on to convict President Nixon of high crimes and misdemeanors, he would have been compelled to leave office by the force of law. In a democratic society, law formalizes the obligations of officeholders to act in a civil way. Law is the ultimate regulatory institution of the civil sphere, the sanction at the base of the medium of civil power, the efficient cause bending state power to civil will. The highest political official in the land, the most powerful bureaucrat, the most persuasive ideologue, and the most fearsome monopolist of social power—in a democratic society, each one of these can be trumped by civil power in its legal form. It is to the operation of this other regulatory institution of the civil sphere that we now turn.

CHAPTER 7

Regulative Institutions (2):
The Civil Force of Law

ARE THERE EVEN more concrete mechanisms by which the subjective and very immaterial entity called civil society, this solidarity that is a "people of individuals," comes to shape struggles for particular power and interest? The communicative boundary of civil society affects noncivil spheres by crystallizing diffuse public opinion, and it gains its effects exclusively through persuasion and influence. As we have seen, however, there are more concrete ways in which civil society exerts its influence. Through the institutions of voting, political party, and office, the criteria of civil society are defined in more hard-headed ways, involving sanction and not only suasion. These institutions compose the regulative as compared with the communicative boundary of civil society, and they compel states to enforce civil obligations vis-à-vis such other noncivil institutions as families, states, religions, and primordial communities. To be fully effective, however, this regulative boundary must be fortified by law.

The Democratic Possibilities of Law

Law is at once the most familiar and the least understood regulative institution. In large part, this is because it has been approached under the tradition of Thrasymachus. Under the aegis of Weber's instrumentalism, Durkheim's functionalism, and Marx's economism, social scientists have approached law as a coercive form of technical regulation: a modern response to demands for functional efficiency, market predictability, and authoritative control. Such an approach has the virtue of distinguishing law from civil institutions of a more communicative kind, but it ignores law's relation to culturally oriented norms and sanctions, the manner in which law sits, in Habermas's felicitous phrase, between *Faktizität* and *Geltung*: between the behavioral level of factual reality and the realm of value.[1]

Of course, law comes in different guises, and in this sense it is misleading to speak of "law" per se. Law often concerns itself with functional adaptation, with establishing the conditions for equilibrium, with creating more efficient means of administration in order to allow actors more effectively to secure material goals or communities to promote their particular values. In modern societies, as Weber has demonstrated, virtually every authoritative decision must eventually be articulated in a rational-legal form.[2] But these noncivil purposes and effects do not exhaust what law is about, as Robert Post has recently pointed out in his insistence on the democratic side to legal regulation.[3] The aspiration toward which democratic law aims is a civil society. In fact, to the degree that the civil sphere gains authority and independence, obedience to law is seen not as subservience to authority, whether administrative or communal, but as commitment to rules that allow solidarity and autonomy. Demands for democracy have often been protests against illegality. For the American revolutionaries, George III embodied anticivil repression. In the *Declaration of Independence*, published in 1776, that British ruler was polluted as much for his denial of law as for his departures from other sorts of democratic behavior.

> He has refused his assent to laws, the most wholesome and necessary for the public good. . . . He has forbidden his Governors to pass laws of immediate and pressing importance. . . . He has obstructed the administration of justice, by refusing his assent to laws for establishing judiciary powers.

More than two centuries later, in the aftermath of a tumultuous contested election in the newly independent Ukrainian Republic, the opposition leader, Viktor Yushchenko, vowed to supporters that, if he won a second presidential run-off election, he would "restore the letter and the spirit of the law."[4]

Though laws certainly are elaborated in complex organizational settings and are backed up by force, they can aspire to a moral status. To the degree that societies are democratic, law can crystallize the seemingly oxymoronic commitment to individuality and collectivity that defines the sphere of civil life. Law can enjoin infringements on the scope of individual action and offer protection for the self's private, interior life. It can, at the same time, restrict the scope of individuality by prohibiting individuals from injuring fellow members of the civil sphere, whether by cheating, lying, or by threatening them with physical force.[5]

For these reasons, law can be a highly significant boundary mechanism for civil society, crystallizing universalistic solidarity by clarifying its application to particular and contingent situations. Through its substantive, hands-on, case-by-case stipulations, the law can become a powerful conduit for civil morality in the universalizing sense I have defined it here.[6] Armed with the law, public representatives can intervene physically to prevent family abuses, such as wife-battering and child molestation. The formal and explicit charge is simply that the abusive family member has broken the law. At a deeper level, however, this intervention is legitimated on the grounds that participants in the familial sphere have not only sphere-specific duties— as father and husband, wife and mother, child and sibling—but also obligations to a wider community defined in civil terms. Because of this double obligation, women and children, who may be relatively powerless in the family sphere, can be made legally equal to males, for they can claim legal membership in an overarching civil sphere. When workers sue their employers for unfair labor practices, or when consumers take producers of defective products to court, they are hoping that the law can create possibilities for justice by mandating a similar extension of solidarity.[7] Whether courts intervene in such disputes depends on where they draw the line between civil and noncivil spheres. Where this line is drawn changes continuously over historical time. That democratic law has the right, indeed the obligation, to intervene on one side of this line does not.

The translation of universalizing solidarity into legal force allows civil society to reconstruct struggles over power, money, and primordial value. Throughout the variety of noncivil spheres, claimants can make the demand for their "civil rights." The substance of these claims varies nowadays, from demands for facilities by disabled persons, for the rights of homosexuals to "civil" unions, for protection from gender and racial bias, for the free access of consumers and citizens to economic and political information, for the rights of employers to be free from the "harassment" of union organizers. Whatever the substance, these are all demands for more symmetry between the claimants' putative legal standing in civil society and their putatively uncivil status in another sphere. Such demands can be aimed at moral persuasion, and they can be broadcast by the communicative institutions of civil life. But they can be made on legal grounds as well. Collective demands can be addressed, in other words, not only in the court of public opinion but in the court of law.

The more differentiated and autonomous the civil society, the more clearly there emerges a more porous legal boundary vis-à-vis noncivil spheres, whose activities become subject to legal-cum-civil regulation. A century and half ago, this legal boundary was much more rigid. "The Supreme Court's decision in *Plessy* had drawn a line *between* the sphere of the legal and the sphere of the social," Angela Harris suggests in recalling how the U.S. Supreme Court upheld Jim Crow laws in *Plessy v. Ferguson*, in 1896.[8] In democratic societies today, by contrast, social conflicts over noncivil goods increasingly involve clashes over just where the legal boundary should be drawn. Lawrence Friedman's analysis of America's "due process revolution," which began in the 1960s and continues today, documents this process. During the course of these decades, state and private spheres alike have gradually been penetrated by egalitarian legal claims. Indeed, boundaries between the legal system and "the general social order" have become so "hopelessly blurred," according to Friedman, that by the late twentieth century, "the legal system [had become] part of the general culture, the general political system, the general economy."[9]

> Spheres of human life, once havens of immunity from law and legal process, were now invaded and (to some degree) conquered [so that] justice is, or ought to be, available in all settings: in hospitals and prisons, in schools, on the job, in apartment buildings, on the streets, within the family. It is a pervasive expectation of fairness.[10]

Powers in the noncivil spheres can be challenged from a position of legal counterpower. Parishioners bring public actions against church ministers, wives against husbands, patients against doctors, students against teachers. Such clashes will not end noncivil hierarchy; such a goal has no place in a plural society. Their effect, rather, is to increase, or at least to make explicit and to open for contention, the immanent boundary tension between civil and noncivil spheres; the result is to allow the former to interpenetrate the latter so that there can be a process I will later call civil repair.[11] "Where a minority bloc is consistently unable to form coalitions with other blocs because of the prejudice those blocs harbor towards it," writes Kenji Yoshino in a review of laws that discriminate against gays and lesbians, the intervention of courts is necessary: "The judiciary is keeping, rather than breaking, faith with the democratic process."[12] In recent American history, the Civil Rights movement of subordinated and disenfranchised black Americans provided a compelling illustration of how such legal forms of civil repair can be made. Half a century before this freedom movement, Justice John Marshall Harlan articulated the legal framework for repairing racial domination in his dissent from the Supreme Court decision upholding Jim Crow apartheid. Harlan maintained that the idealizing legal commitments of America's civil sphere were profoundly in tension with the antidemocratic institutions of the noncivil spheres that bound and often distorted it.

> The white race deems itself to be the dominant race in this country. And so it is, in prestige, in achievements, in education, in wealth and power. . . . But in the view of the Constitution, in the eye of the law, there is in this country no superior, dominant, ruling class of citizens. There is no caste here. Our Constitution is color-blind, and neither knows nor tolerates classes among citizens. In respect of civil rights, all citizens are equal before the law. The humblest is the peer of the most powerful. The law regards man as man, and takes no account of his surroundings or of his color when his civil rights as guaranteed by the supreme law of the land are involved.[13]

Contract law is typically regarded as among the most economically imbedded and least likely legal forms to reflect democratic aspirations of the civil domain. Yet contracts can sustain the institutional boundary for civil society in an unobtrusive way. In doing so, they demonstrate how civil society can articulate claims vis-à-vis another sphere without threatening to obliterate the differentiated nature of its more particularistic, noncivil activities. While Hugh Collins agrees that "pre-contractual obligations require a justification which has sufficient weight to overcome objections based on the protection of freedom of contract and the efficient operation of the market," he insists that there is, in fact, often sufficient weight.

> Such justifications can be established . . . in many instances. Where one party lies to another during the negotiations, or carefully conceals some vital information, then this misconduct can be regarded as forfeiting the protection of freedom to contract and as frustrating the efficient operation of the market. Similarly, where one party deliberately induces another to incur expenditure or to disclose confidential information, without any intention of making a contract, then again we can regard this conduct as an abuse of the freedom to negotiate without incurring obligations.[14]

\Because private transactions are frequently economic, contracts are essential mechanisms in the maintenance of private property systems and capitalist market relations\ It was for this reason that civil society II theorists condemned them and that champions of civil society III have tended to ignore them. This is ironic, for contracts are a primary medium through which civil society actually enters into the economic realm, regulating its fundamental transactions in more universalistic ways. Contracts ensure not only the validity but also the fairness, in civil terms, of private social transactions. The principle that Hugh Collins finds at the basis of British contract law—"the duty to negotiate with care"—expresses this subtle relationship between economic freedom and civil society.[15] Because the parties to a contract "may enter into a relation of dependence during negotiations where the actions of one party may foreseeably cause economic harm to another unless care is taken," a situation in which "promises, statements, and conduct may induce the dependent party to act to his detriment," then "the law is likely to impose a duty to compensate for the losses incurred." This demand for reciprocity can be maintained, however, only if the dependent party's "reliance upon the promises, statements or other conduct" is "reasonable."[16]

Whether between labor and management or producers and consumers, it is the legal institution of the contract that allows negotiation and reciprocity, and questions of justice, to play some role in economic decision making, rather than leaving these phenomena to the power of purely economic criteria or bureaucratic command. Contracts are inimical to socialism only in the authoritarian, antidemocratic versions in which states endeavor to suppress markets and economic negotiation in the name of an overarching and undifferentiated collective good. Indeed, by enforcing a formal element of status equality among economic actors, it might be argued that contracts, first established to benefit private market actors during the seventeenth and eighteenth centuries, actually created a precedent for radical and reformist workers to demand "fair wages" and "just contracts" in the centuries that followed. Durkheim argued for precisely this evolutionary development in his neglected essay on civic morals.[17] This was also what Marshall had in mind when he asserted that the social aspects of citizenship, which undergird the modern welfare state, were built upon earlier, more narrowly focused legal dimensions of civil rights.[18] In light of their harsh personal experiences with the antidemocratic regulation of economic life, it is hardly surprising that, among the critical theorists, it was only the eastern European branch that recognized contract's central role. While they often continued to uphold socialist economics, their experience with political dictatorship made them uniquely sensitive to the institutional underpinnings of democratic life.[19]

Bracketing and Rediscovering the Civil Sphere: The Warring Schools of Jurisprudence

If classical and modern social science has often made little headway in understanding this democratic side of law, there has been a similar gap in legal theory, whose most influential traditions, or schools, have tended to bracket out the law's moral and civil role. Legal formalism, for example, presents law as a system of logically interrelated postulates. It is by providing order and consistency, formalists argue, that law takes on value, regardless of its relation to other spheres or to the broader community. With its heavy emphasis on rationalization, conformity, and obedience, Weber's legal sociology represented, in fact, just such a formalist perspective. Weber highlights and praises the purely logical form of legal restraint, the lack of judicial discretion such formalism allows, and what he viewed as the law's hermetic resistance to extralegal considerations.[20]

As a sometime follower of Thrasymachus, Weber joined this formalist understanding to an emphasis on how the logical and neutral qualities of law allow it to function as an instrument for power.[21] Here the legal approach of the German founder of modern sociology converged with the legal positivism of British jurist John Austin and even, after a fashion, with the legal realism of American pragmatism. These latter approaches also regard the law as reflecting and serving extralegal sources of political, economic, and personal power. Austin famously defines law as the "general command of the sovereign to govern the conduct of society's members."[22] Embracing this so-called imperative theory, Hans Kelsen isolated positive law from morality and emphasized its coercive dimension, describing law simply as a "norm which stipulates a sanction."[23] The realist position, despite its democratic origins in late-nineteenth-century social reform, is perfectly compatible with this anti-idealistic spirit. "The law is full of phraseology drawn from morals," Oliver Wendell Holmes acknowledged in an address to Boston University law students in 1897. But "if you want to know the law and nothing else," he warned, "you must look at it as a bad man, who cares only for the material consequences of which such knowledge enables him to predict, not as a good one, who finds his reasons for conduct, whether inside the law or outside of it, in the vaguer sanctions of conscience."[24]

More sociologically inclined realists turned this pragmatic perspective into an investigation not of the law but of judicial behavior.[25] Some theorists took legal realism in a neo-Marxist direction. The émigré theorist Franz Neumann, in the wake of his experience with Nazi repression, tried to develop a democratic justification for the rule of law; yet the realism of his neo-Marxist perspective made it difficult for Neumann to appreciate law's moral and civil relevance. Aligning himself with Weber, Neumann declared that "the general law has a socially and politically protective function," a "disguising function [that] in a class society and in a competitive economic system . . . conceals the realities."[26] The reason that "judges do not like to admit this simple proposition," Neumann claimed, was because they wished "to veil their power."[27] The contemporary American version of this realist tradition is Critical Legal Studies, one of whose major theoreticians, Duncan Kennedy, has asserted that the communal interests ostensibly represented by law amount to little more than "coercive actions" that threaten "individual freedom" with "annihilation."[28] The contemporary economic approach, the Wealth Maximization School, turns this realism in a conservative direction, but the instrumentality of its theoretical logic make it impervious to law's moral qualities, much less its civil implications. According to Richard Posner, one of this school's most influential intellectual spokesmen, "altruism (benevolence) can be interpreted as an economizing principle." Judge Posner maintains that the "conventional pieties—keeping promises, telling the truth, and the like" are maintained not because they embody civil commitments, but because they maximize wealth: "Adherence to these virtues facilitates transactions (and so promotes trade and hence wealth) by reducing the costs of policing markets through self-protection, detailed contracts, [and] litigation."[29]

What these otherwise antagonistic traditions commonly ignore is the cultural dimension of democratic law, the dimension that anchors itself not only in formal precedent and logic, instrumental rationality, pragmatic negotiation, or coercion, but also in the idealizing, if bifurcated, vision of the motives, relations, and institutions that allow civil society. Such an exclusive "emphasis on fact and strategy," according to Ronald Dworkin, ends up by "distorting jurisprudential issues" and "eliminating just those issues of moral principle that form their core."[30] H. L. A. Hart puts the matter more simply. In a democratic society, Hart wrote, "a great area of the law [is] imbedded in common sense."[31]

In fact, the law's civil aspirations are revealed in the heated polemics between the very warring schools that deny them. Explicitly, their thrust and parry revolve around defending and attacking distinctive theoretical and empirical positions. Implicitly, they reveal their shared commitment to the purifying and polluting binaries of civil society discourse.

In the language Hart chooses to attack legal formalism, for example, we can distinctly hear the echo not only of theoretical but moral critique. Legal formalism "seeks to disguise and to minimize . . . choice," Hart writes. In doing so, it aims "to secure a measure of certainty or predictability at the cost of blindly prejudging what is to be done in a range of future cases." Legal judgments "can only reasonably be settled," Hart asserts, in an anti-formalist, case-by-case manner.[32] In a similar manner, Dworkin accuses legal positivism not merely of being wrong empirically but of harboring barely concealed authoritarian ambitions of erasing the "distinction between law and . . . the orders of a gangster."

> We feel that the law's strictures—and its sanctions—are different in that they are obligatory in a way that the outlaw's commands are not. Austin's analysis has no place for any such distinction, because

it defines an obligation as subjection to the threat of force, and so founds the authority of law entirely on the sovereign's ability and will to harm those who disobey.[33]

Lon Fuller lodges a similar moral claim against legal positivism, suggesting that Austin "confuses fidelity to law with deference for established authority."[34]

In an early symposium on the Wealth Maximization School in *Philosophy and Public Affairs*, Edwin Baker criticizes the emerging school of jurisprudence for violating civil solidarity, "favoring the rich claimant whose use is productive over the poor claimant whose use is consumptive," and Lawrence Tribe pollutes the approach on the grounds that it "anesthetizes moral feeling."[35] Even Frederick Hayek, the foundational theorist of laissez-faire ethics, proves unable to separate his legal reasoning from claims that implicitly evoke civil associations. Attacking pragmatic legal realism for introducing notions of "fairness" and "reason," Hayek actually raises the standard of civil society high: "One could write a history of the decline of the Rule of Law," Hayek writes, "in terms of the progressive introduction of these vague formulas into legislation and jurisdiction." The result has been the destruction of civil society, "the increasing arbitrariness and uncertainty of, and the consequence disrespect for, the law and the judicature [*sic*]."[36]

When Cass Sunstein espouses a realist alternative to such market-driven and formalist approaches, he, too, draws on the discourse of civil society. Indicting strict constructivism for allowing too much free play to private organizations, he claims it runs "afoul of the fundamental constitutional norm against naked interest-group transfers."[37] Raymond Belliotti, who describes himself as a critical pragmatist, constructs the realistic approach as itself anticivil. Attacking realistic insistence on the "entirely arbitrary" and "personal" element in judicial behavior, Belliotti declares, to the contrary, that there is a "rational constraint that judges report and experience when making their decisions"; contrary to the claims of realism, judicial decision making cannot be understood independently of "the meaning and values that judges who participate in the process attribute to it."[38] Owen Fiss, advocating an "interpretive turn" in legal studies that would embrace relativism and deconstruction, defends his approach by evoking the universalism of "bounded objectivity": "An interpretation can be measured against a set of norms that transcend the particular vantage point of the person offering the interpretation. [This] imparts a notion of impersonality."[39]

When Jean Cohen makes the case for the Habermasian "new paradigm" of reflexive law, she emphasizes its purely procedural qualities against communitarian and state-centered jurisprudence. The "application of procedures to procedures," she suggests, allows for "reflective choice," for "conscious awareness on the part of those involved and those affected by a particular area of legal regulation."[40] Explaining how this new paradigm interprets the new constitutionalization of privacy rights, however, Cohen evokes the structured binaries of civil language rather than the pure reflexivity of speech acts. Earlier forms of public regulation were "paternalistic," she argues, creating forms of "domination" and increased "arbitrariness"; the newly reflexive approach, by contrast, ascribes "competence" and "equality" to intimate associates. Only with the new paradigm, she argues, can "reciprocity" be "presupposed" and can legal actors understand that "the rules imposed on us can only be those that we could reasonably be expected to accept."[41]

Even postmodern difference theorists define their jurisprudential status by evoking the universalizing morality of civil equality. When Catharine MacKinnon, the feminist exponent of Critical Legal Studies, argues against the "single-standard rule" of gender neutrality, she does not cite empirical fact but suggests, instead, that such gender-neutral standards actually violate egalitarian morality. The single standard, MacKinnon asserts, suggests that "women are measured according to our correspondence with man, our equality judged by our proximity to his measure . . . according to our lack of correspondence with him."[42]

The Civil Morality of Law

Natural law theorists, of course, have been able to address the civil dimension of law in a less inhibited and contradictory way. Believing that "all people at all times will be embraced by a single and unchangeable law" and that "there will be, as it were, one lord and mast of us all—the god who is the author, proposer, and interpreter of that law," Cicero declared that "whoever refuses to obey it will be turning has back on himself because he has denied his nature."[43] Michael Moore, a contemporary natural law theorist, writes simply that it is the role of law to "find the moral truth."[44] For such natural rights thinkers to see the civic and the moral in law is not particularly difficult. Drawing on an overtly metaphysical worldview, they believe that goodness exists as a natural fact, and that the law has only to find this transcendental norm to itself become a vehicle of moral expression.

This becomes more difficult if one begins with the model of a modern and secular, or at least pluralistic, society. In such a world, the very existence of law suggests that sanctions and punishments are separate from general evocations of moral ideals and religious or ethical obligations. To see that, nonetheless, law remains morally constrained is possible only if social theory has room for a differentiated civil sphere. Certainly law is not the same as "morality," in either the philosophical or everyday sense. Institutional rather than overtly symbolic, specific rather than general, and contingent rather than static, law seems to eschew the structure and sacrality of the discourse of liberty. Law is more regulatory than communicative, and, even among regulative institutions, it is only one among many.[45]

Still, despite these barriers to the self-understanding of modern law, legal theorists themselves, in contrast with social theorists, have often gotten it right. Getting it right depends on recognizing the connection of judicial interpretation to ethical judgment. Such civil sensibility can be present without regard to jurisprudential bent. While he was realist and pragmatic in method, the personal and family background of Oliver Wendell Holmes and the searing experience of the Civil War placed him at the idealistic heart of American civil religion.[46] It was Holmes who famously declared law to be the "witness and external deposit of our moral life."[47] Holmes intuitively understood civil as compared to state power.

> The reason why it is a profession, why people will pay lawyers to argue for them or to advise them, is that in societies like ours the command of the public force is entrusted to the judges in certain cases, and the whole power of the state will be put forth, if necessary, to carry out their judgments and decrees.[48]

In the melodramatic manner of his time and place, Holmes also understood that law is linked both to moral purity and polluting repression, and he connected this binary moral status to American democracy.

The timid and overborne gain heart from her protecting smile. Fair combatants, manfully standing to their rights, see her keeping the lists with the stern and discriminating eye of even justice. The wretch who has defied her most sacred commands, and has thought to creep through ways where she was not, finds that his path ends with her, and beholds beneath her hood the inexorable face of death.[49]

So, too, did Hart's understanding go well beyond his own putative jurisprudential school. If his legal positivism denied to morality a central role, his civil sensibility compelled him, nonetheless, to "distinguish social rules from mere group habits."[50] Insisting that "what is necessary is that there should be a critical reflective attitude to certain patterns of behavior," Hart contended that law "should display itself in criticism," which finds its "characteristic expression" in "the normative terminology of 'ought,' 'must,' and 'should,' 'right' and 'wrong.' "[51] The same can be said for Hart's erstwhile jurisprudential opponent, Lon Fuller. Fuller put himself forward as a proceduralist who insists that law works without reference to substantive values, indeed that it must abjure a "morality of aspiration" if it is to be democratic.[52] This does not prevent him, however, from describing purely procedural constraints in the terminology provided by the discourse of civil society. Procedural fairness, Fuller declares, depends on legal structures that guarantee such values as transparency, autonomy, and reciprocity. "Our whole legal system," he asserts, "represents a complex of rules designed to rescue man from the blind play of chance and to put him safely on the road to purposeful and creative activity." The product of "a centuries-old struggle to reduce the role of the irrational in human affairs," procedurally scrupulous law creates "the conditions essential for a rational human existence."[53]

Such implicit appeals to civil morality certainly validate the position of Ronald Dworkin, the most visible champion of democratic law in the present day. Dworkin insists that good jurisprudence depends on separating the rules that allow efficient policies from the principles of justice that may— or may not—underlie them. Whereas "arguments of policy justify a political decision by showing that the decision advances or protects some collective goal," Dworkin writes, arguments of principle "justify a political decision by showing that the decision respects or secures some individual or group right."[54] Democratic law does not exercise repressive power for the sake of efficiency, but rather to regulate individual and collective action in terms of the principles of civil solidarity.

> The criminal law might be more efficient if it disregarded this troublesome distinction, and jailed men or forced them to accept treatment whenever this seemed likely to decrease future crime. But that . . . would cross the line that separates treating someone else as a fellow human being from treating him as a resource for the benefit of others, and there can be no more profound insult, under the conventions and practices of our community, than that.[55]

Constitutions as Civil Regulation

Democratic constitutions provide perhaps the clearest example of how law can function as a regulative institution of civil society vis-à-vis noncivil activities. This is because constitutions are fabricated documents, self-consciously designed to articulate general principles, to establish moral frameworks that will guide the subsequent individual and institutional life of entire communities. As the "law about law," as meta-law whose principles trump even the most fervent expressions of popular sovereignties, constitutions may well appear to be legal documents of a decidedly undemocratic kind. The very idea of a constitution may seem, in Dworkin's words, "grotesquely to constrict the moral sovereignty of the people themselves— to take out of their hands, and remit to a professional elite, exactly the great and defining issues of political morality that the people have the right and the responsibility to decide for themselves."[56] Although elections have been traditionally understood as the sine qua non of democracy, the argument I have developed in this book is that they represent only one element among several that sustain the relative autonomy of civil society. It is the existence of the fully developed civil sphere that defines broadly democratic life.

In democratic societies, constitutions aim to regulate governing and lawmaking in such a manner that they contribute to solidarity of a civil kind. In his study of constitutional debate in the newly formed Irish free state, Jeffrey Prager, arguing that constitutionalism "represents the claim that the people possess the authority to regulate the relations among all members of the political community," found that when "beliefs and sentiments shift and as membership in the community expands, so too does the meaning of the constitution."[57] As Dworkin puts it, the aim of democratic constitutions is to ensure "that collective decisions be made by political institutions whose structure, composition, and practices treat all members of the community, as individuals, with equal concern and respect."[58] Once a democratic constitution is in place, it stipulates that "the validity of a law depend[s] on the answer to complex *moral* problems, like the problem of whether a particular statute respects the inherent equality of all men."[59] The aim of a democratic constitution is to ensure that the legal decisions are of this kind. As Adam Przeworski, a contemporary political scientist in the tradition of Thrasymachus suggests, constitutions ensure that a democracy becomes something other than a mere "contingent outcome of conflicts."[60] From the other side of the philosophical spectrum, Habermas agrees: "In a constitutional state, the exercise of political power is entrenched in a double code: the regulative mediation of conflicting interests must at the same time be understandable as the implementation of a system of rights."[61]

Regulative institutions would be unnecessary if civil societies were not binary in their normative codes. If people's motives and relations, and the institutions they constructed, were in fact, or could be so construed, as consistently rational, honest, cooperative, and trustworthy, there would be no need to regulate them from without, to build and sustain organizations to issue threats of punishment and promises of future reward. Communicative institutions would be more than enough. As the master blueprint for every legally based social organization, constitutions are particularly concerned with articulating the suspicions about others that mark the dark side of civil discourse; indeed, they are institutions for keeping that dark side under control.

This was precisely the rationale for the U.S. Constitution, which followed by almost a decade the nation's founding under the decentralized legal constraints known as the Articles of Confederation. That first decade of American existence was marred by chaotic and dangerous conflicts among state, nation, organization, and individual, which generated increasing concern about how the new experiment in democracy could survive. The Constitutional Convention was convened to resolve such anxieties. In order to more effectively institutionalize democracy, more constitutional regulation would be necessary.

The convention's guiding spirit was James Madison, and in the long and critical debate over ratification he defended the proposed Constitution by reminding his fellow countrymen that "if men were angels, no government would be necessary."[62] Madison's eloquent defense rests squarely inside the binary discourse of civil society. In urging ratification, he continually evokes fears inspired by the discourse of repression, calling attention to dangerous motives, relations, and institutions. Pointing to what he called a "deficit of better motives" among even democratically inclined citizens—the possibility of succumbing to emotions that threaten the very existence of liberty—Madison decries "zeal," "ambition," and, above all, the "common impulse of passion." These motives, he warns, threaten to undermine cooperative social relations, for they lead to "mutual animosity" and the "violence of faction." Left to their own devices—in the absence of some kind of constitutional regulation—such motives and relations create the "instability, injustice, and confusion" that promote institutions of domination, for in such situations actors are "more disposed to vex and oppress each other than to cooperate for their common good." In order to protect liberty, therefore, "neither moral nor religious motives can be relied on," and spontaneous "communication" will only make things worse. This is precisely why Americans must ratify the Constitution, for it relies on external regulation, not on spontaneous cooperation and good faith. Only carefully constructed "powers of government," Madison insists, can control such "dangerous" tendencies. These powers can be found, moreover, only in a constitution that reflects the republican form of government.[63]

If there is a single constitutional stipulation that aims to assuage Madisonian suspicion about anticivil emotions and relations undermining democratic societies, it can be found in the Fifth Amendment to the American Constitution, which asserts that "no person shall be deprived of life, liberty, or property without due process of law." Virtually from the beginning of the constitutional period, the U.S. Supreme Court interpreted this statute to mean not only that public and state powers cannot act against citizens in an arbitrary manner but that the authority to determine such a danger to civil society rested with the courts and not the state. The notion of "due process," which promotes civil over state power, emerged from the common-law tradition in England. Henry VIII had awarded the Royal College of Physicians the power to license and regulate the practice of medicine in London. These powers included, in addition to the college's right to levy fines, the right to keep one-half of its profits, and Parliament confirmed the legality of doing so. When Thomas Bonham, a Cambridge University doctor, was fined and imprisoned for not obtaining a college license, he brought suit against the college. In his opinion upholding Bonham, published in 1610, Sir Edward Coke established the precedent that courts could overturn "arbitrary" actions of sovereign and Parliament alike. Such a counter, or regulatory, power is necessary, Coke reasoned, to protect the purity of civil discourse against polluting acts of power.

> The censors [of the Royal College] cannot be judges, ministers and parties; judges to give sentence or judgment; ministers to make summons; and parties to have the moiety of the forfeiture. . . . And one cannot be Judge and attorney for any of the parties. . . . In many cases, the common will control Acts of Parliament, and sometimes adjudge them to be utterly void: for when an Act of Parliament is against common right and reason, or repugnant, or impossible to be performed, the common law will control it, and adjudge such Act to be void.[64]

Without such a mandate for court review, constitutional rules about due process would be less regulative than communicative, as Albert Dicey tellingly remarked in *The Law of the Constitution*.

> The restrictions placed on the action of the legislature under the French constitution are not in reality laws, since they are not rules which in the last resort will be enforced by the courts. Their true character is that of maxims of political morality, which derive whatever strength they possess from being formally inscribed in the constitution, and from the resulting support of public opinion.[65]

Dicey drew two contrasts with the French situation. One was with the British Parliament, where the idea of a constitution "has no application" because the nation is, in fact, "ruled by a sovereign Parliament."[66] The latter "can alter the succession to the Crown or repeal the Acts of Union in the same manner in which they can pass an Act enabling a company to make a new railway from Oxford to London."[67]

With us, laws therefore are called constitutional, because they refer to subjects supposed to affect the fundamental institutions of the state, and not because they are legally more sacred or difficult to change than other laws. And as a matter of fact, the meaning of the word "constitutional" is in England so vague that the term "a constitutional law or enactment" is rarely applied to any English statute as giving a definite description of its character.[68]

In the United States, because "it is the duty of every judge throughout the Union to treat as void any enactment which violates the constitution," the restrictions imposed by the Constitution "have the character of real laws, that is, of rules enforced by the Courts." Such a system, "which makes the judges the guardians of the constitution, provides the only adequate safeguard which has hitherto been invented against unconstitutional legislation."[69]

By creating a written and formal document, and by explicitly establishing a separation of powers between the three branches of government, the creators of the U.S. Constitution gave teeth to due process at the highest levels of power. Still, judicial control over state processes did not become an institution in the regulatory sense until 1803, when *Marbury v. Madison* established the Supreme Court's authority for judicial review. Justice James Bradley Thayer, whom Felix Frankfurter called "our great master of constitutional law,"[70] was regarded as a severe opponent of expanded notions of judicial power. Even in his best known argument for judicial restraint, however, Justice Thayer affirmed that the Court could exercise its civil power to guard against the pollution of democratic principles. Because "the people . . . have established written limitations upon the legislature," so must they have the power to "control all repugnant legislative Acts."[71] Normally, courts should not declare legislative acts illegal and should respect legislative power. The founding fathers believed that "courts might disregard such acts," Thayer believed, only "if they were contrary to the fundamental maxims of morality."[72] Such moral threat would emerge if legislative acts were "so monstrous" as to threaten the very autonomy of the civil sphere, for example, "an Act authorizing conviction for crime without evidence, or securing to the legislature their own seats for life."[73] In such a situation, when a government "conflicts with the constitution," then the judiciary itself "must say what the law is . . . and to declare a legislative Act void which conflicts with the constitution, or else that instrument is reduced to nothing."[74] When Supreme Court justices review legislative acts, Thayer cautions, they must give them every benefit of the doubt. They can do so only by attributing to legislators the most idealized motives and relations. They must ignore, for such purposes of constitutional deliberation, what might have been anticivil motivations in actual fact. In setting out his criteria for thinking about the constitutionality of legislative action, Thayer's reasoning vividly reflects the binaries deeply imbedded in democratic law.

> It must indeed be studiously remembered, in judicially applying such a test as this of what a legislature may reasonably think, that virtue, sense, and competent knowledge are always to be *attributed* to that body. The conduct of public affairs must always go forward upon conventions and assumptions of that sort. . . . And so in a court's revision of legislative acts . . . the question is not merely what persons may rationally do who *are* such as we often see, in point of fact, in our legislative bodies, persons [who are] untaught . . . indocile, thoughtless, reckless, incompetent,—but what those other [i.e., idealized] persons, competent, well-instructed, sagacious, attentive, intent only on public ends, fit to represent a self-governing people, such as our theory of government assumes to be carrying on our public affairs,—what *such* persons may reasonably think or do.[75]

The Civil Life of Ordinary Law

It is one thing to agree that constitutional law aims at institutionalizing a democratic civil sphere among the varied and jostling noncivil domains of complex societies. It seems like quite another, however, to demonstrate that this civil society III perspective might also apply to the legal order in its mundane everyday life, to the law of the traffic light, stickup, tax evasion, and burglary. The connection between everyday law and civil society is not immediately obvious. The link becomes visible only if we adopt what Hart once called, following the later Wittgenstein, the internal as compared to the external point of view. If "the observer really keeps austerely to [the] extreme external point of view," Hart writes, the perspective "does not give any account of the manner in which members of the group who accept the rules view their own regular behavior."[76] The result will be to look at everyday law only as a system of sanctions and rewards, unconnected to the actors' subjective moral feelings. In fact, from a purely external perspective, the "description of their life cannot be in terms of rules at all, and so not in terms of the rule-dependent notions of obligation or duty."

> For such an [outside] observer, deviations by a member of the group from normal conduct will be a sign that hostile reaction is likely to follow, and nothing more. His view will be like the view of one who, having observed the workings of a traffic signal in a busy street for some time, limits himself to saying that when the light turns red there is a high probability that the traffic will stop. He treats the light merely as a natural sign *that* people will behave in certain ways, as clouds are sign *that* rains will come. In so doing he will miss out on a whole dimension of the social life of those whom he is watching, since for them the red light is not merely a sign that others will stop: they look upon it as a signal *for them* to stop, and so a reason for stopping in conformity to rules which make stopping when the light is red a standard of behavior and an obligation.[77]

When Paul Kahn undertakes the effort to reconstruct legal scholarship half a century later, he finds a similar example to illustrate his case for an internal approach to legal life.

> From the outside, social practices look like sequences of events that may be explained without reference to the meanings they bear for the participating individuals. . . . This is the way law appears to the alien who happens to find himself temporarily within the jurisdiction. He must negotiate around a set of rules, under a threat of coercion, without understanding the significance of the rules to those who see them as "ours." Law is something done to him, rather than something we do.[78]

Kahn maintains that, to the contrary, it is *"forms of understanding* that make possible the range of behaviors that we characterize as living under the rule of law." To live under the rule of law is "to understand the actions of others and the possible actions of the self as expressions of . . . beliefs." It is only within such beliefs that "law appears as the legitimate and even 'natural' arrangement of our collective life." The aim of legal scholarship must now be to "investigate further the deep structure of law's conceptual universe . . . by offering an interpretation of the . . . imaginative structure of that world."[79]

To take the internal point of view, in other words, is to consider law as a cultural structure. The signifiers of this structure stipulate general forms of good and bad behavior, but the specific forms, their concrete referents or signifieds, vary widely according to the historical specifics of particular societies. Hart and Honoré speak about legal structure as a "fluid and indeterminate language,"[80] and Kahn warns that "the terms reason and will are themselves empty of substantive content" in the sense that "they do not provide a specific program." What this deep structure does, rather, is to "structure the debate . . . by establishing the larger conceptual order within which we deliberate."[81]

For these generalized codes to have their effect, the law is applied and adapted, in often excruciating detail, to putatively significant attenuations of civil responsibility. This is not only to punish and repress, but to construct and, after this construction, to criticize and symbolically expose. This is most overtly the case in highly publicized criminal trials, in which, as Paul Gewirtz observes, "social deviance is explored as well as defined—the twisted deviance of Susan Smith, the apparently brazen evil of the Menendez brothers." Such trials draw symbolic boundaries. By "defining otherness," they mark off the ways the guilty defendant is different from the law-abiding public audience.[82]

By distributing judgments of guilt and innocence, the criminal justice system punishes and symbolizes in a binary manner; and, by so classifying individual and collective actions, seeks implicitly to organize and regulate them.[83] David Garland writes that "penality projects definite notions of what it is to be a person" and shows how "modern courts will insist that individuals generally direct their own actions, have choice, will, intention, rationality, [and] freedom."[84] The possibility of being exposed to legal judgment has an effect that moves beyond persuasion: it compels social action to be sifted through the sieve of civil society. The intention is to keep civil incompetence at bay, and sanctions extend from civil fines and public humiliations to incarceration and, sometimes, to death. The severity of the allocated punishment corresponds to the severity of discursive attribution— of anticivil behavior. From murder in the first degree to manslaughter in the second represents a movement from the most intentional and willed aggression to action that, while irreparably damaging, is deemed to have been of a completely unintended kind.

Solidarity

Such legal attributions of civil purity and anticivil pollution reflect the intertwining of solidarity and autonomy that undergirds civil society.

When Fuller argues that everyday judicial processes belie the notion that "society is composed of a network of explicit bargains,"[85] the alternative reference to which he points is civil solidarity. To legally encode interactions by fair procedures, Fuller argues, is to show that society "is held together by a pervasive bond of reciprocity." Yet in contrast to the ties that bind "a couple deeply in love" or a "small band of men," legal bonds are less diffuse and more differentiated. Large and complex communities cannot depend on intimate communal ties, lifelong knowledge of others' habits, or deep passion. What the legal bonds of civil society reflect, rather, is "a sort of anonymous collaboration among men."

Connecting the law to a solidarity that binds and restricts individualism is also the key understanding of Hart, the determined opponent of Fuller's proceduralism. Hart, too, describes law as "a chain binding those who have obligations so that they are not free to do what they want."[86] However, while the "social morality of societies" requires the "sacrifice of private inclination or interest," Hart warns that such morality can be neither habitual nor primordial. It must be self-conscious, artificially constructed. The aim of the law is "to create among individuals a moral and, in a sense, an artificial equality to offset the inequalities of nature."[87]

In complex and differentiated societies, civil solidarity is sustained by legal rules that abstract away from particular endowments, traditions, and circumstances. In tort law, for example, there is an overarching legal mandate—"no harm to others."[88] But this basic principle must be construed at a high level of generality and impersonality, so that freedom and diversity are not overly constrained. The solidarizing mandate not to harm others does not, in other words, function as a golden rule, as an ethic of brotherly love. It suggests, rather, "that those with whom the law is concerned have a right to mutual forbearance from *certain kinds* of harmful conduct," and to protection from "the *grosser sorts* of harm."[89] These constraints on aggression apply to harm in the physical sense, both to personal safety and to "rules forbidding the destruction of tangible things or their seizure from others."[90] More revealingly, however, they apply to subjective harm, to injuries that reflect substantial departures from expectations for reciprocal consideration. So the law of torts forbids "the free use of violence" but also requires "certain forms of honesty and truthfulness in dealings with others."[91] If one cannot maintain such civil motives and relations, reciprocity is endangered, and legal sanctions follow. In one way or another, those who harm others "are bound to compensate those to whom they have caused harm."[92] The point is to reinforce, via law, the bonds of civil solidarity.

> When the moral code forbids one man to rob or use violence on another even when superior strength or cunning would enable him to do so with impunity, the strong and cunning are put on a level with the weak and simple. Their cases are made morally alike. Hence the strong man who disregards morality and takes advantage of his strength to injure another is conceived as upsetting this equilibrium, or order of equality, established by morals; justice then requires that this moral status quo should as far as possible be restored by the wrongdoer.[93]

CIVIL SOLIDARITY AND CONTRACT LAW

Contracts function to ensure predictability and economic rationality, but as Durkheim suggested long ago, they convey "noncontractual" elements as well. They require parties to demonstrate "due care" for others.[94] In 1889, in the precedent setting *Riggs v. Palmer*, a New York court ruled that an heir who had murdered his grandfather could not receive the bequest that his grandfather had willed to him before his death. This might seem simple common sense, but it is informed by deep cultural structures. Contract law seeks to ensure the long-term effectiveness of individual actions; ruling against the reach of such contractual decisions would have to involve compelling considerations of a more collective kind. By asserting that "all laws as well as all contracts may be controlled in their operation and effect by general, fundamental maxims of the common law," the court stipulated that individuals were not, in fact, free to bargain just as they liked. Contract law had to submit to commonly accepted moral maxims. These most definitely included the idea that to encourage aggression is to undermine the basis for civil relations. "No one," the court declared, "shall be permitted to profit by his own fraud, or to take advantage of his own wrong, or to found any claim upon his own iniquity."[95] No matter how important, contracts cannot be allowed to threaten the basis of civil solidarity.

In 1960, in *Hennngsen v. Bloomfield Motors,* a New Jersey court was asked to decide whether a car manufacturer was liable for more than "making good" on defective parts, as the purchasing contract explicitly stated. Would the manufacturer also be liable for the suffering of persons injured in a crash caused by these defective parts? In its ruling, the court first went out of its way to acknowledge the priority of contracts. Vis-à-vis freely contracted economic activities, it allowed, civil standards have only limited effect, and this is precisely because economic life is itself thought to involve the exercise of certain civil capacities. "The basic tenet of freedom of *competent* parties to contract is a factor of importance," the court declared, and if one party to an economic transaction "does not choose to read a contract before signing it cannot later relieve himself of its burdens."[96] The court went on to insist, however, that market behavior must be limited by more than an economic actor's putative civil competence: "Freedom of contract is not such an immutable doctrine as to admit of no qualification." Even economic actors have obligations of civil solidarity. Fairness to others, not only instrumental consideration of economic calculation, is also involved. How involved, of course, is a matter of interpretation and degree, but the principle is clear: In modern societies that depend on the automobile, the civil boundary of economic life must be subject to special considerations if due care is to apply.

> In a society such as ours, where the automobile is a common and necessary adjunct of daily life, and where its use is so fraught with danger to the driver, passengers and the public, the manufacturer is under a special obligation in connection with the construction, promotion and sale of his cars. Consequently, the courts must examine purchase agreements closely to see if consumer and public interests are treated *fairly.*[97]

To explain why the automobile company was, indeed, required to cover costs to the injured parties, the New Jersey court quoted from an earlier opinion by Justice Felix Frankfurter. In the *United States v. Bethlehem Steel*, Justice Frankfurter had linked the very institutional autonomy of the Supreme Court to its willingness to intervene against economic power.

> Is there any principle which is more familiar or more firmly embedded in the history of Anglo-American law than the basic doctrine that the courts will not permit themselves to be used as instruments of inequity and injustice? More specifically the courts generally refuse to lend themselves to the enforcement of a "bargain" in which one party has unjustly taken advantage of the economic necessities of [the] other.[98]

Still, in a differentiated and plural society, the demand for due care to others, so central to the civil sphere, cannot be allowed altogether to push aside the competitive, instrumental behavior that ties economic efficiency to monetary rewards. The conflict between civil and market justice is adjudicated via the flexibility of the eminently civil stipulation, "reasonable."[99] Contracting parties are negligent or abusive, and thus legally liable, not if they fail to exercise *absolute* care for others members of the civil community, but only if they "fail to take *reasonable* care to avoid inflicting physical injuries on others."[100] The double contingency of demonstrating care, on the one hand, and reason, on the other, illuminates the complex and ambiguous boundary relation between civil and economic society. It also manifests the broader tension between solidarity and autonomy inside the civil sphere itself. This tension is typified when officers of the court face the inevitable question, as Hart puts it, of "What is reasonable or due care in a concrete situation?"

> We can, of course, cite typical examples of due care: doing such things as stopping, looking, and listening where traffic is to be expected. But we are all well aware that the situations where care is demanded are hugely various and that many other actions are now required besides, or are in place of, "stop, look, and listen"; indeed these may not be enough and might be quite useless if looking would not help to avert the danger. What we are striving for in the application of standards of reasonable care is to ensure (1) that precautions will be taken which will aver substantial harm, yet (2) that the

precautions are such that the burden of proper precautions does not involve too great a sacrifice of other respectable interests. Nothing much is sacrificed by stopping, looking, and listening unless of course a man bleeding to death is being driven to the hospital.[101]

When industrial capitalism emerged in the latter part of the nineteenth century, this balance between solidarity and autonomy tilted toward the latter out of deference to the spectacular effects, and demands, of the newly powerful industrial sphere. At the same time, this release threatened to destabilize the balance that allowed civil society to maintain its cultural and institutional independence vis-à-vis economic life. There was growing anxiety about the new industrialists, the so-called Robber Barons, and their newly established monopolies. In 1890, the U.S. Senate passed the Sherman Anti-Trust Act. It is revealing of the tenor of that pro-business time, however, that this "protectionist" effort was not justified in terms of social solidarity.[102] Rather, Congress justified market restrictions by describing the threat that unbound capitalism posed to individual autonomy. The antitrust act held that even as great economic success represented the success of one individual's contractual efforts, it endangered others. It declared, therefore, that "every contract in restraint of trade shall be void." Senator Sherman justified the relevance of civil solidarity to economic behavior in the same manner, not by asserting the priority of collective regulation in itself, but by polluting economic monopolies as antidemocratic. He called them a "kingly prerogative inconsistent with our form of government." In doing so, he recognized the inherent contradictions between civil and economic society. Demanding that similar civilities be respected in both spheres, he advocated legal intervention into the economic sphere in order to ensure this mutual respect.[103]

> If anything is wrong, this is wrong. If we will not endure a king as a political power we should not endure a king over the production, transportation, and sale of any of the necessaries of life. If we could not submit to an emperor, we should not submit to an autocrat of trade, with power to prevent competition, and to fix the price of any commodity.[104]

Still, in a rapidly industrializing capitalist society in which economic innovation was considered to depend on maintaining the independence of markets, courts found it difficult to consistently apply such a broad civil restriction on the nation's economic life. For years after its introduction, the Sherman Act was, in fact, evoked only to regulate the behavior of smaller companies. Only some fifteen years after its creation, in 1904, did the Supreme Court apply legal prohibitions against restraint of trade to the contracts established by one of the huge new corporations. In ruling that the Northern Securities Company constituted an illegal combination in restraint of trade and would have to be dissolved, the Court evoked the necessity to maintain a vital and independent civil sphere. Without application of the antitrust law, Justice Harlan wrote, "the efforts of the national government to preserve to the people the benefits of free competition among carriers . . . will be wholly unavailing . . . thus placing the public at the absolute mercy of the holding corporation."[105] In the American version of civil society, it was more often liberty than equality that justified state regulation of economic life.

Even this new standard, however, could not be consistently applied. In 1911, when the Court upheld a decision to break up Standard Oil, it formulated a "rule of reason."[106] Continuing to fine-tune the balance between civil and economic autonomy, the Court modified the due care provisions of the Sherman Act in an economic direction, albeit in a civilly oriented way. Only contracts that *unreasonably*, or unduly, restrained trade would henceforth be punished as unlawful. This new principle meant that civil standards would be applied to the motives and relations of economic actors only within the established framework of corporate capitalism; they would not be applied to the framework itself. The application of the civil standard of due care was not intended to pollute, and criminalize, the economic facts of size or combination, or the competitive motives of economic acquisition. To do so, the Court concluded, would dissolve the boundary tension between economic and civil life and would threaten the pluralism upon which democracy itself depends. This fine line was underscored a decade later, in 1915, when the Supreme Court found no evidence that U.S. Steel was guilty of the economic "oppression" that earlier had justified its demand to break up Standard Oil. The practices of this giant corporation certainly were intensely economic, but they were not uncivil in terms of the narrow, but justifiable, expectations of economic life. "The business conduct of the Steel Corporation," the Court declared, "has been *fair*"; it had, in fact, been "conspicuously free" from the kind of "brutality, meanness, and unfairness" that often did characterize business life. Because it was free from such anticivil pollution, it was legally without guilt. "We can rest assured," the Supreme Court declared, "that there has been neither monopoly nor restraint."[107]

Individuality

As the effort to balance due care for others with reasonableness indicates, the solidarity that democratic law seeks to establish rests upon the hypothesized existence of idealized actors. Legal agents are imagined to have a natural capacity for autonomy, for the differentiating individuality that specifies solidarity in a democratic, civil way. Despite Lon Fuller's professed proceduralism, his jurisprudential writing paid close attention to such an imagined structure of feeling, acknowledging that democratic law "cannot be neutral in its view of man himself." Democratic law needed to rest on beliefs in the civil qualities of actors; it centered, in fact, on motives, on cultural assumptions about agency, understanding, and responsibility: "To embark on the enterprise of subjecting human conduct to the governance of rules involves of necessity a commitment to the view that man is, or can become, a responsible agent, capable of understanding and following rules, and answerable for his defaults."[108]

Fuller compiled a list of procedural guarantees underlying a democratic legal order. Democratic law is sustained by institutional procedures such as publicity, regularity, generality, clarity, antiretroactivity, and plausibility— not, in his view, by the commitment to substantive ideals and beliefs as such. In fact, these procedures center on an ideal of collective fairness, one that ensures a certain level of acting in solidarity with others. Without this solidarity, the actor's belief in herself as an autonomous, civil individual cannot be sustained. "Every departure from these principles," Fuller writes, would be "an affront to man's dignity as a responsible agent." Maintaining procedural fairness, on other words, is triggered by the need to keep civil values from being polluted. To seek to regulate an individual's actions by "unpublished or retrospective laws, or to order him to do an act that is impossible," Fuller suggests, would be to "convey to him your indifference to his powers of self-determination."[109]

This democratic ideal of self-determination, so critical to civil solidarity, presupposes that individual actors are responsible for their actions. The law can demand responsibility only because it assumes that actors are in full possession of such civil faculties as rationality, sanity, and self-control. This regulating legal ideal is such that if persons are found to have acted in an anticivil manner, to have done harm to others, the law can legitimately punish them; it is hoped, of course, that the very threat will deter rational actors from doing so. If actors are judged not to possess the capacity for self-control, however, they cannot be held responsible for undermining civil solidarity in the legal sense. Intention is the key. The law is a system of moral regulation that discursively constructs autonomy, punishes actors so constructed if they deviate too sharply from this ideal, and allows an escape valve if they seem not to be capable of autonomy at all.[110]

This is not to say that the law is unconcerned with harmful action, that is, with the actual threat to solidarity in and of itself. Civil, as compared with criminal, law often stipulates monetary rewards and punishments that aim to prevent harm, and to make up for it, whether there was intention or not. In terms of criminal responsibility, however, motives are of primary concern. In an influential *Harvard Law Review* article in 1893, Oliver Wendell Holmes differentiated the specifically "malevolent *motive* for action," stressing that legal liability depends more on motive than on whether or not an action creates harm in a purely objective sense: "A man is not liable for a very manifest danger unless he actually intends to do the harm complained of."[111] A century later, Reva Siegel, a feminist legal critic, offers the same kind of distinction in regard to rape. "Many of the *acts* which law regulates," Siegel insists, "do not exist apart from the *language* that defines them."[112] The language she has in mind can only be the discourse of civil society. In a civil society, social relations must be consensual, and it is the application of this cultural ideal that separates innocent actions of passion from sexual crimes. "The *physical act* of sexual penetration," Siegel writes, "is a rape only in circumstances where there is no '*consent*.' " Indeed, it is only the attribution of reason that allows courts to decide whether sexual acts are consensual or constitute rape. "As we attempt to determine whether A has injured B, we sometimes ask whether A *reasonably* believes that B 'consented,' or, in other circumstances, what A 'intended' to do to B, or, in yet other circumstances, whether A proximately 'caused' B's predicament."[113]

As Siegel's very contemporary discussion suggests, for culpability to be established in democratic law, cause is a matter of attributed intention. In deciding responsibility for harm, democratic law seeks to establish whether an action was voluntary. What decides cause is not determinism in the physical sense, but action in relation to a meaningful frame. At stake are civil relationships, the relations among persons that are sustained by civil motives and that create democratic institutions. As Hart and Honoré point out in their treatise, *Causation in Law*, whether a person is the cause of injury in the purely material sense is not of specifically legal concern. That is a matter for physics, not for the laws that sustain civil morality; it is what philosophers of science concern themselves with, as did John Stuart Mill in *System of Logic*. Physical causation concerns factors that form the necessary and sufficient "conditions" for the occurrence of a natural or behavioral event. By contrast, as Hart and Honoré put it, the law "distinguishes causes from mere conditions."[114] In a civil society, legal cause must attribute some part of physical responsibility to human agency: "After it is clearly understood how some harm happened, the courts have, *because of the form of legal rules*, to determine whether such harm can be attributed to the defendant's action [and thus] whether he can properly be said to have caused it."[115]

> We are only in a position to say that he has caused harm, when we have decided that he is responsible. . . . The expression "responsible for" does not refer to a factual connexion between the person held responsible and the harm but simply to his liability under the rules to be blamed, punished, or made to pay.[116]

Legal cause indicates a breakdown in civil relations that can be attributed to a deficit in civil motives. What is critical, as Hart and Honoré write, is "the notion of a person's *reason* for acting."[117] Attributing reason means assessing the degree of self-control and autonomy. Courts apply a criterion known as the standard of "the reasonable man."[118] Only if an actor has the capacity for reason can his anticivil action be considered voluntary, and only if it is voluntary can he be punished.

Someone may discharge a gun by an involuntary movement or pull the trigger in the mistaken belief that it is not loaded; if another person's death is the upshot, these actions of a non-voluntary character are the explanation of the disaster and the cause of it. Such cases, although involving human action, fall under the principles for distinguishing causes from mere conditions.[119]

Extenuating circumstance in a legal sense refers to civil incapacity in a moral sense. In their overview of "the various circumstances which will prevent conduct being consider voluntary," Hart and Honoré point to "lack of control, lack of knowledge . . . pressure exerted by others . . . a physical movement imparted to the actor's body against his will by some other person or thing"—all circumstances indicating some variation of antidemocratic coercion. There are also constrictions of a more complex and mediated kind, for example, an apparently free choice might actually be "made under pressure from the prior wrongful act, or is not a fair choice because the alternative is serious harm, or may be said not to be a 'real' choice because the alternative is neglecting a duty."[120]

Legal authorities will exculpate a person responsible for harm in a physical sense if she is judged to have been incapable of civility when committing it. Such civil incompetence can occur by virtue of emotional, mental, or physiological impairment. If an actor is motivated by an "uncontrollable impulse," or is in a condition of "delirium or frenzy," or in "a depression caused by insanity," or even suffering from "acute anxiety neurosis," courts have often decided that they cannot be punished, on the grounds that their harmful actors were committed "without a full appreciation of the circumstances."[121] Once again, an idealized principle of individual autonomy is at the core of the evaluation.

One necessary condition of the just application of a punishment is normally expressed by saying that the agent "could have helped" doing what he did, and hence the need to inquire into the "inner facts" is dictated not by the moral principle that only the doing of an immoral actor may be legally punished, but by the moral principle that no one should be punished who could not help doing what he did.[122]

While such qualifications typically refer to mediating conditions, particular categories of person can be exempted from punishment in the same way. For example, because "the acts of young children are often unreflective or misinformed," Hart and Honoré suggest, their actions are more resistant to blameworthiness. By contrast, because he is "capable of appreciating what he is doing," an older person may well be held accountable in a legal sense.

> Thus when a boy picked up an incendiary bomb and took it home and later took it to a public thoroughfare and tampered with it, with the result that it exploded and injured a schoolgirl, her injury was held to be caused by the impact of the bomb [and not by the child's action]. But when the defendant left his shotgun in an accessible position in the garage and his thirteen-year-old son fetched it, loaded it, and injured plaintiff's son, this was held a "conscious act of volition" which negatived [sic] causal connection between defendant's alleged negligence and the harm.[123]

To the degree that societies are democratic, the various elements that compose the criminal justice system, from courts and evidentiary rules to policing and places of punishment, are held to similar demands for sustaining civil motives and relations. Idealized as the democratic public in miniature, for example, juries are expected to embody the virtues of the civil sphere. According to the old proverb, they are composed of "nine men brave and true." In their selection and subsequent performance, jury members must exhibit civility. "As a representative institution," Gewirtz writes, the jury's members "are screened and are expected to conform to distinctive and circumscribed role behavior," and "only appropriately unbiased people are supposed to serve on juries and to judge."[124] During a trial, witnesses must take an oath to tell "the whole truth and nothing but the truth," and their honesty and rationality are open to continuous challenge. "When we assert that one person acted as he did because of another's threats," Hart and Honoré write, "our point is that this was his conscious reason." If this motive were doubted, an "honest account" on the defendant's part "would settle the question of its truth or falsity."[125] In his discussion of criminal trials, Fuller points to the performative, symbolic quality of honesty and propriety. "The required intent is so little susceptible of definite proof or disproof," he observes, "that the trier of fact is almost inevitably driven to asking, 'Does he look like the kind who would stick by the rules or one who would cheat on them when he saw a chance?' "[126]

In *Miranda v. Arizona* in 1966, the U.S. Supreme Court introduced a far-reaching reconstruction of policing procedures. This reform had profound organizational, material, and human consequences for the criminal justice system. It was set in motion by a new interpretation, in which the Court majority supplied new social referents, or signifieds, for key terms in the discourse of civil society. The question was how the words "voluntary" and "free" related to confessions in which an accused person incriminated himself. The goal, according to Chief Justice Earl Warren, was to avoid anticivil repression, to "enable the defendant under otherwise compelling circumstances to tell his story without fear."[127]

In declaring unconstitutional existing police methods, Warren polluted them by analogizing them with beatings, hangings, whippings, and prolonged incommunicado interrogations, the kinds of despotic methods employed to extort confessions in antidemocratic societies. Acknowledging that such physical brutality had largely given way to psychological coercion, the chief justice cited *Blackburn v. Alabama* (1960) to the effect that "the blood of the accused is not the only hallmark of an unconstitutional inquisition." In Warren's view, as long as police interrogations continued to be held in secrecy—a prime characteristic of anticivil relations—they would continue to spawn fears that acts of anticivil repression have taken place.

> Interrogation still takes place in privacy. Privacy results in secrecy and this in turn results in a gap in our knowledge as to what in fact goes on in the interrogation rooms.

While such secrecy precluded the justices from having direct evidence about actual interrogations, the chief justice drew accounts from descriptions available in the most widely read police interrogation manuals. From his reading of these manuals, he suggested that contemporary confessions were often still gained by illicit, anticivil methods. Police aimed at creating "an oppressive atmosphere" and gave the accused a sense that there would be "no respite from the atmosphere of domination." In a later case that elaborated *Miranda* rights, when Justice Sandra Day O'Connor voted to strike out a defendant's testimony, she declared that, to be acceptable, a confession must be the "product of a free and rational will."[128]

Even those justices opposed to such restrictions on police methods felt compelled to acknowledge that evidence would be tainted if it were obtained in a coercive, anticivil way. In his *Miranda* dissent, Justice John Harlan argued that the very exigencies of policing inevitably blurred the distinction between methods that rely on liberty and those that evoke repression. "Open and fair as they may be," he argued, "the atmosphere and questioning techniques" of interrogation "can in themselves exert a tug on the suspect to confess."[129] In this light, he suggested, quoting Justice Robert Jackson's early dissent in *Ashcraft v. Tennessee* (1944), that "to speak of *any* confessions of crime made after arrest as being 'voluntary' or 'uncoerced' is somewhat inaccurate." For this reason, he implied, no standard of absolute voluntariness could hold.[130] In his 1997 dissent in *Brewer v. Williams,* a follow-up to *Miranda* that struck down a later confession on similar grounds, Justice Byron White objected on the grounds that rationality extended further than the Court majority thought. "Men usually intend to do what they do," White asserted, and there is nothing in the record to support the proposition that respondent's decision to talk was anything but an exercise of his own free will."[131]

Legalizing Social Exclusion: The Antidemocratic Face of Law

Law addresses the positive ideals of civil society more by implication than by evocation. Rather than pumping up ideals, it concerns itself with demarcating anticivil behavior. The enactment and publication of a legal code crystallizes and threatens anticivil motives, relations, and institutions; its enforcement punishes and stigmatizes them. All of this underscores the binary nature of civil society, the manner in which the civil sphere is simultaneously concerned with inclusion and exclusion, how its regulatory institutions aim to enforce both at one and the same time. To be judged as guilty of illegal behavior and punished is often accompanied by the declaration that the guilty party has acted in a manner that is outside the law. Yet the very application of a guilty verdict actually suggests just the opposite. The activity so stigmatized is very much inside the law once we understand the latter as imbedded in a binary code.

The formal and substantive civility that law stipulates in its positive discourse is continually flouted. To the degree society is democratic, law is an institution of *civil* regulation. Rather than direct state control, it represents the potential for separating knowledge from power. This means that, in a democratic society, the relation between legal norms and social facts— between the law's signifiers and signifieds—is a matter for civil interpretation. It is not a matter of scientific determination or of simple assertion by the state. Only after being interpreted inside the civil sphere can law be forcefully applied. This is where the flouting comes in. Kenneth Karst has written, for example, that the Fourteen Amendment to the American Constitution has created a "principle of equal citizenship" guaranteeing "the right to be treated by the organized society as a respected, responsible participating member," a principle that forbids "the organized society to treat an individual either as a member of an inferior or dependent caste or as a nonparticipant." However, as William Forbath explains, in the decades that immediately followed passage of this post–Civil War amendment, "the language and institutions of the law confirmed the unfree and subjugated character of wage labor," such that "the common law of employment bore many of the 'marks of social caste.' "[132]

Blatant efforts to undermine the legal capacity for civil regulation are endemic in differentiated and stratified societies. Those who have achieved high positions in one or another noncivil sphere, or inside the institutions of civil society itself, can use their disproportionate control of wealth, knowledge, power, race, sex, or salvation to threaten or bribe lawyers, judges, or juries. In an adversarial system, because the talent and resources of legal representation are as critical as they are contingent, representation offers another entryway for manipulation. Such "external" evasions of legal accountability threaten democracy. In such situations, as David Kairys puts it, "law is simply politics by other means."[133] The Critical Legal Studies movement, which flourished in the 1970s and 1980s, was particularly sensitive to the manner in which the law became simply another means. Their scholarly critiques of actually existing law were so one-sided, however, that they barely recognized the possibilities for civil repair, much less the realities of its partial institutionalization. Roberto Unger denied the relative autonomy of law altogether, suggesting that it consisted simply in the "reaffirmation of social division and hierarchy" without any relation to "the ideal aim of the system or rights."[134] During these same decades, external evasion was also the favored topic of legal sociology, which in its American form developed from legal realism and became associated with the anticultural approach of conflict theory. As a pioneer in the field, Richard Schwartz, attested twenty-five years ago, "in turning to legal phenomena, social scientists have been quick to point out the discrepancies between the idealized model of law and the reality of its operation." Schwartz went on to observe that "instead of reflecting a general value consensus, law often implements the value preferences of small groups who are either strategically placed within the system or able to bring power to bear from without."[135]

In the "external" evasion of democratic law, the interests of the wealthy and powerful are barely camouflaged. In the "internal" evasion, the veneer of legality is maintained, but substantively it is stripped away. In this way, the internal evasion of law is more insidious, for it constitutes not merely politics by another means. The nesting of democratic law inside civil society's binary discourse sets the stage for its internal evisceration. The ideal and material hierarchies that sustain noncivil domains project themselves across the boundary of the civil society, and anticivil domination becomes justified by ascriptions of competence and incompetence inside the civil sphere itself. In this manner, the discourse of civil society justifies the pragmatics of domination without compromising the law's semantic integrity. "The power exerted by a legal regime," Robert Gordon writes, "consists less in the force that it can bring to bear against violators of its rules than in its capacity to persuade people that the world described in its images and categories is the only attainable world in which a sane person would want to live."[136]

Under conditions such as economic exploitation, patriarchy, and racial apartheid, the rule of law often seems to be sustained. Like cases can continue to be treated alike, and the principle of respecting voluntary behavior can be scrupulously maintained. What is critical is that the capacities of legal persons are defined asymmetrically. When the ability to be autonomous and rational is attributed unevenly, to apply legal rules consistently inhibits, rather than promotes, real fairness and actual reciprocity in civil life. Anticivil domination is covered with the patina of legality.

If the social process here is a subtle one, the cultural reasoning is circular in a brutal way. Solidarity can be extended, and judicial impartiality maintained, only insofar as parties subject to law are considered full members of the civil community. If judge or jury sees subjects of regulation as less than fully human, they can construe their actions as displaying anticivil qualities and judge them guilty as a result. Hart speaks, for example, about how legal discrimination is often defended "by the assertion that the class discriminated

186

against lack, or have not yet developed, certain essential human attributes."[137] For centuries, the anticivil subjugation of women and nonwhites was justified on the grounds that "women or coloured people lack the white male's capacity for rationale thought and decision."[138] Hart draws from the fictional representations of communicative institutions to elaborate this distortion of the regulative sphere.

> Huckleberry Finn, when asked if the explosion of a steamboat boiler had hurt anyone, replied, "no'm: killed a nigger." Aunt Sally's comment "well it's lucky because sometimes people do get hurt" sums up a whole morality which has often prevailed among men. Where it does prevail, as Huck found to his cost, to extend to slaves the concern for others which is natural between members of the dominant group may well be looked on as a grave moral offence, bringing with it the sequelae *[sic]* of moral guilt.[139]

Where the external approach to legal evasion posits hypocrisy or material interest, the internal approach looks to the limits of socially situated human understanding. The judicial attribution of civil motives and relations cannot extend beyond a lawmaker's empathy, and in a stratified and segmented society such capacity for interpretive understanding is often sharply curtailed. In the early twentieth century, when the British Lord Justice Scrutton acknowledged that "impartiality is rather difficult to attain," he clarified that he was "not speaking of conscious impartiality" but rather about "the habits you are trained in, the people with whom you mix." This differential social mixing, he remarked, leads to "your having a certain class of ideas" which are of such a nature that "when you have to deal with other ideas, you do not give as sound and accurate judgments as you would wish."[140]

If the judges whose rulings articulate the relationship between law and economic society are recruited from or into the upper classes, their ability to apply principles of reciprocity may be undermined by their inability to experience solidarity with members of the lower class, a difficulty in seeing and understanding them as fellow civil beings. In the first century of industrial capitalism, judges applied laws about contract and free association in a grossly uneven manner, effectively restricting substantive economic freedom to the upper classes. They accepted the legality of economic cooperation among early industrialists while polluting the "combinations" among impoverished workers, allowing capitalists free rein while condemning nascent trade unions as "conspiracies" subject to the force of civil and often criminal law.[141] Indeed, in his reflections on impartiality, Lord Scrutton was, in fact, thinking specifically of labor disputes: "It is very difficult sometimes to be sure that you have put yourself into a thoroughly impartial position between the two disputants, one of your own class, and one not of your own class."[142]

Rather than directly, domination more often distorts legal ideals indirectly, via a process that passes through communicative institutions. The apartheid-like regime of Jim Crow legalized the exclusion of African Americans from the social spheres of Southern white society. It did not ensue, however, immediately upon the withdrawal of Northern troops from the American South, when Reconstruction was rescinded in 1876. Rather, the legal repression emerged gradually over the subsequent two decades, preceded and accompanied by shifts in Northern public opinion. The democratic sentiments of abolitionism, which had been enlarged by the Civil War, were waning, and openly racist sentiments were increasingly being expressed north of the Mason-Dixon line. "It was quite common in the eighties and nineties," C. Vann Woodward writes, "to find in the *Nation, Harper's Weekly,* the *North American Review,* or the *Atlantic Monthly* Northern liberals and former abolitionists mouthing the shibboleths of white supremacy regarding the negro's innate inferiority, shiftlessness, and hopeless unfitness for full participation in the white man's civilization."[143] When the law formalizes anticivil constructions, members of polluted social categories—whether determined by class, race, religion, gender, nationality, or sexuality—can more effectively be excluded from membership in civil society. In 1898, the U.S. Supreme Court upheld the taxes and literacy tests that excluded African Americans from the political process, "serenely reasoning that such new regulations measured merit, not race."[144]

> By reason of its previous condition of servitude and dependencies, this race had acquired or accentuated certain peculiarities of habit, of temperament, and of character, which clearly distinguished it as a race from the whites; a patient, docile people; but careless, landless, migratory within narrow limits, without forethought, and its criminal members given to furtive offences, rather than the robust crimes of the whites. Restrained by the federal constitution from discriminating against the negro race, the [plaintiff] discriminates against its char-

acteristics, and the offences to which its criminal members are prone.[145]

Though the rule of law continues, the equality it formally guarantees actually enforces substantive inequality. The interpretation of civil dignity, and thus the power to punish, is distributed in an asymmetrical way. This paradox was first illuminated by the legal effects of stratification in the very society that initiated political democracy, the city of Athens in ancient Greece. Because Athenian law classified residents into the dichotomous categories of citizen and barbarian, differential treatment of victim and wrongdoer often became essential for justice to be "fairly" applied.

> The moral code might forbid Barbarians to assault Greeks but allow Greeks to assault Barbarians. In such cases a Barbarian may be thought morally bound to compensate a Greek for injuries done though entitled to no compensation himself. The moral order here would be one of inequality in which victim and wrongdoer were treated differently [and] repellent though it may be to us, the law would be just only if it reflected this difference.[146]

The importance of the internal meaning reference for those who create legal exclusion is not shared by the excluded. For members of legally subjugated groups, there is no civil society, and the distinction between persuasion and coercion breaks down. The internal, moral reference of the law disappears, and the legal code seems to represent merely the external, coercive power of class, caste, or state. When the law is "used to subdue," Hart explains, its effect is to "maintain in a position of permanent inferiority a subject group." In such a situation, "for those thus oppressed there may be nothing in the system to command their loyalty but only things to fear."[147] For dominated subjects, laws lose their subjective status, becoming standards that "have to be imposed by force or threat of force."[148]

It is hardly surprising that the subjugated often adopt a purely instrumental relation to the law in turn.[149] Morally speaking, they may be justified in doing so; in political terms, however, such actions can have negative effects. In their alienation from civil law, subjugated groups may feel compelled or even entitled to engage in anticivil behavior in order to protect their material and cultural interests or to create the future possibility for their civil inclusion. Legalized social exclusion can compell dominated subjects to engage in aggressive, illegal, and sometimes even violent social actions, with the aim of injuring or destroying members of the dominant group. Such actions are formally anticivil, and they are liable to legal prosecution, but they can also be a tool for reversing the polluting legal categories that have emerged from the distortions of civil society and are imposed by the state. Whether such anticivil actions can be socially productive depends on their interpretation by communicative institutions, on whether the illegal activities of the dominated group are sympathetically constructed as protests and successfully engage public opinion. When such engagement produces a subjective restructuring of collective consciousness, illegal protest actions can change voting behavior, alter the composition of state officials, and eventually change the polluting interpretations of overarching laws. We will examine this complex process of democratic change in Part III when we explore the effects of nonviolent civil disobedience in the African American movement for civil rights.

In the intensely partisan struggles that mark civil life in complex democratic societies, interpreters of the legal order, intellectuals and practitioners alike, frequently argue that civil society's basic law, the Constitution, supports their own political side. The progressive legal scholar Cass Sunstein, for example, has suggested that the Constitution supports government intervention in economic life. Because "the American constitutional regime is built on hostility to measures that impose burdens or grant benefits merely because of the political power of private groups," Sunstein argues, "some public value is *required* for governmental action."[150] But constitutions supply only general principles. They must be applied in practice, and the interpretation of their intent will change with the times.

In the midst of the Great Depression, in 1932, Franklin Delano Roosevelt was elected president of the United States. The regulatory institutions of voting and office were, with his election, effectively responding to an economic crisis that cried out for political change. For five long years, however, another regulative institution of the civil sphere, the Supreme Court, did everything possible to block such change. The Court's majority interpreted government policies supporting working-class organization and protest as promoting anticivil coercion, citing the "commerce clause" that forbade economic interference. This legal blockade shifted only after FDR was elected to a second term. The people had now spoken twice, and public opinion was becoming increasingly sympathetic to labor's plight. In 1937, the Supreme Court abruptly declared that the commerce clause actually did allow the federal government to intervene in the nation's economic life. Officeholders, whether or not they were directly elected, need eventually to be responsive to the source of civil power from which their right to regulation derives.

After the conclusion of this great period of social change, Robert L. Stern, a longtime member of President Roosevelt's Justice Department, reflected on the reasons for the Supreme Court's momentous interpretive shift. If there had been "no change in the membership of the Court," Stern asks, "what had induced Mr. Justice Roberts to switch his vote, after his opinion . . . emphasizing the limitations imposed by the Tenth Amendment upon control of production?" And "what of the Chief Justice, who had joined [Roberts] and . . . nullified the labor relations provisions of the Coal Act?" Stern insists that "the difference in results between the decisions in 1936 and those in 1937" cannot be attributed "to anything inherent in the cases themselves—their facts, the arguments presented, or the authorities cited." What had changed was public opinion, the sea within which every institution of civil society must swim. With evident sarcasm, Stern suggests "perhaps the series of violent strikes had educated Mr. Justice Roberts as to the close relationship between labor relations and interstate commerce." More likely, shifts in the public's opinion threatened the Court's civil power, which depended, in the end, on influence and public belief. Civil legitimation was at stake.

> The consensus among the lawyers speculating on the Court's sudden reversal was that the Chief Justice and Mr. Justice Roberts believed that the continued nullification of the legislative program *demanded by the people and their representatives*—as manifested in the 1936 election—would . . . seriously undermine the independence and prestige of the federal judiciary . . . without preventing the President from attaining his objective."[151]

Legal interpretations by judges are one way of crystallizing changes in civil regulation. Voting and new interpretations of office responsibilities are others. These institutions are not necessarily in friendly relation; rather than cooperating, they often conflict. They must also be responsive to the interpretive reconstructions broadcast by communicative institutions, which themselves stimulate and reflect the public's opinion in an uneven, fragmented, and continuously shifting way. These complexities and contingencies in the structures and dynamics of the civil sphere are exacerbated by the open-ended nature of its boundary relations. The civil sphere does not exist in splendid isolation. It is instantiated in a social world that is often distinctly unfriendly. It is bounded by spheres whose elites can be antagonistic, whose standards of justice seem inimical, and whose goods are sometimes corrosive and encroaching. It is to the systematic consideration of these contradictions of the civil sphere that we now turn. We also will consider how destructive intrusions are subject to civil repair.

CHAPTER 8

Contradictions:

Uncivilizing Pressures and Civil Repair

M Y GOAL IN the discussion thus far has been to give flesh and blood to civil society, a skeletal concept that has hung in the closet of social theory for centuries but has never been considered in a sufficiently complex and empirical way. Theories of modernization, development, and rationalization have assumed that structures of solidarity are broadened in the course of social development, as offshoots of other, more visible, and more familiar structural processes such as urbanization, industrialization, socialization, bureaucratization, and secularization. I have insisted, to the contrary, that the construction of a wider and more inclusive sphere of solidarity must be studied in itself. From the beginning of its appearance in human societies, civil society has been organized, insofar as it has been organized at all, around its own particular cultural codes. It has been able to broadcast its idealized image of social relationships because it has been structured by certain kinds of communicative institutions, and departures from these relationships have been sanctioned and rewarded in more "realistic" terms by institutions of a regulatory kind.

In these discussions of civil culture and institutions, I have walked a delicate line. I have wished, on the one hand, to stress their analytical independence. They must be considered in themselves, as structures in their own right. Their status cannot simply be read off the condition of the spheres

193

that surround civil society; they are not dependent variables. At the same time, I have stressed that, in a concrete sense, these internal modes of organization are always deeply interpenetrated with the rest of society.[1] At every point they are connected to activities in other spheres. They can reach out beyond the borders of civil society to set standards and create images in the noncivil realms. Conversely, what happens in these other spheres, what is possible and what not, fundamentally affects the structure and operation of the culture and institutions of civil society in turn. The tension between the internal and external references of civil society is not merely a theoretical issue but is a central empirical and ideological concern. To the degree that civil society gains autonomy from others spheres, its solidarity can define social relationships in a more consistently universalistic way. The binary structure of the discourse of civil society suggests, however, that even in the most ideal circumstances, this universalism will never be fully achieved. Social reality is far from ideal. The autonomy of civil society is continually compromised and consistently reduced. Noncivil cultural and institutional exigencies permeate civil society, and the discourse of repression is applied far and wide. The world of the "we" becomes narrowed; the world of the "they" becomes larger and assumes multifarious forms. It is not only groups outside of the nation-state that are disqualified from gaining entrance to civil society, but many groups inside it as well.

It is to a systematic model of these boundary processes that our discussion now turns. In this task, what I have called the idealistic approach to civility and the public sphere will not be of much help. Critical republican thinkers have often embraced the utopianism of civil solidarity not only as a regulating idea, or norm, but as a possible representation of society itself. They have suggested the possibility of creating a social system that is thoroughly civil, solidaristic, altruistic, and inclusive, a society that is, whether in fact or in principle, homologous with the civil sphere itself. Writers in this tradition pollute the economic marketplace as a world of necessity, one from which normative ideas of reciprocity are excluded *tout court*. They reject the political world as merely bureaucratic and instrumental, as resting always and everywhere on domination alone. The economic and political worlds are conceived as "systems," as inherently uncivil, as colonizers of the lifeworld and destroyers of solidarity, which is doomed because it is vulnerable to spheres of a stronger, more material kind. In some versions of this approach, religion is also conceived as a dominating sphere, for it grounds understanding in a

194

closed manner that contradicts the open-ended and universalistic dialogue that marks civil understanding.[2]

These approaches are wrong not because they make forceful criticisms of the noncivil spheres. Indeed, I will make generous use of such criticisms in the discussion below. Such approaches err, rather, because they ignore the necessity for functional differentiation and complexity, both in an institutional sense and in a moral one. The more developed the society, the more there emerge different kinds of institutional spheres and discourses. To be sure, the "complete" realization of civil society is restricted by these spheres; at the same time, however, the civil sphere must enter into institutional and moral interchanges with these worlds precisely because they are composed of substances of a very different kind. This interpenetration cuts both ways: civil society can colonize these other spheres, not just be colonized by them.[3] To avoid the idealistic fallacy, we must recognize that civil society is always nested in the practical worlds of the uncivil spheres and we must study the compromises and fragmentations, the "real" rather than merely the idealized civil society that results.[4]

Civil society is instantiated in the real because social systems exist in real space, because they have been constructed in real time, and because they must perform "functions" that go beyond the construction of solidarity itself. Instantiation makes practical but also reduces the ideal of equal and free participation. It compromises and fragments the potentially civil sphere by attaching status to primordial qualities that have nothing to do with one's status in civil society as such. Primordiality is essentializing. It attributes qualities to persons by virtue of their membership in a particular group, one that is thought to be based on unique qualities which outsiders can, by definition, never hope to attain.[5] Such primordial qualities can be analogized to physical attributes like race and blood; yet almost any social attribute can assume such an essentializing position, be it language, race, national origins, religion, class, intelligence, sexuality, gender, and region. In different times and in different places, actors have become convinced that only those possessing certain versions of these qualities have what it takes to become members of civil society. They have believed that individuals and groups who do not possess these essentials must be uncivilized and cannot be included. The truth, of course, is that the very introduction of particularistic criteria is uncivil. Civil primordiality is a contradiction in terms. |

Space: The Geography of Civil Society

Civil society is often idealized by philosophers and by lay members alike as a universalistic and abstract space, an open world without limits, an endless horizon. In fact, however, territory is basic to any real existing society. Territory converts the space of civil society into a particular place. Indeed, civil society can become unique and meaningful only as a particular place. It is not just some place, or any place, but our place, a "center," a place that is different from places outside this territory.[6] Attachment to this central place becomes essentialized. As it becomes a primordial quality, territory divides; it becomes articulated with the binary discourse of civil society. The capacity for liberty becomes limited to those who have their feet on the sacred land, and the institutions and interaction of civil society become distorted and segmented in turn.

Nationalism can be conceived, in this sense, as the socialization of a space that is demarcated by the territorial limits of states. European civility had always been circumscribed by centers, of course, but before the sixteenth century these primordial territories were conceived more locally, as villages, cities, regions, or simply as the physical areas inhabited by extended kinship networks and tribes.[7] In the Renaissance, however, territory began to be viewed nationally. Attachment to place meant connection to the land of the nation. It is important to see that this geographical bifurcation was held to be true no matter how the national territory was defined, whether as a national community of language and blood, as in the German case, or an abstract universal community of ideas, as in postrevolutionary France.[8] No matter how defined, only members of *this* nation were seen as capable of reason, honesty, openness, and civility; members of others nations were not. Membership in other national territories seemed to generate dishonesty, distrust, and secrecy. It made for "natural" enemies. \

This essentializing restriction on universalism has had extraordinary consequences for the real history of civil societies. One consequence has been the continuous intertwining of real civil societies with war, the ultimate expression of relationships of an uncivil kind. Kant believed that democracies would never make war on other democracies; he suggested that the qualities of universalism and reason that characterize such societies would incline them to dialogue rather than force, making it difficult to stereotype and brutalize citizens on the other side.[9] But the democratic quality of other nations is always something very much open to debate, and the territorial bifurcation of civil charisma makes the civility of others much more difficult to discern. This explains why, throughout the history of civil societies, war has been a sacred obligation; to wage war against members of other territories has been simultaneously a national and a civilizing task. Ancient Athens, the first real if limited democracy, whose polis formed the model for every subsequent civil sphere, waged continuous war against its neighboring city-states, fighting against the barbarism that foreign territory implied. For the Italian city-states, military glory was a central virtue, and their publics defended and extended their civil societies by waging war against foreign yet equally civil communities. The imperial expansion of northern European nations from the sixteenth through the nineteenth centuries certainly had economic and geopolitical motives; but it was inspired, as well, by the urgent need to civilize those who were enemies of civilization because they were not fortunate enough to be nurtured in the same part of the earth as they.[10]

It is the great "imperial republics," as Raymond Aron called them, that demonstrate this territorial bifurcation of civility in the most striking way.[11] When the English and French fought against each other from the sixteenth through the nineteenth centuries, they were societies that fundamentally resembled each other, each considering itself to possess a fundamentally civil, if not democratic dimension of social life. Yet elites and common people alike were in each nation convinced that it was only their national territories that allowed them to breathe free. Napoleonic France conceived its conquests as wars of forced national liberation, placing into the same polluted categories the "enslaved" citizens of nations as diverse as Egypt, Germany, Italy, and, potentially, England itself. Or consider the centuries-long military history of the democratic United States, whose every war has been fought as a ritual sacrifice so that the oppressed of other countries may be Americanized and free. This is not to say that many of these wars have not, in fact, been exercises in self-defense or democratic liberation. It is to suggest, however, that the connection between national territory and the binary discourse of civil societies has been striking, and that it has inspired atrocious and punitive wars.[12]

The nationalist understanding of civility, moreover, has also had fragmenting consequences of an internal kind. It has allowed those who have been excluded from civil society to be constructed as "foreigners" and aligned with the territorial enemies of the nations against which wars are waged. Those who are excluded are often seen, in other words, not only as uncivil but as threatening national security. In the United States, this has taken the form of nativism, defined by John Higham as the "intense opposition to an internal minority on the grounds of its foreign connection."[13] In the course of U.S. history, virtually every immigrant group has been subject to such pejorative construction, from Indians to African Americans, from Catholic immigrants to Jews, from Germans in World War I to Japanese in World War II to Islamic and Middle Eastern immigrants today.[14] And one could easily multiply examples from other national climes, of how French anti-Semitism turned Dreyfus into a German spy, of how German Nazism turned the Jewish "nation" into an emblem of the international capitalist conspiracy that purportedly threatened the independence of the German state. Such facts are well-known, but their theoretical implications have not been appreciated. The problem is not just that exaggerated fears of extremists and fundamentalists have so often threatened the tranquility of democratic life. It is an issue of a much more systemic kind.[15]

Because civil society is territorial and spatially fixed, it produces its own enemies. Even in the most civil of societies the discourse of liberty is bifurcated in a territorial manner. In making pollution primordial, this bifurcation makes repression more likely. This is why, in their quest for inclusion into the world of civil society, the excluded so often try to re-represent themselves as patriots. During the rise of German anti-Semitism in Weimar, Jewish organizations widely publicized the fact that tens of thousands of their compatriots had died for the kaiser. Throughout their long struggle for inclusion, champions of the African American community have pointed proudly to the fact that blacks have fought willingly in every major American war, beginning with the Revolution itself. According to T. H. Marshall, it was the patriotic participation of the British working class in World War II that created the cross-class solidarity that formed the basis for the postwar creation of the welfare state.[16]

If nationalism restricts civility by delineating polluted space "outside" the nation, regionalism re-creates a similar if sometimes less violent restriction for space within and sometimes outside it. For it is not only nations that are centers, but very conspicuously cities and regions. Such intranational centers primordialize the discourse of liberty, constructing regional peripheries as lacking the charisma of national civility, as foreign territory inside the nation itself. City and country were for centuries pernicious distinctions of just this kind. The German burgher proverb, "the city air makes us free," was intended to be much more than a sociological observation about the effects of legal rights. Throughout the history of European civil societies, peasants were likened to animals or, in the inimitable phrase of Karl Marx, to "lumps of clay." Regional divisions such as North-South and East-West have always and everywhere carried a surplus of meaning. There is talk of "the American heartland" and *la France profonde*. These regional partitions have fragmented the civil society of nations, its culture, and its regulative and communicative institutions. When they have overlapped with exclusions of other kinds—economic, ethnic, political, or religious—they have formed the basis for repressive closure movements, for the construction of ghettos, for brutal and aggressive exercises in forced incorporation, and for secessionist movements and for civil wars.[17]

This geographical dichotomizing of virtue has also, of course, taken transnational forms. For more than two millennia, the West has provided a primordial anchoring for civility, first in the Greek and then in the European imagination. In *Orientalism*, Edward Said iconically demonstrated how Islamic areas of North Africa and the Middle East became simultaneously "Eastern" and "other" to Europe's imperial powers, preparing and legitimating the grounds for colonial wars of liberation.[18] For hundreds of years, "Europe" and "America" have each primordialized the other, positing democratic virtue in themselves, although since the War of 1812 this has not manifested itself in a war.[19]

Time: Civil Society as Historical Sedimentation

Just as civil societies are always created in real space, so they are always created in real time. The utopian idea of civility suggests a timeless realm when people have always been civil or a future time after history when they will be. Yet every civil society has actually been founded by some particular persons at a particular historical time. Indeed, within every earthly space, different regimes of more and less civil societies have been started over and over again.

What is important about this temporality is that it becomes essentialized. Rather than seen as historical construction, it is treated as a primordial fact. The origins of the community are treated as a sacred time, one that is mythologized in national narratives and replicated by periodic rituals of remembrance. The founders of this community are sacralized as well.[20] A charisma of time attaches to founders because they were there "at the beginning." Myths of origins not only give to these founders pride of place, but they attribute their accomplishment to the primordial characteristics of this founding group: to their religion, their race, their class, their language, and their country of origins if it is different from the nation they founded at a later time. Because the origin myths of civil society narrate the founders' role in terms of the discourse of liberty, the capacity for liberty is essentialized in a temporal way. The primordial characteristics of the founding group are believed to explain the success of the effort to build a democratic nation.[21]

If the characteristics of the founders are equated with the pure categories of civil society, it is only logical—in a cultural sense—that the qualities of those who come after them, insofar as they differ from the founders' own, should be equated with the impure categories of this civil discourse in turn. Temporality, in other words, creates a time order of civility, a rank order of categorical qualities that become the basis for claims of privilege within civil society itself. In American history, each new immigrant group has been considered polluted in certain crucial respects. The inability to speak English properly has been attributed to an incapacity for rationality and clarity. The extended kinship networks that typify some forms of ethnic community have been seen as a manifestation of closed rather than open behavior, as breeding factionalism rather than open competition, as manifestations of secrecy rather than openness and trust. Different religious practices are invariably considered, at least for some time, to be inferior ones, characterized in terms of emotion rather than control and hierarchy rather than equality. The result has not simply been "discrimination," a rather antiseptic and legalistic term, but repulsion and fear. There is a deep suspicion that these later arriving groups are outside the very categories of civil society itself. Can the newly arrived Irish immigrants ever, in fact, become good Americans? Can Jews? Can the newly arrived immigrants from China and Japan? How is it possible, since they are so different from us?[22]

Yet, if peremptory arrival creates such bifurcations, the passing of time can also blur them. Ethnic succession is not simply an economic fact, created by ecological and material pressures that allow one group to leave a niche and another to enter it.[23] It is a cultural learning process that may be tempered by time. Familiarity does not lead to understanding exactly; it leads, rather, to identification, a process that interpolates both space and time. Long-term presence in the essentialized place can cleanse and purify primordial qualities, allowing what were once considered fundamentally different characteristics to be seen, instead, as variations on a common theme. This is not an evolutionary process that happens automatically. Bridging, connecting, and transversing constitute a project, one that is pushed forward by the temporally disprivileged groups themselves. Making use of the communicative and the regulatory institutions of civil society, they demand to be reconsidered in more civil terms. In ethnic literature, for example, writers re-represent their group's primordial qualities in terms of the "common tradition," in both an aesthetic and a moral sense, or they demand the core's extension and revision in turn. In these aesthetic traditions of alterity, alternative framings of primordial traits are proposed; humor, tragedy, and romance are employed to allay danger and create a sense of familiarity. Immigrant social movements and well-known immigrant personalities present themselves as revivifying the national discourse of liberty and their ethnic qualities as complementary analogues of the very characteristics exhibited by the founding groups.[24]

To understand fully the implications of temporality, however, one must see that the origins of a civil community are also reconstructed in a manner that is much less voluntaristic than the "supply and demand" qualities of immigration imply. As the temporal concreteness of civil societies implies, their foundings interrupted and displaced some already existing social organization at some earlier time. They may have emerged from revolutionary upheavals against a more conservative or more radical regime; they may have been founded upon the military conquest of native peoples or resident national groups; they may have involved domination via purchase through commercial treaties or through political acquisition of a less direct type.[25] When the radical English Parliament organized its political revolution against kingship, it did not merely emphasize the expansion of civil society; rather, it presented its revolution as a victory of a different ethnic group, the Anglo-Saxons, over the Royalist bloodline. The French revolutionaries did not only make a universal and democratic insurrection; they proclaimed a victory for the Gauls over the Francs. The American Revolution also involved temporal displacement, not only victory over the Native American aboriginal peoples but over ethnic peoples who were not Anglo-Saxon. Whatever the specific manner of displacement, the primordial characteristics of the dominated group are stigmatized; they are represented in terms of impure categories vis-à-vis the triumphal civil state. Civil society is, at its very origins, fragmented and distorted in what are often the most heinous ways.[26]

These distorted self-understandings of civil society set off chain reactions that often invite "refoundings" of an equally violent type. The repercussions of such posterior reconstructions can produce physical displacement and ghettoization. Apartheid in South Africa occurred after the Afrikaner "refounding" of the earlier settler society founded by English. When the Nazis refounded Germany as an Aryan and supposedly Christian state, it produced not merely physical displacement and coercion but mass extermination. Such refoundings have been particularly acute in the wake of colonialism and postcolonialism. They can themselves produce centuries of struggle for liberation and oppression, which often lead to civil war in turn. This is what happened with America's racial caste system, intrinsic to the founding of a civil society that was, in other respects, of a profoundly democratic type.[27]

The temporal bifurcations of civil societies intertwine with fragmentations based on territory, particularly because both involve constructions that refer to the foundings of national societies. The primordial qualities that societies identify with liberty refer to founders who were "there at the beginning." When excluded national groups re-represent themselves as patriots, as people whose contributions to the nation's security have been unfairly ignored, they are not only symbolically inserting themselves into the particular place of the nation but into its historical time. Because historical memory preserves the charisma of time, it is always disputed by groups who are temporally displaced. Originating events, and later critical episodes as well, are continually reconstituted in order to legitimate a new primordial definition of civility. Groups who have been excluded or dominated reconstrue their nation's history so that civility is described in broader and more expansive ways; groups that are threatened try to maintain more restrictive primordial definitions or even to make them narrower still. Social movements use communicative institutions to convince the public that "history" must be revised; they use regulatory institutions to make this outmoded version of history illegal.

Function: The Destruction
of Boundary Relations and Their Repair

Societies are more than collectivities framed by time and rooted in space. They are enormously complex social systems whose institutions become increasingly specialized, separated from one another not only by the differentiation of their administrative organization and staff, and by material resources and exigencies, but by the normative understandings that inform and regulate them. The possibility of institutional and cultural differentiation into increasingly separate spheres lies, of course, at the very heart of the notion of civil society that I have put forward here. Its capacity for justice, liberty, equality and, indeed, its very existence depend upon the creation of a space that can somehow stand outside spheres of a more restrictive kind. Yet, as I have also suggested in one way or another throughout these first two parts of *The Civil Sphere*, such autonomy must be understood in a dialectical way. The very independence that makes civil society possible makes it vulnerable at the same time.

There is a dangerous and fundamentally illusory tendency in classical and modern social theory to understand functional differentiation as a process that contributes primarily to stability and individuation.[28] Functional differentiation may be integrative and ennobling, but it is by no means necessarily so. If the solidarity and universalism of civil society do, in fact, have the potential to form culture and institutions in one dimension of the social system, the actualization of this potential is challenged, and often blocked, by spheres abutting civil society that have radically different functional concerns and operate according to contradictory goals, employ different kinds of media, and produce social relations of an altogether different sort.[29] The goal of the economic sphere is wealth, not justice in the civil sense; it is organized around efficiency, not solidarity, and depends more upon hierarchy than equality to meet its goals. Polities produce power, not reciprocity; they depend upon authority, not independence; they demand loyalty, not criticism; and they seek to exercise coercive if legitimate forms of social control. The religious sphere produces salvation, not worldly just deserts; it is premised upon a fundamental inequality, not only between God and merely human believers but between God's representatives, his shepherds, and those whom they guide and instruct on earth; and no matter how radically egalitarian or reformed the message, the very transcendental character of reli-

gious relationships demands mystery and deference, not reciprocity or dialogue of a transparent kind. In the family, the species is reproduced not only
in a biological but a moral sense; it is organized more by passion and
unconditional love than self-control and critical questioning, and it depends
fundamentally upon authority and deference.[30]

Each of these noncivil spheres creates function-specific inequalities. Fathers historically assumed power over women and children in families; property owners and managers have organized, led, and commanded employees;
politicians and party bureaucrats have exercised domination over those who
do not hold office in the state; religious notables, whether priests, rabbis, or
sheiks, have exercised control vis-à-vis lay members of their groups. These
privileged accumulations of power may be considered usurpations, but they
are not necessarily so. It is difficult to conceive how such noncivil spheres
could operate in an independent or effective fashion without specialized
experts whose authority allowed them to coordinate and direct institutional
relations, which means, in fact, to "govern" in some manner or way. It is
possible, in other words, to conceive of just and legitimate forms of functional inequalities, insofar as the power over goods and process is acquired
by persons whose distinctive insights and specialized skills effectively produce
the goods in a particular sphere.[31]

The problem is that the privileged accumulations in these other spheres
to one degree or another routinely and systematically become translated into
the sphere of civil society itself. So do the particular goods upon which these
accumulations of power are based. These goods themselves possess a distinctive charisma, as do the powers that have the authority to speak and act
in their name. Money is important not only because of its instrumental
power but because its possession is typically taken to represent a distinctive
and respected achievement in the world of economic life. Grace in the
sphere of salvation, patriarchal authority in the family, and power in the
political sphere should be understood in similar ways. Yet, as a result of such
charisma, these qualities often come to be represented not only as prestigious
possessions acquired in specialized spheres but as qualities that mean something significant, indeed essential, inside civil society itself. Stratification in
these other spheres becomes translated into the bifurcating discourse of civil
society. To be rich often seems to suggest moral goodness; insofar is it does,
wealth is translated into the discourse of liberty. To be poor often exposes
one to degradation, to constructions that pollute an impoverished person in

various ways.[32] In one sense this translation is complicated; analogical threads are woven between different semiotic codes, metaphors, and narratives, and these establish homologous relationships among motives, relations, and institutions in different walks of life. In another sense, however, this translation is very simple. The privileged accumulations of goods in noncivil spheres are used to achieve power and recognition in civil society, to gain access to its discourse and control over its institutions, and to re-represent the elites of other spheres as ideal participants in the interactive processes of civil life.

Forms of Boundary Relations: Input, Intrusion, and Civil Repair

The functional stratification of civil society always and everywhere merges with the stratified instantiations of civil society in time and space. Time, space, and function are analytical distinctions, deciphering distinctive patterns of restriction and opportunity in theoretical terms. In more concrete terms—in terms of empirical institutions, groups, and processes—these three dimensions are not separate even if they are separable. They are simultaneous and overlapping. Polluting temporalities and geographies cannot fail to become articulated with the potentially uncivil inequalities generated by function. The institutional effects of functional processes become intertwined with primordial questions about the capacities generated by race, language, gender, sexuality, ethnicity, time of arrival, and territorial loyalties, often to the nation. This intertwining makes it even more likely that the reactions to these different kinds of conflicts—functional, spatial, and temporal—will be seen primarily as demands for inclusion into civil society as such.

As I have described them, the boundaries between civil and uncivil spheres are objective in the sense that they may exist whether or not particular actors perceive them as such. Yet although they are objective, they are not necessarily understood as just or unjust. There are three ideal-typical ways in which these boundaries can be conceived theoretically, and in which they have been conceived historically: in terms of facilitating input, destructive intrusion, and civil repair. Activities and products from other spheres can be experienced as seriously distorting civil society, threatening the very possibility for an effective and democratic social life. Perceived in this manner, they are feared as destructive intrusions in the face of which civil society can make repairs, via communication, regulation, restructuring, and reform. Yet such interpenetration can also go the other way. The goods and social forms produced by other spheres can be conceived as promoting a more ample civil life. Conservative theorists and politicians and the elites in these noncivil spheres themselves are sensitive to, and are inclined to emphasize, how vital such noncivil "inputs" are to the creation of the good life.[33] Indeed, they frequently argue for loosening controls over the production capacities of such spheres, so that the promotion of such inputs can be expanded. Those on the Left, by contrast, are much more inclined to emphasize the destructive intrusions that these interpenetrations entail and the repairs that must be made as a result. Neither side of this argument can be ignored in the effort to theorize civil society.

⟨That the economic sphere facilitates the construction of a civil society in important ways is a historical and sociological fact that cannot be denied. When an economy is structured by markets, this encourages behavior that is independent, rational, and self-controlled. It was for this reason that the early intellectuals of capitalism, from Montesquieu to Adam Smith, hailed market societies as a calm and civilizing antidote to the militaristic glories of aristocratic life.[34]⟨It is in part for this same reason that postcommunist societies have staked their emerging democracies on the construction of market societies in turn, whether or not in the neoliberal sense. Industrialization and postindustrialism have also frequently been understood in a positive vein. By creating an enormous supply of cheap and widely available material media, mass production has the potential to lessen invidious status markers that separated rich and poor in more restricted economies. It becomes increasingly possible for masses of people to express their individuality, their autonomy, and their equality through consumption and, in so doing, to partake of the common symbolic inheritance of cultural life. Facilitating inputs are produced from the production side as well. As Marx himself was among the first to point out, the complex forms of teamwork and cooperation demanded by productive enterprises can be considered forms of solidarity; persons learn to respect and trust their partners in the civil sphere only after they have learned to do so at work.

Insofar as the economy is conceived as supplying the civil sphere with resources and capacities that promote independence, self-control, rationality, equality, self-realization, cooperation, and trust, the boundary relations between these two spheres is constructed as frictionless, and structural differ-

206

entiation seems to produce integration and individuation in turn. It must be clear to all but the most diehard free marketers, however, that an industrializing market economy also throws roadblocks in the way of the project of civil society. In the everyday language of social science, these blockages are expressed in terms of economic inequalities, class divisions, housing differentials, dual labor markets, poverty, and unemployment. These facts become social problems, however, only when they are viewed as destructive intrusions into the civil realm, as economic criteria interfering with civil ones.

The stratification of the kind and availability of economic products, both human and material, narrows and polarizes civil society. It provides a broad field for the discourse of repression, which pollutes and degrades economic failure. Yet, in empirical terms, there is no inherent relationship between failure to achieve distinction in the economic realm and failure to sustain expectations in civil society; indeed, to ensure a separation is the very point of constructing an independent civil realm. Still, precisely the opposite connection is continually made. If you are poor or lower class, you are often constructed as irrational, dependent, and lazy, both in the economy and in society as such.[35] In this manner, the material asymmetry inherent in economic life becomes translated into projections about civil competence and incompetence. Inside of this translated social language, it becomes much more difficult for actors without economic achievement or wealth to communicate effectively in the civil sphere, to receive full respect from its regulatory institutions, and to interact with other, more economically advantaged people in a fully civil way. Of course, material power as such, power garnered only in the economic realm, can become an immediate and effective basis for making civil claims even without the benefit of translation. For example, though the professionalization of journalism has tended to separate media ownership and the ongoing interpretation that constitutes news, ideologically ambitious capitalists occasionally buy newspapers and television enterprises and fundamentally alter these central communicative institutions in sometimes decisive ways, as the cases of Rupert Murdoch and Silvio Berlusconi attest.

Yet to the degree that the civil sphere exercises an independent force, economically underprivileged actors can be seen as having dual memberships. They are not just unsuccessful or dominated participants in the economy; they have the ability to make claims for respect and power on the basis of their partially realized membership in the civil realm. On the basis of the universalizing solidarity that civil society implies, these subordinated economic actors believe that their claims can find a response. They broadcast appeals through the communicative institutions of civil society; organize social movements demanding justice through its networks and public spaces; and create civil associations, such as trade unions, that demand fairness to employees. Sometimes they employ their space in civil society to confront economic institutions and elites directly, winning concessions in face-to-face negotiations. At other times, they make use of such regulatory institutions as parties, voting, and law to create civil power and to force the state to intervene in economic life on their behalf.

These efforts at repair frequently fail, but they have succeeded often enough to institutionalize a variegated and uneven set of worker rights. In this manner, civil criteria might be said to have entered directly into the capitalist economic sphere. Dangerous working conditions have often been prohibited; discrimination in labor markets has frequently been punished; arbitrary economic authority has sometimes been curtailed; unemployment and its most dehumanizing effects have been mitigated, sometimes to a significant degree; wealth itself has been periodically redistributed according to solidary criteria that are antithetical to those of a strictly economic kind.

Each of the other noncivil spheres has also fundamentally undermined civil society in different times and different ways, especially as they have become intertwined with the segmentations created by time and space. Protestants, Catholics, Muslims, and Jews have been constructed as uncivil and barred from entering into civil life. For most of the history of civil societies, patriarchal power in the family transferred directly into the civil subordination of women. Scientific and professional status has empowered experts and excluded ordinary persons from full participation in vital civil discussions. Political oligarchies have relied on secrecy and manipulation to deprive citizens of information that vitally affects their collective life. The racial and ethnic structures of primordial communities have distorted civil society in terrible ways.

As I suggested in chapter 2, in the course of Western history these intrusions have been so destructive that the social movements organized for repair, and the theorists who have articulated their demands, often came to believe that these blockages were intrinsic to civil society itself. Socialists have argued that civil society is essentially and irrevocably bourgeois, that, as long as there are markets and private property, participants in the economic realm can never be treated in a respectful and egalitarian way. Some feminists have argued that civil societies are inherently patriarchal, that the very idea of a civil society is impossible to realize so long as men are allowed to dominate women. Zionists have argued that European societies are fundamentally anti-Semitic, and contemporary Islamicists have identified anti-Islamic exclusion with the Western idea of democracy itself. Ethnic and racial nationalists have claimed that racism is essential and that the civil realm in white settler societies will always, and necessarily, exclude aboriginals and nonwhites.

In response to these arguments, radical intellectuals, and many of their followers as well, have chosen to exit rather than to exercise voice. They have demanded the construction of an entirely different kind of society, one in which the uncivil nature of the spheres that border civil society would be fundamentally changed. Sometimes these revolutionary demands, and the reactionary efforts to undercut them, have destroyed civil societies. To the degree that national regimes have institutionalized some genuine autonomy for their civil realms, however, these critics have succeeded in creating dramatic reforms. Revolutionary efforts usually have failed, but the claims they lodged have often succeeded in expanding civil society in highly significant ways. The result, rather than exit, has been the incremental but real integration of formerly excluded groups. This inclusion has not been complete by any means, but it has been substantial nonetheless.

To the degree that there is some institutionalization of civil society, economic, political, and religious problems are not treated merely, or sometimes not even primarily, as functional problems, that is, as problems that concern the institutional or cultural processes within a sphere, but rather as problems of "society." They are treated, both by those making the claims and by those on the receiving end, as deficits in civil society itself—forces that threaten social cohesiveness, integrity, morality, and liberty. Inclusion becomes an end in itself, not merely a means for this or that particular repair. Conflicts over distribution and equality become, at the same time, struggles for identity and social recognition, for repairing the fragmentation and distortion of civil life.

It is to the theoretical elaboration of these dynamics, and to their detailed empirical illustration, that we now turn.

PART III

SOCIAL MOVEMENTS
IN THE CIVIL SPHERE

CHAPTER 9

Social Movements as Civil Translations

I N PART I of this book, I introduced "civil sphere" as a new topic for sociological analysis, a concept that can illuminate social solidarity as an independent topic in its own right and throw new light on its often tense boundary relations with other domains. In part II, I gave this abstract idea substantive life. I presented the binary discourses that simultaneously open up universalistic solidarity as a possibility and restrict it as a fact, and I presented the institutions that specify these ideal possibilities, that organize them into one-time-only judgments and sanctions that modulate and control the ongoing flow of social life. In concluding part II, I conceptualized the dynamic forces that bring these civil structures to life. Civil societies are not perfect forms that float in some idealized time and space. There are only actually existing civil societies. Their discourses become instantiated in time and in space, and they take on life inside of institutions that struggle with forces of a decidedly anticivil kind. These contradictions of time, space, and function put the structures of the civil sphere into motion. They establish its dynamics, both internally as symbolic and organizational efforts at self-regulation, and externally as efforts to control its boundary relations with the forces outside.

The dynamics of the civil sphere lead directly to the consideration of social and cultural movements and to modes of incorporation. The contradictions of civil society make it restless. Its relative autonomy promises more than it provides. Its commitments of universalizing solidarity are never fulfilled. Declarations of closure are never fully legitimate. Justifications for the limitations imposed by time and space are continuously questioned. Rationalizations for anticivil institutions and their distributions ring hollow. The core groups of civil society are convinced they are right to be there. Those who are not at center stage are convinced that they have a right to be. Yet the very structures and dynamics that distort civil society provide the symbolic and organizational structures for translating its restlessness into demands for progressive social change. The third and fourth sections of *The Civil Sphere* investigate how such demands proceed, both abstractly and in terms of the world-historical social and cultural movements that have shaped our time.

The Classical Model

Social movements refer to processes that are not institutionalized and to the groups that trigger them, to the political struggles, the organizations, and the discourses of leaders and followers who have formed themselves in order to change institutional rewards and sanctions, forms of individual interaction, and overarching cultural ideals, often in a radical way.

In the history of Western social theory and social science, the most influential approaches to such processes have followed a framework established by the historical understanding of revolutions. Social movements have been identified with, and modeled after, revolutionary movements conceived as mass mobilizations wresting power from an antagonistic state. The revolutionaries' goal, according to this view, is to replace an oppressive form of state power with one directed toward a different end that makes use of similar means.

This classical approach to social movements is permeated by materialism and realism. The intellectuals who organized and ideologized these revolutionary movements viewed them instrumentally, as the most efficient means to achieve the radical redistribution of goods. They accepted as a historical inevitability that these struggles depended upon coercion and violence. According to Sartre, the French Revolution began with a bloody attack on the Bastille; according to Trotsky, the Russian Revolution ended with the storming of the Winter Palace.[1] The success of both these upheavals involved pitched battles, and in the months and years following the revolutionary triumph the new rulers employed every possible means, including violence and repression, to keep their enemies, the former rulers, from ever coming back to power again. Alain Touraine is right: "The old social movements were associated with the idea of revolution."[2]

This association produced a distinctive tactical orientation to power, violence, and control. The essential matter of social movements was the control of power, its central images were those associated with the violence involved in asserting this control: the occupation of the Bastille and Winter Palace, the mass demonstrations violently dispersed by the police, the coercive occupations of factories and the militant general strike. As Touraine has pointed out, these tactics were themselves associated with a strategic emphasis on "the central role [of] institutional arrangements [and] the division of labor [and] forms of economic organization."[3] Yet these tactics and strategies were less reflections of an unavoidable social reality, he suggests, than reflections of the "materialist social thought which has oriented the Western view of society since the eighteenth century."[4] It was because philosophical materialism had created certain "architectonic representations of social life" that these nineteenth-century social movements took "technological and economic resources" to be "the foundations of a building . . . made of forms of social and political organization."[5]

In terms of empirical facts, these revolutionary movements were not without cultural form or ethical content. Rather, it was the theoretical frameworks available to their leaders that limited their self-understanding. Revolutionary leaders conceived these movements as instrumental means whose effectiveness depended upon the deployment of coercion and force. Ideals and practicalities seemed to them thoroughly intertwined, knowledge and power seemed one. Touraine speaks of the intellectual "confusion" that limited the focus of revolutionary actors to the economic field. The "metasocial warrant of these earlier movements," he argues, was defined by the "cultural model" that had been generated by "industrial society," a model that seemed to suggest that significant social change would have "to coincide with the field of economic relations."[6] As a consequence, the revolutionary narrative insisted that only after new forms of economic structure were instituted and technical transformations had allowed goods and services to be redistributed could ethical, moral, and cultural considerations come into play.

As the most powerful ideologist of these nineteenth-century revolutionary movements, Marx did more to establish the classical model than anyone
else, providing the metahistorical narrative that highlighted economic and
material concerns and that relegated morality and solidarity to the status of
issues to be taken up only at a later historical time. Yet before he created
the figure of the revolutionary leader whose actions are dictated by the logic
of industrial society, Marx actually had argued in exactly the opposite way.
He had agreed with other Young Hegelians that revolutionary actors would
have to be transformed in an emotional, moral, and esthetic manner before
any more objective, structural changes could occur. As late as his *Economic
and Philosophical Manuscripts*, Marx insisted that private property could not
be abolished unless alienation—the subjective basis for objectification—
were abolished first: "The supercession of private property is, therefore, the
complete emancipation of all the human qualities and senses . . . from the
subjective as well as the objective point of view."[7]

Only after Marx had thoroughly internalized the theoretical logic of
political economy did this perspective on revolution shift and did he theorize
revolutionary social movements in a manner that excluded the imaginary
and the normative. Adopting the framework of social scientific positivism,
he came to believe that any truly empirical explanation of the workers'
struggle and any effective leadership would have to keep humanism and
subjectivity at bay: ideas and feelings about the utopian future society could
not be allowed to intrude upon the struggle to transform the present one.
Rather than arguing from emancipated subjectivity, Marx now proceeded
from within the rubric of alienated action and external order. In *The Holy
Family*, he wrote that "it is not a question of what this or that proletarian
or even the whole proletariat *imagines* to be the aim."[8] In *The German
Ideology*, he insisted that "communism is . . . not a state of affairs to be
established, an ideal to which reality [will] have to adjust itself."[9] Rather,
"it is a question of what the proletariat *is* and what it consequently is
historically *compelled* to do. Its aim and historical action is prescribed, irrevocably and obviously in its own *situation* in life.[10]

It was from within this perspective that Marx separated socialism, now
conceived practically as a realistic first stage of postcapitalist society, from
communism, conceptualized now as a second stage that could be devoted
to normative action and moral order.[11] If labor would no longer be exploited
in socialism, its instrumental character, the materialism of social life, and

impersonal state control would still remain firmly in place. No wonder that strategic thinking and coercion were so critical in Marx's account of the revolutionary struggle for socialism that he described force as "the midwife of every old society pregnant with the new one."[12] Only in his preface to the posthumously published third volume of Marx's *Capital* did his trusted colleague, Friedrich Engels, admit the possibility that future revolutionary struggles could eschew the military violence of the barricades. In doing so, however, Engels was acknowledging how central force and power had been to the self-understanding of original Marxism and, more generally, to nineteenth-century revolutionary thought.

The Social Science of Social Movements (1): Secularizing the Classical Model

From the classical approach to social movements there emerged the most influential frameworks employed by social scientists, not only for understanding the sociology of revolutionary movements but for studying non-radical social movements as well. In terms of the modern sociology of social movements, one might say that its theorists secularized the classical model, denuding it of revolutionary teleology while maintaining its resolutely rational, distributive, and materialist explanatory frame. Whether inspired by Marx, by Weber, by postwar conflict theorists or by more recent emphases on individual and collective rational choice, the most influential macrosociologists over the last three decades have understood social movements as practical and coherent responses to the uneven social deprivations produced by institutional change. Oberschall put the case plainly in *Social Conflict and Social Movements*, the work that marked the beginning of the most recent secularization phase. Social systems are made up of "positions, strata, and classes," he wrote, which in turn are configured by "the combination of the division of labor with super- and subordination." Everything about social movements is said to follow from these apparently simple facts, more or less unchanged since the beginning of social time.

> Those who are favored have a vested interest in conserving and consolidating their existing share; those who are negatively privileged

seek to increase theirs, individually or collectively. Social conflict results from this clash of opposing interests.[13]

When this secularization of the classical model focused, by contrast, on more microlevel phenomena, it continued to ignore the moral and affective dimensions of collective action, emphasizing instead the constraints of interlocking networks and the availability of organization. Only such factors, it was asserted, could provide social actors with dependable and efficient means to mobilize the resources they needed to achieve success. Effective organizations and structured networks of personal relationships constitute an infrastructure that allows movements not only to gain power but the leverage eventually to shift the distribution of material things. Whether micro or macro, social movements must always be considered purely in the pragmatic key.

Just as classical theorists took their cue from the self-understandings of intellectuals who led nineteenth-century working-class social movements, these modern social scientists were inspired by what they took to be the outlooks of those who led the most conspicuous social movements of their own day.[14] "In the course of activism," McCarthy and Zald wrote in their paradigm-defining essay on resource mobilization, "leaders of movements" strategically create not only tactics but also "general principles," and both tactics and principles are defined with the aim of "overcoming hostile environments."[15] Movements are exercises in calculation; they aim at the "manufacture of discontent" in order to alter the "infrastructure of society." To be successful, these strategic impulses must have recourse to power. "Organizations" supply power in the proximate sense, for they allow movements to "implement . . . goals." But organizations can become powerful only if generalized resources exist, and it is these external conditions of action, conditions that are outside of subjective control, that determine organizational strength and, ultimately, movement success. Meaning and motivation are not the point; rather, "the amount of activity directed toward goal accomplishment is crudely a function of the resources controlled by an organization." If an organization is powerful enough, it can create a "social movement industry," and this cost-efficient form of production will greatly increase the chance of success.[16]

If a social movement for modern macrosociological thinkers resembles a complex maximizing machine, it is hardly surprising that violence and force are treated by them merely as forms of efficient means. Charles Tilly's early historical studies secularized the classical model in exactly this way.[17] He describes violence simply as an effective, more or less routine political resort. "Group violence," he and his coauthors suggest, "ordinarily grows out of collective actions which are not intrinsically violent—festivals, meetings, strikes, demonstrations."[18] Particularly in the nineteenth and early twentieth centuries, group violence was simply the most conspicuously efficient means of "pursuing a common set of interests." Deployment of violence depends on whether or not external social conditions make it cost-effective. Can social actors employ violence to increase the marginal utility of their political acts? Examining the "changing conditions for violent protest in western countries," Tilly describes violence in a mechanistic manner, as a natural outgrowth of urbanization and industrialization.[19] It was because violence was so mundane and rational, Tilly concludes, that "repression works." It follows logically that "the imposition of violent penalties—damage or seizure of persons or objects—on collective action diminishes its frequency and intensity."[20]

The revolutionary model in its secularized form can argue in no other way, despite the often striking incongruity that exists between this model and the contingent, courageous, utopian, and undulating pathway along which successful revolutions actually proceed. Theda Skocpol's effort to explain social revolutions followed exactly the same line.[21] Ideologies, solidarities, and specific regime types are irrelevant in a causal sense. Violent actions, material ends, and determined efforts to seize control of the levers of state coercion must be treated, in her view, as means to ends that are themselves merely means to other ends in turn. Social movement ideologies are not specifications of broader moral concerns but strategies for mobilizing masses. Michael Mann's "organizational materialism," while more pluralistic and antideterminist, offers an approach to social movements via networks of power that differ in result but not in kind.[22]

Given this general theoretical context, it hardly seems surprising that the most influential sociological investigations into the American Civil Rights movement have argued that it was the development of powerful organizations—"movements centers"[23]—that were responsible for the movement's successful mass mobilization. Subjective factors, such as leadership charisma[24] and or the masses' moral aspirations for a new life,[25] are understood by these secularizers of the classical model primarily in functional terms, as highly efficient means to mobilize organizational resources.[26] The permeation of the Civil Rights movement by Christian religious themes and rituals is described by leading social movement sociologists in terms of strategic effects, as having successfully motivated nonconformist political action by linking it with the higher, more legitimate, and more stable social status of church membership.[27] In this way, the passionate idealism and the moral emotivism that permeate powerful social movements are reduced to unconscious strategies; they are treated as cleverly employed devices that "get around" the free rider problem.[28] They are studied as material and nonmaterial commodities that organizations can manipulate to increase their power and support.

The hegemony of this social scientific secularization of the classical model is evident even in efforts to introduce a more cultural approach. Though such efforts ostensibly aim to offer an alternative to this hypostatization of rational choice, they seem often to have had the contrary effect, displacing the symbolic and the utopian with an overweening concern for the practical. Ann Swidler has suggested, for example, that social movements develop cultural innovations because the latter are less expensive than efforts to change the more fundamental role arrangements of institutions. It is because "most movements lack political power," she writes, that so "many social movements revolve around . . . cultural recodings." By turning to culture, movements "reshape the world . . . through redefining its terms, rather than rearranging its sanctions."[29] Though acknowledging the symbolic content of social movement demands, such arguments have the effect of severing the relation between social movement ideology and preexisting discursive traditions. It becomes easier to speak of solidarity as strategy than as shared patterns of representations.

> The cultures of social movements are shaped by the institutions the movements confront. Different regime types and different forms of repression generate different kinds of social movements with differing tactics and internal cultures. Dominant institutions shape the movement's deeper values.[30]

This instrumentalization of the cultural approach, its treatment of symbolic items and themes as a tool kit that organizations can take or leave at will, demonstrates the extraordinary influence that the classical model has continued to exercise over modern social science.[31]

The Social Science of Social Movements (2): Inverting the Classical Model

Yet while the secularization of the classical model dominates contemporary macrosociological approaches to social movements, the role of subjectivity has not gone entirely unrecognized. An increasingly influential network of American social and political scientists led by David Snow has discussed how the cognitive and moral framing of issues plays an important role in generating the discontent upon which social movements thrive.[32] Following in the wake of this challenge, William Gamson, an earlier proponent of resource mobilization, took up themes like collective identity and public discourse.[33] Klandermans has referred to consensus mobilization,[34] and Tarrow has linked radical social movements to collective action frames.[35]

These reactions against the instrumentalizing and decontextualizing limitations of the dominant approach to social movements draw directly and indirectly upon earlier theoretical traditions that were established in reaction to the European theories that informed the classical model. In Europe itself, of course, alternatives to the revolutionary model, alternatives that emphasized the emotional and irrational dimensions of group behavior, were at one time widely accepted. Gustave Le Bon's explorations of crowd behavior represented the most influential example, and it informed Sigmund Freud's studies of group psychology.[36] That these alternatives to the revolutionary model ultimately failed to inform the main paths of future social science can be attributed as much to their rejection of liberal and democratic ideology as to the more empirical objections that were raised. Their undiluted emphasis on the irrationality of subjective motives created an empirical blindness to the strategic and contingent, and this seemingly denied that social movements could be guided by more abstract universalistic and individualistic moral ideals.

While acknowledging and sometimes even focusing on such nonrational elements, some important figures in classical social theory continued to link their theorizing to the project of liberal democracy. Still, these writers rarely focused on mass movements for social change. When such movements did come into their purview, moreover, they were often discussed in a pejorative and pessimistic way. This was the case, for example, with Weber's insistence that democratic movements could succeed only in a plebiscitarian form that depended upon demagogic charisma.[37] Durkheim treated the democratic public meetings and mass movements he admired as analogues to primitive rituals, an equation that gave short shrift to rationality and contingency.[38] Tarde's studies of the interplay of fashion, conversation, newspapers, and public opinion moved in a very different direction. Yet, although his ideas about the microsociology of social movements represented a more liberal, democratic, and culturally oriented alternative to the revolutionary model, they were never incorporated into what later emerged as mainstream sociology.[39]

In the United States, the situation was decidedly different. American pragmatism developed republican and democratic theories about subjective interests and moral identity as alternatives both to the more pessimistic revolutionary model of instrumental motives and material interests and to market-driven theories. Even in the writings of such early American figures as Small[40] and Giddings,[41] individual action is stressed along with the institutional forms that mediate between local moral solidarities and national public spheres. Later thinkers continued these themes but emphasized individual creativity and responsiveness in a more explicitly pragmatic way. Though Park was more influenced by European irrationalist thought, he made certain to distinguish between crowds and publics.[42] Cooley emphasized subjective communication, "enlargement," and "animation,"[43] and Mead provided a systematic philosophy of symbolic understanding and gestural communication.[44]

As this pragmatic alternative to the revolutionary model matured, however, its relevance to macrosociology diminished. On the one hand, responding to the more cynical and more industrialized climate after World War I, Lippman[45] and Dewey[46] decried what they perceived as the decline of the public sphere, the increasingly instrumental manipulation of political life, and the erosion of moral solidarity. In the threatening and unstable climate of the 1930s and 1940s, they joined their European colleagues in the belief that these developments promoted mass society.[47] Alongside this deflation of confidence in moral institutions and collective movements, there emerged strands of pragmatic social science that withdrew from macrosocietal considerations altogether. Herbert Blumer declared, for example, that social movements "can be viewed as societies in miniature, and as such, represent the building up of organized and formalized collective behavior out of what was originally amorphous and undefined."[48]

Blumer's emergentist understanding of social movements, which treated "social organization," "values," and "institutional structure" as "residue[s]" of action instead of acknowledging that they constituted also its very foundations, marked a fundamental narrowing of the possibilities of the pragmatist tradition.[49] Historical and comparative considerations were jettisoned; theorizing about the differential effects of institutional spheres was abandoned. In the work of Turner and Killian,[50] the major American theorists of the post-Blumer "collective behavior" tradition, the attention to contingency illuminates important details about movement organization and construction, about how strain is transmuted into a sense of injustice, about the formation of issue-specific publics and the creation of countermovements and co-optative social control.[51] Yet the institutional and cultural references of these processes are treated as parameters, not as variables. For example, because Turner and Killian presuppose rather than explain the existence of constitutional guarantees for civil freedoms and, more broadly, the strength of a solidary civil community, they conceptualize the public as purely an emergent collectivity constituted by public discussion and debate alone.[52]

Though the disciplinary prestige and influence of this "Chicago school" approach to social movements virtually disappeared under the impact first of functionalism[53] and later resource mobilization theory, it reemerged in the recent interpretive strands of social movement theory I referred to above. Building upon the later Goffman's semiotically inspired theory of frame analysis, this work has been highly innovative. Snow and his collaborators, for example, deepen the kind of detailed reconstruction of interpretive practices that Turner and Killian had begun.[54] Rather than speaking simply of frame alignment as such, they develop a continuum of possible framing practices stretching from those that reinforce preexisting normative rules— frame "bridging" and "amplification"—to more ambitious and original practices, which they call frame "extension" and "transformation." Yet such arguments elaborate the subjective dimension of social movements in an overly microsociological way, treating the interpretive strategies of social movement actors as if they were generated in a purely practical, situationally oriented, here-and-now manner.[55]

Following Blumer's retreat into microsociology, interactional approaches to social movements constitute more an inversion of the instrumentalism and determinism of the classical model than a true alternative to it. In fact, even the most innovative advocates of framing accept the institutional language and macrosociological map that the resource mobilization model laid out. They perceive their contributions, in Klandemans's words, as pointing to subjective and communicative "mediating processes," not as revealing normative and institutional frameworks that exercise control over resource distribution itself.[56] Even as Tarrow has advocated a systematic opening to framing, he has continued to support Tilly's state-centered, power-oriented view of contemporary societies, suggesting that "ideological" and "organizational" approaches to social movements are more complementary than opposed. Interactionists present cultural processes, Tarrow suggests, simply as another kind of strategic resource, as "solutions to the problem that movements need to solve: that is, how to mount, coordinate and sustain collective action among participants who lack more conventional resources and explicit programmatic goals."[57]

The Social Science of Social Movements (3): Updating the Classical Model

The necessity for a historical-cum-theoretical alternative to the classical approach, one that includes cultural meanings and psychological identities but doesn't leave institutions behind, would seem to lead directly to new social movement theory. Originating in Europe but increasingly influential in the United States, this approach is open to contingency and to the subjectivities of actors while exhibiting, at the same time, a strong historical sensibility and institutional focus. Declaring that there has been a world-historical turn toward subjectivity, it connects this transformation in social movements to shifts in macrostructure from industrial to postindustrial society. Historical transformations in material production are said to have made the class-oriented revolutionary movements of an earlier day obsolete; their focus on material needs and their realistic epistemology are seen as having been displaced by new movements oriented to meaning and psychological identity.

It was Alain Touraine who first formulated this new perspective, but his student Alberto Melucci often explored its implications in a more straight-forward way.[58] Melucci's early rationale for the approach reveals its contin-uing emphasis on economic structures as the primary motor of social change. "What changes in the system of production," Melucci asks, "allow us to speak of new class conflicts?" The answer he gives very much follows the classical model. "The mechanisms of accumulation are no longer fed by the simple exploitation of labour force but rather by the manipulation of com-plex organizational systems, by control over information and over the pro-cesses and institutions of symbol-formation, and by intervention in personal relations." In short, there emerged in the 1960s and 1970s a new form of domination, for "the control and manipulation of the centers of technocratic domination are increasingly penetrating everyday life, encroaching upon the individual's possibility of disposing of his time, his space, and his relationships [and] of being recognized as an individual." It was to become more effective at overcoming such forces that social movements changed to a more sub-jective form.

> The movement for reappropriation which claims control over the resources produced by society is therefore carrying its fight into new territory. The personal and social identity of individuals is increasingly perceived as a product of social action. . . . Defense of the identity, continuity, and predictability of personal existence is beginning to constitute the substance of the new conflicts. . . . Personal identity . . . is the property which is now being claimed and defended.[59]

While drawing special attention to the subjective, affective, and cultural dimensions of contemporary movements, new social movement theory does not frame this as a theoretical criticism of the classical model. It suggests, to the contrary, that this revolutionary model was valid for its time and place. The need to shift theoretical and empirical attention responds to new, spe-cifically economic conditions. With new social movement theory, in other words, contemporary social scientists can embrace subjectivity without giving up an instrumental and materialistic approach to the conditions that foster social movements and ultimately determine their success. The mode of production has changed, new kinds of deprivations have emerged, and new social movements are the logical result. Postmaterialist, postindustrial, information-based societies are structural arrangements that have created new forms of stratification, new conflict groups, new patterns of domination, and new perceptions of the goals and interests at stake. It is because "the model of collective action under industrial capitalist conditions is now exhausted," Melucci believes, that new means are required to produce structural change.[60]

> Concrete concepts such as efficacy or success [can] now be considered unimportant. This is because conflict takes place principally on symbolic ground, by means of the challenging and upsetting of the dominant codes upon which social relationships are founded in high-density informational systems.[61]

While Touraine speaks pejoratively of "the revolutionary model," he argues that it is the historical "decline" of revolution as a mode of practice, not the weaknesses of the revolutionary model as a theory, that has allowed contemporary thinkers to give "the central role to social movements and not to institutional arrangements."[62] Though he criticizes the classical model for its myopic focus on institutions, and he sees new social movements as "very distant from the revolutionary model,"[63] it is a specific empirical shift he has in mind, not a general theoretical one. In fact, new social movement theorizing has served as a legitimating bridge between the classical model of social movements and contemporary social life. It has allowed the old theoretical structure to remain in place, changing only its empirical referents.

The perspective I am developing in this book suggests that more fundamental revision is needed. The enormous differences between earlier social movements and those of the present day do not concern the relative weight of material versus ideal factors. Even in early modernity, radical movements in western European and North American societies were oriented to cultural norms and personal identities.[64] Recent historians of the French Revolution—Furet and his collaborators in France and the new cultural historians in the United States—have strongly emphasized cultural factors in that prototypically eighteenth-century, preindustrial upheaval.[65] These studies make it abundantly clear that the classical model profoundly misunderstood the French Revolution, which was less the first ultrarational and thus "modern" movement for radical change than an extension of long-standing republican ideas to a new and unprecedented historical situation, one that encouraged the application to France of a more enlightened, democratic understanding of the French state. In a similar manner, recent studies of nineteenth-century working-class struggles demonstrate that the classical model distorted these early radical movements as well, ignoring the decisive effects of local and folk traditions, of egalitarian refractions of democratic and Christian ideas, and of class-oriented versions of the republican ideology that first crystallized in the quasi-civil societies of the Renaissance city-states.[66]

It is not enough, then, to update the classical model, any more than it is enough to secularize or invert it. Fundamental theoretical revisions must be made in the very understanding of the dynamics of social change, even in its most radical forms. In his concepts of industrial and postindustrial society, Touraine periodizes Western societies and their core values according to successive modes of production, an approach that gives shifting economic culture particular pride of place. Yet "industrial culture" hardly exhausts the influential value systems of nineteenth-century society. From the spheres of religion, family, gender, race, science, and politics there also emerged broad and powerful cultural orientations. Not all of these spheres triggered social movements as powerful as class conflicts, yet each of these spheres did produce massively influential standards of evaluation that created institutional conflicts and often had fundamental effects on social movements in turn. More importantly, however, Touraine neglects the possibility that there existed in the nineteenth century an overarching cultural framework of noneconomic ideas, an interlocking set of political-cum-legal-cum-social discourses that allowed contemporaries to speak of a democratic or civil society. To the degree that such a cultural system and its attendant normative institutions were operative, the universalizing moral and political discourse of the civil sphere permeated the more particular and differentiated spheres of nineteenth-century society, including the industrial, and provided a powerful and critical discursive reference for the social movements of that day.

Displacing the Classical Model: Rehistoricizing the Cultural and Institutional Context of Social Movements

Most of the so-called great revolutions—the English, French, Russian, and Chinese revolutions—were made against an *ancien régime*, traditional order in which government control depended upon habit, custom, charisma, and, in times of crisis, repression and force. In such societies, the masses of persons do not have access to mechanisms that can control the state, either through force of law, public opinion, or publicity, much less through electoral means. The alternative to state control via force is legitimate power, which occurs when obedience is voluntary rather than coerced, when rightness is attributed to power for moral reasons rather than for reasons of habituation or fear. This opportunity for will formation, to use Habermas's term,[67] can be provided only when a civil realm exists that, to some degree, is separated not only from the state but also from the other, noncivil spheres—of religion, science, economy, family, and primordial communities. As I have suggested in earlier chapters, such an independent civil sphere can exist only insofar as the privacy of individual interaction is protected, institutional independence is guaranteed for the creation of law, voting, and public opinion, and normative symbolic patterns make honesty, rationality, individual autonomy, cooperation, and impersonal trust the basic criteria for membership in the binding community that defines "society."

That such civil protections provide only formal rights and opportunities, not their substantive realization, by no means negates their historical importance. Only a handful of modernizing societies succeeded in transforming the structures and cultures of Old Regimes in such civil ways. In these societies, radical social movements demanding the redistribution of fundamental resources did not, in fact, depend primarily on material force; neither did they aim solely at mobilizing the most efficient means. Nor was the emergence, success, or failure of such movements simply a question of the availability of networks and organization. For the challenge was not merely instrumental. They were not mobilizing against state power as such. To the contrary, at least from the early nineteenth century, and often before, radical movements emerged in the midst of, and to some extent were triggered by, the partially realized structures and codes of civil societies, social systems in which civil solidarity was fragmented and institutional independence from noncivil spheres was crippled in systematic ways. In order to succeed, social movements in such societies had to orient themselves not only to the state but to such communicative institutions as the mass media, which could mobilize persuasion rather than force, and to such regulative institutions as law and franchise, which could enforce universalistic civil against oligarchic power.

Because social movements in civil societies have to orient themselves in these ways, the question of legitimacy comes to the fore. Vis-à-vis potential supporters, they must present themselves as typifying sacred values, as the bearers of social, national, and even primordial myth, as cultural innovators who can create new norms and new institutions that will allow resources to be channeled in different ways. The power of such movements depends in the first instance less on organizational command and networks of exchange than on subjective commitments of loyalty and solidarity. Such commitments can be produced only when social movements create and sustain new forms of meaning and more attractive forms of personal and group identity.

Social Movements as Translations of Civil Societies

Only after the cultural and institutional context of eighteenth- and nineteenth-century social movements has been rehistoricized in this way can a coherent alternative to the classical model be presented. I will develop this model more concretely in the case studies that take up the rest of Part III. In what remains of this chapter, I sketch the main lines of the alternative I have in mind.

In every relatively complex society there are differentiated spheres that possess distinctive value regimes, and many if not most social movements emerge and struggle within such spheres to gain justice in a discrete, pluralistic, and self-regulating way.[68] Nonetheless, the most significant idioms, codes, and narratives employed by strong social movements, whether new or old, progressive or reactionary, are independent of their structural position in particular spheres. Indeed, when one examines these tropes one can plainly see that it is their very distance from particular institutional arenas that allows them to offer social movements leverage, that creates the possibility of an escape from immediate institutional demands, that encourages the exercise of agency vis-à-vis institutional constraints that the very existence of a social movement implies.

These transcending, overarching symbolic frameworks refer to the imminent realization of a civil society, a sphere that is separated from other
institutional domains even though it may intrude upon them. If to become
a member of civil society is to participate in the broad and inclusive solidarity
that declares men and women to be brothers and sisters, then inclusion
within it creates binding obligations to institutionalize solidarity and to
increase participation in political decisions about the distribution of social
goods. The benefits of inclusion, in other words, are great. It is no wonder
that there are high hurdles to gain membership, and that every new claim
has been fiercely contested.

Social movements feed off the sense of a wider community. Though
they constitute only one particular group, they either (1) claim to "represent"
the wider society, its desires and best interests—as is the case, for example,
with an environmental or citizens action group—or (2) speak directly to
"society" on behalf of a particular interest, such as a trade union or an
African American or women's group. In order to succeed, social movements
cannot be seen simply as responding to actually existing problems, to the
strains generated by a particular kind of economy, state, geography, law,
family, racial or ethnic system, or scientific domain. Strong movements must
be seen, rather, as responding to problems in this or that sphere by persuasively communicating a broader vision of these problems to the society at
large. Before a social movement develops, whether it be a workers' movement or a women's liberation movement, few actors are aware that the
problems it makes reference to even exist, much less that they can be solved.
What legitimates this construction, indeed what motivates it in the first
place, is the latent reference to the obligations created by civil society.

When one examines the rhetoric of social movements, one sees that
images of "fair and open discussion," of "our day in court," of "society" in
the moral sense seem always to be there. Behind social movements there is
reference to a highly idealized community, one that demands that the universal become concrete. Demands for a concrete universal are made against
the backdrop of a utopian notion of community, according to which rational
actors spontaneously forge ties that are at once self-regulating, solidaristic,
and emancipatory, and are independent of market rewards, religious faith,
family love, state coercion, and scientific truth. Touraine refers to such a
self-regulating and self-constituting community as an imminent reality in
postindustrial society, and he points to its existence as evidence that there is

nothing left of "society" as such.[69] Surely, however, the very language of contemporary social movements suggests that this cannot the case. Self-constituting communities are not realities but rather regulative ideals, ones that have inspired the metalanguage of progressive and reactionary social movements in our time and in the past.

It is the existence of this regulating ideal, and its promised or partial realization in the communicative and regulative institutions at a particular time, that allows protests that emerge in one structural sector to be trans-ferred into the domain of civil society. Problems now concern society itself, not just a particular institution. It is for this reason that they have the potential of creating a "social crisis." Collective action, then, can be understood as a struggle for position vis-à-vis the categorical antipathies of civil life: a struggle to represent others in negative and polluted categories and to re-present oneself in terms of the sacred. To move from a problem in a particular sphere of society to a problem in society as such requires that the leaders of social movements exercise creativity and imagination. This might be called the translation problem, and it is where cultural creativity and political compe-tence both come equally into play.[70] Using an organization effectively means something very different from simply establishing membership rolls, hooking up telephone lines, and raising money. It means learning how to translate experiences from the particular to the general, from the mundane to the civil and back again. Movement intellectuals themselves often conceive their task in quite different terms. Viewing the movement's problems as real, they experience translation from particular to general as something that is always already there, rooted in the materiality of the problem as such. The ambition of these "movement intellectuals," however, is actually to reposition partic-ular demands, to shift them from particular institutions to a location inside of civil society itself. Insofar as they succeed, social movements strike up a conversation with society and draw their members' attention to a more generalized understanding of their cause.[71] When this happens, the social problem and group managing it enter firmly into the public life of the civil sphere.

Successful translation allows movements that emerge as protests in one structural sector—in a particular subsystem, sphere of justice, or segmented community—to be taken up by the civic public. It allows alliances to be welded, mass lines to be formed, and publicity to be made. Domination in a particular sphere is challenged not because it violates a particular institutional culture but because it is constructed as violating the collective representations of civil society. In this way, dominating powers are themselves represented as candidates for exclusion, in terms of the very anticivil categories they employ to justify the subordination of others. In the dynamics of this inverse stigmatizing process, archetypical narrative structures come forcefully into play, inflating the challengers and deflating the powers that be. Movement leaders and organizations, initially seen as lonely and downtrodden activists, are transformed into heroic figures embarking on a romantic quest. Melodrama paints the movement and its opponents in black and white, sentimentalizing the conflict in moralistic and often simplistic ways. Distancing devices like irony and comedy are employed to deflate further the importance of now polluted identities.[72]

Workers and industrial capitalists did not wage a century-long struggle simply over antagonistic material interests, even if one allows for the framing effects of industrial culture. Rather, economic strains were translated into the categories of the civil sphere.[73] Machine destruction, wage demands, strikes, and unionization were conducted in terms of "the rights of Englishmen."[74] The status of workers was upgraded, and they became emblematic of humanity. They now felt entitled to demand full access to such regulatory institutions as the law and the courts, which made critical decisions in the distribution of means. With the help of social movements, the "dark," "soot-covered" workers—the dirty, dependent, violent, and stubborn men who were said to work only with their hands and not with their brains—succeeded in reconstructing their selves and their group in less polluted and more sacred ways.[75] They often succeeded, in fact, in inverting the categorical identification of owners themselves, who were increasingly described as secretive in their motives, dependent in their relations, and authoritarian in their institutions.

Religious emancipation did not work in a much different way. From the late medieval period on, movements were launched against ecclesiastical hierarchy on the basis of the more inclusive rights that were defined as immanent in the civil sphere. In a similar manner, women in families gradually came to reject the identification of their selves with their patriarchy-defined domestic and mothering roles. Like ghettoized Jews, repressed Protestants, or exploited factory hands, women began to experience themselves as having dual membership, as not only members of a family structure in which loyalty, love, and deference were basic criteria but as members of civil society, which demanded criticism, respect, and equality. In the 1960s youth movements, students rejected subordination in schools, families, and work, arguing that neither parental nor knowledge-based authority justified the subordination and objectification they now seemed to experience in schools and homes. Forming their own communities of strong moral and emotional solidarity, they demanded that the larger society treat them in terms of their citizenship roles. Movements for consumer and patient rights can also be seen as expressions of dual membership, as boundary tensions between civil society and the economic and professional spheres create pressure for redefining where civil obligations stop and more specialized interests begin. Dominated ethnic and racial minorities use their dual membership to demand assimilation or to legitimate multiculturalism. For the physically or mentally disabled, for whom polluting categories like irrationality, insanity, and dependence often assume an essentialism that is expressed in physical form, the process of translation is extremely demanding and has only begun to redefine the meaning of these physical qualities. If one considers environmentalism, one can see how nature itself has been redefined. Once "red in tooth and claw," it is now a potentially rational and cooperative partner and being awarded full membership status in civil societies.

Social movements, then, can be seen as social devices that construct translations between the discourse of civil society and the institution-specific processes of a more particularist type. Social movements are practical and historical, yet at the same time they can succeed only if they can employ the civil metalanguage to relate these practical problems to the symbolic center of society and its utopian premises. We are very far from the classical model of social movements, with its realism and materialism and its exclusive concern with overturning the practical power of the state. Yet we are also quite a distance from new social movement theory, which describes symbolic arguments as defensive strategies responding to the isolation and vulnerability of actors confronted with new forms of technical domination.

Politics is a discursive struggle. It is about the distribution of leaders and followers, groups and institutions, not only in terms of material hierarchies but across highly structured symbolic sets. Power conflicts are not simply about who gets what and how much. They are about who will be what, and for how long. Representation is critical. In the interplay between communicative institutions and their public audiences, will a group be represented in terms of one set of symbolic categories rather than another? This is the critical question. Far from being only "symbolic," the answers to it are sometimes a matter of life and death. In the course of social conflicts, individuals, organizations, and large social groups may be transferred from one side of social classification to the other in rapid and often bewildering bursts of shifting historical time. Yet, no matter how new they seem, these categorizations are playing variations on the old and venerable codes of civil life.

CHAPTER 10

Gender and Civil Repair:
The Long and Winding Road
through M/otherhood

I N A PLURAL and differentiated society, there will always be multiple and fundamentally different spheres of culture and practice—markets, families, scientific institutions, and minority sexual, racial, and ethnic communities. Still, as long as a social system contains one putatively civil sphere—one imminently utopian world whose culture and institutions are proclaimed to be civil and democratic—this question can always be posed: What is the relation between the idealizing requisites and demands of the civil sphere and the noncivil spheres that surround it? Posing this question is what stimulates social movements. Answering it is what gives them success.

In the remainder of Part III, I bring this abstract proposition down to earth. In the present chapter, I focus on the boundary relations between family and civil sphere, and the movements it has generated for social change. The aim of this overview is to establish a *prima facie* case for viewing the women's movement in terms of civil society. In the chapters following, I develop a much more detailed discussion of civil society and race. Its aim is to show how our empirical understanding of the Civil Rights movement can, and should, be reconstructed in terms of the civil society theory I am developing here.

For several centuries, the patriarchal gender relations inside families were considered complementary to the utopian claims of the civil sphere, indeed as facilitating inputs to them. When revolutionary democratic expectations challenged this putative reciprocity, patriarchal structures inside the family and patriarchal translations inside the civil sphere itself pushed back, and a compromise formation resulted that made motherhood into a kind of auxiliary civil role. Only in the last century did the new social movements of feminism challenge this compromise. Identifying the restriction of women to family roles as a destructive intrusion of gender inequality into the civil sphere, these feminist movements have pushed, with increasing success, for gender equality and civil repair.

Justifying Gender Domination: Relations between the Intimate and Civil Spheres

It is illuminating of the contradictory nature of civil society and of the infernal, often maddening suppleness that marks its binary symbolic code that, when the egalitarian codes of democracy were first institutionalized on a national scale in seventeenth-century Europe, women could be conceived as having no place. As Blackstone, the first great codifier of democratic law put it, once women were married they ceased to have any civil existence at all: "Husband and wife are one person in law, that is, the very being or legal existence of the woman is suspended during the marriage, or at least is incorporated and consolidated into that of the husband; under whose wing, protection, and *cover*, she performs every thing; and is therefore called . . . a *feme covert* [*sic*]." The fictive social contracts that, according to early modern democratic theory, allowed democratic societies to move from the state of nature into the public world of civil society were represented as having been written by men. With women relegated to the private, invisible sphere of family life, protected first by fathers and later by husbands, what Carole Pateman called the "sexual contract" always accompanied the democratic one.

> In a world presented as conventional, contractual and universal, women's civil position is ascriptive, defined by the natural particularity of being women; patriarchal subordination is socially and legally upheld throughout civil life, in production and citizenship as well as

236

in the family. Thus to explore the subjection of women is also to explore the fraternity of men.[2]

The republican traditions that inspired the first great democratic revolutions were irredeemably masculinist. As Joan Landes pointed out, the very conception of public derived from the Latin *publicus*, meaning "under the influence of *pubes*, in the sense of 'adult men,' [the] 'male population.' "[3] In describing the early American Republic, Mary Ryan explains how female motives were constructed as antithetical to civil ones. "Republican ideology," she writes, "held that the female sex embodied those uncurbed human passions that inevitably subverted the self-control and rationality required of citizens."[4] Under this semantic but also very political distortion, civil wisdom is contrasted with domestic love, and female exclusion is represented as being compelled by the necessity to protect against the enslavement of men. These associations are manifest, for example, in an after-dinner "toast to the ladies" that a male wit offered at a civic occasion in New Orleans, circa 1825: "The fair sex—Excluded by necessity from participation in our labours: we profess equality, [but] the presence of woman would make us slaves, and convert the temple of wisdom into that of love."[5]

However, despite its strangeness and even repugnance to contemporary sensibilities, there is not an objective contradiction between the promises of a democratic society and the subordination and exclusion of women from its civil sphere. It is not something that, in some extrahistorical sense, inherently defies the norms of a plural and differentiated society. To believe this would engage the kind of naturalistic approach to contradiction taken up by the later Marx. Between the belief that there are irredeemable differences between men and women, and the conviction that such differences *unfairly* disqualify women from participating in the civil sphere, there is no more *factual* contradiction than between capitalist market relations and the democratic promises of civil society. It is a matter of interpretation; it depends on context.

Women's Difference as Facilitating Input

In the nineteenth century there were halting and ambiguous advances in the institutionalization of civil society in such domains as class, religion, and to a lesser but still real degree, race. Throughout this time, however, female subordination in the family sphere seemed perfectly compatible with civil equality. Indeed, this subordination was seen as fundamentally contributing to the autonomy and vitality of civil society.

This understanding of boundary relations, not only accepted but actively promoted by women as well as by men, was crystallized by what feminist historians have called the "ideology of separate spheres." As the historian Jeanne Boydston has put it, "the doctrine of gender spheres expressed a worldview in which both the orderliness of daily social relations and the larger organization of society derived from and depended on the preservation of an all-encompassing gender division of labor."[6] In terms of the theoretical model I am developing here, separate sphere ideology legitimated the antidemocratic exclusion of women by constructing them in terms of the negative categories of civil discourse. In 1825, a widely read periodical, *Ladies Museum*, applied this binary code to the men and women of its day.

> Man is strong—woman is beautiful. Man is daring and confident— woman is diffident and unassuming. Man is great in action—woman in suffering. Man shines abroad—woman at home. Man talks to convince—woman to persuade and please. Man has a rugged heart— woman a soft and tender one. Man prevents misery—woman relieves it. Man has science—woman taste. Man has judgment—woman sensibility. Man is a being of justice—woman of mercy.[7]

This binary rhetoric employs gender to specify the general categories of civil discourse. Such engendering provided a pragmatically available *parole* (speech) to the more structural *langue* (language), one that accommodated to functional contradictions of the societies of the day. On the one hand, feminine qualities were conceived as allowing women to manage the intimate sphere, which was vital not so much for the reproduction of labor power as for the reproduction of democratic virtue. These very same characteristics, however, disqualified women from participating in the body politic. John Keane has explained how women's noncivil qualities were understood as resulting from her centrality in the intimate sphere.

> Within this [intimate] sphere, women's functions of child-bearing, child-rearing and maintaining the household are deemed to corre-

spond to their unreason, disorderliness and "closeness" to nature. Women and the domestic sphere [were] viewed as inferior to the male-dominated "public" world of civil society and its culture, property, social power, reason and freedom.[8]

Women's Difference as Destructive Intrusion

Despite this prevailing, anti-inclusive model of facilitating input, the first wave of democratic revolutions had the effect of drawing women along with men into its effervescent wake. The result was a growing suspicion, among some parties, that women may not be so different from men after all. In America, Linda Kerber observes, "The experience of war had given words like independence and self-reliance personal as well as political overtones."

> As the song played at Yorktown had it, the world could turn upside down: the rich could quickly become poor, wives might suddenly have to manage the family economy, women might even shoulder a gun. Revolutionary experience taught that it was useful to be prepared for a wide range of unusual possibilities; political theory taught that republics rested on the virtue and intelligence of their citizens.[9]

The American Revolution had markedly increased the authority and attraction of the liberating side of civil discourse, which intensified efforts to further institutionalize it. For many women, subordination in the separate sphere of the family began to seem an abomination, a destructive intrusion into the normative and institutional core of the newly democratic nation. In one early post-Revolutionary proclamation, Judith Sargent Murray decried the idea that girls should be trained in fashion, flirtation, and charm, with the aim of procuring a successful marriage. She insisted, instead, on the socialization of girls to civil, not specifically feminine, values: "Independence should be placed within their grasp [and] the Sex should be taught to depend on their own efforts, for the procurement of an establishment in life."[10]

But if the dependence of female difference were criticized, then male superiority risked being reframed as a potential threat to the civil sphere.

The argument that began to emerge was not that men were unloving or uncaring—such criticisms would have evoked not civil standards but the values of the noncivil family sphere. Rather, the criticism launched by post-Revolutionary American women drew directly upon the constructions of antidemocratic repression against which Americans had fought the Revolutionary War. When Abigail Adams, wife of the second president, suggested that women ought to have the right to participate in the new system of government, she offered as the reason that "all men would be tyrants if they could."[11] In the late twentieth century, feminist criticism would employ the term "patriarchy," but the civil reference of the category was much the same: the dependent and authoritarian relations that might well prevail between men and women inside the family should not be allowed to intrude upon the relations among men and women in the civil sphere. Now viewed as a destructive intrusion rather than facilitating input, such relations were deemed not only to be noncivil but anticivil, a characterization that implied they should perhaps no longer be allowed even within the intimate sphere itself. When nineteenth-century temperance activists pilloried men for drunkenness, licentiousness, and violence against their children and wives, it was just such civil criteria that were being critically deployed.

At the conclusion of history's first national women's congress, the Seneca Falls Women's Rights Convention in 1848, one hundred persons signed a "Declaration of Sentiments" attacking the threat to civil ideals posed by the ideology and practice of separate spheres and by the underlying principle of innate male-female difference. Asserting that "all men and women are created equal," the document insisted, in a less metaphorical than literal extension of the *Declaration of Independence*, that both sexes were "invested by their creator with the same capabilities." By violating such a civil stipulation, the traditional relations between men and women were condemned as undemocratic, and the polluting language of civil society applied.

> The history of mankind is a history of repeated injuries and usurpations on the part of man toward woman, having in direct object the establishment of an absolute tyranny over her. . . . He has compelled her to submit to laws. . . . He has oppressed her on all sides. . . . He has made her . . . civilly dead. . . . He has taken from her all right in property. . . . He has made her, morally, an irresponsible

being [and] she is compelled to promise obedience. . . . He has created a false public sentiment by giving to the world a different code of morals for men and women, by which moral delinquencies which exclude women from society, are not only tolerated, but [encouraged] to make her willing to lead a dependent and abject life.[12]

"We are a nation and not a mere confederacy," as one suffragist put the matter in 1880. "The theory of a masculine head to rule the family, the church, or the State is contrary to republican principles and the fruitful source of rebellion."[13]

Gender Universalism and Civil Repair

If male superiority and tyranny in the domestic sphere were considered destructive intrusions into the civil one, it followed that there must be a project of civil repair. In the course of the second Great Awakening, women achieved unprecedented equality in the religious sphere, and they also played powerful roles in the growing abolitionist movement. As the nineteenth century progressed, there were, in fact, increasing demands that women be given a civil status appropriate to their capacities. These took the form of demands for education equal to that which men received, equality to men before the law, and, eventually, the right to vote. Activists viewed these policies as steps to deepen the institutionalization of the liberating discourse of civil society. At the Women's Centennial Agenda, the counterconvention to the American Centennial in 1876, the feminist declaration *avant la lettre* charged that "women's degraded, helpless position is the weak point in our institutions today."[14]

To avoid any suggestion of American exceptionalism, and to emphasize the systemic nature of the processes I am describing here, it seems important to note that the other great revolutionary effort to institutionalize civil principles, the French Revolution, initially produced the same movement from separate sphere arguments to universalistic demands for women's rights. In the land of the Enlightenment, it is hardly surprising that the argument over women's civil capacity, which centered on difference versus universality, would focus more attention on the possession of reason. In his essay "On the Admission of Women to the Rights of Citizenship," the liberal Physi-

SOCIAL MOVEMENTS IN THE CIVIL SPHERE

ocrat, the Marquis de Condorcet, emphatically made the link between reason and civic participation central to his argument for the inclusion of women.

> Now the rights of men result simply from the fact that they are sentient beings, capable of acquiring moral ideas and of reasoning concerning those ideas. Women, having these same qualities, must necessarily possess equal rights. Either no individual of the human species has any true rights, or all have the same. And he or she who votes against the rights of another, of whatever religion, color, or sex, has thereby abjured his own.[15]

Rather than viewing female-specific social activities as indicating fundamental difference, and thus as constituting grounds for confinement to a separate sphere, Condorcet dismissed "motherhood and 'other passing indispositions' " as indicating nothing at all about women's civil capacities.[16]

Stimulated by the Revolutionary currents, influential and radical women activists emphasized human universality and the shared capacities that men and women possessed. "The nature of reason must be the same in all," Mary Wollstonecraft declared in her pathbreaking book, *Vindication of the Rights of Woman*. On this basis, Wollstonecraft declared traditional female subordination a threat to the civil values of the Revolution. Addressing herself to the all-male Constituent Assembly, she asked "whether, when men contend for their freedom, and to be allowed to judge for themselves respecting their own happiness, it be not inconsistent and unjust to subjugate women, even though you firmly believe that you are acting in the manner best calculated to promote their happiness?" Such paternalism, she argued, must be criticized as a destructive intrusion into the realm of revolutionary democracy— as long as it was agreed that the intellectual and moral capacities of women are constructed in an equally civil way. "Who made man the exclusive judge," Wollstonecraft demands, "if woman partake with him the gift of reason?"[17]

Assuming that civil, not separate-sphere, standards must apply to male-female relations, such activists attacked male paternalism as uncivil, warning that it presented a destructive intrusion into democratic life. As Wollstonecraft observed:

If women are to be excluded without having a voice, from a participation of the natural rights of mankind, prove first, to ward off the
charge of injustice and inconsistency, that they want reason—else
this flaw in your NEW CONSTITUTION [sic] will ever shew that
man must, in some shape, act like a tyrant, and tyranny, in whatever
part of society it rears its brazen front, will ever undermine morality.[18]

In 1790, Etta Palm, another leading revolutionary activist, similarly asserted that civil values must reconstruct the intimate sphere. In a scathing
speech, she told her male revolutionary confreres, "we are your companions
and not your slaves."[19] Once again, traditional forms of maleness were
reframed as the signifieds of anticivil signifiers—as indicating the failure of
men to exercise rationality, self-control, and honesty. In Wollstonecraft's
words, "men are certainly more under the influence of their appetites than
women; and their appetites are depraved by unbridled indulgence and the
fastidious contrivances of satiety."[20]

The Compromise Formation of Public M/otherhood

It was such confrontations as these that laid the basis for the "feminist"
movement to displace the "woman" movement in the early years of the
twentieth century.[21] That it would take more than a hundred years for such
an assertive female movement to build upon the earliest expressions of
gender universalism demonstrates that, in the early phases of the institutionalization of civil society, most men and women were not persuaded by
representations that female subordination constituted a destructive intrusion
to democracy, much less by the suggestions for its civil repair. Abstract
models of boundary relations are one thing; the messy reality of actual
processes are another. In concrete historical terms, civil repair is never a
linear process, as feminist historians, social scientists, and philosophers have
made increasingly clear, though in thinking about what to make of this
unevenness they have had differing things to say.

In the United States, as Kerber attests, postrevolutionary efforts to apply
civil democratic codes to women often met fierce resistance. "To accept an
openly acknowledged role for women in the public sector," she writes, "was

to invite extraordinary hostility and ridicule."[22] The ideology of natural difference between the sexes and the practice of separate spheres were simply too deeply entrenched. Arguments about female intellectual power and political autonomy were analogically linked to masculine manners. Typical of such responses was a newspaper letter written by a Marylander calling himself "Philanthropos" in 1790 that warned against any overly literal interpretations of the phrase, "All mankind are born equal." Philanthropos was concerned with the separation of spheres. If equality were "taken in too extensive a sense," he argued, "it might tend to destroy those degrees of subordination which nature seems to point out," most particularly the subordination of women to men. Philanthropos suggested an alternative that proved prophetic, pointing the way to a compromise between maintaining separate spheres and furthering civil repair. "However flattering the path of glory and ambition may be," he declared, "a woman will have more commendation in being the mother of heroes, than in setting up, Amazon-like, for a heroine herself."[23]

|What quickly became apparent, in the face of the concerted opposition to gender universalization, was that women would be allowed to enter the public realm only if they remained tethered to their subordinate status and separate sphere. Protected by the ideology of what Kerber called "the Republican Mother," men and women alike justified partial participation in public life on the basis that it would allow women to become better—more virtuous and more democratic—mothers to their male children and to provide more soothing emollients to their already, or at least potentially, civilly virtuous husbands.| Making use of what we would today call gender essentialism, women thus could claim control over a special expertise that allowed them to influence certain domains of public affairs. But the very mothering qualities that legitimated some degree of female public participation confirmed their fundamental difference from men. Republican motherhood was, in fact, merely another kind of "otherhood." What I will call public "m/otherhood" simply put a positive spin on the very anticivil qualities that excluded women from full participation in civil society.

The new role of Republican M/otherhood can be seen as what Robert Bellah once referred to, following Freud, as a "compromise formation," one that responded to a classic situation of role strain.[24] On the one hand, the increasingly strained boundary relations between familial and civil spheres could not be resolved by civic repair; on the other hand, women were unwilling to return entirely to the confines of their traditionally assigned place. The result was the creation of a new role, whose compromise character was revealed by the manner in which it persistently combined "not only" with "but also."

The concept [of Republican Mother] defended education for women not only for their autonomy and self-realization but also so that they could be better wives and better mothers for the next generation of virtuous republican citizens—especially sons.[25]

According to its advocates, the role of Republican M/other would provide sorely needed facilitating inputs to the American civil sphere. As one (male) newspaper editor put it in 1844, the family is "the foundation of public morality and intelligence."[26] Another wrote, "if all is right in the private domain, we need not be concerned for the public."[27] Authority for this civil contribution came from the very emphasis on inherent difference that excluded women from more assertive, and genuinely civil, participation. Public m/otherhood allowed some female activity to be viewed as a facilitating input to civil society, but it stalemated women's efforts to gain actual incorporation into it, as what Mary Ryan calls "the sorry story of a Madam Ranke" suggests. In 1857, in what Ryan describes as a "stalemated attempt to desegregate the male public," Madam Ranke tried to address a meeting of unemployed men who were camped in New York City's Thompkins Square.

When Madam Ranke took the public podium, she was greeted by cries like, "Don't listen to a woman," or alternatively, "Damn it, don't interrupt a woman." The female voice was neither easily blended nor distinctly heard in the embattled sectors of the male public sphere, and Madam Ranke was escorted from the square under a protective escort of women.[28]

Even as Kerber salutes the Republican Mother as a "revolutionary invention," she points, equally emphatically, to its "deeply ambivalent" status. Though sanctioning participation, the new role ensured the continuity of women's uncivil status.

Republican Motherhood legitimized only a minimum of political sophistication and interest. . . . Women were expected to be content to perform their narrow political role permanently and were not expected to wish for fuller participation. Just as planters claimed that democracy in the antebellum South rested on the economic base of slavery, so egalitarian society was said to rest on the moral basis of deference among a class of people—women—who would devote their efforts to service by raising sons and disciplining husbands.[29]

Social and cultural barriers to the civil repair of gender relations generated what Landes calls a "paradoxical" situation in France as well.[30] Even Mary Wollstonecraft found it "difficult to deny the central presumption of her age, that women possess natures different from men."[31] Despite her insistence on the principle of women's rationality, this great proto-feminist believed that most women actually were less rational in practice. Once she abandoned the semantic anchor in civil discourse, which asserted women's putative rationality, it became difficult for Wollstonecraft enthusiastically to recommend the full civil inclusion of women.

> Novels, music, poetry, and gallantry, all tend to make women the creatures of sensation. . . . This overstretched sensibility naturally relaxes the other powers of the mind, and prevents intellect from attaining that sovereignty which it ought to attain to render a rational creature useful to others, and content with its own station: for the exercise of the understanding, as life advanced, is the only method pointed out by nature to calm the passions.[32]

If female activists were themselves so uncertain about the civil qualities of women, French men were that much more so. Such widespread lack of confidence allowed free reign, in France as in America, to the compromise formation of Republican M/otherhood. Women did indeed play active, and at times vitally significant, public roles during the early Revolutionary period. The legendary march of women to Versailles in October 1789, for example, represented a strategically significant moment of women's public participation. Yet, even here, Landes is careful to inform us, the Parisian women only "asserted their right *as women* to participate in public affairs," not their rights as potential citizens.[33] Their aim was to call upon the self-exiled king and to bring him back to Paris.

> They desired to see the king [back] at Paris, where he would find wise women to give him good counsel. They referred to him as "poor man," "dear man," "good papa." The marchers appealed to the king in a paternalist discourse, yet they cried out for "bread and arms."[34]

As a contemporary feminist, Landes pointedly criticizes the emergence of this new kind of otherhood role from the perspective of the civil sphere: "[It] functioned to preserve difference and hence guarantee sexual inequality," despite its connection "to a universalist, egalitarian protest."[35]

> As citizens, women would be educated beyond their limited horizons and wholly self-oriented concerns in order to embrace the larger polity, but ultimately in a *passive* not an active manner. . . . The potential for providing women with a route into the public sphere by way of republican motherhood was undermined by the claims of nature. . . . If women's service to the community was viewed as a function of her mothering role, the most likely consequence was to offer women political representation in a mediated fashion.[36]

In the hothouse atmosphere of revolutionary France, this compromise formation proved much less viable, and ultimately less productive, than it proved to be in the more stable, less radical, American scene. By 1791, the Committee of General Security had recommended that women's rights to active public participation be entirely eliminated. The cultural framing for this recommendation highlighted the uncivil qualities of public behavior that were held to be the inevitable product of women's difference. Because their "moral education is almost nil" and because they are "less enlightened concerning principles," the committee's representative told the Convention, "women's associations seem dangerous."

> Their presence in popular societies, therefore, would give an active role in government to people more exposed to error and seduction.

Let us add that women are disposed by their organization to an over-excitation which would be deadly in public affairs and that interests of state would soon be sacrificed to everything which ardor in passions can generate. . . . Delivered over to the heat of public debate, they would teach their children not love of country but hatred and suspicions.[37]

In the United States, the contradictory effects of the compromise formation were far less dramatic, but they were equally fateful and far-reaching. In fact, as feminist historians have long noted, by framing a limited degree of female participation as a facilitating input to the public sphere, Republican M/otherhood provided legitimation for women to make their sphere less hermetically separate than ever before. Yet, as many contemporary feminists also have insisted on pointing out, the nineteenth-century American women who moved into the public sphere justified their participation not by proclaiming their equal civil competence but by utilizing notions of innate difference and the ideology of separate spheres. One leading temperance activist, Francis Willard, hailed what she called the "omnipotent-weakness which is the incommunicable characteristic of womanhood" to justify women's rights to publicly preach.[38] In the 1870s, women made use of what Ryan calls "an arsenal of weapons and an array of avenues through which to influence public policy." But Ryan immediately adds the following qualification:

> In keeping with the Victorian moral code, [these] female sex reformers used the stereotype of pure womanhood as a point of personal privilege in the matter of prostitution legislation. . . . The politics of prostitution, like female moral reform, was but one rather prickly way to generate gender identity. It placed the woman citizen in a defensive position and identified her by her sexual and reproductive biology. To contemporary feminists, this is an invitation to essentialism and a narrow base on which to mount gender politics.[39]

This public m/otherhood role, I would suggest, actually allowed every subsequent phase of female participation to be justified, and narrated, in an anticivil way. According to the editors of the leading contemporary anthology of feminist history:

At an ever-accelerating pace between 1820 and 1880 . . . women expanded [the] role [of Republican Motherhood] into what might be called "Reformist Motherhood." Instead of influencing the public domain indirectly through the lives of their sons, women began to extend their role as nurturer and teacher of morals from the domestic sphere into the public sphere through church, missionary, and moral reform groups. Women sought to make the world conform more strictly to values taught in the home—sexual responsibility and restraint for men as well as women, self-discipline for those who used strong drink. [Then,] between 1880 and 1920 a new role developed that might be called "Political Motherhood." . . . "Motherhood" was becoming less a biological fact—birthing and nurturing children—and more a political role with ideological dimensions.[40]

During the industrial revolution of the late nineteenth century, another historian has recently observed, Americans "were fascinated by the power and complexity of machines," and "in political debate they used machines as a metaphor for both the electoral system and for parities."[41] Yet the ideology of separate spheres remained alive and well. Its gendered metaphors about civil and uncivil society could be readily adapted to the new technological situation.

Party structures found their ideal opposite in the gentle domesticity attributed to women. Like their English Victorian counterparts, leaders of American opinion hailed the home as "woman's sphere," a place where wives and mothers conserved family bonds and religious devotion. Both men and women of the era described women as "angels of the home." To many, women's selflessness and purity were the very qualities that unfitted them for politics. Politics, however, could not function without the virtues women represented. The institutions of political life might resemble machines, but each party fought for deeply held values. At a fundamental level, elections were disputes about faith and family order. . . . In 1886, New York politician John Boyle O'Reilly expressed his abhorrence at the idea of woman suffrage. "It would be no more deplorable," he declared in a public letter, "to see an angel harnessed to a machine than to see a woman voting politically."[42]

A sociological student of this period, Eyal Rabinovitch, shows how women's public demands for "shelter and protection" for abused women rested on claims that this victimization prevented them from living up to the ideal of true womanhood.[43] Such demands had the paradoxical effect, in other words, of confirming women's "submissive" and "helpless" nature.[44] Rabinovitch writes that even publicly active "women could not directly speak unto men with discursive authority," citing evidence that activist women used such tactics as public prayer, weeping, and silent presence to compel men to alter their public behavior.[45] "Republican mothers . . . went to great lengths to reject any association with civil independence or autonomy," Rabinovitch concludes, "even as they demanded greater respect and recognition as public actors in civic politics." Indeed, women reformers repeatedly associated their own intentions with "sympathy, sentiment, and passion at the expense of autonomy and civic independence."[46]

Public Stage and Civil Sphere

How could this be? How could a clearly particularistic and anticivil understanding of women also function as the basis for launching their public careers? How could unprecedented female public activism have the effect of underscoring, rather than undermining, the second-class position of women? How could this new intervention of women into public affairs actually function to block the civic repair of female subordination?[47]

This paradox certainly underscores the importance of distinguishing between publicness and civil democracy. In the Habermasian tradition most especially, these concepts are blurred, though the confusion widely permeates democratic theory.[48] In terms of the perspective I develop in this book, by contrast, publicness should be seen more in dramaturgical terms. Upon the public stage, performances are projected to audiences of citizens. These performances are diverse, dramatizing a kaleidoscope of ethical positions and political programs. Racists, misogynists, homophobes, and militarists all make their cases. So do movements and ideologies of a more expansive and inclusive kind. During the nineteenth century, in fact, m/otherhood was often publicly employed to legitimate equally particularistic but much less palatable ideological claims. American historians have continually observed how the "distorted . . . manipulation of gender symbolism" was used "to garnish the increasingly stark racial and class partitions of the public."

During the [civil] war women were an honored presence, and female symbols were prolifically displayed amid the pageantry of sectional solidarity. When white dominance was reported in the South, it was portrayed as an act of public purification, a defense of the honor of the ladies. Meanwhile, antiwar Democrats in the North raised cheers to white ladies. Both labor and capital draped their interests in female symbols. The parades of the Workingmen's Party of California mounted wives and daughters in carriages . . . in support of their demand for a family wage, and a countersymbol to Chinese immigration, which they pictured as a flood of bachelors and prostitutes. . . . The upper-class opponents of the Tweed Ring in New York characterized the rapacious city politicians as simian featured Irishmen preying on a demure Miss Liberty.[49]

When Union victory brought black freedom, Democrats around the United States reacted with a race-based appeal for white women's protection, warning of the sexual threat allegedly posed by black freedmen. From the secession movement of the 1850s to the disfranchisement campaigns of the 1890s, southern Democrats drew a strong connection between expansions of federal authority and the sexual violation of white women. Both were encroachments on the patriarchal home; rape and seduction served as consistent metaphors for the perils of excessive government force.[50]

The difference between civil and public was implicitly understood by the major historical actors of the day. Mrs. J. B. Gilfillan was president of the Minnesota Association Opposed to Woman Suffrage. Representing the powerful if ultimately unsuccessful "anti" movement, Gilfillan dramatically evoked difference as the reason to oppose women's voting rights. She did so, however, by emphatically supporting women's public role.

Anti-Suffragists are opposed to women in political life, opposed to women in politics. This is often interpreted to mean opposition to women in public life, which is a profound mistake. We believe in women in all the usual phases of public life, except political life. Wherever woman's influence, counsel or work is needed by the community, there you will find her, so far with little thought of political beliefs. . . . The pedestals they are said to stand upon move them into all the demands of the community.[51]

Those who supported women's right to vote polluted such female "antis" in the most vociferously anticivil terms. Anna Howard Shaw, president of the National American Woman Suffrage Association from 1904 to 1915, contemptuously compared them to "vultures looking for carrion," who "revel in the dark and seamy side of human nature" and "are always emphasizing the small and mean in women."[52] Questioning their sincerity and autonomy, Shaw described the antis as dependent, as mere puppets of powerful male forces, human shields for "liquor interests, food-dopers, child-labor exploiters, white slavers and political bosses." According to her, it was because the antis were selfish, cynical, and irrational, and thus incapable of honest civil behavior—not because of their sincere loyalty to the values of motherhood—that they emphasized the inherent difference of women from men and opposed the voting right.

Its members were mainly well-to-do, carefully protected, and entertained the feeling of distrust of the people usual in their economic class. Their speeches indicated at times an anxious disturbance of the mind lest the privileges they enjoyed might be lost in the rights to be gained. . . . Their uniform arguments were that the majority of women did not want to the vote, therefore none should have it; that "woman's place was in the home," and that women were incompetent to vote.[53]

It is revealing of the influence of the civil sphere that leaders of the "anti" side felt compelled to justify their exclusionary and essentialist arguments, not only by citing separate-sphere arguments about family and children, but also by relating them positively to more universalist claims. When Mrs. Henry Preston (Sarah C.) White addressed the Judiciary Committee of the U.S. House of Representatives in 1914, she defended the antis not as faithful mothers and loyal wives but as "disinterested, public-spirited citizens who give their time and service to questions of public service without the hope of political reward or preference."[54] In fact, alongside their well-publicized commitments to husband, hearth, and home, the antis consistently framed their opposition to voting rights, as Manuela Thurner has shown, as an antidote to the dangers of partisanship. Women would remain more impartial and universalistic, the argument went, if they could stand "apart from and beyond party politics."[55] That women were different from men actually allowed them to keep the dangers of public life at bay. The prominent antisuffragist Mrs. Barclay Hazard offered this justification in her address to the New York State Federation of Women's Clubs in 1907.

> We must accept partisanship, political trickery and office-seeking as necessary evils inseparable from modern conditions, and the question arises what can be done to palliate the situation. To our minds, the solution has been found by the entrance of women into public life. Standing in an absolutely independent position, freed from all party affiliations, untrammeled by any political obligations, the intelligent, self-sacrificing women of to-day are serving the State (though many of them hardly realize it) as a third party whose disinterestedness none can doubt.[56]

Universalism versus Difference: Feminist Fortunes in the Twentieth Century

In her pathbreaking synthetic work, *The Grounding of Modern Feminism*, Nancy Cott recounts the state of affairs for American women at the beginning of the twentieth century. The woman movement of the preceding century had, indeed, brought women into the inlets, nooks, and crannies of public life. However, because these movements had been conducted under the framework of m/otherhood, "the effort to find release from the 'family claim,' which Jane Addams had eloquently described in the 1880s, was being painfully repeated decade after decade."[57]

> Despite the economic changes that had brought women into the paid labor force, despite the improving rates of women's entry into higher education and the professions, and despite the collective and political strengths women had shown through voluntary organiza-

tions, the vast majority of the population understood women not as existential subjects, but as dutiful daughters, wives, and mothers.[58]

By the 1910s, girls and women "swarmed" into what had once safely been male-only arenas—"the street, the factory, store, office, even the barbershop." Yet the interpretive understanding of these places continued to be framed according to the ideology of separate spheres, remaining "terrain culturally understood as male."[59] The boundary relations between the intimate and civil spheres, in other words, was still conceptualized in terms of "facilitating input," even as the behavioral walls separating these spheres were being challenged on the ground. Changing boundary relations required breaking this sense of complementarity. Male-female relations in the intimate sphere would have to be framed as destructive intrusions into the civil sphere. Only such reconceptualization would trigger the project of civil repair.

The time was ripe for the social movement of women to develop a new ideology. This new perspective was feminism, which from the perspective I am developing here can be understood as the ideology of gender's civil repair. Steering sharply away from the shoals of difference and otherhood, "feminists offered," according to Cott, "no sure definition of who woman was."[60] What they sought, rather, was "to end the classification woman" as such. The first explicitly feminist mass meetings took place in New York City in February 1914 at the People's Institute of the Cooper Union. The handbill publicizing the meetings made the following announcement: "Subject: BREAKING INTO THE HUMAN RACE."[61]

With feminism in full gear, and the suffrage amendment passed in 1920, this universalizing ethic led to the fight for an Equal Rights Amendment, the first ERA. Feminists viewed the ERA as a "civic innovation" that would give legal teeth to gender repair. Building on the Nineteenth Amendment and an emerging consciousness of women's equality with men, a constitutional mandate for equality in every aspect of women's lives would have the potential to restructure noncivil spheres in a dramatic way. The noncivil sphere of most urgent concern was the economic. "By the 1910s," Cott writes, "suffragists linked political and economic rights, and connected the vote with economic leverage." Reformers "emphasized that women, as human individuals no less than men, had the right and need to use their talents to serve society and themselves and to gain fair compensation."[62] As members of the civil sphere, women workers shared a common human status with male workers, and it was this common humanity that would provide leverage for repairing gender-triggered economic inequality.

This early effort at civil repair not only failed miserably in the political arena but had the cultural effect of polarizing publicly active women and creating a fateful backlash against feminism. As Cott sees it, the demand for an ERA deepened the antagonism between the traditional defenders of women's difference from men and the more radical arguments for gender universalism. After the success of suffragism and the advent of the category feminism, the compromise formation of public m/otherhood could no longer camouflage the contradictions between civil and intimate spheres. Difference and equality, according to Cott, now "were seen as competing, even mutually exclusive, alternatives." The result was that "the ERA battle of the 1920s seared into memory the fact of warring outlooks among women."[63]

The ERA's purpose was to allow women to have the same opportunities and situations as men. It was triggered by the conviction that women could not continue to emphasize their differences from men without the adverse consequence, usually unintended and often unwished for, of reinforcing civil inequality. The problem was that, while antidifference arguments were becoming widely accepted among America's cultural and political avant-guard, they remained "extraordinarily iconoclastic" among America's mainstream.[64] Difference entered the ERA debate in the pivotal argument over the wisdom of abolishing sex-based protective legislation. Opponents of ERA became outspoken advocates of such protection, "echo[ing] customary public opinion in proposing that motherhood and wage-earning should be mutually exclusive."[65] The outcry showed the vast distance between arguments for public m/otherhood and arguments for genuine civil equality.

> Opponents of the ERA believed that sex-based legislation was necessary because of women's biological and social roles as mothers. They claimed that "the inherent differences are permanent. Women will always need many laws different from those needed by men"; "women as such, whether or not they are mothers present or prospective, will always need protective legislation"; "the working mother is handicapped by her own nature." Their approach stressed maternal nature and inclination as well as conditioning, and implied that the sexual division of labor was eternal.[66]

Despite their deep resonance with the traditional values of the intimate sphere, such particularistic arguments for maintaining separate spheres could be fully justified only if they were also vouchsafed in terms of the overarching civil discourse. Women advocates for the traditionalist position polluted ERA activists as civil incompetents, as "pernicious" women who "discard[ed] all ethics and fair play," as an "insane crowd" who espoused "a kind of hysterical feminism with a slogan for a program."[67] The effect of this equation of feminism with anticivil incompetence was fateful. As the ERA went down to crushing defeat in the 1920s, the victorious difference discourse had the effect of making feminism virtually a dirty word for decades to come.

Without the universalizing ideology of feminism, however, it was impossible to conceive women as fully incorporated into the civil sphere. Even during World War II, when dire objective exigencies propelled women into the public worlds of factory and office, their participation was framed as a facilitating input that preserved sexual difference, not as civil incorporation. So Ruth Milkman demonstrated in *Gender at Work*.

> Accompanying the characterization of women's work as "light" was an emphasis on cleanliness. "Women can satisfactorily fill all or most jobs performed by men, subject only to the limitations of strength and physical requirements," a meeting of the National Association of Manufacturers concluded in March 1942. "However . . . jobs of a particularly "dirty" character, jobs that subject women to heat process or are of a "wet" nature should not be filled by women . . . despite the fact that women could, if required, perform them."[68]

This framework was, of course, merely a new and updated version of public m/otherhood. It had the effect of preserving the gender contradictions between civil and noncivil spheres, not of repairing them.

> There was a contradiction in the management literature on women's war work. It simultaneously stressed the fact that "women are being trained in skills that were considered exclusively in man's domain" and their special suitability for "delicate war jobs." These two seemingly conflicting kinds of statements were reconciled through analogies between "women's work" at home and in the war plants.

"Note the similarity between squeezing orange juice and the operation of a small drill press," the Sperry Gyroscope company urged in a recruitment pamphlet. "Any one can peel potatoes," it went on. "Burring and filing are almost as easy."[69]

Even in the 1950s, amid American boasts about modernity and its social theorizing about modernization, the equation of feminist demands for universalism with anticivil pollution remained widely accepted. "Most women as well as men," the historian Jane Sherron de Hart writes, "still accepted as one of the few unchanging facts of life the conviction that woman's primary duty was to be 'helpmate, housewife, and mother.' "[70]

Feminism could not be revived, nor could the civic repair of gender relations become a realistic political possibility, until universalist arguments about gender relations became much more widely accepted. This happened with the creation of feminism's "second wave," which was stimulated by the effervescence of demands for equalizing the status of African Americans, another group whose inequality had been legitimated by the construction of an essentializing difference. Betty Friedan, whose writings earned her the sobriquet of "mother" to this second wave, equated arguments for difference with the "feminine mystique." Her argument should be taken less as an empirical description of women's status in the 1950s—which had, of course, already been partially reconstructed by modern feminism—than as a culturally sensitive polemic against the extent to which sexual-difference arguments had managed, nonetheless, to sustain their mainstream viability.

The suburban housewife—she was the dream image of the young American women and the envy, it was said, of women all over the world. . . . She was healthy, beautiful, educated, concerned only about her husband, her children, her home. She had found true feminine fulfillment. As a housewife and mother, she was respected as a full and equal partner to man in his world. She was free to choose automobiles, clothes, appliances, supermarkets; she had everything that women ever dreamed of. . . . The words written for women, and the words women used when they talked to each other, while their husbands sat on the other wide of the room and talked shop or politics or septic tanks, were about problems with their children, or how to keep their husbands happy, or improve their children's school, or cook chicken or make slipcovers. Nobody argued whether women were inferior or superior to men; they were simply different. Words like "emancipation" and "career" sounded strange and embarrassing; no one had used them for years.[71]

The social movement called "women's liberation" rejected the mystique of difference and demanded the civil repair of gender relations on the basis of universality. "The first step toward becoming feminists," de Hart writes, "demanded a clear statement of women's position in society, one that called attention to the gap between the egalitarian ideal and the actual position of women in American culture."[72] In 1966, on the basis of such sentiments, the National Organization for Women was formed. The organization's statement of purpose, signed by three hundred women and men, reached back to the universalizing attack on separate-sphere ideology that had marked the long-ago meeting in Seneca Falls. On behalf of women, it demanded "full participation in the mainstream of American society NOW, exercising all the privileges and responsibilities thereof in truly equal partnership with men."[73]

What finally undermined the authority of difference ideology was the persuasive feminist insistence, which itself became hegemonic among broad segments of the public during the 1970s and 1980s, that gender was a social construct, not a natural condition. This contextualization allowed male domination to be labeled as a "sexist" and destructive intrusion into civil equality. Threatening intrusions demanded energetic civil repair. "Given the pervasiveness of sexism," de Hart notes, "many feminists saw no possibility for real equality short of transformation not only of individuals but also of social institutions and cultural values."[74] As with every effort to further institutionalize the idealizing codes of civil society, deepening incorporation and reforming "the system" required deep shifts in boundary relations and fundamental institutional repairs. Thus, "what seemed to be a matter of obtaining equal rights *within* the existing system, in reality demanded changes that *transform* the system."[75] Instead of feminine difference, women would be constructed in terms of civic competence. According to one programmatic statement, published in 1979, feminist transformation involved nothing less than "a reevaluation of women as workers, of women as mothers, of mothers as workers, of work as suitable for one gender and not for the other."

The demand implies equal opportunity and thus equal responsibilities. It implies a childhood in which girls are rewarded for competence, risk taking, achievement, competitiveness and independence— just like boys.[76]

The Ethical Limits of Care

The ERA may once again have been defeated, but this new commitment to gender equality has increasingly permeated the culture and institutions of contemporary life. It is precisely within this context of a less gender-distorting institutionalization of the promises of civil society that we should understand the growing strength over the last three decades of the radical movements that emphasize the separating particularities of "women's culture" and the moral superiority of a female-generated ethics of care. This contemporary development, I am suggesting, must be viewed as emerging from within feminism itself. It has unfolded not as an alternative to civil discourse, but within the very rubric of an underlying belief in the equal civil competence of women and men. As I will suggest in Part IV of this book, it is exactly the same for those movements that have sought to restore the vitality of distinctive ethnic, racial, sexual, regional, and religious culture. Contra such group-centered theorists as Iris Marion Young,[77] justice has not become simply a matter of accepting the politics of difference. The goal is not to allow group cultures to become so distanced from one another that their particularity can be recognized and separation assured. Difference can be positively recognized only if the particular is viewed, to again paraphrase Hegel, as a concrete manifestation of the universal. This becomes possible only if civil discourse is expanded to include subaltern communities, an expansion that de-essentializes and "purifies" polluted identities, recognizing differences as legitimate by constructing them as variations on the theme of a common humanity.[78]

It should not be surprising that some radical advocates of "women's culture" fail to appreciate that its growing legitimacy has actually depended on expanding the civil frame. As civil ideals become more deeply institutionalized, they become more transparent, less visibly taking on a primordial hue. Feminists themselves, however, often have worried about the failure of difference theorists to recognize the continuing reach of civil universalism.

Twenty years ago, Ellen DuBois warned that any single-minded focus on "women's culture" risked ignoring "the larger social and historical developments of which it was a part," and thus failed to "address the limitations of the values of women's culture" itself.[79] It was precisely on such grounds that there erupted, in the mid-1980s, a furious debate inside the feminist community over Carol Gilligan's arguments for a distinctively different female morality in her controversial book *In a Different Voice*.[80] This debate, one part of the broader argument about difference and universalism in the postmodern civil sphere, has not died down to this day.

Against Lawrence Kohlberg's studies of moral development, Gilligan argues that boys have "a self defined through separation," whereas girls have "a self delineated through connection." Women thus feel "a responsibility to discern and alleviate the 'real and recognizable troubles' of this world," while, by contrast, men's imperative "appears rather as an injunction to respect the rights of others."[81] Feminist critics of these claims attacked Gilligan for drawing her data exclusively from women's decision-making processes—primarily decisions about abortion—and for failing to study parallel processes in male decision making. If Gilligan had done so, her critics argued, she might have found that, beyond the differences she discovers, there is an underlying human universality.

> Do not men also in some circumstances find themselves similarly stretched on the rack between selfishness and responsibility? Were we to listen to men during their process of decision on, say, draft resistance, might we note also their similarly anguished contemplation of their responsibility to their families, to the needs of those who depend on them for care?[82]
>
> Gilligan has been attacking a straw man [*sic*]. . . . In childhood and adolescence, there is no trend whatever for males to score at higher levels than females on Kohlberg's scales. . . . There is no indication whatever that the two sexes take different developmental paths with respect to moral thought about abstract, hypothetical issues.[83]

What disturbed Gilligan's feminist critics was the possibility that her argument for difference—despite her own heated denials[84] that it was essentializing or even gendered—might obscure the difference between then and now, between the days of public m/otherhood and the contemporary period of relatively universalist morality. Linda Kerber wrote that "this historian, at least, is haunted by the sense that we have had this argument before, vested in different language [about] the ascription of reason to men and feeling to women."[85] The psychologist Zella Luria asked, "Do we truly gain by returning to a modern cult of true womanhood?"

> Modern women will need *not* to be always caring and interrelated, if indeed they ever were constantly so. And they are also in situations where being abstract and rights oriented is a necessity. My purpose as a feminist is to train women to choose their actions sensibly and flexibly depending on the situation they confront.[86]

Can an ethic of care sustain the discursive kinds of commitments to impartiality, fairness, self-criticism, and inclusion that sustain the civil sphere in a truly democratic society? One influential feminist philosopher, Susan James, has criticized the notion that "the activities typically undertaken by women can be described, without strain, as partial, personal or particular." What she fears is that if "the affections and concerns that go into them are usually directed to particular people and set within specific relationships such as those of mother to child, nurse to patient, secretary to boss, wife to husband," then women could be portrayed as if they "think and behave in ways that are antithetical to the norm of impartiality" that is so essential in constructing a tolerant and democratic world.[87] James points out that, if an ethics of care bases itself on such ties as love, as its advocates have suggested, then there is no theoretical room for compelling commitment to abstract social rules—"for one another's well-being is enough [by itself] to ensure that differences are resolved and that feelings of resentment, frustration or anger are contained."[88] Such an ethic is well and good for the intimate sphere, but can it actually be extended to the civil one?

> To extend these practices (or something like them) beyond the private sphere would be to extend them into a territory where people are not bound by emotional ties and may perceive themselves as having little more in common than the fact they happen to be living under the same political jurisdiction.[89]

Another feminist philosopher, Mary Dietz, wonders whether the motives that bind mother and child, the ties that sustain friendship, and such quintessentially care-giving institutions as families actually provide the appropriate normative standards. Should they be used as models for the kinds of motives, relationships, and institutions that must inform a democratic society? Dietz suggests, to the contrary, that such relationships and institutions might, at least in certain fundamental respects, be anticivil in form.

> Who would not argue that the growth and preservation of children are vital social imperatives, or that the protection of vulnerable human life is important? But surely a movement or a political consciousness committed simply to caring ... offers no standards ... when it comes to judging between political alternatives. . . . The mother and the child are in radically different positions in terms of power and control. The child is subordinate to the mother. . . . In other words, the special and distinctive aspects of mothering emerge out of a decidedly unequal relationship, even if benign or loving. . . . This is an intimate, exclusive, and particular activity. [Because] democratic citizenship, on the other hand, is collective, inclusive, and generalized, [b]ecause it is a condition [in] which individuals aim at being equal, the mother-child relationship is a particularly inappropriate model. . . . Furthermore, the bond among citizens is not like the love between a mother and child, for citizens are, not intimately, but politically involved with each other. . . . Citizens do not, because they cannot, relate to one another as brother does to brother, or mother does to child. . . . Intimacy, love, and attentiveness are precious things in part because they are exclusive and so cannot be experienced just anywhere or by just anyone with just any other. That is why love and intimacy ... must not be made the basis of political action and discourse.[90]

One of the most influential philosophical advocates of this care ethics, Joan Tronto, acknowledges that "we do not care for everyone equally," indeed, that "we care more for those who are emotionally, physically, and even culturally closer to us." As a logical corollary to this particularism and implicit exclusiveness, Tronto admits also that, "in focusing on the preservation of existing relationships," there is "little basis for critical reflection on whether these relationships are good, healthy, or worthy of preservation."[91] Though paternalism and parochialism are unwelcome, they are inevitable "dangers of care."[92] Tronto goes so far as to identify "particularity" as the ethic's central "moral dilemma."[93] By way of solution, she recommends that the care ethic be "connected to a theory of justice,"[94] which would provide a "transformed context"[95] for its application. Yet an ethics of care is consistently put forward as an alternative to just such universalizing theories of justice, not as their complement.

Advocates of an ethics of care have criticized the discourse of civil society as impersonal, mechanistic, and even masculinist. This caricature is produced by a binary logic that merely inverts the simplifying dichotomies of civil discourse itself. The discourse of civil society is not concerned only with individualism; nor does it represent an instrumental and strategic colonization by strategic and abstract forms of rationality. It codes altruism and trust, emphasizes honor and truthfulness over selfishness and deception, demands friendliness and openness, and suggests that social relations should be inclusive, egalitarian, and cooperative. Yet however positive and socially oriented, these qualities do not suggest love, and for this reason they do not denote the lifeworld-centered "ethics of care." The question is not whether love, care, emotional feeling, loyalty, and a relativizing contextualism are good things in themselves. Certainly they often are. Plural societies need such ethical codes. Nor is the question whether women's culture, as distinct from men's, is important to preserve and sustain, often in a separated place. Certainly it is. The question, rather, is whether such qualities can define the sphere of civil justice—indeed, whether identifying ethics by such qualities would make it possible to mark out a relatively autonomous civil sphere at all.

The categorical divisions of the civil sphere have been stable for centuries, but the signifieds of these civil and anticivil signifiers certainly have not. In one historical period, differences of gender, class, race, religion, and sexuality are taken to be primordial differences and criticized or sentimentalized as anticivil by the groups that organize and represent the civil core. At a later historical time, such supposedly natural qualities are seen merely as "constructed," as are the once invisibly primordial qualities that had, up until that time, defined the distinctiveness of civil society's core groups. Reflexivity is not about changing the categories that define the civil sphere; it is about learning how they can be instantiated in new ways.[96]

CHAPTER 11

Race and Civil Repair (1):
Duality and the Creation
of a Black Civil Society

S INCE THEIR FIRST institutionalization in the seventeenth century, the
promises made by the civil spheres of democratic nation-states have
been mocked by gross exclusions and inequalities. These destructive
intrusions have entered into the very construction of civil spheres, distorting
their discourse, institutions, and interaction. Yet insofar as the civil sphere
has retained any autonomy at all, and it often has, it has held out the
continual possibility for civic repair. Those whom civil society has repressed
in the name of a restricted and particularistic conception of civil competence,
it also can save. More precisely, it can offer resources so that they can save
themselves. This is what I want to suggest in these discussions of the great
social movements that have developed around gender and race—that they
can, indeed that they must, be viewed as movements of civil repair.[1]

In making this claim, I am advancing a normative argument that is
designed also to be realistic. When normative social theorists such as Hannah
Arendt or Jürgen Habermas confront the centuries of racial, class, religious,
and gender domination, they have despaired that the civil or public sphere
has disappeared, that it has been colonized into submission. Realists, whether
Marxist or Weberian, disagree; for them, civil society has always been more

or less a chimera. It never existed in the first place. As I see it, by contrast, the question is not whether civil society exists. The question is to what degree. The civil sphere is only one sphere among many. Its promises can only be institutionalized in a partial way.

One must speak, therefore, of the civil sphere and its contradictions—contradictions created not by the total absence of civil society but by the fragmented nature of its institutionalization. As I suggested earlier, these are different from the economic, essentializing contradictions posited by Marx. The contradictions between civil and noncivil spheres cannot be neatly historicized, defined by this particular period or that. Nor do they refer to the strains that are generated from within one particular system alone. Finally, it is not possible to resolve contradictions as such. Future societies will never be without them. The contradictions created by the boundary problems of civil and uncivil spheres are structural, and in that sense are permanent. They are created not only by objective deficiencies but by expectations, by the utopian aspirations of the civil sphere and by the very effort to institutionalize them. This effort can never be completed. In real civil societies, universalism will always be contradicted by particularities of space, time, and function.[2]

One way of thinking about these contradictions is to look at the "duality" they create. In social systems that include a relatively autonomous civil sphere, every actor occupies a dual position. He or she is a subordinate or superordinate actor in a whole series of vertical hierarchies and, at the same time, a member of the horizontal community of civil life. Even when a majority dominates a small minority, this duality allows the possibility of minority access, though of course it does not guarantee it.[3] To speak metaphorically, the dictatorships created by vertical membership in noncivil spheres are surrounded by a horizontal "civil environment." This duality, at once existential, organizational, and cultural, is precisely what is missed by the classical model of social movements and the variations I discussed in chapter 9. For social movements to develop, it is not the allocative system that is crucial—the unequal distribution of resources—but the nature of the integrative, normative environment that surrounds it.[4] If this integrative environment is at least partly defined by the civil sphere, it ensures that conflicts are more than simple battles whose outcomes depend only on instrumental power.[5]

If the cultural and institutional definitions of the nation's integrative community are not civil or not civil enough, then force and violence become decisive, for access is blocked to legitimate procedures, to the means of communication, and to the regulatory institutions that can integrate communities in more expansive and equitable ways. Rather than civil incorporation, this presents a situation of "negative integration," as Gunther Roth aptly described it in his study of the Prussian elite's domination of the German working class in the late nineteenth century.[6] In response to growing class conflict, the German state outlawed the socialist political representatives of the working classes, violently and implacably opposing their political and cultural enfranchisement. Because the environment surrounding class conflict was not nearly civil enough, reform became impossible in Imperial Germany, and revolution the only resort. Much the same could be said for the massive social movements against South African apartheid and the Polish communist regime. In South Africa, only growing violence by the dominated black masses, and the threat of revolutionary destruction, could force reform in an Afrikaner regime that had virtually severed the black majority's connections to civil society.[7] In Poland, despite the resources provided by a free church, private agriculture property, and a doggedly democratic nationalist culture, duality was even less a reality. With institutions of regulation and communication controlled by the *nomenklatura* of the party state, it was only a matter of time before the Solidarity movement was crushed, notwithstanding the original and far-reaching ideology it developed about self-limiting revolution in the civil sphere.[8]

To the degree that there is some autonomy for the civil sphere, it can, in effect, "surround" domination, and things can be different. There can be real, not just putative duality. There must still, of course, be an intense struggle for power, but this power can be gained by civil means. Organizations and resources are crucial, but what these resources provide is access to the means of persuasion, which in turn provides leverage for affecting the institutions of regulation that effectively control the allocation of money and force. It is, in fact, the existence of such duality that explains why the fierce struggles of dominated groups so often are pulled between moderation and radical extremes. On the one hand, the obdurate verticality of exclusion produces alienation from society and the sense that exit is the only option, whether through revolution or withdrawal.[9] Yet, at the same time, the immanent horizontality suggested by implicit civil membership raises the very real possibility of voice, of reform. Duality means that resources for communication are on offer, and the possibility of controlling regulatory institutions is not closed. If the right social circumstances present themselves, civil repair is a real possibility for those who are skillful and strong.

Racial Domination and Duality in the Construction of American Civil Society

To understand how duality works, we must see it not only as a structure but also as a process. It is initiated by destructive intrusions; yet even as these distortions become instantiated in the civil sphere, possibilities for repair emerge. In response to the fragmentation of the civil sphere, and the anticivil domination it legitimates, a counterpublic develops within the dominated group, a kind of mirror image of the dominant segment of civil society that allows the dominated not only to maintain some degree of comity and community but to develop resources for resistance that engage the surrounding civil sphere. The existence of this counterpublic means that at some point it is likely, if not inevitable, that powerful social movements of translation will arise. In this chapter, I will illustrate how duality developed vis-à-vis white American domination of blacks, creating the conditions for civil repair. In the chapters following, I will embark on a detailed analysis of the social movement that emerged to repair this racial distortion of the American of civil sphere. I will show how the Civil Rights movement of the 1950s and 1960s succeeded in translating the particularities of African American domination into the idioms and institutions of the civil environment of the surrounding American society.

As I have suggested throughout this book, categories of repression are built into the very fundaments of the discourse from which the great and liberating experiments of civil society have drawn. Though historically specific societies have filled up these categories in very different manners—providing different kinds of concrete signifieds for the widely shared signifiers—conceptions of racial particularity have been omnipresent.[10] In European civil societies, as Charles Mills has forcefully argued, a "racial contract" was built into the civil foundations. During the so-called age of European exploration, whiteness helped to justify the contradictions of political domination and economic exploitation. Orientalism affected even the most emancipated minds of the northern European Renaissance, and racial-cum-religious ideas obsessed the Spanish in their battle for Reconquest against the North African Moors.[11]

The founding of the American colonies was inextricably tied to racial domination and displacement, actions that helped to create a scale of racial civility whose precise rank ordering was determined by the exigencies of time and place. European settlers colonized American territory over the lands and bodies of native peoples. Yet this colonization was carried out so incrementally and, at the same time, so ruthlessly that "redness"—the supposed color of the native people's skin—did not become thematized as the primary racial distortion of American civil society, despite such assertions as Thomas Jefferson's, in the Declaration of Independence, that Native Americans were "merciless Indian Savages" and John Adams's contention that "Indians" were among those peoples who "cannot bear democracy."[12] It was blackness that became the primary racial distortion, and it did so because of anticivil functional exigencies. By the mid-seventeenth century, Africans were being imported in mass to labor as slaves on plantations in the American South. The planters had tried to make use of the quasi-free labor of Indians and white indentured servants, but, as the sociologist Bert Landry puts it, "unlike Native Americans, Africans were accustomed to agricultural work, and they could not blend into the population as did white indentured servants if they escaped."[13] These considerations made Africans "an ideal inexpensive work force from the planters' point of view." These early functional exigencies specified the generalized racialism of Western culture in a manner that made beliefs about the civic incompetence of blacks intrinsic to America's originating civil discourse. As the literary scholar Houston Baker has suggested, the white American representation of the black minority was an inverted projection of its own claim to reason and civility.

> Black Americans . . . were defined [as] a separate and inverted opposite of a historically imagined white rationality in action. Such a black upside-down world could only be portrayed historically as an irrational, illiterate, owned, nonbourgeois community of chatel . . . sitting bleakly in submissive silence. . . . It would be precisely . . . the "b," or negative, side of a white imaginary of public life in America.[14]

Because domination of slaves was an overriding economic need primarily for America's southern region, this functional exigency soon translated itself into a contradiction of place and even of time, for the southern white planter class supplied a large proportion of the founding fathers of the American democratic state.[15] These contradictions became particularly debilitating with the institutionalization of America's national civil society in the 1770s and 1780s. In justifying their democratic rebellion against England, colonial revolutionaries continually employed the metaphor of slavery to justify their demands for independence. It was to this condition of servitude, they claimed, that their English oppressors were trying to reduce them. The rebellious colonists decried England's increasingly harsh political and economic regulations as an effort to "enslave" them. When Thomas Jefferson asserted, in the Declaration of Independence, that "all men are created equal," he developed a universalizing argument that pointed beyond mere national independence to the abolition of every form of legal servitude. In fact, in the context of this revolutionary atmosphere, some efforts arose to abolish African enslavement even in the southern state of Virginia.[16] Many of the most prominent leaders of the Revolution were themselves abolitionists, and among some fervent supporters of the Revolution there was a widespread belief that postrevolutionary America would wipe slavery out.

These hopes for civic repair were dashed when the American civil sphere was first institutionalized on the national level. In the unstable decades that followed the revolutionary victory, the struggle to define a new, specifically national identity emphasized whiteness as a distinctive solidarity, and in the effort to create a new national constitution the racial contradictions produced by time, place, and function came fatefully to a head. Thus, despite the fact that Benjamin Franklin was president of the Pennsylvania Abolition Society, he declined its invitation to offer an antislavery motion to the Constitutional Convention of 1787. Franklin was afraid to alienate southern delegates whose support would be essential to approving a new constitution.[17] When this geographical bloc pushed through the infamous "three-fifths compromise," it guaranteed that the racial distortions of culture and the destructive intrusions of place, time, and function would become legally specified, crippling the institutions that regulated American civil life.

By so distorting the basic premises of regulatory institutions, the Constitutional Convention ensured, from that time on, that it would be difficult for Americans to eliminate slavery in a civil, democratic way. As the historian Merton Dillon once put it, "because of the three-fifths compromise, the eradication of slavery by peaceful, constitutional means was made exceedingly difficult and unlikely to occur."[18] Indeed, white southern Americans came to view the Constitution as the guarantor of their brutally antidemocratic institution. As an English clergyman visiting the South in the early national period observed, "defenders of slavery began to link that defense to loyalty to the new federal constitution." In fact, he continued, "they now begin to take the position that attacks on slavery were attacks on the Constitution," and thus on the Union itself.[19] Could there be any more compelling example of how racial domination became instantiated in the institutions of civil society?

It was in this way that, triggered by functional exigencies, the anticivil particularism of racial domination eventually became articulated with time and place, enshrined in the origins of the democratic Republic and rooted in its southern region. This particularistic distortion, however, was surrounded by the social system of the northern United States, which became increasingly animated by civil criticism of racial enslavement. This critical reaction was triggered by the social movement of abolitionism, which worked its effects on northern civil society not by leading northern whites to establish solidarity with African American slaves—the racialist culture of the day was much too pronounced for such an identification—but rather by persuasively portraying the white slaveholding South as a threat to northern democracy. As northern communicative institutions broadcast increasingly dire warnings against the polluting threat of the southern "slave power," regulative institutions sought to maintain the integrity of the civil sphere by isolating it, by building a fence around the southern anticivil space. As new states entered the Union, there were battles over whether they would be slaveholding or free. As the South battled to maintain its anticivil institutions of racial domination, its representatives threatened to escape from the North's increasingly restrictive environment by withdrawing from the United States. In the 1850s, as more antislave states were admitted, the South saw the writing on the wall and decided to make good on its threat to secede. Abraham Lincoln and the nascent Republican Party refused to accept secession, and the American nation went to war with itself. Though initiated as a war against secession, the fact that the antislavery movement had pushed the nation into war was formally recognized when Lincoln issued the Emancipation Proclamation, declaring that, on January 1, 1863, all slaves in areas still in rebellion were "then, henceforth, and forever free."[20] The four-year Civil War, one of the bloodiest and most violent in modern history, demonstrated just how fundamentally the American civil sphere was crippled by the racial contradictions of space, time, and function. What could more vividly testify to the fact that the civil solidarity of the nation had completely broken down?

Though postwar constitutional amendments abolished slavery and formally guaranteed African Americans full civil status, the Civil War failed to resolve the destructive intrusion of race. "Reconstruction," the ambitious northern effort to reorganize southern politics and society so that blacks could be included in a substantive way, was shut down after a mere decade.[21] The rollback responded not only to political and economic forces, but to racist cultural understandings that continued to permeate not only the South but the North.[22] Messages testifying to the civil incompetence of blacks were broadcast far and wide by communicative institutions in the North, from the expressive media of traveling "minstrel" shows that featured white men in black face to the cognitive media of news accounts and even purportedly scientific treatises. At Columbia University, then a bastion of the East Coast elite, Howard Odum filed a doctoral dissertation in 1910 that became an influential book, *Social and Mental Traits of the Negro*. Odum justified racial domination by constructing the motives and relations of blacks in terms of the discourse of repression.

> The Negro has little home conscience or love of home, no local attachments of the better sort. . . . He has no pride of ancestry, and he is not influenced by the lives of great men. . . . He has little conception of the meaning of virtue, truth, honor, manhood, integrity. . . . He does not know the value of his word or the meaning of words in general. [Negroes] sneer at the idea of work. . . . Their moral natures are miserably perverted.[23]

It was within this cultural context of anticivil public opinion—the particularistic, essentializing notions broadcast far and wide by the communicative media of the day—that in the latter part of the nineteenth century southern regulatory institutions systematically organized and rationalized forms of domination that culminated in the racial apartheid called "Jim Crow." For our purposes, what is important to understand about this process is that it was not only materially abetted but formally legitimated by the surrounding regulative institutions of the United States. Racial domination, in other words, continued to destructively intrude into the American civil sphere after the Civil War, shaping national culture, institutions, and inter-actions in specific kinds of anticivil ways. In the half century after Recon-struction, the U.S. Supreme Court systematically eroded the new consti-tutional provisions designed to protect black civil rights.[24] In 1896, in *Plessey v. Ferguson*, the white Court declared Jim Crow constitutional by primor-dializing a civil incapacity in blacks. This decision generated the famous dissent by Justice John Marshall Harlan, so revealing because it had such a simple aim—to extricate the founding regulatory document of American democracy from the primordial claims made upon it by the Court's majority. Scolding his colleagues that "the law regards man as man," Harlan reasserted the civil and utopian nature of the Constitution, declaring "our Constitution is color blind and neither knows nor tolerates classes among citizens."[25]

That this democratic sentiment was not shared by the core groups of American civil society is demonstrated by the manner in which office, a critical regulative institution of civil society, was distorted in an equally racial way. In the decade after Reconstruction, for example, there was a drastic decline in the number of prosecutions brought by the federal government against southern noncompliance with the Civil War amendments.[26] Those who held executive office at the national level, moreover, did not hesitate to engage in public rhetoric justifying such anticivil abuse of power. Presi-dent Taft opposed extending voting to blacks by suggesting they were but "political children, not having the mental status of manhood." President Harding affirmed the "fundamental, eternal, and inescapable differences" between blacks and whites, declaring that he would "stand uncompromis-ingly against every suggestion of social equality" for "racial amalgamation there cannot be." President Wilson ordered that a wide range of federal agencies should be segregated in order to avoid what he termed "race mixing."[27]

Truly significant changes in the nation's regulative institutions would not occur until the 1960s. Still, when national politics entered a more progressive period, in the 1930s, regulative power at the national level began to be exercised less overtly in a racist manner. Even the U.S. Supreme Court began to issue decisions that were less anticivil in regard to race.[28] In the southern civil sphere, by contrast, the destructive intrusion of race remained virtually unchanged. Because of the disproportionate power of its southern members, Congress failed to pass a single civil rights measure between 1930 and 1954.[29] It is not an exaggeration to suggest, indeed, that, even in the mid-twentieth century period, African Americans remained almost completely separated from the civil sphere in the southern United States. Aldon Morris describes this distance simply and powerfully when he writes that blacks "were not members of the polity."[30]

/ It was not only in cultural ways that southern whites separated blacks from the reach of the civil sphere, symbolically representing them as devoid of rationality, honesty, and self-control. Southern whites also dominated blacks interactionally. Morris describes the insistence on inequality and deference in personal relations, how blacks "had to address whites in a tone that conveyed respect and [to] use formal titles," and how black males were "advised to stare downward when passing a white woman so that she would have no excuse to accuse him of rape."[31] This corruption of the civil sphere's interactional dimension fed back into the effort to keep blacks from having access to the regulatory institution of office. "In the South," Landry explains, "the idea of blacks engaged in clean work in the front offices of establishments serving a white public was completely repugnant to white sentiments." The result was that "no black individual could occupy a clerical or sales position in white establishments."[32] /

Finally, blacks were also completely separated from southern institutions of communication and regulation. As we will see in our discussion of the civil rights struggles themselves, when white community newspapers did not simply ignore the existence of black society, they distorted its activities in contemptuously anticivil ways. It was the same with regulatory institutions. Blacks were never allowed to hold positions that, in Morris's words, were "vested with authority" in either the private or the public spheres.[33] This exclusion from office was exacerbated by the exclusion of blacks from the legal protections of the civil sphere, for "the courts were controlled by white judges and juries, which routinely decided in favor of whites." The electoral arm of civil society was also unavailable to blacks, who were effectively disenfranchised by such white electoral subterfuges as the poll tax, literacy requirements, and the grandfather clause. It is hardly surprising, given this absence from regulative and communicative institutions, that the southern white community, relatively democratic internally, allowed its police forces to employ "terror and brutality" to mediate its relation to black community life.

Duality and Counterpublics

How was it possible, in such a degraded situation of anticivil domination, for an effective movement for civil repair to emerge? As I suggested earlier, such a possibility is linked to duality. The national civil sphere of American society surrounded the southern system of internal colonization not only socially but spatially. In regard to race, the idealistic promises of the American civil sphere were much more effectively institutionalized in the North, which had earlier waged civil war against the destructive intrusion of southern slavery. It would be a profound error, however, to think that this surrounding national sphere would somehow "act"—on its own, as it were—to resolve the racial contradictions of American civil society. This would be a mistake not only, or even primarily, because of the empirical fact that race also distorted the civil sphere in the North. This would be an error in theoretical, not only empirical terms. Duality must be activated by agents. When the civil sphere is severely distorted, this agency takes the form of social movements and their contingent mobilization of skill, power, and interpretive force. Duality suggests that domination and exclusion exist in some degree of tension with the premises and regulatory force of the partially institutionalized civil sphere. However, in recognizing the importance of duality—the continuing possibility of democratic justice—one must avoid teleology. It is tempting to look down from the perspective of the structure, or system, rather than up from the perspective of the social actors themselves. The problem is the assumption, implicit in Hegel, Durkheim, and Parsons, that because civil societies retain the potential for progressive development, they actually will change in a positive way. They may not change at all, or they may become less democratic.

This insistence on agency and social movements in response to duality leads us directly to the theory of counterpublics, one of the most sociologically relevant ideas to emerge from recent normative discussion about civil society and public life. Drawing from the Gramscian tradition and particularly its sociological application in the Birmingham school of cultural studies, scholars such as Nancy Fraser and Geoff Eley have pointed to the fact that excluded communities develop the capacity for resistance because they have formed counter or "subaltern" public spheres of their own.[34] In terms of the framework I am developing here, these shadow communities of discourse, stimulated by voluntary organizations, create opportunities for developing positive new identities and solidarities in opposition to the polluted and demeaning categories that have been applied to them by dominant core groups. These new discursively created identities become the basis for political resistance and the movement for civil repair.[35]

The idea that there are counterpublic spheres, or subaltern civil societies, allows us to locate the sociological spaces within which critical social movements develop. We can develop a satisfactory discussion of the black civil sphere, however, only if we are sensitive to some of the problems of counterpublic theory as it has been developed thus far. Its origins in neo-Marxist forms of critical theory has been both its strength and its weakness. Fraser and Eley formulate the idea of the counterpublic in relation to Habermas's earliest, neo-Marxist work on the structural transformation of the bourgeois public sphere. As these critics read Habermas, he tied the public values of rationality, dialogue, truth, and transparency—values homologous with the civil discourse of liberty as I have defined it here—to the viability of the public sphere in its exclusively bourgeois form. According to Habermas's early formation, when industrialization intensified the inegalitarian economic contradictions of capitalism, the public sphere and its values were themselves doomed. In opposition to this perspective, counterpublic theorists have pointed out that vigorous public life existed in nonbourgeois communities, that these alternative publics provided vital bases for opposition to capitalism and to such other forms of domination as gender and race, and that, though the bourgeois public did decline, other, more viable public spheres often arose to take its place.

Such arguments provide important insights into the fragmented and conflictual nature of civil society and into the reactions to exclusion I am trying to illuminate here. At the same time, however, they fail to do justice to the universalizing premises of civil norms and the critical implications that follow from them. Underestimating the civil sphere's potential for relative autonomy from the interests of any particular social group, they neglect the degree to which critical social movements are oriented not simply toward gaining resources and power vis-à-vis the civil sphere but to securing a respected place within it. Theorists of counterpublics tend to neglect, in other words, the existence of duality. They ignore the manner in which this structured ambiguity pushes the orientation of social movements not only to conflict, but also to integration.[36]

Counterpublic theorists conceive of the so-called hegemonic public sphere as a kind of empty arena, as a fenced-off space that has the capacity to pacify and contain social conflicts whose goals and ambitions remain fundamentally orthogonal to one another and to the culture and institutions of the wider social world. Thus, Eley identifies the civil public sphere simply as "a setting where cultural and ideological contest or negotiation among a variety of publics takes place."[37] It is precisely because the substantive and universalizing content of the overarching, or environing, public sphere has been emptied out in this manner that the counterpublic can be conceived in such purely agonistic and contingent terms. Fraser calls it a "parallel discursive" arena in which "subordinate social groups invent and circulate counterdiscourses to formulate oppositional interpretations of their identities, interests, and needs."[38]

Such arguments reduce counterpublics to countercultures. As the argument I have been developing in this book suggests, by contrast, counterpublics are built not only upon popular culture per se, but upon refractions of the universalizing representations and practices of the environing civil sphere.[39] When counterpublics succeed, it is not simply because they have engaged in what Fraser calls "agitational activities," utilizing their space of "withdrawal" to launch a "sustained discursive contestation" with the dominant regime.[40] This kind of argument takes us back to the strategic logic of conflict theory, the very perspective which civil society theory was designed to overcome. Alternative publics succeed because their intragroup activities have allowed them to learn the art of translating their particular injustices into the more universal language of civil justice. Counterpublic resources give them the power to project these translations into the surrounding civil sphere. In short, excluded groups successfully transform their subordinate position by making more substantial and more deeply institutionalized— more real and less utopian—the universalistic solidarity promised by the dominant civil sphere.[41]

The Conditions for Civil Repair: Duality and the Construction of Black Civil Society

In light of these considerations, it should not be surprising to learn that the continuing and continuously destructive intrusion of race into American civil society produced a boomerang effect even in the severely distorted southern civil sphere. The very subjugation of the black community gave it a separate space for defending itself against the efforts by whites to construct the African American population in an anticivil way. That this community partially succeeded in doing so, that there eventually emerged within many black communities a vigorous civil sphere and public life, testifies, at least in part, to the limitations placed on the exercise of southern racist power by the surrounding civil sphere. The antidemocratic race dictatorship in the South was not totalitarian, and its subordinate position within the national civic sphere made it even less so. Even in the South, the oppressed black community could, within strict limits, organize itself in a manner that critically responded to the negative symbolic constructions of its white oppressor and, eventually, to its organizational domination as well.

The ability to take full advantage of these opportunities, however, had to wait upon certain social structural developments in African American communities. Before World War I, status within southern black communities was based primarily on race, not on the possibility of achievement defined in more universalistic terms. The black elite, for example, was primarily identified by its mulatto status. As Landry puts it, by virtue of "its white ancestry, skin color, and manners and morals patterned after middle- and upper-class whites," the black elite members were distinguished by their "daily close contact with wealthy whites" in such service positions as barbers, servants, railroad porters, and skilled craftsmen. This status created residential patterns antithetical to the formation of a separate, distinctively black civil sphere, for "whenever possible black elite families sought to live in white neighborhoods, if only on a single block of a street occupied by whites."[42] All this changed during and after World War I, when the dearth of white laborers and the end of European immigration drew massive numbers of blacks from farms to cities. It was this rural-to-urban migration, in the context of continuing racial domination and duality, that created the new urban ghettos in the South and the North, which in turn established the possibility for black civil society.

This newly separate and increasingly complex black civil sphere did not emerge, however, simply from resistance to white domination, as Morris seems to suggest when he argues that the "institutional subordination" of blacks "naturally prevented [them] from identifying with the institutions of the larger surrounding."[43] It emerged, rather, in a much more dialectical and dialogical way, via opposition and refraction, drawing upon the resources provided by black identification with white civil society, not only by its separation from it.

⎮In simple demographic terms, ghettoization compelled the kinds of dense, cross-class interactions that foster solidarity and collective identity. As Morris writes, "irrespective of education and income," blacks "were forced to live in close proximity and frequent the same social institutions."

> Maids and janitors came into close contact with clergy, schoolteachers, lawyers, and doctors. [Because] segregation itself ensured that the diverse skills and talents of individuals at all income and educational levels were concentrated within the black community[,] cooperation between the various black strata was an important collective resource for survival.[44] ⎮

But propinquity was hardly sufficient. Interaction does not take place in an institutional or cultural vacuum. It can lead to solidarity that is primordial and particularistic. Though these impulses certainly were not absent in the African American community, it is critical to understand that, within these segregated communities, interaction was also forcefully structured by resources of a specifically civil kind.

That the solidarity of this newly emerging black civil community would be defined in cosmopolitan and not only in primordial terms was ensured by the fact this dense interaction was informed by highly universalistic cultural themes, by ideals, both sacred and secular, that extended beyond the particulars of race to embrace the utopian norms of civil society itself. Almost from the beginning of their southern servitude, African Americans had embraced and refracted the transcendent symbols of the radical, sectarian Protestantism that had been a vital facilitating input in the formation of the American civil sphere. Until the early years of the twentieth century, the critical social potential of African American Christianity had been hobbled by an other-worldly dimension that regarded the tension between human and divine worlds as more or less unbridgeable, emphasizing compensation in the next world for oppression in this one.[45] When independent black urban communities began forming, however, so did a theological movement that shifted the African-American religious perspective in a more this-worldly direction. This change was stimulated by the "social gospel" movement that had developed within white Protestant churches reacting to industrialization after the Civil War. In white communities, the social gospel argued that good human beings had been corrupted by social structures that henceforth must be changed. Black social gospel took a more radical perspective. Evil had already overtaken the world, and God had commanded humankind, especially black, to wage a social struggle to bring the world back to God.[46] The critical and ethical strains in this later version of black Christianity were palpable. It understood the religious transcendence that Jesus promised in social terms, approaching salvation not as the deliverance from earthly suffering—a condition achieved through prayer, death, and heavenly ascendance—but as the transformation of racial domination in this world. In this way, religious salvation demanded social justice. As a recent sociological student of black spirituality has put it: "Freedom is an explicitly collective endeavor signifying both spiritual deliverance into God's kingdom and worldly deliverance from the material realities of racial oppression. . . . Church hymns were transformed into songs of freedom [and] sermons doubled as political addresses."[47]

It is critical to see that this strand of sacred universalism in African American culture was inextricably intertwined with the secular universalism of American civic life. Beginning in the early years of the nineteenth century, the success of abolitionism had released thousands of freed slaves into the northern white civil society. In his study of black mobilization during Reconstruction, Eric Foner emphasizes the impact on black political thought of this northern civil culture, suggesting that "black political leaders can best be understood as those most capable of appropriating the available political language of American society and using it to express the aspirations of the black community."[48] He describes this emergent black political culture as decidedly universalist, as emphasizing the "rights of citizenship" and "grounded in the republican traditions of the eighteenth century, particularly as expressed in the Declaration of Independence and the Constitution."[49] By emphasizing that African Americans had been cut off from secular civil thinking during slavery, Foner points implicitly to the critical issue of duality. It was, in fact, only during Emancipation and Reconstruction, during the northern physical, political, and cultural invasion of southern white and black society, that the duality of civil society powerfully expressed itself in secular African American thought. One Alabama planter blamed "a shameless class of soldiers"—the invading and occupying forces of the Union

Army—for spreading Republican ideas among his ex-slaves.[50] Republican ideas were also spread by northern officials who administered postwar Reconstruction and by northern teachers who taught thousands of black children in newly constructed schools.[51] It is precisely this powerful cultural interpenetration promoted by duality that was highlighted in 1865 by South Carolina's black Congressman, Richard H. Cain, when he remarked that "the North has sent forth those leading ideas, which have spread like lightning over the land; and the negro was not so dumb and not so obtuse that he could not catch the light, and embrace its blessings and enjoy them."[52]

In discussing the ideas of Frederick Douglass, the onetime slave who became the most influential public voice of African American culture in the abolitionist period, David Greenstone insists on a similar interpenetration in reference to the American liberal tradition, the other reform-oriented manifestation of American civil discourse. Rather than thinking outside or against the liberal tradition, Greenstone insists, Douglass's purpose was "to find a place in it for himself and his people."

> The fact that Douglass recurred to the genus liberalism of founders like Jefferson and John Adams, therefore, is far from surprising. Douglass's was also a founding project: to make sure that the bonds that citizens share would come to include "that class of Americans called Africans."[53]

James Oakes makes a similar point. Acknowledging that, "if any group of Americans might have been expected to repudiate liberalism for its complicity in the defense of slavery, racism, and economic inequality—African-Americans are that group," he insists, nonetheless, that "black political thought" has "never been divorced from the liberal tradition." He concludes that, "from the eighteenth century to the late twentieth, blacks have successfully harnessed the themes of liberalism to the struggle against various forms of inequality."[54]

As these secular traditions became involved in the ups and downs of the continuing black freedom struggle, they became crystallized in folk narratives that constituted another strand of the secular African American protest tradition. Such figures as Denmark Vesey, Nat Turner, Sojourner Truth, Frederick Douglass, W.E.B. DuBois, and Marcus Garvey were symbolized as tragic heroes who fought against overwhelming forces for the just cause.[55]

Looking backward from the Civil Rights movement of the 1960s, this folk tradition of protest was vividly articulated by the Reverend Fred Shuttlesworth, an important leader in 1950s Birmingham and later nationally.

> And of course, we based [the Southern Christian Leadership Conference] on everything that happened in the past—Frederick Douglass, slaves, and Marcus Garvey; everybody who struggled for freedom and who were caught up in the same web. And we were giving it an upward thrust.[56]

The connection between this cultural tradition of rebellion and African American religious belief is exemplified in the evocative letter that the Reverend Ralph Abernathy composed for Martin Luther King, his slain comrade, which Abernathy announced he was sending to heaven:

> It wouldn't be a surprise to me, Martin, if God didn't have a special affair just to introduce his special activist black son to so many others like you that have gone on ahead. . . . Martin, find Frederick Douglass, that great and marvelous human personality who lived in even more difficult times than we live today. Check with Nat Turner, and Marcus Garvey, for they, too, are heroes in our crusade. . . . And don't forget Malcolm X. Look for Malcolm X, Martin. . . . He was concerned about the welfare of his people.[57]

Interpreters of contemporary African American society have found these secular cultural themes to have remained powerfully intact. Houston Baker speaks about the importance of "civic responsibility" in the counterpublics of black southern society, a cultural complex centered on "codes" of "dissent, consensus, tolerance, justice and ethics." In a poignant autobiographical aside, Baker reveals how deeply these cultural values drew upon the idealizations of the surrounding white civil sphere.

> The Constitution of the United States and the American national flag were valued sites of patriotism and pride for the black public sphere. Which of us, for example, who attended those awesomely-scrubbed black urban public southern schools of the 1950s that always smelled of disinfectant, can forget the pride and solemnity with which

each school day began in recitation of the "Pledge of Allegiance" to the flag of the United States of America?[58]

In his closely observed study of African American patrons in a working-class restaurant on the edge of the Chicago ghetto in the 1980s, Mitchell Duneier found adherence to idealized representations of "appropriate or correct behavior" that mirror in critical respects the normative discourse of civil society. At the core of this cultural system, Duneier discovered an ideal of respectability, according to which the black patrons sought to measure their own and others' conduct against a standard of "moral worth" that affirmed the autonomy of the individual—"the reality of a self that existed, not as a function of role or status, but as a mere consequence of one's humanity."[59] In terms of the binary structure of civic discourse, it is revealing that Duneier observes how the "civil attachment" manifest by the black patrons was demonstrated less by their explicit reference to positive ideals than by their vigorous and public opposition to behavior they disdained. The restaurant's patrons located these negative qualities—"pretension, aggressiveness, uncommunicativeness, impatience, flashiness, laziness . . . and perhaps most important a lack of personal responsibility"—less in the culture of the white world than in the social organization and behavior of the new black underclass, which they believed had destroyed the civil solidarity of the "old ghetto" life.[60] It is noteworthy that Duneier connects this minority discourse of civility not only to the historically rooted solidarity of the black community but to the effect of the surrounding white one. He recounts that for these men the " 'white world' functions as vague generality, not unlike someone looking over your shoulder or a 'public' in whose presence it is firmly understood that one should not wash his dirty laundry."[61] At the same time, Duneier insists, this kind of commitment to the universalizing ideals of an environing society does not imply that black patrons accept the legitimacy of white institutions. "To the contrary," he observes, "the black regulars tend to be very cynical about the motives of the powerful institutions [and] elites."[62] Nothing could more clearly express the critical implications of the concept of duality I have in mind.

An increasingly complex network of communicative and regulative institutions mediated between the sacred and secular cultural themes of southern black civil society, on the one hand, and the level of face-to-face civil interaction, on the other. Newspapers that served these communities broadcast interpretations of events that challenged and inverted the polluting characterizations of white society. In her historical study of the black community of Richmond, Virginia, for example, Else Barkley Brown found that the *Richmond Planet* countered the white southern image of African American men as "uncivilized, beastly rapists" by "repeatedly focus[ing] on the sexual perversions of white men with [reports on] cases of rape and incest and spoke of white men in terms designed to suggest their barbarism."[63] Yet because southern blacks faced such scrutiny and control from white society, they could not sustain anything like the dense newspaper network that crystallized black public opinion in the North.[64] This vacuum was filled, in part, by southern distribution of influential northern black papers, such as the *Chicago Defender*, which at one point may have distributed as many as 200,000 copies of its weekly edition in southern black communities.[65] In general, however, public opinion in these communities was crystallized and renewed in other ways. Messages were more often broadcast by expressive institutions, such as clubs and membership societies, which sustained a rich popular culture of music and spectacle. In fact, it was these voluntary associations rather than institutions of mass media that sustained communicative flows in black civil societies. In addition to the myriad of mutual benefit societies and fraternal orders, women's clubs and labor organizations, there were formal salons, like the Acme Literary Society in Richmond, whose goal was to hold "discussions, lectures, and to consider questions of vital importance to our people, so that the masses of them may be drawn out to be entertained, enlightened, and instructed thereby."[66]

It is impossible, of course, for a civil society subject to legal domination by an immensely more powerful government structure to create regulatory institutions in the traditional sense, which distinguish themselves vis-à-vis communicative institutions precisely by exercising government control. This important qualification aside, however, one finds numerous forms of lawlike regulation in black civil societies, from the formal, written constitutions that regulated many voluntary organizations to the informal but strictly observed rules that controlled behavior in recreational, business, and professional life. Eventually, as we will see below, legal organizations actually did emerge, such as the Negro Lawyers Association and the National Association for the Advancement of Colored People (NAACP). Though these black regulatory institutions could neither make nor interpret the law of the state, through their rhetorical pronouncements and courtroom briefs they sought to establish alternative standards of normative regulation for the black community, regulations that were less primordial and more universalistic than those enforced by whites. It is also clear that office institutions in the black community had a marked influence in controlling the organizational exercise of power and money. In economic enterprises, political associations, and in every sort of voluntary organization efforts, persistent efforts were made to prevent the personal and arbitrary exercise of power. The intent was that power should be regulated by civil obligations. The ethical dimension of office was defined less by legally articulated standards than by obligations to wider community solidary. This was nowhere more true, and nowhere nearly as consequential, than in the black church, the central institution in most southern black civil societies.

⎧The black church was more than a site for articulating sacred ideals. It was also an organization with money and power that occupied a physically imposing place. The church was the first independent voluntary organization in the southern black civil community; it was also, by far, the strongest one.[67] On the one hand, this organization can be examined in terms of its external role. Through the weekly sermons of its preachers and its numerous meetings and pronouncements throughout the community, the church broadcast a steady stream of messages that crystallized general values in relation to the contingent, ongoing events of the black civil sphere. In terms of its internal structure, on the other hand, the church constituted a kind of multilevel civil society in microcosm. Inside its organizational space, it promoted solidarity and fellow feeling. It was, in Morris's words, "an institutional alternative to, and an escape from, the racism and hostility of the larger society," and it provided "a friendly and warm environment where black people could be temporarily at peace with themselves while displaying their talents and aspirations before an empathetic audience."[68] This solidarity was stimulated by opportunities for democratic kinds of face-to-face organization. Morris describes the "fluid and informal quality" quality of interaction, which allowed "people to express their feelings and often mingle in informal groups long after service ended."[69]⎫

This interactional and cultural experience of solidarity became institutionally articulated by the numerous standing committees and problem-oriented groups that focused attention on practical matters like fund raising and wider community issues and affairs. The participants in these intrachurch groups were held to strict standards of accountability; they were bound by a sense of duty, not only by practical interests and concerns. These office-like standards for normative behavior were regulated and enforced by the political and economic power exercised by ministers of the black church. Yet this minister, in turn, was elected by, and responsible to, the solidary community constituted by the church members themselves. One influential black minister described the democratic aspect of the selection process in this way: "He had to be nominated to that post. He had to be voted in. He had to be made the pastor. Nobody sent him down. No bishop said here's who you're going to have whether you like it or not. That minister had to make it out of nothing, what we call the rough side of the mountain."[70] Martin Luther King recounted his effort to gain the ministry at Atlanta's Dexter Avenue Baptist Church in this way: "I was very conscious that this time I was on trial."[71]

Duality and Translation: Toward the Civil Rights Movement

There can be no doubt that this black civil community, properly understood as reflection and refraction of the distorted ideals of the surrounding civil sphere, played an enormous role in the civil repair of racism that crystallized in the Civil Rights movement of the 1950s and 1960s. It supplied economic and organizational power and an ideology of solidarity in the struggle against white oppression. As we will see in the following chapter, however, some of the most acute observers of the great events of that time, both academics and movement intellectuals, have conflated this provision of resources with the Civil Rights movement itself, mistaking the mobilization of the ideo-logical and material resources that made successful civil translation possible with the activity of translation itself. In his discussion of the lunch counter sit-in movement in 1960, for example, Morris emphasizes how "the mass-based black church mobilized the resources necessary for collective action." He describes the "telephone lines and the community grapevine;" the "numerous midday and late night meetings" where "the Black community assembled in the churches [and] filled the collection plates, and vowed to mortgage their homes to raise the necessary bail money in case the protesting students were jailed." He speaks of the black lawyers who "pledged their legal services" and the black physicians who "made treatment available to the injured demonstrators."[72] In Bayard Rustin's reflections on the Civil

Rights movement's great success in Birmingham in 1963, this important black intellectual and veteran political activist, who was Martin Luther King's closest advisor during the early years, similarly points to the civil solidarity of the black community, to how it "was welded into a classless revolt."[73] King himself, in an article titled "The Great Lessons of Birmingham," highlights the critical role of the "democratic phalanx" that assembled in Birmingham's streets, where "doctors marched with window cleaners," where "lawyers demonstrated with laundresses," and where "Ph.D.'s and no-D's were treated with perfect equality by the registrars of the nonviolence movement."[74]

The critical question, however, is not what kinds of resources were available but how they were mobilized. This is the transition from counter-public to civil repair. The black counterpublic did not just throw its body against the white oppressor; nor did it simply project the open spirit of the black masses against the closed spirit of southern whites. The black counterpublic was a necessary but not sufficient condition. It supplied material and cultural resources for a movement whose tactics and strategies were defined largely by its possibility of gaining access to the environing civil sphere. Once again, the critical issue is duality. The Civil Rights movement succeeded, in part, because blacks bravely confronted the southern white power structure. It also succeeded because black leaders convinced influential members of the northern civil sphere to enter the confrontation alongside them. In order to achieve such persuasion, they had to find a way to translate their own, primarily black struggle against southern racial domination into the language and idioms of the northern civil community.

In concluding this discussion of the conditions for civil repair, we will briefly examine the black community's uneven but growing understanding of the need for such communicative mobilization. In the decades that marked its gradual emergence, black civil society waffled uncertainly between the options of exit, voice, and loyalty.[75] In the face of the failure of Reconstruction and the closure of opportunities in the South, Booker T. Washington, with his injunction to forget about public protest and to concentrate on educational and economic advancement, advocated a loyalty approach to the surrounding civil sphere. Marcus Garvey's immensely popular Back to Africa campaign embodied an exit strategy that expressed the black community's fatalistic sense of distance from the possibilities of American civil society. However, as black civil society became a more powerful refraction of the surrounding civil sphere, there emerged movements that exercised voice. These efforts sought neither to withdraw from the civil sphere of American society nor to demonstrate loyalty to its contemporary instantiations. What they demanded, rather, was the fuller and more complete institutionalization of its idealistic promises. These demands simultaneously resisted the destructive intrusions of race and reproduced the idealistic principles of the American civil sphere that, at least implicitly, held out the possibility for overcoming them.

The most important expression of this demand for voice was the formation, in 1909 and 1910, of the NAACP. Today, the early activities of the NAACP are primarily remembered as legal ones, and they certainly did represent, as I have mentioned above, a nascent movement toward the democratization of regulative institutions vis-à-vis the white communities of the North and South. In fact, however, the NAACP's role in creating the conditions for civil repair was primarily communicative. This was true in two very different respects.

In the first place, alongside its legal arm, the NAACP established a Publicity and Research Department to change white public opinion about blacks, countering polluting stereotypes through pamphlets, speeches, lobbying, and press releases. Its first director was W.E.B. DuBois, the Harvard-educated sociologist and philosopher who became the most influential black intellectual of the pre–Civil Rights movement era. Believing that racial distortion of the American civil sphere could be overcome through education and persuasion, DuBois created *Crisis*, a monthly magazine that published the works of gifted black poets, artists, and writers.[76] *Crisis* demonstrated the NAACP's ambition both to refract and reach out to the implicit but unfulfilled promises of the surrounding civil society. The editorial section of *Crisis* dedicated itself to the "rights of men, irrespective of color or race, for the highest ideals of American democracy," and in DuBois's maiden editorial he declared his own commitment, and the NAACP's, to explore and to publicize "those facts and arguments which show the danger of race prejudice."[77]

Alongside such activities as these, which were explicitly directed to public opinion, the legal arm of the NAACP, composed of distinguished white and black lawyers, dedicated itself to confronting racial domination by bringing the principles of the American Constitution, the core regulatory institution of the surrounding civil sphere, to bear on destructive civil intrusions in the South. Although these legal efforts achieved a number of important victories in the two decades after the NAACP's foundation, Morris is right that "it would be misleading to present these courtroom battles in a narrowly legal light."[78] The victories, and even the hard-fought losses, served a more symbolic capacity. They provided a kind of demonstration effect for duality, showing black and whites alike that southern white domination was at least potentially vulnerable vis-à-vis the surrounding civil sphere.[79] The NAACP's legal activity achieved its latent function, not its manifest one; failing to overthrow the racist white power, it nonetheless contributed to its "delegitimation."[80]

¦That the NAACP's early legal victories in themselves failed to effectively alter the system of southern racial domination testifies to the fact that law is only one critical element in civil society.⌐To be effective, changes in legal order must either be complemented by shifts in the other regulatory institutions or, at the very least, not directly opposed by them. Furthermore, if the fragmented structures of civil society are to be effectively changed, shifts in regulatory institutions must be related to changes in communicative institutions, to new cultural understandings, and to alterations in face-to-face interactions. This is not to suggest that all the levels and institutions which compose the civil sphere must be articulated, in the sense of working together; it does mean, however, that they cannot work completely at cross-purposes. If more universalistic and civil laws are enacted, how can they go into effect if the regulatory institution of office is not changed in a more civil way? If the officials of the court, such as judges and lawyers, do not support the intent of the new law, how can it be implemented? If administrative officials and police officers do not enforce it, how can the sanctioning power of the legal regulatory institution come into play? How can such legal changes and expanded office obligations be consistently maintained, moreover, if the institution of the franchise is distorted in a manner that produces elected officials whose sensibilities, obligations, and perceptions of interest are not expanded in a more civil way? Finally, how and why would any of these regulatory institutions change if public opinion has not provided a climate that restructures understandings of outsiders' motives and the kinds of relationships and institutions they can sustain?

These theoretical considerations allow us to understand why the NAACP's various strategies failed to alter the southern system of racial domination and why this failure could eventually be remedied only by the emergence of a massive social movement for civil rights. It is not terribly difficult, of course, to understand why the organization's campaign to change public opinion came up short. It was not the case that the opinions of white northerners remained unchanged, for there was, in fact, a gradual but discernable shift in the racial thinking of the white northern elite from the 1930s on. What the NAACP's educational activities lacked, rather, was intensity and scale. The cognitive shift they effected failed to reach the masses of white Northerners. It also failed to generate, even among such white elites, a heightened emotional interest in altering the racial system, and such intensified interest was a fundamental requirement if any identification of white and black sensibilities was to occur. This failure to extend its influence beyond the cognitive, beyond the emphasis on education, was also a critical reason for the NAACP's inability to tap the energies and talents, for both resistance and translation, of the black community itself.[81]

In a country that has historically been obsessed with legalism, as Tocqueville was the first to note, it is more difficult perhaps to understand why the NAACP's legal strategy was relatively ineffective. This is particularly perplexing when one realizes that it was the NAACP that successfully argued *Brown v. Board of Education of Topeka*, the Supreme Court decision that declared school desegregation unconstitutional in 1954. Before the ruling, southern segregationists had expressed great fear about its possible effects. "We will face a serious problem," South Carolina Governor James F. Byrnes warned before the Court's hearings commenced, "should the Supreme Court decide this case against our position."[82] When the ruling was handed down, moreover, it was widely hailed as groundbreaking, a landmark revision of the distorted civil sphere that would radically and permanently alter racial domination in the United States. It did nothing of the kind. Despite the fact that communicative institutions, not only factual and fictional media but public opinion polls, articulated strong public support for the desegregation ruling, the new regulations simply were not enforced.[83] Not only did the highest ranking officer of the nation, President Dwight Eisenhower, never publicly endorse the Court's decision, but, by calling for local and state rather than national action, and by expressing open skepticism about legal remedies for racism, the president actually undermined possibilities for implementation. After the initial publication of their ruling, the Court's own justices acted in a similar way. Not only did they wait almost a year to issue specific instructions for implementing the ruling, but the instructions themselves gave control over the desegregation process to officers of the racist civil society of the South. "Because of their proximity to local conditions and the possible need for further hearings," the justices wrote, "the [southern] courts which originally heard these cases can best perform the judicial appraisal." On these grounds, they claimed it was "appropriate to remand the cases to these courts."[84]

When it became apparent that, under such conditions, the legal regulations demanding desegregation could have no effect, Congress passed the Civil Rights Act of 1957, which established new regulatory institutions and new offices specifically concerned with implementing minority rights. These included the U.S. Civil Rights Commission and the Civil Rights Division of the Justice Department. Yet these efforts too were unsuccessful, and for the same reasons. The officials who held power in southern civil society were again able to block the more civil influence of the North. As David Garrow puts it in his study of voting rights, "recalcitrant, obstructionist judges in most southern jurisdictions all but stifled the Justice Department's attacks on voting-related racial discrimination and harassment."[85]

It was in this context of continuing racial domination and increasing frustration with the regulatory institutions of America's civil sphere that leaders in black civil society turned their protests against racial exclusion in a different direction. From aiming primarily at legal regulations and elite reeducation, they focused on communicative institutions and spoke powerfully to broad masses of people. By skillfully mobilizing nonviolent direct action, they were able to translate their complaints and their selves in a manner that leapfrogged the barriers erected by the anticivil power structure in the South. Taking full advantage of duality, the protest against the destructive intrusion of race developed into the most successful social movement in American history. This is the story about the Civil Rights movement that I will now tell.

CHAPTER 12

Race and Civil Repair (2): The Civil Rights Movement and Communicative Solidarity

THE CIVIL RIGHTS movement has become the most intensively studied subject in contemporary American history, its tens of thousands of significant events and influential social actors serving as the subject of meticulous reconstructions by every discipline of the social sciences and humanities. These studies increasingly have focused on the richness and complexity of the local experiences of African Americans in southern communities, and they bear witness to the extraordinary energy and mundane devotion that made the success of this movement possible, not only the courage to face the terrorism of white violence but the years of door-to-door organizing and neighborhood meetings in homes and churches, the innumerable leaflets and pamphlets, the frustrating string of days in courts, the endless petitions to gain the right to vote and to be treated as human beings. In all these ways, the local and national African American leaders of the Civil Rights movement and the black masses themselves manifested uncommon courage as they marched on a road to empowerment that most visibly began with the Montgomery bus boycott in 1955 and concluded ten years later with demonstrations in Selma and passage of the Voting Rights Act. The march for full empowerment of black Americans, of course, began long before 1955, just as it has continued up to the present day, and it will have to extend long into the future. Still, the decade between 1955 and 1965 was critical; it was then that power was seized, and that seizure of power paved the way for redistributing resources in the years that followed.

As long as there is some autonomy for the civil sphere of society, however, power can be seized only indirectly, by influencing, and only in this sense gaining control over, the discourses and institutions of civil society itself. Blacks could never have seized power directly in the southern states. When they tried, their efforts were put down with overwhelming force.[1] It was duality, not instrumental power, that promised the possibility of justice, and this duality could be activated only by finding a way of reaching over the anticivil domination of white southerners to the other, more civil side. This is why the Civil Rights movement cannot be conceived as being about power in the narrow sense, especially if this term is understood as involving direct, physical, face-to-face confrontations between masses of African Americans and their immediate oppressors on the local scene. The Civil Rights movement, rather, was about influence and persuasion, about achieving a more commanding position in the civil sphere of American society. Only as they were able to gain such influence could civil rights leaders, and the masses they were energized by, achieve power in the more instrumental, regulatory sense.

In the immediate postwar period, as we have seen, it was the inability of regulatory reforms actually to repair the racial distortions of American civil society that triggered the mass mobilization for civil rights. Regulatory reforms in legal institutions were enacted, but they were not sufficiently articulated with the other levels and institutions of the civil sphere. If legal changes are to take effect, they must be complemented by changes in office obligations, by shifts in communicative institutions, and by deep alterations of public opinion. It is for this reason that the civil rights movement always had dual goals. They organized against local racial domination, but in the course of fighting these struggles they tried determinedly to gain national, civil attention as well. They wanted to mobilize public opinion in the northern civil sphere, especially the opinion of members of the northern civil society who were white. By transforming this opinion, they created civil power, influencing the behavior of national officeholders, both in politics and the law, and gaining leverage over social power in turn. With this newfound economic and political power, they could finally control their oppressors, who had been safely insulated in the civil sphere of the white South.

How did this happen? As contemporary historians have noted, local leaders had been conducting battles for racial justice—in effect, little civil rights movements—long before the first big campaign emerged in Montgomery, Alabama, in 1955.[2] What was different about those who assumed leadership in that first battle of the modern Civil Rights movement was precisely their ability to reach outside this local scene. They strategized not only locally but nationally, not only concretely but abstractly, not only in particular but in universal civil terms. In the beginning, this was not so much a strategy as a feeling, a sensibility. There was a lot of fumbling and stumbling, but, from the beginning, the leaders of the Civil Rights movement understood that it was a dualistic direction they must take. What differentiated this new generation was its ability to make the translation, to frame and reframe complaints so that they could leapfrog southern officials and gain the attention of other kinds of whites. Their success at translation was due in part to their skill at reweaving cultural contents, stitching together the tactics of Gandhian nonviolence, Christian narratives of sacrifice and exodus, and the justice rhetorics of American civil society.[3]

These messages, however, were only as good as the communicative institutions that carried them. They were told in the local, particular context; they had to be transmitted to the national, civil one. Such transmission was by no means a foregone conclusion. It depended on the existence and the reach of communicative institutions of an expansively civil kind. That is why we will begin our explanation of the Civil Rights movement with the white journalists who worked for progressive newspapers and magazines. From the beginning, there was a symbiotic interaction between the social dramas staged by civil rights leaders and the "point men" of the communicative institutions who defined their jobs as interpreting such dramas to the civil sphere. That neither could exist without the other was a recognition, at once simple and profound, that became increasingly conscious and consequential as the black movement grew in influence and civil force.

The Battle over Representation: The Intrusion
of Northern Communicative Institutions

That a significant number of journalists and their institutions defined their communicative obligation as interpreting the civil rights dramas to the wider, national civil sphere is something to be sociologically understood. For the fact that protest movements take place does not, in itself, guarantee that they will be represented publicly in the mass media, much less that they will be represented in a civil manner that elicits audience sympathy for the movement and possibly identification with it. In white southern civil society, the communicative media were racist, as distorted in their civil pretensions as white public opinion and southern regulatory institutions.\Southern white newspapers interpreted events in a framework that justified black exclusion from the civil sphere, an interpretive justification that could proceed in two ways.\On the one hand, it could make black exclusion invisible, providing its white audience with deceptive representations of an inclusive, participatory civil sphere. On the other hand, the fact of racial exclusion could be recognized, but the motives and relations of black persons could be constructed in a manner that suggested their inability or unwillingness to participate in civil society, and, indeed, the danger of allowing them to do so.

In his retrospective look at the youthful leaders of the Civil Rights movement, David Halberstam, a former *New York Times* reporter who covered the South extensively in the 1950s and early 1960s, gestures to the first mode of justification when he describes "the old political correctness in those days" as "both very powerful and very pernicious."[4] I will later call attention to the emphatically evaluative character of this declaration; at this point, however, we are concerned simply with Halberstam's description of the white southern media's invisibility strategy, which he describes as "the skillful use of silence at critical times."

> Throughout the South, when blacks gave any demonstration of grievance, there was a decision by consensus—the ruling white oligarchy of the town in concert with the editor of the paper—to take either no note of what had happened, or to write a tiny inoffensive story and bury it somewhere in the middle of the paper.[5]

In terms of representations of the Civil Rights movement, Halberstam describes the results of the invisibility strategy in this way: "If black heads had been cracked during a protest demonstration, then it was . . . unlikely to make the paper[, and] the [white] community would be spared any reports on what had happened."[6]

As the Civil Rights movement heated up, and confrontations between black protesters and southern officials spread throughout the region, representational invisibility gave way to representational distortion. Southern communicative institutions, not entirely but certainly in their vast majority, broadcast representations of the protests that reconstructed the activists' motives and relations in terms of the discourse of repression, employing these constructions to justify segregated institutions in turn. They did so in official editorials, but also by quoting from, and highlighting as factual and perceptive, the observations about ongoing events offered by southern conservatives and racists as they acted to defend white civil society.

In late 1961, for example, at the height of the confrontation between civil rights activists and local officials in Albany, Georgia, the chairman of the Georgia Democratic Party, James Gray, appeared on the local television station, in which he owned a controlling interest, to endorse segregation as "a system that has proved over the years to be peaceful and rewarding." In order to defend this positive evaluation of an obviously antidemocratic institution, Gray described segregation's black critics in polluting, anticivil categories. Rather than portray the activists as rational, independent, and critical, he represented them as "a cell of professional agitators," suggesting deceptiveness, thoughtless conformity, and lack of principle. Linking the demonstrators to the enemies of American democracy and contrasting them with the nation's revolutionary founders, Gray argues that the burgeoning black rebellion "smacks more of Lenin and Stalin than of George Washington, Thomas Jefferson, and Abraham Lincoln." Contrasting altruistic, religiously inspired motives to instrumental and egoistic ones, Gray tells his viewers that Martin Luther King, the leader of the Albany demonstrations, "has learned that martyrdom can be a highly productive practice for the acquisition of a buck." Finally, calling for an end to the disruptions, Gray summed up his advice by offering an overarching binary representation that contrasted white civility with black anticivility. "What we need is tolerance," he asserted, "not tantrum."[7] Seven months later, just before King received a sentence of forty-five days in jail for his misdemeanor arrest during the Albany demonstrations, Gray justified this repressive response to the civil conflict in a special front-page editorial in the *Albany Herald*, the local newspaper which he also owned. Again, he highlighted the antidemocratic motivations of the "agitators," their "craft and cunning" and their secret "plottings." Gray flatly declared, "The Negroes are lying." After so graphically announcing their civil incompetence, Gray went on to link these qualities with American democracy's most hated, anticivil enemies, equating black complaints about segregation with "the Hitlerian tactic of the 'Big Lie.'" Gray concluded by dramatically describing the Civil Rights movement as the polluted and dangerous enemy of everything good. "This sordid effort will fail," he declared, "because its motivation is essentially evil."[8]

One year later, in the midst of the decisive contest in Birmingham, Alabama, Gov. George Wallace used the occasion of the legislature's opening session to broadcast a fierce restatement of this binary. Announcing that "we shall fight agitators, meddlers and enemies of constitutional government," Wallace constructed the movement for black civil rights as an uncivil danger to the Constitution, the central regulatory institution of American democracy. By establishing this binary, he could declare that the struggle against the black movement was "in reality a fight for liberty and freedom."[9] If the core of civil society were really at stake, it is not surprising that, in Wallace's view, the polluted character of the movement activists justified repression. In a widely noted characterization and threat reported by the *Birmingham Post-Herald*, the Alabama governor declared himself to be "tired of lawlessness in Birmingham," and promised that "whatever it takes will be done to break it up."[10] These representations and sentiments were fervently iterated on the local scene. Birmingham's mayor, Arthur Hanes, represented the protest's leader, Martin Luther King, as a "rabble rousing Negro" and "terrorist" and his fellow activists as a "bunch of race agitators." The city's most powerful official drew the same repressive conclusion from this discursive destruction, as had the state's governor, suggesting that the black activists "should be put out of circulation."[11] When members of the city's more moderate white elite finally settled the bloody conflict, Mayor Hanes furiously described them in an equally anticivil way: "They call themselves negotiators. I call them a bunch of quisling, gutless traitors."[12]

Because such symbolic representations had never been successfully challenged before the mid-1950s, they were allowed to stand as cognitive-cum-normative descriptions of the distorted civil sphere in the South. That more expansive representations did not emerge to compete with these restricted ones has a straightforward explanation. Such interpretations were not broadly distributed because journalists from communicative institutions in the surrounding civil sphere, the more civilly oriented northern one, simply were not on the scene in the southern states. This lack of physical presence represented a fundamental lack of attention and concern. The emergence of civil rights as a national social movement changed this situation, or, more accurately, the movement's emergence depended, in some part, on this situation's being changed. From 1956 on, northern journalists were in the South, attracted by the Montgomery movement that caught the national attention and catapulted Martin Luther King into an influential civil position.

Once the northern journalists were there, they took sides, framing their representations of segregation and the struggle against it in ways that attributed civil competence and rationality to the black activists rather than to the southern whites. The newly arrived northern reporters were aware that they were engaged in a battle with the southern press, that they were waging a war against "the treatment of racial news in Southern newspapers," as a reporter for the *New York Post*, Ted Poston, put it in 1966.[13] The battle was over symbolic representation, first and foremost, but it was also a struggle to define and maintain what the northern reporters viewed as their independent professional ethics.[14] For in attacking the southern media's categorical pollution of civil rights activists, northern reporters conflated its anticivil politics with professional irresponsibility. More simply put, they identified racist coverage with the failure to tell the truth, the first and most important commandment of contemporary journalism's ethical code. "The majority of the Southern editors and publishers," Poston declared, "have been cynically defending a myth that they know to be untrue—white superiority, Negro indolence, and a baseless contention that the region's magnolia-scented values would triumph over the moral and legal might of the federal government."[15] Professional irresponsibility and anticivil behavior were considered to be one and the same.[16]

Yet although they disdained the putatively antiprofessional, mythmaking qualities of southern media, these northern reporters did not, in fact, view themselves simply as reporting facts alone. Indeed, just as southern journalism was seen as both antiprofessional and antidemocratic, so did northern

journalists consider their own commitment to truthful observation and accurate reporting as allowing them to become vehicles for expressing the
core values of American civil society. In doing so, they were highly sensitive
to the duality of their social position. In 1962, in the midst of Mississippi's
civil rights upheavals, John Herbers, then manager of the state's United Press
Services wire services and later a southern correspondent for the *New York
Times*, linked the quality of news reporting by northern journalists to their
being outsiders. This external position, Herbers believed, explained their
commitment to the normative legitimacy of desegregation and the regulative
efforts to enforce it. "Most newspapers from outside the region," Herbers
wrote, "have played the Southern integration story from the point of view
that it—the court-ordered change—is morally right, the law of the land and
inevitable."[17] Though Herbers eschews such a morally committed point of
view for his own particular type of communicative institution—"the wire
services cannot do this and they should not be asked to"—he nonetheless
defines his own journalistic role in a manner that emphasizes its commitment
to tracking deviations from the sacred values and regulatory controls of the
civil sphere. "Wire services can and should maintain a vigilant watch for
any violation of individual or group freedoms guaranteed to all citizens of
the United States," Herbers insists, "and report the truth as nearly as it can
be ascertained."[18] From the point of view of this highly influential journalist,
in other words, what is newsworthy, what should be selected and distributed
as accurate and honest social representations, are threats to the ideals of the
civil sphere. Once again, journalism's professional commitment to truth
telling is equated with the commitment to, and maintenance of, transparency: the values of honesty, publicness, and openness that are intrinsic to
the civil sphere itself. /

Nothing more effectively illustrates how duality defined the perspective
and behavior of northern communicative institutions during the Civil
Rights movement. Journalists felt themselves to be vitally connected to the
core of the civil sphere that surrounded Southern racial domination. Thus,
in 1966, when the managing editor of *Life* magazine expressed his hope that
future historians would be able to say that "the press of those critical years
of the mid-1960s was a great press," his criteria for greatness perfectly articulated the requirements for civil solidarity. "Wise and deeply human," it
would be a press that "covered the conflict yet allayed it," whose influence

"changed angry monologues into reasonable dialogues," whose judgment "chipped away at the edges of hatred" and "kept in view the larger cause of a democratic society and thereby helped keep it from being rent apart."[19] In the same committed vein, the executive editor of the *Chicago Daily News* emphasized that reporters could be no more "unbiased" than other American citizens, for "the racial crisis is an issue that no American of this generation can push off into a corner and say with accuracy that it has no personal connection with him."[20] Attacking the "pose of impartiality," the editor insisted that "any decision to disseminate or not to disseminate news is in itself a partisan act."[21] This journalistic involvement was not only moral and political but emotional and psychological. A liberal journalist working for an independent southern newspaper, noting that "intense emotion was involved," acknowledged that "it has been difficult for the professional to keep his reporting and his editorializing separated," reminding his listeners that "reporters and editors and even publishers are human."[22] Herbers agreed. Declaring that "everyone is emotionally involved," he suggested that it was categorical representation—"the way the news is worded"—that triggered the most passionate sentiments.[23]

These emotional and moral commitments created among many northern white journalists a deep sense of psychological identification with the struggles of the southern black community. The managing editor of the *St. Louis Post Dispatch* testified, for example, that northern journalists became more and more deeply involved in the black struggles, recounting how "some of us began to try a little harder . . . to determine the needs, the desires, and the hopes of the Negro community."[24] In fact, it was not entirely accurate to suggest, as I did earlier, that northern journalists took sides in the civil rights struggle only once they were there, in the South and on the scene. Most of them had already taken sides before they arrived; it was precisely their emotional and moral commitments that compelled them to get involved. After describing himself as "a white male, born in rural North Carolina [and] raised in Raleigh," Fred Powledge acknowledges that "for reasons that I never have been able to understand but never thought of as remarkable, I grew up with an intense dislike for segregation."[25] Despite a secure position as a reporter in New England, this sense of emotional revulsion made Powell "desperate to go south and help cover what clearly was going to be the biggest story of my time." Thirty years later, after a distinguished career that included reporting on southern civil rights struggles for the *New York Times*, Powell confesses proudly to his continuing sense of commitment and identification: "I was and am . . . biased in favor of the Movement. More than that, I was and remain completely taken by it. I still believe it is the most important event in American history since Independence."[26]

In his sentimental memoir of the youthful participants in the Civil Rights movement, David Halberstam similarly recounts how intense moral and emotional commitments fused with professional ambition and a sense of historical destiny to compel him to "set off to begin my journalistic career in Mississippi" immediately after graduating from college in 1955. One year after *Brown v. Board of Education*, Halberstam recalls, he had come to believe that "that powerful social forces would now be set into play in the South," and he wanted "to have a chance to cover them."[27] Halberstam set off for his southern journalistic career carrying his earmarked copy of Gunnar Myrdal's *An American Dilemma*, which he describes as "the most important and influential book I had read at the time and probably have read since."[28] Though he claims that there was "very little editorializing in the news columns" that he prepared during his southern stay, and even that the story of the civil rights activists was a story that virtually "told itself," he makes no effort to conceal the intense sense of identification he experienced with the black protagonists of the struggle.[29] Writing of the leaders of the sit-in movement in Greensboro, North Carolina, Halberstam notes how he was "virtually their own age and very much at ease," that he "knew and liked" them, and that he "felt considerable sympathy for their aims and their grievances."[30] Halberstam does not hesitate to describe the deep feelings of admiration he experienced for the youthful sit-in leaders, attributing to them great moral stature. "I was impressed by these young people from the start," he recounts, and he cites their "courage and their dignity and their awesome inner strength."[31] Halberstam closes his narrative by connecting what he calls "the courage and nobility of [such] ordinary people in times of stress" to his own personal commitment to democracy. "No occasion in recent postwar American history," he writes, has provided "so shining an example of democracy at work . . . than what happened in those days in the South."[32]

Translation and Social Drama: Emotional
Identification and Symbolic Extension

Informed by the classical model of social movements and its contemporary variants, recent historians and social scientists have tended to construe the Civil Rights movement as a conflict between two organized groups, a battle whose resolution depended upon one side marshaling sufficient resources, power, and force to dominate the other.[33] Certainly this was not the case. From Montgomery on, the movement's success, both locally and nationally, depended upon its ability to establish a solidaristic relation with the broader, less racially distorted civil sphere, which drew its power from geographical regions outside the South.[34]/Establishing this solidarity depended not on the availability of resources, though these were critically important, but on the movement's ability to translate its particular concerns, whether those of power, money, race, salvation, earthly dignity, or psychological revenge, into the broader idioms, networks, and institutions of civil society. Solidarity depended on identification, identification depended on publicity, and publicity depended on communication of a certain kind./Insofar as this translation cycle was effective, moreover, its communicative phases were continually punctuated by regulatory responses of a more coercive, though equally civil kind, which took the form of interventions by officeholders who potentially wielded great power. Whether these were officers of the court, such as judges, or officers of the state, such as elected politicians, in the course of the Civil Rights movement these officials of the civil sphere periodically were compelled by great movements of public opinion to intervene against those who wielded racial domination and distorted civil society in the South. Sometimes they did so because, as members of the civil sphere, they were persuaded by the translations the Civil Rights movement produced. Sometimes these officeholders intervened for more instrumental reasons; realizing that members of civil society were changing their minds, they were afraid of being subjected to shifts of civil power and, ultimately, losing their jobs.

The northern communicative media functioned as a kind of membrane for the southern Civil Rights movement, creating a semitransparent envelope that mediated messages the movement projected to its far-away civil audience and the responses this audience projected back to it. Andrew Young, centrally involved with King and movement strategy almost from the beginning, spoke about how the civil rights demonstrations aimed to present "a particular injustice before the court of world opinion," a phrase that points to the duality I have been suggesting here. For a local movement of dominated persons to take full advantage of duality, they needed to speak effectively to the court of world opinion, an accomplishment that would depend on skilled and effective translation. "We had to craft a concise and dramatic message," Young wrote, one directed to the broad civil audience and, more specifically, to the initial interpreters of that message: the institutions of communication themselves. The first order of business, then, was to ensure that "the demonstrations be understood by the media."[35] Glenn T. Eskew, a contemporary historian who emphasizes the significance of local civil rights movements and who employs the classical social movement frame, acknowledges that "the mainstream media increasingly played a central role in the movement by broadcasting nationally what previously had been ignored as a local story."[36] With this magnifying and crystallizing membrane in place, "no longer did white violence against civil rights activists escape unnoticed."[37]

But to understand the process of translation and solidarity, to see how symbolic extension and psychological identification were constructed,[38] it is necessary to go beyond the media membrane to the movement itself. Why did the communicative institutions of the North get involved in the South when they had not generally been involved before? It was because of the movement itself. What first attracted journalistic interest, what brought reporters to the South and kept their attention after they arrived, was an extraordinarily compelling social movement, one that was proving itself to be a master of the translating craft. Communicative institutions don't invent the message; they interpret it and make it available to others. As one activist put the matter during planning discussions for the 1965 Selma campaign, "the press could not be expected to stay around and give the movement the national exposure it must have unless there was some action to photograph and write about."[39] This action had to be of a very specific kind. The media were a stand-in for civil society, articulating its requirements and its perspective in the communicative domain. Publicity was not, in itself, a movement goal; what mattered was publicity of a certain type. It was to the discourses and the institutions of the surrounding civil sphere, and to the possibilities of symbolically mediated civil interactions with its members and representatives, that the Civil Rights movement aimed.

In establishing a relationship with the surrounding civil sphere, the Civil Rights movement engaged not only in instrumental but in symbolic action, creating a compelling, arresting, existentially and politically encompassing narrative, a social drama with which the audience, the members of northern civil society, could identify and through which they could vicariously participate.[40] It is a fascinating and highly revealing fact of the academic literature on the movement that even those most interested in portraying civil rights leaders and masses as strategic, purposive, practical, and hard-headed continually employ the term "dramatic" to identify the movement's major events and activities. For example, in his local, "indigenous" approach, Aldon Morris emphasizes the centrality of power and organizational resources in fueling what he calls an "insurgency" by blacks against whites. Yet Morris writes about the 1961 Freedom Rides as an effort by civil rights activists to "provoke dramatic responses," and he attributes the project's success to its having "gripped the attention of protest organizations, Southern segregationists, and the society in general."[41] When Morris describes activists' strategic thinking during the later Birmingham campaign, he recounts that "it was determined . . . that massive daily demonstrations were needed to dramatize the racist nature of Birmingham."[42] In his detailed discussion of the power struggles that ensued, he recounts how "the drama heightened."[43] Despite Morris's own commitment to the classical model, in other words, he implicitly acknowledges that the demonstrations were not simply designed instrumentally to achieve the coercive effect of "prevent[ing] the city from operating normally."[44]

|There are empirical reasons why even those who are most theoretically committed to the classical model seem compelled to employ the term "dramatic." Civil rights activists felt themselves to be participating in an utterly serious morality play, and they tried as hard as they could to ensure that the drama would be presented to the surrounding civil audience in a manner that would evoke sympathy, generate identification, and extend solidarity.| In the late 1970s, James Bevel, one of the movement's most dedicated nonviolent exemplars, retrospectively explained movement "action" in precisely these terms. "Every nonviolent movement is a dialogue between two forces," Bevel wrote, "and you have to develop a drama to dramatize the dialogue to reveal the contradictions in the guys you're dialoguing with within the social context."[45] During the heated days of the social movement itself, participants experienced less a dialogue than a battle,

one that frightened and stimulated both them and the audience who observed and indirectly experienced it.

How could white northern civil society be there, in the South, yet not be there at the same time? When its physical presence was barely tangible, how could its moral presence be strongly felt? How could its representatives be compelled to intervene in a society toward which they had earlier evinced so little interest and on which they had exercised so little control? This could happen only through a process of emotional identification and symbolic extension. When Bevel thought back to the days of heated conflict, he had it right. At the center of the black movement's success was its dramatic quality. Aristotle explained that drama can compel identification and catharsis, the working through of emotions. Tragic drama excites in the audience pity and terror, and sympathy for the protagonist's plight. The progression of protagonist and antagonist can eventually allow catharsis, an emotional working through that affirms not only the existence but the force of higher moral law. The Civil Rights movement was not scripted; it was a social movement, not a text. Nonetheless, the contingent, open-ended nature of its conflicts were symbolically mediated and textually informed. Life imitates art as much as art imitates life.

The Civil Rights movement initiated a deeply serious drama at the heart of American civil society, a drama in which the very meaning and legitimacy of the civil sphere seemed to be at stake. It was a contest of "citizens" and "enemies." The innocent and weak were pitted against the evil and strong, and the forces of good, unexpectedly but persistently, emerged triumphant. This outcome made the process more melodramatic than tragic, yet despite its optimism about ultimate victory, melodrama shares with tragedy an emphasis on suffering and the excitation of pity and terror. In fact, the most dramatic moments in the decade-long struggle of the movement for civil repair were not the ultimate victories but the heartbreaking, if temporary, defeats. The movement's leaders became heroes only because they first were victims, because they came to triumph and power only after experiencing tragedy and domination. The leaders and their followers could be redeemed, and the possibility of civil progress affirmed, if they maintained their civil dignity in defeat; if they refrained from anticivil violence, aggression, dishonesty, and deception; if they kept faith with civil good in the face of anticivil domination and the temptation of despair.

The Montgomery Bus Boycott: Martin Luther King and the Drama of Civil Repair

Dramatic stories need heroes, not only enemies. The abstract discourse of civil society needs to become concrete. When Martin Luther King delivered his first, extraordinary speech as the newly elected president of the Montgomery Improvement Association (MIA) in December 1955 at the Holt Street Baptist Church in Alabama, he fulfilled both these demands. He concretized and embodied a new, race-oriented version of the drama of American democracy, becoming a courageous protagonist in a story about progress that would be narrated not only by King himself but also by grassroots leaders and the masses they inspired. He was taking the first step in a social drama that would break the continuity of political time and thrust the civil sphere into a separated, ten-year-long liminal space.

King was committed to practical things, despite his upbringing as an elite member of the black civil sphere. He was given to socialist leanings; he condemned economic inequality and poverty, and he fiercely resented white domination and privilege. Yet King was also deeply attuned to the symbolic status of protest in civil societies and to the critical duality of civil oppression.[46] For him, symbolic performance was not only a means to some other end, but an end in itself. In 1964, after the success of the Birmingham campaign, he explained what the movement had learned from its earlier failure in Albany. "We have never since scattered our efforts," King remarked, "but have focused upon specific symbolic objectives."[47] The symbolic objectives aimed to connect the particularity of the black movement to the surrounding civil sphere—in King's words, "to appeal to the conscience of the Congress" to "bring the necessary moral pressure to bear" and to "arouse the federal government."[48] Because of this sensibility, King was able to translate what could have been viewed simply as a social, political, and racial conflict over the distribution of resources, centering on aggression and struggles over structural position, into a moral confrontation in which the excluded and denigrated minority won legitimate authority and those who excluded them lost out.

King did not translate only from black civil society to white. He also translated between black and black, mediating between the utopian elements within the black civil sphere and the community's more pessimistic, self-denigrating beliefs. A recent editor of King's papers has described his gift "for dramatizing lofty moral ideas in vivid, down-to-earth word pictures" that "made his oratory irresistible . . . to all segments of the black community."[49] Drawing from the black civil sphere's sacred and secular traditions of universalism, King inspired members of a downtrodden and dominated racial caste to project themselves into the central categories of the surrounding civil society. Those who listened to his rhetoric and followed his actions could envision themselves as actors in the great narratives of historical liberation. They could identify with the Jewish people's exodus from Pharaoh's Egypt—a central biblical parable of black social gospel—or with their newly emancipated racial forebears in the first Reconstruction. As a veteran organizer from the movement's early days recalled, when King "talked about Moses, and leading the people out, and getting the people into the place where the Red Sea would cover them, he would just make you see them. You believed it."[50] Another leader made the mythical identification even more explicit: "Let's face it, a lot of our people thought that Martin Luther King walked on water."[51] One former high school organizer for the 1960 sit-in movements described King's connection to the members of the black civil society this way: "It was clear that they loved him. It was clear that they respected him as a leader and it was clear that they would follow him to the end if he wanted 'em to, you know."[52]

Not by any stretch of the imagination did Martin Luther King create the Civil Rights movement. It existed before him, and after his death as well. I am neither advocating a great man theory of history, nor downplaying the dedication and influence of other black leaders or the critical resistance, over long periods of time, of the members of black civil society themselves.[53] My argument, rather, is that, in order to understand the unprecedented success of the Civil Rights movement between 1955 and 1965, we must understand its discursive achievements, and it is impossible to do so without closely examining the role of Martin Luther King. He was the movement's critical mediating figure, translating between the unkept promises of white civil society and the hopes and anxieties of the black civil sphere.[54] It was in this dualistic role that, more than anyone else, he helped to create the "new Negro" in the South. During the decade-long struggle for civil rights, King often rhapsodized about changes in the identity of his people, who had "replaced self-pity with self-respect and self-depreciation with dignity." King wrote that "in Montgomery we walk in a new way. We hold our heads in a new way."[55] What he was pointing to here was the increasing interconnection between the dominant and dominated civil communities and the alternatives to subordination this allowed. As King mediated and translated the one to the other, the symbolic repertoires of northern white civil society became even more accessible to members of the black civil sphere. After recalling that "it was not easy to communicate effectively with the entire black community in Birmingham," Andrew Young testified that "Martin's arrest put the Birmingham movement in the headlines of the national news, and that in turn aided our efforts to organize locally."[56] Whenever King appeared on the scene of a local civil rights struggle, according to Morris, "a larger number of people were mobilized to protest and fill up the jails."[57]

Even as he crystallized the promise of civil ideals to black Americans and intensified their identification with the nation's civil ideals, Martin Luther King came also to symbolize America's civil promises to whites. It was not only for blacks but for tens of millions of northern whites that King became the most authoritative and compelling interpreter of the civil core of the United States.[58] In an extraordinary departure from the racist history of this democratic nation, a black leader came to represent, and reinterpret, the civil sphere of white society to white people themselves.[59]

How was King able to accomplish this performative action? There is the matter, of course, of his personal gifts. He possessed courage, high intelligence, and sensibilities and strategic abilities that were sharply attuned to the cultural and political currents swirling around him.[60] There was his unusual ability and desire to lead and inspire other men and women. There is also the matter of his background, his roots in African American social gospel, his secure position in the black civil elite, his wide and cosmopolitan learning, and his personal experiences in the northern white civil sphere. Drawing upon all these resources and his own personal gifts, King was able to project, crystallize, and translate the innermost structures of the discourse of American civil society.

King understood the community of the United States as in a state of tension, pulled between the binary forces of good and evil, between civil justice and injustice. This almost tactile sense of the two poles of the civil tradition and of the need to situate the Civil Rights movement in terms of the tension between them, characterized his entrance into the wider civil sphere in Montgomery, Alabama, and it animated every one of his later, much more famous and widely watched interventions as well. As he confided to Glenn Smiley, a civil rights activist for the pacifist Fellowship of Reconciliation in the early days of the Montgomery campaign:

> As we look at the problem, we see that the real tension is not between the Negro citizens of Montgomery and the white citizens, but it is a conflict between justice and injustice, between the forces of light and the forces of darkness, and if there is a victory—and there will be a victory—the victory will not be merely for the Negro citizens and a defeat for the white citizens, but it will be a victory of justice and a defeat of injustice. It will be a victory for goodness in its long struggle with the forces of evil.[61]

The most vivid early public representation of this vision can be found in King's first speech as MIA president. This entire oratory was cast in dualistic terms. Facing the crowded church and the more than ten thousand black Montgomery residents listening with the help of loudspeakers outside, King started with the general and universal. He tells his audience that they have created this protest movement, not because they are black but because they have the status of American citizens: "We are here in a general sense, because first and foremost—we are American citizens."[62] Their status inside the American civil sphere, King insists, is what allows people to use the promise of civil society as a weapon in their struggle: "We are determined to apply our citizenship—to the fullness of its means." From this lofty universalism, King moves immediately to the particularities of time and place: "But we are here [also] in a specific sense—because of the bus situation in Montgomery."

It is from the perspective of this tension between the universal and particular, between the possibilities of the civil sphere and the present state of its instantiation, that King introduces the particular incident that had triggered the Montgomery bus boycott and, indeed, the Civil Rights movement itself:

> Just the other day—just last Thursday to be exact—one of the finest citizens in Montgomery—not one of the finest Negro citizens—but one of the finest citizens in Montgomery—was taken from a bus—

and carried to jail and arrest—because she refused to give up—to give her seat to a white person.

King emphasizes the injustice of this arrest by insisting that Rosa Park's motives for not giving up her bus seat were civil ones. "And since it had to happen, I'm happy it happened to a person like Mrs. Parks," King said, "for nobody can doubt the boundless outreach of her integrity. Nobody can doubt the height of her character; nobody can doubt the depth of her Christian commitment." King now moves back to the universal from the particular, generalizing from this specific incident to the whole situation of southern black people, to their domination and to their feelings that the promises of civil sphere have been betrayed: "And you know, my friends, there comes a time when people get tired of being trampled over by the iron feet of oppression." Speaking graphically and metaphorically about the tension between the promises and the instantiation of American civil society, describing it as an almost physical divide, King tells his audience, "There comes a time, my friends, when people get tired of being thrown across the abyss of humiliation, where they experience the bleakness of nagging despair." Blacks are angry that they have been pushed from the category of civil good, which they deserve both by virtue of their civil status and their personal qualities, to the side of darkness and evil. "There comes a time," King declares, "when people get tired of being pushed out of the glittering sunlight of life's July, and [are] left standing amidst the piercing chill of an Alpine November."

Yet, despite this anger at the manner in which the black community has been pushed outside the category of the good, King wants to affirm that this Montgomery protest will abide by civil norms. "Now let us say that we are not here advocating violence," he declares. "We have overcome that." As putative participants in the civil sphere, blacks need not resort to violence; they can start a social movement. "The only weapon that we have in our hands this evening," King assures his listeners, "is the weapon of protest." Duality is what allows the protest weapon. The affirmation of being outside of civil society but inside it at the same time is, for King, the key to legitimating the civil rights protest and to affirming its identification with the wider civil sphere.

If we were incarcerated behind the iron curtains of a communistic nation—we couldn't do this. If we were trapped in the dungeon of a totalitarian regime—we couldn't do this. But the great glory of American democracy is the right to protest for right.

Yet, even as the MIA stands firmly with the civil mandates of American democracy, King narrates its opponents in the southern white community as defiling democracy in an anticivil way. He insists on the contrast between black civility and white southern anticivility. "There will be no crosses burned at any bus stops in Montgomery," King affirms, referring to the intimidating tactics of the racist Ku Klux Klan. "There will be no white persons pulled out of their homes and taken out on some distant road and murdered," he predicts. He promises that "there will be nobody among us who will stand up and defy the Constitution of this nation." King concludes by appealing explicitly to the utopian nature of civil promises and to the sacred and secular authorities upholding them, authorities admired by black and white Americans alike.

> If we are wrong—the Supreme Court of this nation is wrong. If we are wrong—god Almighty is wrong! If we are wrong—Jesus of Nazareth was merely a utopian dreamer and never came down to earth! If we are wrong—justice is a lie. And we are determined here in Montgomery—to work and fight until justice runs down like water, and righteousness like a mighty stream.[63]

There had been an ongoing protest in Montgomery, but it became transformed when Rosa Parks refused to give up her seat on December 1, 1955. Her arrest triggered the creation of the MIA and the election of King as its leader. Though the movement began and ended as a bus boycott, it reached deep into the heart of the distorted civil sphere. Bus segregation presented racial domination in its most highly visible form, that of civil interaction. Nowhere was the distortion of the promise of civil society so public, tactile, direct, and repetitive.[64] The battle against this anticivil domination involved tactics and strategy, and it depended on money, networks, and organization. But more symbolic elements were also involved. King needed to translate the local battle into a conflict within the broader civil sphere. It was crucial to project southern repression into the reflecting mirror of the surrounding northern civil sphere. Shortly after the initiation of the

Montgomery protest, according to a recent historian of the movement, King began to speak widely in church and community rallies in the North, "not only to raise funds but also to solidify a growing community of black and white activists around the country."[65] He reached into northern and southern black civil society, forging ties with the "established black leadership network of preachers, politicians, educators, and journalists," even as he reached over the racial divide into the most critical sectors of the surrounding white sphere, forging alliances with "white liberals and progressives in pacifist, labor, and religious circles."[66] These initial forays into northern civil society struck many observers as arousing an unexpectedly enthusiastic response. One northern newspaper, describing the atmosphere generated by King's first fund-raiser, in New York City, recorded "the kind off welcome [the city] usually reserves for the Brooklyn Dodgers."[67] This was precisely what King's southern white opponents had blithely ignored—in the words of another student of the Montgomery campaign, "the possibility that their show would not play [as] well to audiences beyond the horizon."[68]

Not surprisingly, less than two months had passed of the Montgomery movement before the northern media directly intervened. They sent journalists to cover the protest, and the reporters' emphatically civil interpretations made Montgomery into an event.[69] The national media projected King's message of redemption and reform back to the northern audience as news. *Newsweek* highlighted King's eloquent effort to universalize the faraway racial struggle. Quoting his statement that "one of the glories of America" was "the right to protest for right," *Newsweek* framed Montgomery in civil rather than racial or economic terms. "This bus situation," King told the magazine, "was the precipitating factor, but there is something much deeper. There is this deep determination . . . to rise up against these oppressive forces."[70] *Time* also placed the black protesters inside the sacred narrative of civic emancipation. Reporting on King's trial in April 1956, the magazine began with a portrait of how racial domination had long denied blacks' civil capacity: "For one hundred years Negroes walked soft and spoke low around Alabama's Montgomery Country courthouse." Now that a real protest had begun, however, things were different, and the debilitating tension between ideals and reality could be criticized. The tramping of their feet "sounded heavy in the dingy downstairs corridors," and their voices "were raised in pain and anger."

A Negro crowd roared hope. . . . After a lifetime of taking it quietly, their emotions welled up and overflowed in their testimony. Some began talking before defense lawyers asked for their names; others could hardly be stopped.[71]

When the bus boycott had triumphed, in December 1956, King congratulated movement activists and followers on their "dignity, sanity, and reasonableness" throughout the campaign.[72] The northern media of communication, following King's lead, employed similarly civil discourse to explain the protest movement's success, writing that broadening solidarity, not divisive conflict or aggression, had been its fundamental goal. The media broadcast this interpretation by configuring King as a dramatic hero. *Newsweek* underscored King's modesty and gentleness in victory, how he advised his followers, "don't go back to the buses and push people around. . . . We're just going to sit where there's a seat."[73] *Time* explicitly constructed this humility as a sign of King's civil capacity, writing that King "was too wise to be triumphant" and quoting his insistence that "all along, we have sought to carry out the protest on high moral standards."[74] Writing retrospectively of King's demeanor when his home was bombed months earlier, in the heat of the dispute, *Time* stressed even more strongly his commitment to the norms and institutions of civil society. The editors described how King had confronted the crowd of furious black supporters who had gathered outside his burned home and who thirsted for revenge. They quoted King's admonition to "please be peaceful" and his insistence on solidarity and its legal regulation:

We believe in law and order. We are not advocating violence. We want to love our enemies. Be good to them. Love them and let them know you love them.

As an indication that King's movement possessed the potential for civil repair, *Time* concluded by quoting a white policeman who had been on the scene: "I was terrified. I owe my life to that nigger preacher and so do all the other white people who were there."[75] In January 1957, a month after the movement's triumph, *Time* completed its civil construction of Martin Luther King. Putting his picture on its cover, they took the first step toward making this symbol into an icon.[76] At the center of American popular culture, such memorialization is reserved only for those figures who elicit the most intense public admiration. In a story titled "Personalities of 1956: Stars in Their Own Orbits,"/Time's editors described King as "what many a Negro—and, were it not for his color, many a white—would like to be."[77] /

King's early performance on the civil sphere's public stage already gave some presentiment of how this black leader could embody central themes not only from the New Testament but from the Old. His iconic representation of these themes deepened with the passage of time. A critical episode in this process of sanctification occurred in the year following the Montgomery victory. While autographing copies of *Stride toward Freedom*, his book-length account of that earlier campaign, King was stabbed in the chest by an emotionally unstable African American woman. Dramatically recounting how the blade had only "narrowly miss[ed] the critical aorta near the heart," *Time* treated the assassination attempt as a premonition of King's mortality and martyrdom. Coming on the heels of the magazine's representation of King as a popular icon, its account of the black leader's mental and physical response to the attack amplified his larger-than-life status./Time called King a "hero." Not only had he "escaped gun and bomb blasts in Alabama," but, while lying gravely injured in a Harlem hospital, King had remained "still conscious and calm." Consciousness and calmness, of course, are central categories that affirm the discourse of the good in American civil society.[78] /

After the great victory in Montgomery, this incident and others equally dramatic and dramatized lay ahead of King. What he had done already, however, was quite enough to create a movement for civil rights. Many practical things became possible after Montgomery. Drawing on church organizations and the little civil rights movements that already were ongoing in cities and villages throughout the South, King and his lieutenants formed the Southern Christian Leadership Conference (SCLC), and large sums of money were raised to staff this network in the North as well as in the South. These organizational efforts created a "material" basis for linking veterans of earlier protests, and for exciting and recruiting younger generations. These new adherents formed a cadre that would organize the massively publicized demonstrations in the years ahead and the hundreds of confrontations that were not selected and highlighted by the national press. These organizational networks were critically important, but it is important to remember that they were made possible by King's translation of the discourse of civil society, by the psychological identification and symbolic extension this mediation allowed for blacks and for whites. King had instantiated a movement of black protest in the symbolic center of the civil sphere for the first time in American history. In doing so, he had made it possible for white Americans to identify with the humiliations and hopes of blacks. Some whites began to feel as if they, too, were participating in the "freedom struggle."

Only with such identification would there develop the possibility of white indignation over southern violation of black rights. As we will see in the chapters following, it was the violation and physical degradation of black activists by southern officials and the shock and indignation this produced that constituted the true dramas of the movement. At the cultural level, this degradation would eventually be experienced by northern whites as a profanation of their sacred values, and the outrage they expressed against it would trigger an effort to protect their traditions in turn. At the psychological level, attacks on black activists were experienced by many northern whites as a violation of their own sense of self, and they expressed outrage in order to affirm their own identities. At the same time, these expressions of shock and indignation were socially oriented symbolic actions. Their aim was to force regulative intervention. Eventually, they succeeded. This dialectic of communication and regulation determined the post-Montgomery movement for civil rights.

CHAPTER 13

Race and Civil Repair (3):

Civil Trauma and the Tightening Spiral

of Communication and Regulation

I N THIS CHAPTER, we will explore more deeply the symbolic extension of interracial solidarity at the heart of the Civil Rights movement, investigating how its tensely wrought dramas triggered a sense of moral violation among members of the surrounding civil sphere that led them to initiate forceful symbolic action for civic repair. We will see how this compensatory symbolic action triggered unprecedented changes in the civil sphere's regulatory institutions, creating overlapping waves of institutional and symbolic activity. However, even as we emphasize the neglected role of symbolic action and communicative institutions, placing them at the center of efforts to change the structure of civil society, we cannot forget the structures of a more coercive kind. To assert the significance of civil power is not to deny political and social forces; it is rather to place them into perspective. When social systems contain civil spheres, the sources and effects of power must be conceived in new ways. Power must be redefined.

Duality and Legal Repair

It was the inability to effect regulatory reform that first stimulated a mass social movement for civil rights, and as this movement unfolded, the challenge of cultural translation necessarily assumed central stage. Yet although the very possibility of regulatory reform depended upon the success of this symbolic effort, the repair of regulatory institutions remained an absolute necessity if changes in popular and elite consciousness was going to affect racial power in an ongoing, long-term way. "Protest could stir the conscience, create concern, [and] focus attention," recalled Charles V. Hamilton, a lawyer and legal scholar who was deeply engaged in the struggle for civil rights. Hamilton goes on to insist, however, that "persuasion had to be codified into rules for future behavior, defining new relationships, spelling out new meanings of rights and obligations, limits and liabilities." This empirical argument about practical necessity points to the contrast between subjective persuasion and external sanctions. If the civil sphere is to construct social solidarity in an effective manner, some kind of complementary relation between communicative and regulative institutions must be attained. Hamilton calls the effects of regulative institutions "concrete outputs"; after successful persuasion, "court decisions had to be rendered, executive decrees issued, [and] legislation passed."[1]

Those who were intimately involved in the communicative struggles of the 1950s and 1960s envisioned just such a symbiotic relationship between their symbolic actions and regulative change. Nelson Benton was a photojournalist whose tape of police brutality at Selma, Alabama, in March 1965 played for more than two minutes on the CBS evening news. Benton later recalled how aides to Alabama's racist governor, George Wallace, had spoken bitterly at the time about there having been just "too much film." They were right. Only a few days after the broadcast, a U.S. District judge cited the film when he issued a critical restraining order against the Selma police. Benton himself drew a direct line between the photographic record and the Voting Rights Act that Congress passed later that summer.[2]

In their own strategic thinking about the Selma protest, civil rights leaders were intent on forging a communicative–regulative connection. "We want to establish in the mind of the nation," Andrew Young told the *New York Times*, "that a lot of people who want to register are prevented from doing so." For him, this communicative effort to change consciousness was the key to reforming the franchise, a central regulatory institution mediating between civil power, on the one side, and state and social power, on the other. "We hope this will lead to a revision of the voter registration laws in this state," Young said. In making this connection, he articulated a spiral relationship between communication and regulation: "We feel that action is needed in the courts and in the streets."[3]

In Martin Luther King's own retrospective analysis of the Selma campaign, he suggested that the connection between symbolic drama and regulatory reform had, in fact, been established precisely as Young proposed. Addressing the kind of thinking that informs classical social movement theory, King suggested that institutional power was not important in itself. "It was not necessary to build a widespread organization," he asserted, "in order to win legislative victories." The object of movement organization is to create compelling social drama, and this can be achieved, King believed, by "sound effort in a single city such as Birmingham or Selma." Selma was successful, in King's view, because the campaign had achieved the status of a collective representation, creating "situations that symbolized the evil everywhere and inflamed public opinion against it." Broadcast by national media, such condensed dramas provided vicarious, symbolically mediated experience far beyond the immediate venue. Such symbolic reach allowed local dramas to produce broad regulatory reform. Recalling how Congress had passed the landmark voting rights legislation in the shadow of Selma, King asserted that where the "spotlight illuminated evil, a legislative remedy was soon obtained that applied everywhere."[4]

As these statements by civil rights activists suggest, voting and lawmaking were the key regulatory institutions over which civil rights activists aimed to exert control.[5] For the racist powers that distorted civil society in the South, disenfranchisement had been a central aim. After the Civil War, however, the South had to pay formal obeisance to the rules that demanded a fully enfranchised civil society. According to the amended U.S. Constitution, every member of the southern civil sphere was, in principle, allowed to participate in deciding who would occupy the most powerful civil offices. To maintain racial domination in this new situation, southern whites created a series of ingenious techniques that effectively prevented their black compatriots from casting their ballots.

It is hardly surprising, then, that registering the disenfranchised became, time and time again, one of the Civil Rights movement's principal aims, from the "Crusade for Citizenship" initiated by the SCLC in 1957 to "Freedom Summer," organized by SNCC in 1964. Neither should it be surprising, however, that such efforts to leap directly from movement organization to local regulatory reform consistently failed. Enfranchisement of southern blacks was not formally assured until the U.S. Congress passed the Voting Rights Act in 1965, and it was not substantially achieved until years after that. As I suggested in chapter 6, while voting typically is considered the sine qua non of democracy, it is just one civil institution among many; sometimes, indeed, it is the last regulative institution to become autonomous vis-à-vis powers in the noncivil domains. If voting is the last civil regulation to take effect, it is because its compulsory power operates with an unalterable finality. Corrupt officeholders can sometimes hold onto their offices even when they are sharply challenged by other institutions in the civil sphere, communicative and regulative. Only when their challengers are able to achieve electoral empowerment is it certain that anticivil political leaders, and the various groups they represent, may finally be removed from control over critical state resources.

A crippled franchise, however, cannot be repaired until mechanisms of legal regulation have themselves been reformed. In terms of organized, concrete sanctions, it is the law that exercises authority over every aspect of civil life, from voting to office to face-to-face relations. Throughout the history of efforts to repair the racial distortion of American civil society, legal reform thus represented the single most important regulatory ambition. For those who have shared this ambition, the legal statutes that underlay the American civil sphere, particularly the constitutional ones, seemed to create an idealized democratic space, a space in principle without racial distortion. Charles Houston, the pioneering NAACP lawyer, believed that in court a black man could "compel a white man to listen."[6] Charles Hamilton, the contemporary legal activist and scholar, expanded on this idea when he asserted that "sound arguments could be presented in a court of law, despite the fact these very same arguments might not be relevant in the halls of Congress."[7] From the idealized perspectives of these legal reformers, the rationality and universality inherent in democratic law compels civility and solidarity, even among hostile parties. Such hopes are not completely unfounded. As we saw in chapter 7, legal regulations codify the utopian aspirations of civil society; their persistent evocation in an institutional arena bounded by professional ethics, precedent, and empirical evidence can have a significant effect on civil repair.

In the dualistic context of American racial domination, these utopian legal aspirations were codified only in federal law, which was, in effect, the law of the northern civil sphere. They were not institutionalized in the legal codes created and enforced by local civil powers in the southern states. It was for this reason that Martin Luther King sharply distinguished, in principle and practice, between state and federal law. King spoke eloquently of "the tragic sabotage of justice in the city and state courts of the South," where "the Negro . . . is virtually certain to face a prejudiced jury or a biased judge, and is openly robbed with little hope or redress." By contrast, he insisted, "the Southern Negro goes into the federal court with the feeling that he has an honest chance of justice before the law."[8] Without a second thought, indeed with fervent moral conviction, King continually broke state injunctions and restraining orders issued by local southern judges. He made it a fundamental tenet of his protest activities, however, never to violate federal law. He would not do so even if he believed that federal injunctions were morally wrong, even if they were issued by overtly racist federal judges whose rulings reflected the civil distortions of southern life. "I don't mind violating an unjust state injunction, but I won't violate a federal one," King told William Kunstler, his legal advisor during the 1962 Albany campaign. Kunstler's recollection is illuminating.

> I constantly stressed the fact that I considered the injunction illegal. While I did not advise King to violate it, I made it quite clear that I did not think he was bound by it. But he was adamant. Since the restraining order bore a federal imprimatur, he was determined not to flout it.[9]

King had organized the Civil Rights movement in response to duality; he wanted it to engage the utopian aspirations of the environing civil sphere, not only in its symbolic but in its organizational manifestations. The 1954 decision against school segregation had demonstrated the civil potential of federal legal codes, despite the fact that officials of the national sphere did not see fit to carry the decision out. Though the Montgomery movement had emerged in response to this regulatory failure, the bus boycott's victory was achieved when the Supreme Court declared unconstitutional Alabama's state and local segregation laws. That decision, moreover, simply denied the appeal by Montgomery and state attorneys of an earlier federal judgment against bus segregation.[10] As a result of these external decisions, the Montgomery judge who had issued pro-segregation rulings against the black protest was compelled publicly to dissolve his earlier regulations. Even as he bowed to these coercive orders, he sought to delegitimate the national civil sphere from which they derived. Constructing the federal authority in an anticivil way, he called the decision by Supreme Court an "evil construction," claiming it was based on "neither law nor reason."[11]

Legal constraint was irreplaceable, and federal legal forces made periodic, and critical, interventions into the local southern scene. Still, it remained very much the case, after Montgomery as before, that civil repair could take legal form only after the social movement for civil rights had succeeded in generating communicative solidarity. As one influential southern editor wrote about the sit-in movement, which emerged in 1960 partly in reaction to the growing frustration with efforts to effect regulatory change, "no argument in a court of law could have dramatized the immorality and irrationality" of segregation in such a powerful way.[12] Laws issue not from deductive logic but from judicial interpretation, and legal interpretation is a subjective action carried out in reference to a cultural frame. Oliver Wendell Holmes might as well have been thinking about the future Civil Rights movement when he wrote, decades earlier, that "the life of the law has not been logic [but] experience," explaining that "the felt necessities of the time, the prevalent moral and political theories," and "even the prejudices which judges share with their fellow-men" have had "a good deal more to do than the syllogism in determining the rules by which men should be governed."[13] Governing rules are deeply affected by public opinion and by the communicative institutions that crystallize opinion in the civil sphere.

Whether or not the fellow feeling of white federal judges was to be extended to the excluded black population in the South depended on how successfully the Civil Rights movement promoted psychological identification and symbolic extension. In the wake of the successful Montgomery campaign, the Republican president and Democratic Congress passed into law the Civil Rights Act of 1957, but federal officials did not even come close to carrying out its limited legal mandates. The Crusade for Citizenship that occupied the SCLC in the years after Montgomery failed miserably in its effort to extend voting rights to disenfranchised southern blacks, for the simple but quite sufficient reason that federal authorities possessed neither the will nor the resources to overcome the extraordinary opposition to franchise expansion that animated southern whites.[14] These and other fundamental repairs of racial domination waited upon compelling performances on the public stage of the surrounding civil sphere. This is precisely what the Civil Rights movement achieved.

The Sit-In Movement: Initiating the Drama of Direct Action

This later phase of the Civil Rights movement emphasized what movement leaders called nonviolent "direct action," for it was only such a provocative but simultaneously civil strategy that could provoke an aggressive, overtly anticivil Southern response. From the beginning of his leadership role in Montgomery, Martin Luther King had been a public advocate of nonviolence, an ethic that, as I have stressed earlier, was fundamental in creating a civil representation for the movement. In the years following Montgomery, moreover, the newly formed SCLC made the teaching of nonviolent tactics and philosophy a primary aim of its organizational development.[15] Yet neither in Montgomery nor in the years immediately following did King and his organization link nonviolence to a determined and provocative strategy of direct confrontation with southern officials. Indeed, it was not King but impatient college students outside the organized movement who, on February 1, 1960, initiated the first sit-in demonstrations at the lunch counter of a Woolworth's store in Greensboro, North Carolina.

There had been sporadic sit-ins at segregated facilities for at least two years preceding Greensboro, just as there had been bus boycotts before Montgomery.[16] What was different about the Greensboro sit-in was that, like the boycott at Montgomery, it succeeded in penetrating the symbolic space of the surrounding civil sphere. It was able to do so because the Civil Rights movement already existed not simply in organizational terms but as a set of collective representations, among them the powerful symbolization of Martin Luther King. In the days after Greensboro, King and other SCLC activists became deeply involved in planning the strategy of the sit-ins and in their public representation. In doing so, they were critical in helping to spread the new protest model to hundreds of other locations throughout the South.

What was new about the sit-in strategy was that it aimed at provoking a repressive response, possibly even a violent one. By doing so, it was able to more persuasively dramatize the civil legitimacy of the black social movement and the anticivil qualities of its southern white enemies. In the words of the historian William Chafe, the sit-ins provided "a new form through which protest could be expressed," a "new language" that more successfully "circumvented those forms of fraudulent communication and self-deception through which whites had historically denied black self-assertion."[17] This new form was far more theatrical than earlier tactics; it was physical and concrete, located in a particular place, at a particular time, involving not only visible but visibly antagonistic historical actors. This agonistic, theatrical form allowed the anger of the black community to be expressed in an embodied, visceral way.[18] This physical dramatization of civil indignation was what the young Robert Moses responded to as he sat in his Harlem apartment in New York City and watched the first televised reports of Greensboro. The future civil rights leader, then a high school mathematics teacher, recalled that "the students in that picture had a certain look on their faces, sort of sullen, angry, determined."[19]

For this new protest tactic to be dramatically successful, however, its aggressiveness had to be carefully encased in a nonviolent form. In fact, this provocative, in-your-face protest was presented to the public as a new kind of civil performance, one that articulated the norm of nonviolent civil interaction. In this artful manner, black anger was translated into the legitimating categories of the civil sphere. The written instructions distributed to sit-in demonstrators in Nashville, Tennessee, twelve days after the triggering Greensboro incident, neatly expressed this demand for civil translation.

> Do show yourself [to be] friendly on the counter at all times. Do sit straight and always face the counter. Don't strike back, or curse back if attacked. Don't laugh out [loud]. Don't hold conversations. Don't block entrances.[20]

As one youthful participant in the Nashville demonstrations later recalled:

My friends and I were determined to be courteous and well-behaved. Most of them read or studied while they sat at the counters, for three or four hours. I heard them remind each other not to leave cigarette ashes on the counter, [and] to take off their hats.[21]

Yet no matter how civil their self-presentation or how self-controlled their restraint, the sit-ins demonstrators aimed to provoke repression. The tactic was effective because it graphically exhibited the binary opposition between civil good and anticivil evil. As the movement of public disruption and disobedience spread, it increasingly provoked southern responses, both official and unofficial, that could be re-presented as violating the fundamental principles of civil society. These considerations lead us from the symbolic action of the sit-ins themselves to the representations of these actions by the communicative media of civil society.

Between the actual events of the Civil Rights movement and their media representations there was a contingent, open-ended relation. The sit-ins, and the black activists who led them, could be represented by the media of mass communication in very different kinds of ways. Conservative local media constructed the demonstrations and their leaders in terms of anticivil qualities that seemed to legitimate, indeed virtually to necessitate, their repression. In Montgomery, the *Advertiser* approvingly quoted the city's police commissioner warning of police reprisals "if the Negroes persist in flaunting their arrogance and defiance."[22] Though arrogance is related to the civil qualities of confidence and autonomy, it shades them in a polluting way, suggesting an aggressive disrespect. The irrational and negative implications of defiance similarly separate it from the civil legitimacy that accrues to critical, independent action vis-à-vis authority.[23]

When the first mass arrests took place in Nashville, local newspapers quoted the advice given to students by James Lawson, a local black leader. Lawson, a minister and experienced advocate of nonviolence who was also a graduate student at Vanderbilt University, told students they should join the demonstrations even if it meant breaking the law. The *Nashville Banner* characterized this statement as "incitation to anarchy." Placing Lawson at the center of an antidemocratic conspiracy of "self-supported vagrants" and "paid agents of strife-breeding organizations," the *Banner* demanded his forceful exclusion from the city, insisting "there is no place in Nashville for [such] flannel-mouthed agitators."[24] As the demonstrations in Nashville continued, Lawson was expelled from Vanderbilt University. When eleven of the Divinity School's sixteen faculty members resigned in protest, the *Richmond News Leader* commented "good riddance."[25] Affirming local understandings, which interpreted the protesters as constituting an anticivil threat, the *News Leader* proclaimed that "Vanderbilt University will be better off." Local media depicted the sit-ins not as a rational, independent response to racial domination but as an irrational, unmotivated, and cowardly siege manipulated by alien, unfeeling, and dictatorial culture and institutions in the North. After sit-in demonstrators were arrested in Raleigh, North Carolina, the local *News and Observer* asserted that "the picket line now extends from the dime store to the United States Supreme Court and beyond that to national and world opinion."[26]

To get a sense of how the northern media represented these same activities, we should recall our earlier discussion of the young David Halberstam's full-throated admiration for the sit-in demonstrators, indeed, his deeply personal identification with them. Journalists like Halberstam had come down to the South as much from political interest as professional ambition. They, and the media institutions they represented, hoped that their interpretations would expose southern racist behavior as violating the legitimate framework of American civil society. For the communicative institutions of the surrounding northern civil society, it was the white opponents of the sit-ins, not the black participants, who were represented as dangerous enemies of democratic life. "Familiar flotsam," *Time* called the white youth who harassed blacks during the sit-ins, reporting how they had heckled and often physically threatened them. In distinctly anticivil terms, *Time* described the whites as "duck-tailed, sideburned swaggerers," identifying the "rednecked hatemongers" with the Ku Klux Klan.[27] In sharp contrast with the local media's applause for Vanderbilt's expulsion of James Lawson, the *New York Times* interpreted the action as a flagrant violation of civil norms and put the story on its front page.[28]

Reporters' interpretations of the sit-ins were motivated not only by their personal inclinations and institutional norms but by frameworks offered to them by the civil rights leaders with whom they identified, especially Martin Luther King. Alone among established leaders of either race, King had responded immediately and enthusiastically to the sit-ins,[29] broadcasting his positive understanding through speeches that were reported throughout the nation, through interviews with various northern media, and through guest appearances on such influential editorial forums as the weekly television show *Meet the Press*.[30] In these broadcasts, King translated the new forms of local protest for the northern audience, deftly weaving them into the moral texture of the surrounding civil society.[31]

King depicted the demonstrators and their opponents in the highly charged language of civil society and its enemies. In his first public commentary on the sit-ins, he told an evening rally in Durham, North Carolina, that "men are tired of being trampled over by the iron feet of oppression."[32] Evoking the rhetoric from his MIA inaugural speech five years before, King symbolically associated the sit-in demonstrators with the righteous motives of a protest movement that had become memorialized as an emblem of justice in the national memory. As for the sit-in movement's local opponents, King drew upon broad and sweeping themes to identify them with civil evil and to insist on their necessary separation from civil good. "The underlying philosophies of segregation are diametrically opposed to democracy and Christianity," he told the audience, "and all the dialectics of all the logicians in the world cannot make them lie down together."[33] King then returned to the student protagonists, describing them, in direct opposition to the claims of their opponents, as mature, rational, and well-intentioned: "What is fresh, what is new in your fight is the fact that it was initiated, led, and sustained by students. What is new is that American students have come of age."[34]

From this coded characterization of the participants, King developed a narrative for understanding the struggle as a whole. He predicted that the sit-in movement was "destined to be one of the glowing epics of our time," that it would occupy one of the "honored places in the world-wide struggle for freedom."[35] Finally, addressing the provocative quality of this new form of protest, he concluded with a ringing assertion that accused southern officials of inverting the relationship between punishment and civil justice.

> Let us not fear going to jail. If the officials threaten to arrest us for standing up for our rights, we must answer by saying that we are willing and prepared to fill up the jails of the South. . . . And so I would urge you to continue your struggle.[36]

This metaphorical admonition to fill up the jails was destined to become a widely broadcast rallying cry for direct action against southern racial domination.[37] Meanwhile, King continued to generate and broadcast legitimating interpretations of the protest movement to the central institutions of the surrounding civil sphere. Three weeks after his Durham speech, as sit-ins erupted throughout the South and tens of thousands of young black students became involved, King cabled the highest official of American civil society, President Dwight Eisenhower. Indignantly demanding regulatory intervention, King called for the president to make good on the unfulfilled promises of the American civil sphere. Evoking the binary discourse of civil society, King dramatically contrasted the "peaceful and non-violent techniques" of the students with the "gestapo-like methods" and "reign of terror" unleashed by police and city authorities. He compared the "incredible assault[s]" of the police officials and their intimidating displays of physical force with the students' "orderly protest."[38] Ten days later, in its first editorial on the sit-ins, the New York Times followed the interpretive framework proffered by King and by agents of the media themselves. Observing that the sit-in movement was "something new in the South," the Times insisted that it should be viewed as "something understandable."[39]

Though the sit-in movement continued for many months, eventually involving some 50,000 protesters across a wide swath of southern states, by the summer of 1960 it already had succeeded in desegregating the lunch counters in key cities. It had done so by creating economic hardships for white store owners, whose black customers honored the protests by boycotting targeted stores. Yet much more than instrumental power and a local "battle of position" were involved.[40] For this local battle had been waged with massive support from the communicative institutions of the northern civil sphere. These institutions broadcast positive and informative "news" about the sit-ins, not only to the national audience but to potential participants on the local scene. These interpretations helped to recruit participants in the local movement and contributed to local organizing by generating infusions of financial and other kinds of material support. Finally, the media representations provided a subtle but very real morale boost to the student protesters themselves, giving them a sense of connection to the civil powers of American society outside the South. In a retrospective interview, James Robinson, CORE's executive director during the sit-in demonstrations, said that he and other leaders had been empowered by the events. Denying a narrowly instrumental understanding of power, Robinson gestured to a sense of participation and inclusion.

Well, it isn't money. It is a sense of power and certainly we got a hold of something. It gave us a great sense of power, because what we did was making a difference to society.[41]

Robinson expressed his astonishment that the demonstrations could have made "that amount of difference in that amount of time," for "when you added it all together, it wasn't enough to make a corporation change its policy." He acknowledged power, indeed, only in the communicative, civil sense. "There certainly was a sense of power," he recalled, when "we got our names in the paper."[42]

But even more important than support for local organizations and activists was the fact that the nationally broadcast representations extended the movement's symbolic reach and deepened the psychological identification it generated in the surrounding civil sphere. Pointing to how the sit-ins pulled "many people, often entire communities, directly into the movement," Aldon Morris wrote in 1984 that the demonstrations had succeeded in making "civil rights a towering issue throughout the nation."[43] A contemporary participant, the historian Howard Zinn, attested in 1964 that the sit-ins "marked a turning point for the Negro American," pointing to the movement's "skill in organization, sophistication in tactics[,] an unassailable moral position[, and] a ferocious refusal to retreat."[44] These analysts are certainly correct in their testimony about the wide ramifications of the sit-ins; they are on shakier grounds, however, in attributing this success to the movement's local effects. Certainly these local effects were great; nonetheless, the southern success of the sit-ins and, even more so, their success on the national scene depended upon the movement's ability to translate local particulars into the generalized language of civil society.

It was, in fact, the power of this symbolic intervention into the environing civil sphere that brought to the Civil Rights movement anticipations of the regulatory intervention that marked its long-term goal. The context was the franchise. Though southern blacks were systematically excluded from exercising their voting power, blacks in the North were not, and by the later 1950s their votes were increasingly tied to the drama of the ongoing movement for civil rights. The most intense period of the sit-in movement, and the communicative mobilization it generated, coincided with the critical winter and spring months in 1960, when Democratic candidates were engaged in a fierce struggle to become their party's presidential nominee.

Despite the risk of losing white votes in what until that time had remained the solidly Democratic South, the white contenders for the Democratic nomination vied with one another to associate themselves publicly with black leaders. Hubert Humphrey, an outspoken liberal, attracted the support of famous sports figure Jackie Robinson, a champion of integration who was in the process of becoming a crossover Republican. Lyndon Johnson, a progressive politician from Texas, posed for an exclusive photograph with a black leader for *Jet*, a leading weekly for the African-American community. Most interesting in retrospect is the orientation to the civil rights movement of John Kennedy.

The least experienced in racial politics of the three candidates, Kennedy became deeply concerned when his brother Robert, the manager of his presidential campaign, announced in early 1960, "we're in trouble with the Negroes."[45] As an aspirant to the highest office in a democratic society, John Kennedy sought civil power. The path to state power, the font of power in an instrumental sense, led through soft power, through influence and trust, not direct control. Kennedy had to gain recognition as a worthy representative of the civil sphere. Only by gaining this recognition could he be trusted with control of the state's coercive power, and only if voters believed that he could be trusted in this way could he win the right to represent the civil sphere inside the state.

In formal terms, civil power is achieved via election by members of the civil sphere. To gain black votes, Kennedy believed that he had to be seen as responsive to the growing movement for civil rights. Robert Kennedy assigned Harris Wofford, a white lawyer with Gandhian inclinations and an old family friend, to be the campaign's full-time liaison with the black community. Wofford had known Martin Luther King since the Montgomery bus boycott and, though he did not occupy a powerful position in the Kennedy campaign, he managed to arrange a breakfast meeting between his old friend and the presidential candidate. The meeting functioned both as a hurried personal introduction between the two increasingly influential civil figures and as a forum to begin discussing what kind of regulatory repair a President Kennedy might eventually propose. "News" of this unprecedented meeting was reported next day in the *New York Times*.

The palpable nature of Kennedy's political interest in King is revealed by the Democratic candidate's upbeat report on the meeting to his staff, which suggested that he had "made some progress" in gaining the protest leader's support.[46] To help solidify this support, the aspirant to high regulatory power felt compelled to go one step further, to identify himself, not just privately, but publicly with King. In fact, it was shortly after their initial meeting that Kennedy made his most direct and public evaluation of the sit-in movement. To a meeting of African diplomats at the United Nations, Kennedy legitimated the most recent, and most aggressive, civil rights protests by placing them within the broad narrative of American democracy. "It is in the American tradition to stand up for one's rights," he declared, "even if the new way to stand up for one's rights is to sit down."[47] The future president did not suggest any concrete course of regulatory intervention and did not make promises of any future actions. Still, his statement illustrates how the communicative mobilization around civil rights had become so powerful that the highest officials of American civil society felt compelled to demonstrate their identification with the movement.

In the almost five months that transpired between this first public statement of identification and the presidential vote, officials in the Kennedy campaign were whipsawed between their private moral support for civil rights and their professional judgment that any further expression of solidarity might forfeit the election by jeopardizing the Democrats' southern white support. Scarcely two weeks before the November vote, King was jailed during a sit-in protest against segregated facilities at an Atlanta, Georgia, department store. Though the county judge released most of the protesters, he denied King bail, sentenced him to four months on a chain gang, and transferred him in shackles to the state's maximum-security prison. Concerned about her husband's life, Coretta King called Harris Wofford, the Kennedy campaign aide, and asked for the presidential candidate's help. In response, Senator Kennedy called Coretta King and offered his sympathy and solidarity. "I know this must be hard for you," Kennedy told her, adding "I understand you are expecting a baby, and I just wanted you to know that I was thinking about you and Dr. King." After making this unprecedented gesture of solidarity, later broadcast via the communicative media to every corner of American society, he concluded by offering the services of his office. "If there is anything I can do to help," he said, "please feel free to call me."[48] That evening, a reporter asked Kennedy if it were true that he had called Mrs. King earlier that day. The candidate reaffirmed his sympathetic identification, replying, "She is a friend of mine, and I was concerned about the situation." Next morning, news of the phone call was reported by the *New York Times*, along with the information, generated by another inquiring reporter, that Kennedy's opponent, Richard Nixon, had offered "no comment" on the King case.[49]

The candidate's brother and campaign manager, Robert Kennedy, shocked and angered by the overtly repressive punishment that southern officials were meting out to King, telephoned not only the local judge but the state's governor, requesting King's immediate release. When word of this quasi-official intervention leaked out, the *New York Times* enthusiastically featured the link between communicative and regulatory power on its front page, citing Martin Luther King's reciprocating statement that he was "deeply indebted to Senator Kennedy, who served as a great force in making my release possible."[50] At the civil rights leader's welcome home celebration in Atlanta, King's father, the influential minister of Ebenezer Baptist Church, expanded on the newly articulated solidarity between the protest movement and the presidential candidate, telling his audience and by implication black civil society more generally, that Senator Kennedy's civic virtue had earned him the black vote. "I had expected to vote against Senator Kennedy," the senior King declared, "but now he can be my President [because] he has the moral courage to stand up for what he knows is right." Martin Luther King senior urged his audience of black citizens to make good use of their regulatory power. "I've got all my votes and I've got a suitcase," King proclaimed, "and I'm going to take them up there and dump them in his [Kennedy's] lap."[51] As rumors of the Kennedy phone calls began spreading through black civil society, the presidential candidate's campaign aides fueled the communicative process by preparing a pamphlet of supportive statements by the King family and black preachers. The Sunday before the election, black ministers and Kennedy supporters distributed two million copies of the pamphlet throughout African American churches in the North.

When Kennedy beat Nixon by less than two hundred thousand votes out of more than sixty-eight million votes cast, it became apparent to journalists and political professionals that African American voters had provided the edge. In 1956, blacks had given Republicans 60 percent of their votes; in 1960, by contrast, blacks voted Democratic by roughly 70 percent to 30. Taylor Branch, the most important historical narrator of this period, frames the significance of this change by suggesting that "this 30 percent shift accounted for more votes than Kennedy's victory margins in a number of key states, including Michigan, New Jersey, Pennsylvania, Illinois, and the Carolinas."[52] The day after the presidential election, the Republican national chairman criticized his party for having taken the black vote for granted.[53] In the days following, the northern media of communication represented Kennedy's victory as depending on the phone calls that had declared friendship and established solidarity between the white leader and Reverend King. Theodore White, whose *Making of the President, 1960* established him as the chronicler and mythmaker of American presidential contests, described the calls as the "master stroke" of the Kennedy–Nixon electoral contest.[54]

The New Regulatory Context

The sit-ins introduced into the Civil Rights movement a new form of direct action, a new and more effective social performance that, by widening symbolic extension and deepening psychological identification, further prepared the ground for regulatory intervention. Yet these civil dramas were still not civil traumas;[55] they would have to become traumatic before the northern civil community felt compelled to demand radical, wrenching institutional change. Though the dramatic confrontations had evoked aggressive responses from the southern officials enforcing racial domination, they had provoked relatively little violence. In this sense, the movement dramas remained more triumphs than tragedies, inspiring in the northern civil audience more a sense of hope and progress than the terror and pity associated with tragedy.[56]

This is not to say that during the sit-in campaign there were not demonstrations of anticivil violence by southern authorities, but that such incidents were either ignored by the local press or judged to be insignificant by those who communicated southern reality to the national civil sphere.[57] Thus, although media representations of the sit-in protests significantly extended symbolic and psychological identification among white members of the northern civil sphere, such representations did not trigger feelings of outrage. Because the movement was unable to spark outrage, it could not be effective in provoking a sustained, intense public attack on southern racial domination.

Only in the year following the sit-in movement, with the Freedom Rides of 1961, was civil indignation more fully expressed. The violently repressive responses to the Freedom Rides initiated a new and much more intensive phase of communicative mobilization. The northern civil audience reacted with anger to southern violence against the movement, with which they had come increasingly to identify. Compelled by this sense of outrage, they engaged in compensatory symbolic action, with the result that there was an extraordinary deepening of regulatory intervention into the southern civil sphere. This was not yet regulatory reform, and only such structural reform would fully repair the racial distortion of American civil society. It was, nonetheless, one major step along the way.

When John F. Kennedy assumed control of the American state in January 1961, he assumed, at the same time, office responsibilities on behalf of the national civil sphere. In both roles, Kennedy was keenly aware that there existed a new situation in regard to black civil rights. Sensing shifts in public opinion, Kennedy as a presidential candidate had demonstrated his responsiveness, and many believed he had been elected president as a result. When he assumed office, expectations for continued sensitivity were intense. Shortly after Kennedy's inauguration, the *New York Times* reviewed the preceding year of protests, noting that the sit-in movement had triggered "stand-ins at theatres, kneel-ins at churches and wade-ins at public beaches." The newspaper declared that the once scattered protests now threatened to "assume the proportions of a national movement."[58] Support for the movement was beginning to crystallize in the northern civil sphere, and it was at once represented and shaped by such newspapers as the *Times*. This communicative mobilization was further articulated and reinforced by public opinion polls. Polling as a communicative institution of the civil sphere had just begun to come into its own. In six of eleven national polling efforts between 1961 and 1965, the American "public" singled out civil rights as the issue that concerned them most, and in three others ranked it second.[59] This did not mean that a majority of Americans sided with the black demonstrators at every moment in every particular demonstration and campaign. To the contrary, the movement significantly polarized public opinion.[60] These poll results did indicate, however, that the movement's civil encounters were closely observed and that arguments over the interpretation of these actions echoed throughout the public and private arenas of civil life.

Indeed, by 1961 the social movement for civil rights had penetrated deeply into the collective consciousness of the civil sphere; it had become one of the primary ingredients animating the amorphous brew of public opinion. Still, though there was broadening support for its goals and increasing identification with its leaders, the northern audience interpreted each campaign and protest as an open-ended drama, and they scrutinized the manner in which protagonists and antagonists contingently displayed their relationship to the overarching framework of civil society and to the project of civil repair. This contingent quality of the movement's relationship to public opinion would never change. Even when it had succeeded in so deepening identification that it was able to secure regulatory intervention and fundamental repair, the movement's relation to public opinion was continuously contested, continuously subject to change.

The public representation of civil opinion via poll data affected the relation between the civil and political spheres in another, quite different way. Crystallizing the moral force of civil opinion, it also provided an opportunity for instrumentalizing it. The possibility for quantifying moral feelings allowed political actors to make more precise, means-ends calculations about the civil effect of their actions. Without doubt, calculations such as these allowed the new Democratic administration to understand with more precision the nature of its quandary.[61] The desire to be responsive to new developments in northern public opinion, as well as their own private moral beliefs, inclined President Kennedy and his staff toward an activist role against racial domination in the South. The cold calculations of power politics, however, told them it would be dangerous to do so. Public activism would risk southern support for the Democratic Party, which could prove disastrous for regulatory repair in the long run. Not only would the Democrats be unable to pass their reformist legislative proposals into law, but the nation's electoral map might shift in a manner that would exclude progressive politicians from executive office for decades to come.[62]

The new administration struggled for a way to offer regulatory intervention in private without making controversial public representations of its support. The head of its Civil Rights Division, Burke Marshall, translated this political inhibition into the seemingly objective language of legal constraint. Emphasizing the limits imposed by federalism, Marshall insisted publicly that federalism imposed severe constraints on government activism in the area of civil rights.[63] If not consciously duplicitous, this argument was thoroughly misleading, for it denied the duality that lay at the core of the civil rights movement's already considerable success. Nonetheless, for instrumental political reasons, public insistence on the limits of federalism remained the Kennedy administration's formal position until its last months in office, an insistence that it consistently violated in the breech. As wielders of political power, the president's staff had good reason to wish that their supportive administrative actions could be hidden from public view. As officers of civil society, however, the same staff were communicatively compelled to become directly and publicly involved.

Even as they consistently tried to push the Civil Rights movement in directions that would not compel them to make this involvement explicit, administrative officers felt bound to broadcast their support for the movement and their commitment to regulatory reform in an unequivocal, if broad and general way. Four months after assuming power, Robert Kennedy, the new attorney general, traveled to the heart of the Deep South to give a major speech on civil rights. "You may ask," Kennedy told his Georgia audience, "will we enforce the civil rights statutes?" To this rhetorical question, he responded, "The answer is: Yes, we will." Contrasting the new administration's interest in civil repair with the passive collaboration in racial domination that had characterized the Eisenhower administration, the new chief legal officer of the United States promised, "We will not stand by and be aloof"; to the contrary, he proclaimed, "We will move."[64] In striking contrast to the alarm these words raised in the South, the *New York Times* praised Kennedy's "resolute speech" on its front page.[65] The communicative institutions of northern civil society had already been aroused; for the first time, they began to anticipate that they would be joined by the nation's regulatory institutions.

The new administration tried to find a way out of its conundrum by organizing a series of semiprivate meetings with civil rights leaders, during which officials announced their intention to intervene actively in the area of black voting rights.[66] During these meetings, administrative officers promised to intensify, without publicity or fanfare, regulatory efforts to compel southern officials to allow blacks voter registration. Though it represented a compromise position, this federal voting rights effort was, nonetheless, a valiant one, headed by an Assistant Attorney General John Doar, who had a long record of defending black civil rights. In a series of visits that resolutely avoided encounters with southern whites, Doar developed material for the government's lawsuits through clandestine personal meetings with disenfranchised blacks. Yet no matter how idealistic, these unpublicized efforts at voter registration were bound to fail, as the Civil Rights movement itself had learned through bitter experience in the years following the Montgomery campaign.

\Simply in terms of administrative and legal power, the federal government had the capacity to force southern officials to register potential black voters. What it lacked was the empowering context of cultural legitimacy.\ Northern civil society would have to be mobilized to a much greater degree before the political calculations of northern leaders were to be altered, and more cautious considerations cast aside. Voter registration eventually would be achieved, and it would demand extraordinary federal intervention. This intervention depended upon massive new enforcement organizations at the national level, not on the daring and courage of individual officers, and it would succeed only insofar as these new enforcement officials were willing to risk potentially damaging public controversy. Regulatory intervention on this scale could not be mobilized until the legislative representatives of civil society passed new and stringent laws and established new, highly ambitious interracial goals. They would not do so until communicative mobilization became much more intense, until psychological identification and symbolic extension were deepened in a significant way.

The civil rights leaders knew all this. Though they were aware of the double political bind faced by the new administration, they knew that the quandary could not be resolved by a strategy that focused exclusively on voting rights. Despite this awareness, they told Kennedy officials that they would give the administration's own reform plan their whole-hearted support. At the same time, however, they told these national political leaders that they would insist on maintaining, and intensifying, their own, highly public and highly controversial struggles to mobilize civil support. Thus, even while Martin Luther King promised to work side by side with the Justice Department in registering voters, he warned the attorney general that earlier SCLC registration efforts had faced threats and harassment, and that assistance from federal police agencies, primarily the FBI, had been hard to find. Robert Kennedy's response made explicit and direct the new connection that was being established between the social movement for civil rights and the surrounding civil sphere. Handing King the telephone numbers, not only of Burke Marshall, but of his own personal assistant, Kennedy told King, "any hour of the day or night, you call."[67]

The Freedom Rides: Communicative Outrage and Regulatory Intervention

It was not only the civil environment that was changing, but the tactics, if not the strategy, of the Civil Rights movement itself. The communicative success of the direct action initiated by the sit-in movement had created a new situation. Civil dramas could be heightened and intensified, it was now understood, if they provoked highly publicized arrests and anticivil repression. Initiated by young and inexperienced activists, this more provocative form of civil protest created a youth-oriented civil rights organization, SNCC; it also pointed to new forms of activism for the established leaders of the Civil Rights movement, most notably for Martin Luther King.

There emerged a distinctive shift in the movement's self-understanding. From the beginning, nonviolent tactics had been fundamental to the successful translation of the black campaign for civil rights. In its earlier, more purely Gandhian form, nonviolence had promised, not only to "civilize" the activists by systematically controlling their physical and verbal aggression, but to educate and pacify the opponents against whom protests were aimed. By treating Southern whites humanely, activists believed, solidarity could be established, and this gesture of solidarity would eventually elicit in movement opponents a sense of moral shame. In December 1956, when the triumph in Montgomery seemed imminent, Martin Luther King had declared at a mass meeting that the movement's goal was not simply to gain victory but "to awaken a sense of shame within the oppressor and challenge his false sense of superiority," and he insisted that "there are great resources of goodwill in the southern white man that we must somehow tap."[68] By 1961, it had become abundantly clear that this second element of the nonviolent strategy rarely worked. Rather than nonviolent demonstrations creating a sense of shame among southern whites, with expressions of goodwill the result, they had triggered resentment, anger, and a desire for revenge.

Instead of the "concrete" other, the immediate partner in interaction, it turned out to be the "generalized" other—the indirect, mediated collectivity—for whom shame became the appropriate response. If there were a white collective consciousness that could experience guilt over racial domination, it animated not the members of the racially disturbed civil sphere in the South, but participants in the northern civil sphere, including the representatives of its communicative and regulative institutions.[69] For reason of both religious belief and civil self-defense, black civil rights leaders continued to uphold such idealistic sentiments as "Love is the force by which God binds man to Himself and man to man." They came to deploy these nonviolent sentiments, however, more as tactic than as strategy, using them to dramatize not the essential humanity of their southern opponents but their opponents' engagement in anticivil repression in defense of racial domination.[70] Nonviolence remained a commitment to civil and religious humanism, but it also became an inflammatory and highly effective tactic for arousing sympathy and identification from the surrounding public sphere. By provoking repression and possibly even violence from the movement's southern opponents, nonviolent tactics could make visible and dramatically powerful the anticivil domination that characterized southern society. "Instead of submitting to surreptitious cruelty in thousands of dark jail cells and on countless shadowed street corners," Martin Luther King wrote, the movement's nonviolent tactics would force the southern "oppressor to commit his brutality openly—in the light of day—with the rest of the world looking on." He was right.[71]

It was this new understanding that motivated the Freedom Rides, the highly provocative bus tour through southern states initiated by CORE in May 1961.[72] Formally, the protest actions aimed at testing laws that banned segregation in interstate transportation, laws that had been significantly strengthened by a U.S. Supreme Court decision, *Boynton v. Virginia*, in December 1960. Yet although CORE activists were thoroughly nonviolent in their tactics, they were perfectly aware that their efforts were likely to trigger physical repression. Through the first seven hundred miles and ten days, however, the bus filled with CORE activists rode through northern Dixie with little incident. This peaceful ride received scant attention from the communicative institutions of the northern civil sphere, let alone from its regulatory institutions. Of the three reporters who accompanied the bus riders at this early point in the protest, all were employed by black newspapers and magazines.

It was white violence against black bodies that altered this situation; only such an explicit dramatization had the power to bring the pain of racial domination and the protest against it back to the front pages and public attention. With the active cooperation of local political and police officials, a group of self-styled white vigilantes launched a ferocious assault on the protesters when their bus pulled up at the station in Anniston, Alabama.

They smashed the bus windows with bricks and axes, ripped open luggage, beat the activists, and set the interior of the bus on fire. A photograph showing flames leaping out the bus's front window and smoke billowing from every side went out over the wire services, eventually appearing, among other places, on the front page of the *Washington Post*.

Because of growing identification with civil rights activists, members of northern civil society reacted with outrage and anger to these depictions of anticivil attacks. By the time the Freedom Ride bus was ready to depart for its next stop, in Birmingham, the threat of continuing repression had attracted a considerable number of northern reporters, who waited in that city's downtown terminal for the bus to arrive. When it finally entered the station, the journalists observed a confrontation even more one-sided and violent than before. With the Ku Klux Klan in the lead and city officials actively collaborating once again, whites brutally bloodied the CORE activists, demonstrating intent to maim if not kill. Their wrath extended to white observers of the scene, including reporters and photographers. As representatives of northern civil society's normative ideals, and as journalists who often identified personally with the activists themselves, reporters reacted to these attacks with intense indignation. Howard K. Smith, a CBS television reporter who described himself as "horrified" by the carnage, offered his "eyewitness account" that very evening on the CBS nightly news. The next morning, narratives describing the violent oppression were broadcast, with barely controlled anger, on the front pages of northern newspapers, including the *New York Times*, which also circulated Smith's television report of the evening before.

This new spasm of civil outrage caused reluctant Kennedy administrators to make their first public regulatory intervention into the civil sphere. In the wake of the Birmingham confrontation, with Freedom Riders hiding out in his church and his home, Fred Shuttlesworth, the local leader of the Civil Rights movement, placed a call directly to Robert Kennedy, making use of the telephone numbers the attorney general had distributed to activists during the private meeting earlier that year. Shuttlesworth told Kennedy that the activists were "trapped" in Birmingham by white locals and southern officials, and that they needed federal protection to continue their protest rides. Kennedy promised to help, and he made the moral connection between African American protest and regulatory institutions physically concrete by establishing a direct telephone link between Shuttleworth's home and various offices in the Justice Department, including his own. In the context of the tense racial crisis and the growing identification of northern citizens with civil rights activists, it should not be surprising that news of this telephone linkage was broadcast on page 1 of the *New York Times*.[73]

Robert Kennedy called Alabama's Democratic governor, John Patterson, a longtime political supporter of the president, demanding that he order state protection for the protesters. Patterson replied that he would not guarantee their physical safety, declaring that the "rabble-rousers" were not "bona fide" interstate travelers and that they had put themselves outside legal protection by breaking Alabama's segregation laws. The governor claimed that, faced with such anticivil demonstrations, "the citizens of the state are . . . enraged."[74] As the officer charged with enforcing standards of the national civil sphere, Robert Kennedy faced a very different kind of outrage from the North. Responding to the Alabama governor's refusal to protect black citizens, he sent his personal assistant down to Birmingham that very night. The stand-off continued, threats of violence mounted, and local officials still refused to intervene. With the *New York Times* headlining "President Can't Reach Governor" on its front page, Robert Kennedy, after consulting with the president, initiated plans for federal marshals to intervene with physical force.[75] Burke Marshall, head of the Civil Rights Division, provided continuous mediation via the direct telephone line. Abandoning his voting rights activities elsewhere in the South, Assistant Attorney General John Doar traveled to the scene.

Faced with these threats of physical intervention, local officials allowed Freedom Ride buses to proceed to their next stop, Montgomery, where a bus boycott six years earlier had triggered the national movement for civil rights. The current protest's symbolic status as a civil drama was demonstrated by the reception the Freedom Riders received when they arrived at the Montgomery bus station. The reception areas inside the station were entirely deserted, as were the parking lot and streets outside. When SNCC leader John Lewis stepped off the bus, he was greeted not by southern citizens, but by a crowd of journalists from the North. As Lewis began an impromptu press statement, however, he was interrupted by armed whites who, having coordinated their plans with local police officials, had until then kept themselves hidden from view. Wielding baseball bats, bottles, and lead pipes, the angry whites proceeded to reap bloody mayhem. They assaulted not only protesters but reporters and photographers for the nation's leading newspapers, television programs, and magazines. Robert Kennedy's personal assistant was beaten into unconsciousness. John Doar described the unfolding scene to Burke Marshall over the direct line. The transcribed words of this civil officer underscore his sense of personal identification with the victims and his outrage over the attacks against them.

> Oh, there are fists, punching! A bunch of men led by a guy with a bleeding face are beating them. There are no cops. It's terrible! It's terrible! There's not a cop in sight. People are yelling, "there those niggers are! Get 'em, get em!" It's awful.[76]

As front page coverage and television time riveted national attention, and Governor Patterson blamed the federal government for the violence, Martin Luther King flew to Montgomery for an evening support meeting at the local church, headed by his SCLC colleague Ralph Abernathy. With the Freedom Riders hiding in the church basement, thousands of unruly white antagonists gathered outside. Outnumbered federal marshals spread themselves in a thin line along the perimeter of the church as the angry white crowd launched bottles and homemade firebombs. Faced with an imminent invasion and the possible loss of life, King placed a direct call to Robert Kennedy, who told King that additional marshals were on their way. King responded, "If they don't get here immediately, we're going to have a bloody confrontation because they're at the door now." When the supplement of federal officials finally did arrive, they used massive volleys of tear gas and the threat of lethal force to push the furious white mob away from the church.

In King's thanksgiving address later that evening to the fifteen hundred demonstrators inside the church, he linked the "hideous action" of the white lawbreakers to the anticivil motives and actions of the Alabama governor. "His consistent preaching of defiance of the law, his vitriolic public pronouncements, and his irresponsible actions," King declared, "created the atmosphere in which violence could thrive."[77] In his entirely different framing of the conflict, Governor Patterson publicly linked anticivil behavior not to violent whites and racist local officials but to "outside agitators coming into Alabama to violate our laws and customs [and] to foment disorders and breaches of the peace."[78] The governor also condemned the federal government. Claiming "its actions encouraged these agitators,"[79] Patterson established a polluting relationship between federal regulatory institutions and the black social movement he condemned. He was right, of course, that a relationship existed, if not in the valuation he placed upon it. Verbal and physical intervention from the highest regulatory institutions of American civil society had given the demonstrators courage and the opportunity to continue the drama of civil protest without risking their lives. In the same manner, symbolic intervention from northern communicative institutions had ensured that if the demonstrators did succeed in carrying the protest drama forward, there would be an audience for it.

This external support from the surrounding civil sphere, both regulatory and symbolic, was fully displayed two days later, when the Freedom Ride bus set out from Montgomery to Jackson, Mississippi. Twelve Freedom Riders were on board, accompanied by sixteen reporters and a dozen National Guard soldiers in full battle dress. Forty-two vehicles followed the bus, including Highway Patrol cars with sirens wailing, FBI spotter cars, and dozens of journalists. In the skies were two helicopters and three U.S. Border Patrol airplanes that supplied periodic reports about the safety of the protesters to the Attorney General's Office in Washington.[80] When the Freedom Riders had begun their protest against racial domination, they had been alone and ignored. Three weeks later, their protest was known throughout the United States, and in the North they were interpreted as heroic representatives of the nation's most cherished civic ideals. This identification had compelled national regulatory institutions to employ physical force to protect the protesters. As the carriers of sacred ideals, nothing could be allowed to harm them in any way.

In the wake of the Freedom Rides, no reforms were made in the legal regulation of the southern civil sphere, despite the extraordinary communicative mobilization the campaign had triggered and the direct intervention it had provoked. The *New York Times Magazine* opened its influential pages to an article by King titled "Time for Freedom," and, in a conspicuous display of public homage, the black leader was feted by Nelson Rockefeller, the powerful New York governor and Republican presidential hopeful.[81] However, while the Interstate Commerce Commission (ICC) strengthened its public commitment to desegregated transportation,[82] the Kennedy administration remained inhibited. Their fears about losing the South had been heightened by publicly exposing their support for the Freedom Rides, publicity that had generated local conservative anger. Trying to prevent further public identification, the attorney general and his staff urged movement activists to avoid demonstrations and to concentrate exclusively on voter registration, going so far as to promise them tax exemptions and draft exemptions if they agreed.[83] In his retrospective analysis of this period, Arthur Schlesinger Jr., one of several prestigious academics who had joined the Kennedy staff, explained that the Democratic administration was still committed to "carrying the mind of the South."[84] Civil rights activists had learned this was not possible, that the key to regulatory reform lay in persuading northern, not southern whites. Southerners would have to be dealt with later, in a more coercive way.

Failed Performance at Albany: Losing Control over the Symbolic Code

The next logical next step in the movement's campaign of mass persuasion was set to unfold in Albany, Georgia, in November 1961.[85] Sit-ins at the lunch counter in Albany's bus station and at other places had begun as a spontaneous outgrowth of the Freedom Rides and continued into the summer of 1962. As the Albany campaign developed, however, it turned into a serious misstep, one that threatened to stall and possibly even to derail the national social movement. What happened in Albany reminds us that even an expansive and skillfully led social movement, in a period when fortune seems to smile broadly upon it, remains an utterly contingent force. Translation is a delicate process that depends not only on resources, speeches, and sympathy, but on getting the staging right. In Albany, they were not made right; the movement's mise-en-scène was clumsy; its messages were not effectively translated. The scenes of protest performance were not transformed by media storytellers into affecting drama. The accomplishments of movement activists were not constructed in a sympathetic and compelling manner. The repressive actions of southern officials were not forcefully constructed as emblems of civil evil. The Albany campaign neither aroused the outrage nor engaged the sympathy of members and officials in the surrounding civil sphere.

In symbolic terms, the civil drama could not be produced because the story's antagonists—white southern officials—failed to follow the script that had worked so well for the movement so many times before. At the beginning of the demonstrations, the earlier dramatic sequence had still seemed firmly in place. Local SNCC activists were arrested at early confrontations, and hundreds of students followed them to jail. The SCLC joined the movement within the month. "When Martin Luther King came to town," the leader of the local movement later recalled, "there was worldwide press immediately present in Albany."[86] Because of King's presence, money poured in from major cities outside the South, and he "bolstered the morale of those people who might have sensed that the movement was really shaky." Describing King's relationship to Albany's African American community, another local black leader recounted, "It was clear that they loved him and that they would follow him to the end if he wanted them to."[87] After his arrival in Albany, with the national media and members of the black civil sphere watching and listening, King gave an electrifying speech, offering a framework for the civil drama that seemed about to unfold. "Don't get weary," he said. "We will wear them down with our capacity to suffer."[88] Shortly after, King was arrested and jailed along with hundreds of protesters.

From this point on, however, the civil confrontation, rather than un-folding, rolled back on itself. The Albany police chief, Laurie Pritchett, tried resolutely and largely successfully to prevent his officers from resorting to violence or any other kind of overtly anticivil behavior. By contrast, some significant acts of violence were committed by members of Albany's black community, and Pritchett immediately brought these departures from the protest movement's civil image to the attention of reporters. One evening, news spread throughout Albany's black civil society that white authorities had beaten a popular woman activist. When veteran movement leaders departed early from the protest meeting that followed, less experienced organizers decided to lead a march to city hall that attracted large numbers of onlookers and quickly turned into a near riot, complete with bricks, bottles, rocks, and threats of incendiary attacks. Andrew Young and other SCLC leaders rushed back to the scene. As they tried desperately, and unsuccessfully, to stop the rioting, Chief Pritchett called out to reporters, "Did you see them [sic] nonviolent rocks?"[89] Later, Pritchett bragged to a hastily assembled news conference that "there was no violence on our part—the officers never took their nightsticks from their belts."

This effort to rewrite the relationship between southern officials and the discourse of civil society was carried further by Georgia's governor, who announced, "I want all trouble-makers to know that I will do whatever is necessary to prevent violence at Albany, Georgia."[90] In an effort to regain control of the translation process, King called a halt to the protests, declaring a public day of penance devoted to self-scrutiny and renewal. Meanwhile, the *New York Times* published a profile lauding Chief Pritchett for his civic mindedness and restraint.[91]

Albany's political officials continued the civil offensive by publicly agreeing to negotiate with the protesters and even indicating that they would be willing to desegregate city facilities. It turned out that they were not. What city officials really wanted was to find a way of stopping the demonstrations without exercising anticivil repression. They wanted to get King and his fellow demonstrators out of jail and out of town as quickly as possible, and along with them the northern news media. Albany officials decided to suspend the protesters' sentences and lower their bail.

Neither King nor his local associates were prepared for the subtlety of this response, which revealed a new capacity to manage self-presentation under conditions of highly charged duality. In the face of King's continuing personal reluctance to leave jail, for example, local officials promised him that, if he would allow himself to be freed, they would also release the hundreds of local activists also being held. With this possibility, and with the SCLC staff urging him to turn his attention to what seemed more pressing movement issues elsewhere, King agreed to leave jail and to depart from Albany immediately thereafter. Whatever the complicating context, it seems clear, in retrospect, that in making this decision King lost sight of his exemplary role.[92]

Federal officials did everything possible to make certain that King would not regain it.[93] When Albany officials reneged on their promises to desegregate public facilities, King reconsidered his earlier decision. Returning to Albany, his protest compelled officials to arrest him and put him back into jail. This time, it was Kennedy officials themselves, acting surreptitiously and in cooperation with local leaders, who arranged King's release, without his knowledge and against his will. The goal was to undermine King's representational power, which derived in good part from his ability to symbolize suffering. This strategy of cultural deflation was intensified by the manner in which local officials explained to northern reporters how exactly King's expulsion from jail had come about. Local police told reporters that, late in the evening, a well-dressed black man had shown up at the jail and posted King's bail, disappearing immediately thereafter. This story was true only on its face. Contrary to its association of King with stealth and corrupting wealth, the messenger had, in fact, no connection to King or the movement; he was an agent of local southern officials working secretly with the Kennedy team.

Robert Kennedy congratulated Albany officials for their willingness to negotiate with protesters, despite the increasingly apparent fact that they had not done so in good faith. *Time* magazine reversed its normal framing of the relation between local protest and the national civil sphere, praising the civil qualities of Albany's police for dealing with the protests "unemotionally and with dignity" and for managing to avoid a "bloody battleground."[94] When King finally left town in late summer, the local demonstrations petered out, and the Albany campaign was represented as a major defeat for the movement against racial injustice. White and black northern reporters wondered aloud about King's civil motives and relationships, suggesting that his earlier successes may have undermined his moral strength. Perhaps he was now too weak, or even too self-centered, to lead the civil rights struggle down the hard path to further communicative mobilization and ultimately to regulatory reform.[95]

Birmingham: Solidarity and the Triumph of Tragedy

Writing thirty-five years after the communicative breakdown at Albany, *New York Times* columnist Russell Baker, an astute observer of the American political scene, still recalled the frustration and bitterness of that time. "By late 1962," Baker wrote, "King seemed to have failed in the attempt to arouse enough public passion to force the Kennedys to intervene."[96] Baker got the problem almost exactly right, except for his casual invocation of the term "force." The challenge was, indeed, to arouse the passion of the northern civil audience, for only if high civil officials were faced with such symbolic mobilization might they be persuaded to intervene. The cultural challenge of arousing passionate indignation had been negotiated time and again in earlier demonstrations, but it still had not yet been fully achieved.

Yet, while Albany had been a devastating setback, the possibility for intensifying communicative mobilization certainly remained. Neither the institutional framework of the surrounding civil sphere nor its deep structures of public opinion had been changed. King was criticized personally during and after Albany; but the communicative media and their civil audience did not, for that, begin to empathize with southern white domination. The collective representation of racial domination had not been altered, even if contingent events were continuously changing in relation to it. At the end of 1962, on the occasion of a study of the Albany campaign marking its one-year anniversary, the *New York Times* headlined the failure of regulatory institutions to act in a responsive, civil manner: "President Chided over Albany, Ga.: Fails to Guard Negro Rights." Though the study had ample criticism for all the parties involved, *Times* reporter Claude Sitton, in his front-page story, chose to quote the report's assertion that the federal government "has hovered about Albany from the beginning [but] incredibly, in this whole time, it has not acted." Emphasizing the study's criticism of federal rigidity, Sutton prophetically remarked that it seemed "the Government will not move in racial controversies unless there is uncontrolled violence."[97]

Though Sutton and other representatives of the northern civil sphere regretted that violence seemed necessary to trigger regulatory intervention, protest leaders not only were thoroughly reconciled to the fact but bound and determined to provoke it. They knew that in order to frame white violence effectively, they would have to exert significantly more control over their own performance than they had in Albany. King and his organization, the SCLC, had always entered civil rights contests haphazardly, leveraging King's prestige and the deference he commanded to exercise— sometimes at the last minute—dramatic power over the flow of events. After Albany, planning for the future in a gloomy atmosphere of possible defeat, the civil rights leaders were determined to leave less to chance.[98]

As the more democratic civil sphere of the North increasingly penetrated the racially distorted civil sphere of the South, symbolically and even organizationally, the significance of duality became widely recognized, and the tensions it produced were more highly charged. More reflexive and self-conscious about civil symbolism, the SCLC for the first time planned, or scripted, a campaign from the start to the putative finish. It drew up a carefully formulated plan called "Project C" for "confrontation" and stipulated three incremental sequences of mobilization that would follow "B Day," when the demonstrations in Birmingham were scheduled to begin.[99] The very choice of Birmingham as the target for this exercise in systematic provocation reveals the movement's heightened self-consciousness as compared with earlier campaigns. Birmingham was picked not because of its potential for civil repair, but for the very opposite reason: it was viewed as a deeply reactionary city whose chief law enforcement officer, "Bull" Connor, had a serious problem containing his temper and maintaining self-control. The protest movement had chosen the drama's prospective antagonist with care. Only if there were a clear and decisive space between civil good and anticivil evil could the conflict in the street be translated into a symbolic contest, and only if it became such a contest could the protest drama gain its intended effect.[100] In the days leading up to the campaign, Ralph Abernathy, King's principal assistant, promised, "We're going to rock this town like it has never been rocked before." Bull Connor retorted that "blood would run in the streets" of Birmingham before he would allow such protests to proceed. King drew upon the book of Exodus, the iconic parable of the Jews' divinely inspired protest against oppression, to provide an overarching narrative for this imminent clash, promising to lead demonstrations until "Pharaoh lets God's people go."[101]

Despite this elaborate initial preparation, at the commencement of the protests the social drama would not ignite; the political play did not develop as planned. The demonstrations began on cue, and King went to jail. Yet Birmingham's black civil society did not rise up in solidarity and opposition, and the surrounding white civil sphere became neither indignant nor immediately involved.[102] Rather than dramatizing the split between local officials and black demonstrators, and the tragic possibilities that might result, the *New York Times* narrated the situation in a more deflated, ameliorating way. Reporting after two weeks of demonstrations, the *Times* argued that Birmingham residents of both races were looking to a newly elected reform mayor, Albert Boutwell, for "a diminution, if not an end, to racial tensions that have grown alarmingly the last few days." On its editorial page, the newspaper suggested that the city's residents should not expect enlightenment to come to Birmingham "overnight," and warned that Martin Luther King "ought not to expect it either."[103]

This dilution of duality did not go unnoticed by the communicative institutions of white Birmingham, whose papers ran such headlines as "Washington Liberals Ponder Wisdom of Demonstrations" and "Birmingham Image Gets Better Press."[104] The ambiguous situation was also seized upon by local clergy, who composed an open letter attacking the protest movement, published in the *Birmingham News* under the headline, "White

Clergymen Urge Local Negroes to Withdraw from Demonstrations." The letter defended the racial status quo by inverting the contestants' relation to civil discourse. Blaming the demonstrators themselves for inciting "hatred and violence, no matter how technically peaceful those actions may be," the clergy praised local police for "the calm manner in which these demonstrations have been handled." The clergy concluded that the protests were not only "untimely," a reference to the unskilled quality of King's translation effort, but "unwise," a phrase that suggested civil incompetence more generally.[105]

As it began to appear that the framework for communicative failure had been established once again, the movement dug in its heels and made a determined, last-ditch response. Martin Luther King made an angry rejoinder to the white clergy's accusations. Weeks later, after the protest movement had regained control of the translation process, King's eloquent twenty-page missive would be hailed as the "Letter from the Birmingham Jail." Against the local clergy's presumption of symbolic legitimacy, King sought to place the protest movement itself at the center of civil cultural power. The tensions in Birmingham, King asserted, occurred not because of black protests but because of the injustice created by white domination, which removed the onus of anticivil pollution from the demonstrators and placed it on southern whites. In such a situation, King insisted, peaceful demonstrations could never be untimely, let alone unwise. Then, in a rhetorically complex series of counterpoints that played skillfully upon the binary chords of civil society, King explained why "we find it difficult to wait." "You will understand" our impatience, he wrote:

> when you have seen vicious mobs lynch your mothers and fathers . . . ; when you have seen hate-filled policemen curse, kick, brutalize and even kill your black brothers and sisters with impunity . . . ; when you suddenly find your tongue twisted and your speech stammering as you seek to explain to your six year-old daughter why she can't go to the amusement park that has just been advertised on television . . . and see her begin to distort her little personality by unconsciously developing a bitterness toward white people . . . ; when no motel will accept you; when you are humiliated day in and day out by nagging signs reading "white" and "colored"; when your

first name becomes "nigger" and your middle name becomes "boy" (however old you are) and your last name becomes "John."[106]

These phrases ostensibly were directed at the local white clergy; implicitly, and much more powerfully, they were addressed to the white audience in the northern civil sphere. When King spoke to his northern audience, he was speaking in the subjunctive mood. Assuming civil solidarity, he asked his listeners to could put themselves in the place of the dominated black other. The Birmingham protests deserved support, he wrote, because "the Negro is your brother." The brotherhood of black and white would be recognized, King predicted, because American democracy, no matter how deeply flawed, remained committed to a transcendent civil ideal: "We will reach the goal of freedom in Birmingham and all over the nation because the goal of America is freedom." In America, King suggested, this institutional goal was rooted in a sacralizing vision that intertwined secular and religious ideals: "We will win our freedom because the sacred heritage of our nation and the eternal will of God are embodied in our echoing demands." Having anchored the framework of racial solidarity in the sacred discourse of civil society, King could conclude by purifying the black protesters whom the white clergy had impugned. He praised them for "their sublime courage" and linked them to the mythical founders of American civil society.

> One day the South will recognize its real heroes. . . . One day the South will know that when these disinherited children of God sat down at lunch counters, they were in reality standing up for the best in the American dream and the most sacred values in our Judeo-Christian heritage, and thusly, carrying our whole nation back to those great wells of democracy which were dug deep by the founding fathers.[107]

This letter, written on scraps of paper and smuggled out of jail over many days, surely constituted one of the most trenchant and persuasive translation efforts in the history of the black struggle for liberation. It would eventually become a classic in the literature of American protest, selling more than forty thousand copies, serialized in popular newspapers and magazines and reproduced in countless academic anthologies. During that low ebb of the movement's fortunes in Birmingham, however, representatives of the civil society's communicative institutions evinced little interest in the document. The dialogue between King and the white clergy could not yet enter the public's central symbolic space. For the moment, then, this brilliant effort at translating particular grievances into universal discourse remained just that, an effort, an action without a script, a script without a play, a frame without an event. The movement had not yet succeeded in ratcheting up the tension. Without dramatic conflict, there was no struggle for interpretation. Without controlling media interpretation—compelling it might be a better term—there could be no projection of anguished injustice. Without this sense of deep injustice, there could be no civil outrage or civil repair.

Still, the leaders of the Birmingham movement were not about to throw in the towel. They hewed persistently to plan. The routine of daily marches, arrests, and nightly mass meetings continued. In hindsight, after victory, not only King but also academic students of the Birmingham campaign would claim much more for these early days of the campaign than they actually produced. King asserted that the nightly round of mass meetings allowed the movement "to generate the power and depth which finally galvanized the entire Negro community."[108] In fact, however, the meetings and demonstrations continued into early May without dramatic effect. Not only did reporters, the eyes and ears of the surrounding civil community, begin to drift away from Birmingham for lack of "news," but it was proving increasingly difficult to mobilize support beyond the core group of dedicated activists, most of whom had already been subject to arrest, often more than once.[109] The problem was that the sequence of demonstration, arrest, and mass meeting was, indeed, becoming routine; it had to be disrupted by an "event," something powerful enough to breach the ongoing social order.

Finally, after intensive discussion and self-doubt, movement leaders made the decision to allow schoolchildren to enter the fray, not only high school students but youngsters in elementary and middle schools. Community leaders had reported that the city's black youth were more stirred up about the ongoing confrontation, and more willing to take risks, than their elders. Allowing these young people to demonstrate would make up for the falling numbers of adult participants—a point that has been emphasized in the scholarly literature by those who follow the classical social movement model of instrumental force.[110] Equally significant, however, it would potentially alter the moral balance of the confrontation. Children would appear more well-meaning, sincere and innocent than the movement's nonviolent but powerful and determined adults, and this vulnerability would throw into sharper relief the irrational, violent repression of southern officials.

This strategic decision, informed both by quantitative and interpretive exigencies, marked the turning point of the Birmingham campaign. When the "children's crusade" began, and hundreds of young people were herded off to jail, the drama sharply intensified and returned the Birmingham campaign to the front pages. Attendance skyrocketed at the mass meetings held nightly inside black civil society, and a sense of crisis was in the air. Local confrontation had once again succeeded in projecting itself into the symbolic space of the wider civil sphere. As Fred Shuttlesworth, the longtime leader of Birmingham's freedom movement, told an overflow crowd at his church on the first night after the children were jailed, "The whole world is watching Birmingham tonight."[111]

It was the pressure created by this intensifying external scrutiny, not simply the objective constraint of the city's jails being filled to overflowing,[112] that finally incited Sheriff Bull Connor to unleash the repressive violence that underlay local white domination. As the children's crusade appeared increasingly persuasive, this sneering official of the white civil sphere simply would not allow them to proceed. Stepping outside the constraints of civil society, he resorted to physical force, turning fire hoses on the protesters, setting police dogs loose on them, and allowing his officers to use electric cattle prods if the demonstrators continued to step out of line. Because of his local power, the sheriff thought he could act with impunity. Yet although he succeeded in gaining local control, he could not control the effect this exercise of unbridled power would have on the audience at one remove. He would ignore duality at his peril.

Bull Connor's forces won the battle but lost the war. Graphic reports of lopsided physical confrontations between civil good and anticivil evil were broadcast over television screens and splashed across front pages throughout the northern civil sphere. When the fiercely rushing water from high-pressure fire hoses swept girls and boys dressed in their Sunday best hundreds of feet across Birmingham's downtown square, pinning them against a brick wall, the civil interpreters from the North transmitted the children's screams of terror and their pathetic efforts to shield themselves from the violent force.[113] When the growling dogs and their police handlers in dark sunglasses lunged forward into the youthful crowd, reporters and photographers recorded the viciousness of the animals and the arrogant indolence of the men, and they captured the fright, helplessness, and righteous rage of their nonviolent victims. An Associated Press photographer caught the moment when a German shepherd sank its teeth into the abdomen of Walter Gadsden, a thin, tall, well-dressed young black man who appeared not only completely submissive in the face of the frightening attack but also deadly calm.[114] Next day, photos of the attacks with fire hoses and dogs were displayed across three columns on the first page of the *New York Times*. The descriptions accompanying the pictures portrayed a stark and moving confrontation between civil protest and repression. The headline read, "Violence Explodes at Racial Protests in Alabama." The captions below the photos just as clearly attributed civil shame. One read, "Police dog lunges at demonstrator during the protest against segregation in Birmingham," the other "Fireman turns high pressure hose on demonstrators who sought to escape at doorway."[115] The emotional resonance these photos generated in the northern civil sphere was palpable and became even more profound with the passage of time. From being symbols that directed the viewer to an actual event, they became icons, evocative embodiments, in and of themselves, of the fearful consequences of anticivil force. In the opinion of one leading historian of the Civil Rights movement, the photo of Walter Gadsden became "perhaps the most remembered and most commented upon visual image of the movement's efforts in the first half of the 1960s."[116]

It is important not to forget that these media messages were representations, not literal transcriptions, of what transpired in Birmingham. Even if the events seemed to imprint themselves on the minds of observers, they had first to be interpreted. The struggle for interpretive control was waged just as fiercely as the struggle in the streets, and its outcome divided just as cleanly along local versus national lines.

Northern reporters quoted Bull Connor as shouting, "I want to see the dogs work" and "Look at those niggers run!" The *New York Times* editorialized that the southern use of dogs and fire hoses constituted "a national disgrace."[117] Birmingham's local news media completely inverted this interpretive frame. Reporting on the fire hosing of demonstrators in Kelly Ingram Park, the *Birmingham News* presented a photograph of an elderly black woman strolling alongside a park path, holding an umbrella to protect herself from the mist produced by the gushing fire hoses nearby. "Just another showery day for Negro stroller," read the caption below the photo, offering the further observation that the woman "appears undisturbed by disturbances in Ingram Park."[118] Dutifully reporting statements by city officials, local reporters broadcast the mayor's condemnation of the "irresponsible and unthinking agitators" who had made "tools" of children and turned Birmingham's whites into "innocent victims."[119] But the linkage of violence to *white* power had already been reported, photographed, and distributed by representatives of the other side. Portraying helpless black victims at the mercy of vicious and inhuman white force, the reports evoked feelings of pity and terror. Claude Sitton wrote the following in the *New York Times*:

> Patrol officers brought up three-foot-long prod poles, usually used for forcing cattle in chutes, and jabbed the demonstrators, giving them repeated electrical shocks. As one of the Negroes flinched and twisted in the grip of the four troopers, an elderly toothless white man shouted from a roadside pasture: "Stick him again! Stick him again!"[120]

For the audience in the surrounding civil sphere, the narrative of tragedy was firmly in place. Their identification with the victims triggered feelings of outrage and moved many to symbolic protest. Angry phone calls were made to congressional representatives, indignant letters fired off to the editorial pages of newspapers and magazines. In the *Washington Post* of May 16, 1963, p. A21, an angry citizen from Forest Heights, Maryland, Ruth Hemphill, poured out her feelings of indignation and shame. Her simple and heartfelt letter eloquently expresses the outrage she evidently shared with many other white Americans. She traces her anger to an identification with black protesters, an empathy that extended her own ethical principles to them as well.

> Now I've seen everything. The news photographer who took the picture of a police dog lunging at a human being has shown us in unmistakable terms how low we have sunk and will surely have awakened a feeling of shame in all who have seen that picture, who have any notion of human dignity.
> This man being lunged at was not a criminal being tracked down to prevent his murdering other men; he was, and is, a man. If he can

355

have a beast deliberately urged to lunge at him, then so can any man, woman or child in the United States. I don't wish to have a beast deliberately urged to lunge at me or my children and therefore I don't wish to have beasts lunging at the citizens of Birmingham or any other place. If the United States doesn't stand for some average decent level of human dignity, what does it stand for?

As fellow members of the civil community, officials of the federal government seemed just as deeply affected as the people over whom they ruled. President Kennedy "voiced dismay" and told an audience at the White House that the pictures made him "sick."[121] Attorney General Robert Kennedy was reported to be "profoundly" disturbed.[122] Emmanuel Cellers, an influential congressman from New York, labeled the actions of Southern officials "barbaric."[123] Whether these high officials actually experienced these emotions, or were making artful presentations in the public sphere, is not the point. What does matter is that in their capacities as officials of the civil sphere, they now felt compelled to make such representations at all.

The widely shared experience of moral outrage set the stage for regulatory intervention. Declaring that "the hour has come for the Federal Government to take a forthright stand on segregation in the United States," Martin Luther King declared to a mass meeting, "I am not criticizing the President, but we are going to have to help him."[124] President Kennedy seemed to be responding to King when he assured the public that he was "closely monitoring events" and sent Burke Marshall to Birmingham. Marshall attended an emergency meeting of the Senior Citizens, a political forum for the city's economic elite. During a heated discussion, an influential former governor of Alabama recommended to his colleagues that they ask Governor George Wallace to declare martial law and "suppress the whole business."[125] This call for repression met with wide approval; only Marshall's presence prevented it from carrying the day. This high official of the northern civil sphere warned these local business leaders that such repression would only make things worse. Despite efforts at suppression, he argued, the black demonstrators would keep protesting, either then or later. If the demonstrations were to be stopped, there must be civil repair, not anticivil suppression. The "central problem" at the "root of the demonstrations," Marshall insisted, was a denial of basic constitutional rights.[126]

As the local negotiations continued, representatives from the surrounding civil sphere—the president and his cabinet secretaries—made calls to stra-tegically placed local businessmen and to corporate executives outside the South who could exercise leverage on the local elite.[127] Eventually, the face-to-face negotiations with Birmingham's whites were extended to include black protest leaders. As this participation proceeded, Fred Shuttlesworth proclaimed the possibilities of civil repair. Purifying the motives and relations of the white negotiators, he attested to reporters, "We do believe that honest efforts to negotiate in good faith are under way."[128] At a press conference in Washington, the president also connected the local negotiations to the ex-pansion of civil solidarity, declaring, "I'm gratified to note the progress in the efforts by white and Negro citizens to end an ugly situation in Bir-mingham."[129] The upshot of these civil interactions, which took place in the eye of the hurricane of communicative mobilization, was a pact signed by black and white representatives that detailed goals and timetables for ending Birmingham's economic segregation.[130] Both sides hailed the agree-ment as a model of civil repair. Fred Shuttlesworth, the local leader, declared: "The City of Birmingham has reached an accord with its conscience. The acceptance of responsibility by local white and Negro leadership offers an example of a free people uniting to meet and solve their problems."[131] President Kennedy also affirmed the pact's civil qualities, highlighting con-sensus, cooperation, and equity. In a widely publicized news conference, he told journalists that, in his view, the "agreement" was "a fair and just accord."[132]

Writing from the classical perspective on social movements, influential social science students of the Birmingham protest have attributed victory to the local movement's successful accumulation of power and resources. Aldon Morris, for example, cites "the collective power of masses generated by the movement," contending that this power allowed the movement to launch an economic boycott that split the city's economic from its political elite, compelling the former to "capitulate" despite the latter's more ideological recalcitrance.[133] Eskew attributes the local movement's victory to its ability to create a split within the local economic elite itself, pitting those with an interest in the service sector, who were more willing to live with racial integration in the interests of a new "consumer society," against the old-fashioned industrial faction, who were rigidly committed to extracting profit from outright domination.[134] The Birmingham movement did, of course, exercise effective power on the local scene, and its success in doing so compelled one part of the white power structure to take sides against another. What we have seen in this chapter, however, is that in thinking about the sources of the movement's power, one must consider not only the vertical relationships of local domination and resistance but the horizontal relationships of solidarity, relationships that potentially included those who wielded great power farther away. It was civil power, not social or political power, that determined the Birmingham movement's success. The protesters' power depended, above all, on influence, not on resources in the narrow sense. They gained control over local regulatory officials because they succeeded in exercising authority over national ones.[135] By achieving identification and extending symbolic identification, "Birmingham" so deeply penetrated the northern civil sphere that it set the stage for fundamental regulatory reform. We take up this topic in the final chapter of our consideration of race and civil repair.

CHAPTER 14

Race and Civil Repair (4):
Regulatory Reform and Ritualization

THE LOCAL REFORMS generated by the denouement of the Birmingham campaign, despite the praise they generated as emblems of civil renewal and repair, do not tell the full story of that civil rights campaign. It was to the community beyond the city, indeed beyond the region, that the demonstrations were aimed, and it was their success in mobilizing this more democratic and potentially much more powerful civil sphere that made Birmingham into "Birmingham"—a watershed in the history of social movements for civil justice in the United States.[1]

"Birmingham" would enter into the collective conscience of American society more powerfully and more indelibly than any other single event in the history of the movement for civil rights. "Images of Birmingham became frozen in time with the fire hoses and police dogs," writes Glenn Eskew, a recent historian of the movement, taking their place right alongside the mythical images of the soon to be martyred president himself.[2] This centrality in the collective consciousness was already apparent to contemporaries at the time. In the days immediately following the Birmingham settlement, a weary President Kennedy summed up this new world of public opinion in a remark that combined realism and resignation, confiding to his majority leader in the Senate: "I mean, it's just in everything. I mean, this has become everything."[3] The president was referring to the new national furor over civil rights. Three months later, a White House official remarked to the Associated Press, "This hasn't been the same kind of world since May."[4] In 1966, after Robert Kennedy had become a U.S. senator deeply involved in the struggle for minority rights, he told an interviewer, "what aroused people generally in the country and aroused the press was the Birmingham riots in May of 1963."[5]

By using the term "aroused" and pointing not only to the people but also to the press, Robert Kennedy gestured to Birmingham's communicative success, its ability to reach over local boundaries and to mobilize a symbolic extension and psychological identification among whites in the North. Nothing could more powerfully demonstrate such arousal than the triumphal speaking tour that Martin Luther King made through northern cities in the days and weeks after the Birmingham success. King was feted by white crowds, with tens and sometimes hundreds of thousands attending rallies in baseball and football stadiums, importuning him for pictures and autographs, showering him with confetti during celebratory ticker-tape parades. Taylor Branch captures the sense of that time remarkably well.[6] In Cleveland, after he was "mobbed at the airport," King "motorcaded like an astronaut" through the city's streets, Branch writes, and "in a whirlwind twelve hours, he gave six speeches and a television interview." In Los Angeles, King spoke to a rally that drew nearly fifty thousand people. "The audience, clutching programs that bore pictures of snarling Birmingham police dogs, filled the seats and aisles of the old Wrigley Field and then spilled across the field and out into the parking lot," Branch writes. In Chicago, King rode "in an open car amid a fleet of limousines, rushing through the streets . . . behind the roar of police motorcycles and the wail of sirens to city hall for an official welcome by Mayor Daley." In Louisville, "the mayor led an escort to the Civic Auditorium." King went on to St. Louis for "yet another giant rally." Later King went to Detroit, where he was invited to attend an interracial march. Branch's account of this last event is worth quoting at length, for it colorfully communicates the aroused and expansive civil solidarity of the time.

> The advance crowd, packed so densely that the city's mounted police could not reach their parade escort stations, spilled out of a twenty-one-block staging area and headed downtown without King and the other leaders. An endless stream of marchers filled almost the full

breadth of Woodward Avenue, the city's main thoroughfare. In a holiday spirit, they raised spontaneous choruses of "We Shall Overcome" and "Battle Hymn of the Republic." One woman wore a gaudy hat in the shape of a birdbath, with a sign saying "Birds of any color can bathe here." To bystanders, strutting marchers shouted, "Come on, get out here. You ain't in Mississippi. Let's walk!" There were countless placards honoring [the slain black NAACP leader] Medgar Evers, and one group of whites carried a banner reading "I'm Ashamed I Live in Dearborn," a wealthy, all-white suburb. When King's motorcade finally intercepted the head of the line at Cadillac Plaza, his name was cried out and the people swarmed forward, knocking aside the police cordon around him. In a deafening chaos, with angry warnings and claustrophobic squeals of terror amid the joyful roar, King linked arms in a line with [local black minister] C.L. Franklin, [white labor leader] Walter Reuther, and [white] Mayor Jerome Cavanagh to keep from being swallowed up and crushed by his own admirers. The tide of people pushed around them with such force that the leaders' legs churned and their bodies moved rapidly down the street without their feet touching the ground. Mayor Cavanagh recalled that the only words he exchanged with King were "Hang on, Hang on." Crowd estimates ranged upward from 125,000. Parents recovered twenty-six children from the lost-and-found. Reporters wrote VJ-day-stories that saturated Detroit's Negro and white newspapers almost equally.[7]

The effect of this dramatic deepening of identification of northern whites with protesting southern blacks, and the profound arousal of civil consciousness that both triggered and reflected it, was to push the elected representatives of the civil sphere decisively in the direction of regulatory reform. When there is an independent civil sphere, powerful state officials face two masters. Authorities in the structure of state power, they are, at the same time, officials of the civil sphere. On one side, they face power-political considerations generated by the need to maintain governmentality, state power, and party position; on the other side, they face demands for moral solidarity and symbolic responsiveness from the civil community. Until Birmingham, the reformist thrust of the Kennedy administration had been paralyzed by the countervailing pressure to maintain the allegiance of the

Democratic Party in the South. After Birmingham, they were much less willing to accept these power-political "necessities," and they became more responsive to riveting moral demands from the civil sphere. As an Associated Press reporter observed in the summer of 1963, translating these theoretical issues into the straightforward language of everyday life, "Birmingham triggered [the] administration's drive for new civil rights legislation."[8]

The First Regulatory Repair: From Birmingham to the Civil Rights Act of 1964

The Kennedy administration drew up detailed legislation that would mandate equal access to all public facilities, desegregation of all public schools, and "fair and full employment" without racial distortion; establish "biracial human relations committees in every city"; and make it illegal for the federal government "to furnish any kind of financial assistance—by way of grant, loan, contract, guarantee, insurance, or otherwise—to any program or activity in which racial discrimination occurs."[9] Even as the administration prepared to submit this legislation to Congress, as the Civil Rights Act of 1963, the *New York Times* broadcast from its front page some strong advice to the most powerful officer of American civil society. It came from Martin Luther King, the leader of the most powerful dissenting movement for its civil repair. Passage of the civil rights bill, King warned, would require something that Kennedy had never been willing to offer before—the "total weight of the President and his prestige."[10] King was demanding that the spiral between communication and regulation be wound more tightly, that, this time, regulatory officials themselves assume some independent responsibility for turning the screws.

Regulatory Reform Enters the Communicative Domain:
The President's Declaration of Identification

In his national television address the following evening, President Kennedy did exactly that, putting his proposals for regulatory reform into a broad context of moral obligation and aligning them with the protest movement for civil repair. In doing so, the president acknowledged the centrality of the black civil rights movement inside northern civil society. Rather than intervening defensively, as he had always done before, the president was now prepared to represent civil power in another, more positive way. In his nationally televised civil rights address, President Kennedy announced his government's intention to reconstruct the racially distorted civil sphere, defending this decision to engage in regulatory repair by making full use of the institutions of civil persuasion. In doing so, he not only announced his identification with the spirit and the goals of the black dissenting movement, but became the spokesman for the movement inside the state. Though Kennedy himself would not be able finally to effect regulatory reform—he would not live long enough—his official and public commitment to civil repair set off a chain reaction that would have been impossible without this decisive and unprecedented act. With the submission of the Kennedy civil rights bill, the symbolic space of communicative mobilization had become transformed into the concrete details of law and organization that underlay regulatory reform. When President Kennedy employed powerful rhetoric on national television to defend this legal proposal, the project of institutional repair entered forcefully into symbolic space. The spiral of communication and regulation was, indeed, becoming ever more tightly wound.

In the formal legislation that Kennedy sent to Congress one week later, the president would observe that "feelings have risen in recent days" about racial injustice because "street demonstrations, mass picketing and parades have brought these matters to the Nation's attention in dramatic fashion."[11] In his speech to the nation, Kennedy similarly linked Birmingham's dramaturgical effect to his administration's decision to pursue ambitious regulatory reform.[12] "The events in Birmingham and elsewhere," Kennedy told his civil audience, have "increased the cries for equality," with the result that "the fires of frustration and discord are burning in every city." Acknowledging that different kinds of responses to this discord were possible, the president insisted, against Southern white officials, that protest "cannot be met by repressive police action." Against the equivocation of many northern political officials, he argued that "those who do nothing are inviting shame." Shame could be avoided, he declared, only if public officials were motivated by the classical civil virtues that combined rationality with calmness and self-control. For "no city or state or legislative body," Kennedy insisted, "can prudently choose to ignore" the heightened civil tension and the social strains that underlay it. If, indeed, a political leader is motivated by such properly civic concerns, the president argued, that leader will choose not to oppose but to identify with the protest movement against racial injustice. Rather than repressing or ignoring it, the truly democratic leader will respond to the movement's demands by creating regulatory reforms that can repair the causes of discord and frustration and, in the very process, ensure that the protest movement's demands continue to proceed along civil lines. Observing that "a great change is at hand," Kennedy declared "our task, our obligation, is to make that revolution, that change, peaceful and constructive for all."

The president had set out what he regarded as the prudential reasons for responding to communicative mobilization with regulatory change. The question remained: Would white Americans, historical carriers of a racially distorted political tradition, be persuaded to respond in such a civil way? To convince them that they should, President Kennedy insisted to his television audience that universalizing, civil principles lay at the foundation of the American nation. In effect, he set himself against the temporal and spatial contradictions that had confounded American civil society from the start. The president questioned primordial restrictions on civil capacity, the limits that had been placed on American democracy two centuries before, when it had been founded by a particular group in a particular time and place.[13] Implicitly countering the restrictive primordial interests of the nation's founding fathers, the president argued that "this nation was founded by men of many nations and backgrounds." If this revisionist emphasis on plurality was accepted, it would have the effect of vitiating the contradictions of time and place. By emphasizing plurality, then, the president pointed beyond the human particularities of the nation's founders to the universal principles they had evoked, to the fact that the nation "was founded on the principle that all men are created equal."

Precisely because universal principles rather than primordial particularities inform American identity, Kennedy insisted, the national community is committed to civil solidarity. If solidarity is at the national core, then "the rights of every man are diminished when the rights of one man are threatened." It is because of this commitment to solidarity, Kennedy declared, that racial domination must be seen as a distorting intrusion in the civil sphere. In a community defined by civil solidarity, "it ought to be possible for every American to enjoy the privileges of being American without regard

364

to his race or his color." Because "this is not the case," it had triggered a radical movement for civil repair.

Kennedy argued that this repair must in part be regulatory; after all, he was speaking in order to introduce new legislation. Declaring that "it is better to settle these matters in the courts than on the streets," the president expressed his belief that "new laws are needed at every level." Yet, the very willingness to engage in regulatory reform, Kennedy continued, depends on a sense of identification and subjective obligation, for the "law alone cannot make men see right." The regulatory and the communicative are intertwined; both ultimately draw upon the civil commitments which Kennedy had insisted on locating at the national core. Transcendental in both the sacred and secular sense, these commitments demand the exercise of ethical self-control and social solidarity.

> We are confronted primarily with a moral issue. It is as old as the Scriptures and is as clear as the American Constitution. The heart of the question is whether all Americans are to be afforded equal rights and equal opportunities; whether we are going to treat our fellow Americans as we want to be treated.

Racial domination is a threat to the civil aspirations of the American nation precisely because it makes this mutual identification impossible. It does so, in effect, by undermining the motivation for solidarity.

> If an American, because his skin is dark, cannot eat for lunch in a restaurant open to the public; if he cannot send his children to the best public school available; if he cannot vote for the public officials who represent him; if, in short, he cannot enjoy the full and free life which all of us want, then who among us would be content to have the color of his skin changed and stand in his place?[14]

For leaders of the black protest movement, whose goal had always been to engage regulatory authorities in the project of civil repair, President Kennedy's speech demonstrated that they were now within striking distance of reaching their goal. For years, they had dedicated themselves to translating the particular grievances of the African American community into the discourse of civil society, into the codes and narratives that they shared with the white audience in the northern sphere. Now they found that the president, the most powerful officer in the civil sphere and the state, was amplifying their message, not only giving them help in the translation process but actually sending the same kind of symbolic interpretations back to them. It is no wonder that, after watching the president's performance in Atlanta, Martin Luther King drafted an immediate response. "I have just listened to your speech to the nation," he wrote to Kennedy. "It was one of the most eloquent, profound, and unequivocal pleas for Justice and the Freedom of all men ever made by any President."[15] The representatives of the communicative institutions of northern civil society responded in the same vein. Northern reporters had been among the first audiences for the black movement's translating efforts, and the movement had succeeded only because, over many years, journalists committed to repairing civil society had continually translated the movement's normative pleading into the language of realistic description. Now the president himself was sharing this factual assessment. It is hardly surprising that Anthony Lewis, a *New York Times* columnist, called Kennedy's televised address "one of the great speeches in the history of the American Presidency."[16]

Filling in the Symbolic and Institutional Space: Ritual Mobilization and Legislative Action

It is a matter of historical debate whether civil rights legislation could have been passed without Kennedy's martyrdom in November 1963 and the accession to the presidency of Lyndon Johnson, a former Senate majority leader and master of the legislative craft. Kennedy himself expressed skepticism about his administration's ability to push the legislation through, looking rather to his second term, and a more powerful electoral mandate, to gain its difficult passage and to put its ambitious organizational mandates into effect.[17] As it happened, the legislation for which the president had offered his historic endorsement, which was approved by the House Judiciary Committee in October 1963, did not become law until July of the following year, when President Johnson employed every ounce of his legislative skill to force an extraordinary "cloture" vote defeating a lengthy filibuster by the Senate's mostly southern conservatives.[18]

The question of what might have been the fate of the Civil Rights Act of 1963 can never be known. That its very introduction represented a fundamental fork in the road, however, is beyond dispute. In fact, despite the momentous events in the two years that followed Kennedy's historic speech—the campaigns mounted, the lives tragically lost, the laws that were eventually made—these later events can be properly understood only if they are seen as amplifying the symbolic and institutional framework that had become crystallized by the early summer of 1963. Virtually everything that followed over the next two years iterated what had come before. Success was not, of course, guaranteed. The narrative of these conflicts was unscripted, their outcome open-ended. On the one hand, the activities had a formulaic quality. On the other, their meaning was assured only if the actors had the strength and skill to succeed. In retrospect, the very success of post-Birmingham activities made them seem teleological and foreordained. Reenacting understandings and relationships that had already been established and were still redolent in institutional memory and symbolic space, the events achieved a ritual-like quality.[19]

The evening after President Kennedy's national civil rights address, Medgar Evers, a veteran NAACP organizer, was murdered in Mississippi. The president ordered that his body be laid to rest with full honors and regalia in Arlington National Cemetery, the iconic heart of the American nation.[20] Such civic memorialization of a black protest leader broke new ground. Yet it followed directly, even predictably, from the symbolic centrality that Martin Luther King had already established in the northern collective consciousness and from the president's public identification with King's movement against racial domination in the South.[21]

Nor was it surprising, although it too was without precedent, that scarcely two months later, when Martin Luther King walked to the platform to address a mixed audience of several hundred thousand persons during the "March on Washington" in late August 1963, NBC and ABC would cut away from the afternoon soap operas to join CBS in live coverage.[22] King had already become a national hero, an iconic representation of the unfulfilled utopian aspirations of whites and blacks alike in the northern civil sphere. The famous "dream" he enunciated in that immortal speech articulated the promise of the civil utopia that King had so powerfully enunciated for the Northern audience so many times before. This time, King's translation across the racial divide was projected live.

What King offered to his tens of millions of viewers on that summer day was a series of rhetorically striking variations on the theme of civil solidarity, which King described as a moral "promissory note" that the framers of the Constitution had issued but on which Americans had "defaulted."[23] Insisting that "the bank of justice is not bankrupt," King declared that, despite its incomplete realization, the ideal of civil solidarity had a transcendental status that could not be destroyed. Emphatically reasserting its normative validity, he embarked on that somber reverie now engraved on the nation's monuments and replayed in its civil places.

> I have a dream that one day on the red hills of Georgia the sons of former slaves and the sons of former slave owners will be able to sit down together at the table of brotherhood. . . . I have a dream that one day the state of Alabama, whose governor's lips are presently dripping with the words of interposition and nullification, will be transformed into a situation where the little black boys and black girls will be able to join hands with little white boys and white girls and walk together as sisters and brothers. . . . I have a dream that one day . . . all of God's children, black men and white men, Jews and Gentiles, Protestants and Catholics, will be able to join hands and sing in the words of the old Negro spiritual, "Free at last! Free at last! Thank God Almighty, we are free at last!"

King delivered this message from the steps of the Lincoln Memorial. He had the authority to do so because of Birmingham and the critical campaigns that had led up to it. The next day, on its front page, the *New York Times* reported that King had "ignited the crowd with words that might have been written by the sad, brooding man enshrined within the memorial."[24] With this analogy, the *Times* reporter crystallized the growing perception of King as a new founding father. After King's death, this founding status would become institutionalized in a national holiday marking his birth.[25]

The assassination of President Kennedy was an utterly contingent event, without which it might not have been possible to institutionalize civil repair. What must be remembered, however, is that the young president's martyrdom rested not only upon his premature death and his Camelot flare, but upon the representation of his death as a sacrifice, the sense that he had died for a higher cause. In the dark days of mourning that followed his murder,

Kennedy's successor, Lyndon Johnson, pushed this representation into the framework of the movement for civil rights. In his first address to Congress, he told the American people, "No memorial oration or eulogy could more eloquently honor President Kennedy's memory than the earliest possible passage of the civil rights bill for which he fought for so long."[26] That Kennedy had, in fact, come only late to his identification with the Civil Rights movement, and that he had not, in fact, fought for legislative repair for "so long," were not relevant in the emotional, symbolically charged atmosphere of that time.[27] Before he had died, President Kennedy had, indeed, publicly cast his legislative and symbolic fate alongside the black movement for civil rights, and President Johnson drew upon this tightening spiral of communication and regulation in framing the larger civil meaning of Kennedy's death. The new president was not alone in drawing this conclusion. Northern reporters and politicians alike interpreted the Kennedy murder as connected to the polarization created by the Civil Rights movement.[28] By restructuring the fractured solidarity that was somehow held to have caused Kennedy's death, civil repair of racial domination would pay homage to the slain leader by restoring peace and tranquility to the world he had left behind.

Taking office with this mythopoeic agenda, Lyndon Johnson pushed regulatory institutions more rapidly down the path that Kennedy already had laid out. Even as he made civil rights legislation his administration's highest priority, Johnson consulted protest leaders regularly and publicly, making them full partners in the project of regulatory repair. As state officials and movement activists worked closely together, the movement began to directly engage opponents of civil repair not only locally, in the south, but in the nation's legislative branch. Within Congress, whose proceedings were immediately broadcast throughout the civil sphere, the opponents of repair could resort to neither physical repression nor outright racist disparagement. Instead, they framed their opposition legally and constitutionally. What they objected to, they proclaimed, was oppressive intervention by the centralized state; what they were defending, they suggested, was grassroots, decentralized democracy. Barry Goldwater, who was about to become the Republican presidential candidate, denounced the civil rights bill as a "threat to the very essence of our basic system," a "usurpation of such power . . . which 50 sovereign states have reserved for themselves."[29] Of course, what Goldwater and other conservatives feared was not state action per se but civil repair of racial domination in the South. This was the very goal for which the Civil Rights movement had fought for so long, and the cause had now been joined by the highest powers of the American state.

The partnership between Johnson and King sustained a long and historic phase of regulatory repair, a period that would be brought to an end by the president's headlong pursuit of the Vietnam War in his second term.[30] In July, after Johnson signed the Civil Rights Act of 1964 into law, he asked civil rights leaders to restrain their public confrontations until after the presidential election in November, and they agreed.[31] King and other movement campaigned vigorously for the president's reelection. Though there were certainly other themes in the Johnson-Goldwater contest, among them the dangers of nuclear war, there seems little doubt that when LBJ received the largest popular mandate of the twentieth century he was regarded, above all, as a champion of black civil rights. Not only in the presidential but also in the congressional elections, support for African American inclusion was by far the most powerful predictor of electoral victory. In the House of Representatives, not one of those who had cast a vote for the civil rights bill was defeated. By contrast, one half of the northern legislators who had voted against the bill lost their seats.[32]

In December of 1964, it was not the victorious white president but the triumphant black civil rights leader whom *Time* selected as its "Man of the Year." In doing so, the magazine cited King's 1963 Birmingham triumph, which had created the context for historic legislative reforms the following year. *Time* characterized King in a manner that pointed directly to psychological identification and symbolic extension, calling him "the unchallenged voice of the Negro people—and the disquieting conscience of the whites."[33]

The Second Regulatory Repair: Rewinding the Spiral of Communication and Regulation

The Civil Rights Act of 1964 and the communicative-regulative spiral that stimulated it established the paradigm for the regulatory repair of southern racial domination. It did not, however, fully achieve it. The law created the political and organizational framework for reconstructing social and economic domination, but it did not explicitly address voting rights. Only if this key regulatory institution were also repaired could local political power in the South finally shift to different hands. To achieve this final step in the repair process, the Civil Rights movement was compelled to return to aggressive direct action. Its leaders maintained their partnership with the highest officers of American civil society, engaging in public consultations that produced such headlines as "President Promises Dr. King Vote Move" and "President Given King's Views on Vote Situation."[34] Even as they did so, however, they planted their feet once again firmly in the symbolic imagination of the northern civil sphere.

Following the model that was by now deeply lodged in the collective consciousness of movement activists and northern whites alike, the protests achieved regulatory reform by generating a dramatic period of communicative mobilization, beginning with Freedom Summer in 1964 and culminating with the cathartic crisis of Selma in the first half of 1965. This intense period of social drama triggered the kind of outrage and symbolic action that was needed for passage of the Voting Rights Act in August 1965.

Freedom Summer: Identification Becomes Concrete

Freedom Summer provided an opportunity for northern whites to participate directly in the symbolic performances they had until then experienced only symbolically. It allowed northern white identification with southern blacks to be experienced interpersonally, and it energetically broadcast representations of this concrete identification back into the northern civil sphere. The project was organized primarily by SNCC, the movement's radical youth arm that had emerged from the 1960 sit-ins. From elite colleges in the North, SNCC recruited more than a thousand volunteers, the vast majority of whom were white, and brought them down to Mississippi to work for three months in segregated black communities throughout the state.[35]

Ostensibly, Freedom Summer was an effort to register new black voters, and SNCC presented it to the media as such. Yet for three long years SNCC activists had been trying to register black voters in Mississippi in the face of great physical danger and with a notable lack of tangible success.[36] They had few illusions that volunteer, part-time white youth would do a better job, and, indeed, they did not. Though volunteers succeeded, over the course of the summer project, in bringing some seventeen thousand black Mississippians to courthouses to fill out voting applications, official registrars accepted only sixteen hundred of the completed applications as valid.[37]

It should not be surprising, then, that the extended debate preceding SNCC's decision to organize the summer project reveals that SNCC organizers aimed less at registering local voters than creating national dramaturgy. As one participant in those discussions recalled, "it was agreed by all" that "publicity was essential for awakening the national conscience and preparing a climate for federal involvement in Mississippi."[38] White volunteers from the North were viewed less in instrumental than expressive terms, less as potential task organizers than as potentially influential collective symbols. Such revivified symbols would be necessary if the spiral of communication and regulation were to be tightened once again. As one participant in these preliminary discussions later explained:

> It was argued that by flooding Mississippi with Northern whites, the entire country would be made dramatically aware of the denial of freedom which existed in the state and that the federal government would be inevitably faced with a crisis of sufficient magnitude that it would have to act.[39]

Bob Moses, SNCC's charismatic leader, put the matter of identification more bluntly to the volunteers themselves during one of their early training sessions. The goal, he said, was "getting the country involved through yourselves."[40]

The activists of SNCC designed and staged this dangerous civil drama with enormous skill. The northern volunteers played their parts with enthusiasm, courage, and sincerity. Local officials reacted with ferocity and often violent repression. Communicative institutions broadcast images and interpretations of this dramatic interaction between black organizers, idealistic white volunteers, and repressive Southern officials back to the northern civil sphere. What they relayed in these reports were deeply affecting interpretations of an heroic and often tragic struggle against racial injustice.

In keeping with the project of identification, the media interpreted the college students who traveled down to Mississippi not as radical or deviant but as representative figures, in fact as young people who typified the most ideal characteristics of northern civil society. The *Saturday Evening Post* broadcast the evaluation by an MIT psychiatrist reporting that the volunteers

were "an extraordinarily healthy bunch of kids, mentally and physically."
Newsweek described the volunteers as "bright," but they also humanized
them by adding that "they are scared and brave all at once." *Look* magazine
brought identification even closer to home, telling its readers that the volunteers "looked disturbingly like the kids next door."[41] The departures of
these young northerners for Mississippi were reported by hometown newspapers with obvious pride, as in the following article, which mixes provincialism, social snobbery, and straightforward identification with the democratic civil sphere.

Stuart Rawlings III in Civil Rights Fight

by

JOAN WOODS, SOCIETY EDITOR

Friends of Stuart Rawlings III, son of the junior Mr. and Mrs.
Rawlings, will be interested to learn he will leave today to
take part in a summer long civil rights movement in Mississippi. . . . During the last week Stuart has been undergoing a
training program in Ohio with 2000 other students from
Stanford, Yale, Harvard, Princeton, Sarah Lawrence and Vas-
sar. They will be part of a group of 1,000 who will tutor
Negroes to enable them to pass voting tests for the November
elections. . . . "We're very proud of him," Kay Rawlings, a
former president of the Junior League, told us yesterday, "but
of course we're scared to death. They're prepared to face
anything."[42]

The young activists experienced their Freedom Summer activities in a
complementary way. They framed their participation as an opportunity to
embody their commitment to the ideal of civil solidarity and to act out their
antagonism to racial domination. As one prospective volunteer wrote on his
application for the summer project:

I have always known that discrimination was wrong and that now is
the time to overcome these obstacles. . . . Until we do, all that we
stand for in democracy and Christianity is negated, mocked while

373

such oppression exists. . . . There is so much to do, so many barriers between men to be broken, so much hate to be overcome.[43]

As idealistic northerners who had strongly identified with the southern movement, volunteers had already experienced the tension that duality produced. The summer project offered them the chance to face that strain more directly and the possibility of doing something about it. As one volunteer put it, "I can no longer escape the tension, the spirit, the anxiety that fills my heart and mind concerning the movement in the South." Another volunteer used a surfing metaphor to link his desire to experience solidarity with his feelings of moral obligation: "I want to do my part. There is a moral wave building among today's youth and I intend to catch it."[44]

In the context of direct and intense interaction, it is not surprising that the identification of white volunteers with black organizers often went beyond moral ideals. As a female volunteer explained to her parents, "You can always tell a CORE or SNCC worker—they're beautiful."[45] As this enthusiastic observation suggests, sometimes the admiration whites experienced for the black leaders became emotional and physical; close friendships developed, and sexual liaisons were not uncommon.[46] As they scattered among small black towns to teach literacy in the Freedom Schools and to bring unregistered black voters to county halls, the white volunteers experienced a powerful sense of identification with, and acceptance by, those whom they were trying to help.

> The women from the church everyday would bring food for all of [us] teachers [at the Freedom School]. . . . It was so touching to be cared for. . . . I felt like I belonged; I felt like they liked me and they wanted me to be there and I, it was so healing, you know, knowing what the divisions were.. . . .And yet somehow you can heal. . . . I think there was a kind of love . . . and a kind of compassion for us that they showed. It was a daily demonstration of love and acceptance. . . . They were feeding us; they were giving us nourishment.[47]

Northern journalists closely monitored the journey of these representative figures, at once idealistic and idealized. The blanket coverage began with the Summer Project's orientation sessions in Ohio.

[Reporters] followed us into the classrooms and dormitories, around the lounges, out along the paths. They asked people to sing that song again for the American public. There was footage, yardage, mileage of every face in the place.[48]

The intervention into the South of the communicative institutions of northern civil society became even more intense, mediating more deeply felt and darker emotions, after three Summer Project volunteers—James Chaney, Andrew Goodman, and Michael Schwerner—were beaten and murdered by southern vigilantes only a few weeks after the organizing began. The response from regulatory institutions in the northern civil sphere was immediate and intense. Expressing the grave public concern, President Johnson ordered the FBI into Mississippi. Federal agents spread throughout the state, and the resources of the Department of Defense were mobilized to search for the missing bodies and material evidence. The investigation continued into August, with daily media reports on progress, or the lack of it, from the "battlefront."[49] Yet, even while northern reporters deployed metaphors of civil confrontation to describe these events, what finally emerged from the summer's media coverage more closely resembled a narrative of sacred pilgrimage.[50] The story invoked powerful tropes of courage and sacrifice, symbolically extending earlier narratives about northern intervention into the racist South. One *Saturday Evening Post* headline, in late July, declared: "At the Risk of Their Lives, Hundreds of Northern Students Are Challenging the Heart of the Deep South." A headline in the *San Jose Mercury* put this narrative of pilgrimage in a more condensed way: "They Walk in Fear, But Won't Give Up."[51]

In the midst of the trauma at the heart of Freedom Summer, President Johnson signed the Civil Rights Act of 1964, but communicative mobilization had already begun to shift civil attention away from the first phase of regulatory reform. What had happened, as the sociologist Doug McAdam put it, was that "in a very real sense, the entire country had visited Mississippi" that summer, "courtesy of the national news media."[52] What Americans had found there provided stark evidence that southern civil society remained in need of further repair. Their symbolic participation in the later confrontations in Selma, Alabama, dramatically underscored this conviction, and the historic legislation to guarantee black voting rights became very quickly the result.

Selma and Voting Rights: Ritualizing the Communications-Regulation Spiral

It would be veteran black demonstrators in Alabama, not white volunteers in Mississippi, who would provide this dramatic final thrust. Though Selma was a tense and heart-stopping movement that depended on continual acts of courage in the face of repression and violence, it constituted, at the same time, a ritual-like process whose performative structure had been perfected in Birmingham and practiced collectively in the many campaigns that had come before. The audience of the northern civil sphere was already primed; it knew what to anticipate; its heart and mind were already involved. The translation techniques were well tested, the crossover language refined. The chief interlocutor, Martin Luther King, had not only proven himself a uniquely powerful director of civic dramas, but had already demonstrated his persuasive powers vis-à-vis the most powerful federal officials. In the months before the Selma campaign, King had been canonized by *Time* magazine, and he had received the Nobel Prize for Peace. His symbolic authority had never been so great.

Just as the SCLC had so carefully strategized the Birmingham campaign, it now engaged in elaborate pre-planning for Selma, plotting a sequence of events that would connect the discourse of civil society to the movement and its enemies in a dramatic and legitimating way. Organizers had chosen Selma because it was a deeply segregated city in which a strong local civil rights struggle had emerged.[53] Selma was chosen also, as Birmingham had been chosen two years earlier, because the city's chief law-enforcement officer—Sheriff James Clark—was an ill-tempered, irresponsible official who often let his emotions run out of control.[54] The Selma organizers knew, as they had known in Birmingham, that this personal failing was essential if their drama about uncivil Southern violence was to unfold. As in Birmingham, the Selma organizers wanted to trigger Sheriff Clark's temper and to put it publicly on display. If they could sustain a nonviolent stance themselves, they could become the protagonists in a civil morality play, one that would be able to provide a wrenching but cathartic emotional-cum-moral experience for the audience far removed.[55]

As they had so often before, within the bounds of their professional ethics northern journalists cooperated with the protest leaders' efforts to produce this performance of civil-versus-anticivil struggle. By now, many were fully aware that the movement's strategy was designed to provoke repression, but they generally refrained from communicating this information to their northern audience. If they had been more forthcoming, their reports might have made movement leaders seem crafty or calculating, which would have undermined the possibilities for civil identification.[56] Revealing such information might also have given the Selma confrontations a fabricated, artificial appearance, undermining the verisimilitude of the performance. It was precisely their ability to sustain the appearance of utter authenticity that allowed the civil dramas to become traumas, and only this traumatizing effect could have triggered outrage, catharsis and symbolic action in response. For similar reasons, the media underplayed the occasional acts of violence that emerged from the demonstrators' side.[57] Finally, as they had done so many times before, the media provided Martin Luther King with a public platform, from which he provided an influential running commentary on the unfolding events.

Because of these conditions, and their own courage and skillfulness, movement leaders succeeded in organizing a profoundly disturbing social drama. Through front-page headlines, evocative photos, and dramatic captions, the northern media of communication framed the black protests and southern white responses in terms of the binary discourse of civil society. The demonstrators were portrayed as peaceful, as devoid of aggressive intent, as seeking merely to exercise their civil right to vote. In their descriptions of southern police officials, by contrast, reporters emphasized their unprovoked aggression and, most of all, their application to the demonstrators of brutal physical force.

By late January, front-page photos of Nazi-like brutality appeared regularly on the front pages of leading papers. One particularly evocative picture showed two police officers pushing a black woman down by her handcuffed hands while a third officer brought a menacing billy club down on her head—"with a whack," as *New York Times* reporter Herbers wrote, "that was heard throughout the crowd gathered in the street."[58] Herbers reported that the woman herself had initiated the confrontation, which had ended so violently, but the *Washington Post*'s photo caption qualified the woman's provocation by marking it as an account rather than a fact and by portraying her aggression as a response to police activity, an exercise of her constitutional rights.

Sheriff James G. Clark, at center, uses his nightstick on a Negro woman as she bites and fights back. The sheriff had thrown her to the ground in an attempt to handcuff her after he said she struck him. The woman was in line at the county courthouse in Selma, attempting to register to vote.[59]

Over the next month, as the nightly church rallies continued and the demonstrations, even as they grew larger, remained doggedly nonviolent, Selma's police forces shed their last vestiges of civil self-control. Violent ambushes were staged in suddenly darkened city streets. Mobs provided violent reinforcement. Not only demonstrators but newsmen were beaten publicly, with little concern for civil presentation, let alone for human life. Influential newspapers reported these events in bold banner headlines. A sense of crisis filled the air. The division between civil good and anticivil evil became ever more sharply etched. Such counterpoint, for example, runs through a three-column *Washington Post* story that topped its front page. This was the lead:

Club-swinging state troopers waded into Negro demonstrators to-night when they marched out of a church to protest voter registration practices. At least 10 Negroes were beaten bloody. Troopers stood by while bystanders beat up cameramen.[60]

Alabama Governor Wallace attributed the confrontations to the willful actions of black demonstrators, characterizing them as "professional agitators with pro-communist affiliations."[61] When the SCLC publicly announced its plans for a dramatic march from Selma to Montgomery, on U.S. 80, Governor Wallace ordered his state troopers "to use whatever measures are necessary to prevent a march."[62] The demonstration went ahead on Sunday, March 7; it had a dirgelike cast. Six hundred marchers linked arms in double-file columns, followed by their medical corps in a procession of four am-bulances. As they came to the crest of a bridge outside town, they could see fifty masked and helmeted Alabama state troopers deployed several lines deep across the four-lane highway. Behind the troopers were several dozen of Sheriff Clark's "possemen," many on horseback. About a hundred white spectators looked on from the sides of the highway, and about half that number of blacks looked on from behind an old school bus further on. The large crowd of newsmen and photographers recorded the agonizing confrontation from their station behind these groups. When the massed group of still but disciplined demonstrators refused to respond to an order to disperse, the commander of the state troopers let his soldiers work their will. Looking more ghoulish than human in their gas masks and riot gear, the troops waded into the defenseless crowd with grisly abandon. The violence of the confrontation, and the bathetic innocence of the victims, were portrayed by the print and television media in eerie, dreamlike sequences that resembled the battle scenes in *War and Peace*. Here is one account:

\The troopers rushed forward, their blue uniforms and white helmets blurring into a flying wedge as they moved. The wedge moved with such force that it seemed almost to pass over the waiting column instead of through it. The first 10 or 20 Negroes were swept to the ground screaming, arms and legs flying, and packs and bags went skittering across the grassy divider strip and on to the pavement on both sides. Those still on their feet retreated.

The troopers continued pushing, using both the force of their bodies and the prodding of their nightsticks. A cheer went up from the white spectators lining the south side of the highway.

The mounted possemen spurred their horses and rode at a run into the retreating mass. The Negroes cried out as they crowded together for protection, and the whites on the sidelines whooped and cheered. The Negroes paused in their retreat for perhaps a minute, still screaming and huddling together.[63] /

This depiction was broadcast the day after the confrontation from the front page of the *New York Times*. On the evening before, ABC television had interrupted its featured movie, *Judgment at Nuremberg*, "for a long film report," the television announcer told his audience, "of the assault on Highway 80, a sequence which showed clearly the quiet column, the flailing clubs, the stampeding horses, the jeering crowd and the stricken, fleeing blacks."[64] This juxtaposition of the fictionalized televised movie and the factual media of news was accidental, but the analogy between historic and contemporary good and evil seemed somehow ordained. "The hideous parallel between Auschwitz and Selma was obvious even to the insensitive," *Ramparts* magazine observed in a later report.[65] Drawing on such earlier metaphors of bloodshed and dark disruption as "Black Monday" and the "St. Valentine's Day Massacre," the anticivil confrontation immediately became symbolized as "Bloody Sunday."

With identification so firmly rooted, these representations could not fail to provoke in the northern civil audience the pity and terror associated with tragedy. Yet this tragic story and these dark emotions were folded inside a more progressive narrative, one that told the story of a deeply flawed but still redeemable civil society.[66] Experiencing pity and terror evoked a cathartic rage, triggering feelings of shame but also a seething desire for repair. A *Washington Post* editorial was aptly titled "Outrage at Selma." Framing Southern actions as outside the boundaries of civil society, the statement termed the Selma events "simply inconceivable," condemned Alabama's "infamous state government that is without conscience or morals," and predicted that "decent citizens will weep for the wronged and persecuted demonstrators [and] for the good name of the nation."[67]

Northern citizens were indeed outraged, and they evidently did weep. Several hundred actually took the first plane to Selma, joining the demonstrators physically and making their solidarity explicit. In a firsthand report in the *Nation* magazine, titled "Midnight Plane to Selma," one television viewer described how the "inhuman" images of violence, which had the "vehemence and immediacy of a dream," had moved him and his wife to the "point [where] my wife, sobbing, turned and walked away, saying 'I can't look any more.' " This account reveals how palpable was the sense of civil solidarity.

> We were in our living room in San Francisco watching the 6 p.m. news. I was not aware that at the same moment people all up and down the West Coast were feeling what my wife and I felt; that at various times all over the country that day and up past 11 p.m. Pacific Time that night hundreds of these people would drop whatever they were doing [and head for Selma to place] themselves alongside the negroes they had watched on television.[68]

These representations of public fury were sent off to communicative institutions; equally intense symbolic actions were directed to regulative institutions. Within forty-eight hours of Bloody Sunday, U.S. senators began reading letters from their angry constituents into the Congressional Record.

Rhode Island Senator John Pastore told his colleagues that "telegrams from horrified citizens—neighbors of mine—pour into me," and said "they reveal the deep felt dismay—the heartfelt resentment that helpless Americans anywhere in America could be subjected to such savagery."[69] Before Wisconsin Senator William Proxmire read a letter from the publisher of a small provincial newspaper in Chippewa Falls, he offered assurances as to the civil quality both of that city's townspeople and of its newspaper. "It is a town in which people are careful and stable in their attitudes. It is a town that is certainly not characterized by emotional reaction," he said. He described the *Chippewa Herald Telegram* as one that "has been, by and large, conservative, careful, and thoughtful in its remarks."

Dear Senator Proxmire,

Never in our experience have [we] received such reaction from normally political, non-emotional leaders of our community and "workingman" alike as we have as a result of the brutality in Alabama. Isn't it possible that this bloody disregard of Americans' constitutional rights can be protected by federal marshals? We and the many citizens who have contacted us are generally not advocates of this type of intervention, but we see no other recourse in this situation. It is not a time for words; it is a time for action.[70]

These senators, who had official power over the regulatory institutions of American civil society, accepted such letters as bona fide representations of the public's shame, anger, and fervent desire to make amends by civil repair. They did so because, after Birmingham, many of them also identified with the protesters, and because they saw and heard Selma through the same representations of an indignant media. Two days after Bloody Sunday, Senator Wayne Morse, from Oregon, gave an angry speech in which he identified himself not as an official but as a member of the television audience who witnessed the violence in Selma.

Last night I sat in my living room, and viewed on my television screen the pictures of the brutality of the Alabama police. . . . As I watched the television screen and saw Negro women beaten to the ground; when I observed the nature of the blows that were struck on the heads and the bodies of Negroes by white, bigoted, racist policemen, I shuddered to think that that could come to pass in any state of my country in the year 1965.[71]

In the days that followed, outraged statements by high regulatory officials permeated public space. Indicating by expression and tone that they were informed by media representations, these statements were broadcast by the media in turn. According to one scholar's estimate, more than a quarter of the members of the House and the Senate made at least one statement protesting the Selma events.[72]

Even before the violent repression, New York Senator Jacob Javits, a Republican, called the southern repression "shocking" because those arrested were simply seeking "the most basic right guaranteed by the Constitution."[73] During a White House press conference, President Lyndon Johnson framed his own reaction to the ongoing Selma demonstration as an instruction in civil solidarity to the American people: "I should like to say that all Americans should be indignant when one American is denied the right to vote."[74] These affirmations of outrage became much more intense in response to the Bloody Sunday events. Senator Javits linked its violence to the antidemocratic tactics of totalitarian regimes, identifying it as "an exercise in terror."[75] Asserting common identity with the protesters and the unimpeachability of their civil status, Texas Senator Ralph Yarborough simultaneously polluted the behavior of the Mississippi authorities and separated himself from it. Declaring "I abhor the violent and brutal attack upon Americans who attempt only to march peacefully," the senator highlighted the contrast between civil and anticivil by repeating that "those Americans who were so brutally attacked yesterday sought only their constitutional right to vote."[76] Minnesota Senator Walter Mondale linked public anger over the profanation of civil ideas to the need for regulatory reform: "Sunday's outrage in Selma, Alabama, makes passage of legislation to guarantee Southern Negroes the right to vote an absolute imperative for Congress this year."[77]

In the midst of this crisis atmosphere, triggered by assertions that there had been a flagrant and dangerous violation of civil society, the nation's highest regulatory official emphatically affirmed the existence of civil solidarity. "I am certain that all Americans everywhere join me," President Johnson declared, "in deploring the brutality with which a number of Negro citizens of Alabama were treated when they sought to dramatize their deep and sincere interest in attaining the precious right to vote."[78] Johnson promised his audience in the national civil sphere that, in contrast to southern repression, their federal officials would respond to the protesters' dramatic performance not with brutality but with recognition. He promised regulatory reform that would allow the racial distortion of the American civil sphere to be repaired in more thorough way.

> The best legal talent in the federal government is engaged in preparing legislation which will secure that right [to vote] for every American. I expect to complete work on my recommendations by this weekend and will dispatch a special message to Congress as soon as the drafting of the legislation is finished.[79]

When, soon after, the Voting Rights Act of 1965 received its first congressional hearings before the Judiciary Committee, the committee's chairman, Emmanuel Celler, connected its likely passage to the massive communicative mobilization in the preceding days.

> Recent events in Alabama, involving murder, savage brutality, and violence by local police, state troopers, and posses have so aroused the nation as to make action by this Congress necessary and speedy. . . . The climate of public opinion throughout the nation has so changed because of the Alabama outrages, as to make assured passage of this solid bill—a bill that would have been inconceivable a year ago.[80]

Congressman Celler was right. The dramatic events of the preceding year, and the year before that as well, had powerfully tightened the spiral of communication and regulation once again. The difference this time around was that Birmingham and its regulative repercussions had already happened. The paradigm was already in place. In fact, while the legislation for voting rights was submitted to Congress only in the immediate wake of Selma, the president and his legal advisors had been drafting the legislation for months, indeed since the summer before Johnson had been elected, virtually by acclamation, to his first full term.[81] As they designed the legislation, these high regulatory officials had continually sought advice from leaders of the black movement for civil rights.[82] President Johnson signed the voting rights legislation law in the first week of August. Its effects in repairing the racial distortion of American civil society were immediately felt, and they have not stopped to this day.[83]

The End of the Civil Rights Movement:
Institutionalization and Polarization

The black protest for civil rights that has been traced in these chapters was arguably the most powerful and effective social movement to unfold inside twentieth-century civil societies.[84] Addressing racial rather than specifically economic citizenship, it put new issues on the table of social protest for the last half of the twentieth century, and it demonstrated new strategies for these later movements to employ. These effects could already be seen in the 1960s in the rebirth of the modern women's movement, the emergence of the popular struggle against the Vietnam War, and the protests of other ethnic and racially dominated groups for the full achievement of their civil rights. The repercussions became only more visible with the passage of time, evident in the social movements of prisoners, homosexuals, and handicapped people, in the new tactics of environmental protest, and even in the assertively nonviolent struggles for the restoration of civil society that marked the massive social movements against communist domination in central and eastern Europe in the 1980s.[85] This is not to mention the movement's effect on the emergence of "multiculturalism," despite the fact that this new mode of incorporation, to the discussion of which we will soon turn, represented an identity-related turning away from the movement's focus on regulatory reform and political life.[86]

But these considerations only address the demonstration effects of the Civil Rights movement, how its prestige and success helped generate protests against other destructive intrusions into civil societies.[87] What about the effect of the movement itself, in terms of its own goals?

/What allowed the American Civil Rights movement to become an exemplary model? First and foremost, there was its success in overthrowing a massively powerful regime of racial domination./The passage of half a century should not dull us to the immensity of this achievement. Our distance from that earlier time, and our awareness of the deep problems of racial exclusion that remain, often make us see the Civil Rights movement as less than it was. In fact, its impact was extraordinary. The civil rights laws of 1964 and 1965, and the organizational interventions that accompanied them, forced significant change in virtually every noncivil sphere of American life, from corporations to universities, from higher education to popular culture, from the choice of residence to participation in political parties, and to the very structure of the state.[88] The white backlash against the black movement crystallized in the late 1960s, with George Wallace receiving large protest votes in northern presidential primaries and Richard Nixon employing his "southern strategy" to gain the presidency in 1968. Yet throughout this decade, the 1964 Civil Rights Act was effecting radical change, most surprisingly, perhaps, in the racial structure of the labor market, through policies that came to be known as "affirmative action." The symbolic power of the Civil Rights movement was such that these policies of racial preference were enforced, despite ideological qualms, by Republican and Democratic administrations alike, and eventually, when political interest waned, by universities, major economic corporations, and the American military on a voluntary basis. The legality of such racial preference systems was, by and large, consistently affirmed by the U.S. Supreme Court. The economic effects of this intrusion of civil regulation into the economic sphere were profound. As Bart Landry demonstrated in his wide-ranging quantitative study of the effects of civil rights legislation on changing economic stratification in the 1960s and 1970s, affirmative action fundamentally altered the shape of black economic life.

> Fortunately, these laws did more than put an end to segregation at lunch counters, restaurants, and hotels; they also made discrimination in employment based on race a crime. And it was new laws mandating equal employment opportunities that had the most far-reaching consequences for black people as a whole and that directly contributed to the growth of the new black middle class. This new legislation and the Equal Employment Opportunity Commission created to implement the law eventually brought access to a greater range of white collar jobs than ever available in the past.[89]

Regulatory reform had been closely intertwined with communicative mobilization throughout the social movement for civil rights. These post-movement shifts in institutional structure, administratively enforced by reg-

ulative bodies, were also accompanied by powerful currents of public opinion, which elaborated and extended the new patterns of interracial
identification that had aided the movement's earlier success. White racial
prejudice hardly disappeared, but among the working and middle classes of
American society, racial distortions of civil solidarity became decidedly less
pronounced. In cultural terms, the civil rights movement had inverted the
relation between white racism and the binary discourse of civil society. For
the first time in American history, it was racialist thinking that occupied the
polluted, antidemocratic side. This inversion has become only more powerful in the years since. Landry calls it a "revolution in values."

> |By 1970, a new normative climate in the area of race relations had
> emerged in the United States—in the South as well as the North.
> Black children born from this time on would know the brutality and
> fear of Jim Crow years only through history books and the stories
> told by parents and grandparents. . . . Whites, South as well as North,
> who discriminated became "racist" rather than regular guys, and
> those who attempted to block the access of blacks could no longer
> count on success, instead running the risk of losing face rather than
> being heroes.[90] /

As white racism became polluted, white Americans increasingly accepted
face-to-face interaction with blacks in the noncivil spheres of education and
work, and to some noticeably greater extent in recreation and private life.[91]
This transformation allowed blacks to move from back stage to front stage
in American institutions. Without such a shift, the economic position of
African Americans in the service-oriented economy of the United States
could not have been changed.[92]

But the decline of the black Civil Rights movement cannot be attributed
simply to the institutionalization of so many of its concrete goals. Its diminution was too rapid for such changes to have an effect. The causes were
more proximate. The movement lost its centrality to the normative core of
American civil society. In part, this was because the national civil sphere
became less responsive to critical idealism. As the early turned into the late
'60s, the fragile equilibrium of the American civil sphere was rent by conservative backlash and radical "front-lash" movements. With this polarization, civil solidarity became a much scarcer resource.[93] Another reason had

to do with the unintended effect of the movement's success. After dismantling de jure segregation in the South, movement organizers, Martin Luther King most conspicuously among them, began confronting the de facto segregation that distorted the civil sphere in the North. De jure racial domination was easier to represent as evil than de facto, which was more indirect and less visible. The representation of de jure segregation as anticivil evil had, moreover, been greatly promoted by its physical location in the South, a region that had long represented, for northerners, a threat to the nation's democratic traditions. When northern whites themselves began to be targeted as anticivil enemies, the possibilities of enthusiastic identification with the movement substantially declined.

Yet another reason for the growing difficulty in sustaining a wide audience for civil repair was change within the black movement itself. Though dominated at the national level by King's SCLC, the movement had always been a delicately balanced coalition. This balance became imperiled when success flooded the organizations, particularly the younger and more radical ones like SNCC, with new supporters and recruits. More important, at the very point when white identification with the black movement reached its high-water mark, some of the most dedicated and effective black activists were becoming not only wary and suspicious of whites but increasingly pessimistic about possibilities for racial justice. The year after Selma and the Voting Rights Act, SNCC expelled its white members and elected as its chairman Stokely Carmichael, the dedicated but increasingly embittered movement intellectual who created the slogan "Black Power."

The cultural implications of the Black Power movement were ultimately far-reaching, for it marked the beginning of a new, multicultural mode of incorporation.[94] These long-term effects, however, were overshadowed by the immediate political controversies it created at the time. The Black Power theme, and the political movement it inspired, indicated a turning away from the themes of democracy and interracial solidarity to nationalism and separatism. This shift, which registered among white and black audiences alike, made it more difficult for protesters against racial domination to translate their demands into the language of civil society. The historian Charles Payne describes Black Power leader Stokely Carmichael's election as "a repudiation of the tradition of Christian nonviolence symbolized by John Lewis," the black leader who had chaired SNCC before.[95] Though Payne resists criticizing the shift to Black Power and maintains that even after his election Carmichael continued working relationships with whites, he observes that Carmichael's emergence as a national SNCC spokesman "symbolized a shift in the organization's self-presentation [to being] more militant on racial issues [and toward] nationalism."[96]

The destructive implications of this more narrow, less civil ideology of black protest were dramatically evident in the pas de deux that unfolded between SNCC and the SCLC in June 1966.[97] Speaking at an evening rally after being arrested earlier that day, Stokely Carmichael declared that black people ought to take charge in the South, that its sheriffs should be black, and that "every courthouse in Mississippi should be burnt down tomorrow so that we can get rid of the dirt."[98] The SNCC chairman shouted, "We want black power," and the crowd took up the chant, yelling "We want black power, we want black power."[99] At a rally the next evening, when another SNCC leader began leading the crowd in this new chant, a leader from the SCLC engaged members of the same crowd in spirited cries of "freedom now, freedom now." If the participants in this rhetorical contest did not fully surmise its implications, their leaders certainly did. King avoided public comment that evening, but he later recalled, "Immediately I had reservations."[100] He considered pulling SCLC out of the march, and northern newsmen wrote about "mounting tension" inside the movement. Finally, King released a public statement pointedly asserting "the term 'Black Power' is unfortunate" because "it tends to give the impression of Black nationalism."[101]

The next evening, in an impassioned and widely publicized speech, King explained his opposition. He told his audience that this new emphasis on power would suggest an instrumental interest in domination, an implication that could obscure the ethical and civil orientation of the movement. Asserting "I am not interested in power for power's sake, but I'm interested in power that is moral, that is right and that is good," King felt compelled to remind his listeners "this is what we are trying to do in America."[102] He also suggested that emphasizing brute power seemed clearly to imply the acceptance of violence, an anticivil connotation that, far from empowering the movement, would end up helping its opponents. Finally, the demand for Black Power, King insisted, implied that black protesters wanted to wage the struggle for freedom by themselves. But it would be foolish to believe that black people could "get our freedom by ourselves," King declared. In the context of white domination over the black minority, it was only duality—the existence of a surrounding democratic civil sphere—that made it possible for blacks to win their freedom. Reiterating the recipe for protest that had been so successful up until that time, King insisted that the black movement must aim at extending solidarity and that the ability to achieve this extension depended on deepening white identification: "There's going to have to be a coalition of conscience, and we aren't going to be free here in Mississippi and anywhere in the United States until there is a committed empathy on the part of the white man."[103]/

King was right to sense that this orientation toward duality was being abandoned. In the late '60s, as the Right became increasingly militant and the Left became splintered between those who wanted to deepen civil society and those who wanted to make revolution, radical groups such as the Black Panther Party followed the trajectory of "Black Power," rejecting interracial solidarity as a goal and conspicuously embracing violence at least as a symbolic means. Even as the project of deepening civil society was being rejected by influential groups inside the white and black Left, large segments of northern white communities were antagonized by the bloody riots breaking out inside urban black ghettos. "The image of the Negro," noted one slightly hyperbolic observer at the time, "was no longer that of the praying, long-suffering nonviolent victim of Southern sheriffs; it was of a defiant young hoodlum shouting 'Black power' and hurling 'Molotov cocktails' in an urban slum."[104] In more measured language, the sociological chronicler of Freedom Summer, Doug McAdam, observes that "interracialism died amid the calls for black power and black separatism," drawing attention to the irony that, less than a year after the idealism of the Mississippi project, "nonviolence was widely repudiated, at least rhetorically, in the wake of Watts."[105]

It was in this context that the progressive center-Left coalition that had undergirded northern identification with the black protest movement broke down. Such liberal media as the *New York Times*, which had been so central to the movement translation, fairly bristled with antagonism to the nationalist and revolutionary turn. For the northern communicative media, the black movement's turn toward violence undermined its claim to embody the principles and structures of the civil sphere. This suspicion was already clearly broadcast in early 1965, when the *Times* reported on the assassination of the Black Muslim militant Malcolm X. Even as some increasingly militant black newspapers extolled the "manhood" of Malcolm against the "hypocrisy" of

King, the *Times* dismissed the nationalist leader's life as "pitifully wasted," citing his "ruthless and fanatical belief in violence." Calling Malcolm a "twisted man," the paper expressed regret that the black leader had turned his "many true gifts" to such "evil purpose."[106] As the polarization of the '60s deepened, such anticivil reframings of black movements and their leaders became more frequent. Long after the heat of that period had subsided, these polluting images of African American militancy lingered, making it more difficult to reignite movements for racial civil repair.

Despite the success of the black protest movement, the racial distortion of America's civil sphere remained; yet because of its great victories, these distorting intrusions took quite different forms. As black economic and political participation became normalized, and symbolic racism declined, the working and middle strata of African American society abandoned inner-city ghettos, leaving an enormous black "underclass" behind.[107] To this day, the social conditions sustaining this continuing racial subjugation—high rates of unemployment, drug addiction, violent crime, crumbling schools, and teenage pregnancy—have not been systematically addressed by the regulative institutions of the surrounding civil sphere. The fictional and factual media of communication, for their part, have tended to pollute this racial under-class.[108] Broadcasting apocalyptic images of black violence and criminality, these symbols have been intermingled with the anticivil representations of black militancy from an earlier time.

Despite the periodic calls for regulatory intervention made by liberal intellectuals and policy elites, the conditions that sustain the racial underclass will not be repaired until a new social movement can arise. Only a pow-erfully affecting social movement could mobilize the increasingly fragmented black community. Only skillful movement intellectuals could translate the particular experiences and conditions of the racial underclass into compelling codes and narratives that can gain psychological identification from the civil sphere outside.

Social scientists and critics speak about repairing this new racial divide primarily in organizational terms, calling for massive state intervention and economic restructuring. But such new forms of regulation depend on the creation of new forms of civil power. The economic, political, educational and demographic subordination of the racial underclass does not, in itself, generate a sense of injustice from those on the outside. These strains must be translated into the language of civil society. Demands for direct organizational intervention, no matter how rational and well-reasoned, are not enough. Social justice requires the regulatory resources of the state, but it is only communicative mobilization in the civil sphere that can bring such intervention about. What has happened up until this time is quite the opposite. The discourse of civil society is being mobilized not on behalf of the racial underclass but against it. In regard to this degraded segmented of the African American community, it seems that the very idea of civil repair has fallen into increasing disgrace.[109]

It is deeply paradoxical that, even as the distance has widened between American civil society and the racial underclass, powerful processes of civil incorporation have not only remained in place, but in many respects have flourished. As they have gained traction, they have challenged otherness in new ways. The Civil Rights movement translated the discourse of civil society into the familiar projects of assimilation and hyphenated American-ism. Black Power militancy, even as it threw up barricades against the social movement for civil repair, initiated a radical cultural restructuring of these familiar incorporative schemes. I discuss these changing modes of incorporation in the fourth and final section of this book.

PART IV

MODES OF INCORPORATION
INTO THE CIVIL SPHERE

CHAPTER 15

Integration between Difference and Solidarity

I N 1974, AFTER twenty years of struggle to make more real the promises of American citizenship, during which efforts that began with black Americans had expanded to include other racial or ethnic minorities and was beginning to open new possibilities for women, a scholar named Peter Adler concluded a widely used anthology called *Intercultural Communication* by offering a definition of "multicultural." Emphasizing the "psychoculturally adaptive," Adler portrayed a protean, ever-changing, integrative actor who had the desire and ability to put himself in the shoes of the other person in a relativizing, crossover, nonjudgmental way. "Multicultural man," he wrote, "maintains no clear boundaries between himself and the varieties of personal and cultural contexts he may find himself in." He is "capable of major shifts in his frame of reference and embodies the ability to disavow a permanent character. . . . He is a person who is always in the process of becoming a part of and apart from a given cultural context. He is very much a formative being, resilient, changing, and evolutionary."[1]

Fifteen years later, delivering her presidential address before colleagues at the Modern Language Association, the feminist literary scholar Catherine Stimpson defined multiculturalism in a decidedly different manner. It means, she said, "treating society as the sum of several equally valuable but distinct racial and ethnic groups."[ ] At that same meeting, the editor of the explicitly multicultural *Heath Anthology of American Literature* defended his textbook's race and gender organization of literary materials by insisting, "I know of no standard of judgment . . . which transcends the particularities of time and place . . . of politics in short."[3] In yet another presentation at the MLA meeting, a Shakespearean scholar justified the need for a multicultural approach to literature by highlighting the boundedness of his particular identity. Reading the work of a black woman author, he explained, "I do not enter into a transcendent human interaction but instead become more aware of my whiteness and maleness, social categories that shape my being."[4]

These juxtaposed quotations suggest more than a shift in disciplinary reference from Eriksonian ego psychology to Foucauldian power-knowledge. They indicate a sea change in social understanding. In the early 1970s, multiculturalism was not yet part of the social imagination, but it connoted compromise, interdependence, a relativizing universalism, and an expanding intercultural community. In our own time, the same term, now absolutely central to the collective consciousness, appears ineluctably connected not with permeability and commonality but with "difference," with the deconstruction and deflation of claims to universalism, with the reconstruction, rehabilitation, and protection of separate cultural discourses and sometimes very separated interactional communities.

Some radical advocates of multiculturalism propose that their particularistic identities determine their actions and being. Promoting a fundamental reorientation of textbooks and pedagogy vis-à-vis the categories of "American" and "race," Molefi Kete Asante, then chair of the Department of African-American Studies at Temple University, justified Afrocentrism on the grounds that, for black Americans, "our Africanity is our ultimate reality."[5] "The idea of 'mainstream American,' " he writes, "is nothing more than an additional myth meant to maintain Eurocentric hegemony. . . . 'Mainstream' is a code word for 'white.' . . . One merely has to substitute the words 'white-controlled' to get at the real meaning behind the code."[6] When Cornell West, the influential black theologian and philosopher, reviews the effects that recent movements for equality have had on contemporary American academic life, he confirms this shift in mentality but demonstrates more sensitivity than Asante to its paradoxical effects. "The inclusion of African Americans, Latino/a Americans, Asian Americans, Native Americans and American women into the cultural of critical discourse," he observes, has "yielded intense intellectual polemics and inescapable ideological polarization that focused principally on the exclusions, silences and blindnesses of male WASP cultural homogeneity."[7]

Convergence between Radicals and Conservatives

This discursive shift from an emphasis on universalism and inclusion to difference and separation seems a strange response to the continuing progress that previously excluded and subordinated groups have made vis-à-vis the core institutions of American society, a progress that, though agonizingly uneven and tragically incomplete, is nonetheless amply documented in statistics about mobility, intermarriage, occupation, and education. What is less paradoxical is that in the course of this transformation, a highly visible conservative intellectual reaction has crystallized, one that is far more suspicious about the motives of multicultural activists than is evidenced by skeptical sympathizers of the movement like Cornel West. Arthur Schlesinger, Kennedy liberal and cosmopolitan thinker of an earlier day, blames multicultural activists for reviving "ancient prejudices."[8] Rather than seeing these thinkers as responding to continuing inequality and exclusion, Schlesinger claims that they have actually introduced divisions where none existed before. By "exaggerating differences," he writes, "the cult of ethnicity . . . intensifies resentments and antagonisms,"[9] thus "producing a nation of minorities [and] inculcat[ing] the illusion that membership in one or another ethnic group is the basic American experience."[10] Samuel Huntington blames the "popularity of multiculturalism and diversity," which he dubs the "deconstructionist movement," for an "erosion of national identity" that is "quite possibly, without precedent in human history."[11] More strident neoconservatives denounce multiculturalism as a new form of racialism, one directed against the white majority. Dinesh D'Souza denounces "the new separatism" and likens it to defending the South African Apartheid regime.[12] For Roger Kimball, multiculturalism, "far from being a means of securing ethnic and racial equality," is "an instrument for promoting ideological separatism based on . . . differences."[13] Hilton Kramer attacks "the new barbarians" who have "already established as a standard practice: the imposition of politics—above all, the politics of race, gender, and multiculturalism—as the only acceptable criterion of value in every realm of culture and life."[14]

In attacking multiculturalism as a new form of racial particularism that denies universalism, the conservative critics of multiculturalism—who are also the most conspicuous intellectual opponents of race- and gender-specific affirmative action programs—go on to make an even more fundamental claim. They argue that this movement has fundamentally undermined the solidarity that has been the basis for American democracy. As Schlesinger sees it, a once united nation has now been torn apart. "The cult of ethnicity," he decries, "has reversed the movement of American history,"[15] and he condemns it for "breaking the bonds of cohesion—common ideals, common political institutions, common language, common culture, common fate—that hold the republic together."[16] Kimball asserts that "what we are facing is nothing less than the destruction of the fundamental premises that underlie . . . a liberal democratic polity."[17]

The claim that multiculturalism undermines the cohesiveness of American society, indeed, the very existence of an American "society" as such, is potentially an extremely damaging ideological charge; after all, the construction of a fuller, more inclusive society is precisely what most of the emancipatory social movements of the last century have been about. What makes this claim so perplexing is that some of the most important intellectual advocates of multiculturalism seem to agree with these conservative critics. They allow that the movements they defend are indeed at odds with the concept of an American community. They promote, instead, an alternative ideal, a social system of insulated but equally empowered groups who, rather than experiencing some shared humanity and solidarity, would simply grant one another the right to pursue distinctive lifestyles and goals.

In this chapter, I will examine this claim on empirical, theoretical, and normative grounds. I will criticize it for ignoring not only the theoretical possibility of a civil sphere, but its real, if fragmented, existence in contemporary American life. We will see that the civil society theory I am developing in this book allows us to cast the debate between radical multiculturalists and fearful conservatives in a very different light.

Recognition without Solidarity?

The most important theoretical articulation of the radical multiculturalist position is Iris Young's philosophical treatise *Justice and the Politics of Difference*.

Speaking as a feminist personally involved in the new social movements of the 1970s and '80s, Young sees modern democracies as neither cohesive societies nor real democracies. Rather, as Young explains it, modern democracies are composed simply of distinct and separate social groups. These groups are defined by particularistic primary identities—she mentions age, sex, race, ethnicity, gender, and religion—and they are always and inevitably organized in a hierarchical way, composed of "social relations . . . tightly defined by domination and oppression."[18] Engaged in mortal conflict with one another, these groups aim at enlarging the field for the expression of their identity interests.

On the basis of this empirical description of contemporary social organization, Young attacks the very idea of "civic impartiality." The notion of an impartial "public" sphere, she asserts, "masks the ways in which the particular perspectives of dominant groups claim universality," and, indeed, actually "helps justify hierarchical decision making structures." The most powerful among such structures is the modern state,[19] whose discourse of universal reason—free and equal citizenship for all—provides a formally abstract but morally empty[20] legitimation for its strategy of excluding politically and humiliating emotionally the members of groups that are not Christian, male, or white.

The universal citizen is . . . white and bourgeois. Women have not been the only persons excluded from participation in the modern civic public. In Europe until recently and in many nations both Jews and working-class people were excluded from citizenship. In the United States the designers of the Constitution specifically restricted the access of the laboring class to the rational public, and of course excluded slaves and Indians from participation in the civic public as well.[21]

The so-called "neutral" state is not only empirically deceptive,[22] Young claims, but ideologically pernicious, making it much more difficult to expose the primordial particularity that underlies domination and to provide for the oppressed an independent voice.[23]

Having ruled conceptually out of bounds any hope for neutral territory and common understanding, Young links justice instead to the full expression of particularity and difference. "The good society," she writes, "does not

eliminate or transcend group difference."[24] To the contrary, "group differentiation is both an inevitable and a desirable aspect of modern social processes." For this reason, justice "requires not the melting away of differences,
but institutions that promote reproduction of and respect for group differences without oppression."[25] Young argues that recent social movements
should be seen in just this way. She reads them simply as emphasizing
difference and particularity—as identity movements in the contemporary
social science sense—suggesting that the discourse of a radical, separatist
multiculturalism is not only rational and morally legitimate but politically
effective as well.

My problem with Young's argument is not with its logical coherence
but with its empirical validity, which is inextricably interrelated with its
moral claims.[26] Does Young have a realistic theory of the cultural and
institutional life of contemporary societies? Of how social movements for
justice actually work? I think not.

Let us examine a claim that is the fundamental meeting point between
the empirical and moral dimensions of her position. Recall that Young asserts
that demands for the recognition of particularity, of difference, will result
not simply in the "reproduction" of difference but in greater "respect" for
them. She cannot, however, defend this proposition empirically or theoretically. Instead, she simply conflates political and moral assertions of the
validity of difference with the empirical achievement of social respect. Following are some examples of short-circuiting:

> By asserting a positive meaning for their own identity, oppressed
> groups seek to seize the power of naming difference itself. . . . Dif-
> ference *now comes to mean* not otherness, exclusive opposition, but
> specificity, variation, heterogeneity.[27]
>
> Asserting the value and specificity of the culture and attributes of
> oppressed groups . . . *results in* a relativizing of the dominant cul-
> ture.[28]
>
> When feminists assert the validity of feminine sensitivity . . . when
> gays describe the prejudice of heterosexuals as homophobic and their
> own sexuality as positive . . . when Blacks affirm a distinct Afro-
> American tradition, then the dominant culture *is forced to discover* itself
> for the first time as specific [and] it *becomes* increasingly difficult for
> dominant groups to parade their norms as neutral . . . and to con-

struct values and behavior of the oppressed as deviant, perverted, or inferior.[29]

These arguments seem more than a bit sociologically naive. At times, Young defends such propositions on normative grounds, as offering a dialogic, "deliberative" approach to the achievement of justice: "A selfish person who refused to listen to the expression of the needs of others will not himself be listened to."[30] But isn't "selfishness"—the self-orientation produced by xenophobic, group-limited perception—exactly what Young herself has identified as the defining characteristic of contemporary social life? When socially marginalized and culturally polluted groups make claims for recognition and respect, can the simple assertion of these claims, in and of itself, change the minds of the very dominant—that is, "selfish"—groups that have made them marginal and polluted? It seems highly unlikely that mere assertion could be so sufficient unto itself.

This is hardly surprising if we acknowledge the existence of a civil sphere and the changing context it provides for political claims. It is not the mere fact of energetic self-identification, much less the simple demand for deliberation, but the construction of the social context within which claims for recognition are made that determines whether the negative understanding of social stereotyping can be ameliorated or reversed. Statements about ourselves and others are interpreted against a background of tacit assumptions. Speakers need to know what language game they are playing before they can properly interpret actions and statements made by the players. If we have different conceptions of the game, we will interpret the same statement differently; for all intents and purposes, we may as well be playing a different game. Insofar as the game is democratic life, the rules for this game are established by the possibility of the very civic impartiality that Young denies *tout court*, that is, by the culture and institutions of civil society.

"We should seek public fairness," Young asserts, "in a context of heterogeneity and partial discourse."[31] Indeed we should. But the factual existence of heterogeneity and assertions of claims for its respect will never, in and of themselves, produce the kind of mutual recognition that Young seeks. It is only the implicit understandings of public culture, articulated in the complex and interlarded relations of civil life, that can valorize representations of heterogeneity in positive and negative ways. Young implicitly acknowledges this all-important fact when she contrasts mere interest group pluralism, which in her view does "not require justifying one's interests as right, or [as] compatible with social justice,"[32] with what she lauds as the preferred politics of difference: "A heterogeneous public, however, is a public, where participants discuss together the issues before them and come to a decision according to principles of justice."[33]

We are back to the civic impartiality from which Young tried so determinedly to escape and to the problem of the nature and scope of common values, the existence of which Young denies and the importance of which conservative critics of multiculturalism have tried so adamantly to assert.[34] As Alasdair MacIntyre once asked,[35] Whose justice and which rationality? What is it about the civil sphere that makes its very existence so important? Does the existence of a public or civic sphere in and of itself suppress or deny heterogeneity, as Young suggests? Must an impartial civil sphere necessarily rest upon the kind of undifferentiated, homogeneous, melted social values that conservatives recommend?

Rethinking the Public Sphere: Fragmentation and Continuity

The conservative critics of multiculturalism are right about one thing. There is already a civil sphere in the United States and in other democratic and democratizing nations as well. Yet the radical champions of multiculturalism are also right, for the civil societies that exist in the present day, and even more so those of earlier eras, remain fragmented and fractured communities, solidary spheres that exclude all sorts of groups from their central cores even while proclaiming liberty and justice for all. What both sides in this argument seem to ignore, in other words, is that the existence of the civil sphere is not a zero-sum, all-or-nothing game. Failure to achieve a full or complete civil sphere should not be seen as an admission of utter failure. To the contrary, it is the contradictions generated by the tension between the ideal and the real that produce the potentially liberating dynamics of contemporary life.

In this civil sphere, actors are constructed, or symbolically represented, as independent and self-motivating individuals responsible for their own actions who feel themselves, at the same time, bound by collective solidarity to every other member of this sphere. The existence of such a civil sphere suggests great respect for individual capacities and, at the same time, trust in the goodwill of others. For how could we grant such a wide scope for freedom of action and expression to unknown others if we did not, in principle, trust in their rationality and goodwill? Trusting in the goodwill of autonomous others is implied in the paradoxical proposition that the "free" members of civil society are at the same time solidaristic with one another. Insofar as such solidarity exists, we see ourselves in every other member of society. Imaginatively taking the place of the other, our actions become simultaneously self-oriented yet controlled in some manner by extraindividual solidarity. In this way, we act simultaneously as members of a community and as rational, self-willed, autonomous individuals. The emergence of this kind of civil realm supersedes but—and this "but" is critically important—does not necessarily suppress more particular commitments we feel as members of primary groups. After all, if we were bound completely by kinship, neighborhood, gender, racial, linguistic, or religious boundaries, we would be something less than autonomous individuals, and we certainly would not exhibit solidarity to the myriad of others occupying the extended territories in which we live.[36]

As I have suggested throughout this book, such an idealistic vision of a civil social order has been a utopian aspiration of communities in different times and places, even while it has generated sharp tensions with other, more restrictive understandings that members of these communities have simultaneously held. As a normative ideal, this utopian vision has been promoted in one form or another by each of the great monotheistic religions, despite the cautionary restriction that members of such a universal religious community must worship one particular deity. We can think of the Athenian Republic as the first great effort to institutionalize elements of such a utopian ideal, despite the fact that access to the Greek public was, in empirical terms, severely restricted. We can see elements of this utopian civic public in myriad other places since. We can find them in the parliaments of medieval kingships in the West; in such aristocratic political demands as the Magna Carta; in what Elias called the "civilizing processes" that radically refined the manners and coarse brutality of medieval knights and courtiers; in the bureaucratic, formal, and homogenizing legal apparatuses created by early modern absolutist regimes; in the Renaissance city-states, such as Florence and Venice, which had vigorous, confrontational, civic-oriented factions and discourses, and even elections, albeit of a highly unequal sort.[37]

None of these were "real civil societies" in the modern sense.[38] When civil societies were first institutionalized on a national scale in such countries as England, the United States, and France, ambitious cultural revolutions created highly universalistic and egalitarian narratives and symbolic codes. Legal institutions formalized individual autonomy and responsibility, protecting free action and demanding reciprocity. In these nations, the civil sphere became so vigorous and expansive that accession to state power could not be legitimated without its blessing, which, as I suggested in chapter 6, is one way to understand the significance of mass electoral systems and the enfranchisement of significant parts of the national populations.

The glorious democratic revolutions did not achieve the full democracy that conservatives applaud, yet neither were they as illusory as radical multiculturalists claim. They marked, rather, one early step in the unending process of institutionalizing civil society. To understand the inherent limits on completing this institutionalization process, we need to recall the model of systematic contradictions presented in chapter 8. Even after the great democratic revolutions, civil society remained only one sphere among others within a broader social system. English, French, and U.S. societies were, and are, also composed of powerful and decidedly noncivil spheres. The family, religious groups, scientific associations, economic institutions, and geographically bounded regional communities still produced different kinds of goods and organized their social relations according to different ideals and constraints. Families, for example, were bound by love and emotional loyalty, not civil respect and critical rationality; they were organized, moreover, in highly authoritarian relations, not only between parents and children, but between husband and wife. The market relations that defined early capitalism emphasized efficiency rather than fairness, competition rather than solidarity, and, once again, hierarchical rather than egalitarian forms of respect. Religious organizations were similarly vertical in their organization, despite the significant horizontal relationships engendered in Protestant sects; they were committed to the highly elitist and exclusionary principle that only those born within a faith, or those converted to it, were to be fully respected and obeyed. Scientific communities also manifested such exclusionary elitism—around truth rather than salvation—although they were even more associational and collegial internally.

{These noncivil spheres did not simply sit outside the boundaries of civil society and conduct with it a courteous and respectful exchange, as the social theory of early liberalism imagined and as contemporary conservatives would so much like to believe today. To the contrary, they invaded civil society from its very inception, penetrating it in systematic and fateful ways. The qualities, relationships, and goods highly valued in these other spheres became translated into restrictive and exclusionary requisites for participation in civil society itself./Familial patriarchy expressed itself in the widely held civil belief that women were not autonomous, rational, or honest enough to participate in democratic politics.[39] The force of market institutions encouraged the belief that economic failure revealed a parallel incompetence in democratic life, hence the long-standing exclusion of the propertyless from full electoral participation and the polluting stereotypes about the irrationality and even animality of the working classes.[40] It is easy to see the conversion of religious into civil competence in much the same way: only members in good standing of certified and dominant confessions could possess the conscience, trust, and common sense required for civil society itself.

But the utopian promises of civil society were also fractured for historical reasons, not just systemic ones. The founders of societies manifest distinctive racial, linguistic, religious, and geographical origins.[41] In the historical construction of civil societies, one finds these primordial qualities established as the highest criteria of humanity, as representing a higher competence for civil life./Only people of a certain race, who speak a certain language, who practice a certain religion, who make love in a certain manner, and who have immigrated from a certain spot on the globe—only these very special persons actually possess what it takes to be members of our ideal civil sphere. Only they can be trusted to exhibit the sacred qualities for participation./

The difficulty for liberal social theory, and for the participants in these actually existing civil societies, is that these contradictory dimensions of formally democratic social systems do not express themselves in a transparent way. To the contrary, these contradictions are hidden by constitutional principles and Enlightenment culture alike. The early democratic social systems were divided into public and private spheres. In the former, civil and democratic principles prevailed for many groups. In the latter, the private spheres, people were relatively free to do what they liked, to whom they liked, and in all sorts of decidedly undemocratic ways.[42] In a famous essay that Kant wrote in 1784, "What Is Enlightenment," he made this distinction the very basis of his defense of autonomous reason. In the public sphere, Kant insisted, all men are enabled, indeed mandated, to challenge authority in the name of autonomy and to act according to the principles of universalism. Yet when these same men are in their private spheres—in the church, the army, or the state—they may not be allowed to exercise these civil rights and they do not have to allow others to exercise them in turn. To the contrary, they must obey noncivil authorities in a highly subservient way, and they have the right to demand obedience to their own commands.[43]

Though this private-public distinction served to protect the civil sphere from obvious and delegitimating fragmentation, it testified, at the same time, to that sphere's profound limitations. When push came to shove, the public world was not nearly so shielded from the vagaries of the private worlds as Enlightenment and constitutional thinking proclaimed. To the contrary, the functional and historical particularities expressed in private life invaded and distorted the understanding of civil life. Jews may have been allowed to practice their religion in the privacy of their homes—although sometimes they were not—but "Jewishness" carried such a stigma that they were excluded from most of the central institutions of public life. The same contradiction of the public promises of civil universalism constrained such other, supposedly private categories as race, gender, sexuality, ethnicity, class position, physical location, and other religious orientations.

Implications for Contemporary Debates

The idea of a contradictory and fragmented civil sphere has clear implications for the present discussion. It suggests, contrary to radical multiculturalists such as Young, that an impartial civil domain does have some traction in Western societies, indeed, that it has enjoyed a real existence for hundreds of years. It also demonstrates, however, and this goes directly against conservative polemics, that the civil sphere's promises of autonomy, solidarity, equality, and justice have never been fully realized. Civil society is not and has never been integrated, cohesive, and fully solidary. Conservatives are deeply mistaken in their suggestion that today's demands for multiculturalism threaten to sidetrack a great success story and that such demands introduce divisive particularities, polarizing a society that has exhibited high levels of solidarity and integration heretofore. The theory of the contradictory civil sphere suggests that multicultural demands for recognition of particularity are justifiable both normatively and empirically, even if, in their radical form, such demands can fundamentally misunderstand what the basis of such recognition might be. For the multicultural critique brings to public attention the debilitating departures from universalism that have corroded civil society from the very beginning of its modern form.

If this proposition is true, much of our thinking about contemporary racial and ethnic conflict in the United States and elsewhere must be recast. Multiculturalism may actually be a new form of social integration that, rather than denying universalism, has the potential to realize it in historically unprecedented ways. Critics on the Left and Right have taken the recent emergence of multicultural discourse, institutions, and practices as marking the end of broad projections of social solidarity. It may actually be the case, however, that it marks the beginning of a radically different, more adequate model, a mode of civil integration whose tenets, still barely visible, will provide the framework for conflicts about the possibilities of justice for decades, if not centuries, to come.

CHAPTER 16

Encounters with the Other

I N THE THREE hundred years since the first democratic institutionalizations of civil society emerged, the crippling of its utopian promises has generated continuous struggle. These have not only been political struggles for power, but legal, cultural, and emotional arguments about definitions of competence and identity, about symbolic representations of the primordial qualities of dominant and excluded groups. The public has never been a dry and arid place composed of abstract arguments about reason. It has always been filled up by expressive images, by narratives, traditions, and symbolic codes. Organizations and social movements have sustained and resisted these cultural structures, engaging in discursive struggles over the legitimating resources they need to expand or restrict civil life.

The Plasticity of Common Identity

Definitions of civic competence are expressed in terms of universal criteria, but these criteria are represented in terms of the concrete historical qualities of particular orientations and groups. "Common identity" is, in historical terms, extremely plastic. Members of subordinate religious sects, social classes, genders, races, sexualities, generations, regions, and ethnicities may look different and act differently from the nation's founders and depart from the

criteria promoted by noncivil elites. Nevertheless, as a result of social movements and less organized and more incremental processes, members of core
groups can be—and often have been—convinced that beneath these differences, and even because of them, there exists a common humanity worthy
of civil respect.

Whether or not members of the core groups become communicatively
convinced that subordinate group members actually share with them a common humanity, and thus are worthy of respect, is critical to the process that
can be called incorporation. Later I will parse this term into more historically
specific and morally evocative subcategories. Here I will use "incorporation"
in a general and abstract, if still obviously evaluative, manner, one that
implies neither evolutionary assumptions about its empirical likelihood nor
preconceptions about the empirical mode through which it may be achieved,
whether conflict, coercion, patronage, or processes of a more democratic
kind. When considered in this manner, it is clear that incorporation is an
issue that no "modern" social system can avoid. It is thrust upon every
society that includes a civil dimension, no matter how crippled or fragmented. Incorporation points to the possibility of closing the gap between
stigmatized categories of persons—people whose particular identities have
been relegated to the invisibility of private life—and the utopian promises
that in principle regulate civil life, which imply equality, solidarity, and
respect among members of society. Whether social movements try to close
this gap or exacerbate it, they make their insistent demands vis-à-vis the
imminent possibilities of this incorporative process.

But incorporation does not only occur in the public arena of social
movements. It is a process that proceeds along extraordinarily complex paths,
extending from micro interactions such as intermarriage to such macro
arenas as labor markets. Insofar as social systems contain a civil dimension,
members of their core groups always face this question: In regard to a
particular category of excluded persons—whether defined by class, region,
gender, race, religion, or national origin—should the gap between utopian
promise and stigmatized actuality be closed? Should the incorporation of
this particular group into civil society proceed?

Exclusionary Solidarity

In later chapters, I will describe different modes of incorporation into civil society, suggesting that there are different ideal-typical paths—at once historical, empirical, and moral—along which the gap between public recognition and private exclusion can be, and has been, closed. To pose the problem in this way is to challenge the manner in which social science typically has conceptualized the problem of out-groups. What differs about the approach I am taking is the notion that out-groups are produced, first and most important, by processes internal to the social system itself. This seems paradoxical. Exclusion results from the very process of constructing, in real time and real space, empirical civil societies, from their instantiation in larger, complex, differentiated, and segmented social systems. It is the contradictions generated by institutionalization that produce exclusion. What particular groups are excluded is historically contingent. That, at any particular historical moment, some groups are relatively more distant from the core is systemic, the result of the very process of instantiating the civil sphere in time, space, and plural institutional domains.

This suggests an almost Marxian logic, one that social scientists have adopted in studies of internal class hierarchies but have rarely applied to understanding outsiders, or "strangers."[1] From Weber and Simmel, through the ecological studies of the Chicago school, to current discussions of ethnicity, immigration, and race, American and European social scientists have tended to conceptualize exclusion differently from the way I am proposing, as resulting from encounters between a relatively well-integrated social system on the one side and an unfamiliar, physically and geographically separated group on the other. Rather than approaching exclusion in terms of endemic social system processes, processes that intertwine with historical and geographic contingencies, exclusion and otherness have typically been understood as a result of external encounters.

Forms of Out-Group Contact

By focusing mainly on encounters between imperial or national societies and "the other," such an approach avoids the fundamental question of how the internal constitution of these collectivities affects the outcome of these encounters.[2] It is precisely such consideration, however, that leads one to recognize the signal importance of the civil sphere. The structure and viability of the civil sphere profoundly affects the motivational, institutional, and discursive frameworks within which strangers are encountered. Such civil mediation will be my principal focus in the considerations that follow. Still, there is no reason to deny the importance of contingent encounters as such. Whether as a result of their own actions or because of developments in their environments, such large collectivities as empires and nation-states continually encounter unfamiliar groups. In the course of these encounters, existing membership in the "home" society—even for subordinated and stigmatized classes, genders, and ethnicities—can provide an insider, privileged status.

One can think systematically about the various ways in which the members of such societies physically encounter such outside groups: (1) through economic or political enslavement of other groups and societies; (2) through military conquest of stable regimes, with the aim of imperial expansion or revolution; (3) through imperial dissolution, reconquest, or upheaval in imperial peripheries; and (4) through economic, religious, or political immigration. Though the first kind of out-group contact is today relatively rare, the other social processes remain very much in evidence. In recent years, out-group contact through immigration has been a particular focus of attention. Revolutions in transportation technology, the emergence of transnational economic institutions, and the decreasing influence of national sovereignty have made it much more likely that mounting Third World poverty, which is itself connected to earlier processes of out-group contact such as imperial conquest and dissolution, will lead to immigration. These push factors are intensified by the pull factor of cultural globalization. When structural opportunities for flight are combined with the effects of an international communicative space saturated by symbolic representations of wealth and poverty—North and South, West and East—the result is unprecedented migration from the world's impoverished southern and eastern regions to northern and western ones.[3]

When social scientists consider nonclass incorporation, they tend to conceptualize the kinds of processes I have just described—globalization, regime breakdown, military conquest, and immigration—as discrete and contingent forms of out-group contact, treating each as the cause of certain

412

behavioral effects. As I have suggested, such an approach ignores the variable internal structure of the social system responding to such outside forces. Certainly, different kinds of out-group contact have distinctive ramifications even if they are not determinate. If we wish to analyze incorporation into American society, it would be folly to ignore the demographic reality that, in historical terms, the American population was formed from revolution (against the British), military conquest (over native Americans and Mexicans), enslavement (of African Americans), and immigration (first Europeans, later Asians and Hispanics). Similarly, if we wish to understand incorporation in France, it is important to know that although France has experienced high immigration flows, for example of Italians and Belgians in the later eighteenth and early nineteenth centuries, its patterns of out-group contact have differed dramatically from those in the United States. The long history of nation-building via imperial expansion within territorial France, the problems created by postwar imperial dissolution of "Greater France" on the African continent, and the much more unstable character of the French revolutionary founding have all been important influences on the manner in which democratic and civil France has responded to contemporary contacts with outside groups. Incorporative patterns in Great Britain and Germany have also been deeply affected by the historical patterns of their contingent encounters with outsiders. Britain has had a long and, compared with France, much less polarized process of democratization, and Germany has historically had a relatively low incidence of immigration. These factors, combined with Britain's "post-colonial melancholia" and the non- and sometimes even counterrevolutionary character of Germany's nation-building, have created populations that, until very recently, were more ethnically and racially homogenous than those in the United States, a demographic fact that has significant comparative implications for the paths these nations have taken to civil incorporation.[4]

Nondemocratic Incorporation

But to recognize such variations in intergroup contact—in the behavioral processes that initially place core groups and out-groups into asymmetrical relationship—is surely not enough to understand the effects that such out-group encounters have on the process of incorporation.[5] We need to know something more, something about the internal structures of the society in relation to which outsiders are placed. It is one thing when outsiders seek to enter rigid "state" societies, and quite another when they encounter social systems that have more independent civil realms.[6] It is not impossible for extensive incorporation to occur in state societies, but it is much less likely, and it will involve much more coercive means.[7]

In response to the dangerous national conflicts that have accompanied the dissolution of the former Soviet and Yugoslavian empires, some contemporary analysts have looked back longingly at imperial forms of organization, whether in the Christian or the Islamic worlds, that were conspicuously multinational and relatively stable.[8] The best that the core groups of empires can offer outsiders, however, is some version of protected guest status. That status can qualify outsider groups for toleration in a restricted legal sense, but it does not engender incorporation in the sense of fuller participation in the communicative processes, interactions, and institutional structures of civil life. Even in this best-case scenario for state societies, in which rights to coexistence are extended to outsiders, the right to integration in a more substantive sense is denied, and hierarchy remains. In the worst-case scenario, empirically far more likely, bureaucratic authoritarian societies such as the former Soviet Union and the contemporary People's Republic of China regulate excluded categories of persons in significantly harsher ways. Political, economic, and cultural subjugation is not untypical; physical dispersion, forced relocation bordering on genocide are not unprecedented.[9]

∖ Yet although such patterns of national "cleansing" are indeed widespread in antidemocratic societies, the rejection of out-group integration is not necessarily tantamount to physical repression or outright annihilation.∕ Even in China and the former Soviet Union, bargains were made between core groups and out-groups which allowed physical copresence and behavioral cooperation to be maintained. Such accommodation may be made for reasons of efficiency. It may develop, as well, because core groups of imperial societies are frequently constrained by the cultural and institutional remnants, or fragments, of a civil sphere, even if badly deformed. Thus, bureaucratic-authoritarian societies often develop what Bryan Turner and Robert Holton call "state administered status-bloc politics."[10] Even while denying authentic forms of recognition, authoritarian regimes can co-opt demands of outside groups by agreeing to employ their primordial categories as criteria for distributing patronage, prestige, and material goods.

Such situations, however, are rarely stable in the long run. The forms of integration they employ are thin rather than thick. Institutional and interactional accommodation may occur, but what is not transformed are the perceptual and affective ties that relate physically copresent members of societies to one another. The Torah distinguishes between obligations that Hebrews owe strangers "sojourning" in their homeland and those who are "dwelling" within it. The first, mere visitors, should be tolerated and not bothered. The second mean to stay, and they must be encountered, recognized, and incorporated: "If a stranger sojourn with thee in your land, ye shall not vex him. But the stranger that dwelleth with you shall be unto you as one born among you, and thou shalt love him as thyself; for ye were strangers in the land of Egypt."[11] Only when subjective ties are thickly and deeply transformed can collective identity be altered and social solidarity expanded in a powerful way. Only such authentic recognition of a common humanity can produce the intertwining of solidarity and autonomy that marks developed civil societies, and only it can lay the basis for the democratic political organizations that depend on this civil solidarity.[12]

When democratic societies employ primordial qualities as criteria for distribution—affirmative action in the United States, the scheduled caste system in India—they can maintain public legitimacy only if citizens perceive this emphasis on particularity as deepening the textures of common humanity.[13] Because state societies have much more rigid and restrictive cultural codes, and communicative and regulative institutions, it is much more difficult to legitimate primordial criteria in this way. Such societies deny the civil sphere autonomy; they block or distort incorporation through the kinds of co-optative and manipulative processes I have described.

Internal Colonialism and the Civil Sphere

Of course, the existence of a more autonomous civil realm does not, in itself, guarantee that incorporation will proceed in a fundamentally democratic way. The systemic and historical contradictions engendered by the institutionalization of civil societies means that civil status for some groups is combined with antidemocratic rule over others. Indeed, even the most democratic civil societies have become implicated in internal colonialism. In the United States, internal colonialism was generated by the constitutional legitimation of slavery between 1789 and 1865 and, later, by Jim Crow laws in the American South.[14] Other examples abound: England's often brutal and exploitative incorporation of the subjugated "British" territory of Ireland; the Apartheid system in post-1948 South Africa; the decades-long occupation of Palestinian territory by the democratic Israeli state; the Western subjugation of native, aboriginal groups in the course of early modern European expansion.[15]

Yet although internal colonialism has been historically significant, and its repercussions continue to be widely felt today, it cannot easily be identified with the out-group domination that occurs in noncivil state regimes.[16] If the dominating regime contains an independent civil sphere, conditions for emancipation are sometimes fostered within the structure of domination itself. In chapter 11, I suggested that subaltern civil societies are marked by duality. In postslavery African American communities, such civil institutions as newspapers and entertainment media flourished, and professional associations created powerful office obligations to the community. In the black townships and proletarian communities of South Africa, thick civil connections also developed, not only culturally but in institutional, often quasi-legal ways.[17] In dominated Palestinian territory, where critical communication is restricted and often distorted, counterinstitutions of office obligation and social regulation have still developed, and distinctively democratic discourses have sometimes emerged.[18] Such nascent civil structures allow subordinated groups to make compelling protests against hegemony. Despite the enormous ideological and material constraints imposed by their exclusion, it is by no means impossible for dominated groups to successfully evoke the liberating discourses and even the communicative and regulative institutions of the hegemonic order. Indeed, in the examples I have cited—racially segregated America, Apartheid South Africa, and the occupied Palestinian territories—fiercely contested, radical, and sometimes successful challenges to internal colonialism have frequently occurred. Of course, these challenges may not themselves be democratic, but rather mirror the repressive civil discourse that justified their own domination.

Though internal colonialism in civil societies is an extreme case, its complexities illustrate the ambiguities that out-group subordination generates in every society that supports a relatively autonomous civil sphere. Because civil societies are sustained by assumptions about enlightened human capacities and rights for participation, protection, and communication, they promise even the most dominated out-group historically unprecedented levels of accessibility and respect. Precisely because such societies possess a relatively independent civil sphere, they are in some manner committed to expanding solidarity, to opposing ascriptive bases for hierarchy, and to projecting common humanity as the criterion for distributing status and rights.

Attention must shift from the mode of intergroup contact to variations in the relationship that develops between out-group and fragmented host society. What is the fit, or lack of it, between the out-group qualities and the primordial distortions of civil society? How will the universalistic dimensions of culture and institutions be applied to the particularities of subordination? These are the questions we now address.

Varieties of Incorporation and Resistance in Civil Societies

A newly encountered out-group defines its collective identity in such terms as language, race, gender, sexuality, religion, ethnic origin, and economic status. Members of the host society primordialize these historically arbitrary characteristics into "essences" that are held to be uniquely capable or incapable of sustaining participation in their civil sphere. Yet, even when this primordialization constructs newly encountered out-groups in terms of the discourse of repression, the resulting representation of domination remains tense; it can never be legitimated fully. This is true even in extremis, as when civil society becomes implicated in internal colonialism. As long as there exists some autonomy for the civil sphere, primordial subordination produces a contradictory situation. Out-group contact may allow civil competence to be deeply primordialized; at the same time, however, the continuing existence of a civil realm maintains the possibility, in principle, that this polluted primordialization can be contested, neutralized, and eventually overturned.

Closing Down the Civil Sphere

As long as a differentiated civil realm remains, so too does the tension I have just described. This contradictory condition creates the possibility for the incorporation of out-groups into civil society. Progressive incorporative movements aim to resolve the contradictions of civil society by more fully including out-groups and expanding the autonomy of the civil realm. But this is only one possibility, for the contradictory situation need not be resolved in an inclusive, progressive way. Antidemocratic movements take a very different path to resolving such contradictions. They promise to eliminate the independence of the civil sphere itself. Because out-group subordination belies the promises of civil life, it threatens members of a society's already established, core groups. Core groups worry that dominated groups can make use of the cultural promises and institutional mechanisms of civil life. When excluded groups do make such efforts, backlash movements form in response. In the very midst of progressive movements toward incorporation, in other words, demands arise for new or renewed forms of exclusion, sometimes even harsher and more permanent ones. It was in the face of significant Jewish assimilation into late-nineteenth-century German, French, and American societies that massive anti-Semitism emerged. It was in response to intensifying European unification, in the late twentieth century, that there developed vociferous and exclusionary anti-immigrant movements.[19]

In the context of civil societies, then, social movements emerge that can successfully block further inclusion and sometimes reverse it. Indeed, backlash movements can threaten the existence of the civil sphere, demanding suppression of the very autonomy that allowed their own movements first to emerge. The goal of such backlash movements is understandable sociologically even if noxious morally. If the civil aspect of society can be restricted or even destroyed, the immanent universalism that creates continuous dissatisfaction with inequality and exclusion can be eliminated; with this elimination, the threats to core-group status will disappear. When the forces of universalism are too weak to mediate exclusion and moderate the subordination of out-groups, civil ties can deteriorate into civil war, for efforts to enforce primordial identities lead to attempts to mobilize noncivil institutions, particularly the state. Stability is possible in so-called plural societies—democratic societies composed of "columnized" primordial groupings.[20] It is empirically more likely, however, that processes of pluralization will engender new forms of domination and, eventually, secession and even civil war. In this manner, the social system can be transformed from a partially realized civil society into a primordial community, from a partially democratic *Gesellschaft* to a modernized, authoritarian *Gemeinschaft*. It was just this kind of countercivilizing process that generated antidemocratic movements throughout the most advanced societies of the twentieth century. These revolutionary fascist movements might well have succeeded in suppressing the civil sphere if their regimes had not been defeated from the outside, by Allied troops in the Second World War.[21]

Opening Up the Civil Sphere

Such a descent to primitivism can be avoided only if excluded groups are incorporated in some manner and to some degree. When out-group representatives demand inclusion, there must be at least some influential core-group members who are responsive to their demands. As intensive symbolic and material conflicts develop between core group and out-group, social movements emerge that challenge the cultural legitimation of exclusion, criticizing stigmatizing interactions and challenging distorted institutions of communication and corrupt institutions of regulation. Such movements demand that core groups reframe their perceptions of out-group identities, rejecting the categories of repression for those offered by the discourse of liberty. They demand that interaction between core-group and out-group members be more respectful; that fictional and factual media representations of out-group activities be more sympathetic and even-handed; and that regulative institutions be more responsive, inclusive, and attentive. These demands of out-group representatives and social movement leaders should be conceived, in the first instance, not as connected with force, but rather as efforts at persuasion. They are translations of the discourse of civil society, which social movements and dissident intellectuals and artists broadcast via communicative institutions to other, more integrated members of the core group. As we have seen in Part III, these translations are often punctuated by efforts at gaining more regulative intervention through court rulings, administrative decrees, and electoral change, efforts that depend upon resources of a more coercive nature.

Discursive struggles over exclusion revolve around two contentious issues, questions that obsess out-group challengers and core group members alike.

1. Is the civil sphere of a particular nation-state really autonomous? How "free-floating" can it be vis-à-vis the historical primordial-ities instantiated in various forms of national stratification? Is the nation's civil realm so closely attached to primordial understand-ings that it should be regarded not as providing a counterweight to stratification but as simply legitimating it?[22]

2. How could the identities of outsiders be understood in relation to the binary discourse of civil society? Are they rational or irra-tional, honest or deceitful, open or secretive, autonomous or de-pendent?

The democratic response to these fateful questions is straightforward. The demeaning contradictions of universalism can be ameliorated, and jus-tice enhanced, only (1) if civil society can be culturally represented and organizationally empowered in a manner that is relatively independent of primordial identities and (2) if core-group members construct outsiders in terms that maintain or restore their full humanity. In 1859, Carl Schurz, a German immigrant to the United States who eventually was elected a U.S. senator, addressed incorporation in these optimistic terms when he argued, in the face of backlash movements against immigration, that the United States was "a great colony of *free humanity* which has not old England but the *world* for its mother country."[23] By not identifying the mother country of American immigrants and founders with England, a particular nation, but rather with the world, Schurz was denationalizing American ethnicity, eras-ing its primordial form. The contradictions between the civil aspirations of America and its historical and geographical specificity were in this way vitiated, and the nation Schurz was defending could be seen as composed of "free humanity" in more than a partial and rhetorical sense.

In real civil societies, however, such ideal, politically correct answers have not been so easily forthcoming. They must, at any rate, always involve as much feeling and speculation as rational common sense, be symbolic and not simply pragmatic, as expressive as scientific. John Higham explained why this must be so in his account of the anticivil American nativism that challenged the waves of American immigrants in the late nineteenth century. "What was worse than the size and the strategic position of the alien pop-ulation," Higham writes, "was its apartness."[24] It was this moral distance that marked the chasm. "The new immigrants lived in a social universe so remote from that of the Americans on the other side of the tracks," Higham writes, "that they knew practically nothing of one another." If core-group members rarely encounter out-groups directly, neither evidence from actual encounters nor personal experience can guide their judgments of civil competence. It is more in response to untested beliefs, to fantasies, hopes, and fears that they place members of outsider groups at different points along the continuum of citizen and enemy.

What are the sociological pathways by which civil reactions to out-groups have been constructed? To the degree that there is incorporation, it has occurred in three ideal-typical ways: assimilation, ethnic hyphenation, and multiculturalism.

Stigmatized Persons and Their Qualities

Assimilation has been by far the most common manner in which the historical expansion and revision of the civil sphere has taken place. For comparative and empirical reasons, therefore, as well as for normative ones, it is important to define assimilation in a precise way. In assimilative incorporation, members of primordially denigrated groups are allowed, and often encouraged, to "pass" into public life. As this notion of passing suggests, such incorporation is not merely the result of regulative institutions guaranteeing excluded groups civil treatment in a procedural sense. The communal life of societies is much too layered and culturally textured for that. Because civil competences are always interlarded with particular identities, any mode of incorporation must focus on the public construction of identities, on how the civic competences of core groups are related to the abilities of subordinate ones. Assimilation is an incorporative process that achieves this extension, or transformation, in a distinctive way. Assimilation takes place when out-group members are allowed to enter fully into civil life on condition that they shed their polluted primordial identities. Assimilation is possible to the degree that socialization channels exist which can provide "civilizing" or purifying processes—through interaction, education, or mass-mediated representation—that allow *persons* to be separated from their primordial *qualities*. It is not the qualities themselves that are purified or accepted, but the persons who formerly, and possibly still privately, bear them. This is the genius of assimilation; it is also, as we will see, its limitation sociologically and morally.

From the perspective of the formal promises of civil society, and often from the perspective of core-group members themselves, this assimilating purification provides for out-group members a civic education, imparting to them the competences required for participation in democratic and civil life. As we have seen, however, civil competence is, in fact, neither practiced nor understood in such a purely abstract way. It is always and everywhere filtered through the primordialities of the core group. Insofar as assimilative processes occur, therefore, persons whose identities are polluted in the private sphere actually are learning how to exhibit new and different primordial qualities in the public sphere. What they are learning, then, is not civil competence per se, but, instead, how to express civil competence in a different kind of primordial way, as Protestants rather than as Catholics or Jews, as Anglos rather than as Mexicans, as whites rather than as blacks, as northwestern Europeans rather than as southern or eastern ones. Civic education is not an opening up to the abstract qualities of Enlightenment rationality per se; civic education means, rather, learning how to embody and express those qualities that allow core-group members persuasively and legitimately to exhibit civil competence. When Eugen Weber wrote that the Third Republic in France turned "peasants into Frenchmen," he was talking about assimilation in exactly this manner.[25] The qualities of peasant life, in and of themselves, remained highly stigmatized by the core groups of France, particularly by Parisian elites. But members of rural France learned how to manifest Frenchness à la Paris, adopting qualities of lifestyle, bearing, language, religion, and thought that, when properly exhibited, gave them a newfound status, a social respect that allowed them to be much more thoroughly incorporated into the civil and democratic life of France.[26]

Assimilation is historically the first and sociologically the most "natural" response to the contradiction between public civility and private particularity that has marked modern mass civil societies from their very beginnings. It is the most natural because incorporation can be achieved without appearing to challenge the established primordial definitions of civic competence. In assimilative incorporation, the qualities that define foreign and different do not change; rather, the persons who are members of foreign, and thus putatively different, out-groups are allowed to shed these qualities in their public lives. They can change from being different and foreign to being "normal" and "one of us."

The plasticity of identity, its cultural and constructed character, allows such assimilative transformation to occur vis-à-vis every conceivable primordial quality. Not only ethnicity and language, but the public identities of stigmatized members of religious, economic, racial, and sexual communities can be reconstructed in an assimilative way. The qualities of these groups remains stigmatized, but they can now be left behind at the door of private life. Those who carry them privately can venture forth into public exhibiting civic competence differently. With assimilation, the split between private and public remains in place; indeed, because the polluted qualities of stigmatized group membership are even more firmly restricted to the private sphere, this split becomes sharper and more unyielding. From a moral point of view, assimilative incorporation is paradoxical. On the one hand, it fails entirely to challenge the myth of transparent civility, leaving in place the illusion, so cherished by members of already established core groups, that primordial characteristics do not belie the substantive validity of the civil sphere. On the other hand, it is precisely this failure to challenge civil transparency that allows out-groups to be massively incorporated in an assimilative way.

Despite its paradoxes, in other words, and even to some degree because of them, assimilative incorporation seems to validate the Enlightenment vision of democratic mass societies. It is for this reason extraordinarily significant in both historical and comparative terms. Insofar as assimilative incorporation proceeds, the notion that all human beings are rational, perfectible, and capable of self-control can be taken seriously, despite the enormous prejudices and distortions that continue to bedevil national social life. Insofar as an out-group is assimilated, its members seem to be treated, in the public sphere, according to the discourse of liberty. They are encouraged to shed those ascriptive qualities that insiders deem inimical to the requirements of modern civil societies and, insofar as they do so, they are treated as representatives of "humanity" rather than as members of a group whose qualities remain stigmatized.

Because the contemporary discourse of difference promoted by postmodern sensibilities has objectified and amalgamated the various phases of modernity, it has become fashionable to attack the incorporation of outgroups into civil society as "merely" acculturation or normalization, to regard it invidiously as simply the stripping of particularist identities and, thus, as a form of repression. Incorporation is reduced to assimilation, and assimilation is reduced to a kind of cultural cleansing. If, under the sign of Foucault, cultural knowledge is falsely equated with structural power, then exclusion of out-group primordial traits from the public arena is understood as simply another form of institutional domination.

Such arguments, however, fundamentally misunderstand assimilative incorporation and civil incorporation more generally. Equating assimilation with domination both eliminates the distinction between state and civil societies and smoothes over the paradoxes that mark civil societies themselves.[27] Affirming the most enlightened principles of human sensibility and confirming democratic against authoritarian morale, assimilation extends some important degree of civil status and participation to persons regardless of primordial origin and private identity. In earlier American history, and in the histories of other democratic nation-states, assimilating out-groups experienced a confirmation of their common humanity, not only its restriction. This is in part because the private-public split allows them to continue to reproduce their primordial cultures in a relatively integral way; it is also because their personhood has been affirmed with their enlarged participation in civil and public life. The paradox, however, is that by failing to challenge negative representations of out-group qualities, by keeping them private and outside of the public sphere, assimilation reproduces demeaning stereotypes in a different way, confirming the substantive restrictions and debilitating contradictions of civil society. We will explore this paradox, and examine the alternative possibilities, in the chapters that follow.

CHAPTER 17

The Three Pathways to Incorporation

I N COMPARATIVE ANALYSES of the United States and France, sociologists, historians, and national intellectuals have argued that incorporation in these nations is different from that in other nations because it proceeds under civic-ideological rather than ethnic-primordial understandings of citizenship.[1] Their revolutionary origins and self-conscious Enlightenment rationales are supposed to have initiated such radical ruptures with tradition that their postrevolutionary civil societies are legitimated not by any primordial particularities but simply by democratic ideology as such.[2] In this chapter, I will demonstrate this is not the case. There are, indeed, highly significant differences between France and the United States, on the one hand, and central and southern European nations, on the other. Nonetheless, neither revolutionary country avoided the primordialization of its civil premises or the struggles over incorporation that issued therefrom. The three pathways to incorporation cannot be parsed into such neatly compartmentalized ways. All three forms are relevant, although certainly not equally relevant, to every national experience.

Even in such a democratic country as the United States, in other words, assimilation has assumed a fundamentally paradoxical form. Though assimilation provided enormous opportunities for participation, it failed to challenge stigmatized qualities, confirming significant restrictions on promises for a democratic life. In the face of increasing immigration and internal stratification, these restrictions produced tensions that allowed out-groups eventually to produce changes in the assimilative model. Eventually, the possibilities for incorporation came to be envisioned in ethnic or hyphenated terms. This change allowed the primordial qualities that instantiated American civil society to be expressed in more plural ways. Recent historical developments have pushed struggles over incorporation into a multicultural mode. This new mode of incorporation remains partial, tentative, and highly contested, but it provides a framework for solidarity that is dramatically different from those that have been available before.

The Assimilative Mode of Incorporation

As the Declaration of Independence symbolically announced in 1776, and as the Constitution legally institutionalized in 1789, the political government of the United States allowed the nation's civil society extraordinary autonomy. Political power in the new nation was to be formally submitted to civil power, which would be generated in an open-ended, democratic way. The implications for incorporation seemed clear. Membership in civil society would be separated from primordiality, and the capacity of newcomers for civil competence would be evaluated in a rational, humanistic way.

Yet as the first censuses of the new Republic demonstrated statistically, and as early nationalistic assertions demonstrated discursively, the founders of this American civil society were predominantly members of particular and specific linguistic, racial, religious, gender, and ethnic communities. Many founders believed, indeed, that it was precisely the primordial qualities derived from membership in these groups that allowed them to establish and maintain their uniquely civil society. In one of the first recorded expressions of primordial suspicions about the civil competence of out-groups, Benjamin Franklin decried the immigration of Germans to Pennsylvania. Describing German qualities in terms that linked them metaphorically to insects and animals, he graphically gestured to their incapacity for a cooperative civil life.

Why should the Palatine Boors [Germans] be suffered to swarm into our Settlements, and by herding together, establish their Language and Manners, to the exclusion of ours? Why should Pennsylvania,

founded by the English, become a Colony of Aliens, who will shortly
be so numerous as to Germanize us instead of our Anglifying them?[3]

In a similar manner, in their effort to gain popular support for ratifying
a new Constitution for American civil society, the authors of *The Federalist*—
John Jay, James Madison, and Alexander Hamilton—sought to reassure
ordinary citizens that this historic democratic document would not be free-
floating vis-à-vis more particularistic communities, despite the fact that it
would impose new civil obligations. To the contrary, these democratic
theorists suggested, the new Constitution would be mediated by solidarities
of much more primordial, restricted, and local kinds.

> Providence has been pleased to give this one connected country to
> one united people—a people descended from the same ancestors,
> speaking the same language, professing the same religion, attached
> to the same principles of government, very similar in their manners
> and customs.[4]

As we have seen, however, civil societies are deeply contradictory. Even
as they stigmatized outsiders and primordialized their civil communities,
America's founding figures were compelled to deny, just as fervently, that
any such primordial stratification existed and to assert the completely free-
floating transparency of America's civil sphere. Membership in the American
community, they declared, could be fully achieved simply with the acquisition of civil status itself. Thus, in a debate over naturalization in 1790, an
ally of Thomas Jefferson's in the House of Representatives argued that "it is
nothing to us, whether Jews or Roman Catholics settle amongst us; whether
subjects or kings, or citizens of free states wish to reside in the United States,
they will find it in their interest to be good citizens." Addressing "the
oppressed of all Nations and Religions," he suggested that they were "welcome to a participation of all our rights and privileges."[5] In much the same
manner, during the Constitutional Convention in 1787, James Madison's
concern about whether outsiders should be included was couched only in
terms of whether or not they accepted the principles of civil society, not in
terms of who or what they were in primordial terms. Though noting the
danger of naturalizing those who had "foreign predilections," he argued,
nonetheless, for inviting "foreigners of merit and republican principles." In

a similar vein, Madison and his friend Thomas Jefferson later pushed through a naturalization bill that required any applicant simply to "make an express renunciation of his title or order of nobility."[6]

The danger to civil society suggested by this second set of statements refers not to primordiality but to antidemocratic beliefs and the authoritarian practices they might inspire. The threat that such commitments represented could be neutralized by conscious declarations of allegiance to civil society itself, pledges of allegiance that members of any primordial community easily could make. The gigantic distance between this more consistently democratic position and the first set of more primordial statements about incorporation reflects the contradictions produced by early institutionalization of American civil society. To articulate and legitimate the democratic aspirations of the new nation demanded, evidently, that these contradictions should somehow be suppressed. An extraordinary example of such suppression can be found in the essays justifying the separation of powers that James Madison contributed to *The Federalist Papers*. In these theoretical statements, which have become famous in the literature on democratic pluralism, Madison focused almost exclusively on political differences, entirely ignoring primordial ones. Ethnic exclusions and the particularistic criteria they implied would have to be made invisible if the principles of civil society were to be institutionalized in an enthusiastic and legitimate way.

It is within the confines of this contradictory frame that the assimilative period of incorporation into American society proceeded. On the one hand, civil society was asserted to be free-floating vis-à-vis particular communities, and the universal civil competence of all human beings was proclaimed. Jefferson had claimed in the Declaration of Independence that it was a "self-evident truth" that "all men are created equal." At the same time, the civil capacities of various out-groups were continually questioned and, on these grounds, strenuous efforts were made to maintain a tight homology between the American civil community and a much more restrictive and primordial one. As I have suggested above, the only possible "solution" to this contradiction was to split private and public life in a radical way.

A German visitor to the United States in the 1830s, Francis J. Grund, starkly described this splitting process even while he extravagantly praised democratic America's incorporative spirit. Grund observed highly separated and particularized German communities. To counterbalance the feeling "that they are strangers in the land of their adoption" and to make "their exile less painful," Grund wrote, German immigrants had adopted a style "of remaining together, and settling whole townships or villages."[7] In several states, Grund reported, there were villages "where no other language is spoken." Indeed, it was almost as if German immigrants had "transfer[red] a part of their country to the vast solitudes of the New World." Grund is describing a situation in which ethnic primordiality was maintained in a radical, highly particularistic way. In almost the same breath, however, he insists that these German immigrants were thoroughly incorporated into American society, describing how members of these segregated German communities rallied "cheerfully round the banner of the American republic." Such contradictory observations can be reconciled when we see how Grund describes the nature of the ties that these new immigrants to Americans so cheerfully embraced: "The Americans present the spectacle of a people united together by no other ties than those of excellent laws and equal justice."[8] The bonds that held these strangers to American society were, in other words, purely of a regulative kind. The strangers were so sharply separated from the core primordial identity of Americans that they hardly bothered to engage them. Their incorporation depended upon purely procedural participation; it consisted in their commitment to the regulative institutions of American civil society.

In the purely assimilative model of early American life, stigmatized primordial identities were maintained in marginalized communities, whose practices remained invisible to the public eye. They flowed beneath the surface of what core-group members took to be the distinctively "American" way of life. Members of primordially stigmatized groups could participate in the discourse and institutions of American civil society insofar as they completely shed these identities upon entering the public domain. Assimilation deepened to the degree that civil participation went beyond procedural participation in regulative institutions to engage communicative processes, which meant participating in such socializing institutions as schools, which provided the cultural resources to participate in discursive struggles over identity construction.

Primordial identifications so reduced civic claims in the first decades of American democracy, however, that even the compromise formation represented by assimilation could proceed only in halting and restricted ways. In terms of national origins, the pool of putatively competent participants was restricted to northwestern Europe. Even within this primordial restriction, moreover, it was much easier for outsiders who shared the founders' Protestant faith than it was for Catholics to make good use of the private-public split upon which assimilative participation depended. During the Reformation, Protestant dissenters had objected to the established Church on civil as well as purely religious grounds, decrying its hierarchical and collectivist institutions, its suffocation of individual autonomy, the licentiousness of the priests.

As Calvinist and Puritan heterodoxies inspired the first democratic revolutions, "popery" became so strongly stigmatized that it was represented as fundamentally anticivil in an essentializing, primordial sense. During the same decade that Grund was extolling the civil participation of German immigrants, for example, Samuel F. B. Morris proclaimed that Catholicism was "opposed in its very nature to Democratic Republicanism."[9] On the basis of this polluting construction, early American "Nativists" went beyond insisting on the private-public split, often demanding overt repression. Declaring that Catholics should be denied access to most regulative institutions, nativists wanted to make citizenship more difficult and to exclude Catholics and foreigners from holding public office.[10] Morris argued that suffrage should be denied to such immigrants for their entire lifetimes. The inclusive and progressive elements of assimilation are demonstrated by the ferocity of those who opposed it, even for immigrants who shared national origins, language, and the Christian faith. In nineteenth-century America, fears of being polluted by interactions with Catholic immigrants triggered massive rioting aimed at denying Catholics access to public schools.[11]

Assimilation rests upon a contradiction between civil solidarity and primordial exclusion, which expresses itself in the homologous split between public and private spheres. These contradictions mark assimilation as a deeply ambiguous social process. On the one hand, it implies that civic bonds can create such powerfully democratic forms of national identity that they can supplant stigmatizing loyalties of more iniquitous kinds. On the other hand, the very nature of assimilation and the social structures that allow it would seem to make such neutralization impossible to achieve.

The first, more optimistic scenario is what inspired Abraham Lincoln when he asserted that, though immigrants did not share the primordial qualities of the founding fathers, they could become "a part of us." Immigrants can become full partners in American civil society because, "when they look through that old Declaration of Independence, they find those old men say that 'We hold these truths to be self evident, that all men are created equal,' is for everyone." Lincoln reasoned that taking the promise of equality seriously demanded that the nation's communal bonds of primordial identification could be defined, somehow, in a thoroughly civil way. The immigrants "have a right to claim it as though they were blood of the blood and flesh of the flesh of the men who wrote the Declaration of Independence," Lincoln argued, and, he concluded, "so they are."[12]

Lincoln is suggesting here that assimilation can not only establish formalistic and procedural incorporation but can broaden civic solidarity in a more substantive, emotional, and discursive sense of the "we." Yet the contradictions that produce assimilation as an incorporative strategy, and the strict public-private split that allows it to succeed, make this kind of broadening unlikely. As the reference to Catholic immigrants suggested above, the fullness of public participation that assimilation promises to members of excluded groups is compromised by the stigma that remains attached to their primordial qualities. For participation not only in regulative but communicative institutions, there would have to be significantly less pollution of outsiders' primordial qualities. Only with such discursive re-presentation can cross-group solidarities be established that allow truly significant public participation and, eventually, real public recognition. Even these cross-group identities, however, may be restrictive and primordial in other ways.

The Hyphenated Mode of Incorporation

In its ideal-typical form, assimilation is not only unsatisfactory in a normative sense but unstable in an empirical one. In social systems that have weaker and less autonomous civil spheres, this instability of assimilation can lead, not to a widening, but to a narrowing of the civil sphere, to its deeper primordialization. In the name of the threatened core groups, social movements arise that demand a more restrictive identification of civil competence and even the destruction of civil society itself.

In social systems with stronger civil societies, by contrast, the instability of assimilation can push incorporation in a more hyphenated, less either/or direction. This positive development involves a double movement. Outsider particularities are viewed in less one-sidedly negative ways; conceived as ethnic rather than foreign, they are more tolerated in private and public life.

At the same time, the possibility of forming stronger and deeper cross-group bonds that bridge, or transcend, these particularities is viewed more positively as well. In this manner, the emergence of ethnicity can be said to hyphenate the essentialized identities of a core group. "Ethnicity" suggests some fluidity in the interchange of outsider and insider primordial qualities; at the same time, it contributes to the creation of a common collective identity that may be neither core nor peripheral. These more fluid exchanges cross various levels of civil society. Culturally, hybrid discourses can emerge from metaphorical bridges between previously separated primordial codes and narratives. At the interactional level, new sites for the public presentation of self can emerge. New opportunities for dialogue and emotional connections arise, which in turn lead to increasing rates of friendship and intermarriage between members of core groups and out-groups.[13]

There are strong and weak versions of this hyphenated approach to incorporation. Both have been metaphorically articulated in the trope of the "melting pot." As the French immigrant Hector St. Jean de Crevecoeur first expressed the notion in 1782, "American individuals of all nations are melted into a new race of man."[14] Insofar as foreign particularities are less negatively perceived, this image paradoxically suggests, they can become hyphenated with core identities and blended into a new race, one that will exhibit only the unique particularity of "America" itself. Emerson expressed this paradox more sharply when he went beyond "melting" to "smelting pot," a shift in poetics that more graphically suggests the liquefaction of both core and out-group qualities, and the creation from "all the European tribes," as Emerson wrote, of a distinctive "new race."[15] When the Jewish immigrant playwright Israel Zangwill popularized the term "melting pot" nearly a century after Emerson, he was supporting the continuation of political asylum to outsiders and open ethnic immigration. Yet Zangwill's call for intermarriage and his characterization of the American experience as "God's crucible" suggested that such openness to outsider particularities would create new, more universalizing ties that eventually would obliterate them. As this historical dialogue demonstrates, ethnic hyphenation is itself an ambiguous model of incorporation. According more positive recognition to outsider qualities, it qualifies this recognition by wishing to absorb these qualities into a high synthesis. This new identity would, it is true, be more solidaristic and thus more complementary to the ideals of civil life, but it would effectively make outsider qualities invisible all the same.

This ambivalence of hyphenation, and the particular kind of instability that attends it, is evident in the extraordinary struggles over incorporation, particularity, and American identity that were sparked by the great inflowing of immigration after the Civil War. The conservative side eventually triumphed, and powerful barriers against outsiders were put into place.

The Civil War helped create a more hyphenated understanding of incorporation. The fight against the South united northern ethnicities in battle and blood, reinforcing a new and more generalized "American" identity, though one that still retained strong aspects of primordiality. In John Higham's historical description of this process, the paradoxes of hyphenation clearly stand out. "All over the country," he reports, "foreign-Americans flocked to the colors," a great coming together under a higher and more universal standard. Ethnic particularities remained evident and pronounced: "Five hundred thousand . . . served the Union armies . . . organized in their own [ethnic] companies, regiments, and even divisions." Yet the shared experiences of sacrifice and victory did much to dissolve the very separations that supplied the Union Army's organizational base: "Everywhere the antiforeign movement of prewar years melted away . . . by absorbing xenophobes and immigrants in a common cause. Now the foreigner had a new prestige; he was a comrade-at-arms."[16] In fighting for the Union, assertively defined under the banner of democracy, legality, and full citizenship, discrete and once stigmatized ethnic identities were re-presented in comradely terms. Following the binary discourse of civil society, they formed the pure and democratic counterpart to the hierarchical, factional, and aggressive other. It was the Confederate enemy, not the new immigrants, who now embodied the antidemocratic discourse of repression.

Of course, assimilation as an incorporative strategy hardly disappeared in the post–Civil War period. Insofar as the hyphenation model involves forming new, extraethnic national bonds, one can, as I have earlier suggested, observe significant assimilative dimensions inside this alternative model itself. More important, the notion of ethnic hyphenation does not in any sense suggest the equal valuation of core and outsider qualities. Significant rank ordering of primordial qualities remains. What hyphenation suggests, rather, is revaluation, a process that allows more fluidity and hybridity, more exchange between the putatively primordial categories that represent civil competence in more and less polluted ways. Because asymmetrical valuation remains, hyphenation, like assimilation, continues to be an ambiguous and

433

unstable social form. The dynamics that produce it and follow in its wake can lead to a more independent civil realm and more recognition for outsider primordial qualities, eventually even to the creation of a less contradictory, more multicultural civil society. These same dynamics, however, can trigger reactions that close civil society down, sharply narrowing the range of primordial identities that are available for expressing civil competence in a positively evaluated way.

After the Civil War, industrialization and territorial expansion triggered massive increases in immigration to the northern and western United States. Certainly the relatively easy availability of free land and wealth, and the federal, decentralized nature of the American political regime affected the possibilities of incorporation in a material way. Of greater significance, how-ever, was the nature of postwar American civil society as it developed outside the defeated southern states. It was the culture, institutions, and interactional possibilities of this ever-changing civil society that mediated the newly intensified struggles over incorporation, creating a new field upon which insider and outsider groups, and their intellectual and artistic interlocutors, could argue, organize, and struggle for symbolic and organizational power. Undergirded by assimilation, the new model of ethnic hyphenation framed these post–Civil War conflicts. Do all particular qualities have to be left at the door of private life? Is it only persons and not their qualities who are allowed to pass into the positively evaluated arena of public life? After the Civil War, for some but not all excluded groups, these questions began to be answered differently than before.

In its earliest forms, hyphenation meant that the primordial criteria defining the American core group expanded. Idealized national origins, for example, increasingly came to include Germany. The particular, idiographic qualities of German culture hyphenated with "old" American qualities, allowing the discourse of liberty to find wider symbolic expression. The "recreational gusto" of the new German immigrants, according to Higham,[17] shocked Americans with more traditional and censorious habits, yet in such post–Civil War urban centers as Chicago they gradually won for themselves a reputation for "thrifty, honest, industrious, and orderly living," qualities that sounded like variations on the discourse of liberty. The card-playing, beer drinking, and Sunday frolics of German newcomers came to be viewed not as licentious or lazy, but as legitimate configurations of democratic virtues. As one Chicago observer remarked in 1893, "The German notion that it is a good thing to have a good time has found a lodgment in the American mind."[18] During this post–Civil War period, the civil competence of religious faiths also began to be more broadly conceived. Though Christianity continued to define its limits, Catholicism became more a viable refraction of Protestantism than its demonic enemy. In large urban centers, second- and third-generation Irish immigrants began to occupy some of the most important regulatory offices of urban civil society, from police officers to politicians. They created political machines for influencing the electoral expression of civil power, and these brought ethnic criteria explicitly into public life.

In the context of this widening of national and religious criteria, reciprocal ethnic exchanges between out-group and in-group became increasingly extensive and widely discussed. Formerly degraded groups reached into the origin myths of American civil society and retold them as hyphenated. In the 1880s in Worcester, Massachusetts, an Irish nationalist society, the Ancient Order of the Hiberians, held an ethnic picnic every Fourth of July, the exuberance of which was publicly presented, not only as a way of maintaining Irish customs, but as an effective way of defending American civil freedoms.[19] In the 1890s, also in Worcester, forty-six hundred of the city's eleven thousand Swedish-Americans attended another publicly reported and overtly ethnic celebration of Independence Day. Festivities began with Swedish Protestant church services and ended with speeches celebrating the democratic and civil character of the United States.

Yet even though possibilities of hyphenation extended the concrete possibilities for legitimate expressions of civil competence, more restrictive understandings of the relation between founding groups and outsiders continued to be energetically asserted, even in regard to earlier and relatively more incorporated immigrant groups. In the centennial celebration of the beginning of the American Revolution in 1875, in Concord and Lexington, Massachusetts, a series of illustrious Anglo-Americans gave ceremonial speeches, but none were scheduled by representatives of Irish or German groups. One of these speakers described the Revolutionary soldiers' stand against the British as "the flower and consummation of principles that were long ripening in the clear-sighted, liberty-loving, Anglo-Saxon mind."[20]

The conflicts between more restrictive and assimilative as compared with more incorporative and hyphenated approaches to civil competence were intensified toward the end of the nineteenth century as the geographical tipping point of immigration shifted decisively from northwest to southern and eastern Europe. Frightened of pollution and displacement by Italians, Russians, Greeks, Slovenians, and Jews from the Slavic Pale, the earlier members of America's core group used the institutions of communication to block incorporation of these new outsiders, asserting narrowly primordial and increasingly restrictive religious, linguistic, and national versions of civil community. Most of the new immigrants would have been more than willing to accept the bargain of assimilation, the procedural participation and public-private split that this restricted model of incorporation could supply. At the same time, however, many of their intellectual, journalistic, and artistic representatives did not hesitate to demand incorporation in a defiantly hyphenated, ethnic way. Representatives of the older American core group fervently opposed these claims. They made persuasive appeals through communicative institutions, and they made use of regulative institutions whenever possible, employing party organization, office power, and legal force to bolster their claims that only certain primordial qualities could manifest civic competence.

Discursive confrontations over whether the civil sphere in the United States was really free-floating and over the "true character" of the recent immigrants often centered on the nation's origin myths. These stories intertwined the primordial qualities of America's founders with heroic accounts of the nation's democratic beginnings. Was it possible to rewind these accounts, to ascribe different primordial qualities to heroic protagonists, and thus to narrate the founding of America differently? It is precisely in these terms that Werner Sollors has interpreted the turn-of-the-century debates that raged around the Statue of Liberty and other iconographic representations of American national identity.[21] In the poem that the abolitionist poet John Greenleaf Whittier wrote for the official dedication of the Statue of Liberty in 1886, he identified the "lightning-flash" welcoming the nation's new immigrants with "Reason's ways and Virtue's aim." Whittier described how such new arrivals would, henceforth, encounter a monumental French construction when they first touched "Freedom's soil" in the United States, and he put a positive, democratic construction on their character by linking it with the Civil War struggle to free America from the primordial restrictions of race, writing that "with freemen's hands we rear the symbol free hands gave." In the stanzas from the poem eventually engraved on the pedestal of the Statue of Liberty, the Jewish poet Emma Lazarus developed a similar interpretation of the icon. Placing it firmly inside the antinomies of civil discourse, she criticized the antidemocratic "pomp" of "ancient lands" for creating fearful and dependent "huddled masses" who wished to flee. With Liberty's "lamp" lifted beside "the golden door," Lazarus confidently predicted, this new iconic representation of America's much more civil society would guide this "wretched refuse" to America, where they finally would be able to "breathe free."

Writers who urged restrictions on incorporation, like New Englander Thomas Bailey Aldrich, broadcast symbolic constructions of the icon, and of immigration more generally, that evoked danger and pollution. Through America's "wide open and unguarded" gates, Aldrich wrote in 1892 in a widely read poem, passes a "wild motley throng" motivated by "tiger passions," a mob obviously unfit for the autonomy and self-discipline that democracy demands. Rather than friendly, trusting, and cooperative, they were a "menace" ready to "stretch their claws," people "strange" and "alien." Faced with such dangerous pollution, it is no wonder that Aldrich urges "liberty, the white Goddess" toward repressive exclusion rather than recognition and incorporation. "With hand of steel," the figure of American civil society should "stay those who to thy sacred portals come to waste the gifts of freedom."

The Statue of Liberty was placed near Ellis Island, where waves of new immigrants first entered the United States. This physical positioning set the stage for fierce discursive confrontations over whether a hyphenated semantic relationship could be established between Ellis Island and Plymouth Rock, where the Puritans had first entered the continent three hundred years before. "The ghost of the Mayflower pilots every immigrant ship, and Ellis Island is another name for Plymouth Rock," declared the Russian Jewish immigrant Mary Antin, whose writings legitimating hyphenation became lightning rods for symbolic confrontation during the last and most heated decade of America's open immigration. Pursuing this juxtaposition of Plymouth Rock and Ellis Island, Antin tried to purify public pollutions of immigrants by constructing a symbolic analogy between the motivations of the nation's earliest and most recent arrivals. Praising "the Pilgrims [as] a picked troop in the sense that there was an immense preponderance of virtue among them," she insisted that this "is exactly what we must say of our modern immigrants, if we judge them by the sum total of their effect on our country." If new immigrants did have civic virtue, of course, their inclusion could not be resisted, and civil society would have to be defined in a much less primordial way. Speaking of "our fathers," of "our faith as Americans," of "our American sensibility," Antin possessively appropriated the national identity, claiming that it is "the love of liberty," not any particular primordial bond, that "unites all races and all classes of men into one brotherhood." In such a free-floating community, membership is established purely by civil ties. "We Americans," Antin concluded, "owe the alien a brother's share."

Denying Antin's claims that the primordial qualities of ancient founders and recent immigrants could be so easily interchanged, opponents of her hyphenated discourse resisted the expansion of civil society. Once again, the relative autonomy of civil society and the character of outsiders were the basic references for debate. A conservative *Atlantic Monthly* journalist, Agnes Repplier, described Antin's reference to "our forefathers" as misguided, arguing that recent immigrants could never lay claim to the "pioneer virtues" of America's founders. Repplier quoted Horace Kallen's emphatically primordial vision to deny a free-floating character to America's civil sphere: "Only men who are alike in origin and spirit, and not abstractly, can be truly equal, and maintain that inward unanimity of action and outlook which makes a national life." Barett Wendell, a New Englander who taught American literature at Harvard, put the matter more bluntly. Antin "has developed an irritating habit of describing herself and her people as Americans," he declared, "in distinction from such folks as [us], who have been here for three hundred years."

During World War I, anti-German and more generally anti-immigrant feeling grew. Faced with radical political agitation in the immediate postwar period, core group fears of being polluted by dark, "anti-American" forces became even more intense. During these years, the post-assimilative, ethnic mode of incorporation came under severe challenge. In October 1915, the *Literary Digest* declared the "hyphenated American" the most vital issue of the day.[22] Theodore Roosevelt thundered that the Republican Party should stand for "unhyphenated Americanism." Contrasting the "German-Americans who call themselves such" with those who identified themselves as "Americans of German origin," Roosevelt attacked hyphenation as "moral treason." As Woodrow Wilson, the Democratic president, campaigned for increased defense appropriations, he discredited those who opposed American entry into the new world war as political radicals with "alien sympathies." Wilson constructed the new immigrants as national enemies, employing the full-blown rhetoric of antidemocratic discourse. Declaring that "such creatures of passion, disloyalty, and anarchy must be crushed out," he justified their repression as a defense of civil society. During the Red Scare that followed the war, such darkly antidemocratic representations of immigrant character seemed to make their expulsion an urgent necessity. In the Palmer Raids, government officials arrested and deported thousands of immigrant radicals without legal justification. Finally, in the early 1920s, as the communicative media broadcast increasingly repressive, anti-immigrant discourse, the regulatory institutions of American civil society promoted drastic restrictions on immigration, which the American state took up. New laws reduced immigration to a trickle and reasserted the primacy of northern European origins as a primordial criterion for regulating what little legal immigration remained.

These historically unprecedented restrictions should be understood more as reactions against the hyphenated approach to incorporating outsiders than as rejections of the possibility for assimilating them, much less of the idea of civic incorporation itself.[23] Still, the immense new immigrant flows, which had increased during the same period as extreme industrialization, made outsider assimilation into core-group primordiality significantly harder than in America's first century. Incorporation could not wait for the separation of private and public to be firmly established or for the gradual shifts in public demeanor that extended participation in socializing institutions produced. As we have seen, moreover, American civil society had itself begun to change. In the decades following the Civil War, when particularistic restrictions on participation became less severe, civil society had become more free-floating, and primordial qualities were increasingly hybrid and fluid and became more easily exchanged. Between the Civil War and the First World War, in other words, hyphenation emerged not only as a more functional but a more culturally attractive model. The civil sphere in America was becoming decidedly more powerful and independent vis-à-vis more particularistic communities and institutions of a less civil kind. In the backlash that broke out against these developments, Americans declared themselves willing to incorporate members of minority groups ("Americans of German origins") but unwilling to positively evaluate outsider qualities ("German-Americans who call themselves such"). In what Higham calls the "tribal twenties," members of America's earliest core groups stridently resisted the idea that their primordial qualities could be hyphenated with those of outsider groups.

Yet even in the midst of these repressive developments, the civil dimension of the nation was reaffirmed in ways that eventually allowed the hyphenated model to forcefully return. Even the assimilative model, after all, placed restrictions on the ways in which communicative institutions could publicly broadcast stigmatizing constructions of out-group qualities. Conservative advocates of backlash policies felt compelled to affirm that America as a national community was ultimately of a civil, not a primordial kind. In the mid-'20s, for example, the racialist thinker Henry Pratt Fairchild acknowledged that American nationality "is not a question of birth, ancestry, or race," and that national solidarity could and should be extended to foreigners who learned to act in a traditional style. Writing about "American fellowship and affiliation," Pratt suggested that although this kind of solidary participation was "natural, easy, and largely unconscious for one who has always lived in America," it was "an achievement for one whose origin is foreign." Whether ascribed or achieved, however, Pratt was compelled to agree the acquisition of such cultural competence would allow community membership to be increasingly widespread, for "America is one and the same for all."[24]

For their part, officials of America's regulative institutions, even in the midst of this most repressive period, refused to eliminate the private-public distinction that separated persons from stigmatized qualities and gave them legal protection against outraged core groups. The U.S. Supreme Court overturned a Nebraska law that had forbidden modern foreign language instruction in elementary and high schools, a scarcely veiled attempt to eliminate the German language. Justice McReynolds, writing for the Court, went out of his way to emphasize that he did not disagree with Nebraska's assimilative aim. Painting civil competence in primordial hues, he expressed his sympathy with the state's desire "to foster a homogeneous people with American ideals, prepared readily to understand current discussions of civic matters."[25] He even affirmed the polluted quality of outsider identities, noting that "the foreign population is very large, that certain communities use foreign words, follow foreign leaders, move in a foreign atmosphere, and that the children are thereby hindered from becoming citizens of the most useful type." For all of this, the justice asserted, language instruction in the United States must remain a private, parental decision. Schools are organized by communities of parents, who must be allowed freedom in their language choice even if this slows acculturation down. In so protecting private particularity, Justice McReynolds referred to the unalterably civic, anti-primordial quality of America's regulatory institutions, asserting that the Constitution "belongs to those who speak other languages as well as those born with English on the tongue."

Two years later, stigmatized religious groups were also offered protection by American regulatory officials, who similarly evoked the private-public split upon which the assimilation model depends. In an effort to eliminate Catholic education, Oregon had passed a law mandating compulsory attendance in public schools. In striking down this ordinance, which had been approved by Oregon's highest state court, the U.S. Supreme Court ruled that privacy rights protected the practice of highly stigmatized primordial qualities, even if this meant protecting this practice against the intrusion of a democratically constituted state. Writing once again for the Court's majority, Justice McReynolds wrote that constitutional freedoms prevented the state from taking actions "to standardize its children." Evoking the autonomy of civil society, and the independence of civil from political power, he declared that "the child is not the mere creature of the state; those who nurture him and direct his destiny have the right, coupled with the high duty, to recognize and prepare him for additional obligation."[26]

In a post-immigration society that remained extraordinarily diverse in demographic terms, such affirmations of the private-public split ensured the deepening of assimilation. Indeed, during this interwar period, America's socializing institutions triggered processes that pointed well beyond the core-group hegemony that conservative victors over immigration had wished to preserve. In public schools, children of immigrant minorities learned not only how to incorporate core-group lifestyles but how to express their own stigmatized ethnicity in more sympathetic, compelling, and legitimate ways. As the politically conservative 1920s gave way to the more progressive political and intellectual life of the '30s and '40s, expressions of hyphenated identity were increasingly broadcast by communicative institutions, and these expressions forcefully shaped public opinion once again. The Slovenian immigrant author Louis Adamic, who declared that "the old American dream needs to be interlaced with the immigrants' emotions as they saw the Statue of Liberty," became a widely popular figure on the national lecture circuit.[27] Adamic founded the Common Council for American Unity, and its journal *Common Ground* attracted contributions from a wide swath of influential writers and intellectuals. Adamic's ambition was to create "an intellectual-emotional synthesis of old and new American." This hyphenation depended on rewinding the nation's founding myths; the tales of ethnic immigration and America's founding, Adamic suggested, would be "made into one story."[28]

Like the Civil War a century earlier, the searing experience of World War II pitted representations of a civil and inclusive America against images of its racist and antidemocratic enemies. This synthesizing surge consolidated the construction of America as an ethnically hyphenated nation, a civic community of hybrid, fluid, exchangeable primordialities. It may well be the case, as Higham has argued, that such a broadly inclusive consolidation could have emerged only after massive migration had been shut off. [29] Certainly, such closure gave out-groups time to further assimilate core-group primordiality. For their part, core-group members had decades to become more familiar with outsiders who once had seemed foreign and strange. By the 1940s, there had gestated a broader, supraethnic "Americanism" that made ethnic contrasts seem far less acute. In the decades before and after the war, it was still impossible for entertainers who wished to achieve mass popularity to use their own, ethnically distinctive names. This assimilative, unhyphenated model still held for Betty Joan Perske, who became Lauren Bacall, for Anna Maria Italiano, who became Anne Bancroft, for Doris von Kappelhoff, who became Doris Day, and for Bernard Schwarz, who became Tony Curtis.[30] In the early 1950s, by contrast, the Beat generation entered the communicative institutions of American civil society with their names intact. Allen Ginsberg, Lawrence Ferlinghetti, Diane DiPrima, and Jack Kerouac were never stigmatized as ethnics.[31] The hyphenated model was by then firmly in place.

Space had been created for out-group ethnicity—for civil competence to be exhibited in ways different from the non-core group's. Yet although negative valences were being neutralized, neither ethnicity nor other peripheral primordialities were positively represented as ends in themselves. Ethnicity was promoted in a nostalgic manner, not prospectively but retrospectively. Oscar Handlin's *The Uprooted*, the paradigm-making history of America-as-immigrant-society published in 1951, begins in a hyphenated manner, asserting the successful retelling of America's origin myth: "Once I thought to write a history of the immigrants in America. Then I discovered that the immigrants were American history."[32] The primordial founding myth that attributed civic competence to one group alone was being fundamentally displaced. Yet, in the 1973 postscript to his book's second edition, Handlin relativized hyphenation by tracing its causes to the decline of actual ethnic differences in the American society of his own day. In the postwar years when he was writing his book, Handlin recounts, ethnicity had seemed "a fading phenomenon, a quaint part of the national heritage, but one likely to diminish steadily in practical importance."

In the very same decade that Handlin published this postscript, ethnicity began to be conceived in a less ambivalent manner. In the mid-1960s, legal immigration from non-core groups was greatly intensified. Incorporation began to proceed along non-ethnic dimensions in ways that allowed a more multicultural, posthyphenation model of inclusion to emerge. The most important of these nonethnic issues was race. It was, in fact, the struggle against racial exclusion from civil society that allowed this new phase of incorporation to occur. By contrast, it had been the successful efforts to maintain and even to extend restrictive racial criteria for incorporation that had allowed the more hyphenated model of incorporation first to succeed, as we will now see.

The Exception of Race:
Assimilation and Hyphenation Delayed

Race had not been terribly important in the struggle for ethnic assimilation before the Civil War, for the very reason that members of nonwhite racial groups had been so thoroughly separated from American civil society. Because the moral character of persons with black, yellow, and red complexions was so deeply polluted, the regulative institutions of American society thoroughly excluded them from participation./The authors of the Declaration of Independence had called the Indians "merciless savages,"[33] and black slaves were widely regarded as subhuman. Because it seemed inconceivable to separate the members of these stigmatized groups from their racial qualities, assimilation was impossible for members of these racially subordinated groups to achieve.[34]/

The post–Civil War amendments to America's regulatory institutions indicated an opening in this racial primordialization of civic membership, but the continuing racial structure of American cultural and psychological life soon reasserted racial categories in an anti-assimilative way. In the southern United States, Jim Crow laws created an apartheid system of internal colonialism. As southern blacks moved to the North in the early years of the twentieth century, segregation was actively promoted de facto rather than de jure, and racially exclusive ghettos were created.[35] Not only blacks and Native Americans, but Asian outsiders were symbolically excluded and institutionally subordinated. Entering the United States mainly as indentured workers, Asian access to full citizenship was opposed on primordial grounds. In 1865, a *New York Times* editorial justified the exclusion of blacks and Chinese by linking together, and polluting, their putatively anticivil characters.

> We have four million of degraded negroes in the South . . . and if there were to be a flood-tide of Chinese population—a population befouled with all the social vices, with no knowledge or appreciation of free institutions or Constitutional liberty, with heathenish souls and heathenish propensities, then we should be prepared to bid farewell to republicanism and democracy.[36]

Racial exclusion became a more demanding political and social project in the post–Civil War period, even as outsider ethnicity was beginning to achieve a more hyphenated position vis-à-vis core group identity. As nonwhite Americans, especially blacks, began to penetrate the institutions of the northern United States, the white racial identities of the new immigrants from southern and eastern Europe, as well as the whiteness of such earlier immigrants as Irish Catholics and German Protestants, played an increasingly important role in aiding exchanges between nonracial ethnic traits. This juxtaposition of increasing immigrant incorporation, on the one hand, with affirmations of racial exclusion, on the other, was forcefully asserted in the Democratic Party platform of 1884. After calling the United States "the land of liberty and the asylum of the oppressed of every nation," the Democrats explicitly excluded the Chinese, who were described as "unfitted by habits, training, religion, or kindred for the citizenship which our laws provide." During that same period, a labor union characterized the Chinese people in violently anticivil terms, as "more slavish and brutish than the beasts that roam the fields," adding that "they are groveling worms."[37] The diverse and sometimes competing dimensions of primordiality are revealed here in a striking way. Even though various European origins and religions were becoming less stigmatized by core group members, racial identity was increasingly evoked as a primordial requirement.

Faced with these disqualifying restrictions, blacks followed immigrant writers in their efforts to use the communicative institutions of American society to broadcast new and more hyphenated versions of the nation's founding narratives. In 1903, W. E. B. Du Bois claimed that the slave ship that "first saw the square tower of Jamestown" was the true American beginning, asking his white readers "How came it yours? Before the Pilgrims landed we were there."[38] In a variety of narrative forms, black writers not only juxtaposed and tentatively equated Jamestown with Plymouth Rock but made efforts to analogize the former with the newer immigrants' arrival at Ellis Island. By equating race with ethnicity, and each with the earliest founding myth of the democratic nation, black writers sought to purify their polluted status and to create pathways for intergroup identification. In a publicity statement that Richard Wright composed for his autobiographical *Black Boy* in 1945, the novelist tried to neutralize the perceived strangeness of his primordial position by developing an analogy between early and later immigrant stories of civil resistance and his own.

[To] those whites who recall how, in the early days of this land, their forefathers struggled for freedom, Black Boy cannot be a strange story. Neither can it be a strange story to the Jews, the Poles, the Irish, and the Italians who came hopefully to this land from the Old World.[39]

These appeals for civil membership were denied by the core group and, increasingly, by hyphenated ethnic minorities alike. Racial criteria were employed to strip interned Japanese-Americans of their citizenship rights, and strict segregation continued to be observed in the armed forces, even as the United States entered World War II to fight against nations that embodied the racial definition of community in a much more primitive and less contradictory way. Still, the narrative of shared sacrifice for utopian civil ideals that crystallized ethnic pluralism during World War II had a formative effect on the relationship of American civil society to race. Because public opinion remained intensely divided, at first it was exclusively the regulative institutions of civil society that intervened to open civil participation to members of stigmatized racial groups. In 1947 the highest office holder in civil society, President Harry Truman, signed an executive order that forcibly integrated the armed forces, allowing minority groups for the first time full access to the levers that controlled the monopoly of violence. In addition to opening up civil participation in an important institution, this reform opened up a new arena for civil interaction on the face-to-face level of everyday life, regardless of the subjective, psychological or cultural feelings of group members on either side. The U.S. Supreme Court made a similar intervention in 1954, when it outlawed racial segregation in the nation's schools. Disregarding strongly held primordial feelings about race, the Court evoked the civil principles of the democratic Constitution and mandated interracial interaction among the nation's school-age children. Citing socio-logical data that showed separate schooling prevented equal access to rea-soning and emotional skills, the Court tried to open up this key socializing institution so that racial assimilation into mainstream American could suc-ceed.

In the face of continuing public support for a racially fragmented civil sphere, however, these postwar regulatory efforts to separate America's civil society from its racial communities failed. Indeed, it was precisely because of these failures, as we have seen, that the legal strategies of the NAACP gave way to the social movement for civil rights. In its highly public cam-paigns for black access to public facilities and the ballot box, the Civil Rights movement made full use of the communicative institutions of American society, particularly the mass media and civil associations, to create new forms of identification that crossed over racial groups. From the cauldron of the Montgomery bus boycott to the wrenching confrontations in Birming-ham and Selma, Martin Luther King performed a pivotal role as an intensely public figure, a symbol of transcendent democratic and religious ideals with whom white Americans in the North experienced an increasingly intense identification. The most charismatic American figure of the postwar period, King led a movement whose narrative of martyrdom and suffering eventually succeeded in reformulating the American drama of democracy[40] in multi-racial, but not multicultural, terms.

Black and white leaders of the Civil Rights movement became American heroes, figures in a drama of collective national redemption in which they—dignified, courageous, critical, self-disciplined, and broadly solidary—represented the discourse of liberty in a poignant and increasingly convincing way. In the course of this drama, they succeeded in neutralizing much of the stigma attached to nonwhite races. This indeed was their goal—to neutralize race, not to make black racial identity positively valued in and of itself.

Because of their efforts, assimilation for racial minorities became possible in the United States for the first time. Blackness as such was not a primordial quality welcomed by white core-group members, but many believed that, for purposes of institutional participation, this quality could now be left aside. For the first time in American history, the members of the black community could create a distance between their public selves and achievements, on the one hand, and the still polluted quality of blackness, on the other. "Color blindness" was the Civil Rights movement's mobilizing theme. It translated local struggles into national public dramas by convincing white Americans that their shared utopian dream of a truly civil society could only be realized in a color-blind way.

The regulatory reforms that followed specified and elaborated this communicative shift, backing up the normative separation of civil obligations from race with political, economic, and, at times, even physical sanctions. Blacks and members of other racial minorities were to be treated simply as members of civil society—as "human beings" in the parlance of the day—rather than as members of a stigmatized race. In a series of new laws extending from the mid-1960s up to the present day, judges and legislators transferred this new and fuller status in civil society to noncivil arenas, declaring discrimination to be illegal in one social sphere after another. Buoyed strongly by less racialized representations in the public sphere, these regulatory efforts have continued to be intensely pursued in the public realms of schools, employment, and municipal facilities, and they have met with significant success. Efforts to enforce Title 7 of the Civil Rights Act of 1964, which banned discrimination in employment, involve thousands of lawyers and administrators in the private and public sectors.[41]

Public and private policies of affirmative action, which have become so controversial in recent years, should be seen primarily in these same assimilative terms. Primordial criteria of race are employed in order to purge the target institution, whether school or workplace, of the public distortions of race. By the mid-1960s, cultural, political, and demographic pressures made it much more difficult for elites and citizens alike to endure the intergenerational transformations upon which earlier assimilative incorporation has depended. Affirmative action was a "forced march" to the creation of racially integrated working and middle classes.[42] It applied to the public spheres of higher education and occupational achievement, leaving private life relatively untouched. As American occupational and education worlds became more integrated, members of different racial groups within the same working, middle, and upper strata tended to become more similar in their manners of acting and feeling.[43] Yet the neighborhoods where black Americans make their homes—the interlinked personal residences that provide the site for such informal activities as friendship, recreation, religious observance, adolescent dating, and marriage—have remained largely separated until this day.[44] Only the residential integration of races would complete the hyphenation process. Racial hyphenation depends not simply on allowing the public separation of blacks from primordial qualities but on altering representations of the qualities themselves. Nonetheless, as I will show below, this process is already well under way.

Even as racial qualities remained relegated to the private sphere, far-reaching changes in white perceptions of race resulted from the Civil Rights movement itself, from the dramatic regulative shifts that followed, and from the substantial changes in the occupational and educational environments of race relations that followed in their wake. Interaction at work and school familiarized whites and blacks with one another, though strong mutual suspicions often remained. Under the limited rubric of assimilation, whites evidenced grudging but increasing respect for the civic competence of black members of the working and middle classes, and the elites.

In the late 1960s and 1970s, communicative institutions were permeated by widely broadcast narratives that separated blacks from the polluted codes of earlier days, normalizing them through representations that emphasized self-discipline, independence, and reasonableness. On network evening television, situation comedies and family dramas employed well-accepted genres to normalize the black situation in a way that allowed whites to extend cultural understanding and emotional identification. *The Jeffersons* portrayed the life and times of what seemed to many whites a surprisingly mainstream, if eccentric, black family, closely imitating the hugely successful portrayal of intergenerational conflict in the white program *All in the Family*. White and black viewers made *The Cosby Show* the single most watched family show

448

of the 1980s, converting the modest and attractive black doctor and bemused family patriarch into a representative figure for broad segments of American life. Herman Gray describes these and other black programs of the time, including *Good Times* (1974–79), *Sanford and Son* (1972–77) and *What's Happening!!* (1976–79).

> These black folk were good-humored and united in racial solidarity, [they] idealize[d] and quietly reinforce[d] a normative white middle-class construction of family, love, and happiness . . . implicitly reaffirm[ing] that such ideals and the values they promote are the rewards of individual sacrifice and hard work.[45]

Allowing white core groups to analogize between their own predicaments and those of their black economic peers, these television narratives supported assimilation, for they suggested that a shared humanity could be separated from the polluted qualities of race. The extraordinary success of the miniseries *Roots* in the late 1970s deepened this process of cross-racial identification and extended the nation's origin myths. Written by Alex Haley, who as a committed 1960s radical had ghostwritten the militantly anti-assimilative *Autobiography of Malcolm X*, *Roots* recast the history of African Americans into the heroic immigrant mold. Gray observes how the television show created a dramatic imaginative movement from polluted to purifying symbolic coding.

> With *Roots* the popular media discourse about slavery moved from one of almost complete invisibility (never mind structured racial subordination, human degradation, and economic exploitation) to one of ethnicity, immigration, and human triumph. This powerful television epic effectively constructed the story of American slavery [on] the stage of emotional identifications and attachments to individual characters, family struggles, and the realization of the American dream.[46]

It was during these same years that black entertainers and sports figures became iconic heroes for masses of white Americans, old and young. Recognized for their prowess in some of the most symbolically representative, if not the most economically or politically powerful, areas of American life, "African Americans" were viewed by an increasing segment of the white core group as "like us" in certain critically important ways.

Although race may still seem to many Americans an indelible marker, which no amount of acculturation can wash away, we would do well to remember that assimilation has always allowed outsider qualities to remain strongly stigmatized; it simply relegates them to the relative invisibility of the private sphere. With hyphenation, there occurs a marked lessening of this pollution, and relationships of symbolic affinity begin to be established between the qualities of insider and outsider groups. Even with hyphenation, however, there is never symmetry; there remain powerful, if less clearly demarcated, hierarchies in the valuations of primordial traits. Hyphenated incorporation does not truly promote the valuing of difference as such. What it does allow is the increasing separation of civil society from existing primordial affinities. Because it also can create a more blended "national" identity, hyphenation is often perceived as a temporary situation, as something that will disappear as members of insider and outsider groups are absorbed into a more universal, if still culturally distinctive national community. Hyphenated incorporation is a process, a means rather than an end. Under both assimilative and hyphenated incorporation, civil societies remained riddled by primordial and asymmetrical conceptions of civil capacities.

The Multicultural Mode of Incorporation

The moral and sociological problem with hyphenation, and equally with assimilation, is that its ambition does not extend to redefining outsider qualities; rather, it allows members of denigrated groups to be separated from those qualities. The anticivil constrictions that have distorted national democracies from their very beginnings can be overcome only by moving beyond hyphenation to a multicultural mode that is different not only in degree but in kind. Only very recently in democratic societies has such a possibility for repair emerged.[47] It opens a new chapter in the history of social integration, and my empirical discussion here is more sketch than historical account, as subjunctive as descriptive.[48] My ambition, in fact, is

primarily theoretical: I want to offer a new understanding of this multicultural mode and to define it in a systematic and comparative way.

The rhetoric generated by this new incorporative mode does not, at first
sight, seem terribly distinctive. It, too, focuses on whether civil society can
be truly universal and whether it can be separated from the primordial
restrictions of particular groups; and these possibilities continue to be discussed in terms of purifying or reconstructing out-groups in civil-discursive
terms. There is, however, a fundamental difference. Instead of trying to
purify the characters of denigrated *persons*, the focus shifts to *qualities*. Within
a putatively multicultural frame, discursive conflicts revolve around efforts
to purify primordial characteristics, not to get rid of them. It is the qualities
of being woman, of being nonwhite, of being gay or lesbian, of being
disabled that core-group and out-group members struggle to resignify and
experience. Insofar as outsider qualities are seen not as stigmatizing but as
variations on civil and utopian themes, they will be valued in themselves.
"Difference" and particularity become sources of cross-group identification,
and it is in this seemingly paradoxical manner that common experiences are
created that transcend the discrete communities composing civil society. The
philosopher of hermeneutics Wilhelm Dilthey argued that social scientific
understanding can never surpass the investigator's own experience of life.[49]
In contrast with assimilation and even hyphenation, multiculturalism dramatically expands the range of imagined life experiences for core-group
members. In doing so, it opens up the possibility not just for acceptance and
toleration but for understanding and recognition. Insofar as such understandings are achieved, rigid distinctions between core and out-group members
break down, and notions of the particular and the universal become much
more thoroughly intertwined.

Multiculturalism can be understood as a moral preference. Yet it is also
very much an empirical process. Even if multicultural incorporation remains
in its infancy and subject to strenuous debate, the outlines of what it might
entail for democratic societies are beginning to become clear. It is set in
motion by discursive and organizational conflicts over incorporation—conflicts that can be resolved, participants come to believe, only by legitimating
their different qualities. It is in societies that have experienced intense racial
and ethnic conflicts, and have deepened civil society by hyphenating core
group identity with primordialities of dominated groups, that such demands

for recognizing particularity begin to appear. In assimilation and hyphenation, the particular is universalized. In multiculturalism, the universal is
particularized. In assimilation and hyphenation, the ambition of out-groups
is to replace ascriptive identification with cultural status based on achievement. In multiculturalism, the ambition is to achieve—to perform and to
display—a cultural status that once appeared to be ascriptively rooted. It is
an achieved ascription, a performed identity, not a passively primordial or
essentialized one. In multicultural incorporation, particular differences do
not have to be eliminated or denied, so the sharp split between private and
public realms recedes. Non-core primordialities become publicly displayed.
They are folded into the "culture of authenticity" that Charles Taylor has
described as one of the most distinctive achievements of modernity. For
Taylor, what the recognition of difference actually means is not separation
and diminution, but sharing and enlarging. It "grows organically out of the
politics of universal dignity," a key principle of civil society, in such a manner
that a "new understanding of the human social condition imparts a radically
new meaning to an old principle."[50]

To the degree that civil society is multicultural, incorporation is not
celebrated as inclusion but as the achievement of diversity. Particularity,
difference, and symmetrical hybridity become the guiding themes of the
day. Minority racial status, peripheral national origins, marginalized religions,
subordinated genders, repressed sexualities, differently abled bodies, minority
languages, even alternative civilizational capacities—all these primordial
qualities become reinterpreted as representing variations on the sacred qualities of civility.[51] Only insofar as such decentering succeeds, according to the
multicultural mode, can there be incorporation. Insofar as it does succeed,
there is a dramatic decrease in the negative identification of previously
subordinated, or subaltern identities. Aspects of these identities begin, in
fact, actually to be embraced by members of the core group. For example,
to gesture toward my analysis in the latter part of chapter 19, whereas the
postwar generation of American Jewish artists and entertainers, from Saul
Bellow to Milton Berle, were intent on translating their particular experiences into universal, non-Jewish terms, such contemporaries as Philip Roth
and Woody Allen publicly display their religious identities and introduce
compelling forms of "Jewishness" into public life, which are sometimes
emulated and incorporated by non-Jews and Jews alike.

A wide range of developments that emerged and began to accelerate during the last decades of the twentieth century can be understood in terms of this multicultural frame.[52] "Black is beautiful" was not a slogan that emerged from the assimilative, race-blind program of the movement for civil rights but from the struggle to get beyond neutrality and invert negative racial identifications. It was expressed strongly and openly, and broadcast widely, because earlier models of incorporation into civil society were already taking effect.[53] Today, "blackness" is vigorously expressed in the world of fashion, and models of male and female beauty have dramatically crossed once forbidding racial lines. Citing "a whole new crop of black models, stylists, [and] photographers," Paul Gilroy sees a "change of climate in the meaning of racialized signs." The "perfect faces on billboards and screens and in magazines are no longer exclusively white," he writes, and "some degree of visible difference from an implicit white norm" often becomes "highly prized as a sign of timeliness, vitality, inclusivity, and global reach." Gilroy concludes from this partial eclipse of hegemonic whiteness that "the old hierarchy" is now "being erased."[54]

Intermarriage rates among phenotypically distinctive racial groups— Asian Americans, blacks, and Hispanic Americans—have steeply risen, though at very different velocities. There can be no better indicator that civil interaction is beginning to break through some of the most restrictive barriers of private life. Indeed, in the United States, ethnicity is increasingly becoming an identity that is selectively pursued. Many Americans now display ethnicity volitionally, rather than for reasons of necessity, as symbols of occasional identity that gain distinction and esteem.[55] Once considered an unchangeable and essentialized identity, the criteria for displaying ethnicity are, increasingly, novelty, attractiveness, and the possibilities for new sociation. Racial and even sexual stereotypes once considered natural are now being disassembled and reappropriated in parts. In advocating performative rather than ontological approaches to gender and sexuality, philosophers are following multicultural pop culture.[56]

As subordinated racial, gender, sexual, and religious ties are transvaluated, they have become fractured and displayed in increasingly hybrid terms. In American universities and among intellectual elites, the centrality of the purely Euro-American artistic canons is being displaced. Central communicative institutions broadcast fictional narratives by "minority" writers which make their own particularities sacred and cast their minority protagonists as heroes and heroines, not victims. Prestigious bodies of women's, black, Hispanic, Native American, homosexual, and subaltern literatures have emerged, and their critical interpreters, themselves often members of these once denigrated groups, have assumed influential intellectual positions on the American cultural scene.

The extraordinarily public debates about multiculturalism and the literary canon, which until recently so politicized this subject, almost invariably portrayed multiculturalism in a separatist, fragmenting light. The leading critical interpreters of their community's own literature, however, have often understood their emphases in a much more universal and incorporative way. Henry Louis Gates Jr., the African American literature professor who has moved to the center of the civil sphere's communicative institutions, defends his efforts to reveal black literature's distinctive qualities against the narrowly assimilative mode.

> Long after white American literature has been anthologized and canonized, and recanonized, our efforts to define a black American canon are often decried as racist, separatist, nationalist, or "essentialist." Attempts to derive theories about our literary tradition from the black tradition . . . are often greeted by our colleagues in traditional literature departments as a misguided desire to secede from a union that only recently, and with considerable kicking and screaming, has been forged.[57]

At the same time, however, Gates argues that black literature is, in fact, neither particularist nor separated from the wider democratic culture.

> Every black American text must confess to a complex ancestry, one high and low . . . but also one white and black. There can be no doubt that white texts inform and influence black texts (and vice versa), so that a thoroughly integrated canon of American literature is not only politically sound, it is intellectually sound as well. . . . The attempts of black scholars to define a black American canon, and to derive indigenous theories of interpretation from within this canon, are not meant to refute the soundness of these gestures of integration.[58]

A similar perspective is expressed by the editor of *Mas*, an avant-guard national Spanish-language magazine.

Multiculturalism has a separatist current (if I'm Latino and you're not, you can't use my secret handshake), and some of it is, alas, necessary for survival—literally, in some streets: culturally, in some salons. It also has an integrationist current. And that means enlarging the barriers erected by chauvinism. In that current, culture is no one's hegemony, not one nationality's, not one class's, not one gender's, not one race's, no one's. It's culture as integration, instead of submission and assimilation. . . . If it's human, it's yours. Take it. Share it. Mix it. Rock it.[59]

The manner in which regulatory institutions enforce these shifts in public opinion has begun to change in complementary ways. When legal rights are extended for fuller civil participation, procedures are now put into place with the express intention of preserving the "authentic" particularities of cultural communities. When access to the ballot box is protected, efforts are made to ensure that voting will allow the expression not only of individual rights but of collective identities, including not just racial but linguistic minorities. Affirmative action was initially justified on assimilative grounds, but in her majority opinion in the 2003 Michigan case *Grutter v. Bollinger*, Justice Sandra Day O'Connor cited diversity as its principal contribution to realizing the "dream of being one nation, indivisible." Whereas in earlier legal opinions, affirmative action has been justified on the grounds of equality, as "remedying past discrimination," this is not "the only permissible justification for race-based governmental action." Things have changed. "Today," Justice O'Connor declared, "we hold that the law school has a compelling interest in attaining a diverse student body." Responding to supporting *amici* briefs submitted to the Court by a wide range of civil associations, she suggests, indeed, that there is now a "compelling state interest that justifies the use of race."[60]

When Congress radically opened up immigration flows in the mid-1960s, it discarded the national origins criteria that had been instituted, four decades earlier, to protect core-group primordiality and to keep the assimilative mode firmly in place. The millions of immigrants who have legally entered American civil society since then, along with the millions more who have entered illegally and stayed, have changed the racial complexion of the United States in a physical sense, but it is the new, more multicultural model that has allowed these post-1960s immigrants to invert social stereotypes. Not long ago, Asian immigrants were subject to virulent pollution; today, their intermarriage with Euro-Americans has approached 50 percent.[61] The incorporation of Central and South American immigrants, the other principal beneficiary of the 1960s regulative change, has proceeded much more rapidly than with earlier Mexican entrants. This time around, however, the Hispanic language has not disappeared. Laws to protect bilingualism have penetrated deeply into American society, and speaking abilities have been maintained beyond the second generation.[62]

None of this is to suggest that demands for assimilative incorporation have disappeared, much less that the institutions that produce and enforce civil power—whether voting, party competition, and office, on the one hand, or law, on the other—have thoroughly converted the multicultural representations circulating so intensively through communicative institutions into new and binding forms of civil regulation. When legal scholar Kenji Yoshino writes that "closeting occurs whenever the state engages in ho-mophobic lawmaking that makes invisibility a prerequisite for gays who wish to enjoy the basic entitlements of a free society," he is speaking, in rather precise terms, about how the assimilative mode continues to rigidly apply on matters of sexuality, and how the asymmetrical results distort the promise of the American civil sphere. Criticizing the "don't ask, don't tell" rule that informs American military policy toward gays and lesbians, Yoshino points to its stigmatizing, anticivil effect: "By forcing only gays to lie about their identities in a culture in which lying is held to be deeply dishonorable, the military inculcates in them a conception of themselves as second-class citizens, not only because of their homosexuality, but also because of their duplicity."[63]

The varieties of civil incorporation I have presented in this chapter are ideal types. It is important to recall Max Weber's admonition that the em-pirical distinctions separating such distinctive types are emphasized for ana-lytical reasons. In practice, assimilation, hyphenation, and multiculturalism blend into one another. It is not a zero-sum game, despite the fact that, as pure types, each of these three modes is different and opposed. Assimilation and multiculturalism are in principle antagonistic, but assimilation can con-tinue to proceed even as multicultural incorporation emerges on the scene. In real historical time, it would be surprising, indeed, if particular commu-nities did not participate in all three of these processes. Members of the American black community continue to strive for assimilation, to find recognition in thoroughly "nonracial" ways. At the same time, as they have come to define themselves as "African Americans," they have developed hyphenated identities. Finally, as members of a "community of color," contemporary black Americans strive to maintain and restore the distinctive and sometimes antagonistic aspects of their racial culture, and demand that it be recognized in a multicultural way.[64]

I began this discussion of the modes of incorporation, in chapter 15, by suggesting that multiculturalism has often been fundamentally misunderstood. Not only social conservatives but also radical intellectuals and activists have described it as a process promoting separation and difference rather than inclusion and solidarity. By placing this new and challenging model of solidarity into the broader framework of civil society, and by systematically relating it to the other modes of incorporation, I have demonstrated, to the contrary, that multiculturalism sits between difference and integration. Multiculturalism frames a new kind of civil society, one in which groups employ its binary discourse to publicly assert the right to be admired for being different. It represents not the diminishing but the strengthening of the civil sphere, a sphere in which collective obligations and individual autonomy have always been precariously but fundamentally intertwined. Multiculturalism is a project of hope, not despair. It can be launched only amid widespread feelings of common humanity, of solidary sympathies that have already been extended significantly to persons, and which now must be extended to their qualities.

CHAPTER 18

The Jewish Question:
Anti-Semitism and the Failure of Assimilation

F ROM THE STANDPOINT of marginalized groups, assimilation is a highly desirable alternative to exclusion and domination, representing a so-ciological opportunity unavailable before the emergence of a rela-tively differentiated civil sphere of society. Nevertheless, as I suggested in the preceding chapter, when civil societies offer out-groups the chance for assimilative incorporation, they are making an offer that is fraught with ambiguity. Inspired by the universalizing dimension of civil society, core groups assert that it is possible to separate the "person" who is a member of the marginalized out-group from the stigmatized "qualities" that pejoratively define that group's differences from the core group itself. The bargain seems to be something like this: Insofar as members of these out-groups agree to keep these negative qualities out of public view, they can practice them freely in their private lives, families, neighborhood groups, circles of friend-ship, love relationships, and places of worship. In the public world, they must learn to behave in a purely civil, universal manner, in this way dem-onstrating their competence, psychologically and interactionally, to become full members of civil society. When proposed in this manner, this sounds like a hard bargain but a fair one. The problem is that it isn't really what's on offer.

Why not? As I suggested theoretically in chapter 8 and as I have tried to demonstrate empirically in my discussions here and in part III, the public sphere of civil society is always permeated by particularistic qualities. Because of the vagaries of time, space, and function, civil capacities from the outset are primordialized, and the ability to perform adequately in civil society is understood as being restricted to those who possess the particular qualities of core groups. For these reasons, assimilation actually presents a rather unfair bargain, requiring an asymmetrical exchange. To gain incorporation, out-groups are, in fact, not required simply to demonstrate "civil" behavior but behavior that is civil from the perspective of the primordialized framework of the core group. They must learn to be Americans, Frenchman, Russians, or Germans. They must learn to exhibit the traits of language, bearing, religiosity, or non-religiosity of the founders of their historically specific, national societies. My point here is not that such learning is impossible. By no means. In the modern period, very high levels of assimilative incorporation have been achieved by scores of formerly marginalized class, religious, ethnic, gender, sexual, and racial groups. What I am pointing to is the asymmetrical nature of the assimilative bargain, and the costs that such a transaction involves.

Because of its delicate and tense balance between negatively evaluated qualities and positively evaluated persons, assimilation is a complex, uneven, and highly unstable mode of incorporation. Historically contingent forces and events can push it "backward," to new forms of excluding and dominating a once partially incorporated group. On the other hand, if assimilation proceeds apace, if the civil sphere becomes more deeply institutionalized and independent of core-group power, then assimilation can create relations between the core group and out-groups that are less asymmetrical, reflecting less polluted cultural representation of outsider qualities. In the first progressive alternative to assimilation—hyphenation—the qualities of excluded groups are seen as in principle complementary to core primordialities. The latter qualities are de-essentialized; their symbolic terms are metaphorically and metonymically linked to signifiers of once foreign primordialities. Even in such a hyphenated form, however, these qualities retain some markedly negative connotations. Purified by their connection to sacred qualities of the core group, they remain subordinated to the hegemonic power. Though softer and much less cruel, therefore, hyphenated incorporation is still conceived, by core group and out-group alike, in an ameliorative, teleological way. It is an acceptable middle point in what remains a progression away from particularistic qualities toward a homogenizing universalism represented either as a variation on core group identity or as a new "higher synthesis" that transcends the particular identities of core and out-group alike.

As this intermediate position suggests, then, hyphenation is also a highly unstable mode of incorporation. Because it retains a rank order of qualities, its openness to abstract "persons" is qualified. Yet just as hyphenation can be pushed backward to assimilation and even to exclusion, it can also be pushed forward to more even-handed, more truly reciprocal understandings of incorporation. This multicultural mode of incorporation becomes available to the degree that civil solidarity has significantly deepened, for it requires not only the tolerance of difference in the legal sense but mutual recognition in the communicative sense, and the latter depends on nothing less than the positive evaluation of outsider qualities—psychologically, interactionally, and culturally. Insofar as incorporation becomes multicultural rather than assimilative or hyphenated, the integration of society appears to be organized around difference and diversity rather than similarity and homogeneity.

Jews and the Dilemmas of Assimilative Incorporation

The deeply troubled and profoundly troubling course of Jewish incorporation into, and their consequent excision from, Western civil societies allows us to consider in much more empirical detail and conceptual complexity the ambiguities of the assimilative mode. By exposing issues of religious rather than racial, economic, or gender exclusion, moreover, this focus allows us to examine the dynamics of incorporation in a case study further removed from contemporary Western political debates.

In the preceding chapter, I used primarily American historical data to elaborate the ideal-typical models of incorporation. Focusing on a single national unit proved useful because it allowed the differences between these modes to be highlighted against a common backdrop, and to be displayed not only analytically but concretely, in narrative chronology. There are, however, distinctive drawbacks to discussing an exclusively American case. The relative historical success of American incorporative struggles can be used to give a seductively evolutionary cast to the modes of incorporation.

In moral terms, one can rank order these modes in an ascending hierarchy; indeed, such ranking is imperative both for normative philosophical argument and for practical social and political struggles alike. In empirical terms, however, to present an evolutionary progression between these ideal-typical models is to commit a basic sociological mistake.

Our consideration of "the Jewish question" in Europe and the United States will amply demonstrate why such a mistake should not be made. In the history of Western societies, no issue has loomed larger for the civil sphere than the incorporation of the Jews. Indeed, for centuries, not only in everyday life but even in some quarters of high social theory, this challenge presented itself as *the* question, one that posed the most fundamental challenge to the civil sphere, even more troubling, perhaps, than the challenges posed by class, gender, and race.[1] These other groups were also constructed as uncivil, and excluded, dominated, exploited, or enslaved; only the Jews, however, were also subject to periodic, massive, and premeditated group murder and, eventually, to a barbaric genocide that brought them to the edge of extermination. "It is not accidental that 'the Jewish question' should have become a major concern from the eighteenth century to the present," Richard Bernstein writes. "Like a red thread running through its many different and sometimes even incompatible uses, there has been an underlying anxiety about the fate of the Jewish people in the modern age."[2]

It is well known, of course, that from the origins of Christianity, and, indeed, because of issues surrounding its origins, the Jewish people were demonized.[3] The anti-Jewish discourse of early Christianity dehumanized Jews by representing them as murderers and as untrustworthy liars. What has not been so clearly understood is that this Christian anti-Semitism can be seen as a "discourse of repression" in civil society terms.[4] As a universalizing cultural code, Christianity saw itself as creating a community of equals in which membership was voluntary and interpersonal relations were trusting and solidary.[5] As Christianity became institutionalized in the Holy Roman Empire, it created elementary forms of what would later become the regulatory institutions of civil society as well. Inspired by shared cultural reference to an impersonal yet sympathetic and righteous God, religious actors were envisioned as having the capacity to engage in ideally oriented communication and to form a solidary society that would be regulated by (canon) law and administered by (church) officials, the most important of whom were subject to collegial self-regulation, including election.

It should not be surprising, then, that in its early and ferocious struggles against Judaism as a hegemonic religion, and in its later, more institutional efforts to deepen and make permanent the isolation of the so-called Jewish heresy, Christianity understood its pollution of Jews as justified not simply by the difference of their religion, but by their failure to fit into a civil frame.[6] The Jews were represented as incapable of participating in the civic life of "Christian" societies, culturally, interactionally, or institutionally. In terms of their motives, Jews were said to be deceitful and hypocritical and motivated by a greedy materialism rather than by morality or ideals. In terms of relations with others, Jews were portrayed as fundamentally and irredeemably egotistical, self-oriented, secretive, and aggressive. In terms of institutions, Jews were held to be tribal and particularistic. It was claimed that the only effective allegiance of Jews was to members of their own community, with whom they conspired against the civil majority; and Jewish institutions were described as archaic and arbitrary, provincial, hierarchical, and divisive rather than solidaristic.[7]

Because these anticivil traits were held to be endemic to Jewishness, Jews were conceived as producing an indelible stain that might ultimately prove resistant even to the continuous Christian effort to convert them. Thus, in terms of the model of incorporation, persons who were or had once been Jews could not be separated from the qualities associated with Jewishness. This symbolic framework explained why Christians could not be allowed to interact with Jews and why, quarantined in ghettos, Jews were neither allowed to occupy office positions nor to enjoy the protections of civil and canon law. Jewishness prevented participation in civil society.

When the first national civil societies were formed, a process that stretched from the mid-seventeenth to the mid-nineteenth centuries, this demonizing, essentialist representation of Jews was increasingly brought into question, as was the legitimacy of the institutional excision of Jews from every legitimate avenue of civic life. Overt, endemic religious exclusion presented an embarrassing denial of civil society's promised solidarity; essentialistic protestations of endemic inferiority seemed to flaunt the universalism of Enlightenment thought. If marginalized Jews were left to organize their own communities, moreover, how could the rule of law be secured? How could emerging nation-states or multinational empires extend their rule in a uniform way?

In this manner, the Jewish question became increasingly significant in social systems that professed to be civil societies, whether they were politically democratic or not.[8] After creating the first democratic and constitutional monarchy, the British invited Jews to return to the land from which they had been expelled four hundred years before.[9] In 1782, Joseph II, king of Germany and Holy Roman Emperor, issued his "Edict of Tolerance" demanding religious tolerance, the encouragement of education, and unrestricted economic activity.[10] Earnest discussions about transforming the status of Jews permeated administrative and intellectual activity in the German states throughout the later eighteenth and early nineteenth centuries. The French formally emancipated Jews in 1790 and 1791.

What is important to see about this amorphous, highly uneven, but nevertheless highly consequential thrust to incorporate Jews is that it was framed by the assimilative rubric of the private/public split I have earlier described. Their incorporation was premised on an exchange. Only if Jews relegated their religious ideas and activities to the invisibility of private life would they be allowed to become fully enfranchised citizens, like every other member of the nation-state. The twenty-fifth and concluding article in the edict of Joseph II stated that "by these favors We *almost* place the Jewish nation on an equal level with adherents of other associations."[11] The adverbial qualification was neither gratuitous nor rhetorical; to the contrary, it was studied and apt. In the edict's first article, the emperor explicitly forbade that Jews "be allowed public religious worship or public synagogues [or] permitted to establish their own press for the printing of prayer books"; in the seventh, he forbade them "to live in rural regions"; in the eleventh, he asserted that Jews "must remain excluded" from "the right of citizenship and mastership" in a craft; in the fifteenth, he asserted that, "considering the numerous openings in trades and manifold contacts with Christians resulting therefrom, the care for maintaining common confidence requires that the Hebrew and the so-called Jewish language and writing of Hebrew intermixed with German be abolished," forbidding "their use in all public transactions." Later in the decade, Joseph II issued an edict compelling Jews "to adopt German-sounding personal and family names, to be chosen from a government-prepared list."[12]

What historical document could more clearly demonstrate the fundamental ambiguities of the assimilation mode? The enlightened thinking that directed the formation of civil societies allowed that, in principle, the person of the Jew could be separated from Jewish qualities. At the same time, the national or imperial communities that carried this universalizing ideology were permeated by primordial particularities, by deeply internalized cultural prejudices attesting to the fundamental incapacities of various groups. As Arthur Hertzberg once wrote, "modern, secular anti-Semitism was fashioned not as a reaction to the Enlightenment and Revolution, but within the Enlightenment and Revolution themselves."[13] These early civil societies were not free-floating; they were founded by men, by white men, by white men of property, by white Christian men of property. In order to enter civil society, it was not enough simply to demonstrate civil capacity as such; one would have to present these capacities by manifesting them in a particular primordial way. As long as core groups pejoratively defined out-group qualities, then, it was extremely difficult to see members of these out-groups as fully human beings.[14]

The attitude of the founders of civil societies toward Jews was that they had to earn incorporation, whether or not they were, in principle, entitled to it. In order to do so—to take "care for maintaining common confidence," in the words of Joseph II—Jews would have to stop being the other and become, as much as possible, like the founders themselves. They would have to learn to act less like excluded Jews and more like the Christians who offered them emancipation. It is important not to understand this paradoxical demand ahistorically, from a contemporary point of view. In the context of a deeply anti-Semitic civilization, to suggest that Jews had the capacity to act like Christians actually was enlightened and progressive, for it reflected the universalistic belief that, somewhere inside themselves, Jews possessed the same fundamental capacities as other persons. In 1785 the Royal Society of Arts and Sciences at Metz sponsored an essay contest anticipating this transformation of Jewish status. Contestants were asked to consider whether it was possible to make the Jews of France not only "happier" but "more useful." The winner, Abbé Henri Baptiste Grégoire, suggested that it was indeed possible, proposing practical activities and moral ideas that would, he believed, markedly improve the capacities of the Jewish people.

> Let us cherish morality, but let us not be so unreasonable as to require it of those whom we have compelled to become vicious. Let us reform their education, to reform their hearts; it has long been observed, that they are men as well as we, and they are so before

they are Jews [and] the great part of their customs are not contrary to civil functions.[15]

Even the most progressive members of Western core groups, however, continued to believe that Judaism, both as practice and belief, would irredeemably poison public life. In order to free their universal personhood from the polluted qualities attached to it, members of Jewish communities would have to learn either to repress or eliminate their Jewishness.

Anti-Semitic Arguments for Jewish Incorporation: The Assimilative Dilemma from the Perspective of the Core Group

Christian Wilhelm von Dohm was a key figure in Prussian intellectual and political life, whose 1781 essay "Concerning the Amelioration of the Civil Status of the Jews" served as a focal point for discussions about the Jewish question, and for policies to affect it, throughout enlightened Europe.[16] In the well-meaning but contorted complexities of this *plaidoyer*, we find a prototypical expression of the distortions and hypocrisies that accompany incorporation into fragmented civil societies. Even for the most conscientious and democratically inclined core group member, assimilating an out-group whose primordial qualities remain deeply repulsive is an awkward, deeply ambivalent business. Discursive struggles over incorporation revolve around the question of whether a nation's civil sphere is truly differentiated, on the one hand, and whether the character of the marginalized out-group is civil enough to merit incorporation, on the other. Dohm is confident of the openness and generosity of Prussian civil society. The problem, for him, is Jewish character.

Dohm's famous essay can be understood, in fact, as a meditation on whether the contemporary degradation of the Jewish people makes it impossible to separate their universal humanity from the qualities of their religion. Concerned with the cultural and psychological requirements of civil society, Dohm asks: Is it inevitable that Jewish motives, relations, and institutions be constructed in terms of the discourse of repression? That they have been so constructed is what has allowed "European states unanimously to deal so harshly with the Jewish nation."[17] The charge had been that the

Jewish religion "contained principles" that made it impossible for Jewish persons to manifest the universal and inclusive solidarity required for civil life, thus preventing Jews "from keeping faith in their actions within the community and with single members of the community." After all, if Jews are indeed motivated by aggression rather than fellow feeling, if they do feel "hatred against those who do not belong to their faith," then they will be deceitful rather than honest in their relations with others, feeling "an obligation to deal crookedly with others and to disregard their rights." If this construction of the "antisocial" Jew were accurate, Dohm allows, then "before the eyes of reason" it would be incumbent that "the rights of citizenship should be withheld entirely only from the Jew and that he should be permitted only partially to enjoy the rights of man."

As a civil Enlightenment thinker recommending Jewish emancipation, Dohm earnestly criticizes this essentialist kind of anti-Semitic thought. He argues that, "according to what has become known about the Jewish religion thus far, it does not contain such harmful principles." To the contrary, "the law of Moses," the most important source of Judaism, "is looked upon by Christians with reverence" and "contains the most correct principle of moral law, justice and order." If Judaism has such a universalist potential, then person and qualities can be separated, and incorporation can be achieved. Concluding that "the Jew is even more man than Jew," Dohm demands that the gates of the ghetto be opened to civil life: "Every art, every science should be open to the Jew as to every other free man. He, too, should educate his mind as far as he is able; he, too, must be able to rise to promotion, honor, and rewards by utilizing his talents."

Yet Dohm is not only a civil intellectual; he also comes from a Christian background and conceives of himself as speaking to a culturally Christian audience. Despite Enlightenment principles and protestations, this primordial religious commitment leads him significantly to restrict his advocacy of Jewish incorporation. Though he insists that, in principle, Judaism is as civil as Christianity, he readily acknowledges that, in practice, Judaism is nothing of the kind. Precisely because of their historical mistreatment by Christian societies, Judaism and Jewishness have become everything their enemies accuse them of being. "In the faith of today's Jews," Dohm writes, there are indeed "some principles" that "exclude them from the other groups of the great civil society." In recounting "the general experience of our states of the political harmfulness of the Jews," Dohm points to their evident incapacity for universal solidarity. In its present historical form, Judaism is defined by "clannish religious opinions." Influenced by the "sophistic conclusions of the rabbis," Jews are filled with such "bitter hatred of all who do not belong to their tribe that they are unable to get used to looking at them as members of a common civil society." These general anticivil motives and relations also manifest themselves in the institutional arena, for Jews have shown a "lack of fairness and honesty in the one field in which they were allowed to make a living—commerce."

That Dohm himself adheres to this denigrating and polluting understanding of Jewish qualities is demonstrated by the fact that what makes him a progressive is not that he denies the reality of this anti-Semitic portrait but that he denies its necessity.[18] The "error" that he finds in anti-Semitic reasoning is not in its ethnography but in its logic: It "states as cause what in reality is the effect, quoting the evil wrought by the past erroneous policy as an excuse for it." Dohm's patronizing elaboration of this position is so revealing of the ambiguities of assimilation that it seems worth considering at some length.

"Let us concede," he begins, "that the Jews may be more morally corrupt than other nations; that they are guilty of a proportionately greater number of crimes than the Christians; that their character in general inclines more toward usury and fraud in commerce, that their religious prejudice is more antisocial and clannish." These facts must still be put in their proper historical context: "This supposed greater moral corruption of the Jews is a necessary and natural consequence of the oppressed condition in which they have been living for so many centuries."

> It is very natural that these conditions cause the spirit of the Jew to lose the habit of noble feelings, to be submerged in the base routine of earning a precarious livelihood. The varied kinds of oppression and contempt he experiences are bound to debase him in his activities, to choke every sense of honor in his heart. As there are almost no honest means of earning a living left to him, it is natural that he falls into criminal practices and fraud.

Dohm escapes from antidemocratic essentialism, in other words, not by disagreeing with the contention that Jews are unfit to join civil society but, instead, by advocating a sociological, rather than specifically religious un-

468

derstanding of this incapacity. "Everything the Jews are blamed for," he explains, "is caused by the political conditions under which they now live, and any other group of men, under such conditions, would be guilty of identical errors." Corresponding with this typically Enlightenment emphasis on the influence of social environment is a reflexive and self-critical acceptance of moral responsibility. "All this is our own doing," Dohm declaims to his Christian audience. What has happened is that "the prejudices which we have instilled and which are still nourished by us in him [the Jew] are stronger than his religion." To continue to punish Jews by pursuing anti-Semitic social policies, then, would be profoundly hypocritical, for "we ourselves are guilty of the crimes we accuse him of."

Because Dohm acknowledges that Christian states are morally responsible, he argues that these civil authorities have an obligation to initiate reforms aimed at incorporating Jews. However, because Jewish degradation is an empirical fact, Dohm makes the paradoxical suggestion that such reforms will have to be directed, first and foremost, not at Christian anti-Semitism but at the beliefs and practices of the Jews themselves. True, giving Jews access to the public sphere might, in itself, have salutary effects on the Jewish character. Face-to-face interaction, for example, could have a civilizing effect on cultural beliefs: "Frequent intercourse and sharing the burdens and advantages of the state equally is the most certain way to dull the edge of the hostile prejudices on both sides." In their present condition, however, Jews are not subjectively ready to participate in civic life. Thus, much more interventionist and restrictive government practices are necessary. Until these initiatives work their effects, Jewish access to the regulatory and communicative institutions of civil society will have to be forcibly restricted. Dohm asks, for example, whether Jewish emancipation would mean that "Jews should be admitted to public office immediately." In principle, he acknowledges, the answer would seem to be yes, for "it seems, in fact, that if they are granted all civil rights, they could not be excluded from applying for the honor to serve the government." Winning such positions, however, would depend on whether Jews "are found to be *capable*." Not only does Dohm express the opinion that "in the next generation this capability will not yet appear frequently," but he insists that "the state should make no special effort to develop it." Reasoning that the duties of office "require that the applicant be far removed from any suspicion of misdemeanors due to greed," he argues that "this will probably not always be the case in the Jews of today and of the next generation." Given the anticivil nature of contemporary Jews, the reformist obligation of the civil state must be to exclude Jews from office: "Impartiality would demand that if a Jewish and a Christian applicant show equal capability, the latter deserves prefer- ence."

In justifying this reformist yet in many respects deeply antidemocratic policy vis-à-vis Jews, Dohm points to what he obviously believes are the prima facie grounds of primordial distinction. "This seems to be an obvious right of the majority in the nation," he writes, "at least until the Jews by wider treatment are changed into entirely equal citizens and all differences rubbed off." Dohm describes himself as speaking in "the interests of civil society,"[19] and it is in terms of this civil interest that he seeks the moral reform of the Jewish character. Incorporation depends on assimilation, not only to civil society but to the particular primordial qualities of a society's core group. Moral re-education would certainly be one area for reconstruc- tive intervention. For example, "besides the holy teachings of his fathers," the government "should take care that . . . the Jew is taught to develop his reason." In this effort to civilize Jewish education, it also "would perhaps be necessary to prevent the teaching of antisocial opinions against men of other persuasions." But moral suasion will not be enough, for Jews may well not voluntarily give up their core beliefs. If differences are to be polished off, the Jewish spirit must be broken. Assimilation demands enlightened coercion. "The too mercantile spirit of most Jews will probably be broken more easily," Dohm concludes, "by heavy physical labor than by the sed- entary work of the public servant." How might this be accomplished? "The government," Dohm suggests, should "try to dissuade the Jews from the occupation of commerce." For example, the state might "restrict the number of Jews active in commerce or subject them to special taxes." The state should be "encouraging them to prefer such kinds of earning a living as are most apt to create a diametrically opposed spirit and character—I mean artisan occupations." Nor should "the Jews be excluded from agriculture." In the same patronizing and particularistic spirit of civic reform, Dohm acknowledges that he would "not wish to see the Jews encouraged to become owners of big estates or tenants." Because such occupation merely "nourishes the spirit of speculation and profit-seeking," it would not prop- erly prepare the Jew for an active civic life. For their own sakes, Dohm would prefer to see the Jews become "peasants working their own land."

Indeed, an enlightened government should consider "settling the Jews of the country on vacant pieces of land."

The same kind of solution to the Jewish question, forced resettlement in far-off agricultural areas, was a response that another and obviously much less well-intended representative of German culture was to offer his compatriots one hundred fifty years later: the Nazi proposals for the Lublin Reservation and Madagascar Plan. That a bold and progressive demand for Jewish emancipation issued by an Enlightenment intellectual would produce proposals not entirely dissimilar to the anti-Semitic program for Jewish exclusion introduced by Adolf Hitler illuminates in a vivid way the structural instabilities of the assimilative mode of incorporation. The German title of Dohm's essay is, in fact, a double entendre. *Über die bürgerliche verbesserung der Juden* can just as easily be translated as announcing its concern for the "civil improvement of the Jews" as being about the "amelioration" of their "civil status."[20] In fact, as we can now see, such a translation would more appropriately suggest the sociological sense of Dohm's work. It would also lead us more directly to the next questions we will consider: Did the Jews themselves want to be improved? If not, what other options did they wish to create?

Initial Jewish Arguments for Self-Change: The Assimilative Dilemma from the Perspective of the Out-Group

The deep subjective ambivalence manifest by Christian core-group representatives about Jewish emancipation translated into the objective contradictions of the incorporative process itself. A century and a half after the initial movements toward emancipation, these contradictions manifested themselves in the violent destruction, rather than the civil inclusion, of a vast swath of European Jewry. Though the contradictions of Jewish assimilation were objective, however, this dire expression of them certainly was not inevitable; it was determined, rather, by a complex of contingent historical processes and events.[21] At any rate, the story of the Holocaust and its causes is not at this point our primary concern, although it inevitably shadows the dark side of the analysis I am developing here. Our concern is more general and systemic. We are concerned with examining Jewish incorporation as a type case of the vagaries of assimilation. In our earlier discussion of incorporative processes in the United States, we observed how, over long periods of time and after bitter and often violent social struggles, the ambiguities of assimilation were resolved in a manner that allowed new modes of civil incorporation. The fate of the European Jews shows that this is by no means necessarily the case. The instabilities of the assimilative mode of incorporation are resolved contingently, not by an inevitable developmental or evolutionary logic. Assimilation can be pushed backward toward primitive modes of domination or forward toward more pluralist forms of inclusion that expand the primordial modes of expression of civil capacities.

We can deepen our understanding of these ambiguities by considering the responses of the actors themselves. In our earlier discussion of incorporation into the United States, the reconstructed statements by core-group and out-group representatives were analyzed from the outside, adopting, as it were, the perspective of civil society itself. The more detailed case study in this chapter allows us to enter much more deeply into the perspectives of the out-group undergoing assimilative change. Our question is, How did the Jewish people themselves respond to the asymmetrical bargain of assimilation? From the perspective of contemporary society, and with the advantage of hindsight, the answer to this question seems rather surprising, for the initial Jewish response to the ambiguous offer of incorporation was highly positive. Eventually, however, the Jewish response became as involuted and ambivalent as the incorporative process itself.[22]

For two thousand years, since the Roman destruction of the Israelites' Second Temple in 70 C.E., the Jewish people had been living on the polluted margins of core societies, at first on the margin of Roman civilization and then, after 379 C.E., when Emperor Theodosius I made Christianity the state religion of the Roman Empire, of Christian civilization broadly conceived. At the same time, Jews continued to conceive of themselves as God's chosen people. When the newly constructed civil spheres of national societies promised Jews, for the first time, "almost" full access to the Christian centers, this was certainly considered by Jews to be a world-historical event. It is no wonder, then, that as soon as the first national civil societies were constructed, Jews began knocking on their doors, asking in a polite but persistent manner to be let into this new, avowedly tolerant and inclusive space. These requests began with the initial success of Cromwell's democratic revolution, when Jews who had earlier been expelled from England petitioned the radical Protestants for the right of return, and they continued for two hundred years, until the gates of every ghetto in western and central Europe had been pried opened.

The formal edicts of emancipation thus assumed for the Jewish people an extraordinary significance. But what of the asymmetry of the bargain upon which this emancipation was premised, the sacrifices which, as we have seen, even the most progressive Christians demanded of Jews—the insistence on self-transformation and the barely concealed anti-Semitic threats? The truth is that, in light of the unprecedented promises of freedom and participation, massive numbers of Jews, including most of their enlightened leaders, were willing, even eager, to overlook the ambivalence and qualifications with which the promises of emancipation were made. According to an old adage, Jews did not walk out of the ghetto, they ran. Two factors were at work. First, Jews wanted out, and assimilation represented the only terms on offer, presenting, in fact, a historically unprecedented opportunity. Second, the Christian demand for Jewish self-transformation appeared attractive, in certain respects at least, to many Jewish leaders themselves. Emancipation was not only a proposition emanating from Christian Enlightenment representatives but from enlightened, antitraditionalist Jewish intellectual and religious figures. Though the latter certainly did not accept the anti-Semitic denigration of Jewish qualities, they did accept the idea that Judaism could and must be changed, that the religion should be transformed in an "enlightened" way.

For both these reasons, then, among the Jewish communities of Western and Central Europe there were initially expressions of great optimism about the possibility of what might be called the deprimordialization of national civil communities. In exchange for the "gift" of this transformed public world—the promise of the first fully transparent and universal civil sphere— Jewish intellectuals and religious leaders agreed to do their part, to both privatize and modernize the world of Jewish religion. That the Christian demand for privatization and modernization was motivated as much by repugnance for Jewish qualities as by belief in the innate reasonableness of the Jewish person was, in the first flush of emancipation, a possibility whose implications were either not seriously considered or else resolutely put aside. After all, in their relations with hostile and suspicious external communities, Jewish tradition had always accepted the necessity for a public/private split. To be "a man in the street and a Jew at home" became the motto for an entire generation of *maskilim*—participants in the Jewish Enlightenment—

in the latter nineteenth century.[23] With the new possibility that the world of the street would assume a much more civil and democratic form, the payoff for keeping Judaism "invisible" to non-Jews would be that much greater. What these early Jewish leaders did not, perhaps could not, foresee was that the contemporary denigration of Jewish qualities would not be transitional, that it would persist into modernity itself, and would make the private/public split impossible to achieve. In truth, Jews would not be allowed to be "men" in public life. Jewish civil participation would become skewed and distorted even as emancipation paradoxically continued apace. In the first flush of the Enlightenment, however, these possibilities were as remote to the early Jewish leaders of emancipation as they were to their philanthropic Christian counterparts.

Such early Jewish optimism, which in retrospect seems naiveté, was no more clearly embodied than in the figure of Moses Mendelssohn. The appearance in Berlin cafe society of this brilliant, self-taught Jewish savant, who had been given formal permission to live in the city, is said to have provided for many German intellectuals a simple and powerful proof of the possibility of Jewish emancipation; Mendelssohn seemed a validation that Jewish persons could be separated from Jewish qualities. It was at Mendelssohn's request that Christian Wilhelm von Dohm wrote his brief for civil inclusion of Jews. It was not, however, simply his own irrepressible character that allowed Mendelssohn to appear unfazed by Dohm's anti-Semitic proposals for restricting Jewish economic and civil participation. In composing his critical response to Dohm, Mendelssohn demonstrated not only an innocent trust in the power of rational discourse; he displayed, as well, a misplaced confidence in the rationality of his would-be Christian emancipators, a confidence that failed to take seriously the strength of their primordial stereotypes about Jews. Mendelssohn refuted Dohm's anticivil framing of the effects of Jewish economic life by explaining that "the pettiest trafficking Jew is not a mere consumer, but a useful inhabitant (citizen, I must say), of the state—a real producer."[24] Applying the universalizing discourse of liberty, in other words, Mendelssohn claimed, contrary to Dohm, that Jewish economic life made Jews autonomous and independent. He further resisted primordial denigration by advising Dohm that the phrase *bürgerliche Aufnahme* (civil admission) would be a much more appropriate description of what Dohm actually intended than his own term, *bürgerliche Verbesserung* (civic improvement).[25]

Yet even as this Enlightenment Jewish intellectual staunchly maintained, against his Christian compatriot, that contemporary Jewish life contained strongly universalist qualities, Mendelssohn was more than ready to live up to what he understood to be his side of the bargain. In doing so, he provided a famous and controversial theoretical grounding for what came to be known as the "reform" of Jewish religion. Mendelssohn claimed that "Judaism knows nothing of a revealed religion," and he insisted that the "immutable truths of God" were not transmitted to the Jews privately, by "direct revelation," much less "forced on the belief of the people, by threats of eternal or temporal punishment." Suggesting in this manner that Judaism was more an ethical and moral system than a metaphysical one, Mendelssohn argued for the inherent complementarity of Jewish qualities with modern civil societies. Rather than a secretive, private, in-turned religion, in his view Judaism was founded on a structure that adumbrated key aspects of contemporary public life. Writing of the Jewish commandments, Mendelssohn claims that God "gave them publicly" to the Jewish people and that, in doing so, God had "recommended" certain principles and ways of life for the Jews' "rational consideration." Far from being an antirational and ethnocentric dogma, then, in Mendelssohn's eyes Jewish principles are "as universal as the salutary influence of the sun, which, while revolving round its orbit, diffuses light and heat over the whole globe." If Judaism so partakes of universal natural laws, it must be viewed as a facilitating input to civilized society rather than a barrier to its realization. Thus, contrary to Dohm's suggestion, the qualities of the Jewish religion need hardly be eliminated or suppressed in the course of building an inclusive civil life.[26]

Ten years after Mendelssohn penned these confident words of advice and inspiration to his fellow Jews and their German emancipators, a Frenchman named Berr Isaac Berr formulated similar sentiments in a public letter he issued to the Jewish congregations of Alsace and Lorraine on the morning that the French National Assembly passed the resolution emancipating the Jews of France. This remarkable missive of gratitude and caution fuses religious and civil language in an argument that simultaneously imitates and underscores the ambivalent, contradictory logic of the Jews' Christian-cum-civic emancipators. Employing the discourse of repression, Berr characterizes pre-revolutionary Jewish ghetto life as "bondage and abasement."[27] Precisely because it had so transformed antidemocratic secular bondage, the French Revolution held out hope to ghetto-bound Jews. "Surely our chains had become the more galling," Berr recalls, "from the contemplation of the rights of man, so sublimely held forth to public view." The French Revolution's decision to extend these revolutionary principles to the Jews recognized how Jewish humanity had been belied by their bondage, a separation of persons from qualities for which Berr believes all Jews should be thankful. "What bounds can there be to our gratitude for the happy event!" he exclaims.

It is revealing, however, that in applauding this imminent recognition of the Jews' universal humanity, Berr also emphasizes the connection between these newly offered universal rights and membership in the primordial community of the French nation, a membership that Berr links to the assumption of new and compelling obligations. "From being vile slaves, mere serfs, a species of men merely tolerated and suffered in the empire . . . we are, of a sudden, become the children of the country, to bear its common charges, and share in its common rights." Berr views the destruction of the ghetto as creating the conditions for solidarity between Jews and Christian Frenchmen, for a horizontal, civil relationship without which domination would inevitably be the Jewish fate. "At length the day has come," Berr proclaims, "when the veil, by which we were kept in a state of humiliation, is rent." Once again, Berr himself recognizes that this promise of civil emancipation is linked to membership of a distinctly primordial kind. "We are now, thanks to the Supreme Being, and to the sovereignty of the nation, not only Men and Citizens, but we are Frenchmen! What a happy change Thou hast worked in us, merciful God!"

What are the "common charges" that emancipated Jews must assume vis-à-vis their new civil-cum-primordial community? Berr recognizes quite clearly that there is a bargain involved, a promise that Jewish persons can become members of the French nation only in return for their commitment to purifying their own Jewish qualities. He calls on his Jewish brethren to "examine with attention what remains to be done, on our part . . . to show, in some measure, our grateful sense for all the favors heaped upon us." The problem Berr comes back to is, in fact, the same one that troubled Dohm, namely the civil competence of the Jews. Recognizing that "the name of active citizen [is] the most precious title a man can possess," Berr warns that "this title alone"—civil status in the legal sense—"is not sufficient." Jews must themselves measure up: "We should possess also the necessary qualifications to fulfill the duties annexed to it."

In order to qualify for civil inclusion, Berr insists that Jewish emancipation must involve not only universalism but a demonstrable shift in primordial affinity. In order to "give signal proofs of [our] glowing patriotism," Jews must "work a change in our manners, in our habits, in short, in our whole education."[28] In demands ranging from his insistence that Jews learn to speak unaccented French to his suggestion that they take up science and manual labor in order to shed their "sloth and indolence," Berr reproduces Christian anti-Semitic stereotypes. This is nowhere more apparent than in his argument about what is "absolutely necessary" for this self-transformation: Jews must "divest ourselves entirely of that narrow spirit, of Corporation and Congregation, in all civil and political matters." Though Berr protests that he intends by this advice no criticism of Judaism as such— "God forbid that I should mean anything derogatory to our professed religion [or] presume to alter [its] dogmas"[29]—he is protesting too much. He realizes that the qualities of Judaism remained deeply stigmatized even among his French emancipators; he is dispensing advice so that his brethren might learn publicly to present themselves as Frenchmen, not as Jews.

The Post-Emancipation Period: Religious and Secular Modes of Jewish Adaptation to the Dilemmas of Assimilation

This enthusiasm for civil inclusion among early Jewish Enlightenment figures had consequences for Jewish religious practices in the modern world. It set off a chain reaction with consequences that could neither be foreseen nor controlled. "Adopt the mores and constitution of the country in which you find yourself," Moses Mendelssohn had advised his religious brethren in 1783, "but be steadfast in upholding the religion of your fathers, too. Bear both burdens as well as you can."[30] But if the Jewish religion was to be maintained, it would not be that of the patriarchs themselves. Bearing both burdens meant that religion would have to change as well. In fact, an extraordinary enthusiasm for religious self-change accompanied the embrace of Enlightenment and assimilation, and it transformed organized Judaism from the turn of the nineteenth century.

Restructuring Organized Judaism

It is true, of course, that this self-change responded in part to outside pressures. Napoleon himself, speaking in 1806 through his appointed commissioner Count Louis Mathieu Molé to the leaders of French Jewry, bluntly demanded loyalty in exchange for emancipation: "Do those Jews who are born in France and who are treated as French citizens regard France as their native country, and do they feel themselves obligated to defend it, to obey its laws, and to submit to all regulations of the civil code?"[31] Yet it was not only in response to the implicitly coercive implications of this question that radical and moderate reformers alike insisted on separating what they called the "spiritual" from the "national" elements of Judaism. They themselves were highly motivated to leave the Jews' traditional pariah status behind. This is clear from the passion with which they hastened to assure their secular national leaders that post-emancipation Jews no longer considered themselves a nation but a religious grouping, an identification that allowed full primordial attachment to their respective nation-states. In 1845, David W. Marks, the first rabbi of the West London Synagogue of British Jews, attested "we unequivocally declare that we neither seek nor acknowledge subjection to any land except the land of our birth." The support which Rabbi Marks expressed for this new primordial attachment was intense: "To this land we attach ourselves with a patriotism as glowing, with a devotion as fervent, and with a love as ardent and sincere as any class of our British non-Jewish citizens."[32] For many Jews, indeed, this shift in primordial loyalty went so far as to compel them to give up the Messianic idea of the return to Palestine, one of the most cherished creeds of the Jewish Diaspora. In 1885, the leaders of American Reform made such a declaration part of their Pittsburgh Platform, which became a guide for the liberal branch of American Judaism for fifty years to come.

> We recognize in the modern era of universal culture of heart and intellect the approaching of the realization of Israel's great Messianic hope for the establishment of the kingdom of truth, justice and peace iamong all men. We consider ourselves no longer a nation, but a religious community, and, therefore, expect neither a return to Palestine, nor a sacrificial worship under the sons of Aaron, nor the restoration of any of the laws concerning the Jewish state.[33]

The issue clearly was not just a pragmatic shift of geopolitical loyalty. As the historian Joseph Blau has put it, nineteenth-century reformers of Judaism wanted an "inner emancipation" that paralleled the outer, political emancipation.[34] For the most radical among them, who started the antitraditionalistic branch of Judaism known as Reform Judaism, this inner emancipation meant subjecting every Jewish religious belief to the test of reason. In 1843, in its "Program for a Declaration of German Israelites," the Frankfort Society of Friends published a streamlined creed that centered on three principles:

1. We recognize in Mosaism the possibility of an unlimited further development.
2. The collection called the Talmud, as well as all the rabbinic writings and statutes which rest upon it, possess no binding force for us either in dogma or in practice.
3. We neither expect nor desire a messiah who is leading the Israelites back to the land of Palestine; we recognize no fatherland other than that to which we belong by birth or civil status.[35]

The same standard of reason was employed by the fifteen American rabbis who prepared the Pittsburgh Platform. Declaring that "we recognize in Judaism a progressive religion, ever striving to be in accord with the postulates of reason," they urged their fellow Jews to reject all moral laws and ceremonies "which are not adapted to the views and habits of modern civilization."[36] The Torah, the Jewish Bible that Christians later included in the Old Testament, itself must be subjected to scientific test: "We hold that the modern discoveries of scientific researches in the domains of nature and history are not antagonistic to the doctrines of Judaism, the Bible reflecting the primitive ideas of its own age and at times clothing its conception of Divine Providence and justice dealing with man in miraculous narratives."[37]

From this postmetaphysical perspective, self-change not only involved giving up the idea of messianic return but any specifically Jewish idea of salvation. Indeed, the Reform movement sublated religious into secular messianism, into the belief in the universal progress of humankind. According to the German Reform leader Ludwig Philippson, whereas Jews formerly "had striven to create a nation, an independent state," their goal now "was to join other nations and reach for the highest rung of development in human society."[38] The very definition of the "new age" was to expand solidarity in a fully horizontal, civil manner, "to form a general human society" which would "encompass all peoples organically." In order to enter fully into this civil sphere, Philippson declared, particularistic definitions of community, including the Jewish one, must be abandoned. It is "the task of the Jews not to create their own nation . . . but rather to obtain from the other nations full acceptance into their society and thereby attain to participation in the general body social."[39]

The Reform leaders' rejection of particularistic definitions of Jewish community, however, did not indicate a desire to erase all distinctions. Their new secular messianism, rather than eliminating the idea of Jewish particularity, reinterpreted chosenness as "the mission of Israel." Though revisers in all the new movements of Judaism promoted a new understanding of Jewish particularity, it was Reform Judaism that came to be identified with the notion of mission. At the Frankfurt rabbinical conference in 1845, David Einhorn articulated this shift.

> The collapse of Israel's political independence was once regarded as a misfortune, but it really represented progress, not atrophy but an elevation of religion. Henceforth Israel came closer to its destiny. Holy devotion replaced sacrifices. Israel was to bear the word of God to all the corners of the earth.[40]

Einhorn and his colleagues, in other words, universalized messianism and added a more human understanding of agency to historical progress; but they hardly rejected the idea of the Jews' divine vocation. Claude Montefiore, a prominent spokesman for Britain's Liberal Judaism—that nation's version of Reform—saw the Jewish mission to carry God's message to humanity as the "one specifically Jewish commandment," defining Jews as a "religious brotherhood" rather than as a nationality or even a people.[41]

In response to such far-reaching change, backlash movements formed within these reforming Jewish communities, movements that eventually became organized as Orthodox and Conservative denominations in contrast to Reform. It is important to understand, however, that for most of the nineteenth century at least, these backlash movements departed from Reform not because they were more pessimistic about the possibility of Jewish incorporation but because their very optimism about this possibility led them to worry deeply about its effects. They resisted not reform per se, much less full inclusion into national citizenship. Rather, they resisted Reformism as threatening the distinctiveness, indeed the very specificity, of Jewishness as such. In his widely read *Nineteen Letters on Judaism*, published in 1836, Samson Raphael Hirsch, one of the intellectual founders of Modern Orthodoxy, wrote that although he respected the "good intentions" of Reformers, he wanted to "weep and mourn" when he examined "the aims to which their efforts are directed."[42] Hirsch claimed, and not without some reason, that the Reformers' rejection of traditional Jewish beliefs and practices seemed to echo the anti-Semitic perspectives of Christian core groups.

In Kantian terms, this disagreement can be described as a struggle over the relationship between the right and the good, between the moral life of the civil public sphere and the ethical life of the private sphere and primary communities. Should "moral" forces and representations exercise control over definitions of the good? From the perspective of Orthodox and Conservative intellectuals, Reformers were all too eager to subordinate Jewish good to civil right. Hirsch claimed that "the champions of contemporary Reform . . . have failed to recognize the good and have erred in their comprehension of the truth."[43] Accusing them of dissolving religion into mere civility, Hirsch resisted this sacrifice—which for Reformers, of course, was not a sacrifice at all—because he viewed certain aspects of traditional Judaism not as primitive and irrational, but as superior religious truth. If one accepts "the eternal ideals of our faith," Hirsch wrote, then Jews certainly must refrain from merging fully into a civil solidarity.[44] In fact, Hirsch viewed Christian core-group spokesmen as strangers and potential enemies. "To take a standpoint somewhere outside of Judaism," he wrote, is "to accept a conception derived from strangers, of the purposes of human life, and the object of liberty, and then to cut, curtail and obliterate the tenets and ordinances of Judaism."[45]

The backlash movement against Reform, in other words, strangely mirrored the antiuniversal, primordial loyalties of the Christian emancipators. Hirsch worried that civil solidarity would bring about "a close union with that which is different and alien, and a severance of the ties that bind us all to Israel's lot."[46] Though professing, "I bless emancipation," and insisting on "the duty of the community no less than that of the individual to obtain for all its members the opportunities and privileges of citizenship and liberty," Hirsch wanted the separation between Jew and civil society to be maintained.[47] For Orthodox and Conservative Jews, religious redemption—

not civil emancipation—remained the ultimate goal. Civil incorporation would make the *Galut* (exile from the land of Israel) more palatable; ultimately, however, Jews must return to the Holy Land to be reunited with God.[48] It was in this peculiar, limited, but nonetheless important sense that the goal of the opponents of Reform was "the avoidance of assimilation," as Baruch Stern, one of Hirsch's successors in the Modern Orthodox movement, put it.[49]

This conflict within the Jewish Reform movement highlighted the ambiguities of incorporation, adumbrating the dilemmas faced not just by Jews but by every assimilating group up to the present day. In the long run, of course, both the unbridled enthusiasm of European Jews for assimilation and their anxieties about the effects of its imminent success turned out to be profoundly misplaced. The Holocaust was proof. Even in the middle term, however, the fervent Jewish commitment to self-change could be said to have had only mixed results.

In Western Europe and the United States, the assimilative exchange, despite its asymmetry, seemed an honest one conducted in good faith. In return for Jewish assiduousness in taking up opportunities to become socialized to their respective civil-cum-primordial communities, openings appeared for Jews to participate in public life. In England, France, Germany, and America, as they took on the coloring of their respective primordial communities, Jews became artists, intellectuals, and professionals, and even, in the case of Disraeli, held the highest positions of civil office. By the later nineteenth century, assimilation had proceeded to the extent that such "incorporated" Jews often demonstrated open antipathy to newer Jewish immigrants, legal and illegal, who came streaming into their countries in response to the sudden rise in anti-Semitic violence in Eastern Europe and Russia. Sometimes they even embraced such anti-Semitic terms as "kike" to stigmatize and distance themselves from these unwelcome newcomers, whom they saw as behaving in an uncultivated manner and as looking and acting "too Jewish."[50]

The barely suppressed fear, of course, was that these raw and unpolished immigrants, with their "typically" Jewish beliefs and practices, would reignite the publicly bracketed but still powerful core-group antipathy to Jewish qualities and would reinforce the stigma that assimilating Jews, whether Reform or Orthodox, were intent on trying to escape. American Jews of Western European origins, writes Gerald Sorin, encouraged the new immigrants to "discard social habits that made them embarrassingly visible and that got in the way of rational and efficient adaptation." [51] Spokesmen for the relatively more incorporated Jewish groups declared the presence of these newer immigrants as "dangerous to the Jews of refinement and culture," asserting that nothing but "disgrace and a lowering of the opinion in which American Israelites are held . . . can result from the continued residence among us of these wretches."[52] In 1895, a statement by a German Jewish public school teacher in Cleveland reflected the unacknowledged but nonetheless real connection between the public universalism of American democracy and the polluted primordiality of Jewishness, which continued to be reproduced in private life. She called upon authorities to protect her immigrant pupils from the influence of their own homes and neighborhoods, describing the latter as filled with "bigoted followers of the orthodox rabbinical law [and] uneducated paupers . . . whose minds are stunted [and] whose characters are warped."[53]

Even in the midst of the very real transformation in the civil status of Western European Jews, in other words, these new members of civil societies manifested a distinctive unease. What Cuddihy aptly termed "the ordeal of civility" can be traced to the awareness, among even the most assimilated Jews, that the public incorporation of their persons in no way mitigated the private stigmatization of their religion's qualities.[54] Properly socialized, Jews could participate in significant if still limited ways in public life. In terms of the everyday private lifeworlds, however, Jews still remained worlds apart, segregated residentially, excluded from primary groups of friendship and clubs, denied opportunities for intermarriage.[55] In the context of this tense duality between public and private orientations, anti-Jewish pollution inevitably circled back into the public sphere, significantly undercutting the incorporation that assimilation had promised to provide if Judaism withdrew into private life.

Religious Conversion

The dilemmas of assimilation also produced "adaptive" responses of a very different kind. Some Jews tried to resolve the harsh dualities of incorporation not only by changing what it meant to be a Jew but by leaving Judaism entirely behind. The most obvious way was converting to Christianity, an option particularly attractive to Jews in German civil societies where access to state positions often remained formally *"judenrein"* (Jewish free).[56] Though Christianity had, in principle, always welcomed Jewish conversion, the fact that earlier Christian societies did not possess constitutionally regulated, formally egalitarian civil spheres had made the prospect of full participation much less likely and conversion much less attractive. With the Enlightened transformation of European societies, the prospect of civil participation became more real, and the incentive became much greater to leave the private stigma of Jewishness entirely behind.[57] If assimilation freed Jewish persons in public but did not change the estimation of their private qualities, then one logical alternative was to change these private qualities by claiming not to be Jewish.

The history of Jewish communities in nineteenth-century central Europe is filled with conversions; in fact, in mid-century Vienna, the city with the highest conversion rate in Europe, one estimate has it that 8 percent of the Jewish population annually made efforts to convert.[58] Heinrich Heine, one of the most famous German poets of the Romantic era, asserted that "the baptismal certificate is the ticket of admission to European culture,"[59] and he was by no means the only talented Jew who was able, as a result of conversion, to enter centrally into the primordial community of his or her national civil society. Still, the very situation that led more than two hundred thousand Jews in the nineteenth century alone[60] to seek conversion seemed also to guarantee that this approach to dissolving the contradictions of incorporation was bound to fail. Converted Jews were not Christians but *Taufjude*—literally, baptized Jews. Jewishness was an underlying, highly polluting quality, not just a formal status, and such qualities were very difficult, if not impossible, to shed. In this respect, these early, highly fragmented civil societies were not so different from the more traditionalist, antidemocratic societies of earlier times.[61] Faced with the Inquisition, many Spanish and Portuguese Jews in the fifteenth and sixteenth centuries chose conversion rather than exile or death. Yet, identified as *conversos* and *Marranos*, they remained forcibly separated not only from Spanish society but from the core groups of other European nations as well.[62] In the nineteenth century, by contrast, conversion did allow Jewish intellectuals to take professorships in German universities and Jewish lawyers to become German municipal officials. Yet the contradictions of assimilation remained. Fourteen years after converting to Christianity for professional reasons, Ludwig Boerne, the

German-Jewish political essayist who became a leader among the political émigrés in Paris in the 1830s, observed that "certain people object to my being a Jew; others forgive me; still others even praise me for it; but everybody remembers it."[63] The separation from the primary groups of Christian society reflected this continuing pollution of Jewish qualities. In Christian eyes, Jews remained Jews, whether they had converted to Christianity or not.

Secular Revolution

If internal religious reform did not alleviate the strain caused by the continuing stigma of Jewish qualities, and if even the conversion to Christianity could not purify it, many Jews began to wonder if post-emancipation European societies really contained any universalism at all. If not, the Jewish orientation to these purportedly civil societies would have to proceed in radically different, much more contentious way.

In the wake of the early Napoleonic reforms that helped open up German civil societies, Heinrich Marx, an ambitious and well-positioned young man in the Jewish community of Trier, pursued a secular education and law degree. In the backlash against Enlightenment beliefs and practices that followed Napoleon's defeat, and which stimulated increasing anti-Semitism in the decades thereafter, Heinrich Marx felt compelled to convert to Christianity to protect his career in the civil service because a new edict prohibited Jews from being advocates or lawyers.[64] Seven years later, Heinrich Marx had his eight children converted to Protestantism. His son, Karl Marx, initially an idealistic and fervent believer in the possibilities of German democracy, personally experienced the repressive and politically intolerant underpinnings of the Prussian state. Along with other disappointed radical democrats, many of them also of Jewish origin, the young Marx became convinced that the contradictions of European civil societies could never be resolved, indeed that they emanated not just from Christian anti-Semitism but from the capitalist economic system in which it was imbedded. In this deepening alienation, Karl Marx was by no means alone. As industrial capitalism began to destabilize and polarize European societies, increasing numbers of Jewish intellectuals opted to escape the dualities of assimilation by dissolving Judaism not in Christianity but in revolutionary socialism.

485

They were converts not to a non-Jewish religion but to a non-Jewish secular faith.

In Marx's extraordinarily controversial "Essay on the Jewish Question," written in 1843 in the midst of his transition from radical democrat to revolutionary socialist, we find striking parallels between his revolutionary critique of capitalism and the ambiguities of Jewish assimilation we have identified thus far. Marx responds to the contradictions of assimilation by generalizing them into a theory of the deeper, fundamentally irresolvable contradictions of capitalist society. He builds upon anti-Jewish stereotypes to develop an anticapitalist critique, and transforms post-Enlightenment religious antagonism into a theory about the empty pretensions of civil solidarity and the selfishness of bourgeois society *tout court*.

In the midst of his brief for revolution, Marx admits to being primarily concerned, as were his Christian and Jewish intellectual predecessors, with "the question concerning the Jew's capacity for emancipation."[65] Like Jewish antitraditionalists before him, he accepts Christian contentions about the anticivil failures of the Jewish community, acknowledging that "we perceive in Judaism a general and contemporary anti-social element."[66] What makes this argument different, however, is that Marx ties this anticivil particularism not to the Jews' religion but to their central participation in economic life. "What is the secular basis of Judaism? Practical need, self-interest. What is the worldly cult of the Jews? Bargaining. What is his worldly god? Money."[67]

But if Christian critics were right that public participation had not cured anticivil Jewish qualities, they are wrong to believe that the contradiction between public ideals and private life has anything specifically to do with Jewish life. Contending that "out of its own entrails, civil society produces the Jew," Marx insists that Christianity itself is uniquely associated with civil society: "Judaism reaches its height with the perfection of civil society, but civil society achieves perfection only in the Christian world."[68] It is not religion, then, but a historically specific form of society that creates the problem. In bourgeois society, the private/public split places the "egoistic independent individual on the one hand and [the] citizen, a moral person, on the other."[69] Neither Judaism nor religion as such establishes "the dualism between individual life and species-life"; rather, "religion is here the spirit of civil society expressing the separation and withdrawal of man from man."[70] Civil society is nothing more than the superstructure, the fig leaf covering capitalist economic life. The hypocritical function of its public/

private division is to shield capitalism from criticism, allowing selfishness and profit-making to take place in the name of universal rights and individual autonomy. Marx confirms that Jewish qualities must be abolished for a good society to be established: "Very well! Emancipation from bargaining and money, and thus from practical and real Judaism would be the self-emancipation of our era."[71] He insists, however, that this abolition of Judaism can occur only through the economic transformation of capitalist society.

> [Only] an organization of society that would abolish the precondi-
> tions of bargaining and thus its possibility would render the Jew
> impossible. His religious consciousness would dissolve like a dull mist
> in the actual life-giving air of society.[72]

In a very real sense, then, Marx continues to insist, as other Jewish reformers had before him, that Jews must change to achieve the emancipation promised by civil society. Jews can abolish dualism and achieve real emancipation only by abandoning religion and working for revolutionary transformation. The Jew must become a revolutionary critic, an anticapitalist thinker, for only in this way can he abolish the real source of his own oppression, both in its religious and nonreligious forms. The Jew must stop being religious and start being a socialist, working in a universal quest on behalf of all oppressed people everywhere. Only "when the Jew recognizes this practical nature of his as futile and strives to eliminate it," Marx advises, can he move away "away from his previous development toward general human emancipation."[73]

Marx can be seen as having created a project that gave to the still excluded Jew an opportunity to actively transform the world that continued to oppress him. He could accept the Enlightenment project and, at the same time, express his anger and resentment at its false promises in a violent and aggressive way. Revolutionary Jews could even participate in the hatred generated by anti-Semitic stereotypes, for Marx affirms that "the social emancipation of the Jew is the emancipation of society from Judaism."[74] As socialists, moreover, these radical Jews could extend this hatred from Jews to Christians and property holders more generally, and they could dedicate themselves to working toward a future solidarity in which these and other false divisions would be permanently overcome.

This is not an effort to explain away revolutionary socialism as a Jewish movement. Still, it is an undeniable fact that the intellectual and ideological clarification of secular radicalism was accomplished by the son of a Jewish convert whose life had been contorted by the contradictory promises of assimilation. For this reason, Marxism can be understood as, among other things, another response to the agonizing dilemmas of Jewish incorporation, providing a major form of self-expression and a promising path of self-transformation for Jews caught in the contradictions of anti-Semitic civil societies. Though adaptive in many ways, this response, like the others we have considered, proved relatively ineffective. Even for those willing to give up their ethnic and religious identity, social radicalism remained a minority option. Participation in revolutionary movements that were often viciously repressed seemed a high cost for incorporation, which was, at any rate, a distant prospect at best. It involved, moreover, not only a radical break with the past in the name of an uncertain future, but participation in a movement from which anti-Semitism had not been entirely expunged. The enemies of socialism were not the only anti-Semites. Socialist movements themselves, though often dominated by Jews, frequently carried powerful anti-Semitic overtones. The intellectual reasoning underpinning this bias is spelled out in the early philosophical argument we have considered by Marx. After the Bolshevik Revolution of 1917, "actually existing socialism" would demonstrate this failure of universalism in a decidedly nonintellectual way.[75]

New Forms of Symbolic Reflection and Social Response in the Fin de Siècle: The Dilemmas of Assimilation Intensify

In the latter part of the nineteenth century, amid these varied responses to the asymmetrical bargain of assimilation and despite the continuing if highly uneven incorporation of Jews into European societies, the obdurate reality of Christian anti-Semitism became ever more difficult to ignore. In the 1870s, mass collective violence against Jews emerged in Russia and other parts of the Pale of Settlement, that broad segment of Eastern Europe and Western Russia where by far the largest group of European Jews had remained segregated in traditional *shtetl* communities. In addition to triggering massive Jewish immigration from the Pale to Western Europe and the United States, these pogroms sent shock waves of horror throughout the Western, less traditional, more assimilated Jewish communities. In the 1890s, partly in reaction to this new wave of Jewish immigration and partly in response to the very gains Jews had been making in these Western societies, anti-Semitic social movements for the first time entered publicly into Western civil life. Certainly the civil spheres of Germany, England, and the United States were further fractured by these developments. However, the most arresting public appearance of this anticivil sentiment against Jews—sentiments that had, up until that time, largely remained confined within the private sphere—was the Dreyfus Affair in France. The public imagination of the age was captured by the accusation in 1894 that Alfred Dreyfus, an earnest French artillery captain, actually was a spy for *la patrie*'s German enemies; by the public persecution of Captain Dreyfus and the distortion of French institutions of communication and regulation it revealed and entailed; and by the massive and contentious public social movements that simultaneously refracted and exacerbated the polarization of French civil society.[76] They symbolized, for many Jews at least, a dangerous narrowing of opportunities to participate, even in an asymmetrical manner, in the universal, public life of post-emancipation societies. In this context, as the situation of Jews became tenser and future incorporation more uncertain, there emerged inside the Jewish civil sphere new forms of Jewish literary and political reflection.

Irony and Absurdity: New Religious and Secular Literary Genres

The shift in Jewish mentality was symbolized by the emergence of an ironic, self-deprecating literary genre that narrated the helplessness of Jewish protagonists in the face of shattered hopes and communal despair. These new antiheroic narratives—which, decades later, were presented as "prototypically Jewish" stories by such neotraditionalist writers as Isaac Bashevis Singer—were broadcast in Yiddish and Hebrew via the communicative institutions of still sharply segregated Jewish civil societies.[77] In the 1880s, for example, one can observe a decided shift in the writing of Sholom Yankev Abramowitz, the Odessan writer who, under the pen name Mendele Mokher Seforim, became a giant of modern Yiddish and Hebrew literature. For twenty years, Abramowitz had modeled his work on Russian authors, devoting himself to upgrading the quality of Yiddish literature so as to modernize and "enlighten" the traditional Jewish communities of the Pale.

Faced with the devastating implications of the pogroms, however, Abramowitz gave up on the project of Jewish integration into Russian society and began writing satirically and critically, though sympathetically, about the passivity and credulity of traditional Jews.[78]

Abramowitz's famous modern parable, "Shem and Japheth on the Train" (1890), is narrated in the first person by Mendele the Bookseller, a pious traditional Jew whose itinerant commercial travels in the Pale appear to have completely cut him off from contemporary events.[79] In the course of an extended train ride filled to overflowing with Jews traveling to what they hope are better lives, Mendele makes the acquaintance of Moshe the Tailor. At first, Mendele patronizes Moshe, describing him as "one of those 'happy paupers' of whom we have many in our midst" who "bow their heads submissively before storms" and who believe "it is their inexorable lot to pass their years in squalor and privation." However, when, at Mendele's request, Moshe recounts his life story, it is Mendele's turn to feel ignorant and humbled, qualities Abramowitz displays in bitingly satiric dialogue. Responding to Moshe's assertion that "I and my family were Jews," Mendele exclaims: " 'What is all this?' . . . 'Do you mean that now you are not a Jew?' "

Moshe's response shocks him.

" 'I am a Jew no longer, for there are no Jews left anymore,' answered the tailor with a smile. 'It seems you do not know what age we are living in.' "

Mendele answers:

"How can I fail to know? Look, here is my calendar. . . . This week's portion of the Law is about Korah, it is the year five thousand six hundred and forty."

This reference to the stability of Jewish tradition betrays Mendele's isolation both from contemporary Jewish efforts at incorporation and the backlash by "enlightened" authorities against Jewish entrance into modern life. Moshe makes this perfectly clear in his tongue-in-cheek monologue, breathlessly recounted by Mendele.

" 'But the Germans think otherwise,' said Reb Moshe quietly. 'The Germans, who perform miracles of science, have turned the clock back a thousand generations, so that all of us at this day are living in the time of the Flood. . . . The non-Semites are hostile toward the Semites; they discover imaginary wrongs. . . . At first these reactionaries were derided by their neighbors, and held to be madmen, but the madder they became, the more followers they found, until this lunacy struck root in the midst of people and rulers alike, and seemed to be a right and proper attitude.' "

Mendele mocks the wonders of German science, and with it modernity itself. The private life of traditional Judaism is impossible and, indeed, irrational. But the carriers of modern enlightenment are irrational in a different and more frightening way. Anti-Semitism is a lunacy that has increasingly wide appeal.

In the hands of Franz Kafka, this sense that the modern world has been turned upside down, that rational pretensions have become lunacy and that madmen rule the world, became secularized and transformed into the prototypical stuff of avant-garde modernism. This Jewish writer transformed his experience of the contradictions of Jewish assimilation into narratives that, broadcast far and wide via the communicative institutions of civil societies, became authoritative sources for understanding the contradictions of modernity more generally. Kafka lived in a marginalized Jewish segment of a small German-speaking community in Prague, itself an outpost of the Austro-Hungarian Empire.[80] He attended a secular German high school, and he wrote only in German. In none of his literary works, moreover, did he ever make explicit reference to Jewish characters or link his fictional representations in any manner to issues of Jewish identity. Yet in his private lifeworld Kafka identified strongly as a Jew and experienced powerfully the anxieties of that status. He had a Bar Mitzvah celebration; socialized almost entirely with Jewish friends; frequented exclusively Jewish resorts; closely followed Jewish newspapers, both in Yiddish and German; and was deeply inspired by Yiddish theater.[81] His private letters to his sisters and intimate friends and the records of his personal conversations reveal an intense preoccupation with the increasingly dismal state of Jewish affairs. Kafka lived out the confusing and dispiriting dualities of Jewish incorporation, this insurmountable paradox serving as a trigger for his art.

Kafka participated publicly and successfully in Prague's economic life, holding an executive job of significant influence and responsibility in the Workmen's Accident Insurance Institute. Yet, during his sixteen-year tenure at the prestigious insurance company, where he was reported to have been "highly esteemed as a staff member and universally popular as a person," Kafka was one of only two Jewish employees among its workforce of approximately two hundred and fifty.[82] The contradiction between public recognition of his personal abilities and the widespread Czech and German degradation of Jewish qualities reinforced Kafka's sense of the contradictions of civil life. When asked to sponsor the application of an Orthodox Jewish friend for employment at his company, Kafka refused, writing that "the institute is off limits for Jews," explaining that "it is incomprehensible how the two Jews that work there managed to get in," and adding, "it will never happen again."[83] At the same time, however, Kafka felt estranged from, and often humiliated by, his Jewish identification. "Most of those who started to write in German," he once wrote to his closest friend, "wanted to get away from their Jewishness. . . . They wanted to get away, but their hind legs still stuck to the fathers' Jewishness, while the forelegs found no firm ground. And the resulting despair served as their inspiration."[84] Surely it was this contradictory splitting of private and public life to which Kafka alluded in the lengthy and bitter "Letter to His Father," the private but oddly polished and formal piece of writing that his mother refused to deliver and that was published posthumously, along with so many of his other literary works, against his own expressed wishes.

> The world was for me divided into three parts; one in which I, the slave, lived under laws that had been invented only for me and which I could, I did not know why, never completely comply with; then a second world, which was infinitely remote from mine, in which you lived, concerned with government, with the issuing of orders and with the annoyance about their not being obeyed; and finally a third world where everybody else lived happily and free from orders and from having to obey.[85]

Kafka may well have experienced such freedom and happiness during his hours of writing after his day job, but it was the combination of enslavement and remoteness that became expressed in his art. In such works as *The Trial* and *Metamorphosis*, he sublimated his wrenching experiences of the antagonism and repression of anti-Semitic society by creating the style that would become known as "Kafkaesque." His representations of the meaninglessness and amorality of civil institutions and their dehumanizing effects on personal life created the aesthetic frame for the absurdism that, beginning with Samuel Beckett, eventually informed avant-garde fiction throughout the twentieth century. His narrative connection of such estrangement with domination and impersonal control adumbrated, and supplied a conceptual vocabulary for, that century's critical political vocabulary as well. It was during the first days of World War I that Kafka wrote the opening sentence of *The Trial*, which became emblematic of so much of that century's social and political life: "Someone must have been telling lies about Joseph K., he knew he had done nothing wrong but, one morning, he was arrested."[86] The first sentences of *The Metamorphosis*, composed at about the same time but on a much more personal and intimate canvass, expresses the same fictional transformation of the Jewish condition and manifests the same universal reference for expressing the cruelty of modern life: "When Grego Samsa awoke one morning from troubled dreams he found himself transformed in his bed into a monstrous insect. . . . 'What has happened to me?' he thought. It was no dream."[87]

Zionism: The Effort to Withdraw from Western Civil Society

The externally oriented response that emerged alongside this dramatic, fictional narrative deflation of Jewish subjectivity was a new kind of Zionism, which, as one influential historian has put it, "became, for the twentieth century, the vital issue in Jewish life."[88] Theodore Herzl's politically oriented Zionism, which emerged as an organized movement in the 1890s, differed from the long-standing Messianic belief in the Jews' return to Israel by its *programmatic* call for Diaspora Jews to leave their respective societies and by its organizational concentration on the practical means for allowing them to do so. Herzl's life experience mirrored the intensifying contradictions of incorporation. An assimilated Hungarian Jew with a secular upbringing, Herzl was working in Paris as a journalist for a Viennese newspaper when the Dreyfus scandal broke out. As Herzl later told the story, his illusions about the possibilities of Jewish assimilation were shattered when he witnessed masses of French citizens marching in the streets shouting "Death to the Jews." Having come face to face with "the profound barbarism of our day," Herzl recommended that Jews should eschew what would, he predicted, be an ultimately futile effort to gain recognition and incorporation; for their own protection, Jews must physically withdraw from European civil societies.[89]

In Herzl's presentation of political Zionism, we find a profoundly pessimistic response to the early Jewish emancipators' enthusiastic demand that their brethren assume their "common charge," that Jews change themselves in response to the imminent opening of Christian civil societies. As Herzl sees it, Jews had, indeed, upheld their side of the bargain. Not only did they sincerely devote themselves to self-change, but they had largely succeeded. Before emancipation, Jews had "slavish habits," but Herzl believes that they had now become autonomous and rational candidates for civil society—persons "strong and free of spirit." It is not only that Jews had become more "civil"; they had willingly taken on the primordial coloring of their respective national states. "We have honestly striven everywhere," Herzl attest, "to merge ourselves in the social life of surrounding communities." This quid received no quo; a stimulus to assimilation, it triggered no incorporating response.

> In vain are we loyal patriots, in some places our loyalty running to extremes; in vain do we make the same sacrifices of life and property as our fellow citizens; in vain do we strive to increase the fame of our native land in science and art, or her wealth by trade an commerce.

Despite their sacrifices, in other words, Jews have not been allowed to enter into solidary relations with their non-Jewish neighbors in civil society: "In countries where we have lived for centuries we are still cried down as strangers." The reason, Herzl suggests, is that these post-emancipation societies are not actually universal in their aims. In matters concerning religion, they are acutely particularistic, ruled by irrational "prejudice," "jealousy," and "intolerance." This is true of every country, "even in those most highly civilized—France itself is no exception." Herzl draws the logical conclusion. There is nothing Jewish persons can do; it is simply a matter of the qualities of Jewish religion as such, for their mere "presence soon produces persecution." In the face of this implacable primordial antagonism, Herzl believes, the very notion of civil incorporation becomes misleading, a dangerous chimera. By putting Jews into closer contact with their Christian enemies, emancipation actually had the effect of exacerbating repression rather than mitigating it: "In the principal countries where anti-Semitism prevails, it does so as a result of the emancipation of the Jews."

In formulating political Zionism, Herzl recapitulates the logic deployed by radical spokesmen for other stigmatized groups in Western civil societies. Generalizing from the demoralizing and often tragic experience of his own community, he concludes that, because the civil sphere is dominated by members of an antagonistic primordial group, civil society as such is irredeemably distorted by particularistic claims. Faced with the anticivil injuries of class, revolutionary socialists argued in a similar manner, that under capitalism the economic and civil spheres cannot be separated. Necessarily rather than contingently reducing the universal to the particular, capitalism cannot be reformed, and revolution alone can realize the possibilities for justice promised by the ideals of civil society. Over the long history of racial oppression in America, many influential African Americans employed the same logic. Believing civil status in the United States to be irredeemably permeated by primordial whiteness, they suggested that exit from the United States was the only viable possibility for obtaining civil freedom. Radical feminists have sometimes also argued this way, suggesting that the universalist ideology of civil society is so undercut by male domination as to be practically meaningless. On this basis, they have suggested that women, whenever possible, should withdraw into all-female societies.

The Crisis of Anti-Semitic Assimilation in the Interwar Period: Resolving the Dilemmas of Assimilation by Going Backward

As I have argued throughout this book, such a maximalist, exit-rather-than-voice strategy to resolve class, race, gender and religious inequality is not usually necessary. Of all the rejectionist movements, only the predictions of European Zionism turned out to be right. Indeed, only exit would have saved European Jews.[90] The qualification "European" is, however, essential. If Zionism is shifted from a claim about an ineradicable, fundamental complicity between anti-Semitism and civil society *tout court* to a historical argument about the fundamental anti-Semitism of European civil societies, then the Jewish maximalist position—the Zionist argument that civil universalism is fundamentally undermined by religious particularity—turns out to have been tragically correct. As the fate of European Jewry demonstrated, there was no mode of adaptation that could resolve "the Jewish question." The religious primordiality of European civil societies simply was too deeply ingrained, too unthinkingly accepted as the only legitimate way of expressing civil capacities. It was not only "Eastern" Jews of the traditional Pale who were decimated by the Holocaust, but "Western" Jews who had been gradually assimilating into more enlightened civil societies. In fact, as the German case would so dramatically demonstrate, the more successful at assimilation the Jews were, the more anti-Jewish antagonism could actually be produced. Individual *persons* could participate in public life, but the *qualities* of Judaism remained despised. The contradictions of assimilation became ever more intense, and European Jews who once were free became enslaved and finally put to death.

The fact that the members of this despised group became the objects of the most heinous mass murder in human history was, however, not a necessary outcome of their contradictory status, even in European society. World War I marked a turning point, and not only because it concluded with the enormously destructive Treaty of Versailles, a "peace" treaty that had the effect of pushing Germany to the brink of Nazism and the next world war. The consequences were even wider than this. The First World War not only reflected but intensified what I called, in chapter 8, the spatial and temporal contradictions of civil societies, those which derive from ethnic origins and express themselves in terms of national particularity. On the one hand, it was during the interwar period that national societies, whether via social democracy or less ambitious, more restricted welfare regimes, began to repair the "functional" distortions of the civil sphere, particularly those that were economic- and class-based. On the other hand, during this same period these very national societies dramatically narrowed the ethnic, racial, and religious options for expressing civil capacity.[91]

Restrictions on Jewish Incorporation in the United States

Struggles over the Jewish question during this interwar period assumed distinctive forms in Continental Europe and the United States, and this parting of ways had enormous consequences for the Jewish relation to civil society. In our discussion thus far, we have not emphasized national differences in how "Christian" core groups constructed their offers of assimilation or in the responses Jews made to its asymmetrical terms.[92] By the 1930s, as the contradictions of Jewish incorporation intensified, it had become unmistakably clear that national differences in responding to the Jewish question were becoming overwhelmingly significant. In light of this development, which in the post–World War II period contributed so powerfully to the ideology of "American exceptionalism,"[93] it is particularly important to recognize that in many, even if not in all respects, American Jews experienced the same intensifying assimilative contradictions as their European counterparts, the same sense of their increasingly tenuous position in civil society.

In the United States, the growing national, ethnic, and religious xenophobia of the fin-de-siècle and interwar periods expressed itself in a massive, historically unprecedented public campaign against free immigration. In the mid-1920s, as a result of this antiliberal mobilization of communicative institutions, America's regulatory institutions for the first time placed highly restrictive limitations on immigrants whose ethnic qualities diverged from the primordialities of the nation's core group. In this decades-long campaign to narrow the American civil sphere, anti-Semitism played a particularly important role. It allowed fears about radical socialism and disorder to be deepened by an anti-Jewish discourse that was itself embroidered by ethnic stereotypes about the nations from which most of the new Jewish immigrants came.[94]

This anti-immigrant social movement did not, in the long run, achieve its intended effect of making assimilation the only viable mode of incorporation, much less of stopping Jewish incorporation into American civil society itself. In the short run, however, it seriously exacerbated the contradictions of assimilation, intensifying prejudices against out-group *qualities* even while individual *persons* in these groups continued to be allowed formally free civil participation. In the early decades of the twentieth century, children of the new Jewish immigrants began to enter in large numbers into the communicative and regulative institutions of American life, for example as science, medical, and law students in elite universities, and as entrepreneurs in the radio and movie industries. In response to such inroads, however, anti-Semitism became increasingly explicit; restrictive quotas on Jewish participation and barriers of all different sorts were imposed for the first time in American institutional life. Though these restrictions were not formalized in legal codes, they were widely known and broadcast throughout the nation's communicative institutions.[95]

This rising tide of anticivil feelings and regulations against Jews, even in the most democratic nation-states, provides a framework for understanding the notorious, and now widely discussed, failure of Allied leaders in World

War II to take action against the Nazis' mass murder of Jews in the final years of the war. In retrospect, after the defeat of the Nazis and the exposure of the European genocide—after the holocaust became the Holocaust—this failure was seen as anomalous. However, when viewed against the backdrop of the growing restrictions on Jewish incorporation, which marked virtually every major industrial society during the interwar period, that failure is not nearly so anomalous as it was later constructed to be. American and British leaders were silent when information about the systematic extermination of the Jews leaked out of Nazi-occupied Europe in 1943 and 1944. Roosevelt and Churchill neither allowed civil institutions wide access to this information nor responded to it by bombing and destroying the Nazi concentration camps, whose locations were well known and whose deadly activities had not, even by that time, yet achieved their full intensity. This abysmal failure can be denounced in moral terms, but the sociological reasons for them should not be overlooked. As Walter Lacquer and others have demonstrated, Roosevelt and Churchill feared that such intervention might have the unintended effect of symbolically transforming the Allied military effort into what might be regarded as a "Jewish war." If Allied military objectives were extended to saving Jews from extermination, these leaders believed, the anti-Nazi war might have become polluted for large segments of the American and British publics, and national élan might suffer drastically as a result.[96]

It should not be altogether surprising, then, that during this interwar period one of the most pessimistic Jewish assessments of the post-emancipation incorporation was launched from inside the United States. Salo Baron was a professor at Columbia, and he was one of only two specialists in Jewish history employed by a secular American university. In 1928, he published "Ghetto and Emancipation," a deeply revisionist evaluation of Jews' relation to the modern world.[97] Baron takes note of the warning signs of anticivility that marked the interwar period, the "growing dissatisfaction with democracy and parliamentarism" and the great popularity of "Fascism" and "Sovietism."[98] In the midst of this crisis, he issues an iconoclastic warning against what he considers the grave dangers of the assimilative mode of incorporation. The Jewish "absorption by the majority," Baron asserts, is a process "that has often proved to be harmful both for the absorber and the absorbed."[99] For the Jews, Baron insists, the Enlightenment and its aftermath brought not progress but dissolution and disillusion. The highly cherished Jewish myth of progress, he claims, is just that: a myth. What Baron proposes is to turn this myth inside out: "A more critical examination of the supposed gains after the [French] Revolution and fuller information concerning the Jewish Middle Ages both indicate that we may have to reevaluate radically our notions of Jewish progress under Western liberty."[100] Baron proceeds to paint a rose-colored romantic picture of pre-Enlightenment ghetto life. Rejecting the previously accepted portrait of the "Dark Ages" before emancipation, he calls for a denunciation of this "lachrymose theory of pre-Revolutionary woe." Most startling, perhaps, is his suggestion that earlier Jewish segregation was self-imposed, an expression of internal Jewish democracy that "grew up voluntarily as a result of Jewish self-government" and defense long before it became a "legal compulsion."[101]

Looking backward from the tensions produced by contemporary assimilation, Baron argues that it was their very separateness that allowed medieval Jews "to live a full, rounded life" and to preserve Jewish nationality. The ghetto, far from being a distorted and repressed community, should be likened to "a corporate governing institution"—"the Jew, indeed, had in effect a kind of territory and State of his own."[102] Reminding us that all pre-modern European societies were made up of such corporate bodies, each with its own rights and duties, Baron advances the claim that Jews were not necessarily worse off than any other non-elite group. Even the draconian restrictions on Jewish occupational life, which Baron acknowledges, are described as having produced a decidedly positive effect. "Paradoxical as it may seem," he insists, "the very restrictive legislation proved in the long run highly beneficial to Jewish economic development," for it "forced them into the money trade, and throughout the Middle Ages trained them in individual enterprise."[103] Having thus redefined medieval Jewish ghetto life as prosperous and democratic—"to most Jews it was welcome"[104]—Baron draws the ironic conclusion that "compared with these advantages, social exclusion from the Gentile world was hardly a calamity."[105] For Baron, emancipation was a "necessity" forced upon Jews by the "modern State," which, after the French Revolution, "could no longer suffer the existence of an autonomous Jewish corporation" or of any other corporations, for that matter.[106] At the end of this bitter exercise in revisionism, Baron observes that "among the younger intellectual leaders of national

Judaism one discovers [today] a note of romantic longing towards the Jewish Ghetto."[107] It is revealing of the interwar situation of assimilating Jews, even in America, that Baron could just as easily have been writing about himself.

Europe's "Final Solution" to the Jewish Question: Resolving the Dilemmas of Assimilation by Eliminating the Jews

Transformed into the dominant metaphor in our time, the Holocaust has been generalized from a contingent event in Jewish-Christian history into a narrative about an evil that has redefined the twentieth century, modern society, and even human nature itself.[108] From a moral and cultural perspective, this generalization is all to the good. From a sociological point of view, however, conflating the Holocaust with the principal contours of modern life is a mistake. Whether it is Horkheimer and Adorno identifying the Nazi destruction of the Jews with capitalist "abstraction" and "industry," or Zygmunt Baumann making the complementary claim, almost fifty years later, that the Holocaust represented the very quintessence of modernity, such efforts have the effect of making invisible the difference between democratic and undemocratic versions of modernity.[109] They ignore the all-important issue of whether a particular social system—capitalist or socialist, modern or postmodern—contains within itself a relatively independent civil sphere. If Germany had managed to maintain its democratic form of government, which allowed the relative independence for the communicative and regulative institutions of the civil sphere, it is unlikely that the systematic mass murder of the Jews could have been carried out. This is simply to say, of course, that if the Nazis had not come to power, the Holocaust would not have occurred, for their coming to power entailed the brutally effective repression of the civil sphere.

Nonetheless, it has been a principal aim of this chapter to demonstrate that the Nazi destruction of the Jews, while constituting a heinous, antihuman, and thoroughly contingent intensification of anti-Semitism, can be seen, at the same time, as markedly continuous with the post-emancipation efforts of Western civil societies to resolve the contradictions of Jewish assimilation by "purifying" stigmatized Jewish qualities. It was the existentialist philosopher Jean-Paul Sartre, with his phenomenological focus on cultural textures and microinteractions, who came closest to getting this right, not the social theorists and social scientists who took the bird's-eye view of macrohistory. Writing in 1944 in the shadow of French collaboration with the Nazi occupation, Sartre makes an argument, in *Anti-Semite and Jew,* not about the evils of modernity but about the particularly insidious manner in which anti-Semitism sharpens the contradiction between civil society and ethnic nationality. What is most striking about this essay is that, despite his role in the Resistance, Sartre speaks as a member of the French national core group that, though not actually committing mass murder, actively collaborated with it. "The Nazi ordinances," Sartre writes, referring to the legal basis of the Nazi occupation of Paris, "only carried to its extreme a situation to which we had formerly accommodated ourselves very well."[110] The situation that Sartre sets out to describe is the deeply ambiguous situation of assimilation, which rested upon the split between public civility and private pollution.

> Before the armistice, to be sure, the Jew did not wear a star. But his name, his face, his gestures, and a thousand other traits designated him as a Jew; walking in the streets, entering a cafe, a store, a drawing room, he knew himself marked as Jew.[111]

In terms of the framework developed here, Sartre is pointing to how, despite the theoretical promises of assimilation, it was empirically impossible for the French to separate Jewish persons from Jewish qualities: "Whatever effort we made [to reach the person], it was always the Jew whom we encountered."[112] The promised universalism of French civil society was undermined by the primordial interests of the national core group: "Anti-Semitism is the expression of a primitive society that, though secret and diffused, remains latent in the legal collectivity."[113]

Affirming the principles of the Enlightenment position, Sartre argues that the Jew, as a person, proved himself to be "perfectly assimilable by modern nations."[114] He notes, for example, how rapidly Jews donned the primordial qualities of their national communities: "He speaks the same language; he has the same class interests, the same national interests; he reads the newspapers that the others read, he votes as they do, he understands and shares their opinion."[115] Yet no matter how closely Jews adopted primordial coloring, no matter how their socialization allowed Jews to achieve high positions in institutions of the public sphere, their invisible stain blocked true civil recognition.

> He may be decorated with the ribbon of the Legion of Honor, he may become a great lawyer or a cabinet minister. But at the very moment when he reaches the summits of legal society, another society—amorphous, diffused, and omnipresent—appears before him . . . and refuses to take him in. . . . The greatest success will never gain him entrance into that society which considers itself the "real" one. As a cabinet minister, he will be a Jewish cabinet minister, at once an "Excellency" and an untouchable.[116]

The problem is not class or modernity. The structured, subjective disposition to stigmatize Jews forces a distance that belies the civil promise of full inclusion. From the experience of Nazism and the widespread collaboration with it, Sartre drew the logical conclusion: "The Jew remains a stranger, the intruder, the unassimilated at the very heart of our society."[117]

It would take the violent destruction of European fascism, and the extensive reconstruction of civil and uncivil societies, for the European project of Jewish incorporation finally to be carried out, for "the Jew" to be converted from a strange intruder into a familiar friend. This task depended upon the intervention of the United States, a nation in which the relation between Western civil society and the Jewish people would, almost immediately upon the conclusion of the Second World War, take a surprising turn.

CHAPTER 19

Answering the Jewish Question in America:

Before and After the Holocaust

I N THE PRECEDING chapter we examined the extraordinary difficulties encountered by the project to incorporate Jewish out-groups into Western civil societies. In the case of the Jews, I suggested, the profound ambiguities of the assimilative mode of incorporation—recognizing the civil status of Jewish persons while continuing to denigrate Jewish qualities— were never resolved. To the contrary, these contradictions became so deep and corrosive as to generate the most heinous mass murder the world has ever known. Considering the Holocaust in the framework of the theory of fragmented civil society demonstrates how misleading it is to insist on the uniqueness of German resistance to Jewish incorporation, much less of German anti-Semitism. The issue is not why Germans disliked Jews so intensely, or even why they had so much trouble with the Jewish question, but why they turned to mass extermination to resolve it. It was the collapse of the civil sphere in Germany, not German anti-Semitism, that allowed the Holocaust to proceed.

That it was problems in the civil sphere that caused the Holocaust, not anti-Semitism, much less such "world-historical" problems as capitalism or modernity, is demonstrated by the uneven but increasingly substantial Jewish incorporation into the modern, capitalist, and often deeply anti-Semitic United States in the latter half of the twentieth century.[1] We will complete our discussion of civil society and the Jewish question by considering this critical case. It will provide one final demonstration of how contingent is the institutionalization of the promises of civil society. Whether these promissory notes are paid does not depend on the presence or absence of Enlightenment ideals. What is decisive is their implementation in a fragmented civil sphere.

Contrary to claims for American exceptionalism, claims that have always carried heavy ideological as well as scholarly weight, the relation of Jews to civil society in the United States was not, until the early 1940s, substantially different from that in Europe.[2] This is not to say, of course, that there was no difference at all. There had never been Jewish ghettos in the United States, a form of direct domination shunned for religious reasons by the radical Protestant dissidents who founded the American nation and for democratic reasons by those who later founded its constitutional state.[3] Demography also mattered. That the new nation was populated by immigrants dispersed over a large territory made it more possible for the civil and religious rights of minorities to be maintained. Still, the Jews' formal status in American civil society was counteracted, more forcefully even than in many European civil societies, by the deep and pervasive Christianity of the American core group, a consensual commitment that provided one of the fundamental sources of primordial identity for the new nation.[4] Despite the relative universalism of Protestant American Christianity, this primordial community polluted the quality of "Jewishness" even as it assured individual Jews that they would be treated fairly as persons. It allowed anti-Semitism to flourish even as the American core group encouraged massive immigration by promising emancipation to the increasingly oppressed members of anti-Semitic European societies.

Keeping Jewish Identity Private: Self-Change and the Utopian Project of Hyphenation

This contradictory character of incorporation suggested to American Jews, as it had to European ones, that they make their polluted identity as invisible and private as possible, and that they learn to express themselves publicly in terms of the primordial idioms of the national core group. In the nineteenth century, the primarily German Jewish immigrants embraced the Reform project of Jewish self-change even more enthusiastically than their European counterparts. Early American Jewish immigrants, according to David Ellenson, "purged 'oriental' patterns of worship from the synagogue, devised a liturgy almost wholly universalistic in orientation, abandoned dietary laws, and rapidly conformed to the cultural patterns and mores of the United States."[5] Yet a similar eagerness to enter into the assimilative bargain also characterized the second, "Eastern" wave of Jewish immigrants in the late nineteenth and early twentieth centuries. Despite their much more traditionalist backgrounds, they, too, "quickly abandoned observance of the Sabbath and dietary laws" and demonstrated a "lack of attachment to either traditional Jewish learning or laws of family purity."[6]

Face to face with the contradictory, civil-cum-primordial American nation, Jews aspired to leave religious particularity behind, not necessarily by becoming completely assimilated to an implicitly "Christian" or WASP nation as much as by entering a new, hyphenated community that was putatively neither Christian nor Jewish but "American."[7] As I have suggested earlier, in chapter 17, hyphenated incorporation actually can take two different forms. One blends core and out-group identities into a putatively higher civil culture that is not, at least explicitly, the original core group's but, nonetheless, remains deeply imprinted by its original primordial values; the other form continues to maintain the two cultural identities but in less rigidly in-group/out-group form. In practice, both forms of incorporation typically exist alongside one another in the hyphenated mode. Hyphenation is less sharply critical of out-group qualities than the assimilative mode, but its continuing primordiality, and implicit hierarchies, still mark it as significantly different from, and less truly inclusive than, multiculturalism.

Jewish immigrants to the United States provided ideal-typical formulations of both hyphenated forms. It was a Jewish playwright, working inside an influential communicative institution of American civil society, who popularized the term "melting pot."[8] Israel Zangwill's play by that name opened on Broadway in 1908.[9] Its hero, a Jewish violinist named David Quixano, is writing a symphony celebrating American freedom. After falling in love with Vera, the daughter of a Russian military officer, David discovers that his own parents, who had been murdered in a Russian pogrom, had been victims of Vera's father. Rather than breaking off his relationship with Vera, however, David decides that he will overcome the anticivil conflicts of the Old World, whether ethnic, political, or religious. In the climactic speech of the play, he cries: "God is making the American. . . . He will be the fusion of all races, the coming Superman."[10] Performed in an atmosphere of increasingly anti-Semitic core-group demands for Jewish assimilation, *The Melting Pot* shows how hyphenated incorporation represented a kind of utopian aspiration for Jewish immigrants. They wanted to be treated not as Jews but as persons, to be allowed to make their Jewish identity sufficiently invisible as to allow them to enter into the nation's civil sphere.[11]

Yet while entirely accepting the demand for self-change, many if not most of these immigrant Jews hoped that incorporation could be accomplished in an ethnic and hyphenated rather than an assimilative way. They wanted to be incorporated not into WASP America but, as Jews, into a new American race. Fifteen years after Zangwill's play, this aspiration toward hyphenation was expressed in an explicitly anti-assimilationist manner by Horace Kallen, whose writings helped lay the philosophical basis for pluralist theory. Just "as in an orchestra every type of instrument has its specific *timbre* and *tonality*" and "its appropriate theme and melody in the whole symphony," Kallen declared, "so in society, each ethnic group may be the . . . instrument," and "its temper and culture may be its theme and melody" in "the symphony of civilization."[12]

The Dilemmas of Jewish Incorporation and Communicative Institutions: Factual and Fictional Media

No more telling illustration of these early Jewish responses to the incorporative dilemma, and the complications it entailed, can be found than the manner in which Jews contributed to establishing the modern communicative institutions of American civil society, in both their factual and fictional forms.[13] The formation of the *New York Times* was, in fact, bound up with the German Reform Judaism of Adolph Ochs, who transformed the newspaper after purchasing it in 1896. Ochs's ambition, in the midst of a period heavily marked by yellow journalism and politically biased reporting, was to create a more detached and objective news vehicle. Ochs chose a new epigraph for the *Times*, the universalistic motto "All the News That's Fit to Print," and succeeded in making the newspaper the principal arbiter of "factual" information about the nature and composition—the motives, relations, and institutions—of American civil life. Ochs's ambition, however, was fueled not only by the commitment to journalistic objectivity but by his personal desire for civil incorporation. This important early effort at making the communicative institutions of the American civil sphere more universalistic and civil society more autonomous can be seen, in other words, as an institutional and cultural corollary of the German Jewish drive for incorporation.

Yet even for wealthy and prominent German Jewish immigrants, the incorporative bargain on offer was never truly reciprocal; it rested on fundamental asymmetries, demanding the continued repression of polluted primordial traits. In *The Kingdom and the Power*, Gay Talese connected Ochs with "the old German-Jewish attitude [of] disenchantment with American Jews who dwelled on the Jewishness," and their "desire that Jews blend into the American scene."[14] It is revealing how the *Times'* hard-won objectivity was sometimes distorted by its failure to provide denigrated out-groups, including Jews, full access to its communicative resources. In the early days of the First World War, for example, Ochs warned his city editor not to give too much space to the American Jewish Committee's effort to aid Jews in the war zones of Europe.[15] The publisher evidently did not see such a news event as "fit to print," given the fragmented nature of the American civil sphere. Ochs felt that he could not allow the *Times* to reconstruct the motives and relations of the American Jewish Committee and its loyalties to European Jews. The publisher's commitment to journalistic neutrality, in this instance, was not only produced but also distorted by his understanding of the requirements of Jewish incorporation. "I don't approve of it," Ochs said of the American Jewish Committee.

> They work to preserve the characteristics and traditions of the Jew, making him a man apart from other men, and then complain that he is treated differently from other men. I'm interested in the Jewish religion—I want to see that preserved—but that's as far as I want to go.[16]

It is thoroughly consistent with the *Times'* sense of vulnerability vis-à-vis core group sensibilities that, in 1939, Ochs' successor and son-in-law, Arthur Hays Sulzberger, urged President Franklin Roosevelt not to appoint

Felix Frankfurter, a Jew, to the Supreme Court. Fearing that the appointment of a Jewish justice would exacerbate anti-Semitism, Sulzberger opposed Roosevelt's effort to universalize one of the central regulative institutions of the civil sphere.[17] A similar anxiety was revealed when, in the early 1940s, the *Times* received reliable information about activities in Nazi concentration and death camps and barely reported it. The paper justified this decision as a legitimate deferral to President Roosevelt's concerns that the anti-Semitic prejudices that crippled American civil society would, upon the publication of this news, undermine wartime solidarity. This fateful decision to bury news about what would later come to be known as the crime of the century betrayed, once again, the *Times'* fear of exposing itself to accusations of "Jewish" loyalties, which might have threatened its status as a civil institution.[18]

Even more decisively than in the institutions of factual communication, Jews were deeply involved in creating the organizational framework and symbolic content of the most powerful fictional medium of early-twentieth-century American civil society—the movies. More than any other mass institution, it was the cinema that created the nation's collective self-understanding, constructing mythical representations of the motives, relationships, and institutions of the nation's religious, racial, ethnic, and economic groups. In the early decades of the century, at a time of intense struggle over increasingly primordial restrictions on civil participation, Hollywood frequently projected images that downplayed the negative and corrosive sides of these conflicts, projecting optimism about the benevolence of America's core group and its possibility for civil interaction with excluded others. In the name of a transparent, universally accessible civil sphere, prejudice and conflict were minimized, and patriotic loyalty exalted.

What makes this popular iconography relevant to the present discussion is how extraordinarily revealing it is of the contradictions of civil incorporation. For these symbolic representations were invented and distributed by marginalized, if institutionally powerful Jews whose primordial identity remained deeply polluted by the very Americans whose commercial loyalty ensured their business success. The major Hollywood studios were founded by first-generation Jewish immigrants, primarily from eastern Europe; the "studio system" that churned out such a prodigious supply of films from the 1920s to the 1940s was supervised by members of the second generation; it was Jewish exhibitors who from 1910 to 1920 transformed storefront theaters into grand cinema palaces; and Hollywood writers and producers were overwhelmingly Jewish.[19]

This deeply paradoxical situation is underscored by the insistent manner in which Hollywood projected sanitized images of a utopian civil society practicing an idealistic, reciprocal form of hyphenated incorporation. Via such purified iconography, Hollywood's Jews re-presented not only the nation but themselves. "What united them," Neil Gabler writes, "was their utter and absolute rejection of their pasts and their equally absolute devotion to their new country," on the basis of which they created a "powerful cluster of images and ideas [that] idealized America on the screen [and] reinvented the country in the image of their fiction."[20]

Although these utopian projections were wildly successful in commercial and popular culture terms, the Jews creating the movies could not fully succeed in making their religion invisible. The continuing negative evaluation of Jewish qualities prevented it. That, in Gabler's apt phrase, "the movies were quintessentially American while the men who made them were not"[21] was a constant anxiety to the anti-Semitic opponents of Jewish incorporation. Seeking a restricted civil sphere, these opponents used a number of pretexts to react aggressively against the "Jewishness" of the movies: if movies appeared too progressive or pluralistic; if they seemed to project implicit aspersions on xenophic and nativist activities and values; if Hollywood's actors, directors, or producers became publicly associated with lifestyles or politics that deviated radically from primordial constraints. From the 1920s sex scandals to the anticommunist witch hunts of the late 1940s and early 1950s, conservative groups complained bitterly about the Jewish influence on film. They demanded that Hollywood be liberated from "the hands of the devil and 500 un-Christian Jews" and from those who "are outside the moral sphere of American culture."[22] These efforts at public denigration and exclusion were not always confined to provincial circles. When the bohemian cosmopolite Scott Fitzgerald met with frustration in his screenwriting career, he complained that Hollywood was "a Jewish holiday, a gentiles [sic] tragedy."[23] The irony was that Jewish Hollywood was intent on creating images that made Jewish identity invisible, and tended to sugarcoat the harsh contradictions of American civil life.[24]

The Dilemmas of Jewish Incorporation and Regulative Institutions: The Law

Because Jews were largely barred from attending or teaching at prestigious law schools and from working at influential law firms, they did not influence the regulative institutions of American civil society nearly so much as did their Gentile counterparts.[25] Nonetheless, on those few occasions when Jews were in a position to exercise substantial regulative power, they did so in a manner that similarly revealed their contradictory, asymmetrical status in civil society.

As a crusading lawyer, Felix Frankfurter became famous for defending civil liberties during the Progressive period, and he worked to ameliorate the inequalities and distortions of the civil sphere as a member of Roosevelt's New Deal "Brain Trust" in the 1930s. Yet once he took up his official duties on the Supreme Court, Frankfurter's opinions demonstrated more commitment to the primordial solidarity of the American nation and more deference to the power of the American state than to excluded individuals, minority group rights, and the normative restriction of political power. In his dissent from the Court's 1944 decision that Jehovah's Witnesses had legitimate religious reasons to object to a compulsory flag salute, Justice Frankfurter publicly identified with his fellow Jews.[26] "One who belongs to the most vilified and persecuted minority in history," he wrote, "is not likely to be insensible to the freedoms guaranteed by our Constitution." Yet it was precisely his identity as a Jew, Frankfurter suggested, that justified his decision, in the case at hand, to subordinate the freedom to be different. "Were my personal attitude relevant," he wrote, "I should whole-heartedly associate myself with the general libertarian views in the Court's opinion." His personal opinions were not relevant, Frankfurter believed, precisely because he was a Jew; as he understood the bargain of incorporation, he was obligated to subordinate every personal feeling and identification. To become a member of American civil society meant leaving Jewish particularity behind. High officials must act in the name of a more general, hyphenated solidarity: "As judges we are neither Jew nor gentile, neither Catholic nor agnostic. [We] are equally bound by our judicial obligation whether we derive our citizenship from the earliest or the latest immigrants to these shores." Three years earlier, before the onset of World War II, the Supreme Court had been less sensitive to minority rights, supporting a statute requiring all students, including the children of Jehovah's Witnesses, to salute the flag. In this case

Frankfurter wrote the majority opinion. According to the recollections of then Chief Justice Charles Hughes, the new Jewish justice had been offered this opportunity "because of Frankfurter's emotional description, in conference, of the 'role of the public school in instilling love of country' based upon his own experiences as an immigrant child."[27]

Justice Frankfurter's regulatory efforts reflected his perception of the public/private split required by the bargain of Jewish incorporation. To become part of civil society, outsiders must learn to exhibit primordial attachment to the nation; to encourage this learning, a state can legitimately require citizens to repress other kinds of primordial attachments, including religious ones.

The Failure of the Project: Jewish Exclusion from American Civil Society

In examining the contradictory position of American Jews, we have seen that, like their European counterparts, most were more than willing to trade self-change for civil incorporation. Through the reorganization of their religious institutions and through their active participation in a wide range of civil institutions, Jews tried to efface their religious identities from the public sphere and to project their enthusiasm for hyphenating and generalizing the traditional values of the American core group.[28]

Yet although their civil circumstances were in certain respects better than those of their European brethren, for many decades American Jews were not more successful in resolving the dilemmas of incorporation. At the turn of the twentieth century, with the great upsurge of nativist and anti-immigrant feeling, there was also a sharp rise of public anti-Semitism. In his widely read polemic *The Passing of the Great Race*, the anthropologist Madison Grant, a member of New York City's old social elite, pleaded for a new racial consciousness that would put a stop to "hybrids." When "the higher races are mixed" with "primitive characters," Grant insisted, there is a reversion to the "lower type."[29] The "cross between [the] European races and a Jew is a Jew." Henry Ford began his fervently anti-Jewish campaign in the *Dearborn Independent,* and the Ku Klux Klan added Jews to their list of "Enemies of America."[30] Stephen Steinberg has described this process in stark but appropriate terms.

Perhaps the most important thing to be said about the period between 1910 and 1920 is that a climate of intolerance toward Jews
had developed in the nation. Manifested in patterns of social discrimination and sustained by an upsurge in anti-Semitic propaganda, anti-
Semitism now figured prominently in American life. Jews, whether
German or Russian, middle-class or lower-class, were lumped together with other aliens who were threatening Anglo-Saxon supremacy.[31]

In chapter 18, I discussed how, in the wake of the First World War,
regulative institutions promoted and legitimated draconian restrictions on
immigration to protect the primordial coloring of U.S. civil society.[32] Stopping the massive waves of Jewish immigrants from eastern Europe and Russia
became of primary concern. Though these new restrictions were often
portrayed by contemporaries as a natural response to excessive numbers,
they actually represented deeply anticivil efforts to block incorporation. It
was in this postwar period that the educational and economic institutions
of U.S. society constructed, for the first time, explicit barriers against Jewish
participation, and for more than two decades afterward these anticivil road-
blocks seemed impregnable. Indeed, they might have continued to remain in
place for an indefinite period of time if it were not for contingent events that
began unfolding far away from the American scene, in Germany in 1933, and
which eventually compelled America's entry into a new world war.

Anticivil Exclusions from Education

The anticivil nature of this backlash was sharply revealed by postwar controversies over access to higher education. Until about 1920, college admission, even to the nation's elite institutions, depended only on the ability to
pass a relatively routine entrance exam. For increasing numbers of Jewish
applicants, this seemed an easy barrier to mount. The children of ambitious
immigrants who displayed simultaneously a hunger for learning and academic achievement, Jewish students took full advantage of the public high
schools in Eastern cities. "The Jew undergoes privation, spills blood, to
educate his child," boasted an editorial in the New York *Jewish Daily Forward*
in 1902. Suggesting that such "capacity to make sacrifices for our children

... as well as our love ... for intellectual effort" reflected "one of the finest qualities of the Jewish people," the editorial claimed "you don't find many German, Irish or Italian children in City College." Whether or not the Jewish immigrants' commitment to education was so distinctive,[33] the facts were not in dispute: Jewish matriculation at the nation's elite institutions was rising rapidly, and in great disproportion to their percentage of the American population. Forty percent of Columbia's students were Jewish in the years before restrictions were imposed; at Harvard, Jewish enrollment was close to 20 percent.

The Ivy League colleges began strenuous efforts to reduce Jewish matriculation. In terms of undergraduate education, the role that such elite institutions played in American society was neither scientific nor particularly democratic. Their primary function was to socialize, and the values they transmitted, while civil in principle, were often primordial in form. This understanding was broadcast by communicative institutions throughout the civil sphere. *Stover at Yale*, a widely read portrait of undergraduate life at Yale, put it in a colloquial, fictional form.

> "Just what does our type take from here to the nation?" said Stover; and then he ... had asked the question that was vital ...
>
> "First, a pretty fine type of gentleman, with good, clear honest standards; second, a spirit of ambition and a determination not to be beaten; third, the belief in democracy."
>
> "All of which means," said Regan, "that we are simply schools for character."
>
> "Well, why not?" said Pike. "Isn't that a pretty big thing?"[34]

In 1922, an article in an academic journal put the issue in a more analytical and expository way. It was titled "Exclusion from College."

> Each student in an American college is there, or is supposed to be there, for some other purpose than acquiring knowledge. He is to be the transmitter to others of ideals of mind, spirit, and conduct. Scholarship is perhaps the most strongly reemphasized of these ideals, but it is not the only one, or even the most generally prized.[35]

It was, in fact, by explicitly bringing "values" into their admissions criteria that such elite colleges moved to protect their primordial ambitions vis-à-vis Jews. In addition to their long-standing but relatively modest academic requirements, they instituted complex procedures that were intended to reveal "the whole man." These included alumni interviews that could supply a firsthand check on qualities that might be invisible in a purely written application and nationwide recruiting goals that would reduce the flow of students from large Eastern cities. Character tests and psychological examinations were also employed for the first time. School principles were asked to evaluate students according to such criteria as "fair play," "public spirit," and "interest in fellows."[36] When justifications for these restrictions were publicly offered, these destructive intrusions into the civil sphere were presented as efforts to maintain democracy. Such decisions, however, usually were made in secret, and their true intent was carefully disguised.[37]

It is the instantiation in time and place that creates the debilitating contradictions of civil society, whose discourse and institutions are rarely renounced as such. The primordial coloration of American democracy is subtle. Rather than explicitly displacing the discourse of civil society, it translates the abstractions of this discourse into more particularistic and familiar terms. Jews were not stigmatized simply because they were held to be anti-Christian, but because their Jewish qualities were constructed as dangerous for civil society itself. In the minds of the anti-Jewish leaders of elite colleges, the fate of Jews was relatively unimportant; it was the ideals and identity of American civil society that were at stake. Jewishness symbolized the antithesis of civil motives and relations. What was insisted on, above all, was the allegedly anti-civil clannishness of Jews, though critics drew from other repressive themes as well. In 1890, in his response to a survey by the *American Hebrew* magazine, the president of Vermont University complained that Jews "have kept themselves together, and apart from others," and another respondent, a Harvard professor, insisted that "the social characteristics of the Jews are peculiar" and "differ from the manners of Americans generally."[38] In a 1922 survey of Harvard students, opinions about Jewish students drew from the discourse of repression in a similar way. One student explained that Jewish students "are governed by selfishness." Another suggested that, because Jews "do not mix," they "destroy the unity of the college." Rather than demonstrate independence and autonomy, another respondent complained, Jewish students merely "memorize their books," with the result "that others with a high degree of common sense, but less parrot-knowledge, are prevented from attaining a representative grade."[39]

By 1920, the student body of Boston Latin School, an elite public school that sent large numbers of graduates to Harvard, had become significantly Jewish. In a revealing memoir published 35 years later, one of the school's non-Jewish students charged that the school's entire atmosphere had been changed as a result, that it had become "fierce and grueling" and that the "solidarity of pupils" was destroyed.[40] In the *Nation*, a writer projected representations that were more complex but essentially no different in kind. Citing the Jews' "pathetic thirst for learning," he explained that the Russian Jew "achieves intellectual or financial success" too early, "before social adjustments have been made." The result was "that there are in fact more dirty Jews and tactless Jews in college than dirty and tactless Italians, Armenians, or Slovaks."[41] According to his relatively progressive perspective, however, it was the arrogance of the American core group, not the dirtiness of the Jews, that was ultimately at fault. The WASP core was not willing to keep the bargain of assimilation; they could not separate persons from their qualities. If Jews are not allowed at least to be Jewish in private, he warned, then even assimilative incorporation would not succeed.

> Anglo-Saxon Americans have small interest in the "melting-pot" except as a phrase. They do not want to be fused with other races, traditions, and cultures. If they talk of the melting-pot they mean by it a process in which the differences of the immigrant races will be carried away like scum, leaving only the pure ore of their own traits. . . . They consider the American a completed product, perfection already attained, and they resent any racial or cultural group which comes among them and persists in believing that it has something worthy of its own.[42]

A variation on this "progressive" version of anti-Semitism was put forward by Harvard University President A. Lawrence Lowell. During the period of elite college retrenchment, Lowell was the only leader to bluntly justify the policy in public. His remarks were briefly scandalous, generating criticism that did not prevent the college from moving ahead.[43] It is revealing of the complex subtlety of civil contradiction that, in confronting his critics, Lowell justified anti-Jewish restrictions as a means to the end of eliminating anti-Semitic prejudice itself. Anti-Semitic feeling among Harvard students, Lowell remarked to concerned alumni, grew in response to the rising influx of Jews. "If every college in the country," he reasoned, would just decide to "take a limited proportion of Jews," then "we should go a long way toward eliminating race feeling among the students, and, as these students passed out into the world, eliminating it in the community." The Harvard president was presenting anti-Semitic restrictions as if they were a strategy for civil repair: "If we do nothing about the matter the prejudice is likely to increase."[44]

By the early 1920s, Jewish matriculation in the nation's elite universities had been pushed back to single-digit figures. It was not only in universities, however, that strenuous efforts were made to put Jews in their place. Christian Americans erected barriers to keep Jews from entering most of the nation's key institutions, and they felt certain that it was the anticivil motives and relations of the Jews themselves that were to blame. Even as the ethnic dimensions of the white core group began to widen—purifying the once-spoiled identities of Irish, Polish, and Italian Catholics from northern, eastern, and southern Europe—the Jewish/Christian split remained entrenched. In the 1920s and '30s, factual and fictional communicative institutions could comfortably project anti-Semitic stereotypes, and social movements and political figures could gain powerful support by linking their opponents to polluted Jewish images and themes.[45]

Anticivil Exclusions from Economic Life

The regulative institutions of American civil society were so distorted that extraordinary economic restrictions on Jews were given full rein. In 1938, the American Jewish Congress published a detailed empirical study of Jewish "non-employment" in New York City, which among all the world's urban areas held the largest number of Jews.[46] The report spoke of the "slowly evolving and now fearfully widespread ranges of economic discrimination."[47] Commission investigators, many of whom were Gentiles, found that economic power-holders were not "reticent in admitting" the scope and effect of anti-Jewish feeling. Interviews with employment agency managers, for example, revealed that "all of them granted that anti-Jewish prejudice is very high." One agency reported that "no applications from Jews were accepted," and another explained that "many companies they serve would not consider a Jewish applicant."[48] Scouring the documents submitted by more than four hundred New York firms, researchers found that almost 90 percent declared that they "preferred Christians."[49] The New York Telephone company went so far as to instruct its recruiters "not to interview Jewish students"[50] at the region's leading technical schools.

The line of causality runs here from civil to economic position. It was not that economic powers were defending their material interests in the face of economic competition; they were defending their thoughts and feelings in an economic way. It is because they constructed Jews as anticivil that they believed them to be unfit for economic life. According to the commission report, employers "point to such objectionable traits as loudness, lack of good breeding, a tendency toward insubordination, aggressiveness, overweening ambition, clannishness, and unscrupulousness." These "characteristics" are cited as demanding Jewish "exclusion from employment on sound principles of personnel management."[51]

The contradictions of the assimilative mode of incorporation are here on full display. It is because the *qualities* of Jewishness are so polluted that the *persons* of Jews do not receive the recognition, and allowed the liberties, that their formal status as members of civil society would imply. Economic life is not only instrumental. It depends on relationships of trust and solidarity, and thus on constructions of the motives and relations of putative others in the civil sphere. Success in the labor market depends on noneconomic ties, even if they are "weak" rather than "strong,"[52] and fragmentation in the civil sphere will reproduce itself by stratifying the economic. The commission put this interdependence in commonsense terms.

There is a direct connection between social and economic discrimination. Countless persons owe their past and present economic opportunities to contacts made in social situations. Jews are largely, if not wholly, excluded by Christians from sharing a common social life.[53]

Just Fate or Dangerous Exclusion?

This interwar extrusion of the Jews from the American civil sphere might well have continued for a very long time. Premonitions of permanent subordination informed the resigned remarks by Harry Austryn Wolfson in the widely read pamphlet, "Escaping Judaism," that he addressed to Jewish college students in 1922. Wolfson, who held the first chair in Judaic studies at Harvard, analogized the quality of Jewishness with the stigma of physical deformity: "All men are not born equal. Some are born blind, some deaf, some lame, and some are born Jews." Just as those suffering from such incurable handicaps "have to forgo many a good thing of life," he lamented, so "to be isolated, to be deprived of many social goods and advantages, is our common lot as Jews." Even in that early postwar period, the American situation seemed so hopeless that Wolfson pleaded with Jewish students to "submit to fate" rather than "foolishly struggle against it."[54] Sixteen years later, the author of *Jews, Jobs, and Discrimination* betrayed similar worries. "Regardless of all personal qualities," Jacob X. Cohen lamented, "Jewishness throws one into a lower caste." It seems that nothing can save the Jew except leaving his religion behind. Cohen observes that "in an effort to traverse the vicious barrier many consciously and systematically drop Jewish associations."[55]

How different was this from the Jewish condition in Europe in the middle of the preceding century, when the doors opened by Enlightenment and emancipation were slammed shut by the continuing primordial restrictiveness of Christian civil society?[56] Among American Jews there was, in fact, a massive effort to flee their religious fate. Throughout these decades, ambitious American Jews changed their names, dropped their Jewish friendships, became Unitarians, or started attending a Christian church. Cohen makes pointed reference to such "twentieth-century Marranos" and describes these American *conversos* as living "in dread of discovery."

After 1933, when the Nazis seized power in Germany, some influential members of the American core group began to see anti-Jewish domination in a critical new light.[57] Protests against Jewish exclusion, of course, had always sought to frame it as antidemocratic and un-American. However, as the military ambitions of Hitler became more evident, America's homegrown anti-Jewish practices were increasingly presented as threatening the very survival of the American state. In 1938, on the first page of *Jews, Jobs, and Discrimination*, Cohen framed his findings in a manner that implicitly analogized American practices with Nazi Germany. "Many discriminatory employers," he reported, "feel that for an establishment to be *Judenrein* [Jewish free] is a kind of tangible asset."[58]

The extent of this new concern was demonstrated by the decision of the editors of *Fortune* magazine to devote a special section in their February

1936 issue to the topic of "Jews in America."[59] Straddling the sensitive boundary between market and civil sphere, *Fortune* was a critical communicative institution in American civil society. It was owned by Time Inc., whose publisher, Henry Luce, the son of Christian missionaries, had been educated at Yale. *Fortune's* editors began with the observation that "the 'Jewish Problem' has become violently acute in recent years." "Faced with the unbelievable record of Nazi barbarities," they asserted, "any man who loathes Fascism will fear anti-Semitism." Reassuring their readers that America was, indeed, fundamentally different than its anticivil enemies, *Fortune's* editors distinguished prejudice from anti-Semitism. Though they acknowledged that the former was present in America, they insisted that the latter was exclusively "German in manufacture," as could be seen "in the light of Hitler's career." Yet the manner by which this leading business magazine chose to validate its assertion that America was not anti-Semitic seemed actually to demonstrate that the opposite was the case.

The journalistic ambition of this special issue was to challenge the factual accuracy of anti-Semitic claims that some overreaching Jewish conspiracy controlled America's economic life: "The fact is this. . . . There is no basis whatever for the suggestion that Jews monopolize U.S. business and industry." The manner and tone of the report reveal, however, that anti-Semitism in American was actually alive and well. *Fortune's* reporting assuaged its fearful Christian readers by claiming to have unearthed facts that "were totally unexpected . . . by non-Jews." The magazine's reporters discovered that from heavy industry to banking, from the learned professions of law and medicine to high judicial and political office, the key American institutions had virtually no Jewish imprint at all. The manner in which such assurances eerily echoed the Nazi ambition of making German institutions *Judenrein* was an irony that escaped *Fortune's* editors, who breathlessly repeated their findings about American institutions being Jewish free.

> They do not run banking. They play little or no part in the great commercial houses. . . . The absence of Jews in the insurance business is noteworthy. . . . They have an even more inconspicuous place in heavy industry. . . . The coal industry is almost entirely non-Jewish. . . . Rubber is another non-Jewish industry. . . . Shipping and transportation are equally non-Jewish.

If Jews were so absent, what then was the problem? It was the attitudes of Jews themselves. According to *Fortune*'s editors, Jews have "notoriously" tended "to agglomerate." In the few industries and professions open to them, they could be seen "clannishly crowding together." Faced with such behavior, "the non-Jew . . . is more than ever impressed with the exotic character of this unusual people." The "true difference" between Jewish and non-Jewish Americans is "cultural." It has to do with civility. Because of centuries of mistreatment, Jews have "the underlying feeling of foreignness." Ever the eternal "stranger," they are so enmeshed in their particularity that they reject participation and inclusion in the civil sphere.

> All other immigrant peoples accept the culture of the country into which they come. The Jews for centuries have refused to accept it and are now, in any case, unable to accept it when they would.

It is because of this Jewish refusal of American civil society, according to *Fortune*, that Nazism remained a threat to the American state, for such narrow clannishness confirmed the paranoia of anti-Semites. "Granted," the editors acknowledge, "there is a strong reason . . . for believing that Fascism can be defeated in this country;" nonetheless, "it still remains true that the future of the Jew in America is puzzling." The critical question is this: "Can the universal stranger be absorbed in the country which has absorbed every other European stock?" The question can be answered affirmatively only if Jews become more civil. "The first condition of their success will be the quieting of Jewish apprehensiveness and the consequent elimination of the aggressive and occasionally provocative Jewish defensive measures." It was not enough for *Fortune*'s putatively rational non-Jewish editors to refute the paranoia of anti-Semites. Jews themselves would have to be changed. A century and half after the Enlightenment, in the nation that saw itself as the open and democratic alternative to Europe, one hears the echoes of Christian von Dohm.

Responding to Nazism and Holocaust: America's Decision to Be "With the Jews"

In less than one decade, this situation changed remarkably. Though in 1945 the vast majority of American Jews continued to live, work, and communicate in strongly segregated primordial communities, there began a seismic shift in civil discourse, one that eventually resulted in major institutional change. Despite the continuing strength of anti-Jewish feeling in right-wing groups, feelings that fueled the anticommunist hysteria of the McCarthy years, by the mid-1950s Jews and mainstream Gentiles alike came to believe that the Jewish dream of hyphenated incorporation into American society was becoming a reality. By the early 1960s, Jews were postwar America's newly favorite ethnic group. In the decades following, Jewishness was constructed, not only by cultural elites but their mass audiences, as a widely admired and distinctive quality of American civil life.

What caused this transformation was not some developmental process triggered by the modernization of American society, much less the modernization of its Jews. The civil sphere does not expand in an evolutionary way, any more than how and whom it excludes is determined in advance. Whether and how the ideals of civil society are instantiated is an open question, a contingent matter of historical, not genetic time. What changed the civil status of America Jews was an unexpected and deeply unwanted military confrontation, one whose repercussions on American civil society could scarcely have been foreseen.

When the United States entered the battle against German, Japanese, and Italian fascism, the anti-Jewish restrictions on American civil society remained fully in force.[60] In order to legitimate this bloody and ferocious struggle, however, the United States had to proclaim itself a healthy civil society. As our earlier discussion has suggested, while the war was actually being conducted, this idealizing nationalist discussion could not be extended explicitly to the nation's Jews. Indeed, during the first three years of American fighting, with the ultimate battle against Nazism in doubt, anti-Semitic feelings actually rose in strength.[61] It was only after the war's conclusion that the American nation began to repair the civil status of Jews. Neither the victory nor postwar geopolitics made the difference. It was the now unavoidable and extraordinarily weighted knowledge that the principal American enemy in that wartime battle, the German Nazis, had had as their own principal enemy the Jews.

Revelations of the Nazi concentration camps, transmitted with graphic immediacy by communicative institutions, created shock waves that reverberated among core groups of American civil society. As with Christian and secular core groups in Europe, these images of massive and systematic murder

forced into public view the ugliest underside of civil life and strongly contradicted its idealizations. These challenges were handled differently in the
postwar Western democracies. What every reaction shared, however, was
the tendency to deflect responsibility for anti-Semitic exclusion away from
the nation as such to social actors that were more narrowly defined, to more
marginal groups that had been directly or indirectly associated with the Nazi
movement. In Germany, as Bernhard Giesen has shown, this meant blaming
the "deranged" and "abnormal" vanguard group directly associated with the
Fuhrer himself.[62] In France, it meant accusing only those who publicly had
collaborated, the relatively small group of "anti-French" leaders of Vichy.[63]
In both the German and the French cases, this deflection of responsibility
away from national core groups had the corollary effect of making the Jewish
question external, and largely irrelevant, to the postwar reconstruction of
those national societies.

Like Europeans, Americans interpreted the mass murder of Jews as the
logical result of anti-Semitism in particular and anticivil prejudice in general,
and they, too, employed narratives forged in wartime to project blame far
away from themselves.[64] What differed in the American case was that this
interpretation also became, paradoxically, the foundation for reconsidering
the Jewish question inside of American society itself.

In the face of revelations of anti-Jewish mass murder, American core-
group leaders rejected any possible similarities between the anti-Semitic
German nation and their own. To take responsibility for the American
history of anti-Semitism, to engage in self-critical recognition and repudiation, would have equated the sacred discourse of American civil society
with the degraded impurity of its defeated German enemy. To have allowed
such a juxtaposition would have been culturally incoherent.[65] It would have
challenged a wartime identity constructed in the fiery cauldron of sacrifice.
Nazism had been narrated as the "dominant evil of our time," its barbarism
and violence represented most distinctively in terms of racial and religious
hate. That Nazism embodied the very paradigm of anticivil evil had formed
the presupposition of America's four-year prosecution of the world war.
After the prosecution was successful, only one symbolic logic made sense:
postwar American society must be defined in relation to anti-Semitism in
the same manner as the American war effort had been oriented to Nazi
Germany.[66]

According to such cultural reasoning, anti-Semitism now became the enemy of Americanism. Faced with the revelations of what would eventually be represented as the Holocaust, Americans transformed their deeply anti-Nazi feelings into "anti–anti-Semitism."[67] During wartime, the American horror of Nazism had little explicit connection with the nation's domestic religious strife; the horror had been connected, instead, to civil values and primordial antipathies of a nonreligious kind. In the postwar period, the profane symbols that silhouetted the sacred national identity changed. The anti-Nazi repulsion became enlarged to include, and eventually to center upon, a horror for those who hated Jews, and these necessarily included not only Europeans who hated Jews but Americans as well.[68]

Americans came to believe that being "against the Nazis" necessarily meant being "with the Jews." In France and Germany, such an identification could not be made. Important members of core groups in Continental Europe had themselves directly or indirectly collaborated with anti-Jewish murderers. In order retrospectively to insulate their recovering, post-Nazi national identities from such polluting association, such groups had to separate themselves entirely from the Jewish question in the postwar period.[69] It was possible for Americans, by contrast, to view themselves in a sharply different way. Because they did not perceive themselves, and were not perceived by others, as even indirectly associated with Nazi collaboration, Americans could enter the postwar period by embracing rather than separating themselves from the Jewish question. Indeed, in order powerfully to project their wartime collective identity into the postwar period—to adapt and sustain the high national morale of cultural and social triumph—Americans actually felt compelled to embrace the Jews.

Beyond the Assimilative Dilemma: The Postwar Project of Jewish Ethnicity

This complex, historically contingent chain of reactions opened up the possibility for redefining the social relationships between Christian and Jewish Americans. Vis-à-vis the Jewish question, it created, for the first time in the history of Western civil societies, the conditions for transcending the asymmetries of assimilation.[70] The private antipathy toward Jewish qualities that had long distorted the civil orientations of American life began to dissipate; explicit expressions of anti-Semitism were publicly condemned and began gradually but persistently to disappear. Only days after the cessation of hostilities in World War II, in response to an appeal from the National Council of Christians and Jews, the three candidates for mayor in New York City pledged to "refrain from appeals to racial and religious divisiveness during the campaign." One of them made explicit the connections of this public anti–anti-Semitism to the meaning of America's triumph in the anti-Nazi war, and the *New York Times* published this appeal.

> This election will be the first held in the City of New York since our victory over Nazism and Japanese fascism. It will therefore be an occasion for a practical demonstration of democracy in action— a democracy in which all are equal citizens, in which there is not and never must be a second-class citizenship and in which . . . the religion of a candidate must play no part in the campaign.[71]

Progress toward establishing civil relations between Christian Americans and Jews was woven into the patriotic postwar narratives projected by the fictional and factual media of communication.[72] In the 1945 box-office hit *Pride of the Marines*, the Jewish protagonist chides his friends for their pessimism about eliminating postwar prejudice. He cites the ideals that had sustained their fighting during the anti-Nazi war: "Ah, come on, climb out of your foxholes, what's a matter you guys, don't you think anybody learned anything since 1930?"[73] Later, as the film's closing music turns into "America the Beautiful," the hero comes back to the link between the anti-Nazi fight and postwar civil repair: "Don't tell me we can't make it work in peace like we do in war. Don't tell me we can't pull together. Don't you see it guys, don't you see it?" *Better Homes and Gardens*, a magazine central to the domestic space of middle- and upper-class housewives, framed civil repair of the Jewish question in a similar way. Its 1947 feature titled "Do You Want Your Children to Be Tolerant?" proclaimed that "the old indifference and local absorption cannot continue" and warned that Americans must not "relapse into our before-the-war attitudes and limitations."[74] In a *Better Homes* story later that year, "How to Stop the Hate Mongers in Your Home Town," the writer observed "I suspect that many a decent German burgher, hearing tales of Nazi gangs, likewise shrugged off the implications of uncurbed racial and religious persecution."[75] That same year, a movie promoting anti–anti-Semitism, *Gentleman's Agreement*, won the Academy Award for best picture, for which another similarly inclined movie, *Crossfire*, had been nominated as well. Explaining the success of *Gentleman's Agreement*, the *Saturday Review of Literature* asserted that "the Jewish people are the world symbol of [the] evil that is tearing civilization apart," suggesting that the film's success "may mean that the conscience of America is awakening."[76] In the year following, the *Saturday Evening Post* profiled "the story of the Jewish family Jacob Golomb." Describing the Golombs as "just nice folks who lead busy, fruitful, decent lives," the writer reported that, despite their being "members of a race with a long history of persecution," the family had "kept their faith" with the belief "that the United States really was, *or would soon be*, the land of the genuinely free."[77] Four years later, America's most popular photo magazine published "*Life* goes to a Bar Mitzvah: A Boy Becomes a Man."[78]

Members of American core groups became interested not so much in allowing Jewish persons to separate from Jewishness as with recognizing the civil legitimacy of Jewishness as such. This core-group movement beyond the narrow restrictions of the assimilative mode of incorporation reflected and triggered shifting orientations among Jewish activist groups. In November 1945, the American Jewish Committee changed not only the name but the mission of its principal publication. The *Contemporary Jewish Record* had spoken to Jews about Jewish things. Its successor, *Commentary*, was given a much broader scope. Encouraged to write broadly about national and international issues and to address a wide civil audience, the magazine became an increasingly influential voice on the American scene.[79] Jewish civil activists now became deeply concerned, moreover, not only with public speech and behavior, but with private opinions and beliefs. Jewish and non-Jewish groups, both private and public, began to turn their attention to the newly emerging communicative institution of public opinion polls. They devoted vast resources to creating and evaluating opinion surveys measuring anti-Jewish feelings and to designing educational campaigns to transform them.[80]

These radical postwar shifts were institutional as well as discursive. By 1950, anti-Jewish quotas had been successfully exposed and often defeated,[81] and deep pathways for continuing civil repair were put into place. For the first time in American history, Jewish groups could publicly mobilize the communicative and regulative institutions of civil society. Jewish civil associations had begun to organize against quotas in the latter part of the war, but they entered the public sphere as aggressive political advocates only in

1945. In the years immediately following, they held news conferences, wrote editorials, and issued detailed proposals for legal and political change. This advocacy was effective because the civil audience was primed. During the same month that New York's mayoral candidates announced their anti–anti-Semitism, the *American Mercury*, a leading popular magazine, published an article, "Discrimination in Medical Colleges."[82] The story was replete with graphs and copious documentation, but the facts of anti-Semitic practices had, of course, already been well known for a long time. What changed now was its public representation. This mass magazine declared the behavior of the nation's elite medical institutions to be "spurious" when judged according to "democratic or sheerly human" criteria, denouncing such practices as "un-American." A few months earlier, when the president of Amherst College publicly defended Jewish quotas in college admissions, the *New Republic* responded that "we can no longer afford the luxury of these obsolete myths of racial differentiation," adding "if you don't believe it, ask Hitler."[83] In 1949, *Collier's* magazine devoted a story to the practice of restricting fraternity membership to "full-blooded Aryans." They reported that for "scores of college men" such restrictions suggested "a false and undemocratic sense of superiority" that was "a little nauseating in this day." Such reactions explain, according to *Collier's*, why "the anti-discrimination movement is hopping from campus to campus."[84]

This incorporative movement, at once the discursive cause of shifts in civil institutions and their effect, created the conditions for a new hyphenation between "American" and "Jewish," triggering the same kind of search for common values, intertwined roots, and overlapping narratives that, in earlier periods of American history, had marked a newly enshrined ethnic status of non-Jewish European immigrant groups. Less than one week after the Japanese surrendered, on September 2, 1945, judges in Atlantic City awarded the title of "Miss America" to Bess Myerson, a second-generation Jewish woman from the Bronx whose family still spoke Yiddish at home.[85] At the end of that same month, on the last day of the major league baseball season, Hank Greenberg hit a grand-slam home run in the ninth inning that won the pennant for the Detroit Tigers, and with that, Greenberg, the most prominent Jewish athlete of his time, became an American hero as well.[86] In the years that followed, the Zionist effort to create a Jewish state, one that became home to many Jews who had fled anti-Semitic Europe, became identified in the national imagination with the history of America itself, with the founding narrative of the "first new nation" settled by immigrants fleeing from earlier forms of European religious discrimination.[87] The extraordinary success of Leon Uris's novel *Exodus*, which sold four million copies during the 1950s and formed the basis for box office movies, television films, and song, demonstrated and also crystallized this once unlikely convergence of Jewish and American fates.

Alongside this Zionist-American representation of "fighting Jews" who won independence through courage and heroism, there emerged other, equally familiar forms of ethnic sentiment and appreciation. In 1946, an inspirational and upbeat self-help book called *Peace of Mind* raced to the top of the *New York Times* best-seller list, sold more than a million copies, and was translated into ten languages. Its author, a Boston Reform rabbi named Joshua Loth Liebman, offered his readers counseling of a human, not specifically Jewish kind. That Christian Americans would seek "helpful insights about human nature that psychology has discovered" from a Jew who mined "the truest religious insights and goals of the ages" would have been unthinkable in the prewar years.[88] Later, in such best-selling autobiographical memoirs as *Only in America* and *For Two Cents Plain*, Harry Golden, publisher of the *Carolina Israelite*, reconstructed New York's turn-of-the-century "Lower East Side" as a golden era in which Jewish ethnicity was so seamlessly connected with national legend and myth that one historian of postwar America called him the "Jewish Will Rogers."[89] Such sentimental narration provided opportunities for revising Jewish-Christian relationships not only from the Jewish but from the non-Jewish side. *Fiddler on the Roof*, which became one of the longest running musicals in Broadway history, offered a similarly emotional and revisionist representation of Jewish history. Starting from the fiction that immigration to the New World redeemed Old World suffering, *Fiddler* narrated Jewish life in the *shtetls* of anti-Semitic Europe, and even the long-term effects of the pogroms, in an ultimately uplifting and ethnic way.

Yet although this dramatic embrace of hyphenation transformed civil society's relation to the Jewish question, it did not eliminate the asymmetries of incorporation. Even while Judaism was equated with Americanism, it remained subordinated to it. There was still the order of hierarchy, the subtle aura of patronizing benevolence that lay just beneath the surface of American construction of ethnicity. Jewish persons might now be fully admitted into the American mainstream, but there still remained the ever-present danger of appearing "too Jewish."[90] The anthropologist Karen Brodkin recalled, in a bitter but revealing way, how this danger marked her postwar childhood.

> My parents moved to the suburbs in 1949. . . . We lived where Jews had not been allowed to live a few generations earlier. . . . My parents bought me a storybook, *The Happy Family*, where life began in the kitchen and stopped at the borders of the lawn, where Mom, Dad, the kids, and the dog were relentlessly cheerful, and where no one ever raised their voices except to laugh. It was my favorite, and I desperately wanted my family to look like the one in the book. When I became an adolescent, my goal in life became to have a pageboy hairstyle and to own a camel-hair coat, like the pictures in *Seventeen* magazine. I thought of storybook and magazine people as "the blond people," a species for whom life naturally came easily, who inherited happiness as a birthright, and I wanted my family to be like that, to be "normal." My childhood was divided between everybody I knew and the blond people.[91]

In 1959, Ruth Handler, a Jewish woman in Los Angeles, created the Barbie doll, the tall, blond, pug-nosed, buxom, and blue-eyed icon that embodied the primordial WASP stuff that Jews had never been allowed to be.[92]

In the early postwar world of high culture, even as Jewish intellectuals and artists were transforming their once lowly social status, they still felt compelled to transcend the "particularism" of their Jewish identities if they were to succeed. In the 1950s, Jewish persons stood at the center of the American avant-garde, but not *as* Jews; they did so, rather, as carriers, creators, and definers of humanistic culture. Lionel Trilling and his fellow "New York intellectuals" placed the existential idea of authenticity at the center of American civil discussion.[93] During the interwar period, many of these figures had published in the *Menorah Journal,* an assertively "Jewish" publication concerned not only with religious but with social and ethical questions. Yet when Trilling looked back to this earlier participation from the vantage point of the postwar years, he claimed that, for contributors to the *Menorah Journal,* the "idea of Jewishness . . . had nothing to do with religion."

We were not religious. . . . Chiefly our concern with Jewishness was about what is called authenticity, [with] the individual Jewish person recogniz[ing] naturally and easily that he *is* a Jew and 'accepts himself' as such, finding pleasure and taking pride in the identification.[94]

Similar concerns for separating Jewish persons from their qualities were evidenced by a wide range of Jewish writers who became central to the communicative institutions of that time. J. D. Salinger, Norman Mailer, and Saul Bellow fictionalized the new postwar Jewish consciousness in secular narratives that revolved around the tensions between alienation and community, conformity and individuality.[95] Writing as secularized Jewish persons, their art translated historically religious qualities into broad reflections on humanity and modernity as such. In much the same manner did the Jewish social theorist Philip Rieff translate the "true" theoretical significance of Sigmund Freud. The interest in psychoanalysis that inspired so much postwar thinking, Rieff asserted, derived not from the great Jewish thinker's obsession with libido but from his humanistic commitment to the idea of moral responsibility.[96]

As we observed in chapter 18, concerns with alienation and authenticity can be seen as Jewish responses to tensions generated by the asymmetrical bargain of incorporation. Even as Jewish artists were allowed for the first time to move into the very mainstream of a national high culture,[97] these concerns still could not be expressed in anything other than a non-Jewish way. Arthur Miller acknowledged that, after fictionalizing anti-Semitism in his 1945 novel *Focus*, "I gave up the Jews as literary material."[98] In his 1949 play *Death of a Salesman*, which came to be regarded as a classic of twentieth-century American drama, the characters were not recognizably Jewish in any way. When Saul Bellow looked back at his first two novels, The *Dangling Man* (1944) and *The Victim* (1947), he described a different literary reaction but revealed a similar insecurity vis-à-vis mainstream uneasiness with Jewish qualities. Explaining the meticulous, self-consciously Flaubertian style of these early works, as compared to the earthy and melodic language that emerged later in *The Adventures of Augie March* (1953), Bellow acknowledged that he had been "timid" and "felt the incredible effrontery of announcing myself to the world (in part I mean the WASP world) as a writer and an artist." Pointing to his student days in the 1930s, Bellow said, "it was made clear to me when I studied literature in the university that as a Jew and the son of Russian Jews I would probably never have the right feeling for Anglo-Saxon traditions, for English words." His response, in *Dangling Man* and *The Victim*, was that "I had . . . to demonstrate my abilities, pay my respects to formal requirements."[99] It was the same with the newly prominent Jewish comedians. No longer isolated in the Catskills, their routines, no matter how "typically Jewish," were still comedy that never spoke its name.[100] As Herman Wouk graphically suggested in his best-selling 1955 novel, *Marjorie Morningstar*, Jews were not yet truly inside the institutions of America's core groups, and their desperate desire to be so not only underscored their vulnerability but reinforced continuing anti-Semitic frames. Though universities effectively dropped their quotas by the late 1950s and early 1960s, the large corporations and law firms remained segregated religiously for decades after. So did primary relations generally, as revealed by patterns of residence, friendship, and marriage.[101]

All of this underscores the instability of hyphenated incorporation. Because it represents a lessening of antagonism to out-group qualities, it allows the persons who are members of these marginalized groups to gain civil incorporation in a much more substantial way. Still, the orientation to these qualities, while definitely changed, remains highly ambivalent; the qualities are still rank-ordered below those of the core group, even if they can now be productively hyphenated with them. This unevenness prevents incorporation from proceeding in a truly effective and egalitarian manner. The instabilities of hyphenation can be resolved by moving backward toward the narrower terms of the assimilative mode or by legitimating out-group difference in a manner that moves toward multiculturalism. Not only can the instabilities push in either direction, but they can be resolved in different ways for different groups at different times.

Making Jewish Identity Public:
The Multicultural Mode of Jewish Incorporation

In the context of the commitment by American core groups, after Nazism and the Holocaust, to be "with the Jews," and the intense identification of Americanism with Jewishness that flourished in its wake, it should not be entirely surprising that the instabilities of Jewish American incorporation were pushed in a multicultural direction. In fact, Jewish intellectuals and artists were among the first to thrust particularity into the center of the national discussion about integration. At the same time that "Black Power" challenged the incorporative strategies of the Civil Rights movement during the mid-1960s, Jewish intellectuals and artists, and eventually radicalized students as well, began demanding the right to be recognized as different, to be incorporated without changing their identities in any significant way.[102]

Looking back from the vantage point of 1969, the Jewish sociologist Peter Rose suggested that, in the immediate postwar period, "for the majority of Jewish young people, things looked bright and the future even brighter" because "they had made it *into* American Society and, in this sense, they 'had it made,' or, at least, they thought they did."[103] Two decades later, however, Jewish incorporation had taken a new turn: "Few anticipated the day when Christian Americans or, at least, some middle-class Christian Americans, would begin to want to 'think Jewish'—or, at least, think 'thinking Jewish' was in."[104] If thinking Jewish was in, then the mode of incorporation had indeed begun to change; for the first time, the primordial "givens" of civil society could be expressed in a religiously multicultural way. As Rose understood it, in the postwar period "the Jew became everyman"; twenty years later, through "a curious transposition," according to Rose, "everyman became the Jew."[105]

When Charles Stember analyzed his surveys of the American public in 1962, he noted that "anti-Semitism in all its forms" had "massively declined in the United States," that "significantly fewer people than formerly believed that Jews as a group had distinctive undesirable traits" or "thought Jews were clannish, dishonest, unscrupulous."[106] Stember went beyond his data, however, when he went on to interpret these findings as evidence that Americans now viewed Jews as not "having any distinctive traits or characteristics at all, whether bad or good."[107] The discourse of civil society is binary. Rather than becoming unmarked, Jewish qualities had moved from the polluted and repressive to the purified and liberating side.

By the early and middle 1960s, being "with the Jews" shifted from anti-anti-Semitism to philo-Semitism. Rather than simply being open to full civil participation by Jewish persons and tolerating Jewish qualities, Christian Americans began to find Jewish qualities attractive in themselves. American primordiality was being opened to "Jewishness." In the nation's elite popular culture, in matters of emotion, ideas, and aesthetics, communicative institutions played the chords of civil discourse in a new key. In 1966, in "Notes on Cult: or, How to Join the Intellectual Establishment" in the *New York Times Magazine*, Victor Navasky jokingly assured his readers that "rumors to the contrary notwithstanding, you don't have to be Jewish to be an intellectual."[108] In 1968 in the *Atlantic*, Calvin Trillin published an apocryphal story about a thoroughly assimilated Jewish American named Lester Drentluss, who comes to realize, during the course of the 1960s, that he is not, in public terms, nearly "Jewish" enough.

> Although Lester was Jewish, he felt left out. [H]e began to spot some signs of a trend . . . a boom in Jewish novels here, a Jewish Lord Mayor of Dublin there. He noticed an increasing use of Jewish mothers by comedians and of Jewish advisers by politicians. Scotch-Irish professors seemed undisturbed about being included in the category of "Jewish intellectuals." The gentile movie stars who failed to convert to Judaism repented by donating their talents to Bonds for Israel benefits. The subway graffiti had begun to include phrases like "Media Is a Yenta" and "Kafka Is a Kevetch." Lester's final decision came in February, 1965, while he was reading an article in *Life* magazine about Robert Lowell, the New England poet. "Do I feel left-out in a Jewish age?" Lowell was quoted as saying. "Not at all. Fortunately, I'm one-eighth Jewish myself, which I do feel is a saving grace." . . . Robert Lowell had been right; it was a Jewish world.[109]

Shifts in popular culture echoed, and also triggered, these high cultural themes. When Barbra Streisand asked, in her 1968 hit film *Funny Girl*, "is a nose with deviations a crime against the nation?" it was understood as a rhetorical question: her conspicuous "Jewish nose" had by that time become an object of admiration, if not beauty, for millions of her non-Jewish fans.[110] New and powerful tropes emerged about Jewish openness and warmth. The most striking were representations of an endearing "Jewish mother" who embodied a sometimes overwhelming physical and emotional indulgence, parenting qualities that were taken as notably lacking in the culture of America's WASP core group. The 1964 best-seller that brought this trope into the popular imagination was Dan Greenberg's *How To Be a Jewish Mother: A Very Lovely Training Manual*.[111] In this new emotional context, the prohibitions against Jews as neighbors and marriage partners, which Christian Americans had upheld for centuries, were rapidly fading.[112] An African American comedienne, Caryn Johnson, changed her stage name to Whoopi Goldberg, thinking, quite rightly it turned out, that such a public transformation would be of real benefit to her career.[113]

I will examine this new situation in more detail by focusing on the unprecedented Jewish self-representations created by a novelist, Philip Roth, and a filmmaker, Woody Allen. After considering the wider effects of these symbolic constructions, I will return, in conclusion, to the repercussions of multiculturalism on the Jewish community itself, and how this new mode of incorporation brought a new set of tensions in its wake.

Making the Good Jew "Bad": Philip Roth's Confidence

By his own construction at least, the literary career and real life of Philip Roth present a mirror of the changing Jewish position in American society, both in the sense of reflecting it and providing an opportunity for reflection upon it.[114] Growing up in a Jewish neighborhood in Newark, New Jersey, in the 1930s and '40s, Roth experienced the near-total segregation of primary relationships and the radical disjunction of private and public life that characterized American Jewish efforts at incorporation in the assimilative mode. In *I Married a Communist* (1999), Roth's Jewish narrator, Ira Ringold, recalls the repulsion for Jewish qualities that permeated this period. He does so via a retrospective account of *Focus*, the now largely forgotten novel published by Arthur Miller in 1945. In Roth's retelling, Miller's story concerned the fate of "a cautious, anxiety-ridden conformist" named Mr. Newman. A Gentile who worked as a personnel officer in a big New York corporation, Newman is "too cautious to become actively the racial and religious bigot he is secretly in his heart." After Newman is fitted for a new pair of glasses, however, he confronts an experience that reveals, to employ terms drawn from the present discussion, how the hatred for Jewish qualities effectively prevented the civil incorporation of Jewish persons.

> After Mr. Newman is fitted for his first pair of glasses, he discovers that they set off "the Semitic prominence of his nose" and make him dangerously resemble a Jew. And not just to himself. When his

crippled old mother sees her son in his new glasses, she laughs and says, "why, you almost look like a Jew." When he turns up at work in the glasses, the response to his transformation is not so benign: he is abruptly demoted from his visible position in personnel to a lowly job as a clerk, a job from which Mr. Newman resigns in humiliation. From that moment on, he who himself despises Jews for their looks, their odors, their meanness, their avarice, their bad manners, even for "their sensuous lust for women," is marked as a Jew everywhere he goes.[115]

As Roth has told the story both in fiction and in fact, when he left Newark to enroll at Bucknell University, at the end of the 1940s, and later for graduate work in writing at the universities of Iowa and Chicago, he was making a sociological transition, not only a geographical one, entering a nonreligious world of "humanistic" learning that promised the opportunity of escaping from his particularistic and segregated roots. As an aspiring writer, he majored in English literature, becoming a follower of the Trillings and Bellows of the postwar period. In *Letting Go* (1962), his first novel after the short story collection *Good-bye Columbus* (1959), Roth displayed the sophisticated irony and distancing tone that distinguished the newly arrived, highly influential Jewish intellectuals in that hyphenated time. By the novel's conclusion, however, when Roth's protagonist tells his mentor, an established older writer, that he finally has found his "voice" as a novelist, Roth is announcing his transition to a different kind of Jewishness, to a much more explicit, robust, and complex public representation of Jewish life. In the controversial stories that culminated in his 1969 novel, *Portnoy's Complaint*, and in the string of books he published from *The Breast* (1972) to *The Anatomy Lesson* (1981) and *Zuckerman Bound* (1985), Roth projected a Jewish voice that had never been heard before.[116] Introducing both a new kind of Jewish character and a new kind of Jewish author—which seem, for Roth, invariably intertwined—Roth's fictional constructions of core and outgroup relations marked the transition to what later would be called the politics of difference.

The Roth author-character was brash, vulgar, assertive—in a word, decidedly uncivilized. Most important, he was openly, sometimes revoltingly "Jewish" in an often self- and group-demeaning, thoroughly public way. Alexander Portnoy's accusing self-pitying takes up the whole of *Portnoy's*

Complaint, which is one long, first-person *spiel* from Portnoy's prone position on his psychoanalyst's couch. On the surface, Portnoy's life looks rosy. He is well educated, has a devoted family, and at thirty-three has a promising and respectable position. Yet rather than feel grateful to his Jewish mother and appreciative of his loving family, Portnoy feels fear and loathing toward them, certain they are responsible for all his personal torments and travails. He lashes out at his overbearing mother as castrating and at his "Philistine" father as weak, accusing them of being "the outstanding producers of guilt in our time!" Linking the guilt he suffers from compulsive masturbation to the historic crimes against the Jewish people, Portnoy asserts the former, not the latter, to be a much more significant and proximate source of his pain.

> Who made us so morbid and hysterical and weak. . . . Is this the Jewish suffering I used to hear so much about? Is this what has come down to me from the pogroms, the persecution? From the mockery and abuse bestowed by the goyim over these two thousand lonely years?[117]

Rather than present his characters' Jewishness through the lens of some suprareligious shared humanity—the strategy that inspires Bellow's great middle period work—Roth's protagonists achieve their humanity via their intense and contradictory Jewishness. *Portnoy* took Roth almost ten years to complete, with several fragments and partially completed manuscripts strewn along the way. He would later write that he was not able to complete the novel "until I found, in the person of a troubled analysand [Alexander Portnoy], the voice that could speak in behalf of both the 'Jewboy' (with all that word signifies to Jew and Gentile alike about aggression, appetite, and marginality), and the 'nice Jewish boy' (and what that epithet implies about repression, respectability, and social acceptance)."[118]

In many quarters, *Portnoy* was accorded an immensely enthusiastic reception, with a biographical spread in *Life* before publication, talk show appearances after, and applause in high-toned reviews along the way. Critics praised Roth for continuing the radical thrust of modernism by exposing private, previously hidden and repressed thoughts and desires, for bringing the private self into the literary public sphere. Inside the Jewish community, however, Roth's effort to reconfigure the line between public and private was viewed in an entirely different way. His new Jewish voice, aesthetic ambitions, even his religious credentials were harshly, sometimes violently criticized. In the United States, in an essay widely read in the Jewish community, one reviewer claimed that "anti-Jewish stereotype" was at the core of Roth's book, and asserted that "there is little to choose" between "Roth's interpretation of what animates Portnoy" and "what the Nazis call *rassenschande* (racial defilement)," that Roth's construction of his protagonist was "straight out of the Goebbels-Streicher script."[119] In Israel, Gershon Sholem, a widely admired cultural historian of medieval Jewry, published an essay attacking *Portnoy* as "the book for which all anti-Semites have been praying." At the "center" of "Roth's revolting book," Sholem fulminated, "stands the loathsome figure whom the anti-Semites have conjured in their imagination and portrayed in their literature."[120]

Roth responded to his Jewish critics with a series of searching essays that illuminated the relationship between his fictional representations and the ambiguous, rapidly changing civil status of American Jews.[121] As Roth understood the Jewish community's charges against him, he was accused of having committed the sin of informing on the private, usually hidden worlds of Jewish life.

> I had informed on the Jews. I had told the Gentiles what apparently it would otherwise have been possible to keep secret from them: that the perils of human nature afflict the members of our minority.[122]

The not entirely pristine perils of their own human natures—the complex, often down-and-dirty realities of motive and desire—were precisely what assimilating Jews had always tried to keep from public view in their ongoing effort at self-change. Undergoing "the ordeal of civility,"[123] Jews had felt compelled to present themselves as wholly and completely capable of performing the exacting exercises in rationality, self-control, and other-oriented moral obligation required for participation in civic life. Roth argues that, even in the postwar war decades of Jewish hyphenation, America's most influential Jewish writers distorted their fictional reconstructions of human motives and relations under the constraint of this civilizing imperative. "The Jew in the post-holocaust decades," he wrote in 1974, "has been identified in American fiction with righteousness and restraint, with the just and measured response rather than with those libidinous and aggressive activities that border on the socially acceptable."[124] Roth saw his fiction as violating this unwritten civilizing constraint on Jewish self-presentation. It was for this reason, he believes, that he had been so vehemently ostracized from the Jewish community:

> Going wild in public is the last thing in the world that a Jew is expected to do—by himself, by his family, by his fellow Jews, and by the larger community of Christians whose tolerance for him is often tenuous to begin with, and whose code of respectability he flaunts or violates at his own psychological risk, and perhaps at the risk of his fellow Jews' physical and social well-being.[125]

In his own defense, Roth evokes both moral and aesthetic criteria. For the first time in American history, he suggests, it is not only possible but necessary for the true Jewish self, the self that assimilation and even hyphenation had made private and invisible, to make its noisy and distinctive appearance on the public stage. He starts with the aesthetic criteria of modernism itself. Citing Trilling's own protest against mass society's "acculturation of the anti-cultural," Roth justifies his iconoclasm in general social and artistic, rather than religious or ethnic, terms. He describes it as providing an alternative to "that deadening 'tolerance' that robs—and is designed to rob—those who differ, diverge, or rebel of their powers."[126] Fiction does not help people be "upright citizens," Roth argues; neither is it designed to "guarantee the appropriateness of our feelings" or to "affirm the principles and beliefs that everybody holds."[127] What distinguishes such art is precisely that it frees the self from such "circumscriptions that society places upon feeling," allowing the self "to experience in ways not always available in day-to-day conduct; or, if they are available, they are not possible, or manageable, or legal, or advisable."[128]

Whatever the truth of these aesthetic observations, it seems safe to say that, for Roth, they ultimately gain their power for reasons closer to home. Roth's most sustained and compelling response to his Jewish critics is not about art or even the responsibilities of the artist. It is about the obligations of the Jewish artist in the context of what Roth regards as the drastically transformed position of American Jews. Drawing a sharp contrast between the experience of his own generation of Jewish Americans and the older generation of assimilating and hyphenating American Jews, Roth makes the large claim that, in contemporary American society, Jews no longer need to change themselves, or even the public image of themselves. Roth charges that his critics in the Jewish community are "ashamed of what I see no reason to be ashamed of, and defensive where there is no cause for defense."[129] It is precisely because he is not ashamed or defensive about Jewish qualities, precisely because he does not accept the need to distance these qualities from Jewish persons, that Roth has insisted on making his complex and ambivalent protagonists flamboyantly and, for many, disturbingly Jewish.[130] Criticized for identifying one of his early characters, a misanthropic and self-seeking Army sergeant, as a Jew, Roth acknowledges that the character's "moral complexities are not exclusively a Jew's," but he asserts, nonetheless, "I never for a moment considered that the characters in the story should be anything other than Jews."[131]

Roth links his aesthetic commitment to the public presentation of Jewish qualities to the sociological transformation of Jewish incorporation. He accuses his Jewish critics of thinking in terms of an outdated, traditional model of Jewish-Gentile relations, in terms of a pre-Holocaust world that has largely disappeared. Failing to recognize "the success of the struggle against the defamation of Jewish character in this country," Roth asserts, his Jewish critics cannot accept the fact that "neither defamation or persecution are what they were elsewhere in the past."[132] In a 1961 speech at Loyola University in Chicago, a leading Jesuit institution, Roth ruefully presents his own perception of the times in which Jews live: "I find that I am suddenly living in a country in which the Jew has come to be—or is allowed for now to think he is—a cultural hero."[133]

In the context of this astonishing recognition by American popular culture, Roth believes that it is no longer necessary for Jews to worry about "putting on a good face."[134] If not only Jewish persons but Jewish qualities are purified, why should the putatively anticivil motives of Jewish people be hidden? Indeed, Roth claims that only by presenting Jewish idiosyncrasies as sociologically normal—as public—can Jews fight against the "restriction of consciousness as well as communication" that anti-Semitism still can create.[135] Only by being themselves in public—not only a Jew at home but a Jew in the street—can Jews participate fully in the world of civil communication that characterizes democratic societies. This, of course, was the utopian promise offered by the early Christian and Jewish civic reformers.

What Roth understands is that it could be made good only by rejecting the asymmetrical bargain they had earlier undertaken.

The Universality of Jewish Difference: Woody Allen as Cultural Icon

In 1973, in *The Masks Jews Wear*, Eugene Borowitz made an observation that seemed to confirm the wisdom of Philip Roth's choice to go public with the once-denigrated qualities of Jewish life.

> Today [humanity] needs people who are creatively alienated. To be satisfied in our situation is either to have bad values or to understand grossly what [persons] can do. . . . Creative alienation implies sufficient withdrawal from our society to judge it critically, but also the way and flexibility to keep finding and trying ways of correcting it. I think Jewishness offers a unique means of gaining and maintaining such creative alienation. This was not its primary role in the lives of our parents and grandparents.[136]

Whether, in fact, creative alienation has anything specifically to do with Judaism or Jewishness is not our concern here. What does hold our interest is Borowitz's claim that a specifically Jewish quality, now positively represented by the liberating discourse of civil society, can and should become a universal aspiration for the broader non-Jewish world—for "humanity." In making this claim, Borowitz registers the same sense of historical transition as Philip Roth, and derives from it the same confidence. Roth would undoubtedly have found the term "creative alienation" soporific and the idea of its contributing to the American ethos conventional and cloying. Still, Borowitz's prescription of the Jewish experience as a therapeutic tonic for non-Jewish America echoes Roth's insistence that Jewish dissimulation should be a thing of a past and that the aesthetic representation of Jewish motives and relations can deepen the texture of civil life. In fact, the transparent simplification of Borowitz's proposal puts its sociological implications into sharp relief. Jewish difference can be publicized rather than repressed because, for the first time, it has come to be regarded as a rich and important variation on the universal traits of humankind.

In the latter decades of the twentieth century, Woody Allen's films, and Allen himself, became artistically vivid and socially iconic representations of this transformation in the mode of incorporation, both for Jews and non-Jews alike. What could more powerfully portray the transition from assimilation to multiculturalism than this new and unabashedly conspicuous Jewish figure in the communicative medium that immigrant Jews had created in an effort to hide their particularity behind the gauze of American pastoral?

Woody Allen's comic presentation can be traced directly to the "new Jewish literature" of Mendele and other Jewish writers of the middle and later nineteenth century, to the satiric, despairing, doggedly unsentimental and ironically self-critical genre they created in response to the schizophrenic promises and disappointments of post-emancipation Jewish life.[137] In the interwar period, when American Jews struggled with, and often were defeated by, the dilemmas of assimilation, Jewish comedy was segregated, projecting images into the margin of the mainstream from the Catskills and other specifically Jewish resorts and clubs.[138] In the postwar period of hyphenation, Jewish comedians moved into the center of the communicative institutions of civil society. In the 1950s and early 1960s, the television "comedy hours" of Sid Caesar and Milton Berle provided weekly rituals of family entertainment, and symbolic media for face-to-face civil interaction, for tens of millions of non-Jewish Americans, even as they were hailed by critics for their cutting-edge originality in artistic terms. But this Jewish comedy by Jewish comedians was presented without any explicit reference to their Jewishness as such.

As a high school student, Woody Allen started his professional career by contributing material to these closeted Jewish comedians. When he began writing, directing, and acting in his own movies, however, the mode of presentation dramatically changed. Allen's films are permeated by his public obsession with "the Jewish question" What is a Jew? Are they really different, or is it only Christians who think they are? Does this difference mean that Jews are inferior, that they will inevitably be persecuted and excluded from civil society? Caught in the asymmetries of incorporation, Jews themselves, of course, have always worried about such questions. What made Woody Allen's worries so atypical was that, rather than keeping these anxieties and speculations private and separated, he exhibited them in the public square, and millions of non-Jewish Americans paid to see.[139] In making these once-private Jewish obsessions public, Woody Allen's art broke down the often iniquitous barrier between the civil presentation of a public self and the "true self" of private life. In doing so, he emphatically announced that self-change need no longer be exchanged for Jewish incorporation.

Rather than denying or hiding the stereotypes about Jewish qualities promoted by anti-Semitism, Allen seems, at first glance, to acknowledge their truth. His literary persona is a bundle of weaknesses, uncertainties, and insecurities. He presents himself as besieged by self-deprecating doubts about his masculinity and, if not his intelligence, then his ability to cope in a rational, self-controlled, and competent manner with the relations and institutions of contemporary life. At the same time, however, Woody Allen is never simply the laughable *schlemiel* of Hebrew-Jewish literature or the pathetic and foolish bumbler of anti-Semitic lore. The power of the Woody Allen character is his ability to nudge the distinctive images of Jewish character from the negative into the positive discursive frame. In the midst of laughter and the often intense discomfort produced by the shock of self-recognition, Allen's neurotic self-recrimination morphs into a tolerance for ambiguity, his obsessive doubt into a becoming modesty, the constant questioning of his own commitments into an ironic and mature reflexivity. The Woody Allen figure is not only funny but endearing and wise. His stories portray him as engaged in a *Bildung*, a developmental learning process that increases his competence to understand and to successfully navigate the complexities of modern society. These abilities make his character central, not marginal, to contemporary civic life.[140]

There is no better illustration of this Roth-like duality of self-presentation than *Annie Hall* (1977), an Academy Award–winning film that became powerfully emblematic and influential in matters of speech, fashion, and emotional style for more than a decade. *Annie Hall* is a multicultural transformation on the fable "Jew meets Goy," drawing broadly and graphically upon American religious and ethnic stereotypes even while revising them in a radical way. In the character of Alvy Singer, Allen presents himself as the "typical Jew," speaking obsessively and fearfully about the injuries of his race and anxieties about his character. He meets and falls for Annie Hall, portrayed by Diane Keaton, just after she has arrived in New York City. Tall, thin, light haired and open eyed, Keaton is the prototypical American WASP, as the tortured and hilarious Thanksgiving dinner scene in her small northern Wisconsin hometown reveals, with her grandmother's open anti-Semitism, Allen's visual and visceral fantasies of Jew hatred, and the mutual discomfort of all concerned.

The central concern of *Annie Hall* is the possibility of civil relations between Christians and Jews. The key statement in this regard is Annie's spirited riposte to Alvy, "You're a real Jew!" Until the mid-1960s, such an expressive identification of Jewish particularity would have been purely pejorative, not only to non-Jewish but Jewish ears. It would have communicated the feelings of unease and disgust toward Jewish qualities, and the sense of their separateness, that blocked the extension to Jewish persons of civil solidarity. In Diane Keaton's mouth, however, the expression signifies something entirely different. Woody Allen's Jewish difference is recognized, even emphasized, but it is now a positive identification, a source of admiration, an object even of emulation.

As this hermeneutical transformation suggests, in *Annie Hall* the traditional relation of Jew and non-Jew has been inverted. There is neither the assimilative representation of domination and degradation nor the hyphenated image of sameness and complementarity. The symbolic recoding of Jew and Gentile allows a new narrative to develop, one in which it is the civilized Jew who brings the primitive Gentile into the realm of civic life. It is now the *goyim* who feel stupid and inferior to the Jew, not the other way around. Woody Allen is not simply Diane Keaton's lover but her tutor, her mentor in the intricate learning of things sophisticated. Metaphorically speaking, Allen brings Keaton from Wisconsin, the negative geographical representation of the Christian core group, to New York, a location at once physical and semiotic that is presented, here and elsewhere in Allen's films, in an idealized way. Alvy encourages Annie in her aesthetic interest in photography; he introduces her to the higher intellectual realms of philosophy and classical literature; he sponsors her social mobility by encouraging her to take night-school classes in composition.

In *Annie Hall*, Woody Allen transforms the standard narrative of American civil society not by changing the plot but by changing the religious and cultural identities of its principal characters. The heart of this cinematic *Bildungsroman* is the transition of an innocent from the periphery to center, from provincialism to cosmopolitanism, from particularity to universalism. What has changed in this standard narrative is that it is the Jew who does the *Bildung* and the Gentile who makes the journey.

This valorization of Jewish difference creates something else that is new as well. The psychological end point of Annie's journey is not the standard American version of "health, happiness, and apple pie." Annie is being tutored in a more complex and ambiguous, specifically Jewish kind of knowledge. Sigmund Freud insisted that the goal of psychoanalysis, what anti-Semites called the "Jewish science," is not happiness; its aim, rather, is to substitute for the irrational fantasies of neurosis the realistic unhappiness of normal health. Annie Hall becomes less cheerful as her journey progresses. What she learns is not how to become happy but how to enter more deeply and surely into the problematic and uncertain nature of her self. She begins psychoanalysis, starts writing fiction, and becomes increasingly ironic, skeptical, and wise. In the closing scene, she demonstrates her hard-won reflexivity and intelligence not only by separating from Allen but by offering him emotional advice. Rather than being shattered by this rejection, Allen demonstrates his own deepening maturity by accepting and ruefully reflecting upon it, demonstrating a psychological integrity that even Annie does not yet possess. It is Allen, after all, who has written the story, cast the characters, and created the film. It is Allen, the Jewish character, who provides the film's voiceover narration and who, at critical moments, steps outside the mise-en-scène to explain to us, in his own authoritative words, what is really going on.[141]

In *The Melting Pot* (1908), Israel Zangwill's utopian representation of hyphenated incorporation, the Jewish hero enthusiastically gives up his religious identity to marry his Gentile lover and enter fully into American society. Seven decades later, in *Annie Hall*, the hero confidently maintains his Jewish identity, deploying it not to marry his Gentile lover but to transform her. Rather than move toward traditional Christian-American values, this rite of passage moves into the character and culture of Jewishness. It is the non-Jew, not the Jew, who must give up an earlier identity in order to learn how to enter into the heart of American civil life.[142]

The Dialectic of Differentiation and Identification: A Crisis in American Jewry?

In the multicultural mode of incorporation, difference gains recognition not because it is separate and distinctive per se or because recognition is merited in normative terms, but because core group members have learned to perceive difference as a variation on shared humanity. The identities of once-marginalized groups come to be viewed both as legitimately and importantly different from the core group's and, at the same time, as fundamentally the same. It is for this reason that I have so strongly resisted the notion, suggested by conservative opponents of multiculturalism and radical proponents alike, that multiculturalism produces a less integrated and more divided society. Multiculturalism is a mode of incorporation, not a form of disintegration. In comparison with other modes, it is better able to combine integration and justice: it requires, and helps to produce, thicker and deeper forms of mutual identification and less unfair forms of civil solidarity.

Yet this paradox is what makes the multicultural mode of incorporation unstable in its own way. The instabilities of assimilation and hyphenation have to do with asymmetries of super- and subordination, with sacrificing justice for integration. By widening horizontal solidarity—expanding the primordial symbols through which civil discourse can be expressed—multiculturalism addresses the suppressed vertical strains of hegemonic integration. The process, however, does not produce nirvana, a tranquil equilibrium. By expanding the range of the primordial variation of civil ideals, it produces horizontal rather than vertical strains, highlighting problems of boundary definition and identity. Thematizing cultural issues like meaningfulness and authenticity, the multicultural mode of incorporation makes them criteria for the distribution of resources of a more material kind.

A dialectic of differentiation and identification characterizes multicultural societies. In the contemporary United States, we observe confident assertions of Jewish difference and demands to go beyond the putative blandness of integration, not defensive or aggressive responses to the failure of assimilation or the promises of hyphenation. In terms of religious organization, observant Jews have abandoned almost entirely the assimilative project of religious reform. Not only in Reform but in Conservative synagogues, there has been a marked return to such traditional religious practices as chanting and singing prayers, an upsurge of Hebrew rather than English in religious services, and a new emphasis on ritual observance, not only of Friday-night candle lighting and bread-breaking on *shabat* but of other holy occasions marked in the ancient Hebrew calendar. Among cosmopolitan and highly integrated Jews there has emerged a movement of neo-Orthdoxy that revives some of the most traditional aspects of premodern Jewish life—from living together near *shul* to davenning and dietary laws.[143] When Nathan Glazer published his interpretive sociological treatise *American Judaism* fifty years ago, his prediction that Judaism was well on its way to becoming an ethnic rather than religious identity seemed like a provocative insight that was thoroughly compatible with the evolutionary spirit of the tenets of modernization theory that reigned in that day. Thirty years later, when the now-classic book was revisited by Jewish scholars, it was roundly criticized for not foreseeing such a revival in orthodoxy and religiously Jewish ways. In his introduction to the book's second edition, Glazer remarked, in reference to such criticisms, that "certainly something has happened that was not envisioned in *American Judaism*."[144]

But it is not only the relatively small minority of religiously observant Jews who have demonstrated a new interest in differentiation. The Jewish day schools that have mushroomed throughout American society are more concerned with maintaining a sense of Jewish cultural difference than they are devoted to reviving Jewish religiosity. Throughout the American university system, it has primarily been secular Jews who have pressed for the creation of specifically Jewish studies departments and programs. Before the 1960s, only Salo Baron at Columbia and Harry Wolfson at Harvard directed such programs. In 1945, twelve positions existed in American universities, and in 1965 there were sixty. In 2003, the Association for Jewish Studies in the United States reported some sixteen hundred members.[145] In these university settings, and in all kinds of other secular institutions, observant and nonobservant Jews alike have felt entitled to make public demands for cultural recognition and for institutional attention to their distinctiveness. They expect to be paid when they refuse to work Jewish holidays, whether they actually attend religious services or simply remain at home; they demand the right to dress in traditional ways and the opportunity to eat kosher food in public dining places.

Twenty years ago, Charles Silberman was already drawing attention to "the ease with which Jews now display their Judaism in public." Observing that the mainstream communal organizations of American Jewry were facing criticism for "not being Jewish enough," he pointed to a broad and deep "rediscovery of particularism" among American Jews.[146] It is striking that those participating in this new revival of Jewishness, whether religious or secular, have by and large accepted rather than rejected the pluralism of civil society.[147] This should not be surprising. It was the deeply democratic turbulence of the 1960s that did so much to trigger the multicultural mode of incorporation. If there was a single seedbed event that announced the renewal of Jewish particularity in a public and political way, it was the "new Jews" movement promoted by the largely secular radical students of that day. In 1969, several hundred members of Concerned Jewish Students threatened a sit-in to disrupt the General Assembly of the Council of Jewish Federations. When a spokesman for the student group, Hillel Levine, was given a chance to address the assembly, he denounced its priorities for favoring "a greater mobilization of resources to combat one crack-pot anti-Semite than to deal with the Jewish illiteracy of millions of Jews."[148] In a collective publication that came out of this movement, a prophetic document filled with the apocalyptic spirit of those times, James Sleeper described the "American Jewish community" as undergoing a "spiritual Hiroshima" and decried "the transformation of the Hebrew spirit into an increasingly dispensable appendage of middle-class aesthetics and culture."[149]

When, for the first time in American history, Jews are demanding and succeeding in civil assertions of difference, how is it that that so many influential voices in American Jewry have, in recent decades, expressed anxious concern about the continuing viability, even the bare existence, of Judaism in America? Why has there been such continuous discussion in Jewish magazines and journals about the crisis of Judaism? Why do social scientific students of contemporary Jewish life talk about whether Judaism in America will soon disappear, not only as a viable religion but as a distinctive ethical and ethnic orientation?[150]

It is because of the continuing dialectic between difference and identification. If difference can be recognized only when there is increased solidarity between core and out-group, it should not be surprising that, even as they begin to cultivate their differences, Jewish Americans would come to feel more like non-Jewish Americans and the latter more like them.[151] It is, after all, an increasingly positive evaluation of Jewish qualities that allows incorporation to go beyond the asymmetries of assimilation and hyphenation. In a multicultural setting, the spaces between Jew and non-Jew—institutional, cultural, and interactional—become smaller and more permeable than ever before. Institutionally, Jews have entered the higher echelons of once-segregated law firms and corporations, and they are the executive officers of formerly anti-Semitic elite universities. Culturally, opinion surveys show that Jews "affirm general values that make them virtually indistinguishable from certain sectors of the general public."[152] But it is perhaps in the dramatic shift in intermarriage rates—at the face-to-face, interactional level of civil society—that the effects of the extraordinary transvaluation of Jewish qualities can best be seen. In 1965, less than 10 percent of Jews married non-Jews; thirty years later, slightly more than half were doing so. For pessimistic observers, this remarkable trend set alarm bells ringing about a demographic crisis that could be a "Holocaust of our own making" and would jeopardize the Jewish community's "very survival."[153] The optimists in this demographic-cum-cultural debate, in which camp are included most academic observers, caution that intermarried Jews are not more inclined to abandon Judaism, that the non-Jewish partner often converts to Judaism, and that at least half of the children from intermarriage are raised as Jews.[154]

However the particulars of this argument are ultimately decided, from the perspective of civil society and the Jewish question, the broader implications of this rising tendency for Jewish-Christian intermarriage are clear. What could more clearly signal the positive evaluation of Jewish qualities than the growing Christian interest in marrying Jews? What could more graphically demonstrate how multicultural incorporation points to increasing solidarity, to deepening sentiments of respect and affection between members of core groups and out-groups?[155]

CHAPTER 20

Conclusion:

Civil Society as a Project

I N THIS BOOK, I have presented a new theory of society by defining a
new sphere, its cultural structures, its institutions, and its boundary
relations with discourses and institutions outside it. With this theory, I
have tried to create a new social fact and to examine it empirically in a series
of case studies. If this new theory is productive, and the case studies illuminating, we will better understand our society and ourselves, and we will
see more clearly the possibilities of justice. Nothing is more practical than a
good theory.

For a good part of the last two centuries, many social theorists, activists,
and ordinary persons interested in the project of social improvement have
been preoccupied with a particular form of critical thinking called Marxism
and, more recently, with critical theory. Their concerns have lain less with
thinking through the possibilities of justice broadly construed and the institutions it might necessitate than with justice as it might be realized in the
form of socialism and with the equal distribution of economic resources.

The purpose of this book has been to examine a more fundamental
question, one overlooked in this narrower focus, that has to do with the
foundations of social criticism per se, and I have sought throughout to
broaden our understanding of these foundations. The death of the socialist
dream is not the end of critical thought, deep institutional reform, or cultural

discourse in a utopian vein. It is not this or that institutional form that marks the critical strand of democratic life. Civil solidarity—that is the real utopia. It lies beneath every particular demand for institutional reform, every historically specific demand for cultural reformation. The utopia of a truly civil solidarity informs every manifestation of the restless and critically demanding spirit that marks democratic life. It is the general language of every specific, historically delineated form of reformist speech.

Utopianism is not over. To the contrary, it is being continuously redefined. We do not know where this restless spirit will lead. We cannot guess what new evil the intrusive spirit of civil hermeneutics will interpret and construct next. The civil sphere's utopian discourse is not an entirely free-floating signifier, but neither is it rigidly defined. In the centuries since it assumed a national form, there has never been certainty about where this spirit will alight.

For now at least, the worker-centered dream of dramatically transforming civil society into socialism has faded. In its moderate form, the dream transmogrified into social democracy and reformist liberalism. In its radical form, it was a totalizing vision, a kind of big-bang version of civil repair. It may return again someday in another, less totalizing form, one that is less inclined toward an abstract equality that trumps justice in its other, plural ways. That might be a good thing.

For now, we are living in a world of smaller and more discrete utopian dreams, of family, of conjugal and erotic love, of the kingdom of god on earth, of the perfect market, of equilibrated nature, or a pure liberal state. These are sphere-specific demands, and their advocates often want to be civil-sphere free. Rather than resenting civil injustice, they celebrate and idealize the qualities of noncivil life, sometimes as indispensable facilitating inputs to the good society, often as superior forms of justice in themselves, and it is the civil sphere itself that often seems to intrude. There does, in fact, need always to be adjustments in boundary relations between civil and uncivil spheres. Institutions change. Industrial becomes postindustrial, sex becomes more detached from love, women from husbands and men. The scope of private life becomes enlarged even as civil controls on arbitrary authority take hold. Boundary relations need to be adjusted for new historical times. The discourse of civil society is a pattern of signifiers. About its particular and specific signifieds, history will decide.

But shifting involvements always shift again. We live in relatively conservative, chastened, and sometimes frightened times, but the spheres outside civil society still cannot be seen as merely benign, much less as purely facilitating inputs to democratic life. They will inevitably be seen as destructive intrusions as well. Civil society is a project. It is a restless aspiration that lies deep in the soul of democratic life.

Great utopian projects of democracy rocked Western and Eastern societies in the last decades of the twentieth century. In the world of intellectual life, one major result was the revival of "civil society." We must take hold of this concept before it is too late. We must make civil society into a major focus of empirical and theoretical thought and thus to everyday social life.

That has been my ambition here. In Part I, I retrieved "civil society" from the cobwebs of earlier social theory. Once it made good sense to think of civil society as all the realms outside the state. Later, during the earlier days of industrial capitalism, many were afraid that civil society had disappeared, or been narrowed to mimic the selfishness of economic life. It is this vision that, in modern social science, allowed the spirit of Thrasymachus free rein. Realism is the salve for disappointment. But civil society has not disappeared. It is not everywhere, but it is not nowhere, either. Rather than dancing on its grave, we need to transform the idea of civil society in a critical way. It needs to be recentered on the promise of a community of individuals, centered on solidarity of a distinctively civil kind. Civil society is not everywhere except the state. A differentiated sphere of justice, it contends with and often conflicts with the value demands of spheres.

In Part II of *Civil Sphere*, we left the world of high theory to discover the imbedded discourse and institutions of everyday social life. Rather than an abstract deduction of philosophers, the normative stipulations of civil society turn out to be the language of the street, the television, novels, polls, parties, politics, office, and scandal. This rich and textured language is not only about utopia but about the evils that impede it. It turns out, in fact, that ideal inclusion is always shadowed by pollution and exclusion. The evils of modernity are not anomalies. Postmodernity will not overcome them. They are systemic products of the search for civil justice and the good life.

But if we cannot overcome binarism, we can fundamentally change its referents. There will always be two goalposts, but we shift them, even in the middle of play. This is what concerned us in Parts III and IV. The civil sphere is a promise, and this promise can be redeemed. Outsiders demand the expansion of the discourse of liberty. Stigmatized individuals and groups, polluted by the discourse of repression, can be purified and redeemed. If leaders are skillful, followers are brave, and the stars are right, movements for civil repair can succeed. But often they do not. History can go backward. The cracks in civil society split open. The golden bowl can drop and split into parts. It can be thrown down and shattered. The discourse of repression can triumph, and barbarism can rise in its place.

Though the empirical studies in *Civil Sphere* concern movements inside of nation-states or regions, its theoretical reflections have been developed without reference to scale. They refer to a way of imagining and organizing a society, not to a particular expanse. They do not necessarily refer to city, nation, or region. It is possible, indeed, for the imagining and the organizing of civil society to go beyond the territory of the nation-state. As the scale of other institutions, interactions, and discourses expands, so might the organization of the civil sphere.

If it were possible to organize a global sphere, the systematic problem of earthly war would cease, for civil virtue could not be demonstrated by exterminating the other side. It would be extraordinarily difficult to achieve this new resting place for the spirit of civil utopia. There would have to be a world state or something like a state for civil communication to become regulation on a global scale and for civil repair to proceed. Still, a more global playing field has already emerged.

Even if were able to establish a global civil sphere, and to extend the goalposts of civil society to the other side of the earth, the binary nature of civil discourse and the contradictions of time, place, and function would not go away. Certainly, they have not done so in the nation-state. The spirit of civil society will always be restless. Its boundary relations will continue to be dynamic, and it will be as liable to exclusionary integration as it is within the nation-state. The contradictions would still be alarming, and struggles over civil repair would still be contingent and dramatic.

In a world of increasingly dangerous weapons and political tactics, such a globalized civil sphere may be the only way to proceed. Without a global range, the promises even of civil society in its national form may die. Only the civil sphere can regulate force and eliminate arbitrary violence. It does so through persuasion and civil power and, if necessary, by dispensing force to defend democratic solidarity and to keep the aspirations of civil society alive. As violence becomes global, so must the civil sphere.

We cannot foresee how the life and times of the civil sphere will proceed.

At the beginning of the last century we could not have predicted that the fledgling feminist struggle would eventually create massive movements of civil regulation to free women from male power; or that gays and lesbians would demand civil unions and eventually their full freedoms as equal and autonomous human beings; or that masses of nonwhite people would over-throw every great colonial power in the name of civil aspirations for inde-pendence, so that they could create civil power to regulate their own states. Nor could we have anticipated the horrifying scale of military technology and how difficult it would still be, at the beginning of the twenty-first century, to regulate violence in the name of civil life.

What we can know for certain is that the discourse and structure of the civil sphere will remain. It will still be restless, and its dynamism will be dangerous and contradictory. But the discourse of liberty will continue, and the hopes for civil repair will remain. Civil society is a project. It inspires hope for a democratic life.

NOTES

CHAPTER 1

1. Rawls, *Theory of Justice*, esp. pp. 3–54 and 118–192.

2. Alexander, *Meanings of Social Life*.

3. Rawls, *Political Liberalism*, esp. pp. 1–32.

4. Habermas, *Theory of Communicative Action*.

5. For an elaboration of this criticism, see Alexander, "Habermas' New Critical Theory." See also Cooke, *Re-Presenting the Good Society*.

6. For example, Habermas, "Further Reflections on the Public Sphere," esp. pp. 441–446; and Habermas, *Between Facts and Norms*, pp. 299–308 and 352–384.

7. Walzer, *Spheres of Justice*. For a revealing analysis of tensions between such hermeneutic philosophies of justice and the more universalizing sort represented here by Rawls and Habermas, see Warnke, *Justice and Interpretation*. For a much more developed discussion of the issues I am signaling here, and their relation to the themes of this book, see Alexander, "Theorizing the Good Society."

8. E. Durkheim, *Division of Labor in Society*. More generally, see Alexander, *Antinomies of Classical Thought*.

9. For these theoretical sentiments as highlighted by the theoretical shifts in Durkheim's later work, see Smith and Alexander, "Introduction: The New Durkheim," pp. 1–40.

10. Marshall, *Class, Citizenship, and Social Development*.

11. Parsons, *System of Modern Societies*.

12. Alexander, "Contradictions in the Societal Community."

13. For example, Foucault, *Discipline and Punish*.

14. For his later reconsiderations of the self, see Foucault, "About the Beginning of the Hermeneutics of the Self"; and Z. Bauman, *Postmodern Ethics*.

15. For a critical discussion along these lines, see C. Taylor, "Foucault on Freedom and Truth."

16. For example, M. Weber, *Protestant Ethic and the Spirit of Capitalism*.

17. Alexander, *Classical Attempt at Synthesis*.

18. Freud, *Civilization and Its Discontents;* Elias, *Civilizing Process*.

19. Eisenstadt, "The Axial Age"; and Alexander, "Fragility of Progress."

CHAPTER 2

1. Seligman, *Idea of Civil Society*.

2. Hirschman, *Passions and the Interests*.

3. Franklin, *Autobiography and Selection from Other Writings*. Franklin's equivalence of capitalistic thrift with virtue was related to the influence of Puritanism by Max Weber in *Protestant Ethic and the Spirit of Capitalism*, pp. 48–57, and derided by Lawrence in his *Studies in Classic American Literature,* pp. 9–22, for the same association. Neither Weber nor Lawrence, however, highlighted the association of Franklinian virtue with democratic and civil life. See Morgan, *Benjamin Franklin*.

4. See Dumont, *From Mandeville to Marx*.

5. For the manner in which Hodgskin's critique of Ricardo and his innovative concepts adumbrated and facilitated Marx's own radical political economy, see Elie Halévy, *Thomas Hodgskin (1787–1869)*.

6. Polanyi, *Great Transformation*.

7. Keane, *Democracy and Civil Society*.

8. Jean Cohen, *Class and Civil Society*.

9. Easton and Guddat, *Writings of the Young Marx on Philosophy and Society;* and Alexander, *Antinomies of Classical Thought*, pp. 11–40.

10. Jean Cohen, *Class and Civil Society,* pp. 5, 24.

11. K. Marx, "Contribution to the Critique of Hegel's Philosophy of Right."

12. Adam Ferguson, *An Essay on the History of Civil Society*, appeared in 1767; in the German translation that appeared the following year, "civil society" was written as *Burgerliche Gesellschaft* (Bobbio, "Gramsci and the Concept of Civil Society," p. 80).

13. Hegel, *Philosophy of Right*, Part III, section ii: a–c. In addition to Jean Cohen's *Class and Civil Society*, see the argument about Hegel in Jean Cohen and Arato, *Civil Society and Political Theory*, pp. 91–116. For other arguments that develop the non-egoistic interpretation of Hegel, see Pelczynski, *State and Civil Society: Studies in Hegel's Political Philosophy;* and Reidel, *Between Tradition and Revolution*. The problem with these interpretive discussions is that they are so concerned to save Hegel from Marx—and, quite rightly, to provide an alternative to the reductionistic implications of civil society II—that they tend to credit Hegel with too much originality, suggesting, at least by implication, that he virtually invented the nonindividualistic

conception of civil society from whole cloth. As the present discussion suggests, however, this underplays the Scottish, British, and French contributions to the earlier creation of civil society I and neglects the importance of discussions by Hegel's non-German contemporaries such as Tocqueville.

14. It was Keane who was the first to present this historical account of strong state versus civil society theory, in "Despotism and Democracy," pp. 35–71.

15. For the historical origins and traces of this conservative conflation, see Polanyi's *Great Transformation*, pp. 135–200, and Hirschman's *Passions and the Interests*, pp. 100–113; for comparisons between historical and contemporary conservative conflations, see Hirschman, *Rhetoric of Reaction: Perversity, Futility, Jeopardy*; and Somers and Block, "From Poverty to Perversity."

16. For a discussion of the disappearing public in the writings of the American pragmatists, see chapter 9 of this book; and for a discussion of Putnam's claims about democratic declension, see the section on "Civil Associations" in chapter 5.

17. Gramsci, *Selections from the Prison Notebooks*, e.g., pp. 12–13 and 234, 263, 268. See also Jean Cohen and Arato, *Civil Society and Political Theory*, pp. 142–174.

18. Alexander, "Bringing Democracy Back In." This intellectual critique of big-state theory from a progressive, civil society perspective first appeared in a series of philosophical articles written by eastern Europeans, e.g., Kolakowski, "Hope and Hopelessness"; Michnik, "New Evolutionism"; Tesar, "Totalitarian Dictatorships."

19. See, for example, Sztompka, *Trust*; Seligman, *Problem of Trust*; and for an earlier and still important treatment, see Barber, *Logic and Limits of Trust*.

20. E.g., Habermas, *Knowledge and Human Interests*; Rorty, *Philosophy and the Mirror of Nature*; MacIntyre, *After Virtue*; Nussbaum, *Fragility of Goodness*; Taylor, *Hegel* and *Sources of the Self*.

21. Keane, *Democracy and Civil Society*, pp. 3, 14. The same kind of broad, civil society approach informs such later work by Keane as *Civil Society: Old Images, New Visions*, e.g., pp. 6, 17–19, 53–55. This book presents, at the same time, an informative overview of the wide-ranging international discussions that the revival of civil society has triggered. M. Emirbayer and M. Sheller take up a CSI approach that resembles Keane's, defining it as including "willed communities" and "voluntary associations, on the one hand, and families, schools, churches, and other cultural or socializing institutions, on the other" ("Publics in History," p. 152).

22. Arato, "Civil Society against the State," p. 23.

23. Jean Cohen and Arato, *Civil Society*.

24. For a development of this criticism, see my review of Jean Cohen and Arato, "Return to Civil Society."

25. E.g., Habermas, *Between Facts and Norms*, pp. 352–387. As my argument unfolds, it will become clear that although with the idea of civil society III I am calling for a sharp analytic separation between civil society and these other spheres, I am in no sense arguing for their empirical separation. The different possibilities

for empirical separation and overlap are explored throughout the rest of this book and are presented systematically as a model of "the contradictions of civil society" in chapter 8.

26. A. Wolfe, *Whose Keeper?*

27. Seligman, *Idea of Civil Society.*

28. Pateman, "Fraternal Social Contract," in Keane, *Civil Society and the State.*

29. Shils, "Virtue of Civil Society."

30. Walzer, "Rescuing Civil Society."

31. Perez-Diaz, "Public Sphere and a European Civil Society."

32. Putnam, *Making Democracy Work* and *Bowling Alone*. For a critical discussion of Putnam's ideas in relation to the civil society III alternative which I am proposing here, see the section "Civil Associations" in chapter 5 of this book.

33. Though the cultural and institutional sources of the civil sphere and their interrelation with noncivil spheres form the main topic of this book, I will not have the opportunity to explore such historically specific interactional practices. Such an examination would build upon Freud's understanding, in *Civilization and Its Discontents*, of civilization as a distinctive kind of psychological structure; Elias's analysis of the historical origins of the mannerisms marking civility, in *Civilizing Process* (the dark side of which he explored in "Violence and Civilization"; cf. Keane, "Uncivil Society," in *Civil Society*, pp. 115–156); and Erving Goffman, a great theorist of civil face-to-face relations in contemporary social science, in, e.g., *Presentation of Self in Everyday Life* and *Interaction Ritual*. For contemporary empirical studies of the interactional level of civil society, see Phillips and P. Smith, "Emotional and Behavioral Responses to Everyday Incivility" and "Everyday Incivility"; N. Eliasoph and P. Lichterman, "Culture in Interaction"; and G. Fine and B. Harrington, "Tiny Publics."

34. For the religious origins: Troeltsch, *Social Teaching of the Christian Churches*; Jellinek, *Declaration of the Rights of Man and of Citizens*; M. Weber, " 'Churches' and 'Sects' in North America; and Taylor, *Sources*, esp. pp. 127–142. For individualism in the Renaissance, Reformation, and Enlightenment: J. Burckhardt, *Civilization of the Renaissance in Italy*, esp. pp. 143–174; Greenblatt, *Renaissance Self-Fashioning*; Erikson, *Young Man Luther*; M. Walzer, *Revolution of the Saints*; and Gay, *Enlightenment: An Interpretation*. For the sources of individuality in romanticism, see Taylor, *Sources*, pp. 368–390, and his book *Ethics of Authenticity*. For the eleventh-century roots of English individualism and its reflection in citizenship law, see Somers, "Citizenship and the Place of the Public Sphere"; and Colin Morris, *Discovery of the Individual: 1050–1200*. For medieval parliaments and Western feudalism, see M. Weber, *Economy and Society*, pp. 1038–1039, and, for their relation to individualism in modern times, pp. 1381–1469; and Bendix, *Kings or People*, pp. 200–217. For the distinctiveness of Western cities and individuality, see M. Weber, "The City," 1212–1372. For religious sect activity and individuality, see P. Miller, *Life of the Mind in*

America; and M. Weber, " 'Churches' and 'Sects' " and "The Protestant Sects and the Spirit of Capitalism," *From Max Weber*, pp. 302–322. For individualism and romantic love, see Bloch, "Untangling the Roots of Modern Sex Roles."

35. Somers, "Citizenship and the Place of the Public Sphere."

36. B. Anderson, *Imagined Communities*; Greenfeld, *Nationalism*; and Brubaker, *Nationalism Reframed*. For discussions that emphasize solidarity but are less focused specifically by the national reference, see M. Weber, *City*, and Bendix, *Kings or People*.

37. Polanyi, *Great Transformation*, pp. 168, 73, and 154.

38. Ibid., pp. 146, 154. At the same time that Polanyi insisted on the purely pragmatic and practical origins of these protest movements, however, he said that they "almost invariably" also involved such concerns as "professional status," "the form of a man's life," and "the breadth of his existence" (p. 154).

39. For discussion of the noneconomic, religious, and political-cultural origins of the collective obligations that generated earlier working- and middle-class critiques of industrial capitalism, see R. Williams, *Culture and Society: 1780–1950*; E. P. Thompson, *Origins of the British Working Class*; Sewell, *Work and Revolution in France*; Joyce, *Visions of the People*; Wilentz, *Chants Democratic*; and Biernacki, *Fabrication of Labor*. More generally, see Hess's discussion of "the semantics of stratification" in his *Concepts of Social Stratification*, pp. 1–9 and 168–174.

40. Walzer, *Spheres of Justice*.

41. Boltanski and Thevenot, *De la justification*.

42. Though this is the same kind of critique as the one Ronald Dworkin leveled against Walzer when *Spheres of Justice* first appeared ("To Each His Own"), I do not agree with Dworkin's argument that the alternative is Rawlsian universalism. Dworkin fails to recognize Walzer's hermeneutic achievement vis-à-vis Rawls, which was, per my argument in chapter 1, to ground justice in cultural meaning. For the most developed statement of this position, see Walzer, *Interpretation and Social Criticism*.

43. In chapter 8, I will develop a model of the temporal, spatial, and functional contradictions of civil society and the three ideal-typical forms of boundary relations that mediate them.

CHAPTER 3

1. Dewey, *Democracy and Education*, p. 87.

2. I will also consider traditional political approaches to democracy in chapter 6.

3. T. Parsons, "Evolutionary Universals in Society."

4. Parsons, *System of Modern Society*.

5. Lerner, *Passing of Traditional Society*.

6. S. M. Lipset, *Political Man*, and *First New Nation*.

7. Despite its elegance and systematic power, Niklas Luhmann's approach to

democracy exhibits just this kind of anachronistic complacency. For example, in his "Politics as a Social System," he writes: "A political system's ability to absorb social conflicts has to increase when society becomes more complex and conflict-ridden. The political system then changes these conflicts from being cases of outright opposition to being cases of regulated, articulate struggles to influence the decision-making centers" (p. 149).

8. In addition to the contributors to the debates about justice and civil society cited in chapters 1 and 2, above, see the series of synthetic works by David Held beginning with *Models of Democracy* and *Political Theory and the Modern State*, and the turn toward "deliberative democracy" in political theory, e.g., Seyla Benhabib, "Toward a Deliberative Model of Democratic Legitimacy"; Joshua Cohen, "Procedure and Substance in Deliberative Democracy"; Bohman, *Public Deliberation: Pluralism, Complexity, and Democracy*; and Gutmann and Thompson, *Democracy and Disagreement*.

9. B. Moore, *Social Origins of Dictatorship and Democracy*.

10. Rex, *Key Problems of Sociological Theory*.

11. Dahrendorf, *Class and Class Conflict in Industrial Society*; and R. Collins, *Conflict Sociology: Toward an Explanatory Science*.

12. Skocpol, *States and Social Revolutions*; P. Evans, Rueschemeyer, and Skocpol, *Bringing the State Back In*; and Rueschemeyer, E. H. Stephens, and J. D. Stephens, *Capitalist Development and Democracy*.

13. In the outpouring of studies devoted to power structure research, which involves arguments about such topics as class versus elite formations in cities and nations, and manager versus property control in corporations, there is scarcely any indication that in many capitalist societies these structural issues and the conflicts they produce are nested within a democratic political order. (For a more detailed discussion of this point, see chapter 6.) Although the kind of criticism I am making here has typically been the staple of conservative critiques of Marxism, in the recent efflorescence of democratic political theory it has been levied by a growing number of post-Marxist critics of critical theory. As I indicated in chapter 2, for example, Jean Cohen has forcefully argued that the exclusive Marxist focus on class relations is fundamentally mistaken because it misconstrues civil society as a realm without independent normative mediation either in a legal constitutional or in a more broadly cultural sense *(Class and Civil Society)*. Claude Lefort has put the argument in even more polemical terms, wondering why there is so little enthusiasm for the analysis of political freedom and democracy among social and political scientists: "Political sociologists and scientists find the preconditions that define their object and their approach to knowledge in this mode of appearance of the political, without ever examining the form of society within which the division of reality into various sectors appears and is legitimated" ("The Question of Democracy," p. 11).

14. One of the leaders of this realistic turn in sociology, Randall Collins, called

norms and values "dubious constructions" and asserted that the very concept of a norm should "be dropped from sociological theory" ("On the Micro-Foundations of Macro-Sociology," 991, 991 n. 3).

15. Rex, *Key Problems*.

16. Przeworski, *Capitalism and Social Democracy*. Certainly social democratic theorists like Rex and Przeworski analyze democracy and theorize about it in a decidedly more appreciative manner than orthodox Marxist critics, who assumed its merely formal character. They conceive of it, however, primarily as an economic adaptation to the growing power of the proletariat, a power whose possibility, they acknowledge, Marx himself did not sufficiently recognize. Thus, for Przeworski, democracy has succeeded because it allows class conflict to proceed without the destabilizing intervention of physical force (p. 140). Such an approach recapitulates the necessitarian logic of earlier modernization theory, minus the idealization. The particularity of democracy is not conceptualized, and its specific structural and historical requisites are assumed rather than explained. What is most fateful in the continuity between Marx and neo-Marxists, as Jean Cohen has written in *Class and Civil Society* (p. 5), is their dislike of the institutions of modern civil society and their reduction of these institutions to mere bourgeois culture and capitalist relations.

17. Marcuse, *One-Dimensional Man*.

18. Foucault, *Discipline and Punish* and *History of Sexuality*. It is paradoxical that Foucault's radically relativistic work on the omnipresence of systematic and debilitating discipline throughout modern society became so widely accepted precisely among those critical intellectuals who were themselves committed to the expansion of democracy, individual autonomy, and social progress. In this regard, it is worth quoting from Charles Taylor's radical humanistic response to Foucault:

> Free participatory institutions require some commonly accepted self-disciplines. The free citizen has the *vertu* to give willingly the contribution which otherwise the despot would coerce from him, perhaps in some other form. Without this, free institutions cannot exist. There is a tremendous difference between societies which find their cohesion through such common disciplines grounded on a public identity, and which thus permit of and call for the participatory action of equals, on the one hand, and the multiplicity of kinds of society which require chains of command based on unquestionable authority on the other." (*Human Agency and Language*, p. 83)

For another, complementary response, see Walzer, *Company of Critics*, pp. 191–209.

19. Giddens, *Power, Property, and the State*; and Bogard, *Simulation of Surveillance*.

20. Sennet, *Fall of Public Man*; and Habermas, *Structural Transformation of the Public Sphere*.

21. Bourdieu concentrates almost exclusively on vertical rather than horizontal

social ties, and he insists that symbolic boundaries are modeled on—and in a real sense derive from—social, typically economic, hierarchies (see, e.g., *Outline of a Theory of Practice*; *Distinction: A Social Critique of the Judgment of Taste*; and *La Noblesse d'État*). Writing from within the tradition of ideology-critique, Bourdieu consistently portrays moral universalism as a false and misleading cover for self-interest. He conceives of social codes not as rules stipulating civil and uncivil criteria but as hegemonic vehicles for domination that issue from, and lead back to, the interest of the powerful. Democracy, and the kind of systematic possibilities for civil repair that it generates, cannot be conceptualized if the possibilities of moral universalism and trans-sectional solidarity are denied in principle. See Alexander, "The Reality of Reduction."

22. Edelman, *Symbolic Uses of Politics*; J. B. Thompson, "Sources of Social Power," in *Studies in the Theory of Ideology*, pp. 1–33.

23. Dahrendorf, "In Praise of Thrasymachus."

24. Plato, *Republic*, Part I, chap. 3, p. 18.

25. Aristotle, *Politics*, bk. 4, sec. E, chap. 14.

26. Montesquieu, *Spirit of Laws*, bk. 2, chap. 6.

27. Madison, no. 51, in A. Hamilton, Madison, and Jay, *Federalist Papers*, pp. 320–325.

28. "The dispute between Thrasymachus and Socrates," Hannah Pitkin writes, "has modern parallels central to political and social concerns," citing such "modern versions" of Thrasymachus as Marxist and legal realist arguments about values as camouflages for social interests (*Wittgenstein and Justice*, p. 170). In such modern discussions, deference has often been paid to Thrasymachus in the name of the value-freedom that purportedly informs the empirical stature of contemporary social science. Robert Dahl pioneered power studies in contemporary American political science. In writing about the *Republic*, he suggests that the two Greeks "are talking right past one another" because "Socrates evidently intends his argument to be primarily *normative*, while Thrasymachus pretty clearly means his observation to be essentially *empirical*," that "Socrates met Thrasymachus' attempt to describe how rulers generally *do* act by indicating how good rulers *ought* to act," and that Thrasymachus "represented an early Greek attempt to find naturalistic explanations for political behavior" (*Modern Political Analysis*, po. 105–106, emphasis in original). I do not accept this distinction. Though certainly not identical, the is and ought are inevitably intertwined; Socrates and Thrasymachus offer not only competing political ideals but contrasting perspectives on action and order in an empirical sense, contrasts that have major explanatory implications. For a *locus classicus* of arguments against any radical separation of is from ought judgments in modern social science, see Leo Strauss's critique of Max Weber's methodology of social science, "Natural Right and the Distinction between Facts and Values."

29. K. Marx, "Manifesto of the Communist Party."

30. M. Weber, "Appendix II: Parliament and Government in a Reconstructed Germany," in *Economy and Society*.

31. Michels, *Political Parties*.

32. Lipset, Trow, and Coleman, *Union Democracy*. See also Lipset's introduction to *Political Parties: A Sociological Study*.

33. Mansbridge, *Beyond Adversary Democracy*, pp. 278–289.

34. Keller, *Beyond the Ruling Class*; Etzioni-Halévy, *Fragile Democracy* and *Elite Connection*. For a critical discussion of approaches that emphasize the homogeneity of modern elites, see chapter 6 of this book.

35. Waltzer, *Spheres of Justice*.

36. Habermas, *Communication and the Evolution of Society*; Bobbio, *Future of Democracy*; Keane, *Democracy and Civil Society*, p. 3; Held, *Models of Democracy;* Lefort, "Question of Democracy," p. 19. (See also, in this regard, the affirmation of the narrowly procedural position by the Lukacian political theorist Heller, "On Formal Democracy"); and Alford and Friedland, *Powers of Theory*, e.g., pp. 430–431. Friedland has since moved toward a more cultural approach to politics, e.g., Friedland and Hecht, *To Rule Jerusalem*; and Friedland and Mohr, "Cultural Turn in American Sociology."

37. Alexander, *Real Civil Societies*.

38. Sloterdijk, *Critique of Cynical Reason*.

39. For structures of feeling, see R. Williams, *Long Revolution*, pp. 63–64. For the worlds of common sense and perception that make living together possible, see M. Oakshott, *On Human Conduct*, esp. Parts I and II. For habits of the heart and self-interest broadly understood, see Tocqueville, *Democracy and America*, bk. 2, chap. 8. Tocqueville distinguished between simply *"l'intérêt"*—"egoistic" or "brutal" self-interest—and *l'intérêt bien entendu,* which became known in English as "self-interest rightly understood" and recently has been translated as "self-interest properly understood." (For the former, see *Democracy in America,* Vol. 2, trans. Reeves, Bowen, and Bradley; for the latter, see the Goldhammer translation, Vol. 1. While Goldhammer's translation is, in general, more contemporary and more precise, it seems unfortunate that he has chosen to render differently a phrase that, in English, has become a classic theoretical term. In the following, I quote from Goldhammer's translation, which contains both Vols. 1 [1835] and 2 [1840].) Broadly understood, self-interest, according to Tocqueville, refers to "the disinterested, spontaneous impulses that are part of man's nature" (p. 611), as compared with the conscious and calculated estimates of material well-being upon which the market sphere and political-economic theories are based. It suggests motives and relations that "are disciplined, temperate, moderate, prudent, and self-controlled" (p. 612). It is the influence of "mores," Tocqueville believes, that allows self-interest to be broadly understood. "Mores" has been the accepted English translation for Tocqueville's *les meurs*. Tocqueville refers to mores as "one of the great general causes to which the

persistence of the democratic republic in the United States can be attributed" (p. 331). He defines them as "habits, opinions, usages, beliefs" (p. 356), and he is at pains to distinguish this dimension from more physical and institutional causes and to place upon them greater causal power in the creation of democracies: "Physical causes, law, mores: these are without a doubt the three major factors that have governed and shaped American democracy, but if I were asked to rank them, I would say that physical causes matter less than laws and laws less than mores" (p. 356). For a modern social scientific statement of this point of view, see Pizzorno, "On the Rationality of Democratic Choice."

40. Tocqueville suggests that "in the strict sense," mores refer to "habits of the heart," though he wishes to widen the term to refer "also to the various notions that men possess, to the diverse opinions among them, and to the whole range of ideas that shape habits of mind" (p. 331). In their collective study of American individualism, Robert Bellah and his colleagues suggest that Tocqueville's understanding of the patterned subjectivity that is the heart of institutions goes back to "the concept of the 'heart' in Pascal" and is "ultimately biblical." Since "both the Old and the New Testament speak of the heart as involving intellect, will, and intention as well as feeling," then Tocqueville's "notion of 'habits of the heart' perhaps goes back ultimately to the law written in the heart (Rom. 2:15)" (*Habits of the Heart*, p. 312 n. 28).

41. Shils, "Nationalism, Nationality, Nationalism and Civil Society."

42. Shils, "Primordial, Personal, Sacred, and Civil Ties."

43. Habermas, *Structural Transformation*, p. 27. For individual and society as markers in a language game, in Wittgenstein's sense, see n. 59 below.

44. Ackerman, *Foundations*.

45. J. Prager, "Totalitarian and Liberal Democracies."

46. In *Class, Citizenship, and Social Development*, Marshall drew upon the long democratic tradition of Fabian socialism. The tension-in-balance that defined Marshall's ideas later became the starting point for the significant sociological extensions of citizenship theory created by Reinhard Bendix in *Nation Building and Citizenship*, and Parsons in "Full Citizenship for the Negro American?" Bruce Ackerman provided an ambitious philosophical statement of this Marshallian perspective (*Social Justice in the Liberal State*). For a sociological extension and restatement of this Marshallian position, see Janoski, *Citizenship and Civil Society*.

47. Locke, *Second Treatise on Government*, bk. 2, sec. 6.

48. Ferguson, *Essay on the History of Civil Society*.

49. Adam Smith, *Theory of Moral Sentiments*. For an elaboration of this Smithean discussion of impartial spectator, see Boltanski, *Distant Suffering*.

50. See notes 39 and 40.

51. Arendt, *Human Condition*; Wolin, *Politics and Vision*; Habermas, *Structural Transformation of the Public Sphere*; Unger, *Knowledge and Politics*; MacIntyre, *After*

Virtue; Walzer, *Spheres of Justice;* Sandel, *Liberalism and the Limits of Justice.* In his later writings, of course, Habermas has explicitly denied being a republican theorist, suggesting that his discourse ethics position transcends the liberal/republican divide, e.g., his "The Three Normative of Democracy." This self-disqualification seems viable, however, only if the republican position is rather narrowly conceived. In his theory of the public sphere, Habermas continues to identify democracy with a form of public active participation that presupposes fundamental orientations of reciprocity and cooperation that are antithetical to political partisanship and economic participation.

52. Seyla Benhabib expresses similar reservations about the writings of such philosophical republicans, suggesting that they are afflicted by a "nostalgic trope," and, in light of this criticism, that the public should be seen not as an idealized social or political condition, but as a "regulative ideal" (*Reluctant Modernism of Hannah Arendt*, pp. 203–206). For the relationship between public opinion and the status of the public as a regulative ideal, see my discussion in the section titled "The Public and Its Opinion" in this book's chapter 5.

53. Bellah et al., *Habits of the Heart;* Bell, *Cultural Contradictions of Capitalism,* pp. 220–282.

54. Rousseau, *Social Contract* (1762), bk. 2, chaps. 1–3.

55. Durkheim, *Division of Labor in Society*; Parsons, "Durkheim's Contribution to the Theory of Integration of Social Systems"; Parsons, *System of Modern Societies*; and also Smelser, *Social Change in the Industrial Revolution.*

56. Hegel, *Phenomenology of Spirit,* e.g., chap. 6; Simmel, *Conflict;* and Walzer, *Obligations,* pp. 3–23. This critical interrelation between conflict and integration in Simmelian theory was thoroughly obscured by the insistence of those in the realist tradition that Simmel should be seen as a "conflict theorist" (e.g., Coser, *Functions of Social Conflict*). For a more culturally oriented refutation of this perspective and a discussion of the modes of complementarity between Simmel and Parsons, see D. Levine, "Simmel and Parsons Reconsidered." In *The Evolution of Rights in Liberal Theory,* Ian Shapiro criticizes the debate "over 'community' versus 'no community' " between Aristotelian and Hegelian philosophers, on the one side, and Kantian liberals, on the other, as "no more . . . than a beguiling opposition of gross concepts." Every political theory, he argues, makes "substantive judgments about how communities ought to be organized and governed [and] assumes accounts of how they are formed and reproduced, and of what their goals and purposes might be, and of how they should limit community action, both internally, and with respect to the individual actions of members." "Because this is so," Shapiro suggests, "the argument should not be over whether community, but rather of what sort" (p. 296).

57. For a systematic and insightful early discussion of these ideas of symbolic code and base, see Parsons, "On the Concept of Political Power." A parallel contrast between the communicative as compared to the instrumental dimension of politics

informs Habermas's key concepts, beginning with the labor versus interaction contrast in his *Theory and Practice*, pp. 142–169, and continuing through the various
modes of normative justification in *Theory of Communicative Action*. If Parsons had
little sense for normative-philosophical theorizing, Habermas has demonstrated little
sense of the complexities of empirical theorizing in social science, particularly those
involved in the cultural analysis of normative action.

58. C. Levi-Strauss, "Structural Analysis in Linguistics and in Anthropology,"
p. 50. Levi-Strauss invokes the strict semiotic sense of the term "arbitrary," the
contemporary equivalence of which would be "constructed" as compared to naturally occurring or "realistic." Thus, when he first insisted on the arbitrary character
of signs, Ferdinand de Saussure (*Course in General Linguistics*) argued that the meaning
of a linguistic term can be understood only relatively—in terms of its difference
from, or relation to, a paired term—rather than by its verisimilitude. For a broad
discussion of this sense of arbitrary vis-à-vis more materialistic thinking, see Sahlins,
Culture and Practical Reason. For the consequences of this position for contemporary
conceptions of culture, see Alexander, "On the 'Relative Autonomy' of Culture";
and Alexander and Smith, "Strong Program in Cultural Sociology."

59. The notion that the discourse of civil society is a structure, in the sense of
the linguistic tradition initiated by Saussure, is homologous with the notion that it
is a language, as Wittgenstein first conceived it in *Philosophical Investigations*. Both
perspectives argue against the idea of discourse as a congeries of speech acts in the
formal-pragmatic terms of Habermas. In Wittgenstein's language game, the definitions of words do not refer to real qualities in the pragmatic sense. They are not
"ostensive," a term by which Wittgenstein designated an approach to meaning that
locates it outside of words; they are not constative but performative, in the terms
that Austin developed later, in *How to Do Things with Words*, which carried Wittgenstein's language philosophy into a new key. The words of a language game define
qualities relationally, as parts in a structural whole. The larger "game" of civil society
must already be known before the meaning of any activity within it can be assigned
meaning or sense. As I will suggest in chapter 4, in the language of the civil sphere,
such qualities as rationality, autonomy, and cooperation are not real attributes of
"democratic actors" but symbolically generated attributions. Wittgenstein articulated
this point in an important series of passages about naming, color, and standards of
evaluation: "One has already to know (or be able to do) something in order to be
capable of asking a thing's name. . . . The meaning of a word is its use in the language.
. . . Let us imagine samples of colour being preserved in Paris like the standard
metre. We define: 'sepia' means the colour of the standard sepia which is there kept
hermetically sealed. Then it will make no sense to say of this sample either that it
is of this color or that it *is not*. . . . This sample is an instrument of the *language* used
in *ascriptions* of colour. In this language-game it is not some*thing* that is represented,
but is a *means of representation*" (secs: 30, 43, 50). The presuppositional status of this

language game—the fact that it is a game with rules and a language rather than situationally directed speech—is not accessible to the understanding of those who speak and use it. In her sustained effort to demonstrate the relevance of this perspective to political philosophy and democracy, Pitkin emphasizes this point with reference to concepts that do significant work in the language of civil society:

> In Wittgensteinian terms one might say "individual," "society," "culture," "state," are, first of all, concepts; they are words in our language. That does not mean that society is not real but a mere concept, any more than it means that the individual is not real but a mere concept. Individuals are real and so is society, but they are not separate entities of the same kind, and both are dependent on our conceptualization. We are tempted to suppose that society is a mere concept while individuals are really real because individual persons have tangible, visible physical bodies. But deeper reflection easily reveals that our concept of the individual person is by no means equivalent to that of his physical body; rather, it is every bit as complex, as abstract, as conceptual, as our concepts of society or culture. What an individual is depends as much on the grammar of the "individual" as what a society is depends on the grammar of "society." Once that fact has penetrated into our habits of thought, new ways of investigating old issues about individuals and social wholes become accessible. (p. 195)

60. A. Farge, *Subversive Words*, pp. viii–ix.

61. See, e.g., Kant, "What Is Enlightenment?" This is not to say, however, that that such Enlightenment philosophers envisioned even such abstractly defined ideals as having a truly universal reach. For a critique of Kant's restricted conception of the reach of enlightenment rationality, see my discussion in chapter 15, n. 43.

62. See my discussion, in this regard, of Habermas, Rawls, Durkheim, and Parsons in chapter 1. In their major theoretical elaboration of civil society theory, *Civil Society in Political Theory*, Jean Cohen and Arato have been both inspired and limited by this Habermasian framework, as I argued in chapter 2. Suggesting that such normative criteria as transparency and autonomy are at the heart of empirical discourse in the civil sphere, their analysis tends to remain restricted by the rational ideals of philosophers and the idealized norms of such regulative institutions as civil law. The cultural particularities that actually inform public speech as a social process, and the manner in which it bifurcates, particularizes, and divides as much as it transcends and unifies, is not for them a major concern. Among the philosophical descendants of Habermas, Benhabib and Cooke have moved closer to a conception of culture as an independent process. Benhabib notes the narrative structure of democratic discourses in *Reluctant Modernism of Hannah Arendt* (e.g., p. 125) and their identity-creating properties in *Claims of Culture*. Criticizing crititcal theory's

abstract approach to rationality, in *Re-Presenting the Good Society*, Cooke argues for a more concrete and imagistic understanding of transcendental criticism. Against Habermas's own version of critical theory, Cooke suggests that "shifts in perception do not come about solely—or, indeed, even primarily—as a result of the exchange of reasons through argumentation; typically they are prompted by experiences in other, nonargumentative contexts" (p. 111). She describes such contexts as cultural: "Regulative ideas such as [Habermas's] idea of the ideal speech situation are fictions: fabricated myths." Rather than describing an actual method or practice for arriving at truth, they operate "in a metonymic fashion, signaling in a partly symbolic, partly substantive, partly imaginative way something that cannot be fully represented in language or rendered fully transparent to our knowledge and practices" (p. 115). From this perspective, "critical social thinking may be described as regulative ideas that have an imaginary, fictive character and re-present an idealized social condition" (pp. 115 and 161).

63. L. Hunt, *Politics, Culture, and Class in the French Revolution*.

64. Bloch, *Visionary Republic*; Bercovitch, *American Jeremiad*; Middlekauff, "Ritualization of the American Revolution."

CHAPTER 4

1. The theoretical logic that underlies this manner of conceptualization goes back to the interchange model developed by Talcott Parsons and such colleagues as Neil Smelser (e.g., *Economy and Society*). Building upon Durkheim and Max Weber, as well as Keynes's macroeconomic model, this theorizing made it possible to conceptualize solidarity as an independent sphere with boundary relations to other subsystems (see Alexander, *Modern Reconstruction of Classical Thought*, pp. 73–118). This new possibility for empirical theorizing was later developed in a more normative and philosophical direction by Habermas in *Theory of Communicative Action*. I do not employ this Parsonian model in the theory I am developing here, for reasons I have outlined elsewhere, e.g., Alexander, *Modern Reconstruction*, pp. 241–254; "After Neofunctionalism"; and "Contradictions in the Societal Community."

2. The "new utilitarianism" can be taken broadly or narrowly. In the narrow sense, it is exemplified in the resurgent rational choice theories in political science and sociology, which take economic theory as their model. For a foundational document, see Coleman, *Foundations of Social Theory*. For less rigidly defined approaches, see such collections as M. Brinton and V. Nee, eds., *The New Institutionalism in Sociology*. In the broader sense, this new utilitarianism is exemplified by the kinds of realistic approaches discussed in chapter 3 under the rubric of the Thrasymachus tradition (cf. my critical discussion in chapter 6 of the political sociology of parties and power). For an example of the new utilitarianism more broadly defined, which contrasts directly with the position I am outlining here, see Michael Mann's hope

that "if I could, I would abolish the concept of 'society' altogether," *A History of Power from the Beginning to A.D. 1760*, p. 2.

3. There has been little work on institutional elites in the civil sphere. This reflects the tight connection between elite theorizing and the tradition of Thrasymachus, which, by conceptualizing elites in terms of instrumental rationality, can understand them only as threats to democracy rather than as sources of possible support. The most important recent work on elites and civil society is the discussion of movement intellectuals by Eyerman and Jamison in *Social Movements*. For earlier, more structurally oriented work, see the writings by Keller and Etzioni-Halévy cited in chap. 3, n. 34, and also R. Aron, "Social Class, Political Class, Ruling Class."

4. For the theoretical background to the empirical model of culture I am presenting here, see Alexander, "Analytic Debates: Understanding the Relative Autonomy of Culture," and, more recently, Alexander, *Meanings of Social Life*. The roots of this approach reach into linguistic, literary, and anthropological theory, but they also grow from the classical sociological tradition. There is a "structure" and a "narrative" to the discourse of civil society (cf. Barthes, "Introduction to the Structural Analysis of Narratives"). Structure refers to the binary discourse that describes those who are in and those who are out, and it can be conceived in terms of the legacy of the Durkheimian and Saussurian traditions. In his later and more culturally sensitive work, Durkheim tried to theorize a secular equivalent of "religious society." He argued that the binary sacred versus profane classification, totemlike symbols, and subjectively experienced solidarity were not only keystones of primitive but modern social structures and classification (cf. Smith and Alexander, "The New Durkheim"). The linguistic tradition that created semiotics took up this Durkheimian insight. For the sources of binary cultural analysis in the general linguistic tradition, see Saussure, *Course in General Linguistics*; for the widely influential Slavic version of structuralism, see Jakobson, *On Language*; for the anthropological, see Levi-Strauss, *Savage Mind*, and Sahlins, *Culture and Practical Reason*; for the social-semiotic version, see Barthes, *Mythologies*, and *Fashion System*. The narrative element of contemporary civil discourse can be taken back to Weber's historical investigations of salvation religions (e.g., *Economy and Society*, pp. 399–634). Weber understood that developed religions introduced a fateful tension between this world and the next, which could be resolved only through salvation, and that, henceforth, a focus on eschatology and theodicy dominates the religious consciousness of the age. The binary categories of sacred and profane upon which Durkheim based his religious sociology provide the reference points for the journey of salvation that Weber describes.

For contemporary social scientific understanding, the challenge is to translate the understanding and relevance of these two strains of classical thinking into a framework relevant to the culture of secular societies. Social scientific discussions of culture in contemporary societies overlook the dualistic, sacred-versus-profane quality of symbolic systems. Whether framed as values, discourses, or ideologies, culture has been treated in a one-sided way as normative ideals about the right and the good. Certainly, political culture is normative and evaluative, but it is as concerned with defining evil as with the good, and inspires purifying conflict as much as creating the foundations for order.

In a manner that is complementary to the cultural sociology I am employing here, cognitive psychology, and cognitive science more generally, has emphasized the role of structured categories in perception, the role of such relational structures as binaries, and the importance of analogical processes in relating preexisting categorical structures to perceptual inputs. See, e.g., Lakoff, *Women, Fire, and Dangerous Things*, and D. Hofstadter, "Analogy as the Core of Cognition."

5. For thematizations of civilized and uncivilized in the history of social theory, see Freud, *Civilization and Its Discontents;* Elias, *Civilizing Process;* and such discussions as Cuddihy, *Ordeal of Civility*, and M. Rogin, *"Ronald Reagan."* Though Rogin places concern for the projection of unworthiness at the center of the political process and links it to the cultural process he calls demonology, it might be useful to indicate how his approach, shared in sometimes less sophisticated forms by a wide range of critical cultural studies, differs from the one I pursue here: (1) Because his conception of motive is psychological, Rogin provides no independent analysis of symbolic patterns; (2) Because he focuses exclusively on overt practices of violent domination—particularly of American whites over Native Americans—Rogin fails to tie demonology to either the theory or the practice of civil society, a structure that can allow the inclusion as well as the exclusion of social groups. (3) Because Rogin studies oppressed groups exclusively, he locates demonology as the practice of political conservatives, whereas it also informs liberal and progressive forces.

6. In his investigation of "othering" in ancient Greek political philosophy, with special reference to aliens, slaves, and women, Paul Cartledge writes that "beginning at the highest level of generality, the Classical Greeks divided all humankind into two mutually exclusive and antithetical categories: Us and Them, or, as they put it, Greeks and barbarians. In fact, the Greek-barbarian antithesis is a strictly polar dichotomy, being not just contradictory but jointly exhaustive and mutually exclusive. Greeks + barbarians = all humankind. . . . Thus whereas Greeks were ideally seen as not-barbarians, barbarians were equally envisaged as being precisely what Greeks were not" (*Greeks*, p. 11).

7. The position I develop here is not antagonistic to the notion that exigencies of time and space create open-ended, contingent relations between social "signifieds" and the set of structured symbolic "signifiers" that I refer to as the discourse of civil society. Cultural theory—in linguistics, literature, anthropology, philosophy, and sociology—has articulated this openness by constructing paired conceptual terms and specifying that both sides are present in any speech act: metaphorical *and*

metonymic, semiotic *and* poetic, *langue* (language) *and parole* (speech), code *and* message, language structure *and* speech-genre, syntactic-semantic *and* pragmatic, structure *and* agency, constative *and* performative. See, e.g., Jacobson, *On Language* and *Language in Literature*; Bakhtin, *Speech Genres and Other Late Essays*; Sahlins, *Historical Metaphors and Mythical Realities*; Charles Morris, *Foundations of the Theory of Signs*; Austin, *How to Do Things with Words*; and Alexander, "Cultural Pragmatics." For an empirical discussion of how the contingencies of time, space, and functional differentiation articulate with the structure of civil society discourse, see chapter 8 of this book; for how such ideological configurations as Left and Right function as "shifters" that mediate and specify the structure of civil society discourse vis-à-vis pragmatic interests and contingent events, see chapter 6.

In its most polemical form, e.g., in the foundational work of Saussure and Levi-Strauss, structuralism emphasizes static and homeostatic (synchronic) rather than dynamic and conflictual (diachronic) approaches to cultural life. The cultural-pragmatic approach that informs this book, by contrast, embraces both sides of the conceptual dualities discussed above, dualities which emerged in the dialogue with structuralism in its pure form. Even within structure qua binary there is an immanent conception of endemic cultural tension and strain. Because each side of the binary constituting sociocultural language gives rise—indeed, necessitates—its moral, cognitive, and affective antithesis, it triggers an ongoing, dialogical process of assertion, comparison, and counterassertion.

By contrast, social scientific traditions of cultural analysis understand cultural dynamics and conflict in terms of the tension between internally integrated cultural patterns and a society that fails to supply the resources necessary to fulfill or institutionalize them. In liberal or conservative versions, this leads to discussions about the failure of socialization and the breakdown of social control, which focus primarily on the social rather than cultural sources of conflict and strain and give an unreal picture of the opportunities for creating an integrated and nonconflictual society. In more radical analysis, this understanding leads to studies of hegemony and dominant ideologies, on the one hand, and resistance, on the other.

The thinker who gave structuralism its name, Roman Jakobson, understood instability and dynamism as immanent to the binary structure of culture itself, which he described, in fact, as "dynamic synchrony" (*On Language*, p. 64). In concert with such an understanding, Bakhtin developed a dialogical approach to genre, and Derrida his theory of difference (in his essay "Différance"). Derrida insists that assertions about the meaning of a text, while necessarily referring to an extant structured binary, always also entail relations of difference, such that even actions that cite, or accept, existing meaning structures as their rationales—thus claiming meaningful equivalence, identity, and true translation—must be understood, in fact, as making claims for analogy. It is in this moment of *différance* that there emerges the idea of performative action, first developed philosophically by Austin and critically reworked by Derrida (in "Signature, Event, Context"), and later by Butler (e.g., "Critically Queer"). See also Alexander, Giesen, and Mast, *Social Performance*.

8. The focus on the particular and diverse cultural traditions of democratic nations has generated a vast field of scholarship, the most influential works of which have singled out specific religious, social, and intellectual movements, influential thinkers, and great books as critical to this or that tradition, or even to the democratic or progressive tradition per se. To consider only the political-cultural historiography of America, for example, one can trace the debate between those who emphasize Lockean liberalism (e.g., Hartz, *Liberal Tradition in America*, and Appleby, *Capitalism and a New Social Order*); those who emphasize Puritanism (e.g., P. Miller, *Life of the Mind in America;* and Bloch, *Visionary Republic*); and those who emphasize Republicanism (e.g., Bailyn, *Ideological Origins of the American Revolution;* and Pocock, *Ancient Constitution and the Feudal Law*). For an overview of these discussions of American cultural-political history, see Hesse, *American Social and Political Thought*, pp. 3–61.

When one surveys even a small part of this historiography, however, the danger of concentrating on particular causal sequences at the expense of broader hermeneutic constructions soon becomes apparent. On the one hand, diverse historical movements contributed to the emergence of democratic discourses and practices and each has been responsible for particular emphases, constructions, and metaphors in national and regional configurations of democracy. On the other hand, it is evident that there is an overarching structure, or "whole," of democratic discourse that is more general and inclusive than any of these particular "parts." As I will suggest in the course of this book, such a structure preceded early modern and modern movements, and had already taken shape in ancient Greece.

9. Rorty, *Contingency, Irony, and Solidarity*, pp. 190–192.

10. At this early point in our discussion, the structure of civil discourse can only be presented schematically. It will be developed in a more historically and institutionally situated manner in the empirical elaborations presented in later chapters. This cultural structure has not been deduced from some a priori, abstract theory of action, culture, or democratic society, whether empirical or normative. It has been developed, rather, through the hermeneutic reconstruction of a wide range of empirical materials, and its variations have been subjected to controls in a series of comparative and historical studies. My first inkling about such a noncontingent binary structure came as I studied fifty hours of condensed videotape at the Vanderbilt Television Archives in 1985, a compilation that presented, sequentially, every story mentioning the word "Watergate" on *CBS Evening Television with Walter Cronkite* between the break-in at the Watergate building in June 1972 and President Nixon's resignation in August 1974. This inkling became a conviction as I read more widely in the ideological history of the American, English, and French revolutions,

and as I researched other crises that had been sparked by political and social polarization in American history in preparation for a book on the Watergate crisis that,
in the end, appeared only as an article. This conviction took the form presented
here in the late 1980s, when I developed a cultural-sociological theory that included
a late Durkheimian version of structuralism. A paper about this cultural structure
circulated as a manuscript among graduate students with whom I worked in the
UCLA "Culture Club" and was first published as "Morale e Repressione"; in a
longer form as "The Deceptiveness of Morality"; and, still more fully, in "Citizen
Enemy." Philip Smith and I documented the manner in which this cultural structure
played a central role in a series of scandals and crises in American history: the
Nullification Crisis of 1832; the Bank War that rocked Washington in the 1830s; the
scandals that enveloped Presidents Johnson and Grant in the mid-nineteenth century; the scandals of the Teapot Dome in the mid-1920s; Watergate in the early
1970s; Iran-Contra in 1986; and representations of Michael Gorbachev and *glasnost*
in 1987–1988 (see Alexander and Smith, "Discourse of American Civil Society").
Since that time, empirical investigations have explored this cultural structure in
nationalist rhetoric in American history textbooks (Magnuson, "Ideological Conflict
in American Political Culture"); the rhetoric of racial conflict between African
American and white citizens in Los Angeles and Chicago, as recorded in the white
and black newspapers of both communities during racial conflicts in the second half
of the twentieth century (R. Jacobs, "Civil Society and Crisis" and *Race, Media,
and the Crisis of Civil Society*); British popular and official rhetoric during the Falkland
Islands war (P. Smith, "Codes and Conflict"); and American, British, French, and
Spanish popular and official rhetoric during the Suez Crisis, the Gulf and the Iraqi
wars (P. Smith, *Why War? The Cultural Logic of Iraq, the Gulf War and Suez*, and
Alexander, "Bush, Hussein, and the Cultural Preparation for War"); popular and
official argumentation in Hong Kong during the transition crisis (Ku, "Boundary
Politics in the Public Sphere"); fascist and communist variations of civil rhetoric (P.
Smith, "Barbarism and Civility"); studies of class conflict and constitutional crisis in
contemporary Brazil (Baiocchi, "Civilizing Force of Social Movements"); and in
the framing of anti-American rhetoric among certain leading European intellectuals
(Heins, "Orientalizing America").

11. Which is to say that between the sides and the levels of civil society discourse
there exists a powerful intertextuality, in Kristeva's sense in, e.g., "Bounded Text."

12. To fully encompass the discursive dimension of the nature of everyday social
life, the binary element of semiotic analysis must be complemented by a narrative
element. Narrative transforms the dualities of structure into patterns that order lived
experience in a chronological way. For the philosophical background to narrative
analysis, see Ricoeur, *Time and Narrative*; and Entrikin, *Betweenness of Place*. For the
connection of narrativity to ontological and metaphysical themes in Western history,
see Frye, *Anatomy of Criticism*; and White, *Metahistory*. For recent narrative ap-

proaches in cultural sociology, see Somers, "Narrating and Naturalizing Civil Society"; Wagner-Pacifici, *Moro Morality Play*; Kane, "Theorizing Meaning Construction"; P. Smith, "Semiotic Foundations of Media Narratives"; Sherwood, "Narrating the Social"; and the citations in note 10.

13. Until the twentieth century, confession was, apparently, principally a Western institution, one that emerged in tandem with the gradual social recognition of the centrality of individual rights and self-control in the organization of political and religious societies. At least from the medieval period on, criminal punishment was not considered to be fully successful until the accused had confessed his or her crimes, for only such confession could demonstrate that rationality had been achieved and individual responsibility assumed. In this manner, the discourse of civil society becomes tied to public confessions of crimes against individuals in the civil collectivity and, indeed, of crimes against the collectivity itself. This helps explain why such great efforts are expended to extort fraudulent confessions in those situations where coercive force has obliterated civility, e.g., in show trials, as well as in instances of political brutality in democratic societies. See Foucault, *Discipline and Punish*, pp. 36–47, and *History of Sexuality*, Vol. 1, pp. 58–65. For a detailed exposition of the Foucauldian position and its relation to the traditions of sociological theory, see Hepworth and Turner, *Confession*. For a subtle investigation of confession that relates the emphases of civil discourse to contemporary legal practices, and is informed by semiotic and poststructuralist literary theory, see P. Brooks, *Troubling Confessions*.

14. The notion that there is a discourse of repression that constitutes the hidden, other side of a discourse of emancipation is developed, in a certain manner, by Foucault in his reconstruction of the conflicts between Victorian and sexological, especially Freudian, approaches to sexual behavior in *History of Sexuality*, Vol. I. In Part II, "The Repressive Hypothesis," Foucault suggests that the purpose of Victorian pollution of an aberrant eros was not really to suppress it, purely and simply, but actually "to give it an analytical, visible, and permanent reality" such that it was "made into a principle of classification and intelligibility, established as a *raison d'être* and a natural order of disorder." The result, then, was "not the exclusion of these thousand aberrant sexualities, but the specification . . . of each one of them," i.e., "to strew reality with them and incorporate them into the individual" (pp. 44–45). I am saying something of the same about the specification of anticivil qualities by the civil sphere. Though these qualities are purported to embody heinous moral antipathies, qualities that civil democracies wish to, and could in principle, dispense with, they are, in fact, valued as alternatives that define and highlight the purity of civil forms. They are, in this way, necessary for both discursive and institutional reasons. My approach differs from Foucault's, of course, in terms of the substantive, i.e., civil/uncivil, contents that I attribute to the emancipating and repressive discourses, but in other ways as well. First, I suggest that the internal structuring of

this dichotomous discourse provides the possibility for relative autonomy vis-à-vis structures of domination rather than, as Foucault would have it, necessarily being intertwined or instantiated inside them—"interlocking, hierarchized, and . . . highly articulated around a cluster of power relations" (p. 30). Second, though the anticivil discourse of repression is not used merely or simply for the purposes of actual suppression, it certainly did, and does, motivate, promote, and legitimate brutality, domination, murder, and annihilation. Third, even while being symbiotically tethered to the repressive discourse, the discourse of liberty provides leverage for actual emancipation, even if still constrained in semiotic terms. In these emancipation processes, which I will discuss in Parts III and IV, the dark side of civil discourse is not eliminated, but the construction of any particular group or individual can be shifted from anticivil to civil. Such leverage is possible because of what I have described as the nondetermined relation between symbolic signifiers and social signifieds—the relative autonomy of culture vis-à-vis social structure, an autonomy which the power-knowledge linkage informing Foucault's most influential writings was designed to deny.

In his final lectures ("Hermeneutics of the Self," pp. 202–204), Foucault suggested that although the philosophy of consciousness in postwar Europe "had failed to take into account the formative mechanisms of signification and the structures of systems of meaning," his own alternative strategy had been to emphasis "objects of knowledge" only insofar as, "at the same time," they became "objects of domination." Announcing an "autocritique," Foucault acknowledged this had been an overly restrictive response: "I insisted, I think, too much on the techniques of domination." He admitted that, "while what we can call discipline is something really important . . . it is only . . . one aspect of governing people in our society," and he suggested that "I would like in years to come to study government . . . starting from the techniques of the self." Foucault justified this new focus on the self because "for the government of people in our societies everyone had not only to obey but also to produce and publish the truth about oneself." The problem, however, was that, despite this insight, Foucault did not allow techniques of selfhood to connect with meaning and signification. He could conceive truth speaking and emancipation only as self-oriented, rather than as social and solidaristic, as involving only matters of resistance against social discourses rather than as being stimulated by them. My position here is quite different. Government can respect the self, I would suggest, only if there is an independent civil sphere and if the structure of civil discourse can be separated, in principle, from domination.

15. In Aristotle's discussion of such efforts at justification, he puts together references from the three different levels of civil discourse:

The name of citizen is particularly applicable to those who share in the offices and honors of the state. Homer accordingly speaks in the *Iliad* of a man being treated "like an alien man, without honor," and it is true that those who do not share in the offices and honors of the state are just like resident aliens. To deny men a share [may sometimes be justified, but] when it is done by subterfuge its only object is merely that of hoodwinking others.

Aristotle's translator, Ernest Barker, footnotes this discussion with a comment that illustrates the rule of homology I am suggesting here, according to which concepts like honor, citizenship, and office are effectively interchangeable: "The Greek word time which is here used means, like the Latin *honos*, both 'office' and 'honor.' The passage in the Iliad refers to honor in the latter sense: Aristotle himself is using it in the former; but it is natural to slide from one into the other" (*Politics of Aristotle*, p. 109). See my connection of office status and civil pollution in chapter 6.

16. See Shils, "Center and Periphery" and "Charisma, Order, and Status."

17. The role of the sacred and profane in structuring consciousness, action, and cosmology in early human societies is widely understood. See, for example, the classic exposition by Émile Durkheim, *Elementary Forms of Religious Life*. For this focus in the Durkheimian tradition more generally, see Parkin, *Dark Side of Humanity*, and A. Riley, " 'Renegade Durkheimianism' "; for a provocative treatment of archaic religion by Mircea Eliade, see *Sacred and the Profane*; for an exposition of taboo theory by Franz Steiner, see *Taboo*; and for an analysis of dirtiness and cleanliness, or purity, in premodern dirt symbolism by Mary Douglas, see *Purity and Danger*. The challenge for a cultural sociology of contemporary society is to find a way to translate these understandings of pollution and purity in "primitive" religious processes into a secular frame of reference. This task was launched in the reformulation of Durkheim's sacred/profane scheme by Roger Caillois, *Man and the Sacred*, and in closely related discussions by Georges Bataille, e.g., *Literature and Evil*. For contemporary discussions, see the references in note 10, and also V. Zelizer, *Pricing the Priceless Child*; L. D. Edles, *Symbol and Ritual in the New Spain*, and the work on symbolic boundaries by Michele Lamont, who in a series of closely argued comparative empirical studies has found the moral binary worthy/unworthy at the center of racial and economic stratification in France and the United States: *Money, Manners, and Morals* and *The Dignity of Working Men*. In his introduction to a historical inquiry into the origins of the link between moral purity and pollution, on the one hand, and political persecution, on the other, Barrington Moore observes that "human beings kill and torture other human beings who, on account of their different religious, political, and economic ideas, appear as a threatening source of 'pollution' " (*Moral Purity and Persecution in History*, p. ix). In a Weberian fashion, Moore traces the origins of this binary to Western monotheistic religions and their secular revolutionary successor movements, and he suggests it has today spread throughout the world. It seems to me, however, that anthropological understandings

place the purity/pollution binary at the very beginnings of human social organization and thought.

18. Hegel, *Philosophy of Right*, p. 108.

19. For the omnipresence of cultural framing within even the most mundane political process, see Bellah, "Civil Religion in America"; Bennett, "Imitation, Ambiguity, and Drama in Political Life"; and B. Schwartz, *Abraham Lincoln and the Forge of National Memory*.

20. For a discussion of the role of the myth of origin in archaic societies, which has clear implications for the organization of mythical thought in secular ones, see Eliade, *Sacred and the Profane*. For contemporary discussions of secular society that employ notions of origin myth to understand emerging collective identity, see Apter, "Mao's Republic"; Apter and Tony Saich, *Revolutionary Discourse in Mao's Republic*; E. Ringmar: *Identity, Interest, and Action*; and Giesen, *Intellectuals and the Nation*. For myth and critical theory, see Cooke, ch. 3, n. 62.

21. Bailyn, *Ideological Origins of the American Revolution*; Pocock, *Ancient Constitution and the Feudal Law*.

22. Henry Smith, *Virgin Land*; Cawelti, "From Rags to Respectability."

23. Higham, *Strangers in the Land*; B. Wolfe, "Uncle Remus and the Malevolent Rabbit"; Slotkin, *Regeneration through Violence*; Cameron, *American Samurai*; and Gibson, *Warrior Dreams*.

24. The counterpositioning of heroic enactors of liberty with criminals who act out of uncontrolled passion was a major plotting device in the "action detective" genre that emerged in pulp fiction in the late nineteenth century, whose popularity has continued unabated in the present day. See Cawelti, *Adventure, Mystery, and Romance*; and Noel, *Villains Galore*. This long-standing genre, for example, provided the legitimating symbolic framework for the Federal Bureau of Investigation throughout most of the twentieth century. When Americans looked at FBI Director J. Edgar Hoover, they saw "not a spokesman for a partisan political philosophy, but a suprapolitical national hero" modeled on the action genre (Powers, *G-Men*, p. xii). Powers emphasizes the binary nature of the discourse that sacralized Hoover's actions: "For the mythological process to produce a Hoover-style hero, there had to be a universally understood formula within the culture for dealing with the sort of villain who had come to represent the public's fears" (p. xiv). In the popular-culture/political-culture hybrid of the twentieth century, the criminals pursued by "officials" were persistently portrayed as subject to "gang rule," which posed the danger that this form of repressive social organization would spread to "still wider areas of life" (p. 7). For their part, the G-men pursuing these criminals were portrayed both as "rebelliously individualistic" and as the upholders of rational law, as involved in "an epochal struggle between lawful society and an organized underworld" (p. 94).

25. P. Smith, "Codes and Conflict," and *Why War?*; also references in notes 17 and 20–24.

26. Alexander, "Watergate as Democratic Ritual."

27. Keynes, *Economic Consequences of the Peace*; Skidelsky, *John Maynard Keynes*, pp. 354–402.

28. For an insightful fictional representation of this tendency in American culture, see P. Roth, *Plot against America*.

29. For a sweeping historical overview of how "civil society" and "fanaticism' have been deeply intertwined, indeed constitute nothing less than "conjoined histories" in political thought from the Greeks to modern times, see D. Colas, *Civil Society and Fanaticism*.

In the deeply controversial manifesto *The Concept of the Political*, which Carl Schmitt produced on the eve of the Nazi seizure of power, we are offered a sophisticated rationalization for a violently antidemocratic state and its ambitions for wider domination. In a manner that, at first glance, seems eerily to adumbrate the position I am putting forward here, Schmitt emphasizes the inevitability of the discursive binary friend/enemy. The differences between our positions, however, are dramatic and telling, not only normatively but theoretically and empirically. Schmitt traces the origins of the friend/enemy binary to the state's struggle for power and domination, not to the semantics of moral language or the civil sphere's symbolic construction of solidary boundaries that could, in principle, place moral regulations over state power and violence. "It is the state as an organized political entity," he writes, "that decides for itself the friend/enemy distinction" (pp. 29–30). Rejecting a cultural position theoretically, a democratic position normatively, and the possibility for an autonomous civil sphere empirically, Schmitt insists that, for a "realist," politics could not involve "symbolic wrestlings" or "intellectual controversy" (p. 33). These were concerns only for a weak-kneed liberalism mistakenly focused "almost solely on the internal struggle against the power of the state," a move that makes of the state "a compromise and of its institutions a ventilating system" (70). As compared to a democratic liberalism that seeks to control the state, Schmitt insists that politics is inevitably associated with violence and war. It is the "fighting collectivity" that demands the division between friends and enemies, so that it can provide the "real possibility of physical killing," a "real enemy" that can be attacked with "the utmost intensity." For further discussion of Schmitt, see chapter 5, n. 55.

30. R. Smith, *Civic Ideals: conflicting Visions of Citizenship in U.S. History*, p. 4. In his systematic and empirically rich exposure of the ascriptive and exclusionary dimensions that shadow the better known and "official" democratic, liberal, and republican strands, Smith's work supports the general thrust of the approach I am developing here. There are two differences worth noting. One is that Smith sees the negating, antithetical civil ideals as existing outside of liberalism and republicanism, as representing a third tradition that is ascriptive, particularistic, and antidemocratic. The approach I have developed here suggests, to the contrary, that the

antidemocratic, repressive elements of civic ideals are postulated directly within democratic discourse itself. Second, the source from which Smith reconstructs the content of civil ideals is different from the one I employ here, and so is his explanation for their form. In locating the roots of the contradictory and paradoxical logic of American political culture in legal and legislative decisions, he does not construct it as a relatively autonomous discourse but sees it as the result, in the first instance, of "the imperatives of state building" (p. 39) vis-à-vis a complex and divided social structure. These imperatives express themselves, according to this notion, in the need that political leaders have to maintain their power by manipulating the masses; they suggest themes of peoplehood that can satisfy the masses' need for psychological security and moral worth (pp. 32ff.). In his essay "The Dynamics of Democratic Exclusion," Charles Taylor observes that "there is something in the dynamic of democracy that pushes toward exclusion," but he, too, locates the source of this paradox in something outside, rather than inside, democratic civil discourse. In his case, it is the need for democracies also to maintain "something like a common identity . . . to form an entity and have a personality" (p. 143).

CHAPTER 5

1. Douglas, *How Institutions Think*. Compared with those following the classical Weberian approach to organization, contemporary "neo-institutionalists" have downplayed purely instrumental-pragmatic concerns and incorporated more culturally oriented concepts. See, for example, J. W. Meyer and Rowan, "Institutionalized Organizations," and DiMaggio and Powell, "Iron Cage Revisited." Nonetheless, even those who articulate such an institutional approach tend to homologize patterns of organization and culture, such that culture qua meaning—the internal patterning of symbols via codes and narratives—fails to achieve relative autonomy vis-à-vis organizational restraints. See, for example, Friedland and Alford, "Bringing Society Back In." For further discussion of these issues, see chapter 6.

2. In her empirical analysis of elites and public opinion, Susan Herbst has emphasized just this specifying, multilevel process: "Interest groups are more than simple surrogates for public opinion. . . . They translate opinion, but during this translation process they also help to give public opinion a more solid and comprehensible form" (*Reading Public Opinion*, p. 53. For the conceptual distinction between influence and authoritative control or power, see Parsons's important essays on influence and power as generalized media of exchange in *Politics and Social Structure*, pp. 352–438, distinctions that were later elaborated and modified by Jürgen Habermas in *Lifeworld and System*, esp. pp. 266–282. If this distinction is not made—if communicative institutions are not conceptually differentiated from coercive control, whether in states or organizations—then power can be conceptualized only as hegemony in the

Gramscian sense or power-knowledge in the Foucauldian. In neither case is it possible to conceptualize an independent civil sphere and, thus, democracy as I have conceived it here.

3. Arendt, *Human Condition*, p. 57.

4. Habermas, *Structural Transformation of the Public Sphere*. For more recent versions of this critical republican position, see the normative work on deliberative democracy (chap. 3 n. 8) and the continuing wave of empirical analyses aimed at reforming putatively passive public opinion, e.g., Fishkin, *Voice of the People*.

5. M. Weber, "The City," and Sennett, *Classic Essays on the Culture of Cities* and *Rise and Fall of Public Man*.

6. Walzer, *Revolution of the Saints;* and Mayhew, *Public Spirit*.

7. Diana C. Mutz makes the same point in her empirical study of the transformation of the public from direct relationship to impersonal public opinion, which constitutes a kind of "generalized other" in the sense of George Herbert Mead (*Impersonal Influence*).

8. For a similar criticism of Habermas and Arendt, and the suggestion of the idea of the public as a regulating ideal, see Benhabib, *Reluctant Modernism of Hannah Arendt*, pp. 203–206, and Cooke, *Re-Presenting the Good Society* (chapter 3, n. 62, above).

9. Tocqueville, *Democracy in America*, Vol. 1, Part I, chap. 8, p. 40.

10. Bryce, *American Commonwealth*, pp. 499–505.

11. Tocqueville, *Democracy in America,* Vol. 1, Part II, chap. 7, p. 293.

12. Gallup and Rae, *Pulse of Democracy*, p. 8. For a comparison of Bryce and Gallup that evaluates their conflicting writings on public opinion in terms of empirical accuracy, rather than as reflecting the binary discourse of civil society, see *Voice of the People*, pp. 71–81.

13. Durkheim, conclusion to *Division of Labor in Society*.

14. For example, Tarde, "Opinion and Conversation." For an illuminating reconstruction of Tarde's public opinion theory in terms of contemporary media and symbolic action theory, see Katz et al., "Press-Conversation-Opinion-Action."

15. John Dewey wrote, in *The Public and Its Problems*: "The confusion which has resulted in the size and ramifications of social activities has rendered men skeptical. . . . Men feel that they are caught in the sweep of forces too vast to understand or master. Thought is brought to a standstill and action paralyzed" (p. 135). Lippmann, *The Phantom Public*, wrote: "The public citizen today has come to feel rather like a deaf spectator in the back row [who] cannot quite manage to keep awake. . . . He is being swept along by great drifts of circumstance. . . . He does not know for certain what is going on, or who is doing it. . . . His sovereignty is a fiction" (p. 13).

16. But see the recent work by Susan Herbst and Diana Mutz cited in notes 2 and 7.

17. It has been common for democratic theory to maintain a sharp distinction

between factual or normative truth, on the one side, and fictional-aesthetic experience on the other. The roots of this tension can be traced back to Plato's suspicion of theater and rhetoric, expressed for example in his *Gorgias*, but in terms of modern debates it begins with Nietzsche's embrace of the aesthetic-expressive and his sharp rejection of universalizing morality, as in *The Birth of Tragedy* and *The Genealogy of Morals*. In contemporary times, this distrust has been most forcefully and influentially expressed by Habermas in his polemic against Hans Georg Gadamer ("A Review of Gadamer's Truth and Method"). In that essay, he insists on associating hermeneutic analysis, or expressive understanding, with tradition, and he portrays the latter as antimodern and antidemocratic; hermeneutic analysis, he argues, is antithetical to theorizing that embraces the normative aspiration of rationality, autonomy, and social emancipation. For an important alternative philosophical argument, one which embraces fiction as a source of ethical-moral instruction, see Booth, *The Company We Keep*. There has been a revisionist movement within the Habermasian tradition to widen his normative theory to embrace the aesthetic and symbolic, most energetically by rethinking some of Habermas's key concepts via the philosophy of Hannah Arendt. In *The Reluctant Modernism of Hannah Arendt*, for example, Benhabib argues that "the term *communicative action* does not quite capture the conceptual issues that Arendt, as opposed to Habermas, had in mind." Thus, "instead of *communicative action*, I shall use the terminology of the *narrative model of action*," which depicts "action embedded in a 'web of relationships and enacted stories' " and combines "the constative as well as the expressive." The "rational core" of this model, Benhabib writes, "cannot be as clearly extricated as Habermas would like" (p. 124). For another example of this culturally oriented revisionism, see Cooke, *Re-Presenting the Good Society* and also Maria P. Lara, *Moral Textures*.

18. Fass, "Television as a Cultural Document: Promises and Problems"; Glover and Kaplan, "Guns in the House of Culture?"; Seyhan, "Ethnic Selves/Ethnic Signs"; Mukerji, "Monsters and Muppets"; T. Rose, "Rewriting the Pleasure/Danger Dialectic"; Lembo, *Thinking through Television*, particularly the empirical analyses of "plausibility" and "narrative-based viewing," pp. 168–185; and Long, *Book Clubs*.

19. The normative rationalism that has broadly informed Habermas's philosophy of the public sphere has obscured the fact that at one important moment in his normative reconstruction of Western history, he actually paid special attention to the aesthetic domain. The sentimental novel, he wrote, allowed "self-clarification of private people focusing on the genuine experiences of their novel privateness," explaining that "the psychological novel fashioned for the first time the kind of realism that allowed anyone to enter into the literary action as a substitute for his own, to use the relationships between the figures, between the author, the characters, and the readers as a substitute relationship for reality." The notion of a "substitute relationship for reality," which allows readers to enter into literary action, is complementary to the argument that I am developing here, though it is hardly limited

to the genre of literary realism. The explicitly cultural focus of the present discussion allows me to view such aesthetic projections and identifications as an ongoing and vital dimension of civil discourse and public opinion formation; the restrictions of Habermas's rationalist perspective, by contrast, compel him to speak of such literary identifications as merely a *"training ground* for a critical public reflection," as a "literary *precursor* of the public sphere" (*Structural Transformation,* pp. 29, 50, emphasis added). An alternative, less determinately rationalist perspective on the relation between fiction and emancipation, still broadly within the Marxist-critical tradition, can be found in Raymond Williams's analysis of the fiction of protest against industrial society in nineteenth-century England, in his essay titled "A Nineteenth Century Tradition." For nineteenth-century fiction as realistic, and thus reflecting industrialism, see Jameson, *Political Unconscious;* for a contrasting view and an analysis of Austin's art as a fictional reconstruction of variable moral capacities, see Lara, "Narrative Cultural Interweavings: Between Fact and Fiction," in *Moral Textures,* pp. 92–104. For nineteenth-century novelist art and narratives about purity and corruption, see P. Brooks, *Melodramatic Imagination.* For a critical argument against reading "realism" as fiction that allows transparent access to truthful observation rather than as itself a meaning-genre, see Jakobson, "On Realism in Art."

20. Goodwin, *Team of Rivals,* p. 161. See also W. L. Miller, *Arguing about Slavery,* pp. 333–335. For a discussion of moral empathy and the romantic movement in fiction, see G. Hartmann, "Sympathy Paradox."

21. Peter Brooks, *Realist Vision,* pp. 8, 13.

22. Long, *American Dream and the Popular Novel.*

23. Sherwood, "Narrating the Social."

24. In his essay "From the Polluted Homosexual to the Normal Gay," Steven Seidman has emphasized the importance of fictionalized reconstructions of homosexuality in American film, and he demonstrates how shifts in such filmic representations have helped to undermine the repressive "closet" metaphor in gay and lesbian life (*Beyond the Closet,* pp. 123–162). One observer of American television commented that "*Will and Grace* has taken the classic four-character sitcom format of *I Love Lucy* and made gay characters an indispensable part of TV Land" (Bob Smith, "From Billy to Willy"). For the contrast between assimilative and multicultural, see chapter 17.

25. *Roots* ran from January 23 to January 30, 1977, on eight consecutive nights, and was watched by some 130 million viewers, the largest audience recorded for a television show up until that time. That same year, the book on which the epochal TV series was based, Haley's autobiographical *Roots: The Saga of an American Family,* was awarded a special Pulitzer Prize and the National Book Award.

26. Huff, "Viva!"

27. Wright, *Six Guns and Society.*

28. Bazin, *What Is Cinema?*

29. Darnton, "Writing News and Telling Stories"; R. Jacobs, "Producing the News"; Herbst, *Reading Public Opinion*, p. 64; Lembo, "Narrative-Based Viewing"; M. Schudson, *Sociology of News*, pp. 177–193.

30. "For many people deeply involved in politics," Susan Herbst reports, "the phenomena of public opinion and mass media are largely conflated" (*Reading Public Opinion*, p. 5).

31. This continuum of flexible responsiveness has been stretched further in recent years by the gradual appearance of new Web-based sources of event-responsiveness, such as blogs. On the one hand, blogs are even more rapid responders than daily news institutions, and thus create a new source of civil mediation. On the other hand, blogs are not informed by professional reporting norms of neutrality. Because they have an overtly personal or ideological character, their constructions of factual reality are less forceful interventions into the civil sphere, even as they constitute a new source of intervening construction.

32. Ronald Jacobs has conducted a series of detailed empirical analyses of how American news media in both white and black communities and in different metropolitan areas have reported on critical events by constructing them in terms of the binary discourse of civil society, and of the repercussions of such representations on powerful elites and institutions. See R. Jacobs, "Civil Society and Crisis" and *Race, Media, and the Crisis of Civil Society*.

33. Habermas, *Structural Transformation*, pp. 181–221. Habermas writes: "The disintegration of the electorate as a public becomes manifest with the realization that press and radio . . . have practically no effect; within the framework of the manufactured public sphere the mass media are useful only as vehicles of advertising" (p. 217). See C. Wright Mills, *Power Elite*; Bourdieu, *On Television* and "Return to Television." For a broad overview of democratic theory and media theory, see Alexander and Jacobs, "Mass Communication, Ritual, and Civil Society."

34. Alexander, "The Mass News Media in Systemic"; Schudson, *Discovering the News*.

35. Describing the origins of commercial media in the American colonial period, Michael Schudson (*The Good Citizen: A History of American Civic Life*) writes that "the newspapers advanced a public discourse [that] helped promote a colonies-wide consciousness." He argues that "the public realm that commercialism and commercial sentiments shape is different from one dominated by political principle or partisan engagement, but it is not necessarily retrograde. The newspapers' neutral space was revolutionary in its own way. That the printers' ambitions were commercial rather than political may have been a critical step in a growing toleration for conflicting points of view" (p. 38). Paul Starr has also documented this positive link between commercial media and civil society in his exhaustive social history, *The Creation of the Media: Political Origins of Modern Communications*. About the rise of the penny press in the 1820s and 1830s: "Depending entirely on revenue from readers and

NOTES TO PAGES 83–84

advertisers, the publishers of penny papers proclaimed their independence of any political party and represented themselves as the unfettered champions of the public in reporting the news. . . . In their quest for circulation, they became the first papers in the United States to publish extensive coverage of local news" (pp. 132, 134–135). About the origins of mass circulation magazines in the 1890s:

> The broadened audience for magazines . . . created the preconditions for the turn toward muckraking in the first decade of the new century. . . . It made sense at least for some magazine publishers to use muckraking as a sensation-creating, circulation-building strategy. In late 1902, when it began publishing Ida Tarbell's series on John D. Rockefeller's takeover of the oil industry, *McClure's* opened a new era in political journalism. . . . S. S. McClure put his investigative writers on long-terms salaries, paying them for their research rather than merely for the copy they produced; Tarbell's fifteen Standard Oil articles, produced over five years, cost McClure . . . $4000 each. No publisher could have afforded that investment without the mass circulations then achievable. . . . Muckraking was, therefore, as much a product of the rise of the early mass media as it was a result of the distinct political outlook of the Progressive era. (pp. 260–262)

36. According to Pulitzer Prize-winning media critic David Shaw in "Journalism Is a Very Different Business," contemporary American journalists speak about "the Wall" "that has traditionally separated the business side of the news and editorial side of a good news organization":

> Journalists can be a bit self-aggrandizing, even self-righteous, at times about their mission as truth-tellers—particularly in contrast with what they regard as the bean counters on the business side. Reporters and editors speak of their "mission" and "sacred trust" and make it sound like some sort of mystic priesthood, with rights and rituals incomprehensible to the nonjournalist.

37. Perhaps the most vivid exemplification of this capacity for the representation of society as such are televised "media events," the liminal moments in which news media create the sense of "time out of time," a break from routine programming that represents what is taken to be a dramatic, society changing event. See D. Dayan and E. Katz, *Media Events*.

38. For an analysis of the role that media autonomy, based on professional ethics, played in the construction of a more civil society, see my discussion of the role of northern journalists in the origins of the Civil Rights movement in chapter 12.

39. Tocqueville, *Democracy in America*, Vol. 1, Part 2, chap. 3, p. 212.

40. Congressman quoted in Schudson, *Good Citizen*, p. 105.

41. Benjamin Franklin quoted in Schudson, *Good Citizen*, p. 34.

42. In other words, whether the putative public is a "mass" or an independent and individuated force is as much a matter of construction via the discourse of civil society as it is of a reality that is independent of cultural coding. This binary construction mass-versus-public also occurs within the world of social theory, where it provides antagonistic narratives about democracy and civil society. It is a critical pivot in arguments about the possibilities for democracy in complex capitalist societies. For the manner in which C. Wright Mills's insistence on massification justified his exclusive concentration on elite power rather than on civil communication and regulation, see chapter 6 of this book. If, by contrast, the force of public opinion polls is recognized, their civil power can be undermined at a second remove by claiming that the structure, resources, and interpretation of polling are tied to the power and interests of anticivil actors. This is the theoretical logic that informs the arguments employed by such widely different thinkers as, for example, Bourdieu, "L'opinion publique n'existe pas," and L. Mayhew, *New Public*, e.g., pp. 189–209.

43. Gallup and Rae, *Pulse of Democracy*, p. vi.

44. Ibid., p. vii.

45. Ibid., p. 8.

46. Ibid., p. 26.

47. Ibid., p. 144.

48. Ibid.

49. Ibid., p. 14.

50. Ibid.

51. Gallup, *Guide to Public Opinion Polls*, p. 85.

52. Lang and Lang, *Battle for Public Opinion*.

53. Alexander, "Watergate as Democratic Ritual."

54. See chap. 4, n. 11.

55. On typification as a mode of action connecting micro and macro social worlds, see Alexander, "Action and Its Environments." The concept of typification was developed by Alfred Shutz in his dialogue with Husserl and Max Weber, in *Phenomenology of the Social World*, pp. 139–214.

56. Ku, "Boundary Publics in the Public Sphere," "Revisiting the Notion of 'Public' in Habermas's Theory," and *Narratives, Politics, and the Public Sphere*.

57. William Drozdiak, "Cresson Meets Enemy: Public Opinion Polls," *International Herald Tribune*, June 28, 1991, Sec. A, p. 1.

58. Dick Polman, "Public's Support of War Faltering," *Philadelphia Inquirer*, August 14, 2005, Sec. A, pp. 1, 18.

59. Sam Dillon, "Mexican Party Reported to Quash Polls Predicting Its Defeat," *New York Times*, July 17, 2000, Sec. A, p. 9. For a cultural-sociological analysis of the dynamics of the emerging civil sphere in Mexico that draws from and develops

the framework I have been developing here, see Luis Escala-Rabadan's "The Symbolic Construction of Human Rights Discourse in Mexico's Media, 1978–1996."

60. Hedrick Smith, *New Russians*, pp. 84ff.

61. Ibid., p. 88. After the Soviet Union was dismantled, there ensued a utopian but chaotic and destabilizing period of privatization and democratic experimentation. Standards of living declined, previously unknown men became billionaires overnight, and the Russian military drastically declined in its power and prestige. In this context, it is hardly surprising that polls, often organized by these same institutions, began to crystallize the public's increasingly antidemocratic opinions, registering distrust, low expectations, superstition, hero worship, aggressive feelings toward minorities, and the growing pollution of democracy itself. It was in this symbolic context that Vladimir Putin first rose to the presidency. Placing increasing restraints on Russia's communicative and regulative institutions, Putin was reelected by a landslide vote, and began a campaign to suppress the independence of Russia's noncivil elites. See Richard Pipes, "Flight from Freedom."

62. Majid Al-Haj and Elihu Katz, "Peace: Arab and Jewish Attitudes," *Jerusalem Post*, August 4, 1989, p. 8.

63. This distinction recalls the antithesis between functional and communicative interests that Jürgen Habermas developed in *Theory of Communicative Action*. My approach differs because of the cultural-performative perspective I bring to bear: the critical issue is not whether an organization actually *is* civil but whether it must enter into the civil sphere to justify its aims and interests. Its ambitions may, in fact, be anticivil, and its discourse may employ highly polluting rhetoric. The issue is not whether speech is *really* strategic—being really strategic, in Habermas's perspective, means it cannot be truly communicative—but whether actors in the civil sphere must present their strategic interests in terms of an ethical discourse such that the attribution, e.g., of being "Machiavellian," pollutes them and prevents their strategic interests from being realized.

64. See Herbst's study of how congressional staffers relate to public opinion:

> Staffers find that the public and public opinion are fairly amorphous entities, and some staffers exhibit a fair degree of impatience with knowledge levels among the general public, so lobbyists seem to them a reasonable and appropriate stand-in for the public. In response to my open-ended question about the meaning of "public," one staffer said: "I immediately think of interest groups. That's how we gauge our public opinion. . . . I rarely am clueless about where that constituency is because of the interest groups keeping me informed. . . . I would have to say that from a public opinion standpoint, we don't really care what the average Joe thinks. I don't say that as if we're not representing them, but we're representing the people who

represent them. It's one step removed from the general public." (*Reading Public Opinion*, p. 53)

Herbst concludes that, for these political elites, "lobbyists are perceived to crystallize or clarify the content of intensity of vague public moods" (p. 53).

65. For a broader theoretical understanding of this specifying and translating of general civil codes, see my discussion of the role that ideological "shifters" play in the construction and destruction of civil power, in chapter 6.

66. Quoted in Skocpol, *Boomerang*, pp. 1 and 116, emphasis added.

67. Ibid., pp. 4–5 and 75.

68. Ibid., commentator quoted on p. 10.

69. Ibid., p. 136.

70. Ibid., p. 141.

71. Ibid., pp. 134, 76.

72. Ibid., p. 136.

73. Ibid. Though Skocpol's careful empirical analysis supplies the data from which this analysis is drawn, she herself would not agree with the discursive focus and the emphasis on communicative institutions that I present here. She presents, instead, a more "structural" focus, suggesting (1) that the fiscal resources and strategy available to Clinton forced him to offer a complex plan without financial incentives to the middle class and (2) that the nature of civil associations had changed in a manner that made citizen involvement in progressive movements more difficult. "The changing organizational and resource patterns in U.S. politics and society make certain kinds of political communication, mobilization, and alliance formation more or less feasible," she wrote, with the result that "President Clinton's options for explaining his health care reform plan to his fellow citizens . . . were sharply limited by the groups and technologies at work in the contemporary U.S. civic life" (pp. 83–84). For criticism of the kind of state- and resource-centered approach that Skocpol has introduced into the contemporary analysis of politics, see my discussion of the tradition of Thracymachus in chapter 3 and chapter 6.

74. The campaign for the Patient's Bill of Rights was pushed by such issue-oriented civil associations as "Public Citizen." Its Web site (http://www.citizen.org/), headlined by the banner "Protecting Health, Safety, and Democracy," justifies the Bill of Rights by polluting health maintenance organizations in strikingly anticivil terms: "When death or serious injury occurs because of an HMO's decision to deny necessary or appropriate medical care, the patient or surviving family members should have the right to go to court to seek redress and the insurer should be held accountable for the consequences of negligent or reckless decisions."

75. Tocqueville, *Democracy in America*, Vol. 2, Part II, chaps. 5–7.

76. Durkheim, *Division of Labor in Society*, pp. xxxi–lix.

77. Arendt, *On Revolution*; Habermas, *Structural Transformation*, pp. 35–43.

78. Kornhauser, *Politics of Mass Society*; C. Wright Mills, *Power Elite*.

79. Banton, "Voluntary Associations."

80. Sills, *International Encyclopedia of the Social Sciences*, p. 363.

81. Putnam, *Making Democracy Work,* "Bowling Alone," and *Bowling Alone*.

82. Jean Cohen, "Does Voluntary Association Make Democracy Work?" p. 268.

83. This purely associational, CSI emphasis on nonstate groups as, in themselves, carriers of democracy and civil society has also been articulated by contemporary sociologists in the language of networks. Harrison White, for example, speaks of publics as "interstitial social spaces which ease transitions between specific domains [by] decoupling actors from the pattern of specific relations and understandings embedded with[in] any particular domain and network" ("Where Do Languages Come From?" *Pre-Print Series*, Paul F. Lazarsfeld Center for the Social Sciences, Columbia University, 1995, p. 4). Drawing attention to the relevance of this network approach of White, and connecting it more explicitly with the Habermasian idea of deliberative publics, Emirbayer and Sheller define publics as "interstitial networks," or as "open-ended flows of communication that enable socially distant interlocutors to bridge social network positions, formulate collective orientations, and generate psychical 'working alliances,' in pursuit of influence over issues of common concern" ("Publics in History," p. 156.) Despite its technical quality, however, this broad formulation shares the problem common to CSI approaches and, specifically, to the voluntary associations approach to civil association I am discussing here. The approach applies to any communicative process inside any sphere in society, whether economic, religious, ethnic, familial, or governmental, as long as there is mobilization of communication among those who inhabit structural network positions. This definition has, in other words, nothing specifically to do with democratic theory, much less with the discourse codes that inform the kinds of solidarity community that sustain citizenship. It does not, for example, differentiate the kind of publicity that might characterize influential market innovation from civil association.

84. See Putnam, *Bowling Alone*, p. 48. The reference is to Tocqueville's discussion in *Democracy in America,* Vol. 2, Book II, chap. 5, of how "Americans of all ages, all conditions, and all minds are constantly joining together in groups" (p. 595). (This and all following quotations from Tocqueville are from the Goldhammer translation.)

85. Tocqueville, *Democracy in America*, Vol. 2, Part II, chap. 5, p. 596.

86. Ibid., Vol. 1, Part II, chap. 4, p. 216.

87. Ibid., p. 220.

88. Ibid., p. 222.

89. Ibid., p. 220, emphasis added.

90. Ibid., pp. 220–222.

91. Ibid., chap. 9, pp. 352–353.

92. Robert Gannett makes a complementary argument in his analysis of Tocqueville's discussion of the state's role in America as compared to England, from a draft chapter for *Democracy in America* not included in the published version of Tocqueville's book: "Central governments need not automatically usurp associational incentive or authority, Tocqueville thus argued, provided that they remain mindful of their proper role of giving short-term '*help*,' not commanding long-term '*obedience*' " ("Bowling Ninepins in Tocqueville's Township," p. 14; emphasis in original). The critical issue for Tocqueville's view of the state, in other words, is whether it was civil in its orientation.

93. Schudson, *Good Citizen*, pp. 48–66.

94. Lipset et al., *Union Democracy*, p. 4.

95. Ibid.

96. Ibid., p. 5.

97. Sills, *International Encyclopedia*, pp. 368–369.

98. Putnam, "Bowling Alone," p. 32. In the book version of this argument, there is a similarly damaging admission, followed by the introduction of a major residual category that belies the entire thrust of Putnam's argument about the causal line from association to social capital to democracy:

> Social capital . . . can be directed toward malevolent, antisocial purposes, just like any other form of capital. . . . Therefore it is important to ask how the positive consequences of social capital—mutual support, cooperation, trust, institutional effectiveness—can be maximized and the negative manifestations—sectarianism, ethnocentrism, corruption—minimized. . . . Of all the dimensions along which forms of social capital vary, perhaps the most important is the distinction between bridging (or inclusive) and bonding (or exclusive). Some forms of capital are . . . inward looking and tend to reinforce exclusive identities. . . . Other networks are outward looking and encompass people across diverse social cleavages. . . . It would obviously be valuable to have distinct measures of the evolution of these various forms of social capital over time. However[,] like researchers on global warming, we must make do with the imperfect evidence that we can find. . . . Exhaustive descriptions of social networks in America . . . do not exist. I have found no reliable, comprehensive, nationwide measures of social capital that neatly distinguish "bridgingness" and "bondingness." In our empirical account of recent trends in this book, therefore, this distinction will be less prominent that I would prefer. (*Bowling Alone*, pp. 22–24)

99. Putnam, *Making Democracy Work*, p. 125.

100. Ibid., pp. 128, 130.

101. Ibid., pp. 125–126. As Jean Cohen writes, "Without other mediations, there

is no reason to expect that the forms of reciprocity or trust generated within small groups would extend beyond the group, or, for that matter, that group demands would be anything other than particularistic" ("Does Voluntary Association Make Democracy Work?" pp. 269–270). For an extended empirical criticism of Putnam's claims about the consequences of voluntary associations for Italian democracy, see Mabel Berezin's argument that the areas of greatest voluntary organization were also the most likely to become Fascist during the interwar period (M. Berezin, "Uncivil Society: Putnam's 'Italy' and the Other Side of Association," unpublished paper presented at the Conference on the Discourses of Civil Society,' University of California at Los Angeles, Center for Modern and Contemporary Studies, June 12, 1998).

102. Schudson, *Good Citizen*, p. 42.

103. Ibid., p. 43.

104. In "Democratic Liberalism and the Challenge of Diversity in Late-Twentieth-Century America," Robert Wuthnow presents empirical data for an alternative reading of shifts in American associations, suggesting that, in complex societies, home and neighborhood have become more "loosely coupled" from work and formal associations, one result of which is that civil associations have a more professionalized, less voluntary staff. Current jeremiads about the supposed decline of such face-to-face groupings and their deleterious effects on democracy, of course, extend considerably beyond Putnam's singular crusade. As I have suggested several times here, such alarmist claims have always been the stock-in-trade of both radical and conservative republican critics of modern societies. In *Democracy on Trial*, for example, J. Elshtain asserts that "it is no longer possible for us to speak to one another," and that "we quite literally inhabit our own little islands of bristling difference where we comport with those just like ourselves." In *Trust: The Social Virtues and the Creation of Prosperity*, Francis Fukuyama similarly opines that "the moral communities that made up American civil society at midcentury, from the family to neighborhoods to churches to workplaces, have been under assault, and a number of indicators suggest that the degree of general sociability has declined." Both of these conservative proclamations are quoted in Wuthnow, "Democratic Liberalism," p. 20.

105. Putnam, "Bowling Alone," p. 20.

CHAPTER 6

1. M. Weber, "Bureaucracy," pp. 214–215.

2. Skocpol, "Bringing the State Back In," "On the Road toward a More Adequate Understanding of the State," and *States and Social Revolutions*.

3. Weber, "Bureaucracy," p. 230. Weber continues: "One has to remember that bureaucracy as such is a precision instrument that can put itself at the disposal of

quite varied—purely political as well as purely economic, or any other sort—interests in domination" (p. 231). It is this proposition that allows Weber to open his theory of modern rationalization to democracy, a process he conceptualizes, however, in its most minimal sense as plebiscitarian caesarism. He developed this connection between his bureaucracy theory and democratic politics in "Parliament and Government in a Reconstructed Germany," esp. pp. 1403–1405 and 1438.

4. It was Weber who first systematically distinguished between economic, political, and symbolic ("status") forms of power in his foundational essay, "Class, Status, and Party." This distinction was elaborated for elite and class theory by such thinkers as C. Wright Mills in *The Power Elite* and as a model of "social power" by Mann in *Sources*.

5. For representative analyses, see, e.g., Domhoff, *Who Rules America* and *Powers That Be*; and Miliband, *State in Capitalist Society*.

6. In addition to the works cited in note 5, see, for example, Michels, *Political Parties;* and Poulantzas, "The Problem of the Capitalist State" and "The Capitalist State."

7. Downs, *Economic Theory of Democracy*, p. 36.

8. Crick, *In Defense of Politics*, p. 23.

9. Polsby and Wildavsky, *Presidential Elections*, p. 3.

10. M. Weber, "Class, Status, and Party," p. 194.

11. Michels, *Political Parties*, pp. 65, 70.

12. Duverger, *Political Parties: Their Organization*, p. 4.

13. Key, *Southern Politics in State and Nation*, pp. 303–304.

14. Polsby and Wildavsky, *Presidential Elections*, p. 27.

15. Polsby, "Coalition and Faction in American Politics."

16. Lipset, "Elections: The Expression of the Democratic Class Struggle."

17. The classic text here is Bendix and Lipset, *Class, Status, and Power*, first published in 1953 and subsequently reprinted several times.

18. Lipset, " 'Fascism'—Left, Right, and Center," and, partly in response, R. F. Hamilton, *Who Voted for Hitler?*

19. Bell, "Interpretation of American Politics," p. 21.

20. Lipset and Ladd, *Politics of Unreason*, p. 23.

21. Freidland and Alford, "Bringing Society Back In," pp. 421–422.

22. C. Brooks and J. Manza, "Social and Ideological Bases of Middle-Class Political Realignment," pp. 204–205.

23. See nn. 5 and 6, and also Zeitlin, "Corporate Ownership and Control."

24. C. Wright Mills, *Power Elite*, p. 303.

25. Ibid., p. 298.

26. Ibid., p. 302.

27. Ibid., pp. 309, 315.

28. Rokkan et al., *Citizens, Elections, Parties*, p. 143.

29. Euripides, "The Suppliant Women," pp. 206–207, quoted in Arblaster, *Democracy*, pp. 21–22.

30. Keyssar, *Right to Vote*, p. 2, emphasis in original. Keyssar is here adopting a narrower, strictly Aristotelian definition of democracy than the broader one I suggest in this book.

31. Ibid., p. 9. The reasoning is not any different in the contemporary efforts by the Chinese Communist Party to restrict electoral participation in contemporary China:

> The regime . . . claims that popular elections above the village level will not work because the *suzchi* (quality, character) of the people is too low. The masses are ignorant, and would be too easily swayed by passion or bias. Therefore, they continue, we, the masters of the regime, have to be in control. The logic is not only humiliating to the Chinese people but oddly circular: we must, the regime says, run things in our own repressive way because the people are ignorant, and the people are ignorant in large part because we keep them from being informed. (P. Link, "China: Wiping Out the Truth," p. 39)

32. Shklar, *American Citizenship*, p. 2.

33. Ibid., p. 15.

34. Ibid., pp. 16, 27.

35. Ibid., p. 38.

36. Quoted in Keyssar, *Right to Vote*, p. 5.

37. Montesquieu, *Spirit of the Laws*, Vol. 2, p. 155.

38. See Little, *Religion, Order, and Law*.

39. Blackstone, *Commentaries on the Laws of England, 1765–1769*, Vol. 1, p. 165.

40. Quoted in Dinkin, *Voting in Provincial America*, p. 36.

41. Quoted in Keyssar, *Right to Vote*, p. 19.

42. Ibid., p. 35.

43. Ibid., p. 36.

44. Dinkin, *Voting in Provincial America*, p. 54.

45. Ibid., p. 56.

46. Ibid., p. 57.

47. Ibid., p. 93.

48. Quoted in Gillette, *Right to Vote*, p. 42, emphasis in original.

49. Ibid., p. 87.

50. Quoted in U.S. Commission on Civil Rights, *Voting in Mississippi*, p. 3.

51. Quoted in Gorfman, Mandley, and Niemi, *Minority Representation*, p. 8.

52. Quoted in U.S. Commission on Civil Rights, *Voting in Mississippi*, p. 6, emphasis added.

53. Aldrich, *Why Parties?* p. 1, emphasis added.

54. Mouffe, *Democratic Paradox*, p. 101.

55. This is a critical distinction. For example, though Carl Schmitt was a keen observer of how friend/enemy rhetoric permeated contemporary politics in such works as *The Concept of the Political*, he embraced polarization and irrationality not only in an empirical manner but normatively as well. Ultimately, I believe, the normative weakness of Schmitt's political theory is connected with the empirical inadequacies of his political sociology. He views the binary distinction friend/enemy as a reflection of power-political forces rather than of concerns about a meaningful life. For this reason, he could not conceive the possibility that a differentiated civil sphere and the power it generates can or should place democratic moral limits on social and state power. For further criticism of Schmidt, in relation to the framework presented here, see chapter 4, note 29, this volume.

56. Popkin, *Reasoning Voter*; Paige, *Rational Public*; Aldrich, *Why Parties?* p. 21.

57. "By privileging rationality," Mouffe observes, "both the deliberative and the aggregative perspectives leave aside a central element which is the crucial role played by passions and affects in securing allegiance to democratic values." Such rational subjects can be imagined, she adds, only if they are "abstracted from social and power relations, language, culture and the whole set of practices that make agency possible" (*Democratic Paradox*, p. 95).

58. It has often been argued, for example, that the American conflict over slavery was marked by rational debates which are impossible in contemporary mass society, where "performance" rules. For an interpretation of the Lincoln-Douglas slavery debates that challenge this specific claim and, more generally, challenges Habermas's theory that politics was more democratic and reflexive in the nineteenth century, see Schudson, "Was There Ever a Public Sphere?" For Abraham Lincoln as a performative figure, and a storyteller par excellence, see Goodwin, *Team of Rivals*, e.g., pp. 164–166.

59. See chap. 8.

60. Quoted in Dinkin, *Voting in Provincial America*, p. 112.

61. Quoted in Altschuler and Blumin, *Rude Republic*, p. 137.

62. Leviero, "President Likens Dewey to Hitler," p. 1.

63. Quoted in Abramson, Aldrich, and Rohde, *Change and Continuity in the 1992 Elections*, p. 58.

64. Wilgoren and Halbfinger, "Kerry and Dean, All Forgiven."

65. Sears et al., "Self-Interest vs. Symbolic Politics," p. 680.

66. Zaller, *Nature and Origins of Mass Opinion*, pp. 22–23.

67. Jakobson defined shifters as a linguistic element that links the local and situated

references of speech acts to the more general and abstract code. Shifters are necessary, in Jakobson's words, "since we are far from confining our speech to events sensed in the present by the speaker himself" ("Shifters and Verbal Categories," p. 387).

68. Stokes writes:

> For the average person, the affairs of government are remote and complex, and yet the average citizen is asked periodically to formulate opinions about those affairs. At the very least, he has to decide how he will vote, what choice he will make between candidates offering different programs and very different versions of contemporary political events. In this dilemma, having the party symbol stamped on certain candidates, certain issue positions, certain interpretations of political reality is of great psychological convenience. [This] involves subtle processes of perceptual adjustment by which the individual assembles an image of current politics consistent with his partisan allegiance. With normal luck, the partisan voter will carry to the polls attitudes toward the new elements of politics that support his long-standing bias." ("Party Loyalty and the Likelihood of Deviating Elections," p. 127)

69. R. MacIver, *Web of Government*, p. 216.

70. Berelson, Lazarsfeld, and McPhee, *Voting*, pp. 88–117; Campbell et. al., *Elections and the Political Order*, pp. 125–158; W. E. Miller and Shanks, *New American Voter*, pp. 120–133.

71. Green, Palmquist, and Schickler, *Partisan Hearts and Minds*, pp. 4, 6.

72. Ibid., pp. 6, 8, 205–206, emphasis in original.

73. Berelson et al., *Voting*, p. 223. In terms of disciplinary developments, an important corrective to this approach is the cognitive psychology of partisanship and party politics, which is broadly informed by cognitive science. For example, in *Moral Politics: How Liberals and Conservatives Think,* George Lakoff focuses not on anxiety as a putative emotional trigger for partisanship but on the divided structures of thinking which "define incompatible moral worlds" that raise "the deepest questions of who we are" (p. 222). Though this approach generally complements the perspective that informs this work, the partisan constructs that Lakoff identifies—strict father (Republican) versus nurturing parent (Democrat)—suggest that the frames of political rhetoric are built up directly from family feelings. This overlooks the possibility that there is an institutionalized culture in the civic sphere, such that contemporary frames of partisan political cognition are imbedded in sets of highly structured ideological shifters that are relatively stable over long periods of historical time. Lakoff's approach also neglects the manner in which such deeply institutionalized cognitive-cum-cultural structures not only sustain partisanship, and thus political separation, but also allow partisans to speak to others in a manner that can

create a wider audience, expand the authority of a particular position, and sustain wider solidarity. Lakoff focuses, in this sense, only on shifters, not on the more general cultural structures within which shifters are imbedded and which allow, on many occasions, a common language to be spoken by partisans on different sides.

74. Campbell et. al., *Elections and the Political Order,* p. 126; Berelson et al., *Voting,* p. 225.

75. Berelson et al., *Voting,* p. 83.

76. In Nancy Fraser's "From Redistribution to Recognition? Dilemmas of Justice in a 'Postsocialist' Age," she presents a philosophical mediation between more recent identity politics and earlier class politics, arguing that recognition and distribution are equally significant matters of political struggle. She suggests, however, that struggles for recognition are cultural and that those over distribution are not. Though it is certainly true that participants in economic and political struggles often believe that their fights are about means, not meanings, it is central to the argument I am developing here that distribution struggles are imbedded in cultural assumptions about motives, relations, and institutions in the civil sphere.

77. Mouffe, *Democratic Paradox,* p. 13.

78. Ibid., p. 103. Mouffe does not actually investigate the culture or the institutions of this common symbolic space. For example, liberty and equality are by no means the only positive discursive principles at work in liberal democracy, and the entire series of sacred symbols is balanced by those on the negative side. Mouffe's poststructural and deconstructive framework allows her to see the place of *difference* in political language, but her residual Gramscianism leads her to locate the impetus for conflict purely in social divisions of wealth and power, not in the cultural antinomies that structure civil life.

79. R. Hofstadter, *Idea of a Party System,* p. 10.

80. Quoted in ibid., p. 2.

81. Ibid.

82. Quoted in ibid., pp. 251–252.

83. Ibid., p. 251.

84. Ibid., emphasis in original.

85. Ibid.

86. A. Hamilton, *Federalist Papers,* Number 57.

87. For a discussion of the systematic opportunities for corruption that the boundary between economy and state offers to high-level state officials, see Rose-Ackerman, *Corruption and Government: Causes, Consequences, and Reform,* pp. 27–38. Rose-Ackerman writes:

"Grand corruption" occurs at the highest levels of government and involves major government projects and programs. Governments frequently transfer large financial benefits to private firms through procurement contracts and the award of concessions. Bribes transfer monopoly rents to private investors with a share to the corrupted officials. Privatization processes are vulnerable to corrupt insider deals." (p. 27)

88. Weber, *Economy and Society*, p. 1418. I am grateful to Ates Altinordu for pointing this passage out to me.

89. It is notable that when contemporary political scientists conceptualize the institutions that create accountability in democratic societies, they focus exclusively on elections and party competitions. Their emphasis on strategic motivations, sanctions and rewards, and the organizational environments of rational actions makes it difficult to conceptualize obligation of office, let alone the moral dimensions of civil society to which it relates. See, e.g., the contributions in Przeworski, Stokes, and Manin, *Democracy, Accountability, and Representation*.

90. Banfield, *Moral Basis of a Backward Society*, p. 89.

91. Ibid., pp. 19, 89.

92. Aristotle, *Politics*, pp. 195–198.

93. In liberal versions of the CSII understanding, office universalism is located inside government, not civil society, interpreted as a controlling device vis-à-vis the particularism and plurality of the civil sphere: "Where the distinction between civil society and government is marked . . . there must always exist a boundary between them, because each is defined in opposition to the other. Government fails if it embodies merely particularist values. A police officer betrays his office if he does not treat citizens equally, but gives favor to members of his own group . . . if the common good is conflated with, and understood to be conflated with, particularist goods . . . Without independence from civil society, government cannot protect basic rights." N. Rosenblum and R. Post, *Civil Society and Government*, p. 11. What is elided by such a Hegelian conception is what sustains the universalism of governmental office. It can only be the civil power generated from within the civil sphere, which according to the CSIII perspective employed here, has the potential for generating universalizing civil power through its regulatory institutions.

94. For a valuable discussion of the critical role that scandals play in affecting the symbolic power at the heart of politics, see John Thompson, *Political Scandal*. However, because Thompson adopts the conflict approach of Pierre Bourdieu, he does not conceptualize the democratic dimension of this scandal-creating process, neglecting the significance of an autonomous civil sphere for allowing communicative institutions to be independent of power and for defining the meaning of this sphere that constructs and scandalizes "deviance." Bourdieu's neo-Marxist approach has been corrosive even of culturally oriented attempts to understand the structures and processes of democratic societies. Homogenizing every form of power by instrumentalizing them as so many different forms of "capital," and every institutional

domain as an isomorphic "field" of Hobbesian power and strife, Bourdieu singularly fails to distinguish between democratic and undemocratic societies. See Alexander, "The Reality of Reduction."

95. Office obligation clearly structures positions of authority in organizations other than the state. Though these positions do not depend on civil power, they are, nevertheless, subject to weaker forms of civil control in both the communicative and regulative sense. These weaker controls can be regarded as manifestations of the "civil repair" processes I speak about in chapter 8.

96. For the idea of an "ethic of responsibility," as compared to both a more fundamentalist ethic of "absolute ends" and a purely instrumental, means-oriented ethic of strategy, see Weber's discussion in "Politics as a Vocation."

97. Mosher, *Democracy and the Public Service*, pp. 7–8, emphasis added.

98. See chap. 5, n. 1.

99. Selznick, *Leadership in Administration*, for an approach to organization that emphasizes value.

100. Lipset, Trow, and Coleman, *Union Democracy,* pp. 268–269. The quotations that follow are also from these pages.

101. See M. Weber, *Protestant Ethic*, pp. 79ff. In the chapter "Conclusions: Confucianism and Puritanism," in his book *The Sociology of China*, Weber offers an enlightening contrast between office in the traditional patrimonial bureaucracy of the Chinese Empire and office in the more potentially democratic sense that emerged in the Protestant Reformation. It is not sufficiently appreciated that Weber's investigations into comparative religion are as potentially relevant to an empirical theory of democracy as they are for questions about the origins of capitalism, which is their explicit focus. See Alexander and Loader, "Max Weber on Church and Sect in North America: An Alternative Path toward Rationalization."

102. For a critical discussion of this fissure in Weber's work, see Alexander, *Classical Attempt at Synthesis.*

103. Walzer, *Spheres of Justice*, p. 129.

104. Walzer, *The Revolution of the Saints*, which is one of the few explicit empirical applications of Weber's religious theory to the question of the origins of democracy. In his discussion of the corresponding shift in secular office obligations, in *Spheres of Justice,* Walzer cites Mosher, *Democracy and the Public Service,* pp. 53–98.

105. Walzer, *Spheres of Justice*, p. 149.

106. Ibid., p. 155.

107. Weber introduced the idea of heteronomy as a critical distinction between Western and non-Western patrimonial systems in *Economy and Society*, pp. 1158–1211. It seems significant that he concluded this long historical discussion with one of his rare analyses of the relationship between religion and democratic political forms in modern life, "Sect, Church, and Democracy," pp. 1204–1211.

108. Tellenbach, *Church, State, and Christian Society*, p. 48.

109. Ibid., p. 50.

110. Ibid., p. 72.

111. Ibid., p. 149 and passim.

112. Doyle, *Venality*.

113. Ibid., p. 153.

114. Ibid., p. 3.

115. Ibid., pp. 3–4.

116. Doyle, "4 August, 1789," p. 145.

117. Quoted in Doyle, *Venality*, p. 2.

118. Tagliabue, "Opening New Era, Poles Pick Leader."

119. "Mr. Giuliani's Thunderbolt."

120. J. Thompson, *Political Scandal*, p. 12.

121. De Dampierre, "Thèmes pour l'étude du Scandale," quoted in J. Thompson, *Political Scandal*, p. 273.

122. For an insightful case study of a recent British scandal that takes up the kind of cultural pragmatic approach I am suggesting here, emphasizing the relation of office pollution to social dramas of purification, see Cottle, *The Race Murder of Stephen Lawrence: Media Performance and Public Transformation*. For a related discussion in this vein, see M. Jacobs, "The Culture of the Savings and Loan Scandal on the No-Fault Society." For more micro-studies that take a complementary cultural approach to scandals, see Nichols, " 'Whistleblower' or 'Renegate': Definitional Contests in an Official Inquiry" and "Social Problems as Landmark Narratives." For an institutionalist approach that analyzes "Scandal and Crisis as Catalysts" for organizational reforms to combat corruption, see Rose-Ackerman, *Corruption and Government*, pp. 209–213.

123. Tara York, " 'Contamination by Corruption.' "

124. J. Warren, "No Gloating, Just Sadness."

125. Skelton, "Pity Quackenbush?"

126. *Los Angeles Times*, March 7, 1991, A21, quoted in R. Jacobs, *Race, Media, and the Crisis of Civil Society*, p. 84.

127. R. Jacobs, *Race, Media, and the Crisis of Civil Society*, p. 85.

128. *Los Angeles Times*, March 12, 1991, quoted in R. Jacobs, *Race, Media, and the Crisis of Civil Society*, p. 86.

129. Bailyn, *Ideological Origins of the American Revolution*.

130. J. Madison, Number 48, *Federalist Papers*, quoting p. 309.

131. Kutler, *Wars of Watergate*, pp. 473–744.

132. Quoted in ibid., p. 474.

133. Quoted in ibid., p. 475.

134. Ibid., p. 477.

135. In the final version that was ratified in 1789, the U.S. Constitution separated the impeachment process into two phases, corresponding to the two separate houses

of Congress. Technically, "impeachment" referred to the indictment of a sitting president for "high crimes and misdemeanors," and it required a majority vote in the House of Representatives. If impeached, the president would then face trial in the Senate. If he were convicted in this trial, which required a majority vote, he would be removed from office.

136. See Alexander, "Three Models of Culture and Society Relations" and "Watergate as Democratic Ritual"; also Lipset and Raab, "An Appointment with Watergate." In the following, I draw from "Watergate as Democratic Ritual."

137. A. Lewis, introduction to *Not Above the Law*, p. 13.

138. Quoted in Alexander, "Watergate as Democratic Ritual," p. 165.

139. Ibid., pp. 169–171.

140. Ervin, *Whole Truth*, p. 211.

141. Quoted in Alexander, "Watergate as Democratic Ritual," p. 165.

142. Ibid.

143. Jaworski, *Right and the Power*, p. 139.

144. Representative William Cohen, quoted in Stanley Kutler, *Wars of Watergate*, p. 521.

145. Kutler, *Wars of Watergate*, p. 518.

146. Representative Robert McClory, quoted in Kutler, *Wars of Watergate*, p. 528.

147. For an analysis of the third and last presidential impeachment in U.S. history, in terms of the broad civil society model I am developing here, see Jason L. Mast's discussion of the polarization that triggered the Republican indictment of President Bill Clinton in 1998: "The Cultural Pragmatics of Event-ness: The Clinton/Lewinsky Affair," pp. 115–145 in Alexander, Giesen, and Mast, *Social Performance*. Despite the substantive social conflicts involved, it is revealing that the articles of impeachment focused on such civil-discursive issues as deceit. In contrast with the two earlier impeachment episodes, Mast demonstrates, the hearings about Clinton in the House of Representatives did not achieve a ritual status; they had, by contrast, an often comic and partisan cast. The reason was sociological; there did not exist a widespread sense, in the broad political center, that Clinton's actions did, in fact, threaten the fundaments of the civil sphere. It is not surprising, then, that when the indictment reached the Senate, it was met with easy defeat. In striking contrast, the conviction of President Johnson was defeated by only one vote, and the conviction of Nixon had been considered a certainty.

CHAPTER 7

1. J. Habermas, *Between Facts and Norms*.

2. M. Weber, *Economy and Society*, pp. 29–37, 215–222.

3. See Post, *Constitutional Domains*, which distinguishes between the instrumental, communal, and democratic aspects of law.

4. Quoted in P. Finn and D. Williams, "Yushchenko Vows to Prosecute." He did win.

5. Because "the essential problematic of democracy thus lies in the reconciliation of individual and collective autonomy," Post observes, there is "a paradox at the center of democracy," which ensures that "laws attempting to establish democracy are intrinsically contestable." It "can always be maintained either that [laws] have overly stressed the preconditions of social cohesion and hence have impaired the individual autonomy necessary for democratic legitimacy, or, conversely, that they have overly stressed individual autonomy and hence have impaired the social cohesion that is equally necessary for democratic legitimacy" (*Constitutional Domains*, 7–8). For a discussion of this tension in terms of legal rights to privacy in recent U.S. court decisions and their broader relation to democratic theory, see Jean Cohen, *Regulating Intimacy*.

6. Those who particularly emphasize the critical and liberating force of democratic law are often loath to acknowledge its relation to overarching worlds of cultural values. Among recent philosophers of law, Habermas has been particularly fierce in this regard, proclaiming that law must be understood in an entirely procedural manner if is to be democratic, and lambasting every cultural approach to law, even the most liberal- or Left-republican, as communitarian. Arguing against the "republican tradition that binds the citizens' political practice to the ethos of an already integrated community," Habermas proclaims that his "discourse theory breaks with an ethical conception of civic authority." He asserts that "democratic will-formation does not draw its legitimating force from the prior convergence of settled ethical convictions" but from "communicative presuppositions that allow the better arguments to come into play in various forms of deliberation and, on the other, procedures that secure fair bargaining conditions." Jurisprudential decisions about the "collective good," Habermas objects, are not derived from "the hermeneutic appropriation of 'constitutive traditions' " (*Between Facts and Norms*, pp. 278–279). The inadequacies of such a position are rooted in general problems of democratic theorizing that I discuss throughout this book, namely, that the normative commitment of democratic theorists to rational engagement, deliberation, and undogmatic, pragmatic decision making have often made them allergic to the empirical connection of democratic practices with cultural structures and culturally oriented theories. Though Habermas's discussion of law reproduces the same ambiguities about culture that have come to characterize the rest of his later work, his principal argument is that law fills the gap in solidarity created by disenchantment: "How can disenchanted, internally differentiated and pluralized lifeworlds be socially integrated if, at the same time, the risk of dissension is growing, particularly in the spheres of communicative actions that have been cut loose from ties of sacred authorities and released from bonds of archaic institutions?" (p. 26). Modern law is a "conscious organization" (p. 42), which "displaces normative expectations from morally unburdened individuals unto the

laws," which in turn "draw their legitimacy from a legislative procedure" (p. 83). In the modern legal medium, "the actor's self-interested choice is released from the obligatory contexts of a shared background" (p. 119).

At first glance, the approach of Robert Post, a leading figure in American First Amendment jurisprudence, would seem to assert the same untenable distinction between democratic legal reasoning and cultural commitment. Post identifies instrumental law with Weberian rationalization, communal law with culture, and democratic law with autonomy and reflexivity. He thus argues that democratic law is distinguished from communal law because of its refusal to sanction, a priori, any given set of cultural values held by particular communities. "Within community," Post argues, persons "are conceived as thickly embedded within a constitutive skein of social norms that simultaneously defines their identity and invests them with dignity," whereas "within democracy, persons are represented as autonomous" and "they are imagined as beings who seek to determine their own fate and who are consequently able to transcend both the constitutive norms that happen to define them and the managerial purposes that constrict them" (p. 10). Yet, while anticommunitarian in normative terms, the demarcation that Post proposes is not, in fact, anticultural in the empirical sense. Particular attention should be paid, in the preceding definition, to such words as "conceived," "represented," and "imagined." Post acknowledges that "the social order of democracy exists only because of our commitment to the *value* of self-determinism" and that "if we inquire into the origins of this antecedent commitment . . . it becomes immediately clear that . . . it arises because it happens to *be imbedded in a culture* that desires to foster the end of self-government." It is in this manner, and for this reason, that a supraindividual cultural language constitutes an unavoidable background to self-determination in a purely pragmatic or rationalist sense: "It would be self-defeating for democratic authority to expand to the point of displacing the very culture that fosters the unique *value* necessary for the maintenance of democratic social order." Though "democracy *imagines* persons as just such autonomous agents who continually choose their purposes and ends," Post suggests, "choices have significance only within the context of an anterior horizon of commitments," and for this reason it remains a presupposition of democratic law that "persons who do not already have an identity are incapable of meaningful choice." Despite the critique of communalism, then, "democracy presupposes community, which alone can fashion persons with the identity capable of giving content to the value of autonomy." Such a "conclusion in fact requires us to distinguish two distinct senses in which community is relevant for law. On the one hand, community is a particular social order thematized and established by the law with discrete and ascertainable boundaries. . . . On the other hand, however, community is also a comprehensive social milieu that makes possible the very existence of the rule of law . . . Community in this larger, more embracing sense is a prerequisite for the institution of law itself" (14–15, 17–18, emphasis added). For a particularly powerful argument for the cultural basis of American constitutional law, see Michelman, "Law's Republic"; this article served as one of the principal foils for Habermas's anticultural criticism.

7. For an historical reconstruction of the shifting boundary relationship between labor practices and the ideals of the civil sphere, see Forbath, "Caste, Class, and Equal Citizenship." Forbath traces the movement from the more "hands-off" interpretations of the nineteenth and twentieth centuries to the more regulative, interventionist interpretations that legitimated such pro-labor legislation as the Wagner Act in the 1930s.

8. A. Harris, "Equality Trouble," p. 1967, emphasis added.

9. Freidman, *Total Justice*, p. 33.

10. Ibid., pp. 42–43.

11. See chap. 8, below.

12. K. Yoshino, "Assimilationist Bias in Equal Protection," p. 507.

13. Quoted in Siegel, "In the Eyes of the Law," p. 228.

14. H. Collins, *Law of Contract*, p. 173.

15. Ibid., and more generally pp. 171–206.

16. Ibid., p. 173. In his later work, Collins calls the contract "a form of communication system," suggesting the "contract 'thinks' about the relation between people in a particular way." He writes that "the contract thinks, for instance, about a promise, whether it was made, what the promise intended by the commitment, and whether the promise has been kept" (*Regulating Contracts*, pp. 15–16).

17. Durkheim, *Professional Ethics and Civic Morals*.

18. T. H. Marshall, *Class, Citizenship, and Social Development*.

19. Heller, "On Formal Democracy."

20. M. Weber, "Categories of Legal Thought." On formalism more generally, see Belliotti, *Justifying Law*, pp. 3–16. Luhmann takes a similarly formalist position in his approach to law as a purely self-referential, and thus self-regulating, "auto-poetical system." See "The Autonomy of the Legal System."

21. The formalism of Weber's legal sociology complements his generally instrumental, noncultural approach to the other regulative institutions of civil society, such as office, voting, and political parties; his failure to discuss the communicative institutions of civil life; and his emphasis, more generally, on state rather than civil power. These difficulties reflect Weber's failure to integrate his political with his religious sociology, as I suggested in Alexander, *Max Weber: The Classical Attempt at Synthesis*.

22. Austin, *Province of Jurisprudence Determined*, chap. 1.

23. Kelsen, *General Theory of Law and the State*, pp. 58–63, 143–144.

24. Holmes, "Path of the Law," p. 171.

25. Frank, *Law and the Modern Mind*; and Lewellyn, "Some Realism about Realism."

26. F. Neumann, *Rule of Law*, p. 213.

27. Ibid., p. 229.

28. D. Kennedy, "Structure of Blackstone's Commentaries," p. 205.

29. Posner, "Utilitarianism, Economics, and Legal Theory," p. 123.

30. Dworkin, "Jurisprudence," p. 4.

31. Hart and Honoré, *Causation in the Law*, p. 123.

32. Hart, *Concept of Law*, p. 126, emphasis added.

33. Dworkin, "The Model of Rules I," p. 19.

34. Fuller, *Morality of Law*, p. 63, emphasis added.

35. C. E. Baker, "Ideology of the Economic Analysis of Law," p. 3; Tribe, "Policy Science," p. 66, emphasis added.

36. Hayek, *Road to Serfdom*, p. 78, quoted in Fuller, *Morality of Law*, p. 65.

37. Sunstein, *After the Rights Revolution*, p. 139, emphasis added.

38. Belliotti, *Justifying Law*, p. 9.

39. Fiss, "Objectivity and Interpretation," p. 232.

40. Jean Cohen, *Regulating Intimacy*, pp. 151, 159.

41. Ibid., pp. 197–199.

42. MacKinnon, *Feminism Unmodified*, p. 34.

43. Cicero, *Republic and the Laws*, bk. 3, p. 69.

44. M. S. Moore, "A Natural Law Theory of Interpretation," p. 39.

45. This failure to thematize the differences between law and morality vitiates the strong position advanced by Patrick Devlin in his well-known book *The Enforcement of Morals*. Writing "as a judge who administers the criminal law and who has often had to pass sentence in a criminal court," this judge of the Queen's Bench and former Lord of Appeal was keenly sensitive to the inner life of law, and how it had necessarily to rest for its effectiveness on commitments of a moral kind: "I should feel handicapped in my task if I thought that I was addressing an audience which had no sense of sin or who thought of crime as something quite different" (p. 4). In his interpretation of this moral connection, however, Devlin took an old-fashioned organic view of culture that posited homogeneity, consensus, and collective community: "Society . . . is held by the invisible bonds of common thought. If the bonds were too far relaxed the members would drift apart. A common morality is part of the bondage. The bondage is part of the price of society; and mankind, which needs society, must pay its price" (p. 10). However, it is neither society nor morality as such to which law refers, but the civil sphere and a very particular kind of anti-particularistic morality. See Post's remark that although "the Devlin model of law and culture usefully describes many phenomena within our legal system," it "undertheorizes both law and culture" ("Law and Cultural Conflict," p. 487).

46. See Menand, *Metaphysical Club*, pp. 58–69.

47. Holmes, "The Law," and "The Path of the Law," pp. 26, 170.

48. Holmes, "The Path of the Law," p. 167.

49. Holmes, "The Law," pp. 27–28.

50. Hart's relationship to legal positivism is deeply ambiguous, as my reconstruction of his position here and elsewhere in this chapter suggests. In reference to the relationship between Hart and the nineteenth-century founder of legal positivism, John Austin, Dworkin observes that "Hart rejected Austin's account of legal authority as a brute fact of habitual command and obedience." Instead of this thin and power-oriented approach, according to Dworkin, Hart "said that the true grounds of law lie in the acceptance, by the community as a whole, of a fundamental master rule." The consequence is a radically different understanding. Of that "master rule," Dworkin says: "Propositions of law are true, when they are true, not just in virtue of the commands of people who happen to enjoy habitual obedience, but more fundamentally in virtue of social conventions which represent the community's acceptance of a scheme of rules" ("Legal Theory and the Problems of Sense," p. 11). See also Frederick Hayek's remark that Hart's work represented "in most regards . . . one of the most effective criticisms of legal positivism" (quoted in N. Lacey, *A Life of H.L.A. Hart*, p. 381).

51. Hart, *Concept of Law*, p. 56.

52. Fuller, *Morality of Law*, p. 30. For the exchange, see Fuller, "Positivism and Fidelity to Law"; and H. Hart, "Positivism and the Separation of Law and Morals." For a discussion of the complexities of their relationship, which was sparked by the personal encounters that led to this exchange, see Lacey, *Life of H.L.A. Hart,* 197–202.

53. Fuller, *Morality of Law*, p. 9.

54. Dworkin, "Hard Cases," p. 82.

55. Dworkin, "Jurisprudence," p. 11. Dworkin's argument parallels the distinction that Post makes between instrumental and democratic law and the connection between the latter and the community. See n. 6, above.

56. Dworkin, "Introduction: The Moral Reading and the Majoritarian Premise," p. 4. John Hart Ely has argued to the contrary, suggesting that there is an "antidemocratic" quality of constitutions, or at least of the activist interpretation of constitutions, and concluding that, in order to counteract such antidemocratic tendencies, one needs to approach constitutions primarily as a guarantee for access to politics and voting. In issuing findings against the results of elected legislatures and officials, he argues, constitutional judges ignore the democratic will. See Ely, *On Constitutional Ground*, pp. 6–18.

57. J. Prager, "Free State Constitution and the Institutionalization of Value Strains," p. 68.

58. Dworkin, "Introduction," p. 17.

59. Dworkin, "Taking Rights Seriously," p. 185, emphasis added.

60. Przeworski, "Democracy as a Contingent Outcome of Conflicts," pp. 59–80.

61. Habermas, "Struggles for Recognition in Constitutional States," p. 128.

62. The following quotations are drawn from Numbers 10 and 51 of A. Hamilton et al., *Federalist Papers*, pp. 77–84 and 321–325.

63. In *The Cultural Study of Law*, Paul Kahn suggests that "the claims of reason are central to the cultural practice of law," observing that "the underlying structure of the debate" about American law "remains remarkably constant: my reason against your desire."

> The problem for a democratic order under law is to determine the collective will by reason, rather than desire. Politics is conceived as a struggle between good and evil, represented by reason and desire. . . . What is reasonable is universal and, therefore, good for all. Desire, on the other hand, is particular and private. Without reason, desires . . . are in conflict with each other, both within the individual and across various groups. A politics of desire is rule by special interest groups or, in Madison's term, factions. A system of law captured by factional interests and individual desire has only the appearance of law's rule. (pp. 17–18)

64. Quoted in Fuller, *Morality of Law*, p. 100, emphasis added.

65. Dicey, *Introduction to the Study of the Law of the Constitution*, p. 126.

66. Ibid.

67. Ibid., p. 118.

68. Ibid.

69. Ibid., p. 128.

70. Frankfurter, "Note on Advisory Opinions," p. 1004.

71. Thayer, "Origin and Scope of the American Doctrine of Constitutional Law," p. 139.

72. Ibid., p. 133.

73. Ibid., p. 134.

74. Ibid., p. 139.

75. Ibid., p. 149, emphasis added.

76. Hart, *Concept of Law*, p. 87. In this section and the following, I draw extensively from cases that Hart presents in his philosophical writings about law. Two decades ago, Ruth Gavison wrote about "legal philosophy as we find it *after* Hart has transformed it" (introduction to *Issues in Contemporary Legal Philosophy*, p. 1, emphasis in original). Lacey speaks of Hart's "worldwide reputation as the foremost legal philosopher writing in English in the twentieth century," observing that *The Concept of Law* "remains, forty years after its publication, the main point of reference for teaching analytical jurisprudence" (*Life of H.L.A. Hart*, pp. 219, 224). No doubt Hart would not immediately have accepted the reconstruction of his thought I am developing here. Ordinary-language philosophy, whether in the person of Wittgen-

stein in Cambridge or of J. L. Austin in Oxford, did not see itself as related to the Continental linguistic tradition that created semiotics and eventually connected with, and stimulated, the cultural turn in the social sciences today—and Hart was deeply affected by both Wittgenstein and Austin (*Life*, 112–151). From the cultural pragmatic perspective, however, these theoretical traditions are complementary. Austin's philosophy of the performative has, posthumously, entered directly into the heart of discussions about culture, action, and society, and it informs the position I am taking here. See chap. 4, n. 7.

77. Hart, *Concept of Law*, p. 87, emphasis in original.

78. Kahn, *Cultural Study of Law*, pp. 35–36.

79. Ibid., emphasis added.

80. Hart and Honoré, *Causation in the Law*, p. 1.

81. Kahn, *Cultural Study of Law*, p. 17. Rather than take his cultural-theoretical orientation from analytic language philosophers, Kahn follows Clifford Geertz, as did Robert M. Cover in "*Nomos* and Narrative," the foreword to "The Supreme Court, 1982 Term" in the *Harvard Law Review* twenty years before:

> We inhabit a nomos—a normative universe. We constantly create and maintain a world of right and wrong, of lawful and unlawful, of valid and void. The student of law may come to identify the normative world with the professional paraphernalia of social control. The rules and principles of justice, the formal institutions of the law, and the conventions of a social order are, indeed, important to that world; they are, however, but a small part of the normative universe that ought to claim our attention. No set of legal institutions or prescriptions exists apart from the narratives that locate it and give it meaning. . . . Once understood in the context of the narratives that give it meaning, law becomes not merely a system of rules to be observed, but a world in which we live . . . trajectories plotted upon material reality by our imaginations. . . . Law is a resource in signification[, and] the creation of legal meaning . . . takes place always through an essentially cultural medium." (pp. 4–5, 8, 11)

82. Gewirtz, "Victims and Voyeurs, p. 151.

83. "The complexities . . . are usually not apparent . . . because police and prosecutors structure their accounts of case to fit into legal categories. These categories are simple, often dichotomous (guilty/not guilty; sane/insane; intentional/not intentional; reckless/not reckless; voluntary/involuntary) and deny the ambiguities and uncertainties of the world of experience" (M. McConville et al., *Case for the Prosecution*, p. 12).

84. Garland, *Punishment and Modern Society*, p. 268.

85. The quotations in this paragraph are from Fuller, *Morality of Law*, pp. 20–22.

86. Hart, *Concept of Law*, p. 85.

87. Ibid., pp. 167, 160.

88. Hart and Honoré, *Causation in the Law*, p. 59.

89. Hart, *Concept of Law*, p. 160, emphasis added.

90. Ibid., p. 167.

91. Ibid.

92. Hart and Honoré, *Causation in the Law*, p. 59.

93. Hart, *Concept of Law*, pp. 160–161.

94. For contract in the context of civil morality, see above, pp. 155–157. Also see Durkheim, *Division of Labor in Society*, bk. 2, chap. 7, e.g., p. 129.

95. Quoted in Dworkin, *Taking Rights Seriously*, p. 23.

96. Ibid., emphasis added.

97. Ibid., p. 24, emphasis added.

98. Ibid.

99. For the notion that allowing market efficiency to determine monetary results may, in a pluralistic society, be considered justice, see Walzer, *Spheres of Justice,* and my discussion of the broader implications of this position in chapter 1.

100. Hart, *Concept of Law*, p. 129, emphasis added. See chapter 1 for my discussion of how Rawls's philosophy displays a similarly flexible insertion of the adjective "reasonable" in his effort to reconcile the plurality of primordial meanings—meanings that are not "reasonable" for the actor—with democratic justice.

101. Hart, *Concept of Law*, p. 129. Reasonableness is also the decisive qualifier in assigning noneconomic liability, even in cases of office abuse. On November 13, 2000, the U.S. Supreme Court agreed to consider a police officer's claim that he had "qualified immunity" to protect himself against a complaint accusing him of using excessive force when he arrested a protestor at a political event. Under the defense of qualified immunity, an officer or other public official cannot be held liable, according to the *New York Times*, "if they reasonably believed at the time that their conduct was lawful." At the same time, however, the Fourth Amendment to the U.S. Constitution guarantees that all persons should be free of "unreasonable seizure." The Ninth Circuit Court decision, the one subject to Supreme Court review, had decided that this constitutional reasonableness clause trumped the civil qualifier guaranteeing immunity. "An officer cannot have an objectively reasonable belief that the force used was necessary (entitling the officer to qualified immunity)," the Court had ruled, "when no reasonable officer could have believed that the force used was necessary (establishing a Fourth Amendment violation)." Linda Greenhouse, "Court to Decide Fine Point on Use of Force by Police."

102. "Protectionism" was the term Karl Polanyi employed to describe the movement by "society" to control an earlier form of industrial capitalism in Great Britain.

See chapter 2, where I suggest that Polanyi did not put institutional or cultural teeth into his historical account, an effort that would have implied thematizing a specifically civil sphere of society.

103. As this example of major reform legislation indicates, the distinctions that Post makes between instrumental and democratic law must be seen as analytical, not concrete, as he himself acknowledges. In the antitrust case I discuss here, it could be suggested that the state made laws to ensure the better functioning of the economic sphere—the "instrumental" meaning of law in Post's sense. It is clear, however, that this functional concern can be understood only within the framework of concerns about the vitality of the civil sphere, which imposes a normative, democratic, and antieconomic obligation. As Post suggests, despite their being "in tension with one another in significant respects," the different forms of law "also presuppose and depend upon one another in ways that are fundamental and essential" (*Constitutional Domains*, p. 2). The passage of the Sherman Anti-Trust Act represents a case study of institutional interaction with the civil sphere. Legal regulation emerged from the confluence of voting, party, and office obligations, which were constrained and stimulated by civil institutions of a more communicative kind, and also by social movements. I explore similar kinds of multiple interactions between communicative and regulative institutions in my discussion of the Civil Rights movement in chapters 11–14 and of the pivotal role of social movements in civil society in chapter 9.

104. Quoted in J. Strouse, *Morgan: American Financier*, pp. 302–303.

105. Ibid., pp. 533–534.

106. Ibid., 622 n. 7.

107. Ibid., p. 624, emphasis added. Cf. Dworkin, *Taking Rights Seriously*, pp. 27–28.

108. Fuller, *Morality of Law*, p. 162.

109. Ibid. We find here echoes of Durkheim's insistence that a pluralistic and modern society can be integrated only by the "cult of the individual." See Durkheim's "Individualism and the Intellectuals," pp. 43–57.

110. How large or small this escape valve is and what constitutes incapacity and intention are subject, of course, to continuous change; that there is such a valve, and that it is related to the idea of capacity and intention, is not.

111. Holmes, "Privilege, Malice, and Intent," pp. 118, 119, emphasis added.

112. Siegel, "In the Eyes of the Law," p. 227, emphasis added.

113. Ibid, emphasis added.

114. Hart and Honoré, *Causation in the Law*, p. 23.

115. Ibid., emphasis added.

116. Ibid., pp. 62, 61.

117. Ibid., p. 22, emphasis added.

118. Fuller, *Morality of Law*, p. 71.

119. Hart and Honoré, *Causation in the Law*, p. 39.

120. Ibid., p. 134.

121. Ibid., pp. 145–146.

122. Hart, *Punishment and Responsibility*, p. 39.

123. Hart and Honoré, *Causation in the Law*, p. 144.

124. Gewirtz, "Victims and Voyeurs," p. 152.

125. Hart and Honoré, *Causation in the Law*, p. 31.

126. Fuller, *Morality of Law*, pp. 72–73.

127. Quoted in P. Brooks, "Storytelling without Fear? Confession in Law and Literature?" p. 116. All subsequent quotations by Warren are from this chapter. For a much more elaborate discussion of confession in this context, see Brooks, *Troubling Confessions: Speaking Guilt in Law and Literature*. The normative upshot of Brooks's literary investigation is to suggest that confession is a trope that is induced by the manner in which American law is imbedded inside the discourse of civil society; confession cannot, in other words, be viewed simply as a factual, self-willed action:

> How can someone make a false confession? Precisely because the false referentiality of confession may be secondary to the need to confess: a need produced by the coercion of interrogation or by the subtler coercion of the need to stage a scene of exposure as the only propitiation of accusation, including self-accusation for being in a scene of exposure. . . . Guilt can in any event always be produced to meet the demand for confession, since there is always more than enough guilt to go around, and its concealment can itself be a powerful motive for confession. One might want to say that confession, even if compelled, is always in some sense "true" as a performative, indeed as a performance, but this does not guarantee that it is not false as a constative, as a relevant "fact." (pp. 21–23)

128. Quoted in P. Brooks, "Storytelling Without Fear?" p. 131.

129. Ibid, emphasis in original.

130. Ibid., p. 125.

131. Ibid.

132. Karst, "Supreme Court 1976 Term," quoted in Forbath, "Caste, Class, and Equal Citizenship," p. 20.

133. Kairys, "Legal Reasoning."

134. Unger, *The Critical Legal Studies Movement*, p. 24. For other paradigmatic early statements, see D. Kennedy, "Form and Substance in Private Law Adjudication"; and Klare, "Judicial Deradicalization of the Wagner Act." See also the contributions in Kairys, *The Politics of Law*, and in Spitzer, *Research in Law and Sociology*, Vol. 3. In a skeptical essay, Robert Gordon points to how the critical movement's antagonism to earlier functionalist reasoning caused its practitioners to "collapse

'Needs' into 'Interests' and 'Domination,' " with the result that "the function of law then becomes that of responding to some balance of interests" or "to maintain the power of a dominant class or group." From this perspective, "modern American legal history is in part the story of how . . . 'liberal legalism' arose and developed [and] started to decay under attacks from without and the pressure from its own internal contradictions—ultimately leaving us where we are now, living in its ruins, no longer believing in its mediating powers." ("Critical Legal Histories," pp. 71–72, 74, 115). In its more recent form, this self-consciously critical approach to law has taken its bearings from a mixture of cultural Marxism and Foucault, morphing into what Austin Sarat and Thomas Kearns call the "critical cultural studies of law" ("The Cultural Lives of Law," p. 11). Revealing in this regard is Sarat's Foucauldian critique of Paul Kahn's more Geertzian approach to legal culture in his review essay of the cultural study of law, "Redirecting Legal Scholarship in Law Schools." The empirical focus within the new critical studies movement has increasingly shifted to extranational themes of postcoloniality, e.g., Darian-Smith and Fitzpatrick, *Laws of the Postcolonial*, and Fitzpatrick and Tuitt, *Critical Beings: Law, Nation and the Global Subject*. In his discussion of punishment practices, David Garland remarks on the manner in which such approaches elide with the "sociology of" approach to law, with the result that they "underemphasize questions of meaning": "The tendency of most sociologies in this area is to argue that penal systems have some kind of hidden social rationality" such that "the interpretive task is to show how penal processes in fact display the logic of power-knowledge techniques, of economic relations, or of modes of social organization, and thus reveal their external determinations and social functioning" (*Punishment and Modern Society*, p. 193).

135. R. Schwartz, "Moral Order and Sociology of Law," pp. 577–578. See Habermas's remark that "the sociology of law insists on an objectivating view from the outside, remaining insensitive to the symbolic dimension whose meaning is only internally accessible" (*Between Facts and Norms*, p. 66).

136. R. Gordon, "Critical Legal Histories," p. 109.

137. Hart, *Concept of Law*, p. 158.

138. Ibid., p. 159. For this asymmetrical construction of female capacity, see chapter 10 of this book; for the law's distorted construction of African American capacities, see chapter 11.

139. Ibid., p. 196.

140. T. E. Scrutton, "The Work of the Commercial Courts," p. 8, quoted in F. Neumann, *Rule of Law*, pp. 235–246. Cf. Adams, "The Modern Conception of Animus."

141. Horowitz, *Transformation of American Law, 1780–1860*, p. 3. Cf. Bendix, *Nation-Building and Citizenship*, pp. 80–87.

142. T. Scrutton, "Work of Commercial Courts," p. 8, quoted in F. Neumann.

143. Woodward, *Strange Career of Jim Crow,* p. 70.

144. A. Harris, "Equality Trouble," p. 1937.

145. *Williams v. Mississippi*, quoted in A. Harris, "Equality Trouble," p. 1963.

146. Hart, *Concept of Law*, 161.

147. Ibid., p. 197.

148. Ibid.

149. Perhaps it is the identification with their subjects, then, that leads legal theorists most concerned with the excluded often to develop an externalist, objectivizing view themselves.

150. Sunstein, *After the Rights Revolution*, p. 164, emphasis added.

151. Stern, "Commerce Clause and the National Economy, 1933–1946," pp. 681–682, emphasis added.

CHAPTER 8

1. For the distinction between analytic and concrete autonomy, see A. Kane, "Cultural Analysis in Historical Sociology."

2. I summarize here criticisms I have made of elements of the critical republican tradition at various points in the preceding, beginning in chapter 1, when I juxtaposed Walzer's pluralistic and cultural view of multiple justice spheres with the more totalizing perspectives of Rawls and Habermas, and extending to my discussion, in chapter 5, of how the demand for small, face-to-face publics had made thinkers insensitive to the democratic achievements and possibilities of symbolically mass-mediated civil spheres.

3. For an extended discussion of civil society as colonizing the political and economic spheres, in explicit contradiction of Habermasian theory, and an empirical illustration of this process in terms of the democratic movement against authoritarianism in South Korea, see S. Park, *Culture, Civil Society, and Political Change.* For an important related argument, see Edles, *Symbol and Ritual in the New Spain.*

4. Alexander, *Real Civil Societies.* For general discussions of social and cultural differentiation in a sociological sense, see Alexander and Colomy, *Differentiation Theory and Social Change;* for how such complexity creates the conditions for differentiation in a moral sense, for plural modes of conflict resolution and ideas of justice, see Walzer, *Sphere of Justice;*

5. Shils, "Primordial, Sacred, Civil, and Personal Ties." For a discussion of "everyday essentialism," see chapter 4.

6. For a philosophical analysis of the contrast between abstract space and idiographic place, see Entrikin, *Betweenness of Place.* For sociological approaches, see Shils, "Center and Periphery"; and Friedland and Boden, *NowHere.*

7. Norbert Elias speaks of the emergence of national identification as the "com-

plete fading of humanist or moral connotations," a "reduction" and "subordination of moral or humanistic values under national ones," and "a shift in priority from humanist and moral ideals and values applicable to people in general to nationalist ideals which placed an ideal image of country and nation above general human and moral ideals." He adds that it "can be observed in the outlook of the middle classes of most European countries between the eighteenth and twentieth centuries." Elias says of these people's turn from universalism that "the core of their we-image and their we-ideal was formed by an image of their national tradition and heritage," such that they "based their pride and their claim to a special value either on their nation's ancestry or on seemingly unchanging national achievements, characteristics and values." (*Germans*, pp. 134–137.)

8. In their discussions of the relationship between primordial identities and the more universalistic understandings that give fuller access to legal, political, and social rights, students of the relationship between nationalism and citizenship, e.g., Brubaker in *Citizenship and Nationhood in France and Germany*, have emphasized the distinction between *Jus sanguinis* and *Jus soli*. The problem with such a distinction is that it obscures how national boundaries, even those with more open citizenship regimes, continue to essentialize space and, thus, primordialize citizenship. Benedict Anderson's treatment, in *Imagined Communities*, of the arbitrary and excluding quality of national boundaries in and of themselves is more consistent with the position I am developing here, as are Brubaker's later writings on the construction of nations, e.g., *Nationalism Reframed*. A larger problem, of course, which I mentioned earlier, is that neither Brubaker nor Anderson conceptually differentiates the idea of a civil society from a national regime; this is a persistent shortcoming of studies of nationalism and nation-building, which generally fail to thematize democracy.

9. Kant, "Perpetual Peace."

10. On the pervasiveness of war in civil regimes, see Walzer, *Revolution of the Saints* and *Just and Unjust War*; R. Aron, *Clausewitz: Philosopher of War*; and M. Shapiro, *Violent Cartographies*. For historical discussions, see Kaiser, *Politics and War*; Fussell, *Great War and Modern Memory*; Hanson, *Wars of Ancient Greeks and Their Invention of Western Military Culture, Carnage and Culture*, and *Soul of Battle*; P. Kennedy, *Rise and Fall of the Great Powers*; Goubert, *Course of French History*, pp. 91–92, 199–314; Lacouture, *De Gaulle, The Rebel, 1890–1944*; and Meinecke, *Age of German Liberation, 1795–1815*, pp. 102–128.

11. Aron, *Imperial Republic*.

12. In addition to the citations in notes 9 and 10, see, e.g., D. Little, *American Foreign Policy and Moral Rhetoric*; Slotkin, *Regeneration through Violence*; Dower, *War without Mercy*; Marvin and Ingle, *Blood Sacrifice and the Nation*.

13. Higham, *Strangers in the Land*, p. 4. For an exploration of this internal stratification and its relation to civil society, see Part IV.

14. A. Harris writes:

In the years following World War I, many state and local governments took steps to discriminate against aliens, and to make it easier to punish aliens and citizens suspected of ideological disloyalty, and to keep schools and churches from passing on "foreign" values. . . . Legislators justified these statutes by the need to protect the country from "clannish" and politically dangerous aliens, and whiteness as civilization, fitness for self-government, and the rule of law were accordingly contrast in public opinion with images of the German nation as "anti-democratic and barbarous." ("Equality Trouble," p. 1976)

15. For anti-Semitism and the nation-state, see H. Arendt, *Anti-Semitism*. The most interesting contemporary discussion of the German Nazi's essentializing anti-Semitism is Daniel Goldhagen, *Hitler's Willing Executioners*, though I do not accept his exceptionalist perspective on the origins of the Jewish genocide for reasons I will explain in chapter 19. For French anti-Semitism, see Marrus and Paxton, *Vichy France and the Jews*, pp. 1–72 and passim; Soucy, "Nature of Fascism in France"; and M. Burns, *Dreyfus, A Family Affair: 1789–1945*. For the notion of ethnocentrism as an abnormality rather than a systemic contradiction of civil life, i.e., as representing the kind of "extremism" and psychological paranoia of deviant, fundamentalist religion, see Lipset and Raab, *Politics of Unreason*.

16. T. H. Marshall, *Class, Citizenship and Social Development*.

17. For regionalism, see Agnew, *Place and Politics* and *Place and Politics*; Agnew and Smith, *American Space / American Place*; and Friedland and Hecht, *To Rule Jerusalem*. For Marx, see "The Eighteenth Brumaire of Louis Bonaparte." For the idea of *la France profonde*, the primordial, mythical, inner core of the French nation that has been contrasted with Parisian and cosmopolitan France, see E. Weber, *Peasants into Frenchmen*. For an analysis of the idea of overlapping, or isomorphism, as a condition for exclusions, see Dahrendorf, *Class and Class Conflict in Industrial Society*; and for closure theory, see Brubaker, *Citizenship and Nationhood*, pp. 21–31. For a theoretical discussion of inclusion and exclusion in American history in terms of isomorphic categories of repression, see Alexander, "Core Solidarity, Ethnic Outgroup, and Social Differentiation." For a discussion of overlapping exclusions in the American construction of African American ghettos, see Massey and Denton, *American Apartheid*.

18. Said, *Orientalism*. See also Doty, *Imperial Encounters*; I. Neuman, *Uses of the Other*; and Matsuda, *Empire of Love*.

19. Dijkink, *National Identity and Geopolitical Visions*; Diner, *America in the Eyes of the Germans*; Kuisel, *Seducing the French*; and Heins, "Orientalism."

20. Mircea Eliade has written powerfully, in *The Sacred and the Profane,* about founding myths and the charisma that attaches to founding times and their places in early societies. In terms of more complex societies, Paul Connerton, in *How Societies*

Remember, has conceptualized founding rituals and anniversaries and the construction of national memories around primordial time. Bernhard Giesen has discussed primordial conceptions of national founding figures in "The Trauma of Perpetrators," pp. 113–143. See also the citations in notes 13–15, above. For a broader discussion, see chapters 15–17.

21. In the United States, the most strident recent intellectual assertion of the primordial basis for civil qualities has been Samuel Huntington, whose work *Who Are We?* represents a type case of the dangers of theoretical reduction I am criticizing here. On the one hand, Huntington acknowledges democratic discourse in America as central, describing the American Creed as "liberty, equality, law, and individual rights" (xv, xvii) and defining the national American commitment in civil terms, as "a set of universal principles of liberty and democracy" (p. 10). However, Huntington immediately qualifies this civic commitment—the American nation's and evidently his own—by employing arguments that are putatively historical, but more accurately might be termed mythical, to mark out restrictions on the capacity to practice the American creed. He describes the creed as "the product of the distinct Anglo-Protestant culture of the founding settlers of America" (p. xv). It was this "culture," he insists, that "produced the Creed," explaining that "America is a founded society created by seventeenth- and eighteenth-century settlers almost all of whom came from the British isles," and that it was "their values, institutions, and culture [that] provided the foundation for *and shaped* the development of American in the following centuries" (p. 38, emphasis added). Huntington believes that the "key elements" of Anglo-Protestant culture are "the Christian religion, Protestant values and moralism, a work ethic, the English language, British traditions of law, justice, and the limits of government power, and a legacy of European art, literature, philosophy, and music" (p. 40). At another point, he suggests that these elements include also "the responsibility of rulers, and the rights of individuals," the "dissenting Protestant values of individualism," and the "duty to try to create heaven on earth" (p. xvi). To so define the capacity for democracy in terms of the putative qualities of its founders, however, merely reproduces some of the more primordial and restrictive myths of American history. It also obscures historical variation. It has often been argued, for example, that the Revolution actually constituted a second founding of the United States, placing a more secular and civil, or creedal, set of commitments alongside those of its founding religious and ethnic groups. There is an arbitrary quality to Huntington's choice of founding characteristics. Why is whiteness not included, or, indeed, racism, as part of the American core founding culture, when elsewhere in his discussion Huntington acknowledges that these, too, were beliefs shared by those who founded the new nation? Do the qualities Huntington does choose have clear referents? What does "Protestant" mean? Huntington identifies it with dissent and individualism. How does this relate to the fact that, when they arrived in the New World, the Puritans set up religiously

exclusive colonies? Is dissent an inherently Protestant or even Christian commitment, or does it have roots in humanism and Enlightenment thinking as well? In fact, Huntington's distinction between America's putative "culture" and its "creed" is forced. Why is the creed defined in terms of universal principles of civil society and the culture in particularistic terms? Are not both equally cultural? In particularizing American political culture, Huntington simplifies and homogenizes it.

Huntington also fails to demonstrate the continuity between the WASP core group and the twentieth-century political culture, a continuity that is central to his claim that the core primordiality remained intact until the late twentieth century when, supposedly for the first time, it was powerfully challenged by multicultural fragmentation. The shakiness of this empirical claim is demonstrated by Huntington's evident uncertainty as to just how long the "Anglo-Protestant" hegemony lasted. He says on one page "almost four centuries" and, on the next, "three hundred years" (pp. 59–60). Rather than an empirical demonstration of the unchanging quality of American culture over one or the other of these time lines, Huntington tries to define America as a settler rather than an immigrant society, a move that allows core culture to be set at the beginning and unmodified, in principle, by later temporal additions: "Settlers and immigrants different fundamentally. Settlers leave an existing society, usually in a group, in order to create a new community, a city on a hill, in a new and often distant territory. They are imbued with a sense of collective purpose. . . . Immigrants, in contrast, do not create a new society. They move from one society to a different society" (p. 39). The bottom line is Huntington's exclusionary assertion that the primordial qualities of America's foundings are essential to the practice of civil society: "The Creed is unlikely to retain its salience if Americans abandon the Anglo-Protestant culture in which it has been rooted. A multicultural America will, in time, become a multicreedal America, with groups with different cultures espousing distinctive political values and principles rooted in their particular cultures" (p. 340). For a powerful critical essay on Huntington's book, see A. Wolfe, "Native Son."

22. For a discussion of how Christian Europeans and Americans constructed post-emancipation Jews as "new arrivals" to Western civilization, and hence as barbaric and uncivilized, see Cuddihy, *Ordeal of Civility* and *No Offense*. See also chapters 18 and 19.

23. See, e.g., the argument by Bonacich, "A Theory of Ethnic Antagonism."

24. See Sollors, "Of Plymouth Rock." See also my discussion in chap. 19.

25. For an approach to racial and ethnic stratification that emphasizes such factors exclusively, at the expense of considerations of the civil sphere itself, see Schermerhorn, *Comparative Race Relations*.

26. See D. Horowitz, "Immigration and Group Relations in France and America," and G. Noiriel, "Difficulties in French Historical Research on Immigrant."

27. On apartheid as a refounding, see Kuper, "Heightening of Racial Tension";

and P. Van den Berghe, *South Africa*. For the problem of colonial and postcolonial refoundings, see, e.g., Chatterjee, *Nation and Its Fragments*; and Mamdani, *Citizen and Subject*. For a theoretical and empirical discussion of gender, race, and religion as distortions of the American founding civil society, see my discussions in Parts III and IV.

28. For such positive statements about differentiation, see Durkheim, *Division of Labor in Society*, bk. 1; Parsons, *Societies* and *System of Modern Societies*; and Luhmann, *Differentiation of Society*. For critical discussions that emphasize the frequent link between differentiation, conflict, and injustice, see Rueschemeyer, *Power and the Division of Labor*; Alexander, "Differentiation Theory"; and Colomy, "Uneven Differentiation and Incomplete Institutionalization."

29. For the classical statement of this conflictual view of such plural spheres, see M. Weber, "Religious Rejections of the World and Their Directions." See S. N. Eisenstadt, *The Political System of Empires,* for a work that emphasizes how functional differentiation creates conflicts between spheres over scarce resources, normative definition, and social and political control. For a more recent statement about the conflict between spheres from a neoinstitutionalist perspective, see R. Friedland and R. Alford, "Bringing Society Back In." For a philosophical perspective on the conflict between spheres, see Walzer, *Spheres of Justice.*

30. Though these arguments are presented in a universalizing manner, I do not intend them to be understood in an ahistorical or transhistorical way. I am offering them contextually, in terms of the debate about the harmonic or conflictual nature of social differentiation. The manner in which individual spheres define themselves and are defined by others varies according to the nature of the boundary relationships that are institutionalized between civil and noncivil spheres in a particular historical period, as the following discussions will demonstrate.

31. This is, of course, the counterintuitive and still controversial assertion that is at the core of Walzer's *Spheres of Justice*. Though I accept Walzer's insight in this regard, I believe he did not adequately recognize the systematic consequences of the cultural power generated by sphere-specific charisma, how it invariably creates crippling intrusions vis-à-vis the civil sphere, and how the civil sphere must engage in a continuous process of civil repair as a result. This process does not "respect" but systematically "violates," in Walzer's terms, the independence and autonomy of noncivil justice spheres. This is to repeat the reservations I expressed about Walzer's position in chapters 1 and 2.

32. For sociological investigations of stigma and working-class life, see Goffman, *Interaction Ritual*, pp. 47–95; Sennett and Cobb, *Hidden Injuries of Class*; and Sennett, *Corrosion of Character* and *Respect in a World of Inequality*. See also Hays, *Flat Broke with Children.*

33. For modern social science discussion, see, for example, the literatures on the positive relationship between market capitalism and political democracy, e.g., M.

Friedman, *Capitalism and Freedom*, pp. 1–21; and Lipset, "Economic Development and Democracy." For the correlation between Protestantism and democracy, see, e.g., B. Nelson, "Weber's Protestant Ethic." For the correlation between the nuclear family and democracy, see, e.g., Goode, *World Revolution and Family Patterns*. For the correlation between state-building and democracy, see, e.g., Huntington, *Political Order in Changing Societies*. In more contemporary terms, since the transitions of the late 1980s such arguments have been made by "neoliberal" advocates of restructuring, who have argued that only the big bang of free market capitalism can sustain political democracies..

34. See chap. 2.

35. See K. Polanyi, *Great Transformation;* Somers and Block, "From Poverty to Perversity"; and S. Hayes, *Flat Broke with Children.*

CHAPTER 9

1. Sartre, *Critique of Dialectical Reason*, pp. 351–363; Trotsky, *Russian Revolution,* pp. 304–410.

2. Touraine, "Beyond Social Movements," p. 143.

3. Touraine, "Social Movements, Revolution, and Democracy," p. 280.

4. Touraine, "Waning Sociological Image of Social Life," pp. 33–34.

5. Ibid., p. 38, emphasis added.

6. Touraine, *Self-Reproduction of Society*, p. 323.

7. Marx, "Economic and Philosophical Manuscripts," p. 160. For a detailed textual reconstruction of this early subjective moment in Marx's thinking and the transition to objectivism described below, see Alexander, *Antinomies of Classical Thought*, pp. 15–74.

8. Marx, "Holy Family," p. 368, emphasis in original.

9. Marx, *German Ideology*, pp. 58–59.

10. Marx, *Holy Family*, p. 368, emphasis in original.

11. Marx, "Critique of the Gotha Programme," pp. 13–48.

12. Marx, *Capital, Vol. 1*, p. 751.

13. Oberschall, *Social Conflict and Social Movements*, p. 33.

14. "By the early 1970s, many sociologists had either been active in or were sympathetic to the movements they studied. Dismissive of the pejorative tone and empirical inaccuracy of prior accounts, their orientation was structural, rationalistic, and organizational. Protestors were simply pursuing existing group and individual interests" (Goodwin, Jasper, and Polletta, "Why Emotions Matter," pp. 4–5 in *Passionate Politics: Emotions and Social Movements*).

15. McCarthy and Zald, "Resource Mobilization and Social Movements," p. 1212.

16. Ibid.

17. Jean Cohen and A. Arato, *Civil Society and Political Theory*, pp. 504ff.

18. Tilly, Tilly, and Tilly, *Rebellious Century, 1830–1930*, p. 46.

19. Ibid., p. 3

20. Ibid., p. 285. Faced with the growing influence of more culturally oriented social movement theory, which I discuss in the sections following, and more generally with the cultural turn in the social sciences, Charles Tilly has developed his position in less starkly instrumental styles of thinking. Whether the theoretical logic of his position has actually shifted is another question. See note 57 below.

21. Skocpol, *States and Social Revolutions*.

22. Mann, *Origins of Social Power I*.

23. A. Morris, *Origins of the Civil Rights Movement*, pp. 40–76.

24. This factor is emphasized by Taylor Branch in his *Parting the Waters*.

25. The challenge to resource mobilization theory from the perspective that emphasized the moral and ideological concerns of activists and their relation to broader sociocultural change was launched most forcefully by Eyerman and Jamison in *Social Movements*. See especially pp. 120–145. This was followed up by Eyerman and Jamison, *Music and Social Movements*; and Eyerman, "How Social Movements Move." See the discussion, in note 57, below, of the new countermovement in American social movement studies, which has begun to explore emotions and culture in a similar way. Unfortunately, there has as yet been little apparent overlap between these European and American challenges to instrumentalism.

26. A. Morris, *Origin of the Civil Rights Movement*, pp. 91–93. It was in his own investigation of the Civil Rights movement, *Political Process and the Development of Black Insurgency, 1930–70*, that Doug McAdam developed a new version of the resource mobilization approach. For an extended critical discussion of the instrumental and strategic character of this political process model in the empirical context of the Civil Rights movement, see chapter 12, note 33; for a discussion of McAdam's polemical relation to the cultural elements of framing theory, see note 57 below.

27. D. Friedman and McAdam, "Collective Identity and Activism," p. 163.

28. Ibid., pp. 166–169.

29. Swidler, "Cultural Power and Social Movements."

30. Ibid., p. 37.

31. For the metaphor of culture as a tool kind, see Swidler, "Culture in Action."

32. Snow et al., "Frame Alignment Process, Micromobilization, and Movement Participation"; Snow and Benford, "Ideology, Frame Resonance, and Participant Mobilization."

33. Gamson, "Political Discourse and Collective Action," "From Structure to Action: Comparing Social Movement Research Across Cultures," and "Social Psychology of Collective Action."

34. Klandermans, "Formation and Mobilization of Consensus" and "The Social Construction of Protest and Multiorganizational Fields."

35. Tarrow, "Mentalities, Political Cultures, and Collective Action Frames" and *Power in Movement.*

36. Le Bon, *Crowd;* Freud, *Group Psychology and the Analysis of the Ego.*

37. M. Weber, "Parliament and Government in a Reconstructed Germany."

38. Durkheim, *Elementary Forms of Religious Life*, pp. 236–245.

39. Tarde, "Opinion and Conversation." See also chap. 5, n. 14.

40. Small and Vincent, *Introduction to the Study of Society*, pp. 325–326.

41. Giddings, *Scientific Study of Human Society*, p. 134.

42. R. Park, *Crowd and Public and Other Essays*, p. 80.

43. Cooley, *Social Organization*, p. 150.

44. Mead, *Mind, Self, and Society.*

45. Lippman, *Public Opinion.*

46. Dewey, *Public and Its Problems.*

47. See these concerns, for example, in Lasswell, *Democracy through Public Opinion.*

48. Blumer, "Collective Behavior," p. 214.

49. Ibid..

50. R. Turner and Killian, *Collective Behavior.*

51. For a more general account of this development from Blumer to Turner, see Alexander and Colomy, "Social Differentiation and Collective Behavior."

52. R. Turner and Killian, *Collective Behavior*, pp. 179–198.

53. Smelser, *Theory of Collective Behavior.*

54. Snow et al., "Frame Alignment Process."

55. "Framing scholars," observes J. E. Davis, "tend to focus only on external threats to alignment and tend not to systematically explore the preexisting meanings" ("Narrative and Social Movements," p. 9).

56. Klandermans, "Social Construction of Protest," p. 77.

57. Tarrow, *Power in Movement*, p. 7. These remarks indicate how, as framing theory has gained influence, the theorists who had tied social movements exclusively to resources and opportunities responded by trying to demonstrate how framing concepts, and the putatively cultural focus they represented, could be incorporated into their own more strategic and realist approach. These efforts, in my view, have not been entirely effective. Though they gesture toward reform and synthesis, they have often had the effect simply of introducing residual categories or ad hoc arguments, without shifting theoretical presuppositions in a significant way. In an avowedly revisionist article on the Civil Rights movement, for example, Doug McAdam accuses frame analysis of an "ideational bias" and calls for future research to focus on "the *strategic* framing efforts of movement groups" ("The Framing Function of Movement Tracts," p. 338, emphasis added). Even as Charles Tilly has introduced such promising concepts as performance and repertoire, and the idea that movements need to demonstrate "worthiness" (e.g., "Social Movements as Historically Specific Clusters of Political Performance"), he has continued to emphasize super- and

subordinate power over the translation of general and widely shared civil shared meanings. He weighs in, for example, against the "widespread idealism" of contemporary social science, rejecting the idea that there is something "abstract we might call 'the Culture',," and emphasizing, instead, the "causal mechanism" imbedded in "concrete social relations" that actually "*produce* the repetition of cultural patterns," i.e., "invention, network ramification, emulation, and adaptation" ("Epilogue: Now Where?," pp. 411, 419, 408, emphasis added). In *Stories, Identities, and Political Change*, though he gestures to the existence of ideational elements in social movements, Tilly suggests that social movement narratives are "mystification," that activists choose only those stories that "pay off," that stories cannot function as "causal structures," and that the task of students of social movements is to "tunnel under" stories to find real social structural causes (pp. 89, 88, 37, and 26ff). For examples of other such efforts at revision, see Johnston and Klandermans, *Social Movements and Culture*; the citations in notes 34–35, above; and the work by Swidler in note 29.

Francesca Polletta's critical evaluation of these defensive efforts is apt. Though she acknowledges that "in recent years, scholars of social movements have certainly paid attention to culture," she objects that "several things are missing from this picture." Asserting that "treating culture as the subjective perceptions that people bring to objective structures . . . makes it difficult to understand political opportunities," she points to the paradox that "political opportunities" is, in fact, "the key term in many accounts of movement emergence." What is missing, she suggests, is the understanding that "objective political opportunities *are* cultural": "Something as seemingly non-cultural as a state's level of repression reflects not only numbers of soldiers and guns but the strength of constitutional provisions for their use and traditions of military allegiance. These are features of institutional politics; all are cultural; none exist just in insurgents' heads. . . . What is missing here is a recognition that culture shapes what people perceive as effective as well as what they perceive as morally right" (emphasis added; "Why Stories Matter," and for a fuller statement, *It Was Like a Fever*).

Polletta is part of a small but significant countermovement inside American sociology that is challenging the hegemony of resource mobilization and framing theory. Arguing against "the instrumentalist bias of reigning models," for example, Polletta and E. Amenta ask, "Under what circumstances are people likely to battle for their dignity . . . rather than for material benefits?" They suggest that the conditions that would inspire such battles "are likely to be cultural as much as structural, to include distinctive ways of seeing the world as much as formal rules and resources" ("Second that Emotion?" pp. 308–309). In *The Art of Moral Protest: Culture, Biography, and Creativity in Social Movements*, James Jasper suggests that "protest is like religious ritual" in that "it embodies our moral judgments, so that we can express allegiance to moral visions," and he emphasizes the importance to social movements of "moral shocks" and "locating a villain" (pp. 14, 106–107). Some have tried to connect this emergent understanding to broader issues in cultural sociology, e.g., A. Kane, "Finding Emotion in Social Movement Processes"; Polletta, " 'It Was Like a Fever' "; and Polletta and Jasper, "Collective Identity and Social Movements." See also the contributions in J. E. Davis, *Stories of Change*. What remains is to connect this emerging perspective to macrosociology and democratic theory, to describe the broader institutional and cultural context within which movements forge their meanings and reach beyond themselves to connect to audiences in the civil sphere.

58. For a detailed examination of Touraine's approach to new social movements, with special focus on its relation to the civil society theory I am developing here, see Alexander, "Collective Action, Culture, and Civil Society."

59. Melucci, "New Social Movements," pp. 217–218.

60. Melucci, "Social Movements and the Democratization of Everyday Life," p. 246.

61. Ibid., p. 248.

62. Touraine, "Social Movements, Revolution, and Democracy," p. 281.

63. Touraine, "Triumph or Downfall of Civil Society," p. 232, emphasis added.

64. This argument has been forcefully made by Calhoun, "Culture, History, and the Problem of Specificity in Social Theory."

65. Furet, *Interpreting the French Revolution*; L. Hunt, *Politics, Culture, and Class in the French Revolution* and *New Cultural History*; Sewell, *Work and Revolution in France* and "Ideologies and Social Revolutions"; and K. Baker, *Inventing the French Revolution*.

66. E. P. Thompson, *Making of the English Working Class*; Sewell, *Work and Revolution in France*; G. S. Jones, *Languages of Class*; Joyce, *Visions of the People*; Vernon, *Politics and the People*; Montgomery, "Labor and the Republic in Industrial America"; Wilentz, *Chants Democratic*; and Tucker, *French Revolutionary Syndicalism and the Public Sphere*.

67. Habermas, "Morality, Society, and Ethics," pp. 155–156.

68. Walzer (*Spheres of Justice*) and Boltanski and Thevenot *(De la Justification)* present the most important such sphere-specific accounts of social process and change.

69. A. Touraine, "Triumph or Downfall of Civil Society?" and "The Waning Sociological Image of Social Life"; and Alexander, "Collective Action, Culture, and Civil Society."

70. In the strict philosophical sense, ordinary linguistic and cultural action rests upon continuous translation, since it proceeds according to analogies between the signifiers and signifieds in relational codes. "The meaning of any linguistic sign is its translation into some further, alternative sign," Jakobson argues in "On Linguistic Aspects of Translation" (in Jakobson, *Language and Literature*, p. 429), and "no linguistic specimen may be interpreted by the science of language without a translation of its signs into other signs of the same system or into signs of another system."

Translation in the more commonsense understanding should not be seen as fundamentally different: "The translator recodes and transmits a message received from another source. Thus translation involves two equivalent messages in two different codes"(ibid., p. 430). In both senses, translation is analogical, not literal; it is a matter of imagining and convincing. Its meaning, in other words, is performative, not constative. For a performative, specifically Derridean philosophical perspective on translation, see N. Sakai, *Translation and Subjectivity: On "Japan" and Cultural Nationalism.* Sakai stresses, for example, that for every translation there is "an essentially mixed audience among whom the addresser's relation to the addressee could hardly be imagined to be one of unruffled empathetic transference."

> To address myself to such an audience by saying "we" [is] to reach out to the addressees without either an assurance of immediate apprehension or an expectation of uniform response from them. "We" are rather a nonaggregate community; for the addresses would respond to my delivery with varying degrees of comprehension. . . . Addressing does not guarantees the message's arrival at the destination [but] designates a relation, which is performative in nature. (p. 4)

For an analytic-philosophical discussion on how "radical" is the "indeterminacy of translation," see W. V. Quine, "Translation and Meaning," pp. 119–168 in Quine, *Quintessence: Basic Readings from the Philosophy of W. V. Quine.* On "artfulness" as a challenge for successful social movements, see Jaspers, *Art of Moral Protest,* pp. 64–67.

71. "We use the term movement intellectual to refer to those individuals who through their activities articulate the knowledge interests and cognitive identity of social movements" (Eyerman and Jamison, *Social Movements: A Cognitive Approach,* p. 98).

72. Alexander and Jacobs, "Mass Communication, Ritual, and Civil Society."

73. Pizzorno, "Political Exchange and Collective Identity in Industrial Conflict."

74. Bendix, *Nation-Building and Citizenship,* pp. 61–71.

75. See, e.g., Forbath, "Caste, Class, and Equal Citizenship" and the references in n. 66.

CHAPTER 10

1. William Blackstone, cited in "Documents: The Law of Domestic Relations: Marriage, Divorce, Dower," in *Women's America: Refocusing the Past,* ed. Linda K. Kerber and Sharon De Hart, p. 49, emphasis in original.

2. Pateman, "Fraternal Social Contract," p. 121.

3. Landes, *Women and the Public Sphere in the Age of the French Revolution*, pp. 2–3.

4. Ryan, "Gender and Public Access," p. 266.

5. Ibid.

6. Boydston, *Home and Work*, p. 142.

7. Ibid., cited on pp. 142–143.

8. Keane, "Introduction" to *Civil Society and the State*, p. 21, emphasis added.

9. Kerber, *Women of the Republic*, p. 189.

10. Murray, *Gleaner*, I, nos. 17, 167, 168 and III, nos. 91, 219, cited in Kerber, *Women of the Republic*, p. 205.

11. Quoted in Kerber, *Women of the Republic*, p. 277.

12. *Declaration of Sentiments*, Seneca Falls, New York, July 19–20, 1848, reprinted in "Documents: Claiming Rights II," in *Women's America: Refocusing the Past*, pp. 207–208. Emphasis added.

13. Quoted in R. Edwards, *Angels in the Machinery*, p. 11.

14. S. B. Anthony, "Declaration of Rights for Women by the National Woman Suffrage Association." Reprinted in "Document: The Women's Centennial Agenda, 1876," in *Women's America: Refocusing the Past*, p. 261.

15. Quoted in Landes, *Women and the Public Sphere*, p. 114, emphasis added.

16. Ibid., p. 115.

17. Ibid., p. 127.

18. Ibid., emphasis added.

19. Ibid., p. 119, emphasis added.

20. Ibid., p. 131.

21. Cott, *Grounding of Modern Feminism*, pp. 1–10.

22. Kerber, *Women of the Republic*, p. 279.

23. Ibid., cited on p. 281.

24. Bellah, *Beyond Belief.*

25. Kerber, "Republican Mother and the Woman Citizen," p. 117.

26. Quoted in Ryan, "Gender and Public Access," p. 273.

27. Ibid.

28. Ibid., p. 270.

29. Kerber, "Republican Mother and the Woman Citizen." See also Crane, *Ebbtide in New England.*

30. Landes, *Women and the Public Sphere,* p. 2.

31. Ibid., p. 13.

32. Ibid., quoted on p. 132.

33. Ibid., p. 109, emphasis added.

34. Ibid., pp. 109–110.

35. Ibid., p. 123.

36. Ibid., p. 138, emphasis added.

37. Ibid., quoted on p. 144.

38. Quoted in Rabinovitch, "Gender and the Public Sphere," p. 362.

39. Ryan, "Gender and Public Access," p. 281.

40. Kerber and De Hart, "Many Frontiers of Industrializing America 1880–1920," pp. 265–266.

41. Edwards, *Angels in the Machinery*, p. 3.

42. Ibid., pp. 3–4.

43. Rabinovitch, "Gender and the Public Sphere," p. 355.

44. Ibid.

45. Ibid., p. 356.

46. Ibid., p. 362.

47. Kerber notes the blocking quality of the motherhood trope explicitly:

> Republican motherhood . . . was one of a series of conservative choices that Americans made in the postwar years as they avoided the full implications of their Revolutionary radicalism. In America responsibility for maintaining public virtue was channeled into domestic life. By these decisions Americans may well have been spared the agony of the French cycle of revolution and counterrevolution. . . . Nevertheless the impact of this choice was to delay the resolution of matters. . . . When the war was over, Judith Sargent Murray predicted a "new era in female history." That new era remained to be created [b]ut it could not be created until the inherent paradox of Republican Motherhood was resolved, until the world was not separated into a woman's realm of domesticity and nurture and a man's world of politics and intellect. The promises of the republic had yet to be fulfilled. (*Women of the Republic*, 287)

48. For a sustained argument against overlapping and overburdened meanings of the term "public," see Weintraub, "Public/Private."

49. Ryan, "Gender and Public Access," p. 278.

50. Edwards, *Angels in the Machinery*, p. 6.

51. Quoted in Thurner, "Better Citizens without the Ballot," p. 40, emphasis added.

52. Ibid., quoted on p. 34.

53. Ibid.

54. Ibid., quoted on p. 38.

55. Ibid., quoted on p. 41.

56. Ibid., quoted on p. 48.

57. Cott, *Grounding of Modern Feminism*, p. 40.

58. Ibid.

59. Ibid., p. 7.

60. Ibid., p. 8.

61. Ibid., p. 12.

62. Cott, "Equal Rights and Economic Roles," p. 378.

63. Ibid., p. 385.

64. Cott, *Grounding of Modern Feminism*, p. 179.

65. Cott, "Equal Rights and Economic Roles," p. 384.

66. Ibid., p. 383.

67. E. M. Smith, "What Is Sex Equality and What Are the Feminists Trying to Accomplish?" p. 96, cited in Cott, "Equal Rights and Economic Roles," p. 383.

68. Milkman, *Gender at Work*, p. 60.

69. Ibid., p. 61.

70. De Hart, "Conclusion: The New Feminism and the Dynamics of Social Change," p. 590.

71. Friedan, *Feminine Mystique*, pp. 18–19.

72. De Hart, "New Feminism," p. 597.

73. Ibid., quoted on p. 600.

74. Ibid., p. 606.

75. Ibid., emphasis in original.

76. Bardwick, *In Transition*, p. 26, cited in de Hart, "The New Feminism," p. 606.

77. I. Young, *Justice and the Politics of Difference*.

78. Calhoun, "Politics of Identity and Recognition," p. 341.

79. Quoted in Kerber, "Some Cautionary Words for Historians," p. 308.

80. Gilligan, *In a Different Voice*.

81. Ibid., p. 100.

82. Kerber, "Some Cautionary Words for Historians," pp. 305–306.

83. Greeno and Maccoby, "How Different Is the 'Different Voice'?" p. 312.

84. E.g., Gilligan, "Reply."

85. Kerber, "Some Cautionary Words for Historians," p. 306.

86. Luria, "Methodological Critique," p. 320, emphasis in the original.

87. S. James, "Good Enough Citizen," in *Beyond Equality and Difference*, p. 55.

88. Ibid., p. 58.

89. Ibid.

90. Dietz, "Citizenship with a Feminist Face," pp. 57–58.

91. Tronto, "Beyond Gender Difference to a Theory of Care," pp. 659–660.

92. Tronto, *Moral Boundaries*, p. 170.

93. Ibid., p. 141.

94. Ibid., p. 171.

95. Ibid., p. 158.

96. Benhabib writes:

The requirement that needs and their interpretations become the focus of discursive argumentation has the consequence that those traditions and practices, the semantic content of which defines the good life and happiness, are thematized. In practical discourses, a certain conception of justice is revealed to rest on a certain understanding of our needs, the cultural traditions which justify them, and the socialization patterns which shape them. If the subject matter of discourses is not artificially restricted, if the process of self-reflection reaches these presuppositions, then issues of justice and the good life flow into one another. . . . It is ultimately the process of discourse . . . that establishes the truth and falsehood of our needs. . . . A genuinely fluid and unrepressed relation to inner nature consists in the capacity for constant critical reevaluation and reconsideration of our most cherished needs. (*Critique, Norm, and Utopia*, pp. 336–338)

CHAPTER II

1. I will not discuss the destructive intrusions of religion and ethnicity in these chapters on social movements. I will consider them, instead, in the context of the modes of incorporation I discuss in Part IV. This is not to say that religious and ethnic exclusions have not generated social movements for civic repair, but that, at least in relatively recent times, the efforts to repair these exclusions, in western European and North American societies, have generally occurred in other ways. There are civil repair processes that have stimulated vigorous social movements to which I do not devote chapter-length discussions here. In terms of nineteenth-century repair, there is the working-class movement; for the last half of the twentieth century, there is the environmental movement and the struggle for sexual freedom. I have discussed the class movement several times in preceding chapters. For the beginning of an approach to the sexual rights and environmental movements in the terms I am developing here, see the section on "Sexuality, Difference, and Civil Society," in Alexander, "The Long and Winding Road"; and Alexander and Smith, "Social Science and Salvation." Nationalist and anticolonial movements present complex situations, but they are typically in some part also movements for civil repair.

2. The concept of institutionalization has been central to the tradition of normative functionalism that, for modern sociologists, is associated with Talcott Parsons's work. It refers to the relation between idealized cultural norms and social structural processes of organization and interaction. In his "theorem of institutionalization," Parsons worked with the regulating ideal of a perfect equilibrium, a hypothetical situation in which "ego" and "alter" accepted the same norm and in which sanctions for deviance and rewards for conformity were legitimate and accepted on all sides.

Though he was aware that this ideal was rarely achieved, distance from such equilibrium was viewed as unfavorable for action and social systems. (See, e.g., Parsons and Shils, *Toward a General Theory of Action*, pp. 197ff, and "Integration and Institutionalization the Social System." Also see Alexander, *Modern Reconstruction of Classical Thought*, pp. 183–192 and 219ff; and Alexander, "Contradictions in the Societal Community.") Against this Parsonian idea, S. N. Eisenstadt introduced a fundamentally different idea of institutionalization, according to which every effort to bring ideals down to earth through internalization and organizational design would produce new strains in turn. For Eisenstadt, equilibrium was neither possible nor desirable, and it was for this reason that his macrosociological theory centered on the notion of "contradiction" and strain and, in this manner, assumed a more complementary relationship to Marxian work (see, e.g., Eisenstadt, *Political System of Empires*; and Alexander, "The Fragility of Progress"). In *The Structural Transformation of the Public Sphere*, Habermas's most important, neo-Marxist work on the public sphere, he employs the idea of incomplete institutionalization in much the same manner. Chapter 11, for example, is titled "The Contradictory Institutionalization of the Public Sphere in the Bourgeois Constitutional State" (p. 78). Earlier we find such statements as: "Not that this idea of the public was actually realized in earnest in the coffee houses . . . but as an idea it had become institutionalized and thereby stated as an objective claim. If not realized, it was at least consequential" (p. 36), and, later: "In France too arose, although not before roughly the middle of the eighteenth century, a public that critically debated political issues. Before the Revolution, however, it could not effectively institutionalize its critical impulses, as was possible in contemporary England" (p. 67).

3. On this idea in terms of the power of nonconforming, minoritarian ideas, see Moscovici, Mugny, and Van Avermaet, *Perspectives on Minority Influence*. As a social psychologist, however, Moscovici and his colleagues do not refer to the institutional or cultural climate that makes such minority influence possible.

4. For the relation of allocative and integrative systems, see Parsons and Shils, "Values, Motives, and Systems of Action." This emphasis on the integrative, not the allocative dimensions as critical to the stimulation of social movements was the seminal argument that Alain Touraine raised in his struggle against Marxian forms of critical sociology. At the same time, however, he engaged in a subtle but virtually invisible battle with the manner in which Parsons had defined the relation between social and cultural integration. Against Parsons, Touraine insisted that the "norm component" of integration—the level of culture most directly related to organizational and allocative functions—tends to be in tension with the more generalized value element. It is this conflict, he argued, that sets the stage for social movements to demand radical structural change in the service of value consistency. See Alexander, "Collective Action, Culture, and Civil Society."

5. In his later writings, Habermas implicitly introduces this idea of duality into his public sphere theory:

> As both bearers of the political public sphere and as *members of society*, citizens occupy two positions at once. As members of society, they occupy the roles of employees and consumers, insured persons and patients, taxpayers and clients of bureaucracies, as well as the roles of students, tourists, commuters, and the like; in such complementary roles, they are especially exposed to the specific requirements and failures of the corresponding service systems. Such experiences are first assimilated "privately," that is, are interpreted within the horizon of a life history intermeshed with other life histories in the contexts of shared lifeworlds. The communicative channels of the public sphere are linked to the thick networks of interaction found in families and circles of friends as well as to the looser contacts with neighbors, work colleagues, acquaintances . . . in such a way that the spatial structures of simple interactions are expanded and abstracted but not destroyed. Thus the orientation to reaching understanding that is predominant in everyday practice is also preserved for a *communication among strangers* that is conducted over great distances in public spheres whose branches are quite complex. (*Between Facts and Norms*, pp. 365–366, emphasis in original)

This passage is particularly revealing because it demonstrates how, in the later writings, Habermas's empirical sense for the civil sphere outruns his theoretical apparatus. Because he refuses to allow cultural structures and the discursive solidarity they can sustain, Habermas must figure out a way to conceptualize the universalizing moment of duality in another way. He insists, first, that experience is assimilated privately, in actual groups and without reference to regulating ideals, and that it is the objective spatial expansion of communication that pushes outward, not the culturally induced sensibility of actors themselves. This objectively motivated reach is complemented by the metalinguistic assumption that there is always an orientation toward reaching understanding in everyday practice. These two putative practically-given realities are what allow an opening toward otherness and to strangers over a great distance.

6. G. Roth, *Social Democrats in Imperial Germany*.

7. Fredrickson, *White Supremacy*.

8. See Ash, *Polish Revolution*; and M. Kennedy, *Professionals, Power, and Solidarity in Poland*.

9. Hirschman, *Exit, Voice, and Loyalty*. The explanatory power of this important book is limited by its commitment to building an actor-centered and propositional model. The three options Hirschman outlines should be viewed as options that are

made available to actors caught within the contradictions between civil and noncivil spheres.

10. This is not, of course, confined to those societies that have maintained civil aspirations in a democratic sense. In Imperial China, which valued civility highly but not democracy, inferior race was also an indicator of barbarism, and it was defined by departures from the skin color yellow that moved in lighter and darker directions. See Dikoetter, *Discourse of Race in Modern China*, pp. 10–17 and passim.

11. Charles W. Mills, *Racial Contract*, pp. 11, 18, 25; Clendinnen, *Ambivalent Conquests*; and E. Said, *Orientalism*.

12. These statements are quoted in Charles W. Mills, *Racial Contract*, pp. 28 and 57, respectively.

13. Landry, "Enduring Dilemmas of Race in America."

14. H. A. Baker Jr., "Critical Memory and the Black Public Sphere," p. 7.

15. For the spatialization of racial thought, see Charles W. Mills, *Racial Contract*, pp. 42–52.

16. Dillon, *Abolitionists*, pp. 3–34.

17. Ibid., p. 16.

18. Ibid., p. 18.

19. Ibid., p. 74.

20. Though Dillon (*Abolitionists*, p. 256) notes strategic reasons for Lincoln's decision—to divide the Confederacy, to persuade Europe to cut off its aid to the South, to assuage the Radical Republicans in Congress—he rightly emphasizes "Lincoln's own advancing antislavery sentiment and his awareness of the swelling popular demand that this become an antislavery war, that the base of Southern power be altered, and the cruel anachronism of slavery be swept from America." Dillon adds, "For the creation of such sentiment abolitionists . . . could take much credit." For the antislavery commitment as the critical stimulus for the formation of the Republican party in the 1850s, and for the revival of Abraham Lincoln's political career, see Goodwin, *A Team of Rivals*.

21. For the failures of Reconstruction generally, see Foner, "Reconstruction and the Black Political Tradition."

22. For the continuing culture of racism, see Fredrickson, *Black Image in the White Mind*, p. 197.

23. Quoted in Landry, "The Enduring Dilemmas," p. 201.

24. McAdam, *Political Process*, pp. 71–79.

25. Quoted in Tomberlin, "Common Thread," p. 101. See also chap. 7 of this book.

26. McAdam, *Political Process*, p. 72.

27. Ibid., quoted on pp. 107, 72.

28. Ibid., p. 84.

29. Ibid., p. 86.

30. A. Morris, *Origins of the Civil Rights Movement*, p. 2.

31. Ibid., pp. 2–3.

32. Landry, *New Black Middle Class*, p. 54. Landry describes this as an economic exclusion, rather than an office exclusion. In terms of the theoretical model I am developing here, however, it is clearly the distortion of the possibility of civil interactions with blacks that led white businessmen to block the opportunity for filling positions of responsibility, either in the front office or back. That the inter-penetration of economic domination and civil exclusion has not been sufficiently explored is an issue I discussed in chapter 8.

33. For this and following quotations, see A. Morris, *Origins of the Civil Rights Movement*, p. 2.

34. Fraser, "Rethinking the Public Sphere"; and Eley, "Nations, Publics, and Political Cultures."

35. For a more elaborate reformulation vis-à-vis neo-Marxist counterpublic the-ory, see R. Jacobs, *Race, Media, and the Crisis of Civil Society*.

36. These difficulties are signaled by the frequency with which theorists of the counterpublic invoke the Gramscian notion of hegemony to describe the relation of the publics of dominant and subordinate groups. The origin of this failure can be traced back to Gramsci himself. As I suggested in chapter 2, this brilliant neo-Marxist thinker had a very underdeveloped sense of civil society in its democratic sense. Gramsci viewed civil society as fundamentally structured by ruling-class ideology and interests, and he understood contentions within it rather instrumentally, as struggles in an all-out "war of position." I have argued, to the contrary, that insofar as the civil sphere has autonomy, its premises and institutional arrangements can never be fully captured by a dominant group. This is the broader theoretical frame-work within which I introduced the concept of duality. It can be argued, I think, that it is precisely such a Gramscian sensibility that leads counterpublic theorists to misread Habermas's ambiguous arguments about the status of the normative frame-work of rationality, transparency, truth, and dialogue. Though Habermas does seek to tie these values to particular bourgeois commercial interests—emphasizing, for example, how the early bourgeois press had a material interest in factual, undistorted information—he also argues that these civil norms emerged for more general polit-ical and cultural, i.e., systemic reasons. In terms of the latter, Habermas explains the development of a democratic, publicly centered social and cultural system as devel-oping not from class interests per se but from a political-cum-cultural opposition to the structures and norms of an absolutist, patrimonial state. Moreover, as Habermas shed his neo-Marxist orientations, he pursued with great determination the latter, more systematic effort to tie democracy to broader structural developments of modernization rather than to any one of modernity's particular social forms. It is for

this reason that, in later replies to his critics, Habermas traces the discursive commitments of rationality, transparency, and so forth, not to the emergence of the bourgeoisie but to "the entire spectrum of cultural and societal rationalization processes" ("Further Reflections on the Public Sphere," p. 442). For an insightful discussion of the difference between Gramscian and Habermasian perspectives on civil society, see Jean Cohen and Arato, *Civil Society and Political Theory*, pp. 142–158. For an emphasis on the importance of integration from a modified Habermasian perspective, see the arguments of Maria Pia Lara in *Moral Textures*.

37. Eley, "Nations, Publics, and Political Cultures," p. 306.

38. Fraser, "Rethinking the Public Sphere," p. 123.

39. For refraction as a concept in social and cultural theory, see Evans-Pritchard, "The Nuer Conception of the Spirit in Its Relation to the Social Order"; and Alexander, "Three Models of Culture and Society Relations," in which I extrapolate from Evans-Pritchard's concept to contemporary sociocultural conflict.

40. Fraser, "Rethinking the Public Sphere," pp. 124, 129.

41. It must be added, however, that although Eley and Fraser fail to make shared normative ideals and practices central to their discussion of counterpublics, neither do they rule this possibility completely out. Despite her embrace of hegemony theory, Fraser suggests that whether counterpublic theory completely "preclude[s] the possibility of an additional, more comprehensive arena in which members of different, more limited publics talk across lines of cultural diversity" is an "empirical question" rather than a "conceptual" one (p. 126). For his part, Eley acknowledges that, "in one sense," working-class movements can indeed be seen as refractions on the "dominant model" of Enlightenment thought. If this were the case, it would suggest that emphasizing counterpublics is simply a way to sensitize the researcher to, in Eley's words, the "historical specificity and autonomous forms of expression" exhibited by critical social movements (304–305). These suggestions by Fraser and Eley contradict the idea that counterpublics are entirely separated from, and antagonistic to, the prevailing norms and practices of the surrounding civil society.

42. Landry, *New Black Middle Class*, pp. 29, 32.

43. A. Morris, *Origins of the Civil Rights Movement*, p. 5.

44. Ibid., p 3.

45. The distinction between this-worldly and otherworldly refers, of course, to Max Weber's ideal-typical fourfold differentiation of religion, the other dimension being ascetic versus mystical. See Weber, "Religious Rejections of the World and Their Directions."

46. For the origins of black Christianity in the period of southern enslavement, see Genovese, *Roll, Jordan, Roll*. For a detailed and evocative overview of black Christianity in the post–Civil War period, particularly as providing resources for the

Civil Rights movement, see Branch, *Parting the Waters*, pp. 1–26. For a discussion of black social gospel in relation to its white counterpart, see S. Burns, "Overview . . . The Proving Ground," esp. pp. 24–25. For a broad historical overview, see Luker, *Social Gospel in Black and White*.

47. Pattillo-McCoy, "Church Culture as a Strategy of Action in the Black Community," pp. 770–771.

48. Foner, "Reconstruction and the Black Political Tradition," p. 59.

49. Ibid., pp. 59, 60.

50. Ibid., quoted on p. 59.

51. Ibid. For the effects of schools and their teachers, see the monumental work of the first Afro-American historian, G. W. Williams, *History of the Negro Race in America from 1619–1880*. I am grateful to Ron Eyerman for bringing this to my attention. More generally, see Eyerman, *Cultural Trauma*.

52. Quoted in Foner, "Reconstruction and the Black Political Tradition," p. 60.

53. Greenstone, *Lincoln Persuasion*, p. 190.

54. Oakes, "Liberal Dissensus."

55. For the notion of the black protest tradition, see A. Morris, *Origins of the Civil Rights Movement*, p. 88. Eyerman and Jamison speak about this protest tradition as carried in black popular song in *Music and Social Movements*. Henry Louis Gates and others have identified the secular origins of this protest tradition in the "slave narratives" of freedmen. More than one hundred of these narratives were published before 1865, and ex-slaves had published more than six thousand such narratives, via interviews, essays, and books by 1945. Gates emphasizes that these narratives were initially formulated and presented in the "rhetoric and oratory" of "the anti-slavery lecture circuit" and "were often direct extensions of their speeches" (introduction to *Classic Slave Narratives*, pp. ix, xi). The stories about resistance, in other words, first appeared in communicative institutions of northern civil society.

56. "Interview with Fred Shuttlesworth," in A. Morris, *Origins of the Civil Rights Movement*, p. 88.

57. Abernathy, "Our Lives Were Filled with Action," quoted in A. Morris, *Origins of the Civil Rights Movement*, p. 88.

58. H. A. Baker, "Critical Memory," p. 23.

59. Duneier, *Slim's Table*, pp. 65, 92. There is a close connection between Duneier's focus on civil ties and the theoretical writings of his teacher Edward Shils.

60. Ibid., p. 66.

61. Ibid., p. 100.

62. Ibid., p. 74.

63. Brown, "Negotiating and Transforming the Public Sphere," p. 143.

64. The importance of black newspapers in the North has been virtually ignored by students of black civil society. For an important exception, see R. Jacobs, *Race, Media, and the Crisis of Civil Society: From Watts to Rodney King*. Jacobs demonstrates

the centrality of these communicative media to the maintenance of the black counterpublic and to black criticism of the regulative institutions of white civil society.
As Jacobs convincingly demonstrates, the black media interpreted ongoing events
in terms of the binary discourse of civil society.

65. R. Jacobs, personal communication.

66. Quoted in Brown "Negotiating and Transforming the Public Sphere,"
p. 142.

67. For a broad and evocative discussion of the formation of the southern black
Baptist Church in the period after the Civil War, see T. Branch, *Parting the Waters*,
pp. 1–68.

68. A. Morris, *Origins of the Civil Rights Movement*, p. 6.

69. Ibid., p. 7

70. Ibid., quoted on p. 9.

71. Ibid., p. 10.

72. Ibid., p. 205.

73. Quoted in Eskew, *But for Birmingham*, p. 233.

74. Ibid., quoted on p. 234. Eskew himself objects to these arguments by A.
Morris, Rustin, and King on the grounds that they paint a rosy halo that obscures
the manner in which continuing class divisions in black communities obstructed
cooperation with the Civil Rights movement, even in Birmingham. Aside from
deemphasizing the importance of the translation process himself, Eskew's neo-
Marxist argument assumes that to emphasize the existence of a strong civil dimension
in black communities is to suggest that class divisions failed to exist. This is not the
case; indeed, black civil society existed alongside many other intracommunity divisions as well.

75. Hirschman, *Exit, Voice, and Loyalty*.

76. A. Morris, *Origins of the Civil Rights Movement*, pp. 13–14.

77. These quotations from *Crisis* are cited in D. L. Lewis, *W.E.B. Dubois*,
pp. 410–411.

78. A. Morris, *Origins of the Civil Rights Movement*, p. 26. For the court victories,
see pp. 14ff.

79. For the role of demonstration effects in earlier periods of democratic revolution, see Bendix, *Kings or People*.

80. For a discussion of this delegitimating role, see A. Morris, *Origins of the Civil
Rights Movement*, pp. 26ff. The distinction between latent and manifest functions
was classically articulated by Robert K. Merton.

81. For the role of emotions in social movements, see Goodwin et al., *Passionate
Politics*.

82. Quoted in A. Morris, *Origins of the Civil Rights Movement*, p. 27.

83. For public opinion polls at the time, see A. Morris, *Origins of the Civil Rights
Movement*, p. 28.

84. Ibid.

85. Garrow, *Protest at Selma*, p. 5.

1. That southern whites defeated with physical force earlier and more direct black efforts to gain power is demonstrated by the correlation between local community organizing and black lynchings in the South between the 1890s and the 1950s. See Payne's discussion in *I've Got the Light of Freedom*, pp. 7–15 and p. 444 n. 2. Payne (pp. 34ff) shows that during the efforts to register black voters in the Mississippi Delta region, whites responded, both in their official capacities and as members of racist groups, with threats and eventually with armed violence. Though these efforts were not sufficient to intimidate every organizer, Payne's research reveals that they were, in fact, usually sufficient to put a strong damper on the ability of the most courageous organizers to effectively reach into the wider black civil community—for the simple fact that ordinary people were afraid for their livelihoods and their lives. Payne's account of a series of lynchings in Mississippi between 1930 and 1950 shows "how tenuous Black life was." He writes: "The point was that there did not have to be a point; black life could be snuffed out on whim, you could be killed because some ignorant white man didn't like the color of your shirt or the way you drove a wagon. Mississippi Blacks had to understand that viscerally" (*Light of Freedom*, p. 15). It is important, for the present argument, to realize that this pattern remained unchanged even *during* the days of the Civil Rights movement. In the early 1960s, before the movement's success finally compelled direct federal intervention in the South. the pattern of lynchings continued, despite massive organizing on local levels throughout the South.

2. I use the terms "big" and "little" not to denigrate the latter but to get to the kind of distinction Robert Redfield made when he introduced the distinction between big and little traditions in premodern societies (*Little Community, and Peasant Society and Culture*). While acknowledging the integrity of local traditions, Redfield pointed to the broader patterns of culture and regulation over extended periods of time.

Payne's fine-grained research into local movements in the Mississippi Delta can be read as descriptions of the delimited effects of the grassroots efforts by local movements of southern blacks to achieve self-defense, voting, and more social equality—insofar as these movements were not connected to the larger, national, extralocal scene. As Payne shows, there were continuing waves of such efforts from the 1890s on. These local movements contributed to the morale of the dominated black communities in the counterpublic spheres from which they sprang. In this way, they helped to lay the basis for the "big" organizing efforts of the SCLC, the Student Nonviolent Coordinating Committee (SNCC), and the Congress of Racial

Equality (CORE) in the years to come. At the same time, one must emphasize, in a manner that Payne does not, that these earlier confrontations on the local level usually had little "echo" effect outside their immediate region. They typically were not reported by the white press, and until the late 1950s and early 1960s the causes for which they struggled were not usually picked up and carried by progressive groups outside, nor even by movements in other regions of Mississippi, let alone in other southern or northern states. For a contrasting illustration of the tight connection between grass roots struggles on the local level and the nationally organized civil rights movement at a later time, and how that interaction allowed such local struggles eventually to be memorialized in the civil society of the American nation, see the photographic and documentary exhibition by Sue (Abram) Sojourner, "The Some People of That Place: 1960s Holmes Co. Mississippi—The Local People and Their Civil Rights Movement," Haverford College, Haverford, Pennsylvania, February 1–28, 2006. According to the exhibit catalog: "All photographs were taken in Holmes County, Mississippi, in 1968–1969, which was five years after the first local people began organizing and attending Freedom Meetings, and started making voter registration attempts . . . Sue Sojourner and her late husband Henry Lorenzi lived and worked for five years as civil rights workers in Holmes. They were called 'white outside agitators' by the local whites. While they mostly worked to help local leaders to build a grassroots organization for voter registration, political education, and running for public office, Sue Sojourner also realized the importance of documenting that historic time with camera, pen, and tape recorder. Thirty years later, she assembled 'The Some People' exhibition for the Tweed Museum of Art at the University of Minnesota–Duluth. Since 1999, the show has grown and traveled to colleges, universities, community centers, and historical and philanthropic institutions in the South, Midwest, and East."

3. For the concept of reweavings, see Lara, *Feminist Narratives*.

4. Halberstam, *Children*, p. 723.

5. Ibid.

6. Ibid. "To know that period of the South," recounts Eugene Patterson, a journalist who worked for the *Atlanta Constitution* during the Civil Rights movement, "is to know that it was frozen in silence." This remark is reported in Raines, *My Soul Is Rested*, p. 368. Raines compiled this book of interviews from many of the primary actors in the Civil Rights movement. Like Halberstam, Raines, who eventually assumed positions as editorial page editor and then as managing editor of the *New York Times*, represents another in a long string of now-prestigious journalists who began their careers by remaining in, relocating, or returning to the South to cover movement activities for progressive newspapers.

7. Quoted in Branch, *Parting the Waters*, p. 554.

8. Ibid., p. 600.

9. Quoted in Dorman, *We Shall Overcome*, p. 154. Like the other progressive

northern journalists who published widely read books on the movement, Dorman drew upon his daily reporting on the Civil Rights movement events for a northern newspaper, in his case the Long Island paper *Newsday*.

10. Quoted in Eskew, *But for Birmingham,* p. 282.

11. Quoted in Dorman, *We Shall Overcome,* p. 166.

12. Ibid., p. 161.

13. Poston, "American Negro and Newspaper Myths." Poston's remarks, and those of several others quoted below, occurred in the context of a national symposium titled "The Racial Crisis and the News Media," sponsored by the Freedom of Information Center of the University of Missouri and cosponsored by the Anti-Defamation League of B'nai B'rith. The very existence of such an event at the height of the growing national polarization over civil rights demonstrates the centrality of media representation during that time.

14. In addition to its cultural and professional implications, or, more accurately perhaps, precisely because of them, this "war" also had a physical dimension. "Mississippi could be deadly," recounts Claude Sitton, a former wire services and *New York Times* reporter, about his years covering the movement in the South. He continues, in an interview with Raines:

> They'd kill ya over there. And they did. . . . People were killed up there at Oxford when Jim Meredith was admitted. I was there. . . . One of 'em, a French reporter, was actually executed. I mean, he was shot in the back of the head. He was taken down right off the campus . . . made to kneel behind a tree, and was shot in the back of the head . . . pure out-and-out execution. . . . It was like crossin' no-man's-land to get from a motel off the campus where I was filing my story by telephone, through the rioters, and then up to the administration building where they had Meredith. (*My Soul Is Rested,* p. 380)

Richard Valeriani, an NBC News correspondent during those years, recounts how a white southerner assaulted him during a conflict in Montgomery, Alabama:

> The townspeople were out in force. They harassed anybody trying to cover it, sprayed black paint on the lenses of the cameras, and generally jostled us and intimidated us. . . . Somebody walked up behind me and hit me with an axe handle. Luckily he came up with a roundhouse swing rather an overhead swing, so that it caught me in the back of the head, where all the bone is, rather than the top of the skull. And there was a loud clunk . . . Somebody walked up to me . . . and said, "Do you need a doctor?" And I, in a daze . . . said, "Yes, I think I do. I'm bleeding." And then he looked at

me, he stared me in the face with this ugly look, and he said, "We don't have doctors for people like you." (*My Soul Is Rested*, pp. 371–372)

15. Poston, "The American Negro," p. 63.

16. This identification of professional autonomy with the maintenance of the ideals and structures of an independent civil sphere is a tendency that journalists share with other institutional elites in complex societies that contain a vital civil sphere. See Alexander, "Mass News Media in Systemic, Historical, and Comparative Perspective."

17. Herbers, "Reporters in the Deep South," p. 227.

18. Ibid.

19. G. P. Hunt, "Racial Crisis and the News Media," p. 11.

20. Fanning, "Media: Observer or Participant," p. 107.

21. Ibid., p. 108.

22. Boone, "Southern Newsmen and Local Pressure," p. 47.

23. Herbers, "Reporters in the Deep South," p. 225.

24. Bertelson, "Keeper of a Monster," p. 61.

25. Powledge, *Free at Last?* pp. xix–xx.

26. Ibid., p. xx.

27. Halberstam, *Children*, p. 721.

28. Ibid.

29. Ibid., p. 725.

30. Ibid., pp. 724–725.

31. Ibid., p. 725.

32. Ibid., pp. 726–727. In the autobiographical introduction to his own book on the Civil Rights movement, Howell Raines similarly offers personal testimony to the awe he experienced for civil rights activists' "sacrifice and unfathomable courage," acknowledging his intense identification and admiration for what he regards as the transcendent moral vision of Martin Luther King: "If he had lived, Martin Luther King, Jr., would see a South still burdened with inequities in housing, education, and distribution of wealth. But I believe he would look beyond these problems to see a region changed in a way that millions of us who lacked his vision would have thought impossible twenty years ago. He would see a South where we are all free at last to become what we can" (*My Soul Is Rested,* pp. 23–24). The phrase "free at last" reproduces the conclusion of King's "I Have a Dream" speech, delivered at the March on Washington in 1963, a speech that has since become one of the immortal documents of the American civil tradition. See chapter 14.

33. Though one finds this strategic and power-centered approach throughout the three disciplines that have been responsible for the brunt of contemporary research into the movement for civil rights—sociology, history, and political sci-

ence—it becomes articulated in terms of different disciplinary exemplars and theories.

Aldon Morris, a sociologist, introduces his study of the origins of the Civil Rights movement—invaluable in so many respects—with the explanation that his book is about how "black protest" was generated simply by "American racism and exploitation," not by the possibilities that the civil sphere surrounding this domination implied. Ignoring duality and solidary communication, Morris asserts that "the word that best expresses the spirit of this period was 'confrontation.' " Drawing metaphors from war rather than from fragmented civil relations, he promises to discuss the early "battles" of the movement and how these battles "forced" authorities to capitulate. These battles were based on the ability of organizers to "transform indigenous resources into power resources" and to apply them, in an instrumental fashion, "in conflict situations to accomplish political ends." What the movement had to face in order to make these accomplishments was "state power and widespread repression," without, evidently, any possibility of interpenetration by an environing civil sphere (*Origins of the Civil Rights Movement,* pp. ix–xii).

Among sociological treatments of the Civil Rights movement, the study most often cited alongside A. Morris's pioneering work is Doug McAdam's *Political Process and the Development of Black Insurgency, 1930–70.* Because McAdam employed fewer primary source materials—Morris conducted a number of extraordinarily valuable interviews with movement participants less than twenty years after the movement's denouement—*Political Process* has been less influential in the historiography of the Civil Rights movement. Yet its more explicitly conceptual focus has made it more influential in transforming the Civil Rights movement into a valuable sociological case study for discussions about the viability of the classical model in contemporary social movement theorizing and research. Though McAdam develops a revision of the classical model that focuses less exclusively on resources than on "opportunities," his account of the Civil Rights movement follows the same focus on power and self-interest at the expense of communication, solidarity, and duality, and is just as relentlessly instrumental in the logic it employs. According to McAdam, it is the "structural power" (*Political Process,* p. 37) of excluded groups that provides them with their "leverage" for social change, power they deploy as "negative inducements" (p. 30) vis-à-vis opponents. Shifts in the "power discrepancy" between these protest groups and their opponents make success more likely, thus allowing "net increases in the political leverage" and "raising the cost of repression" (p. 43), a cost that can independently be raised by the employment of nonviolent protest methods (pp. 39, 56). If elites eventually do respond to protests from below, it is only because they have calculated the costs of continuing their efforts to repress it, which at an earlier point were equally rational. If positive responses are forthcoming from the dominators, these represent an effort at "cooptation" that can cut the cost of "disruption" by forcing protest into "institutional channels" (p. 28). Shifts in public opinion may play a role by leading elites to make new calculations about the costs of repression (p. 159). This recalculation also may be encouraged by "cognitive liberation" within some segments of the ruling elite. Stimulated not by symbolic change but in response to changing social conditions (p. 49), this cognitive shift has the effect of creating more "optimistic" calculations of risks versus gains (p. 34). It is important to add, however, that some of McAdam's later empirical work on the Civil Rights movement, especially his *Freedom Summer*, seems to fundamentally contradict the kind of theoretical logic that informs this earlier agenda-setting writing and his later conceptually oriented discussions.

The most recent sociological approach to the Civil Rights movement, building upon McAdam's political process model but focusing it on a different empirical cause, takes the refusal to acknowledge the autonomy and influence of the civil sphere in a new direction. This is the argument that the federal government's civil rights reforms emerged not simply from local power politics but as a response to the international conflict of the Cold War. In "The Effect of the Cold War on African-American Civil Rights: America and the World Audience, 1945–1968," John David Skrentny connects McAdam's political process model to a neoinstitutionalist perspective, arguing that it was fear of losing international legitimacy, and ultimately power, that led certain collective actors, particularly the State Department and the president, to be sensitive to racial domination and eventually to argue for its repair. Though pointing to a normative environment—the "world acceptance of rights" (p. 262)—Skrentny locates this environment not inside the civil sphere of northern society but, rather, outside the nation-state. It was, he writes, only "American engagement with *that* audience" (p. 262, emphasis added)—the world audience—that caused reforms to be made. In fact, it was not even the American state structure per se but only certain groups within it, those responsible vis-à-vis its foreign environment. Thus, because Congress was "notoriously isolationist in the first half of the twentieth century," it "showed less engagement and less sensitivity for the world audience and was the most conservative of the three branches of government on civil rights" (p. 246). Skrentny explains the difference between southerners and northerners on the race issue as stemming from the fact that "local audiences in the Deep South states tended not to be concerned with world opinion" (p. 243); only because they had no engagement with foreign policy, in other words, did Southern officials lack interest in racial justice. This differential engagement with the extranational community explains why federal officials chose not to resort to repression and violence. "This being the case, the White House handled demonstrations and violence with conciliation and positive rights gains, rather than repression" (pp. 262, 263).

Skrentny downplays, in other words, the existence of the northern white civil sphere, and the role within it of public opinion, and communicative and regulative institutions. Like so many other sociological approaches to social movements, he ignores the democratic dimension of political life. But this theoretical denial leads to some empirical problems. Eisenhower and Nixon, for example, are presumed to be as responsive to the movement as Kennedy and Johnson (pp. 251, 261), and early Kennedy as responsive as later Kennedy. Despite occasional qualifications, Skrentny even suggests that the reformist impulses of the Supreme Court and the antireformist politics of the bloc of conservative congressmen and senators are linked to their differential relation to this foreign threat (p. 279 n. 31). He does not consider the possibility that the demands of the Cold War were continually referenced not because of instrumental concerns with losing prestige but because the rhetoric of international competition provided a particularly provocative symbolic container for the much more deeply institutionalized cultural themes of American civil life. Ultimately, as I have suggested in chapter 6, the instrumental and sometimes elitist logic of neoinstitutional theory does not differentiate between democratic and antidemocratic organizations. Skrentny treats the U.S. state as a bureaucratic oligarchy—like any other organization—influenced not by its members but by other oligarchic organizations competing with it from outside.

Within the historical discipline, a similar kind of "classical model" has inspired many recent students of the movement to concentrate on local histories of grassroots organizing at the expense of national movements and nationally known leaders. Two of the most important such studies are Payne's *Light of Freedom* and Eskew's *But for Birmingham.* In the historiographic essay attached as an appendix to *Light of Freedom* (pp. 437–438), Payne excoriates what he calls "uncritical top down" history as "King-centric" and "Kennedy-centric," and as "White History, history where the patterns of selection and emphasis are consistent with the underlying vision of history that has always been most comfortable to the socially privileged." For a brief discussion of the theoretical and empirical limitations of this approach, see note 2 above, which I amplify in notes in chapters 13 and 14. For his part, Eskew views his own densely researched monographic account of Birmingham as an alternative both to "top down" and "bottom up" studies (*But for Birmingham,* p. 343 n. 18), a perspective that might have allowed him to capture the ambiguity of social movements which are structured by duality. In fact, Eskew does acknowledge, at certain points, the role of interpretive processes, publicity, and symbolic mediation. Nonetheless, he resolutely portrays the outcome of the Birmingham conflict in terms of the movement's instrumental power vis-à-vis the elite's, a power that eventually allowed the local movement to win by splitting the economic from the political elite (see chap. 13). Such an argument amounts to the kind of "last instance" argument suggested by Friedrich Engels in his late efforts to simultaneously defend causal complexity and Marxian economic determinism. Eskew emphasizes, for example, the movement's successful appeal to the material interests of one fragment of the city's capitalist class, the postindustrial fragment that, he believes, felt it could dispense with the racial servility demanded by the objective interests of the old industrial elite. He describes "Bull Connor's brutal attempt to suppress the protests," an attempt that ultimately was not successful, as the logical product of "Birmingham's industrial heritage with its peculiar socioeconomic and political composition" (p. 12). Simultaneously speculative and resolutely determinist, this argument also leads Eskew to argue that the Birmingham campaign, and indeed the Civil Rights movement more generally, actually failed as a radical movement. He sees it as a bourgeois movement led by representatives of the "old Negro leadership class" that reinforced, rather than truly challenged, the power structure of American society. The movement demanded "incorporation into an inherently unequal system, as opposed to transforming the system to make it more equitable" (p. 312). In terms of the perspective I am developing here, however, this judgment fails to address the real if fragmented status of the civil sphere and the possibility for reforms to substantively repair it.

In political science, the approach to the Civil Rights movement that corresponds to the theoretical logic of the classical model in sociology and the local model in history is rational choice theory. Dennis Chong's work illustrates how this approach—often called the collective action model—has been applied to the movement for civil rights. See D. Chong, "All-or-Nothing Games in the Civil Rights Movement" and *Collective Action and the Civil Rights Movement*.

Taken together, these three disciplinary approaches to the Civil Rights movement constitute a kind of social scientific application of the narrow version of counterpublic theory that I criticized in the preceding chapter. The problem is the failure to conceptualize properly that "duality" not only allows dominated actors to reach outside their particularized public but provides them, to one degree or another, with the resources to make these appeals effective. By describing his sociological approach as an "indigenous" perspective, Morris implicitly makes the connection between the classical social movement model he develops, the "bottom up" new local history, and the treatment of the black counterpublic as an entirely separate, purely antagonistic force vis-à-vis white civil society.

34. In a literal sense, these regions were not simply northern; this designation, rather, is a metaphor for those regions that, unlike the old southern Confederacy, did not experience slavery. This includes regions to the West and North of the old southern bloc.

35. A. Young, *Easy Burden*, pp. 207–208.

36. Eskew, *But for Birmingham*, p. 23. Eskew misleadingly suggests, however, that the media's role became more important as the movement developed. The media were central from the beginning, for it was the duality of racial oppression that made the Civil Rights movement possible, and the media were a signal expression of the environing civil sphere.

37. Eskew, *But for Birmingham*, p. 23.

38. For an extended theoretical discussion of how emotional identification and

cultural extension are central to expanding moral understanding in a fragmented social order, see Alexander, "Social Basis of Moral Universalism."

39. Quoted in Garrow, *Protest at Selma*, p. 224. This important early work by a political scientist, whose later biography of Martin Luther King, *Bearing the Cross: Martin Luther King, Jr. and the Southern Leadership Conference,* won the Pulitzer Prize, demonstrates how local and national foci must be combined if the quintessential duality of the Civil Rights movement is to be understood. In this discussion of the relative importance of local versus national, both among actual social actors and among historians and social scientists themselves, the term "national" must be conceptually reinterpreted as a cipher for "civil." As I have suggested throughout this book—see esp. chapters 3 and 8—in democratic or even democratizing societies, reference is often made to the immanent obligations of the civil sphere by speaking of the nation. The latter can assume a concrete identity that provides material for mythical narratives, icons, and metaphors of collective identity. Such references can, in other words, evoke universalistic, not "nationalistic" or particularistic criteria. Throughout the Civil Rights movement, for example, references to "American" traditions and values were often much less particularistic and anticivil than universalistic and civil.

40. As I mentioned in chapter 4, the theoretical rationale for this performative perspective is presented in Alexander, "Cultural Pragmatics" and elaborated in Alexander, Giesen, and Mast, *Social Performance.*

41. A. Morris, *Origins of the Civil Rights Movement,* pp. 231–232. Overflowing with richly textured empirical reconstructions of primary data, including in-depth interviews with movement participants, this book remains a vital resource for any theoretical reflection on the Civil Rights movement.

42. Ibid., p. 258.

43. Ibid., p. 265.

44. Ibid.

45. Ibid., p. 260.

46. Unfortunately, this has not been as true for many of the contemporary social scientific interpreters of King's leadership. Garrow, however, is the critical exception. In *Protest at Selma,* for example, he describes King as an astute symbolic leader who allowed the movement access to both communicative and regulative institutions. In this regard, Garrow may have been influenced by August Meier's pioneering "On the Role of Martin Luther King." Now largely forgotten, this interpretation was published in the immediate wake of the Selma demonstrations in May 1965. Emphasizing the "paradox" of King's public role, Meier called King a "conservative militant." Without providing a broader, macrosociological framework that could explain their relevance, Meier drew attention to the issues of duality and dramaturgy that later became central to Garrow's empirical discussion and are at the heart of my own theoretical analysis here.

King's career has been characterized by failures that, in the larger sense, must be accounted triumphs. The buses in Montgomery were desegregated only after lengthy judicial proceedings conducted by the NAACP Legal Defense Fund secured a favorable decision from the U.S. Supreme Court. . . . King's subsequent major campaigns—in Albany, Georgia; in Danville, Virginia; in Birmingham, Alabama—ended as failures or with only token accomplishments in those cities. But each of them, chiefly because of his presence, dramatically focused national and international attention on the plight of the Southern Negro, thereby facilitating overall progress. . . . Essentially, this pattern of local failure and national victory was recently enacted at Selma, Alabama. King is ideologically committed to disobeying unjust laws and court orders . . . but generally he follows a policy of not disobeying Federal Court orders. . . . He [has sometimes] expressed a crude, neo-Marxist interpretation of history romanticizing the Populist movement as a genuine union of black and white common people, ascribing race prejudice to capitalists playing white workers off against black. Yet, in practice, he is amenable to compromise with the white bourgeois political and economic Establishment. . . . With intuitive, but extraordinary skill, he not only castigates whites for their sins but, in contrast to angry young writers like Baldwin, he explicitly states his belief in their salvation. . . . King first arouses the guilt feelings of whites, and then relieves them. . . . Like a Greek tragedy, King's performance provides an extraordinary catharsis for the white listener. (Meier, passim)

47. Garrow, *Protest at Selma*, p. 321.

48. Ibid., pp. 35, 39, emphasis added.

49. Quoted in S. Burns, "Overview: The Proving Ground," p. 12.

50. Septima Clark, quoted in A. Morris, *Origins of the Civil Rights Movement*, p. 98.

51. Dr. William Anderson, president of the Albany Movement in 1961, quoted in A. Morris, *Origins of the Civil Rights Movement*, p. 244.

52. Cornell Reagon, quoted in A. Morris, *Origins of the Civil Rights Movement*, p. 244.

53. The argument that acknowledging the critical importance of King necessarily downplays the importance of the grassroots level has been advanced by some of the most influential new "local historians." In addition to Eskew and Payne, see, for example, Clayborne Carson's dismissal of the notion that national leaders and organizations "played a decisive role in mobilizing Southern Blacks," in "Civil Rights Reform and the Black Freedom Struggle," p. 22. Carson argues (p. 24) that King's activities were entirely separate from those of local leaders, who developed movements that were distanced and completely independent of his own. This kind of

one-sided emphasis, it seems to me, is no better than the exclusively national emphasis that such local historians seek to depose. As I suggest throughout these chapters, indeed, both the local and the national references are necessary if duality is to be understood.

From a sociology of knowledge perspective, it might be speculated that such historical interpretations can be seen as carrying forward into academic work an argument that was ongoing within the various circles of the Civil Rights movement during the early and middle 1960s, when SNCC and other increasingly radical groups complained bitterly, if usually privately, about the attention that King received, the credit outsiders gave him, and the manner in which outside resources were funneled to SCLC rather than to other organizations. In fact, it was just such a critique of King's supposedly unhealthy influence that the veteran organizer Ella Baker made in her pivotal arguments in April 1960, which led the young people who had organized the sit-ins to withdraw from the SCLC and organize their own organization, SNCC. (For Baker's role in this historical development, see Payne, *Light of Freedom*, pp. 92–100.) In this sense, contemporary historians take one side or the other in that earlier debate, in which some of them actually participated, directly or indirectly.

Relating this historiographic dispute to the empirical circumstances in Montgomery, S. Burns ("Overview: The Proving Ground," pp. 1–10) identifies four equally important groups of people that determined the success of the local movement: (1) Mobilizers, the handful of charismatic leaders generated by the national movement, e.g., King and Abernathy; (2) Organizers, the dozens of local ministers, secular leaders, and women activists; (3) Activists, the several thousands of persons engaged in organizing activities at the microlevels of family, neighborhood, church, and workplace; and (4) Followers, the majority of the black population, about twenty thousand persons, who never or at least rarely attended mass meetings but who refused, nonetheless, to ride busses during the boycott. It is striking that, even in this eminently sensible account of the relationship between national and local elements, Burns makes no mention of the absolutely central role of the surrounding civil sphere.

54. The concept of "charismatic" does not get to these. Though King certainly exercised charismatic authority over the black masses, most never encountered him directly. This direct relationship to charismatic authority was, of course, even less the case for northern whites. The political sociology of leadership must find a new way to understand the very concept of charisma, one that relies less on psychological force than on semiotic mediation. See the argument along these lines advanced by P. Smith, "Culture and Charisma: Outline of a Theory."

55. King, "Our Struggle," quoted in S. Burns, "Overview: The Proving Ground," p. 12.

56. A. Young, *Easy Burden*, p. 225.

57. A. Morris, *Origins of the Civil Rights Movement*, p. 244.

58. See the polls cited in McAdam, *Political Process*, attesting to the centrality of the civil rights issue during the first half of the 1960s. For King's role in affecting this communicative institution, see below.

59. To understand King as the dominant American of his time and to illustrate this understanding in a compelling narrative history is the singular achievement of Taylor Branch in *Parting the Waters*.

The importance to the project of civil repair of a black leader becoming the subject for enthusiastic white identification suggests parallels with the relation of Nelson Mandela to many whites in South Africa during and after the transition from Apartheid. There is, however, a critical difference between the two cases. Martin Luther King inspired this identification during the course of "normal" social movement politics inside civil society. In South Africa, by contrast, the vast majority of whites refused any identification with the black anti-Apartheid movement, giving support, instead, to an overtly racist white leadership that imprisoned and silenced the movement's key leaders and engaged in systematic, anticivil terrorism that eventually led to a low-level guerrilla war. South Africa did not, in other words, allow the development of an antiracist social movement inside its civil sphere. George M. Frederickson draws attention to this counterintuitive contrast between the two national situations of racial domination in his comparative study:

> Although blacks were of course an overwhelming numerical majority in South Africa, they were until 1994 even more of a minority in terms of their access to political, social, and economic power than the African-American fraction . . . of the total population of the United States . . . It was the unholy achievement of South African white domination to have made blacks even more powerless relative to whites than were African-Americans after the abolition of slavery. . . . Territorial and political segregation served to make a numerical minority into a functional polity. (*Black Liberation*, p. 6)

The example of South Africa makes it clear that, even when the surrounding sphere is democratic, simply publicizing injustice is, in and of itself, not enough to provoke identification and repair. There needs to be some differentiation among elements of the dominating society, which fragments the core group in terms of region, history, political order, and values. In the United States, it was critical that there had been a centuries-long split between the North and the South precisely over the issue of tolerating slavery and formal racial domination. Though South Africa was by no means without such divisions, the internally democratic white society was more homogeneous on the race issue. The conflict between the overwhelming Dutch Afrikaner majority and the much smaller British minority had been settled after World War Two, and Apartheid constructed as a result. In South

Africa, the whites who created and enforced racial domination were, in effect, the same as the white civil audience who viewed this oppression as an audience. Precisely the opposite was the case in the United States. Whereas the white audiences in the northern United States came to identify with black protests against the white racial domination and expressed their indignation in the public sphere, in South Africa white emotional identification moved in the other direction as conflict intensified, toward support for those who carried racial oppression out. As a consequence, deployment of white violence did not create indignation among the majority of white South Africans, much less motivate them to join blacks in an effort at civil repair. The transition from Apartheid to an interracial democracy occurred not because of persuasion but because the continuing violence and resistance of black freedom fighters forced the white elites to contemplate the very real possibility that their institutions and ways of life would not survive the unfolding conflict. It was only after this transition from above that a dramatically effective solidarizing process between blacks and whites began to occur, in part under the aegis of the Truth and Reconciliation Commission. See, e.g., T. Goodman, "Performing a 'New' Nation."

The importance of an independent mediating element between dominating core group and dominated mass is what the rational choice perspective means when it insists on the importance of "third parties." In his article on the Civil Rights movement, Chong suggests that "non-violence is almost certain to be ineffective if it is not able to find support among the third parties to the conflict." Chong points out that in South Africa the state was not "subjected to the same domestic pressures and constraints on the use of violence against blacks as American authorities were during the 1950s and 1960s" ("All or Nothing Games in the Civil Rights Movement," p. 696). But rational choice theory can explain neither when and where third parties exist, nor how they actually influence social movements. Its instrumental assumptions about action and the external, objective status of order make it simply another variant of the classical model, unable to conceptualize the nature and function of the civil sphere.

60. See Garrow, *Bearing the Cross,* for an account of King's personal courage. Garrow recounts that "the emotional trauma" of King's first arrest, in Montgomery in 1956, "heightened the growing personal tensions King was feeling. He had not wanted to be the focal point of the protest in the first place" (this and following quotations from pp. 56–58).

> [King] stressed to everyone that he as an individual was not crucial to the protest, that if something happened to him, or should he step aside, the movement would go on. . . . But others thought King had everything to do with it. The obscene and threatening phone calls continued apace, and they took their toll.

Quoting King's own recollection that "I felt myself faltering and growing in fear," Garrow narrates what he calls "the most important night of [King's] life, the one he always would think back to in future years when the pressures again seemed to be too great."

Finally, on Friday night, January 27, the evening after his brief sojourn at the Montgomery jail, King's crisis of confidence peaked. He returned home late after an MIA meeting . . . and he was about to retire when the phone rang and yet another caller warned him that if he was going to leave Montgomery alive, he had better do so soon.

The caller warned, "Nigger, we are tired of you and your mess now. And if you aren't out of this town in three days, we're going to blow your brains out, and blow up your house." After hearing the call, King went back to bed but was unable to sleep. He went down to the kitchen, made himself some coffee, and sat down at the kitchen table to think things through.

I was ready to give up. With my cup of coffee sitting untouched before me I tried to think of a way to move out of the picture without appearing a coward. . . . I sat there and thought . . . you've got to call on that . . . power that can make a way out of no way. And I discovered then that religion had to become real to me, and I had to know God for myself. And I bowed down over that cup of coffee. I never will forget it. . . . I prayed a prayer, and I prayed out loud that night. I said, "Lord, I'm down here trying to do what's right. I think I'm right. I think the cause that we represent is right. But Lord, I must confess that I'm weak now. I'm faltering. I'm losing my courage. And I can't let the people see me like this because if they see me weak and losing my courage, they will begin to get weak." And it seemed at that moment that I could hear an inner voice saying to me, "Martin Luther, stand up for righteousness. Stand up for justice. Stand up for truth. And lo I will be with you, even until the end of the world." I heard the voice of Jesus saying still to fight on. He promised never to leave me, never to leave me alone. No never alone. No never alone. He promised never to leave, never to leave me alone.

King believed that this critical religious experience gave him the courage to continue as a leader, despite his belief that death was certain. "Almost at once, my fears began to go," he recalled later, "and my uncertainty disappeared" (p. 58).

From the moment of this personal crisis, King carried with him the conviction that eventually he would be assassinated. This represented an accurate social understanding of the repercussions of his leadership, which was so visible, and created such tension, in the dualistic context of American society. Though King's religious faith allowed him to channel this fear into the narrative of martyrdom and redemption, he continued to experience episodes of panic and depression for the rest of his life, living with the certainty of an early death.

61. Quoted in S. Burns, "Overview: The Proving Ground," pp. 24–25.

62. These quotations are from the transcription made from a recording of King's speech, dramatically presented and interpreted in Branch, *Parting the Waters,* pp. 138–141.

63. Branch's description of the scene that followed, with its religious intonation and its teleological revelation of King's eventual sacrifice, is worth reproducing here:

> The crowd retreated into stunned silence as he [King] stepped away from the pulpit. . . . The applause continued as King made his way out of the church, with people reaching to touch him. . . . The boycott was on. King would work on his timing, but his oratory had just made him forever a public person. In the few short minutes of his first political address, a power of communion emerged that would speak inexorably to strangers who would both love and revile him, like all prophets. He was twenty-six, and had not quite twelve years and four months to live. (*Parting the Waters,* p. 142)

64. A. Morris suggests that "buses became the first target of the movement because members of the black community had begun to see bus discrimination not as a private misery but as a public issue" (*Origins of the Civil Rights Movement,* p. 48).

65. S. Burns, "Overview: The Proving Ground," p. 5.

66. Ibid.

67. Quoted in Branch, *Parting the Waters,* p. 185.

68. Ibid.

69. For the performative distinction between routine occurrences and events, see Mast, "The Cultural Pragmatics of Event-ness."

70. *Newsweek,* March 5, 1956. Quoted in Lentz, *Symbols,* p. 26.

71. *Time,* April 2, 1956. Quoted in Lentz, *Symbols,* p. 27.

72. Quoted in *Eyes on the Prize: America's Civil Rights Years, 1954–1965* (documentary film, first broadcast on PBS, 1987), Part 1.

73. *Newsweek,* November 26, 1956, quoted in Lentz, *Symbols,* p. 31.

74. *Time,* November 26, 1956, quoted in Lentz, *Symbols,* p. 31.

75. *Time,* February 18, 1957, quoted in Lentz, *Symbols,* p. 36. The cultural power of this early construction of the incident—the power of its civil society frame—is

demonstrated by the fact that, thirty years later, an academic historian of the Montgomery movement, Stewart Burns, offered a supposedly factual description that represented the incident in exactly the same symbolic way:

> This was the most dramatic and public but not the only time that he [King] almost single-handedly steered the civil rights movement from turning violent. Acting spontaneously in the heat of the moment, he gracefully transformed the Montgomery protest's first direct encounter with violence into a public declaration of commitment to nonviolent principles, grounded in Christian faith. His action and words set a defining tone for the next decade. ("Overview: The Proving Ground," p. 17)

76. For the distinction between symbol and icon, see C. Peirce, "Logic as Semiotic." Iconic representation converts representation into a physical form, as in a statue. When Peirce suggests, however, that this physical form embodies, not a conventional representation, but the literal meaning of an object, he conflates the iconic and symbolic. See Alexander, "Standing before Giacometti's *Standing Woman.*"

77. *Time*, January 7, 1957, quoted in Lentz, *Symbols*, p. 34.

78. This incident is subtly recounted in Lentz, *Symbols*.

CHAPTER 13

1. C. Hamilton, "Federal Law and the Courts in the Civil Rights Movement," p. 112.

2. Nelson Benton, interviewed by Howell Raines, in *My Soul Is Rested*, p. 386.

3. Quoted in Garrow, *Protest at Selma*, p. 40, emphasis added.

4. King, *Where Do We Go from Here*, p. 158, quoted in Garrow, *Protest at Selma*, p. 225, emphasis added.

5. The Civil Rights movement also aimed at achieving office control. Its activists, however, were not as reflexive about this regulatory institution. They often folded their interest in office regulation into their focus on legislative and legal activity.

6. Quoted in McNeil, *Groundwork*, P. 219; cited in C. Hamilton, "Federal Law," p. 106.

7. C. Hamilton, "Federal Law," pp. 106–107.

8. Ibid., quoted on p. 109.

9. W. Kunstler, *Deep in My Heart*, p. 102, quoted in A. Morris, *Origins of the Civil Rights Movement*, p. 247.

10. A. Morris, *Origins of the Civil Rights Movement*, p. 63; Branch, *Parting the Waters*, p. 188.

11. Quoted in Branch, *Parting the Waters*, p. 196.

12. Ralph McGill, the pioneering reformist editor of the *Atlanta Constitution*, quoted in Payne, *Light of Freedom*, p. 78.

13. Quoted in C. Hamilton, "Federal Law," p. 107.

14. A. Morris, *Origins of the Civil Rights Movement*, pp. 108–116. Though Morris defends the importance of the SCLC's "crusade" as an organizing and preparatory vehicle, he acknowledges its failure as a vehicle for actually registering voters.

15. A. Morris (*Origins of the Civil Rights Movement*, pp. 157–166) provides a vivid and detailed account of the organizational network through which nonviolence, as a tactical strategy, was transmitted to the MIA from the beginning of the Montgomery bus boycott. Nonviolence as a political tool had been developed in the American context by the Fellowship of Reconciliation (FOR), during World War I. During the early 1940s, FOR spawned the Congress for Racial Equality to carry nonviolence into the field of civil rights activism. When, at the insistence of King, the Montgomery movement publicly presented itself as committed to nonviolence, CORE and FOR sent experienced representatives to help the MIA organize workshops to train volunteers in nonviolent techniques, among them Bayard Rustin, who was to remain a vital associate of King's until the end of his life. From that point on, nonviolent workshops were organized throughout the South under the auspices and by CORE and FOR.

Morris has suggested the term "movement halfway houses" (*Origins of the Civil Rights Movement*, pp. 139–174) for such organizations, and he has documented how these institutions—which included the American Friends Service Committee, the War Resisters League, the Southern Conference Educational Fund, and the Highlander Folk School, located in Monteagle, Tennessee—brought "a battery of social change resources" to the emerging Civil Rights movement. Morris defines movement halfway houses as institutions "only partially integrated into the larger society" (*Origins of the Civil Rights Movement*, p. 139). In doing so, Morris follows the classical perspective that frames social movements as engaging in a power struggle against an antagonistic society. From the perspective developed here, however, such halfway houses can be understood differently—as prototypes of "duality." It is their connection to the surrounding civil sphere of northern society, not just their separation from it, that allowed them to play a small but vital role in the southern black movement. Their utopianism reflected the ideal strains of the surrounding civil sphere, their political radicalism the possibilities for dissent that a partially institutionalized civil sphere inspires.

The career of Myles Horton, the founder of the Highlander Folk School, provides a concrete illustration of this duality. After growing up amid the poverty of Appalachia, Horton left the South to enroll at Union Theological Seminary in New York, where he studied with Reinhold Niebuhr, the influential theologian of white Social Gospel. Niebuhr's thinking was later to profoundly influence Martin

Luther King. Horton was also deeply affected by John Dewey, the critical pragmatist philosopher. When Horton left New York in 1930, he studied for a year at the University of Chicago with the pioneering sociologist Robert Park, who himself had been affected by the settlement house movement that challenged urban poverty, ethnic domination, and powerlessness in northern cities. Horton traveled to Denmark to study its "folk schools," and he returned to the South to put these ideas into practice in the mountains of Tennessee, starting his Highland Folk School in 1932.

During the 1930s, the Highland school concentrated on labor organizing, but in his work with Southern labor unions Horton realized that their patterns of racial segregation "just kept blocking everything" (quoted in A. Morris, *Origins of the Civil Rights Movement,* p. 144). Believing that integrating the school was the "right thing to do," Horton made interracial civility an institutional policy from 1940 on. In the next two decades, Highlander offered training in social activism to a number of figures who became prominent in the Civil Rights movement, including Septima Clark, a grassroots NAACP activist; E. D. Nixon and Fred Shuttlesworth, leaders in Montgomery and Birmingham, respectively; Rosa Parks, whose refusal to move to the back of the bus sparked the Montgomery bus boycott; and James Bevel, Diane Nash, and John Lewis, who subsequently helped initiate the sit-in movement and the Freedom Rides and were instrumental in later civil rights campaigns. Eventually, Highland's staff and former students conceived and sponsored a network of "citizen schools" for illiterate and impoverished southern blacks. The schools offered instruction in basic reading and writing skills, and Horton recalled that he and his colleagues also promoted the schools to blacks on the basis of "them becoming full citizens and taking their place in society and demanding their rights and being real men and women in their own right" (quoted in *Origins of the Civil Rights Movement,* p. 151). In the reading clinics, readers practiced on such documents as the "United Nations Declaration of Human Rights." Martin Luther King was another civil rights activist who maintained close relations with Horton during the movement's early days.

16. Branch, *Parting the Waters,* p. 272. There had been a successful mass boycott movement in Baton Rouge, Louisiana, in June 1953. See A. Morris, *Origins of the Civil Rights Movement,* pp. 17–25.

17. Chafe, *Civilities and Civil Rights,* pp. 138–139.

18. Ibid., p. 139. For the role of agonism in creating fusion between audience and actors in successful social performance, see Alexander, "Cultural Pragmatics."

19. Quoted by H. Zinn in *SNCC,* partly reprinted in Leon Friedman, *Civil Rights Reader,* p. 44.

20. Ibid., p. 46.

21. Ibid.

22. Quoted in Branch, *Parting the Waters,* p. 283.

23. This kind of criticism from southern opponents of the Civil Rights movement points to the broader theoretical issue of the relationship between "civility" and the kind of interpersonal behavior that is legitimately demanded of participants in civil society. Civility suggests control over aggression and courtesy, certainly qualities that are at a premium in maintaining universal respect for others, yet it can and often does also imply deference. Deference maintains authority rather than equality and is more an aristocratic than a democratic quality. Certainly it suggests cultural ideals that belie the ability to engage in criticism, which is a fully legitimate motive in the discourse of civil society. One can debate this issue in theoretical terms, comparing, for example, the conservative emphasis on civility and deference in the discussions of Edward Shils ("Primordial, Personal, Sacred, and Civil Ties") with the insistence on frankness and criticism in Michael Walzer's understanding of Puritanism's contribution to civil society, in *The Revolution of the Saints*. In the context of the present discussion, however, the issue can be approached in a more empirical manner. One of the principal historians of the sit-in movement, William H. Chafe, observed that white civility, to both blacks and other whites, was central to the ideology of the "culture of white progressivism" in North Carolina. He goes on to describe this culture, however, as functioning to camouflage paternalistic and ultimately exploitative racial relations.

> Civility is the cornerstone of the progressive mystique, signifying courtesy, concern about an associate's family, children, and health, a personal grace that smoothes contact with strangers and obscures conflict with foes. Civility was what white progressivism was all about—a way of dealing with people and problems that made good manners more important than substantial action. Significantly, civility encompassed all of the other themes of the progressive mystique—abhorrence of personal conflict, courtesy toward new ideas, and a generosity toward those less fortunate than oneself. (*Civilities and Civil Rights*, p. 8)

From the viewpoint of the subordinate in this relationship of civility, there lurked a significant element of very uncivil domination. Blacks "understood the other side of civility," Chafe writes, "the deferential poses they had to strike in order to keep jobs, the chilling power of consensus to crush efforts to raise issues of racial justice."

> As victims of civility, blacks had long been forced to operate within an etiquette of race relationships that offered almost no room for collective self-assertion and independence. White people dictated the ground rules, and the benefits went only to those who played the game. (*Civilities and Civil Rights*, p. 9)

It was not surprising, therefore, that within the protected context of black civil society, a critical attitude toward the value of deference prevailed.

> If the etiquette of civility precluded honesty in direct contacts with whites, it could not suppress that honesty—that protest—within the black community itself. In churches, schools, pool halls, and corner gatherings, another culture existed—one of assertion rather than deference. Sometimes blacks said they wanted a separate world where whites could never enter. Other times they voiced a determination to share fully the benefits of the white world. Always there was the mocking humor of blacks making fun of whites who thought they knew their "niggers" but never could understand what black people were all about. The result of these gatherings was an agenda of demands. (*Civilities and Civil Rights*, p. 9)

24. Quoted by Zinn in Leon Friedman, *Civil Rights Reader*, p. 48.
25. Ibid.
26. Quoted in Chafe, *Civilities and Civil Rights*, p. 120.
27. Quoted in Lentz, *Symbols*, p. 45.
28. Branch, *Parting the Waters*, p. 280.
29. Ibid., p. 276.
30. Ibid., p. 293.
31. For the concept of "moral texture" as the ambition of speech acts in the public sphere, see Maria Pia Lara, *Moral Textures*.
32. Branch, *Parting the Waters*, p. 275.
33. Ibid.
34. Ibid.
35. Ibid., p. 276.
36. Ibid.
37. Ibid.
38. Quoted in A. Morris, *Origins of the Civil Rights Movement*, p. 204.
39. Ibid., quoted on p. 288.
40. I refer to "battle for position" to evoke the Gramscian approach to civil society, in which the latter is regarded simply as a milieu within which dominated groups battle against classes and intellectuals who exercise power in a purely hegemonic manner. Aldon Morris applies just this framework (e.g., *Origins of the Civil Rights Movement*, p. 212) to explain the sit-in movement triumph. For a critical theoretical discussion of this understanding in terms of counterpublic theory, see chapter 11, above.
41. Interview in A. Morris, *Origins of the Civil Rights Movement*, p. 229.
42. Ibid., p. 230.
43. Ibid., p. 213.

44. In Leon Friedman, *Civil Rights Reader*, p. 51.

45. Wofford, *Of Kennedys and Kings*, p. 47, quoted in Branch, *Parting the Waters*, p. 306. As I mentioned earlier, Branch's historical reconstruction of what he calls "America in the King Years" provided a new understanding of the centrality of the social movement for civil rights and particularly its leader, Martin Luther King. Branch also reveals the personal, political, and organizational connections, beginning in 1960, between black civil rights leaders and politicians at the highest levels of national power. For Branch's account of the campaign for the Democratic nomination in 1960, see *Parting the Waters*, pp. 304ff.

46. Quoted in Branch, *Parting the Waters*, p. 315.

47. Ibid.

48. Ibid., p. 362.

49. Ibid., p. 365. That Kennedy was not, in fact, a personal friend of Mrs. King's, that he had neither met nor spoken with her before that phone call, underscores the importance that Kennedy placed upon establishing a public semblance of identification. From a performance perspective, it is not the backstage motives of the politician that are of concern but the presentation he makes of them on the front stage.

50. Quoted in Branch, *Parting the Waters*, p. 369.

51. Ibid., p. 366.

52. Ibid., pp. 374–375.

53. Ibid., p. 375.

54. Ibid., p. 378.

55. For the process by which social traumas are constructed, see Alexander, "Toward a Theory of Cultural Trauma," pp. 1–30 and passim.

56. For a discussion of "triumph" versus "tragedy," progressive versus tragic narratives, and heroes versus victims, see the contributions by Giesen, Eyerman, and me in *Cultural Trauma and Collective Identity*. See also Eyerman, *Cultural Trauma;* and Giesen, *Triumph and Trauma*.

57. It is a fascinating testimony to the separation of signifier and signified that the violence of sit-in opponents "missing" from contemporary reports assumed great importance retrospectively, appearing as graphic descriptions in accounts that were composed in the shadow of later developments. In his discussion of the months-long sit-in campaign, Howard Zinn, writing in 1964—after the Freedom Rides and the Birmingham campaign, during the bloody incidents of Freedom Summer—highlighted the overtly violent responses of civil officials, particular a truly repressive, yet by and large unrepresentative, incident in Orangeburg, South Carolina. Zinn's account is melodramatic and detailed, creating a sense of pathos, pity, and terror (Zinn in Leon Friedman, *Civil Rights Reader*, pp. 49–50). Following Zinn's account, A. Morris (*Origins of the Civil Rights Movement*, p. 209), who otherwise emphasizes organizational power as compared to dramaturgical force, writes that, in the sit-ins

at Orangeburg, "hundreds of students" not only were arrested but "brutalized." Branch (*Parting the Waters*, p. 283) draws from, and elaborates upon, Morris's account of Orangeburg, writing of how "local police and units of special state agents" intercepted the demonstrators "with massed force, firing tear gas and water hoses" upon the "doused, choking students." My point here is not that these accounts are inaccurate but that they are metaphorical; the emphasis in such retrospective accounts of the sit-in movements seems to be at clear odds with contemporary ones, and this reconfiguration can be explained by the increasing importance of public outrage, the process I am describing here.

58. Branch, *Parting the Waters*, p. 386.

59. McAdams, *Political Process*, p. 159.

60. A majority of northern white Americans usually responded positively in response to such questions as "Do people have the right to demonstrate for civil rights?" They also typically would support the demonstrators' side in the immediate aftermath of the intense, often violent confrontations that marked particular campaigns. When questioned more generally about specific movement methods, however, there existed much more equivocation. (See Garrow, *Protest at Selma*, pp. 155–159.) In this early period of reports from national surveys, however, the results were rarely controlled for region; nor were they controlled for education. Correlating responses with these factors would have provided more statistical insight into the demographic correlates of the influential expressions of public indignation that I refer to here.

61. In *Numbered Voices: How Opinion Polling Has Shaped American Politics*, Susan Herbst has pointed to how precisely this quantification of public opinion can contribute to such mean-ends calculation in the political process. By putting this quantification into the context of Max Weber's rationalization theory and Frankfurt School thinking about reification, however, she overemphasizes its instrumental effects and loses contact with the deep civil references of public opinion, a reference that she actually emphasizes and helps to elaborate in her later work, *Reading Public Opinion: How Political Actors View the Democratic Process*.

62. This anxiety turned out to be well founded, though the backlash against Democratic actions on civil rights was to take several more years before its effects could be fully experienced on the national stage. When President Lyndon Johnson signed the Civil Rights Bill in 1964, he told his staff, "I think we just gave the South to the Republicans," and Bill Moyers, his aide at the time, recalls Johnson lamenting that he had delivered the South to the Republicans "for your lifetime and mine" (quoted in T. Branch, *Pillar of Fire*, p. 404). The conservative candidacy of Barry Goldwater marked the Republican Party's first effort to take advantage of this white backlash against Democratic identification with black civil rights. After four more years of Johnson's hard-driving reform policies, three Republican Presidents were elected because they employed what Richard Nixon in 1968 called the "Southern

strategy." In the decades following, the only Democrats who could gain election to the presidency were southerners themselves—Johnson, Carter, and Clinton.

63. See Branch, *Parting the Waters*, pp. 405–406.

64. Ibid., quoted on pp. 414.

65. Ibid., p. 415.

66. Ibid., pp. 403–407.

67. Ibid., p. 407.

68. Garrow, *Bearing the Cross*, p. 81. For Garrow's other, post-Montgomery presentations of nonviolence, see *King's Stride toward Freedom* and his "Nonviolence and Racial Justice," pp. 165–167.

69. The concept of the generalized as compared to the concrete other was articulated by the American pragmatist social philosopher George Herbert Mead, who called it a requirement for social participation. According to Mead, the developing personality learns to generalize from early encounters with such concrete actors as parents, siblings, and teachers to an "other" that represents the society as such. As this generalized other becomes internalized, it becomes the psychological vehicle that allows people to "take the role of the other" in such a way that they can act cooperatively in a complex society. Though in his philosophical writings Mead did not link the generalized other explicitly to democracy, as compared with society as such, the link between this so-called symbolic interactionist perspective and the normative political tradition has been made by Jürgen Habermas in "Individuation through Socialization: On George Herbert Mead's Theory of Subjectivity." See also the elaboration of Mead's insight in relation to democratization in A. Honneth, *The Struggle for Recognition: The Moral Grammar of Social Conflicts*. Seyla Benhabib made use of this Meadian distinction to develop a feminist twist on democratic political theory in *Situating the Self: Gender, Community, and Postmodernism in Contemporary Ethics*.

70. These quotes are from James Lawson, one of the leaders of the Nashville sit-in movement, from a speech he delivered in April 1960, to what turned out to be the founding conference of SNCC. See Branch, *Parting the Waters*, p. 291.

71. Quote from King, *Why We Can't Wait*, p. 37, quoted in Garrow, *Protest at Selma*, pp. 224–225. It is instructive to note that a similar dynamic came into play during the abolitionist struggle against slavery in the antebellum period, more than a century before. M. Dillon writes that the abolitionists struggled to convince Northerners that slavery was not "a remote institution that did not concern them" (*Abolitionists*, p. 40). They soon found that speeches focusing on religious and moral ideals were not sufficient. There remained a "vast emotional gulf" (p. 84) between themselves and their northern audience. To close this gap, to stimulate identification on the part of the northern audience, the abolitionists became more performative in their strategies. They created and distributed highly dramatic narratives of suffering and redemption, including the firsthand accounts written by freed blacks that later

came to be called "slave narratives." As Dillon puts it, "Abolitionists tried to create emotional involvement by presenting Northerners with poignant and moving accounts of suffering" (p. 84). The thousands of printed tracts and orations were "dramatizations of the plight" of the slaves that "held whites spellbound" (p. 84), arousing pity, hope, and rage as forcefully as television would a century later. The extraordinary popularity of Harriet Beecher Stowe's *Uncle Tom's Cabin*, published in 1853, represents a case in point. This "literary sensation of the era" created a profound, if in contemporary terms somewhat patronizing, sympathy for the slave. Reproduced in musical waltzes, stage productions, and even in traveling dioramas, its effect was such that "fugitive slaves and their rescuers [became] folk heroes" (pp. 191–192). This epic symbolic narrative is often credited with psychologically preparing northerners for their declaration of war against southern secession in 1860 (p. 254).

But the abolitionists also found ways to compel southern officials to actually engage in public repression, not just in literature but in fact. In addition to the stories produced by fictional media of communication, the factual media—northern newspapers—carried reports of courageous but ill-fated abolitionist efforts at emancipation and disruption. In 1837, for example, a crusading Illinois newspaper editor named Lovejoy was murdered by an angry pro-slavery crowd. This murder "created enormous resentment" throughout the North (Dillon, *Abolitionists*, p. 93). In the subsequent decades leading up to the Civil War, the abolitionists found various ways to "maneuver their opponents into taking ever more extreme and outrageous action." The result of this combination of factual and fictional representations was to effect a "momentous revolution in Northern sentiment with respect to slavery" (p. 93).

72. Garrow (*Protest at Selma*, p. 2) and other historians of the Civil Rights movement locate the shifting understanding of nonviolent tactics much later—in the aftermath of the Albany campaign, which led to the movement in Birmingham. From what we know of the new tactics employed in the Freedom Rides, this later date seems highly implausible. We must keep in mind, moreover, that nonviolence was always a response to duality, that it looked not only to the immediate opponent but to the surrounding civil sphere. What this mid-movement shift represented, in other words, was less a new strategic understanding than a new tactical orientation to duality.

For the following discussion of the initial days of the Freedom Ride, see Branch, *Parting of the Waters*, pp. 417–425; Smith quotes on p. 425.

73. Branch, *Parting the Waters*, p. 426.

74. Ibid., p. 427.

75. Ibid., p. 441.

76. Ibid., p. 447.

77. Ibid., p. 462.

78. Ibid., p. 463.

79. Ibid.

80. Ibid., p. 471; and A. Morris, *Origins of the Civil Rights Movement*, p. 233. Both these accounts apparently rely on Zinn, *SNCC*, p. 51.

81. Branch, *Parting the Waters*, pp. 490, 488.

82. Ibid., p. 485.

83. Ibid., pp. 478–481; and A. Morris, *Origins of the Civil Rights Movement*, 235–236.

84. Schlesinger, *A Thousand Days*, p. 935, quoted in A. Morris, *Origins of the Civil Rights Movement*, p. 235, emphasis added.

85. A. Morris, *Origins of the Civil Rights Movement*, p. 243.

86. Ibid., p. 244.

87. Ibid.

88. Eskew, *But for Birmingham*, p. 44.

89. Branch, *Parting the Waters*, p. 618.

90. Ibid.

91. Ibid.

92. For the nature of "exemplary" action in the context of social movements, see Eyerman and Jamison, *Music and Social Movements*. They draw this notion from Hannah Arendt. For a philosophical account of "exemplary universalism" that complements the cultural-sociological approach I am developing here, see A. Ferrara, *Reflective Authenticity*.

93. This account draws from Branch, *Parting the Waters*, pp. 601–602.

94. Eskew, *But for Birmingham*, p. 52.

95. Ibid., pp. 46–47; Branch, *Parting the Waters*, p. 557.

96. R. Baker, *New York Review of Books*, April 9, 1998.

97. Branch, *Parting the Waters*, p. 680.

98. Ibid., p. 632.

99. A. Morris (*Origins of the Civil Rights Movement*, pp. 250–267) discovered the degree of planning and conscious orchestration in his interviews with Birmingham veterans in the early 1980s. As Eskew's research shows, however, Morris overestimates the extent to which the SCLC were able to implement these plans (*But for Birmingham*, pp. 261ff). The actual campaign, in contrast to the planned one, was continually in danger of imploding. It was repeatedly saved by skillful leadership, risk-taking, and plain luck. What neither Eskew nor Morris sufficiently emphasizes is that, regardless of whether it could be carried out, the simple fact of elaborate pre-planning reveals the heightened self-consciousness about the relation of the movement to the phenomenon of duality. The reason for this lack of emphasis is that both authors view the Birmingham struggle in terms of the classical model of social movements, ignoring the central importance of the boundary relationship between civil and uncivil spheres.

100. In the social science literature on the Birmingham campaign, and on the

Civil Rights movement more generally, an argument has emerged over the extent to which movement leaders consciously calculated and encouraged tactics that would provoke repressive violence, and to what degree representatives of the northern media were collusive in this strategy. For example, in speaking about such planning at Selma, in 1965, Garrow (*Bearing the Cross*, p. 54) remarks that "the SCLC leadership believed that its efforts would appeal favorably to more persons if the strategic and tactical considerations underlying those efforts were not made public" and, examining the writings of *New York Times* reporter John Herbers, he suggests that they do "not indicate that he understood fully just how conscious and well-calculated was the SCLC effort to evoke public nastiness and physical violence from [Selma] Sheriff Clark and other officials." Writing six years later, Morris condemns such a "simplistic explanation" and goes on to insist that "Garrow and others are incorrect when they say that the SCLC's main strategy in Birmingham was to have the demonstrators beaten by 'Bull' Connor and his police force, thereby to elicit federal intervention and the nation's outrage and sympathy" (*Origins of the Civil Rights Movement*, pp. 252, 258). "To the contrary," Morris argues, "the Birmingham movement was designed to generate the necessary power needed to defeat local segregationists by using the economic boycott and mass demonstrations" (p. 258).

In one sense, this empirical argument recapitulates the theoretical conflict between the classical social movement approach of Morris and the more civil society orientation of Garrow. There is another sense, however, in which both interpretations suffer from being too closely involved in the events they are writing about. It is true that, during the heat of the moment, public revelations about conscious incitement of violence may have delegitimated the translation efforts of the civil rights campaigns; at the minimum, such disclosures would have created substantial interpretive challenges in their own right. Almost four decades removed from these confrontations, however, it seems unnecessary to view such interpretations as "outing" the movement in a manner that could lead to its delegitimation. Quite to the contrary, the leaders' conscious and unconscious awareness of the importance of the need for dramaturgy, and their skill in producing it, are to be admired. In constructing an effective dramaturgy, they demonstrated sharp insight into the duality of injustice in societies that contain a relatively autonomous civil sphere, and what this implies for social movements in civil societies that seek fundamental social change. It seems reasonable to suggest that it would have been highly implausible if participants and observers of the civil rights campaigns were not aware of the provocative quality of nonviolent direct action, a tactic that was widely discussed at the time, and of its potential for stimulating violence in response. Northern and southern media representatives were aware of the strategy; if the northern reporters did not write explicitly about it, or at least not very often, it was because their civil sympathies extended so strongly to the black protesters' side.

101. A. Morris, *Origins of the Civil Rights Movement*, p. 262.

102. Eskew, *But for Birmingham*, pp. 259–263.

103. Branch, *Parting the Waters*, p. 737.

104. Ibid.

105. Ibid., pp. 737–738.

106. Ibid., quoted on p. 739.

107. Ibid., quoted on pp. 742–744. King recalls here the rhetorical inversion Senator Kennedy made in his presidential campaign.

108. Quoted in A. Morris, *Origins of the Civil Rights Movement*, p. 263.

109. Branch, *Parting the Waters*, p. 754.

110. E.g., Eskew, *But for Birmingham*, p. 262.

111. Quoted in Branch, *Parting the Waters*, p. 757.

112. Following the classical model of social movements, this objective constraint is the reason Eskew offers for Bull Connor's turn to repression. See Eskew, *But for Birmingham*, p. 266.

113. Branch, *Parting the Waters*, pp. 760–761.

114. This description follows the probing account in Branch, *Parting the Waters*.

115. Garrow, *Protest at Selma*, pp. 139–140, 167.

116. Ibid., p. 166.

117. Ibid., pp. 139 and 141.

118. Quoted in Eskew, *But for Birmingham*, p. 272.

119. Branch, *Parting the Waters*, pp. 761–762.

120. Quoted in Garrow, *Protest at Selma*, p. 140. The quotation following from the letter to the *Post* is on p. 168.

121. Quoted in Branch, *Parting the Waters*, p. 764, and Garrow, *Protest at Selma*, p. 141.

122. Quoted in Garrow, *Bearing the Cross*, p. 141.

123. Ibid., quoted on p. 142.

124. Branch, *Parting the Waters*, p. 780.

125. Eskew, *But for Birmingham*, p. 279.

126. Quoted in Branch, *Parting the Waters*, pp. 774–778.

127. Branch, *Parting the Waters*, p. 778.

128. Ibid., quoted on p. 783.

129. Ibid., quoted on p. 783.

130. Eskew, *But for Birmingham*, pp. 294–295.

131. Ibid., p. 295.

132. Branch, *Parting the Waters*, pp. 783, 800.

133. A. Morris, *Origins of the Civil Rights Movement*, p. 250.

134. Eskew, *But for Birmingham*, p. 326 and passim. Despite their shared orientation to the classical model, Morris and Eskew are fully aware that the effect of the local victory, and even its causes, were much broader than simply a shift in local power relations.

135. It is precisely this all-important relation between local and national that the new local history underplays. Payne (*Light of Freedom*), for example, devotes his massive study to the proposition that grassroots organizing in the Mississippi Delta proceeded without much reference to national developments, that the publicity generated by the national movement had virtually no effect on the local movements, and that the interventions of outside regulative forces were ephemeral and had virtually no lasting effect. Yet in the interstices of his account one can find periodic acknowledgment that such connections did, in fact, have great effect on the status of the local movements that Payne describes.

What is different about the 1950s is not the presence of Blacks willing to resist but the fact that as the state [of Mississippi] became less isolated, politically and economically, as Black organizations . . . became able to draw on a wider range of resources, it was possible for some of these [local] leaders to survive long enough to begin making a difference. (p. 47)

[In 1961, SNCC organizer Bob] Moses was arrested and charged with interfering with an officer. Before the trial, Moses placed a collect call to [Assistant Attorney General] John Doar at the Justice Department, deliberately speaking loudly enough to be overheard. . . . Hearing Moses talk to the Justice Department seemed to unnerve the local authorities. Moses was given an amazingly light sentence. . . . This timidity was partly a result of local whites looking over their shoulder. (pp. 116–117)

As terrorists, the perpetrators of white violence in Greenwood [Mississippi] in the early sixties fall far short of their racist forefathers. . . . There are relatively few cases where perpetrators of violence operate openly. Most trouble took place at night. . . . The days were past when whites would, in broad daylight, boldly stride into the home of any Black who had offended custom and drag that person out. . . . The changing patterns of violence are partly a reflection of the structural changes that had taken place in the South's relationship with the rest of the nation. There was no way to be sure that violence wouldn't stir up a reaction from Washington. (p. 202)

The victories that affected the daily life of the average person began in the summer of 1964, with the public-accommodations bill. After that came the Voting Rights Act of 1965, bringing federal registrars to the South. The same period saw a decline in the frequency of both economic and physical reprisals and increasingly vigorous federal prosecution of those who persisted in violence. (p. 272)

The federal government was moving in the direction of more visible and aggressive protection of [local] civil rights workers [because] the summer of 1964 had exposed the worst state in the South [i.e., Mississippi] to the scrutiny of the entire nation. (p. 315)

CHAPTER 14

1. The administrative director of the SCLC, Wyatt T. Walker, wrote on behalf of the organization in early June 1963: "We believe that Birmingham will prove to be a watershed in the history of the nonviolent revolution in America" (quoted in Eskew, *But for Birmingham*, p. 314).

2. Eskew, *But for Birmingham*, p. 318.

3. From a recorded conversation with Carl Albert on June 12, 1963. Quoted in Branch, *Parting the Waters*, p. 828.

4. Quoted in the *Birmingham News*, August 18, 1963, and cited in *But for Birmingham*, p. 392 n. 24.

5. Quoted in Eskew, *But for Birmingham*.

6. Branch, *Parting the Waters*, pp. 603–806.

7. Ibid., pp. 842–843.

8. Quoted in the *Birmingham News*, August 18, 1963, and cited in *But for Birmingham*, p. 392 n. 24.

9. Quotations drawn from "President Kennedy's Report to Congress Outlining a Civil Rights Bill (June 19, 1963)," in Leon Friedman, *Civil Rights Reader*, pp. 245–260.

10. Quoted in Branch, *Parting the Waters*, p. 822.

11. "President Kennedy's Report to Congress," p. 259.

12. The following quotations are drawn from "Address to the Nation on Civil Rights, President John F. Kennedy (June 11, 1963)," in Leon Friedman, *Civil Rights Reader*, pp. 64–67.

13. See chap. 8.

14. The rhetorical question about whether a white American would be willing to have his skin color changed and stand in the place of a black American palpably illustrates the philosopher John Rawls's idea that justice demands that citizens should wear a "veil of ignorance" about the position they occupy in society, for this knowledge separates citizens from one another and impedes the social solidarity necessary for justice. With this veil in place, Rawls argues, citizens can return, in their imagination, to the "original position," in which they might occupy the place of the least privileged members of society. That President Kennedy couched this proposal symbolically, in terms of the discourse of civil society and its most recent dramatic reproduction, provides an empirical illustration of the argument I made in chapter 1: The Rawlsian philosophical understanding of solidarity can be empirically translated only by a cultural-theoretical understanding of the discourse of civil society.

15. Quoted in Branch, *Parting the Waters*, p. 824.

16. Ibid., quoted on p. 64.

17. Ibid., pp. 884–885.

18. For the close working relationship that developed, immediately after Kennedy's assassination, between King and the newly inaugurated president, Lyndon Johnson, and how this relationship focused on translating communicative into regulatory power, see Nick Kotz, *Judgment Days*.

19. There has been debate among historians of the Civil Rights movement about the relative significance of "Birmingham" as compared with the Selma demonstrations that followed two years later and that triggered the Voting Rights Act. David Garrow, in *Protest at Selma: Martin Luther King, Jr. and the Voting Rights Act of 1965*, argues that in Birmingham, as compared with Selma, there was "no widespread national outcry, no vocal reaction by the nation's clergy, and no immediate move by the administration to propose salutary legislation" (p. 144). Garrow rests this argument on the fact that the relationship between the Selma protest and congressional action was virtually immediate, whereas a whole series of events intervened between Birmingham and the passage of the first civil rights bill in 1964. Though Adam Fairclough may have been the first to take strong issue with this conclusion (*To Redeem the Soul of America*, pp. 133–135), the alternative narrative has most recently been taken up by Eskew, who argues in his lengthy treatment of Birmingham that "the key here is the historical context of race reform," adding that "Kennedy's civil rights bill—even as proposed legislation—signified a turning in the governmental policy of the executive branch" (*But for Birmingham*, p. 393 n. 27). Although Garrow describes in an exemplary manner the intertwining of symbolic drama and legislative enactment that followed Selma, he does not do justice to the historical context from which it emerged, to how "Selma" can be seen as an iteration—an imitation and repetition—and not only as an innovation. As the present discussion has demonstrated, creating a spiral of communication and regulation was an ambition of the Civil Rights movement from the very beginning. The strategy for accomplishing it emerged with the sit-in movements in 1960 and became apparent with the Freedom Rides after the Kennedy administration took office. It was only as a result of Birmingham, of course, that the regulatory part of the civil "double helix" came fully into play. It crystallized the dramatic formula for Selma. Selma, then, was more symbolic reenactment than innovation. As Eskew implies, it was Kennedy's June 1963 legislative intervention that marked the critical, paradigm-creating regulatory response to protest, despite the fact that the intervention did not achieve fruition during his administration.

20. Branch, *Parting the Waters*, pp. 827–833.

21. The space that by this time separated northern regulatory institutions from the southern can be seen from the fact that, even as Medgar Evers was memorialized in Arlington, his accused killer—"son of an old Delta family, self-anointed defender of segregation and a member of the Greenwood [White] Citizens' Council" (Payne, *Light of Freedom*, p. 288)—was making a mockery of his murder trial in Mississippi.

An observer at the trial recalled that "the accused killer appeared to enjoy himself immensely."

> He rested his legs on another chair while he drank soda pop, scowled at Negro newsmen, and waved gaily to white friends. At one point, a bailiff had to escort him back to his place when he strode over to chat with members of the jury [and] with a courtly flourish . . . offered cigars to Prosecutor William L. Waller. (quoted in *Light of Freedom*, p. 289)

The trial ended in a hung jury. When the accused killer returned home to Greenwood, its white citizens gave him a rousing parade. With these events as background, it is instructive to recall that Greenwood was a town where SNCC had some of its most extended and significant grassroots organizing experiences, a fact that demonstrates the difficulties of focusing on local civil rights conflicts at the expense of the wider national movement.

22. Branch, *Parting the Waters*, p. 881.

23. Quoted from Martin Luther King, Jr., " 'I Have a Dream' Speech (August 28, 1963)," in Leon Friedman, *Civil Rights Reader*, pp. 110–113.

24. Ibid., p. 110, and Branch, *Parting the Waters*, p. 887.

25. In the years since, King's sacrality at the center of the new, more racially integrated collective consciousness of the American civil sphere would expand. Thirty-five years after the March on Washington speech, a *New York Times* news story discussed the controversy generated by the highly unusual sale by King's family of the leader's personal papers to the Library of Congress. Drawing an implicit analogy between secular and religious sacrality, the story noted that "the last time the library made a purchase was in 1930 when it spent $1.5 million to buy a rare book collection that included one of the three perfect copies of the Gutenberg Bible." This communicative representation testifies to the universalization of King's civil status, not only beyond his particular time and race but beyond place as well: "The pending sale of Dr. King's papers has once again raised the question of the King family's trying to capitalize financially on the legacy of one of the towering figures of the 20th century and an icon to many Americans of all races" (*New York Times*, October 30, 1999, p. A9).

26. Quoted in Garrow, *Bearing the Cross*, p. 144.

27. Branch, *Parting the Waters*, pp. 918–919.

28. Branch, *Pillar of Fire*, p. 197.

29. Ibid., p. 357.

30. See Kotz, *Judgment Days*.

31. Branch, *Pillar of Fire*, p. 388.

32. Ibid., p. 522.

33. Ibid., p. 197. It was about this same time, in November 1964, that the director

of the FBI, J. Edgar Hoover, joined in the symbolic contestation over whether King was fit to be a member in good standing, let alone a hero, of American civil society. For the first time in his long and secret campaign to vilify the black leader, Hoover went public with his accusations about King's anticivil motives and relations. Speaking to a group of women reporters in Washington D.C., Hoover called King "the most notorious liar" and "one of the lowest characters in the country," representing King and his movement as being "controlled" by communist advisors (quoted in Branch, *Pillar of Fire*, p. 526). One week later, in an address to a large public banquet, Hoover warned his listeners, with scarcely veiled reference to King, to beware of zealots who "think with their emotions, seldom with reason" and who have "no compunction in carping, lying, and exaggerating with the fiercest passion, spearheaded at times by Communists and moral degenerates" (quoted in Branch, *Pillar of Fire*, p. 530). Hoover was scarred by racial prejudice and deeply suspicious of any social movement for civil repair. For years, he had directed the FBI to conduct secret surveillance of King's personal and political life. In order to obtain legal cover for these activities, recent evidence suggests, Hoover may have blackmailed Robert Kennedy, the highest legal officer of the United States, by threatening to reveal embarrassing details about his brother Jack's personal life. See R. Mahoney, *Sons and Brothers: The Days of Jack and Robert Kennedy*.

Under Hoover's direction, the FBI composed and mailed numerous threatening messages to King and to newspaper editors and powerful politicians. On one occasion, the FBI went so far as to mail King and his wife what agents called a "suicide package"; it contained spliced recordings from surveillance of King's extramarital sexual encounters and the written recommendation that King kill himself in order to avoid the public humiliation that would befall him upon the tapes' release (Garrow, *Bearing the Cross*, pp. 372–373; and Branch, *Pillar of Fire*, pp. 526–537). In the face of this threat to his personal and public integrity, King simply moved on, in effect calling Hoover's bluff. Hoover's "revelations" about King were publicly aired in November 1964. In response, King publicly accused the director of behaving in a shockingly anticivil way. Calling the accusations "irresponsible," King noted that Hoover "has apparently faltered under the awesome burden, complexities, and responsibilities of his office." In the light of Hoover's putative inability to perform critical regulatory functions, King suggested that "I cannot engage in a public debate with him" and concluded "I have nothing but sympathy for this man who has served his country so well" (quoted in Garrow, *Bearing the Cross*, pp. 360–361).

In any event, Hoover proved incapable of blocking the historic movement for racial repair. In that time of heightened civil effervescence and the threat of newly crystallized civil power, high officials in the American state were responsive to public opinion and rebuffed even this most powerful of bureaucratic oligarchs, despite the vast regulatory power he directed and the still substantial well of civil respect at his command. Hoover's failure cannot be seen only structurally, as arising from the differentiation of civil and political spheres in a democratic society. It was also performative, the result of the FBI Director's declining authority, on the one hand, and King's personal courage and skill on the other. The public was unresponsive to Hoover's charges because of the empathy King had earned from a public audience who received his performances with identification and respect. For a discussion of how such empathy can serve as a resource for political leadership—how the people's moral judgment enters into the world that the tradition of Thrasymachus describes as responsive to power and interest alone, see J. Kane, *The Politics of Moral Capital*.

34. Branch, *Pillar of Fire*, p. 705n, and p. 582.

35. The best scholarly study on this organizing effort is Doug McAdam's *Freedom Summer*. In the following, I draw heavily from the participant interviews McAdam conducted and from his archival research. McAdam himself is interested primarily in the effect of the experience on the white youth themselves and the way they carried the politics of radical democracy and direct action back to their universities in the North, which fed into the creation of the white New Left. My interest here is different though related, namely the effect of this white participation on northern engagement with the black movement.

36. For a detailed, almost ethnographic account of these organizing efforts, which began in Mississippi in 1962, see Payne, *I've Got the Light of Freedom*. Payne demonstrates that, despite their failure to achieve any statistically significant increase in voter registration, the massive efforts of SNCC and other organizations—even in those early years there were more than forty full-time SNCC field organizers in the state—were significant in other ways, e.g., raising consciousness, increasing self-confidence, imparting skills. Though the organizing did not have the radical effect for which the SNCC organizers had hoped, it helped prepare large numbers of individuals who had been profoundly marginalized for broader participation in southern civil society. Once regulatory reforms were initiated at the extralocal, national level, these SNCC organized groups played a key role in demanding implementation of the 1964 and 1965 laws (*Light of Freedom*, pp. 317–337).

37. McAdam, *Freedom Summer*, p. 81.

38. Ibid., quoted on p. 38.

39. Ibid.

40. Quoted in Branch, *Pillar of Fire*, p. 351. From the point of view of many SNCC leaders, this strategy of using white volunteers to generate a more northern connection was not taken as an indication of the wider possibilities for white identification with black protesters which were available by 1964. They came to the opposite conclusion. If the presence of whites was necessary for generating higher levels of publicity, they reasoned, this fact, far from demonstrating the growing potential for white sympathy with the movement, showed just how racist American

society continued to be. This kind of thinking affected even a leader as moderate in his politics as SNCC's fabled Bob Moses, who in 1965 declared to students at University of California in Berkeley that "before the summer project last year we watched five Negroes murdered in two counties in Mississippi with no reaction from the country."

> We couldn't get the news out. Then we saw that when three civil rights workers were killed, and two of them were white, the whole country reacted, went into motion. There's a deep problem behind that, and I think [that] you can begin to understand what that problem is—why you don't move when a Negro is killed the same way you move when a white person is killed. (quoted in Payne, *Light of Freedom*, p. 284)

Such frustration with the still substantial racial distortions of white civil society was entirely understandable for activists who had dedicated their lives to civil repair in the South and were still taking great risks to fight it at the time of Freedom Summer. Less so is the extent to which contemporary scholarship suffers from the same lack of perspective (e.g., Payne, *Light of Freedom*, p. 300). Is the theoretically and empirically compelling question why, in 1964, racism continued to affect public opinion, or why, by the summer of 1964, its effects were finally being substantially diminished, and to such large effect? Why did northern public opinion narrate the white and black solidarity that seemed to inform Freedom Summer in such an enthusiastic manner? Yes, there was continuing racial distortion in news coverage and public opinion, but from 1956 onward the success of the Civil Rights movement depended on, and produced, increasing identification and expanding solidarity.

41. Quoted in McAdam, *Freedom Summer*, p. 150.

42. Ibid., quoted on p. 151.

43. Ibid., quoted on p. 45.

44. Ibid., quoted on p. 46.

45. Ibid., quoted on p. 68.

46. Ibid., pp. 93–96, 143–145.

47. Ibid., quoted on p. 89. Payne's research indicates that the solidarity was reciprocal. Despite the growing disaffection with whites experienced by some SNCC organizers, "the volunteers were generally accepted, and accepted with affection" by black people across Mississippi (Payne, *Light of Freedom*, pp. 306ff).

48. Quoted in McAdam, *Freedom Summer*, p. 68.

49. For a detailed discussion of the federal activities, see Branch, *Pillar of Fire*, pp. 361–385.

50. Developed in the literature of religious life, pilgrimage refers to the physical

voyage by seekers or penitents from the terrain of the mundane to the territory of the sacred. The goal of the journey is to come into direct contact with sacred space, which embodies the sacred ideals and personages of religious life. Pilgrimage is often repetitive and ritualized. Victor Turner generalized from this religious process to develop a cultural concept of pilgrimage that can be applied to secular processes ("Pilgrimages as Social Processes").

51. Quoted in McAdam, *Freedom Summer*, p. 150.

52. Ibid., p. 118. It was not, of course, the "entire country" but primarily the members of northern civil society who visited Mississippi in the solidarity-enhancing manner that McAdam suggests. Southern whites, informed by much more racially distorted communicative media, drew very different lessons from the same events.

53. Garrow, *Bearing the Cross*, p. 34.

54. Ibid., pp. 40, 42.

55. The ritualized quality of the Selma campaign can be seen in the degree to which this sequence of confrontation, shame, identification, and regulatory attention had become reified and explicit. Shortly after its denouement, Martin Luther King published a reconstruction of the Selma events in the *Saturday Review of Books*, a widely read liberal weekly. Though his article "Behind the Selma March" (April 3, 1965, pp. 16–17, 57) was post-hoc, it presented the protest as an organized, step-by-step exercise, one that seemed more like choreography than contingent political struggle. The aim of Selma, as King defined it, was to "dramatize the existence of injustice" by mounting "a confrontation with injustice [that] would take place in full view of the millions looking on throughout this nation." In detailing how this was to be accomplished, King described four precisely defined, sequential steps: (1) "Non-violent demonstrators go into the streets to exercise their constitutional rights"; (2) "Racists resist by unleashing violence against them"; (3) "Americans of conscience in the name of decency demand federal intervention and legislation"; and (4) "the Administration, under mass pressure, initiates measures of immediate intervention and remedial legislation."

56. David Garrow drew attention to this conundrum more than two decades ago. Commenting about the manner in which King's February 1965 arrest was reported by John Herbers, a *New York Times* reporter, Garrow writes:

> Although Herbers did not indicate that he understood fully just how conscious and well-calculated was the SCLC effort to evoke public nastiness and physical violence from Sheriff Clark and other officials, he did write: "Dr. King's arrest was at least two weeks behind schedule, according to a blueprint his organization drew up before the first of the year." That remark was virtually the only public acknowledgment of the SCLC's highly confidential strategic planning throughout late 1964 and 1965. . . . The SCLC

believed that its efforts would appeal favorably to more persons if the strategic and tactical considerations underlying those efforts were not made public (*Protest at Selma,* p. 54).

See also chapter 13, n. 100.

57. Garrow, *Protest at Selma,* p. 45.

58. Ibid., quoted on p. 44.

59. For Herbers's account, see Garrow, *Protest at Selma,* p. 44; for the *Washington Post* caption, see ibid., p. 54.

60. Ibid, p. 61.

61. Ibid., quoted on p. 62.

62. Ibid., quoted on p. 72.

63. Ibid., quoted on p. 75.

64. Ibid., quoted on p. 78.

65. Ibid., quoted on p. 272.

66. For the role of progressive as compared with tragic narratives, see Eyerman, *Cultural Trauma;* and Alexander, "The Social Basis of Moral Universalism."

67. Quoted in Garrow, *Protest at Selma,* p. 87.

68. Ibid., quoted on p. 85.

69. Ibid., quoted on p. 177.

70. Ibid., quoted on pp. 177–178.

71. Ibid., quoted on p. 294.

72. Ibid., p. 172.

73. Ibid., quoted on p. 49.

74. Ibid., quoted on p. 51.

75. Ibid., quoted on p. 81.

76. Ibid., quoted on pp. 81–82.

77. Ibid., quoted on p. 82.

78. Ibid., quoted on pp. 89–90.

79. Ibid., quoted on p. 90.

80. Ibid., quoted on p. 113.

81. Ibid., pp. 36ff. See also Kotz, *Judgment Day.*

82. Ibid., e.g., pp. 49, 55, 57, 70.

83. See *Protest at Selma,* pp. 180–211, for a detailed account of the dramatically empowering effects of the voting rights law in the first decade after its passage. In my earlier discussion, I maintained that, before the Civil Rights movement began, it had become clear to reformers that civil repair could not be achieved simply by the passage of reformist laws. Thus, disappointment with the results of the Supreme Court's 1954 school desegregation decision had been one of the primary triggers for the Montgomery movement in 1955, and the same frustration registered within the movement over the paltry effects of the civil rights reforms passed by Congress in 1957. In the context of the massive communicative mobilization that had taken

place by the summer of 1965, federal officials were no longer hesitant to organize the kind of massive intervention and surveillance of southern political society that repairing black voting rights would entail.

> By the first week of August, when it was clear that President Johnson would be signing the bill within a few days, the administration's preparations for implementation were all but complete. Civil Rights Commission Chairman John Macy reported that some six dozen commission personnel would undergo a three-day training session in preparation for serving as [voting registration] examiners, and Attorney General Katzenbach informed the White House that [the] Justice [Department] was ready to complete the formalities for suspending all "tests and devices" in covered jurisdictions and for beginning the assignment of examiners as soon as the Voting Rights Act was signed into law. Justice also was ready to file suits challenging the poll taxes of Alabama, Mississippi, Texas, and Virginia, as called for by section 10 [of the legislation]. Following President Johnson's signing . . . on Friday, August 6, the federal implementation effort quickly sprang into action. Some four dozen Civil Service personnel headed South after completing their training session that day, and early Saturday afternoon the first [lawsuit] was filed in Jackson, Mississippi. . . . The first day's effort . . . had produced impressive results: 1,144 black applicants had been "listed" by the examiners. [By] late October . . . the number of individuals registered by the federal examiners had topped 56,000, while 110,000 more had been registered by local officials in the six states and several dozen North Carolina counties covered by the act (ibid., pp. 180–184)

For a statistical demonstration of the empowering effects of the Voting Rights Act of 1965, with data stretching from the mid-1960s to 1984, see Andrews, "The Impacts of Social Movements on the Political Process."

84. In comparison with the labor movement, which began in the early nineteenth century and achieved legitimation in the United States only in the 1930s, the civil rights struggle achieved its goals in a much more compact period of time. As for second-wave feminism, the Civil Rights movement might be said to have made it possible.

85. McAdam (*Freedom Summer,* pp. 161–198) makes a compelling case for the direct connection between Freedom Summer and the student movements of the '60s, including the protest for student power, the peace movement, and the women's movement. In his reports on the protest movements that swept through central and eastern Europe in 1989, *The Magic Lantern: The Revolution of '89 Witnessed in Warsaw, Budapest, Berlin, and Prague,* Timothy Garton Ash notes the exemplary influence of the earlier American movement for civil rights. For a broad discussion of the effects

of the "rights revolution" on American society over the last three decades, see Michael Schudson, *The Good Citizen*.

86. See Part IV, chaps. 15–19.

87. The notion of "demonstration effect" was first developed by Robert Merton in his studies of scientific innovation and later employed in a historical context by Reinhard Bendix in *Kings and People*.

88. For a balanced empirical presentation, see Patterson, *Ordeal of Integration*, pp. 15–82; Farley, "Racial Issues"; and Alba and Nee, *Remaking the American Mainstream*, pp. 215–270.

89. Landry, *New Black Middle Class*, p. 72.

90. Ibid., pp. 78, 83.

91. Landry, *New Black Middle Class*, p. 72.

92. In his discussion of the pre–civil rights barriers that blacks faced in gaining entrance to the all-important level of clerical, lower middle class employment, Landry demonstrates this connection between patterns of cultural recognition and stratificational position. "The difficulty blacks experienced in being hired for clerical work," he writes, "had a significant impact on their class structure and especially on the development of a middle class" (*New Black Middle Class*, p. 56).

> In the South, where most black workers could still be found, cultural norms dictated that no black individual could occupy a clerical or sales position in white establishments, since these occupations were associated with a social status to which black workers could not aspire. The idea of blacks engaged in clean work in the front offices of establishments serving a white public was completely repugnant to white sentiments and effectively prevented blacks from occupying such positions. (p. 54)

The fact that they were forced, for cultural reasons, to remain economically backstage severely compromised black stratification when compared to white, for "clerical and sales workers constituted the single largest category within the white middle class" (p. 43). Landry found that this situation dramatically changed after the normative and regulatory shifts triggered by the Civil Rights movement. Looking at economic shifts between 1973 and 1982, he reported that "although blacks won additional jobs in each of the four occupational groups of the middle class, clerical workers accounted for almost 50 percent of the gain" (p. 197).

93. For the idea that societies move in pendulum swings between periods of intense public involvement and more nonpolitical, private concerns, see Hirschman, *Shifting Involvements*.

94. See part IV, below.

95. Payne, *Light of Freedom*, p. 376.

96. Ibid., p. 376. In sociological terms, of course, it is perfectly understandable

why, in the context of the social tensions and heightened expectations of the '60s, younger members of the black protest movement would become increasingly militant and radicalized. The political effects of this radicalization, however, are another matter.

97. The following discussion draws from Garrow's detailed account of this brief but fateful period in his King biography, *Bearing the Cross* (pp. 481–485). In comparison with Payne's discussion (*Light of Freedom*, pp. 375–380), Garrow's pays closer attention to King's public responses to Carmichael's growing militancy. Payne suggests only that King had "private misgivings" about the Black Power slogan when it was first presented, and that, in public, King "stressed the more pragmatic elements of the slogan and noted that there was nothing wrong with racial pride" (*Light of Freedom*, p. 377). According to Garrow's account, however, this was evidently not the case.

98. Quoted in Garrow, *Bearing the Cross*, p. 481.

99. Ibid.

100. Ibid., quoted on p. 482.

101. Ibid.

102. Ibid., quoted on p. 484.

103. Ibid.

104. This statement was made by James L. Sundquist, writing in a Brookings Institution publication in 1968. Quoted in Garrow, *Protest at Selma*, p. 295 n. 10.

105. McAdam, *Freedom Summer,* p. 5.

106. "Malcom X," *New York Times*, Feb. 22, 1965, p. 20.

107. William Julius Wilson argued that the underclass is the paradoxical result of the success of the Civil Rights movement in his *The Truly Disadvantaged: The Inner City, the Underclass, and Public Policy*. In *American Apartheid,* Massey and Denton are right, however, to quarrel with Wilson's argument that cultural racism no longer plays a significant role in racial domination. This criticism gains support from such ethnographic works as Elijah Anderson's *Streetwise: Race, Class, and Change in an Urban Community*. But Massey and Denton suggest that residential segregation remains as extreme as in pre–civil rights days. However, even if black working- and middle-class communities are not yet integrated with white residential communities and often remain thoroughly separated from them, labeling this continuing residential segregation "apartheid" ignores the fact that the African American community has become geographically dispersed and economically stratified in an unprecedented manner, in part because of the Civil Rights movement's effects on economic and educational life.

108. For an interpretive reconstruction of this polluting representation of the contemporary black underclass and its contribution to sustaining underclass poverty, see Patterson, *Rituals of Blood*.

109. It is primarily social conservatives and conservative communitarians who

employ civil society discourse in regard to race. James Q. Wilson, for example, argues against state intervention by blaming the existence of the underclass on the members of that class themselves. By introducing observations about the supposed decline of "impulse control" and the erosion of respect for authority, Wilson seems, at least, to impugn the motives and relations of members of the black underclass, in this way suggesting that their lack of interactional civility is responsible for the decline of their communities (see, e.g., Wilson, *Thinking about Crime*). For a contrasting social science perspective on African American underclass men that emphasizes their rationality, autonomy, and discipline, see M. Duneier, *Sidewalk*.

CHAPTER 15

1. Adler, "Beyond Cultural Identity," pp. 369–371, emphasis added

2. Stimpson, "On Differences," pp. 43–44.

3. Quoted in Kimball, "Periphery v. the Center," p. 75.

4. Ibid., p. 69.

5. Quoted in Schlesinger, *Disuniting of America*, p. 65.

6. Ibid., quoted on p. 305.

7. C. West, "The New Cultural Politics of Difference," in Russel Ferguson, Martha Gever, Trinh T. Minh-Ha, and Cornel West, eds., *Out There: Marginalization and Contemporary Cultures*, p. 584.

8. Schlesinger, *Disuniting of America*, p. 15.

9. Ibid., p. 102.

10. Ibid., p. 112.

11. Huntington, *Who Are We?* pp. 137, 143. For a critical discussion of Huntington's views, see chapter 8, no. 21.

12. D'Souza "Big Chill?" p. 30.

13. Kimball, "Periphery v. the Center," p. 82.

14. Ibid., quoted on p. 316.

15. Schlesinger, *Disuniting of America*, p. 112.

16. Ibid., p. 138.

17. Kimball, "Periphery v. the Center," p. 65.

18. I. Young, *Justice and the Politics of Difference*, pp. 32–33.

19. Ibid., p. 107.

20. Ibid., p. 100.

21. Ibid., p. 110.

22. Ibid., p. 114.

23. Ibid., p. 116.

24. Ibid., p. 163.

25. Ibid., p. 47.

26. Edward Said's critique of radical multiculturalism is relevant in this regard.

Victimhood . . . does not guarantee or necessarily enable an enhanced sense of humanity. To testify to a history of oppression is necessary, but it is not sufficient unless that history is redirected into intellectual process and universalized to include all sufferers. . . . Great antiauthoritarian uprisings made their earliest advances, not by denying the humanitarian and universalist claims of the general dominant culture, but by attacking the adherents of that culture for failing to uphold their own declared standards, for failing to extend them to all, as opposed to a small fraction, of humanity. ("Politics of Knowledge," pp. 187–188).

27. I. Young, *Justice and the Politics of Difference*, p. 171, emphasis added.

28. Ibid., p. 166, emphasis added.

29. Ibid., emphasis added.

30. Ibid., p. 106.

31. Ibid., p. 112.

32. Ibid., p. 190.

33. Ibid.

34. Writing from inside the Habermasian tradition's emphasis on public life, Seyla Benhabib has taken strong issue with arguments such as Iris Young's. Going beyond this tradition of discourse narrowly defined, Benhabib emphasizes the critical role of background culture as providing, and limiting, the universe of possible understandings for either restrictive or expansive multicultural claims. See her *Claims of Culture*.

35. MacIntyre, *Whose Justice?*

36. For complementary elaborations, see Benhabib, *Claims of Culture*.

37. For references to the historical discussions of such processes, see chap. 2, n. 34.

38. Alexander, *Real Civil Societies*.

39. See chapter 10, above.

40. See chapter 6, above.

41. As I stressed in chapter 8, these are, of course, only putatively primordial qualities. Qualities are not primordial in and of themselves; they are construed as such. Any human quality can be treated in a primordial manner, although certain characteristics have historically been more likely to be singled out as critical by core groups.

42. In his early and more critical writings, Talcott Parsons made precisely this sociological observation:

American society is ostensibly built upon a philosophy of "natural rights," with its universalistic standards of the equality of all men. Legally, therefore, all elements of the population, regardless of "race, creed, or color," are equal. Actually, however, the community which espoused this principle has to a considerable extent been a closed community, and has never been willing to apply it in actual life. It became a community of "White, Protestant, Anglo-Saxon" origin, with a relatively well articulated but mostly implicit and informally enforced cultural pattern. ("Sociology of Anti-Semitism," p. 110)

43. Kant, "What Is Enlightenment?" Kant carefully distinguishes between "the public use of one's reason," which he describes as "the use which a scholar makes of it before the entire reading public," and the "private use . . . which he make of this reason in a civic post or office."

> For some affairs which are in the interest of the commonwealth a certain mechanism is necessary through which some members of the common-wealth *must remain purely passive* in order that an artificial agreement with the government for the public good be maintained or so that at least the destruction of the good be prevented. In such a situation it is not permitted to argue; one must *obey*. (pp. 134–135, emphasis added)

Kant refers to such members of the commonwealth who must remain passive and obey authority as "unit[s] of the machine," and he includes among them: (1) military officers, who should not "argue concerning the utility or appropriateness of [a] command"; (2) citizens, who should not engage in "rash criticism" of taxes imposed on them; (3) the clergyman, who "is obliged to teach his pupils and his congregation according to the doctrine of the church which he serves, for he has been accepted on that condition," and, as "a member of an organization," he "is not free and ought not to be, since he is executing someone else's mandate" (pp. 135–136). Presumably this list of "private," organizational obediences would include every other area of nonscholarly and nonreading life, e.g., family, ethnic, economic, and legal associations. Kant has, in effect, adapted his democratic commitments to the contradictions that develop from instantiating the civil sphere in time, place, and function. He is employing the negative side of civil society discourse—the discourse of repression—to describe and prescribe the motives, relations, and institutions of a very wide swath of modern life. For a critical discussion of these contradictions in the Enlightenment split between private and public, with special attention to gender, see Landes, *Women and the Public Sphere in Eighteenth Century France* and *Feminism, the Public and the Private*.

CHAPTER 16

1. For Simmel's concept of the "stranger," its productive relation to classical, modern, and postmodern conceptions of estrangement, and its inadequacies vis-

à-vis the perspective I am developing here, see Alexander, "Rethinking Strangeness."

2. This social scientific tendency has been continued in postmodern studies inspired by Foucault, which have tended to treat all encounters with "subalterns" as having essentially the same quality, whether or not the encounter is generated by dominant orders that are democratic. Such an undifferentiated approach characterizes "postcolonial" literary and social scientific studies of sexuality, gender, race, and class. See, e.g., Spivak, "Can the Subaltern Speak?" and H. Bhabha, "Signs Taken for Wonders."

3. Lapeyronnie, *L'Individu et Les Minorités: La France et la Grande-Bretagne face à leurs immigrés*, pp. 29–62.

4. Gilroy, *Post-Colonial Melancholia*. For comparative discussion of France, Germany, Great Britain, and the United States, see *L'Individu et les Minorites*; D. Horowitz and Noiriel, *Immigrants in Two Democracies*; Favell, *Philosophies of Integration*; Geddes and Favell, *Politics of Belonging*; Joppke, *Immigration and the Nation State;* and Joppke and Morawska, *Towards Assimilation and Citizenship*. Recently, as the relative homogeneity of postwar European civil spheres has been severely strained—for example, by the influx into Britain and France of immigrants from their former colonies—primordial restrictions of time and place have intertwined with functional inequalities of class to raise significant new difficulties of incorporation.

5. Moving from objective patterns of out-group contact (conceptualized as causes) to patterns of incorporation (conceptualized as effects) is not a compulsion only of structure-oriented social scientists. It reflects the common sense of everyday life and can even structure the perceptions of those who make use, in every other respect, of an interpretive approach. For example, in the midst of an otherwise imaginative and culturally oriented effort to explain how "the terms 'American' and 'American culture' have undergone some dramatic transformations" and expansions— an account of which I will make extensive use below—Werner Sollors links these changes, *en passant*, to "the changing ethnic composition of the United States" (" 'Of Plymouth Rock and Jamestown and Ellis Island,' " p. 107). Sollors points, in other words, to the objective relations of in-group and out-group alone, to quantitative aspects of intergroup contact, rather than to the importance of shifting internal cultural perceptions, that is, to qualitative shifts in internal conceptions that might be related to new developments in civil communication and moral regulation. This very widely shared emphasis on external factors is homologous with the manner in which earlier sociologists of "modernization" viewed expanded social solidarity merely as the reflection of structural developments like increasingly efficient transportation, the rise of mass communication, increased economic mobility, and urbanization.

6. To utilize such a distinction between "state" and "civil" societies is to return to the theory of "civil society I" (e.g., V. Pérez-Díaz, *The Return of Civil Society* and "The Public Sphere and a European Civil Society"), which I situated historically,

and criticized, in chapter 2. As I suggested in that earlier discussion, however, while civil society I blurs important empirical and normative issues, it remains useful for discussions of transitions between formally democratic and nondemocratic societies, and for the kinds of broad ideal-typical distinctions between nations and empires I am proposing here. In terms of civil society I, "state societies" are authoritarian social systems in which the autonomy of the civil sphere, in both its cultural and institutional dimensions, has been sharply curtailed. "Civil societies" are social systems in which such the civil dimension has some independent power to shape noncivil domains, including the state. According to this definition, civil societies may not necessarily be formally democratic, but they must have institutionalized some autonomy for the civil domain. The misleading aspect of employing "civil society" in this dichotomous ideal-typical sense is that it obscures the fact that democratic social systems are by no means exclusively civil, but contain, as I have suggested throughout this book, powerful noncivil domains that sharply contradict it.

7. For an example of such forced incorporation, see the analysis of compulsory nationalism in Soviet society in Brubaker, "Nationhood and the National Question in the Soviet Union and Its Successor States: An Institutionalist Account."

8. Maria Rosa Menocal's account, in *The Ornament of the World: How Muslims, Jews, and Christians Created a Culture of Tolerance in Medieval Spain*, gains an especially acute relevance in light of the current enmity and violence between these religious groups inside and in between contemporary modern nation-states.

9. See Kuper, *Prevention of Genocide.*

10. B. Turner and Holton, "Status Politics in Contemporary Capitalism," in *Max Weber on Economy and Society.*

11. Lev. 19:33–34.

12. Such thick recognition, and its more democratic connotations, are clearly what Charles Taylor has in mind in his historical and philosophical discussions of the multicultural model in *The Ethics of Authenticity* and "The Politics of Recognition."

13. When Justice Sandra Day O'Connor wrote the majority opinion in *Grutter v. Bollinger* case, which upheld affirmative action by a 5-to-4 margin, she described the University of Michigan law school's program as being necessary "in order to cultivate a set of leaders with legitimacy in the eyes of the citizenry: Effective participation by members of all racial and ethic groups in the civil life of our nation is essential if the dream of one nation, indivisible, is to be realized" (Linda Greenhouse, "Justices Back Affirmative Action").

14. Woodward, *Strange Career of Jim Crow.*

15. Hechter, *Internal Colonialism*; Kumar, *Making of English National Identity*; Kimmerliing and Migdal, *Palestinian People*; and Nash, *Red, White, and Black.* See also the references in chap. 8, nn. 15 and 27.

16. This distinction is precisely what is usually not made by those who employ the internal colonialism model. For example, in *Racial Oppression in America*, R.

Blauner emphasized primarily the similarities between the American system of racial domination and traditional colonialism. Blauner suggests, for example, that the Black Panther Party, at that time a major political force in northern California, was engaged in an anticolonial struggle. Yet in suggesting not only similarities but homologies Blauner overreaches, for reasons I discuss above. The claim for homology first emerged among Jean-Paul Sartre and his students, such as Franz Fanon and Albert Memmi, and reflects the Marxist approach, civil society II, that sees civil society as eliminated by capitalism. The inability to distinguish the specificity of internal colonialism in civil as compared to state societies has led this tradition either toward a strident revolutionism or fatalistic resignation. In the former, there has been a dangerous tendency to romanticize violence and to denigrate civil conflict, which is the subject of Raymond Aron's critique of Sartre's later philosophy in Aron's *History and the Dialectic of Violence.*

17. For an overview and critical discussion of the South African literature that developed civil society theory in relation to these segregated township communities, see D. Glaser, "South Africa and the Limits on Civil Society."

18. Friedland and Hecht, *To Rule Jerusalem;* and Kimmerling and Migdal, *Palestinian People.*

19. For anti-Semitic movements in the context of civil society, see chapter 18. For the emergence of anti-immigrant and exclusionary nationalism in response to European immigration, see Berezin, *Democracy and Security.*

20. See Kuper and Smith, *Pluralism in Africa.*

21. The structural significance of these threats to civil society, and the real possibility of their long-term success, has rarely been taken seriously in normative and empirical writings on democracy.

22. This claim, that civil impartiality is merely a legitimation of primordiality, is offered in the radical multiculturalist literature I discussed in chapter 15. That civil universalism represents a hypocritical and disingenuous camouflage for group interest is central to civil society II theorizing, and it runs from Marx to Nietzsche to Foucault. The argument represents a performative contradiction in that it stimulates critical social intervention even as it conceptualizes, in theoretical terms, no space for democratic struggle in theoretical terms. Pierre Bourdieu presents the most powerful recent sociological version of this performative contradiction in social science theory. See chapter 3, note 21. The self-contradictory qualities of civil society II arguments usually trigger the introduction of ad hoc reasoning to allow critical thought and action, e.g., suggesting that all domination produces resistance by subordinate groups. The concept of "resistance" is only a residual category unless the civil conditions that allow and encourage resistance, and not only domination, are theorized in a systematic, civil society III way.

23. Quoted in Fuchs, "Thinking about Immigration and Ethnicity in the United States," p. 45, emphasis in original.

24. Higham, *Strangers in the Land*, p. 213.

25. E. Weber, *Peasants into Frenchmen*.

26. To speak of "exhibiting" or "manifesting" civil qualities suggests not only a theoretical emphasis on self and agency but a sense of the complexities of the self, one whose relation to social values must be conceptualized more fully than any simple notion of value internalization and externalization implies. This complexity is suggested by M. Archer in *Being Human: The Problem of Agency*. As Erving Goffman suggests in *The Presentation of Self in Everyday Life*, actors generally try to "present" only such elements of their selves as embody consensual social values; more precisely, they make publicly available only those parts of their identities which they hope will be regarded by interactional partners or third-party observers as typifying dominant, institutionalized values. This front-stage behavior, Goffman observes, may be very different from behavior backstage. While Goffman's dramaturgical sociology of public interaction has, thus, an extraordinary relevance to the interactional dimensions of civil exclusion and incorporation, Goffman himself never historicized his theory in this way. Rather than view the normative criteria mediating interactions culturally or comparatively, he described them as generic to human behavior as such. Neither did he relate his notion of the fragmented self to the notion of the fragmented public sphere, with its split between public and private life.

27. The writings about out-group exclusion by Zygmunt Bauman, the leading sociological theorist of postmodernity, demonstrate how the conflation of knowledge and power makes it difficult to conceptually distinguish incorporation in state as compared with civil societies. Baumann equates George Orwell's "memorable image of a jackboot trampling the human face," which "trample[d] the strangers in the dust" and "squeeze[d] the strange out of the human," simply with "the modern state—that which legislated order into existence and defined order as the clarity of binding divisions, classifications, allocations and boundaries." The "order-building" project of the modern state, he insists, "was a war of attrition waged against the strangers and the strange." It is no wonder then, that for Bauman, assimilation means "annihilating the strangers by devouring them and then metabolically transforming them into a tissue indistinguishable from one's own." Nor is it surprising that Baumann should equate such assimilative incorporation with "the strategy of exclusion—vomiting the strangers, banishing them from the limits of the orderly and barring them from all communication with those inside [with] confining the strangers within the visible walls of the ghettos or [with] expelling the strangers beyond the frontiers of the managed and manageable territory" ("Making and Unmaking of Strangers," pp. 1–3, emphasis eliminated). In *Modernity and the Holocaust*, Bauman views the Germans' physical annihilation of millions of Jews and other out-groups as exemplifying state treatment of the stranger in the modernist period.

CHAPTER 17

1. For example, A. Smith, *National Identity*, pp. 11–14, and Nairn, "Breakwaters of 2000."

2. In the *The First New Nation*, Lipset developed this thesis in comparative studies of revolution, counterrevolution, and democracy as responses to modernization. A comparable figure in France would be Dominique Schnapper, e.g., *La France de l'intégration: Sociologie de la nation en 1990* and *Community of Citizens: On the modern idea of Nationality*. The most recent argument in this tradition is R. Brubaker, *Citizenship and Nationhood in France and Germany*, which problematizes the traditional distinction between *jus sanguinis* (citizenship according to birth) and *jus soli* (according to territory). Donald Horowitz's systematic comparative work on French and American integration policies argues, in a similar vein, for the civic nationalism of America and France, but, within this rubric, emphasizes the importance of immigration and ethnicity ("Immigration and Group Relations in France and America").

3. Quoted in K. Thompson, "Identity and Belief," p. 20, emphasis eliminated.

4. Quoted in Higham, *Strangers in the Land,* p. 3.

5. Quoted in Fuchs, "Thinking about Immigration and Ethnicity in the United States," pp. 40–41.

6. Ibid., quoted on p. 42.

7. Ibid., quoted on p. 43.

8. Ibid.

9. Quoted in Sollors, "Of Plymouth Rock," p. 236.

10. Higham, *Strangers In the Land,* p. 6.

11. Tyack, "Preserving the Republic by Educating Republicans."

12. Quoted in Fuchs, "Thinking about Immigration," p. 43.

13. See references in chap. 14, n. 88; also Alba, *Ethnic Identity*.

14. Quoted in K. Thompson, "Identity and Belief," p. 19.

15. Quoted in Fuchs, "Thinking about Immigration," p. 41.

16. Higham, *Strangers in the Land*, pp. 12–13

17. Ibid., p. 25

18. Quoted in ibid.

19. Fuchs, "Thinking about Immigration," p. 46.

20. Ibid., quoted on p. 42.

21. Sollors, "Of Plymouth Rock," pp. 212–223. All quotations from original sources in this and the following three paragraphs are drawn from this article.

22. Quotations here and elsewhere in this paragraph from Higham, *Strangers in the Land*, p. 198.

23. Indeed, as Higham points out, during the Progressive period, democratic reformers faced in two different directions. As members of the American core group, they often supported repressive restrictions against immigration; at the same time,

as advocates of civil repair, they were instrumental in broadening the political and economic dimensions of incorporation:

> The logic of democracy . . . pointed to a respect for the integrity and importance of all people, toward a cooperative concern with the problems of every group. [Yet] most progressives, while convinced of the solvent power of democracy, applied it largely to political and economic inequalities. That it might reform relationships among men of varying creeds or colors or cultures did not impress them. (*Strangers in the Land*, p. 119)

24. Quoted in Sollors, "Of Plymouth Rock," p. 239.

25. Quoted in Fuchs, "Thinking about Immigration," p. 47.

26. This regulatory intervention, which defended assimilation on the grounds of the private right to be different and to be thus protected from standardization, demonstrates, once again, why democratic and authoritarian incorporation must not be conflated.

27. Here and following in this paragraph, quoted in Sollors, "Of Plymouth Rock," p. 226.

28. Noting this forward-looking development in the social imaginary of the 1930s is not to suggest, however, that such movement beyond assimilative incorporation proceeded evenly or, for many excluded groups, at all. For the deepening exclusion of Jews that marked this prewar period, see chapter 19. For the manner in which even some central policies of the New Deal deepened the exclusion of African Americans, see Katznelson, *When Affirmative Action Was White: An Untold History of Racial Inequality in Twentieth-Century America*.

29. Higham, "Cultural Responses to Immigration," pp. 55–57.

30. Sollars, "Of Plymouth Rock," p. 213.

31. Ibid., p. 235.

32. For this quotation, and the following from Handlin's second edition, see K. Thompson, "Identity and Belief," p. 21

33. This infamous phrase occurs in a list of charges the Declaration made against the British king: "He has endeavored to bring on the inhabitants of our frontiers . . . the merciless savages, whose known rule of warfare, is an undistinguished destruction of all ages, sexes and conditions." The historical context of this accusation lay in American opposition to the 1763 treaty that concluded the French and Indian War, in which the British sought, as a compromise with the native Americans, to limit colonial settlement beyond the Appalachians. Knowing the colonists' strong opposition to any such limitation, the Indians often sided with the British after hostilities began in 1775. But whatever the pragmatic reasons for the tension between colonists and Indians, it is the cultural evocation of anticivil stereotype that is so shocking today.

34. Passing represented an exception that proved the rule, for it was possible only for African Americans who phenotypically presented as white. From the core group's perspective, in other words, it was not African Americans who were allowed to assimilate. The denial of assimilation is further illustrated by the fact that African Americans had to be extraordinarily careful not to allow any vestiges of their former racial identity to be practiced in their private lives. The result was self-abnegation, the obliteration of earlier family and friendship ties, often at the cost of great personal duress. For a fictional account of such a struggle, see Nella Larson, *Passing*. This situation is homologous with the behavior of homosexuals during what Steven Seidman has called "the closet years" of the twentieth century, in *Beyond the Closet: The Transformation of Gay Identity*. Not only was normative heterosexuality mandated in the public sphere, but it was also prescribed in private life. Homosexual experiences could only be pursued in arenas that were literally invisible.

35. Massey and Denton, *American Apartheid*.

36. Quoted in Fuchs, "Thinking about Identity," p. 50.

37. Quoted in Higham, "Cultural Responses to Immigration," p. 25.

38. Quoted in Sollors, "Of Plymouth Rock," p. 229. Whereas the English pilgrims had first arrived in Plymouth Rock in 1620, in what would eventually become the Massachusetts Bay Colony, the first Africans encountered North American soil in 1619, when their slave ship arrived in Jamestown, in what would later become Virginia.

39. Quoted in Sollors, "Of Plymouth Rock," p. 232.

40. Sherwood, "Narrating the Social."

41. Horowitz, "Immigration and Group Relations in France and America," p. 16.

42. As I mentioned earlier, neither affirmative action policies nor civil rights mandates more broadly have affected the condition of the racially segregated underclass (chapter 14 and the discussion in notes 92, 107). Indeed, by allowing the dispersal of blacks throughout the mainstream occupational structure, affirmative action seems actually to have contributed to the break-up of the cross-class racial ghetto, which until the 1960s had prevented the creation of an economically and racially separated underclass.

43. For the lifestyle and self-understanding of African American elites who were the recipients of affirmative action projects over the last three decades, see R. Zweigenhaft and G. Domhoff, *Blacks in the White Elite: Will the Progress Continue?* For the lifestyle and self-understanding of the middle classes, see M. Pattillo-McCoy, *Black Picket Fences: Privilege and Peril among the Black Middle Classes*.

44. Massey and Denton, *American Apartheid*.

45. H. Gray, *Watching Race*, p. 77.

46. Ibid., p. 78. For shifting media representations of race, and reference to *Roots* in this context, see chap. 5.

47. Writing in 1994, the American political theorist Amy Gutmann observed that "it is hard to find a democratic or democratizing society these days that is not the site of some significant controversy over whether and how its public institutions should better recognize the identities of cultural . . . minorities" (*Multiculturalism,* p. 3). Almost a decade later, a leading Italian sociologist of ethnicity confirmed:

> There is currently broad interest in the social and political consequences of 'cultural' heterogeneity, with multiculturalism evoked (or feared) in most political and intellectual debates on the future of Western polities. A quick search at Amazon.com reveals that, currently, there are 777 books in English about multiculturalism, ranging from theoretical treatises to self-help manuals, from historical works to biographical novels. The search engine of Google returns 276,000 Internet pages linked to multiculturalism. These figures are significant when it is considered that the term was hardly ever used prior to 1989. (G. Sciortino, "From Homogeneity to Difference? Comparing Multiculturalism as a Description and a Field for Claim-Making," p. 264)

48. In chapter 19, in my discussion of shifting modes of Jewish incorporation in postwar America, I will develop a richer empirical analysis of the contrast between assimilative and hyphenated modes, on the one hand, and multicultural modes on the other.

49. Dilthey, "Construction of the Historical World."

50. C. Taylor, "The Politics of Recognition," p. 39. This same commitment to combining the recognition of difference with commitment to democratic principles, particularly legal constitutional ones, informs the philosophical writings of Will Kymlicka, e.g., *Multicultural Citizenship: A Liberal Theory of Minority Rights.* Kymlicka's theorizing draws attention to how multicultural understandings of incorporation have encouraged new approaches to dominated aboriginal groups and internal colonies radically separated from core groups. At the same time, his focus is too concentrated on such distinctive "nations" to relate directly to the issues I am engaging here.

51. C. Gray, "Disability as Ability."

52. The question of the national distribution and specific path of this multicultural mode in contemporary societies—or, for that matter, of the assimilative and hyphenative modes—is impossible to address here. The controversial quality of this new model, which is hegemonic for some parties and anathema to others, has sometimes caused it to be evoked a model for incorporation in situations where, in fact, even the much more restrictive form of assimilation is difficult to obtain. In contemporary Germany, for example, intellectuals and politicians on the Left often speak about creating a multicultural society, yet it is only recently that nonethnic

German minorities have become eligible for simple citizenship, and their ability to become "true Germans," the basic ideal of assimilation, is still widely and publicly debated. See, for example, L. Rapaport, *Jews in Germany after the Holocaust: Memory, Identity and Jewish-German Relations*. In France, though assimilation is deeply established and citizenship has for centuries been much more easily available, the *républicain* model resists even hyphenating the primordial qualities of Frenchness, and the possibilities for certain forms of multicultural expression, particularly the religious, are denied in what is sometimes a repressive way. This restrictive *républicain* approach to assimilation is exemplified in *l'affaire du foulard*, a decades-long controversy which has resulted in state enforcement of nonreligious dress in public schools. See F. Gespard and F. Khosrokhavar, *Foulard et la République*. Yet, in both Germany and France the multicultural mode of incorporation is not only increasingly discussed but manifest in different ways. While Britain has much more thoroughly engaged the multicultural mode, it has often taken different specific forms than in the United States.

53. At a conference commemorating the history of African-American cultural awareness marking Black History Month at Columbia University, in March, 2005, Kwame Brathwaite, president of the New York chapter of the National Council of Arts, traced its origins back to the Harlem Renaissance in the 1920s and its crystallization to the "Black is Beautiful" movement of the 1960s, "which celebrated African culture and established a benchmark for aesthetics that recognized beauty in non-European physical features" (Ernest Beck, "Black is Beautiful and It's History, Too," *Columbia News*: The Homepage of the Public Affairs Office and its publication, *The Record*, March 9, 2005). Beuford Smith, of Kamoinge Artists, an association of black photographers that had "grown out of the Black Arts Movement of the 1970s to advance awareness of contemporary black artists using photography," recalled that "The Negro Woman" exhibition in 1965–1966, which had "focused on the black female body" and "presented images of women with 'natural' hairstyles," had caused an outcry because it raised issues about being black" (ibid.).

54. Gilroy, *Against Race*, p. 21.

55. See Gans, "Symbolic Ethnicity"; and Waters, *Ethnic Options*.

56. Butler, *Gender Trouble* and *Excitable Speech*.

57. Gates, "Whose Canon Is It, Anyway?" p. 197.

58. Ibid.

59. Fernandez, "P.C. Rider," pp. 322–325.

60. "Excerpts from Justices' Opinions."

61. Farley, "Racial Issues"; and Alba and Nee, *Remaking the American Mainstream*, pp. 90–94, 132–133, 262–267.

62. Portes and Rumbaut, *Legacies*.

63. Quoted in Yoshino, "Assimilationist Bias in Equal Protection, pp. 542, 548.

64. There is a "new assimilationist" literature in American sociology that has

quite rightly reasserted the normative and empirical importance of outgroup integration into American society. It is unfortunate, however, that, even as they suggest
that an improved version of that tried and true term "assimilation" is needed, those
who are developing this new approach continue to employ it in a manner that elides
the distinctions among the modes of incorporation that I have emphasized here. For
example, in "The Revival of Assimilation in Historical Perspective," the introductory essay to Peter Kivisto's edited collection *Incorporating Diversity: Rethinking Assimilation in a Multicultural Age*, Kivisto argues that "any effort to make sense of the
analytical utility of assimilation must be pursued first by recognizing the three
incontrovertible facts . . . (1) there is little consensus about what we mean by the
term; (2) it remains highly contentious; and (3) it is back in vogue" (p. 4). After
reviewing the new normative literature in political philosophy, which emphasizes
multiculturalism, Kivisto concludes with the critical remark that "a distinctly sociological theory of assimilation that locates multiculturalism within it . . . has yet to
be articulated" (p. 22). In a similar manner, in "The Return of Assimilation? Changing Perspectives on Immigration and Its Sequels in France, Germany, and the United
States," Rogers Brubaker argues that, in the new empirical literature emphasizing
integration, the emphasis is "not identity, but similarity," that "assimilation is a matter
of degree," and of "becoming similar *in certain respects*" (p. 534, emphasis in original);
yet Brubaker goes on to conclude, in a manner at once ambiguous and critical, that
this recent work is "agnostic" about the "directions" and "modalities" of assimilation, and even about its "desirability" (p. 540). In their important synthetic empirical
study, Alba and Nee demonstrate that the primordial core of American society has
been fundamentally reshaped. Yet, they continue to use the old concept: "Through
assimilation, the mainstream has become diverse in the ethnic origins of those who
participate in it; and the ethnic majority group, which dominates the mainstream
population, has been reconstituted" (p. 284). The critical issue here, what is up for
grabs empirically and theoretically, is what has allowed ethnic and other outgroup
qualities to have reconstituted this mainstream? What precisely do Alba and Nee
mean by mainstream and reconstitution? Their own discussion paradxically stresses
the continuity of American incorporative patterns, and seems to suggest that both
nothing and everything has changed. They write, for example, that "historically,
the American mainstream, which originated with the colonial northern Europeans
settlers, has evolved through incremental inclusion of ethnic and racial groups that
formerly were excluded and accretion of parts of their cultures to the composite
culture." As for this "composite culture," which they identify with the mainstream,
it is "made up of multiple interpenetrating layers and allows individuals and sub-
populations to forge identities out of its materials to distinguish themselves from
others in the mainstream—as do, for instance, Baptists in Alabama and Jews in New
York—in ways that are still recognizably American" (pp. 12–13). But what it means
to be recognizably American is precisely what needs to be explained, and it changes

according the mode of incorporation. In "Dealing with Diversity: Mapping Multiculturalism in Sociological Terms," Douglas Hartmann and Joseph Gerteis regret that there is "a lamentable absence of appropriate data to provide for common empirical grounding" in studies of incorporation, but suggest, quite rightly in my view, that "perhaps the first and most fundamental problem is the lack of theoretical clarity about what we mean by multiculturalism" (p. 219).

CHAPTER 18

1. It is extraordinary that the place of Jews in Western or democratic society has rarely been considered a central topic for systematic social theories either of the more sociological or the more philosophical kind, whether their focus is justice, democracy, the West, civil society, or alterity. "Non-Jewish historians," J. L. Talmon once wrote, "do not really know how to treat the Jews, and so they barely mention them. They do not know where to place Jewish history or how to handle it within the scheme of world history or even of their own national history" ("Suggestions for Isolating the Jewish Component in World History," p. 8). John Higham agreed, writing that "to general American historians, anti-Semitism has never seemed a subject of major importance" ("American Anti-Semitism Historically Reconsidered," p. 237). Except for such isolated cases as Hannah Arendt and Zygmunt Bauman, neither social theory generally nor sociological theory specifically has considered the Jewish question as a central and illuminating type case.

2. Bernstein, *Hannah Arendt and the Jewish Question*.

3. Of course, as Joshua Trachtenberg has written, "anti-Jewish prejudice is older and more extensive than Christendom" (*The Devil and the Jews: The Medieval Conception of the Jew and Its Relation to Modern Anti-Semitism*, p. 6). Trachtenberg cites Dio Cassius's "blood-curdling description of the Jewish revolt in North Africa at the time of Trajan: 'The Jews were destroying both Greeks and Romans. They ate the flesh of their victims, made belts for themselves out of their entrails, and anointed themselves with their blood' " (*The Devil and the Jews*, p. 128). Even in this non-Christian discourse, however, the "civil" is held up as a criteria for anti-Jewish thought. In the third century B.C., for example, Philostratus wrote that "the Jews have long been in revolt not only against the Romans, but against humanity; and a race that has made its own life apart and irreconcilable, that cannot share with the rest of mankind in the pleasures of the table nor join in their libations or prayers or sacrifices, are separated from ourselves by a greater gulf than divides us from Sura or Bactra of the distant Indies" (quoted in D. Prager and Telushkin, *Why the Jews? The Reason for Anti-Semitism*, p. 83).

4. The now nearly canonical distinction between theological and racial anti-Semitism may well be partly true, but it is only partly true. First, it is certainly wrong to think of negative, suprareligious identifications of Jews only as a nine-

teenth-century phenomenon that developed with the emergence of nationalism in a political form. The case of the Spanish Jews who converted because of the Inquisition demonstrates the fallacy of this sharp division, for even after living for centuries as Christians, these "Conversos," or "Marranos," did not succeed in neutralizing anti-Jewish feelings and activities. The medieval Spanish laws of *limpieza de sangre* evoked "purity of blood" arguments to prevent the rise to power of even the descendants of converts from Judaism to Catholicism.

> For most of the population, the conviction began to spread that Jewish ancestry or "race," not professed religious belief, defined who was a Jew. The resentment of the Christian populace was clearly evident in the preamble to these . . . ordinances: "We declare the so-called conversos, offspring of perverse Jewish ancestors, must be held by law to be infamous and ignominious, unfit, and unworthy to hold any public office or any benefice within the city of Toledo, or land within its jurisdiction, or to be commissioners for oaths or notaries, or to have any authority over the true Christians of the Holy Catholic Church." (Gerber, *Jews of Spain*, p. 127)

Second, Jews were always thought of by others, and so conceived of themselves, as a nation, as a people with an identity that included more than religion in the theological sense. Third, and perhaps most important for the present discussion, whatever the signified (the religious, racial or national group referent) of anti-Jewish discourse, the signifiers (the symbolic discourse of anti-Semitism) displayed a remarkably coherent structure in terms of the substantive abuses it evoked.

5. This perspective on the distinctiveness of the Christian community, as open to border-crossing and ruled by ethics rather than blood, is the base line for Weber's very ambivalent understanding of Judaism as, at least in its post-exilic form, a tribal and particularistic "pariah" religion. See M. Weber, *Ancient Judaism*, pp. 336–355 and 405–417.

6. Weber's conceptualization of ancient Judaism (see n. 5) can be seen has having articulated just such a conviction about the anti-civil orientation status of Jews. In this manner, and despite his liberal and cosmopolitan commitment to the full participation of modern Jews in modern Germany, Weber's historical sociology implicitly placed responsibility for Jewish exclusion, in some real part, upon the Jews themselves.

> Ancient Judaism was granted an honored place in the intellectual and economic history Weber wrote of the West because it had given birth to an ethic of moral rationalism that would have decisive consequences for the course of modern civilization. However, in the Weberian narrative Judaism attached the truth claims of that moral rationalism too closely to the narrow nationalistic concerns of the Jewish people. Ancient Judaism bound God's

will to a specific ethnic group. As a result, the universalism inherent in prophetic teaching could not be unleashed.

In Weber's view, Judaism did not seek a just and egalitarian society; it focused instead upon the fate of Israel and God's vindication of the people [of] Israel in the face of the hostility and indifference of the nations. It was Christianity that allowed the prophetic teachings of moral rationalism to transcend the confines of a single tribe. It was Christianity that made these teachings available to the entire world. In making these claims, Weber reveals himself to be embedded in the cultural and religious context of his day. His views and attitudes toward Jews and Judaism cannot be understood apart from the partisan world of German scholarship and Protestant religiosity that formed him . . . They embody certain attitudes representative of the modern world's attitudes towards Jews and Judaism. (D. Ellenson, *After Emancipation*, pp. 93–94)

7. In addition to the preceding citations, see Darrell J. Fashing, *Jewish People in Christian Preaching*; A. P. Rubin, *Scattered among the Nations: Documents Affecting Jewish History 49–1975*; L. Poliakov, *The History of Anti-Semitism, Vol. I: From the Time of Christ to the Court Jews;* and Jeremy Cohen, *Essential Papers on Judaism and Christianity in Conflict: From Late Antiquity to the Reformation*. In terms of the narrative origin of these anticivil qualities, early and later Christian leaders cite the "fact" that Jews killed Christ. "The Jews were obviously incarnations of the Devil," Prager and Telushkin explain, "for who else could murder God?" (*Why the Jews?* p. 92). "It was not only one group of Jews that was guilty of murdering God," they continue, "but all Jews then and forever: the New Testament put into the mouths of the Jews present at the Crucifixion, 'let the blood be on our heads and the heads of our children' [Matthew 27: 25]." This narrative about origins points to murder, the most anticivil act possible, and it provides a narrative justification for the broad construction of Jewishness as inimical to the qualities that compose civil society. Paul writes (1 Thess. 2:15), for example, that because the Jews "both killed the Lord Jesus, and the prophets, and have persecuted us," they "are adversaries to all men." Similar sentiments are attributed, in John, to Christ himself: "You are of your father the devil, and your will is to do your father's desires. He was a murderer from the beginning and has nothing to do with the truth, because there is no truth in him. When he lies, he is expressing his own nature, for he is a liar and the father of lies" (John 8:44). According to John Chrysostom, the fourth-century saint and father of the Eastern Orthodox Church, "The synagogue is also a cave of pirates and the lair of wild beasts. . . . Living for their belly, mouth forever gaping, the Jews behave no better than hogs and goats in their lewd grossness and the excesses of their gluttony. They can do one thing only: gorge themselves with food and drink" (quoted in *The History of Anti-Semitism*, p. 25).

8. As I suggested in Part II, the electoral system is only one of the regulatory institutions of the civil sphere, although it is the critical one for defining democracy in the political sense. As the present discussion demonstrates once again, there can be quite a highly developed civil sphere, and internal civil dynamics, without democracy. The dialectics of civil discourse may be quite robust, many of the institutions of communication and regulation may be functional, and facilitative and destructive tensions between civil and noncivil spheres may be at work.

9. England expelled the Jews in 1290. In 1655 Menasseh ben Israel petitioned to readmit the Jews to England, and Oliver Cromwell responded by appointing a commission, the Whitehall Conference, to decide the matter. When they failed to come to a resolution, Cromwell decided to "authorize the tacit and unofficial readmission of the Jews" to England. After the restoration of the monarchy, the Jews petitioned the king, and Charles II granted a "formal written statement of toleration." In 1673, the Jews were granted religious liberty. (Quotations from E. Barnavi, *A Historical Atlas of the Jewish People From the Time of the Patriarchs to the Present*, p. 140.)

10. Joseph II, "Edict of tolerance (January 2, 1782)," in Mendes-Flohr and Reinharz, *Jew in the Modern World*, pp. 36–40.

11. Ibid., p. 40, emphasis added. The quotations that follow in this sentence are drawn from the 1782 edict, ibid.

12. Mendes-Flohr and Reinharz, *Jew in the Modern World*, p. 40 n. 1.

13. Hertzberg, *French Enlightenment and the Jews*, p. 7.

14. The most striking illustration of this deep tendency toward primordialization, which so glaringly contradicted the civil pretensions of rationalist thought, can be found in the anti-Semitism of such philosophers as Voltaire, Diderot, and d'Holbach, who believed Jews to be "hopelessly and irretrievably alien" (Hertzberg, *French Enlightenment and the Jews*, p. 286). In Voltaire's 1771 *Lettres de Memmius à Ciceron*, he constructed Jews as the ultimate anticivil force, "the worst of men, hating all others and in turn hated by them"; he praised Cicero for acknowledging that Jews "are, all of them, born with raging fanaticism in their hearts, just as the Bretons and the German are born with blond hair," and he concluded that "I would not be in the least bit surprised if these would not some day become deadly to the human race." The following year, in *Il faut prendre une partie*, Voltaire addressed the Jews in a manner that similarly cast them as uniquely unqualified for membership in civil society: "You seem to me to be the maddest of the lot. The Kaffirs, the Hottentots, and the Negroes of Guinea are much more reasonable and more honest people. . . . You have surpassed all nations in impertinent fables, in bad conduct, and in barbarism" (quoted in Hertzberg, *French Enlightenment and the Jews*, p. 301). Hertzberg describes Voltaire's ideas as "the major link between the anti-Semitism of classical paganism and the modern age" (p. 285). For an English sample of Voltaire's thinking, see his "Jews."

15. Grégoire, "Essay on the Physical, Moral, and Political Reformation of the Jews," p. 50.

16. Liberles writes:

> Although discussions on the Jews were already intensifying by the late 1770s, [Dohm's] treatise served as the basis for extensive debate on the question of the Jews during the years to come. . . . [It] marked a significant transition in the discussion on the status of the Jews . . . and it was in Dohm's formulation that the French Enlightenment adopted the question and, in less than a decade, passed the first acts of Jewish emancipation in the National Assembly. ("Dohm's Treatise on the Jews," pp. 29–42)

17. Dohm, "Concerning the Amelioration of the Civil Status of the Jews," pp. 27–34. Unless otherwise indicated, all quotations from Dohm are from this selection (emphasis added).

18. "Indeed, his [Dohm's] attitude towards contemporary Jews was contemptuous. [They] revealed scorn and distance. . . . His program sought to make the Jews what they were not, while supplying no measure of appreciation for who they were" (Liberles, "Dohm's Treatise on the Jews," pp. 36, 41).

19. Quoted in Liberles, "Dohm's Treatise on the Jews," p. 39. This phrase can be found in the second edition of Dohm's treatise, published in 1783, which included some of the critiques that it had generated and Dohm's responses to them.

20. On this revealing paradox in the original German title, see Liberles, "Dohm's Treatise on the Jews," p. 38.

21. In this respect at least, the critics of Daniel Goldhagen's controversial book, *Hitler's Willing Executioners,* are correct. In the first place, Germany was not the only society to exhibit an "exterminating" strand in its anti-Jewish thought. In the second, no matter what the quality or quantity of anti-Semitism in the German cultural complex, this discursive structure cannot, by itself, be considered the cause of the Nazi's mass murder of Jews; every cultural configuration is effectuated in terms of more specific, conjunctural factors, as we will see in our discussion of the Holocaust at the end of this chapter. In my view, however, there is, at the same time, something importantly right about Goldhagen's approach in more general and theoretical rather than explanatory terms. This is his effort to counter the social structural emphasis in recent "Holocaust studies" by making anti-Jewish feelings and attitudes more central, that is, by bringing meaning back into the consideration of anti-Jewish social action. To bring meaning back in, however, does not mean to engage in a one-sided cultural explanation. See Alexander, "Why Cultural Sociology Is Not Idealist."

22. For recent discussions, see Robertson, *"Jewish Question,"* especially his dis-

cussions, titled "The Meaning of Assimilation," "Self-Hatred," and "Hyperaccul-turation," on pp. 233–378; and the contributions to Timms and Hammel, *German-Jewish Dilemma*.

23. The phrase is from Judah Leib Gordon's "Awake My People!" which was composed in 1863, after the liberation of the serfs by Czar Alexander II, and published in Hebrew in the journal *Hakarmel* in 1866. It is revealing that less than a decade later, Gordon was already expressing bitterness over the assimilation process in his Hebrew poem "For Whom Do I Toil?" published in *Hashahar* in 1871. Scholars of Jewish history continue to debate Gordon's true intent in the earlier poem. See Stanislawski, *For Whom Do I Toil?*

24. Mendelssohn, "Response to Dohm" (1782), pp. 38–42. Unless otherwise noted, all following quotes from Mendelssohn are from this excerpt.

25. Mendes-Flohr and Reinharz, *Jew in the Modern World*, editors' n. 1, p. 42.

26. In a less widely known but similarly revealing argument published in the same year, the *Haskalah* poet, linguist, and exegete Naphtali Herz Wessely published his *Divrei Shalom v'Emert* (Words of Peace and Truth), the first systematic work in the Hebrew language on Jewish education from a self-consciously enlightened per-spective. Wessely called on his fellow Jews to support Joseph II's Edict of Tolerance and demanded schools for Jewish children where German would be taught. His emphasis was on extrareligious solidarity, and this inspired him to accept the bargain of assimilation. According to Joshua Barzilay, Wessely believed that the "acquisition of human knowledge demands instruction in subjects which are necessary to man's relationship with man, namely, a training in general subjects and ethics, i.e., secular studies common to the human race" and he "came to the conclusion that he who studies Torah without acquiring common human knowledge, will, when he grows up, become a burden upon society" ("Naphtali Herz [Hartwig] Wessely," p. 463). Though Wessely's ideas were fiercely opposed by orthodox Jews, such as Ezekiel b. Judah Landau of Prague and Gaon Elija of Vilna, sections of *Words of Peace and Truth* were translated into French, German, Dutch, and Italian.

27. Berr, "Letter of a Citizen to his Fellow Jews (1791)," pp. 118–121. Unless otherwise noted, this and following quotations are made from this selection. Beer was one of six Jews whom the Jewish community of Alsace and Lorraine chose to present this case for civil protection and rights before the National Assembly, and he served later as a representative in the Assembly of Jewish Notables and the Parisian Sanhedrin (p. 121 n. 1).

28. The quotations in this sentence do not appear in the selection of Beer's letter from which I have been quoting in *The Jew in the Modern World*. They can be found in the reprint of the text of the whole letter: "Letter of M. Berr-Isaac-Berr to his Brethren, in 1791, on the rights of active Citizens being granted to the Jews," in Rivkin, *Readings in Modern Jewish History*, p. 251.

29. Quoted in Rivkin, *Readings in Modern Jewish History.*

30. Mendelssohn, *Jerusalem,* p. 133.

31. Quoted in M. Diogene Tama, *Transactions of the Parisian Sanhedrin,* trans. F.D. Kirwan, London, 1807, pp. 133–134.

32. Quoted in J, Blau, *Modern Varieties of Judaism,* p. 124.

33. Quoted in M. A. Meyer, *Response to Modernity: A History of the Reform Movement in Judaism,* New York and Oxford: Oxford University Press, 1988, pp. 387–388.

34. *Modern Varieties of Judaism,* p. 89.

35. Quoted in M. Meyer, *Response to Modernity,* p. 122. In *The Reform Movement in Judaism,* David Philipson describes this Frankfort reform movement as "one of the most striking episodes of the drama of Jewish religious development."

> The men who formed the society were actuated by the conviction that there must be many Jews throughout Germany who were ripe for a new expression of the principles of Judaism, since the changed political and social status, the acquisition of secular knowledge, in short, the complete break between their external fortunes and the conditions of the life of their ancestors must make them feel the impossibility of fitting the rabbinical interpretation of the religion to the modern Jewish environment. It was also felt that if they would make a short, sharp, and definite declaration of what they considered the essential principles of the faith, this would encourage all who entertained like sentiments to do the same, and the concerned movement away from rabbinical Judaism (many of whose enactments were disregarded by a multitude of contemporaneous Jews) and toward a modern Judaism would be begun. (p. 118)

The desire to measure Judaism by the standards of reason and science was, in fact, already an established movement by the time of these organizational efforts to reform Jewish practice. The *Wissenschaft des Judentums* (Science of Judaism), whose forerunners were already active in Jewish student circles in Berlin in 1819, was devoted to "factual accuracy, normative neutrality and the quest for truth" in Jewish studies. Many of the most vocal founders of German Reform Judaism were also in the *Wissenschaft* (p. 209).

36. Quoted in M. Meyer, *Response to Modernity,* p. 388.

37. Ibid., quoted on p. 387.

38. Ibid., quoted on p. 124.

39. J. Blau, *Modern Varieties of Judaism,* p. 124.

40. Quoted in M. Meyer, *Response to Modernity,* p. 138.

41. Ibid., quoted on p. 216.

42. Hirsch, *Nineteen letters on Judaism,* p. 114.

43. Ibid.

44. Ibid., p. 106.

45. Ibid., p. 114.

46. Ibid., p. 106. For a discussion of this conservative anxiety about the threat assimilation posed to the religious authority of Jewish religious leaders and community, see N. Stolzenberg and D. Myers, "Community, Constitution, and Culture."

47. Ibid., p. 110.

48. Ibid.

49. Quoted in J. Blau, *Modern Varieties of Judaism*, p. 82. In *The Emergence of Conservative Judaism: The Historical School in Nineteenth Century America*, Moshe Davis writes that the American Reform movement was centered in western European immigrants and "hoped to bring back within the Jewish fraternity countless contemporaries who had rejected the traditional view and looked upon ritual practice as obsolete." Orthodoxy, by contrast, emerged from the eastern European immigration. Only as "a native Orthodox group developed," however, "did it enter the struggle in the main arenas of American Jewish life." Nevertheless, "even at the beginning its position was clear, consistent, and always mindful of the great dangers to Judaism present in the emancipated society of America" (p. 12).

50. The etymology of the epithet "kike" is much debated and far from certain. One version has it that when illiterate eastern European immigrants arrived at Ellis Island, they signed their names with a circle—roughly "*kikel*" in Yiddish—rather than with the customary "x," which might have been mistaken for a cross. For the notion of "too Jewish" as a criticism that fearful, more incorporated Jews applied to themselves, and not only to newcomers, see Kleebatt, *Too Jewish?: Challenging Traditional Identities*.

51. Sorin, *Time for Building*, p. 62.

52. These remarks are from late-nineteenth-century American Jewish newspapers, and are quoted in Sorin, *Time for Building*, pp. 56 and 50.

53. Quoted in Sorin, *Time for Building*, p. 162. It should be noted, however, that "despite a strained, ofttimes bitter, relationship with eastern European Jews," the more incorporated Jews who had immigrated from western Europe provided "significant aid, including jobs, social welfare, philanthropy, and political support" to the new eastern immigrants, and they eventually strongly opposed efforts to close off such immigration (p. 10).

54. Cuddihy, *Ordeal of Civility*. This present interpretation differs from Cuddihy's by stressing the continuing stigmatization of Jewish qualities as responsible for concerns about the civilizing process, rather than simply Jewish concerns about their own ability to perform in a "civil" manner.

55. This multilayered model of assimilation as allowing integration in more public arenas while maintaining strict segregation in private life corresponds to the socio-

logical approach to the topic developed by M. Gordon, *Assimilation in American Life: The Role of Race, Religion, and National Origins*. In the decades since this work appeared, difference theory and multicultural arguments have bloomed, and it has been sharply criticized for an overemphasis and seeming complacency about assimilation. Yet the multidimensionality and texture of Gordon's approach remains relevant for the kind of person/quality distinction I am developing here. He did, in fact, envision "cultural pluralism" as an option in principle, though he did not think it a likely option for American society in the empirical sense. What Gordon did not envision, of course, was that a fundamentally new mode of incorporation would emerge to challenge assimilation and hyphenation and that this challenge would be strongly legitimated as offering new possibilities, even as assimilation and hyphenation proceeded apace.

56. Almost all of western and central Europe kept state positions off-limits to Jews until the revolutions of the 1840s. In Germany and Austria, however, there developed such strong backlashes against these developments that they reverted to *"judenrein"* civil service relatively soon after. Many more positions were included in this category in Germany than in the United States, e.g., professorial positions in universities. Farther east, e.g., in Russia, where many more Jews lived, state positions remained closed to Jews until much later than that.

57. For a discussion of the various reasons for and against conversion to Christianity in this milieu, see Hertz, *Jewish High Society in Old Regime Berlin*.

58. Rozenbilt, "Jewish Assimilation in Habsburg Vienna," p. 237. For complete statistics on Jewish conversions to Christianity in the nineteenth century, see Table XV in Mendes-Flohr and Reinharz, *Jew in the Modern World*, p. 715.

59. Heine, "Ticket of Admission to European Culture." For a similar rationale, see the now widely known letter of Abraham Mendelssohn to his daughter upon her confirmation into the Lutheran church.

> The outward form of religion . . . is historical, and changeable like all human ordinances. . . . We, your mother and I, were born and brought up by our parents as Jews, and without being obliged to change the form of our religion have been able to follow the divine instinct in us and our conscience. We have educated you and your brothers and sister in the Christian faith, because it is the creed of most civilized people, and contains nothing that can lead you away from what is good . . . even if . . . the example of its founder [is] understood by so few, and followed by still fewer. By pronouncing your confession of faith you have fulfilled the claims of *society* on you, and obtained the *name* of a Christian. Now *be* what your duty as a human being demands of you . . . unremittingly attentive to the voice of your conscience, which may be suppressed but never silenced. ("Why I Have Raised You as a Christian," pp. 257–258, emphasis added)

Two years after writing this letter, Abraham Mendelssohn, the great Jewish Enlightenment figure's son, himself embraced Christianity "because it is the religious form acceptable to the majority of civilized human beings" (quoted in Mendes-Flohr and Reinharz, *Jew in the Modern World*, p. 258 n. 1).

60. According to Todd M. Endelman, the number of Jews in the modern period who converted to Christianity—a process he ironically describes as "radical assimilation"—was much greater even than this, numbering several hundred thousand (*Radical Assimilation in English Jewish History, 1656–1945*, pp. 1–2). "To study drift and defection," he writes, "is to focus attention [on] radical responses to pressures and attractions to which all Jews were exposed [and it] would be foolish to ignore its relevance to the problem of Jewish integration into the modern world" (p. 6).

The gradual, multigenerational character of the process of Jewish disaffiliation has worked to mask the extent of the phenomenon everywhere. For subtle and undramatic transformations, however great their cumulative impact, aroused less interest, both at the time and in historical retrospect, than dramatic and decisive ruptures. This obscuring of the extent of drift and defection has been particularly acute in the case of English Jewry, among whom dramatic bursts of outright apostasy—so characteristic of the Central European Jewish experience—were noticeably absent. In addition, succeeding waves of Jewish immigration from the continent in the nineteenth and twentieth centuries periodically swelled the size of the community and thus masked the decline occurring among families long settled in the country. The number of newcomers easily outstripped the number of those lost through various forms of radical assimilation. Consequently, conversion, intermarriage, and disaffiliation never became burning issues of communal concern (except, perhaps, during the interwar period) in the way they did elsewhere. Nevertheless, considerable leakage occurred, although without fanfare for the most part, if not in one generation, then in the next. . . . Scores of once-prominent Jewish families ceased to be Jewish between the mid-eighteenth century and World War II. Harts, Frankses, Goldsmids, Gompertzes, Montefiores, Cohens, Jessels, Franklins, Beddingtons, and Sassoons, to name only a few examples from the Georgian and Victorian periods, disappeared from the ranks of the communal notability. . . . The departure of these families, once pillars of the Jewish establishment, indicates that radical assimilation was not an extraordinary event, a phenomenon on the periphery of Jewish life, but rather a common occurrence, eating away at the maintenance of group solidarity. (p. 6)

61. "In German lands," writes Elisheva Carlebach, "from the sixteenth century, this belief in the indelible power of baptism began to erode in the case of Jewish

converts. Christians believed that the Jewish nature of these converts inhered so deeply that no baptismal chrism could configure it" (*Divided Souls*, p. 1). The present discussion reinforces the skepticism that I expressed, earlier in this chapter, about the contention that anti-Semitism switched from the more ideologically focused "religious" to the more primordially focused "racial" in the course of the nineteenth century.

62. In *Hebrews of the Portuguese Nation: Conversos and Community in Early Modern Amsterdam*, Miriam Bodian discusses the feeling of ethnic or racial unity experienced by former Jews in Portugal and in the diasporic groups that formed in Amsterdam in the sixteenth and seventeenth centuries, where the Portuguese former Jews who later created a new Jewish community in Amsterdam referred to themselves as a "*Nacion.*" Bodian shows how the 1449 *limpeiza de sangre* law, stipulating that Jewishness passed through the blood, marked a shift in both the treatment of conversos by local authorities and also in the former Jews' self-understanding.

63. Boerne, "Because I Am a Jew," pp. 259–260. Boerne lost his position as an official in the Frankfurt Police Department when the anti-Jewish restrictions of the pre-Napoleonic era were reimposed after the defeat of France at Waterloo in 1815. He converted to Lutheranism in 1818 so as to reassume the position but became a political journalist instead.

64. Heinrich's actual birth name was Hirschel ha-Levi Marx. His father had been a rabbi who was preceded by generations of Talmudic scholars. See Levinson et al., "Karl Heinrich Marx," *Encyclopedia Judaica 11*, p. 1075.

65. K. Marx, "On the Jewish Question," p. 243.

66. Ibid.

67. Ibid.

68. Ibid., pp. 245, 247.

69. Ibid., p. 241.

70. Ibid., p. 231.

71. Ibid., p. 243.

72. Ibid.

73. Ibid.

74. Ibid., p. 248.

75. Despite official early Soviet policy condemning anti-Semitic manifestations, according to Bernard D. Weinryb ("Anti-Semitism in Soviet Russia"), the Soviet communist party increasingly fanned anti-Jewish feelings. According to Deutscher, the typical party member "often looked upon the Jews as the last surviving element of urban capitalism," and, despite the structures of Jewish equality that the early Soviet leadership had erected, "enmity towards the Jews was almost unabated in the last years of Stalin's life" (I. Deutscher, *Stalin,* p. 589). When we consider that such antisocialist propagandists as the Nazis used the term "Marxism" to denote "a sinister, worldwide 'Jewish' plot against their national interests" (Levinson, "Karl Heinrich

Marx," p. 1075), we see a close parallel with the earlier converts to nonsecular religion. Marx and his comrades in the revolutionary secular religion were still considered not only Jews but emblematic ones at that.

76. For a nuanced treatment of the Dreyfus Affair and its effects on Jewish identity and politics, see Hyman, *From Dreyfus to Vichy: The Remaking of French Jewry, 1906–1939*, who argues against the representation of French Jews as overly assimilated, offering a broader view of Jewish identity instead. See also A. Rodrigue, "Rearticulations of French Jewish Identities after the Dreyfus Affair."

77. For a discussion of the emergence of classical Yiddish literature and its transition to the younger generation of writers, see M. Krutikov, *Yiddish Fiction and the Crisis of Modernity, 1905–1914*. This reference to the sharply segregated civil spheres provides an illuminating contrast with the "subaltern publics" theorized within the neo-Habermasian critical tradition. While constituting relatively self-regulating civil societies, these Jewish communities were cut off from viable participation in the civil spheres of the imperial and national communities that controlled their ultimate fates. There were few links between segregated Jewish civil societies and those to whose hegemony they were subject—no possibility for persuasion, for influence, for communication, much less for social movements or legal challenge. As I suggested in my earlier discussion of this theoretical issue (see chapter 16), what is critical to understand about unequal social positions is whether, and to what degree, inequality occurs as a contradiction within a "civil" hegemony or as a colonial relationship outside it. The former was true for the subordination of women in the early centuries of national civil societies, for the economic domination of the proletariat, and even for racial domination of the African American minority in the United States during but especially after slavery. Domination outside civil hegemony was much more the case for these radically segregated Jewish civil societies, as their ultimate fates starkly revealed.

78. Looking backward, in an interview in 1889, Abramovitz recalled his fateful switch from writing in Hebrew to writing in Yiddish in this revealing manner:

> Here I am observing the ways of our people and seeking to give them stories from a Jewish source in the Holy tongue, yet most of them do not even know this language and speak Yiddish. What good does a writer do with all his toil and ideas if he is not useful to his people? This question—for whom do I toil?—gave me no rest and brought me into great confusion. (Quoted in K. Frieden, *Classic Yiddish Fiction: Abramovitsch, Sholem Aleichem, and Peretz*, p. 25)

In *A Traveler Disguised: A Study in the Rise of Modern Yiddish Fiction in the Nineteenth Century*, Dan Miron discusses the historical conditions that gave rise to Abramovitz's later Yiddish work and the reflections of these new conditions inside his literary work itself. Describing "the mood prevailing in the 1880s and the early 1890s among Russian-Jewish intellectuals," Maron writes:

> Shocked into disillusion with the once-believed-in liberalism of the czarist regime, these intellectuals went into a fit of nationalistic enthusiasm. Many *maskilim* [i.e., members of the Jewish enlightenment] of long standing gave up their ideological commitments in the two or three years immediately following the pogroms. A chauvinistic, highly sentimental literature began to appear, in which the mistakes of the *Haskala* were endlessly harped upon. . . . Declarations of loyalty to the common people and to the long-abused fathers and forefathers . . . as well as sentimental expressions of longing for one's childhood *shtetl* were also not lacking. (pp. 105–106)

As Miron emphasizes, however, Abramowitz by no means completely identified with this new and sentimental nationalism. To the contrary, it is "ironic juxtaposition" that characterizes his fictional reconstructions of the new and more depressing Jewish situation, a "dialectic of assertion and doubting, of saying and unsaying" (pp. 105–106). What allowed this new ironic genre, in other words, was "the ability of Abramovitsh [*sic*] to separate himself into two independent entities: one, the Abramovitsh of Odessa, the well-dressed gentleman, the member of the educational profession, etc.; the other, an old-fashioned Jewish bookpeddler, Mendele Moykher-Sforim" (p. 92). It was this "separation of Mendele from Abramovitsch" that allowed the author to create the kind of "theatrical internal duality" of his stories, in which the "troubled consciousness" of his favorite protagonist, Mendele, is split into "two different persons engaged in a dispute or a discussion" (pp. 93–94).

79. In 1879, Abramowitz adopted the pseudonym Mendele Moykher Sforim, which roughly translates as "Mendele the Itinerant Bookseller" ("Mendele Moykher Sforim," *Encyclopedia Britannica Online,* January, 2006).

80. Though "Kafka was in many respects an isolated and unique figure," writes Hillel J. Kieval, "on a deeper level . . . his life epitomized the very processes that were transforming Jewish life in Bohemia and Moravia" ("The Lands Between," pp. 49–50).

> Until the late 1840s, linguistic and ethnic boundaries in the Czech lands were relatively fluid [and] intellectuals in the Hapsburg lands imagined a society in which democracy, national rights and full emancipation for religious minorities coexisted. These were heady, if uncertain, times for Jewish students in Prague and Vienna. Some aligned with the young literary and national movements of the Czechs, the Hungarians, and the South Slavs. . . . But the efforts of Jewish students and intellectuals to promote Czech nationalism in the 1840's foundered on the shoals of hostility, misunderstand-

ing, and popular violence . . . directed mainly against the businesses and homes of Jews [and] Bohemian and Moravian Jewry [who] were prompted to narrow their vision of that community into which they hoped to integrate. . . . If Bohemian and Moravian Jewish culture had been colored largely by the German-Jewish alliance of the late 18th century . . . the new Czech-Jewish orientation was highly nuanced, increasingly alienated from Austrian-German liberalism, and self-consciously bilingual . . . By the first decade of the 20th century, German-Jewish culture in the Czech lands was in full retreat. But it was not dead. Jewish parents in Prague, Brno and other large cities continued to send their children in significant numbers to German schools and universities. . . . No one with Kafka's personal history, having emerged from that peculiar cultural mixture that was Prague, can be considered to have been simply a German writer. (pp. 44–49)

Referring to the relationship between emerging Czech nationalism and the minority of Christian Germans and German-speaking Jews in Prague in the late nineteenth century, Ernst Pawel writes:

The spread of pan-German nationalism, with its anti-Semitic cast, soon drove a wedge between them. By the 1890s, they had split into distinctly separate and mutually antagonistic camps, though the differences between them were largely lost on their Czech fellow citizens. To the Young Czech nationalists, the Jews were Germans. To the Germans, the Jews were Jews; the racial doctrines which an Austrian corporal was to translate into genocide half a century later were already sprouting in the subsoil of Austro-Hungarian politics. Caught between the lines, trapped in the shrinking no-man's-land between crusading armies headed for a showdown but both equally committed to their Jew-baiting extremism, Bohemia's Jews found themselves in a unique quandary that was to shape the attitude of Kafka and his generation in fatally decisive ways." (Pawel, *Nightmare of Reason*, p. 31)

See also H. Kieval, *The Making of Czech Jewry: National Conflict and Jewish Society in Bohemia, 1870–1918.*

81. For an investigation of the role that Kafka's encounter with the Yiddish theater of the East had for simultaneously stimulating his artistic production and his deeper interest in Jewish history and literature, see Robertson, *Kafka: Judaism, Politics, and Literature*, pp. 1–37.

82. Pawel's evaluation draws from comments by Kafka's fellow employees, both executive colleagues and subordinates, in *Nightmare of Reason*, p. 189.

83. Pawel, *Nightmare of Reason*, p. 181.

84. Ibid., p. 99.

85. Franz Kafka, "Letter to His Father," p. 195. For the sort of interpretive controversy this letter has stimulated, see, e.g., Flores, *The Problem of "The Judgment": Eleven Approaches to Kafka's Story*, In his foreword to the collection, Flores calls *The Judgment* "Kafka's seminal story" and observes that "it contains in miniature the essence of his themes and techniques as developed in his later work."

86. Kafka, *Trial*. For the timing of Kafka's composition of this sentence, see Pawel, *Nightmare of Reason*, p. 322.

87. Kafka, *Metamorphosis*, p. 7.

88. Blau, *Modern Varieties of Judaism*, p. 145.

89. Herzl, "Solution to the Jewish Question (1896)." All quotations are from this selection.

90. For the idea of "exit," see Hirschman, *Exit, Voice, and Loyalty*.

91. I am referring here, of course, to the manner in which the major industrial societies responded to the interwar economic crisis by increasing social rights to the working classes, though most had already begun to do so before. It is critical to understand, however, that this kind of "social" incorporation is not necessarily connected to incorporation along other lines, e.g., religious, ethnic, or racial. In fact, economic incorporation, via the legal and political recognition of trade unions for example, actually can increase racial domination, strengthening the racial core group by empowering its lower class component. In his first book, *Power, Racism, and Privilege: Race Relations in Theoretical and Sociohistorical Perspective*, William Julius Wilson made just this point, suggesting that American trade unions and working-class groups were critical in the racial formation of the late nineteenth and twentieth centuries. This is another illustration of how the failure to allow for the separate historical trajectories of the three dimensions of citizenship and to apply them to nonclass groups markedly weakens T. H. Marshall's classic account in *Class, Citizenship, and Social Development*.

92. This simplifying assumption has been made for heuristic reasons, so that a theoretical model of the contradictions of Jewish incorporation in Western civil society could be developed. There were, of course, national variations, and no conclusions about the fate of Jews in any particular context could be made in a deductive manner from the more general model I have developed here. Only in the 1930s, however, did these national variations become matters of life and death. The genocide against Jews, the conditions for which developed in the 1930s, created two completely divergent paths for the relation of Jews to modern civil society.

93. For an influential example of this ideology of American exceptionalism as it informed historical work, see Hartz, *Liberal Tradition in America*.

94. See chapter 19 below.

95. For a contemporary discussion of the restrictions on Jews in higher education, see J. X. Cohen, "Jews, Jobs, and Discrimination: A Report on Jewish Non-

Employment," pp. 18–22. For more recent studies of the restrictions that emerged in the interwar era, see Rosovsky, *Jewish Experience at Harvard and Radcliffe*; Oren, *Joining the Club: A History of Jews and Yale*; and the comprehensive first chapter, "The 'Jewish Problem' in Higher Education," of S. Steinberg's *The Academic Melting Pot: Catholics and Jews in American Higher Education*, pp. 5–31. More generally, see chapter 19.

96. See Lacquer, *Terrible Secret*.

97. Though this revisionism was generally directed, as the following discussion makes clear, against the Enlightenment account of modern Jewish progress, Baron was also targeting, more specifically, the Jewish historians of the *Wissenschaft des Judentums*, such as Graetz and Dubnow.

98. Baron, "Ghetto and Emancipation," p. 12.

99. Ibid.

100. Ibid., p. 2.

101. Ibid., p. 5.

102. Ibid., p. 6.

103. Ibid., p. 9.

104. Ibid.

105. Ibid.

106. Ibid., p. 10.

107. Ibid.

108. Alexander, "Social Basis of Moral Universalism."

109. Horkheimer and Adorno, *Dialectic of Enlightenment*, p. 169; Bauman, *Modernity and the Holocaust*. See my criticisms of Bauman's equation of incorporation in state and civil societies in chapter 16.

110. Sartre, *Anti-Semite and Jew*, p. 77.

111. Ibid., pp. 77–78.

112. Ibid., p. 77.

113. Ibid., p. 69.

114. Ibid., p. 67.

115. Ibid., p. 78.

116. Ibid., pp. 79–80.

117. Ibid., p. 80.

CHAPTER 19

1. In 1942, a group of distinguished American social scientists published a book called *Jews in a Gentile World: The Problem of Anti-Semitism*, edited by I. Graeber and S. Henderson Britt. In his contribution to that volume, "The Sociology of Anti-Semitism," Talcott Parsons wrote that "the question frequently raised these days, in view of the violent form anti-Semitism has taken in many countries of Europe,

particularly in Germany, is whether anti-Semitism is likely to become as widespread and as extreme in the United States as in those countries." Parsons answered in the negative, pointing to the fact that "the causes bringing about social disorganization . . . are quite different here and in Germany." In Parsons's opinion, however, these differences did not extend to anti-Semitic sentiments. To the contrary, "it would be difficult to demonstrate that there are any important differences in anti-Semitism as it is found here and in Germany" (p. 118).

2. The notion that the history of America offers an exception to the repressive social structure of Europe and to the fate of virtually every group within it has been a fixture in the ideological self-understanding of Americans since John Winthrop admonished his fellows voyagers on the Mayflower, before the Puritans landed on Plymouth Rock, that they must be like a "City on the Hill." The specific term "American exceptionalism," however, seems to have first emerged within Marxist intellectual discourse as a way to explain why socialist workers movements did not emerge in the United States as they had in Europe. Seymour Martin Lipset is the social scientist who most systematically elaborated this perspective in the modern period, beginning with his book *The First New Nation* (1965). In 1969, in "The American Jewish Community in a Comparative Perspective," Lipset applied this perspective to American Jews: "To understand the American Jew, it is necessary to be sensitized to factors in American life which used to be discussed . . . as the problem of 'American exceptionalism.' . . . The orientations towards men and groups stemming from equalitarian values and the structure of a society composed of many ethnic-religious groups, have given American Jews opportunities for acceptance as individuals such as have never existed in any predominantly Gentile society in history" (p. 31). (For a later iteration of this position, see Lipset, "A Unique People in an Exceptional Country.") This theme broadly informed the influential 1974 collection edited by Marshall Sklare, *The Jew in American Society*, to which many contemporary experts on American Jews contributed. In one of his section introductions, Sklare writes:

> In their native European countries the Jews generally constituted a group whose rights—if granted at all—were subject to challenge. . . . Furthermore, whatever the legal status of the Jews it was clear that their position in society was controversial. . . . However, America offered Jews something more than opportunity: it offered unambiguous acceptance as a citizen. Such acceptance also meant that Jews were offered the opportunity to contribute to the national culture on an equal basis. All of this was in sharp contrast to . . . much of modern Jewish experience. . . . In the United States participation in the life of the larger society has generally been welcomed." (pp. 51–52, 68)

This understanding remains the framework informing most, though by no means all, popular and scholarly discussion of Jewish experience in the United States. Most recently, see A. J. Karp, *Jewish Continuity in America: Creative Survival in a Free Society*.

3. In their introduction to *Insider/Outsider: American Jews and Multiculturalsim*, David Biale, Michael Galchinksy, and Susannah Heschel point to the absence in America of "the corporate traditions of European monarchies and the state sponsored churches of many European nations" (p. 2). For other discussions of the status of American Jewry as the exception to the European rule, see, e.g., Handlin, "The Acquisition of Political and Social Rights by the Jews in the United States"; Halpern, "America Is Different," esp. pp. 69, 71, 74; Katznelson, "Between Separation and Disappearance"; and Soyer, *Jewish Immigrant Associations and American Identity in New York, 1880–1939*. Though the effect of such historical literature is often (see my discussion in note 2) to produce an exaggerated and sometimes one-sided emphasis on the success of Jewish incorporation in the United States, to note the differences between Europe and the United States denies neither the facts of anti-Semitism nor Jewish segregation in American history, both voluntary and involuntary (see, e.g., L. Wirth, *The Ghetto*). It is to suggest only that ghettoization in the sense of state-enforced direct domination has generally been absent.

4. On the pervasive Protestant Christian culture in America, see R. Laurence Moore, *Religious Outsiders and the Making of Americans,* and, more generally, the classical writings of the American cultural historian Perry Miller, e.g., *Errand into the Wilderness* and *The Life of the Mind in America*.

5. Ellenson, *After Emancipation*, p. 34.

6. Ibid.

7. As I reiterated in the conclusion to the preceding chapter, these three modes of incorporation are ideal types. In a historically specific situation, they can be mixed together, such that they exist to some degree or another even if one form may predominate.

8. I draw here from Ellenson, *After Emancipation*, p. 34.

9. Zangwill, *Melting Pot*.

10. Quoted in Ellenson, *After Emancipation*, p. 34.

11. The Morgenthau family immigrated to the United States from Germany at the close of the Civil War. In a memoir, Henry Morthenthau III recalled that "when I was a child in the 1920s, growing up on the West Side of Manhattan, being Jewish was something that was never discussed in front of children. . . . It was instead a kind of birth defect that could not be eradicated but (with proper treatment) could be overcome. . . . The cure was to be achieved through a vigorous lifelong exercise of one's Americanism." When he was five years old, Morganthau remembered coming home from Central Park, where a young friend had asked him about his religion. After asking his mother, "What is my religion?" there "came a deliberate

pronouncement: 'If anyone ever asks you that again, just tell them you're an American.' The conversation was over, never to be reopened" ("Central Park West," pp. 19, 24).

12. Kallen, *Culture and Democracy in the United States,* pp. 124–125 (emphasis in original).

13. For a concise overview of the roles that Jews played in twentieth-century American journalism and movies, see Whitfield, *American Space, Jewish Time,* pp. 129–170.

14. G. Talese, *The Kingdom and the Power,* p. 93.

15. Talese, *Kingdom and the Power,* pp. 168–169. For an account of the American Jewish Committee's efforts to deal with the rise of Nazism in the 1930s, see Arad, *America, Its Jews, and the Rise of Nazism.*

16. Talese, *Kingdom and the Power,* p. 168.

17. Ibid., p. 91. In this, Sulzberger was hardly alone: "The report that Roosevelt intended to appoint Professor Felix Frankfurter to the Supreme Court provoked a delegation of distinguished and wealthy Jews to scurry to Washington to urge the president against the nomination in 1939, out of the fear that it would intensify anti-Semitism" (Whitfield, *American Space, Jewish Time,* pp. 4–5).

18. In his fifty years with the *Times,* A. M. Rosenthal served as reporter, managing editor, and op-ed columnist. When he joined the staff in the 1940s, the editors asked him to replace his Jewish-sounding given name, "Abraham," with the more ambiguous "A. M.," an Anglicization that continued to mark his byline until he retired (Talese, *Kingdom and the Power,* pp. 58–60).

19. See Gabler, *An Empire of Their Own,* pp. 1–7; and Lester Friedman, *Hollywood's Image of the Jew,* pp. 1–55. In their special issue "Jews in America" in 1936, the editors of *Fortune* magazine concluded that although "Jewish control of the great moving-picture companies is less than monopolistic[, Jews] do exert pretty complete control over the production of pictures. . . . Of eight-five names engaged in production either as executives in production, producers, or associate producers (including independents), fifty-three are Jews. And the Jewish advantage holds in prestige as well as in numbers." For a fuller discussion of *Fortune*'s highly ambivalent statement about Jews during the 1930s, see below.

20. Gabler, *Empire of Their Own,* pp. 6–7.

21. Ibid., p. 7.

22. Ibid., quoted on p. 2.

23. Ibid.

24. In the silent film era of the teens and 1920s, according to L. D. Freidman, when "America discovered its Jews and its national cinema" (*Hollywood's Image of the Jew,* p. 57), Jewish images were heavily framed by "racist stereotypes" (p. 27). Moreover, in the 1930s, "in the first decade of the sound era Jews virtually disappeared from America's movie screens," in the sense that "Jewish characters" were

robbed "of all telltale ethnic traces: names, mannerisms, issues" (p. 57). See also Whitfield, *American Space, Jewish Time*, pp. 155–156. That the creators of Hollywood movies were reluctant to highlight Jewish qualities did not, of course, mean that their industry was conservative in a political sense. See, e.g., Birdwell, *Celluloid Soldiers*.

25. It was precisely because they were excluded from those already in existence that Jews began to establish their own law firms and banks beginning in the 1920s (see Sowell, *Ethnic America*, p. 93). As for the other regulatory institutions—the electoral system and "office"—Jews were not yet able to participate, qua Jews, in either until after World War II, for reasons I will suggest below.

26. Ellenson, *After Emancipation*, p. 39.

27. Ibid.

28. See chapter 18 for the manner in which American Reform Jews organized the Pittsburgh Platform, which powerfully introduced Reform Judaism into the United States.

29. Grant, *Passing of the Great Race*, p. 16 (quoted in Selzer, *"Kike,"* p. 78). After World War I, Grant played a significant role in formulating the newly restrictive anti-immigrant legislation.

30. Quoted in Oren, *Joining the Club*, p. 70.

31. Steinberg, *Academic Melting Pot*, p. 9. See, more generally, the description of this period in Goren, *American Jews,* pp. 60–73.

32. During World War I, as the "progressive" President Woodrow Wilson threw his support to this restrictive backlash movement, he continued to support the principle of inclusion in a manner that clearly illustrated the WASP core's identification of its culture as national rather than group-specific. "There are no minorities in the United States," Wilson insisted, just as "there are no national minorities, racial minorities, or religious minorities." In fact, "the whole concept and basis of the United States precludes them" (quoted in Strober, *American Jews,* p. 215). Assimilation allows incorporation into civil principles as they are mediated by the primordial qualities of the core group.

33. There is some evidence to think it was. In *Joining the Club: A History of Jews at Yale*, the most fully researched and authoritative history of the relationship between Jews and an elite educational institution, Oren tries to explain why Jewish children entered Yale in much higher numbers than the children of Catholics, despite the fact that the groups shared New Haven's immigrant slums.

> The largest single group of ghetto Jews at Yale came from the slums that stood just a few blocks from the campus. . . . From a physical standpoint, the Jewish ghettos in American were not unique, but in terms of industriousness and intellectual activity, the Jewish slum neighborhoods had few rivals. Respect for scholarship had been an integral part of Jewish culture

for centuries. In Europe the study of the Talmud (commentary on religious law)—not for the purpose of achieving any particular goal but wisdom, often for its own sake—was the accepted norm of Jewish life, and the reputation of a Jewish community rested on the talents of its greatest scholars. In America the thirst for knowledge continued in the Jewish ghettos, including the one in New Haven. . . . Though the religious drive would falter, the searing passion for a better understanding of one's world remained. . . . Education was seen as the basis of personal fulfillment and economic advancement. (pp. 31–33)

For a discussion of why this contrast between local Catholics and local Jews continued into the middle of the twentieth century, see Oren's discussion of the findings of the Connecticut Commission on Civil Rights (pp. 193–197). For other attestations to the Jewish commitment to education, see Glazer, *American Judaism,* p. 80, and *The American Jews,* p. 5.

34. Johnson, *Stover at Yale,* p. 199. This novel first appeared in *McClure's Magazine* in 1911. Quoted in Oren, *Joining the Club,* p. 34.

35. Quoted in Steinberg, *Academic Melting Pot,* p. 16.

36. Ibid., p. 20.

37. For a discussion of the elaborate, drawn-out process by which the administrators and governors of Yale College introduced newly restrictive, anti-Jewish procedures—while euphemistically camouflaging them as "reforms"—see Oren, *Joining the Club,* pp. 19–101. In 1922, when the rise of Jewish students at Yale had climbed to 13 percent, far less than at Columbia or even Harvard, Dean Robert Corwin sent Yale President James Angell an advisory "Memorandum on Jewish Representation in Yale," in which he suggested "there seems to be no question that the University as a whole has about all of this race that it can well handle, that the number of applicants for admission is increasing and seems likely to increase still further" and that "many feel that the saturation point has already been passed" (p. 49).

38. Quoted in Steinberg, *Academic Melting Pot,* p. 18

39. Ibid., p. 24.

40. F. Russell, "Coming of the Jews," quoted in Steinberg, *Academic Melting Pot,* p. 15.

41. Gannett, "Is America Anti-Semitic?" quoted in Oren, *Joining the Club,* pp. 70–71.

42. Ibid., p. 71.

43. Steinberg, *Academic Melting Pot,* pp. 21–28; and Oren, pp. 50–52.

44. Quoted in Oren, pp. 50–51.

45. Goren writes:

The frenzied nativism of the 1920s intensified anti-Jewish agitation. . . . At congressional and legislative hearings, at public meetings, and in the organs of the Ku Klux Klan, immigrant Jews were portrayed as architects of the Russian Revolution and as agents of world communism preparing to seize control of America. . . . Henry Ford added his powerful voice to the anti-Semitic campaign in his *Dearborn Independent,* a weekly he distributed through his thousands of dealerships, featuring accounts of cabals of Jewish bankers maneuvering to gain control of the economy. . . . One influential State Department report described the Jewish immigrants . . . as "of the usual ghetto type . . . filthy, un-American and often dangerous in their habits . . . abnormally twisted, [their] dullness and stultification resulting from the past years of oppression and abuse." . . . The situation deteriorated in the 1930s. . . . The confluence of economic distress and anti-Semitism provided a fertile field for demagogues preaching hate. . . . The German-American Bund represented a direct connection between Nazi Germany and rising domestic anti-Semitism; the Bund received funds, organizational leadership, and propaganda material from the German government. . . . Charles E. Coughlin was a Roman Catholic priest whose nationwide broadcasts and newspaper, *Social Justice,* won an immense following. His anti-Communist crusade and his populist rhetoric relied on . . . stereotypes of the Jews. . . . By 1938 he was justifying the Nazi persecution. . . . Important Catholic diocesan papers supported Coughlin's position and encouraged the Christian Front, an organization propagating anti-Semitism. Between 1939 and 1941, when the United States entered the war, some isolationists attacked the Jews as "the most dangerous force pushing the nation into war" and were echoed in Congress by Senators Burton K. Wheeler and Gerald Nye. (*American Jews,* pp. 81–85).

46. J. X. Cohen, *Jews, Jobs, and Discrimination.* I quote from the third edition.

47. Wise, foreword to *Jews, Jobs, and Discrimination,* pp. 3–4.

48. Ibid., p. 8.

49. Ibid., p. 10.

50. Ibid., p. 13.

51. Ibid., p. 6.

52. For the importance of weak ties in the labor market, see Granovetter, *Getting a Job.*

53. Wise, *Jews, Jobs, and Discrimination,* p. 7.

54. Wolfson, "Escaping Judaism," pp. 1, 50–51.

55. Cohen, *Jews, Jobs, and Discrimination,* p. 25. The following quotations are also from this source and page.

56. Although the denigration of American Jews did not typically extend to violence—by contrast, for example, with the more than four thousand recorded lynchings of African Americans—the threat of physical violence was never entirely removed. In April 1913, Leo Frank, a Jewish industrialist who had been raised in Brooklyn, was arrested in the murder of a 14-year-old girl in a factory he had managed in Atlanta, Georgia. Despite flimsy evidence, in a situation marked by "a frenzy of anti-Jewish agitation," Frank was convicted of murder. Every appeal was rejected, including by the U.S. Supreme Court. When, in 1915, the governor of Georgia, convinced of Frank's innocence, commuted his death sentence to life imprisonment, it set off a new wave of anti-Semitic attacks in the press, economic boycotts, and threats of violence against local Jews. On August 16, 1915, a mob kidnapped Frank from prison and lynched him. See Goren's account of Frank's case in *American Jews*, pp. 61–62.

57. This is certainly not to say, of course, that important figures in the American core group had not opposed anti-Semitism before this time, despite how widespread these anti-Jewish feelings were. In *Send These to Me*, John Higham shows that Left-leaning intellectuals, artists, academics, and journalists—many from the old elites and core groups of American society—set out to oppose the rising flood of nativism in the 1920s. Far from being stimulated by the rise of Nazism to reconsider anti-Semitic feelings, such civil activists were already deeply opposed and viewed the rise of Nazism in this context.

58. Higham, *Send These to Me*, p. 3.

59. *Fortune,* February 1936. This special section stimulated such widespread interest that it was subsequently reprinted in pamphlet form by Random House, and sold for $1. Later, *Digest and Review* procured the rights to reprint the book and published a slightly condensed version. The following quotations are from the *Fortune* article, which ran on pages 79–85, 128–30, 133–144; they were maintained in the *Digest and Review* condensation as well.

60. For a broad and systematic analysis of poll data on American anti-Semitism before, during, and after World War II, see Stember, "Recent History of Public Attitudes."

61. Stember concludes that "hostility against Jews actually increased from the beginning of the period"—his data analysis begins in 1938—"until the final phase of the war" (p. 210). His detailed analysis (pp. 130–133) demonstrates, for example, that Americans who responded that they would "support" or "sympathize" with "a campaign against Jews" rose from slightly more than 30 percent of the nation in 1939 to well over 40 percent in June 1944, and that, at that late date in the war, less than 30 percent of Americans responded that they would "oppose a campaign against the Jews." In 1943, according to Jonathan D. Sarna *(American Judaism: A History)*, "an official government study found substantial amounts of Judeophobia in half of the forty-two states it surveyed, and as late as 1944 fully 60 percent of Americans

claimed to have heard 'criticism or talk against the Jews' in the previous six months' "
(p. 266).

62. Giesen, "The Trauma of Perpetrators."

63. Stanley Hoffman speaks of "the post-World War II representation of Vichy as a reactionary clique which the occupier and the circumstances had coerced into collaborating" ("Foreword," p. ix). Moving away from this distinctly self-congratulatory understanding meant coming to terms with how widespread was initial French support for the harshly anti-Semitic rhetoric and policies of the Vichy government, which ruled "un-occupied France" from the German victory in 1940 until the Allied liberation of France in 1944. At least among French intellectual and cultural elites, this coming to terms actually began with the work of such outsiders as the American historian Robert O. Paxton, whose pivotal research explores what he and Marrus called "the autonomous French anti-Jewish project of 1940–42" (p. 369). Hoffman attests that "when Robert Paxton's *Vichy France* [his earlier book] was published in France, in 1973, it was not very well received. The tone of comments and reviews ranged from what the French call *gêne*—let us translate it as embarrassment—to hostility. . . . What hurt was the stark picture of the regime's eagerness for collaboration" (p. ix). What was so controversial about such revisionist work was its demonstration of the relatively widespread popularity that the Vichy project enjoyed among French elites and masses, support that markedly subsided after the summer of 1942, when Vichy began carrying out the mass deportations for Germany's Final Solution.

> The Vichy regime, reacting against the Third republic whose legitimacy had vanished in defeat, launched France on what many French people believed was a permanent new tack, the program called the National Revolution: authoritarian, traditionalist, pious, and neutral in the war between Hitler and the Allies. . . . The Vichy regime wanted to solve in its own way what it saw as a "Jewish problem" in France. . . . The regime initially sought the re-emigration of recently arrived Jews it deemed refractory to French culture, the submergence of longer-established Jews, and their ultimate assimilation in to a newly homogeneous French nation. (xvi–xvii)

As these and later revisionist historians inside and outside France have demonstrated, moreover, this deeply anti-Semitic support for the Vichy project occurred against a background of decades of increasingly virulent anti-Jewish French social and cultural movements (see, in this regard, Marrus and Paxton, "The Roots of Vichy Anti-Semitism," in *Vichy France and the Jews*, pp. 25–71). Tony Judt discusses the fragile position in the French Third Republic of Leon Blum, the Jewish socialist leader who briefly became prime minister in the 1930s (*Burden of Responsibility*, pp. 29–86).

64. In what came to be viewed as an iconographic representation of such framing, less than three weeks after the U.S. Army's liberation of the death campus, the *Picture Post* juxtaposed photos of dead or tattered and starving Jewish victims at Buchenwald with pictures of well-dressed, apparently well-fed German citizens from the surrounding towns. In an accompanying story, titled "The Problem That Makes All Europe Wonder," the *Post* described "the horror that took place within the sight and sound of hundreds of thousands of seemingly normal, decent German people" and asked, "How was it possible?" Alongside another widely circulated photo in the same issue—displaying a representative American GI standing guard, and seeming to pass judgment, on the entire scene—the *Post* advocated a civil response to the revelations that clearly demarcated the postwar mission of the United States: "It is not enough to be mad with rage. It is of no help to shout about 'exterminating' Germany. Only one thing helps: the attempt to understand how men have sunk so far, and the firm resolve to face the trouble, the inconvenience and cost of seeing no nation gets the chance to befoul the world like this again" (quoted in B. Zelizer, *Remembering to Forget*, pp. 128–129).

65. In the vocabulary of cultural theory, such a juxtaposition would have created a "metonymical" association that would have upended the "metaphorical" analogies that had formed America's anti-Nazi, war-fighting core, which had aligned the sacred and profane sides of discourse of civil society with the geopolitics of war. For a foundational discussion of the restrictions imposed by analogies of cultural logic, see Levi-Strauss, *The Savage Mind*. For a more contemporary social scientific analysis of such cultural-logic pressures, and their resistance to apparently factual anomalies, see Sahlins, *The Culture of Practical Reason*; for the empirical application of this sense of the tension between metonomy and metaphor to a period of intense social upheaval and change, see Sahlins, *Historical Myths and Mythical Realities*. On the language of cultural theory more generally, see chapter 4.

66. One month after the discovery of the Nazi camps, former U.S. Undersecretary of State Sumner Welles framed the polluting power of the revelations in a representative manner. He acknowledged American responsibility, but only in a limited and indirect way, citing not the nation's prewar anti-Semitism but its isolationist foreign policy. At the same time, despite the evasive ambiguity of such framing, Welles asserted that America, indeed all "free peoples," were compelled for moral reasons to undertake a program of compensation to the Jewish people.

> The crimes committed by the Nazis and by their accomplices against the Jewish people are indelible strains upon the whole of our modern civilization. They are stains which will shame our generation in the eyes of generations still unborn. For we and our governments, to which we have entrusted power during these years between the Great Wars, cannot shake off the responsibility for having permitted the growth of world conditions

which made such horrors possible. The democracies cannot lightly attempt to shirk their responsibility. No recompense can be offered the dead [but] such measure of recompense as can be offered surely constitutes the moral obligation of the free peoples of the earth as soon as their victory is won. ("New Hope for the Jewish People," pp. 511–513)

67. "Anti–anti-Semitism" represents a turn upon Clifford Geertz's phrase, "anti-anti-relativism," which he introduced to indicate that, while not advocating relativism as an epistemological principle, he was, at the same, against antirelativism ("Distinguished Lecture"). Geertz cites, as his guide, the phrase "anti-anti-communism," widely used among progressive Americans in the late '40s and early '50s who, though not pro-communist, strongly opposed the anti-communism that demagogue Joseph McCarthy was projecting at that time. For an earlier, and more detailed discussion of this postwar "anti-anti-Semitism" and how it confronted not only anti-Jewish sentiments but institutional discrimination as well, see Alexander, "On the Social Construction of Moral Universals: The 'Holocaust' from War Crime to Trauma Drama." In that analysis, I also reconstruct the shifting representation of the Nazis' mass murder of the Jews from a heinous atrocity associated with a specific historical event—World War II—to a crime against humanity that was constructed as leaving an indelible and tragic marking, not only on the twentieth century but, more broadly, on modernity as such. I trace, as well, some of the social implications of this transformation, and its institutional causes and effects. This much later separation of Holocaust representations from specific associations with Nazism and World War II, while inverting the association I am emphasizing here, marks a process that could only have initially been stimulated by it.

68. When Leonard Shapiro writes, in *A Time for Healing: American Jewry since World War II*, that "the war saw the merging of Jewish and American fates" such that "Nazi Germany was the greatest enemy of both" (p. 16), he is correct in a literal but not a symbolic sense. Though the fates of Jewish and non-Jewish Americans indeed merged during the war, sharing as they did the same enemy, their sense of this merging—their connectedness via a subjectively shared solidarity—did not emerge until the completion of the war and the revelations of the death camp.

69. As Giesen has shown in "The Drama of Perpetrators," only the "third generation" of postwar Germans were able to accept national responsibility for the Holocaust. His reasoning is that only groups who themselves had no actual connection with the Holocaust were, paradoxically, free to participate fully in its traumatic effects. This seems as well to have been true in France.

70. In 1985, Charles E. Silberman, one of the most acute nonacademic observers of this radical reconstruction of Jews in American society, described the "profound change that has occurred in the position of Jews in American society since the end of World War II" as "wholly unlike anything that any Jewish community has ever

encountered before" (*A Certain People: American Jews and Their Lives Today*, p. 22). Though Silberman himself emphasizes the contrast with America's early treatment of its Jews, it has often been just this kind of appreciation—the sense of a world-historical shift in postwar America—that has caused some observers retrospectively to reread the entire history of Jewish/non-Jewish relations as having been equally unique. In regard to the period before 1945, however, an emphasis on American exceptionalism is not warranted. It misleadingly attributes to American culture and social structure what was, in fact, the result of America's unique role in, and reaction to, the fight against Nazism and its mass murder of the Jews.

71. *New York Times*, October 1, 1945, p. 32.

72. In the following discussion of the magazine literature, I draw from Alexander, "On the Social Construction of Moral Universals."

73. For this film as well as the following discussion of *Gentleman's Agreement*, I draw from Short, *Feature Films as History*.

74. Buck, "Do You Want Your Children to Be Tolerant?" *Better Homes and Gardens*, February 1947, p. 33.

75. Carter, "How to Stop the Hate Mongers in Your Home Town," *Better Homes and Gardens*, November 1947, p. 45.

76. *Saturday Review of Books*, December 13, 1947, p. 20.

77. Perry, "Your Neighbors: the Colombs." *Saturday Evening Post*, November 13, 1948, p. 36, emphasis added.

78. *Life Magazine*, October 13, 1952, p. 96.

79. Harap, *In the Mainstream*, p. 11; and E. Shapiro, *A Time for Healing*, pp. 23–24.

80. Such surveys formed the background for the massive compilation and analysis in Stember.

81. Dinnerstein, "Anti-Semitism Exposed and Attacked, 1945–1950."

82. *American Mercury*, October 1934, pp. 391–399.

83. *New Republic*, August 20, 1945, pp. 208–209.

84. Whitman, "College Fraternity Crisis"; *Collier's*, January 8, 1949, pp. 34–35.

85. E. Shapiro, *Time for Healing*, pp. 8–10.

86. Ibid., pp. 10–15. In 1979, a *Village Voice* writer, Andrew Kopkind, recalled that for his Jewish family in New Haven, Connecticut, Myerson and Greenberg were "secular saints" because "for the first time, the Jews had successfully crossed over from ethnic favorites to national heroes" (quoted on p. 15).

87. For this trope, see S. M. Lipset, *First New Nation*. For the American reaction to Israeli's founding and later wars, see P. Rose, *Ghetto and Beyond*, pp. 3–18; and E. Shapiro, *Time for Healing*, p. 204.

88. Quoted in Sarna, *American Judaism*, pp. 272–273. See also Heinze, "*Peace of Mind*" (1946).

89. Golden, *Only in America* and *For Two Cents Plain*. Both books were published with forewords by the American poet and Lincoln biographer Carl Sandburg, with whom Golden shared progressive and, in the South, highly unpopular racial views. The "Jewish Will Rogers" phrase is by Leonard Shapiro, in *A Time for Healing*, p. 256.

90. For reflections on this American-Jewish concern see the contributions in Kleeblatt, *Too Jewish?* This book accompanied an exhibition curated by the Jewish Museum in Brooklyn that traveled around the country and concluded in the Hammer Museum in Los Angeles. This theme could not have been exhibited, I would suggest, during the 1950s and early 1960s, when the assimilative and hyphenated modes of incorporation were dominant.

91. Brodkin, *How Jews Became White Folks*, p. 10.

92. Handler first encountered the model for Barbie on a visit to Switzerland in 1955, and she found a three-dimensional, adult-looking comic-book character named Lilli sold in German tobacco shops (Ramos, "Barbie Doll Revolutionized Toy Industry").

93. On this phenomenon, see Bloom, *Prodigal Sons;* and E. Shapiro, "Jewishness and the New York Intellectuals." For Trilling, see, e.g., *Liberal Imagination*.

94. Trilling, "Afterword," pp. 319, 320, 322, as quoted in Harap, *In the Mainstream*, p. 5 (emphasis in original). Trilling's public rejection of any connection between his writing and his Jewish "particularity" first emerged in the waning days of the World War II when he declared, in a symposium of younger Jewish literati, that he would "resent it" if any critic were to "discover" in his work "either faults or virtues which he called Jewish" (quoted in *In the Mainstream*, p. 10).

95. For discussion of the New York intellectuals and their Jewishness, see Harap, *In the Mainstream*, pp. 1–22, 173–174; Pinsker, *Jewish-American Fiction, 1917–1987*, pp. xi, 31–38; Podhoretz, *Ex-Friends*, pp. 11–15, 219 and passim; Clayton, *Saul Bellow*, pp. 43–46; and Bloom, *Saul Bellow*, pp. 107–110.

96. Rieff, *Freud*.

97. This ascending movement was symbolized on November 6, 1959, when the *Times Literary Supplement* heralded "A Vocal Group: The Jewish Part in American Letters." In his survey of Jews and American literature in the twentieth century, Harap calls the 1950s "the Jewish decade" (*In the Mainstream*, pp. 21–52).

98. Quoted in Harap, *In the Mainstream*, p. 23.

99. These statements were first published in *Paris Review* in winter 1966 and were quoted by Harap in *In the Mainstream*, p. 106. Though it is true that, in describing the life and times of Augie March, the prototypical child-of-immigrants–urban Jew, Bellow found a much less constrained and original artistic voice, it is also the case that in none of the succession of great novels that followed did Bellow concentrate on explicitly Jewish themes. As Philip Roth later observed about that 1953 novel:

You could, in fact, take the Jew out of the adventurous Augie March without doing much harm to the whole of the book, whereas the same could not be said for taking Chicago out of the boy. [Bellow] connects Augie's health, cheeriness, vigor, stamina, and appetite, as well as his enormous appeal to just about everyone in Cook County, if not in all creation, to his rootedness in a Chicago that is American to the core, a place where being Jewish makes of a boy nothing more special in the Virtue Department than any other immigrant mother's child. ("Imagining Jews," pp. 225–226)

Indeed, Bellow himself would later object that being called an "American Jewish writer" was a "put-down," describing the "label" as "vulgar, unnecessarily parochializing and utterly without value" (quoted in J. Epstein, "Saul Bellow's Chicago," and in Harap, *In the Mainstream*, p. 102).

100. Of Milton Berle, one of the major television comedians of the 1950s who hosted his own Sunday evening comedy hour, Anthony Lewis writes that he "went so far as he could in denying his heritage; he changed his name from Beringer, had his nose 'bobbed' ('a thing of beauty and a goy forever'), and became a Christian Scientist ('for about twenty years')" ("The Jew in Stand-Up Comedy," p. 61). The discrete but intense use of plastic surgery in the 1950s and early 1960s to alter Jewish features, particularly the Jewish nose, demonstrates in the most palpable physical manner how Jewish self-change continued as the other side of the now much more fully realized bargain of assimilation and hyphenation. Exploring "the contradiction that frames the anxiety about the body of the Jew in the Diaspora—a body marked as different even in its sameness," Gilman ("Jew's Body") writes: "The Jew's nose makes the Jewish face visible in the Western Diaspora. That nose is 'seen' as an African nose, relating the image of the Jew to the image of the Black. It was not always because of any overt similarity in the stereotypical representation of the two idealized types of noses, but because each nose is considered a racial sign and as such reflects the internal life ascribed to Jew and African no less than it does physiognomy" (pp. 60–61).

101. N. Glazer, "New Perspectives in American Jewish Sociology," p. 13; Stember et al., *Jews in the Mind of America*, p. 209.

102. African-American philosopher and social critic Cornel West sees "the Jewish entrée into anti-Semitic and . . . exclusivistic institutions of American culture" as a development that "initiated the slow but sure undoing of the . . . WASP cultural hegemony and homogeneity" ("The New Politics of Difference," pp. 124–125). The relationship between the process of Jewish incorporation and the black Civil Rights movement that I discussed in Part III is complex and often controversial. The postwar atmosphere decidedly did not extend to being "with the Negroes," to employ the identity term of that time. Despite President Truman's consequential decision to admit blacks to the armed forces, the nation's struggle to oppose the

legacy of Nazism primarily extended to its most public, bitter, and deeply wounded enemy, the Jews, and not to any other group. Yet scarcely a decade after the conclusion of the war, America's white elites began to respond sympathetically to the black struggle in Montgomery and to the charismatic leadership of Martin Luther King. The ten years between war's end and Montgomery had been a decade of intensive discursive and institutional change vis-à-vis Jews, of public and open agitation against anti-Jewish quotas, and of demands to reconstruct the primordial givens of American civil life. It seems clear that these developments not only informed but helped trigger the black incorporation process that followed immediately in its wake. It is well known, of course, that American Jews as individuals, and American Jewish organizations as well, were conspicuous in their support for the black Civil Rights movement, providing human and material resources and technical advice to black leaders and movements and visible examples of public responsiveness on the white side. It is equally well known that during the late 1960s this coalition broke down. Yet although the emergence of a more difference-centered multiculturalism on both sides had something to do with this—what would later pejoratively be called "identity politics"—much more powerful was the general process of polarization that characterized the cultural politics and political culture of that time.

103. P. Rose, "The Ghetto and Beyond," p. 12, emphasis in original.

104. Ibid., p. 12.

105. Ibid., p. 13.

106. Stember, "The Recent History of Public Attitudes," p. 208.

107. Ibid., p. 211.

108. Quoted in M. Gordon, "Marginality and the Jewish Intellectual," p. 487.

109. Trillin, "Lester Drentluss."

110. The radical implications of this multicultural reconstruction can be appreciated only against the centuries-long approbation that had been levied against this polluted quality of the Jews' alleged physiognomy (see n. 101). In *Reshaping the American Mainstream*, Alba and Nee observe "the decline in the frequency of rhinoplasty, intended to give Jews a less ethnic appearance at the very moment when Jewish-Christian marriages are soaring in number suggests that the mainstream standards of physiognomic attractiveness have expanded" (p. 284). For discussion of Jewish-Gentile intermarriage rates, see below.

111. For discussions of this phenomenon, see Bellman, "The Jewish Mother Syndrome"; Bienstock, "The Changing Image of the American Jewish Mother"; Blau, "In Defense of the Jewish Mother"; Rothbell, "The Jewish Mother: Social Construction of a Popular Image." Jewish feminists later criticized this representation and emphasized its misogynistic implications (e.g., Prell, "Rage and Representation"), but I am emphasizing another dimension here. In her entry on "Stereotypes" in *Jewish Women in America: An Historical Encyclopedia* (pp. 1328–1329), Riv-Ellen

Prell observes that although it was only in the postwar era that the Jewish mother "became the central image" of Jewish representation, it had existed in the American imagination since the first decades of the twentieth century. There is no doubt, as well, that the ethnic mother image played a similar role in the civil reconstruction of other denigrated out-groups.

112. Stember, "The Recent History of Public Attitudes," p. 209; Silberman, *Certain People*, p. 287; Glaser, "Jewish Sociology," p. 13.

113. E. Shapiro, "Jewishness and the New York Intellectuals," p. 256.

114. In a prescient early assessment, Allen Guttmann observed that, "of Jewish writers a generation younger than Saul Bellow and Norman Mailer, [Roth] is the most talented, the most controversial, and the most sensitive to the complexities of assimilation and the question of identity. Roth's first collection of a novella and five stories, *Goodbye, Columbus* (1960 [actually 1959]), received the National Book Award, the praises of those writers generally associated with *Partisan Review* and *Commentary*, and considerable abuse from men institutionally involved in the Jewish community" (*The Jewish Writer in America: Assimilation and the Crisis of Identity*). For later critical overviews, see Cooper, "Confessions of Philip Roth."

115. P. Roth, *I Married a Communist*, pp. 153–154.

116. Cooper comments about this shift in Roth's authorial voice that begins with *Portnoy's Complaint*: "From now on, his characters could sound like the Jews among whom he had been most comfortable in his youth and like those popular comics now teaching rising inflection to the general population" (p. 100). In *The Facts: A Novelist's Autobiography*, Roth speaks about the self-inhibiting restrictions he felt compelled to place on his early writings out of deference to his "apprentice's literary models, particularly from the awesome graduate-school authority of Henry James" and from the "detached irony" of Flaubert (p. 157). It is instructive to compare this with Bellow's parallel confession of early restriction on self-expression, in which Bellow notes specifically his fear of appearing too Jewish, and of the corresponding need to disprove anti-Semitic claims that Jews would never be able to master English prose. Coming to maturity a generation later, Roth's fears—even when he also mentions Flaubert—do not have that anti-Semitic reference. The mode of incorporation has changed.

117. P. Roth, *Portnoy's Complaint*, pp. 36–37.

118. P. Roth, "In Response to Those Who Have Asked Me," p. 35.

119. Syrkin, quoted in *Philip Roth and the Jews*, p. 109, and in Harap, *In the Mainstream*, p. 141.

120. Quoted in Cooper, *Philip Roth and the Jews*, p. 110.

Over the years, reviewers and critics have had a strange response to Philip Roth, one unparalleled in their responses to other writers. It can be found in the titles of their essays, in the drawings that accompany them, in the extent to which these writers have laid aside moderation and taken positions—almost as if their subject were not a writer but some force let loose among them. [Roth's] scalpel has touched a nerve the critic can no longer pretend is not there, or if always acknowledged to be there, not as well insulated as the critic might once have thought. (ibid., pp. 288–289)

121. The early essays in which Roth replied publicly to his critics were collected in Roth's 1975 book *Reading Myself and Others*. This ambivalent, fraught, and sometimes tortured relationship between Roth and the Jewish community has continued to smolder to the present day. In part this is because Roth has been a singularly outspoken public intellectual, continually intervening on highly partisan political issues both in America and abroad. More important, however, it is because Roth's fiction has continued to narrate his post-assimilationist obsession with the Jewish question. At the time of this writing, for example, his 2004 novel, *The Plot against America*, Roth narrates, via a series of not entirely unbelievable contingencies, how the famous aviator Charles Lindberg won the Republican nomination in 1940 and proceeded to upset President Franklin Roosevelt in the general election. President Lindberg then pursued an alliance with Nazi Germany and initiated anti-Semitic measures across the United States before being killed in a mysterious airplane accident that allowed Roosevelt to return to power and restored the progressive path toward Jewish incorporation.

122. P. Roth, "Writing about Jews," p. 161.

123. Cuddahy, *Ordeal of Civility*.

124. Philip Roth, "Imagining Jews," p. 224.

125. Ibid., p. 222.

126. P. Roth, "Some New Jewish Stereotypes," p. 145.

127. P. Roth, "Writing about Jews," p. 151.

128. Ibid., p. 151.

129. Ibid., p. 150.

130. In 1959, in one of the best early critical evaluations of Philip Roth's work, Theodore Solotaroff favorably compared the vitality of Roth's fiction with that of earlier American Jewish novelists and, in doing so, revealed precisely the social considerations I am suggesting here: "The really surprising and elating achievement of Roth's work . . . is the way he has triumphed over the major disabilities of his subject. . . . The Jewish writer's judgment as well as his imagination is likely to find itself being dictated to by his world, which makes so much of morality as well as the main chance that the writer begins to worry about the Jewish heritage, the need for good public relations, the fate of the six million" (reprinted in "Philip Roth and the Jewish Moralists," pp. 13–14).

131. P. Roth, *Reading Myself and Others*, p. 157. The character Sergeant Nathan Marx appears in "Defender of the Faith," published in *Goodbye, Columbus and Five Stories*.

132. P. Roth, "Writing about Jews," p. 165.

133. P. Roth, "Some New Jewish Stereotypes," p. 137.

134. P. Roth, "Writing about Jews," p. 164.

135. Ibid., p. 163.

136. Borowitz, *Mask Jews Wear*, p. 209.

137. See chapter 18.

138. Lawrence Epstein writes in *The Haunted Smile*:

> Though anti-Semitism delayed a fuller assimilation of America's Jews, while they waited they were able to develop a full range of cultural and communal activities, safe from the psychological demands of gentile society and the emotional and sometimes physical demands of dealing with anti-Semites. One principal resource was a ten-by-twenty-five-mile strip of the Catskill region a hundred miles northwest of New York City . . . There, in a thousand hotels and bungalow colonies, Jews could escape the heat of the city and the tensions of trying to fit into the wider American society. They could be themselves. They could eat all they wanted, play all day, relax, look for husbands and wives or more transient romantic partners, and, most of all, laugh. . . . After the war, the Catskill resorts would begin a slow decline, due mostly to a growing acceptance of Jews by the wider society." (pp. 109, 124; see, more generally, pp. 104–125)

139. So did masses of non-Jewish people outside the United States, particularly in Europe, where there emerged a devoted and influential audience for Allen's films. In this manner, the new multicultural take on Jewishness became widely projected throughout the global civil sphere, even if this framework could not have been initiated in a civil sphere outside the United States. It was in the United States that Jewish incorporation first entered a multicultural stage. This complex, uneven and combined play of origin and reception applies, more broadly, to the entire range of multicultural phenomena I have investigated in Part IV. The diffusion of such American patterns as multiculturalism is significant, and there is a "systematic" basis for moving from assimilation to hyphenation and multiculturalism as well—the more repressive modes create instabilities, and the deepening of civil societies allows more variations to be played on primordial forms. Still, there is no warrant for seeing the modes of incorporation as stages in a developmental sense. It is instructive in this regard to compare contemporary Jewish life in American with other national civil spheres. Though there is some discussion of "multiculturalism" in France (see., e.g., Lapeyronnie, *L'Individu et les Minorités*), the principal mode of incorporation remains

assimilation. In France, assimilation is organized around the civil-cum-primordial framework *républicanisme*, an orientation to democratic capabilities that insists upon the subordination, indeed the relative invisibility, of ethnic, racial, religious and other identity-related group particularities vis-à-vis the collectively shared, civil values of the national republic, the "liberty, equality, and fraternity" enshrined by the French Revolution. This *républicain* commitment to assimilation is shared by both center-Left and center-Right, as demonstrated by the more than decade-long state resistance to allowing Muslim girls to wear headscarves to school. Because democratic France does not make space for a multicultural civil sphere, French Jews are much less inclined to publicly exhibit their religious or cultural differences. They are less likely to demand to make specifically "Jewish" demands for recognition in the public sphere. See in this regard Tony Judt's revealing discussion of Raymond Aron as a "thoroughly assimilated . . . Frenchman of Jewish origin with none of the objective or subjective traits of membership in a distinctive Jewish community" (*Burden of Responsibility*, pp. 174–175). Aron remained a vocal and committed supporter of Israel, and because of the restrictive context of French republicanism, he was continually called upon to defend the legitimacy of such support, to explain, in Judt's words, why he, "a nonpracticing, assimilated French Jew, felt unable to break his links with Judaism and Israel, particularly in view of his criticisms of Israeli politics" (p. 177). The assimilative mode of incorporation had so restricted the supply of linguistic resources that Aron could not find a way to justify his support in a legitimate and public manner. "In the final analysis I don't know," he replied: "maybe out of loyalty to my roots and to my forefathers [but] I cannot say more" (p. 177).

140. Virtually every interpreter of the relationship between Woody Allen and Judaism asserts the seamless, unchanging continuity between his comic persona and the iconic figures of Yiddish tradition, such as the *Schlemiel*. See, e.g., Lester Friedman, *Hollywood's Image of the Jew*, p. 274; Whitfield, *American Space, Jewish Time*, p. 36; L. Epstein, *Haunted Smile*, p. xv; Boyer, "*Schlemiezel*"; Wade, *Jewish American Literature since 1945*, pp. 4–5, 139; Berger, *Jewish Jesters*, p. 6 and passim. Such an emphasis, however, makes it difficult to understand the changing reception of Jewish comedy in post-emancipation civil societies, in which modes of incorporation shift and the performance of humor changes in response. For example, even as "traditional" a Yiddish-American writer as Isaac Bashevis Singer protested, "I don't feel I write in the tradition of the 'little man' because their man is actually a victim" (quoted in *Jewish American Literature since 1945*, p. 4). Earl Rovit more accurately describes "the initial Jewish adaptation to the American scene" as "a *naïve* attempt to re-create the old conditions of city life in this baffling New World," as humor that "remained defensive and private, a reserve for one's own bitter amusements in the homely curses muttered under the breath in Yiddish that the customer or employer couldn't possibly understand" ("Jewish Humor and American Life,"

p. 240, emphasis added). In the post-emancipation period, as Jews for the first time experienced the opportunities and dilemmas of incorporation, the tropes of Jewish humor changed, becoming public and making links with non-Jewish national traditions and with broader civil values. "The Yiddish *schlemiel*-figure and the *schnorrer*," Rovit writes, "have their native American counterparts in such eighteenth- and nineteenth-century folk creations as Brother Jonathan and Poor Richard, on the one hand, and The Confidence Man, on the other" (p. 204).

141. The standard critical interpretation of *Annie Hall* is distorted by the "traditionalistic" perspective on what might be called "tropic reproduction" that I described in note 140. Even Lester Friedman, in his far-reaching and scholarly treatment of Jews in film, reads *Annie Hall* as if it simply represented the frustrations and failure of the bumbling *schlemiel* in modern guise. As a result, he interprets the movie as about a love affair "doomed to failure" because of the "cultural and emotional differences" between Annie and Alvy (*Hollywood's Image of the Jew*, p. 280, and, more generally pp. 272–284; see also L. Epstein, *The Haunted Smile*, pp. 187–208). In fact, as I have suggested here, almost exactly the opposite is the case.

142. Describing Woody Allen as not merely a celebrity but a "demi-mythical" figure in American popular culture, Alan Spiegel argues that he attained this "ultimate pop accolade . . . not by underplaying Jewish looks, manners, and backgrounds . . . but precisely by exaggerating these characteristics almost to the point of iconic abstraction" ("The Vanishing Act," p. 258). Lawrence Epstein, in *The Haunted Smile*, writes about how "Gentile audiences" have learned through Woody Allen's films that "they identified with Jews in a profound way" (p. 199). In 1979, two years after *Annie Hall*, Elizabeth Hardwick, a native of Kentucky, was asked by an interviewer whether she considered herself a "Southern writer." The reasons she offered exemplify the new centrality of Jewish qualities I am pointing to here: "Even when I was in college 'down home,' I'm afraid my aim was—if it doesn't sounds too ridiculous—my aim was to be a New York Jewish intellectual. I say 'Jewish' because of their tradition of rational skepticism; and also a certain deracination appeals to me—and their openness to European culture [and] the questioning of the arrangements of society called radicalism" (quoted in *In the Mainstream*, p. 19).

143. For a detailed and sympathetic discussion of the "late twentieth-century awakening" within American Judaism, see Sarna, *American Judaism*, pp. 323–355. Sarna's discussion, however, is narrowly focused. Because it concentrates primarily on religiosity, it underplays the broader movement toward Jewish particularity shared by non-observant and observant American Jews alike, and that corresponds to broader shifts in the mode of incorporation.

144. Glazer, *American Judaism: Second Edition, Revised with a New Introduction*, p. xxiv.

145. Sarna, *American Judaism*, p. 329. For an influential early survey and analysis of Jewish studies in American universities, see Band, "Jewish Studies in American

Liberal Arts Colleges and Universities." For a broad discussion of the Jewish studies movement in contemporary American universities, see E. Shapiro, *A Time for Healing*, pp. 79–93, where Shapiro emphasizes the decidedly nonreligious character of this movement, how broadly it appeals, how central the Holocaust has been to its development, and how it relates to a new comfort with public expressions of Jewish identity.

> Often the most popular Jewish studies undergraduate courses were in the history and literature of the Holocaust. Courses in Jewish feminism were also well received. Jewish studies appealed to Gentiles as well as to Jews, particularly in colleges outside the Northeast. Among those motivated to take these courses were Gentiles who wished to learn about the Jewish background of Christianity and non-Jews who were involved romantically with Jews. Most students enrolled in Jewish studies courses, and virtually all the Jewish studies majors, however, were Jews curious about their roots. A willingness of American Jews to take courses in Jewish studies indicated . . . a willingness of the young to go public with their Jewishness, a trait their parents had not exhibited. Some sought in Jewish studies a vicarious Jewish experience. Studying Jewish culture and Judaism was an alternative to living Jewish lives." (p. 81)

146. *A Certain People*, pp. 224, 207, and 206.

147. The exception, of course, would be Hassidic communities that practice radical and antimodern forms of geographical, economic, cultural, and to some extent political withdrawal from civic life.

148. Quoted in Silberman, *Certain People*, p. 207. Note how the same criticism of the misplaced attention to anti-Semitism in a post-assimilation era was made during the same period by Philip Roth.

149. Sleeper, "Introduction," in Sleeper and Mintz, *New Jews*, p. 7.

150. See, e.g., the contributions in Bayme, *Facing the Future*.

151. The same can be said, of course, for other American minority groups whose relationship to the majority has been reconstituted under the multicultural mode. Among nonwhite racial groups, women, and gays and lesbians, there has been increasing discussion about whether incorporation comes at the expense of difference even inside a multicultural society. For a recent and insightful sociological study of this dialectic, see Seidman, *Beyond the Closet*. It is this new and deepening dialectic between difference and identification that explains recent claims for the revival of the idea of "assimilation" in recent American sociology, despite the tendency for that term to conceal what is really new about the multicultural mode. See chapter 17, note 64.

152. Ellenson, *After Emancipation*, p. 41.

153. This statement was made by Rabbi Sol Roth, professor at Yeshiva University and newly elected president of the Rabbinical Council of America, who called for the elimination "from leadership roles in Jewish public life of all those who marry out of their faith and rabbis who perform marriages between Jews and non-Jews" (quoted in Yaffe, "Intermarriage Abettors").

154. For positions on, and overviews of, these often highly charged demographic debates, see Sklare, "Intermarriage and Jewish Survival" and *America's Jews*, pp. 201–206; Bergman, "American Jewish Population Erosion," pp. 9–19; A. Schwartz, "Intermarriage in the United States"; Goldsheider, *Jewish Continuity and Change*; Silberman, *Certain People*, pp. 293–297; and Glazer, "New Perspectives in American Jewish Sociology."

155. In the most recent and ambitious synthetic overview of the incorporation of out-groups into American life, Alba and Nee confirm these shifting statistics on Jewish-Gentile intermarriage, and argue that such "intermarriage cannot be understood simply as an assimilation of the Anglo-conformity type, a passing of minority individuals into the religion of the dominant group." After noting that about one-third of the Jewish-Christian couples participate in Jewish congregations and "raise their children as Jews," and that even some among "those who have adopted a Christian religious identity also participate in some Jewish rituals," they observe that "the once sharp religious boundary has been blurred, in the sense that rituals from both traditions are practiced."

> What is especially telling is that, in a society that once defined itself as Christian, even Protestant, and evinced substantial anti-Semitism, Christian and Jewish families accept that their sons and daughters marry across a historical religious chasm and raise their children in the other religion. This can occur on a large scale only if the chasm has been filled in. (*Remaking the American Mainstream*, p. 283)

BIBLIOGRAPHY

Abernathy, Ralph. 1979 [1970]. "Our Lives Were Filled with Action." In *Martin Luther King, Jr.,* ed. C. Eric Lincoln, pp. 219–227. New York: Hill and Wang.

Abramowitz, Shalom [Mendele Mocher Sforim]. 1975 [1890]. "Shem and Japheth on the Train." In *Modern Hebrew Literature,* ed. R. Alter, pp. 15–38. West Orange, N.J.: Behrman House.

Abramson, Paul R., John H. Aldrich, and David W. Rohde. 1995. *Change and Continuity in the 1992 Elections.* 2nd ed. Washington, D.C.: Congressional Quarterly Press.

Ackerman, Bruce. 1980. *Social Justice in the Liberal State.* New Haven, Conn.: Yale University Press.

———. 1991. *We the People.* Vol. 1: *Foundations.* Cambridge, Mass.: Harvard University Press.

Adams, Brooks. 1906. "The Modern Conception of Animus." *Green Bag* 19: 12–33.

Adler, Peter. 1974. "Beyond Cultural Identity: Reflections on Cultural and Multicultural Man." In *Intercultural Communication: A Reader,* ed. Larry A. Samovar and Richard E. Porter, pp. 262–380. Belmont, Calif.: Wadsworth.

Agnew, John A. 1987. *Place and Politics: The Geographical Mediation of State and Society.* Boston: Allen and Unwin.

———. 2002. *Place and Politics in Modern Italy.* Chicago: University of Chicago Press.

Agnew, John A., and Jonathan M. Smith, eds. 2002. *American Space/American Place: Geographies of the Contemporary United States.* New York: Routledge.

Alba, Richard D. 1990. *Ethnic Identity: The Transformation of White America.* New Haven, Conn.: Yale University Press.

Alba, Richard D., and Victor Nee. 2003. *Remaking the American Mainstream: Assimilation and Contemporary Immigration.* Cambridge, Mass.: Harvard University Press.

Aldrich, John H. 1995. *Why Parties? The Origin and Transformation of Political Parties in America.* Chicago: University of Chicago Press.

Alexander, Jeffrey C. 1980. "Core Solidarity, Ethnic Outgroup, and Social Differentiation: A Multidimensional Model of Inclusion in Modern Societies." In *National and Ethnic Movements,* ed. Jacques Dofny and Akinsola Akiwowo, pp. 5–28. Beverly Hills, Calif.: Sage.

———. 1981. "The Mass News Media in Systemic, Historical, and Comparative Perspective." In *Mass Media and Social Change,* ed. E. Katz and T. Szecsko, pp. 17–52. London: Sage.

———. 1982. *Theoretical Logic in Sociology.* Vol. I: *Antinomies of Classical Thought: Marx and Durkheim.* Berkeley: University of California Press, Routledge Kegan Paul.

———. 1982. *Theoretical Logic in Sociology.* Vol. III: *The Classical Attempt at Synthesis: Max Weber.* Berkeley: University of California Press, Routledge Kegan Paul.

———. 1984. *Theoretical Logic in Sociology.* Vol. IV: *Modern Reconstruction of Classical Thought: Talcott Parsons.* Los Angeles: University of California Press.

———. 1984. "Three Models of Culture and Society Relations: Toward an Analysis of Watergate." *Sociological Theory* 3: 290–314.

———. 1985. "Habermas' New Critical Theory: Its Promise and Problems." *American Journal of Sociology* 91: 400–434.

———. 1987. "The Dialectic of Individuation and Domination: Weber's Rationalization Theory and Beyond." In *Max Weber, Rationality, and Modernity,* ed. Scott Lash and Sam Whimster. London: Allen and Unwin.

———. 1987. *Twenty Lectures: Sociological Theory after World War II.* New York: Columbia University Press.

———. 1988. "Action and Its Environments." *Action and Its Environments: Towards a New Synthesis,* pp. 301–333. New York: Columbia University Press.

———. 1990. "Analytic Debates: Understanding the Relative Autonomy of Culture." In *Culture and Society: Contemporary Debates,* ed. Jeffrey Alexander and Steven Seidman, pp. 1–27. New York: Cambridge University Press.

———. 1990. "Differentiation Theory: Problems and Prospects." In *Differentiation Theory and Social Change,* ed. Jeffrey Alexander and Paul Colomy, pp. 1–16. New York: Columbia University Press.

———. 1990. "Morale e Repressione." *Mondoperai* 12: 127–130.

———. 1991. "Bringing Democracy Back In: Universalistic Solidarity and the Civil Sphere." In *Intellectuals and Politics: Social Theory in a Changing World,* ed. C. Lemert, pp. 157–176. London: Sage.

———. 1991. "The Deceptiveness of Morality." In *Due Dimensioni Della Societa l'Utile e la Morale,* ed. C. Mongardini, pp. 41–50.

———. 1992. "The Fragility of Progress: An Interpretation of the Turn toward Meaning in Eisenstadt's Later Work." *Acta Sociologica* 35: 85–94.

———. 1992. "Citizen and Enemy as Symbolic Classification: On the Polarizing Discourse of Civil Society." In *Cultivating Differences: Symbolic Boundaries and the Making of Inequality,* ed. Michele Lamont and Marcel Fournier, pp. 289–308. Chicago: University of Chicago Press.

———. 1992. "General Theory in the Post-positivist Mode: The 'Epistemological Dilemma' and the Search for Present Reason." In *Postmodernism and Social Theory,* ed. Steven Seidman and David Wagner. New York: Blackwell.

———. 1993. "The Return to Civil Society." *Contemporary Sociology* 22 (6): 797–803.

———. 1995. *Fin-de-Siècle Social Theory: Rationality, Reduction, and the Problem of Reason.* New York: Verso.

———. 1996. "Collective Action, Culture, and Civil Society: Secularizing, Updating, Inverting, Revising and Displacing the Classical Model of Social Movements." In *Alain Touraine,* ed. M. Diani and J. Clarke, pp. 205–234. London: Falmer.

———. 1998. *Neofunctionalism and After.* London: Blackwell.

———. 1998. "Bush, Hussein, and the Cultural Preparation for War: Toward a More Symbolic Theory of Political Legitimation." *Epoch* 21: 1–13.

———. 2000. "This Worldly Mysticism: Inner Peace and World Transformation in the Work and Life of Charles 'Skip' Alexander." *Journal of Adult Development* 7 (4): 267–272.

———. 2000. "Contradictions: The Uncivilizing Pressures of Space, Time, and Function." *Soundings* 16 (autumn): 96–112.

———. 2000. "Theorizing the Good Society: Hermeneutic, Normative, and Empirical Discourses." *Canadian Journal of Sociology* 25 (3): 271–310.

———. 2001. "The Long and Winding Road: Civil Repair of Intimate Injustice." *Sociological Theory* 19 (3): 371–400.

———. 2001. "Towards a Sociology of Evil: Getting beyond Modernist Common Sense about the Alternative to the Good." In *Rethinking Evil, Contemporary Perspectives,* ed. Maria Pia Lara. Berkeley: University of California Press.

———. 2002. "On the Social Construction of Moral Universals: The Holocaust from Mass Murder to Trauma Drama." *European Journal of Social Theory* 5 (1): 5–86.

———. 2003. "The Strong Program in Cultural Sociology: Elements of a Structural Hermeneutics." In *The Meanings of Social Life: A Cultural Sociology,* Jeffrey C. Alexander, pp. 11–16. New York: Oxford University Press.

———. 2003. "Watergate as Democratic Ritual." In *The Meanings of Social Life: A Cultural Sociology,* pp. 155–178. New York: Oxford University Press.

———. 2003. *The Meanings of Social Life: A Cultural Sociology.* New York: Oxford University Press.

————. 2004. "Cultural Pragmatics: Social Performance between Ritual and Strategy." *Sociological Theory* 22 (4): 527–573.

————. 2004. "Rethinking Strangeness." *Thesis Eleven* 79: 87–104.

————. 2004. 'Towards a Theory of Cultural Trauma." In *Cultural Trauma and Collective Identity*, Jeffrey C. Alexander, Ron Eyerman, Bernhard Giesen, Neil J. Smelser, and Piotr Sztompka, pp. 1–30. Berkeley: University of California Press.

————. 2005. "Why Cultural Sociology Is Not Idealist: A Response to McClennan." *Theory, Culture, and Society* 22 (6): 19–29.

————. 2005. "Contradictions in the Societal Community: The Promise and Disappointments of Parsons' Concept." In *After Parsons*, ed. V. Lidz, R. Fox, and H. Bershady, pp. 93–110. New York: Russell Sage.

————. Forthcoming. "Iconic Experience in Art and Life: Beginning with Giacometti's 'Standing Woman.' " *Theory, Culture, and Society*.

————, ed. 1988. *Durkheimian Sociology: Cultural Studies*. New York: Cambridge University Press.

————, ed. 1998. *Real Civil Societies: Dilemmas of Institutionalization*. London: Sage.

Alexander, Jeffrey C., and Colin Loader. 1985. "Max Weber on Church and Sect in North America: An Alternative Path toward Rationalization." *Sociological Theory* 3 (1): 1–6.

————. 1989. "The Cultural Grounds of Rationalization: Sect Democracy versus the Iron Cage." In *Structure and Meaning: Relinking Classical Sociology*, Jeffrey C. Alexander. New York: Columbia University Press.

Alexander, Jeffrey C., and Paul Colomy. 1988. *Action and Its Environments*. New York: Columbia University Press.

————, eds. 1990. *Differentiation Theory and Social Change: Comparative and Historical Perspectives*. New York: Columbia University Press.

Alexander, Jeffrey C., and Ronald Jacobs. 1998. "Mass Communication, Ritual, and Civil Society." In *Media, Ritual and Identity*, ed. T. Liebes and J. Curran, pp. 23–41. London: Routledge.

Alexander, Jeffrey C., Ron Eyerman, Bernhard Giesen, Neil Smelser, and Piotr Sztompka, 2004. *Cultural Trauma and Collective Identity*. Berkeley: University of California Press.

Alexander, Jeffrey C., and Philip Smith. 1993. "The Discourse of American Civil Society: A New Proposal for Cultural Studies." *Theory and Society* 22 (2): 151–207.

————. 1996. "Social Science and Salvation: Risk Society as Mythical Discourse." *Zeitschrift fur Soziologie* 25 (4): 251–262.

————. 2005. "Introduction: The New Durkheim." In *The Cambridge Companion to Durkheim*, ed. Jeffrey C. Alexander and Philip Smith. New York: Cambridge University Press.

————, eds. 2005. *The Cambridge Companion to Durkheim*. New York: Cambridge University Press.

Alexander, Jeffrey C., Bernhard Giesen, and Jason Mast, eds. 2006. *Social Performance: Symbolic Action, Cultural Pragmatics, and Ritual*. New York: Cambridge University Press.

Alford, Robert R., and Roger Friedland. 1985. *The Powers of Theory: Capitalism, the State, and Democracy*. New York: Cambridge University Press.

Allen, John W. 1957 [1928]. *A History of Political Thought in the Sixteenth Century*. London: Methuen.

Allen, Woody. 1982. *Four Films of Woody Allen*. New York: Random House.

Altschuler, Glenn C., and Stuart M. Blumin. 2000. *Rude Republic: Americans and Their Politics in the Nineteenth Century*. Princeton, N.J.: Princeton University Press.

American Anti-Slavery Society. 1995 [1848]. *Declaration of Sentiments*. Seneca Falls, N.Y., July 19–20. Reprinted in "Documents: Claiming Rights II." In *Women's America: Refocusing the Past*, ed. Linda K. Kerber and Jane Sherron De Hart. Oxford: Oxford University Press.

American Mercury. 1934. October, pp. 391–399.

Anderson, Benedict R. 1983. *Imagined Communities: Reflections on the Origin and Spread of Nationalism*. London: Verso.

Anderson, Elijah. 1990. *Streetwise: Race, Class, and Change in an Urban Community*. Chicago: University of Chicago Press.

Andrews, Kenneth T. 1997. "The Impacts of Social Movements on the Political Process: The Civil Rights Movement and Black Electoral Politics in Mississippi." *American Sociological Review* 62 (5): 800–819.

Anthony, Susan B. 1995 [1876]. "Declaration of Rights for Women by the National Woman Suffrage Association." Republished in "Document: The Women's Centennial Agenda, 1876." In *Women's America: Refocusing the Past*, ed. Linda K. Kerber and Jane Sherron De Hart. Oxford: Oxford University Press.

Appleby, Joyce O. 1984. *Capitalism and a New Social Order: The Republican Vision of the 1790s*. New York: New York University Press.

Apter, David E. 1987. "Mao's Republic." *Social Research* 54: 691–729.

Apter, David E., and Tony Saich. 1994. *Revolutionary Discourse in Mao's Republic*. Cambridge, Mass.: Harvard University Press.

Arad, Gulie Ne'eman. 2000. *America, Its Jews, and the Rise of Nazism*. Bloomington: Indiana University Press.

Arato, Andrew. 1981. "Civil Society against the State: Poland 1980–81." *Telos* 47: 23.

Arblaster, Anthony. 2002. *Democracy*, 3rd ed. Buckingham, England: Open University Press.

Archer, Margaret S. 2000. *Being Human: The Problem of Agency*. New York: Cambridge University Press.

Arendt, Hannah. 1951. *Anti-Semitism*. New York: Harcourt Brace.

———. 1951. *The Origins of Totalitarianism*. New York: Harcourt, Brace.

———. 1958. *The Human Condition.* Chicago: University of Chicago Press.

———. 1963. *On Revolution.* New York: Viking.

Aristotle. 1962. *The Politics of Aristotle,* trans. Ernest Barker. New York: Oxford University Press.

Aron, Raymond. 1969. "Social Class, Political Class, Ruling Class." In *European Journal of Sociology* 1 (2): 260–81.

———. 1974. *Imperial Republic: The United States and the World, 1945–1973.* Englewood Cliffs, N.J.: Prentice-Hall.

———. 1975. *History and the Dialectic of Violence.* New York: Harper and Row.

———. 1983. *Clausewitz: Philosopher of War.* London: Routledge and Kegan Paul.

Ashcroft, Bill, Gareth Griffiths, and Helen Tiffin, eds. 1995. *The Post-Colonial Studies Reader.* London: Routledge.

Austin, John 1954 [1832]. *The Province of Jurisprudence Determined; The Uses of the Study of Jurisprudence.* London: Noonday.

Austin, J. L. 1957. *How to Do Things with Words.* Cambridge, Mass.: Harvard University Press.

Bailyn, Bernard. 1967. *The Ideological Origins of the American Revolution.* Cambridge, Mass.: Harvard University Press.

Baiocchi, G. 2006. "The Civilizing Force of Social Movements: Corporate and Liberal Codes in Brazil's Public Sphere." *Sociological Theory* 24.

Baker, C. Edwin. 1975. "The Ideology of the Economic Analysis of Law." *Philosophy and Public Affairs* 5: 3.

Baker, Houston A., Jr. 1995. "Critical Memory and the Black Public Sphere." In *The Black Public Sphere: A Public Culture Book,* ed. Black Public Sphere Collective. Chicago: University of Chicago Press.

Baker, Keith. 1990. *Inventing the French Revolution: Essays on French Political Culture in the Eighteenth Century.* New York: Cambridge University Press.

Baker, Russell. 1998. "Bravest and Best." *New York Review of Books* 6, April 9.

Bakhtin, Mikhail Mikhailovich. 1986. *Speech Genres and Other Late Essays.* Trans. Vern W. McGee, and edited by Caryl Emerson and Michael Holquist. Austin: University of Texas Press.

Band, Arnold J. 1966. "Jewish Studies in American Liberal Arts Colleges and Universities." *American Jewish Year Book.* 67: 3–30. New York: American Jewish Committee.

Banfield, Edward C. 1958. *The Moral Basis of a Backward Society.* New York: Free Press.

Banton, Michael. 1968. "Voluntary Associations." In *The International Encyclopedia of the Social Sciences,* ed. David L. Sills, p. 357. New York: Macmillan.

Barber, Bernard. 1983. *The Logic and Limits of Trust.* New Brunswick, N.J.: Rutgers University Press.

Bardwick, Judith M. 1979. *In Transition: How Feminism, Sexual Liberation, and the Search for Self-Fulfillment Have Altered Our Lives.* New York: Holt, Rinehart, and Winston.

Barnavi, Eli. ed. 1992. *A Historical Atlas of the Jewish People from the Time of the Patriarchs to the Present.* London: Hutchinson.

Baron, Solo. 1928. "The Ghetto and Emancipation: Shall We Revise the Traditional View?" *Menorah Journal* (June): 1–12.

Barthes, Roland. 1972. *Mythologies.* Trans. Annette Lavers. New York: Hill and Wang.

———. 1977. "Introduction to the Structural Analysis of Narratives." In *Image, Music, Text,* trans. Stephen Heath. New York: Hill and Wang.

———. 1983. *The Fashion System.* Trans. Matthew Ward and Richard Howard. New York: Farrar, Straus, and Giroux.

Barzilay, Joshua. "Naphtali Herz [Hartwig] Wessely." *Encyclopedia Judaica* 16: 461–463.

Bataille, Georges. 1989. *Theory of Religion.* Trans. Robert Hurley. New York: Zone Books.

———. 1990 [1957]. *Literature and Evil.* London: Boyars.

Bauman, Zygmunt. 1989. *Modernity and the Holocaust.* Ithaca, N.Y.: Cornell University Press.

———. 1993. *Postmodern Ethics.* London: Blackwell.

———. 1995. "Making and Unmaking of Strangers." *Thesis Eleven* 43: 1–16.

———. 1998. "On the Postmodern Uses of Sex." *Theory, Culture, and Society* 15 (3): 19–34.

Bayme, Steven, ed. 1989. *Facing the Future: Essays on Contemporary Jewish Life.* Hoboken, N.J.: KTAV.

Bazin, André. 1967. *What Is Cinema?* Berkeley: University of California Press.

Beilharz, Peter. 2000. *Zygmunt Bauman: Dialectic of Modernity.* London: Sage.

Bell, Daniel. 1976. *The Cultural Contradictions of Capitalism.* New York: Basic Books.

———, ed. 1963. "Interpretation of American Politics." In *The Radical Right,* pp. 47–74. New York: Doubleday.

Bellah, Robert N. 1970. "Civil Religion in America." *Beyond Belief: Essays on Religion in a Post-Traditional World,* pp. 168–189. New York: Harper and Row.

———. 1970. *Beyond Belief: Essays on Religion in a Post-Traditional World.* New York: Harper and Row.

Bellah, Robert, et al. 1985. *Habits of the Heart: Individualism and Commitment in American Life.* Berkeley: University of California Press.

Belliotti, Raymond A. 1992. *Justifying Law: The Debate over Foundations, Goals, and Methods.* Philadelphia: Temple University Press.

Bellman, Samuel I. 1965. "The Jewish Mother Syndrome." *Congress Bi-Weekly* (December 22): 3–5.

Bendix, Reinhard. 1964. *Nation-Building and Citizenship: Studies of Our Changing Social Order*. New York: Wiley.

———. 1978. *Kings or People: Power and the Mandate to Rule*. Berkeley: University of California Press.

Bendix, Reinhard, and Seymour M. Lipset, eds. 1953. *Class, Status, and Power: Social Stratification in Comparative Perspective*. New York: Free Press.

Benhabib, Seyla. 1986. *Critique, Norm and Utopia: A Study of the Foundations of Critical Theory*. New York: Columbia University Press.

———. 1992. *Situating the Self: Gender, Community, and Postmodernism in Contemporary Ethics*. New York: Routledge.

———. 2002. *The Claims of Culture: Equality and Diversity in the Global Era*. Princeton, N.J.: Princeton University Press.

———. 2003. *The Reluctant Modernism of Hannah Arendt*. Lanham, Md.: Rowman and Littlefield.

———. 1996. "Toward a Deliberative Model of Democratic Legitimacy." *Democracy and Difference: Contesting the Boundaries of the Political*, pp. 67–94. Princeton, N.J.: Princeton University Press.

Bennett, W. Lance. 1979. "Imitation, Ambiguity, and Drama in Political Life: Civil Religion and the Dilemmas of Public Morality." *Journal of Politics* 41: 106–133.

Bercovitch, Sacvan. 1978. *The American Jeremiad*. Madison: University of Wisconsin Press.

Berelson, Bernard B., Paul F. Lazarsfeld, and William McPhee. 1954. *Voting: A Study of Opinion Formation in a Presidential Campaign*. Chicago: University of Chicago Press.

Berezin, Mabel. 1998. "Uncivil Society; Putnam's 'Italy' and the Other Side of Association." Unpublished paper presented at the Conference on the Discourses of Civil Society, University of California at Los Angeles, Center for Modern and Contemporary Studies, June 12.

———. Forthcoming. *Democracy and Security: Populism in the New Europe*. Cambridge: Cambridge University Press.

Berger, Arthur Asa. 2001. *Jewish Jesters: A Study in American Popular Comedy*. Cresskill, N.J.: Hampton Press.

Bergman, Elihu. 1977. "The American Jewish Population Erosion." *Midstream* 13 (8): 9–19.

Bernstein, Richard J. 1996. *Hannah Arendt and the Jewish Question*. Cambridge, England: Polity.

Berr, Isaac. 1995. "Letter of a Citizen to His Fellow Jews [1791]. In *The Jew in the Modern World: A Documentary History*, ed. Paul Mendes-Flohr and Jehuda Reinharz. New York: Oxford University Press.

Bertelson, Arthur B. 1967. "Keeper of a Monster." In *Race and the News Media*, ed. Paul L. Fisher and Ralph L. Lowenstein. New York: Frederick A. Praeger.

Bhabha, Homi. 1995. "Signs Taken for Wonders." in *The Post-Colonial Studies Reader,* ed. Bill Ashcroft, Gareth Griffiths, and Helen Tiffin, pp. 29–35. London: Routledge.

Biale, David, Michael Galchinsky, and Susannah Heschel, eds. 1998. *Insider/Outsider: American Jews and Multiculturalism.* Berkeley: University of California Press.

Bienstock, Beverly Gray. 1979. "The Changing Image of the American Jewish Mother." In *Changing Images of the Family,* ed. Virginia Tufte and Barbara Myerhoff. New Haven, Conn.: Yale University Press.

Biernacki, Richard. 1995. *The Fabrication of Labor: Germany and Britain, 1640–1914.* Berkeley: University of California Press.

Birdwell, Michael E. 1999. *Celluloid Soldiers: The Warner Bros. Campaign against Nazism.* New York: New York University Press.

Birmingham News, August 18, 1963.

Blackburn, Robin, ed. 1972. *Ideology in Social Science; Readings in Critical Social Theory.* London: Fontana.

Blackstone, William, Sir. 1979. *Commentaries on the Laws of England: a Facsimile of the First Edition of 1765–1769,* Vol. 1. Chicago: University of Chicago Press.

———. 2000. "Documents: The Law of Domestic Relations: Marriage, Divorce, Dower." In *Women's America: Refocusing the Past,* 5th ed., ed. Linda K. Kerber and Jane Sherron De Hart. New York: Oxford University Press.

Blau, Joseph L. 1966. *Modern Varieties of Judaism.* New York: Columbia University Press.

Blau, Zena Smith. 1967. "In Defense of the Jewish Mother." *Midstream* 13: 42–49.

Blauner, Robert. 1972. *Racial Oppression in America.* New York: Harper and Row.

Bloch, Ruth. 1978. "Untangling the Roots of Modern Sex Roles: A Survey of Four Centuries of Change." *Signs* 4 (December): 37–58.

———. 1985. *Visionary Republic: Millennial Themes in American Thought 1756–1800.* New York: Cambridge University Press.

Bloom, Alexander. 1986. *Prodigal Sons: The New York Intellectuals and Their World.* New York: Oxford University Press.

Bloom, Harold, ed. 1986. *Saul Bellow.* New York: Chelsea House Publishers.

Blumer, Hebert, and Alfred McClung Lee. 1951 [1939]. "Collective Behavior." In *Principles of Sociology.* Herbert Blumer and Alfred McClung Lee. New York: Barnes and Noble.

Bobbio, Norberto. 1987. *La Democracia Socialista.* San Antonio: Ediciones Documentas, 24.

———. 1987. *The Future of Democracy: A Defense of the Rules of the Game.* Trans. Roger Griffin, edited by Richard Bellamy. Minneapolis: University of Minnesota Press.

———. 1988. "Gramsci and the Concept of Civil Society." In *Civil Society and the State,* ed. John Keane. London: Verso.

Bodian, Miriam. 1997. *Hebrews of the Portuguese Nation: Conversos and Community in Early Modern Amsterdam*. Bloomington: Indiana University Press.

Boerne, L. 1995 [1832]. "Because I Am a Jew I Love Freedom." In *The Jew in the Modern World: A Documentary History,* ed. Paul Mendes-Flohr and Jehuda Reinharz. New York: Oxford University Press.

Bogard, William. 1996. *The Simulation of Surveillance: Hyper-control in Telematic Societies*. New York: Cambridge University Press.

Boltanski, Luc. 1999. *Distant Suffering: Morality, Media, and Politics*. New York: Cambridge University Press.

Boltanski, Luc, and Laurent Thevenot. 1991. *De la Justification: Les économies de la grandeur*. Paris: Gallimard.

Bonacich, Edna. 1972. "A Theory of Ethnic Antagonism: The Split Labor Market." *American Sociological Review* 37: 547–559.

Boone, Buford. 1967. "Southern Newsmen and Local Pressure." In *Race and the News Media,* ed. Paul L. Fisher and Ralph L. Lowenstein. New York: Frederick A. Praeger.

Booth, Wayne C. 1988. *The Company We Keep: An Ethics of Fiction*. Berkeley: University of California Press.

Borowitz, Eugene. 1973. *The Mask Jews Wear: The Self-Deceptions of American Jewry*. New York: Simon and Schuster.

Bourdieu, Pierre. 1977. *Outline of a Theory of Practice*. Cambridge, England: Cambridge University Press.

———. 1980. "L'opinion publique n'existe pas." In *Questions de Sociologie,* pp. 222–235. Paris: Editions de Minuit.

———. 1984. *Distinction: A Social Critique of the Judgment of Taste*. Cambridge, Mass.: Harvard University Press.

———. 1989. *La Noblesse d'État*. Paris: Editions de Minuit.

———. 1998. *Acts of Resistance: Against the Tyranny of the Market*. New York: Free Press.

———. 1998. "On Television." In *Acts of Resistance: Against the Tyranny of the Market*. New York: Free Press.

———. 1998. "Return to Television." In *Acts of Resistance: Against the Tyranny of the Market,* pp. 70–77. New York: Press.

Boydston, Jeanne. 1990. *Home and Work: Housework, Wages, and the Ideology of Labor in the Early Republic*. New York: Oxford University Press.

———. 1995. "The Pastorialization of Housework." In *Women's America: Refocusing the Past,* ed. Linda K. Kerber and Jane Sherron De Hart. Oxford: Oxford University Press.

Boyer, Jay. 1993. "The *Schlemiezel*: Black Humor and the *Shtetl* Tradition." In *Semites and Stereotypes: Characteristics of Jewish Humor,* ed. Avner Ziv and Anat Zajdman. Westport, Conn.: Greenwood.

Branch, Taylor. 1988. *Parting the Waters: America in the King Years, 1954–63.* New York: Simon and Schuster.

———. 1998. *Pillar of Fire: American in the King Years, 1963–65.* New York: Simon and Schuster.

Brinton, Mary C., and Victor Nee, eds. 1998. *The New Institutionalism in Sociology.* New York: Russell Sage Foundation.

Brodkin, Karen. 1998. *How Jews Became White Folks: And What That Says about Race in America.* New Brunswick, N.J.: Rutgers University Press.

Brooks, Clem, and Jeff Manza. 1997. "The Social and Ideological Bases of Middle-Class Political Realignment in the United States, 1972–1992." *American Sociological Review* 62 (April): 191–208.

Brooks, Peter. 1984 [1976]. *The Melodramatic Imagination: Balzac, Henry James, Melodrama, and the Mode of Excess.* New York: Columbia University Press.

———. 1996. "Storytelling Without Fear? Confession in Law and Literature?" In *Law's Stories: Narrative and Rhetoric in the Law,* ed. Peter Brooks and Paul Gewirtz. New Haven, Conn.: Yale University Press.

———. 2000. *Troubling Confessions: Speaking Guilt in Law and Literature.* Chicago: University of Chicago Press.

———. 2005. *Realist Vision.* New Haven, Conn.: Yale University Press.

Brown, E. Barkley. 1995. "Negotiating and Transforming the Public Sphere: African American Political Life in the Transition from Slavery to Freedom." In *The Black Public Sphere: A Public Culture Book,* ed. Black Public Sphere Collective. Chicago: University of Chicago Press.

Brubaker, Rogers. 1992. *Citizenship and Nationhood in France and Germany.* Cambridge, Mass.: Harvard University Press.

———. 1996. *Nationalism Reframed: Nationhood and the National Question in the New Europe.* New York: Cambridge University Press.

———. 1996. "Nationhood and the National Question in the Soviet Union and Its Successor States: An Institutionalist Account." In *Nationalism Reframed: Nationhood and the National Question in the New Europe,* pp. 23–54. New York: Cambridge University Press.

———. 2001. "The Return of Assimilation? Changing Perspectives on Immigration and Its Sequels in France, Germany, and the United States." *Ethnic and Racial Studies* 24 (4): 531–548.

Bryce, James. 1922 [1896]. *The American Commonwealth.* Abridged ed. New York: Macmillan.

Buck, Pearl S. 1947. "Do You Want Your Children To Be Tolerant?" *Better Homes and Gardens,* February, p. 33.

Burckhardt, Jacob. 1958 [1860]. *The Civilization of the Renaissance in Italy.* New York: Harper and Row.

Burns, Michael. 1991. *Dreyfus, A Family Affair: 1789–1945.* New York: Harper Collins.

Burns, Stewart. 1997. "Overview . . . The Proving Ground." In *Daybreak of Free-dom: The Montgomery Bus Boycott,* ed. Stewart Burns, pp. 1–38. Chapel Hill: University of North Carolina Press.

———, ed. 1997. *Daybreak of Freedom: The Montgomery Bus Boycott.* Chapel Hill: University of North Carolina Press.

Butler, Judith. 1990. *Gender Trouble: Feminism and the Subversion of Identity.* London: Routledge.

———. 1993. "Critically Queer." *GLQ* 1: 17–32

———. 1997. *Excitable Speech: A Politics of the Performative.* London: Routledge.

Caillois, Roger. 1959. *Man and the Sacred.* New York: Free Press.

Calhoun, Craig. 1992. "Culture, History, and the Problem of Specificity in Social Theory. In *Postmodernism and Social Theory,* ed. S. Seidman and D. Wagner, pp. 244–288. Cambridge, Mass.: Blackwell.

———. 1995. *Critical Social Theory: Culture, History, and the Challenge of Difference.* Cambridge, Mass.: Blackwell.

———. 1995. "The Politics of Identity and Recognition." *Critical Social Theory: Culture, History, and the Challenge of Difference.* Cambridge, Mass.: Blackwell.

Cameron, Craig M. 1994. *American Samurai: Myth, Imagination, and the Conduct of Battle in the First Marine Division, 1941–1951.* New York: Cambridge University Press.

Campbell, Angus, et. al. 1966. *Elections and the Political Order.* New York: John Wiley and Sons.

Carlebach, Elisheva. 2001. *Divided Souls: Converts from Judaism in Early Modern Germany, 1500–1750.* New Haven, Conn.: Yale University Press.

Carson, Clayborne. 1986. "Civil Rights Reform and the Black Freedom Struggle." In *The Civil Rights Movement in America,* ed. C. Eagles. Jackson: University Press of Mississippi.

Carter, Hodding. 1947. "How to Stop the Hate Mongers in Your Home Town." *Better Homes and Gardens,* November, p. 45.

Cartledge, Paul. 1993. *The Greeks: A Portrait of Self and Others.* Oxford: Oxford University Press.

Cawelti, John G. 1968. "From Rags to Respectability: Horatio Alger." In *The National Temper: Readings in American History,* ed. Lawrence W. Levine and Robert Middlekauff, pp. 207–222. New York: Harcourt, Brace, and World.

———. 1976. *Adventure, Mystery, and Romance: Formula Stories as Art and Popular Culture.* Chicago: University of Chicago Press.

Chafe, William H. 1980. *Civilities and Civil Rights: Greensboro, North Carolina, and the Black Struggle for Freedom.* New York: Oxford University Press.

Chatterjee, Partha. 1993. *The Nation and Its Fragments: Colonial and Postcolonial Histories.* Princeton, N.J.: Princeton University Press.

Chong, Dennis. 1991. "All-or-Nothing Games in the Civil Rights Movement." *Rationality and Society* 30 (4): 677–697.

———. 1991. *Collective Action and the Civil Rights Movement*. Chicago: University of Chicago Press.

Cicero, Marcus T. 1998. *The Republic; and, The Laws*. New York: Oxford University Press.

Clayton, John Jacob. 1968. *Saul Bellow: In Defense of Man*. Bloomington: Indiana University Press.

Clendinnen, Inga. 1987. *Ambivalent Conquests: Maya and Spaniard in Yucatan, 1517–1570*. Cambridge, England: Cambridge University Press.

Cohen, Jacob X. 1938. *Jews, Jobs, and Discrimination: A Report on Jewish Non-Employment*. New York: American Jewish Congress.

Cohen, Jean L. 1982. *Class and Civil Society: The Limits of Marxian Critical Theory*. Amherst: University of Massachusetts Press.

———. 1999. "Does Voluntary Association Make Democracy Work?" In *Diversity and Its Discontents: Cultural Conflict and Common Ground in Contemporary American Society*, ed. Neil Smelser and Jeffrey C. Alexander. Princeton, N.J.: Princeton University Press.

———. 2002. *Regulating Intimacy: A New Legal Paradigm*. Princeton, N.J.: Princeton University Press.

Cohen, Jean L., and Andrew Arato. 1992. *Civil Society and Political Theory*. Cambridge: MIT Press.

Cohen, Jeremy, ed. 1991. *Essential Papers on Judaism and Christianity in Conflict: From Late Antiquity to the Reformation*. New York: New York University Press.

Cohen, Joshua. 1996. "Procedure and Substance in Deliberative Democracy." In *Democracy and Difference, Public Deliberation: Pluralism, Complexity, and Democracy*, ed. James Bohman, pp. 95–119. Cambridge: MIT Press.

Cohen, Sarah B., ed. 1983. *From Hester Street to Hollywood: The Jewish-American Stage and Screen*. Bloomington: Indiana University Press.

Coleman, James S. 1990. *Foundations of Social Theory*. Cambridge, Mass.: Harvard University Press.

Collins, Hugh. 1993. *The Law of Contract*. London: Butterworths.

———. 1999. *Regulating Contracts*. New York: Oxford.

Colas, Dominique. 1997. *Civil Society and Fanaticism: Conjoined Histories*, trans. Amy Jacobs. Stanford, Calif.: Stanford University Press.

Collins, Randall. 1975. *Conflict Sociology: Toward an Explanatory Science*. New York: Academic Press.

———. 1981. "On the Micro-Foundations of Macro-Sociology." *American Journal of Sociology* 86: 984–1014.

Colomy, Paul. 1990. "Uneven Differentiation and Incomplete Institutionalization:

Political Change and Continuity in the Early American Nation." In *Differentiation Theory and Social Change,* ed. Jeffrey C. Alexander and Paul Colomy, pp. 119–162. New York: Columbia University Press.

Connerton, Paul. 1989. *How Societies Remember.* Cambridge: Cambridge University Press.

Cooke, Maeve. 2006. *Re-Presenting the Good Society.* Cambridge, Mass.: MIT Press.

Cooley, Charles H. 1909. *Social Organization: A Study of the Larger Mind.* New York: Charles Scribner.

Cooper, Alan. 1996. "Confessions of Philip Roth." In *Philip Roth and the Jews,* pp. 133–150. Albany: SUNY Press, 1996.

———. 1996. *Philip Roth and the Jews.* Albany: SUNY Press.

Coser, Lewis A. 1956. *The Functions of Social Conflict.* New York: Free Press.

Cott, Nancy F. 1987. *The Grounding of Modern Feminism.* New Haven, Conn.: Yale University Press.

———. 1995 "Equal Rights and Economic Roles: The Conflict over the Equal Rights Amendment in the 1920s." In *Women's America: Refocusing the Past,* ed. Linda K. Kerber and Jane Sherron De Hart. Oxford: Oxford University Press.

Cottle, Simon. 2004. *The Racist Murder of Stephen Lawrence: Media Performance and Public Transformation.* Westport, Conn.: Praeger.

Cover, Robert M. 1983. "The Supreme Court 1982 Term, Foreword: Namos and Narrative." *Harvard Law Review* 97 (1): 4–68.

Crane, Elaine Forman. 1998. *Ebb Tide in New England: Women, Seaports, and Social Change, 1630–1800.* Boston: Northeastern University Press.

Crick, Bernard. 1962. *In Defence of Politics.* Harmondsworth, England: Penguin.

Cuddihy, John M. 1974. *The Ordeal of Civility: Freud, Marx, Levi-Strauss, and the Jewish Struggle with Modernity.* New York: Basic Books.

———. 1978. *No Offense: Civil Religion and Protestant Taste.* New York: Seabury.

Dahl, Robert A. 1991. *Modern Political Analysis.* Englewood Cliffs, N.J.: Prentice-Hall.

Dahrendorf, Ralf. 1959. *Class and Class Conflict in Industrial Society.* Stanford, Calif.: Stanford University Press.

———. 1968. "In Praise of Thrasymachus." In *Essays in the Theory of Society,* ed. R. Dahrendorf, pp. 129–150. Stanford, Calif.: Stanford University Press.

Dampière, Eric de. 1954. "Thèmes pour l'étude du Scandale." *Annales* 9 (3): 330.

Darian-Smith, Eve, and Peter Fitzpatrick, eds. 1999. *Laws of the Postcolonial.* Ann Arbor: University of Michigan Press.

Darnton, R. 1975. "Writing News and Telling Stories." *Daedalus* 104 (2): 175–93.

Davis, J. E., 2002. "Narrative and Social Movements: The Power of Stories." In *Stories of Change: Narrative and Social Movements.* Albany: State University of New York Press.

————, ed. 2002. *Stories of Change: Narrative and Social Movements*. Albany: State University of New York Press.

Davis, Moshe. 1963. *The Emergence of Conservative Judaism: The Historical School in Nineteenth Century America*. Philadelphia: The Jewish Publication Society of America.

Dayan, D., and E. Katz. 1992. *Media Events: The Live Broadcasting of History*. Cambridge, Mass.: Harvard University Press.

De Hart, Jane Sherron. 1995. "Conclusion: The New Feminism and the Dynamics of Social Change." In *Women's America: Refocusing the Past,* ed. Linda K. Kerber and Jane Sherron De Hart. Oxford: Oxford University Press.

Derrida, Jacques. 1988. "Signature, Event, Context." In *Limited, Inc.,* pp. 1–23. Evanston, Ill.: Northwestern University Press.

————. 1991. "Différance." In *A Derrida Reader: Between the Blinds,* ed. Peggy Kamuf, pp. 59–79. New York: Columbia University Press.

Deutscher, Isaac. 1966. *Stalin, A Political Biography*. Harmondsworth, England: Penguin Books.

Devlin, Patrick. 1965. *The Enforcement of Morals*. Oxford: Oxford University Press.

Dewey, John. 1927. *The Public and Its Problems*. New York: Henry Holt and Company.

————. 1966 [1916]. *Democracy and Education*. New York: Free Press.

Dicey, Albert V. 1889. *Introduction to the Study of The Law of the Constitution,* 3rd ed. London: Macmillan and Co.

Dietz, Mary G. 1998. "Citizenship with a Feminist Face: The Problem with Maternal Thinking." In *Feminism, the Public and the Private,* ed. Joan B. Landes. New York and Oxford: Oxford University Press.

Dijkink, Gertjan. 1996. *National Identity and Geopolitical Visions: Maps of Pride and Pain*. London: Routledge.

Dikoetter, Frank. 1992. *The Discourse of Race in Modern China*. Stanford, Calif.: Stanford University Press.

Dillon, Merton L. 1974. *The Abolitionists: The Growth of a Dissenting Minority*. DeKalb, Ill.: Northern Illinois University Press.

Dilthey, Wilhelm. 1976. "The Construction of the Historical World in the Human Sciences." In *Dilthey: Selected Writings,* ed. and trans. Hans Peter Rickman, pp. 168–245. Cambridge, England: Cambridge University Press.

DiMaggio, Paul J., and Walter W. Powell, eds. 1991. "The Iron Cage Revisited: Institutional Isomorphism and Collective Rationality in Organization Fields." *The New Institutionalism in Organizational Analysis,* pp. 63–82. Chicago: University of Chicago Press.

Diner, Dan. 1996. *America in the Eyes of the Germans: An Essay on Anti-Americanism*. Trans. Alison Brown. Princeton, N.J.: Markus Wiener.

Dinkin, Robert J. 1977. *Voting in Provincial America: A Study of Elections in the Thirteen Colonies, 1689–1776.* Westport, Conn.: Greenwood.

Dinnerstein, Leonard. 1981–1982. "Anti-Semitism Exposed and Attacked, 1945–1950." *American Jewish History* (September–June): 134–149.

Dohm, Christian Vilhelm, Von. 1995. "Concerning the Amelioration of the Civil Status of the Jews (1781)." In *The Jew in the Modern World: A Documentary History,* ed. Paul Mendes-Flohr and Jehuda Reinharz. New York: Oxford University Press.

Domhoff, G. William. 1967. *Who Rules America: Power and Politics.* Englewood Cliffs, N.J.: Prentice-Hall.

———. 1978. *Powers That Be: Processes of Ruling Class Domination in America.* New York: Random House.

Domhoff, G. William, and Hoyt B. Ballard, eds. 1968. *C. Wright Mills and the Power Elite.* Boston: Beacon Press.

Dorman, Michael. 1964. *We Shall Overcome.* New York: Dial Press.

Doty, Roxanne. 1996. *Imperial Encounters: The Politics of Representation in North-South Relations.* Minneapolis: University of Minnesota Press.

Douglas, Mary. 1966. *Purity and Danger: An Analysis of Concepts of Pollution and Taboo.* New York: Praeger.

———. 1986. *How Institutions Think.* Syracuse, N.Y.: Syracuse University Press.

Dower, John W. 1986. *War Without Mercy: Race and Power in the Pacific War.* New York: Pantheon.

Downs, Anthony. 1957. *An Economic Theory of Democracy.* New York: Harper and Row.

Doyle, William. 1995. "4 August 1789: The Intellectual Background to the Abolition of Venality of Offices." In *Officers, Nobles, and Revolutionaries: Essays on Eighteenth Century France,* pp. 141–154. London: Hambledon.

———. 1995. *Officers, Nobles, and Revolutionaries: Essays on Eighteenth Century France.* London: Hambledon.

———. 1996. *Venality: The Sale of Offices in Eighteenth-Century France.* Oxford: Clarendon Press.

D'Souza, Dinesh. 1992. "The Big Chill? Interview with Dinesh D'Souza." In *Debating P.C.: The Controversy over Political Correctness on College Campuses,* ed. Paul Berman, pp. 29–39. New York: Vintage.

Dumont, Louis. 1977. *From Mandeville to Marx on Mandeville: The Genesis and Triumph of Economic Ideology.* Chicago: University of Chicago Press.

Duncan, Graeme, ed. 1983. *Democratic Theory and Practice.* Cambridge: Cambridge University Press.

Duneier, Mitchell. 1992. *Slim's Table: Race, Respectability, and Masculinity.* Chicago: University of Chicago Press.

———. 1999. *Sidewalk.* New York: Farrar, Straus, and Giroux.

Durkheim, Émile. 1957. *Professional Ethics and Civic Morals*. Trans. Cornelia Brook-field. London: Routledge and Kegan Paul.

———. 1963 [1912]. *The Elementary Forms of Religious Life*. New York: Free Press.

———. 1973. "Individualism and the Intellectuals." In *Emile Durkheim on Moral-ity and Society,* ed. R. N. Bellah, pp. 43–57. Chicago: University of Chicago Press.

———. 1984 [1893]. *The Division of Labor in Society*. New York: Free Press.

Duverger, Maurice. 1962 [1951]. *Political Parties: Their Organization and Activity in the Modern State,* 2nd ed. Trans. Barbara North and Robert North. New York: John Wiley.

Dworkin, Ronald M.. 1977. "Hard Cases." In *Taking Rights Seriously*. Cambridge, Mass.: Harvard University Press.

———. 1977. "Jurisprudence." In *Taking Rights Seriously*. Cambridge, Mass.: Har-vard University Press.

———. 1977. "The Model of Rules I." In *Taking Rights Seriously*. Cambridge, Mass.: Harvard University Press.

———. 1977. "Taking Rights Seriously." In *Taking Rights Seriously*. Cambridge, Mass.: Harvard University Press.

———. 1977. *Taking Rights Seriously*. Cambridge, Mass.: Harvard University Press.

———. 1983. "To Each His Own." *New York Review of Books* 30 (6): 6.

———. 1987. "Legal Theory and the Problems of Sense." In *Issues in Contemporary Legal Philosophy: The Influence of H.L.A. Hart,* ed. R. Gavison, pp. 9–42. New York: Oxford University Press.

———. 1996. *Freedom's Law: The Moral Reading of the American Constitution*. Cam-bridge, Mass.: Harvard University Press.

———. 1996. "Introduction: The Moral Reading and the Majoritarian Premise." *Freedom's Law: The Moral Reading of the American Constitution,* pp. 1–38. Cam-bridge, Mass.: Harvard University Press.

Eagles, Charles, ed. 1986. *The Civil Rights Movement in America: Essays by David Levering Lewis et. al.* Jackson: University Press of Mississippi.

Easton, Lloyd, and Kurt H. Guddat, eds. 1967. *Writings of the Young Marx on Philosophy and Society*. New York: Doubleday Anchor.

Edelman, Murray. 1964. *The Symbolic Uses of Politics*. Urbana: University of Illinois Press.

Edles, Laura. 1998. *Symbol and Ritual in the New Spain: The Transition to Democracy after Franco*. New York: Cambridge University Press.

Edwards, Rebecca. 1997. *Angels in the Machinery: Gender in American Party Politics from the Civil War to the Progressive Era*. New York: Oxford University Press.

Eisenstadt, S. N. 1963. *The Political Systems of Empires*. New York: Free Press.

———. 1982. "The Axial Age: The Emergence of Transcendental Visions and the Rise of Clerics." *European Journal of Sociology* 23 (2): 299–314.

———. 1999. *Fundamentalism, Sectarianism, and Revolution: The Jacobin Dimension of Modernity.* Cambridge, England: Cambridge University Press.

———, ed. 1986. *The Origins and Diversity of Axial Age Civilizations.* Albany, N.Y.: State University of New York Press.

Eley, Geoff. 1992. "Nations, Publics, and Political Cultures: Placing Habermas in the Nineteenth Century. In *Habermas and the Public Sphere,* ed. Craig Calhoun, pp. 289–339. Cambridge: MIT Press.

Eliade, Mircea. 1957. *The Sacred and the Profane: The Nature of Religion.* Trans. Willard. R. Trask. New York: Harcourt, Brace.

Elias, Norbert. 1982 [1939]. *The Civilizing Process.* Trans. Edmund Jephcott. New York: Pantheon.

———. 1984. "Violence and Civilization." In *Civil Society and the State: New European Perspectives,* ed. John Keane. London: Verso.

———. 1996. *The Germans: Power Struggles and the Development of Habitus in the Nineteenth and Twentieth Centuries.* Cambridge, England: Polity.

Eliasoph, Nina, and Paul Lichterman. 2003. "Culture in Interaction." *American Journal of Sociology* 108 (4): 735–794.

Ellenson, David. 2004. *After Emancipation: Jewish Religious Responses to Modernity.* Cincinnati, Ohio: Hebrew Union College Press.

Elshtain, Jean, B. 1995. *Democracy on Trial.* New York: Basic Books.

Ely, John H. 1996. *On Constitutional Ground.* Princeton, N.J.: Princeton University Press.

Emirbayer, Mustafa, and Mimi Sheller. 1999. "Publics in History." *Theory and Society* 28: 145–197.

Endelman, Todd M. 1990. *Radical Assimilation in English Jewish History, 1656–1945.* Bloomington: Indiana University Press.

Entrikin, J. Nicholas. 1990. *The Betweenness of Place: Towards a Geography of Modernity.* Baltimore, Md.: Johns Hopkins University Press.

Epstein, Joseph. 1971. "Saul Bellow's Chicago." *New York Times Book Review* (May 9): 12.

Epstein, Lawrence. 2001. *The Haunted Smile: The Story of Jewish Comedians in America.* New York: Public Affairs.

Erikson, Eric. 1958. *Young Man Luther: A Case Study in Psychoanalysis and History.* New York: Norton.

Ervin, Sam J., Jr. 1980. *The Whole Truth: The Watergate Conspiracy.* New York: Random House.

Escala-Rabadan, Luis. 2002. The Symbolic Construction of the Human Rights Discourse in Mexico's Media, 1978–1996. Ph.D. diss. Univ. of California, Los Angeles.

Eskew, Glenn T. 1997. *But for Birmingham: The Local and National Movements in the Civil Rights Struggle.* Chapel Hill: University of North Carolina Press.

Etzioni-Halévy, Eva. 1989. *Fragile Democracy: The Use and Abuse of Power in Western Societies*. New Brunswick, N.J.: Transaction.

———. 1993. *The Elite Connection: Problems and Potential of Western Democracy.* London: Polity.

Euripides. 1972. *Orestes and Other Plays*. Trans. Philip Vellacott. Harmondsworth, England: Penguin Books.

———. 1972. "The Suppliant Women." In *Orestes and Other Plays*. Trans. Philip Vellacott. Harmondsworth, England: Penguin Books.

Evans-Pritchard, E. 1953. "The Nuer Conception of the Spirit in Its Relation to the Social Order." *American Anthropologist* 55 (2): 201–214.

Evans, Peter, Dietrich Rueschemeyer, and Theda Skocpol, eds. 1985. "On the Road toward a More Adequate Understanding of the State." *Bringing the State Back In*. New York: Cambridge University Press.

Evans, Peter, Dietrich Rueschemeyer, and Theda Skocpol, eds. 1985. *Bringing the State Back In*. New York: Cambridge University Press.

Eyerman, Ron. 2001. *Cultural Trauma: Slavery and the Formation of African American Identity*. New York: Cambridge University Press.

———. 2005. "How Social Movements Move Emotions and Social Movements." In *Emotions and Social Movements,* ed. H. Flam and D. King, pp. 41–56. London: Routledge.

Eyerman, Ron, and Andrew Jamison. 1991. *Social Movements: A Cognitive Approach*. Cambridge, England: Polity.

———. 1998. *Music and Social Movements: Mobilizing Traditions in the Twentieth Century*. New York: Cambridge University Press.

Eyes on the Prize: America's Civil Rights Years, 1954–1965. Part I. (PBS, 1987)

Fairclough, Adam. 1987. *To Redeem the Soul of America: The Southern Christian Leadership Congress and Martin Luther King, Jr.* Atlanta: University of Georgia Press.

Fanning, Lawrence S. 1967. "The Media: Observer or Participant." In *Race and the News Media,* ed. Paul L. Fisher and Ralph L. Lowenstein. New York: Frederick A. Praeger.

Farge, Arlette. 1994. *Subversive Words: Public Opinion in Eighteenth Century France*. Trans. Rosemary Morris. Cambridge, U.K.: Polity Press.

Farley, Reynolds. 1999. "Racial Issues: Recent Trends in Residential Patterns and Intermarriage." in *Diversity and Its Discontents: Cultural Conflict and Common Ground in Contemporary American Society,* ed. Neil J. Smelser and Jeffrey C. Alexander, pp. 85–128. Princeton, N.J.: Princeton University Press.

Fasching, Darrell J., ed. 1984. *The Jewish People in Christian Preaching*. New York: Edwin Mellon.

Fass, Paula S. 1976. "Television as a Cultural Document: Promises and Problems." *Television as a Cultural Force,* ed. Richard Adler, pp. 37–58. New York: Praeger.

Favell, Adrian. 1999. *Philosophies of Integration: Immigration and the Idea of Citizenship in France and Britain.* New York: St. Martin's.

Ferguson, Adam. 1966 [1767]. *An Essay on the History of Civil Society.* Edinburgh: University of Edinburgh Press.

Fernandez, Enrique. 1992. "P.C. Rider." In *Debating P.C.: The Controversy over Political Correctness on College Campuses,* ed. Paul Berman. New York: Vintage.

Ferrara, Alessandro. 1998. *Reflective Authenticity: Rethinking the Project of Modernity.* London: Routledge.

Fine, Gary, and Brooke Harrington. 2004. "Tiny Publics: Small Groups and Civil Society." *Sociological Theory* 22 (3): 341–356.

Finley, M. I. 1972. *The Peloponnesian War.* Harmondsworth, England: Penguin.

Finn, Peter, and Daniel Williams. 2004. "Yushchenko Vows to Prosecute Political Crimes if Elected." *Washington Post,* December 9, A22.

Fishkin, J. S. 1997. *The Voice of the People: Public Opinion and Democracy.* New Haven, Conn.: Yale University Press.

Fiss, Owen M. 1988. "Objectivity and Interpretation." In *Interpreting Law and Literature: A Hermeneutic Reader,* ed. Sanford Levinson and Steven Mailloux. Evanston, Ill.: Northwestern University Press.

Fitzpatrick, Peter, and Patricia Tuitt, eds. 2004. *Critical Beings: Law, Nation, and the Global Subject.* London: Ashgate.

Flores, Angel, ed. 1977. *The Problem of The Judgment: Eleven Approaches to Kafka's Story.* New York: Gordian.

Foner, Eric. 1984. "Reconstruction and the Black Political Tradition." In *Political Parties and the Modern State,* ed. Richard L. McCormick, pp. 53–69. New Brunswick, N.J.: Rutgers University Press.

Forbath, W. 1999. "Caste, Class, and Equal Citizenship." *University of Michigan Law Review* 98 (1): 1–91.

Foucault, Michel. 1979. *Discipline and Punish: The Birth of the Prison.* Trans. Alan Sheridan. New York: Vintage.

———. 1980. *The History of Sexuality.* Vol. 1: *An Introduction.* Trans. Robert Hurley. New York: Vintage.

———. 1993. "About the Beginning of the Hermeneutics of the Self." *Political Theory* 21 (2): 198–227.

Frank, Jerome. 1930. *Law and the Modern Mind.* New York: Tudor.

Frankel, Jonathan, and Steven J. Zipperstein. 1992. *Assimilation and Community: The Jews of Nineteenth-Century Europe,* Cambridge, England: Cambridge University Press.

Frankfurter, Felix. 1924. "A Note on Advisory Opinions." *Harvard Law Review* 37: 1002–1009.

Franklin, Benjamin. 1952. *The Autobiography and Selection from Other Writings.* New York: Liberty Arts.

Fraser, Nancy. 1992. "Rethinking the Public Sphere: A Contribution to the Critique of Actually Existing Democracy." In *Habermas and the Public Sphere,* ed. Craig Calhoun, pp. 109–142. Cambridge: MIT Press.

———. 1997. "From Redistribution to Recognition? Dilemmas of Justice in a 'Postsocialist' Age." In *Justice Interruptus: Critical Reflections on the "Postsocialist" Condition,* pp. 11–40. New York: Routledge.

Frederickson, George M. 1971. *The Black Image in the White Mind: The Debate on Afro-American Character and Destiny, 1817–1914.* New York: Harper and Row.

———. 1981. *White Supremacy: A Comparative Study in American and South African History.* New York: Oxford.

———. 1995. *Black Liberation: A Comparative History of Black Ideologies in the United States and South Africa.* New York: Oxford University Press.

Freud, Sigmund. 1959 [1922]. *Group Psychology and the Analysis of the Ego.* Translated and edited by James Strachey. New York: Norton.

———. 1961 [1930]. *Civilization and Its Discontents.* Translated and edited by James Strachey. New York: W.W. Norton.

Friedan, Betty. 1995 [1976] "The Problem That Has No Name." In *Women's America: Refocusing the Past,* ed. Linda K. Kerber and Jane Sherron De Hart. Oxford: Oxford University Press.

———. 1997 [1963]. *The Feminine Mystique.* New York: W.W. Norton.

Frieden, Ken. 1995. *Classic Yiddish Fiction: Abramovitsh, Sholem Aleichem, and Peretz.* Stonybrook: State University of New York Press.

Friedland, Roger, and Robert Alford. 1991. "Bringing Society Back In: Symbols, Practices, and Institutional Contradictions." In *The New Institutionalism in Organizational Analysis,* ed. Paul J. DiMaggio and Walter W. Powell, pp. 232–263. Chicago: University of Chicago Press.

Friedland, Roger, and Deirdre Boden, eds. 1994. *NowHere: Space, Time, and Modernity.* Berkeley: University of California Press.

Friedland, Roger, and Richard Hecht. 1996. *To Rule Jerusalem.* New York: Cambridge University Press.

Friedland, Roger, and John Mohr. 2004. "The Cultural Turn in American Sociology." In *Matters of Culture: Cultural Sociology in Practice,* ed. R. Friedland and J. Mohr, pp. 1–70. New York: Cambridge University Press.

Friedman, Debra, and Doug McAdams. 1992. "Collective Identity and Activism: Networks, Choices, and the Life of a Social Movement." In *Frontiers in Social Movement Theory,* ed. Aldon D. Morris and Carol McClurg Mueller. New Haven, Conn.: Yale University Press.

Friedman, Lawrence M. 1994. *Total Justice.* New York: Russell Sage.

Friedman, Leon. 1967. *The Civil Rights Reader: Basic Documents of the Civil Rights Movement.* New York: Walker.

Friedman, Lester D. 1982. *Hollywood's Image of the Jew.* New York: Frederick Unger.

Friedman, Milton. 1962. *Capitalism and Freedom.* Chicago: University of Chicago Press.

Frye, Northrop. 1957. *Anatomy of Criticism.* Princeton, N.J.: Princeton University Press.

Fuchs, Lawrence H. "Thinking about Immigration and Ethnicity in the United States." In *Immigrants in Two Democracies: French and American Experience,* ed. Donald L. Horowitz and Gerard Noiriel, pp. 39–65. New York: New York University Press.

Fukuyama, Francis. 1995. *Trust: Social Virtues and the Creation of Prosperity.* New York: Free Press.

Fuller, Lon L. 1958. "Positivism and Fidelity to Law—A Reply to Professor Hart." *Harvard Law Review* 71: 630–672.

———. 1969. *The Morality of Law.* New Haven, Conn.: Yale University Press.

Furet, Francois. 1981 [1978]. *Interpreting the French Revolution.* Trans. Elborg Forster. New York: Cambridge University Press.

Fussell, Paul. 1975. *The Great War and Modern Memory.* New York: Oxford University Press.

Gabler, Neal. 1988. *An Empire of Their Own: How the Jews Invented Hollywood.* New York: Crown.

Gadamer, Hans-Georg. 1975. *Truth and Method.* Trans. Garrett Borden and John Cumming. New York: Seabury.

Gallup, George. 1948. *A Guide to Public Opinion Polls.* Princeton, N.J.: Princeton University Press.

Gallup, George, and S. Forbes Rae. 1940. *The Pulse of Democracy: The Public-Opinion Poll and How It Works.* New York: Simon and Schuster.

Gamson, William A. 1988. "Political Discourse and Collective Action." *International Social Movement Research,* Vol. 1, *From Structure to Action: Comparing Social Movement Research Across Cultures,* ed. Bert Klandermans, Hanspeter Kriesi, and Sidney Tarrow, pp. 54–76. Greenwich, Conn.: JAI Press.

———. 1992. "The Social Psychology of Collective Action." In *Frontiers in Social Movement Theory,* ed. Aldon D. Morris and Carol McClurg Mueller. New Haven, Conn.: Yale University Press.

Gannett, Lewis S. 1923. "Is America Anti-Semitic?" *Nation* 116 (March 21): 3–4.

Gannett, Robert T., Jr., 2003. "Bowling Ninepins in Tocqueville's Township." *American Political Science Review* 97 (1): 1–6.

Gans, H. 1979. "Symbolic Ethnicity: The Future of Ethnic Groups and Cultures in America." *Ethic and Racial Studies* 27 (2): 228–247.

Garland, David. 1990. *Punishment and Modern Society: A Study in Social Theory.* London: Oxford University Press.

Garrow, David J. 1957. "Nonviolence and Racial Justice." *Christian Century* 74 (February 6): 165–167.

————. 1958. *King's Stride toward Freedom: The Montgomery Story*. New York: Harper and Brothers.

————. 1978. *Protest at Selma: Martin Luther King, Jr., and the Voting Rights Act of 1965*. New Haven, Conn.: Yale University Press.

————. 1993 [1986]. *Bearing the Cross: Martin Luther King, Jr. and the Southern Leadership Conference*. London: Vintage.

Garton Ash, Timothy. 1983. *The Polish Revolution: Solidarity*. New York: Scribner.

————. 1990 *The Magic Lantern: The Revolution of '89 Witnessed in Warsaw, Budapest, Berlin and Prague*. New York: Random House.

Gates, Henry L., Jr. 1992. "Whose Canon Is It, Anyway?" In *Debating P.C.: The Controversy Over Political Correctness on College Campuses*, ed. Paul Berman, pp. 190–200. New York: Vintage.

————, ed. 1987. *The Classic Slave Narratives*. New York: New American Library.

————. 1987. "Introduction." In *The Classic Slave Narratives*. New York: New American Library.

Gavison, R. 1987. "Introduction." In *Issues in Contemporary Legal Philosophy: The Influence of H.L.A. Hart*, ed. R. Gavison. New York: Oxford University Press.

Gay, Peter. 1966. *The Enlightenment: An Interpretation*. New York: Norton.

Geddes, Andrew, and Adrian Favell, eds. 1999. *Politics of Belonging: Migrants and Minorities in Contemporary Europe*. Brookfield, Vt.: Ashgate.

Geertz, Clifford. 1973. *The Interpretation of Cultures: Selected Essays*. New York: Basic Books.

————. 1984. "Distinguished Lecture: Anti Anti-Relativism." *American Anthropologist* 86 (June): 263–278.

Genovese, Eugene D. 1974. *Roll, Jordan, Roll; The World the Slaves Made*. New York: Pantheon.

Gerber, Jane S. 1992. *The Jews of Spain: A History of the Sephardic Experience*. New York: Free Press.

Gespard, Françoise, and Farhad Khosrokhavar. 1995. *Foulard et la Republique*. Paris: Decouverte.

Gewirtz, Paul. 1996. "Victims and Voyeurs: Two Narrative Problems at the Criminal Trial." In *Law's Stories: Narrative and Rhetoric in the Law*, ed. Peter Brooks and Paul Gewirtz. New Haven, Conn.: Yale University Press.

Gibson, James William. 1994. *Warrior Dreams: Paramilitary Culture in Post-Vietnam America*. New York: Hill and Wang.

Giddens, Anthony. 1981. *A Contemporary Critique of Historical Materialism, Vol. I: Power, Property, and the State*. London: Macmillan.

Giddings, Franklin H. 1924 [1896]. *The Scientific Study of Human Society*. Chapel Hill: University of North Carolina Press.

Giesen, Bernhard. 1998. *Intellectuals and the German Nation: Collective Identity in the German Axial Age*. New York: Cambridge University Press.

———. 2004. "The Trauma of Perpetrators: The Holocaust as the Traumatic Reference of German National Identity." In *Cultural Trauma and Collective Identity,* Jeffrey C. Alexander et al., pp. 113–143. Berkeley: University of California Press.

———. 2004. *Triumph and Trauma.* Boulder, Colo.: Paradigm.

Gillette, William. 1965. *The Right to Vote: Politics and the Passage of the Fifteenth Amendment.* Baltimore, Md.: Johns Hopkins University Press.

Gilligan, Carol. 1982. *In a Different Voice: Psychological Theory and Women's Development.* Cambridge, Mass.: Harvard University Press.

———. 1986. "Reply." *Signs* 11 (2): 324–333.

Gilman, Sander L. 1996. "The Jew's Body: Thoughts on Jewish Physical Difference." In *Too Jewish?: Challenging Traditional Identities,* ed. Norman Kleeblatt, pp. 60–73. New York: Jewish Museum; New Brunswick, N.J.: Rutgers University Press.

Gilroy, Paul. 2000. *Against Race: Imagining Political Culture beyond the Color Line.* Cambridge, Mass.: Harvard University Press.

———. 2005. *Postcolonial Melancholia.* New York: Columbia University Press.

Glaser, Daryl. 1997. "South Africa and the Limits of Civil Society." *Journal of Southern African Studies* 23(1): 5–25.

Glazer, Nathan. 1957. *American Judaism.* Chicago: University of Chicago Press.

———. 1987. "Revisiting a Classic: Nathan Glazer's *American Judaism.*" *American Jewish History* 77 (2).

———. 1989. *American Judaism.* 2nd ed., with a new introduction. Chicago: University of Chicago Press.

———. 1989. "New Perspectives in American Jewish Sociology." In *Facing the Future: Essays on Contemporary Jewish Life,* ed. Steven Bayme, pp. 3–22. New York: American Jewish Committee.

———. 1997. *We are All Multiculturalists Now.* Cambridge, Mass.: Harvard University Press.

Glover, David, and Cora Kaplan. 1992. "Guns in the House of Culture? Crime Fiction and the Politics of the Popular." In *Cultural Studies,* ed. L. Grossberg, C. Nelson, and P. Treichler, pp. 213–223. New York: Routledge.

Goffman, Erving. 1956. *The Presentation of Self in Everyday Life.* New York: Doubleday Anchor.

———. 1967. *Interaction Ritual: Essays on Face-to-Face Behavior.* New York: Pantheon.

Golden, Harry. 1958. *Only in America.* Cleveland: World.

———. 1959. *For Two Cents Plain.* Cleveland: World.

Goldhagen, Daniel. 1996. *Hitler's Willing Executioners: Ordinary Germans and the Holocaust.* New York: Alfred A. Knopf.

Goldscheider, Calvin. 1986. *Jewish Community and Change: Emerging Patterns in America.* Bloomington: Indiana University Press.

Goode, William J. 1963. *World Revolution and Family Patterns.* New York: Free Press.

Goodman, Tanya. 2005. "Performing a 'New' Nation: The Role of the TRC in South Africa." In *Social Performances,* ed. Jeffrey C. Alexander, Bernhard Giesen, and Jason Mast. New York: Cambridge University Press.

Goodwin, Doris Kearns. 2005. *Team of Rivals: The Political Genius of Abraham Lincoln.* New York: Simon and Shuster.

Goodwin, Jeff, James Jasper, and Francesca Polletta, eds. 2001. *Passionate Politics: Emotions and Social Movements.* Chicago: University of Chicago Press.

Gordon, Judah Leib. 1871. "For Whom Do I Toil?" In *Hashabar* 2.

Gordon, Milton M. 1964. *Assimilation in American Life: The Role of Race, Religion, and National Origins.* New York: Oxford University Press.

————. 1969. "Marginality and the Jewish Intellectual." In *The Ghetto and Beyond: Essays on Jewish Life in America.* ed. Peter Rose, pp. 477–491. New York: Random House.

Gordon, Robert W. 1984. "Critical Legal Histories." *Stanford Law Review* 36: 57–125.

Goren, Arthur A. 1982. *The American Jews.* Cambridge, Mass.: Harvard University Press.

Goubert, P. 1988. *The Course of French History.* Trans. Maarten Vitee. London: Routledge.

Graeber, Isacque, and Steuart Henderson Britt. 1942. *Jews in a Gentile World: The Problem of Anti-Semitism.* New York: Macmillan.

Gramsci, Antonio. 1971. *Selections from the Prison Notebooks of Antonio Gramsci.* New York: International.

Granovetter, Mark. 1974. *Getting a Job: The Importance of Contacts and Careers.* Cambridge, Mass.: Harvard University Press.

Grant, Madison. 1916. *The Passing of the Great Race; or, The Racial Basis of European History.* New York: C. Scribner.

Gray, C. 2003. "Disability as Ability: Narratives of Disability and the Movement from Deficiency to Difference." Master's thesis, UCLA Department of Sociology.

Gray, Herman. 1995. *Watching Race: Television and the Struggle for "Blackness."* Minneapolis: University of Minnesota Press.

Green, Donald, and Ian Shapiro. 1994. *Pathologies of Rational Choice Theory: A Critique of Applications in Political Science.* New Haven, Conn.: Yale University Press.

Green, Donald, Bradley Palmquist, and Eric Schickler. 2002. *Partisan Hearts and Minds: Political Parties and the Social Identities of Voters.* New Haven, Conn.: Yale University Press.

Greenberg, Dan. 1964. *How to Be a Jewish Mother: A Very Lovely Training Manual.* Los Angeles: Price, Stern, Sloan.

Greenblatt, Steven J. 1980. *Renaissance Self-Fashioning: From More to Shakespeare.* Chicago: University of Chicago Press.

Greenfeld, Liah. 1992. *Nationalism: Five Roads to Modernity*. Cambridge, Mass.: Harvard University Press.

Greenhouse, Linda. 2003. "Justices Back Affirmative Action by 5 to 4, but Wider Vote Bans a Racial Point System." *New York Times,* June 24, p. A1.

Greeno, C., and E. Maccoby. 1986. "How Different Is the 'Different Voice'?" *Signs* 11 (2): 310–316.

Greenstone, J. David. 1993. *The Lincoln Persuasion: Remaking American Liberalism.* Princeton, N.J.: Princeton University Press.

Grégoire, Abbe Henri Baptiste. 1995. "An Essay on the Physical, Moral, and Political Reformation of the Jews." In *The Jew in the Modern World: A Documentary History,* ed. Paul Mendes-Flohr and Jehuda Reinharz. New York: Oxford University Press.

Grofman, Bernard, Lisa Mandley, and Richard G. Niemi. 1992. *Minority Representation and the Quest for Voting Equality.* Cambridge, England: Cambridge University Press.

Guttmann, Allen. 1971. *The Jewish Writer in America: Assimilation and The Crisis of Identity.* New York: Oxford University Press.

Gutmann, Amy, and Dennis Thompson. 1996. *Democracy and Disagreement.* Cambridge, Mass.: Harvard University Press.

Habermas, Jürgen. 1971. *Knowledge and Human Interests.* Trans. Jeremy J. Shapiro. Boston: Beacon.

———. 1973. *Theory and Practice.* Trans. John Vietel. Boston: Beacon.

———. 1977. "A Review of Gadamer's Truth and Method." In *Understanding and Social Inquiry,* ed. Fred R. Dallmayr and Thomas A. McCarthy, pp. 335–363. Notre Dame, Ind.: University of Notre Dame Press.

———. 1979. *Communication and the Evolution of Society.* Trans. Thomas McCarthy. Boston: Beacon.

———. 1984. *The Theory of Communicative Action.* Vol. 1. Trans. Thomas McCarthy. Boston: Beacon Press.

———. 1987. *The Theory of Communicative Action.* Vol. 2: *Lifeworld and System: A Critique of Functionalist Reason.* Trans. Thomas McCarthy. Boston: Beacon Press.

———. 1989 [1963]. *The Structural Transformation of the Public Sphere: An Inquiry into a Category of Bourgeois Society.* Trans. Thomas Burger. Cambridge: MIT Press.

———. 1992. "Further Reflections on the Public Sphere." In *Habermas and the Public Sphere,* ed. Craig Calhoun, pp. 421–461. Cambridge: MIT Press.

———. 1992. "Individuation through Socialization: On George Herbert Mead's Theory of Subjectivity." In *Postmetaphysical Thinking: Philosophical Essays,* trans. William Mark Hohengarten, pp. 149–204. Cambridge: MIT Press.

———. 1992. *Postmetaphysical Thinking: Philosophical Essays.* Trans. William Mark Hohengarten. Cambridge: MIT Press.

———. 1993. "Morality, Society, and Ethics: An Interview with Torben Hviid

Nielsen." In *Justification and Application: Remarks on Discourse Ethics,* trans. Ciaran Cronin. Cambridge: MIT Press.

———. 1993. "Struggles for Recognition in Constitutional States." *European Journal of Philosophy* 1 (2): 128–155.

———. 1996. *Between Facts and Norms: Contributions to a Discourse Theory of Law and Democracy,* trans. William Rehg. Cambridge, Mass.: MIT Press.

———. 1998. "Three Normative Models of Democracy." In *The Inclusion of the Other: Studies in Political Theory,* ed. Ciaran Cronin and Pablo de Greiff, pp. 239–252. Cambridge, Mass.: MIT Press.

Halberstam, David. 1998. *The Children.* New York: Random House.

Halévy, Elie. 1903. *Thomas Hodgskin (1787–1869).* Paris: Société Nouvelle de Librairie et d'Edition.

Haley, Alex. 1976. *Roots: The Saga of an American Family.* Garden City, N.J.: Doubleday.

Halpern, Ben. 1975. "America Is Different." In *The Jew in American Society,* ed. Marshall Sklare, pp. 67–89. New York: Behrman House.

Hamilton, Alexander, James Madison, and John Jay. 2003 [1788]. *The Federalist Papers,* ed. Clinton Rossiter. New York: Penguin.

Hamilton, Charles V. 1986. "Federal Law and the Courts in the Civil Rights Movement." *The Civil Rights Movement in America,* ed. C. Eagles. Jackson: University Press of Mississippi.

Hamilton, Richard F. 1982. *Who Voted for Hitler?* Princeton, N.J.: Princeton University Press.

Handlin, Oscar. 1955. "The Acquisition of Political and Social Rights by the Jews in the United States." *American Jewish Yearbook.*

Hanson, Victor D. 2001. *Carnage and Culture: Landmark Battles in the Rise of Western Power.* New York: Doubleday.

———. 1999. *Soul of Battle: From Ancient Times to the Present Day, How Three Great Liberators Vanquished Tyranny.* New York: Free Press.

———. 1999. *Wars of The Ancient Greeks and Their Invention of Western Military Culture.* London: Cassell.

Harap, Louis. 1987. *In the Mainstream: The Jewish Presence in Twentieth Century American Literature, 1950s–1980s.* New York: Greenwood.

Harris, A. 2000. "Equality Trouble: Sameness and Difference in Twentieth-Century Race Law." *California Law Review* 88: 1925–2015.

Harris, George. 1899 [1896]. *Moral Evolution.* Boston: Houghton, Mifflin.

Hart, H.L.A. 1958. "Positivism and the Separation of Law and Morals." *Harvard Law Review,* 71: 593–630.

———. 1961. *The Concept of Law.* Oxford: Oxford University Press.

———. 1968. *Punishment and Responsibility: Essays in the Philosophy of the Law.* Oxford: Oxford University Press.

Hart, H.L.A., and A. M. Honoré. 1958. *Causation in the Law*. Oxford: Oxford University Press.

Hartmann, Douglas, and Joseph Gerteis. 2005. "Dealing with Diversity: Mapping Multiculturalism in Sociological Terms." *Sociological Theory 23* (2): 210–240.

Hartmann, Geoffrey, H. 1997. "Sympathy Paradox: Poetry, Feeling, and Modern Cultural Morality." *The Fateful Question of Culture,* pp. 141–164. New York: Columbia University Press.

Hartz, Louis. 1955. *The Liberal Tradition in America: An Interpretation of American Political Thought since the Revolution.* New York: Harcourt, Brace.

Hayek, Frederick A. 1944. *The Road to Serfdom.* Chicago: University of Chicago Press.

Hays, Sharon. 2003. *Flat Broke with Children: Women in the Age of Welfare Reform.* New York: Oxford University Press.

Hechter, M. 1975. *Internal Colonialism: The Celtic Fringe in British National Development, 1536–1966.* Berkeley: University of California Press.

Hegel, Georg W. F. 1952 [1821]. *The Philosophy of Right.* New York: Oxford University Press.

———. 1977 [1807]. *The Phenomenology of Spirit.* Trans. A. V. Miller. Oxford: Clarendon.

Heine, Henreich. 1995. "A Ticket of Admission to European Culture." In *The Jew in the Modern World: A Documentary History,* ed. Paul Mendes-Flohr and Jehuda Reinharz, pp. 258–259. New York: Oxford University Press.

Heins, Volker. 2006. "Orientalising America? Continental Intellectuals and the Search for Europe's Identity." *Millennium* 34 (2): 433–448.

Heinze, Andrew R. 2002. "*Peace of Mind (1946):* Judaism and the Therapeutic Polemics of Postwar America." *Religion and American Culture* 12 (winter): 31–58.

Held, David. 1987. *Models of Democracy.* Stanford, Calif.: Stanford University Press.

———. 1989. *Political Theory and the Modern State.* Stanford, Calif.: Stanford University Press.

Heller, Agnes. 1988. "On Formal Democracy." In *Civil Society and the State: New European Perspectives,* ed. John Keane, pp. 129–145. New York: Verso.

Hepworth, Mike, and Bryan S. Turner. 1982. *Confession: Studies in Deviance and Religion.* London: Routledge and Kegan Paul.

Herbers, John. 1965 [1962]. "The Reporters in the Deep South." In *Reporting the News: Selections from Nieman Reports,* ed. Louis M. Lyons. Cambridge, Mass.: Harvard University Press.

Herbst, Susan. 1993. *Numbered Voices: How Opinion Polling Has Shaped American Politics.* Chicago: University of Chicago Press.

———. 1998. *Reading Public Opinion: How Political Actors View the Democratic Process.* Chicago: University of Chicago Press.

Hertz, Deborah. 1988. *Jewish High Society in Old Regime Berlin*. New Haven, Conn.: Yale University Press.

Hertzberg, Arthur. 1990. *The French Enlightenment and the Jews: The Origins of Modern Anti-Semitism*. New York: Columbia University Press.

Herzl, Theodore. 1995. "A Solution to the Jewish Question [1896]". In *The Jew in the Modern World: A Documentary History*, ed. Paul Mendes-Flohr and Jehuda Reinharz, pp. 533–538. New York: Oxford University Press.

Hess, Andreas. 2000. *American Social and Political Thought: A Concise Introduction*. Edinburgh: Edinburgh University Press.

———. 2001. *Concepts of Social Stratification: European and American Models*. London: Palgrave.

Higham, John. 1955. *Strangers in the Land: Patterns of American Nativism, 1860–1925*. New Brunswick, N.J.: Rutgers University Press.

———. 1966. "American Anti-Semitism Historically Reconsidered." In Charles Stember et al., *Jews in the Mind of America*, pp. 237–258. New York: Basic Books.

———. 1975. *Send These to Me: Jews and Other Immigrants in Urban America*. New York: Atheneum.

Hirsch, Samson R., Rabbi (Ben Uziel). 1969 [1838]. *The Nineteen Letters on Judaism*, prepared by J. Breuer (based on the translation by Rabbi Dr. B. Drachman.) Jerusalem: Feldheim.

Hirschman, Albert O. 1970. *Exit, Voice, and Loyalty; Responses to Decline in Firms, Organizations, and States*. Cambridge, Mass.: Harvard University Press.

———. 1977. *The Passions and the Interests: Political Arguments for Capitalism before Its Triumph*. Princeton, N.J.: Princeton University Press.

———. 1982. *Shifting Involvements: Private Interest and Public Action*. Princeton, N.J.: Princeton University Press.

———. 1991. *The Rhetoric of Reaction: Perversity, Futility, Jeopardy*. Cambridge, Mass.: Harvard University Press.

Hobbes, Thomas. 1962 [1651]. *Leviathan*. New York: Collier.

Hoffman, Stanley. 1995 [1981]. "Foreword." In *Vichy France and the Jews*, Michael R. Marrus and Robert O. Paxton. Stanford, Calif.: Stanford University Press.

Hofstadter, Douglas R. 2000. "Analogy as the Core of Cognition." In *The Best American Science Writing*, ed. James Gleick, pp. 116–144. New York: Harper Collins.

Hofstadter, Richard. 1969. *The Idea of a Party System: The Rise of Legitimate Opposition in the United States, 1780–1840*. Berkeley: University of California Press.

Holmes, Oliver Wendell. 1920 [1894]. *Collected Legal Papers*. New York: Harcourt, Brace, and Company.

———. 1920 [1894]. "The Path of the Law." In *Collected Legal Papers*. New York: Harcourt, Brace, and Company.

―――. 1920 [1894]. "Privilege, Malice, and Intent." In *Collected Legal Papers*. New York: Harcourt, Brace, and Company.

Holquist, Michael. 1990. *Dialogism: Bakhtin and His World*. London: Routledge.

Holton, Robert J., and Bryan Turner. 1989. *Max Weber on Economy and Society*. London: Routledge.

Honneth, Axel. 1995. *The Struggle for Recognition: The Moral Grammar of Social Conflicts*. London: Polity.

Horkheimer, Max, and Theodor W. Adorno. 1972 [1947]. *The Dialectic of Enlightenment*. Trans. John Cumming. New York: Herder and Herder.

Horowitz, Donald L. 1992. "Immigration and Group Relations in France and America." In *Immigrants in Two Democracies: French and American Experience,* ed. Donald L. Horowitz and Gerard Noiriel, pp. 3–35. New York: New York University Press.

Horowitz, Donald L., and G. Noiriel, eds. 1992. *Immigrants in Two Democracies: French and American Experience*. New York: New York University Press.

Horowitz, Morton J. 1977. *The Transformation of American Law, 1780–1860*. Cambridge, Mass.: Harvard University Press.

Huff, Richard. 2005. "Viva! For 'Lopez' and Latinos." *Daily News,* January 27, p. 84.

Hunt, George P. 1967. "The Racial Crisis and the News Media: An Overview." In *Race and the News Media,* ed. Paul L. Fisher and Ralph L. Lowenstein. New York: Frederick A. Praeger.

Hunt, Lynn. 1978. *Revolution and Urban Politics in Provincial France: Troyes and Reims, 1786–1790*. Stanford, Calif.: Stanford University Press.

―――. 1984. *Politics, Culture, and Class in the French Revolution*. Berkeley: University of California Press.

―――, ed. 1989. *The New Cultural History: Essays*. Berkeley: University of California Press.

Huntington, Samuel P. 1961. *Political Order in Changing Societies*. New Haven, Conn.: Yale University Press.

―――. 2004. *Who Are We? The Challenges to America's National Identity*. New York; London: Simon and Schuster.

Hyman, Paula. 1979. *From Dreyfus to Vichy: The Remaking of French Jewry, 1906–1939*. New York: Columbia University Press.

Jacobs, Mark. 2005. "The Culture of Savings and Loan Scandal in the No-Fault Society." In *The Blackwell Companion to the Sociology of Culture,* ed. Mark Jacobs and Nancy Hanrahan, pp. 364–380. Oxford: Blackwell.

Jacobs, Ronald N. 1996. "Civil Society and Crisis: Culture, Discourse, and the Rodney King Beating." *American Journal of Sociology* 101 (5): 1238–1272.

―――. 1996. "Producing the News, Producing the Crisis: Narrativity, Television, and News Work." *Media, Culture and Society* 18 (3): 373–397.

————. 2000. *Race, Media, and the Crisis of Civil Society: From Watts to Rodney King.* Cambridge: Cambridge University Press.

Jacoby, Russell. 1999. *The End of Utopia: Politics and Culture in an Age of Apathy.* New York: Basic Books.

Jakobson, Roman. 1987. "On Linguistic Aspects of Translation." *Language in Literature,* ed. Krystyna Pomorska and Stephen Rudy. Cambridge, Mass.: Harvard University Press.

————. 1987. "On Realism in Art." *Language in Literature,* ed. Krystyna Pomorska and Stephen Rudy, pp. 19–27. Cambridge, Mass.: Harvard University Press.

————. 1990. "Shifters and Verbal Categories." In *On Language,* ed. Linda R. Waugh and Monique Monville-Burston. Cambridge, Mass.: Harvard University Press.

James, Susan. 1992. "The Good Enough Citizen." In *Beyond Equality and Difference: Citizenship, Feminist Politics, and Female Subjectivity,* ed. Gisela Bock and Susan James. New York: Routledge.

Jameson, Fredric. 1981. *The Political Unconscious: Narrative as a Socially Symbolic Act.* Ithaca, N.Y.: Cornell University Press.

Jamison, Andrew, and Ron Eyerman. 1994. *Seeds of the Sixties.* Berkeley: University of California Press.

Janoski, Thomas. 1998. *Citizenship and Civil Society: A Framework of Rights and Obligations in Liberal, Traditional, and Social Democratic Societies.* New York: Cambridge University Press.

Jasper, James. 1997. *The Art of Moral Protest: Culture, Biography, and Creativity in Social Movements.* Chicago: University of Chicago Press.

Jaworski, Leon. 1976. *The Right and the Power: The Prosecution of Watergate.* New York: Reader's Digest Press.

Jellinek, Georg. 1901. *The Declaration of the Rights of Man and of Citizens.* Trans. Max Farrand. New York: Holt.

"Jews in America." 1936. *Fortune Magazine,* February.

Johnson, Owen. 1968 [1911]. *Stover at Yale.* New York: Macmillan.

Johnston, Hank, and Bert Klandermans, eds. 1995. *Social Movements and Culture.* Minneapolis: University of Minnesota Press.

Jones, Arnold H. M. 1957. *Athenian Democracy.* Oxford: Basil Blackwell.

Jones, Gareth Stedman. 1983. *Languages of Class: Studies in English Working Class History, 1832–1982.* New York: Cambridge University Press.

Joppke, Christian. 1999. *Immigration and the Nation State: The United States, Germany, and Great Britain.* New York: Oxford University Press.

Joppke, Christian, and Ewa Morawska, eds. 2003. *Towards Assimilation and Citizenship: Immigrant in Liberal Nation States.* New York: Palgrave Macmillan.

Joseph II. 1995. "Edict of Tolerance [January 2, 1782]." In *The Jew in the Modern*

World: A Documentary History, ed. Paul Mendes-Flohr and Jehuda Reinharz. New York: Oxford University Press.

Joyce, Patrick. 1991. *Visions of the People: Industrial England and the Question of Class, 1848–1914.* New York: Cambridge University Press.

Judt, Tony. 1998. *The Burden of Responsibility: Blum, Camus, Aron, and the French Twentieth Century.* Chicago: University of Chicago Press.

Kafka, Franz. 2005 [1925]. *The Trial,* trans. David Wyllie. Project Gutenberg Ebook (www.gutenberg.org).

———. 1979. "Letter to His Father." In *The Basic Kafka,* ed. Erich Heller, pp. 186–236. New York: Washington Square.

———. 1996. *The Metamorphosis.* Prague: Vitalis.

Kahn, Paul W. 1999. *The Cultural Study of Law: Reconstructing Legal Scholarship.* Chicago: University of Chicago Press.

———. 2000. "Redirecting Legal Scholarship in Law Schools." *Yale Journal of Law and the Humanities* 12 (winter): 129–150.

Kairys, David. 1982. "Legal Reasoning." In *The Politics of Law: A Progressive Critique.* New York: Pantheon.

Kaiser, David. 1990. *Politics and War: European Conflict from Philip II to Hitler.* Cambridge, Mass.: Harvard University Press.

Kallen, Horace M. 1970 [1924]. *Culture and Democracy in the United States: Studies in the Group Psychology of the American People.* New York: Arno.

Kane, Anne. 1991. "Cultural Analysis in Historical Sociology: The Analytic and Concrete Forms of the Autonomy of Culture." *Sociological Theory* 9 (1): 53–69.

———. 1997. "Theorizing Meaning Construction in Social Movements." *Sociological Theory* 15 (3): 249–276.

———. 2001. "Finding Emotion in Social Movement Processes: Irish Land Movement Metaphors and Narratives." In *Passionate Politics: Emotions and Social Movements,* ed. Jeff Goodwin, James Jasper, and Francesca Polletta, pp. 251–266. Chicago: University of Chicago Press.

Kane, John. 2001. *The Politics of Moral Capital.* Cambridge: Cambridge University Press.

Kant, Immanuel. 1949 [1795]. "What Is Enlightenment?" In *The Philosophy of Kant: Immanuel Kant's Moral and Political Writings,* ed. C. J. Friedrich, pp. 263–270. New York: Modern Library.

———. 1986 [1795]. *Perpetual Peace,* ed. Lewis White Beck. Indianapolis, Ind.: Bobbs-Merrill.

Karp, Abraham J. 1998. *Jewish Continuity in America: Creative Survival in a Free Society.* Tuscaloosa: University of Alabama Press.

Karst, K. 1997. "The Supreme Court 1976 Term." *Harvard Law Review* 92.

Katz, Elihu, et al. 1998. "Press-Conversation-Opinion-Action: Gabriel Tarde's Public Sphere." In *Paul Lazarsfeld: (1901–1976) La Sociologie de Vienne à New York,* ed.

De Jacques Lautman and Bernard-Pierre Lecuyer, pp. 433–454. Paris: L'Harmattan.

Katznelson, Ira. 1995. "Between Separation and Disappearance: Jews on the Margins of American Liberalism." In *Paths of Emancipation: Jews, States, and Citizenship,* ed. Pierre Birnbaum and Ira Katznelson. Princeton, N.J.: Princeton University Press.

———. 2005. *When Affirmative Action Was White: An Untold History of Racial Inequality in Twentieth-Century America.* New York: Norton.

Keane, John. 1988. *Democracy and Civil Society: On the Predicaments of European Socialism, the Prospects for Democracy, and the Problem of Controlling Social and Political Power.* London: Verso.

———. 1998. *Civil Society: Old Images, New Visions.* Stanford, Calif.: Stanford University Press.

———, ed. 1988. *Civil Society and the State: New European Perspectives.* London: Verso.

———. 1988. "Despotism and Democracy: The Origins and Development of the Distinction between Civil Society and the State, 1750–1850." In *Civil Society and the State: New European Perspectives,* pp. 35–71. London: Verso.

Keller, Suzanne. 1963. *Beyond the Ruling Class: Strategic Elites in Modern Society.* New York: Random House.

Kelsen, Hans. 1946. *General Theory of Law and State.* Trans. Anders Wedberg. Cambridge, Mass.: Harvard University Press.

Kennedy, Duncan. 1976. "Form and Substance in Private Law Adjudication." *Harvard Law Review* 89 (8): 1685–1778.

———. 1979. "The Structure of Blackstone's Commentaries." *Buffalo Law Review* 28: 205.

Kennedy, Michael D. 1991. *Professionals, Power, and Solidarity in Poland.* New York: Cambridge University Press.

Kennedy, Paul. 1987. *The Rise and Fall of the Great Powers: Economic Change and Military Conflict from 1500–2000.* New York: Vintage Books.

Kerber, Linda K. 1980. *Women of the Republic: Intellect and Ideology in Revolutionary America.* Chapel Hill: University of North Carolina Press.

———. 1986. "Some Cautionary Words for Historians." *Signs* 11 (2): 304–310.

———. 1995. "The Republican Mother and the Woman Citizen." In *Women's America: Refocusing the Past,* ed. Linda K. Kerber and Jane Sherron De Hart. Oxford: Oxford University Press.

Kerber, Linda K., and Jane Sherron De Hart. 1980. "The Many Frontiers of Industrializing America 1880–1920." In *Women's America: Refocusing the Past,* ed. Linda K. Kerber and Jane Sherron De Hart. Oxford: Oxford University Press.

———, eds. 1995. *Women's America: Refocusing the Past.* Oxford: Oxford University Press.

Key, Vladimir, O. 1950. *Southern Politics in State and Nation.* New York: Alfred A. Knopf.

Keynes, John Maynard. 1919. *The Economic Consequences of the Peace.* London: Macmillan.

Keyssar, Alexander. 2000. *The Right to Vote: The Contested History of Democracy in the United States.* New York: Basic Books.

Kieval, Hillel J. 1988. *The Making of Czech Jewry: National Conflict and Jewish Society in Bohemia, 1870–1918.* New York: Oxford University Press.

———. 1990. "The Lands Between: The Jews of Bohemia, Moravia, and Slovakia to 1918." In *Where Cultures Meet: The Story of the Jews of Czechoslovakia,* ed. Natalia Berger, pp. 23–51. Tel Aviv: Beth Hatefutsoth.

Kimball, Roger. 1992. "The Periphery v. the Center: The MLA in Chicago." In *Debating P.C.: The Controversy over Political Correctness on College Campuses,* ed. Paul Berman, pp. 61–84. New York: Vintage.

Kimmerling, Baruch, and Joel Migdal. 2003. *The Palestinian People: A History.* Cambridge, Mass.: Harvard University Press.

King, Martin Luther, Jr. 1956. "Our Struggle." *Liberation* (April).

———. 1964. *Why We Can't Wait.* New York: New American Library.

———. 1965. "Behind the Selma March." *Saturday Review of Books* (April 3): 16–17, 57.

———. 1967. *Where Do We Go From Here: Chaos or Community?* New York: Harper and Row.

Kivisto, Peter, ed. 2005. *Incorporating Diversity: Rethinking Assimilation in a Multicultural Age.* Boulder, Colo.: Paradigm.

Klandermans, Bert. 1988. "The Formation and Mobilization of Consensus." In *International Social Movements,* Vol. 1 of *From Structure to Action: Comparing Movement Participation across Cultures,* ed. Bert Klandermans, Hanspeter Kriesi, and Sidney Tarrow, pp. 173–197. Greenwich, Conn.: JAI Press.

———. 1992. "The Social Construction of Protest and Multiorganizational Fields." In *Frontiers in Social Movement Theory,* ed. Aldon D. Morris and Carol McClung Mueller, pp. 71–103. New Haven, Conn.: Yale University Press.

Klare, Karl E. 1978. "Judicial Deradicalization of the Wagner Act and the Origins of Modern Legal Consciousness, 1937–1941." *Minnesota Law Review* 62 (3): 265–399.

Kleeblatt, Norman L., ed. 1996. *Too Jewish? Challenging Traditional Identities.* New York: Jewish Museum; New Brunswick, N.J.: Rutgers University Press.

Kolakowski, Leszek. 1971. "Hope and Hopelessness." *Survey* 47 (3): 37–52.

Kornhauser, William. 1959. *The Politics of Mass Society.* Glencoe, Ill.: Free Press.

Kotz, Nick. 2005. *Judgment Days: Lyndon Baines Johnson, Martin Luther King, Jr., and the Laws That Changed America.* Boston: Houghton Mifflin.

Kristeva, Julia. 1980. "The Bounded Text." *Desire in Language: A Semiotic Approach to Literature and Art,* pp. 36–63. New York: Columbia University Press.

Krutikov, M. 2001. *Yiddish Fiction and the Crisis of Modernity, 1905–1914.* Stanford, Calif.: Stanford University Press.

Ku, Agnes. 1998. "Boundary Politics in the Public Sphere: Openness, Secrecy, and Leakage." *Sociological Theory* 16 (2): 172–190.

———. 1999. *Narratives, Politics, and the Public Sphere: Struggles over Political Reform in the Final Transitional Years in Hong Kong (1992–94).* London: Ashgate.

———. 2000. "Revisiting the Notion of 'Public' in Habermas's Theory: Towards a Theory of Politics of Public Credibility." *Sociological Theory* 18 (2): 216–240.

Kuisel, Richard F. 1993. *Seducing the French: The Dilemma of Americanization.* Berkeley: University of California Press.

Kumar, Krishan. 2003. *The Making of English National Identity.* New York: Cambridge University Press.

Kunstler, William M. 1966. *Deep in My Heart.* New York: William Morrow.

Kuper, Leo. 1960. "The Heightening of Racial Tension." *Race* 2 (November): 24–32.

———. 1981. *Genocide: Its Political Use in the Twentieth Century.* New Haven, Conn.: Yale University Press.

———. 1985. *Prevention of Genocide.* New Haven, Conn.: Yale University Press.

Kuper, Leo, and M. G. Smith, eds. 1969. *Pluralism in Africa.* Berkeley: University of California Press.

Kutler, Stanley I. 1990. *The Wars of Watergate: The Last Crisis of Richard Nixon.* New York: Alfred A. Knopf.

Kymlicka, Will. 1995. *Multicultural Citizenship: A Liberal Theory of Minority Rights.* Oxford: Oxford University Press.

Lacey, Nicola. 2004. *A Life of H.L.A. Hart: The Nightmare and the Noble Dream.* New York: Oxford University Press.

Lacouture, Jean. 1993. *De Gaulle, The Rebel, 1890–1944.* New York: Harper Collins.

Lakoff, George. 1987. *Women, Fire, and Dangerous Things: What Categories Reveal about the Mind.* Chicago: University of Chicago Press.

———. 2002. *Moral Politics: How Liberals and Conservatives Think.* Chicago: University of Chicago Press.

Lamont, Michele. 1992. *Money, Morals, and Manners: The Culture of the French and American Upper-Middle Class.* Chicago: University of Chicago Press.

———. 2000. *The Dignity of Working Men: Morality and the Boundaries of Race, Class, and Immigration.* Cambridge, Mass.: Harvard University Press.

Landes, Joan B. 1988. *Women and the Public Sphere in the Age of the French Revolution.* Ithaca, N.Y.: Cornell University Press.

———, ed. 1998. *Feminism, the Public, and the Private.* New York: Oxford University Press.

Landry, Bert. 1987. *The New Black Middle Class*. Berkeley: University of California Press.

————. 1991. "The Enduring Dilemmas of Race in American," In *America at Century's End*, ed. Alan Wolfe, pp. 185–207. Berkeley: University of California Press.

Lang, Gladys E., and Kurt Lang. 1983. *The Battle for Public Opinion: The President, the Press, and the Polls during Watergate*. New York: Columbia University Press.

Lapeyronnie, Didier. 1993. *L'individu et les Minorités: La France et la Grande-Bretagne face à leurs immigrés*. Paris: Presses Universitaires de France.

Laqueur, Walter. 1980. *The Terrible Secret: Suppression of the Truth about Hitler's "Final Solution."* Boston: Little, Brown.

Lara, Maria Pia. 1998. "Narrative Cultural Interweavings: Between Fact and Fiction." *Moral Textures: Feminist Narratives in the Public Sphere*, pp. 92–104. Cambridge, U.K.: Polity Press.

————. 1998. *Moral Textures: Feminist Narratives in the Public Sphere*. Cambridge, U.K.: Polity Press.

Larsen, Nella. 1929. *Passing*. New York: Alfred A. Knopf.

Laslett, Peter. 1963. "Introduction to Locke." In John Locke, *Two Treatises on Government*. New York: Cambridge University Press.

Lasswell, Harold D. 1941. *Democracy through Public Opinion*. Menasha, Wis.: George Banta.

Lawrence, D. H. 1970 [1923]. *Studies in Classic American Literature*. New York: Viking.

Le Bon, Gustave. 1960 [1895]. *The Crowd: A Study of the Popular Mind*. New York: Viking.

Lefort, Claude. 1988. *Democracy and Political Theory*, trans. David Macey. Minneapolis: University of Minnesota Press.

Lembo, Ron. 2000. *Thinking through Television*. New York: Cambridge University Press.

Lentz, Richard. 1990. *Symbols, the News Magazines, and Martin Luther King*. Baton Rouge: Louisiana State University Press.

Lerner, Daniel. 1958. *The Passing of Traditional Society: Modernizing the Middle East*. Glencoe, Ill.: Free Press.

Lévi-Strauss, Claude. 1967. *The Savage Mind*. Chicago: University of Chicago Press.

————. 1963. "Structural Analysis in Linguistics and in Anthropology." In *Structural Anthropology*, Vol. 1, trans. Claire Jacobson and Brooke Grundfest Schoepf. New York: Basic Books.

Leviero, Anthony. 1948. "President Likens Dewey to Hitler as Fascists' Tool." *New York Times*, October 26, p. 1.

Levine, Donald N. 1985. *The Flight from Ambiguity: Essays in Social and Cultural Theory*. Chicago: University of Chicago Press.

———. 1991. "Simmel and Parsons Reconsidered." *American Journal of Sociology* 96 (5): 1097–1116.

Levinson, Shneier Salman, et al. "Karl Heinrich Marx." *Encyclopedia Judaica* 11: 1075.

Lewellyn, K. N. 1931. "Some Realism about Realism." *Harvard Law Review* 40.

Lewis, Anthony. 1977. "Introduction." In James Doyle, *Not Above the Law: The Battles of Watergate Prosecutors Cox and Jaworski, a Behind-the-Scenes Account*. New York: William Morrow.

———. 1983. "The Jew in Stand-Up Comedy." In *From Hester Street to Hollywood: The Jewish American Stage and Screen,* ed. Sarah Blacher Cohen, pp. 58–70. Bloomington: Indiana University Press.

Lewis, David L. 1993. *W.E.B. Dubois: Biography of a Race, 1868–1919*. New York: Henry Holt.

Liberles, Robert. 1998. "Dohm's Treatise on the Jews: A Defense of the Enlightenment." *Leo Baeck Institute Year Book* 33.

Lidz, Victor, Renee Fox, and Harold Bershady, eds. 2005. *After Parsons: A Theory of Social Action for the Twenty-First Century*. New York: Russell Sage.

Liebman, Joshua Loth. 1946. *Peace of Mind*. New York: Simon and Schuster.

Life Magazine. 1952. "*Life* Goes to a Bar Mitzvah: A Boy Becomes a Man." October 13, p. 96.

Lippman, Walter. 1922. *Public Opinion*. New York: Harcourt Brace.

———. 1925. *The Phantom Public*. New York: Harcourt Brace.

Lipset, Seymour M. 1962 [1911]. "Introduction." In Robert Michels, *Political Parties: A Sociological Study of the Oligarchical Tendencies of Modern Democracy*. New York: Free Press.

———. 1960. *Political Man: The Social Bases of Politics*. New York: Doubleday.

———. 1965. *The First New Nation: The United States in Historical and Comparative Perspective*. New York: Vintage.

———. 1969. "The American Jewish Community in a Comparative Perspective." In *The Ghetto and Beyond: Essays on Jewish Life in America,* ed. Peter I. Rose, pp. 21–32. New York: Random House.

———. 1981 [1960]. "Elections: The Expression of the Democratic Class Struggle." In Seymour M. Lipset, *Political Man: The Social Bases of Politics,* pp. 230–278. Baltimore, Md.: Johns Hopkins University Press.

———. 1981 [1960]. "Economic Development and Democracy." In Seymour M. Lipset, *Political Man: The Social Bases of Politics,* pp. 27–63. Baltimore, Md.: Johns Hopkins University Press.

———. 1981 [1960]. " 'Fascism'—Left, Right, and Center." In Seymour M. Lipset,

Political Man: The Social Bases of Politics, pp. 127–179. Baltimore, Md.: Johns Hopkins University Press.

———. 1990. "A Unique People in an Exceptional Country." In *American Pluralism and the Jewish Community,* ed. S. M. Lipset, pp. 3–30. New Brunswick, N.J.: Transaction.

Lipset, Seymour M., and Earl Raab. 1970. *The Politics of Unreason: Right Wing Extremism in America, 1790–1970.* New York: Harper and Row.

———. 1975. "An Appointment with Watergate." In *Why Watergate?* ed. Paul Halpern, pp. 17–35. Pacific Palisades, Calif.: Palisades.

Lipset, Seymour M, Martin A. Trow, and James S. Coleman. 1956. *Union Democracy: The Internal Politics of the International Typographical Union.* Glencoe, Ill.: Free Press.

Little, David. 1969. *American Foreign Policy and Moral Rhetoric.* New York: Council on Religion and International Affairs.

———. 1969. *Religion, Order, and Law: A Study in Pre-Revolutionary England.* New York: Harper and Row.

Locke, John. 1952 [1694]. *The Second Treatise on Government: An Essay Concerning the True Original, Extent, and End of Civil Government,* ed. Thomas Peardon. Indianapolis, Ind.: Bobbs-Merrill.

Long, Elizabeth. 1985. *The American Dream and the Popular Novel.* Boston: Routledge and Kegan Paul.

———. 2003. *Book Clubs: Women and the Uses of Reading in Everyday Life.* Chicago: University of Chicago Press.

Los Angeles Times, March 7, 1991.

Los Angeles Times, March 12, 1991.

Luhmann, Niklas. 1982. "The Autonomy of the Legal System." In *The Differentiation of Society,* trans. Stephen Holmes and Charles Larmore, pp. 122–137. New York: Columbia University Press.

———. 1982. *The Differentiation of Society,* trans. Stephen Holmes and Charles Larmore. New York: Columbia University Press.

———. 1982. "Politics as a Social System." In *The Differentiation of Society.* trans. Stephen Holmes and Charles Larmore. New York: Columbia University Press.

Luker, Ralph E. 1991. *The Social Gospel in Black and White: American Racial Reform, 1885–1912.* Chapel Hill: University of North Carolina Press.

Luria, Z. 1986. "A Methodological Critique." *Signs* 11 (2): 320

Machiavelli, Niccolo. 1950 [1531]. *The Discourses.* New Haven, Conn.: Yale University Press.

MacIntyre, Alasdair. 1981. *After Virtue: A Study in Moral Theory.* Notre Dame, Ind.: University of Notre Dame Press.

———. 1988. *Whose Justice? Which Rationality?* Notre Dame, Ind.: University of Notre Dame Press.

MacIver, Robert M. 1947. *The Web of Government.* New York: Macmillan.

MacKinnon, Catherine A. 1987. *Feminism Unmodified: Discourses on Life and Law.* Cambridge, Mass.: Harvard University Press.

Magnuson, Eric. 1997. "Ideological Conflict in American Political Culture: The Discourse of Civil Society and American National Narratives in American History Textbooks." *International Journal of Social Policy* 17 (6): 84–130.

Mahoney, Richard D. 1999. *Sons and Brothers: The Days of Jack and Robert Kennedy.* New York: Arcade.

Malin, Irving. 1973. *Contemporary American-Jewish Literature; Critical Essays.* Bloomington: Indiana University Press.

Mamdani, Mahmood. 1996. *Citizen and Subject: Contemporary Africa and the Legacy of Late Colonialism.* Princeton, N.J.: Princeton University Press.

Mann, Michael. 1986. *The Sources of Social Power.* Vol. 1: *A History of Power from the Beginning to A.D. 1760.* Cambridge: Cambridge University Press.

Mansbridge, Jane J. 1980. *Beyond Adversary Democracy.* Chicago: University of Chicago Press.

Marcuse, Herbert. 1960 [1941]. *Reason and Revolution; Hegel and the Rise of Social Theory.* Boston: Beacon Press.

———. 1963. *One-Dimensional Man: Studies in the Ideology of Advanced Industrial Society.* Boston: Beacon Press.

Marrus, Michael R., and Robert O. Paxton. 1995 [1981]. *Vichy France and the Jews.* Stanford, Calif.: Stanford University Press.

———. 1995 [1981]. "The Roots of Vichy Anti-Semitism," in *Vichy France and the Jews,* pp. 25–71. Stanford, Calif.: Stanford University Press.

Marshall, Thomas H. 1965. *Class, Citizenship, and Social Development.* New York: Free Press.

Marvin, Carolyn, and David W. Ingle. 1999. *Blood Sacrifice and the Nation: Totem Rituals and the American Flag.* New York: Cambridge University Press.

Marx, Karl. 1962 [1867]. *Capital.* Vol. 1. Moscow: International.

———. 1962 [1875]. "Critique of the Gotha Programme." In *Karl Marx and Frederick Engels: Selected Works II,* pp. 13–61. Moscow: International.

———. 1962 [1848]. "The Eighteenth Brumaire of Louis Bonaparte." In *Karl Marx and Frederick Engels: Selected Works I,* pp. 247–345. Moscow: International.

———. 1963 [1843] "Contribution to the Critique of Hegel's Philosophy of Right, Introduction." In *Karl Marx: Early Writings,* ed. T. B. Bottomore, pp. 41–60. New York: McGraw-Hill.

———. 1963 [1844]. "Economic and Philosophical Manuscripts." In *Karl Marx: Early Writings,* ed. T. B. Bottomore, pp. 61–219. New York: McGraw-Hill.

———. 1963 [1843]. "On the Jewish Question." In *Karl Marx: Early Writings,* ed. T. B. Bottomore, pp. 216–248. New York: McGraw-Hill.

———. 1967 [1845]. "The Holy Family." In *Writings of the Young Marx on Philosophy and Society,* ed. L. Easton and K. Guddat, pp. 361–398. New York: Doubleday.

————. 1970 [1846]. *The German Ideology*. Moscow: International.

————. 1962 [1848]. "Manifesto of the Communist Party." In *Karl Marx and Friedrich Engels: Selected Works*, Vol. I, pp. 18–48. Moscow: International.

Massey, Douglas S., and Nancy A. Denton. 1993. *American Apartheid: Segregation and the Making of the Underclass*. Cambridge, Mass.: Harvard University Press.

Mast, Jason. 2005. "The Cultural Pragmatics of Eventness: The Clinton/Lewinsky Affair." *Social Performances: Symbolic Action, Cultural Pragmatics, and Ritual*, ed. Jeffrey C. Alexander, Bernhard Giesen, and Jason Mast. New York: Cambridge University Press.

Matsuda, Matt K. 2005. *Empire of Love: Histories of France and the Pacific*. New York: Oxford University Press.

Mayhew, Leon H. 1984. *The Public Spirit: On the Origins of Liberal Thought: An Address to the Librarians Association of University of California, Davis*. Davis, Calif.

————. 1997. *The New Public: Professional Communication and the Means of Social Influence*. New York: Cambridge University Press.

McAdam, Doug. 1982. *Political Process and the Development of Black Insurgency, 1930–70*. Chicago: University of Chicago Press.

————. 1988. *Freedom Summer*. Cambridge: Cambridge University Press.

————. 1996. "The Framing Function of Movement Tracts: Strategic Dramaturgy in the American Civil Rights Movement." In *Comparative Perspectives on Social Movements: Political Opportunities, Mobilizing Structures, and Cultural Framings*, ed. Doug McAdam, John McCarthy, and Mayer Zald. New York: Cambridge University Press.

McCarthy, John D., and Mayer N. Zald. 1977. "Resource Mobilization and Social Movements: A Partial Theory." *American Journal of Sociology* 83 (6): 1212.

McConville, Michael, Andrew Sanders, and Roger Leng. 1991. *The Case for the Prosecution: Police Suspects and the Construction of Criminality*. London: Routledge.

McNeil, Genna Rae. 1983. *Groundwork: Charles Hamilton Houston and the Struggle for Civil Rights*. Philadelphia: University of Pennsylvania Press.

Mead, George H. 1964. *Mind, Self, and Society*. Chicago: Chicago University Press.

Meier, August. "On the Role of Martin Luther King." *New Politics* 4 (1): 52–59.

Meinecke, Friedrich. 1975 [1905]. *The Age of German Liberation, 1795–1815*, trans. Peter Paret and Helmuth Fischer. Berkeley: University of California Press.

Melucci, Alberto. 1980. "The New Social Movements: A Theoretical Approach." *Social Science Information* 19 (2): 217–218.

————. 1988. "Social Movements and the Democratization of Everyday Life." In *Civil Society and the State: New European Perspectives*, ed. John Keane. London: Verso.

Menand, Louis. 2001. *The Metaphysical Club: A Story of Ideas in America*. New York: Farrar, Straus, and Giroux.

Mendelssohn, Moses. 1983 [1783]. *Jerusalem, or, on Religious Power and Judaism.* Trans. Alexander Altman. Hanover, N.H.: University Press of New England.

———. 1995 [1782]. "Response to Dohm." *The Jew in the Modern World: A Documentary History,* ed. Paul Mendes-Flohr and Jehuda Reinharz, pp. 38–42. New York: Oxford University Press.

———. 1995. "Why I Have Raised You as a Christian: A Letter to His Daughter [1820]." In *The Jew in the Modern World: A Documentary History,* ed. Paul Mendes-Flohr and Jehuda Reinharz. New York: Oxford University Press.

Mendes-Flohr, Paul, and Jehuda Reinharz. 1995. *The Jew in the Modern World: A Documentary History.* New York: Oxford University Press.

Menocal, Maria Rosa. 2002. *The Ornament of the World: How Muslims, Jews, and Christians Created a Culture of Tolerance in Medieval Spain.* Boston: Little, Brown.

Meyer, John W., and B. Rowan. 1991. "Institutional Organizations: Formal Structure as Myth and Ceremony." In *The New Institutionalism in Organizational Analysis,* ed. Paul J. DiMaggio and Walter W. Powell, pp. 41–62. Chicago: University of Chicago Press.

Meyer, Michael A. 1988. *Response to Modernity: A History of the Reform Movement in Judaism.* New York: Oxford University Press.

Michelman, Frank. 1988. "Law's Republic." *Yale Law Journal* 97 (8): 1493–1537.

Michels, Robert. 1962 [1911]. *Political Parties: A Sociological Study of the Oligarchical Tendencies of Modern Democracy.* Trans. Eden Paul and Cedar Paul. New York: Free Press.

Michnik, Adam. 1976. "The New Evolutionism." *Survey* 22 (3/4): 267–277.

Middlekauff, Robert. 1972. "The Ritualization of the American Revolution. In *The National Temper: Readings in American History,* 2nd ed., ed. Lawrence W. Levine and Robert Middlekauff. New York: Harcourt, Brace, and World.

———. 1982. *The Glorious Cause: The American Revolution 1763–1789.* New York: Oxford University Press.

Miliband, Ralph. 1969. *The State in Capitalist Society: An Analysis of the Western System of Power.* New York: Basic Books.

Milkman, Ruth. 1987. *Gender at Work: The Dynamics of Job Segregation by Sex during World War II.* Urbana: University of Illinois Press.

———. 1995. "Gender at Work: The Sexual Division of Labor during World War II." In *Women's America: Refocusing the Past,* ed. Linda K. Kerber and Jane Sherron De Hart. Oxford: Oxford University Press.

Miller, Perry. 1939. *The New England Mind: The Seventeenth Century.* Cambridge, Mass.: Harvard University Press.

———. 1956. *Errand into the Wilderness.* Cambridge, Mass.: Belknap.

———. 1965. *The Life of the Mind in America, from the Revolution to the Civil War.* New York: Harcourt, Brace, and World.

Miller, Warren E., and J. Merrill Shanks. 1996. *The New American Voter*. Cambridge, Mass.: Harvard University Press.

Miller, William L. 1996. *Arguing About Slavery: The Great Battle in the United States Congress*. New York: Alfred A. Knopf.

Mills, Charles W. 1997. *The Racial Contract*. Ithaca, N.Y.: Cornell University Press.

Mills, C. Wright. 1956. *The Power Elite*. New York: Oxford University Press.

Miron, Dan. 1973. *A Traveler Disguised: A Study in the Rise of Modern Yiddish Fiction in the Nineteenth Century*. New York: Schocken.

Montesquieu, Charles de Secondat, Baron de. 1949 [1748]. *The Spirit of the Laws*. Trans. Thomas Nugent. New York: Hafner.

Montgomery, David. 1980. "Labor and the Republic in Industrial America: 1860–1920." *Le Movement Social III*: 201–215.

Moore, Barrington. 1966. *The Social Origins of Dictatorship and Democracy: Lord and Peasant in the Making of the Modern World*. Boston: Beacon.

———. 2000. *Moral Purity and Persecution in History*. Princeton, N.J.: Princeton University Press.

Moore, Michael S. 1985. "A Natural Law Theory of Interpretation." *Southern California Law Review* 58: 279.

Moore, R. Laurence. 1986. *Religious Outsiders and the Making of Americans*. New York: Oxford University Press.

Morgan, Edmund S. 2002. *Benjamin Franklin*. New Haven, Conn.: Yale University Press.

Morganthau, Henry. 1982. "Central Park West." *Moment* 7 (4): 18–24.

Morris, Aldon D. 1984. *The Origins of the Civil Rights Movement: Black Communities Organizing for Change*. New York: Free Press.

Morris, Charles W. 1938. *Foundations of the Theory of Signs*. Chicago: University of Chicago Press.

Morris, Colin. 1972. *The Discovery of the Individual: 1050–1200*. New York: Harper and Row.

Moscovici, Serge, Gabriel Mugny, and Eddy Van Avermaet, eds. 1985. *Perspectives on Minority Influence*. New York: Cambridge University Press.

Mosher, Frederick C. 1968. *Democracy and the Public Service*. New York: Oxford University Press.

Mouffe, Chantal. 2000. *The Democratic Paradox*. London: Verso.

"Mr. Giuliani's Thunderbolt." 1994. *New York Times,* October 25, p. A20.

Mukerji, Chandra. 1997. "Monsters and Muppets: The History of Childhood Techniques of Cultural Analysis." In *From Sociology to Cultural Studies: News Perspectives,* ed. Elizabeth Long, pp. 157–184. New York: Blackwell.

Murray, Judith Sargent. 1992. *The Gleaner*. Schenectady, N.Y.: Union College Press.

Mutz, Diana C. 1998. *Impersonal Influence: How Perceptions of Mass Collectives Affect Political Attitudes*. New York: Cambridge University Press.

Nairn, T. 1995. "Breakwaters of 2000: From Ethnic to Civic Nationalism." *New Left Review* 214: 91–203.

Nash, Gary B. 1992. *Red, White, and Black: The People of Early North America.* Englewood Cliffs, N.J.: Prentice-Hall.

Nelson, B. 1973. "Weber's Protestant Ethic: Its Origins, Wanderings, and Foreseeable Futures." In *Beyond the Classics? Essays in the Scientific Study of Religion,* ed. Charles Glock and Phillip Hammond, pp. 71–130. New York: Harper and Row.

Neumann, Franz. 1986. *The Rule of Law: Political Theory and the Legal System in Modern Society.* Heidelberg, Germany: Berg.

Neumann, Iver B. 1999. *Uses of the Other: "The East" in European Identity Formation.* Minneapolis: University of Minnesota Press.

New Republic, August 20, 1945.

New York Times. October 1, 1945.

New York Times. November 26, 1956.

New York Times. January 7, 1957.

New York Times. February 18, 1957.

New York Times. August 25, 1989.

New York Times. October 25, 1989.

New York Times. October 30, 1999.

New York Times. "Excerpts from Justices' Opinions on Michigan Affirmative Action Cases." June 24, 2003, p. A24.

Newsweek. March 5, 1956.

Newsweek. November 26, 1956.

Nichols, L. 1991. " 'Whistle Blower' or Renegade: Definitional Contests in an Official Inquiry." *Symbolic Interaction* 14 (4): 395–414.

———. 1997. "Social Problems as Landmark Narratives: Bank of Boston, Mass Media and 'Money Laundering.' " *Social Problems* 44 (3): 324–341.

Nietzsche, Friedrich W. 1956 [1872, 1887]. *The Birth of Tragedy and the Genealogy of Morals,* trans. Francis Golffing. New York: Anchor.

Noel, Mary. 1954. *Villains Galore: The Heyday of the Popular Story Weekly.* New York: Macmillan.

Noiriel, Gerard. 1992. "Difficulties in French Historical Research on Immigration." In *Immigrants in Two Democracies: French and American Experience,* ed. Donald L. Horowitz and Gerard Noiriel, pp. 66–79. New York: New York University Press.

Nussbaum, Martha C. 1986. *The Fragility of Goodness: Luck and Ethics in Greek Tragedy and Philosophy.* New York: Cambridge University Press.

Oakes, James. 1995. "The Liberal Dissensus." Manuscript, quoted in M. Dawson, "A Black Counterpublic? Economic Earthquakes, Racial Agenda(s), and Black Politics." In *The Black Public Sphere: A Public Culture Book,* ed. Black Public Sphere Collective, pp. 205–206. Chicago: University of Chicago Press.

Oakeshott, Michael. 1975. *On Human Conduct.* Oxford: Oxford University Press.

Oberschall, Anthony. 1973. *Social Conflict and Social Movements*. Englewood Cliffs, N.J.: Prentice-Hall.

Oren, Dan A. 2000. *Joining the Club: A History of Jews and Yale*. New Haven, Conn.: Yale University Press.

Page, Benjamin I., and Robert Shapiro. 1992. *The Rational Public: Fifty Years of Trends in Americans' Policy Preferences*. Chicago: University of Chicago Press.

Park, Robert E. 1972 [1904]. *The Crowd and Public and Other Essays*, ed. Henry Elsner, trans. Charlotte Elsner. Chicago: University of Chicago Press.

Park, Sunwoong. 1996. Culture, Civil Society, and Political Change: The Transition to Democracy in South Korea. Ph.D. diss., Univ. California, Los Angeles.

Parkin, Robert. 1996. *The Dark Side of Humanity: The Work of Robert Hertz and Its Legacy*. Amsterdam: Harwood.

Parsons, Talcott. 1942. "The Sociology of Anti-Semitism." In *Jews in a Gentile World: The Problem of Anti-Semitism*, ed. Isacque Graeber and Steuart Henderson Britt, pp. 101–122. New York: Macmillan.

———. 1946. "Certain Primary Sources and Patterns of Aggression in the Western World." *Psychiatry* 10: 167–81.

———. 1966. "Full citizenship for the Negro American?" In *The Negro American*, ed. K. Clark and T. Parsons. Boston: Houghton Mifflin.

———. 1966. *Societies: Evolutionary and Comparative Perspectives*. Englewood Cliffs, N.J.: Prentice-Hall.

———. 1967. "Durkheim's Contribution to the Theory of Integration of Social Systems." In *Sociological Theory and Modern Society*, pp. 3–34. New York: Free Press.

———. 1967. "Evolutionary Universals in Society." In *Sociological Theory and Modern Society*, pp. 490–520. New York: Free Press.

———. 1969. "On the Concept of Political Power." In *Politics and Social Structure*, pp. 352–404. New York: Free Press.

———. 1969. *Politics and Social Structure*. New York: Free Press.

———. 1971. *The System of Modern Societies*. Englewood Cliffs, N.J.: Prentice-Hall.

Parsons, Talcott, and Edward Shils. 1967. "Values, Motives, and System of Action." In *Toward a General Theory of Action*, pp. 47–234. Cambridge, Mass.: Harvard University Press.

———. 1992. "Integration and Institutionalization of the Social System." In *Talcott Parsons on Institutions and Social Evolution*, ed. Leon Mayhew, pp. 117–129. Chicago: University of Chicago Press.

———, eds. 2001 [1951]. *Toward a General Theory of Action*. New Brunswick, N.J.: Transaction.

Parsons, Talcott, and Neil J. Smelser. 1956. *Economy and Society: A Study in the Integration of Economic and Social Theory*. New York: Free Press.

Pateman, Carole. 1988. "The Fraternal Social Contract." In *Civil Society and the State: New European Perspectives,* ed. John Keane, pp. 101–128. London: Verso.

Patterson, Orlando. 1997. *The Ordeal of Integration: Progress and Resentment in America's "Racial" Crisis.* Washington, D.C.: Civitas.

———. 1998. *Rituals of Blood: Consequences of Slavery in Two American Centuries.* Washington, D.C.: Civitas.

Pattillo-McCoy, Mary. 1998. "Church Culture as a Strategy of Action in the Black Community." *American Sociological Review* 63: 767–784.

———. 1999. *Black Picket Fences: Privilege and Peril among the Black Middle Classes.* Chicago: University of Chicago Press.

Pawel, Ernst. 1984. *The Nightmare of Reason: A Life of Franz Kafka.* New York: Farrar, Straus, and Giroux.

Payne, Charles M. 1995. *I've Got the Light of Freedom: The Organizing Tradition and the Mississippi Freedom Struggle.* Berkeley: University of California Press.

Peirce, Charles. 1985. "Logic as Semiotic: The Theory of Signs." In *Seminotics: An Introductory Anthology,* ed. Robert Innis, pp. 1–23. Bloomington: Indiana University Press.

Pelczynski, Z. A., ed. 1984. *The State and Civil Society: Studies in Hegel's Political Philosophy.* New York: Cambridge University Press.

Pérez-Diaz, Victor. 1993. *The Return of Civil Society: The Emergence of Democratic Spain.* Cambridge, Mass.: Harvard University Press.

———. 1998. "The Public Sphere and a European Civil Society." In *Real Civil Societies: Dilemmas of Institutionalization,* ed. Jeffrey C. Alexander. London: Sage.

Perry, George Sessions. 1948. "Your Neighbors: The Colombs." *Saturday Evening Post,* November 13, p. 36.

Philipson, David. 1931. *The Reform Movement in Judaism.* New York: Macmillan.

Phillips, T., and Philip Smith. 2004. "Emotional and Behavioral Responses to Everyday Incivility: Challenging the Fear/Avoidance Paradigm." *Journal of Sociology* 40 (4): 378–399.

———. 2003. "Everyday Incivility: Towards a Benchmark." *Sociological Review* 51 (1): 85–108.

Pinsker, Sanford. 1992. *Jewish-American Fiction, 1917–1987.* New York: Twayne.

Pipes, Richard. 2004. "Flight from Freedom: What Russians Think and Want." *Foreign Affairs* 83 (May): 9–15.

Pitkin, Hannah F. 1972. *Wittgenstein and Justice: On the Significance of Ludwig Wittgenstein for Social and Political Thought.* Berkeley: University of California Press.

Pizzorno, Alessandro. 1978. "Political Exchange and Collective Identity in Industrial Conflict." In *The Resurgence of Class Conflict in Western Europe since 1968,* Vol. 2, ed. Colin Crouch and Alessandro Pizzorno. New York: Holmes and Meier.

———. 1985. "On the Rationality of Democratic Choice." *Telos* 63 (spring): 41–69.

Plato. 1965. *The Republic.* Trans. Francis MacDonald Cornford. New York: Oxford University Press.

Pocock, J.G.A. 1967. *The Ancient Constitution and the Feudal Law: A Study of English Historical Thought in the Seventeenth Century.* New York: Norton.

Podhoretz, Norman. 1999. *Ex-Friends: Falling out with Allen Ginsberg, Lionel and Diana Trilling, Lillian Hellman, Hannah Arendt, and Norman Mailer.* New York: Free Press.

Polanyi, Karl. 1944. *The Great Transformation: The Political and Economic Origins of Our Time.* Boston: Beacon.

Poliakov, Leon. 1965. *The History of Anti-Semitism.* Vol. I: *From the Time of Christ to the Court Jews.* New York: Vanguard Press.

Polletta, Francesca. 1998. " 'It Was Like a Fever . . . ' Narrative and Identity in Social Protest." *Social Problems* 45 (2): 137–159.

————. 2005. "Why Stories Matter." Unpublished manuscript.

————. 2006. *It Was Like a Fever: Storytelling in Protest and Politics.* Chicago: University of Chicago Press.

Polletta, Francesca, and Edwin Amenta. 2001. "Second that Emotion? Lessons from Once-Novel Concepts in Social Movement Research." In *Passionate Politics: Emotions and Social Movements,* ed. Jeff Goodwin, James Jasper, and Francesca Polletta. Chicago: University of Chicago Press.

Polletta, Francesca, and James Jasper. 2001. "Collective Identity and Social Movements." *Annual Review of Sociology* 27: 283–305.

Polsby, Nelson W. 1978. "Coalition and Faction in American Politics: An Institutional View." In *Emerging Coalitions in American Politics,* ed. Seymour M. Lipset, pp. 103–126. San Francisco: Institute for Contemporary Politics.

Polsby, Nelson W., and Aaron B. Wildavsky. 1974. *Presidential Elections: Strategies of American Electoral Politics,* 3rd ed. New York: Scribner.

Popkin, Samuel L. 1991. *The Reasoning Voter: Communication and Persuasion in Presidential Campaigns.* Chicago: University of Chicago Press.

Portes, Alejandro and Rubén G. Rumbaut. 2001. *Legacies: The Story of the Immigrant Second Generation.* Berkeley: University of California Press.

Posner, Richard A. 1979. "Utilitarianism, Economics, and Legal Theory." *Journal of Legal Studies* 8: 123.

Post, Robert C. 1995. *Constitutional Domains: Democracy, Community, Management.* Cambridge, Mass.: Harvard University Press.

————. 2003. "Law and Cultural Conflict." *Chicago-Kent Law Review* 78: 485–508.

Poston, Ted. 1967. "The American Negro and Newspaper Myths." In *Race and the News Media,* ed. Paul L. Fisher and Ralph L. Lowenstein. New York: Frederick A. Praeger.

Poulantzas, Nicos. 1972. "The Problem of the Capitalist State." In *Ideology in Social*

Science; Readings in Critical Social Theory, ed. Robin Blackburn, pp. 238–253. London: Fontana.

———. 1976. "The Capitalist State: A Reply to Milibrand and Laclau." *New Left Review* 95: 63–83.

Powell, Walter, and Paul DiMaggio, eds. 1991. *The New Institutionalism in Organizational Analysis.* Chicago: University of Chicago Press.

Powers, Richard G. 1983. *G-Men: Hoover's FBI in American Popular Culture.* Carbondale: Southern Illinois University Press.

Powledge, Fred. 1991. *Free at Last? The Civil Rights Movement and the People Who Made It.* Boston: Little, Brown.

Prager, Dennis, and Joseph Telushkin. 1983. *Why the Jews? The Reason for Anti-Semitism.* New York: Simon and Schuster.

Prager, Jeffrey. 1985. "Totalitarian and Liberal Democracies: Two Types of Modern Political Orders. In *Neofunctionalism,* ed. Jeffrey C. Alexander, 179–209. Beverly Hills: Sage.

———. 1986. *Building Democracy in Ireland: Political Order and Cultural Integration in a Newly Independent Nation.* New York: Cambridge University Press.

———. 1986. "The Free State Constitution and the Institutionalization of Value Strains." *Building Democracy in Ireland: Political Order and Cultural Integration in a Newly Independent Nation.* New York: Cambridge University Press.

Prell, Riv-Ellen. 1990. "Rage and Representation: Jewish Gender Stereotypes in American Culture." In *Uncertain Terms: Negotiating Gender in American Culture,* ed. Faye Ginsburg and Anna Lowenhaupt Tsing. Boston: Beacon.

———. 1997. "Stereotypes." In *Jewish Women in America: An Historical Encyclopedia,* ed. Paula E. Hyman and Deborah Dash Moore. New York: Routledge.

Przeworski, Adam. 1985. *Capitalism and Social Democracy.* New York: Cambridge University Press.

———. 1988. "Democracy as a Contingent Outcome of Conflicts." In *Constitutionalism and Democracy,* ed. Jon Elster and Rune Slagstad. Cambridge, UK; New York: Cambridge University Press.

Przeworski, Adam, Susan C. Stokes, and Bernard Manin, eds. 1999. *Democracy, Accountability, and Representation.* New York: Cambridge University Press.

Putnam, Robert D. 1993. *Making Democracy Work: Civic Traditions in Modern Italy.* Princeton, N.J.: Princeton University Press.

———. 1995. "Bowling Alone: America's Declining Social Capital." *Journal of Democracy* 6 (1): 65–78.

———. 2000. *Bowling Alone: The Collapse and Revival of American Community.* New York: Simon and Schuster.

Quine, V. W. 2004. "Translation and Meaning." In *Quintessence: Basic Readings from the Philosophy of W. V. Quine,* ed. Roger Gibson. Cambridge, Mass.: Harvard University Press.

Rabinovitch, Eyal. 2001. "Gender and the Public Sphere: Alternative Forms of Integration in Nineteenth-Century America." *Sociological Theory* 19 (3): 344–370.

Raines, Howell. 1977. *My Soul Is Rested: Movement Days in the Deep South Remembered*. New York: G.P. Putnam.

Ramos, Belem. "Barbie Doll Revolutionized Toy Industry." Available at Border land/Barbie_doll.htm.

Rapaport, Lynn. 1997. *Jews in Germany after the Holocaust: Memory, Identity and Jewish-German Relations*. New York: Cambridge University Press.

Rawls, John. 1971. *A Theory of Justice*. Cambridge, Mass.: Harvard University Press.
———. 1993. *Political Liberalism*. New York: Columbia University Press.

Redfield, Robert. 1960. *The Little Community; and, Peasant Society and Culture*. Chicago: Chicago University Press.

Rex, John. 1961. *Key Problems of Sociological Theory*. London: Routledge and Kegan Paul.

Ribalow, Harold U., ed. 1950. *This Land, These People*. New York: Beechhurst.

Ricoeur, Paul. 1984. *Time and Narrative*, Vol. 1. Trans. Kathleen McLaughlin and David Pellauer. Chicago: University of Chicago Press.

Riedel, Manfred. 1984. *Between Tradition and Revolution: The Hegelian Transformation of Political Philosophy*. Trans. Walter Wright. New York: Cambridge University Press.

Rieff, Philip. 1979. *Freud: The Mind of the Moralist*. Chicago: University of Chicago Press.

Riley, Alexander T. " 'Renegade Durkheimianism' and the Transgressive/Left Sacred." In *The Cambridge Companion to Durkheim*, ed. Jeffrey C. Alexander and Philip Smith, pp. 274–301. New York: Cambridge University Press.

Ringmar, Erik. 1996. *Identity, Interest, and Action: A Cultural Explanation of Sweden's Intervention in the Thirty Years War*. New York: Cambridge University Press.

Rivkin, Ellis, ed. 1957. *Readings in Modern Jewish History*. Cincinnati, Ohio: Hebrew Union College Jewish Institute of Religion.

Robertson, R. 1985. *Kafka: Judaism, Politics, and Literature*. Oxford: Clarendon Press.
———. 1999. *The "Jewish Question" in German Literature, 1749–1939: Emancipation and Its Discontents*. Oxford: Oxford University Press.

Rodrigue, A. 1996. "Rearticulations of French Jewish Identities after the Dreyfus Affair." *Jewish Social Studies* 2 (3): 1–24.

Rogin, Michael. 1987. *"Ronald Reagan": The Movie, and Other Episodes in Political Demonology*. Berkeley: University of California Press.

Rokkan, Stein, with Angus Campbell, Per Torsvik, and Henry Valen. 1970. *Citizens, Elections, Parties: Approaches to the Comparative Study of the Processes of Development*. New York: McKay.

Rorty, Richard. 1979. *Philosophy and the Mirror of Nature*. Princeton, N.J.: Princeton University Press.

———. 1989. *Contingency, Irony, and Solidarity*. New York: Cambridge University Press.

Rose, Peter I. 1969, ed. *The Ghetto and Beyond: Essays on Jewish Life in America*. New York: Random House.

Rose, T. 2000. "Rewriting the Pleasure/Danger Dialectic: Black Female Teenage Sexuality in the Popular Imagination." In *From Sociology to Cultural Studies*, ed. Elizabeth Long, pp. 1185–1202. Malden, Mass.: Blackwell.

Rose-Ackerman, Susan. 1999. *Corruption and Government: Causes, Consequences, and Reform*. London: Cambridge University Press.

Rosenblum, Nancy, and Robert Post. 2002. *Civil Society and Government*. Princeton, N.J.: Princeton University Press.

Rosovsky, Nitza. 1986. *The Jewish Experience at Harvard and Radcliffe*. Cambridge, Mass.: Harvard University Press.

Roth, Guenther. 1963. *The Social Democrats in Imperial Germany; A Study in Working-Class Isolation and National Integration*. Totowa, N.J.: Bedminster.

Roth, Philip. 1959. *Goodbye Columbus and Five Short Stories*. New York: Modern Library.

———. 1962. *Letting Go*. New York: Random House.

———. 1969. *Portnoy's Complaint*. New York: Random House.

———. 1972. *The Breast*. New York: Holt, Rinehart, and Winston.

———. 1975. "Imagining Jews." In *Reading Myself and Others*, pp. 215–246. New York: Farrar, Straus, and Giroux.

———. 1975. *Reading Myself and Others*. New York: Farrar, Straus, and Giroux.

———. 1975. [1974] "In Response to Those Who Have Asked Me: 'How Did You Come to Write That Book, Anyway?' " In *Reading Myself and Others*, pp. 33–41. New York: Farrar, Straus, and Giroux.

———. 1975. "Some New Jewish Stereotypes." In *Reading Myself and Others*, pp. 137–147. New York: Farrar, Straus, and Giroux.

———. 1981. *The Anatomy Lesson*. New York: Farrar, Straus, and Giroux.

———. 1985. *Zuckerman Bound*. New York: Farrar, Straus, and Giroux.

———. 1988. *The Facts: A Novelist's Autobiography*. New York: Farrar, Straus, and Giroux.

———. 1998. *I Married a Communist*. Boston; New York: Houghton Mifflin.

———. 2004. *The Plot against America*. Boston: Houghton Mifflin.

Rothbell, Gladys. 1986. "The Jewish Mother: Social Construction of a Popular Image." In *The Jewish Family: Myths and Reality*, ed. Steven Cohen and Paula Hyman. New York: Holmes and Meier.

Rousseau, Jean-Jacques, 1968 [1762]. *The Social Contract*. London: Penguin.

Rovit, Earl. 1967. "Jewish Humor and American Life." *American Scholar* (spring): 237–245.

Rozenbilt, M. L. 1992. "Jewish Assimilation in Habsburg Vienna." In *Assimilation and Community: The Jews of Nineteenth-Century Europe,* ed. Jonathan Frankel and Steven J. Zipperstein. Cambridge: Cambridge University Press.

Rubin, Alexis P., ed. 1995. *Scattered among the Nations: Documents Affecting Jewish History 49–1975.* Northvale, N.J.: Jason Aronson.

Rueschemeyer, Dietrich. 1986. *Power and the Division of Labour.* Stanford, Calif.: Stanford University Press.

Rueschemeyer, Dietrich, Evelyne H. Stephens, and John D. Stephens. 1992. *Capitalist Development and Democracy.* Chicago: University of Chicago Press.

Russell, Francis. 1955. "The Coming of the Jews." *Antioch Review* 15 (1): 15.

Russell, Jeffrey Burton. 1988. *The Prince of Darkness: Radical Evil and the Power of Good in History.* Ithaca, N.Y.: Cornell University Press.

Ryan, Mary P. 1992. "Gender and Public Access: Women's Politics in Nineteenth-Century America." In *Habermas and the Public Sphere,* ed. Craig Calhoun. Cambridge: MIT Press.

Sabine, George H. 1963 [1937]. *A History of Political Theory.* New York: Holt, Rinehart, and Winston.

Sahlins, Marshall. 1976. *Culture and Practical Reason.* Chicago: University of Chicago Press.

———. 1981. *Historical Metaphors and Mythical Realities: Structure in the Early History of the Sandwich Islands Kingdom.* Ann Arbor: University of Michigan Press.

Said, Edward. 1978. *Orientalism.* New York: Random House.

———. 1992. "The Politics of Knowledge." In *Debating P.C.: The Controversy over Political Correctness on College Campuses,* ed. Paul Berman. New York: Dell.

Sakai, Nooki. 1997. *Translation and Subjectivity: On "Japan" and Cultural Nationalism.* Minneapolis: University of Minnesota Press.

Sandel, Michael. 1982. *Liberalism and the Limits of Justice.* Cambridge: Cambridge University Press.

Sarat, Austin, and Thomas Kearns. 1998. "The Cultural Lives of Law." In *Law in the Domains of Culture,* ed. Austin Sarat and Thomas Kearns, pp. 3–20. Ann Arbor: University of Michigan Press.

Sarna, Jonathan D. 2004. *American Judaism: A History.* New Haven, Conn.: Yale University Press.

Sartre, Jean-Paul. 1948. *Anti-Semite and Jew.* Trans. George J. Becker. New York: Schocken.

———. 1976 [1960]. *Critique of Dialectical Reason, Theory of Practical Ensembles.* Trans. Alan Sheridan-Smith, and edited by Jonathan Ree. London: New Left Review Book.

Saturday Review of Books. 1947. December 13.

Saussure, Ferdinand de. 1966. *Course in General Linguistics.* Trans. Wade Baskin, and edited by Charles Bally and Albert Sechehaye. New York: McGraw-Hill

Schermerhorn, Richard Alonzo. 1970. *Comparative Race Relations.* New York: Random House.

Schlesinger, Arthur M. 1965. *A Thousand Days: John F. Kennedy in the White House.* Boston: Houghton Mifflin.

Schlesinger, Arthur M.. 1991. *The Disuniting of America.* New York: W.W. Norton.

Schmitt, Carl. 1996 [1932]. *The Concept of the Political.* Trans. George Schwab. Chicago: University of Chicago Press.

Schnapper, Dominique. 1991. *La France de l'intégration: Sociologie de la nation en 1990.* Paris: Gallimard.

———. 1998. *Community of Citizens: On the Modern Idea of Nationality.* New Brunswick, N.J.: Transaction.

Schudson, Michael. 1978. *Discovering the News: A Social History of American Newspapers.* New York: Basic Books.

———. 1992. "Was There Ever a Public Sphere? If So, When? Reflections on the American Case." In *Habermas and the Public Sphere,* ed. Craig Calhoun, pp. 143–163. Cambridge: MIT Press.

———. 1992. *Watergate in American Memory: How We Remember, Forget, and Reconstruct the Past.* New York: Basic Books.

———. 1998. *The Good Citizen: A History of American Civic Life.* New York: Martin Kessler.

———. 2003. *The Sociology of News.* New York: Norton.

Schwartz, Arnold. 1974. "Intermarriage in the United States." In *The Jew in American Society,* ed. Marshall Sklare, pp. 303–331. New York: Behrman House.

Schwartz, Barry. 2000. *Abraham Lincoln and the Forge of National Memory.* Chicago: University of Chicago Press.

Schwartz, R. 1978. "Moral Order and Sociology of Law: Trends, Problems, and Prospects." *Annual Review of Sociology* (4): 577–601.

Sciortino, Giuseppe. 2003. "From Homogeneity to Difference? Comparing Multiculturalism as a Description and a Field for Claim-Making." *Comparative Social Research* 25: 263–285.

Scrutton, T. E. 1921. "The Work of the Commercial Courts." *Cambridge Law Journal* 1 (8).

Sears, David O., et al. 1980. "Self-Interest vs. Symbolic Politics in Policy Attitudes and Presidential Voting." *American Political Science Review* 74 (3): 670–684.

Seidman, Steven. 2002. "From the Polluted Homosexual to the Normal Gay." *Beyond the Closet: The Transformation of Gay and Lesbian Life.* New York: Routledge.

Seligman, Adam B. 1992. *The Idea of Civil Society.* New York: Free Press.

———. 1997. *The Problem of Trust.* Princeton, N.J.: Princeton University Press.

Selzer, Michael. 1972. *"Kike": A Documentary History of Anti-Semitism in America.* New York: World.

Selznick, Philip. 1957. *Leadership in Administration; A Sociological Interpretation.* Evanston, Ill.: Row, Peterson.

Sennett, Richard. 1977. *The Fall of Public Man.* New York: Alfred A. Knopf.

———. 1998. *Corrosion of Character: The Personal Consequences of Work in the New Capitalism.* New York: Norton.

———. 2003. *Respect in a World of Inequality.* New York: Norton.

———, ed. 1969. *Classic Essays on the Culture of Cities.* Englewood Cliffs, N.J.: Prentice-Hall.

Sennett, Richard, and Jonathan Cobb. 1972. *The Hidden Injuries of Class.* New York: Alfred A. Knopf.

Sewell, William H., Jr., 1980. *Work and Revolution in France: The Language of Labor from the Old Regime to 1848.* New York: Cambridge University Press.

———. 1985. "Ideologies and Social Revolutions: Reflections on the French Case." *Journal of Modern History* 57: 570–585.

Seyhan, A. 1996. "Ethnic Selves/Ethnic Signs: Inventions of Self, Space, and Genealogy in Immigrant Writing." In *Culture/Contexture: Explorations in Anthropology and Literary Studies,* ed. E. Valentine Daniel and Jeffrey M. Peck, pp. 175–194. Berkeley: University of California Press.

Shapiro, Edward S. 1989. "Jewishness and the New York Intellectuals." *Judaism* 38: 282–292.

———. 1992. *A Time for Healing: American Jewry since World War II.* Baltimore, Md.: Johns Hopkins University Press.

Shapiro, Ian. 1986. *The Evolution of Rights in Liberal Theory.* Cambridge: Cambridge University Press.

Shapiro, Michael J. 1997. *Violent Cartographies: Mapping Cultures of War.* Minneapolis: University of Minnesota Press.

Shaw, David. 1999. "Journalism Is a Very Different Business—Here's Why." *Los Angeles Times,* December 20, section V, p. 3.

Sherwood, Steve. 1994 "Narrating the Social: Postmodernism and the Drama of Democracy." *Journal of Narrative and Life History* 4 (1/2): 69–88.

Shils, Edward. 1975. "Center and Periphery." *Center and Periphery: Essays in Macrosociology,* pp. 3–16. Chicago: University of Chicago Press.

———. 1975. "Charisma, Order, and Status." *Center and Periphery: Essays in Macrosociology,* pp. 256–275. Chicago: University of Chicago Press.

———. 1975. "Primordial, Personal, Sacred, and Civil Ties." *Center and Periphery: Essays in Macrosociology,* 111–126. Chicago: University of Chicago Press.

———. 1991. "The Virtue of Civil Society." *Government and Opposition* 26 (1) (winter): 3–20.

————. 1997. "Nationalism, Nationality, and Civil Society." In *The Virtue of Civility,* ed. Steven Grosby, pp. 188–224. Indianapolis, Ind.: Liberty Fund.

Shklar, Judith N. 1991. *American Citizenship: The Quest for Inclusion.* Cambridge, Mass.: Harvard University Press.

Short, K.R.M., ed. 1981. *Feature Films as History.* Knoxville: University of Tennessee Press.

Shutz, Alfred. 1967. *The Phenomenology of the Social World.* Trans. George Walsh and Frederick Lehnert. Evanston, Ill.: Northwestern University Press.

Siegel, Reva B. 1996. "In the Eyes of the Law: Reflections on the Authority of Legal Discourse." In *Law's Stories: Narrative and Rhetoric in the Law,* ed. Peter Brooks and Paul Gewirtz. New Haven, Conn.: Yale University Press.

Silberman, Charles E. 1985. *A Certain People: American Jews and Their Lives Today.* New York: Summit.

Sills, David L., ed. 1968. *The International Encyclopedia of the Social Sciences,* vol. 16. New York: Macmillan.

Simmel, Georg. 1955 [1908]. *Conflict.* Trans. Kurt H. Wolff. Glencoe, Ill.: Free Press.

Skelton, George. 2000. "Pity Quackenbush? Sorry, He Did It to Himself." *Los Angeles Times,* June 29, Metro Section, p. 3.

Skidelsky, Robert. 1983. *John Maynard Keynes: A Biography.* London: Macmillan.

Sklare, Marshall. 1970. "Intermarriage and Jewish Survival." *Commentary* (March): 51–58.

————. 1971. *America's Jews.* New York: Random House.

————, ed. 1974. *The Jew in American Society.* New York: Behrman House.

Skocpol, Theda. 1979. *States and Social Revolutions: A Comparative Analysis of France, Russia, and China.* Cambridge: Cambridge University Press.

————. 1985. "Bringing the State Back In: Strategies of Analysis in Current Research." In *Bringing the State Back In,* ed. Peter Evans, Dietrich Rueschemeyer, and Theda Skocpol, pp. 3–43. New York: Cambridge University Press.

————. 1985. "On the Road toward a More Adequate Understanding of the State." In *Bringing the State Back In,* ed. Peter Evans, Dietrich Rueschemeyer, and Theda Skocpol, pp. 347–366. New York: Cambridge University Press.

————. 1996. *Boomerang: Clinton's Health Security Effort and the Turn against Government in U.S. Politics.* New York: W. W. Norton.

Skrentny, John D. 1998. "The Effect of the Cold War on African-American Civil Rights: America and the World Audience, 1945–1968." *Theory and Society* 27: 237–285.

Sleeper, James. 1971. "Introduction." In *The New Jews,* ed. James A. Sleeper and Alan L. Mintz. New York: Vintage.

Sleeper, James A., and Alan L. Mintz, eds. 1971. *The New Jews.* New York: Vintage.

Slesinger, Tess. 1934. *The Unpossessed.* New York: Simon and Schuster.

Sloterdijk, Peter. 1987. *Critique of Cynical Reason*. Trans. Michael Eldred. Minneapolis: University of Minnesota Press.

Slotkin, Richard. 1973. *Regeneration through Violence: The Mythology of the American Frontier, 1600–1860*. Middletown, Conn.: Wesleyan University Press.

Small, Albion W., and George E. Vincent. 1894. *An Introduction to the Study of Society*. New York: American.

Smelser, Neil. 1959. *Social Change in the Industrial Revolution: An Application of Theory to the British Cotton Industry*. Chicago: University of Chicago Press.

———. 1962. *Theory of Collective Behavior*. New York: Free Press of Glencoe.

Smelser, Neil, and Jeffrey C. Alexander, eds. 1999. *Diversity and Its Discontents: Cultural Conflict and Common Ground in Contemporary American Society*. Princeton, N.J.: Princeton University Press.

Smith, Anthony D. 1991. *National Identity*. London: Penguin.

Smith, Adam. 1976. *The Glasgow Edition of the Works and Correspondence of Adam Smith*, Vol. 1: *The Theory of Moral Sentiments*, ed. D. D. Raphael and A. L. Macfie. Oxford: Clarendon Press.

Smith, Bob. 2000. "From Billy to Willy." *Advocate* 817/818 (August 15): 82.

Smith, Ethel M. 1929. "What Is Sex Equality and What Are the Feminists Trying to Accomplish?" *Century Monthly Magazine* 118 (May): 96.

Smith, Hedrick. 1990. *The New Russians*. New York: Random House.

Smith, Henry Nash. 1970 [1950]. *Virgin Land: The American West as Symbol and Myth*. Cambridge, Mass.: Harvard University Press.

Smith, Philip. 1991. "Codes and Conflict: Towards a Theory of War as Ritual." *Theory and Society* 20: 103–138.

———. 1994. "The Semiotic Foundations of Media Narratives: Saddam and Nasser in the American Mass Media." *Journal of Narrative and Life Narrative* 4 (1–2): 89–118.

———. 1998. "Barbarism and Civility in the Discourses of Fascism, Communism, and Democracy: Variations on a Set of Themes." In *Real Civil Societies: Dilemmas of Institutionalization*, ed. Jeffrey C. Alexander. London: Sage.

———. 2000. "Culture and Charisma: Outline of a Theory." *Acta Sociologica* 43 (2): 101–111.

———. 2005. *Why War? The Cultural Logic of Iraq, the Gulf War, and Suez*. Chicago: University of Chicago Press.

Smith, Rogers. 1997. *Civic Ideals: Conflicting Visions of Citizenship in U.S. History*. New Haven, Conn.: Yale University Press.

Snow, David, et al. 1986. "Frame Alignment Processes, Micromobilization, and Movement Participation." *American Sociological Review* 51 (August): 464–481.

Snow, David, and Robert D. Benford. 1988. "Ideology, Frame Resonance, and Participant Mobilization." *International Social Movement Research* 1: 197–217.

Sollors, Werner. 1992. " 'Of Plymouth Rock and Jamestown and Ellis Island,' Or, Ethnic Literature and Some Redefinitions of 'America.' " In *Immigrants in Two Democracies: French and American Experience,* ed. Donald Horowitz and Gerard Noiriel, pp. 205–245. New York: New York University Press.

Solotoroff, Theodore. 1959. "A Vocal Group: The Jewish Part in American Letters." *Times Literary Supplement.* November 6. Issue 3010. (The American Imagination Supplement).

———. 1973. "Philip Roth and the Jewish Moralists." In *Contemporary American-Jewish Literature: Critical Essays,* ed. Irving Malin. Bloomington: Indiana University Press.

Somers, Margaret R. 1991. "Narrating and Naturalizing Civil Society and Citizen-ship Theory." *Sociological Theory* 13 (3): 229–274.

———. 1993. "Citizenship and the Place of the Public Sphere: Law, Community, and Political Culture in the Transition to Democracy." *American Sociological Review* 58 (5): 587–620.

Somers, Margaret, and Fred Block. 2005. "From Poverty to Perversity: Ideas, Mar-kets, and Institutions over 200 Years of Welfare Debate." *American Sociological Review* 70 (2): 260–287.

Sorin, Gerald. 1991. *A Time for Building: The Third Migration, 1880–1920, Vol. III of The Jewish People in America.* Baltimore, Md.: Johns Hopkins University Press.

Soucy, R. 1968. "The Nature of Fascism in France." In *Fascism: An Anthology,* ed. Nathanael Green, pp. 275–300. New York: Crowell.

Sowell, Thomas. 1981. *Ethnic America: A History.* New York: Basic Books.

Soyer, Daniel. 1997. *Jewish Immigrant Associations and American Identity in New York, 1880–1939.* Cambridge, Mass.: Harvard University Press.

Spiegel, Alan. 1983. "The Vanishing Act: A Typology of the Jew in the Contem-porary American Film." In *From Hester Street to Hollywood: The Jewish-American Stage and Screen,* ed. Sarah B. Cohen. Bloomington: Indiana University Press.

Spitzer, S. 1980. *Research in Law and Sociology, Vol. 3.* Greenwich, Conn.: JAI Press.

Spivak, Gayatri. 1995. "Can the Subaltern Speak?" in *The Post-Colonial Studies Reader,* ed. Bill Ashcroft, Gareth Griffiths, and Helen Tiffin, pp. 24–28. London: Routledge.

Stanislawski, Michael. 1988. *For Whom do I Toil? Judah Leib Gordon and the Crisis of Russian Jewry.* New York: Oxford University Press.

Starr, Paul. 2004. *The Creation of the Media: Political Origins of Modern Communications.* New York: Basic Books.

Steinberg, Stephen. 1974. *The Academic Melting Pot: Catholics and Jews in American Higher Education.* New York: McGraw-Hill.

———. 1974. *The Academic Melting Pot: Catholics and Jews in American Higher Edu-cation.* New York: McGraw-Hill.

Steiner, Franz. 1956. *Taboo*. London: Cohen and West.

Stember, Charles Herbert. 1966. "The Recent History of Public Attitudes." In C. H. Stember, *Jews in the Mind of America*, pp. 31–234. New York: Basic Books.

———. 1966. *Jews in the Mind of America*. New York: Basic Books.

Stern, Robert L. 1946. "The Commerce Clause and the National Economy, 1933–1946." *Harvard Law Review* 59: 645–693.

Stimpson, Catherine R. 1992. "On Differences: Modern Language Association Presidential Address 1990." In *Debating P.C.: The Controversy over Political Correctness on College Campuses,* ed. Paul Berman, pp. 40–60. New York: Vintage.

Stokes, Donald E. 1966. "Party Loyalty and the Likelihood of Deviating Elections." In *Elections and the Political Order,* ed. A. Campbell et al. New York: John Wiley and Sons.

Stolzenberg, Nomi Maya, and David N. Myers. 1992. "Community, Constitution and Culture: The Case of the Jewish Kehilah." *Michigan Journal of Law Reform* 25, 633–670.

Strauss, Leo. 1953. "Natural Right and the Distinction between Facts and Values." In *Natural Right and History,* pp. 35–80. Chicago: University of Chicago Press.

Strober, Gerald S. 1974. *American Jews: Community in Crisis*. Garden City, N.Y.: Doubleday.

Strouse, Jean. 1999. *Morgan: American Financier*. New York: Harper Collins.

Sunstein, Cass R. 1990. *After the Rights Revolution: Reconceiving the Regulatory State*. Cambridge, Mass.: Harvard University Press.

Swidler, Ann. 1986. "Culture in Action: Symbols and Strategies." *American Sociological Review* 51 (April): 273–286.

———. 1995. "Cultural Power and Social Movements." In *Social Movements and Culture,* ed. Hank Johnston and Bert Klandermans, pp. 25–40. Minneapolis: University of Minnesota Press.

Sztompka, Piotr. 1999. *Trust: A Sociological Theory*. New York: Cambridge University Press.

Tagliabue, J. 1989. "Opening New Era, Poles Pick Leader: Forty Years of One-Party Rule Ends as Parliament Elects a Solidarity Premier." *New York Times,* August 25, p. A8.

Talese, Gay. 1969. *The Kingdom and the Power*. New York: World.

Talmon, J. L. 1972. "Suggestions for Isolating the Jewish Component in World History." *Midstream* 18 (3): 8–36.

Tama, M. Diogene. 1807. *Transactions of the Parisian Sanhedrim*. Trans. F. D. Kirwan. London: C. Taylor.

Tarde. Gabriel de. 1969. "Opinion and Conversation." In *On Communication and Social Influence,* ed. Terry N. Clark, pp. 277–318. Chicago: University of Chicago Press.

Tarrow, Sydney. 1992. "Mentalities, Political Cultures, and Collective Action

Frames: Constructing Meaning through Action." In *Frontiers in Social Movement Theory,* ed. Aldon D. Morris and Carol McClurg Mueller, pp. 174–202. New Haven, Conn.: Yale University Press.

———. 1994. *Power in Movement: Social Movements, Collective Action, and Contentious Politics.* Cambridge: Cambridge University Press.

Taylor, Charles. 1975. *Hegel.* Cambridge: Cambridge University Press.

———. 1985. *Human Agency and Language.* New York: Cambridge University Press.

———. 1986. "Foucault on Freedom and Truth." In *Foucault: A Critical Reader,* ed. David C. Hoy, pp. 69–102. Oxford: Blackwell.

———. 1989. *Sources of the Self: Making of Modern Identity.* Cambridge, Mass.: Harvard University Press.

———. 1992. *The Ethics of Authenticity.* Cambridge, Mass.: Harvard University Press.

———. 1994. *Multiculturalism: Examining the Politics of Recognition.* Edited by Amy Gutmann. Princeton, N.J.: Princeton University Press.

———. 1994. "The Politics of Recognition." In *Multiculturalism: Examining the Politics of Recognition,* ed. Amy Gutmann, pp. 25–73. Princeton, N.J.: Princeton University Press.

———. 1998. "The Dynamics of Democratic Exclusion." *Journal of Democracy* 9 (4): 143–156.

Tellenbach, Gerd. 1970 [1939]. *Church, State, and Christian Society at the Time of the Investiture Contest.* Trans. R. F. Bennett. Oxford: Basil Blackwell.

Tesar, Jan. 1981. "Totalitarian Dictatorships as a Phenomenon of the Twentieth Century and the Possibilities of Overcoming Them." *International Journal of Politics* 11 (spring): 85–100.

Thayer, James B. 1893. "The Origin and Scope of the American Doctrine of Constitutional Law." *Harvard Law Review* 7: 129–156.

Thompson, E. P. 1964. *The Making of the English Working Class.* New York: Pantheon Books.

Thompson, John B. 1984. *Studies in the Theory of Ideology.* Cambridge, England: Polity.

———. 2000. *Political Scandal: Power and Visibility in the Media Age.* Cambridge, England: Polity.

Thompson, Kenneth. 1993. "Identity and Belief." In *The United States in the Twentieth Century: Culture,* ed. Jeremy Mitchell and Tichard Maidment. London: Hodder and Stoughton.

Thurner, Manuela. 1993. "Better Citizens without the Ballot: American Anti-Suffrage Women and Their Rationale During the Progressive Era." *Journal of Women's History* 5 (1): 33–60.

Tilly, Charles. 1994. "Social Movements as Historically Specific Clusters of Political Performances." *Berkeley Journal of Sociology* 38: 1–30.

———. 1999. "Epilogue: Now Where?" In *State/Culture: State Formation After the Cultural Turn,* ed. George Steinmetz, pp. 407–419. Ithaca, N.Y.: Cornell University Press.

———. 2002. *Stories, Identities, and Political Change.* Boulder, Colo.: Rowman and Littlefield.

Tilly, Charles, Louise Tilly, and Richard Tilly. 1975. *The Rebellious Century, 1830–1930.* Cambridge, Mass.: Harvard University Press.

Time, April 2, 1956.

Time, November 26, 1956.

Time, January 7, 1957.

Time, February 18, 1957.

Timms, Edward, and Andrea Hammel, eds. 1999. *The German-Jewish Dilemma: From the Enlightenment to the Shoah.* Lewiston, N.Y.: Edwin Mellon Press.

Tocqueville, Alexis de. 1945 [1840]. *Democracy in America,* Vol. II. Trans. Henry Reeve, rev. Francis Bowne, ed. Phillips Bradley. New York: Random House.

———. 2004 [1835, 1840]. *Democracy in America,* Vols. I and II. Trans. Arthur Goldhammer. New York: Library of America.

Tomberlin, Joseph A. 1993–1994. "A Common Thread: African-Americans, the Civil Rights Movement, and the United States Supreme Court." *Mississippi Quarterly* 47 (Winter): 91–104.

Touraine, Alain. 1977. *The Self-Production of Society,* tr. Derek Coltman. Chicago: University of Chicago Press.

———. 1984. "The Waning Sociological Image of Social Life." *International Journal of Comparative Sociology* 25 (1–2): 33–34.

———. 1985. "Social Movements, Revolution and Democracy." In *The Public Realm: Essays on Discursive Types in Political Philosophy,* ed. Reiner Schurmann. Buffalo: State University of New York Press.

———. 1992. "Beyond Social Movements." *Theory, Culture, and Society* 9: 143.

———. 1992. "Triumph or Downfall of Civil Society." In *The Public Realm: Essays on Discursive Types in Political Philosophy,* ed. Reiner Schurmann. Buffalo: State University of New York Press.

Trachtenberg, Joshua. 1961. *The Devil and the Jews: The Medieval Conception of the Jew and Its Relation to Modern Anti-Semitism.* Cleveland, N.Y.: World; Jewish Publication Society.

Tribe, Lawrence H. 1972. "Policy Science: Analysis or Ideology." *Philosophy and Public Affairs* 2: 66.

Trillin, Calvin. 1968. "Lester Drentluss, A Jewish Boy from Baltimore, Attempts to Make It through the Summer of 1967." *Atlantic Monthly,* January, p. 43.

Trilling, Lionel. 1934. "Afterword." In Tess Slesinger, *The Unpossessed.* New York: Simon and Schuster.

————. 1950. *The Liberal Imagination: Essays on Literature and Society*. New York: Harcourt Brace.

Troeltsch, Ernst. 1960 [1911]. *The Social Teaching of the Christian Churches*. Chicago: University of Chicago Press.

Tronto, Joan C. 1987. "Beyond Gender Difference to a Theory of Care." *Signs* 12 (4): 644–663.

————. 1993. *Moral Boundaries: A Political Argument for an Ethic of Care*. New York: Routledge.

Trotsky, Leon. 1959 [1932]. *The Russian Revolution: The Overthrow of Tzarism and the Triumph of the Soviets*. New York: Doubleday.

Tucker, Kenneth. 1996. *French Revolutionary Syndicalism and the Public Sphere*. New York: Cambridge University Press.

Turner, Ralph, and Lewis Killian. 1972. *Collective Behavior*. Englewood Cliffs, N.J.: Prentice-Hall.

Turner, Victor. 1974. *Dramas, Fields, and Metaphors: Symbolic Action in Human Society*. Ithaca, N.Y.: Cornell University Press.

————. 1974. "Pilgrimages as Social Processes." *Dramas, Fields, and Metaphors: Symbolic Action in Human Society*, pp. 166–230. Ithaca, N.Y.: Cornell University Press.

Tyack, D. 1999. "Preserving the Republic by Educating the Republicans." In *Diversity and Its Discontents: Cultural Conflict and Common Ground in Contemporary American Society*, ed. Neil Smelser and Jeffrey C. Alexander, pp. 63–83. Princeton, N.J.: Princeton University Press.

Unger, Roberto. 1975. *Knowledge and Politics*. New York: Free Press.

————. 1986. *The Critical Legal Studies Movement*. Cambridge, Mass.: Harvard University Press.

United States Commission on Civil Rights. 1965. *Voting in Mississippi: A Report*. Washington, D.C.: U.S. Government Printing Office.

Van den Berghe, Pierre L. 1965. *South Africa: A Study in Conflict*. Middletown, Conn.: Wesleyan University Press.

Van den Berghe, Frederic. 1997–98. *Une Histoire critique de la sociologie allemande: alienation et reification*. Paris: La Decouverte/MAUSS.

Vernon, James. 1993. *Politics and the People: A Study in English Political Culture, c. 1815–1867*. New York: Cambridge University Press.

Voltaire. 1995 [1756]. "Jews." In *The Jew in the Modern World*, compiled and edited by P. Mendes-Flohr and J. Reinhaz, pp. 304–305. New York: Oxford University Press.

Wade, Stephen. 1999. *Jewish American Literature since 1945: An Introduction*. Edinburgh: Edinburgh University Press.

Wagner-Pacifici, Robin. 1986. *The Moro Morality Play: Terrorism as Social Drama*. Chicago: University of Chicago Press.

Walzer, Michael. 1965. *The Revolution of the Saints: A Study of the Origins of Radical Politics.* Cambridge, Mass.: Harvard University Press.

———. 1970. *Obligations: Essays on Disobedience, War, and Citizenship.* Cambridge, Mass.: Harvard University Press.

———. 1977. *Just and Unjust Wars: A Moral Argument with Historical Illustrations.* New York: Basic Books.

———. 1984. *Spheres of Justice: A Defense of Pluralism and Equality.* New York: Basic Books.

———. 1987. *Interpretation and Social Criticism.* Cambridge, Mass.: Harvard University Press.

———. 1988. *The Company of Critics: Social Criticism and Political Commitment in the Twentieth Century.* New York: Basic Books.

———. 1994. *Thick and Thin: Moral Argument at Home and Abroad.* Notre Dame, Ind.: University of Notre Dame Press.

———. 1999. "Rescuing Civil Society." *Dissent* 46, 1: 62–67.

Warnke, Georgia 1992. *Justice and Interpretation.* Cambridge, England: Polity.

Warren, Jennifer. 2000. "No Gloating, Just Sadness—and Some Lessons." *Los Angeles Times,* June 29, A27.

Waters, Mary C. 1990. *Ethnic Options: Choosing Identities in America.* Berkeley: University of California Press.

Weber, Eugen J. 1976. *Peasants into Frenchmen: The Modernization of Rural France, 1870–1914.* Stanford, Calif.: Stanford University Press.

Weber, Max. 1927 [1904–05]. *The Protestant Ethic and the Spirit of Capitalism.* New York: Scribner's and Sons.

———. 1946. "Bureaucracy." In *From Max Weber: Essays in Sociology,* trans. and ed. Hans Gerth and C. Wright Mills, pp. 196–266. New York: Oxford University Press.

———. 1946. "Class, Status, and Party." In *From Max Weber: Essays in Sociology,* trans. and ed. Hans Gerth and C. Wright Mills, pp. 180–195. New York: Oxford University Press.

———. 1946. "Religious Rejections of the World and Their Directions." In *From Max Weber: Essays in Sociology,* ed. Hans Gerth and C. Wright Mills, pp. 323–359. New York: Oxford University Press.

———. 1951. "Conclusions: Confucianism and the Puritanism." *The Sociology of China,* pp. 226–249. New York: Free Press.

———. 1952 [1917–1919]. *Ancient Judaism,* ed. and trans. Don Martindale. New York: Free Press.

———. 1958. "The Protestant Sects and the Spirit of Capitalism." In *From Max Weber: Essays in Sociology,* ed. Hans Gerth and C. Wright Mills. New York: Oxford University Press.

———. 1978. "The Categories of Legal Thought." In Max Weber, *Economy and Society*, Vol. 2, pp. 641–901. Berkeley: University of California Press.

———. 1978. "Appendix II: Parliament and Government in a Reconstructed Germany." *Economy and Society*, Vol. 2, pp. 1381–1469. Berkeley: University of California Press.

———. 1978. "The City." *Economy and Society*, Vol. 2, pp. 1212–1372. Berkeley: University of California Press.

———. 1978. *Economy and Society*, Vols. 1 and 2. Edited by Guenther Roth and Claus Wittich. Berkeley: University of California Press.

———. 1985 [1906]. " 'Churches' and 'Sects' in North America: An Ecclesiastical Socio-Political Sketch." *Sociological Theory* 3 (1): 7–13.

Weeks, Jeffrey. 1998. "The Sexual Citizen." *Theory, Culture, and Society* 15 (3): 35–52.

Weinryb, Bernard D. 1970. "Anti-Semitism in Soviet Russia." In *The Jews in Soviet Russia since 1917*, ed. Lionel Kochan, pp. 288–320. London: Oxford University Press.

Weintraub, Jeff. 1997. "Public/Private: The Limitations of a Grand Dichotomy." *Responsive Community* 7 (2): 13–24.

Welles, Sumner. 1945. "New Hope for the Jewish People." *Nation*, May 5, pp. 511–513.

West, Cornel. 1990. "The New Cultural Politics of Difference." In *Out There: Marginalization and Contemporary Cultures*, ed. Russell Ferguson, Martha Gever, Trinh T. Minh-ha, and Cornel West, pp. 19–139. Cambridge, Mass.: MIT Press.

White, Harrison. 1995. "Where Do Languages Come From? Switching Talk." Pre-Print Series, Paul F. Lazarsfeld Center for the Social Sciences, Columbia University.

White, Hayden. 1973. *Metahistory: The Historical Imagination in Nineteenth-Century Europe*. Baltimore, Md.: Johns Hopkins University Press.

Whitfield, Stephen J. 1988. *American Space, Jewish Time*. Hamden, Conn.: Archon.

Whitman, Howard. 1949. "The College Fraternity Crisis." *Collier's*, January 8, pp. 34–35.

Wilentz, Sean. 1984. *Chants Democratic: New York City and the Rise of the American Working Class, 1788–1850*. New York: Oxford University Press.

Wilgoren, Jodi, and David M. Halbfinger. 2004. "Kerry and Dean, All Forgiven, Joined to Unseat a Common Foe." *New York Times*, March 11, A26.

Williams, George W. 1882. *History of the Negro Race in America from 1619–1880*. New York: Putnam's Sons.

Williams, Raymond. 1958. *Culture and Society: 1780–1950*. New York: Harper and Row.

———. 1958. "A Nineteenth Century Tradition." In *Culture and Society: 1780–1950*, pp. 3–158. New York: Harper and Row.

———. 1965. *The Long Revolution*. 3rd rev. ed. New York: Harper and Row.

Wilson, James Q. 1983. *Thinking about Crime*. New York: Basic Books.

Wilson, William Julius. 1973. *Power, Racism, and Privilege: Race Relations in Theoretical and Sociohistorical Perspectives*. New York: Macmillan; Free Press.

———. 1987. *The Truly Disadvantaged: The Inner City, the Underclass, and Public Policy*. Chicago: University of Chicago Press.

Wirth, Louis. 1929. *The Ghetto*. Chicago: University of Chicago Press.

Wise, Stephen J. 1930. "Foreword." In *Jews, Jobs, and Discrimination: A Report on Jewish Non-Employment*, ed. Jacob X. Cohen. New York: American Jewish Congress.

Wittgenstein, Ludwig. 1953. *Philosophical Investigations*. Trans. G.E.M. Anscombe. London: Macmillan.

Wofford, Harris. 1980. *Of Kennedys and Kings: Making Sense of the Sixties*. New York: Farrar, Straus, and Giroux.

Wolfe, Alan. 1989. *Whose Keeper? Social Science and Moral Obligation*. Berkeley: University of California Press.

———. 2004. "Native Son: Samuel Huntington Defends the Homeland." *Foreign Affairs 83* (3): 120–125.

Wolfe, Bernard. 1968. "Uncle Remus and the Malevolent Rabbit." In *The National Temper; Readings in American History*, ed. Lawrence W. Levine and Robert Middlekauff, pp. 190–206. New York: Harcourt, Brace, and World.

Wolfson, Harry A. 1922. "Escaping Judaism." Menorah Society Pamphlet No. 2. New York: Menorah Press.

Wolin, Sheldon S. 1960. *Politics and Vision: Continuity and Innovation in Western Political Thought*. Boston: Little, Brown.

Woodward, C. Vann. 1974. *The Strange Career of Jim Crow*. Rev. 3rd ed. New York: Oxford University Press.

Wouk, Herman. 1955. *Marjorie Morningstar*. Garden City, N.Y.: Doubleday.

Wright, Will. 1975. *Six Guns and Society: A Structural Study of the Western*. Berkeley: University of California Press.

Wuthnow, Robert. 1999. "Democratic Liberalism and the Challenge of Diversity in Late-Twentieth Century America." In *Diversity and Its Discontents: Cultural Conflict and Common Ground in Contemporary American Society*, ed. Neil J. Smelser and Jeffrey C. Alexander, pp. 19–36. Princeton, N.J.: Princeton University Press.

Yaffe, Richard. 1980. "Intermarriage Abettors Should be Ousted from Leadership, Roth Urges." *New York Jewish Week*. Manhattan Edition (July 6): Vol. 193 (6): 2.

York, Tara. 2003. "Contaminated by Corruption." *New Haven Register*. July 2, p. A1.

Yoshino, Kenji. 1998–1999. "Assimilationist Bias in Equal Protection: The Visibility Presumption and the Case of 'Don't Ask, Don't Tell.'" *Yale Law Journal* 108: 485–571.

Young, Andrew. 1996. *An Easy Burden: The Civil Rights Movement and the Transformation of America*. New York: Harper Collins.

Young, Iris Marion. 1990. *Justice and the Politics of Difference*. Princeton: Princeton University Press.

Zaller, John R. 1992. *The Nature and Origins of Mass Opinion*. New York: Cambridge University Press.

Zangwill, Israel. 1909. *The Melting Pot: A Drama in Four Acts*. New York: Macmillan.

Zeitlin, Maurice. 1974 "Corporate Ownership and Control: The Large Corporation and the Capitalist Class." *American Journal of Sociology* 79 (5): 1073–1119.

Zelizer, Barbie. 1998. *Remembering to Forget: Holocaust Memory through the Camera's Eye*. Chicago: University of Chicago Press.

Zelizer, Viviana. 1985. *Pricing the Priceless Child: The Changing Social Value of Children*. New York: Basic Books.

Zerubavel, Eviatar. 1991. *The Fine Line: Making Distinctions in Everyday Life*. New York: Free Press.

Zinn, Howard. 1964. *SNCC: The New Abolitionists*. Boston: Beacon.

Zweigenhaft, Richard, and G. William Domhoff. 2003. *Blacks in the White Elite: Will the Progress Continue?* Boulder, Colo.: Rowman and Littlefield.

INDEX